TRANS BODIES, TRANS SELVES

TRANS BODIES, TRANS SELVES | A RESOURCE BY AND FOR TRANSGENDER COMMUNITIES

SECOND EDITION

Edited by

Laura Erickson-Schroth

OXFORD
UNIVERSITY PRESS

Oxford University Press is a department of the University of Oxford. It furthers
the University's objective of excellence in research, scholarship, and education
by publishing worldwide. Oxford is a registered trade mark of Oxford University
Press in the UK and certain other countries.

Published in the United States of America by Oxford University Press
198 Madison Avenue, New York, NY 10016, United States of America.

Library of Congress Cataloging-in-Publication Data
Names: Erickson-Schroth, Laura, editor.
Title: Trans bodies, trans selves : a resource by and for transgender communities /
[edited by] Laura Erickson-Schroth.
Description: Second edition. | New York, NY : Oxford University Press,
[2022] | Includes bibliographical references and index.
Identifiers: LCCN HYPERLINK "callto:2021033767" 2021033767 (print) |
LCCN HYPERLINK "callto:2021033768" 2021033768 (ebook) |
ISBN 9780190092726 (paperback) | ISBN 9780190092740 (epub)
Subjects: LCSH: Transgender people. | Gender nonconformity. | Gender identity.
Classification: LCC HQ77.9 .T714 2022 (print) | LCC HQ77.9 (ebook) |
DDC 306.76/8—dc23
LC record available at https://lccn.loc.gov/2021033767
LC ebook record available at https://lccn.loc.gov/2021033768

9 8 7 6 5 4 3 2 1

Printed by Sheridan Books, Inc., United States of America

CONTENTS

SECTION 1
WHO WE ARE   1
SECTION EDITOR: SAND C. CHANG

FOREWORD
Kai Cheng Thom

As I write this foreword in March of 2020, the novel coronavirus, COVID-19, is overturning our world: Socioeconomic, political, and healthcare systems across the globe are in crisis as they struggle to adapt to the pandemic. Among the most heavily impacted by the upheaval are traditionally marginalized communities, including the trans, nonbinary, genderqueer, and other gender-variant people whom this book seeks to empower.

Already at risk of reduced access to the social determinants of health, such as stable housing, income, and social support, trans communities will likely feel the reverberations of this crisis for years to come—particularly the disproportionate number of us who are chronically ill, disabled, racialized, and survival sex workers.

Yet if there is anything I know to be true about trans people—vulnerable, fractious, politically divided as we can be (I write this with the exasperated affection of a woman who has spent her whole adult life living and working in trans social services)—it is that we possess the capacity to unite, care for one another, and grow in the midst of struggle. For this is what we have always done, for generations upon generations, stretching back to the beginning of European colonization—and in many places, further back still: We have lived and loved each other in a world that was not made for us to survive in.

***

I came out to myself as a trans girl about a decade and a half ago, when I was fourteen. The sheltered child of a Chinese migrant family in Vancouver's East Side (the poor part of town, but not the *really* poor part was how we thought of it), I had no language or concept for what I was except the meagre resources I could find on the pre-social media era of the Internet.

Like many trans youth of color, I was isolated, ostracized at school, a survivor of physical and sexual abuse, and deeply traumatized. Queer and trans community saved my life—not the teachers at school who were either too timid or bigoted to stand up for me, not the doctors or counselors who diagnosed and pathologized me. Peer outreach workers, community organizers, activists, and sex workers were the people who found me, saw me, and gave me the words to name what I was and demand what I needed.

Trans community also gave me vision—made me start thinking about a society that people like me, everybody, could belong in. A society where I wasn't stared at or threatened in public, where my friends didn't always seem to be in danger. And trans community gave me history and possibility: The legacy of radical trans activists like Sylvia Rivera and Marsha P. Johnson, who started the Street Transvestite Action Revolutionaries (STAR) House for runaway queer kids.

In this book, you will find such powerful words, vision, history, and possibility. The first edition of *Trans Bodies, Trans Selves* was a groundbreaking work that sought to place the ownership of knowledge about trans bodies and culture directly in the hands of trans people and our allies. This was—and still is—a radical project, for within the dominant colonial, cisnormative culture, trans people have long been reduced to the product of mental illness or sexual fetish, specimens to be studied and cured (if not outright reviled and shunned). Psychiatrists, psychologists, and other "experts" have attempted to define who we are and gatekeep our access to legal and medical transition.

Trans Bodies, Trans Selves stands within the activist lineage that dares to recognize the rich depth and brilliance of our culture, to imagine that *trans people* are the rightful experts in our own identities, bodies, and experiences. The second edition of the book, which you are currently reading, has been expanded and updated so as to be even more inclusive of the vast diversity of perspectives that make up our communities.

***

In the years since I first came out as an adolescent, I have spent my whole professional lifetime working with and for trans people. I've been a peer educator, sex worker, queer event planner, author, speaker, arts facilitator, and (former) clinical social worker and family therapist, to name just a few jobs I've had. In each role, I specialized in working with trans people—an experience I consider both an immense privilege and an intense, at times overwhelming, responsibility. Through it all, I have come to believe that while trans people are just as human as anyone else (what a concept!), we also have unique gifts to offer one another and broader society.

It is often said in the field of transgender health that there is "no one way to be trans," and this is true. Any sweeping generalization about trans people is likely to ring false for at least some segment of our community. Yet it is also true that the oppression and discrimination leveled toward us have the effect of pushing us toward the extremes of the human condition: Trans people know trauma. We know pain. We know survival. We know connection, care, loss, and betrayal. We know joy.

I have supported trans individuals in courtrooms where the presiding legal officials refused to recognize their chosen names and pronouns—their basic humanity. I have sat with countless trans therapy clients as they wept, broken-hearted over a world that didn't seem to want them, and expressed self-harmful or suicidal intent. I've worked through endless trans community conflicts over intimate partner violence, assault, and abuse. I've tried to look up old sex worker friends from adolescence only to find them gone from this world, murdered in their own homes.

And I have also watched trans friends dance with gorgeous abandon, voguing like legends from a mythical world. I've seen my communities rally around trans siblings in crisis, struggling with psychosis or chronic illness. I've been transported and transformed by trans art, theater, literature, and innovation. I've been humbled and inspired by the scope of trans scholarship, community organizing, and institution-building. No one knows how to survive like trans people. No one knows how to thrive like trans people.

***

Trans Bodies, Trans Selves is a vast wealth of scientific, cultural, and historic knowledge. The material here spans a dizzying array of medical facts, lived experiences, and opinions. Yet each one is, in its way, a testimony to the strength and beauty of who we are—our refusal to disappear and our commitment to life.

If you are reading this book as an ally, I urge you to acknowledge our resilience and self-determination, that you might work with us as partners rather than would-be saviors. And if you are reading it as a trans or gender-questioning person, then I remind you of the legacy of dreamers, fighters, creators, and change-makers that stands behind us. No matter where you come from, or what you believe about being trans, no matter what challenges you face, know that you are a vital part of something bigger.

The second edition of *Trans Bodies, Trans Selves* is a book that will come out into a tempestuous world, full of uncertainty and change. But then, trans people have been coming out into just such a world for as long as I can remember. And if there is anything I have learned from trans community, it is that change comes with the potential for growth as well as loss. In the midst of the crisis, we discover who we are—our courage, our will to live, the hope that gives birth to whole new ways of living and being with one another.

I write this to the future of trans community: You hold a map to transformation in your hands. It is a map of where we have been, and where we might go. It is a map to remaking yourself, yes, but also remaking our world. And together, I do believe that we might make a world where all of us—everyone—can finally belong.

ACKNOWLEDGMENTS
Laura Erickson-Schroth

It has been incredibly exciting for me to take part in the creation of a second edition of *Trans Bodies, Trans Selves (TBTS)*. When I started working on the first edition, I had no idea it would reach so many people, and certainly couldn't have imagined there would be a second. The process of this new edition has been wildly different from that of the first.

I began brainstorming for the first edition of *TBTS* in 2009. At the time, the *Diagnostic and Statistical Manual of Mental Disorders (DSM)* still considered trans people to have "gender identity disorder." *Orange is the New Black* and *Transparent*, both now off the air, wouldn't premiere for another few years. I had never heard the term "nonbinary" used to describe anyone. Hashtags had just been invented and Instagram didn't yet exist. In order to find collaborators for *TBTS*, I attended conferences, asking people who were good speakers to contribute, and reached out to authors of books I read. Somehow, hundreds of amazing writers, editors, artists, and photographers answered the call.

The creation of this second edition has been leaps and bounds more organized. Before a single word was written, we had a full editing team in place. We had an idea of the scope of the project and a template to work from. While this, in some ways, made the creation of the second edition easier, it also made it immensely harder. There were higher expectations now. We could no longer say that we left things out simply because it was a first attempt. At the same time, the amount of potential material now seemed endless. There were thousands of new organizations, websites, social media accounts, books, and articles. And we couldn't possibly include all of them. So we did our absolute best.

I have learned so much—and such different things—from the creation of the first and second editions of *TBTS*. And I am extremely grateful to everyone who gave of their time and energy to make these projects happen. This list is very long and includes all of the contributors to both editions, all of the donors to our first edition fundraising campaign, the second edition Editing Team, our editor at Oxford (Dana Bliss), and all of the former and current board members of the nonprofit, Trans Bodies, Trans Selves.

There were four original board members of TBTS—me, Amanda Rosenblum, Jonah A. Siegel, and A. Robin Williams. Amanda organized forums across the United States and Canada to gather information on what community members thought was important to include in a book like this. She also wrote to law firms and asked them to take us on pro-bono so that we could become a nonprofit, and found support at Cleary, Gottlieb, Steen, and Hamilton. Establishing TBTS as a nonprofit meant that we could channel the funds from book sales to start our now-robust book donation program that has partnerships with organizations like LGBT Books to Prisoners.

Current board members of TBTS include myself, Ikaika Gleisberg, Kevin Johnson, Stephanie Luz-Hernandez, and Kelsey Pacha. Past board members have included delfin bautista, Tamar Carmel, Sand C. Chang, Skyler Cruz, Cecilia Gentili, Zil Goldstein, Laura Jacobs, Scott Loren Moore, Nick Mwaluko, Naim Rasul, Dena Simmons, and Jessica Lina Stirba.

For this second edition of *TBTS*, I would be remiss not to thank the LGBT Community Center National History Archive for providing us with some key historical photos that would have been nearly impossible to find otherwise. I would also like to send my sincere appreciation to donors Kate Poole, Margot Seigle, Naomi Sobel & Becky Silverstein, and Sam Vinal for their support, which allowed TBTS to pay chapter authors for their time and effort.

In addition to the camaraderie of the many, many folks involved in TBTS, there are two things that have gotten me through this second edition process. The first is my partner, Abby, who makes life an incredible joy to live. The second is the knowledge that this book has made an impact on thousands of people across the world. Every year the TBTS team tables at the Philly Trans Wellness Conference, and every year we hear from transgender and gender expansive (T/GE) people, parents, partners, friends, and service providers that this book changed their lives. That is why we do what we do.

HOW TO READ THIS BOOK

We don't expect you to read this book in one sitting or from beginning to end. Instead, we invite you to start with your favorite chapter or flip through to a page that piques your interest. If you're looking for a basic primer, we suggest that you start with Chapter 1, "Our Selves," which provides an overview of important terminology and concepts.

The main text of this book is made up of 23 chapters, each written by different authors. They all have their own styles, but we have tried to keep the text accessible by avoiding the use of technical terms or jargon, as well as defining terms and phrases that may not be as familiar to everyone. Many of these terms appear in the book's Glossary.

Quotes from the Trans Bodies, Trans Selves survey are in italics. We've interspersed them throughout the book to bring in as many voices as possible.

Short pieces by over 150 contributors add personal experiences and opinions to each chapter, and artwork demonstrates the creative side of our communities.

Sidebars with extra information appear in page margins, adding details about resources such as books, TV and film, support groups, and nonprofit organizations, as well as defining terms.

Each chapter contains endnotes that include research articles, essays, books, and other materials that provide more detailed information and can be used for further reading. An index in the back of the book may help you to find specific information you are looking for.

We've standardized language as much as possible, using the phrase transgender and gender expansive (T/GE) throughout. We chose this phrase to include as many people as we could who identify as part of transgender, nonbinary, and gender nonconforming communities. We understand this language may not encompass the broad range of terms readers identify with, and expect that this nomenclature will continue to evolve in the coming years.

We write from the point of view of "we" to invite you to be in community with us. When we describe individuals whose genders we do not know, we use "they/them."

We have made some deliberate choices about language in this book. For example, due to histories of colonization, we have chosen to capitalize Black and Brown, but not white. Language is ever-evolving, and the choices we have made now are not necessarily those we would make five or ten years from now. They are made with good intentions, however, and with the hope that as many of our readers as possible will see themselves reflected in these pages.

INTRODUCTION

It has been seven years since the publication of the first edition of *Trans Bodies, Trans Selves*. Between 2014 and 2021, there have been massive changes in the visibility and politics of transgender and gender expansive (T/GE) communities.

As we write this introduction, our communities are being profoundly impacted by the global COVID-19 pandemic. This crisis has amplified the effects of systemic racism, sexism, xenophobia, transphobia, and poverty that already existed, heightening our fear and concern for our lives and livelihoods. Some of us have been met with state violence as we protest in the streets; others have experienced increased interpersonal violence in our homes or while incarcerated. Many of us continue to struggle to pay for housing and other basic necessities, while others grapple with anxiety, depression, addiction, and other mental health issues. Yet, we have also been struck by the increase in community visibility online and the expanding mental health supports and resources. As we move into an uncertain future, T/GE communities are coming together to provide support, care, and mutual aid to one another.

The landscape of understanding and self-description by T/GE communities has evolved, ever in conversation with our culture and social systems. The National Center for Transgender Equality (NCTE) U.S. Trans Survey (USTS) was released in 2015, with data from over 28,000 respondents. This marks the largest quantitative sample ever of transgender people in America, increasing almost fivefold from NCTE's National Transgender Discrimination Survey (NTDS) in 2012 (6,745 respondents). Thirty percent of USTS respondents identified as nonbinary, while "nonbinary" was not yet popular enough to even be included as an option in the NTDS. Compassionate media representation of T/GE children and their families has increased. Gender exploration is portrayed as the norm, rather than the exception, for younger generations, in shows like "I Am Jazz" and MTV's "Are You the One: Come One, Come All." Figures such as Janet Mock, Laverne Cox, and many others have propelled T/GE identities into mainstream media, sharing stories beyond simply gender transitions. We have experienced a growing social consciousness around intersectionality, the many issues that impact our communities' access to resources, and intracommunity discussions about language, politics, and approaches to liberation.

We have also experienced a resurgence of anti-trans, racist, homophobic, xenophobic, classist, and ableist politics. We write to you during a time when trans and gender expansive first-person perspectives have proliferated, but in an intensely trans-negative context. The completion of this project is a testament both to the resilience of each individual contributor and to the energy of our communal resistance, hopeful for a better world for T/GE people in the fullness of all our identities. The participants who made this project possible collaborated on chapters, created art, shared poetry, coded vast amounts of data, and edited tens of thousands of words, often within the context of demoralizing loss or threat of loss. On behalf of the Editing Team and Board, we are proud and grateful for contributors' immense commitment to our communities during a time of such threat to our personal and collective safety.

The Trans Bodies, Trans Selves Board and Editing Team present the second edition of this volume as a living document, one that attempts to represent as many diverse voices of T/GE people as possible. *Trans Bodies, Trans Selves* is an aspirational and evolving document, and we expect it to change, perhaps radically, with each iteration. We have chosen to use the pronouns "we/us" throughout the book to underscore that this is a text by and for T/GE communities; however, we do not purport to represent all T/GE people in this volume. It is vital to name that not every person's voice is represented, as there is no one universal T/GE experience. In several chapters, contributors actively disagree, and their disparate viewpoints can be seen as a representation of the many dynamic conversations and perspectives within our communities.

Jennifer Finney Boylan wrote the Foreword (titled Introduction) to the first edition of *Trans Bodies, Trans Selves*. In this second edition, we have invited Boylan to write the

Afterword, putting into perspective the years that have passed, and we asked a new author, Kai Cheng Thom, to bring her voice to the Foreword. We are considering this a new tradition that will invite a sense of continuity and perspective across editions.

In the first edition, we wanted to give voice to our communities' experiences and provide much-needed information to providers, caregivers, families, and friends. In the second edition, we continue to empower people to share their expertise and personal experiences and share this with our providers and loved ones. Our first edition survey had 3,500 respondents—the largest qualitative sample (that we know of) ever collected from trans and gender expansive people. For the second edition, we collected data from over 2,400 respondents, and went through the process to have the survey approved for academic publishing. We have made a commitment to empowering trans scholarship, and are making this data available exclusively to T/GE people for research and academic publishing. So often, non-trans people create, comment on, and contextualize our experiences without being part of our communities. It is important to us that we can describe and analyze systemic patterns in our own lives as we articulate our needs and observations.

Unlike many resource compendiums, the publishing of *Trans Bodies, Trans Selves* is coordinated by a nonprofit organization (also called Trans Bodies, Trans Selves!) The TBTS nonprofit is managed by a tireless team of volunteers who serve three-year terms. The board recruits all contributors for the book, manages the survey, and performs educational and outreach activities at conferences around the country. Royalties from the book go directly to the nonprofit, supporting our book donation program and outreach work. For the second edition, we have engaged in fundraising efforts in order to compensate chapter authors for their time, experience, and labor. We feel it is in line with our values to pay trans community members for their work, and wish that we had the funds to do so for everyone who contributed in any way.

The second edition of *Trans Bodies* is meant to provide a comprehensive look at issues that affect trans and gender expansive people, from medical care to legal support to social transition, and much more. We endeavored to lift up new voices and to acknowledge how power and privilege affect our access to self-determination and self-description. This text is meant as a primer, with sidebars in each chapter that point to resources and ideas for further research.

An effort was made to select short pieces, quotes, and art that represent the diversity of trans communities. We have inevitably failed at this goal. Most of the authors live in the United States or Canada. Many are middle or upper class, and many are white. There are stories that are not told here—voices that are not heard. If one of these voices is yours, please consider sending your suggestions for the next edition of this book to info@transbodies.com.

As you read through various chapters and stories, we hope that you find parts of yourself reflected. We hope that you take in knowledge that can help you and others to live more comfortably and fully in this world. We hope that the words and images here invite self-reflection and exploration of the questions that matter most to you. We feel honored to accompany you on your path, regardless of where you are. As trans people, we have always been here, and we will continue to persist.

–The TBTS Editing Team
Tamar Carmel
Sand C. Chang
Alan Dunnigan
Laura Erickson-Schroth
Ikaika Gleisberg
Sha Grogan-Brown
Kevin Johnson
Kelsey Pacha
Anneliese Singh

SECTION 1
WHO WE ARE

OUR SELVES

Mira C. Jourdan and Harper B. Keenan

1

INTRODUCTION

(Mira and Harper)

What does it mean to be trans? A common understanding of transgender, or trans for short, is that a person's gender differs from the sex they were assigned at birth. However, many see the idea of being trans as more complicated—as an active process of challenging the formal structures that govern how gender is defined. For different people, and in different times, places, and contexts, gender itself can be a broad entity or a very narrow one, and in various ways, understandings of "trans" can seem too expansive or too restrictive.

Trans can be a creation story or the culmination of a story. It can be a history, a means of survival, a way of being, or a personal or political identity. It may be a response to an already-existing conversation about gender, or a wholly new dialogue about gender. Trans can create an experience of bonding and connection, or a difference that sets one apart. In other words, "trans" has no singular meaning, which itself highlights and expands our understanding of the incredible complexity of gender.

> *Depending on the context, I describe myself as a woman or a trans woman. The term MTF is convenient shorthand, and I sometimes use it when discussing trans issues with other trans people, but I was never male, so the literal translation does not apply.*[*]

We know what being trans is, for ourselves, because we have lived it. We can speak to our individual experiences and to our personal analyses of the systems that impact our lives and people in our communities, but when it comes to saying anything worth saying about our *collective* selves, we may struggle. Is there such a thing as a collective trans consciousness?

This chapter's authors, Mira and Harper, have marked the sections where each was a primary author. The two come from different backgrounds, and they describe the process of working together as generative, particularly in moments of disagreement. See their bios in the Contributors section of the book.

---

[*] Quotes in this book, unless otherwise noted, come from the Trans Bodies, Trans Selves online survey.

Julian Harris. (Zackary Drucker)

It would be impossible to try to speak to the infinite ways that trans people exist in the world. There is no way to do that well. We all have our own vantage points and biases. Dialogues within trans communities have the opportunity, however, to demonstrate our vast complexity.

Transgender, or trans, is a complex concept, but it is often used as an umbrella term to describe people whose gender identity differs from their sex assigned at birth.

I like the term genderqueer because it implies engagement in the process of queering gender. While some people with nonbinary gender identities do not consider themselves trans, I strongly resonate with the concept of having changed my gendered interactions with the world through coming out as a gender other than my assigned one.

Dialogue in trans communities is born from generations of conversations among people whose ways of being have challenged dominant conceptions of the meaning of gender. Obviously, there have been more contributions to that dialogue than are possible to record here. Important threads within the conversation in the context of the United States have included questions such as "Is transness inherently politically transgressive?" and "Is being trans a psychological or medical condition?" Within just these two threads, there are countless opinions and experiences.

Historically, those who identified as transsexual were binary trans individuals who were interested in surgical interventions, while those who identified as transgender were less likely to be binary or to desire these interventions. This distinction has diminished, however, and many people who would have previously considered themselves transsexual now use the word transgender.

When I transitioned, my counselor thought I was well-prepared. So did my physician. When I started living full-time, my learning curve became a shuttle launch—vertical!! I was fortunate in that I had a number of colleagues who took me under their wing like a younger sister and helped me along. What I found is that learning about privilege, politics, and then being homeless tempered me in ways I never could have imagined! I found a voice I never had. I found a strength I never had. I found a backbone I never had. Maybe even a level of courage I never had before. I would not wish this journey on my worst enemy! At the same time, I wouldn't trade it for anything!

Self Portrait. (Noah Jenkins)

"I WILL LOVE MYSELF. UNAPOLOGETICALLY."
– Noah Jenkins

People who don't fit into dominant conceptions of gender have probably always existed, but there is a lot we will never know because of the confines of how and by whom the past has been recorded. The terms used to describe what gender means have, like all language, changed over time. In a U.S. context, much of our vocabulary related to trans identity has historically been produced by non-trans doctors and psychologists—people like Magnus Hirschfeld and Harry Benjamin.[1]

The term transsexual is still widely used in languages other than English and can vary in meaning, sometimes signifying something similar to the term transgender in English and sometimes indicating a more binary identity and desire for surgery.

BECOMING A TRANS BODYBUILDER IN INDIA

Aryan Pasha (he/him) is a transman, lawyer, and bodybuilder from Delhi, India. In 2018, he was the first transman in India to become a bodybuilding champion.

TBTS: How Do You Identify? When and Where Did You Come Out and Begin Your Transition?

AP: I identify as a transman. I was born in Delhi, India to a Muslim family, and fortunately, they never stopped me or harassed me because of my gender. I was six years old when I refused to wear a girl's uniform in school. My father knew that I meant it—because I was a very stubborn and pampered child as I am the first-born. Everyone in my family agreed. They changed my school, and from day one, I started going to school in a boy's uniform. No one knew that I was born female except a few of my teachers who were very supportive. I started my medical transition in 2010 at the age of 18 with the help of my mother who stood by my side, and she convinced my dad to help me to start my SRS procedure the following year.

I officially came out to my friends on my 25th birthday. I invited around 30 people, and I told them who I am and what I've gone through during my transition and while growing up. They all became very emotional—a few of them even started crying! The good thing is I lost no one's friendship after coming out.

TBTS: What Community Did You Find in India? What Was Your Relationship Like with the Trans Community There?

AP: In my area, I was one of the youngest transmen to start transitioning, so I was very young when I met other trans activists. It led to a lot of attention—some positive and some negative. Here in India, the trans rights moment is led by transwomen. In the beginning, it was a little bit difficult to adjust to this. Some of them tried to pull my leg and make fun of me (being so young), but after some years they became solid supports, who always stood by me and the other transmen of India. I got so much love from my community. In April 2019, I got engaged to one of the most famous trans rights activists in India, Laxmi Narayan Tripathi. So for me, the trans community here has become my second, chosen family.

TBTS: Why Bodybuilding? What Challenges Do You Encounter as a Transman while Preparing for Bodybuilding Competitions?

AP: I was always into sports like speed skating, cricket, and basketball. Later on, I left sports entirely to pursue a law degree, but something was missing in my life. I realized that I needed physical activity for my mental health, so I joined a gym. Bodybuilding slowly became a hobby and then became a passion.

At first, I had a difficult time building muscle because my body doesn't produce testosterone naturally. Sometimes, I got demotivated and depressed because I did not have as many gains compared to my brothers and friends, but I persisted and got better. I asked my trainer about participating in a competition, and he told me I wasn't ready yet at least twice. Finally, I stopped listening to him and started preparing for my first competition. I initially prepared for Trans FitCon, an all-trans competition in the United States, but I couldn't get a visa, so I looked into competitions in India with cis men.

At that time, winning was not on my mind; I just wanted to participate and tell the world that I'm trans and that I can give tough competition. I wanted to prove to everyone that I am muscular enough to compete with the other men. Initially, I was afraid people might disqualify me or protest if they found out. I wrote to different bodybuilding federations, informing them that I'm trans and on hormones, but the dosage is equivalent to the normal testosterone level of a cis man. I participated in Musclemania India in December 2018 and I got second place. After that I participated in International Bodybuilding & Fitness Federation, India in March 2019 and secured third place in men's physique.

TBTS: What Would You Like Everyone to Understand about Trans Bodies?

AP: Transgender people are no different from cisgender people. We are also human beings. Our brain works like any other human being. I feel blessed to be born transgender because I am lucky to have experienced two genders in one life.

MTF and FTM are sometimes used to mean "male to female" or "female to male." Some trans people utilize these terms, but others feel they are inaccurate or offensive.

Nonbinary and genderqueer are terms some people use who see themselves as outside of binary male and female genders.

The acronyms AMAB (assigned male at birth) and AFAB (assigned female at birth) can be useful shorthands.

There was a shift toward self-definition in trans communities in the early 1990s, when the word "transgender," originally coined by Virginia Prince in the 1970s, came into widespread use in public discourse. Although difficult to trace precisely, the use of this term was initiated in part by U.S.-based trans activists and public intellectuals like Holly Boswell and Leslie Feinberg.[2] At the time, the word transgender was intended not only as an umbrella term to describe those whose genders do not easily fit within a binary system, but also as a political statement—a push toward a world with less formalized, less systematic gender regulation. Feinberg specifically argued that the binary regulation of gender was a product of colonialism and capitalism.[3] Importantly, although Feinberg was a staunch anti-capitalist, to claim the term transgender for oneself today does not necessarily suggest any specific political stance. There are trans people all along the political spectrum.

Some trans people see a direct link between their gender identity and their politics. Others see their trans identity largely in isolation from other identities or affiliations. They may even maintain active membership in and engagement with organizations or groups that are antagonistic toward transness. Like most communities, every individual trans person decides for themselves where they fit on this spectrum and what is right for them.

Sometimes it's what's not said—binary as default. Your identity just isn't even on the radar. Sometimes it's well-meaning, fumbling inclusivity. Like this white dude reads a Medium article and thinks he knows all about you. Sometimes it's subtle aggression, often masking fear—teasing at your expense, being casually dismissed or singled out, getting left out of opportunities; you're treated differently and you don't know why (you know why but you can never prove it). The whole skewed fabric of the universe. I hear microaggressions about gender and class every day. Race and sexuality less frequently (because people are more careful about speech). But the same shitty assumptions are there. It's banal dehumanization, paper cut by paper cut. You're never quite at the center of things.

Support the T. Monte, Liam, Andromeda, and Shayne. (Brayden Asher Misiolek | roguestud.io)

Trans people are diverse, and we will never resolve the contradictions between our many views. We can all agree, however, on certain things. Trans people are real. There are many, many ways that people conceive of their own genders. This expansiveness can be creative, and it can also be a source of frustration. Trans people should not be forced to earn recognition of who they are, nor be forced to perform a narrowly prescribed gender role to be able to stay alive, to be safe, or to access community integration, legal recognition, or medical services they need. Although we are all very different, there is strength in common advocacy.

A trans man/guy is someone who was assigned female at birth and identifies as male, while a trans woman/girl is someone who was assigned male at birth and identifies as female.

SUNSHINE

Aliya Rae (no pronouns) is a Queer Psychic residing in so-called Colorado. Queer Magic is real. I love you. I need you.

because I'm not androgynous
I am still she
because I am scared
I won't show all of me
I still get mad at ma'am
because it's not who I am
although my long hair and filled out figure
have me made to be

because I'm not getting surgery
or doing HRT
because I'm not in transition
that is clear to see
but I will always change and grow
and only my safe people will know
for I can't truly show
Me

I am queer
the loosest term I could find
I am pansexual and nonbinary
and it's not all in my mind
I am valid
I am real
this is a lot to reveal
but this is my truth
so please be kind
I'm not "hey lady," "go girl,"
and I am not "yas queen"
I am a human being
who needs to be seen
I don't use she or her
even though I am "femme"
yes I am sure
I'm not they or them
And I'm not some foolish confused teen

please be a friend
I'm not falling into trend
If you don't accept that
then this is our end
I will always honor
and stay true to myself
this isn't a chapter
in a book on a shelf
I hope this is easy
for you to comprehend

My pronouns are my name
I have no shame
I use Aliya & Aliya's, this isn't some game
This helps me feel free
I hope you can see
This really is how I be me

CELEBRATING OUR COMPLEXITY

A Name to Call Ourselves: Language as a Site of Creativity and Constraint

(Harper)

> *I generally use the term trans or trans man when describing myself. It is easier for other people to understand. If I am really being honest with myself, I am more genderqueer than anything, but queer is so ambiguous that a lot of people who don't use that word are uncomfortable with it. It's easier to put myself in a box. I get more respect that way.*

One of the many beautiful things about trans communities is that hardly anyone agrees on exactly what it means to be trans. Yet, we seem to continue to find ways of connecting with one another, creating community, and making kin without building strictly enforced borders around ourselves. In doing so, we demonstrate that it is indeed possible

Transgender Lives: Your Stories is an interactive campaign created by *The New York Times* to allow transgender people to tell their own stories in their own words.

Caprice, 55, Chicago, IL, 2015. (Jess T. Dugan). From "To Survive on This Shore: Photographs and Interviews with Transgender and Gender Nonconforming Older Adults," a project by Jess T. Dugan and Vanessa Fabbre.

to find some sense of mutuality without formally policing the bounds of what makes us who we are.

I have many trans daughters. They fill me with joy.

For those of us who do not fit neatly into institutionally prescribed categories of gender, language is both a site of creativity and constraint. At a basic level, we may need language in order to become legible to others (and, perhaps, even to ourselves). For generations, language has been one among many sites of creativity within trans communities. Over the last several decades, we have seen a continued proliferation of new words coined as trans and queer communities reach toward the difficult task of articulating ourselves.

Some of these newer words include nonbinary (identifying outside the gender binary), bigender (moving between two genders), and demiboy/demigirl (partially male or partially female). These words add to a long list of words in dozens of languages that groups all over the world have used to describe gender between and beyond male and female since time immemorial, including *bakla* (Tagalog), *muxe* (Zapotec), and *we'wha* (Zuni). This new language allows for new modes of self-expression and communication, but also raises questions about maintaining connections to history and lineage. For each new word, we wonder: Where did this word come from? What does it offer? Will this word allow for new forms of freedom, or erase the struggles and traditions of the past? These kinds of questions are germane to linguistic change.

Many people within and outside of trans communities describe their genders in ways that are unique and personal to them. And, of course, the language of transness is not solely found in words, but in other creative modalities such as movement, art, and style. Working to learn from this multiplicity of expression can be a generative and joyful process.

I am a trans-masculine nonbinary person, but I also use the word "tumtum" to explain my gender. I am a Jewish person and tumtum is a classical Jewish gender found in the Talmud meaning "hidden."

Gender identity signifies a person's internal sense of their gender, while gender expression is how we express ourselves to the outside world and gender roles are the gendered expectations placed on us by the societies in which we live.

Those who identify as cross-dressers typically identify with their gender assigned at birth and enjoy dressing as another gender either alone or with partners or friends.

Drag queens and drag kings perform gendered acts on stage. Their gender identities off-stage fall across the gender spectrum and do not necessarily line up with their stage genders.

THE MAN THAT I AM

Julian Paquette (he/him) is a poet and a queer trans man. He is also an advocate for LGBTQ-2SAI + people and works through Ambit Gender Diversity Consulting Company in Victoria, British Columbia (Canada).

A man who likes to listen to the rain on dark nights. Candlelight. A guy who soaks his beans before cooking them and also eats sprouts. And meat. I do like. Even though death saddens me, it tastes so good in my mouth. A man who sometimes cries. Gets mad. Drives a truck. Bikes. Likes beer. Nachos. Kissing. Laughter. And kids. I like kids and think they're cute. A guy who uses the word *cute*. Who hasn't learned how to fix cars or pipes. Who is strong and becoming stronger. One of those decent guys. A poet type.

Many communities around the world have a "third gender" or "third sex." Some third genders include the *Kathoey* of Thailand, *Fa'afafine* of Samoa, and *Hijras* of India/Pakistan.

Every year, the Trans 100 recognizes one hundred trans people doing service for trans communities.

Trans/Portraits: Voices from Transgender Communities, edited by Jackson Wright Shultz (Dartmouth College Press, 2015), shares the stories of over 30 trans people from various backgrounds.

In wider societies where the meaning of gender is defined by legal and medical systems, creative generativity is frequently constrained. As trans people seek access to basic resources—things such as medical care, public benefits, or legal identification—we often find that our ways of talking about ourselves do not translate to these contexts.[4,5] In situations like these, when we are unable to define and describe ourselves on our own terms, we are often forced to work with the language of the system as a matter of practical necessity. Gendered checkboxes on paperwork and gendered facilities in public spaces become sites where human complexity is erased and confined. The gendered nature of public systems can be a source of frustration and a regularly exhausting nuisance to many trans people, but it is also sometimes life-threatening. In situations such as medical emergencies or police interactions, in which the fragility of human life can quickly come into stark relief, trans people too often find ourselves in danger when our trans status is disclosed or discovered.

I identify as bakla—I'm Filipino, it's the one word I know that closely correlates to my gender identity. In western terms, I suppose I fit somewhere between nonbinary and genderfluid.

In the United States, many trans people have resisted the institutional categorization of our bodies, arguably for as long as systematic categorization has taken place. At the same time, trans people have also fought for inclusion within administrative systems that define and regulate gender, both out of material necessity and out of a desire for recognition. Within trans communities, questions of inclusion are often fraught. Who exactly gets to be included, and how? Does inclusion depend on some form of exclusion? What are the costs and benefits of inclusion, both short- and long-term? Why do we want to be included anyway? Is inclusion politically useful? Do we want to be included in the system as it is, or work to change the way society is organized altogether? Is there anything in between?

1. androgynous	27. gender bender	52. monogender	77. stone butch
2. bent	28. gender defender	53. multigender	78. stone femme
3. berdache	29. gender gifted	54. neither	79. stud
4. bigender	30. gender outlaw	55. neutrois	80. switch third
5. biogirl	31. transcender	56. new man	81. tomboy
6. boi	32. gender variant	57. new woman	82. tomgirl
7. both	33. genderbent	58. no-op	83. trans
8. boydyke	34. genderf**k	59. none of the above	84. transexual
9. brother	35. genderqueer	60. none of your business	85. transfag
10. bull dyke	36. goy	61. nongender	86. transfeminine
11. butch	37. grrl	62. omnigender	87. transgender
12. cross-dresser	38. gynandroid	63. other	88. transgenderist
13. drag king	39. human	64. othergendered	89. transgirl
14. effeminate	40. intergender	65. pangender	90. transman
15. either	41. intersex	66. prettyboy	91. transmasculine
16. epicene	42. MTF (male to female)	67. queen	92. transperson
17. FTM (female to male)	43. MTFTM	68. queer	93. transsensual
18. faerie	44. male	69. questioning	94. transsexual
19. fairy	45. male-assigned	70. self-defined	95. transwoman
20. female	46. male-bodied	71. shaman	96. two-spirit
21. femaleassigned	47. man	72. shapeshifter	97. undecided
22. female-bodied	48. me	73. sir	98. undeclared
23. femme	49. merm	74. sissy	99. undefined
24. fluid	50. metamorph	75. soft butch	100. unspecified
25. fourth gender	51. mixedgendered	76. static gendered	101. womyn
26. freak			

Two Spirit is newer, but a feeling that's always been present for me. It's entirely linked to my Indigenous identity, and encompasses attraction, gender, & how I love in my experience. Queer and whatever-the-hell-it-is are what I use when talking about it in a more understandable sense for western concepts. My being is fluid, but always some balance of feminine and masculine deep in my soul.

Two Spirit is an umbrella term used by some indigenous people from North America to describe themselves as well as their ancestors who embodied both masculine and feminine spirits and characteristics.

VISIBILITY

(Harper)

The past decade has seen a rapid increase in trans visibility. Trans people are increasingly featured in popular mass media, from Laverne Cox's role on Netflix's *Orange is the New Black* to FX's series *Pose*, a depiction of New York City's drag ball scene in the 1980s, featuring multiple trans people of color as main characters. These two specific examples also represent important initial shifts away from the common portrayal of trans experience primarily through the bodies of white actors who do not publicly identify as trans. These depictions have begun to move trans characters from peripheral roles to center stage, and from presenting trans people through tropes of victimhood to complex portrayals of trans humanity.

As the nature of global media changes, new avenues for visibility have emerged. More and more, trans people can broadcast their voices to a wide audience without mediation or

GLAAD's Transgender Media Program is a resource for trans media advocacy.

Jamison Green. (Zackary Drucker)

approval. Although this presents challenges and raises new questions, the Internet and social media have also afforded trans people from a variety of walks of life a less-filtered public voice. Forums such as podcasts, YouTube, Instagram, and Twitter provide a platform for a new kind of celebrity, including trans and gender nonconforming people around the world who produce media for a range of purposes such as musical entertainment, performance art, gaming tips, fashion advice, and social commentary. These forms of media may be especially impactful in facilitating trans learning and community-making for those trans people who tend to be most isolated, including youth and people who live in rural areas.

Do you lead trans trainings? You may want to check out *The Teaching Transgender Toolkit: A Facilitator's Guide to Increasing Knowledge, Decreasing Prejudice & Building Skills* (by Eli R. Green & Luca Maurer, published by Out for Health & Planned Parenthood of the Southern Finger Lakes).

Trans people and trans lives have recently been at the center of many political movements. Some of this participation has taken place in grassroots organizing. The Black Lives Matter Global Network, first formed in 2013, holds the affirmation of trans people and a commitment to dismantling trans-antagonism among its guiding principles. The Transgender, Gender Variant, and Intersex Justice Project (TGIJP) in San Francisco and the Sylvia Rivera Law Project in New York are trans-led organizations that prioritize the support of incarcerated trans people as work integral to broader social change. There are many other U.S.-based, trans-led organizations working toward trans justice, including the TransLatina Network, Brown Boi Project, El/La Para Trans Latinas, the Transgender Law Center, and the National Center for Transgender Equality, to name just a few. Over the last several years, out trans people have won election to governmental offices across the United States. In 2017, Phillippe Cunningham and Andrea Jenkins, who now both sit on the Minneapolis City Council, made history by becoming the first openly transgender Black people to hold public office. The same year, Danica Roem, an out white trans woman, joined the Virginia state House of Delegates.

Cisgender, or cis, is typically used to describe those whose gender identities match the genders they were assigned at birth.

Trans people exist in all walks of life. Some of us are professors, prisoners, doctors, teachers, lawyers, refugees, actors, artists, athletes, and activists. Some of us are unemployed. Some of us are homeless. Some of us are without adequate medical care. Many of us are parents, caregivers, elders, siblings, partners, and children. Although trans visibility is on the rise as trans people are increasingly featured in media, trans people also remain invisible in many ways. Will the public's interest and care for trans people extend beyond the rhetorical level and lead to material change? In other words, will those who celebrate trans art and media commit to ensuring that all trans people have homes, food, jobs, and quality medical care?

Who We Are

"What if I'm Wearing 200 Vests??" Tikva Wolf is a freelance author and illustrator focusing on the topics of healthy communication and relationship dynamics, as well as polyamorous, queer, and gender issues. Wolf's work is used as an aid by therapists and educators, has been translated to several different languages, and is a part of the Kinsey Institute's archive collection. (TikvaWolf.com)

BEYOND THE BINARY

(Harper)

As a nonbinary person I feel like more of a debate topic than a person.

For some people, trans or not, the idea of a gender binary is confining. And, for some people, trans or not, the gender binary is an important part of how they understand themselves, and how they want to be seen. There are wonderful arrays of words developed all over the world that describe gender outside of "male" and "female." Although language to describe gender has broadened in recent years, the meaning of "transgender" has itself also become increasingly institutionalized and regulated. For example, in developing plans for how to support trans students, schools may allow individual students to select a different gendered bathroom than the one that aligns with their assigned birth sex, but typically do little to change how gender is regulated for all children.[6]

I am in school, and I am so grateful that all of my teachers ask for pronouns at the beginning of each semester. They don't always remember to use they/them pronouns for me, but their willingness and openness makes me feel more comfortable.

Perhaps the only simple truth about gender is that it is never simple. As "transgender" has become more commonly used, it is frequently understood to refer to an individual who has permanently transitioned from one discretely defined gender to another. Although that framing is certainly how some trans people understand and describe themselves, it is not representative of the full complex spectrum of trans experience as articulated by trans people.

It has been mostly positive, but confusing to find my place. Sometimes I worry that people don't see me as trans, don't see me as queer. Not discrimination, but

The gender binary is the concept that there are two and only two genders—male and female. The gender binary is built into our communities and systems of government.

Pronouns are the words we use to describe other people when we are not saying their names. Many trans people use gendered pronouns (he/him, she/her). Others prefer gender-neutral pronouns, including they/them.

Spanish, like other romance languages, is gendered. Spanish speakers have come up with a number of ways to get around this, including substituting the letters x or e for the feminine *a* or masculine *o* (e.g., Latina/o → Latinx, ellas/os → elles).

there have been unfortunate moments where my white queer friends/peers don't respect or minimize my Latinx identity.

In recent years, the term nonbinary has been increasingly taken up by individuals as a way of more explicitly articulating gender beyond the male/female binary. Some people who describe themselves as nonbinary also identify as trans and some don't. There may sometimes be tension between people who use different words to describe their genders, just as there are sometimes tensions across any set of differences within any community or relationship. On some level, this is simply a part of the human condition. The existence of nonbinary people does not preclude the existence of trans people who identify as men or women, and vice versa.

GENDER NEUTRAL PRONOUNS. (FORGE. WWW.FORGE-FORWARD.ORG)

Subjective	Objective	Possessive adjective	Possessive pronoun	Reflexive	Pronunciation
She	Her	Her	Hers	Herself	pronounced as it looks
He	Him	His	His	Himself	pronounced as it looks
Ze	Zim	Zir	Zirs	Zirself	pronounced as it looks
Sie/Zie	Hir	Hir	Hirs	Hirself	pronounced: zee, here, here, heres, hereself
Zie	Zir	Zir	Zirs	Zirself	pronounced: zee, zere, zere, zeres, zereself
Ey	Em	Eir	Eirs	Eirself	pronounced: A, M, ear, ears, earself
Per	Per	Pers	Pers	Persself	pronounced as it looks
They	Them	Their	Theirs	Themself	pronounced as it looks

Put simply, there is room for all of us. Tensions may emerge, however, especially in relation to public legibility and access to material resources. For example, in the United States, where legal and medical systems often serve as gatekeepers to transition, there are many people who desire surgeries to align their self-concept with their bodies, but who may not meet a surgeon's evaluative criteria for surgery because they do not identify strictly as a gender different from the one they were assigned at birth. Challenges such as these only further reveal our collective need to more carefully imagine the meaning of gender justice.

THRIVING AS RESISTANCE

keaton gaughan (he/they) is a queer, nonbinary transmasculine person currently residing in Portland, Oregon who is still trying to figure out his place in this world. keaton is at peace with this struggle and has decided to pursue a master's degree in gender and women's studies—a process through which they hope to gain some clarity as well as grow as a writer, a feminist, and a human being.

My nonbinary identity can be understood as a neither here nor thereness. "Nonbinary" is as much a political statement as it is a personal articulation of my gender. Nonbinary identities can exist anywhere within/beyond/in contrast to the gender spectrum.

So, why are we still trying to affix such identities with language? If labels require stasis, what happens if my gender is never going to be stagnant?

Descriptors that resonate with me are: nonbinary, transmasculine, queer. These words represent putting my body and my self on the line and resisting a singular identification whenever possible. My gender identity is an act of resistance, a refusal, and a promise to keep it queer for as long as I exist in this visibly altered, beautiful, hybrid body.

I'd like to problematize the idea of passing—especially for nonbinary people. A common misconception is that ALL trans people simply want to pass as the opposite [binary] gender that they were assigned at birth. This overgeneralization is a thinly veiled act of violence that effectively erases the existence of nonbinary genders and those that embody them.

Not All of Us Revel in the Instances in Which We Pass—Even If They Do Assure Our Safety

These days, because I pass as a masculine figure, it is no less difficult to be seen for who I am—a **nonbinary trans**masculine **person**—than it was when I was being read as female. For example, when strangers assume that I am a cisgender man (based on the gender my *clothed* body signifies), an entire 20 years of my life has just been erased, rendering me complicit in a partial yet persistent erasure of my most enduring self. Defaulting to ONLY he/him pronouns in reference to me is yet another way that my nonbinary identity and all of its complexities are erased in one single interaction.

Which begs the possibly unanswerable question of: *How does one translate context-specific/historically and geographically dependent meanings of certain queer experiences to an audience with no possible frame of reference? How does one put experiences into words when the words have yet to be created?*

At this point, I've come up with far more questions than I have answers. Despite the hardships that come alongside living out my authentic gender and all of its queer glory, I've recently been feeling much lighter, happier, and significantly more invested in my life than ever before. I've also come to understand that in order to survive, my gender must be something that is internally validated. People will always misperceive us—but you are valid, your gender is valid, and I see you.

TRANS PEOPLE AND SEXUALITY

(Mira)

A common Trans 101 talking point is that gender identity and sexuality are two different things. However, this approach, which attempts to strictly delineate these concepts, can also be limiting. Some people may experience gender and sexuality as two unrelated aspects of who they are, but others may view them as more interconnected.[7] For example, gay men and straight women (cis or trans) may both be attracted to men, but their experiences of their sexuality may not be quite the same. Within these groups there are also different cultural elements, practices, and beliefs.

Understanding trans people's relationships to sexuality is complicated if the conversation is framed around heterosexual cisgender identities. Trans people are often expected to choose from among labels created and used primarily by someone else. Sometimes, the existing terms fit, and using them is easy. However, when trans people do use these terms in their conventional ways, others sometimes react with confusion. For example, a trans woman may identify as straight (attracted to men) and have her identity rejected or invalidated by others, or taken to mean something different than she intends.

Sometimes, within our communities, we work to "queer" or broaden the language related to sexuality. This is an attempt to create words that we feel fit us better, and to include trans and nonbinary identities. We may use terms that help us to explain our sense of attraction or orientation outside of the traditional lens of the "same" or "opposite" gender.

> *I am both trans and gender-expansive. More precisely, I am a masculine-of-center trans woman dripping with feminine masculinity who rejects the antiquated notion that she has to be extremely femme in order to be accepted by a binary world.*

Trans sexuality is infinite in its variety. Studies show that diverse sexualities, outside of lesbian, gay, or straight, may be more common among trans people.[8] It may also be more common for trans people to identify with asexual or aromantic identities—identities that are understood poorly even within the broader LGBTQ community. Polyamory and kink practices are likely to also be more common among trans people.[9] One strength of much of the research in this area is that it is free form and qualitative, inviting participants to describe their experiences in their own words.

Gender identity is generally thought of as a person's understanding of their own gender, while sexuality is used to describe who they are attracted to.

There are numerous versions of the acronym LGBTQ, the most common of which expands to mean "lesbian, gay, bisexual, transgender, and queer or questioning."

Queer is a complicated term that was initially used in a derogatory manner but has been reclaimed. As an adjective, it can function as an umbrella term to describe nonheterosexual sexualities or to connote a political stance against compulsory heterosexuality. As a verb, it can signify turning things on their head by looking at them through a nonheterosexual lens.

Those who identify as pansexual often describe themselves as having the ability to be attracted to people of many different genders.

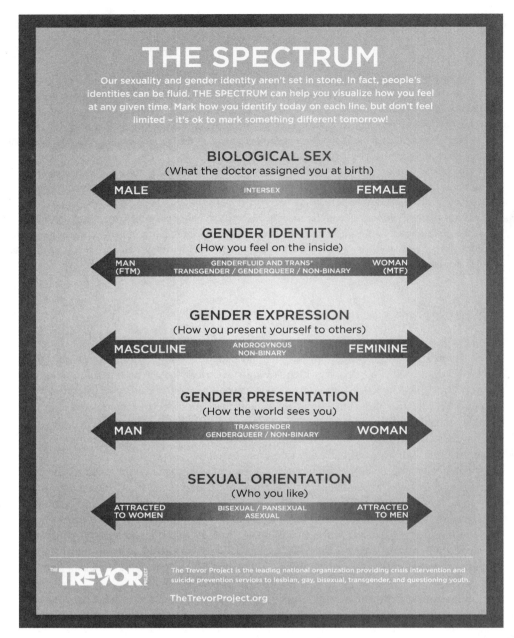

The Spectrum. (The Trevor Project)

TONGUE-TIED

Sav Zwickl (they/them) is a queer nonbinary researcher and community worker living in Melbourne, Australia. They have a Master of Sexology and are currently completing a PhD in Gender, Sexuality, and Diversity Studies, with a focus on capturing and conveying the diverse stories of nonbinary people living in Australia. Sav is also involved in research focused on transgender and gender-diverse health care and well-being, and providing peer support to LGBTIQA + young people. They also love spontaneous road-trips, Netflix binges, and true-crime podcasts.

I have been tongue-tied my entire life, choking on words that don't even exist. I keep asking myself: What is this? This thing that consumes me, that refuses to loosen its grip? I am failing without the words and flailing without steady ground.

Looking back on my life now, I realize I was always walking two parallel paths; I just thought it was one. While I was pouring all my energy into denying my queer sexuality, I didn't realize I was also vehemently denying my queer gender—because of a failure of words.

"Gay," though completely terrifying, was in my vocabulary. "Gender" wasn't on my radar at all. Gender, if I knew the word then, wasn't something up for debate or questioning; it was a given. And so, I grappled with my sexuality in the shadows of a deep, dark depression, all the while, ignoring the excruciation of puberty in a body that wasn't quite mine.

It took me nearly 10, incredibly lonely, years to come out by way of, "I am gay," scrawled in nervous cursive on a tear-stained Post-It Note. Those three words set me free in many ways. They gave me space to explore my queer sexuality and also dabble with my queer gender—though I didn't know it at the time. The lesbian stereotype gave me room to be and walk and talk in a different way, something outside the confines of heterosexual gender norms.

It took me close to another 10 years to realize that "gay" is not my word, not my place. I exist in lonely, uncharted space, where everything is disjointed, half-thoughts. My gender is so queer. I am not a woman, and I have never, for even a moment, been comfortably woman. Where am I, then? What am I, then?

I question my sanity every day, pushing myself for answers and validation. How do you know you are not a woman? I push myself further—but how? Really, truly, how? Or, for that matter, the only obvious alternative—how do you know you are not a man? Does that leave you on middle ground?

I have been tongue-tied my entire life, choking on words that don't even exist. It is just a feeling. I just know.

UNEQUAL RISK AND RESILIENCY FACTORS: DISPARITIES AMONG TRANS COMMUNITIES

(Mira)

Trans people may be perceived and treated differently based on other intersecting identities, such as race, class, legal status, ability, and other cultural markers. The experience of having one identity cannot be divorced or separated from the experience of embodying other identities. The serious risks that trans people face, including poverty and murder,[10,11] do not apply to all trans people equally. Having other marginalized identities, such as being a person of color, greatly increases these risks. Seventy to ninety percent of murders of trans people are of Black and Latina trans women[12] and sex workers make up 62% of the murders of trans people globally. Limited data regarding HIV infection in trans communities suggests the same pattern, with HIV mostly affecting poor, urban, Black and Latina trans women.[13]

> *I've had MANY close friends either come out as trans, or begin transition. It's been intense, as many have a large amount of obstacles to overcome. But it's also been amazing to see them become authentic into themselves. During my time in college, many of those I knew who transitioned have also killed themselves after complications (social, environmental, or otherwise). Many of those have been trans women—which I think should be addressed by those who are doing work in supporting trans communities.*

Intersectionality is a term first used by Kimberlé Crenshaw to point out "the problematic consequence of the tendency to treat race and gender as mutually exclusive."[14]

Protective factors such as privilege associated with a class identity and wealth also have a different impact depending on race, and have been entrenched by generations of accumulated impacts of processes such as racism. This is particularly true in the United States, where racial disparities in wealth are not only extreme but progressively worsening over time.[15] Thus, particularly in the United States, risk may be very strongly centered on specific groups of people, such as impoverished Black trans women who are engaged in survival sex work. Little effort is expended, however, on either supporting this population or on deterring those who inflict violence specifically on them.

> *I've been homeless, and also that stage of marginal housing where you're tenuously couch surfing, and also that stage of marginal housing where you are begrudgingly being let stay in a room for an always-about-to-end period of time. It's stressful, and painful, and traumatic, and harder now that I'm definitely no longer passing as cis, even though people don't know how to parse me exactly. Being visibly divergent from the normalized, no matter what form that takes for you, gives you less margin for error. People are less patient, less understanding, less helpful.*

Misgendering someone takes place when we refer to someone by the wrong pronouns or other gendered words. This can be done intentionally or unintentionally.

Less inclined to hire you, less inclined to care. You sort of have to decide if you want to cut yourself to ribbons or have the world do it. Only that isn't exactly it, right? Because even if I hid the transness, the world would still be cutting into me about it. It's worth the fight to me to be visibly nonbinary. I have sometimes barely survived, but if I'd have always hid, I don't think I would have made it this far.

TRANS IDENTITY IN THE POLITICAL SPHERE

(Mira)

The increased public visibility of trans and gender-diverse people in the past decade is remarkable. Although Caitlyn Jenner's legacy is complex, 17 million viewers watched her come out on national television, instantly changing the number of Americans who had ever knowingly listened to a trans person tell their story by almost two percentage points.[16] Many large companies in the United States now have official trans inclusive policies, even if they do not always meet these obligations in reality.

Intersex people are those whose bodies, at birth, differ from strict binaries. Some identify themselves under the trans umbrella and some do not.

> *I'm from the city, but I work in rural outlying counties in the South. Going stealth puts a weight on my soul. I have to be stealth now to remain employed, but it feels like I dishonor myself and my story. One day I want to be out and proud and inspiring to other queer folx, and I hope the heaviness doesn't get to be too much until I feel safe doing that.*

Trans political visibility has a fraught relationship with the visibility of lesbian and gay communities. Our bodies have always been present in more mainstream LGB movements, from the earliest community actions such as the Stonewall Riot to the push for marriage equality. Trans rights have at times, however, followed a different path. Many LGBTQ people seek some degree of societal acceptance, and there are many political changes that could potentially benefit all LGBTQ people, but there are also unique issues for trans communities. One obvious example is legal recognition of sex/gender markers (including nonbinary and intersex-friendly options). Others include the battle over trans health care and the unique ways in which trans bodies are politicized.

Portrait of Josh Vettivelu. Activist Portrait Series. (Syrus Marcus Ware)

With respect to trans health care, insurers continue to argue that surgeries such as bottom and top surgery (and sometimes even hormone therapy or psychotherapy) are not medically necessary, even though this viewpoint is soundly rejected by major health professional organizations.[17] Interestingly, as trans health care becomes more readily available, multiple sources of evidence suggest that trans people do not seek out *more* care (on a per capita basis). Surprisingly, trans people are very conservative in their medical choices. Many trans people find medical procedures unnecessary or find that risks outweigh benefits. Others, in collaboration with their healthcare providers, choose carefully among options for the ones that are least harmful and most helpful.[18] However, these choices remain policed and regulated by those who are not trans themselves, often without incorporating scientific evidence.

Beyond medical choices, trans bodies are objectified and demeaned, in the physical sense, and in the public eye. The idea that "the personal is political"[19] is intimately true for us. Trans people find one of their most personal physical features, their genitalia, a topic of public discussion. This is done to trans people with an intensity and an invasiveness to which bodies that are not trans are rarely subjected. It is even argued that trans people may prey upon or victimize others in the bathroom, even in the absence of any evidence in support of this claim.[20]

This political conversation is harmful in that it not only centers a cis perspective on trans bodies, but it pits trans and gender-diverse people against one another, in the classic mode of wedge-driving within minority communities by the majority. Trans people who "pass" are often pitted against trans and gender-diverse people who do not, and it is cis people and oppressive institutions who benefit. This is the typical design of this kind of structure, and overcoming it requires political dialogue, action, and bridge-building both within trans and gender-diverse communities and with cis allies.

In the past, transition-related surgeries were often referred to as sex reassignment surgeries but now are more often called gender-affirming surgeries.

Top surgery can be any surgery done on a person's chest, including breast augmentation, although the term is typically used to refer to surgeries that create a masculine appearing chest.

Bottom surgery can describe any surgery performed on the genital area.

Ms Ty 2017. Charcoal and Gesso on Canvas. (Devon Reiffer)

The idea of "passing" is a complicated concept. There are many people who are not able to pass, or to be "read" as their identified gender, in all situations. For a large number of people, passing is a matter of safety. For those who have a choice, choosing not to pass can sometimes be a political act.

Some people choose to live "stealth," not revealing their trans status to others. In many cases, safety is a major concern.

We have a continual opportunity to subvert and replace this way of talking, thinking, and relating with one that celebrates and centers our diversity. Trans people who are highly accepted by society can choose, where appropriate and safe for them, not to disappear into the broader society but to broaden the tent and build inclusion for trans and gender-diverse people whom society does not yet know how to celebrate. Trans people who have safety can agitate for safety for all, leveraging the mutual understanding they have with their cis loved ones that all are deserving of the safety they have. In this way, every act of trans visibility can be a political act of defiance, celebration, and the building of resilience for future trans bodies.

Like all communities that are historically marginalized but are coming into their own, we do not always stand up for one another in the ways we should. At times, within trans communities, we engage in what authors including Elizabeth "Betita" Martinez and Julia Serano[21] call "oppression Olympics," where we attempt to hierarchically define the level of oppression each subgroup experiences. We have the opportunity to break old stalemates and build a framework for broader inclusion. We can leverage our common experiences and desire for empowerment to build bridges and pull marginalized people into conversation. Speaking out about our intersecting identities can also help to break up this hierarchy. Additionally, those of us with economic privilege or social acceptance can be visible advocates for the welfare of others.

THE RURAL STRUGGLE FOR TRANSGENDER PEOPLE

Neil P. Allen (he/him)

Living in rural areas can be challenging for everyone who lives there—from a lack of public transportation, to inaccessibility of communication services, to few resources. For those who are transgender, it can be even more isolating, and the challenges can seem unsurmountable.

In rural areas, there's rarely any form of public transportation or taxi services. If there are taxi services, the cost of using them makes them a luxury and services such as Uber aren't trusted or allowed. There are often few local agencies and no LGBTQ centers nearby, which can make finding carpools or rides more difficult.

The cell phone coverage can be spotty in rural areas and there is often little to no Internet access beyond the center of town. The ability to provide access to these services, which many believe to be essential utilities, is often beyond the budgets of these small towns and counties. And, it's often made more difficult due to the geography.

Access to transgender-specific medical care and support can be limited. Medical professionals who perform surgeries and other services that are needed for transitions are often far away from rural areas with no way to get to them without a driver's license or car. Local doctors and mental health professionals are often unfamiliar with treatments for transgender people and they're frequently too busy with their large patient loads to get additional training.

In addition, trans people in rural areas may not know another trans or LGBQ person in or around where they live and may not feel safe allowing others to know about their gender identity. Even if there are events and support groups, they may not attend for fear of being outed to their families or in the community.

Transgender students are especially vulnerable because they are often bullied and not supported by the administration. They can be denied access to the bathrooms and locker rooms that match their gender identity. They may not have gay straight trans alliance groups to turn to for support, and their teachers and guidance counselors may not be allowed to be supportive.

Many challenges exist and there's still much heavy work needed to create spaces where transgender people feel safe, and which meet the wide-ranging needs of the rural community. The good news is that pockets of groups are forming to provide much-needed support and sharing of resources to reduce the isolation and challenges.

ADDRESSING INFIGHTING

(Mira)

Ways of being trans are infinite, and different trans people have different goals that do not always align. Friction can result from the fact that trans advocates have finite resources and society is willing to pay only a certain amount of limited attention to trans causes. Unfortunately, anger, frustration, shame, and resentment can build within communities, allowing opposing forces to grow stronger.

Internal attacks can take many forms, but one common theme is the policing or oversight of others' identities. In situations where resources are limited, individuals sometimes attempt to speak for others, even extending their views to the point of telling others what it is like to be them.

I feel sometimes like feminist communities still view me with a bit of skepticism, or with a sense that I haven't really earned my womanhood wings. When #metoo was first becoming a social phenomenon, I felt reluctant to join, either as someone who has been harassed and catcalled (both as a woman and as a trans person) or as an ally, because I felt like I would be seen as not *really* understanding women's experiences, or as co-opting women's issues and voices in an effort to validate myself. I'm sure some of that, maybe a lot of it, is due to my own self-doubt, and I'm working on trying to unpack that.

At times, members of our communities purposefully attempt to invalidate the experiences of others. For example, some binary trans people insist that, unless someone has feelings of gender dysphoria and goes through medical interventions, they are not truly trans. People with this view sometimes call those they feel are not really trans words such as "transtrenders," signifying that they believe these individuals are saying they are trans only because it is "trendy." It is one thing to believe that gender dysphoria is important to one's own experience of being trans. It is a very different thing to impose that stance on others. Backlash to these types of limiting views can be just as harsh, creating terms such as "truscum" (pronounced like "true scum") to refer back to the binary trans people making judgments about others' identities. It is nearly impossible to have generative conversations if each side has already labeled the other with disparaging terms.

Some people identify as "male to trans," or MTT. These individuals may see themselves as trans and not ever fully female because they see gender as at least partially biologically based. Although this identity may feel right to them, it becomes problematic when they insist that others not be allowed to identify as female either.

Gender policing involves attempting to control or regulate another person's gender identity or expression, and can be done by both cisgender and transgender people.

Gender dysphoria is a phrase, often used in a medical context, that signifies distress related to a person's gender identity not lining up with their assigned sex.

Untitled. (Zackary Drucker)

There are also those who decide to "de-transition," returning to their birth-assigned gender after spending some time identifying as trans. Some may call themselves "ex-trans." People may choose this option for a variety of reasons, including a genuine feeling that their assigned gender fits them better, but also due to circumstances where it becomes unsafe or too difficult to live as a trans person in their particular situation.

Robust collaboration among trans people, which builds on core, common values but celebrates and embraces a diversity of advocacy perspectives and priorities, will not be easy, but is needed to avoid the risk of diverting trans advocacy into a means of hurting trans people.

The identity that feels most affirming is trans guy or simply trans. I know many AFAB trans men want to lose all traces of their female assignment and be affirmed as male/man. In my journey, it feels important to hold space for my female experiences as well as male identity! I want to be known as TRANS through and through.

When infighting occurs, there can be a variety of responses. Some people walk away from advocacy because it is too fraught with conflict. Others become siloed, only participating in smaller groups where all members agree. Some people choose to compromise, though this can result in "watered down" advocacy that centers the needs of trans people with dominant identities. The most successful advocacy groups work to establish core, common beliefs, and to support co-advocacy across lines of difference.

"TRANS" IS MY GENDER MODALITY: A MODEST TERMINOLOGICAL PROPOSAL

Florence Ashley (they/them) is a transfeminine jurist and bioethicist from Canada.

Currently, no word exists in our vocabulary for the broad category that includes being trans and being cis. This terminological blind spot interferes with clinicians, theorists, and transgender people's ability to speak about important realities at a higher level of generality. The absence of this higher order term has tended to reproduce a strict dichotomy between cis and trans, which has hindered discussions on the gendered experiences of intersex people as well as those nonbinary people who do not consider themselves trans. Whereas the gay-straight binary, which renders invisible bisexual, pansexual, and other queer people, can be avoided through discussions couched in terms of sexual orientation, no analogous notion exists in relation to trans and cis people.

To address this gap, I propose the adoption of a new term: *gender modality*. Gender modality refers to how a person's gender identity stands in relation to their gender assigned at birth. It is an open-ended category that includes being trans and being cis and welcomes the elaboration of further terms that speak to the diverse experiences people may have of the relationship between their gender identity and gender assigned at birth. The cis-trans binary is challenged by some nonbinary people—especially agender people—some intersex people, some gender creative youth, and some people who were raised in a fully gender neutral manner.

Whereas I typically define cis and trans as the presence or absence of correspondence between gender identity and gender assigned at birth, I chose to define gender modality through "standing in relation to" because the all-or-nothing nature of "correspondence" may be too constraining for the nuances gender modality wishes to capture.

I chose the word modality because it is a "manner or state of being, as distinct from its substance or identity" (Oxford English Dictionary). Gender modality is about modalities of gender, about different ways of being our gender that do not alter its fundamental essence. The terminology recognizes the difference between, say, trans and cis women, while at the same time recognizing that this difference is not one that makes trans women any less or worse women. Whereas trans and cis women have a different gender modality, they share the same gender identity: woman.

Discrimination against trans people is often described as discrimination based on gender identity. It would be even more accurate, however, to say it is discrimination based on gender modality, given that trans people face discrimination because their gender identity doesn't correspond to the gender they were assigned at birth—that is, because of their gender modality. A richer and more accurate vocabulary enhances our collective capacity to describe and improve our material circumstances. I believe that the notion of "gender modality" fits this bill perfectly.

TRANS SPIRITUALITY AND BARRIERS TO RELIGIOUS INCLUSION

(Mira)

In the United States, the fight for trans inclusion is often pitted against the right to religious freedom. Particularly among certain evangelical Christian movements, the focus has been on actively regulating society in a way that accords with that movement's interpretation of the religion. Some people within these communities have instead called their religious communities back to a life-affirming vision of their religion. For example, Rev. Mark Wingfield seemed to surprise even himself when he began learning from trans people and sharing his learning with his Southern Baptist community.[22]

> *I am from rural Georgia and have lived in rural and small-town Alabama for about a decade. I don't feel safe to be myself here, and my partner and I take measures to protect ourselves and our home because we are perceived as an interracial lesbian couple and many people around here do not like that. Because of my conservative Christian upbringing (which was largely consistent with the cultural norms in the region, though slightly more intensive than the local average) I still struggle to accept who I am and express that authentically because I still have a nagging feeling that something is "wrong" with me.*

Some trans people are, themselves, religious, and religion can be a powerful protective factor in the lives of trans people.[23] Religions are not one-dimensional. There are movements throughout most facets of the Christian church to include trans people. Some of these groups work on a grassroots level, but a number of sects or denominations have official policies that are trans-affirmative. There are also clerics or imams who are inclusive of trans people, and the same is seen in most other religions. Atheist groups, or those oriented around secular philosophy, can also be places of community for trans individuals.

TRANS OUR WHOLE LIVES

(Harper)

Gender frames how people understand us even before we are born. Considerable efforts have been put toward developing technologies for "sex-selected sperm," that is, laboratory processes intended to increase the likelihood of conceiving a human embryo with a specific chromosomal makeup. Preimplantation genetic testing and hormone treatment are offered to prospective parents seeking to avoid producing intersex children. The popularity of "gender reveal parties," celebrations of prenatal sex assignment, is on the rise. By the time our births are narrated by shouts of "It's a boy!" or "It's a girl!" gender has already played a role in shaping the trajectory of a child's life.

The process of legally documenting gender typically begins within a baby's first hours in the breathing world. Most birth certificates require a gender designation. Although some locales, such as New York City, Colorado, and Washington State, are making moves toward including a third gender option on birth certificates and other legal documents, there are fervent debates within trans communities as to whether we are better off with more options or without legal gender categories at all.

> *I think the isolation I feel as an ethnically adrift child of a refugee with no community and no culture and the ways I've had to come to accept not-knowing through that has beaten down a path for my not-knowing regarding gender and its performance. I feel sometimes that I have an easier time navigating gender than some of my peers because I'm so used to not having information about myself that it almost no longer bothers me regularly.*

Some terms trans people use as self-identifiers emerge from the intersections of race and gender. For example, trans women who are also Latinx sometimes refer to themselves as Translatina.

Gender is a core discipline baked into the social curriculum of childhood. In other words, gender is a system that teaches children how to make sense of themselves and other people, and it is in constant interaction with other systems of social sorting, such as race, dis/ability, and class. These systems extend far beyond the law. From placing pink bows on nearly-bald infants, to handing action figures or dolls to one child and not another, to off-hand comments at the grocery store (e.g., "What a sweetheart. She's gonna be a real heart-breaker!" or, "Hey little man! He's a little bruiser, isn't he?"), infinite everyday exchanges between adults and children teach young people about what gender means. Gender never exists in a vacuum: Any individual's understanding of gender will be informed by count-less experiences in our social and geographic environments. As people are disciplined into gendered structures, we are also disciplined into hierarchically produced structures of race, ability, class, and sexuality.

Transmasculine and transfeminine are terms that are sometimes used to describe those who fall toward the masculine or feminine end of the gender spectrum.

I am in high school. The school refuses to change my name on documents. All of my teachers call me by the right name and I've even had one of them be more supportive than I could've asked for. People use homophobic, transphobic, sexist, and racist slurs all the time in my school. Most teachers don't stop them. I normally don't have things said to me specifically, but I have to hear them every day.

As people grow up, nearly everyone—trans or not—breaks from gendered expectations at some point. Sometimes, those breaks are celebrated. In 2012, the Kickstarter for Goldie Blox, a toy set designed to introduce girls to the basics of engineering, made nearly $1 million in preorders. There has also been a recent explosion of children's books intended to complicate conceptions of gender, including *I Am Jazz*, *Julian is a Mermaid*, and *Sparkle Boy*, each of which has been eagerly purchased by many families, school librarians, and classroom teachers across the United States. Sometimes, it can seem like transness and gender transgression are only widely celebrated when they are made prof-itable. At the same time, there are also countless examples of children and young people made to feel shame for transgressing systems of gender, which has too often had violent or deadly consequences. Perhaps with increasing frequency, trans young people experience both intense celebration *and* degradation.

Kaiden Hayward (FTM: He/him/his) and his girlfriend Katelyn Ashton (Cis: She/her/hers) laughing together at a tailgate event at Penn State University.

Blake Brockington, a young Black trans man who lived in North Carolina, participated in a variety of trans activist projects and was named homecoming king at his high school. As he entered the foster system after experiencing rejection in his birth family, and as his transness garnered greater publicity, Brockington faced a deluge of online and street harassment. In 2015, at the age of 18, he took his own life. On the morning of his suicide, he wrote on his Tumblr page, "I am so exhausted."[24]

Exhaustion is an all-too-common experience for transgender and gender nonconforming (TGNC) youth (and adults), whose bodies and self-expression regularly stand in the crosshairs within national debates. Most TGNC youth grow up with parents who are not trans themselves, which can sometimes lead to isolation within our own families. Some organizations, such as NativeOUT, Somos Familia, and Asian & Pacific Islander Family Pride, support families of queer and TGNC youth, in part by framing strong familial connections as a longstanding tradition within Indigenous and/or other communities of color, emphasizing that all families have always included people who embody a variety of genders.

> *QTPOC groups have made me feel a greater sense of belonging than I have ever imagined possible for a person in life.*

THROUGH BI, TRANS, AND NON-BINARY TO NONBINARY

Oshee Eagleheart (they/them) is an experiment in living outside the gender boxes, identifying as transgender, nonbinary, pansexual, and Radical Faerie. They is a gender diversity educator and writer who loves to talk about sex and gender and is writing a book with the working title Beyond Men and Women: Gender Diversity and the Healing of Our World.

"I'm not a man or a woman!" That was the huge epiphany I had in my early fifties, at a workshop for men and women, having arrived there believing I was a man. Sobbing uncontrollably for all the times I'd betrayed and compromised my core identity, I committed myself to living outside the "man" and "woman" boxes from that moment on. Ever since, I've identified as transgender—the label that felt closest to describing this human being who doesn't belong in either gender box.

Fifteen years later, I'm still searching for an English word that defines my gender. I grew up believing what everyone told me: that I was a boy. I didn't feel like a boy, but it never occurred to me that I could be anything else. With no gender-nonconforming role models and no words for my kind of being, I thought I wasn't good at being a boy, that there was something terribly wrong with me. I envy people who identify with their assigned gender, or who've always known they are "the opposite" gender, but that's not my story.

In my forties I came out as bisexual—which for me was as much about identity as orientation—and started cross-dressing. When my therapist asked whether I thought I might be transgender, I assured him I wasn't, because I thought transgender meant changing sex from one to the other. I soon learned that the word had a much broader definition.

When I started writing about gender, after that epiphany fifteen years ago, I called prevailing beliefs, attitudes, and social conventions "binary" and "binarism." But I didn't think anyone would know what I was talking about if I told them I was nonbinary.

Then, a couple of years ago, I began hearing people claim nonbinary as their gender, even in news stories in the media; it seemed like its time had come. "Transgender" has served me well for 15 years, but the term is increasingly being applied only to people transitioning from one sex to the other. Tired of explaining that I'm not transitioning, I've started saying that I'm nonbinary.

Now, with the most recent U.S. administration having threatened to define sex and gender as strictly binary, it feels all the more important for me to proudly identify as nonbinary. The label almost fits, except that it says what I'm not, without saying who I am. So, my search for the perfect label continues.

(Mira)

In a world where trans history is too often erased, trans elders can impart important knowledge and experience both within and outside trans communities. They are also vital members of our activist and social communities.

> *My youngest sibling came out as nonbinary a year or so after I came out and moved away! I was so proud! They're 13 years younger than me, and I think my*

SAGE: Advocacy & Services for LGBT Elders is an organization with in-person locations in New York City and a 24/7 national hotline (877-360-LGBT (5428)).

long-term gender weirdness and suddenly leaving the family paved the way for some of the family to be more accepting. I'm so so glad that they haven't had to hide and suffer the way I did, and that I can be a big brother for them.

Trans elders face unique challenges.[25] Having grown up in an era in which trans people were ostracized, even for those who most valiantly fought that ostracization, isolation can become a significant issue later in life. Many trans elders have lost friends and loved ones, and may find it difficult to access LGBTQ spaces that are designed for younger people. Trans elders may also face new barriers unique to late life, such as rejection in care settings like nursing homes, where they may be forced to go "back in the closet" in order to access care.[26] Adding to the healthcare aspects of this challenge are legal aspects, including maintaining autonomy in end-of-life decisions and control over how one is represented after death (e.g., ensuring that we are named and recognized in a way that is consistent with our gender and not our sex assigned at birth).

GRIOT Circle is based in New York City and serves LGBTQ elders of color. According to the GRIOT Circle website, a *griot* is "a storyteller in western Africa who perpetuates the oral tradition and history of their village or family."

I was diagnosed with breast cancer in 2015. Through the process of determining the best course of surgery and treatment and the realization that if I removed my breasts that I could always have the body I wanted, I began to explore more deeply what that means for me.

The challenges and opportunities of trans youth and elders highlight that being trans is not the domain of young adults. Trans advocacy must be "cradle to grave," because we were all young once, and, hopefully, most of us will grow old one day.

I think I began my journey while poor/working class but am currently probably upper class. The difference and influence of both are hard to track since a lot of other things changed as well, but being poor, underage, and dependent I always felt like we couldn't afford for me to be doing this weird gender thing. It was a lot harder to be out because stress was much higher, and I didn't have the time or clarity of mind to think about my identity or put that weight on my single mother.

WHERE DO WE GO FROM HERE?

(Harper and Mira)

Being trans is complicated. It certainly doesn't mean the same thing to everyone. And yet, when we think about the trans and gender nonconforming people in our lives, and even those we have never met, we often feel some sense of kinship as we each live with the simultaneous beauty and struggle of being trans. Sometimes, as is the case in any community, we disagree with one another. Sometimes, those conflicts can be frustrating, exasperating, or painful. They may induce fear or shame. Conflict can seem risky, especially when it takes place in public, given the precarious nature of trans survival in a world that too often rejects us. Maybe, though, there are other ways of thinking about it. Where do these conflicts come from? How did we find ourselves arranged in collision with one another? What gets in the way of our ability to connect with each other? What does that tell us about where we should go from here? Are there ways in which conflict can be generative, bringing us all into closer conversation about the meaning of trans justice?

I have several people in my life who are "accepting," but grow frustrated with being corrected or told that somebody uses a different name or pronouns than they expected. It's things as simple as a groan or a sigh of frustration that make it clear that the person considers you a burden for your identity.

As we spend time talking through ways in which our perspectives converge and diverge from one another, we can challenge one another, help one another to refine our ideas, and, occasionally, transform them. In order to make meaning together, we have to work from a foundation of care and respect, a willingness to listen without seeking to control, and an

Trans Sketch. (Misha Grifka Wander)

authentic desire to support one another. In other words, it is not quite so simple as inviting *any* divergent set of perspectives into debate, which is sometimes proposed as a solution to controversy. What we know is that we cannot avoid conflict in trans communities. It exists, just like all of us, and it can't be ignored. As trans people find themselves increasingly the subject of public conversation (whether we like it or not), we are faced with a set of choices: What should we do with our questions and disagreements? Which ones jeopardize trans livelihoods or the expansion of trans knowledge? Which of them are generative and useful to the project of ensuring trans survival? Which invite deeper thinking and teach us something about gender, justice, or both?

NOTES

1. Stryker, S. (2008). *Transgender history.* Berkeley, CA: Seal Press Books.
2. Boswell, H. (1991). The transgender alternative. *Chrysalis 1*(2), 29–31.
3. Feinberg, L. (1992). *Transgender liberation: A movement whose time has come.* New York: World View Forum.
4. Spade, D. (2008). *Documenting gender.* UCLA: The Williams Institute. https://escholarship. org/uc/item/995307dm.
5. Spade, D. (2015). *Normal life: Administrative violence, critical trans politics, and the limits of law.* Durham, NC: Duke University Press.
6. Meyer, E., & Keenan, H. (2018). Can policies help schools affirm gender diversity? A policy archaeology of transgender-inclusive policies in California schools. *Gender and Education, 30*(6), 736–753.
7. Galupo, M. P., Mitchell, R. C., & Davis, K. S. (2017). Face validity ratings of sexual orientation scales by sexual minority adults: Effects of sexual orientation and gender identity. *Archives of Sexual Behavior, 47*, 1241–1250.
8. Herman, J. (2016). LGB within the T: Sexual orientation in the National Transgender Discrimination Survey and implications for public policy. In *Trans Studies: The Challenge to*

Hetero/Homo Normativities. UCLA: The Williams Institute. https://escholarship.org/uc/item/4n7727j7.

9. Balzarini, R. N., Dharma, C., Kohut, T, Holmes, B. M., Campbell, L., Lehmiller, J. J., & Harman, J. J. (2018). Demographic comparison of American individuals in polyamorous and monogamous relationships. *Journal of Sex Research*, *56*(6), 681–694. doi: 10.1080/00224499.2018.1474333.

10. James, S. E., Herman, J. L., Rankin, S., Keisling, M., Mottet, L., & Anafi, M. (2016). *The Report of the 2015 U.S. Transgender Survey.* Washington, DC: National Center for Transgender Equality.

11. Fedorko, B. & Berredo, L. (2017). The vicious circle of violence: Trans and gender-diverse people, migration, and sex work. *TGEU.* http://transrespect.org/wp-content/uploads/2018/01/TvT-PS-Vol16-2017.pdf.

12. Wirtz, A. L., Poteat, T. C., Malik, M., & Glass, N. (2018). Gender-based violence against transgender people in the United States: A call for research and programming. *Trauma, Violence, & Abuse*, *21*(2), 227–241. doi: 10.1177/1524838018757749.

13. Weiss Wiewel, E., Torian, L. V., Merchant, P., Braunstein, S. L., & Shepard, C. W. (2016). HIV diagnoses and care among transgender persons and comparison with men who have sex with men: New York City, 2006–2011. *American Journal of Public Health, 106*, 497–502.

14. Crenshaw, K. (1989). Demarginalizing the intersection of race and sex: A Black feminist critique of antidiscrimination doctrine, feminist theory and antiracist politics. *University of Chicago Legal Forum, 3*, 139–168.

15. Collins, C., Asante-Muhammed, D., Nieves, E., & Hoxie, J. (2017). The road to zero wealth. *Institute for Policy Studies.*

16. Kissell, R. (2015, April 25). Bruce Jenner interview ratings: 17 million watch ABC special. variety.com/2015/tv/news/bruce-jenner-interview-ratings-17-million-watch-abc-special-1201479968.

17. Transcend Legal. (2018). Medical organization statements. transcendlegal.org/medical-organization-statements.

18. Herman, J. L. (2013). Costs and benefits of providing transition-related health care coverage in employee health benefits plans. williamsinstitute.law.ucla.edu/wp-content/uploads/Herman-Cost-Benefit-of-Trans-Health-Benefits-Sept-2013.pdf.

19. Hanisch, C. (1970). "The Personal is Political." In S. Firestone & A. Koedt (Eds.), *Notes from the second year: Women's liberation.*

20. Wang, T., Solomon, D., Durso, L. E., McBride, S., & Cahill, S. (2016). State anti-transgender bathroom bills threaten transgender people's health and participation in public life. *Fenway Institute.* fenwayhealth.org/wp-content/uploads/2015/12/COM-2485-Transgender-Bathroom-Bill-Brief_v8-pages.pdf.

21. Serano, J. (2007). Whipping girl: A transsexual woman on sexism and the scapegoating of femininity. Berkeley, CA: Seal Press Books.

22. Wingfield, M. (2016, May 13). Seven things I'm learning about transgender persons. baptistnews.com/article/seven-things-im-learning-about-transgender-persons.

23. Dowshen, N. F., Johnson, C. M., Kuhns, A. K., Rubin, L. M., & Garofalo, D. R. (2011). Religiosity as a protective factor against HIV risk among young transgender women. *Journal of Adolescent Health, 48*, 410–414. doi:10.1016/jadohealth.2010.07.021

24. Garloch, K. (2015, March 28). Charlotte-area transgender teens' suicide rocks community. *The Charlotte Observer.* https://www.charlotteobserver.com/news/local/article16655111.html

25. Porter, K. E., Brennan-Ing, M., Chang, S. C., dickey, l. m., Singh, A. A., Bower, K. L., & Witten, T. M. (2016). Providing competent and affirming services for transgender and gender nonconforming older adults. *Clinical Gerontologist*, *39*(5), 366–388.

26. Wheeler, D. (2016). LGBT seniors are being pushed back into the closet. *The Atlantic.* https://www.theatlantic.com/health/archive/2016/08/lgbt-seniors/497324/.

RACE, ETHNICITY, AND CULTURE

Romeo Romero and Sy Simms

2

INTRODUCTION

Experiences of being trans or gender expansive are informed by our racial and ethnic identities, and by histories of colonialism. Many people think of gender identity and racial identity as two separate experiences, taking the approach that someone may be transgender *and* white, or nonbinary *and* Asian. However, by separating our identities, and thinking of trans identity as a nonracial experience, we assume more similarity between trans people than may actually be there. The idea of a universal "transgender experience" flattens the diversity within our communities.

> *As an Indian person, I find that there are very few stories in American society that center on Asian queer stories at all, and of those most of them focus on East Asian cis gay men. As a South Asian trans person, it's quite rare for me to find someone like myself in real life, and even rarer in media. American media, while it does increasingly try to discuss queer stories, still naturally centers white and cis people, while major Indian media is only recently and only very slowly (and with a great deal of backlash) beginning to attempt to tell the stories of gay people. Thus when I do find someone who is both South Asian and trans (either in real life or in media) I find myself wanting to cling to their story and discuss with them all the parts of my identity that a white cis person might not understand, such as interactions with Asian family, cultural traditions, language, and a great deal more.*

The authors of this chapter describe themselves as "a Black transmasculine genderqueer person who is five generations out of chattel slavery in the South" and "a genderfluid Boricua Jew, of Afro-Taino/Spanish ancestry who has been shaped by a double-diasporic connection to both a colonized island people and a people who have just recently assimilated into whiteness."

Gender is worn differently in every community, and what constitutes non-normative gender can shift based on cultural and ethnic context. The gender differences across the many cultures of our world are vast and complex. Gender roles and expectations of "women" and "men" are not universal truths, but rather cultural ones. Further, the gender norms of western society have been exported and violently enforced throughout colonial history. The violence that trans people in western culture now face, for defying a dominant two-gender culture, is the same violence that seeks to eradicate the gender diversity in Indigenous cultures across the globe. As a community, we cannot lose sight of the ways that trans liberation is inherently an antiracist, anti-imperial, and anticolonial endeavor.

> *I am white and Arab. My gender expression and identity caused white communities to alienate me (I always presented as male, even as a little kid). Arab communities weren't much better. Women tended to be a lot more accepting or at least kind to me. Arab men were the most aggressive. After 9/11, things got a lot harder. I was a kid when it happened, so I didn't fully understand what was happening. I just knew that people started treating me and my family different. We started getting pulled over more. At the airport, my family and I would (and still do) get pulled aside for extra screening all the time. The pat downs always outed me to TSA workers. Then I'd get mocked and ridiculed. Stuff like that happened outside airports, too. Now that I've transitioned, I get read as more intimidating because I'm an Arab man.*

A note from the authors: "We, as authors, do not represent the entirety of trans people of color's experiences, and reject the idea that we could ever speak for all trans people of color. We hope to provide stories, histories, and perspectives that open more questions and reflection for the reader, rather than to give facts, definitions, or certainties."

Support the T. (Brayden Asher Misiolek | roguestud.io)

ACKNOWLEDGING OUR TRANSCESTORS

The term *trans people of color* (or *TPOC* for short) denotes the specific experience of people who are targeted both by racism and cissexism because gender and race are tied together in a way that cannot be separated.

Although it is no longer illegal to "cross-dress" in the United States, sex work continues to be criminalized, and dressing in feminine clothing often leads to profiling of trans women as sex workers, whether or not they engage in that economy.

In almost every culture, storytelling has been used to teach people about who we have been and who we can become together. Trans people come from many different races, ethnicities, and cultures. However, we share many similarities in our histories and relationships to colonialism, oppression, and the struggle for collective liberation. Trans people of color make up a racially diverse community of people who have faced marginalization and alienation for both race and gender identity. Many trans people of color see ourselves as deeply connected with one another, and have chosen to come together across our many differences and to define ourselves as a people in our own right. This connection, community, and identity that is rooted in being trans people of color has most famously been traced back to a particular moment in LGBTQ history: The Stonewall Riots of 1969.

In the 1960s there were laws that barred LGBTQ people from openly congregating in public spaces, as well as purchasing alcohol in bars and wearing "cross-gender" clothing. In resistance to these laws, queer and trans people across the country fought back through direct action against police enforcement. In 1966, the Compton Cafeteria Riot took place in San Francisco after the police tried to arrest a trans woman for cross-dressing and sex work. The queer and trans patrons fought back against the arrest.[1] One year later, demonstrations took place at the Black Cat Tavern in Los Angeles after undercover police raided the bar. It was during this time of queer uprising that the Stonewall Inn existed as a hotspot for queer and trans people in New York City.

The Stonewall Inn was a Mafia-owned bar and worked around existing laws by maintaining itself as a private men's club, charging high prices in order to make a profit off of queer and trans people who were looking for spaces to exist together. Marsha P. Johnson, Sylvia Rivera, Miss Major, and Stormé DeLarverie are three trans women of color and a Black butch lesbian, respectively, who frequently patronized the Stonewall Inn to find belonging and refuge from the stares, sneers, and slurs of the transphobic world around them. One day in June 1969, patrons like them headed toward the bar, just as they always had.[2]

BRUJX AND REMEDIES

Stephanie Luz Hernandez (she/her) is a therapist based in Oakland, California and a member of the Trans Bodies, Trans Selves board of directors.

Romero pirul canto y flor
herein lies the memory
of a song forgotten a heartbeat drum
ancestral remembrance
& family chosen Life
at the intersections
the borderlands colonized imposed
gender undone
Cempasuchil scent with copal smoke
we honor our transcestors
Marsha P Johnson Sylvia Rivera
& all our 2-spirit elders
Close your eyes you are not alone
you are loved
beautiful queers of color
our healing is our legacy
for future generations

In that one night, the Stonewall Inn went from being a sanctuary to a war zone. The police raided the bar unexpectedly. This was not the first time that the police had entered the bar, but they were typically paid quickly and business resumed as usual. On this evening, things were different. They had no interest in acting peacefully, and instead started rounding up the patrons, arresting them on the spot. However, the people of the bar started resisting arrest. The physical struggle between the patrons and the police escalated. A police officer hit a drag queen in the face. Someone threw the first bottle, and what ensued after that is a riot that would go down in history as the beginning of our movement. The riots lasted three days and spread to surrounding neighborhoods until the whole city was aware that something big was happening.

Although the Stonewall Riots were an important moment in our history, what is more important is how queer and trans people of color did the hard work of mobilizing and caring for their people in the aftermath. Marsha, Sylvia, Miss Major, and Stormé organized people together to continue resisting the police and the violence that was inflicted upon their community. Marsha and Sylvia formed an organization called STAR (Street Transvestite Action Revolutionaries), which was designed to support drag queens and trans women of color who were unable to access food, clothing, and stable housing. Miss Major has continued to be an activist and organizer for trans communities, most notably serving as the executive director of the Transgender Gender Variant Intersex Justice Project (TGIJP). Stormé continued to volunteer as an LGBTQ community street patrol worker as well as work at LGBTQ bars and clubs.

One year after the riots, STAR participated in the first march to commemorate the struggle of the Stonewall Riots. Originally called the Christopher Street Liberation Day parade, but now known as "Pride," this tradition of marching continues every year in thousands of cities around the world. It is because of their bravery in the face of oppression, and their commitment to uplifting and caring for their community when no one else would, that we now consider these activists our transcestors.

The mass-shooting at the Pulse Nightclub in Orlando in 2016 is a reminder that queer and trans POC safe havens are frequently under attack, and that history repeats itself. May the 49 lost members of our community rest in power.

The Black Trans Prayer Book (produced by J Mase III and Lady Dane) "is an interfaith, multi-dimensional, artistic and theological work that collects the stories, poems, prayers, meditations, spells, and incantations of Black Trans & Non-Binary people."

Reclaim Pride 2019. (Colin Laurel)

POETS AND ARTISTS IN TPOC COMMUNITIES

Adelina M. Cruz
Alan Pelaz
ALOK
Amir Rabiyah
Anthony J. Williams
Arielle Twist
Benji Hart
Black Trans Prayer Book
Bo (Luengsuraswat) Rittapa
Cam Awkward Rich
D'Lo
Dee Dee Watters
Demian Diné Yazhi
Ebo Barton
Elena Rose
Fabian Romero
Hinaleimoana Kwai Kong Wong-Kalu
Ignacio Rivera
J Mase III
jia qing wilson-yang
Joshua Alan
Joshua Jennifer Espinoza
Kai Cheng Thom
Kay Ulanday Bartlett

Lady Dane
Mey Rude
Micha Cárdenas
Nepantla (Journal for Queer Poets of Color)
Nori Reed
Ryka Aoki
Sins Invalid
Star Amerasu
StormMiguel Florez
Toni Newman
Tourmaline
Venus Di'Khadijah Selenite
Vivek Shraya
Wu Tsang

Though there have been great successes in securing rights for LGBTQ people today, we continue to see the persistence of violence, poverty, food insecurity, and many other struggles that STAR fought so hard against—the same struggles that continue to disproportionately affect trans people of color. Historically, trans people (and particularly trans women of color) have been pushed out of queer and trans movements that focus on legal recognition. White, wealthy lesbians and gays have often organized around attainable and acceptable goals, such as marriage equality, property ownership, and other platforms that would encourage inclusion into a middle-class ideal. Their work has left issues of poverty, police brutality, street violence, racism, access to safe public spaces, and incarceration on the back burner.

Thanks to the archival work of Tourmaline,[3] there is a publicly accessible video of Sylvia Rivera giving a speech to a large crowd of overwhelmingly white cis gay people at the 1973 Christopher Street Liberation Day parade. Sylvia passionately demanded recognition and support for trans people of color in jail. Fifty years later, her words still resonate as true as ever. In 2019, at the 50th anniversary of the Stonewall Riots at the Stonewall Inn, a Black trans woman, who has chosen to remain anonymous, gave a similar speech to a predominantly white audience during a drag show. She asked, "Where is your rage?" and was subsequently threatened by the white owners of the bar that they would call the police on her.[4] As the experiences of trans people of color and the experiences of the wealthier white gay and trans communities continue to diverge, it is no surprise that we are in a moment where it is necessary to reclaim our places in the movement that would not have started without us.

TRANS IN COLOR: RACE, ETHNICITY, AND CULTURE

Dani Barnhill-Farrell (he/they) is a trans activist, writer, and founder of Trans in Color and TBuddy. He lives in the DMV area (District of Columbia, Maryland, Virginia) with his wife, where he makes it his mission to positively influence trans men around the world.

As a trans man of color, I was discouraged by the lack of resources available in our community specifically for transmasculine people of color. I struggled with finding a community where I could not only feel accepted but also get advice and develop a sense of brotherhood with those experiencing the same day-to-day triumphs and hurdles. So, in 2017, I created two organizations dedicated to the empowerment of transmasculine people of color: *Trans in Color* and *TBuddy*. They both provide mental, emotional, and transitional support.

Trans in Color offers weekly support groups, biweekly podcasts, and bimonthly articles in *FTM Magazine*. We also conduct clothing drives, provide housing assistance, look for trans-friendly physicians and mental health professionals, assist with voter registration, and help with health insurance navigation. We have a team member on board who is a tattoo artist and offers free and low-cost tattoos to cover top surgery and self-harm scars.

Unfortunately, in the black community, mental health is not always prioritized because of the negative stigma that surrounds it. To ease the negative connotation, *TBuddy* was formed. *TBuddy* is a free, 24/7 service offered to transmasculine individuals by transmasculine individuals. We provide support, encouragement, and love because so many of us are missing out. These free services are offered via phone, text, Skype, or in person.

I believe both organizations are important because there is a war on people of color in America and a war on transgender people in America—just imagine being affected by both. In addition to the pressure of being black and trans, transmasculine people are underrepresented within the LGBTQ + community and often struggle with finding a support system.

Many transmasculine people of color have been alienated and disowned by their families. We are here to give them the courage and support to grow despite the adversities we face—because finding it within the mainstream community has proven to be difficult. We do this to share transmasculine success and transmasculine struggle with others who can relate. We are here to save and protect the lives of trans youth and adults of color in our community.

NAMING OURSELVES

There is power in naming ourselves as a community, particularly because of the ways our labor and creativity so often become co-opted. Kimberlé Crenshaw initially coined the term *intersectionality* to describe the ways in which Black women were made invisible and marginalized in both white feminist spaces and male-led movements for Black liberation.[5,6] The word *intersectionality* highlights the space that people occupy when they hold multiple marginalized identities at once. Often, we can become lost between the two (or more) identities that we hold, which can make it difficult to find community on the basis of either identity. For Black women, this looks like navigating the racism of the white feminist movement and the sexism of Black liberation movements. For trans people of color today, we enter into trans communities that are predominantly white, exposing us to both explicit and unintentional forms of racism. In our communities of color, it is common for many trans people to lose the support of their families and friends for not conforming to expected gender roles.

> *Intersectionality to me means how different aspects of my identity and status overlap. I feel that my ethnicity, gender and sexual orientation overlap in the sense that I always feel in between, othered, non-existent, or pressured to "pick a side." I often hear "Are you black or white?" (I'm both). "Are you gay or straight?" (I'm aroace). "Are you a boy or a girl?" (I'm nonbinary).*

People of color learn from an early age what it is like to be systematically isolated from mainstream society. Once we come out as trans, we often also feel pushed away from our communities of color. It can often feel like we have to choose between our identities, rather than existing in our wholeness. The term *trans person of color* helps us name this

Black Trans Media 50,000 Years of Resistance mural created by Olympia Sudan, Mikayla Capozzi, Donna Rymes, Jia Hurd, Ifunaya, Maddox Guerilla, Xenophyrous, DonChristian Jones, and Sasha Alexander.

intersection where we exist, between our trans and racial identities, without giving up any parts of ourselves.

> *I am a mixed (Native American/white) nonbinary teenager, who is autistic, in a very Christian area. For my differing beliefs, I have been forced out of school and had stones physically pelted at me as I walk home. I do not feel safe as any sort of minority, and if I add being trans and gay into the mix, I have no doubt I'd probably get killed. This sort of complete intersection puts my life in danger just that much more. My status as autistic intersects with my gender in the way that sometimes, it feels cloudy. I have difficulty understanding my gender and what it means to me, and I feel that my autism colors my experience in both my gender and in all situations. My status as very poor combines with my status as trans and puts my chances at surgery at a very low one, since I can barely afford my own other medicines. I feel like my age hits it where people don't believe me/take my gender seriously because they believe it's a teenage fad, like being goth or punk.*

The term "trans" does not inherently address all people who fall outside of the western colonial binary of man/woman. Because of the way language changes over time and space, there are people across history who have used different words to describe themselves (including transsexual, transvestite, etc.). There are also people in our current historical moment who identify with genders that have always existed (Two Spirit, *Hijra*, third gender, *Māhū*, *Fa'afafine*, *Ashtime*, and many more) who do not identify with being trans. Finally, there are people who break the gender binary through being explicitly gender-nonconforming, androgynous, and/or illegible to mainstream notions of gender, and those who face transphobic violence, but may continue to identify with their gender assigned at birth. We recognize all of these ways of being and more.

EMBRACING COMPLEXITY

A. Ikaika Gleisberg (they/them) is a member of the Trans Bodies, Trans Selves board of directors.

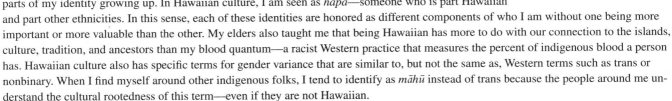

Like many other trans and nonbinary folks, my own identity is a complex amalgamation of different parts that are constantly shifting with each passing year. The terms I have used to describe myself have changed over time and are both a reflection of how I see myself and shaped by how others see and interact with me. The racial and ethnic identities I inhabit, and how others perceive me in different geographic locations, also contribute to the terms I use to describe who I am.

Although my ethnic background is complex and consists of over 10 different ethnicities, I primarily identify as Hawaiian (*Kanaka 'Ōiwi*), Chinese, and German because these were the most culturally salient parts of my identity growing up. In Hawaiian culture, I am seen as *hapa*—someone who is part Hawaiian and part other ethnicities. In this sense, each of these identities are honored as different components of who I am without one being more important or more valuable than the other. My elders also taught me that being Hawaiian has more to do with our connection to the islands, culture, tradition, and ancestors than my blood quantum—a racist Western practice that measures the percent of indigenous blood a person has. Hawaiian culture also has specific terms for gender variance that are similar to, but not the same as, Western terms such as trans or nonbinary. When I find myself around other indigenous folks, I tend to identify as *māhū* instead of trans because the people around me understand the cultural rootedness of this term—even if they are not Hawaiian.

When I left the islands and moved to San Francisco, I noticed that many people outside of Polynesian communities do not understand what *māhū* means. I also started to realize how my different ethnic identities were usually whittled down to more general racial categories. For instance, one day I was at a laundromat in my neighborhood—the Mission District in San Francisco—when a Latina who worked there started a conversation with me in Spanish. After I muddled through my response in Spanglish, she remarked that she was sad for me that I have been robbed of my language and culture. Although what she said was true, I realize that she saw my generic "brownness" as Latino. On one hand, I felt seen and part of the larger community in my neighborhood, even if their language and culture was different than mine. On the other hand, being seen as Latino in a rapidly gentrifying city led to escalating police harassment, especially when I was walking home alone or with friends who are white women.

Geographic location and culture contribute greatly to how we see the connections between our race, ethnicity, and gender identity. On one hand, I acknowledge and respond to the various privileges that get mapped onto my body, especially if I am seen by others in a Western context as a white cisgender man. On the other hand, I feel the complexity of my identity and its cultural significance being erased and have to continuously work at its preservation and mine.

The main areas I see my gender intersect with other aspects of my identity would be my religion and my disability. I am ethnically and religiously Jewish, and I choose to wear a kippah full-time, something which my community has been supportive toward when I transitioned from FTM but that I worry may be less accepted as my presentation becomes more femme again. I am someone with disabling mental illness who works with a service dog; I often feel like I need to "pick" a marginalized identity for safety, particularly at work, like showing up as my full self in all my queerness & craziness will be too much for people to handle. It's hard to know how legitimate these fears are, however, & how much they are internalized oppression.

"Trans people of color" is an explicitly political term. TPOC communities create space for us to exist in all of our wholeness, a space for us to call home. In TPOC spaces, we get to be both/and at the same time. There is something powerful about naming "trans people of color," and organizing our communities around this shared experience. It is a statement and a commitment toward solidarity between trans people of all marginalized racial and ethnic groups (including Black, Indigenous, Latinx, East and South Asian, Pacific Islander, and Middle Eastern trans people). However, we are also cognizant and wary of this term being used to group us together into a monolithic category that doesn't honor the complexity of our differences. There is so much diversity in our cultures, histories, communities, and struggles, both between and within each racial group. This is to say that not every trans person of color experiences the world like every other trans person of color. But, also that not all Black trans people, or Latinx trans people, would experience the world similarly, either. Endless factors shape who we are, which is why we move away from using "trans person of color" as a descriptor of a certain kind of person, and instead use it as a statement of our *chosen* collectivity around our *shared* experiences of oppression.

I knew I was trans when I was 19, living in Indiana. But the idea of becoming a black man in the Midwest was really hard. I also didn't have the resources to transition then. I waited until I was 33 to actively transition. I am glad I waited. I got the chance to transition with insurance that could help me and in a major city with lots of resources.

Because the majority of trans people of color do not have access to political, economic, and social power or agency (because of systems of racism, colonialism, and cissexism), we continue to be in a struggle for freedom that is intricately linked to the trans and racial parts of our identities. For us to live free, we must live in a world without domination, subordination, oppression, borders, prisons, and all forces that keep trans people of color on the margins. For us to live free, we cannot leave anyone behind.

THE STRUGGLE CONTINUES: THE REALITIES OF OPPRESSION AND MARGINALIZATION

When we think about the ways that systems of oppression (racism, classism, sexism, etc.) function, they do not exist in a vacuum, isolated from one another. Rather, they function in a deeply interconnected web. Racism, classism, sexism, and all forms of oppression are tangled up in one another. As trans people of color, we have to navigate the compounded effect of existing at the intersection of gender-based and race-based discrimination. We endure similar hardships as white trans people, including difficulties of legally changing our names and gender markers, accessing trans-affirming health care, and fighting for our pronouns to be used and recognized. We are, however, also targeted by racism at every point along those struggles. For example, to obtain gender confirmation surgery, many trans people need to find a trans-competent therapist. Trans people of color, however, also need to find a therapist who is culturally competent and able to understand the cultural values that inform who we are as people. Because of these experiences, trans people of color move through the world in a way that is distinct from both white trans people and cis people of color.

Raquel Willis Speaking to the Crowd at the Black Trans Lives Matter March, Brooklyn, NY, June 14, 2020. (Cole Witter)

THE WORLD IS NOT COLORBLIND: MY WHITENESS AS PROTECTION IN A RACIST WORLD

Anonymous

I am white. My race definitely intersects with my gender identity, because it has afforded me a lot of privilege as a trans person: Most of the before/after pictures of transition-related surgeries that you can find online are of white people.

My Black trans partner gets a lot of transphobic harassment in public, and I am a white trans person, and I hardly ever experience transphobic harassment in public. White people have more access to medical care and other costly resources, including transition-related expenses. Other white people are more likely to listen to me and respect me than they are a person of color, when we are talking about any issue –trans-related or not. Gender and sexuality alliances (GSAs) and trans-specific spaces that are dominated by white people are more accessible to me as a white trans person than they would be to a trans person of color.

Binders, breast forms, make-up, underwear, packers, gaffs, and other items are often sold in one "flesh colored" tone, which is really white people's skin color, so I can easily access items that match my skin. Trans people of color are murdered at a much higher rate than white trans people, so I don't generally have to worry as much about being killed for my gender identity. When trans people are portrayed in a positive light in popular media, they are most often white, so I can see myself represented more frequently because I am white.

And I'm sure there are *many* more examples that just aren't coming to mind right now!

I must recognize where I do have privilege. My whiteness, my masculinity, and my being afab mean that I look more like what society seems to expect nonbinary people to look like.

Trans people of color also experience the multiplied effects of both transphobia and racism through increased police brutality, racial profiling, wealth disparities, and other forms of racism.[7] Trans people of color face a disproportionate amount of violence compared to the rest of the queer community, and this number is even higher for transgender women of color (TWOC). Of the deaths that we remember on Transgender Day of Remembrance (TDOR) every year, most are Black/Latinx trans femmes and trans women.

While there are a number of challenges that come with being trans, I am otherwise a fairly well off and healthy white man living in a liberal area. As a result,

Transgender Day of Remembrance (TDOR), which takes place every year on November 20, was started in 1999 by Gwendolyn Ann Smith as a vigil to honor the memory of Rita Hester, a transgender woman who was killed in 1998.

Code-switching is when a person changes the way they speak or express themselves to fit into a particular social context. People of color often code-switch when they move between communities of color and white settings.

I've been able to easily access all of the medical care I want, not worry about employment or housing discrimination, and generally stay safe from many of the dangers and fears facing other trans people.

Trans people of color in the United States face significantly fewer opportunities for safe housing, job security, education, access to health care, and other basic needs, and finding supportive services that can help mitigate some of these stressors can be an additional challenge. For example, schools in communities of color generally have less funding than schools in wealthier white communities, so are less equipped to provide supportive services. With increased levels of funding, schools are better able to afford student groups such as gender and sexuality alliances (GSAs) and trainings for school staff to learn more about issues related to gender and sexuality. Students of color face disproportionate disciplinary consequences across the country in part due to racial bias. Schools in communities of color are more likely than wealthier white schools to have school police officers.[8] Therefore, when a trans student of color demands to use the correct bathroom, or gets in a fight with someone who was bullying them for being trans, they are at a higher risk of being arrested at school than a white trans student whose school does not have a school police officer present. If that student of color is pushed out of their home, in addition to being pushed out of school, they are at an increased risk of experiencing homelessness. Being forced into public space increases the risk for hyper-surveillance, racial profiling, police brutality, and engaging in survival economies. This young person now has a far more difficult time accessing basic health care, housing, food security, and employment.

I am white, and it is my white privilege that has allowed me to not examine this intersection critically. White privilege has also shielded me from much of the violence that has befallen my trans sisters of color. I have received a fair share of violence early in my transition—people defacing my art/property, being publicly shamed—but these things did not physically impact me, and now I do not fear for my safety as a function of my trans identity. It has afforded me a high degree of security and freedom to live my life unencumbered.

FITNESS AS A HEALING MODALITY

Ilya Parker (he/they) is a nonbinary transmasculine person of color currently living in Chapel Hill, North Carolina. He is also a writer, social justice advocate, and owner of Decolonizing Fitness. He is a Licensed Physical Therapist Assistant and Medical Exercise Coach with over 13 years of rehabilitative and functional training experience.

I am a black queer trans masculine person (and yes, "labels" matter when you are carving space for yourself in a world that wants to deny your existence). I am reminded of the ways this world seeks to pathologize and remove me from my body daily. Many times, I've heard: "You Can't Be a Trainer . . . You Don't Even Look Like You Work Out."

What does that even mean? What we're literally saying here is that because someone doesn't embody the typical "fitness standards of beauty" (which also conveniently align with normative "European ideals of beauty") that they are automatically removed from being viewed as a valid personal trainer. The current fitness industry has caused many trans and queer folks so much grief due to gender-based violence, homophobia, and inaccessibility of affirming and inclusive services. We are living in a time where trans folks are more visible than ever, yet we're still being violently targeted by people in our own communities.

Remember. Erasure equals violence. When you never see folks who look, sound, and move like you, you think you are abnormal . . . . Society reinforces this, and then you internalize the hatred that is extended toward you. Trans and queer people need to be in physical and virtual spaces where we are met with compassion. We need to be encouraged and supported when we engage in movement practices that allow for us to embrace all of who we are. This is where Decolonizing Fitness comes in.

For me to "decolonize" means to break free from systems, schools of thought, practices, and so on that cause us harm, that restrict our individual/collective power, and that remove our right to self-determination . . . as whole, complex, beautiful humans. Fitness can be reclaimed and utilized as a healing tool to help our most marginalized folks reconnect with their bodies in ways that feel healing and liberating. So when I use the words, "decolonizing fitness," I'm literally naming the ways to reinvent, reimagine, and restructure fitness practices into something that is supportive, affirming, and empowering.

I have embedded in my fitness practice a grassroots, community-based healing justice framework. To me, healing justice means creating a space where we are able to liberate our ideas of health and healing from what we have been conditioned to believe about ourselves through systematic oppression. The goal is to experience health and healing from our own autonomy, not from trying to achieve an ideal created by a mainstream that excludes and erases us. We all possess tools for healing. Healing is a collective effort. It can be rooted in African and Indigenous practices. It can also have components from conventional medicine. It can be as simple or as complicated as we want it to be. Healing is about listening to our bodies while respecting and honoring the collective.

For trans folks of color, learning how to soften or hide their true self through code-switching is a necessary tool for survival. Some parts of an individual's identity as a person of color might have to be hidden or shifted in order to been seen as "safe" or less threatening to white people. For example, in familiar communities of color, it would be acceptable to greet someone by saying, "What's good?" In a professional, white workspace, it would be more acceptable to say, "Hi, how are you doing?" People of color who can navigate white society and successfully code-switch are often given more credit and access to resources, but they often have to withstand microaggressions from their white and cis peers. Over time, these microaggressions can be just as harmful as acts of more overt violence or harassment.

I am Chinese and Jewish and appear very ethnically ambiguous. Often people assume I am Latinx. Since I've been presenting more masculine I've been able to see first hand some very aggressive and shitty treatment from, especially, old white men. I get bumped and shoved around a lot, where I never did when femme presenting. I am aware now that I may be a target of police aggression in a way I never was before. I've been threatened with anti-Semitic threats on social media because of my Jewish last name, and experienced some anti-Semitism from partners' families. I'm fortunate in my socioeconomic status—I have a lot of education and am financially fairly well off. This affords me a lot of shelter and protection from racism and mistreatment for the most part.

Microaggressions are the everyday verbal, nonverbal, and environmental slights, snubs, or insults, whether intentional or unintentional, that communicate hostile, derogatory, or negative messages toward a particular group.

HOW ONE PERSON CHOSE THEIR NAME

I changed my name twice. The first time, I hastily changed it to a western gender-neutral name in an attempt to blend in as the new semester started at my University. I was five months on T, and just beginning to pass as a cisgender guy. I had already lived a good chunk of my life paranoid and anxious about standing out as an androgynous person, so at that point blending in was what I wanted most. I was scared and felt guilty about changing my name, particularly in regards to the burden it put on others. My parents did not react well to the name change, and I allowed them to continue calling me by my birth name. My mother particularly did not take a liking to my new name as she, a non-native speaker of English, could not pronounce it easily. Other than my parents, though, my peers and professors accepted the name change well, and changing it at the beginning of a new semester served me well in transitioning smoothly into my new name. After about a year of using my new name, the discomfort of realizing that I had given up a large part of myself, namely my culture, in choosing a western name (my birth name worked both in English and in Japanese), I began brainstorming a new name. I did not come up with any names that I liked that worked in both languages, so I made the decision to go with a Japanese name of my liking. It was gender neutral, had minor similarities to my birth name, sounded pretty, had beautiful characters, and most importantly, my mother (who gave me my birth name) approved of it. And thus, after about a year and a half of using a western gender-neutral name, I changed it once again, this time to a name that both I and my mother are satisfied with. This time, I changed it about mid-semester, and unlike the first time around, I was confident and happy about it. I announced my new name to my classes and friends, and though at first people messed up, eventually they all got accustomed to my new name. Though pronunciation was an issue for many, it was something I had prepared for and did not bother me too much. The best part of it all was that I could now fully embrace myself in Japanese spaces, including those with my mother, and still feel connected with my gender.

Out Numbered. "A comic style digital art painting depicting the feeling of overwhelming scrutiny when trans in every day life and trying to find a way to overcome it with art when it all feels way too much." Josephine Baird is an independent scholar, activist, performer and visual artist. She speaks and performs regularly worldwide and has appeared in a number of films. She has recently started drawing again as a way to express herself when words failed her.

Code-switching is not just a matter of language. For trans people of color in particular, gender-presentation is often linked to clothing, and privilege can be afforded or denied based on how we dress. For many trans folks, what we wear on our body becomes a way to feel seen in our gender. There is an even higher level of scrutiny, however, for trans people of color to conform to gender expectations than for white trans folks. There are specific negative stereotypes associated with trans people of color when we do not wear clothes that conform to white, middle-class ideals. For example, trans people of color, and especially trans women of color, in the workforce are often seen as "not professional enough," unless they wear very conservative clothing. Failing to comply with mainstream gender norms can lead to harassment, discrimination, and other forms of violence.

As a mixed, white passing Latinx person who is often not read as trans, I have come into even greater privilege than I once experienced. What has been particularly distinct and often really uncomfortable/imposter syndrome type feeling is when men I perceive as straight/white/cis give me the "NOD." I've received this gesture of "being in the boys club" from men I have perceived as POC/Non-white, but the boys club NOD is very particular to cis straight white men.

In addition to the physical and economic struggles that trans people of color face, we also face ostracization and ignorance within the white LGBTQ community. Although trans people of color have and continue to play a crucial role in movements for queer and trans rights, there is a disproportionate amount of positive media portrayal, visibility, and representation for white LGBTQ people. Up until the airing of the television series *Pose* on FX in 2018, accurate portrayals of trans people of color in mainstream media/television were virtually nonexistent. Where representation did exist, it often villainized gender

Some media/films featuring trans people of color include:

free cece (2016)
Happy Birthday Marsha (2018)
KUMU HINA (2014)
Leitis In Waiting (2018)
MAJOR! (2015)
Mohammed To Maya (2012)
Paris is Burning (1990)
POSE (TV series; 2018)
Trans in Color (Podcast)
We Want the Airwaves (Podcast)

nonconformity. For many years, characters were either one-sided, limited in their depth, rarely survived to the end of the show, or were portrayed as murder victims (particularly in cop shows). Many folks look to pop culture/media for "possibility models" of how to be in the world. Not having access to a reflection of ourselves is harmful to trans people of color's identity formation. This lack of representation is not only present in media, but in physical queer spaces as well. Many people in leadership within queer-based organizations are white or white-passing. If and when trans people of color take on leadership roles, they are often pushed out of the organization before they can make meaningful change.

> *Personally, as a light-skinned "white-passing" biracial person, who also "passes" (despite my efforts and desires) as a cis woman, and "passes" as straight especially when with my spouse who is a cis white man, I have lots of complicated feelings about being misidentified by strangers and not seen as who I really am. "Passing" is a funny term because historically it was used for Black people who chose to pass as white and leave their family and culture behind in order to avoid the oppression that others faced. And while there are many safeties and privileges that come with "passing," I am in no way trying to "pass" and there is lots of pain that comes with not being seen as who I am. I would never try to equate the pain of being misidentified with the pain of racist or transphobic violence, but there is pain there. I also think that the binary isn't just seen in our culture regarding gender but also regarding race. People have this idea that race is real and either you are white or Black or somewhere in-between. But in reality these terms could never encapsulate the nuance of human experience. And so in many ways I feel like I am that nuance.*

"Possibility model" is a phrase coined by Laverne Cox. She prefers this over "role model" because she likes the idea that, instead of expecting others to model their lives after her, she is showing them it's possible to live their dreams.

QTPOC ST. LOUIS

Tim Lumpkins (he/him) is the Director of Communications for Metro Trans Umbrella Group in St. Louis, Missouri.

I am a Black, queer, masculine-presenting trans person, living in St. Louis, Missouri.

I started my physical and social transition over a decade ago. Because of my appearance, I am often read as a cisgender man. Because of my relationships with women, I am often read as straight. Because of the intersections of my identities and the misperception that I am "one of the boys," I have experienced micro-aggressions and witnessed toxic behavior that I used to think was unique to me.

A few years ago, however, I began to understand that I was just one of the hundreds of queer and/or trans folks of color in St. Louis who was struggling at times to deal with the weight of living and working in a society that looks down on you because of your race, who you love, and how you identify. Luckily, there is a place for us.

QTPOC (Queer Trans People of Color) St. Louis was created by and for queer and trans activists of color in the wake of the killing of Mike Brown in Ferguson. They created this space because there was often no real safe space for queer and trans folks in the movement for racial equity. QTPOC St. Louis was birthed from the need for community and kinship with others who held multiple marginalized identities. I attended some of the first meetings and the room was filled with the love of dozens of folks of color who were able to show up as their full selves. I didn't know that there were so many of us here and QTPOC St. Louis reminded me that I'm not alone.

In the years since, QTPOC St. Louis has evolved as the needs of the community have evolved. In addition to meetups, QTPOC St. Louis has organized events and been there for our community. In 2019, they held their first *kiki* so that we could have a bit more joy in our lives. And QTPOC St. Louis was there when a young trans woman needed help paying off her high school graduation fees and buying a dress for her senior prom.

As people who hold so many identities that are often pushed aside, queer and trans people of color need these spaces. And as an emerging leader of QTPOC St. Louis, I am proud that I am helping to create more spaces with my queer and trans siblings.

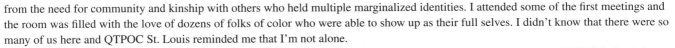

Just as it can be difficult to find POC representation in queer and trans communities, it can be equally as hard to find queer and trans representation in communities of color. Although many queer people have played key roles in movements for racial justice, their queerness is often covered up or they are asked to lead from the shadows. Bayard Rustin, an openly gay Black man was the orchestrator behind Martin Luther King's March on

Washington for Jobs and Freedom, but was asked to take a back seat when news of his sexuality became "an issue."[9] Within our own cultures, we are taught to abide by certain roles and scripts. When we break from the norms of our communities, the people we know, love, and respect often try to tear us down and force us to conform.

> *I absolutely cannot perform gender without being black. The Black (capital B as in culture) in me cannot fade and it is in direct conflict with how I live my life at times. I also grew up in a Black church. I know lots of homophobic people and transphobic people and I have had to unlearn a lot of that for myself. Race can't be removed from my equation of identity because that's what people think they know first about me. My gender is passable as cis.*

COLONIALISM AND THE IMPORTANCE OF SOVEREIGNTY

It is important to name the role of colonialism in the lives of trans people of color. In the United States, colonialism is the structure and process by which European settlers stole land and enslaved people to (continuously) build an empire of a nation-state. These settlers acquired their wealth through the genocide of peoples indigenous to Turtle Island (an Indigenous name for North America), the Caribbean, and Oceania, the enslavement of peoples from Africa, and the destruction of the natural world. Technologies of colonialism, including racism and gender oppression, were and are used to maintain control over Black and Brown people. Because of this history, all life in the United States is infused with colonialism and white supremacy.

> *I'm black. I think the way gender plays out in the black community doesn't allow for softness or tenderness. Black women are expected to be strong and black men stronger. This leads to people (i.e., white people) fearing me and ready to challenge me at any moment.*

MY INTERSECTIONALITY

Naiymah Sanchez (she/her) is a community activist.

I am a proud Afro-Latina of trans experience who struggled with gender from a young age. My blossoming was a little abnormal, but I used Halloween to help navigate the challenge of a "boy" identifying as a girl. I socially transitioned as a pre-teen, and my family wasn't too shocked. They just thought that I was feminine and ultimately would come out as gay. Back then, in the late 1990s/early 2000s (I'm telling my age) there was significant confusion. Gender identity and sexual orientation were seen as the same thing. My family never expected me to say that I was comfortable expressing myself as a girl. They were, however, receptive to my wishes. They just wanted me to be safe and healthy.

I have always felt safe and a sense of community in my Latinx neighborhood. Being unique was a bonus in life, and people honored my willingness to live my truths. I was able to find community outside of the Latinx community within youth groups that were queer-focused and served other youth of color. That gave me a sense of not being alone.

The activism I am involved with is intersectional but makes sure that gender identity is a focal point. I came into advocacy work nine years ago when I was offered a position with Galaei (a queer Latinx organization). It was my first job in the nonprofit sector, and it showed me how marginalized communities of color are—especially trans communities of color. I then became the program coordinator for the Trans Health Information Project, and my voice has been loud ever since. I want to be clear that we (humans) all experience intersectionality, whether it's around impactful issues or likes and dislikes. For me, my intersectionality is that I'm a person who is formerly incarcerated; I'm a survivor of sexual violence; I have experienced police profiling, overpolicing, and police mistreatment; I am spiritual and love pizza; I'm a former sex worker and a descendant of slaves. See how my intersectional identities may add to historical trauma? Oh, and I didn't add that I'm trans! I highlight the importance of intersectionality to build a bigger movement toward liberation.

I keep a positive mindset (in the face of challenges and objections to trans people's mere existence) by knowing that everything we are doing today is making it better for us tomorrow. Eventually, we will dismantle the systems of oppression.

About trans bodies, I want people to understand that there is no guide for being trans. There is no right and wrong way to be trans. It's about how you feel and see yourself. We all need to protect trans bodies and support trans rights initiatives. Finally, while we trans folks may have a unique identity that differs from others, it doesn't make us any less human.

Jamie Pandit (@justjamiep). "I am Jamie. I am a transgender woman. I exist. We exist."

The erasure of Indigenous peoples and the exploitation of Black people continue to be central to the functioning of the empire. It is a message that is reinforced in every institution, including schools, churches, and banks. And yes, even gender is colonial. Gender serves as a tool for forcibly assimilating Indigenous peoples. It is the container by which colonialism can be absorbed into the body. To learn whiteness, one needs to learn how to do gender in a western way. This is evidenced by the way Native children were stolen from their families and put in boarding schools to learn to be "civilized." The boys were forced to cut their hair and wear white men's clothes. The girls were taught how to be subservient, good housewives. These gender roles were enforced through psychological, physical, and sexual abuse. Through the Indian Allotment Act of 1887, nations that were historically matriarchal, egalitarian, and/or collectives were disbanded. People were forced into nuclear families with a man as a state designated head-of-household.

> *I am keenly aware of the binary of gender identity being a result of colonialism. My identity doesn't fit there, but I am not aware or connected to the parts of my ancestry that may have had more words for myself. I don't want to appropriate any other group's identities.*

This history is relevant because understanding the structure of colonialism helps us to understand how we continue to be influenced by the social and cultural forces around us. To be specific, trans people of color, as we know ourselves today, would not exist without the introduction of colonialism into our world. The term "trans people of color" was created in resistance to both white supremacy and cisheteropatriarchy. This label would be irrelevant if colonialism never existed, or if our people did not experience such extreme violence that divorced us from our traditional ways of knowing and being. Indigenous cultures across the globe each had (and should continue to have) the sovereignty to define gender on their own terms and in their own way. When operating in sovereignty, many Indigenous cultures did/do not subscribe to a strict gender binary.[10] The Bugis people (Indonesia) have five genders: the *makkunrai, oroané, bissu, calabai*, and *calalai*. Navajo people have four genders:

man, woman, masculine *nádleeh,* and feminine *nádleeh.* In many parts of India, *hijras* are recognized as a third gender. Many Indigenous peoples in North America recognize one or more kinds of Two Spirit people (those who embody both the masculine and feminine).

"Colonialism is a structure, not an event."[11]

> *My Indigenous identity is very much tied into my gender and sexuality. The latter two are an expression of anti-colonialism to me, because of how pervasive anti-Indigenous racism was and still is in society as a whole. My gender and sexuality truly have no English description.*

Not only was/is there common language and understanding around multiple genders in many Indigenous cultures, but the people who embodied these genders were/are often given a sacred place in society. Historically, many people who embodied the masculine and feminine at the same time were seen as healers or prophets. This is very different from the plight of trans people in the United States, where we face some of the deepest marginalization. Although some Indigenous peoples are able to retain cultural memory, many others have not. Our histories have been taken from our peoples. Because of this forced forgetting, we may never know the expansiveness of gender prior to colonization. The potential is gone because the only way we have to understand it now is through the lens of whiteness. For those of us who have been disconnected from our Indigenous languages and traditions, speaking in English and adopting western norms and values creates a barrier to understanding our own cultures.

EXPRESSING GENDER IN KOREAN

I am a second-generation Korean-American, and I find that it intersects with my gender identity in very specific ways. Korean language is structured in a way that is very hierarchical in terms of age and gender. The one I find myself facing the most is in terms of titles with peers. Boys have different terms for older brother and older sister than girls do, which leaves you with four different "titles" that assume the gender of both the person being addressed and the person who is addressing the other person. With my peers, I find ways to subvert things in subtle ways, and have created my own "gender neutral" term for older sibling—"hyungnni" combining hyung (older brother to a boy) and unni (older sister to a girl). I also find that some primarily Korean spaces I enter don't even have the context to understand my physical presentation as being queer or trans, so they just fit me within the context that they do know.

> *I'm Jewish, so with most sects of Judaism my transness isn't . . . . that big of a deal because we recognize six different genders in Rabbinic texts. Transtorah can explain it better than I can, but it means that I can even label myself using a traditional term—Tumtum.*

In addition to being stripped of our traditional knowledge and ways of doing gender, many communities of color have begun to internalize the homophobia and transphobia of the colonizing culture. There is a stereotype that communities of color are more homophobic/transphobic than white communities. Of course, this stereotype is not true across the board, and homophobia/transphobia exists in all communities regardless of race. It is true, however, that many communities of color have been taught, through processes of assimilation, that cisgender identities and behaviors are moral and "right." By using a lens of colonialism, it is possible to contextualize internalized gendered violence within communities of color as a learned behavior from oppressive forces. We learn how to conform to gender roles, along with roles of power and dominance.

> *I am a light-skinned Latinx individual. My race intersects with my gender a lot, both culturally and racially. I was very close to my family and it was very hard*

being rejected by my parents. My parents were my tie to my Latinx heritage. They are immigrants and I was born here far away from my ancestors. So it was tough coming out and jeopardizing those connections. But of course, I had to come out. Racially, I have been stopped by the police so much more after I began being read as a man.

In many communities of color, queerness is often seen as something that only white people do. Thus, some people of color identify as something other than trans or queer. For example, transmasculine people of color may describe themselves as studs or masculine of center (MOC). These different ways of defining gender-nonconforming POC experience come from both a resistance to being forced into white queer identities and a desire to be visible to communities of color by embodying Brown and Black ways of doing gender.

A "WHITE PEOPLE THING"

As a black person from a poorer upbringing, I'm transitioning near a lot of uneducated family members who don't understand what transitioning is. So many other black people think I'm just a butch lesbian or "experimenting with my biology." I've also been told "only white people transition," by my mother or that "trans people don't look the same as us" and "you can always tell when someone is trans."

I am biracial—black and white—and my race often feels erased in the same way my gender is. Separately, they are both ignored or not thought about, but together my identity is even more erased. For example, those few who know what nonbinary people are tend to think of it as a "white people thing."

Even though communities of color have internalized mainstream western gender ideals, there are a number of queer theorists who suggest that in a white-dominated society, people of color will always fail at performing white genders.[12,13,14,15,16] To be seen as a Black woman in the United States is something very different than to be seen as a white woman. To be seen as a Black man is different than to be seen as a white man. The same is true across all marginalized races. We have different assumptions about what gender looks and feels like, and what expectations and roles we place on people of different races with the same gender. Even when people of color are presenting as their genders assigned at birth, they are still failing at performing white gender. They will always fail at being "perfect white women" or "perfect white men."

I'm Blaxican, that's African American plus Mexican, ethnically and Black, Native American, and White racially, or just Black Mestizo for short. This intersects with my gender by us people of color being colonized into Eurocentric views of gender and me entirely tossing that mess out of the window to be myself and never compare myself to what the white standard of gender is.

It is a huge disservice to all people of color in the United States to deny us an opportunity to understand our Indigenous roots—that we are all Indigenous to somewhere and have all been deeply affected by colonial violence. Without understanding this history, we sometimes get lost trying to assimilate into a power structure that wasn't built for us and will never serve us. At the core of many Indigenous cultures is a relationship with land, a relationship with other human beings, and a relationship with all things at once. In losing that, we are destroying our earth, as we destroy our own bodies. For many trans people of color, honoring our true genders is so much more than a transition from one gender to another. It is an act of resistance and liberation from a gender binary that was violently forced upon our peoples. Knowing that our ancestors did not experience gender the way that we are told to experience it in the United States opens up possibilities for us to make different choices around our gender identities and expressions. Part of honoring our true genders is a move away from whiteness and toward our own sovereignty.

AN INDIGENOUS TRANS PERSPECTIVE

I'm mixed white and indigenous, both ethnically and culturally, and I'm white-passing and have attended predominantly white schools, so I experience a lot of white privilege. As an indigenous person in the LGBT + community, I have a rather unique experience. One aspect is my acute awareness of the appropriation and stereotyping of indigenous cultures that exists both within and outside of the LGBT + community (non-native people calling themselves Two Spirit is one glaring example). Additionally, being bi and nonbinary in a culture that strongly emphasizes the duality of the female and male (with gendered partner dances, strongly defined gender roles—including dress—both in secular and ceremonial life, and much more) can sometimes be frustrating, especially when the predominantly non-native LGBT + community loves to talk about how "native american cultures recognize more than just male and female" and "binary gender is a western concept." It's true that some native cultures had roles beyond male and female, and in general I've seen my indigenous community try to be inclusive of LGBT + people, but they're learning just as much as any other group, and the intense focus on the male/female binary can be alienating (for example, our heritage language, which we're trying to revitalize, has an unavoidable gender binary built into the kinship terms, so one cannot, for example, be a child or sibling or parent, but must be a son or a daughter or a brother or a sister or a mother or a father).

I'm half white half native. I'd say being native affects my gender identity, but because of colonialism i have no connections to my family or my culture. my dad is dead so we can't explore that together, but i can tell u on a spiritual level how it feels and what it means to me just without words that match my heritage. I can tell u that colonialism and being raised by a white parent who literally stole me from my brown parent that there are intense psychological and cultural traumas there. that i felt lonely and unable to come out or even really feel or see myself for who I was because of white supremacy. even though my white parent didn't MEAN to do any of that, it still happened. I have been suffocated by whiteness my whole life.

EMBODYING A NEW WORLD

The future is trans, and a trans future is a beautiful future. A trans future is a future where trans people, particularly trans people of color, no longer exist on the margins. We seek a future that dismantles binary ways of thinking and creates space for the expansiveness of all humans. We are so much more than victims of a system that continues to try to enact genocide upon us and to keep us from existing. We do not have to be defined by our marginalization. We get to control our own narratives.

In my native language, which is Malay, there are only gender neutral pronouns. When my dad, who doesn't know about my identity, speaks in English and sometimes refers to me with he/him pronouns, it's always satisfying!

Make Trans Dreams A Reality. (Colin Laurel)

There are so many gifts to embodying a trans-of-color space. For example, we have more opportunities for deep connection because of the ways that our struggles straddle so many different communities. We are in a position to teach the rest of society how to choose to live in truth, even if we are afraid. We are cultural creators, and some of the most brilliant theorists. In spite of—or because of—our pain, trans people of color have created ballroom culture, art, and some of the most powerful movements for justice. We are drivers of joy and creativity. We are nothing less than courage and magic.

I am indigenous Australian. Within that culture I'm known as a Sistergirl. I am widely accepted in that community.

THE LEGACY OF HOUSE/BALLROOM CULTURE

Trans people of color have been innovators of art, music, dance, and style for decades. One example of this is House/Ballroom culture, which came about in the 1980s in New York and consisted mostly of Black and Latinx queer and trans people.[17] This community was and still is based on competitions between "houses" in categories such as beauty, fashion, dance, and more. Houses are not just social communities; they are formed as chosen families, often with house "mothers" and "fathers" that care for the "children" not just in the ballroom scene but in everyday life. The House/Ballroom Communities have played pivotal roles in the survival and resilience of trans communities of color.

Unfortunately, House/Ballroom culture is an example of how trans and/or people of color communities have created art that is seen as valuable in society even when we, as people, are not. The 1990s fascination with voguing is a great example of how something that came out of our communities was appropriated and repackaged for the masses by pop star Madonna.

More recently, House/Ballroom culture has been more accurately and respectfully depicted in the television series POSE, in which trans characters are played by trans actors and relevant social issues and significant events in LGBTQ history are portrayed through the lens of these communities.

Trans future is potential. We can hold space for ourselves to move through the world in a way we haven't experienced before—without being riddled with pain/oppression/torture/trauma/violence. Trans futures are about possibilities of joy, love, and empathy. They are about the gracefulness of living in a world where all those things are present.

> *I feel that I have been fortunate to come from a culture where a "Two-Spirit" ideal was already a feature of their history. At the very least it has offered me a way to feel more comfortable with exploring gender as a spectrum rather than a binary. On the other hand, I present as caucasian. People observing me from the outside would never know I had come from the Kanien'keha culture unless I told them. For this reason, I have found that how I choose to express my gender or sexuality is generally more easily accepted by my peers and by society, because I'm at least white still. White people can identify with me on that level. I am fully aware that this entire process of expression is much more difficult for those of PoC background due to societal relations with race and ethnicity. To me, Intersectionality is a necessary aspect of our community's fight for inclusivity and acceptance. It must be included in any discussions about LGBT + rights, or we're only doing a fraction of our job.*

To be a trans person of color is to exist in a time and space that is not understood by mainstream society. We are both returning to a way of being that was nearly destroyed by colonialism, while simultaneously creating new genders and new ways of understanding ourselves that have never existed before. We are in a process of constant self-creation, and, in that process, we are simultaneously confusing and expanding the world around us (confusion is a necessary part of learning).

> *My gender identity and expression absolutely intersect especially with my race. I do not present with androgyny the way white people do—slim and elven or fae like. I do not wear androgynous or men's clothing the way white people do. I have a swagger and sex appeal and ability to wear bright colors that no white person could pull off.*

When we are owning ourselves, feeling ourselves, being unapologetically ourselves, we show the world what is possible. Even though many of us navigate feelings of insecurity, imposter syndrome (the experience of feeling you do not belong and that, soon, everyone else will realize it), and not feeling good enough, we still wake up every day and survive. That is something to celebrate. Every time we are able to see each other without requiring each other to leave parts of ourselves at the door, we give each other the strength to continue this work. We find validation from each other to keep reminding ourselves that we are real, necessary, and powerful.

> *It was really hard making the move to being a black man with the way our society treats us. I was very afraid to make that move. But, I got the chance to meet older and younger black trans men who have been living life. I finally felt comfortable moving forward and I am glad that I finally did.*

IVRI

Lior Gross (they/them) is a connector who applies their knowledge of ecology as a framework for justice by building critical community connections and fostering diversity for resilience through education. They are also part of the Nonbinary Hebrew Project, an online resource that has been working on a gender-expansive Hebrew grammatical system.

Ivri can be a direct translation of "one who crosses over," but it is also used throughout the Torah to refer to the Jewish people, and ivri is the word commonly transliterated as Hebrew. Our language, *ivrit,* is inherently nonbinary in name, and I have been working to create a parallel nonbinary Hebrew grammar system. In Margaret Moers Wenig's essay on "Balancing on the Mechitzah," ivri is posited as a word to use for trans folks when speaking in Hebrew, to use for embryonic beginnings, and to refer to the past as well as the present process of undergoing or surpassing. Ivri has existed for the biblical history of the language itself, and it carries great holiness because it is the name of my people.

As Jews, we are suspended in the in-between, and we honor that (for more, read "The Holiness of Twilight" on TransTorah.org). We are a people shaped by the Diaspora but longing for home, a people of *keva* (structure) and *kavannah* (intention), a people with a global holy language but with beautiful local renditions, born from regional language, customs, and food. We are a people who love to question and to doubt, a people with an ancient legal category for that which defies categories (*bria b'ifney atzmah*, a being created unto its own). We are inherently a people in and of transition, a people immersed in the society around us and yet also on the margins, a people rarely seen and often misunderstood, a people with a tenacious gift of survival. We are a people who sanctify twilight as the best time to pray and also a people who seek to litigate how to tell what twilight is.

We are a people who made six ancient gender categories, so trans and intersex folks can have honored roles in our society. We are a people grasping for some degree of control in the face of intergenerational trauma, while bowing in humility at the oneness and the ineffability of the divine. We flirt between the two prayers in our pockets, one of smallness and one of grandeur (from the teaching of Rabbi Simcha Bunim of Pshish'cha). We hold our holy texts in one hand and our commentators in the other as we seek to understand, and we agree that we never will.

No wonder so many of the major American Jewish Movements (Conservative, Reform, Reconstructionist) passed decrees in 2016 explicitly welcoming trans Jews, and so many trans rabbis are thought-leaders and world-shakers in our communities. After all, we are a people who are traditionally radical, with our roots in resilient nonbinary thinking (for more about Option 3 mindsets, check out Rabbi Benay Lappe's Eli Talk and SVARA).

I have been performing my Judaism for a long time, but I never truly lived it until I surrendered to my personal—and our Jewish—nonbinary-ness. I could not be spiritually vulnerable until I learned that I am a reflection of the divine image as well, and until I felt held and seen as such. I find gender affirmation through wrapping *tefillin*, wearing a *kippah* and *tzitzit*—not because these are men's actions in very traditional spaces, but rather because these rituals honor my trans body as a Jewish one. As I study Talmud, pray in synagogue, and host Shabbat dinners, I am queering Judaism and letting it queer me.

In my morning blessings, I give thanks to be made an ivri, to be put in a Jewish life and in a trans body. I cannot and will not separate my nonbinary-ness from that experience, for the Torah is written on parchment between two poles, held aloft, dancing black fire timelessly spelling my personal name and our Jewish name: ivri.

When we live in our truth, we are actually teaching the world about how to be in touch with their own potential and to create themselves in their own image, rather than living in the script written out for them. We are leaders of our world, and all people can benefit from our wisdom. We are leading our world into a different way of allowing people to be people—messy, complicated, beautiful, unique people. We are leading the movement toward being a different world: one that is not stuck in boxes, not stuck in cages, and not stuck in borders. We are decolonizing ourselves. When we don't allow the restrictiveness of white supremacy to define us, and when we define ourselves, we are enacting a kind of sovereignty that was supposed to have been taken from us. Instead we said, *No, that's not taken from us. I am in charge of myself.* We start with sovereignty over our own bodies, but we do not stop there. We demand to also be in charge of our own communities, and to be in charge of our own nations. We demand to be in relationship with the land and the earth, and with all things that are sovereign. In the refusal to be what colonialism says that we are, we enter into the bigger project of decolonization that is necessary for the health of our world.

Being in indigenous spaces in Tonala, Jalisco, I was able to get an incredible message from an elder that, yes, women are sacred, but also intersex and two-spirit people are sacred. Since then, I hold my head up to the stars knowing my own power with femininity and masculinity and reconnected with myself in ways I have never known were possible. I have traditional Mexican indigenous healers and brujos in my lineage and these ancestors are guiding me. I feel them radiating how proud they are of me being able to be me and honor myself, others, and the universe.

TPOC-CENTERED/LED ORGANIZATIONS

Abuela Taught Me (New York City)
API Chaya (Seattle)
Arianna's Center/ Trans Latina T Services (Florida)
Audre Lorde Project (New York City)
Black and Pink (National)
Black Excellence Collective (Minneapolis and New York)
Black LGBTQIA + Migrant Project, Transgender Law Center (National)
Black Trans Media (New York)
Black Transwomen, Inc. and Black Transmen, Inc. (National)
Brown Boi Project (New York City)
Cultivate QTPOC Healing Practice (Boston)
El/La Para TransLatinas (San Francisco)
GAPIMNY: Empowering Queer and Trans Asian Pacific Islanders (New York)
Garden of Peace Project (Pennsylvania)
Gender Justice LA (Los Angeles)
Griffin-Gracy Educational Retreat & Historical Center (Arkansas)
Interlocking Roots (National)
Intersex Justice Project (National)
Keeping Ballroom Community Alive Network (National)
Kween Culture Initiative
Marsha P Johnson Foundation
Montana Two Spirit Society (Montana)
My Sistah's House (Memphis)
National Queer and Trans Therapists of Color Network
NQAPIA—National Queer Asian Pacific Islander Alliance (National)
Organización Latina de Trans en Texas (Texas)
Out Now (Springfield, Massachusetts)
PARIVAR South Asian Collective (San Francisco Bay Area)
QTPOC Mental Health (Online)
Saint James Infirmary (San Francisco)
SONG: Southerners on New Ground (SouthEast Region)
Soul Fire Farm (Upstate New York)
Southern Fried Queer Pride (Atlanta)
Sylvia Rivera Law Project (New York City)
TGI Justice Project (California)
The Compton's Transgender Cultural District (San Francisco)
The Fund for Trans Generations
The Network/La Red (Boston)
The NW Network (Seattle)
The Queer & Trans People of Color Birthwerq Project (National)
The Solutions Not Punishment Collaborative (Atlanta)
Trans(Forming) (Atlanta)
Transgender Law Center (National)
Trans and Queer People of Color Collective Charlotte (North Carolina)
Trans Sistas of Color Project (Detroit)
Trans Women of Color Collective (Washington, DC)
Trans Women of Color Solidarity Network (Seattle)
Transcend (for TGNC API) (Chicago)
TransLatina Coalition (National)
Transwoman Empowerment Initiative (New Mexico)
U.T.O.P.I.A.—United Territories of Pacific Islanders Alliance (Seattle & Portland)

Bittu K. Rajaraman is a non binary trans masculine Associate Professor of Biology and Psychology. He is also an activist who works to imagine and create a world without hierarchies of class, caste, gender, race and ableism.

A liberatory trans future is not possible without abolishing nation-states, borders, and prisons; ending youth oppression and supporting intergenerational leadership; valuing art and cultural production; sex workers rights; housing accessibility and wealth redistribution; disability justice; transformative/healing justice; decolonization and the end of imperialism; reproductive justice for people of all genders; restoration of the earth; and the end of capitalism. All of these things are inherently connected, and all of these things negatively impact our trans communities. A trans future is thus inherently destabilizing because we are creating a departure from all that structures our current world. In this instability, we get to move in a way that allows for the recognition of self and others and that sees people as the whole of who they are. A liberatory trans future means that we are all going to rise up (and out and around) together and figure out how to be in relationships with one another, ourselves, and the world we live in. To build a trans future, we need to already be practicing, and we need to do it together.

A CLOSING BLESSING

We give thanks to the trans women of color who mother our movements, the ones who did/do the hard, care-based organizing that is necessary to ensure that no one gets left behind and everyone can access what they need. May all queer and trans people continue to remember who we are as a people, and how this movement came to be.

NOTES

1. Stryker, S. & Silverman, V. (Directors and Producers). (2015). *Screaming Queens* [Motion picture]. San Francisco, CA: Frameline.
2. Tourmaline & Wortzel, S. (Directors). Shields, M. & Wagner, A. (Producers). (2018). *Happy Birthday Marsha!* [Motion picture]. New York, NY. (No studio)
3. Lovetapescollective. (2017). "L020A Sylvia Rivera, 'Y'all Better Quiet Down' Original Authorized Video by LoveTapesCollective, 1973 Gay Pride Rally NYC" https://vimeo.com/234353103.
4. Chisholm, N. J. (2019). Black trans woman heckled, nearly arrested at Stonewall Inn. *Colorlines.* https://www.colorlines.com/articles/black-trans-woman-heckled-nearly-arrested-stonewall-inn
5. Crenshaw, K. (1989). Demarginalizing the intersection of race and sex: A Black feminist critique of antidiscrimination doctrine, feminist theory and antiracist politics. *University of Chicago Legal Forum, 1989*(1), 139167. http://chicagounbound.uchicago.edu/uclf/vol1989/iss1/8
6. Crenshaw, K. (1993). Mapping the margins: Intersectionality, identity politics, and violence against women of color. *Stanford Law Review, 43*(6), 1241–1299.

7. National Center for Transgender Equality. (2015). *The Report of the 2015 U.S. Transgender Survey.* https://transequality.org/sites/default/files/docs/usts/USTS-Full-Report-Dec17.pdf

8. Scott, J., Moses, M. S., Finnigan, K. S., Trujillo, T., & Jackson, D. D. (2017). Law and Order in School and Society: How Discipline and Policing Policies Harm Students of Color, and What We Can Do about It. *National Education Policy Center.*

9. Kates, N., & Singer, B. (Directors). (2003). *Brother Outsider: The Life of Bayard Rustin* [Motion picture]. United States: Question Why Studios.

10. b. binaohan. (2014). *decolonizing trans/gender 101.* biyuti publishing.

11. Wolfe, P. (2006). "Settler colonialism and the elimination of the native." *Journal of Genocide Research*, *8*(4), 387–409. https://doi.org/10.1080/14623520601056240.

12. Cohen, C. (1997). Punks, Bulldaggers, and Welfare Queens: The radical potential of queer politics? *GLQ*, *3*, 437–465.

13. ALOK. (2019). Trans is Natural. https://www.alokvmenon.com/blog/2019/7/5/trans-is-natural

14. Rifkin, M. (2011). *When Did Indians Become Straight?: Kinship, the History of Sexuality, and Native Sovereignty.* Oxford: Oxford University Press.

15. Somerville, S. B. (2000). *Queering the Color Line: Race and the Invention of Homosexuality in America.* Durham, NC: Duke University Press.

16. Snorton, C. R. (2017). *Black on Both Sides: A Racial History of Trans Identity.* Minneapolis: University of Minnesota Press.

17. Bailey, M. M. (2011). Gender/racial realness: Theorizing the gender system in ballroom culture. *Feminist Studies*, *2*(2), 365–386. http://www.jstor.org/stable/23069907

IMMIGRATION

Maria Carmen Hinayon

3

INTRODUCTION

The lived experiences of transgender and gender expansive (T/GE) people are multilayered and multifaceted, and so are their stories of immigration. Nevertheless, common themes underlie the immigration/migration circumstances for T/GE people as they leave their countries of origin. This chapter is U.S.-focused and discusses factors that may affect a person's experience in migrating to the United States, as well as the ways U.S. laws may create challenges for some T/GE people seeking asylum or a safer life.

FACTORS THAT AFFECT A MIGRATION EXPERIENCE

Both my parents and I are immigrants, as are my sisters. It means that my gender plays out differently in the different languages I speak. It's harder to convince people to refer to you a certain way when you don't do it yourself. It's really hard to break a decades-long habit of using feminine conjugations for myself in Russian. The Eastern European family dynamic of unconditional love and support is something I don't want to give up so for me my parents' difficulty in accepting my gender is an obstacle rather than a reason to cut them off. I think American culture is a lot more individualistic so it's easier to set hard lines. Finally, the struggle with legal documents is exacerbated by being an immigrant because there's MORE OF THEM. It's exhausting realizing that even five years after legally changing my name, I'm not done.

The author of this chapter does not represent herself as an expert in immigration law. This chapter contains legal information only and should not be construed as legal advice.

Many factors can affect a T/GE person's experience of leaving a home country and establishing a life in a new country. For many, this experience can be very stressful. Scholars have named this *acculturative stress*[1]—a specific type of stress that immigrants experience as they navigate their new environment and culture.

T/GE people migrate for various reasons. Experts have identified four main categories of immigrants,[2] which include: (1) voluntary immigrants seeking employment, advanced education, or reconnection with family members; (2) refugees who were involuntarily displaced by war, persecution, or a natural disaster; (3) asylum seekers who voluntarily leave their country to escape violence or persecution; and (4) people who relocate temporarily for a specific purpose with the intent of returning to their home country.

I am an immigrant to the United States. I actually moved here because I felt there would be more freedom to dress and express myself how I wanted, but I don't think it has affected my gender identity beyond feeling more free to express it fully.

The sense of *choice* or *willingness* one has can greatly affect their experience of adjustment. Some of us, if given other options, would not have chosen to leave our friends, families, or communities but made a difficult decision in order to live safely or access necessary medical care. Meanwhile, some of us may have had a relatively positive experience in our home countries but for other reasons, such as better opportunities, chose to come to the United States. Studies suggest that people who migrate voluntarily experience about 50% less acculturative stress than refugees.[3]

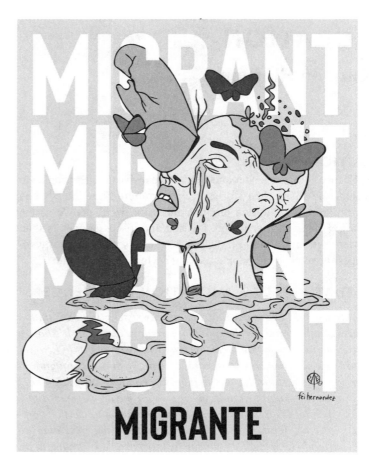

Migrante. (Féi Hernandez)

MY INTERSECTIONAL ACTIVISM

Diego Barrera (he/him) is a transgender immigrant from El Salvador. He does activism work around sexual violence specific to the trans community and the Latino community.

I've been in the United States for 15 to 16 years now. I can only think of one other Trans Latinx person in Northwest Arkansas, and that person is not out and doesn't put themselves out there as much as I do. The Trans community here focuses more on the white part of our community—the white identities of Trans-ness. It is important to talk about what it is like to have three different identities: to be an immigrant, to be Trans, and to be Salvadoran. The majority of the community here is Mexican, so coming here as a Salvadoran I faced two different cultures: the American culture and the Mexican culture. I had to assimilate to both and let go of the Salvadoran language (the *voseo*) to be able to fit into both.

A lot of people don't think about intersectionality. I have that perspective, and I know what it's like to be an immigrant, to be undocumented, and to be Trans. For example, if you are Trans here and either born in the United States or documented, you can change your documents such as your driver's license or birth certificate. However, if you are an immigrant—especially an undocumented immigrant—you can't change any of that. Being Salvadoran, my experience is especially different because although the Mexican government doesn't fully embrace Trans identities, the Salvadoran government is worse and will probably not budge. They won't even accept queer people. So, even though I present very masculine, all my documents still say female, and they all still have my birth name. Just a few weeks before writing this, the gangs in El Salvador said they would kill all the Trans people there. That they would eliminate us.

I think it is very unique to not only be an immigrant, but a Salvadoran immigrant. So I speak out about that, bringing awareness to what it is like to have multiple identities. I also speak out against sexual assault and domestic violence, because I have experienced both. Having multiple identities increases your chances of being victimized even more.

For the victims who lost their lives at the Pulse shooting back in 2016, I hosted the first queer event in Springdale, Arkansas, a bilingual vigil. It was the only vigil that fully recognized the identities of the survivors of Pulse. The majority of the victims were Latinx, and the shooting took place on Latin night. After the vigil, some youth approached me and talked about how unique it was to see a queer event in Springdale of all places. The need to have a space, where multiple identities are recognized, is why *InTRANSitive* started. *InTRANSitive* is a Trans migrant-led organization in Arkansas that works on providing education and on celebrating Trans resilience. I wanted to make sure that we are aware of all the intersections of having multiple identities, acknowledge what that looks like, and serve as advocates.

Mary Harris Jones, an Irish immigrant and activist from the 1890s, once said, "Remember the dead and fight like hell for the living." The reason why I put myself out there, which is scary and depressing at times, to be viewed only through the lens of "Oh, there is the trans guy that makes everyone mad," is that I've been in spaces where young Trans people break down crying because of how difficult their life is for being Trans and for being of color and I thought here I am and it hurts me, but I'm not at that level.

The more I put myself out there— through all the different work that I do—the more I help to change the minds of people so that these young people can grow up in a world where they can just go about their lives and not have to repeatedly come out or not have to be kicked out of their homes, to be raped or assaulted in any way. I don't necessarily do it to make people come out and be visible. Although I wish people would do that, we know as activists that not everybody can. So, those of us who can and are willing to, do so to create a future for descendants better than the one we have.

Premigration factors, such as access to resources and support, both social and financial, can greatly affect a T/GE person's experience of migration. Those of us who have struggled with poverty, torture, or persecution have faced much greater stressors overall than those of us who came to the United States simply to seek better opportunities. Access to support and resources as well as legal protections after getting to the new country are also crucial. Language can be a barrier. Having a support system in the new country, such as family, friends, and community makes a world of positive difference. Many T/GE people do not have access to these kinds of resources or support because of intersectional discrimination, isolation, and rejection, including from our own family members.

I am a second-generation South Indian immigrant. My identity growing up as a Brown girl was always othered from the "norm" of white children— whiteness, white girlhood, and therefore "normal" girlhood was characterized by pale skin, thin hair, slight features, etc.; none of which I possessed. Presently, I identify with the term tritiya prakriti, *which is an identity dating back to ancient India, and encompasses a large number of sexual and gender minorities.*

Scholars have suggested a Four Fold Model[4] to describe an immigrant person's experience of adjusting to their new country. This model includes: (1) assimilation (adopting the cultural norms of the dominant or host culture); (2) separation (rejecting the dominant or host culture and instead preserving the culture of origin); (3) integration (adopting the norms of the dominant or host culture while also maintaining the culture of origin); and (4) marginalization (rejecting both the culture of origin and the dominant or host culture). Here, the term "marginalization" is used to refer to a loss of ties to a culture rather than its customary meaning that refers to systemic or individual oppression of a person or group (i.e., marginalized communities). In this model, one's sense of freedom and choice is significant. When people feel coerced to assimilate into dominant or mainstream culture at the expense of sacrificing their own identity and culture, their immigration experience can be greatly and negatively impacted.

I have a deferred American citizenship. Given this Administration [Trump], I have no idea what will happen to my status. It frightens me terribly!

T/GE people coming to the United States may face intersectional discrimination and oppression stemming from racism, xenophobia, misogyny, transphobia, and/or homophobia. It is important to open our minds to this multilayered and compounding nature of oppression so that we may fully understand the lived experiences of T/GE people. For example, T/GE immigrants of color will experience racism and colorism, on top of transphobia, homophobia, misogyny, and anti-immigration sentiments.

My first-generation identity was relevant in two ways. First, I felt a pressure to be traditionally successful as a reflection of my family. Bringing embarrassment to my parents, or throwing away their sacrifices, was never an option. Second, in Farsi, there are no gendered pronouns and, without malicious intent, Iranians tend to misgender people when speaking English. I think this made me a little more forgiving. Additionally, because my own Farsi skills were poor, it was difficult for me to explain my transition to relatives, and I often had to rely on others to explain things for me, especially my mother. I didn't have any control over the timing or the narrative; my grandparents didn't find out I had changed my name until three years after the paperwork had been filed, and five years after I'd started using my new name informally.

TRANS IMMIGRATION AND THE LAW

Trans and gender expansive (T/GE) people occupy a precarious position in U.S. immigration law.[5] We are oftentimes misunderstood, stereotyped, and discriminated against in the immigration process and in society overall. Yet, we are a class of persons for whom immigration relief is often needed given the harsh realities of violence, persecution, and discrimination that pervade our everyday lives. These inequities are certainly true for many of us in the United States, and in many cases they are harsher in countries outside the United States.

I'm a naturalized citizen but have not attempted to do anything with it yet. Too expensive to make changes. Like hundreds of dollars to make changes.

Dismantle Prisons, Abolish ICE. (Asharah Saraswati / Art Twink)

The National Center for Transgender Equality (NCTE) estimates that there are between 15,000 and 50,000 undocumented transgender adults in the United States,[6] a number that is likely underreported. T/GE people, especially transgender women of color, experience disproportionately high rates of violence and persecution globally. Thus, many seek refuge (or asylum) in countries such as the United States to escape serious threats to their lives and safety and to freely live as their authentic selves under the protection of trans-affirming laws in some U.S. states (such as California).

I'm an immigrant myself. Being a stranger in the US makes me feel even queerer. And I also feel like a stranger in my own country, because the transphobia is worse than in the US.

U.S. immigration law is complex, and it would take several book volumes to explain it all in depth. This chapter strategically focuses on several aspects of immigration law that more often intersect with T/GE people and our unique experiences. There are many ways a person can obtain and maintain legal presence in the United States. It is important for T/GE people to seek the advice of a legal professional to explore all immigration options.

Every year, the LGBT Asylum Program at East Bay Sanctuary Covenant in Berkeley, California provides legal assistance and psychological support to over 550 people fleeing violence and persecution in their home countries.

A CONVERSATION WITH MAYA JAFER

Maya Jafer (she/her) is a transgender woman from India now based in Hollywood, California. She is an actress, Bollywood dancer, comedian, and activist. She is known for her roles on "Mohammed to Maya," an award-winning documentary, and the TV show, "Transparent."

Transitioning has not only changed me physically, but it has forced me to grow, evolve, and mature emotionally, intellectually, and especially spiritually. I came from a strict religious Muslim family in South India. My father was extremely devout and forced us kids to follow every aspect of Islam. If we didn't, he would physically and emotionally abuse us. He thought that was his role as a parent. I never was, at heart, a religious person, Islamically. But I did follow a lot of the rules out of fear of my father. So I carry a lot of resentment around him and religion in particular. Being trans or gay was out of the question. I never came out in India.

I came to the United States in 2000 on a student visa. There, I quickly realized I was transgender, but I didn't come out or transition at that time because it was a lot bigger deal and more expensive then. In 2008, the market crashed, and I had more free time on my hands because I was laid off. I started seeing a therapist for free at the LGBT center. The first thing I told her was that I was trans, but that we weren't going to talk about that. I just wanted to talk about my father and the abuse. She convinced me to go to a transgender support group just once, and it was the perfect time for me. Everything fell into place.

One day, it hit me that I could be a very beautiful Indian woman. I had many blocks in my mind that prevented me from considering transition in the past: that I would never look like a woman, that I would be mistreated, that I'd be disowned—like many people in third world countries are. But I realized that I'm trying to fix everything from the outside when the root cause of my unhappiness is that I'm not being true to myself. I'm always going to be unhappy until I address this issue. So that was the moment I decided I was going to transition, and even though all those blocks were there, they didn't feel as daunting.

On May 27, 2009, I had my estrogen shot, and then I had some procedures I could afford. On April 10, 2010, I started living as a woman full-time. On February 10, 2011, I had gender confirmation surgery. Jeff Roy from UCLA was looking for a Bollywood dancer transwoman for a project he was doing. He joined me in Thailand when I was having surgery, and he made a short film about my transition. A year later, we had a documentary feature called "Mohammed to Maya," which has been shown in festivals all over the world. All of this happened without my family knowing. I knew what their answer would be.

While the documentary was becoming more popular, my brother contacted me. He had been taking care of my mother, who has dementia, since my father died in 2004. He wanted me to take care of her. I said yes and then realized I'm a woman and they still have no idea. I wrote both of my siblings a very long e-mail coming out. I didn't hear from them for seven days, and then I got the worst e-mail of my life. My brother said the only way I could be part of the family is if I reversed the process and became a man. My sister stopped talking to me altogether. They told me that I had gone against Islam, that I dishonored the family, that I was going to Hell, and that Allah hates me now.

I knew they wouldn't support me, but I didn't think they would disown me! I became more depressed with suicidal thoughts. I got 20 to 30 panic attacks a day. With his words, my brother also took away my main anchor, Allah. Even though I wasn't a religious person, I still had faith in Allah, and I prayed frequently—not the full ritual but when lying in bed, I connected with my God. I realized I had no one, so I had to quickly reestablish my relationship with God, which was tainted with trauma from my father.

That's where spirituality came in. I had to fake it until I make it, as they say, by believing that God had brought me to that point and that God would bring me through it. I didn't choose to be transgender. I tried to change it, but I couldn't. I began to believe that even if everyone hates me, God still loves me. That's where my spirituality began. Through all of the ups and downs of my transition, I gained a new life, new friends, and a new chosen family.

I still see myself as Muslim, but I'm not a religious Muslim. I'm a spiritual Muslim with a Buddhist approach to life. I believe in peace, respect, and equality. Now, I'm happier than ever. I still struggle with depression, but I have medication and a sense of peace. When I look in the mirror now, I see myself. I feel like a complete human being.

TERMINOLOGY RELATED TO IMMIGRATION AND THE LAW

Citizenship (being a U.S. citizen) is obtained by birth (being born on U.S. soil or elsewhere to at least one U.S. citizen parent) or is obtained by naturalization.

Naturalization is the legal process by which a noncitizen acquires U.S. citizenship after meeting certain eligibility requirements and pledging allegiance to the United States as their country.

Permanent Residents (also known as "green card holders") are noncitizens who are authorized by the government to permanently reside and work in the United States. After satisfying certain requirements, which include continuous U.S. residence within a period specified by law, permanent residents are eligible to acquire U.S. citizenship through naturalization.

> "UndocuQueer" is a term that has grown in popularity since the early 2000s and refers to a movement to advocate for the people who exist at the intersection of LGBTQ and undocumented immigrant identities/experiences.

Nonimmigrant Residents are those who are legally authorized to reside in the United States temporarily and with certain conditions, which may or may not include work authorization.

Undocumented Immigrants are those who are physically present in the United States without formal legal authorization. They either entered the United States without going through the legal process of immigration, or they have violated the terms of their visa, such as overstaying its time limit.

Deportation is the legal process by which an immigrant is removed from the United States, either because they are undocumented or because they are a documented immigrant who has been convicted of a crime.

Refugees are those who flee violence and persecution and are unwilling or unable to return to their home country because they fear serious harm.

Asylum is a form of immigration relief given to refugees who are already in the United States or seeking admission at a port of entry. An *Asylee* is a person who is seeking or was granted asylum.

IDENTITY DOCUMENTS DURING IMMIGRATION

> *I am a recent immigrant to the United States, and I have not changed my name legally yet because I am worried that I may run into trouble if my green card doesn't match my other documents.*

> Immigration Equality is an LGBTQ immigrant rights organization that assists LGBTQ people with immigration issues, including asylum and detention.

T/GE people can change their name and gender marker on immigration-specific identity documents such as a U.S. passport or green card by presenting either (1) an amended birth certificate or court-ordered name and/or gender change, or (2) a medical certification from a licensed physician (doctor) attesting that the person underwent gender transition pursuant to the medical standards of care approved by the World Professional Association of Transgender Health (WPATH). Proof of "sex reassignment surgery" is no longer required for this purpose. If the person has not legally changed their name, they may still change their gender marker through a medical certification letter. They may be required to provide a recent photograph reflecting their current appearance.

Untitled. Chucha Marquez is a Queer, Chicanx print maker, digital illustrator, and social media whiz. They were born and raised in the South Bay and are currently based out of Oakland, California. Chucha's artwork is inspired by current and historical struggles for social justice and liberation, especially within the context of gender and sexuality, immigration, feminism, current events, and solidarity work.

SAMPLE MEDICAL CERTIFICATION LETTER FOR GENDER MARKER CHANGE ON U.S. PASSPORT OR GREEN CARD

The U.S. Department of State website (travel.state.gov) includes a sample medical certification letter for physicians to use in helping their clients to apply for gender marker changes. Below is the exact text of the sample letter. A certification that a person "has had appropriate clinical treatment for transition" results in a passport that is valid for ten years for adults and five years for those under 16 years of age, while a certification that a person "is in the process of transition" results in a passport that is valid for two years.

Sample Letter:

[Licensed Physician's Letterhead]

[Physician's Address and Telephone Number]

I, (physician's full name), (physician's medical license or certificate number), (issuing U.S. State/Foreign Country of medical license/certificate), am the physician of (name of patient), whom I have treated (or whose medical history I have reviewed and evaluated).

(Name of patient) has had appropriate clinical treatment for transition to (specify new sex male or female).

Or

(Name of patient) is in the process of transition to (specify new sex male or female).

I declare under penalty of perjury under the laws of the United States that the foregoing is true and correct.

[Signature of Physician]

[Typed Name of Physician]

[Date]

My legal status in the US has to match my French passport, and my female gender marker. It is frightening because I never know who is going to take issue with the fact that I look male but am legally female.

IMMIGRATION AND CRIMINAL JUSTICE

Noncitizens, even if they have legal status, are subject to deportation if they are found to have engaged in criminal acts. Even minor criminal offenses classified as misdemeanors can lead to deportation if they are considered violent crimes, moral turpitude offenses (involving fraud or dishonesty), or drug-related offenses.

Trans and gender expansive (T/GE) people, especially transgender women, experience high rates of arrests due to discriminatory policing and profiling. Even when they have not committed crimes, trans defendants often plead guilty or no-contest ("nolo contendre") in exchange for lesser sentences (such as avoiding jail time) and/or to avoid any interaction with the criminal justice system, where transgender people experience disproportionate violence and discrimination.

In some cases, T/GE people are ill-advised by criminal defense lawyers about the immigration consequences of their pleas, which have the same effect as "convictions" in immigration law. If you have been given bad advice and accepted a plea without proper counseling, you may have legal options. "Misinformed" pleas (wherein the person taking the plea was not given all of the relevant information) can be vacated as instructed by the U.S. Supreme Court in *Padilla v. Kentucky*, 559 U.S. 356 (2010).

The Queer Undocumented Immigration Project (QUIP), is a program of United We Dream, which seeks to organize and empower undocumented LGBTQ immigrants.

IMMIGRATION RELIEF BASED ON PERSECUTION IN A COUNTRY OF ORIGIN

There are various forms of relief under U.S. immigration law for refugees. Refugees are those who have been forced to flee their country due to persecution, war, or violence. They cannot, or are unwilling to, return to their country of origin because of a well-founded fear of persecution and harm based on their race, religion, nationality, political opinion, or membership in a particular social group.

A *particular social group* experiences violence and persecution based on common and immutable characteristic/s that is/are fundamental to their identity. T/GE people, by virtue of our gender identity and gender nonconformity, have been identified as a particular social group within the protection of immigration law.

For example, in *Hernandez-Montiel v. INS*, 118 F.3d 641 (9th Cir.1997), the Court held that "gay men with female sexual identities" constitute a particular social group eligible for immigration relief. Geovanni Hernandez-Montiel, originally from Mexico and described by the Court as a "gay man who dressed and behaved as a woman" experienced repeated sexual assaults and physical violence from the Mexican police and civilians. Although the Court's observation seems to conflate gender identity and sexual orientation, it clarified the protected status of transgender people as asylees in *Avendano-Hernandez v. Lynch*, 800 F.3d 1072 (9th Cir. 2015). In that case, the U.S. Appeals Court held that "transgender persons are often especially visible, and vulnerable, to harassment and persecution due to their often public nonconformance with normative gender roles." Erin Avendano-Hernandez, a transgender woman, experienced sexual assault and physical violence from the Mexican police, her own family, and members of the local community.

T/GE people also experience persecution and violence because of political activism and community work. Being outspoken about political opinions can increase visibility, which, in turn, increases vulnerability to backlash, retaliation, and targeted violence. For example, a 2012 REDLACTRANS report titled, *The Night is Another Country*, highlights the violence against transgender human rights defenders in Latin America, and points to their identity and activism as main motives for the crimes committed against them. In 2011, the treasurer of *Colectivo Unidad Color Rosa* in Honduras was shot seven times by

Illegal. (Art by Emulsify)

two males identified by a witness as members of the *Policia National Preventiva*. About 60% of transgender human rights activists in Guatemala and Honduras report having been arbitrarily detained. One activist described being held with 300 men and being raped and beaten all day.[7]

In establishing eligibility for immigration relief based on persecution as a member of a particular social group, asylees often need to prove they belong to that group. This means that T/GE refugees may be scrutinized and asked for proof to establish their gender identity and/or sexual orientation. It is important to understand that non-western and Indigenous cultures have different views of gender identity and sexual orientation, which go beyond the rigid binary conception of male and female. Thus, advocates must keep an open mind in understanding the specific backgrounds and experiences of their clients and be strategic in exploring and presenting the legal theories of their case based on the immigration relief sought.

T/GE refugees who have been "firmly resettled" in another country outside the United States are not eligible for immigration relief on the basis of persecution. Thus, if a T/GE refugee has been granted permanent residence or citizenship in another country (other than the country of origin) and/or has permanent housing or work authorization in another country, they are ineligible to receive refugee status in the United States.

ASYLUM

Asylum is a discretionary form of immigration relief granted to refugees in the United States under the Immigration and Nationality Act § 208. A T/GE refugee may seek asylum upon entry to the United States (affirmative asylum) or as a defense to prevent deportation (defensive asylum).

Aside from belonging to a particular social group, T/GE asylees must prove by credible evidence that they have a "well-founded fear" of persecution and violence if returned to their country of origin, and that their persecutor/s are government actors or private individuals/groups that the government is unwilling or unable to control. Oftentimes, asylees do not have or have difficulty obtaining documentation and corroborating evidence to support their claims of persecution and violence. Thus, the asylee's own testimony is

The National Immigrant Justice Center focuses on serving low-income immigrants, including asylum seekers, binational same-gender couples, survivors of violent crimes, and LGBTQ immigrant detainees.

Justice for Roxsana. (Familia: Trans Queer Liberation Movement) Roxsana Hernandez was an immigrant from Honduras who died in ICE custody in 2018.

crucial, if not the only, evidence and must be "believable, consistent, and sufficiently detailed to provide a plausible and coherent account of the basis for [their] fear." [*Matter of Mogharrabi*, 19 I. & N. 439 (B.I.A. 1987)]. A testimony that is credible and corroborated by evidence increases the likelihood that an application will be granted. When there is not clear evidence that an individual was persecuted, an attorney also has the option of providing background information on a country that can support individual testimony. This might include reports such as those produced by Amnesty International.

REFLECTING ON HISPANIC HERITAGE MONTH AS A TRANS WOMAN

Úmi Vera (she/her) is the Campaign and Organizing Director for Familia: TQLM.

I am a trans woman, born in southeast Los Angeles, California, and raised in Portland, Oregon. I am also the daughter of Mexican immigrant parents who are descendants of Tepehuan O'dami indigenous peoples. Currently, I am the campaign and organizing director at Familia: Trans, Queer Liberation Movement (Familia:TQLM), and cofounder and incoming board chair of the Association of Jotería Arts, Activisms and Scholarship (AJAAS).

Familia: TQLM is a national organization creating a cultural political home for Latinx trans and queer immigrants. For over five years, we have spearheaded some of the most radical campaigns in the immigrant rights and the LGBTQ rights movements. #Not1More, #EndTransDetention, #AbolishICE, and #Justicefor-Roxana, have all been campaigns led by women, gender nonconforming/trans and queer, working-class and poverty-surviving people of color—many of whom are immigrants.

Hispanic Heritage Month is nationally recognized between September 15 and October 15. I want to relate a few thoughts and ideas on family equity for all. Hispanic Heritage Month happens to begin on the date of the independence of Costa Rica, El Salvador, Guatemala, Honduras, and Nicaragua, and it precedes Mexico's Independence Day as well. All of these countries have experienced multiple struggles to gain their independence from more than one European invader. And similar to the United States, colonial powers continue to be reformed generation through generation—still impacting some of the most vulnerable communities, who just so happen to be the same communities who have led and continue to lead pertinent social change.

OK . . . take it all in::breath::

We can do this together::exhale::

What does family equity mean to you?

What does family equity mean for all of us?

Families we are born into or have chosen are vastly diverse. As gender nonconforming/trans and queer communities creating families, you have your personal understanding of this fact. With the many individuals it takes to raise a family, you are fostering radical community support networks. You are also part of a movement resisting institutionalized oppressive ideas of which families are allowed to exist with human rights protections and which are not. And thank you!

As you may imagine all of the realities that exist for us here as GNC/trans and queer folks, they also exist for our migrant siblings in their home countries. Familia: TQLM began with a *familia* and parent support network, further building into the multigenerational approach to community building and organizing we have now. This space allows for an unlearning of mono-religious colonial ideas of the binary, and more importantly holds space to reclaim our gender identities, our sexualities, and ourselves.

With our elders and our young, the ways we always have, we have successfully organized for the closure of one trans/GNC detention center in Santa Ana, California, and continue surviving ripples that will scar for generations to come due to forced migration/displacement, detention, and deportations. We have borne witness to countless deaths in these for-profit detention centers, one of them being Honduran trans immigrant woman Roxsana Hernandez.

We also don't have all the answers within just our movement alone. Over the years we have formed a national trans and queer migrant justice coalition with the Black LGBTQ + Migrant Project (BLMP), the Transgender Law Center (TLC), and Familia: TQLM community members. When the U.S./Mexico border is an epicenter of this country's dialogues on immigration, we must also all recall that the southern borders are global migration routes.

During Hispanic Heritage Month and for the rest of the year, I ask that we think about what family equity means for all of us. Ask what it means for your collective families, and you individually to listen, honor, and respect the leadership of historically marginalized peoples. For this month reminds us of the many generations of resisters before us and the fact that we walk a journey having us soon-to-be trancestors and queer ancestors ourselves.

What does family equity mean to you?

What does family equity mean for all of us?

The application process for asylum may vary depending on whether you are an affirmative or defensive asylum applicant. Affirmative asylum involves an applicant who is physically present in the United States and files for asylum within a year of entry. (There are some exceptions to the one-year deadline, including mental health issues.) The asylee must complete USCIS Form I-589 and submit their supporting documents and evidence. They may include their spouse and any unmarried children (under 21 years old) in the application. If no decision has been made within 150 days of filing, the asylee may apply for temporary work authorization by completing and filing USCIS Form I-765.

Defensive asylum involves an applicant who is facing removal proceedings. As a defense to prevent deportation, the applicant requests the Immigration Judge grant them asylum by demonstrating that they satisfy the same legal requirements as an affirmative asylum applicant. In cases where an affirmative asylum application is denied and the applicant no longer has legal authority to stay in the United States, the applicant is referred to the Immigration Court for deportation, but may renew their request for asylum, turning it into a defensive asylum application.

Asylum seekers who present at a U.S. port of entry, rather than already living in the United States, are placed in expedited removal proceedings by the U.S. Customs and Border Protection (CBP) and referred to "credible fear" interviews with an asylum officer. If the asylum officer determines that the asylee has a significant possibility of being eligible for asylum, they are referred to Immigration Court to undergo a defensive immigration process. Otherwise, they are ordered removed and will be deported. If an asylum officer determines that an asylee is not eligible for asylum, the asylee can still appeal to an Immigration Judge. It is important to consult with a knowledgeable immigration attorney when applying for asylum or appealing an asylum case.

Bellevue Hospital's Program for Survivors of Torture in New York City welcomes LGBTQ immigrants and provides medical, mental health, and legal services, including expert documentation for asylum cases.

WITHHOLDING OF REMOVAL

Withholding of removal is a form of immigration relief granted to refugees under the Immigration and Nationality Act § 241(b)(3) and a defense to prevent deportation. There is no one-year deadline to apply for withholding of removal the way there is to apply for asylum. Withholding of removal is similar to asylum, but with a few key differences. Although the same grounds for obtaining asylum apply to withholding of removal, the burden of proof is higher—the refugee must demonstrate that it is more likely than not that they will be persecuted if returned to their country of origin. Thus, even when the T/GE applicant experienced past persecution or violence, their application for withholding of removal may still be denied if there are changed circumstances in their country of origin and the threat of persecution no longer exists or, if they can relocate to another area of the country of origin, where they will be safer.

Chicago LGBT Asylum Support Partners, also known as CLASP, assists asylum-seekers resettling in Chicago with housing and legal referrals, social support, and public transit funds.

In contrast with someone granted asylum, a person granted withholding of removal must pay an annual renewal fee for work authorization, is entitled to receive fewer government benefits, and cannot travel outside of the United States. It is also not a permanent relief and has no pathway to permanent residence or citizenship. The government may still deport the refugee to a country other than the country of origin. Withholding of removal must be granted, however, if the refugee qualifies. This means it is available to those convicted of nonserious criminal offenses or those who for other reasons do not qualify for asylum.

LETTER TO A GRANDFATHER NOT LONG GONE

Yanin Alexa Kramsky (they/them) is a PhD candidate at the University of California, Berkeley interested in spatial politics, critical social and queer theory, and climate justice. Yanin holds a Master of Environmental Science from Yale University and a Bachelor of Science from Art Center College of Design. Yanin's lifelong pursuits revolve around understanding the complex web of identity and environment.

You took your secrets to the grave and I assimilated well.

Hope funneled through a worn emigration route one month before U.S. borders closed to Soviet Jews. Political asylum was an instance: A Resident Alien card amid unsorted documents on a table; an assimilation agent mispronouncing my name, my dead name; Los Angeles circa 1989. I assimilated well—into a fraught girlhood, postponed boyhood, and 1.6 million melding stories of Jewish refugees who fled the Soviet Union. Ukraine.

Political asylum was Odessa gone. Memories—WWII, evacuation, imprisonment, political dissidents, political psychiatry—funneled through a worn emigration route one month before U.S. borders closed to Soviet Jews. You cloaked your stories in happy endings and took your secrets to the grave.

Old headlines fan the flames of my hunger for clues and a narrative to call my own. A laptop rests amid unsorted notes on a table with two tabs open: 1. A patchwork history, and 2. Present day. One: I situate your stories in political jargon that determined my fate, in shifting policies broadcast on Voice of America, and rushed exit visas hitting the shoddy beams holding up this country's descending immigration ceiling. Two: I read headlines threatening a border wall and the deportation of Dreamers—their fate suspended in the wavering hands of power. A collision of suppressed past and reckless future. An eroding genealogy of volatile immigration policies exposing secrets that still sting. Hundreds of thousands of undocumented livelihoods editorialized without a break. I sit with a dizzying awareness of simultaneous marginalization and colonization—uprooted by exclusion from my homeland, only to be re-rooted in a dry landscape encrusted with cyclical narratives of displacement suffered by those who belong.

August 1989. I sit on dry sand looking into the future you imagined. I'm nearly three years old and can easily attune to your soft laughter. Its apprehension is lost to the wind. Sand is grasped firmly in your hand—a plan—yet several grains fall through. A confused girlhood and hesitant boyhood. A diagnosis of gender dysphoria, unplanned. Three tabs open: 3. Iniquitous national debates unsuccessfully aimed at undermining transgender rights. I assimilated well, but couldn't feign ignorance. I find companionship and solace in a longstanding struggle. I stand anchored in US history. My own transition solidifies in the thick air of resistance. A mote carried by a legacy of yearning. I catch the grains of sand slipping through your fingers. Your unfettered hope provides more opportunity than you imagined. You cast a net that caught me in all my forms. I take your hand.

This long-standing struggle permeates the mundanities of everyday life. Slipping between genders and cultures, I ruffle the feathers of humanity. It throws back a blanket of assumptions I struggle to find my way through. "Third culture kid," "nonbinary kid," and every other phrase carved from a language used by a nation that prides itself on homogenizing difference. I take refuge in newly forming language, testing its stronghold. But justifications stick to the tip of my tongue and linger there. How can I pull empathy through this rigid mesh woven of category and judgment that entraps me? Invisibility encroaches. I navigate humanity's discomfort and wear its postulations awkwardly. Mishaps are inevitable. Assimilation casts its net selectively. This time I can go unnoticed. I assimilate well, grip your weathered hand, and keep my secrets, too.

Assimilation casts its net selectively. Children in immigration detention centers await asylum. The drone of footsteps and bureaucracy is disrupted by clanging. The mundanities of everyday life are suspended by waiting. They'll grow up forgetting the details, but will feel them in their bones. Old headlines and human rights discourses won't provide answers; they won't scratch the surface of justice deeply enough to make a gash that demands attention. I look out at a dry landscape swelling with memories. It is a landscape of congealing stories waiting to be unearthed and grasped fully; stories ready to be complicated by undisciplined, raw feeling; stories that can no longer serve the self-proclaimed victors of humanity. Pressed by the weight of one another's stories, I impatiently wait for the eruption that is bound to shake history.

August 2016. One fist clenched tight and the other hand trembling. You ask questions about my life and I craft stories with happy endings. Uninhibited tears are interrupted by soft laughter. Your lessons force their way through the contradiction. I'm nearly 30 years old and savor every instance. We close our eyes and dig through memory. You hold my cold palm and I press my fingers into comfort. You swallow stories that land on the tip of your tongue that you think might scare me. Instead, we meet at a bicycle path where I fall over and over again with naive abandon. Riding reluctantly beside the Great Wall of Los Angeles, I'm distracted by colorful, staggering images of those who came before us—an imprint imploring cultural remembrance. Your focus never leaves my bicycle. Too busy protecting me, you run out of time to leave your own mark. But you're reflected in the portraits of other grandfathers, painted with the brushstrokes of unceasing sacrifice and the colors of tenacity. You are painted among grandparents who will continue shielding their grandchildren's ears from the clanging; whose grandchildren will continue tending to the deep, tired roots that twist and turn for answers—for justice that is never too deep to stop seeking. We open our eyes. Yours are transparent revealing all secrets.

You say you took your secrets to the grave, but I protect them.

DEFERRAL OF REMOVAL BASED ON THE CONVENTION AGAINST TORTURE

The United Nations Convention Against Torture and Other Cruel, Inhuman, or Degrading Treatment or Punishment (CAT) prohibits the United States from returning a refugee to any country in which they will likely be tortured. The process for requesting CAT protection is similar to asylum and withholding of removal. The refugee must prove that it is more likely than not that they will be subjected to torture if returned to their country of origin. To constitute torture, the acts must involve cruel and inhuman treatment of the victim who is under custody or control of the torturer. Torture can involve infliction of severe physical and mental suffering, sexual assault, or deprivation of food, water, or sleep.

The Queer Detainee Empowerment Project, based in Brooklyn, New York, is a community organizing project that offers detention center visitation and postrelease support to LGBTQ people.

Artwork. (Diego Matéo Barrera)

CAT protection offers fewer benefits than asylum, does not confer permanent legal status and pathways to citizenship in the United States, and does not guarantee release from detention. The government may also remove the refugee to a safe third country that will grant them refugee status. However, deferral of removal based on CAT is mandatory and must be granted even when the refugee was convicted of particularly serious crimes. There is no one-year deadline to apply for CAT relief.

Among the three forms of immigration relief based on persecution, asylum grants the most benefits to the refugee and has a clear pathway to permanent residency and citizenship. But when asylum fails, a transgender refugee may still be eligible for withholding of removal or deferral of removal under CAT. An advocate may request some or all of these forms of relief, simultaneously or subsequently, as part of their strategy.

COMMUNITY-BASED RESOURCES FOR TRANS IMMIGRANTS

ACLU Immigrants' Rights Project
Dedicated to expanding and enforcing the civil liberties and civil rights of noncitizens and to combating public and private discrimination against immigrants.

Familia Trans Queer Movement
Works at local and national levels to achieve the collective liberation of trans, queer, and gender nonconforming Latinxs through building community, organizing, advocacy, and education.

Immigration Equality
Works to ensure immigration rights for lesbian, gay, bisexual, and transgender people and those living with HIV.

Lamba Legal Transgender Rights Tool Kit
A legal guide for transgender people and their advocates.

Mariposas Sin Fronteras
Supports LGBTQ people in immigration detention.

National Center for Lesbian Rights Immigration Project
Advocates in court for LGBTQ (not just lesbian) asylum seekers and immigrants.

The Queer Detainee Empowerment Project
Provides direct services and community organizing, supporting LGBTQIA + and HIV + immigrants in detention centers in the United States.

Seeking Asylum in the U.S. to Escape Trans Discrimination
A free documentary on YouTube exploring the lives of transgender Latinx migrants.

OTHER FORMS OF IMMIGRATION RELIEF

The Center for Human Rights at Weill Cornell Medical College in New York City is a group of volunteer medical professionals and trainees who conduct free forensic medical and psychological exams for asylum seekers.

In addition to immigration relief based on persecution in a country of origin, there are a number of other forms of immigration relief that may apply to T/GE immigrants to the United States. These include family-based immigration relief (wherein a person is sponsored by a relative who is a U.S. citizen or green card holder) as well as relief based on being the victim of a crime. Victims of human trafficking can apply for a T-Visa and those who are victims of certain crimes and cooperate with law enforcement can apply for a U-Visa.

T/GE immigrants may also be eligible for protection based on the Violence Against Women Act (VAWA), regardless of gender identity, by submitting USCIS Form I-360 with supporting documentation. VAWA allows victims of family or domestic violence, where the abuser is a U.S. citizen or green card holder, to apply for a green card confidentially without their abuser being notified. The victim must be a spouse, ex-spouse, child under 21 years old, or parent of the abuser.

CONCLUSION

T/GE immigrants can have a broad range of experiences prior to, during, and after migrating from one country to another. Aside from the legal factors that can greatly affect T/GE experience, social, economic, cultural, and personal aspects shape the unique and individualized journey of T/GE immigrants and how they live and thrive in a new culture or environment.

NOTES

1. Berry, J. W. (1992). Acculturation and adaptation in a new society. *International Migration, 30*, 69–85.
2. Schwartz, S. J., Unger, J. B., Zamboanga, B. L., & Szapocznik, J. (2010). Rethinking the concept of acculturation: Implications for theory and research. *American Psychologist, 65*(4), 237.
3. Berry, J. W. (2003). *Conceptual Approaches to Acculturation*. In K. M. Chun, P. Balls Organista, & G. Marín (Eds.), *Acculturation: Advances in theory, measurement, and applied research* (pp. 17–37). American Psychological Association.
4. Berry, J. W. (1997). Immigration, acculturation, and adaptation. *Applied Psychology, 46*(1), 5–34.
5. Immigration Law, Policies, and Procedures were current at the time of drafting of this chapter. These rules may change from time to time especially when there is change of Administration. Please refer to current law, policies, and procedures at the USCIS website: https://www.uscis.gov/.
6. National Center for Transgender Equality (n.d.). Our Moment for Reform for Transgender People and Immigration. https://transequality.org/issues/resources/our-moment-reform-immigration-and-transgender-people.
7. REDLACTRANS. The night is another country: impunity and violence against transgender women human rights defenders in Latin America 2012. http://redlactrans.org.ar/site/wp-content/uploads/2013/05/Violencia-e-impunidad-English.pdf.

4

DISABILITY
Sarah Cavar and Alexandre Baril

INTRODUCTION

Because of cisgenderism and ableism, trans and gender expansive (T/GE) people are often categorized as having a mental illness, and therefore a disability. Searching the Internet for the terms "trans" and "disability," yields a disproportionate number of results about trans mental health issues. This shows that one of the primary connections often established between trans and disabled experiences is that T/GE people are thought of as having mental illness, also called mental disability. Although research suggests that our communities experience higher rates of mental disability[1,2] as a result of daily social oppression and minority stress, it is far from the only critical connection between trans and disabled experiences.

T/GE people and disabled people have bodyminds in conflict with dominant norms. Both groups face medical, psychological, legal, and social barriers not only in asserting our identities, but also in being seen as legitimate by medical and legal authorities as well as the general public. The categories "trans" and "disabled" are built to ensure the maintenance of certain social norms, which can only exist if positioned against a trans, disabled "other."

Trans and gender expansive communities have often sought to gain legitimacy by excluding disabled people, and disability communities have often tried to gain recognition through a sex/gender "normality" that excludes sexual and gender minorities. This reproduction of a logic of exclusion prevents both communities from seeing and highlighting the intricate links between transness and disability.[3,4,5,6]

My gender dysphoria is deeply intertwined with my experience of embodiment, which is impacted deeply by being autistic, having chronic pain, having PTSD, being fat. How my gender is read by others is inextricable from my fatness.

A significant proportion of T/GE people are disabled, and T/GE and disabled people share similar experiences in terms of our history of pathologization, the regulation of our identities and bodies through material and normative systems of power, and our daily struggles with the medical/psychiatric system. These similarities open up the possibility of forging strong alliances between us, and indeed coalitions have been growing and evolving rapidly in the past few years. Allyship between T/GE and disabled people has been emerging through specific nascent communities, many of which are online, as well as through research, activism, social media, and art.

Being sick also makes transition tough in many ways. Hormones and surgery are more complicated, and even stuff like finding clothes is complicated by the braces I need to wear, which sucks when it's already so tough to find clothes that fit me!

WHAT IS DISABILITY?

Disability, like gender, is a socially constructed category––one initially invented and constantly reinvented by people and institutions––that can be understood using a variety of "models." To date, medical and social models of disability have predominated.[7,8] The medical model, one of the oldest models and still the most common today, understands disability as something that affects individuals' bodyminds and promotes the need for

Leila smiles while sitting on a couch and resting their chin against their cane. Leila is an artist, activist, and organizer living in the Pacific Northwest. (Disabled and Here. www.affecttheverb.com/disabledandhere)

medical intervention and "cure." The social model of disability, put forward by disability activists in the 1970s, understands disability as a social construction whose definition changes based on time, place, and circumstance.[9,10]

Social construction takes place when a society gives meaning to an object or identity and then views that meaning as naturally occurring rather than created by the society.

The social model of disability distinguishes between impairment and disability. While impairment is a natural variation, disability is the meaning placed on that variation based on the environment. This means that what is considered "disabling" depends on the accessibility of the space. It is the space, not the body itself, that has a problem in need of fixing. According to this model, an impairment that involves the inability to use your legs to walk is not an inherent "problem" that requires an individual cure. Being a wheelchair-user only becomes a disability in the absence of appropriate ramps, elevators, and other architectural and social adaptations.

> *I have worked with a service dog for several years but still not allowed myself*
> *to claim the word disabled until last year, when my mental illness forced me*
> *to miss four months of work due to residential treatment, followed by another*
> *three of intensive outpatient & reduced hours. I feel like I try to keep these parts*
> *of my identity separate because I don't know how to reconcile them.*

Since its inception, disability studies has focused on the experiences of the "healthy" (not chronically or mentally "ill") disabled, as well as those disabled people who experience the social privileges of whiteness, masculinity, cisgender identity, and heterosexuality.[11,12] This has come at the expense of chronically ill people as well as mentally disabled people (including those deemed "mentally ill" and those deemed "intellectually" or "developmentally" disabled), who occupied, until recently, the outskirts of disability rights conversations. Although there is some burgeoning awareness of the exclusions perpetuated by/ within disability studies, and some proposals for more inclusive reflections in the larger field of critical disability studies, further work is urgently needed.

WHAT IT'S LIKE GROWING UP TRANSGENDER AND DEAF

Blake Culley (they/them)

Around seven or eight months ago, I started posting vlogs on my Instagram. I talked about my transgender journey. I identify as AFAB, which means Assigned Female at Birth, and nonbinary. For me, it means that I do not identify with either gender: man or woman. Sometimes, I am one or the other, both, or neither of them.

I didn't realize I was transgender until I was 28 years old. Why so late? I had no access to information about trans people, which is already limited to begin with. Much of the already available info I saw was for hearing (non-Deaf) people. There are so many, many, many, many—I'm not kidding—many vlogs in spoken English. I saw hearing transgender people explain their transgender journey in depth, along with the situations they faced and much more. I would have loved to know more about it, but I couldn't understand, and most of the time I was limited to automatic captioning, which isn't ideal. I became very frustrated. That's why I did not realize I was transgender until a later age.

Anyway, the point is that many deaf people find it difficult to have that access, and that kind of information is vital! I decided to start my own vlogs using American Sign Language and become open with the Deaf community. I talk about my transgender journey, the struggles I've faced as trans, and the situations I've encountered that I've never imagined before as a trans person.

The only downfall is that I can only share about my personal experiences, and I can't share about other Deaf trans experiences. Those experiences are their stories, and I can only share about mine.

So many people have contacted me with overwhelming support, and I've learned so much from them, too, about things I'd never thought of before. I have gotten tremendous support from the Deaf community and some hearing people, who read my transcripts because they don't know ASL. Many people say they have learned so much from me and learned about different perspectives. There are some deaf trans people out there who thought they were the only ones. They reached out to me asking for support and advice on what to do next in their trans journey (how to talk to their parents and family, etc.) It has been an amazing opportunity to share my vlogs about my personal transgender journey with you all.

A head injury impaired my memory and cognitive abilities [. . .] [so] people find it easier to dismiss my gender because of my disability. For people who don't want to acknowledge my gender identity, they have an easy excuse to just call me crazy and leave it at that.

Critical disability studies and its related disciplinary fields, such as Crip Studies, Mad Studies, and Deaf Studies, is broadly understood today as including people with

Lydia X. Z. Brown and Shain Neumeier are nonbinary trans, asexual, and queer disabled advocates. Lydia is a disability justice organizer, scholar-activist, writer, strategist, educator, and attorney focused on addressing and ending interpersonal and state violence targeting disabled people at the margins of the margins, especially disabled people living at the intersections of race, class, sexuality, gender, language, and nation. Shain is an attorney and advocate focused on addressing and ending coercive and involuntary treatment, guardianship, and institutionalization as used against disabled, queer, trans, fat, and young people. (© Katie Miller)

physical, mental/psychological, cognitive, and learning disabilities, as well as people with chronic diseases, illnesses, or other health conditions, such as HIV/AIDS, chronic fatigue, fibromyalgia, and multiple chemical sensitivity. We can experience stable or degenerative illnesses and disabilities that may manifest with mild, moderate, or severe symptoms and that may be visible or invisible. The field of critical disability studies invites us to go beyond the mainstream idea of what disability looks like (e.g., limited to wheelchair users and blind and D/deaf people). Instead, it creates a category large enough to include the realities and experiences of all individuals facing surveillance, regulation, pathologization, and discrimination in ableist and sanist societies.

TRANS AND DISABLED

My gender intersects with my ability, as a mentally ill and chronically ill person that uses a walking aid when needed. I have trouble trusting medical professionals even more now than I did when they perceived me as a cis woman who that was "lying about her pain." It has affected my ability to get jobs and to be cautious about passing at work.

According to the 2015 U.S. National Transgender Survey,[13] 39% of those surveyed reported a disability, compared to 15% of the general population. Of this 39%, 28% identified as being a "person with a disability." In a large study of T/GE Canadians, 55% reported having a disability or chronic illness.[14] The majority of T/GE disabled people live with mental disabilities, and, in the U.S National Transgender Survey, report experiencing mental disability at a rate about six times higher than that of the general population.

"Sanism" is ableism toward mentally disabled people, who are perceived as "insane."

I have a chronic pain condition that affects my mobility [. . .] I worry a great deal about finding jobs in the future, since disability and transgender identity individually both can contribute to difficulty in finding employment. With both of them together, I worry that I will be seen as a very unemployable person.

Although the majority of trans people who report being denied equal treatment by various medical, legal, and other institutions feel they have been discriminated against due to their gender identity or gender expression, it is notable that 14% of participants in the U.S. National Transgender Survey feel they were denied equal treatment on the basis of disability. Other research projects confirm increased discrimination related to multiple factors of marginalization, including race, class, sexual orientation, age, and ability.

At the moment, I am in the middle of something of a battle with my school and their housing policy, for my suitemates felt uncomfortable sharing a bathroom with a trans woman. They placed a deadbolt on my bathroom door, allowing my suitemates to lock me out of the public section (sinks) of the bathroom. Aside from the clear human rights violation which this created, it also created a health risk as I have a traumatic brain injury (TBI), and that is where I keep my counter seizure medication.

Another large quantitative survey of T/GE people conducted in the United States shows that those of us who are also disabled are at least twice (and sometimes three times) more likely to experience discrimination while trying to access health care and social services than nondisabled people.[15] We also face higher risks of physical and sexual harassment on the basis of disability as compared to the general population.[16] It appears that our T/GE identities increase the likelihood that we will face ableism and our disabilities increase our chances of facing cisgenderism. This reveals the importance of an intersectional approach to understanding oppression.

I do consider myself disabled, although it is with undiagnosed chronic widespread pain. Being gender nonconforming and gay make going to doctors very intimidating because I have no idea whether they've ever had experience interacting with people like me before.

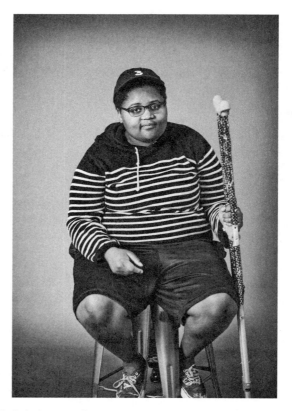

Dani Som (Sommerville) led advocacy efforts to expand the accessibility of Ferndale Pride (MI). He was a recipient of the Spirit of Detroit Award (2015). Prior to his death in 2019, he was quoted in an interview: "I just want people to know that your disability, mental illness, or neurodivergence is just as beautiful an identity as your trans one — embrace all of your medical quirks!" (Brayden Asher Misiolek | roguestud.io)

WHY DISABILITY SHOULD MATTER IN TRANS STUDIES

Statistics confirm that a significant percentage of T/GE communities are disabled, but very few research projects have documented the specific realities of T/GE disabled people. This gap leaves researchers poorly equipped to understand the complex realities of those of us who live at the intersection of two systems of oppression: cisgenderism and ableism. This lack of research raises several questions: Do these disabilities predate transition? Do they have medical causes? Are our disabilities caused by difficult lived experiences resulting from cisgenderism? Are disabled people, who experience various forms of non-normative embodiment, more prone to question their gender identity than nondisabled people? Responses to these questions are urgently needed in order to adequately address the specific needs of those of us living with disability and chronic illness.

> *Having had a traumatic brain injury made it a tad difficult to come out to my parents because it will always leave open the question, "Is this who she is, or is it simply brain damage?" It is a tool that is useful to open doors for issues of rights, but also one which may or may not hinder the views of others on the validity of my identity.*

TRANSNESS: A LONG HISTORY OF PATHOLOGIZATION

Trans people and disabled people (if we were to imagine that these are mutually exclusive categories, a myth that this chapter aims to deconstruct) share an ongoing history of pathologization. There is no way to talk about the history of T/GE people—or about queer history in general—without mentioning medical and psychiatric institutions. These institutions are arbiters of social norms, and their pathologizing of gender dysphoria, trans identity, and other instances of gender nonconformity highly influence social perception. Similarly, the view that disability ought to be cured and eradicated continues to impact our lives, because transition is painted as a cure-all for the so-called "disorder" of gender dysphoria.

Sky looks to the side while standing in front of a vine-covered red wall with a cane and prosthetic leg. Sky is an Indigenous Two-Spirit environmental and social justice activist. (Disabled and Here. www.affecttheverb.com/disabledandhere)

Pathologization occurs when our behavior, embodiment, desires, and interactions are transformed into "symptoms" and "diagnoses." Though we all experience states of anxiety sometimes, "generalized anxiety" becomes a "disorder" when a psychiatrist is able to look at it in terms of a set of unhealthy "symptoms" that are treated as abnormal and in need of treatment/cure.

> *I have severe PTSD. Because of this, numerous doctors have accused me of using transitioning as a coping mechanism, or else have asked if I have dissociative identity disorder. It's devastating to be treated like my gender identity is an illness or a symptom.*

The importance of pathologization and its consequences in T/GE life cannot be overstated. The presence or absence of particular diagnoses can quite literally transform a T/GE person's identity, making the difference between legal and medical recognition and total erasure. At the same time, a pathological view of transness enables ableist, sanist dismissal of trans identity as "insane" or "delusional."

MY INVISIBLE CHRONIC ILLNESS

Grey Ellis (they/them) is a chronically ill artist, ex-party queer, and a current collaborator on youth liberation work. They have spent 10 years in doctors' offices being told their debilitating illness isn't real. They like to read, watch campy films, grow plants, work in collectives, and build accessible spaces for intergenerational queer and trans community building.

I realized in 2016 that I had been chronically ill for 26 years. I had learned from a young age to maintain my health with careful plans to make sure I ate the right foods for my body regularly, and make sure I slept nine hours every night, in order to never put myself in the nebulous "danger zone" of my health, which I could never quite articulate but that I always knew was lurking right beyond my quietly regimented routines. The adults in my life could not recognize or name what was wrong with me.

I had gone through dozens of doctors, tests, nutritionists, physical exams, body work, chiropractors, and therapists since I was 13 years old. I had been tested for anemia and mono more times than I could count. I had been told to take antacids for severe vomiting. I had been asked if the cognitive impairment that accompanies fatigue was just in my head. No expert believed my illness was real. They consistently dismissed me or gave up on me for a decade. I did everything I could to manage my illness that I couldn't name, but every year it got worse.

Three years ago, my health spun wildly out of control. No matter how much I rested, exercised, hydrated, or ate "healthy" meals, I would still end up bedridden for weeks to months—unable to cognitively process new information and unable to muster the energy to leave my bed, my room, or my house. It was a struggle to make it to the bathroom or the kitchen. In this condition it's hard to work for enough money to pay your rent; you can't attend events or be in public. You can only maintain community with people willing to silently sit or lie in bed with you and fetch you meals or glasses of water.

With my declining health, I lost access to dozens of people I had considered supportive. I lost people I thought were my queer and trans family. Many people don't want to or don't know how to slow down to sit with or care for the sick. Many don't want to see someone they once knew as able-bodied suddenly become severely disabled. Some people don't want to face the truth that they are only temporarily able-bodied, even if that means discarding a community member you once loved and celebrated. Being disabled in this way means grieving the body and the life that you once knew. I slowly began building new support networks with other chronically ill folks from all over the continent.

A few months later, a naturopathic doctor finally diagnosed me with chronic active Epstein-Barr, also known as chronic fatigue syndrome or myalgic encephalomyelitis. Two years later an acupuncturist also diagnosed me with a heat pathogen stuck in my body since childhood. But just as my illness was not believed, my diagnosis is not believed. While I was actively having an asthma attack, a doctor told me that I was a fool to believe in my diagnosis and that chronic active Epstein-Barr is not a real disease.

Anyone with a mystery chronic illness will tell you that the medical-industrial complex fails us gravely, even as it provides life-saving aid. As a white person, I know doctors are more likely to believe and, therefore, give better medical care to people who are white. As a nonbinary person, I know that doctors and nurses who claim to help have often violated and misgendered me. Doctors ask me if there is trauma surrounding my rejection of my assigned-at-birth gender that could've made me sick. Medical professionals would rather blame me because I'm trans, because I'm queer, or because they assume I'm lying. Other chronically ill people have believed me, have witnessed my pain, have been some of the kindest, gentlest, and most creative people I've ever met.

I urge you to believe the chronically ill and disabled: They are intimately acquainted with the human condition. They know so much about living in a body, about healing, and about pain.

TRANSSEXUALISM, GENDER IDENTITY DISORDER, AND GENDER DYSPHORIA: AN OVERVIEW

In 1980, the *Diagnostic & Statistical Manual of Mental Disorders (DSM)-III*, published by the American Psychiatric Association (APA), introduced the term "transsexualism." Among those diagnosed, some would be further classified by sexual orientation. Notably, this change happened a mere seven years after the formal depathologization of "homosexuality" by the APA. In the *DSM-III-R* (published in 1987), transness was further parsed by how closely it adhered to the diagnostic criteria the APA had recently created; those who presented too few symptoms to qualify for a "transsexualism" diagnosis were often diagnosed with GID NOS, or "gender identity disorder, not otherwise specified." In the *DSM-IV* and *DSM-IV-TR*, the APA's language transitioned alongside contemporary terminology, swapping out "transsexualism" for "gender identity disorder" (GID).[17]

The *DSM*'s fifth and current edition, published in 2013, lists "gender dysphoria" rather than "gender identity disorder" as a diagnosis.[18] Similarly, the 11th edition of the *International Classification of Disease* (ICD) published by the World Health Organization (WHO) moved its diagnosis of "gender incongruence" from its subsection on mental illnesses to its subsection on sexual health.[19] This shifts the focus of pathologization from trans *identity* to *gender dysphoria/incongruence*, which many see as a sign of decreased stigma. Although the official diagnosis may be beneficial for some—by providing a recognized narrative to justify their transition to themselves or others, or facilitating access to insurance and healthcare coverage in some (but not all) national contexts—the medicalization of T/GE identities has had wide-ranging and often negative effects on many of us.

Portrait of My Immune System. "I have Lupus, an autoimmune disease named after a wolf bite. I like to imagine my immune system as a wild canine fighting to protect me against the toxins and traumas of the world." "I am a chronically ill and disabled, trans non-binary rabbi and painter. I live in Oakland with my partner, kid, and many animals." (Elliot Kukla)

NEW TERMS, NEW WAYS OF PATHOLOGIZING: RAPID-ONSET GENDER DYSPHORIA

Being autistic, people make fun of us in general, and when we identify as being LGBT at all it is chalked up to us being autistic rather than being LGBT. In addition to being mentally ill, it makes ableist detractors of the trans movement keen to blame my transness on being autistic/mentally ill/whatever else have you.

With the public presence of our communities in the media and the increasing number of young people controlling their own coming out narratives, new terms, often based on cis-genderist, ableist presumptions, have been created by medical professionals and researchers in order to better understand and manage our communities. One new term is "rapid-onset gender dysphoria" (ROGD), most often applied to teenagers who were assigned female at birth (AFAB). From the "rapid-onset gender dysphoria" perspective, AFAB teenagers are not really trans or gender nonconforming; rather, they are vulnerable "girls" negatively influenced by their peers and T/GE-related online trends. Deemed a "social contagion," this so-called disorder is even likened to anorexia nervosa in the way it "spreads" among friend groups and appears to be accompanied by increased use of trans-affirming social media.

Several critiques have been made regarding ROGD, from scholars demonstrating how research data and methods reveal ROGD to be bad science,[20] to international organizations, such as the World Professional Association for Transgender Health (WPATH), stating that ROGD is not a true or formal diagnosis,[21] to researchers, activists, and organizations warning of the potential negative impacts of these interpretations of T/GE identities. It is worth mentioning that the material included in the paper that first mentioned ROGD was provided by parents in an online survey,[22] and therefore reflected the parents' views and did not include the views of the young people being studied or anyone else in their lives.

I'm disabled with severe PTSD from a lifetime of neglect, abuse, and trauma. It definitely colors how people accept or *don't* accept my gender, in that they

*sometimes are like, "Oh you're ace [asexual]/trans because you were raped,"
when NO, I would be trans even if I had a perfect life.*

Though ROGD is not included in the *DSM*, the dangers posed by this "diagnostic category" are immense. It represents a new way of pathologizing T/GE identities and bodies in an era of increasingly democratized access to trans-affirming educational and social media. Now that information on T/GE topics has become more widely accessible, ROGD emerges as a reactionary way of "quarantining" a small number of people deemed *truly* trans, while dismissing others as self-diagnosed victims of friends, social pressures, and media influences. Self-identifying as T/GE or disabled without medical/psychiatric approval challenges the systems that try to control and organize social identities and non-normative bodyminds. Indeed, many T/GE and disabled people are confronted with dismissal, distrust, and fear of self-diagnosis. This opposition to self-diagnosis brings to light the fears that medical and psychiatric institutions have of self-determined and non-normative bodyminds.

ABLE-BODIED NORMATIVITY AND CISNORMATIVITY

Cis- and able-bodied- normativity are pervasive, often invisible forces that structure our everyday lives. All people, regardless of gender or ability, interact with these forces constantly from the time we are born. From day one, we are placed into pink or blue onesies and hoped to be "healthy," that is, to have bodyminds that conform to social norms. Cis and/or abled people experience the privileges of being able to overlook––or never notice in the first place––the same systems we as trans and disabled people cannot ignore.

> *I am disabled. Many spaces made for LGBTQIA + people are not made with disabled people in mind [. . .] I'm constantly debating whether to use a cane or my wheels when I really need them, just to access spaces where my queerness will be seen and celebrated, and give up on my disability being seen or respected for the night.*

Because all systems of normativity need an "other" to be compared to, ableism and cisnormativity do the simultaneous work of normalizing everyday oppression of trans disabled people, *and* presenting trans, disabled bodyminds as forever "inherently" abnormal.

BODILY NORMATIVITY: HOW ABLEISM AND CISGENDERISM INTERSECT

The various forms of normativity (based on abled and/or cis bodies/identities) that structure the world in which we live are built on the same assumption that there is a normal way to have a bodymind and that those who do not conform are odd, frightening, infuriating, or simply pathological. This is crucial in maintaining an ableist social system; it is the logic that drives the oppression of disabled people. Able-bodied normativity assumes that bodies and minds worthy of participating in society will have the same needs; we are presumed to move, talk, and think in the same ways and at the same pace.

> *I think that when I use my cane and I am visibly queer people are more aggressive. Too much discomfort for them I think. It also affects my ability to get medical care –my disability and gender are not taken seriously.*

Cisnormativity can be defined as the normative aspects of the cisgenderist system. In this case, it presumes all those who enter a given space will experience their gender identity in a way that reflects the ways in which they are gendered in a cis society, and, in turn, the sex/gender they were assigned at birth. For example, the absence of all-gender restrooms in a building presumes everyone will identify fully with either manhood or womanhood and have genitalia that appear to match both that internal identity and the social roles assigned at birth.

> *Being white passing has made it easier to get away with presenting as butch from a young age because white women are not held to as rigid standards of*

gender as women of color (especially black women) or the same double binds around being seen as too masculine but too feminine at the same time.

These norms, which are reinforced by material conditions that challenge our existence as T/GE disabled people, have two major functions: (1) They affirm the superiority of so-called normal bodyminds, and (2) they keep stigmatized people out of social life. In other words, these normative systems naturalize some identities and bodyminds while pathologizing and marginalizing others. Despite being socially constructed, gender and disability, as well as cisgenderism and ableism, are all too real. That is, these socially constructed systems have material impacts on our daily realities. Both able-bodied normativity and cisnormativity put the burden of assimilation onto pathologized bodyminds rather than on the inaccessible and rigidly normative spaces around us. As T/GE disabled people, we end up taking the blame for being different, rather than the powerful institutions that create hierarchies and differential treatment. For example, we may be faulted for being unable to walk, or for needing audio transcription or a quiet space in highly social settings. In this way, the system of power, whose conditions work best for the abled, may go unchallenged and remain invisible. As T/GE people, we may also be seen as burdensome (a stereotype associated with disabled people) for expecting cis people around us to respect our name and pronoun preferences. Meanwhile, to misgender a cis person, or to call them by an incorrect name, is considered deeply wrong and elicits sincere apologies.

Both disability and transness are thus socially constructed by the norms that produce their opposites. Disability becomes apparent when contrasted with the able body, and transness when contrasted with the cis body. These binary categories exist, in part, thanks to developments in medical technology––and corresponding diagnoses (which change frequently according to cultural norms) ––to "treat" or "cure" non-normative bodyminds.

I do have a disability and consider myself disabled. I have a few mental illness-related disabilities and this intersects with my gender identity. I have a dissociative disorder, so I have alters or, as I prefer to call them, headmates. Other people sometimes inhabit this body, so collectively, we are genderfluid.

Many of us choose to reclaim one or more of the identities assigned to us by these oppressive social systems, and many more use the clinical language of disability and/or gender as a way of communicating our experiences to others more easily (trans people, for instance, may use the term *dysphoria* while also challenging its inclusion in the *DSM*). Others (re)invent labels and categories to gain more autonomy in self-definition. Some use different labels depending on social context. No matter what language we use to share our experiences, there is pressure for it to be understandable to a society built on cis- and able-bodied-normativity.

RUNNING WITHOUT LIMITS

Amber Desjardins (she/her), 29, is a disabled, nonbinary trans woman athlete and activist. She lives in Upstate New York, where she trains for races.

I am a disabled person. I have Cerebral Palsy. I am a trans woman. I am a disabled runner. This means that I run races in a wheelchair pushing myself the distance of a race. Most races, I am the only athlete who is in a wheelchair, so I compete against those on foot. I am also an activist both locally in my hometown in Upstate New York and on the state level for the LGBTQIA + community, the mental health community, and my disabled community.

I started my running journey three years ago. I struggled with depression and with where I fit in. I was really struggling with my body image and physical health. I had gained a good number of pounds that were making getting around difficult. I had a hard time accepting that and slipped into a deeper depression. Things became very bleak. I sought hormone therapy, but because of my physical health at the time I couldn't take hormones to help my transition. I needed a change. I needed a healthier lifestyle. I needed happiness. I needed to find it.

A friend noticed this and felt very uncomfortable with the path I was taking. They suggested I get involved in sports, especially running. I have always loved sports. I dreamed of playing soccer and basketball as a kid. I didn't because of the lack of resources, so I felt left behind. I pursued my childhood dream—turning it into an adult dream of being a disabled athlete by running.

At the time, I only had a hospital-style wheelchair not built for running or going quickly. I trained for a bit, but I wasn't consistent. With some encouragement, I signed up for my first race: The Burlington Color Run in Vermont. That race was a lot of fun. You get powdered paint thrown at you at paint stations. Who doesn't like being colorful while you run? Life was looking up for me. I was living a healthier lifestyle. I lost a little bit of weight and was soon cleared by my doctor to start hormone replacement therapy.

The following year, I ran 12 races in the same wheelchair. I knew I needed a new, better, more fitting chair that would enable me to run faster and easier. I worked with a few friends to get a sport wheelchair and got it. Then I signed up for my first major race and 5k. I signed up for the Freihofer's Run for Women in Albany, New York. There, people from around the world participated—from elite runners to casual runners like me. I finished the race and surpassed my personal best time by 20 minutes. Why am I sharing this? Well, simple. That was my hardest race to date. The first mile and a half was all uphill. It was a challenge . . . a huge challenge way over my head. I took that challenge on.

Living a disabled life has challenges. We have obstacles, things we have to overcome. Life isn't easy but at the end of the day we need to keep pushing. Keep fighting. Push through those obstacles so when we cross our own finish lines—not just in a race—we can be happy. We can rest our head on our pillow at night knowing that we pushed our limits. We can show people that despite our disabilities we can do amazing things.

Now, I'm happier than I have ever been. I'm not focused on my weight anymore; I just focus on being healthy in the body I have. It's not about the size you are but the heart and determination within that makes a person amazing.

(DE)GENDERED, (DE)SEXUALIZED, AND HYPERSEXUALIZED SELVES

I've often been the only male-presenting person in a room of people who have similar experiences as me (PTSD from sexual assault). More than once I've been told I'm a good step-stone friend to feeling safe with men again, and I'm glad that I've been able to help them, but it also kinda feels like they might see me as not REALLY a man.

In his pioneering work on gender, sexuality, and disability, Eli Clare[23,24,25] demonstrates how gender recognition goes hand in hand with able-bodied norms. Feminine and masculine individuals need to move, talk, occupy space, and mobilize gender codes that can sometimes only be accessed if they are able-bodied. In other words, according to the dominant heterosexist and ableist structures, a woman living with cerebral palsy, for example, who uses a cane to walk, who has tremors and twitches in her body, and who has a non-normative elocution tone/pace is considered less feminine than an able-bodied woman. Because disabled people are often degendered (seen as not having a gender), T/GE disabled people are more disadvantaged in their transition and in their search for gender recognition.[26] A T/GE disabled or neurodivergent person might be unable, find it difficult, or refuse to perform ableist/sanist gendered norms/codes. Failing to conform to cisnormative norms prevalent in healthcare settings might increase forms of gatekeeping regarding transition, or delay or even prevent transition. A disabled person who wants to start transitioning might be delayed or delegitimized based on ableist assumptions about disabled people as genderless or asexual, or as having more important health issues that are unrelated to gender (finding a cure for their chronic illness, for example). These degendering processes, rooted in cisnormativity and able-bodied normativity, pose further challenges to T/GE disabled life.

Chronic pain makes it difficult to dress how I want sometimes. I don't have the energy or grip strength to apply makeup most times, and occasionally pain in my shoulders and back keeps me from wearing my binder. This tends to make me feel less authentic.

Gatekeeping is the act of controlling or limiting access to something. When used in trans communities, gatekeeping typically refers to the process by which medical and mental health systems control access to transition-related health care.

T/GE and disabled people experience a wide range of stereotypes regarding the ways in which we do or do not have sex, ranging from perceived asexuality to perceived

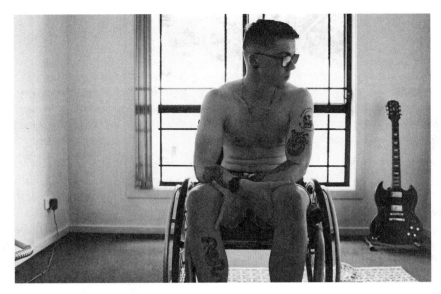

Az is a 23 year old trans-man from Australia. He enjoys weight-lifting and spending time with his dog, and believes you can always adapt your goals to make them possible. (Azrael Cosgrove / @wheelyboy_az)

hypersexuality. Physically disabled people, especially those with visible mobility aids, are often assumed to be inherently both asexual and undesirable. Intellectually and mentally disabled people are not considered to be sexual beings because it is presumed that none are capable of sexual consent.[27,28] Although there is a thriving community of autistic people on the asexual spectrum, it is also essential to acknowledge sexual diversity among disabled and neurodivergent people.[29] The assumption that disabled people, especially mentally disabled people, not only *do not* but *should not* have sex, denies their sexual agency, leads to a dangerous lack of sexual education for this group, and therefore increases our vulnerability to sexual abuse.[30] At the same time, people with mental and cognitive disabilities are vilified for their perceived hypersexuality and "uncontrollable" sexual desires. Hypersexuality is sometimes even associated with certain mental disabilities (such as borderline personality disorder), which reinforces existing stigmas.[31]

An asexual/hypersexual binary system of representation is also enforced on T/GE people. Little information exists on attitudes and sexual stereotypes associated with T/GE people outside the gender binary. Many T/GE people on the masculine spectrum experience desexualization at the hands of popular and sexual media, while T/GE people on the feminine spectrum may be vilified as potential assailants of cisgender women or turned into pornographic fetishes.[32] Like their disabled counterparts, T/GE people are viewed as the objects of sex and sexual theorizing, rather than as active sexual subjects. Trans women, for example, are often cast as hypersexual predators requiring surveillance and control, while trans men's sexualities are routinely erased and ignored.

The asexual/hypersexual binary system of representation leads to disturbingly frequent attacks on the reproductive rights of our T/GE and disabled communities.[33] Those who live at the intersections of ableism and cisgenderism experience, therefore, a greater risk of being deemed "unfit" to reproduce and of experiencing forms of "stratified reproduction." These violations of reproductive rights take many forms, including a lack of relevant education, lack of support regarding reproductive issues, or even forms of sterilization. In many countries, T/GE people are forced to undergo surgical interventions, such as forced sterilization, in order to obtain civil status and documents that match their gender identity. Both T/GE and disabled communities have faced, and continue to face, forced sterilization, violating our reproductive rights, and revealing another crucial intersection between our communities.[34] Depending on the legal context, AFAB T/GE people can also be exposed to misogynistic healthcare providers who refuse to proceed with surgical procedures such as

Some people who are on the autism spectrum or have brains that are different from the statistical majority identify as being "neurodiverse" or "neurodivergent." These terms may be used in contrast to the majority, which can be labeled "neurotypical."

tubal ligations or hysterectomies, valuing patients' ability to conceive over their reproductive autonomy. This is both a misogynistic process *and* a cissexist one: It misgenders the patient and uses the presumed gender as a means of discrimination.

> *There were times my pelvic floor issues were so bad I could barely walk or sit or stand, and sex was impossible. But because I'm trans and queer, it was very very difficult to find any physical therapists or specialists who wouldn't misgender me or see it as a "women's issue." This kept me from getting help for a long time and worsened my symptoms.*

Another experience shared by T/GE and disabled people is the daily invasive questions received about one's body and sexual practices. Both groups face questions about if and how they are able to have sex (and about their genitalia in general) in situations where it is irrelevant and inappropriate.[35] Such questions stem from normative cis and able-bodied assumptions that there are "normal" or "correct" ways to have sex, and that those who deviate from these norms are perpetually open to personal interrogation on the subject. Some T/GE and disabled people experience frequent fetishization by those attracted to our bodies. This reinforces the idea that to find non-normative bodyminds desirable is not a normal variation in desire but a fetish that deserves to be pathologized and diagnosed as a paraphilia in the *DSM*.

> *I have EDS [Ehlers-Danlos Syndrome] and POTS [postural orthostatic tachycardia syndrome] which means I can't always chest bind [or] have top surgery [. . .] People also tend to desexualize and fetishize me more [than cis, abled people], both as a trans person and as a cane user.*

ENFORCING NORMATIVITY THROUGH CURES AND TREATMENTS

> *I hated to be called handsome, sir, guy, etc. [. . .] I'd get into screaming matches with anyone who said [facial hair] made me look like a man. And at the time I wasn't aware of it being tied to my gender, I was just told, "That's just how autism is."*

The contexts of medical and psychiatric treatment for disability include both implicit and explicit pressures to conform to prescribed gender roles as a key component of "cure" and "recovery." These pressures are particularly insidious in relation to mentally disabled people, whose disabilities carry implications of "irrationality" and of not being in their "right minds." This means that gender conformity can be positioned as the rational alternative to supposedly "crazy" trans identification. For example, if you are a T/GE person experiencing dysphoria in relation to your chest and menstrual periods who then begins restricting your diet in order to shrink your chest and stop menstruating, professionals treating eating disorders may be quick to dismiss your trans identification as being part of the eating disorder. As a result, cisnormativity is normalized as part of the eating disorder treatment.[36]

> *As a wheelchair user with caregivers who do not support my new gender identity completely, I am limited in the ways I can outwardly express gender, and I cannot access medicalized gender confirmation without their support.*

As many T/GE disabled people testify, we fear that our disability (particularly if it is a mental disability) or neurodivergence will be used to dismiss our transness, or to delay or deny us access to hormones and surgeries.[37] Spaces designed to treat deviations from social, psychological, and bodily norms (such as hospitals, psychiatric facilities, and group homes) frequently function as sites of gender-policing. In these institutions, casual cisgenderist forms of violence (such as misgendering) occur as part of the gender-policing mechanisms understood to help cure patients, and subsequent anger on the part of patients is further pathologized.

Shannon Schaffer (no pronouns) spends most of Shannon's time thinking about mental health, reality shows, and Shannon's dog, Barry. To practice self-care, Shannon frequents coffee shops too cool for Shannon and writes emo poetry with colorful pens.

When I'm not sick, I'm queer, and right now I'm focused on my health. I go to my partial hospitalization program and rarely am concerned with people using my correct (lack of) pronouns. I hear my psychiatrist's attempt at being gender-conscious, but I'm more worried about what they're prescribing me. I suggest to the therapists that we share our pronouns more often, and I only realize weeks later that they didn't take my suggestion. I've had to come to terms with the fact that my mental health identities strip me of all other identities because "health comes first," right?

Throughout my life, my queer, nonbinary, and sick identities haven't been connected through experiences, but connected through time. I'm able to perform my queer identities with others when needed, but once I'm alone my sickness takes over. My queered version of time exists until my sick timeline discards everything else: switching between being queer in public and sick at home. Now, however, my mental health has overrun all my identities in every environment.

Even though I know my sickness isn't the only thing about me, it's all I think about, all I'm affected by, and all I can talk about—to the point where I struggle to put into words my relationship to gender. My health puts up a barrier to my experiences of all other identities. I believe illness can be queered, but I haven't been able to experience that myself. I am queer and ill and, for me, they aren't connected.

My mental health is consuming and everything else is not. My illnesses bombard my brain with thoughts or emotions that keep me from being able to focus. I know that someday this phase of being engulfed in my own illnesses will be over, but I'm not sure that I want it to be. Chaos can be comforting. Something I've learned since the onset of my diagnoses is that it's unrealistic to work against my mental health. As I'm re-learning now, I can only use skills to regulate, to tolerate, to be mindful, and to be effective.

Maybe one day I'll be able to mentally connect my queer, nonbinary, and sick identities (and maybe it'll be soon), but until then I'll just quietly and proudly display them in the form of pins on my sleeves. I consider this narrative the beginning of that process. When I'm not sick, I'm queer and (maybe) one day I'll be both.

AT THE NEXUS OF TRANSNESS AND DISABILITY: DENIAL OF HEALTH CARE

I am disabled and in a wheelchair. In addition, my spouse is deaf. Because I have high medical needs and an intersex body and medical records and insurance from when I had the wrong gender assignment, I feel very vulnerable. I avoid medical care because I am afraid of how I will be treated.

BARRIERS AND GATEKEEPERS

As T/GE people, we are typically required to "correctly" embody the diagnosis of gender dysphoria and undergo a period of surveillance by medical authorities (to ensure "psychological stability") before being permitted to transition. When describing our gender dysphoria "symptoms," we are often expected to regurgitate a narrative that cis professionals are already familiar with, which is difficult to do without consulting resources shared by other trans people.[38] Although such surveillance is problematic for all of us, it is particularly challenging for those of us who are also disabled, because disability can make appearing "correctly" trans more difficult due to heterosexist, cisgenderist, and ableist norms. A trans woman or transfeminine person with hand tremors may be unable to apply makeup; one with autism or sensory processing disorder may be limited in the styles of women's clothing she can wear because of her sensitivities. Similarly, if someone with sensory processing disorder or autism is unable to bind their breasts, they may have less chance of being seen as legitimately dysphoric and thus may not qualify for top surgery. The use of various mobility aids can also limit gender presentations that gatekeepers deem acceptable.

I am disabled, both physically and mentally. My dissociative disorders directly affect my gender identity, so they do intersect both inherently and because of the effect this fluctuation causes—people are less likely to believe in my gender identity because of this fluctuation. My physical disability also intersects with my gender identity because it impedes my ability to express my gender in the way I would prefer, which affects how people perceive and treat me.

The diagnostic criteria T/GE people are required to uphold in order to have access to the health care and services we need are not only rooted in sexist societal gender roles and expectations, as well as cisnormative double standards, but also, in ableist expectations. These requirements have long existed at the expense of nonbinary people who seek medical transitions,[39] but also at the expense of those of us in T/GE communities who are disabled. We face major gatekeeping practices used by medical and psychiatric authorities as well as by insurance companies. These diagnostic criteria and requirements privilege "passing," binary, and able-bodied trans people at the expense of those who do not fit into these categories. The gatekeeping system presumes that healthcare providers know more about their patients' inherent goals and desires than the patients themselves.

DENIAL OF HORMONES

Autistic trans people often can't get hormones or have surgery because autistic people are said to not know what they want or who they are.

T/GE people who seek hormones always run the risk of having them denied. This is particularly true for disabled and older T/GE people.[40] The withholding of hormones may occur for multiple reasons, including adopting a nonbinary identity, being otherwise nonconforming according to the expectations of their provider, or being considered too old or not healthy enough for receiving "risky" hormonal treatment. In order to access hormonal treatment, a T/GE person (especially those of us with mental disabilities) may therefore be forced to resort to lying about their gender identity and lived experiences.

In a 2017 study, researchers Riggs and Bartholomaeus[41] found that the trans men they interviewed tended to hide their emotional and mental disabilities from healthcare practitioners in order to avoid being delegitimized and to avoid experiencing further

"I chose to live open and visible as a transgender woman, while also having a chronic illness like multiple sclerosis, because it is a very important tool to normalize us in society, as well as to give Trans*people with disabilities hope for a happy and fulfilled life. Neither disabilities nor being trans* defines us." (Hannah Herr)

gatekeeping during their transition process. In other words, to avoid negative impacts on their transition, they pretended not to have mental health issues. Among many T/GE disabled people who share their testimonies online, writer and activist Sam Dylan Finch writes about his experience being denied a standard dose of testosterone due to his psychological disability.[42] These are only two of many examples demonstrating the extent to which, in the current cisgenderist and ableist context, members of our communities who are also disabled people are placed in difficult situations. We are forced to prioritize one aspect of our lived experiences over another (gender identity over mental health, for example), or to compromise one part of our lives in order to be able to fully live another. T/GE disabled people should not have to face these difficult and sometimes even impossible choices, and both our mental health needs and our gender-related needs should be considered simultaneously and equally.

> I have ADHD. Most people don't realize how much of a disability severe ADHD can be. It impacts all my executive functioning. If I hadn't had people willing to help me with all the paperwork when changing my documentation, I wouldn't have been able to do it. I couldn't track or comprehend everything the system needed me to do. I can't always get my T prescription because my insurance requires me to jump through so many hoops, and I can't track the hoops. It also impacts my impulse control. I would try any drug to try to forget about my dysphoria without a second thought.

DENIAL OF SURGERY

Gatekeeping practices involve the monitoring of T/GE people, not only for gender conformity, but also for conformity to particular standards of sanity and ability. It is an established fact that ableist cultures lead to high rates of unemployment among disabled people,[43,44] and the expectations that T/GE people maintain employment or full-time study also contribute to a culture of ableism regarding transition and surgery requirements. These rules assume that all T/GE people will have the ability to be hired, keep a job, or be a full-time student, and that productivity is a necessary part of doing gender "correctly."[45,46] In addition, the belief that one must meet markers of supposed mental "stability" before transitioning is founded on forms of ableism and sanism and relates to a cisgenderist perception of transition as self-mutilation. T/GE people with mental disabilities run the risk of having their surgeries deferred for long periods or simply denied, based on the argument that they don't have mental capacity to make the informed decision to potentially "damage" their body. It is important to note that although mental disabilities could involve short periods of time during which judgment is blurred, mental disabilities don't prevent disabled people from making informed decisions at other times. Removing the agency of T/GE people with mental disabilities to make surgical choices is therefore anchored in ableist and sanist ideologies, and also in cisgenderist forms of transition gatekeeping.

DISMISSAL OF INTERSECTING IDENTITIES

For T/GE people with disabilities, their disabilities may be questioned because of their T/GE identity, or vice versa. Often, once healthcare practitioners become aware of a person's trans identity, all "symptoms" or mental disabilities are interpreted through the lens of gender. T/GE people are seen as depressed, anxious, suicidal, or socially withdrawn because of their "gender dysphoria," and not because of mental disabilities or neurodivergence. On the flip side, autistic, genderqueer activist Lydia Brown writes about their experience with their trans identity sometimes being attributed to their autism.[47] Their gender identity is frequently brushed aside, and emphasis is placed instead on disability/neurodivergence. Healthcare professionals frequently fail to take health and disability issues into consideration by focusing on gender identity alone, or they fail to acknowledge gender-related issues by focusing only on mental health and mental disabilities.

The little research that exists has shown that T/GE disabled people are more likely to experience various forms of discrimination (including outright refusals of treatment) in medical contexts, and that they are more likely to report negative experiences with their healthcare providers than T/GE and disabled groups, respectively.[48,49]

I have a crippling mystery joint condition, autism, and several mental illnesses, so I do consider myself disabled. Because of this, I'm very rarely taken seriously. People often assume I'm not intelligent enough to know my identity because of my autism, or my identity is a delusion caused by my mental health issues.

<hr>

DEAF, TRANS, AND DISABLED

Rhys McGovern (he/they)

About five years ago, I was struggling with increasing trouble with my balance. On good days, I was fine, with legs that worked and carried me safely where I needed to go. The rest of the time, the floor pitched and rolled under my feet, and walls became islands of stability as I lurched my way along. One day, when I was walking home from the train, the sidewalk shifted and curled away from me, ungluing gravity and sending me spinning. I stopped at a crosswalk, stuck, too afraid that I would fall in the middle of the road to try and cross it. My partner had to come and pick me up –less than a block away from home. As I sat on the curb, humiliated and sick, I remember thinking that the road had never looked so wide and dangerous. I wondered when my perspective had shifted so much that a side street could stretch to the width of a highway. I wondered if this was just a moment or the rest of my life, waiting for help from someone else, unable to make it the last block home.

I started losing my hearing when I was in college, and I preferred using a videophone (VP) to the telephone even back when I wasn't yet fluent in ASL. Shortly after I got my VP number, I called my parents . . . and they hung up on me. I called them back immediately, sure it had been a mistake. They said that it was too uncomfortable to talk through another person—Couldn't I just talk while I called them? I could always sign the rest of the time. The next time I called, I asked the interpreter to sign everything my parents said, and spoke for myself to respond to them. In order to cover occasional pauses while the interpreter caught me up, I said that I was cooking while we talked. It didn't feel comfortable or connected, but at least we were talking.

(switch to using wheelchair)

Beyond the edges of the Deaf community, hearing loss is considered an affliction. It evokes pitying looks and cloying comments about *bravery* and *perseverance*. It summons ranks of doctors and audiologists with well-funded statements about spoken language and auditory rehabilitation and the dangers of signing. It is something to be overcome, never embraced, but ASL has been my lifeline. It gives me a way to communicate that doesn't rely on my increasingly blurry hearing, and the Deaf community gives me space to feel frustrated with losing full access to sound, as well as reassurance that life without it can still be full and happy. ASL and Deaf spaces allow me to feel safe, and whole, and capable. And yet when I first shared that I was losing my hearing with one of my education professors, he asked, "Why not just get a cochlear implant? Wouldn't you rather hear?"

Wheelchairs are always portrayed as ponderous objects carrying passive and incapable people, but in my wheelchair, the whole world speeds up. What takes ten unsteady minutes to walk takes two easy minutes to roll. Protracted, impossible distances suddenly snap toward me like a rubber band. My freedom has wheels, but people say "wheelchair bound." When I sit, I am supposed to lose myself below the waist. When I go grocery shopping in my chair, and stand to reach the cream cheese, I grow a sign on my back that says, "Ask me personal questions, I'm obviously faking." There is no space in the concept of "wheelchair user" for me to wedge my functional-legged, dizzy, joyful self into.

No matter what I'm doing, there are parts of me left unseen. Standing up, my need for a wheelchair ghosts into the background. Sitting down, my legs disappear. When I sign, my hearing family beats a retreat. When I talk, my hands ache to communicate. I balance so many separate parts, sometimes I think I might collapse, folding into myself like a demolished building, until all that is left is a rubble-littered crater and a cloud of dust.

I live in the gray spaces outside of what people expect: I look able, but I'm not. I sound hearing, but I'm not. It's easiest for me to show you what you think you already see, but then I know you're not really seeing me. As uncomfortable as it is to share my whole self, the moments I do are the moments I really connect with other people. What is missed when we stop at face value? What parts would you share?

As a person living at an intersection of gender variance, hearing loss, and disability, I find myself pulled in many directions by a world that is not built for me. Living at this intersection sometimes feels suffocating as I am constantly reminded of the ways in which I fall short. But that weight is lifted by the people who have gathered around me through the trans, Deaf, and disabled communities. With every person who mirrors a facet of my lived experience, I feel myself finding more comfort in my identity.

FORGING PATHWAYS BEYOND "CURE"

Understanding transness and disability, not only as opposites of cisness and able-bodiedness, but as positive and fulfilling parts of life in their own right, requires imagining alternative futures for T/GE and disabled identities and bodies. Many members of our communities are moving beyond "cure" and instead thinking in terms of transition and disability, embracing the unique potential of our non-normative bodyminds. In doing so, we create new words and pioneering scholarship that speak to our lived experiences.

> *Knowing that I'm not a woman means I don't have to distance myself from woman-coded things in order to be myself. I know now that I can and should demand to be treated as myself regardless of what I'm wearing. I actually wear more dresses now than I ever did before growing into myself as trans and non-binary. I'm also fat, and neurodivergent, and disabled, and the disability has a varying visibility on the surface day-to-day. Those things I can't change, and I have only a limited ability to adjust how the world at large reads those things in me. But I would be lying if I said I don't play off them. My cane is wrapped in rainbow tape, for instance. My presentation goal is to be unparsable. I don't want cis people to know what they are seeing when they look at me. I want them to be unable to answer the question, "So, what ARE you?" and I'm getting there. I'm getting there.*

EMERGING COMMUNITIES, EMERGING IDENTITIES: NEUROQUEER AND AUTIGENDER

> *There's this term "neuroqueer," that is, one cannot separate one's gender/sexuality from one's neurology. It fits me, although I don't use it much. I cannot separate how I conceive of my gender identity and how I feel alienated from traditional masculinity/maleness without factoring in that I am autistic and have never fit into neurotypical spaces.*

Autistic people, as well as other neurodivergent people, have developed our own terminologies to describe our unique relationships with gender and identity. For many, it is essential to acknowledge the connection between gender and neurodivergence, leading to the creation of the umbrella term neurogender. Autism is a subcategory under the vast umbrella of neurodivergence, and autigender is a subcategory of the neurogender umbrella.[50] Autigender people experience their gender as intrinsically linked to their autistic identity. Both neurodivergence and gender are shaped by social conditions and expectations, and "social skills" and "gender roles" are often difficult to separate. For example, autistic women (and T/GE people who are marked as women by medical authorities) may be, under the guise of "therapy," trained in the "social skills" of quietness and feminine dress, thereby reinforcing gender roles.

> *My parents never really commented on any of my gender expression beyond, "That's just your autism."*

Terms like "autigender" have been created by and for autistic and other neurodivergent T/GE people, in order to represent our complex relationships to gender.[51] Neurogender and autigender people are often met with anger and prejudice, even by some T/GE people who view such new forms of gender identification as threatening to trans respectability. For this reason and many others, further research about neurogender and autigender communities, as well as the amplification of these communities' voices, is critical.

> *To me, a person's gender has always been whatever they want it to mean. However, my autism also means that I cannot always understand why most cisgender people simply accept that their gender is constant, fixed and aligned with their biological sex. It seems silly to me that someone told a child, "You're*

a boy, so that means you have to be this," or "You're a girl, so that means you have to be that," and the child just accepted it without question.

FORMING COMMUNITIES THROUGH ACADEMIA AND ACTIVISM

Hearing a lecture by a trans autistic person was the first time I'd heard a trans person describe their experience growing up that actually resonated for me.

Both inside and outside formal "academia," T/GE and disabled people are furthering scholarship and knowledge at the intersection of transness and disability. Several disabled T/GE scholars straddle the line between academic and nonacademic work, including Eli Clare, whose scholarship, rooted in working-class experiences, includes prose and poetry, as well as A. J. Withers and Alexandre Baril who propose auto-ethnographic methodologies and essays. Lydia Brown, a trans and multiply disabled blogger at *Autistic Hoya*, brings activism and academia together seamlessly, showing that, as with gender, the "binary" between activism and academia does not exist. These scholars write for popular media, publish academic articles and books, and are well-known for their activism. There is also a subset of T/GE disabled former academics who commit to posting their work online for free. This is especially important for those who fear that fields of study (particularly Trans Studies in this case) have been "depoliticized" now that they have been assimilated into academic settings. One such former academic is Rachel Anne Williams, a blogger at *Trans Philosopher*. Both Brown and Williams illustrate the ways in which academic activists use social media to make an impact.

FORMING COMMUNITIES THROUGH SOCIAL MEDIA AND ART

I have lost complete vision in one eye. After a stroke about two years ago, I had no major additional deficits. I do not drive now, due to fear of having a stroke while driving and possibly killing myself and others. I have very severe osteoarthritis pain and am limited in my physical activities. Before this I was much more able to endure long travel to trans-related conferences, etc. I am much more home-bound and very sedentary, since physical activity causes increased pain.

There are many T/GE disabled activists whose work is primarily featured on social media. The Internet allows disabled people with mobility and/or speech variations the unprecedented possibility to share ideas without face-to-face contact. The importance of this mode of communication is outlined by Johanna Hedva in their article on their experience as the "sick woman" who needs to stay in bed as protest marches carry on outside, but nevertheless carves out their own space of defiance and survival.[52] Hedva is a genderqueer writer who also bridges the gaps between academia, activism, and social media.

I have bipolar disorder, ADHD, and have had past issues of serious substance abuse. Because of this, I have had to navigate the mental health system as a transgender person. This makes things difficult sometimes, like finding a therapist/psychiatrist that doesn't insist that the root of my problems is actually my gender (which happened a couple of times). Being hospitalized was also made even more stressful due to the lack of privacy and the fear of other people in the ward finding out about my gender.

Sam Dylan Finch is a social media activist and a blogger at *Let's Queer Things Up*. He writes about his experience as a psychologically disabled person navigating the process of medical transition as well as about being trans while institutionalized.

Mel (Amanda) Baggs, who is genderless and uses sie/hir pronouns, has been a prominent disabled social media activist for well over a decade.[53] In 2007, sie created the video, *In My Language*, compelling viewers to engage with hir on hir terms rather than viewing hir in terms of the norms with which they were familiar. Baggs was also part of the

Kay Ulanday Barrett (www.kaybarrett.net). (Micah Bazant)

Loud Hands Project, which aimed to promote and destigmatize stimming (or making self-stimulatory movements such as hand-flapping) common among autistic people, because it is so frequently met with hostility by neurotypicals. For years, Baggs blogged on Tumblr, a platform where many people living at the intersections of T/GE identity and disability/illness found community.

Perhaps most famous at the artistic intersection of transness and disability is *Sins Invalid,* a group that produces performance art centering non-normative bodies (primarily disabled bodies). The scarcity of such groups, however, illustrates the novelty of most T/GE disabled community and artistic projects. Individual trans/disabled creators, especially creators of color, are also pioneering projects that speak to their lived experiences. Kay Ulanday Barrett, a "disabled pin@y-amerikan transgender queer" writer, artist, and activist, is also making critical contributions to trans disabled culture and visibility.

REJECTING "NORMALCY"

> *As a working class Femme I put together fabulous outfits for under $5 by hustling at thrift stores, estate sales, garage sales, and dollar stores. My Femme presentation also intersects with my disability. As a disabled person, there are many days I can't leave the house looking how I want to look, and I also have tics that make me look distinctly odd to ableds. I also use a cane part-time. I decide to rock this for the most part, though it can be tough to be read as androgynous when I'm not wearing makeup or cute clothes.*

Rather than suggesting that disability is simply an "extra risk" one takes when living as T/GE, or that transness is an unnecessary and confusing addition to a disabled life, we must acknowledge that oppressive social norms create the experiences we call "transness" and "disability" as distinct categories. In so doing, we can refuse to frame deviation as an avoidable risk and do what disabled and T/GE communities have been doing for

Amythest Schaber (neurowonderful) is an autistic activist who blogs and posts informational videos on YouTube.

decades: celebrate the joys of living among like-bodyminds in a state of joyful defiance. Rather than viewing disability as something that must be made palatable using gender-conformity and understanding transness as something that can be "cured" by transition, life at the intersection of transness and disability insists on defying cisnormativity and able-bodied normativity.

WITHIN THE IN-BETWEEN

Annette (A) Powell (they/them) has: lived and worked in three different countries; earned a B.A. in English and M.Ed. in Counseling Psychology; been a champion horse rider, bartender, waitress, admin assistant, education facilitator, and peer supporter. They are a person's child who is a queer questioner, advocate, adventurer, animal lover, Buddhist, parent, sibling, friend, and counselor working on self-love, self-compassion, and peaceful ease.

Truth is I don't fall into a category . . . I can't even jam myself into one. I know I'm not a boy, but not sure I'm totally a girl. I feel like I'm a little bit of both and not enough of either.

I've been waiting my whole life to finally feel like a woman, but that didn't even happen after being pregnant and giving birth. Breastfeeding and postpartum depression left me traumatized and not ethereally enamored with my child.

When I first heard the term nonbinary a couple of years ago, I thought, "yep, that fits." Then I saw Asia Kate Dillon in *Billions* and thought, "crap, I'm not that either." They seemed androgynous, and I am not.

That's the thing . . . I don't have a thing. I hate make-up. I'm not into most "girly" things. I wanted to play with dinkies, not Barbies. I was happiest at the barn, smelling of horse manure. I've asked out more guys than had guys ask me out. I don't want a penis, but I would like to know what it feels like to thrust myself into a woman. I think that's more about power than gender though one can never fully separate the two. If I could just find where I fit, I think I'd feel better, feel OK about being me . . . who doesn't really seem to fit anywhere.

A hereditary neuropathy slowly took away the feeling in my feet throughout my twenties. My leg braces often break down the skin on my feet without my awareness. So in order to keep my feet, I had to choose to use a wheelchair in my early thirties.

I felt it neutralized my gender. People no longer saw a full-functioning, sexual adult. They looked at me as an incapable, sexless child. People pat me on my head, talk down to me, they don't know (or care) whether I'm a boy or girl.

One would think I'd experience a release being freed from gender expectations. Though neither gender fully resonated with me, I did gain value from being seen as an attractive, able-bodied female. Men wanted to date me, people gave me free things, getting a job was easier, and so much more. I didn't like losing that power. I might not have fully identified as a woman, but I certainly wanted the benefits from being seen as one.

My days are filled with moving things out of the way of my wheelchair: garbage cans, chairs, boxes; telling businesses that their accessible door opener is off; advocating for trainings to be held in actual wheelchair-accessible locations; convincing someone I can do the job I'm trained to do; dealing with people's assumptions about who I am based on how my body appears; and hearing medical people tell me what's wrong with me and what they think is best for my body.

I think that's why I'm not currently in a place where I feel safe enough to ask people to use they pronouns instead of she . . . to cut off all my hair . . . to get a tattoo on my forearm. I'm just starting to explore my gender identity. I don't have the extra strength, energy, or confidence to delve into correcting pronouns, navigating more awkward, intimate conversations, or having people look at me with confusion and contempt.

I already struggle with a sense of raw exposure and judgment from a difference I can't hide. My gender identity is something I can choose to reveal or not. Sometimes I experience power from knowing my truth without sharing it. Other times I feel alone in it. Most times I'm weighed down with shame about it.

I'm terrified to fully be myself while I'm excited to finally start embracing all of who I am. It's a complex layering of roads to journey on, and who knows what I'll find in the in-between?

BEING AN ALLY: T/GE AND DISABLED ACCESSIBLE SPACES AND EVENTS

I am a disabled person, and often it feels like my gender/sexuality takes a back seat to my disability. A lot of queer spaces are not accessible, but crip spaces are typically very queer friendly. It has changed who I feel my community is.

When we think about accessibility, we often reduce it, from a layperson's point of view, to accessible architectural design that makes it easier for wheelchair users, as well as

D/deaf and blind people to navigate diverse environments. There are, however, many more dimensions of accessibility that need to be addressed. These include paying attention to accessible communication, attitude (creating an actively welcoming space for disabled people), and sensory environments (low-noise options; scent-free spaces). In addition, a truly accessible space or event should not only be welcoming and convenient for people with diverse disabilities (physical, mental, sensorial, learning disabilities, etc.), but also to a wide variety of marginalized populations whose participation is hindered when spaces and activities cater to the needs of a universal and abstract individual, often imagined as male, white, middle-class, able-bodied, cisgender, and heterosexual, instead of around the needs of real, embodied individuals living under oppressive power structures. To give only one example, an organized event requiring participants to pay $100 (such as a conference) is inaccessible to socioeconomically disadvantaged people.

> *I can't be broken into neat little boxes. I'm disabled and fat and neurodivergent and mixed. I often end up in circumstances where there isn't any winning. Most often, a space will be wonderful for queer people . . . at least abled queer people . . . but not have accessible seating at all and so I can't be in that space. There's a monthly event I would love to go to in my city, but I had to stop going when they added strobe lights to the show and I started having seizures. They didn't care enough to change it no matter how much noise I made. It gets exhausting to have to fight two times the battles on half the energy.*

Although they may be champions of accessibility for disabled people, disability activists often forget T/GE accessibility when planning events. While gearing up to host a conference or meeting, disability activists may want to identify gender-neutral washrooms and send maps identifying these washrooms to the participants ahead of time. It is also important to redesign (even if only with temporary signs) gender binary bathroom symbols, to include garbage cans in both washrooms (people of all genders may need to dispose of sanitary products), to hire web designers to create gender nonbinary registration forms, to use gender neutral language in documents and on websites, and to offer name tags providing blank spaces for pronouns. These small actions make a huge difference in creating spaces and events accessible to T/GE people. Ensuring that there are trans people taking active leadership roles in the planning process for disability-related events, and ensuring that there are disabled people in active leadership roles when planning T/GE events, can improve allyship all around.

> *In queer spaces I feel safe in expressing my gender freely, yet unsafe due to my disability and the exclusion that I face from those spaces as someone that uses a cane. We have meetings that may have no elevator or ramp to get to.*

T/GE communities often leave behind the access needs of various disabled people. Given that all oppressions are connected, and because a significant number of T/GE people are also disabled, it is surprising and disappointing that disabled T/GE people remain on the margins of T/GE scholarship, activism, and communities because of inaccessible structures. Making an event accessible to people with various disabilities requires long-term, advance planning.

Here are some tips to make T/GE spaces and events more accessible for those of us who are disabled:

- Carefully planning in advance who will be invited and who will participate in order to identify their needs (such as providing simultaneous sign language interpretations, quiet recovery spaces, plugs for recharging electric wheelchairs, audio-description for blind people, accessible paper copies for D/deaf people and people with learning disabilities, and avoiding the use of chemicals that can potentially trigger sickness [such as scented products]).

DisAbled Women's Network/ DAWN Canada, has developed toolkits with concrete suggestions to help plan and host accessible events, not only for people with various disabilities, but for other marginalized communities, such as LGBTQ, racialized, and Indigenous communities, as well as those with diverse religious affiliations or from different age groups.

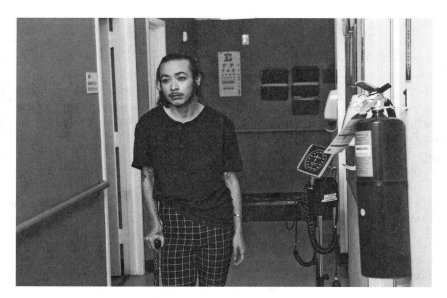

A genderqueer person with a cane walking down a hallway in a hospital. (Zackary Drucker, The Gender Spectrum Collection, VICE/Broadly)

- Making note of your event's accommodations in an easily accessible place online, in a format compatible with screen-readers;
- Including accessibility needs in the budget for each event;
- Renting the equipment needed to make the event accessible to all attendees;
- Purchasing food for the event that can be eaten by people with a variety of intolerances, allergies, and other dietary needs;
- Scheduling the event while taking into consideration the different temporalities experienced by various disabled people ("crip time," as we sometimes call it). This could include flexible start/end times, as well as not penalizing people for arriving late or leaving early.

For concrete suggestions on how to commit to mixed ability organizing and create accessible events (as well as learn about the history of disability activism), check out *Skin, Tooth, and Bone: The Basis of Movement is Our People*, a disability justice primer from Sins Invalid.

Being a part of queer disability justice communities has been immensely important for all aspects of my identity, especially my relationship to my sensuality/ sexuality, which is a really important part of my femme-ness. My disability is invisible but impacts every day of my life, which adds to the constant coming out process that I'm always doing with new people. I'm not sure how else to explain the connection except that it's there because my disability and my femme-ness both exist within me together.

Good planning for hosting accessible events is clearly a central component to the cultivation of disabled-positive spaces and events in T/GE communities. Considering accessibility, not only for disabled people but also for a large variety of people within our T/GE communities, will necessarily involve reimagining our scholarship, activism, art, and (social) media production and participation. Examples include academic articles and monographs that use jargon without including simplified-language versions, gatherings or protests that do not account for the needs and realities of disabled people, self-produced YouTube videos made by T/GE people that do not include subtitles, or art exhibitions about T/GE issues that fail to provide audio-description. Although these events and activities improve the lived experiences of T/GE people and help create solidarity in our communities, they are often produced, organized, and disseminated in a way that excludes disabled people. Our aim is not to call out the T/GE people who work toward greater recognition and social justice for T/GE communities; their work has been, and continues to be, crucial to our survival. Rather, our goal is to (re)open conversations between communities that have been historically distanced from each other (T/GE and disabled communities). Our communities are not separate or exclusive, but rather have a lot in common. Conceptualizing accessibility in the spirit of allyship has enormous potential for facilitating engagement with these vital and urgent conversations.

NOTES

1. Bauer, G. R., & Scheim, A. I. (2015). *Transgender people in Ontario, Canada: Statistics from the Trans PULSE Project to inform human rights policy.* London, ON. http://transpulseproject.ca/wp-content/uploads/2015/06/Trans-PULSE-Statistics-Relevant-for-Human-Rights-Policy-June-2015.pdf

2. Valentine, S. E., & Shipherd, J. C. (2018). A systematic review of social stress and mental health among transgender and gender non-conforming people in the United States. *Clinical Psychology Review, 66,* 24–38.

3. Baril, A. (2015a). Needing to acquire a physical impairment/disability: (Re)thinking the connections between trans and disability studies through transability. *Hypatia, 30*(1), 30–48.

4. Baril, A. (2015b). Transness as debility: Rethinking intersections between trans and disabled embodiments. *Feminist Review, 111,* 59–74.

5. Withers, A. J. (2012). *Disability politics and theory.* Halifax, NS: Fernwood Publishing.

6. Withers, A. J. (2014). Disability, divisions, definitions, and disablism: When resisting psychiatry is oppressive. In B. Burstow, B. A. LeFrançois, & S. Diamond (Eds.), *Psychiatry disrupted: Theorizing resistance and crafting the (r)evolution* (pp. 114–128). Montreal/Kingston: McGill-Queen's University Press.

7. Wendell, S. (2001). Unhealthy disabled: Treating chronic illnesses as disabilities. *Hypatia, 16*(4), 17–33.

8. Withers, A. J. (2012). *Disability politics and theory.* Halifax, NS: Fernwood Publishing.

9. Clare, E. (2017). *Brilliant imperfection: Grappling with cure.* Durham, NC: Duke University Press.

10. Kafer, A. (2013). *Feminist, queer, crip.* Bloomington: Indiana University Press.

11. Erevelles, N. (2011). *Disability and difference in global contexts. Enabling a transformative body politic.* New York: Palgrave Macmillan.

12. Wendell, S. (2001). Unhealthy disabled: Treating chronic illnesses as disabilities. *Hypatia, 16*(4), 17–33.

13. James, S. E., Herman, J. L., Rankin, S., Keisling, M., Mottet, L., & Anafi, M. (2016). *The Report of the 2015 U.S. Transgender Survey.* Washington, DC: National Center for Transgender Equality. https://transequality.org/sites/default/files/docs/usts/USTS-Full-Report-Dec17.pdf

14. Bauer, G., K, A., Pyne, J., Redman, N., Scanlon, K., & Travers, R. (2012). *Improving the health of trans communities: Findings from the Trans PULSE Project.* Ottawa, ON. http://transpulseproject.ca/wp-content/uploads/2012/04/Trans-PULSE.-Rainbow-Health-Ontario-Conference.-Plenary-2012-vFINAL.pdf

15. Kattari, S. K., Walls, E. N., & Speer, S. R. (2017). Differences in experiences of discrimination in accessing social services among transgender/gender nonconforming individuals by (dis)ability. *Journal of Social Work in Disability & Rehabilitation, 16*(2), 116–140.

16. James, S. E., Herman, J. L., Rankin, S., Keisling, M., Mottet, L., & Anafi, M. (2016). *The Report of the 2015 U.S. Transgender Survey.* Washington, DC: National Center for Transgender Equality. https://www.transequality.org/sites/default/files/docs/USTS-Full-Report-FINAL.PDF

17. Drescher, J. (2015). Out of *DSM*: Depathologizing homosexuality. *Behavioral Sciences, 5*(4), 565–575.

18. American Psychiatric Association (APA). (2013). *Diagnostic and statistical manual of mental disorders (DSM-5).* 5th ed. Arlington, VA: American Psychiatric Publishing.

19. World Health Organization (WHO) (2018). *International Classification of Diseases.* https://www.euro.who.int/en/health-topics/health-determinants/gender/gender-definitions/whoeurope-brief-transgender-health-in-the-context-of-icd-11

20. Ashley, F., & Baril, A. (2018). Why "Rapid-onset Gender Dysphoria" is bad science. *The Conversation,* March 22, 2018. http://theconversation.com/why-rapid-onset-gender-dysphoria-is-bad-science-92742

21. World Professional Association for Transgender Health (WPATH) (2018). *WPATH Position on "Rapid-Onset Gender Dysphoria (ROGD)."* https://www.wpath.org/media/cms/Documents/Public%20Policies/2018/9_Sept/WPATH%20Position%20on%20Rapid-Onset%20Gender%20Dysphoria_9-4-2018.pdf

22. Littman, L. (2018). Rapid-onset gender dysphoria in adolescents and young adults: A study of parental reports. *Plos One, 13*(8). doi:10.1371/journal.pone.0202330.

23. Clare, E. (2009). *Exile & pride: Disability, queerness and liberation (Second edition with a new Afterword by Dean Spade).* New York: South End Press.

24. Clare, E. (2013). Body shame, body pride. Lessons from the disability rights movement. In S. Stryker & A. Z. Aizura (Eds.), *The Transgender Studies Reader 2* (pp. 261–265). New York: Routledge.

25. Clare, E. (2017). *Brilliant imperfection: Grappling with cure.* Durham, NC: Duke University Press.

26. Baril, A. (2018). Hommes trans et handicapés: une analyse croisée du cisgenrisme et du capacitisme. *Genre, sexualité & société,* 1–26. https://journals.openedition.org/gss/4218

27. Gill, M. (2015). *Already doing it: Intellectual disability and sexual agency.* Minneapolis: University of Minnesota Press.

28. Marshall, Z., Burnette, M., Lowton, S., Rainbow, Smith, R. D. T., Tiamo, J., Udegbe, O., & Vo, T. (2014). A Conversation about art and activism with trans and genderqueer people labelled with intellectual disabilities. In R. Raj & D. Irving (Eds.), *Trans activism in Canada: A reader* (pp. 125–135). Toronto, ON: Canadian Scholars' Press.

29. Kim, E. (2011). Asexuality in disability narratives. *Sexualities, 14*(4), 479–493.

30. Gill, M. (2015). *Already doing it: Intellectual disability and sexual agency.* Minneapolis: University of Minnesota Press.

31. Mangassarian, S. Lekeisha, S., & O'Callaghan, E. (2015). Sexual impulsivity in women diagnosed with borderline personality disorder: A review of the literature. *Sexual Addiction & Compulsivity, 22*(3), 195–206.

32. Serano, J. (2007). *Whipping girl: A transsexual woman on sexism and the scapegoating of femininity.* Berkeley, CA: Seal Press.

33. Kafer, A. (2013). *Feminist, queer, crip.* Bloomington: Indiana University Press.

34. Marshall, Z., Burnette, M., Lowton, S., Rainbow, Smith, R. D. T., Tiamo, J., Udegbe, O., & Vo, T. (2014). A conversation about art and activism with trans and genderqueer people labelled with intellectual disabilities. In R. Raj & D. Irving (Eds.), *Trans activism in Canada: A reader* (pp. 125–135). Toronto, ON: Canadian Scholars' Press.

35. Serano, J. (2007). *Whipping girl: A transsexual woman on sexism and the scapegoating of femininity.* Berkeley, CA: Seal Press.

36. Thapliyal, P., Hay, P., & Conti, J. (2018). Role of gender in the treatment experiences of people with an eating disorder: A metasynthesis. *Journal of Eating Disorders, 6*(18). doi:10.1186/s40337-018-0207-1.

37. Baril, A. (2018). Hommes trans et handicapés: une analyse croisée du cisgenrisme et du capacitisme. *Genre, sexualité & société,* 1–26. https://journals.openedition.org/gss/4218

38. Spade, D. (2003). Resisting medicine, re/modeling gender. *Berkeley Women's Law Journal, 18,* 15–37.

39. Spade, D. (2003). Resisting medicine, re/modeling gender. *Berkeley Women's Law Journal, 18,* 15–37.

40. Ansara, Y. G. (2015). Challenging cisgenderism in the ageing and aged care sector: Meeting the needs of older people of trans and/or non-binary experience. *Australasian Journal on Ageing, 34,* 14–18.

41. Riggs, D. W., & Bartholomaeus, C. (2017). The disability and diagnosis nexus: Transgender men navigating mental health care services. In C. Loeser, V. Crowley, & B. Pini (Eds.), *Disability and masculinities: Corporeality, pedagogy and the critique of otherness* (pp. 67–85). London, UK: Palgrave Macmillan.

42. Finch, S. D. (2017). When you're too mentally ill to transition. https://letsqueerthingsup.com/2016/06/20/too-mentally-ill-to-transition/

43. Clare, E. (2009). *Exile & pride: Disability, queerness and liberation (Second edition with a new Afterword by Dean Spade).* New York: South End Press.

Who We Are

44. Withers, A. J. (2012). *Disability politics and theory.* Halifax, NS: Fernwood Publishing.

45. Kafer, A. (2013). *Feminist, queer, crip.* Bloomington: Indiana University Press.

46. Spade, D. (2003). Resisting medicine, re/modeling gender. *Berkeley Women's Law Journal, 18*, 15–37.

47. Brown, L. X. Z. (2017). Ableist shame and disruptive bodies: Survivorship at the intersection of queer, trans, and disabled existence. In A. J. Johnson, J. R. Nelson, & E. M. Lund (Eds.), *Religion, disability, and interpersonal violence* (pp. 163–178). Cham, Switzerland: Springer International Publishing.

48. James, S. E., Herman, J. L., Rankin, S., Keisling, M., Mottet, L., & Anafi, M. (2016). *The Report of the 2015 U.S. Transgender Survey.* Washington, DC: National Center for Transgender Equality. https://www.transequality.org/sites/default/files/docs/USTS-Full-Report-FINAL.PDF

49. Kattari, S. K., Walls, E. N., & Speer, S. R. (2017). Differences in experiences of discrimination in accessing social services among transgender/gender nonconforming individuals by (dis)ability. *Journal of Social Work in Disability & Rehabilitation, 16*(2), 116–140.

50. Walker, N. (2015). Neuroqueer: An introduction. http://neurocosmopolitanism.com/neuroqueer-an-introduction/

51. Hack, S. (2017). Anonymous asked: What exactly is autigender? I've seen it used a few times now but there's several definitions and it's really confusing. https://candidlyautistic.tumblr.com/post/163767993845/what-exactly-is-autigender-ive-seen-it-used-a

52. Hedva, J. (2016). Sick woman theory. http://www.maskmagazine.com/not-again/struggle/sick-woman-theory

53. Baggs, M. (2013). A bunch of stuff that needed saying. https://ballastexistenz.wordpress.com/2013/04/18/a-bunch-of-stuff-that-needed-saying/

5

RELIGION AND SPIRITUALITY
Kelsey Pacha

INTRODUCTION

There are as many unique varieties of religious and spiritual experience among transgender and gender expansive people as there are unique experiences of gender. Transgender and gender expansive people may identify with the religious tradition we grew up in, change our religious affiliation, identify as atheist, agnostic, humanist, spiritual but not religious, or we may create our own spiritual practices outside of an established tradition. Although the relationship between religious institutions and transgender people has often been characterized by discrimination and abuse, there is also a long history of gender expansive mythology, leaders, and resilience that stretch back to the origins of organized spiritual practice.

> *My spirituality/faith has definitely helped me to accept and celebrate my gender as a calling from God. Even more specifically, to see my gender journey from being socialized female to embodying genderqueerness to now emerging from second adolescence into adulthood where I am deciding what kind of man I want to be as such a special, and unique, vocation from God.*

In this chapter, we highlight ways that trans people have reclaimed our spirituality within our authentic genders and honored our authentic genders through spiritual expression. We explore religious affiliation and practices among trans and gender expansive people in the United States, consider how our religious experiences may affect our well-being, and look at how major world religions engage with trans, nonbinary, and gender expansive people. This chapter will mostly speak to a North American experience, though we will discuss the impact of race, ethnicity, colonialism, culture, education, and generational differences on our experiences.

The first all-transgender Gospel Choir, Transcendence Gospel Choir, was created in a United Church of Christ (UCC) church.

> *I was not raised particularly religious, so I was spared the angst of navigating my gender identity intersecting with my faith. I have been atheist since before I knew the word for it. However, I have recently begun exploring the idea of (secular) spirituality, with regard to my wholeness as a person and how I relate to myself and others. I am developing rituals of loving to support myself through hard times and to heal myself through trauma.*

Although the words "religion" and "spirituality" may be paired together often in this chapter, they refer to distinct concepts. Religion is used to describe institutions that organize belief systems in texts, ritual, and other practices. Spirituality refers to an individual quest for meaning, which may happen in the context of a religion, but does not have to, and which may concern itself with religious beliefs, but may also be decidedly nonreligious. Both religion and spirituality ask questions about ultimate purpose, values, and transcendence. We sometimes use the term "faith tradition" or "faith community" to refer to an established religious or spiritual community.

> *I always knew I was different, just not how different. Growing up in a church that presented identifying as any sort of trans/queer as a choice, I figured everyone felt the way I did but was better at not wanting to act on it.*

We hope to explore the bountiful examples of how nonconforming gender expressions and identities have been connected to mystery, holiness, and wholeness throughout human

Divine Love is Our Birthright. (Féi Hernandez)

history. We attempt to offer context for how traditions around the world have represented and revered transgender and gender expansive people, as well as divine figures. Often these representations have been distorted or even erased by white supremacist, colonizing forces. We endeavor to lift up individuals and communities who reclaim the sacred history of transgender and gender expansive people, and to offer resources for further exploration. Reading this chapter may bring up strong emotions. Whatever an individual's experiences are with religion and/or spirituality, that experience is valid, and we hope it is reflected in these pages.

OUR SACRED CONNECTIONS

Many different kinds of practices could be called "spiritual," whether they involve interacting with supernatural beings, remembering ancestors, or simply connecting to ourselves and others. Whether we are heavily involved with a faith community or have never been involved with one, there are many ways we can use spiritual practices for healing and to honor the ways we are living into our authentic genders. These include using ritual to mark stages of transition, meditation, creating altars, and other practices.

> It is important for me to have ways to engage with my spirituality. I read tarot cards, say prayers, and light candles.

Many of us come from traditions that mark stages of our life using ritual. For example, Roman Catholics may receive sacraments recognizing stages of their faith, such as baptism, first communion, confession, and confirmation, as they grow up. These rituals represent the ways individuals grow into deeper relationship with their faith. We might recreate some of these rites of passage to mark stages of our transition, whether social, medical, legal, or any combination thereof. Many different kinds of rituals may be helpful to us as we change our expression, heal, and form new relationships.

> *I pray every morning giving thanks for being created the gender that I am. When I put on the male garments for my religion every morning, I feel my gender is affirmed. When I sit in the men's section, I feel affirmed. When I lead rituals as a man, I feel affirmed.*

> *I prayed before surgery. I had my first vial of T prayed over by my pastor before I injected it.*

Many faith traditions use naming/renaming ceremonies to signify when someone moves to a new stage in their spiritual life. In Judeo-Christian traditions, for example, Jacob takes the name Israel after wrestling with God. In the Christian New Testament, Saul uses his Greek name, Paul, after he converts to Christianity and begins spreading the Gospel.

> *When I converted to Judaism, I had chosen a Hebrew name for myself and began using it all the time. When I transitioned, I chose a masculine Hebrew name starting with the same initial. I have had nothing but positive reactions to my new name, even though some people struggle to pronounce it correctly.*

> *I kind of want to get baptized into my new name. I don't know if that's a thing or how I would do it. I've also started thinking of God with gender neutral or feminine terms when I talk to and picture them.*

Perhaps we invite friends to witness us speaking our name aloud for the first time, do a special set of practices before writing our name for the first time, or receive a blessing before going to court for a legal name change. These rituals may or may not be spiritual in nature but use symbols and ritual acts, such as donning new garments or interacting with the elements (i.e., earth, air, water, and fire). Perhaps we combine a releasing ceremony with a renaming—releasing ourselves from past identities, expectations, and even relationships. Some people have created rituals to bless their bodies before, during, and after surgery, or to honor scars. We can ritualistically change our clothes or jewelry, cut or style our hair, or wash off words written on our bodies that don't resonate with our identity. An increasing number of transgender and gender expansive people are using herbs or naturopathic medicine to not only aid in their transitions and overall health, but also in ritualized fashion to heal emotional wounds, protect against negativity, and explore their spiritual journeys.

Others, regardless of religious/spiritual beliefs, use altars as meditative sites, to honor revered figures, prepare offerings, and to house treasured objects.

Faith-based organizations, such as the Freedom Center for Social Justice and Soulforce, not only provide spaces for T/GE people to lead, but also work for social justice in a broader context.

> *I have secret objects that give me strength. My first piece of leather is special to me. My kink mentor made it for me! It's a thick wrist band which I shift from one arm to the other as my gender identity shifts throughout the day. I also have prayer totems, which I set up to help me focus my thoughts before I sleep. And a small bag of tokens that I carry with me when I travel. I set them up into an altar to remember the love of the friends who gave them to me. These items do not belong to any particular tradition, I just find them useful aids. I sometimes*

Stud. Charcoal and Gesso on Canvas. (Devon Reiffer)

pray but the words are of my own making, and not to any gods—I just send my intentions into the "verse."

Practices such as meditation, prayer, positive affirmations, altar building, using card decks, and creating vision boards may help us focus our attention and reframe our experiences in an affirming light. We may use mindfulness meditation to get more space between our thoughts and emotional reactions, to act more intentionally, or to be more present in our bodies. We may speak aloud to deceased loved ones, whether or not we believe they can hear us, or we may speak intentions aloud.

I pray daily and I have always included in my prayers that I can have the confidence and love I need to be my true self.

I found some prayers written by Rabbi Elliot Kukla, which I say before and after every important moment of my transition, even taking my hormone pills. I also found a few prayers for when we have to misgender ourselves and other trans experiences, so I use those to help me feel connected to Judaism and loved by G-D.

We may repeat positive beliefs about ourselves, even if they are goals that we are trying to live up to. Some people may consult an angel, tarot, or other spiritual card deck in a nonspiritual way to help organize their thoughts, or as a journal or conversation prompt. We may create a vision board to help remind us of goals in our life. All of these practices may help us feel calm, centered, and focused. None of them needs to be connected to religious or spiritual beliefs to be helpful.

JOURNAL PRAYER

Edward Olivera lives in New York City and journals daily about his spiritual journey as a trans femme, steering clear of all gatekeepers, and is an amateur classical pianist.

". . . present your bodies, a living sacrifice, holy, acceptable to God . . ."

—Rom.xii.I

I know there is a change taking place within me as well as outwardly in my appearance, making of me a new person. The clothes have been a big part of this transformation, but more than that is the acceptance, self-acceptance and self-love that generates a better human being, more helpful and mindful of others, caring and loving I would hope, nurturing of others and all things, a feminine creativity, earth mother, spiritual queen, queer empress over my demense. Protective and motherly, soft and gentle, all the things I was made for. If this is God's will may I be directed in the right ways of change and discovery, of my evolution to a more complete human being, of both sexes if need be or of neither. There is no confusion now, only waiting and learning and seeing with new eyes. This is my spiritual path, my devotion, and it is creative and fun too. I will no longer be the scared boy that inhabited me for so long but will love and nurture him and care for him and become what he was always meant to be. I pray for release from his fears.

WHAT DO WE KNOW ABOUT TRANS AND GENDER EXPANSIVE PEOPLE'S INVOLVEMENT IN RELIGION?

A majority of trans-identified Americans were raised in religious households, with higher percentages of trans people of color reporting having been part of a faith community at some point in their lives.[1] Some trans people stay with the religion they grew up in, feeling supported through gender transition. More and more faith communities are developing supportive networks and inclusive curricula, as well as releasing supportive theological and policy statements on trans affirmation. For some trans people, their faith life is a critical source of support and discernment on their gender journey, and there has never been any conflict between these parts of their lives.

> *I always knew that I was trans. I just have not always had the words for it. When I was in my mid 20s, I met an older African-American trans man and I knew that he was just like me. I was not ready to admit to myself or anyone else that I was trans. It was not until I started attending the church that I am a part of now. My church is open and affirming. I was able there to take the steps that I needed to be my authentic self.*

> *I met my first trans adult when I started going to church at age 9. Her name was Rosa, she sang in the choir, and I was entranced by her. I don't know how she felt about her voice, but to me seeing a woman sing as a bass was beautiful, and I still think of her as I sing in my own choir now."*

Large numbers of trans Americans disaffiliate from—or leave—their childhood religious traditions due to rejection or a fear of rejection based on their gender identity or expression.[12] Rejecting behaviors include conversion therapy, public outing and humiliation, exorcisms, or being outright ordered to leave a community. Some trans and gender expansive people perceive a conflict between their religious and gender identities, which may cause psychological distress such as depression, low self-esteem, anxiety, and internalized transphobia.[3] There is also evidence that transgender and gender expansive people experience disproportionate amounts of religiously and spiritually-based rejection compared to both LGB people and the general population.[4,5]

I don't like religion because the church community I grew up in was blatantly racist and xenophobic, and that's the strongest memory I have of them as a child. So now, I perhaps unfairly have negative opinions of religion as a whole.

I am Atheist. When I was 6, I began praying every night to magically wake up with the right body. A "female" body. I would wake up disappointed every day. After some time, I wondered what I did to deserve such punishment. I felt like God hated me, and for years I hated him right back. Then I began my search for a different God. By age 17, my faith was completely gone. My Atheism is, in a way, based on my gender identity.

Studies have found that there are links between religious affiliation (the religion one is a member of), religiosity (which can include how often one attends religious services and how important religious beliefs are in one's life), and whether a family rejects its queer and trans youth. Family rejection includes behaviors such as disowning, shunning, and forcing a person to leave home. Family rejection is correlated with homelessness, substance abuse, survival sex work, and cycles of abuse.[6]

I am and have always been and will always be a man because I was born with a penis, end of story. Anything else to my family is considered sinful heresy of the highest order. I'm not even exaggerating.

Although many trans and gender expansive people later find supportive faith communities, many still experience rejecting behaviors even in these faith spaces.

I describe myself as agnostic. I believe there could be a God(s) or higher power(s) out there, but I don't really practice a certain religion. I have definitely been rejected from quite a few churches since I came out, but it doesn't really bother me. If they want to believe that God hates me because of my identity, that's on them.

I'm pagan—specifically Asatru, which celebrates the traditions and lore of pre-Christian Scandinavia. There's a surprising amount of gender fluidity in the sagas, performed both by gods and heroes, so the faith fit me quite well. My communities have been eager to embrace me and are fantastic about pronoun use and PERSONAL validation . . . however, some folk behave differently on social media (sharing transphobic memes and defending them as "funny," for example) and have caused me to cut several ties. No religion is a monolith, I suppose!

Other factors can affect an individual's experience of religious acceptance and rejection. Older transgender people are more likely to have grown up with a childhood religion, while younger transgender folks are more likely to have been raised atheist, agnostic, or simply not affiliated.[7] Older trans folks may prefer to be part of accepting versions of the institutional religion they grew up in, while younger folks may gravitate toward individual spiritual practices or "nontraditional" spiritual communities. Some geographical regions, such as the American South, tend to have a more openly religious (in this case, Christian) society, which places additional pressure on people to identify as religious, and can make nonbelievers, regardless of gender, feel stigmatized.[8] Some studies suggest trans people of color (TPOC) may negotiate their religious and spiritual identities differently from white trans people, perhaps because faith communities led by people of color often serve as more than simply spaces for spiritual expression, but also as insulation against a white supremacist society. For example, some trans people of color may attend a rejecting POC-led religious or spiritual

People who have had negative experiences with religion and spirituality may seek out mental health support to heal from rejection and abuse. Therapists and other practitioners who are well-versed in LGBTQ identities and spirituality can be found in therapy databases such as the GAYLESTA or Spiritual Emergence Network websites.

Emani Love (she/her). (Brayden Asher Misiolek I roguestud.io)

The iAmClinic of Denver focuses on healing the mental health harm done by anti-LGBTQ religion.

community while also attending an accepting, but mixed race, or mostly white, religious community.[9,10] Although some religious and spiritual groups began as explicitly trans-supportive spaces, some of these communities may not be as responsive to people based on other identities, such as their race, age, or ability.

THE BLACK TRANS PRAYER BOOK

J Mase III (he/him) is a poet, educator, and founder of awQward, and Lady Dane Figueroa Edidi (she/her) is a poet, educator, author, and priestess.

In a world steeped in anti-Blackness, transphobia, and transmisogyny, very few Western faith spaces have a deep understanding of the ways unexamined theologies can spread anti-Blackness and transphobia. Said faith spaces are at the root of the founding of the United States. As Black trans people, we are often the target of criminalization, homelessness, murder, and joblessness. Even if we may not consider ourselves religious or spiritual, harmful faith institutions are often involved in making laws and crafting opinions that harm our lives and our economic circumstances.

Through the creation of the #BlackTransPrayerBook, we cultivate a tool for healing; we create a place to hold and process our spiritual pain; we write a work that holds faith spaces accountable to the anti-Blackness and transphobia they perpetuate; and we fuel the resiliency of Black trans people.

This interfaith project, which we organized, facilitated, and coedited, brings together Black trans poets/artists/theologians to collectively create a book of prayers, meditations, poems, and stories that center the spiritual realities of Black trans people. In order to build community as we craft this offering, we hosted a four-day writing retreat, with collaborators from all over the United States. We committed to creating not just a book, but a movement in theological work that centers Black Liberation and Trans Liberation theologies.

Some trans people perceive antagonism or hostility from the LGBTQ community toward religion because of its systemic harm toward queer and trans people, and feel they cannot be honest about their religious and spiritual needs because it is looked down upon by their queer and trans peers.

> *I feel a strong need for religious and spiritual life, which often clashes with the dominant secular culture of many LGBTQ communities. However, I have neglected this area of my life because of my experiences growing up as an evangelical Christian, believing that sex was reserved for marriage and never*

knowing it was possible to identify and live as a different gender. Since my family still believes this way and does not affirm my gender or sexual orientation, I find it very painful to reconcile my desire for religious life with the pain it has caused me and so many other LGBTQ people. I have attended a few affirming Christian churches and Buddhist meditation groups but still have not found a community that feels like home. I imagine this will be a lifelong challenge as I attempt to find a different, more affirming understanding of religion than the one that shaped me growing up.

Despite all odds I am still a Christian, but I've experienced love despite who I am and it's made me feel good about it. However, I can still feel the judgment from others around me who don't approve. Also, sometimes I refrain from telling people I'm Christian because some people hold grudges against the church for how they've been treated due to their identity and LGBT status.

For some people, religion is so integrated within their culture or family that they continue to participate in religious practices, such as daily prayer, dietary practices, or seasonal celebrations, regardless of their investment in the religious belief system. Some people may change their gender presentation and be involved in practices based on the sex they were assigned at birth rather than their current gender identity. Some people may feel like they cannot live their true gender full-time because of the way their gender transition may affect their connection to their families. For example, some Mormon trans or gender expansive people may feel that they must maintain a connection to their biological sex in order to be connected with their families in the afterlife. For this reason, it is important not to generalize about a faith tradition's stated acceptance of transgender people, or to make assumptions about how a person negotiates their gender identity, religion, or any other identity. There is no wrong or right way for a person to express their gender in connection with their spirituality.

I have kept my intersex body and transition status a secret for decades. If somehow people were to find out, I would lose everything because my religious community is anti-LGBT and strictly separates men and women. My spirituality has always given me strength because I believe I was created the way I am and that I am good the way I am. I am not a sin. I am not a mistake. I am not a defect. I am not evil. It hurts me very much that when "religious" people say anti-LGBT things they are talking about me.

My family were fundamentalist Christians, and they forced me to wear long hair and dress in feminine clothing. I would get physically punished if they caught me wearing pants to church or school, but sometimes I snuck out in them anyway. Wearing a dress made me feel like I was crossdressing in church, and that felt more disrespectful than pants could possibly be.

Qualitative research on trans people and religion suggests that transgender and gender expansive people create individualized spiritual identities in order to protect themselves from anti-trans religious messaging and to express themselves authentically. This can include combining elements of several traditions, attending services of multiple communities, creating one-of-a-kind spiritual practices, or adhering to a rejecting tradition while not accepting its anti-trans beliefs. In creating our own unique spiritual paths, trans people maintain our connection to the health-promoting aspects of religion, like community support and meaning-making, while protecting ourselves from religiously based harm.[11,12]

I have used various kinds of rituals to help me heal spiritual wounds and step into new parts of my gender journey, such as creating an altar and praying to ancestors, doing guided meditation with spiritual teachers and friends, and getting myself grounded before important transition-related events, like having reiki before surgeries.

I am a Catholic nonbinary person. This has generally led me to ignore most harmful/toxic things from this community about my queerness/transness; however, it has also allowed me to invest my energy in Christian queer activism and holding Christian/Catholic communities accountable for their anti-queer/anti-trans violence. This means that I've met Christian and faithful queer/trans kids who see a possibility of being both spiritual and queer at the same time—a possibility that I was significantly lacking as a teenager.

In recent years more and more faith communities are becoming welcoming and inclusive, meaning that more people experience little to no rejection in their childhood faith communities and feel congruent in both identities.

Transfaith is a national nonprofit "working to support transgender spiritual/cultural workers and their leadership in community."

My faith is very important to me. When I was discovering my sexuality, I never questioned the existence of God. Rather, I tried to figure out if God was OK with my sexuality. I had to reconcile the two. I did manage to do so and after that, gender identity just kind of flowed along. I did not have to do the same level of searching and questioning. I am considering becoming a pastor, and I think my gender identity will certainly play into that. I want to be a safe place, a supportive person for all queer youth in the church. I recognize that I am created in God's image and that thus, God created me genderqueer. I think it is a beautiful thing, and I don't see it as a mistake in any way.

A MESSAGE FROM THE FLIGHT DECK

Al Cole (they/he) is an engineer by day and a poet by night. They enjoy beer and board games, often at the same time.

Ladies and gentlemen, on behalf of the crew I ask that you please direct your attention to the monitors above as we review the emergency procedures. While we wait for death, please take a moment to review the holy book in the seat pocket in front of you. You are on the one known planet in our solar system that supports carbon-based lifeforms. There are no exits. Take a minute to locate the friend closest to you. Note that the nearest friend may not look like you. Please discontinue the use of all electronic devices at this time and go outside. Federal law prohibits tampering with, disabling, or destroying the earth.

Should the earth experience a gradual increase in temperature, stay calm and listen for instructions from the scientific community. Facemasks will drop down from above your seat. If you are traveling with children or someone that is acting like a child, secure your mask first before assisting them. In the unlikely event of the rapture, leave your sins behind. We ask that you make sure that all xenophobia, homophobia, misogyny, and racism is stowed away safely during the flight around the sun. We appreciate your attention. On behalf of everyone worldwide, we thank you for not being an asshole.

RELIGIOUS TRADITIONS' EVOLVING STANCES ON TRANSGENDER AND GENDER EXPANSIVE PEOPLE

Although it is impossible to fully summarize every religious tradition's views about transgender and gender expansive people, some broad characterizations of prominent world religions can be made by looking at gender in their social networks, historical contexts, theology, bioethics, and policy statements, as well as the presence of trans and gender expansive faith leaders and trans resource networks. It is difficult to retrospectively project the label "transgender" onto people from times and places vastly different than our own.

However, by looking at ancient texts and artifacts, we know many religions' histories and texts contain important figures who defied the gender norms of their culture and contributed significantly to their traditions.

Judaism

There is a long history of acceptance for transgender and gender expansive people in the Jewish tradition. There is also a robust tradition of rabbis, religious leaders, and other commentators wrestling with Jewish sacred texts orally and in writing, particularly around issues of biological sex.

The Hebrew language contains words for at least six genders. *Androgynos* and *tumtum* are two such terms. Androgynos most often referred to people with indeterminate biological sex, perhaps most analogous to intersex people. Some writers believe the term androgynos is an umbrella term that encompasses several categories of gender expansive people, including people whose sex is completely unique to them and separate from binary sex designations, those who are both male and female simultaneously, and those who possess some elements of either binary sex in various combinations. Tumtum referred to people whose biological sex is unknown because their genitalia are covered or otherwise ambiguous.[13,14]

> *I have no gender, I'm just a dyke and that's enough for me. That being said, I also grew up very poor and still lead the life of a working class person, which I think explains why I'm drawn to the leatherdyke scene a lot. My Jewishness is also a big part of it. We have six genders in Rabbinic texts, many are still up for vague debate but I still low-key identify as Tumtum.*

The Trans Torah website includes rituals and blessings for transition, videos, and essays by Jewish T/GE people.

Rabbinical commentaries, such the Talmud and Midrash, expound upon the original text of the *Torah* and *Tanakh*, applying it to the time in which the writers were living and offering interpretations of ambiguous passages. Some rabbinical writings challenge the notion that God created binary gender in the story of creation in Genesis. In fact, several commentators contend that God created one human being, the *adam* (sometimes translated as "humanity" from Hebrew), as *androgynos*. The midrash Genesis Rabbah interprets Genesis 1:27, translated in English as "So God created humankind in his image, in the image of God he created them; male and female he created them," as referring to one unified creature who was both male and female. In this interpretation, humanity was

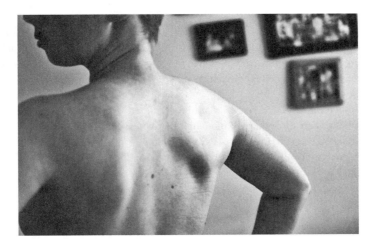

Framed Photographs. (Teddy G. Goetz, 2020)

created before gender, and therefore the gender binary was put into place by humans, not by God.[15,16] Readers see this in subsequent verses Genesis 2:21–23 as Adam creates Eve, the first woman, out of his rib.

In Jewish tradition, eunuchs—people assigned male at birth who were castrated as children—are also acknowledged as beloved children of God, and often influential actors in sacred history. In the ancient Near East, eunuchs were often royal courtesans. It was believed that a lack of sex drive would make eunuchs more trustworthy confidantes to rulers. Eunuchs are significant figures in Ancient Hebrew texts, the early Christian church, and in early Muslim history. In the writings of Isaiah, God instructs eunuchs not to mourn their position in society and promises those who keep God's commandments that they will be given "a monument and a name better than sons and daughters."[17] This verse certainly can be interpreted as celebrating nonbinary people, and all identities beyond male or female.

LIVING WATERS

Gabriel Stein-Bodenheimer (he/him) is a Jewish trans man. When he's not teaching English (or grading papers), Gabriel can be found writing poetry and memoir, going to the movies, and hanging out with his wife Tayja and their beloved pet, Grammarcat.

On the path accompanying the rushing and frothy waters of Lithia Creek, I resolved to medically transition. I wanted, in all parts of my life, to be seen as a man. But there was an insistent feeling that I did not have permission to make decisions about my body. I feared I was making the wrong decisions about my life. How could I trust my intuition and desires? Especially in an American culture of institutional gatekeepers that does not trust trans people with our own lives. As I walked the creekside trail, I began to sing an old song, *mikolot mayim, mayim rabim, adirim mishberei yam. Above the many voices of the waters, the thunder of the sea.* I sang the melody without the words; I sang the words and pressed all my fears into the soft, malleable melody. From that afternoon forward, I sang that psalm whenever my anxieties threatened to deflate my resolve.

As the date of my top surgery approached, I grew increasingly excited, and with equal, opposite intensity, increasingly anxious. I was afraid of regretting surgery, and afraid, too, of losing the erotic sensation in my nipples. In my transmasculine support group, it was suggested that I might be interested in a ritual.

I thought of the mikveh.

People use this Jewish ritual of immersion for all kinds of reasons, such as conversions or milestone events. What sets the mikveh apart from a soak in a jacuzzi are the three ritual dunks in *mayim hayim*, living waters. I wanted to sanctify my body—both the body that existed and the body that soon would be. Traditionally, the mikveh insists on separate spaces for men and women; my best friend Rachel, a cis woman, was permitted to accompany me.

We arrived, and Betsy the mikveh lady, a middle-aged Orthodox woman with a brown wig and blue skirts, answered the door. She led me to a dressing room with 1970s-era blonde-wood paneling. Betsy explained the laws of the mikveh, how I needed to shower and scrub away all dirt, lotions, and hair product, remove any piercings, remove anything that might get in the way of the water's contact with my skin. The purpose is to immerse entirely. "When you're ready," she said, "open the second door, which leads to the mikveh." Rachel would be there, waiting for me.

Seven steps, a sacred number, descended into a square pool lined with cerulean blue tiles and filled with chest deep water. Rachel stood on a wood platform and read from a document we had written together with intentions and blessings, drawn primarily from the TransTorah ritual guide. "Water is God's gift to living souls/To clear us, to purify us/ To sustain us and renew us," we read together.

Before the first immersion, I said the Shema. I dunked, pulling my body into a fetal position beneath the water, feeling the force of my curling inward guide me down to the pool's depths and the buoyancy of my body resisting. "Kosher!" Rachel cried out, witness to my first successful immersion. Water droplets on my lips, I said in Hebrew, "Blessed are You, Creator of all Life, who has sanctified us with the mitzvot and commanded us concerning immersion."

"Amen," said Rachel, "This immersion is for the present, the time of transition, the in-between time. A time of adjustment, from one perfection to another. This is a liminal time: decisions have been made. Now you can surrender to your choices and be blessed. There is nothing to do but be carried and held by us, the water, and then by a blessing for the holiness of in-betweens." We sang *mikolot mayim,* over and over, full voiced, full hearts, Rachel carrying the melody while I wept for the beauty of it, the release of fear, the real sense of giving myself permission and the holiness imbued in human choices that expand and create the world.

I dunked again, drawing my legs toward my chest and letting my body drop into the waters. "Kosher!" exclaimed Rachel. The last immersion, Rachel instructed: "Here is your intention for your time alone in the water. This is your moment to let go of anything you want to let go of, are ready to let go of, that you have not already released, and your time to invoke and draw anything that you want to carry with you from this ritual, as you bask in the warmth of these embracing waters." I stood in the water for a long time, praying for guidance and comfort, for healing of body and mind, for acknowledging the holiness of this moment and the transformative holiness of the next day's surgery. I felt the water envelop my body. I felt its presence, my wrestling with it, the meanings society gave it, and my readiness and trepidation to change it.

At last, I gave my body permission to relax and immersed, letting the waters flow over my head. Rachel confirmed, "Kosher!" We sang the *Shehecheyanu*, "Blessed are You, Source of Life, who has kept us alive and sustained us and enabled us to reach this moment." Then I walked out of the mikveh.

Two years later, the scars from my surgery had healed and my beard became a full chin strap. Rachel called to schedule a time to go to the mikveh before her wedding. "A man cannot be a witness for a woman's mikveh," Betsy the mikvah lady explained. I waited for Rachel at a bar down the street.

There are many strands of Judaism practiced in America, including Orthodox, Conservative, Reform, and Reconstructionist. Each branch represents a different interpretation of how strictly Jewish law, *halakha*, found in the Torah, must be adhered to in modern life. One's biological sex is incredibly important in determining a person's obligations under Jewish law. Many American Jewish communities have been LGBTQ-affirming since the 1970s, drawing upon the aforementioned ancient tradition of gender nonconforming representation to provide affirming spaces.

Orthodox Judaism views Jewish law as completely binding, meaning strict binary gender roles ordained by God must be upheld. This includes an assumption of cisgender, heteronormative, monogamous family structures, traditional gender roles, and separate religious obligations and spaces for men and women. At an official level, Orthodox and ultra-Orthodox communities tend not to be supportive of transgender and gender nonconforming people, though Orthodox transgender people and supportive allies certainly exist (such as Joy Ladin, the first openly transgender professor at an Orthodox Jewish institution). Given that much of Orthodox practice is predicated on male and female identities, nonbinary people may have a difficult time finding or creating space for themselves. Modern Orthodox communities may be more open to transgender and gender expansive people, because they tend to be less insular than other Orthodox communities.

The Conservative, Reform, and Reconstructionist Jewish denominations do not interpret the *Tanakh* as strictly as Orthodox communities. All three denominations have passed resolutions affirming the full acceptance and equality of transgender and gender expansive people (Conservative in 2016, Reform in 2015, and Reconstructionist in 2017). The Conservative movement's resolution stated that welcoming and including people of all gender identities is supported by the tradition's belief that all people are created in God's image (*b'tzelem Elohim*), and the rabbinic tradition's emphasis on *kvod habriyot,* or human dignity. Due to the denomination's power structure, which provides for synagogues to act autonomously, not every Conservative Jewish community may be welcoming. The Reform statement urges its communities to use gender-neutral language, to provide trainings on gender, and to advocate for the rights of trans people in society. Conservative, Reform, and Reconstructionist Jewish camps and other youth programs have taken steps to provide inclusive and affirming spaces for transgender, gender expansive, and questioning youth. The first Jewish seminary to accept LGBTQ students was Reconstructionist, and their curriculum and other materials include depictions of LGBTQ people.

Balancing on the Mechitza: Transgender in Jewish Community is a collection of essays edited by Noach Dzmura (North Atlantic Books, 2010).

In her book, "*Becoming Eve: My Journey from Ultra Orthodox Rabbi to Transgender Woman*" (Seal Press, 2019), Abby Stein writes about her experiences as the first openly trans woman raised in a Hasidic community.

Contemplation. "During the early part of my transition the upheavals and challenges were cause for constant reflection; much of it in isolation." Robin is a Canadian transgender artist living in British Columbia, Canada. She primarily paints in acrylic and oils though has recently started sculpting. Her gender transition has been an ongoing process that started ten years ago and has faced many challenges, many of which she has captured in her work. (Robin Rose)

Deuteronomy 22:5 states, "A woman should not put on the apparel of a man; nor should a man wear the clothing of a woman. For whoever does these things is *to'evah* [often translated as "abomination," this Hebrew word is better understood as "forbidden"] to God." Although this verse seems to condemn cross-dressing, many scholars believe it is meant to prevent the ancient Hebrew people from participating in the pagan rituals of neighboring tribes. Law books of the Torah (Numbers, Leviticus, and Deuteronomy) repeat prohibitions against mixing unlike things, including fabric in clothing, seeds in fields, and certain kinds of foods, in order to distinguish the monotheistic tribe of Israel from its polytheistic neighbors.

Orthodox strands of Judaism turn to biological sex as definitive proof of one's gender and therefore do not usually support gender transition (including gender confirmation surgery), sometimes citing Leviticus 22:24, which prohibits castration for males and animals. Some Jewish traditions state that one's gender identity is only validated if one undergoes a surgery that creates a body that conforms to binary standards (i.e., a trans woman is not considered a woman under Jewish law until she receives surgeries that make her anatomy more like a cis woman's.) Other Jewish communities support trans people who would like to access surgery but do not believe surgery is mandatory to validate trans people's identities.

Transgender and gender expansive people have contributed significantly to the tradition of analyzing, re-evaluating, and reclaiming Jewish sacred texts. Resource compendiums like *Trans Torah* include rituals, prayers, essays, and text studies by trans, gender nonconforming, and nonbinary people, while the book *Torah Queeries* includes weekly commentary on the Torah written by LGBTQ Jewish people.

I am Jewish, and work in an LGBTQ + Jewish organization. These aspects of my identity are intertwined and cannot be separated. My Judaism is queer, and my queerness is Jewish. I have faced pushback from members of the Jewish community for many years, but I don't always believe that my faith requires the consent of faith leaders in my tradition. My faith at times can be largely individual, and I don't feel pressure to conform to the expectations of others.

Trans Jewish people may be involved in Jewish LGBTQ organizations such as Keshet, Eshel, or The World Congress of GLBT Jews; attend LGBTQ groups at their synagogue; participate in Queer Seders at LGBTQ community organizations; or be members of a fully LGBTQ synagogue. Several LGBTQ-led synagogues, such as Congregation Beit Simchat Torah (CBST) in New York City, Sha'ar Zahav in San Francisco, and Beth Chayim Chadashim in Los Angeles, have existed since the early 1970s. CBST is not associated with any Jewish denomination, while Beth Chayim Chadashim is a Reform congregation. Gender-inclusive Jewish summer camps, like Camp Towanga, also offer open and affirming spaces for transgender and gender expansive youth.

Christianity

Christianity has a rich history of gender expansive sacred figures in its scripture, history, and theology. Eunuchs are mentioned in historical narratives of ancient Israel, by prophets, and by Jesus in parables as special examples of God's love and mercy. Jesus mentions eunuchs in Matthew 19, saying, "For there are eunuchs who have been so from birth, and there are eunuchs who have been made eunuchs by others, and there are eunuchs who have made themselves eunuchs for the sake of the kingdom of heaven." This verse can be interpreted in several ways depending on theological tradition, but it is important to realize Jesus is acknowledging and affirming people who occupied a third gender space in society, regardless of their journeys into that gender expression. The first Christian convert in the book of Acts was an Ethiopian eunuch, different in both ethnicity and gender from Jesus's followers (Acts 8: 25–39), which some see as a widening of the people deemed as acceptable to God's community, particularly in contrast to the many conversations in the New Testament about who can become a Christian and how they can signify that through their bodies (i.e., whether Gentiles should get circumcised or observe Jewish dietary laws).

Medieval tales of Christian saints include several stories of women who prayed to become male in order to escape marriage and pursue monastic life in full service to God. There are approximately 20 versions of this type of tale, including the stories of Thecla, Ununcumber, Pelagius-Margarita, and Paula. Some even argue that the tale of Joan of Arc fits this structure. These stories of gender transgression are steeped in a patriarchal culture that believed a woman who attempted to become more male was, by definition, attempting to become more holy. Their historical purposes notwithstanding, an important takeaway for some transgender and gender expansive people is that, in these stories, God can change someone's gender to suit a higher spiritual purpose. Despite the impact of gender expansive people on Christianity, patriarchal and colonizing powers within Christian institutions have rewritten and even erased the presence of these figures. They have also erased the memory of the trans and gender expansive people in cultures colonized by the Christian West.

Q Christian Fellowship's mission is "cultivating radical belonging for LGBTQ + Christians and allies." They offer a guide for Christian parents of newly out LGBTQ people.

Many theological tenets of Christianity inherently celebrate and affirm trans and gender expansive people. In Matthew 22: 37–39, Jesus is asked what commandment of Jewish law is the greatest. He responds by restating a section of the Torah called the Shema, replying, "You shall love the Lord your God with all your heart, and with all your soul, and with all your mind . . . and you shall love your neighbor as yourself." Many Christian communities emphasize this commandment above all others that may cast judgment on people for any reason, recalling that Jesus built community with people from a variety of backgrounds—from Roman tax collectors to sex workers to the sick and poor. Additionally, in Christianity, humans are said to have been created in the image of God, in the fullness of all our identities. St. Paul wrote that within a Christian community, "There is no longer Jew or Greek, there is no longer slave or free, there is no longer male or female; for all of you are one in Christ Jesus," (Galatians 3:28). Once individuals become believers, human designations of class, race, and gender disappear and become less important than their new identity as children of the Christian God.

Queer Grace is a "curated encyclopedia of information and ideas around the life of LGBTQ + people and Christian faith."

Queer Christian theology is a branch of Christian theology that deconstructs traditional theological conventions about gender, sexuality, and other identities. It is a perspective that reimagines God in the image of queerness and reveals the ways Christian theology is inherently complicated with regard to binary gender and heteronormative sexuality. For example,

Wisdom, Reclamation, Wholeness. Part of a series portraying a reclaimed queer tarot deck. "Wholeness" (2016) "represents myself and two of my closest trans guy friends home with my family for the holidays (corresponding to sacrament of Matrimony.)" "Reclamation" (2016) is "a self-portrait of me as a faith leader reclaiming my faith journey." "Wisdom" (2017) "represents my altar." (Kelsey Pacha)

queer theologians have argued that if Jesus was not created through the union of egg and sperm, he must have been created through parthenogenesis, an asexual reproductive process that would have given him either XX or XO chromosomes, suggesting that he might not have been a cisgender man. Others have interrogated the relationship between the three persons—father, son, and Holy Spirit (often represented as female)—who exist within one God. Queer theology invites individuals to reclaim sexual and gender fluidity as transcendent and holy, vanquishing the many centuries of shame and hiding that have existed within Christianity.

I was raised Catholic, and it was bad, but today I have my own relationship with the universe that isn't informed by organized religions at all, and I'm happy with it. God is queer and no one can tell me any different.

The organization Queer Theology invites LGBTQ people to "join us in uncovering and celebrating the gifts that LGBTQ people bring to the Church and the world and the ways in which Christianity has always been queer."

GNOSTICISM

Vivian Taylor (she/her) is climate activist, a theologian, and a now pacifist Iraq War veteran. She lives in North Carolina and is working for there to be a good future for everyone.

I grew up a Southern Baptist in small-town North Carolina. I sometimes had a confrontational relationship with my faith. I spent much of my time in a high school youth group arguing with my fundamentalist peers over evolution, abortion, and LGBT rights. At the same time, Christianity and my church community were extremely important to me. I both loved and hated being a Christian.

I never regularly attended a Baptist church again after I graduated high school. It wasn't an easy break, I still felt a deep connection to Christianity.

In college, I majored in religion and spent several semesters studying Gnosticism. Gnosticism was great. Gnosticism is the idea that the world isn't quite real and that the world in its fakeness is immoral, unjust, or chaotic. It's kind of a "fuck you" to reality. Gnosticism is thoroughly and intentionally weird. While there's Christian Gnosticism, there's also Gnosticism attached to any other philosophy or religion. There's groovy queer gender and sexual stuff associated with Gnosticism, and there's all kinds of supernatural entities. There's a strong idea that God is unknowable, so religious authorities who act like they know everything are either hucksters or fools. It's almost exactly right for a 19-year-old, queer, comic-book-nerd trans girl.

As cool as I found Gnosticism, I'm a fairly orthodox Episcopalian these days, a regular old mainline Protestant. Gnosticism is deeply "anti-body." When I was young, I think I was ashamed of having a body that was assigned male at birth. Thanks to all the anti-trans stuff in the culture, I was afraid having a trans body made me less than, so Gnosticism also became an escape from the bodily reality of transness.

As I've gotten older, I've learned to love trans bodies. The more trans people I meet, the more I love our people. I've come to see what a blessing and privilege my own body is. I have gone from being angry and embarrassed about my body to being deeply grateful to God for it.

The Episcopal Church is not perfect, but it's trying to be a place that in St Paul's words, recognizes and treats trans people as true co-heirs with Christ and members of the Body of Christ along with everyone else. I don't know all the secrets of the cosmos, but I know I want to be part of a loving community that says thank you for life.

Queer theology also questions using paternal imagery and male pronouns for a God who must be beyond the human limits of binary gender. Though Christianity has a long history of masculinizing God, using he/him/his pronouns and referring to God as father, more and more churches are using gender neutral pronouns for God. Justin Welby, the Archbishop of Canterbury (the symbolic head of the Anglican Communion), stated in 2018 that God cannot be defined by gender, and is neither male nor female. This stance not only offers more room for transgender people to see themselves as created in the image of an agender or nonbinary God, but also reinforces the idea that gender is a human constraint.

I identify as Christian. It conflicted with my gender identity until I found queer theology and my church I go to now. I was more rejected from a nondenominational church, I wasn't allowed to lead (which I found out after I left). I have been embraced at a church in an urban area that is led by trans individuals. It has made me feel strong in my identity and faith.

The Metropolitan Community Church, a Christian denomination created by and for LGB people in the 1970s, has long been a safe haven for many trans people, although even MCC has, at times, struggled to be consistently welcoming to T/GE people.

For me, my gender most intersects with my religion. I am a Christian and fully believe that God themself is far beyond our constructs of gender and They created me with this androgynous/nonbinary spirit and I love it!

Most mainline Protestant denominations have come out firmly in support of transgender and gender expansive people in the fullness of their authenticity. The Episcopal, ELCA Lutheran, Presbyterian, and American Baptist churches have released statements affirming the right of transgender and gender expansive people to participate in all aspects of worship and daily life of the church, including as ordained faith leaders. The United Church of Christ was the first denomination to release such a statement in 2003. Out transgender and gender expansive pastors, music and youth ministers, religious educators, and chaplains exist in almost all of these denominations, living out their vocation to serve and providing a beacon of hope for young transgender and gender expansive Christians in their communities.

Some Christian denominations are in an in-between space with regard to trans inclusion. Depending on a denomination's polity (power structure), gender inclusivity may vary widely in individual churches, and certain regions of the country might be more accepting. For example, the Religious Society of Friends (also known as Quakers), encompasses several traditions that have splintered off due to various theological issues, including affirmation of LGBTQ people.

I am a pastor. I transitioned while serving the same church for a decade in a denomination that is not very supportive. But my local congregation is supportive.

Some Christian communities outright condemn transgender and gender expansive identities in their official policies, like the Roman Catholic Church, Southern Baptist Convention, Church of Jesus Christ of Latter-Day Saints (Mormonism), Jehovah's Witness groups, and Christian Science churches. Orthodox Christianity—also known as Eastern Orthodox Christianity—is a communion made up of several Orthodox denominations, such as the Greek Orthodox and Russian Orthodox churches. In the United States, the Assembly of Canonical Orthodox Bishops of the United States of America holds annual meetings and sometimes distributes policy statements on issues. Although this body has not released a policy statement about transgender people, several prominent bishops and other clergy have stated that gender transition is a challenge to God's purpose for humanity and should be condemned. Because each denomination (and often individual churches) operates independently of one another, there may be congregations that are openly inclusive of transgender and gender expansive individuals. Almost all Christian denominations, including those officially opposed to gender inclusivity, include at least one denomination-wide LGBTQ network that provides theological resources, such as Bible studies, affirming/welcoming church curriculum, as well as opportunities to organize, including annual conferences and activist trainings. In-person support groups may exist locally (e.g., for transgender and gender expansive Mormons in Utah) and many exist online.

I am Muslim, and I am a practicing Muslim. I have gained much strength from the legacy and tenacity of Muslim trans women, past and present. My mosque openly supports trans women praying with cis women, and I've given talks at queer Muslim women's retreats and been invited to write on my experiences for Muslim women's editorials. I think the young Muslim community is very open. Previous generations of Muslims are more accepting on average than those same generations of Christians.

I am a trans Muslim, which is a hard thing to be, but it fits me and I love it.

Islam

The landscape for transgender, gender expansive, and nonbinary people in Islam is complex. Like other traditions, Islam places a heavy emphasis on gender segregation in prayer

Openly transgender people serve as fully ordained clergy, youth ministers, and other positions within the United Methodist Church. In fact, a vote to block transgender people from becoming ordained failed at the UMC's General Conference, their governing body, in 2008. The church is starkly divided, however, and ongoing debates continue. Currently, there are sanctions for clergy who perform "same-sex" wedding ceremonies and LGB clergy are not permitted to serve openly, though many do so within "reconciling" congregations. UMC policies on LGBTQ inclusion will be debated at the 2022 General Conference.

and other faith expressions, as well as on a heteronormative family model. There is, however, a well-documented history of gender nonconforming people interacting with the earliest Muslim communities, including the Prophet Muhammad. It is important to name the impact of Islamophobia, xenophobia, and racism in preventing Americans from seeing the accepting parts of Muslim communities around the world.

Despite some controversy about whether being transgender is acceptable (*halal*) or prohibited (*haram*) in Islam, one study showed that a majority of American Muslims (64%) surveyed believe there is more than one way to interpret Islamic teachings. More than half (52%) believe traditional understandings of Islam must be reinterpreted to address modern issues, gender transition among them.[18] Some Muslims believe anyone who professes the *shahadah*—the Islamic statement of faith, which says, "There is no god but Allah and Muhammad is the messenger of Allah"—is Muslim, regardless of gender identity or expression. Some trans-identified Muslims feel all that matters is their relationship with Allah and dedication to the five pillars of Islam—any existing dictate about gender is culture-dependent. LGBTQ-inclusive and mixed-gender Muslim communities emphasize the concept of *ummah,* the community of all Muslims regardless of particular lineage, nationality, race, or other identity, believing it transcends a particular focus on gender as the most important determinant of belonging.

Islamic scripture, theology, law, and tradition are defined by their expression in Arabic, a binary-gendered language with no gender-neutral pronoun, although a few words are gender-neutral.[19] Although Allah is referred to with male pronouns, some Muslims believe Allah is beyond gender. Sufism, a mystical branch of Islam, explores the connections between body, spirit, soul, and Allah. Ibn' Arabi, a prominent Sufi thinker, contended that not only is Allah beyond gender, but gender itself only describes a kind of spirit—male the active, female the passive—which can animate creation but does not define individuals. The seeming duality of gender in humanity is merely an illusion that must be questioned in order to grasp the awesome reality of a nondual, nongendered Allah.[20]

Axios is an organization of LGBTQ Eastern and Orthodox Christians "for an Orthodox Church worthy of the 21st century."

Orthodoxy in Dialogue is an Orthodox Christian blog and informational website for Eastern Orthodox Christians to engage with progressive ideas including discussions about gender and sexuality.

Asifa Lahore - "Britain's First Out Muslim Drag Queen." (photo by Christine Hayter, editing by Metin Osman)

Muslims turn to the sacred text revealed to the prophet Muhammad, the Qu'ran, for guidance on ethical issues and how to live out Islamic law in daily life. The Qu'ran ostensibly mentions transgender and gender expansive people in a few places, revealing perhaps three categories of gender-transgressive people in premodern Muslim societies. These are the eunuch or *khasi, mukhannath,* and the many third genders that existed in cultures where Islam spread by trade. According to the Qu'ran and Hadith (sayings of the Prophet), the khasi and mukhannath interacted with the Prophet and his wives.

Mukhannath is a term that refers to gender nonconforming people assigned male at birth. There are many mentions of the mukhannath's contributions to Islamic communities through their relationships with Islamic leaders (Hit, a *mukhannathun*, was welcomed into the Prophet Muhammad's home and friends with the Prophet's wife Umm Salama[21]), poetry (Al-Marini[22]), and music (Tuwais[23]). Mukhannath were represented as effeminate and assumed to be the passive partners in anal sex, which was believed to be their inherent nature. They often enjoyed special status in society, given that they could access both male- and female-only spaces. However, their effeminacy was later criminalized in Islamic jurist decisions in the Abbasid period (750–1258 CE), because their gender nonconforming behavior was seen as evidence of homosexuality and an affront to the heterosexual mandate within families. Gender nonconformity became forbidden within the tradition, because it was believed this would prevent homosexuality. During this same period, a class of women who dressed and acted like males, the *mutarrajjulat*, were often royal courtesans and concubines. Their gender expression was not seen as indicative of homosexual behavior or non-female gender identity, but merely a performance. Trans and gender expansive people helped guard and steward sacred sites, such as *Masjid-e-Nabvi*.[24] There are also tales of Muslim adherents changing genders, such as the legend of *Khurafa*.[25]

As the world's second-largest religion, Islam has interacted with and in some cases, supplanted indigenous cultures around the world for centuries. Some of the indigenous belief systems Islam later replaced believed people could hold multiple genders and featured deities that were androgynous or "dual-gendered." Muslim communities have responded in a variety of ways to the existence of third gender designations. Muslims have a long history, for example, of interacting with *hijras* in India, *kathoey* in Thailand, and *mak nyah* in Malaysia.

Many of the third gender communities in Muslim-majority countries have experienced religious oppression ranging from housing discrimination to criminal fines to violence. Some scholars believe that the appearance of Islamic traders in these regions is what caused an accepted social category of sacred gender transgressors to disappear—in part because Islamic law limited the public roles available to women in society. Whereas these gender transgressors were formerly viewed as taking part in a holy practice, under Islamic influence, they were later seen as an affront to Allah. Furthermore, by deviating from their destinies as mothers/wives or husbands/fathers, their behavior made them immoral. For example, the Bugis of South Sulawesi have five genders in their society—the equivalent of cisgender men and women, *calalai* (perhaps equivalent to transmasculine people), *calabai* (perhaps equivalent to transfeminine people), and *bissu*, people who embody masculinity and femininity and are believed to be intermediaries between humans and the gods. Their gender duality is viewed as evidence of a supernatural power to connect the material and spiritual realms. Bissu are shamans and priests, formerly serving as royal confidantes and healers. Though bissu existed prior to Islam's arrival in Indonesia in the 13th century, many were run out of their villages and their land and positions were stolen by the Islamic movement Darul Islam, which came to power following Indonesia's independence from Dutch colonial rule in 1949.[26]

In some Muslim-majority cultures, gender nonconforming and/or LGBQ people are encouraged to undergo medical transition to pass as gender-conforming men or women in society, regardless of whether they identify as a gender different from the one they were assigned at birth or experience gender dysphoria. This forced medical transition creates

The Muslim Alliance for Sexual and Gender Diversity (MASGD) works to support, empower, and connect LGBTQ Muslims.

The Muslims for Progressive Values LGBT Resources page has links to video lectures on LGBTQ issues within Islam, connections to over 20 LGBTQ Muslim groups around the world, and dozens of writings by Muslim scholars on LGBTQ issues.

The Muslim Youth Leadership Council has an online resource called, "I'm Muslim and My Gender Doesn't Fit Me," designed for trans Muslim youth.

a complicated situation in which LGBQ people are not affirmed in society, and sexual reassignment surgery[27] is viewed as a way to remedy the theological and social quandary gender nonconformity and/or homosexual behavior creates. In 1983, Ayatollah Khomeini issued a fatwa, or legal decision, that stated people could obtain sex reassignment surgery if they were confirmed to identify as "the opposite" sex. Currently, Iran performs a high percentage of all sex reassignment surgeries in the world. Although the dynamics as they relate to sexuality may be complex, this policy also provides opportunities for many trans people to receive the care they need to be their authentic selves.

Gender diversity is certainly present in Islamic history, scripture, and in Muslim communities around the world. There are, however, few current communities that are openly accepting of transgender and gender expansive people. Some Muslims report a lack of safe space to talk about gender diversity within Muslim communities; thus many communities exist online on message boards, listservs, and blogs. There are some LGBTQ-supportive Muslim communities in the United States, including the Muslim Alliance for Sexual and Gender Diversity, which hosts a retreat for LGBTQ Muslims and their partners every year. There are eight LGBTQ-inclusive Muslim masjids in several urban areas of the United States, including Chicago, Illinois, Atlanta, Georgia, and Berkeley, California, as well as outside the United States in Canada, Great Britain, Germany, and South Africa.

Queer Crescent Healing is an LGBTQI Muslim organization with healing programs and events.

WONDER WOMAN: A WORTHY TRANS GODDESS?

Margo King is an "aspiring" MTF, 57, who studies various spiritualities, believes in the Goddess, and seeks to help others in the transgender community.

Wonder Woman is my Goddess guide and direction. She has been known in comic books since the 1940s. She came from an island of Amazonian women and was chosen to save the world from the Nazis of World War II. Since then, Her exploits have taken Her from comics into television, movies, feminist magazines, and spiritual movements. Named "Diana" (The Roman equivalent of Artemis), Her emergence into a Goddess figure expanded as the writers revealed Her mother, Hippolyta, had a "fling" with Zeus, making this daughter as much a Goddess as Athena!

So how could one take a comic book character and make Her into a Goddess all Her own? Flash forward into the 1970s, and Lynda Carter brings Diana to life on the television set. Wonder Woman appears on the first cover of Ms. Magazine. Carter's take on Wonder Woman was considered "campy" at first, yet as time marched on, the show and actress achieved iconic status. In an interview, Carter recalled, "I've discovered that the archetype of Wonder Woman really lives in all of us. She had the goddess within. It's who we really are." Carter has also been a vocal supporter of LGBT equality and has participated in the New York Pride Parade.

Admiring the character of Wonder Woman brings out the Goddess from within. One finds stories online of cancer-stricken children dressed in the Wonder Woman costume, using their "inner Goddess" as their strength to fight the deadly affliction. Many a marathon or race has women in some kind of Wonder Woman running outfit, inspiring them to head toward the finish line. Since the 2017 movie (featuring Gal Gadot) was released, Halloween brings more girls dressing as Wonder Woman than some famed Disney princesses. Boys have also taken to loving the character. Unlike Batgirl, or Supergirl, Wonder Woman has no male counterpart that She would imitate! Hence, many boys wear Wonder Woman costumes on Halloween because She inspires them, too!

In my personal dealings with Wonder Woman, transgender identity and spirituality intertwine. My own journey in finding myself came while watching the Wonder Woman pilot episode on TV. I instantly found myself in awe of the character—not in masculine fascination but as a reflection of what I wished I could be. I so wanted to BE Her! It was a pivotal moment where I knew I was different. She inspires me to be the woman I was meant to be.

Can we connect Wonder Woman to various forms of Spirituality? If you look at the Tree of Life in Kabbalah, the various triads conform perfectly with Her costume and powers. The Supernal Triad can be formed with Her tiara (star) and earrings (sometimes shown as two red stars). Another triad aligns with Her eagle breastplate (which covers the heart where spirit is contained), and Her bracelets (which serve as protection of the God-self). One of Wonder Woman's tools is a golden lasso, which when placed over a person, makes them tell the truth. Truth, beauty, love, kindness, are all traits we can even see from the Christian view of Mother Mary. Wonder Woman often wears a magnificent cape, which could easily appear to resemble one Mary or even Goddess Isis would wear.

Barbara Ardinger's book, *Goddess Meditations* reveals a method of channeling Wonder Woman in a Meditation. This meditation is designed to bring forth your inner courage and strength. Wonder Woman tells the meditator she is strong and wonderful and that she can do whatever she wants. At the end, she can feel as if Diana is walking with her with all the courage and strength she can hope for!

There are religious items, such as a Wonder Woman candle, incense, and even a rosary to be found! A Facebook page aptly titled, "Church of Wonder Woman" reveals an altar, complete with statue and candle, that can be placed inside your home! I have one, and it does help to meditate before Her image.

Goddesses can come to you in any form. Why couldn't She come to you in a modern Goddess appearance? Today's superhero explosion in pop culture may just show us the new mythology of God/Goddess worship. I've been a spiritual seeker for a long time, and a Goddess came to me in a personal vision: A cloaked woman came forth and handed me a chalice, and She told me that I was Hers! Her aura gave a feeling that many who have passed and returned to life have reported: Pure love!

Lynda Carter played the part of Wonder Woman as a Goddess who loved all, even Her enemies. Although the modern-day movie version shows Gal Gadot as a warrior, there's a scene of Her in a cloak that looked quite like my vision!

As a Transgender woman, and a spiritual seeker looking for my inner strength, Wonder Woman has brought that all to me, and still guides me. I honor Her by being the woman I long to be by Her inspiration. I see nothing wrong with thinking of Diana/Wonder Woman as my personal image and reflection of the Goddess, within and without. Hail Diana!

Hinduism

Hinduism is one of the oldest religions in the world, and the third-largest world religion behind Christianity and Islam. Hinduism does not necessarily have a centralized institutional body, but rather comprises practices, rituals, and images that are woven into daily life. Depending on when and where one is born, an individual or their family may worship a particular deity or set of deities, whose myths and genders may vary among geographical locations. Some scholars contend that the Hindu view of various deities goes beyond binary gender—that the enduring reality of gods and goddesses is not connected to male- or femaleness, but is seen as both and much more.

Hindus believe that every person has an eternal soul, called an atman, which reincarnates into various bodies throughout many lifetimes. In some traditions, an individual's atman is identical to Brahman, the supreme spirit. Some traditions understand the atman to be the same in all beings, and like Brahman, transcending gender. Gender can be seen as a human construct, although some understand Brahman to be both male and female, or binary male or female.[28] The ultimate spiritual goal is to discover and liberate one's atman from the limitations of one's human body and ego, freeing oneself from the cycle of rebirth and death.

In some strands of Hinduism, it is believed that every being and thing on Earth is composed of a combination of masculinity and femininity. The amount of masculinity and femininity present in a person determines their role in society and in relation to the divine in these traditions. This is called the "double nature." To reach their ultimate spiritual potential, a person must discover their unique and true nature through their interactions with others. Honoring a balance of masculinity/femininity as closest to divine nature is clear in the stories of deities such as Ardhanarishvara, an androgynous combination of the god Shiva and the goddess Parvati, who are husband and wife. Ardhanarishvara is often artistically represented as half-male and half-female, symbolizing the divine inseparability between the masculine and feminine energies of the universe. Thus, Ardhanarishvara is seen as encompassing and surpassing all dichotomies, whose unitive perfection represents the origin of all creation.[29]

In several Vedic texts, people whose nature was balanced between masculine and feminine were called *tritiya-prakriti,* meaning the "third nature" or "third gender." The third nature was considered one more variation of the human experience among reincarnated souls who experience many lives. One who had lived in both male and female bodies may carry subconscious expressions of their former lives in their mind or spirit, which may not match with their current incarnation. In many places where Hinduism is practiced, those possessing the third nature are considered holy, with special spiritual, creative, and social responsibilities, and often are part of a Hindu sect that is devoted to one deity.[30] There are over a dozen categories of people mentioned in Vedic texts who embody the third nature. *Hijras,* for example, appear in ancient texts and are recognized as a unique gender category

Sarbat ("equality for everyone") is an LGBTQ group for practitioners of the Indian religion Sikhism.

Being 3. Jam Bridgett is a Black queer artist and writer just outside of Toronto, exploring themes like self-discovery, identity and community. Find them online @yikesjamaica.

today. In current society, hijras may be looked down upon, and forced into sex work and homelessness due to discrimination. Despite the prejudice they experience, they are still called upon to give blessings and participate in special spiritual ceremonies.

Third nature/third gender people sometimes devote their lives to gender-transcendent deities. Bahuchara Mata, a goddess of fertility and chastity, is considered the patron saint of hijras. Bahuchara Mata is seen as the manifestation of the maternal aspects of Shakti. The legend of Bahuchara Mata is that she and her sisters were attacked on a caravan journey, and rather than surrender to their attackers, they cut off their breasts and bled to death. One of the attackers, Bapiya, was thereafter made impotent, and repented to Bahuchara by taking on female dress. He was then forgiven for his transgression. The *jogappa* of Southern India worship the goddess Yellamma (also known as Renuka). Jogappa often serve as dancers or sex workers in the goddess' temple, and manage Yellamma's temple maidservants. In Southern India, the *aravanis* (Ali third gender sect) worship the god Aravan. The arvanis are famous for the festival Koovakam, which celebrates the life of Aravan. According to legend, Aravan was willing to die in order to secure victory in battle, but wanted to experience sex before his death. The god Krishna manifested as a woman named Mohini, who married and had sex with Aravan before his death. Thousands of LGBTQ people attend the 15-day Koovakam festival, reenacting Aravan's marriage and death, ritualistically dancing, and attending seminars on transgender rights and health care.

Although ancient Vedic texts and South Asian cultures have acknowledged the existence of third gender people as integral parts of Hindu worship, these spiritual beliefs are influenced heavily by culture. As with other traditions originating in countries colonized by the West, the acceptance of third gender people declined sharply with the

Are you South Asian and looking for confidential support? Try the Desi LGBTQ Helpline online or at 908-367-3374.

The Gay and Lesbian Vaishnava Association (GALVA) offers information and support for LGBTI Vaishnavas & Hindus.

rise of Western influence. British colonial forces not only criminalized non-procreative sexual behavior between people of any gender, but also saw hijras and other third gender people as contributing to immoral sexual practices. Their legal prohibitions challenged, and in some cases, destroyed existing third gender communities in India and other surrounding areas. Although there are no institutional Hindu theological statements made on transgender people, several countries with sizable Hindu populations (such as India and Nepal) recognize the rights of third gender people to employment, health care, and appropriate legal identification. These rights may still be unevenly administered, and do not erase social stigma that causes many gender expansive people to be homeless, unemployed, and/or exploited. Several organizations for transgender and gender expansive Hindu people exist, such as the Gay and Lesbian Vaishnava Association and Trikone, a support network for LGBTQ people of South Asian descent. These organizations offer community-building events such as an inclusive Diwali, support groups, and online resources.

Buddhism

In speaking about Buddhism, it is essential to recognize its ancient cultural context as opposed to more recent Western importation of Buddhist practices to places like the United States. Trans acceptance is often dependent on the cultural context of the Buddhist community; for example, a traditional Japanese Buddhist temple may not be welcoming to transgender people, while an American sangha may have its own LGBTQ sitting group. And the reverse may also be true—a seemingly progressive American Buddhist temple may not be welcoming to transgender individuals while Buddhist communities in countries that recognize more than two gender categories may have sacred roles for trans and gender expansive people.

Many out transgender and gender expansive Buddhist teachers lead retreats at prominent centers like Spirit Rock Meditation Center or disseminate dharma talks and meditations online.

Exploring your faith? Check out *I Am Divine, So Are You: How Buddhism, Jainism, Sikhism, and Hinduism affirm the dignity of queer identities and sexualities* by Devdutt Pattanaik and Jerry Johnson (HarperCollins India, 2017).

The American branch of Sokka Gakkai International (SGI), a Mahayana community, has an LGBTQ network called Courageous Freedom, which produces resources for LGBTQ Buddhists and supports LGBTQ initiatives.

One of the basic teachings of Theravada Buddhism, the Three Marks of Existence, asserts that human experience is marked by impermanence, suffering, and the nonexistence of a stable self. Impermanence, the idea that everything in life is temporary, causes suffering. The third mark, the "no-self," states that there is no stable soul or essence within any living being. Therefore our sense of identity—our social location, history, and personality—are a false self, and the notion of gender identity can be contentious for some Buddhists. Some Buddhists may see the desire to change one's identity or transition in any way as just another fleeting desire that will not bring lasting happiness. Others insist that in order to follow the path of the Buddha, every person must live authentically, with the ability to be present in practice.

In Mahayana Buddhism, Avalokiteshvara, the bodhisattva of compassion and mercy, is often seen as transgender. Some believe the male Avalokiteshvara morphs into the female Kuan Yin when overcome by compassion for women and children. Likewise, Kuan Yin can transform back into her male form when called on to protect her followers—changing gender based on what serves his/her devotees best.[31] The gender transformation of this figure underscores that ascended bodhisattvas in some way transcend gender once they surpass the human form.

Buddhist texts acknowledge the existence of people who transgress gender norms in society. The Vinaya, a set of rules for monks, acknowledges the existence of *pandakas*— people who did not fit into normative gender and sexual categories in modern-day India. These include people born with ambiguous sex characteristics and people whose sex and gender seem to change according to the moon cycle.[32] The Pali Canon, the words of the Buddha in Theravada, contains a story about a male follower named Soreyya, whose infatuation with a Buddhist elder causes him to transform into a woman. He marries a man and bears several children before changing back to a man and asking forgiveness for his transformation.[33]

Social rules about gender roles, sexual morality, the sacredness of the body, and the spiritual destiny of families may impact how Buddhist beliefs are applied to a person's

Oracle of the Southern Marsh. "It is my most humble honor to bring the divine forms of black and queer/trans, and especially black, queer/trans people/beings/creatures into a tangible and visual existence through art and poetry. Revealing the infinitely expansive divinity of our existence is my life's purpose. (Malachi Lily. www.maggielily.com. IG @theholyhawkmoth)

gender identity and expression. For example, some Japanese communities believe a person's body must be totally preserved after death in order for them to be spiritually accessible as an ancestor to their living relatives. Any change to the person's body during their lifetime, particularly the sex organs that help propagate the family line, may endanger their own fate in addition to failing at their gender-specific family obligations. Thus, gender confirmation surgery may be problematic.[34]

Many scholars believe Buddhism is neutral on transgender identity and gender nonconformity, and because centralized institutional authorities don't necessarily exist for the tradition, it is difficult to make any declarations about whether a given Buddhist community will be accepting of trans and gender expansive people. Inclusion and acceptance are largely dependent on the culture in which individuals practice, globally and within the American Buddhist context. American communities tend to support trans and gender expansive people, allowing trans people to study at their monasteries and schools, become ordained, teach, and participate in community.

Other Spiritual/Religious Communities

Although there has not been a nationally representative study of transgender and gender expansive people's religious identities, some evidence suggests trans people are more likely to be wiccan or pagan[36] and twice as likely as the general population to identify with a non-Judeo-Christian tradition.[37] There is also evidence that transgender and gender expansive people may combine elements of multiple traditions to best express their individualized belief systems and honor their sacred experiences.[38]

Michael Dillon, later known as Lobzang Jivaka, was the first trans man to undergo a phalloplasty in 1945. Dillon, a physician, British aristocrat, and Navy officer, became a Buddhist monk near the end of his life, fleeing to India after being outed as trans in global newspapers when he received his inheritance from his aristocratic family. While in India, Dillon studied with a guru who attempted to block his monastic ordination because he was transgender. He published several works on Buddhism before dying in India in 1962.[35]

I've always wanted to be a woman, but for most of my life, my gender iden-
tity was mixed up with my sexuality, and I thought that desire was just a
fetish, that I was perverted. When I began addiction treatment and began to
address my mental health issues, especially lifelong depression, I also began
a spiritual journey to find out how to be happy. Eventually, I developed a
healthy relationship to my sexuality and shifted my attention to the idea of
authenticity, of finding out who I really am, because feeling a lack of integrity
has always been a very painful experience. I studied A Course in Miracles
diligently for 10 + years, and I also learned about the Hindu goddess Kali.
For two years, every morning when I studied and meditated, I prayed to Kali,
saying simply, "Kali, please remove all that is not real." Eventually, I dis-
covered blogs written by trans women explaining their own experiences and
transitions. Once I knew that it was actually possible to transition and live as
me, I began my journey.

Earth-Based Communities. Many trans and gender expansive people are involved in earth-based traditions, broadly referred to as neo-Paganism, which encompasses a wide range of practices that predate many current major world religions. These include traditions of various lineages such as Celtic or Alexandrian Wicca, or Orisha-based traditions such as Yoruba, Hoodoo, or Santeria. In these traditions, a follower may choose to work with one or more gods, goddesses, or other deities, who may overlap with figures from multiple traditions. These deities may combine male and female genders or even alternate in how their gender manifests depending on the situation. Some people feel these pantheons reflect their own multifaceted gender existing in one being. Others appreciate how these traditions uplift femininity and goddess worship, providing an alternative to more patriarchal, male-centered religions.

The LGBTQ Religious Archives Network (LGBT-RAN) "is an innovative venture in preserving history and encouraging scholarly study of LGBTQ religious movements around the world."

I have begun to reach out to more spirits in nature, similar to Wiccan practices.
This is mainly because growing up, crying to the Christian God to let me be
normal, or to show me the way to stop feeling like a stranger in my own body,
to no avail, made me think any spirit or minor deity should get a chance to help
me along my way.

I grew up indoctrinated into Christianity, and as I realized that I was queer and
later nonbinary, it became incredibly difficult for me to continue within that
religion. I now practice as a Norse Pagan, and I find so much freedom here.
The other pagans I interact with are either queer themselves or super open and
accepting of my queerness—hell, most of our gods are canonically queer in one
way or another.

Some people also appreciate the grassroots nature of Pagan communities, which are less structured, not requiring profession of faith to belong, and often rely on consensus-based, rather than hierarchical, decision-making. A central tenet of neo-Pagan traditions is "Harming none, do what you will"—meaning as long as it doesn't harm anyone else, every person should pursue the path that feels most authentic to them without judgment. Queer and trans-centric covens and other circles exist in-person and online. Although neo-Pagan and other Earth-based traditions have a less patriarchal structure than many other religions, controversies over the participation of trans people may still exist. Because of their history as a female-led and female-focused fellowship, there have been tensions over allowing transgender people to access historically cis female-only spaces. For example, at Pantheacon 2011, America's largest Pagan conference, controversy erupted over the exclusion of trans women in a ritual only open to people who were assigned female at birth.

THE ROLE OF RITUAL IN MY TRANSITION

Kai Koumatos (he/him)

I was 14 years old when my mother died. She was 42 years old. As the eldest daughter in a Greek-American family, I highly identified with her, so for many years I feared also dying at 42 years old. My parent's death derailed the discovery of my true gender identity through my late thirties. I mistook my gender dysphoria for psychological wounding. I felt broken, never experiencing a sense that I belonged anywhere in the world. I worked to heal my wounds for years until I met several trans men and discovered that the "wrongness" I had felt for so long had nothing to do with the tragedies of my childhood losses and everything to do with my misaligned gender identity.

Transitioning at this stage in life required re-evaluating my past and making new meaning out of what I have always known. It has been a deeply healing process, because many of my discoveries have answered questions I have been struggling with for years. However, it has also involved a reimagining of my identity. For most of my adult life, I crafted my sense of self on a foundation of womanness, feminism, and fat acceptance. I was a size-acceptance activist and educator. I worked hard to embrace my fat body as beautiful and valuable in a world that regularly teaches the opposite, so it was quite difficult when my body size threatened my path of transition.

When I consulted a plastic surgeon for top surgery, the surgeon relentlessly insisted that she was not comfortable performing the surgery on someone with a body mass index as high as mine. Despite all of my arguments, she was unwilling to proceed and recommended that I talk to my doctors about weight loss options and come back to her in a year. I fell into a deep depression of anger and sadness.

Although I was ready to fight for my rights to transition as a fat man, my most recent lab work showed that my blood sugar was rising to unhealthy levels. To my surprise, I started considering weight loss surgery to target this. While I researched the advances of the last 10 years, I continued to struggle with my decision. I attended a weight loss surgery orientation, and I found the bariatric program was completely ill-suited for my life and values. They implied that there was something wrong with being fat, which I simply didn't believe. I rebelled and struggled with the program—at times leaving completely and returning several times—over the course of two years.

I eventually realized that I didn't have to want bariatric surgery to decide that it was the best option for my physical and emotional health. I also discovered the deep connection between my fat identity and my femaleness, which was a big turning point in my struggle. I began letting go of my identity as a fat person. My hope for a stronger future body with less pain slowly began to grow.

As I turned 42 years old, I began working with a Jungian therapist. He showed me how I had transformed my suffering into a sacred calling, and provided me with a new language and narrative for my life. As he explained, "The shaman chooses to go into the underworld, die, gain wisdom, and then bring that wisdom back to the community." I started to embrace the death I had always feared. I prepared for the surgery, determined to use it as an opportunity for a deep and powerful ritual transformation.

Ritual has been an important part of humanity for longer than we've had written history. I believe it is a powerful tool for transformation—in part because it engages every aspect of our selves. In ritual, our conscious, analytic selves are engaged in planning and words; our nonverbal selves respond to the actions and symbolism of the behavior; and our spiritual selves create meaning. The whole ritualistic experience can be enacted in the presence of or with the help of a divine energy: either God, the Goddess, the Great Spirit, or whathaveyou. Transitioning is filled with important moments of transformation, and ritual can help us mark these moments in our lives.

I planned for my surgery very carefully—in ritualistic fashion. I created jewelry of skulls and coins. I wrote a loosely scripted guided meditation, and I finished my will. I was ready to die, leave behind the pieces of me that I no longer needed, and then, hopefully, return to my new life. In the presurgery ward, my dear friend and fellow witch began my guided meditation about 15 minutes before the surgery was to begin.

I fell into a deep state of relaxation. I traveled to the Hellenic Underworld, to the River Styx. In books, the river is usually depicted as dark and gloomy, but I found myself on what felt like a long stretch of ocean covered in a light fog. As the water gently lapped at the sand beneath my feet, Charon, the ferryman of Hades, came out of the mist, guiding his long boat toward the shore. Suddenly he was with me, not frightening and dangerous but familiar and welcoming. We embraced like old friends, and I paid for my passage with the coins from the jewelry I was wearing. I boarded his boat and crossed the river.

On the shore, I had intended to first seek Hades and Kore, the ruling deities of the underworld. But as I stepped from the boat, I saw my mother and father waiting for me with open arms. Because they had both died before I had any inkling that I was trans, I never found the right way to tell them. I don't remember saying any words, but they responded to my nervous energy: "You are no different than you have always been. You are the same wonderful child we have always loved."

It was a more affirming response than I could have ever hoped for. As I stepped back from their embrace, I felt that I was wearing huge armor made up of big interlocking pieces that covered my torso. I pulled off my breasts and my belly and handed them to my mother, "I have no need for these anymore," I said. She took them willingly as my father moved around to my back. He pulled other large pieces off of my shoulders, saying, "And you've carried these pieces for us for long enough." They were proud of the work I had done on their behalf and freed me from the need to be anything but who I am. My next memory was in the recovery ward after my operation.

I don't remember the rest of my visit, but I know that the ritual succeeded in all the ways I needed it to. I returned from the land of the dead, leaving behind all traces of my female self. My self-fulfilling prophecy was complete. Just like my mother, the female identity I created in her image died as I always feared it would. But after all the times I've transformed death into wisdom and healing, I should have known that this death was nothing to fear. I returned to the world, no longer feeling a duality of self. Now, I can just be Kai, and I know exactly where he belongs in the world.

I'm a Hellenic Polytheist—I worship Greek gods. Aphrodite has helped ease my gender dysphoria. Apollo was there as a protector of boys to accept me as a boy and protect me, and somewhat as a father figure when my own dad didn't accept me as his son.

The Radical Faeries are a Pagan, intentionally queer spiritual movement founded in the late 1970s by several gay men. Radical Faeries embrace the sacred in connecting to the Earth, the divine feminine, gender nonconformity, communal living, playfulness, sex positivity, and the distinct contributions queer, trans, and gender expansive people have to make to humanity. Radical Faeries are nonhierarchical and have several networks of groups around the world, as well as sanctuaries, sacred spaces open for retreats, ritual, and full-time living.[39]

I am Pagan. I felt an overwhelming urge to "express my feminine" that came in the form of a call from the Goddess. Literally, She told me to stop hiding behind the mask, and to honor the feminine in me. I started dressing more (still at home, but not just in the bedroom), wore light makeup and nail polish to work, and spent "a year and a day" honoring the Divine Feminine.

The Center for LGBTQ & Gender Studies in Religion (CLGS) offers resources for trans inclusion in religion.

Eastern traditions. Although "Eastern" traditions are an imperfect distinction (and assume a western perspective), there are several spiritual and philosophical traditions arising out of South and East Asia that have distinctive views on gender. These traditions' spiritual beliefs are deeply intertwined with cultural and social mores, and have no centralized authority that speaks for their believers. For Confucianism and Daoism, a binary oppositional understanding of gender, described in the yin/yang dualism, is foundational to each tradition. Yin is understood as the feminine (receptive, soft, dark, cold) manifestation of universal energy, while yang is the masculine (active, hard, light, hot) part of universal energy. Yin and yang are seen as interdependent, complementary forces whose combination creates balance and the cycles of life (e.g., seasons). Yin is associated with being female, and yang associated with being male. It is believed that everyone has a combination of yin and yang, which is always flowing and changing. Nothing is pure yin or yang, as evidenced in the tai chi (yin–yang) symbol, wherein yin includes a dot of yang and vice-versa. Depending on where you come from, these philosophies can support gender fluidity, or reinforce heteropatriarchal norms. Daoism is seen by some as less patriarchal, as it uses feminine imagery for the divine and has invited female leadership, while Confucianism may be interpreted as more patriarchal. Confucianism places great importance on hierarchy, one's ancestors, the wishes of one's elders, and propagation of the family line. Thus, gender transition may be seen as a threat to continuing the family name.

Some scholars believe that karmic religions (religions that believe in multiple cycles of lives and the continuing consequences of decisions across lifetimes), such as Hinduism, Buddhism, Sikhism, and Jainism all acknowledge third genders in their ancient texts. Jain texts mention three genders—male, female, and *napumsakalinga* (neither male nor female). Whether one incarnates as one of these three genders is the result of karma from previous lives. The *Digambara* Jain sect believes women must be reborn as men through an exemplary life in order to achieve freedom from the cycle of

Tony, 67, San Diego, CA, 2014. (Jess T. Dugan). From "To Survive on This Shore: Photographs and Interviews with Transgender and Gender Nonconforming Older Adults," a project by Jess T. Dugan and Vanessa Fabbre.

birth and rebirth, while the *Svetambara* Jain sect does not believe gender is a factor. The Digambara also believe the 19th *Tirthankara* (enlightened being) Mallinatha was male, while the Svetambara venerate her as female. In Sikhism, *Ik Onkar*, the one supreme reality, is genderless. The soul is also seen as ultimately genderless, moving from body to body in the cycle of birth and rebirth.

Shinto, a spiritual tradition which comes out of Japan, describes a collection of local deities called *kami*. Kami rule particular places, objects, and living beings, and are worshipped at shrines around Japan. Many of the kami are explicitly gender expansive, such as the *shirabyoshi*, female or transgender half-human, half-snake deities. Shamans or priests of this kami, also called shirabyoshi, were often women or gender expansive people who performed ritual dances in men's clothing for ceremonial celebrations. *Inari Okami*, one of the most prominent kami, who is connected to fertility, rice, tea, and prosperity, is represented variously as male, female, and androgynous depending on context.

The Konkokyo LGBT Kai Facebook group offers a space for LGBTQ Shintos.

SHINTO AND TRANS IDENTITY

Shigeru Nic Sakurai (they/them)

Shinto, the ancient spirituality of Japan, originates reverence for nature, for ancestors, and for the infinite kami (spirits/deities.) Although Shinto could be understood as an ethnic religion particular to Japan, its conceptual and spiritual roots are embedded in shared values that naturally spring forth from humanity and our environs. As a distinctively Japanese spirituality, Shinto has been used in recent centuries as a tool for ultranationalist factions in Japan to promote their agendas. For me, however, as a transgender and nonbinary person of Japanese descent, Shinto is a religion that can promote great inspiration and empowerment.

An expansive understanding of gender is strewn throughout Shinto history. The Kojiki, or Record of Ancient Matters, is the oldest surviving history of Japan, written circa 712 CE. The Kojiki describes the first seven creator kami as genderless. Humans are seen as created by but also descended from kami, and a person can become enshrined as kami after they die. So, one interpretation is that the original progenitors of humanity are genderless. To put it as a slightly hyperbolic, monotheistic corollary: God is nonbinary. Some of the most well-known deities in the Shinto pantheon have also been represented as various genders (depending on the local tradition, or changing over time) or as multiple genders within one deity.

For example, Inari Okami is one of the most commonly enshrined kami, and has been represented as man, woman, nonbinary, animal, or even as a collective of several spirits. Perhaps you have seen the famous pathways full of vermillion gates at the Inari shrine in Kyoto. These gates are called torii, and they are often seen as a symbol of Shinto. Torii welcome and guide the spirits and humans to commune with one another. Significantly, these are gates that are always open and can never be shut. For me, they represent a radical welcome we should seek to promote.

For me, Shinto is queer. What I mean by that is that Shinto defies the ability to be easily defined and categorized, particularly by Western scholars who use a monotheistic or Christian-centric lens for defining what counts as a "religion." Even the most orthodox understandings of Shinto are quite unorthodox for Western religious thinking. Official sources on Shinto describe the religion as having no defined canon of scripture, no creed, and no dogma. Shinto has no founder and does not emphasize "faith" or "belief." Indeed, many people who practice Shinto rituals and pray at Shinto shrines are not formally members, and might consider themselves atheists. Shinto has no formal way to "convert" or "become" Shinto, and has little interest in defining its membership in these ways.

Orthodox sources on Shinto emphasize the importance of adaptation of the tradition over time, asserting that Shinto's essence requires that it continually seek a deeper and truer form that fits both to tradition and to what harmony looks like within contemporary realities. Shinto is always moving and never fixed. Shinto values are situated in specific circumstances and contexts, not to be thought of as a morality of absolutes or rules-based thinking. Shinto centers the principles of living with an authentic, sincere, true, and kind heart, in harmony with community, nature, ancestors, and the divine.

Sometimes transgender people are seen as individualistic or even antisocial to communitarian values (like those of Japan.) But if our communities value gender plurality, then our identities need not be exceptional, but simply part of a larger whole. If communities can recognize that trans people have existed since time immemorial among our honored ancestors and in our spiritual heritage, perhaps it can be understood that trans people are simply living with integrity, true to our hearts. Westernization and colonization have erased the gender variations that were seen as simply a part of humanity, and have made gender variation into an individualistic expression at the margins of communitarian thinking. By seeking to understand our heritage, perhaps gender diversity may again be integral to community.[40]

Indigenous communities. Many cultures throughout the world have acknowledged the existence of gender expansiveness in their spirituality. In North America, the term "Two Spirit" has often been used to describe the various ways transgender and gender expansive Native Americans were identified in their tribal cultures, from the Cheyenne to the Ojibwa. The term "Two Spirit" was adopted at the 1990 Basket and the Bow Conference for LGBTQ North American Indigenous people to describe individuals whose gender and sexuality transcend Eurocentric descriptors.[41] Two Spirit is an umbrella term that covers over 200 names for trans, gender expansive, and/or LGBQ people, and refers to the idea that LGBTQ people walk between the worlds of gender, taking on masculine and feminine qualities in various combinations. Some communities see the term, "Two Spirit," as first and foremost a spiritual one and believe Two Spirit people have special powers to walk between humanity on Earth and the spiritual realm. Several tribes, including the Navajo and Zuni, believe Two Spirit people were present at the beginning of the world and reincarnate into each generation.[42] Two Spirit people are often asked to give blessings, to play matchmaker to couples, and to bestow a secret spiritual name unto children. Certain spiritually significant ceremonies cannot happen without a Two Spirit person's presence and guidance.[43] Although this very positive view of transgender and gender expansive people may resonate with many non-Native American trans people, it is very important to not appropriate the term "Two Spirit" as our own if we do not identify with an Indigenous culture from the Americas. Cultural appropriation refers to the act of a person who is a part of a dominant culture—for example, a white trans person whose ancestors colonized North America—taking elements from the nondominant culture—in this case, the Native American identity "Two Spirit"—and making it part of one's identity without respecting that culture's context.

New religious movements. Many trans and gender expansive people have found spiritual homes in New Thought traditions, such as Centers for Spiritual Living or Churches of Religious Science. New Thought doctrine emphasizes individual spiritual discovery and the power of attention and intention in helping people heal and manifest their desires. These communities have historically been inclusive of LGBTQ people, though the level of education and welcome may depend on each individual community. The Baha'i faith does not make any kind of explicit statement on the morality of gender expansive identities. Their highest authority, the Universal House of Justice, stated in 2002 that Baha'i scriptures did not appear to address gender transition in any explicit way, and thus, a person who was questioning their gender identity did not need to consult their local Baha'i assembly. Rather, they should consult a physician.[44]

A PRAYER FOR THIS CURRENT MOMENT

Rev. Dr. Kerr Mesner (he/him) is a queer/transgender spiritual director, minister, facilitator, consultant, and activist. He is passionate about spiritual journeys, creativity, contemplative practices, and radical approaches to anti-oppressive education. The following prayer was written after attending a protest resisting the U.S. government's brutal treatment of families trying to immigrate to the country. Kerr invites you to substitute any language within the prayer with words that feel more resonant with your truth.

Holy One of Many Names,

May we trust in our knowing—the knowing that emerges from our bodies and hearts and minds and spirits.

May we trust in our communities—the communities that we know about—those that we have forged through choice, and love, and solidarity—as well as that invisible web of sibling connection that binds us all together.

May we trust in love. Hard-won love of self—forged through the fire of our gender journeys—the love of those relationships that strengthen us and nourish us—and the love of that which is greater than us.

May we lean into the power of our knowing—*our* trans wisdom.

May we lean into the power of our communities—a web built of steel strong strands across our world.

May we lean into our love for self, for other, and for the Spirit that sustains us when we most need it.

And reader . . . may you know that *you* are loved, that *you* are part of this web community, and that the gift of *who you are* makes all the difference in the world.

Amen.

Unitarian Universalist Association. The Unitarian Universalist Association is a spiritual community where humanists, Pagans, Christians, and even atheists gather in community fellowship to discern their values and participate in social justice. The UUA developed from two Christian traditions—the Unitarians and the Christian Universalists, who later joined and developed a multifaith community whose only beliefs required for membership are in the Seven Principles, which include a belief in the inherent worth and dignity of every person; justice, equity, and compassion in human relations; and a free and responsible search for truth and meaning.[45] The UUA has worked for the inclusion of transgender people since the 1990s and has welcomed transgender people to lead their ministries since 2002. They report that most of their congregations are welcoming to transgender people. The UUA provides trans-affirming youth ministry, camp, religious education, and sex education programs.[46]

Spiritual but not religious. A growing number of people in America, especially young people and LGBTQ people, are identifying as "spiritual but not religious" and pursuing spiritual paths beyond membership in any organized fellowship or belief in God(s).[47] Spiritual but not religious folks may use a range of divinatory and healing practices, such as reiki, law of attraction, astrology, tarot, and other energy work at various times. They may view these practices as part of an overall spiritual journey or simply as recreational activities. They may also use spiritual practices such as meditation, yoga, burning incense, reading sacred text, chanting, and many other practices to strengthen their mind-body connection and stay present in the moment. These practices may reflect beliefs about supernatural figures and spiritual laws or be secular in nature. Transgender people may be part of recovery groups (including 12-Step) that profess belief in a Chosen Power as part of their steps out of addiction or codependency. This Chosen Power may refer to God, one's Higher Self or Ideal Self, laws of nature, or the physical universe.

> *I am a little spiritual, not religious, but I feel it is hardly relevant to my identity. I've been through conversion therapy, which is tough. I've had several religious individuals reject me, be afraid of me. I have a very strong bias against religion at this point in my life.*

> *I'm not religious in an organized sense, nor was I raised within a religion. I've read a great deal of mythology and studied some other religions, including goddess-based religion. I try to keep this perspective day to day. Transitioning gives me perspective on religion, not the other way around.*

HOW TO FIND AN INCLUSIVE FAITH COMMUNITY

Over the past decade, more and more faith communities have stated their welcome for transgender and gender expansive people. It is easier than ever to find out whether a community is trans-affirming or not, simply by looking at their website. Organizations such as Believe Out Loud, Gaychurch.org, and Church Clarity have "Find a Church" functions where you can search for communities that welcome LGBTQ people. These sites tend to index mostly Judeo-Christian communities. Several communities, like the Episcopal Church and the Unity Church, have search functions to find LGBTQ-friendly groups within their denomination. Many LGBTQ community centers also offer resource lists on their websites with local LGBTQ-inclusive spiritual communities.

Although it's wonderful to have such a wide range of potential inclusive faith communities available, it's important to realize that just because a community is named a safe space on one of these sites, doesn't mean it will be the perfect fit for an individual. Sometimes these faith community databases are not updated when leadership changes, which can affect the church's commitment to continued learning about LGBTQ matters. Other times, a church may have done a lot of work around sexuality, but is not ready to be inclusive to transgender and gender expansive people.

Some transgender and gender expansive people may choose to be part of a faith community that is not openly affirming of transgender and gender expansive people. This may be for cultural reasons, because it's not safe to be out, or simply because the other beliefs of the community resonate. It may be a good idea to have safe, affirming people you can call on to support you if you hear messages that upset you or comments that challenge your identity. There may be books or other resources written by affirming people or trans people in your tradition to which you can turn for support if you need it.

If you are searching for a new faith community, it may be helpful to ask yourself some questions about what you're ultimately looking for. Here are some questions to help you get started:

- What am I looking for in a faith community in terms of its:
    - Belief system?
    - Spiritual practices?
    - Fellowship?
    - Social justice/activism?
- Does the faith community have a clear statement of welcome to trans and gender expansive people on its website?
- Does its building/other physical location have a rainbow or trans flag outside?
- Are they a member of their tradition's LGBTQ and ally network?
- Does this community participate in my area's Pride events?
- Do I know anyone who is part of this faith community? Could I meet with a representative of the community to ask questions?
- Do I know any transgender and gender expansive people who have attended a service or other ritual?
- Can I be part of a faith community whose belief system is not affirming of transgender and gender expansive people? If so, what do I need to take care of myself if I experience rejecting behaviors?

It may be helpful to have a buddy visit multiple communities with you to reflect on the experience. Often, faith leaders or other staff members are willing to meet with visitors as part of a welcome ministry or answer questions via email.

CONCLUSION

I have always been both spiritual and religious in some way, even since earliest childhood. I have been a member and/or practitioner of many different religions during my lifetime. I feel that this constant exploring, questioning, and deep reflection is similar to the whole process of gender exploration. Perhaps the same people who do the one are more likely to be led into doing the other. In many cultures of the world, gender-variant people historically held esteemed roles as shamans, priests, priestesses, and mediums who had a special gift in accessing the spirit world. I think that a large percentage of religious professionals, persons serving in the clergy or in religious or monastic orders, across all world religions, are members of sexual or gender minorities, because they tend to be spiritually gifted.

Some transgender and gender expansive people have never left the religious tradition we grew up within. Some of us were never raised with a religion or spirituality and are not interested in pursuing it. Some begin spiritual practices later in life. Some of us have been greatly hurt by churches, faith leaders, religious family members, and religious people in our communities. Many of us have reinterpreted and reclaimed aspects of ancestral traditions, unpacking the ways that patriarchal, colonizing forces erased their support of gender and sexual diversity. All over the world, trans and gender expansive people have been shamans and healers, walking in multiple worlds of gender and between the physical and spiritual realms.

I don't subscribe to any religions that currently exist but I also don't deny that something ethereal might exist. I like the idea of life after death because it makes that finality less scary. I also like the idea that spiritual beings don't have genders so something really happy and comforting might be waiting after we escape the flesh prisons.

Coming from a science background, I am not particularly religious. However, I feel religion is a deeply personal thing and I respect and look up to those who follow such a path. How nice to have such guidance in your life. Deep in me, I do cling to spirituality (Two Spirits comes to mind). I would like to think that love in the world is among us. That we are loved for our differences, that helping others does reap rewards, we are not alone. When a person can tell me they pray for me, it means the world to me! Something so deep and valued to them, and they are including me in their prayers—wow!

Some transgender and gender expansive people view their gender journey as a calling from God, a vocation just like becoming ordained as a spiritual leader. Others see the process of discovering their gender as inherently spiritual, as it points to transcendent knowledge present beyond the evidence of the body—a reality beyond physicality. Some folks might see their gender journey as another way they are meant to learn spiritual lessons, including exploring the relationships between the body, mind, and spirit. Others may find themselves reinterpreting the way they perceive God's gender based on their own gender evolution. Still others may find gratitude for the ways their gender journey developed spiritual gifts, including courage, prophecy, self-knowledge, hope, or compassion. Regardless of how we connect more deeply to ourselves and that which is beyond ourselves, transgender and gender expansive people are tremendously capable of spiritual creativity and resilience. Through our journeys to claim our authentic selves, we express the unique beauty of the transcendent.

NOTES

1. James, S. E., Herman, J. L., Rankin, S., Keisling, M., Mottet, L., & Anafi, M. (2016). *The Report of the 2015 U.S. Transgender Survey*. Washington, DC: National Center for Transgender Equality.

2. Mikalson, P., Pardo, S., & Green, J. (2013). *First Do No Harm: Reducing Disparities for Lesbian, Gay, Bisexual, Transgender, Queer and Questioning Populations in California*. The California LGBTQ Reducing Mental Health Disparities Project.

3. Levy, D. L., & Lo, J. R. (2013). Transgender, transsexual, and gender queer individuals with a Christian upbringing: The process of resolving conflict between gender identity and faith. *Journal of Religion & Spirituality in Social Work: Social Thought, 32*, November, 60–83. doi:10.1080/15426432.2013.749079.

4. James et al.

5. Mikalson et al.

6. Ryan, C., Huebner, D., Diaz, R. M., & Sanchez, J. (2009). Family rejection as a predictor of negative health outcomes in White and Latino lesbian, gay, and bisexual young adults. *Pediatrics, 123*(1), 346–352. doi:10.1542/peds.2007–3524.

7. Pew Research Center. (2013). *A Survey of LGBT Americans Attitudes, Experiences and Values in Changing Times*. Washington, DC: Pew Research Center.

8. Barton, B. (2010). 'Abomination'—Life as a Bible Belt Gay. *Journal of Homosexuality, 57*(4), 476.

9. McQueeney, K. (2009). "We Are G-D's Children Y'all": Race, gender, and sexuality in lesbian- and gay-affirming congregations." *Social Problems, 56*(1), 151–173. doi:10.1525/sp.2008.56.1.151.

10. Minwalla, O., Rosser, B. R. S., Feldman, J., & Varga, C. (2005). Identity experience among progressive gay Muslims in North America: A qualitative study within Al-Fatiha. *Culture, Health & Sexuality, 7*(2), 113–128.

11. Wilcox, M. M. (2002). When Sheila's a lesbian: Religious individualism among lesbian, gay, bisexual, and transgender Christians. *Sociology of Religion, 63*(4), 497–513. doi:10.2307/3712304.

12. Kidd, J. D., & Witten, T. (2008). Understanding spirituality and religiosity in the transgender community: Implications for aging. *Journal of Religion, Spirituality & Aging, 20*(1–2), 29–62.

13. *Talmud, Tractate Yevamot 82a-84a*.

14. *Mishna, Tractate Bikkurim, 4:1, 4:5*.

15. Ladin, J. (2018). *The Soul of the Stranger: Reading God and Torah from a Transgender Perspective, Ladin*. Brandeis University Press, 20.

16. Bereishit Rabbah 8, retrieved from Sefaria. https://www.sefaria.org/Bereishit_Rabbah.8.1?lang=bi

17. Isaiah 56: 3–5, New Revised Standard Version.

18. Pew Research Center. (2017). *U.S. Muslims Concerned About Their Place in Society, but Continue to Believe in the American Dream*. Washington, DC.

19. Kugle, S. A. (2010). *Homosexuality in Islam: Critical reflection on gay, lesbian, and transgender Muslims*. Oneworld, 243.

20. Ibid.

21. Muslim Youth Leadership Council, *I'm Muslim and My Gender Doesn't Fit Me: A Resource for Trans Muslim Youth*, 6. https://www.advocatesforyouth.org/wp-content/uploads/2019/05/Im-Muslim-My-Gender-Doesnt-Fit-Me.pdf

22. Conner, R. P., Sparks, D. H., & Sparks, M. (1998). *Cassell's encyclopedia of queer myth, symbol, and spirit: Gay, lesbian, bisexual, and transgender lore* (1st ed). Cassell, 50–51.

23. Ibid., 328.

24. Tauqeer, Atif. Saudi plan to bar transgender persons from performing Umrah is un-Islamic: Ghamidi, *The Express Tribune*, Pakistan. November 27, 2016.

25. Tauqeer, Atif. Saudi plan to bar transgender persons from performing Umrah is un-Islamic: Ghamidi, *The Express Tribune*, Pakistan. November 27, 2016.

26. Kate Lamb. (2015, May 12). Indonesia's transgender priests face uncertain future. *Al-Jazeera America*. http://america.aljazeera.com/articles/2015/5/12/indonesias-transgender-priests-face-uncertain-future.html

27. I use the term "sexual reassignment surgery" rather than "gender confirmation surgery" because it is unclear whether those who access this surgery are affirming their authentic gender or protecting other kinds of identities related to sexuality or gender nonconformity.

28. Ruth, V. (2012). Hinduism and Homosexuality. In D. L. Boisvert & J. E. Johnson (Eds.), *Queer religion*. Praeger, 11.

29. Conner, R. P., Sparks, D. H., & Sparks, M. (1998). *Cassell's encyclopedia of queer myth, symbol, and spirit: Gay, lesbian, bisexual, and transgender lore* (1st ed). Cassell, 67.

30. Danielou, A. (1987). *While the Gods Play*. Inner Traditions, 173-176. https://www.simonandschuster.com/books/While-the-Gods-Play/Alain-Danielou/9780892811151

31. Conner, R. P., Sparks, D. H., & Sparks, M. (1998). *Cassell's encyclopedia of queer myth, symbol, and spirit: Gay, lesbian, bisexual, and transgender lore* (1st ed). Cassell, 78.

32. Likhitpreechakul, P. Homophobic law has NO BASIS in Buddhism, *The Nation*, Opinion, April 3, 2015. http://www.nationmultimedia.com/detail/opinion/30257329.

33. Bhikkhu Bodhi (Ed.). (2005). *In the Buddha's words: An anthology of discourses from the Pāli canon*. Wisdom Publications.

34. Post, S. G. (2004). Body. *Encyclopedia of bioethics*. New York: MacMillan Reference USA, 328.

35. Michael Dillon/ Lobzang Jivaka and Susan Stryker, *Out of the Ordinary: A Life of Gender and Spiritual Transitions*, ed. Jacob Lau and Cameron Partridge, 1st edition (New York: Fordham University Press, 2016), 230–231.

36. Herek, G. M., Norton, A. T., Allen, T. J., & Sims, C. L. (2010). Demographic, Psychological, and Social Characteristics of Self-Identified Lesbian, Gay, and Bisexual Adults in a US Probability Sample. *Sexuality research & social policy : journal of NSRC : SR & SP*, 7(3), 176–200. https://doi.org/10.1007/s13178-010-0017-y

37. Pew Research Center. (2013). *A survey of LGBT Americans: Attitudes, experiences, and values in changing times*. Washington, DC: Pew Research Center, 91, http://www.pewsocialtrends.org/files/2013/06/SDT_LGBT-Americans_06-2013.pdf.

38. Kidd, J. D., & Witten, T. M. (2008). Understanding Spirituality and Religiosity in the Transgender Community: Implications for Aging. *Journal of Religion, Spirituality & Aging*, 20(1–2), 29–62. https://doi.org/10.1080/15528030801922004

39. Rad Fae (North America) http://www.radfae.org/ and Folleterre (Europe) https://www.folleterre.org/en/ are two resources about Radical Faerie history and gatherings.

40. "An Outline of Shinto Teachings," a 1958 pamphlet published by Jinja Honcho (The Association of Shinto Shrines), Kokugakuin University, and the Institute for Japanese Culture and Classics, which was compiled by the Shinto Committee for the IXth International Congress for the History of Religions.

41. McLeod, A. "History of Two-spirited People in Manitoba," in Alley Yapput, Two-spirited Outreach Project. Final Report, Ottawa: Egale Canada Human Rights Trust, 2004, 5, Two-Spirited Collection, box 1, folder 1-7, University of Winnipeg Archives.

42. Baum, R. M. (1993). Homosexuality and the traditional religions of the Americas and Africa. In Arlene Swidler (Ed.), *Homosexuality and World Religions* (pp. 1–46). Trinity Press International, 8.

43. Brown, L. B. (Ed.). (1997). *Two Spirit People: American Indian Lesbian Women and Gay Men* (1 edition). Routledge, 10.

44. Universal House of Justice. (2002, December 26). *Transsexuality*. Bahai Library Online. https://bahai-library.com/uhj_transsexuality

45. Unitarian Universalist Association. (2014, November 24). *Unitarian Universalism's Seven Principles*. UUA.Org. https://www.uua.org/beliefs/what-we-believe/principles

46. Unitarian Universalist Association. (2021). *Welcoming Congregations Program*. Unitarian Universalist Association. https://www.uua.org/lgbtq/welcoming/program

47. Pew Research Center. (2015). *America's Changing Religious Landscape*. Pew Research Center. http://www.pewforum.org/2015/05/12/americas-changing-religious-landscape/

6

SEX AND GENDER DEVELOPMENT

E. Kale Edmiston, Laura Erickson-Schroth,
Miqqi Alicia Gilbert, T. Evan Smith, and
Anastacia Tomson

INTRODUCTION

In a Western and colonial understanding of gender, many people assume that there are two genders: male and female, and that both our sex and gender depend on our genitals. Research in a variety of fields, however, including psychology, genetics, sociology, and anthropology, suggests that sex and gender are not the same. Today, our "sex" typically describes our anatomical and biological characteristics—usually our genitals and our genetics. "Gender" most often refers to our social roles or behaviors. Sex and gender are not completely separate concepts, however, and social and biological factors play an important role in defining both our sex and our gender. In this chapter, we will discuss various influences on gender and sex development, including biological, sociocultural, and familial factors. The aim of this chapter is not to clearly "determine" what exactly "causes" a transgender or gender expansive (T/GE) identity to emerge or be experienced; rather, it is to engage a critical lens regarding many possible factors and call attention to the impossibility of the very question. We hope that this can help broaden understanding, and not limit or confine how being trans is conceptualized. Challenging assumptions and rigid determinations that do not fit for the vast majority of us is a necessary step toward a decolonized framework for trans bodies and trans lives.

CURIOSITY ABOUT OUR ORIGINS

There are many potential explanations for why a person might be transgender. There is a great deal of variation in how important these explanations are for individual transgender people and our understanding of our transgender identity. Importantly, there is no one explanation for why someone might be transgender. Instead, many factors likely contribute to how any person understands their gender. More work needs to be done to understand gender identity development from transgender perspectives. It is also important to remember that undue emphasis on understanding why someone is transgender, but not why someone might be cisgender, assumes that cisgender identity is the default. The "why" can frame transgender identities as a problem or disorder rather than part of the diversity of human experience.

> I have felt different from my peers since I could remember, but being neurodivergent and gender nonconforming and Jewish all blended together, and I can't say if my feelings of difference were one or the other.

OUR GENDERED WORLD

How do we see ourselves? To what kinds of people do we feel similar? What do we feel comfortable being called? All these aspects make up our gender identity, our inner sense of being male, female, something in-between, or something entirely different. Unlike gender identity, gender roles are not determined by our inner sense of ourselves. Instead, they are defined and enforced by society. Gender roles give us rules about how we are supposed to behave and what kinds of opportunities and responsibilities are available to us.

Onsen. "Onsen are traditional Japanese hot springs where navigating segregated areas can be challenging for those who identify outside traditional genders." Cai Quirk is a trans/genderqueer photographer and musician from upstate New York currently finishing a double degree at Indiana University.

I'm originally from a rural farming environment and it has certainly played a role in my gender identity. Growing up, I was taught traditionally feminine roles in the household (cooking, cleaning, sewing, emotional labor, etc.) and learned some "outside" more masculine tasks. The adults in my life who farmed seemed to have more blurred gender roles, because some tasks just had to get done and it didn't matter so much what your gender was.

Gender roles may also help shape our ideas about what characteristics are "feminine" and "masculine." Often, feminine or masculine traits are thought of as natural or innate to people with certain types of bodies and are therefore taboo or off limits to people with other kinds of bodies. This way of thinking results in gender stereotypes, which describe how men and women "should" look, behave, and feel. Gender stereotypes differ from culture to culture, and they have a great deal of influence on how we think about ourselves and behave. In the United States, gender expectations are largely based on white, western, colonialist ideals. These ideals do not fit for the vast majority of people, yet they are reinforced. On the other hand, people who do not fit these ideals are typically excluded or punished.

EVOLUTION OF MY GENDER ACCEPTANCE

Logan (they/them) is a demiguy living in Sacramento.

Age 4: one of my earliest memories. My first "big girl bed." A pink canopy bed. Threw a tantrum because it was all pink and not blue. I sat on the floor in front of my mirror watching tears stream down my face.

Age 5: cut off my own hair.

Age 8: asked for a blue bike and blue helmet for Christmas, threw tantrum when I got a pink bike and purple helmet.

Age 13: started wearing my brother's old clothes.

Age 14: began role-playing as a gay man online.

Age 16: people began assuming I was a lesbian, which confused me because I never identified with that.

Age 17: learned about the pregnant man, learned that trans men exist, and wondered if that's what I was.

Age 19: read a magazine article about androgynous style and shopping in the men's section. Felt validated and bought my first men's shirt at Target.

Age 22: decided that if I wanted to have a boyfriend I would have to start acting/dressing more femininely; liked the reaction and attention I got but felt fake, felt like I was being inauthentic.

Age 23: experienced the worst depressive episode of my life.

Age 24: cut my hair short and told my partner at the time that I always wanted to be a gay man (my way of explaining a feminine man). They were the first person to tell me I could be.

Age 26: decided I should figure out my gender identity; did a lot of self-reflection.

Age 27: came out as nonbinary, chose a name that I wanted to use someday.

Age 28: came out as transmasculine/demiguy and began asking people to use the name Logan.

HOLDING COMPLEXITY: BIOPSYCHOSOCIAL THEORIES OF GENDER DEVELOPMENT

Historically, gender development researchers emphasized the differences between biological and social theories—known as the "nature versus nurture" debate. But biological, psychological, and sociological stances on gender development are all simply different perspectives. Understanding that biology influences us does not mean rejecting the concept of social influences. Each perspective prioritizes different facets—and none has the full picture.

Gender is influenced by many factors, including biology, psychological experiences, and social interactions. Theories that incorporate all of these factors are called biopsychosocial theories. Within a biopsychosocial model, we can move away from either/or arguments and make space for a variety of T/GE people's identities and experiences.

Gender: What Everyone Needs to Know is a quick-read paperback that explores the history of gender as a concept; the role of biology, psychology, and culture in gender; and gender norms over time and across the globe. (Laura Erickson-Schroth and Benjamin Davis, Oxford, 2021).

An example of a biopsychosocial theory is Milton Diamond's biased-interaction theory of gender development.[1] According to this theory, early biological factors (possibly including genetics or fetal hormones) set us up to interact with our environments in certain ways. They give us temperaments or predispositions. Although these early biological factors do not decide our gender identities, they influence our preferences and aversions.

We then compare ourselves to others to decide whether we are like them or different from them, and this helps us to form our gender identities. Whether our gender identities come about in exactly this way or not, it is likely that they are influenced in some way by biology as well as our social environments.

A transgender psychologist, Jaimie Veale,[2] proposes the identity-defense model of gender variance, in which biological factors and early childhood influences determine whether, and to what degree, a gender-variant identity develops, and then personality and environmental factors determine whether defense mechanisms are used to repress the gender variance. Veale argues that our biological factors, as well as our defense mechanisms or coping strategies, determine whether we are going to identify as transgender, cross-dressers, or drag artists.

THROUGH THE LENS(ES) OF QUEER THEORY

What we now call queer theory began with a set of texts written from the late 1970s into the 1990s by scholars including Gloria Anzaldua, Judith Butler, Cathy Cohen, Michel Foucault, C. Jacob Hale, Gayle Rubin, Eve Kosofsky Sedgwick, Jack Halberstam, and Michael Warner. Queer theory presented new ways to conceptualize sex, gender, and sexuality.

Queer theorists claim that current U.S. culture is characterized by heteronormativity, in which nonheterosexual identities are seen as bad, unnatural, or immoral. Behaviors that

Dr. Jaymie Campbell is a Senior Trainer for the Transgender Training Institute and has taught over 100 trainings on sexuality.

boost the status of reproductive heterosexuality—monogamy, sex during marriage, and sex for the purpose of procreation—are given higher social status and material benefits (e.g., tax deductions for married couples). Behaviors that threaten or challenge reproductive heterosexuality are socially degraded and deemed sick or undesirable. This concept, that sexual desires and practices are cultural concepts and not biological facts, can also be applied to gender identity.

> *I figured when I came out as bisexual, traditional masculinity had no place for me already, so I was free to experiment and pass it off as, "Oh, I'm bisexual." That was never really enough to make me feel right. After I started getting closer with nonbinary people, I started to see myself and my story in them and theirs. After a while, I felt like I needed to put a name to how I was feeling about gender and free myself from "man" as a label. When I did, I was immediately relieved. And excited! It was like a whole new world opened up for me.*

GENDER FRAGMENTS

Miriam Eric Suzanne (she/her) is a writer, musician, designer, and web developer—working with OddBird, Teacup Gorilla, Grapefruit Lab, and CSS Tricks. She's the author of the novel, Riding SideSaddle, *and an award-winning playwright.*

We have a story in my family. My brother is young, nursing his favorite doll.

"I'm going to be a mommy when I grow up."
"Boys grow up to be daddies."

Mom is only trying to be accurate, but he sets down the doll, and never looks back. *Cis doesn't mean simple*, he tells me now, a father of two. If I had that story, maybe everything would make sense. Maybe I could string this together into a narrative: beginning, middle, and end.

I never felt like a girl. What do girls feel like? I didn't always know, and dream of wearing dresses. I wasn't consistent, insistent, or persistent.

I was frustrated.

I tell myself I'm too masculine. I tell myself a beard will protect me. I use my beard as a beard, to throw us all off the scent. I tell myself: If you don't try you can't fail. I tell myself it's only a body. I tell myself nothing fits right.

Mom writes:

"I saw your photo in heels. Are you exploring bisexuality?"
"Which sex is the gay one?"

Mom can talk for hours about the fluid nature of god as mother and father—masculine and feminine together. Her congregation uses all the pronouns, and all the metaphors.

"You understand, then. My gender, like your god. These pronouns don't fit right."
"Oh. I'm not sure I can think of my son that way."

Finally, I announce that I'm trans. I still don't know what that means. Grandma asks how often I wear dresses. It depends on the weather. She seems happy with that.

"What pronouns should we use?"
"She . . . or they?"
"I don't like they. Are you going to have surgery?"
"I don't . . . think so?"
"Will you still date women?"
"Will women date me?"

Grandma has a friend on T. Transition looks hard. Expensive. Awkward.

"I hope you don't transition. You look so good as a boy."

Have you seen Michelle Pfeiffer in Batman Returns? Transition is basically like that.
All my old raincoats become skin-tight catsuits.

Trying on clothes to see if they fit is way better than trying on clothes to see if your gender fits. I didn't know there was a difference, until everything changed.
I can finally hate my body for the normal reasons.

CREATING AND LEARNING GENDER

Characteristics of femininity and masculinity do not come from a biological or innate starting point. Scholars call this the social construction of gender, meaning that we construct—or create—gender by telling men and women how to act. The feminist philosopher Judith Butler argues that gender is a product of culture, and its meaning is created by people. Butler calls gender a performance.[3] This "performance," however, is not the same thing as acting. We learn and repeat others' behaviors, internalize them, and interpret them as our sense of self. Gendered behaviors repeat over generations, influencing our cultures' current understanding of gender.

There is significant evidence that our gender identities are influenced by social factors. Some feminist theorists argue that gender functions as a system of social control. This system pressures individuals to conform to sexist and cisnormative societal expectations. This approach to understanding gender acknowledges the unequal power dynamics at play in the way gender is reinforced.

Regardless of our sex or gender, we all have a wide array of characteristics that might be considered feminine or masculine. In our sexist society, many of the traits that are perceived as "feminine" are often devalued, favoring "masculine" traits. Fighting sexism

Cisnormativity refers to the assumption that all people are cisgender and/or that cisgender identity is normal and natural.[4]

means recognizing the value of femininity and allowing people to act in ways that are masculine, feminine, or something else entirely, regardless of their bodies.

> *I remember around the age of 7 telling my mom to call me a "gal" because I saw myself as different than a "girl." Later, I just saw this as early internalized misogyny. I often felt that social behavior (including femininity) didn't come naturally to me like it did to others. (I believe this is interwoven with my anxiety and possible nondiagnosed autism.) I also remember being extremely sensitive to statements (either from religion or society) on what it meant to be a girl/woman and what it meant I should be doing. I often experienced (what I now think of as dysphoria) extreme anguish at essentialist statements that declared a certain nature to men and women.*

DECONSTRUCTING AND RECONSTRUCTING TRANS NARRATIVES

A strictly social constructionist view of gender identity development is seemingly invalidating to many transgender people. If gender is not innate and we all learn gender by constant external reinforcement, then it would not be possible to develop a gender identity that differs from the socially acceptable norms associated with an assigned sex. Early theories of transgender identity ascribed to the idea that T/GE people were "trapped in the wrong body." This narrative assumes that there is a disconnect between our bodies and our minds and is closely related to many biological theories of transgender identity. This theory, however, is also ultimately unsatisfying for many of us, because it assumes a male–female sex binary can be mapped onto a specific type of body. The model doesn't account for the diversity that exists within our T/GE communities. The "trapped in the wrong body" theory also creates problems for both cis and T/GE feminists, because it assumes that there is such a thing as a "woman's body," as well as some sort of innate characteristic that can be attributed to a female identity (e.g., "I know that I am a woman because I liked to play with dolls as a child.")

> *I realized that my gender didn't align with my assignment at birth at a fairly young age, second or third grade, but I lacked the vocabulary to discuss it. It would be several more years, eighth or ninth grade, until I found any of the words that eventually come to describe me. But at that point I didn't recognize myself in those words, because I didn't fit into any of the "traditional" narratives.*

In contrast, T/GE scholars and writers (particularly T/GE feminists), including Sandy Stone, Julia Serrano, Kate Bornstein, and Talia Mae Bettcher have developed their own theories for understanding trans identities that contest both the "trapped in the wrong body" model and the completely social constructionist model of gender identity. In particular, Bettcher, a transfeminist philosopher, offers a framework for understanding T/GE identity in the context of Lugones's "multiple worlds of sense."[5] Here, terms such as "woman" can take on multiple meanings in different contexts. This allows T/GE people to have the opportunity to describe sex and gender on our own terms and not rely on theories of sex and gender created by cisgender people for cisgender people.

> *Until quite late in high school, I don't believe that I experienced much if any gender questioning. I am still trying to contextualize my gender history, but my current best guess is that I really was a boy, but I don't think I was ever a man.*

BIOLOGICAL ORIGINS

Few topics are as divisive as that of the biological basis of T/GE identity. For some, the thought of a biological explanation for our experiences offers comfort and affirmation. Some people believe that identifying the biological origins of transgender identity would mean greater acceptance of transgender individuals. The promise of a biological explanation of T/GE identity could prove that T/GE experience is predetermined by factors

Kate, 69, New York, NY, 2017. (Jess T. Dugan). From "To Survive on This Shore: Photographs and Interviews with Transgender and Gender Nonconforming Older Adults," a project by Jess T. Dugan and Vanessa Fabbre.

beyond the control of the individual. However, this way of thinking about our origins suggests a T/GE identity is less desirable than a cisgender identity—encouraging some to think it is okay to be transgender, but only as long as we fit the "born this way" trope.

Similar arguments were made about gay identity in the last half of the 20th century. Biologists such as Simon LeVay[6] attempted to identify a biological basis for gay identity in men. It wasn't this research, however, that swayed popular opinion on gay acceptance. Studies showed that greater acceptance of gay people happened as more and more people came out of the closet.[78] Once more heterosexual people realized that they had gay friends and family members, the popular discussions surrounding gay people changed. This was the result of activism from within gay communities, not the efforts of scientists.

In contrast, some of us may find the idea of a biological explanation—or even the search for one—pathologizing. Biologists study illnesses to prevent or cure them. However, ideas about what constitutes an illness are culturally determined. Why study the biological basis of transgender identity if it is not an illness? Doing so potentially reinforces the damaging idea that we are "sick." Additionally, as scientists uncover biological clues to the development of transgender identity, there is potential for tests to develop that might gatekeep access to essential rights and services for trans people. The irony is that in a world where biological evidence would not be used against transgender people, the same evidence would not be needed in the first place. The validity of an individual's identity should not rest on any biological basis. Regardless of biological evidence, our identities are valid and there is nothing inherently wrong, broken, or defective about us.

> I used to hear cis people talk about transness as if you're trapped in the wrong body. And I never felt that. It wasn't until I started listening to trans people speak about their own experiences with gender that I realized that the narrative of being in the wrong body isn't the only narrative.

LABELING BODIES AT BIRTH

After conception, the initial cells that grow into a person can develop in various ways. Cells may grow into a uterus, a vagina, a penis, testes, breasts, or other organs typically

ALOK (they/them) is a gender non-conforming writer and performance artist. As a mixed-media practitioner, ALOK explores themes of gender, race, trauma, belonging, and the human condition. They are the author of Femme in Public (2017) and Beyond the Gender Binary (2020). (Eivind Hansen)

used to classify sex. Our genetics influence how our bodies will look and function. But these are not the only factors that shape our bodies and identities.

At birth, we are assigned a sex (usually male or female). Healthcare providers determine sex by looking at the baby's external genitalia—if the external genitalia look like a vulva, the baby is assigned female, and if the external genitalia look like a penis and scrotum, the baby is assigned male. The determination of sex is far more complex and intricate, however, than simply looking at genitalia. In reality, there are many biological factors to consider when assessing sex. These factors do not always align with one another or operate within a binary framework of sex.

I never really considered gender until I had the chance to see that gender could be so different from sex.

CHROMOSOMES AND GENES

Chromosomes are long strands of DNA made up of thousands of genes. Most people have two copies of 23 different chromosomes, making a total of 46 chromosomes, although some individuals have more or fewer than 46 chromosomes. Our first 22 pairs of chromosomes are numbered 1 through 22, but the last pair—the so-called sex chromosomes—are named for their shapes: X and Y. The X chromosome is much larger, containing about 2,000 genes, while the Y chromosome has only 78 genes.

When someone has two X chromosomes (XX), that person typically develops as female. When someone has one X and one Y chromosome (XY), that person typically develops as male. Scientists are still discovering why these combinations usually lead

Genes are small pieces of genetic material that are usually located on a chromosome. They contain information that the body uses to make specific proteins or express specific traits. The total human genome is estimated to have about 20,000 genes.

to female and male development. Most T/GE people have the chromosomes that are expected based on their birth-assigned sex, although there may be slightly higher rates of chromosomal differences in transgender compared to cisgender people.

ENDOGENOUS HORMONES

Estrogen and testosterone, two dominant sex hormones, are both present in most individuals and affect our bodies throughout our lives—even before we are born. Hormones influence primary sex characteristics during embryonic development and assist with the development and maintenance of secondary sex characteristics during puberty.

Puberty is a time of change, when our bodies develop from being relatively gender-neutral to looking more typically male or female. During puberty, estrogen levels begin to cycle monthly in most people assigned female at birth. Testosterone levels increase in both sexes, but more so in most people assigned male at birth.

When I was a kid, the word tomboy seemed to fit the differences I noticed. In fourth grade (about age 9), I noticed the differences more acutely. That kept ramping up toward and through puberty.

As we go through puberty and enter adulthood, the hormones surging through our bodies every day have powerful effects on our thoughts and mood. Popular media sources such as magazines and television often lead us to believe that testosterone is a male hormone and estrogen is a female hormone, and they may link these hormones to masculine or feminine behaviors. The truth is that both males and females have testosterone and estrogen in their bodies, and the levels of these hormones vary considerably between people of the same sex.

Until the 1970s, many scientists thought that differences in adult hormone levels could be responsible for our feelings about our gender identities. They even thought that homosexuality might be caused by differences in hormone levels—specifically, that gay men (and trans women) might have lower levels of testosterone than cis men. These notions have been shown to be untrue. Some groups also believed that lesbians and trans men might have higher levels of endogenous testosterone than cis women. Although there is no evidence of this among lesbians, there is some debate about testosterone levels in certain trans men.

Many researchers believe that although it is possible intrauterine hormones (those we are exposed to as fetuses in a uterus) may affect our gender identity, it is unlikely that adult hormone levels have much of an effect. One possible exception is a medical condition

Endogenous hormones refer to hormones that our bodies make. Exogenous hormones come from outside the body either through medications or environmental contaminants.

Primary sex characteristics are present at birth and refer to the genitals and internal reproductive organs. Secondary sex characteristics are the changes that occur during puberty—usually under the influence of hormones.

We Have Never Asked Permission. Glori Tuitt is a New York City based Painter and Illustrator. Mining the collective history of queer representation, she sees herself as intermediary and visual translator, assembling new hybrid archetypes and narratives, ultimately seeking to both humanize and deify trans existence.

called polycystic ovary syndrome (PCOS). In PCOS, people assigned female at birth have higher than typical levels of testosterone, increased body hair, acne, irregular periods, and problems with fertility. The name comes from the cystic appearance of the ovaries when an ultrasound is done.

Some studies suggest that trans men may have higher rates of PCOS than cis women. Most of these studies, however, were done in small groups of transgender people, and most people with PCOS are not trans. PCOS is relatively common, affecting 5%–10% of people assigned female at birth. It is possible that PCOS could affect the way we understand our gender identity, but it does not explain why most of us are trans.

If you have PCOS, or symptoms of PCOS, you may want to talk about it with your healthcare provider. Some of the effects, such as increased body hair and irregular periods, may be desirable, but others, such as acne and a tendency toward diabetes, are not.

INHERENTLY VARIABLE

Sam Sharpe (they/them) is a PhD studying drought adaptation across grass populations. They believe strongly in the importance of scientific literacy, science communication, and the capacity of biology to empower, rather than invalidate, queer and transgender identities. In their free time, Sam enjoys running marathons, baking rainbow cakes, and taking selfies with cute plants.

Although I did not become a scientist because I am transgender, it has only been through my engagement with biology that I have been able to understand my own experience of gender. Assigned female at birth, I came into awareness with a strong conviction that I should be a boy. Seeing no path forward with that knowledge, I spent nearly 20 years trying unsuccessfully to live as a girl. My relationship with biological sex and gender was further complicated by a hormonal condition I developed as a teenager, which has caused my body to have both male and female secondary sex characteristics. At 25, I have come to identify as nonbinary and transmasculine.

As a gender nonconforming scientist, I am both visibly other and do not exist. In my field, anyone who deviates from the cisgender heterosexual white male default is presumed less capable and less objective. My graduate work takes place at a state institution in a state that refuses to acknowledge transgender identities. As a biologist, I struggle to reconcile my love for my work with the knowledge that the phrase "biological sex" and the widespread misconceptions about its meaning are constantly weaponized to invalidate trans people.

Most of the science that makes headlines about the neurobiology and genetics of trans people makes me squirm. The specific category of transgender is a modern, Western parameter, but the physiological or psychological variations that inspire gender variability are not. If our society was less obsessed with the deviance of those who step outside our narrow gender roles, would we be so determined to pin transgender identities to a particular piece of gray matter or stretch of DNA?

My body and my personhood pose an inherent challenge to medical, scientific, and institutionalized understandings of sex and gender. I have neither changed my biological characteristics to match my gender, nor am I comfortable arguing that my anomalous physiology has caused my unconventional gender. Most human traits are variable, and as an evolutionary biologist, I have seen no evidence to suggest that a transgender or gender nonconforming identity falls outside the inherent variation of our species. I don't need a specific gene or neurological pattern to tell me that I and others like me are biologically valid and real in who we understand ourselves to be.

GONADS

Before they become ovaries or testes, gonads are called a gonadal ridge, a structure that persists until at least the seventh week of gestation. In the presence of the SRY gene, a hormone called Testis Determining Factor (TDF) drives development of gonads into testes. In the absence of TDF, ovaries typically develop.

The SRY gene is typically located on the Y chromosome, but in some cases, the genetic code for the gene might be found on an X chromosome, leading to the development of testosterone-producing testes in a person with XX chromosomes.

INTERNAL REPRODUCTIVE ORGANS

The internal reproductive structures remain undifferentiated in the growing embryo until approximately the eighth week of gestation. At this stage, these tissues include two sets of tubal structures, named the mesonephric and paramesonephric ducts. The mesonephric ducts (occasionally referred to as Wolffian ducts) are capable of further differentiating into the epididymis, vas deferens, and seminal vesicles. The paramesonephric (or Mullerian) ducts have potential to become the uterine tubes, uterus, and cervix.

trans-masculine bodies

When we know what's going on with our own bodies, we're able to tell others what's going on with our bodies—including what we like and don't like. Knowing your body can also keep you from accidentally getting pregnant or getting an STI. These diagrams are of people who were female-assigned-at-birth and have not taken hormones or had surgery.

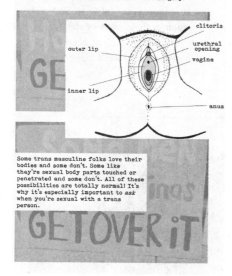

Some trans masculine folks love their bodies and some don't. Some like they're sexual body parts touched or penetrated and some don't. All of these possibilities are totally normal! It's why it's especially important to *ask* when you're sexual with a trans person.

These are the medical terms for our sexual bodies parts. It's good to know these terms so that if anything is wrong you can tell a doctor or healer about it.

If getting your period freaks you out, but you can't/don't want to take testosterone, you might be able to take continuous birth control. It's another way to not get your period. You can get it from a doctor's office.

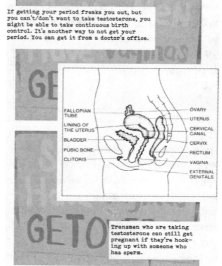

Transmen who are taking testosterone can still get pregnant if they're hooking up with someone who has sperm.

trans-feminine bodies

Knowing how our bodies work is powerful—it means we know when something isn't working right and can tell a doctor or healer about it. These diagrams are of people who are male-assigned-at-birth and have not changed their sexy bits through hormones or surgery.

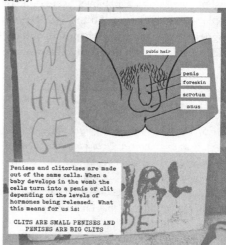

Penises and clitorises are made out of the same cells. When a baby develops in the womb the cells turn into a penis or clit depending on the levels of hormones being released. What this means for us is:

CLITS ARE SMALL PENISES AND PENISES ARE BIG CLITS

The head, or glans of the penis is the most sensitive bit because it has the most nerve endings, like a clit.

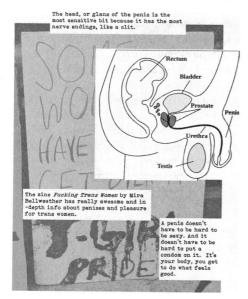

The zine *Fucking Trans Women* by Mira Bellweather has really awesome and in-depth info about penises and pleasure for trans women.

A penis doesn't have to be hard to be sexy. And it doesn't have to be hard to put a condom on it. It's your body, you get to do what feels good.

fill in the blank: sexy body words

For some people using the "medical" terms that are connected to a gender they don't identify with is really uncomfortable. No problem—this is where we get to make up our own words. Language is powerful and we can use it as a tool to feel more comfortable in our own skin.

What words do you use to talk about your body?

What words would you want a hot date to use?

word bank

cock	penis	clik
clit	vagina	boycunt
dick	parts	
pussy	genitals	---------
bits	funparts	
junk	stuff	---------
ass	fronthole	
hole	backhole	---------
bonus hole	jam	---------

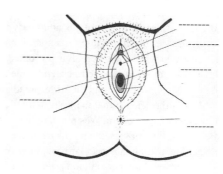

perception

You get to choose how you want your body to be talked about and touched. Many trans folks talk about feeling like their orgasms change and how they want to be touched changes after taking hormones. Lots of MTFs (but not all) want their penises talked about and treated as clits. Lots of FTMs (but not all) want their clits talked about and treated as cocks. People who are genderqueer or have non-binary identities might want either of these or something completely different.

Practice by jerking off. What do you like? What don't you like? It's not what you have, it's how you use it.

toys/prosthetics

Toys or prosthetics can be a way to feel more comfortable with your body when you're having sex. Some transmen don't want their clit or vagina touched, but can cum wearing a strap-on. Some transwomen aren't into penetrating with their bits, but really get into wearing a strap-on.

Trans Sex Zine Pages. (Damon Constantinides)

Whether or not the paramesonephric ducts will develop or not is determined by the presence or absence of a hormone known as anti-paramesonephric or anti-Mullerian hormone. This hormone is often produced by the testes. The development of the mesonephric ducts requires testosterone. In the presence of testosterone, the mesonephric ducts become the epididymis, vas deferens, and seminal vesicles.

EXTERNAL GENITALIA

Our external genitalia (penis, scrotum, vulva) develop in utero alongside our other organs. Until an embryo is nine weeks old, the external genitalia are undifferentiated—no sex-specific structures can be identified, and all genitalia have followed a common thread of development up until this point.

Even after differentiation begins, some common processes remain. In the absence of androgens, most specifically, dihydrotestosterone (DHT), the external genitalia will develop into labia minora, labia majora, and a clitoris. This process is not fully understood, but it appears to occur independently of ovarian hormone production. Thus, a vulva can develop even in the absence of ovaries, or in combination with nonfunctional ovaries. When DHT is present, the genital tubercle will elongate to form a penis. There are numerous situations in which development of the external genitalia will not necessarily neatly follow one of the above two pathways, which can result in genitalia that are not easily identifiable as either a vulva, or as a penis and scrotum.

Taken together, the development of sexual and reproductive organs is a complex process involving many players, including genes, hormones, and receptors. Importantly, all of these developmental processes describe only characteristics of the reproductive tract (and, eventually, secondary sexual characteristics), but not of the brain or the identity of an individual.

Surgery on ambiguous genitalia in a newborn is never a medical emergency, contrary to what many healthcare providers have told parents. Surgeries to change the appearance of external genitalia should be withheld until the individual is able to choose for themself.

INTERSEX PEOPLE

Though this book is geared toward T/GE communities, discussions of sex and gender development often lead to questions about intersex people—those whose bodies do not align with a binary sex system. Intersex people have been the subjects of research into gender and sexuality for some time, and they have not always had a voice to speak for themselves.[9] The Intersex Society of North America (ISNA), an advocacy group for intersex people, wrote that "people with intersex conditions ought to be treated with the same basic ethical principles as everyone else—respect for their autonomy and self-determination, truth about their bodies and their lives, and freedom from discrimination. Physicians, researchers, and gender theorists should stop using people with intersex conditions in 'nature/nurture' experiments or debates."[10]

> *Being a religious minority I always knew that we didn't fit in and that didn't mean there was anything wrong with us. So being intersex and not fitting in, even as a child, I knew that didn't mean there was anything wrong with me.*

Intersex and transgender experiences are not the same. Although understanding the biology of intersex people may provide some insights into biological factors in transgender experience, we should be cautious about using intersex research to explore the experiences of transgender people who are not intersex. There is some overlap, however, between intersex and T/GE communities. Some intersex people consider themselves to be part of transgender communities because their bodies or gender identities differ from what is considered typical (cisgender). Some intersex people may "transition" when they find that the gender they were assigned at birth doesn't align with their gender identity. On the other hand, there are intersex people who do not wish to be categorized as or lumped together with T/GE communities. Therefore, self-determination is key, and we must always respect any given person's autonomy in describing their gender, body, or identity.

Parents of intersex children may feel strong social pressure to choose a gender for their child. The sex of their baby is often one of the first questions new parents are asked, so it can be hard or embarrassing for many parents who do not have a simple answer.

Intersex Initiative, founded by Emi Koyama, is a "national activist and advocacy organization for people born with intersex conditions."

InterACT maintains a list of intersex support and advocacy groups around the world.

Parents may also worry that if they do not choose quickly, their child will be teased or ostracized for being different. However, choosing a binary gender for your child and sticking to it even if the child raises objections can be harmful long-term.

BORN PURPLE

Er. A. Vickie Boisseau CPS (herm) is the New England Director of Organization Intersex International, a Peer Support Specialist, Intersex activist, and co-founder of Intersex Day of Awareness, which was started in 2002 at the University of Montana in Missoula.

A healthy baby was born this fine afternoon . . .
To two grateful parents who lived by the lagoon.
There was a flutter of activity when they thought that the
      baby wasn't healthy at all.
Doctors were sought from all over the country . . .
To see what was wrong with this fine healthy baby.
One doctor said, "The penis is too short."
Another one said, "The clit is too long,"
So they decided to change little baby Mark into lovely Susan Long.
They sliced and they diced a vagina to make,
Who cares what Susan thinks, our reputation is at stake.
Then the Phys got into a tizzy
Teaching little Susan why she was pretty.
You're a girl; there is no doubt in that.
You can talk all you want, but a fact is a fact.
In doubt she walked,
Not being able to talk,
Hiding her pain
Just trying to be sane.
Until she found others that had what she had.
They said, "I was like you. I got real mad."
They walked and they walked
As sisters they talked.
Now he finally came out
By telling others what it is all about.

VARYING EXPERIENCES OF BEING INTERSEX

There are many ways in which people can be classified as intersex. We can't describe them all here, but knowing about some common body types that fall outside of the male–female binary can help us understand a little more about the diversity of human bodies.

Klinefelter syndrome is a variation in which an individual is born with XXY chromosomes, rather than XX or XY. Most people with Klinefelter's syndrome appear male and identify as male, and they often do not discover the presence of this condition until later in life, if ever. They may have problems with infertility or signs of decreased testosterone, such as small penises, more breast tissue, and decreased body hair or muscle mass compared to other men. As many as one in five hundred men may have Klinefelter syndrome. There are cases of people with Klinefelter identifying as transgender, but there is little evidence that rates of transgender identity are increased.

Congenital Adrenal Hyperplasia (CAH) occurs when the adrenal glands produce hormones differently due to blockages in enzyme pathways—sometimes leading to more androgen exposure than usual. In one type of CAH, people with XX chromosomes are born with genitals that look more masculine than is typical for girls. The degree of difference

The Intersex Society of North America (ISNA) is "devoted to systemic change to end shame, secrecy, and unwanted genital surgeries for people born with an anatomy that someone decided is not standard for male or female."

No Gender, No Problem. "This is a self portrait I made back in 2016 based off of a selfie of me that I feel really good about." "I'm a 23 year old nonbinary trans person living in the Delta Mississippi. I created and help run some online trans support groups that are very important to me. My focuses in life are making art, helping people, and finding ways to combine the two." (Silas Julian)

in their genitals from the typical XX person depends on the amount of androgens their adrenal glands produce in utero. A person with CAH may have a large clitoris or labia that are fused together and look more like scrotum, although they have the same internal organs as other XX people, including a uterus and ovaries. Most people born XX with CAH are raised as girls. Many researchers who study brain organization theory are interested in people with CAH and XX chromosomes (often called "CAH girls"), and there have been numerous studies of CAH girls and their interests, abilities, and play habits for the express purpose of testing whether they are more "masculine" than other girls. Although most CAH girls raised as girls grow up to identify as cisgender, a little over 5% do not identify as female—higher than the percentage of transgender people in the general population—suggesting that hormones in utero can affect later gender identity.

> *I have non-typical congenital adrenal hyperplasia. It is the central part of who I am. I identify and present as a male but that cannot exist without attention to my intersex experience. My gender identity would not exist without my intersex identity.*

When someone with XY chromosomes has androgen insensitivity syndrome (AIS), the body produces androgens, but the androgen receptors in the body's cells cannot recognize the hormones, so they cannot have an effect on the body. In partial androgen insensitivity syndrome (PAIS), the body's receptors may respond somewhat, but not completely, to androgens. People with PAIS have a wide variety of bodies and gender identities. In complete androgen insensitivity syndrome (CAIS), the body's receptors do not respond at all to androgens, and the person's body appears female on the outside, including their genitals. Babies born with CAIS are typically assigned female at birth. Girls with CAIS often do not learn of their condition until they fail to menstruate at puberty. The majority of those with CAIS identify as women.

In 5-alpha reductase deficiency (5-ARD), the body cannot convert testosterone into another androgen called dihydrotestosterone (DHT) because the enzyme that performs this conversion, 5-alpha-reductase, does not function. DHT typically masculinizes the genitals while the fetus is developing. An XY baby with 5-ARD may have mostly female-appearing genitals, and those with this variation are often raised as girls. At puberty, testosterone in the body increases, and their bodies begin to masculinize in a way similar to typical male puberty, with facial hair growth, deepening of their voices, and enlargement of their genitals. Some people with 5-ARD continue to live as women, but more than half transition to male when they go through puberty.

Androgens refer to hormones that are associated with the development of male characteristics. These include testosterone along with other hormones such as dihydrotestosterone (DHT) and androstenedione.

Enzymes are molecules that help convert one substance to another.

Sex and Gender Development

M. Killian Kinney (they/them) is a queer, nonbinary, currently able-bodied, neurodiverse atheist working to improve the well-being of gender diverse individuals through practice and research. Mx. Kinney is a doctoral candidate at Indiana University School of Social Work, a visiting scholar at the Center for Disease Control and Prevention Health Law Program, a trainer in trans-affirming health care, and has been a social worker in gender health clinics and mental health organizations.

Although the literature on transgender experiences has increased, it has often done so through a binary frame, perpetuating nonbinary erasure. When nonbinary experiences are included, a narrow representation of nonbinary identities is often presented—affluent, slender, androgynous, able-bodied, white, AFAB, youthful, and young adult. Frequently, this visibility just highlights microaggressions, discrimination, victimization, and adverse health outcomes, including suicidality, depression, and anxiety. As such, there is a dearth of research that truly understands the unique experiences of nonbinary individuals, especially how they relate to well-being.

So what if your well-being comes with a caveat? The prevailing topics in well-being theories were reviewed and critiqued, finding gaps in the understanding of marginalized populations. Expressly, an assumption of equity and the missing context of a hostile sociopolitical climate, limit their usefulness. Research shows nonbinary individuals face gender-based discrimination across personal and professional settings, much of it in part due to their gender identities and gender expressions not conforming to social norms. A new holistic well-being framework addresses adversity while drawing our attention to resilience and thriving at individual, community, and systems levels.

In response to the identified gaps in well-being theory and in nonbinary literature, I am conducting a participatory action PhotoVoice project with nonbinary individuals. The project explores their gendered experiences and well-being, centering community voices. The primary findings will include a community-created conceptualization of well-being, promotive and corrosive factors to well-being, and community recommendations for applying these findings for the benefit of nonbinary communities. I hope this will contribute to a greater understanding of the unique gendered experiences of nonbinary individuals and find ways to bolster well-being through social awareness and trans-affirming practice and policies. Ultimately, an exploration of well-being led by nonbinary community members will contribute to a shift from predominantly studying adverse outcomes toward promoting thriving.

GENETICS OF TRANS IDENTITY

There have been some early studies of specific genes that could be connected to trans identities. Some of these "candidate" genes include genes for hormones, hormone receptors, and enzymes. A few small studies have shown average differences in some of these genes between cisgender people and people who identify as trans or are diagnosed with gender dysphoria, but there is considerable overlap between the groups. Most traits of a person (sometimes referred to as "phenotypes") are complex and influenced by both our genes and our environments.

In order to determine whether genes are contributing factors to a specific outcome, researchers look at the family history of an individual. Once researchers know that genes contribute to a particular trait, they try to identify the specific genes that are associated with the outcome. Some of these studies try to compare the occurrence of certain genetic differences between a group of people with the trait and a group without the trait.

Twin studies are very good for determining whether genes contribute to an outcome (i.e., if something is heritable) because identical twins share nearly 100% of their genes, fraternal twins share 50% of their genes, and both have family environments that are likely to be similar.

I was around 21 years old when my brother came out to me as a transgender man. This revelation led me to really examine my own gender for the first time, and I realized I had no idea what gender even meant. It's taken over two years of questioning already, and while I still haven't gotten it all figured out, I've come to realize I have always had issues with gender dysphoria growing up, and my current identity of nonbinary just fits so comfortably. I can finally feel moments of gender euphoria every now and then.

If we are trying to prove that transgender identity is heritable, it is important to know the way researchers define "transgender," which can be controversial. It is often based on an individual being diagnosed with gender dysphoria and is rarely based on an individual self-identifying as transgender. The definitions of transgender used by researchers are very specific, and therefore, so are the results. Much like the search for the "gay gene" in the 1990s, results from genetic studies of transgender people have been both limited

Dr. Kylan Mattias de Vries (he/they) is a trans educator/scholar/activist in Gender, Sexuality, & Women's Studies at Southern Oregon University. Kylan co-created a Transgender Studies certificate that began Fall 2020. (Danny LeClaire)

and inconclusive. At this point, none of the genes found to be associated with being transgender or having gender dysphoria have been replicated in follow-up studies.

Future genetic studies will likely focus on epigenetics. Epigenetics are changes in gene activity that do not change our DNA but are still heritable. Scientists who study epigenetics look at the way our genes can change without the underlying structure of our DNA shifting. These changes can sometimes occur during our lifetimes, so that our genes are actually changing while we are alive. Environmental factors such as diet, stress, or nutrition often shift gene activity. At the time of this writing, there has been only one, unreplicated study[11] that suggested that endocrine system disrupters, such as the chemical insecticide DDT, could contribute to epigenetic changes associated with being transgender. Future studies on epigenetics and other areas of genetics may clarify the ways in which our unique genetic makeup plays a role in our gender identity.

Most research studies of families of trans people look exclusively at people who consider themselves transsexual or those diagnosed with gender dysphoria. The results, therefore, may not apply to all of us. Findings from family studies reveal that trans participants are more likely to have a sibling who is transgender. This association could be due to genetics, hormones, or even to the way we are raised. Identical twins may both be transgender, but there are also many identical twin pairs where one person is transgender and the other is not, suggesting there are factors other than genes that influence our gender identity.

THE BRAIN AND GENDER

Scientists who work in the field of "brain organization theory" suggest that the same hormones that influence the development of internal reproductive organs and external genitalia may also cause changes in the brain that lead people to think in certain ways about their gender as adults.

Critics of brain organization theory argue that gender is not something that can exist before birth because it is created by society. They argue that although we might have predispositions to think and behave in certain ways because of our genes or hormones, we would not feel male or female without society to tell us what male and female are.

The differences we observe in the brains of adult humans are likely caused by the complex interaction of many factors across development, including genetics, hormones, and the social environment. This is because our brains change based on the type of environments to which we are exposed.

ON BEING IN ACADEMIA AND RESEARCH

Keanan Gabriel Gottlieb (he/him) is an LGBTQ health research analyst and patient advocate in Nashville, Tennessee. His professional interests include transgender health and emergency medicine. He also enjoys scuba diving and learning to play the bagpipes.

I am a research analyst at a large academic medical center in the South. I am one of the few out trans employees at my institution and one of the most visible trans people, given that my sole focus is LGBTQ health. I am, to my knowledge, the only trans person on my research teams, which creates a sense of responsibility.

My colleagues have not asked me to be the voice for all trans people, but I still feel a responsibility to my participants and communities to be that voice. However, as a white butch trans guy with no other marginalized identities, my experiences and identities often differ dramatically from our research participants' identities and experiences. Even though I am not ultimately responsible for the study, if there is a problem with any aspect of it, I feel like I have let down my community.

I do not always know whether to come out or not to my colleagues on my team or at conferences. I am proud of being trans and am not stealth, but I tend to come out in subtle ways, and I am not interested in being a spectacle or tokenized. It is important, however, for people to know there are trans researchers who contribute to trans health research in a unique way.

There are also smaller trans health research studies that our interns and medical students conduct. I have provided feedback for many of these studies, but I am not directly involved with the research and do not receive authorship. Some of these studies, however, do not have any trans authors. I am conflicted about these circumstances because it is not possible for me to be on all of these studies, and many of them address significant gaps in the literature, but I also want to be involved with every trans health study conducted at my institution. Part of this desire is because I enjoy my work, but there should also be at least one trans person involved with every trans health study. Because I am the only out trans researcher working on trans health at my institution, this role would automatically become my responsibility.

Ultimately, it is vital for academic medical centers to hire trans researchers at every level of research, provide support for trans researchers, remember that trans people are not a monolith, give credit to trans collaborators and participants, and compensate trans participants appropriately.

THE "TRANSGENDER BRAIN"

In recent years, numerous studies have looked at differences in brain structure and function between transgender and cisgender people, with varying results; some showed possible differences and some not. There are many reasons that the brains of transgender people might be different from the brains of cisgender people. These neurobiologic differences may be caused by genetic or prenatal hormone influences. Hormone therapy also likely affects the brains of those of us who choose to transition with hormones. In addition, although many people do not realize it, stress, trauma, depression, and anxiety, all of which occur more often among transgender people than cisgender people, can also affect the structure and function of our brains. If we are to compare the brains of transgender people and cisgender people we must take these factors into account. Most studies of transgender people do not collect information about stress, trauma, or psychiatric diagnoses. The studies that do collect this information exclude transgender people who have ever been depressed. This means that the research published about the brains of transgender people does not represent the majority of us, given that rates of depression among transgender people are very high.

I grew up poor. Poor means powerless and always being under stress and afraid because there is no safety net and your basic needs are unmet. You are focused on surviving, not on thriving. You are always working and can never rest,

everything is hard and other people don't know what you go through without
simple things they take for granted, like having insurance to be able to go to
the doctor. The same is true with having an intersex body that doesn't match
your assigned gender or the gender you correct it to, you feel powerless, always
under stress, afraid, there is no safety net and your basic needs are unmet.

The first studies of transgender neurobiology were published in the 1990s. Since then, scientists have associated almost every brain region with transgender identity. Few findings have been replicated, however, and several studies show conflicting findings. Most studies of transgender people's brains have sought to understand if transgender people have brains more like cisgender people who share their gender identity or more like people who share their assigned sex.

The first studies of the "transgender brain" involved brains donated to science after people died. These studies looked at the hypothalamus, counting specific types of cells and comparing them between cisgender people and transgender women. The brains of transgender women had either similar numbers of brain cells as those of cisgender women or cell counts between cisgender women and cisgender men. However, all of the transgender women in these studies had taken estrogen before their deaths, so it is possible that this affected their brain structure. In fact, in a follow-up study, researchers found that one of the parts of the hypothalamus from these studies, the BSTc, is similar in cisgender men and women until puberty, when it is possible that hormones or other factors affect its size. And, like most studies of human brain tissue, the sample sizes in these studies are very small and we have very little information on the lives of the people who donated their brains. Therefore, any results from these studies have to be interpreted cautiously.

More recent studies involve magnetic resonance imaging (MRI), which allows us to look at the structure and function of the brain in living people. Although individual imaging studies have found differences in the size or function of parts of the brain in transgender versus cisgender people, findings are inconsistent from study to study and no differences have been replicated.

The relationships between hormone levels and the structure and function of the brain are extremely complex. Some studies look at the effects of hormones on transgender people's brains by scanning our brains before and after we begin hormone therapy. This research generally finds that the brains of transgender people on hormone therapy become more like the brains of cisgender people of the same gender identity. Some, but not all, of these studies have shown correlations between hormone levels and these brain changes. Importantly, because starting hormone therapy is also a time of social change, research should also consider social factors related to transition and how these factors might affect the brain. For example, one study looked at how transgender people's brains responded to being socially rejected.[12] The scientists found that brain regions that activate during social rejection are active longer for transgender people than for cisgender people. These studies offer a more complex look at how the experience of being transgender might relate to the brain.

> *I felt different from my peers, but it was either the result of or the cause of the*
> *ruthless bullying I experienced from kindergarten onward. It probably hindered*
> *me from understanding that I was trans, since I felt different from my peers but*
> *assumed it was from my status as a punching bag. However, as an adolescent*
> *I knew that my femininity was different than girls my age. They embodied it,*
> *thought nothing of it, chose gestures and presentation effortlessly. I dressed and*
> *performed as feminine with agonizing precision.*

Research on trans people's brains has also sought to understand experiences of gender dysphoria. Some studies have scanned the brains of transgender people while they complete tasks that trigger gender dysphoria. For example, one study focused on transgender men who experienced gender dysphoria related to their chests. Researchers compared their brain response to being touched on the chest versus being touched on the foot.[13] The researchers found that the part of the brain associated with body representation was less

Many early studies of trans people's brains focused on the hypothalamus—a part of the brain that helps to control hunger, thirst, sleep, and temperature, and secretes a number of hormones. The hypothalamus is a target of research into gender identity because there are parts of the hypothalamus that are different in cisgender men and cisgender women, and because the hypothalamus controls sexual behavior in rodents.

Nova Donnell is a proud LGBTQ+ activist based in Los Angeles, CA. She believes in using her positivity and uplifting voice to inspire dialogue that ignites change for all women. (Lewis C. Tran)

active when transgender men were touched on the chest versus on the foot; while, for cisgender people, there was no difference in response to being touched on the chest versus the foot. This difference in responsiveness of the area of the brain related to body representation could indicate a brain basis for the experience of gender dysphoria.

> I did not notice any differences or confusion about my gender growing up. Part of it is that I don't have any consistent issues with the gendered parts of my body now, and did not back then either. Most of my issues were related to my weight and fatphobia. I didn't notice how uncomfortable I could be in my body until I realized I was trans.

It is important to remember that neuroscience is nowhere near being able to identify transgender people based on the structure or function of our brains because these studies look at average differences between groups of people. If scientists were able to identify a brain difference between cisgender and transgender people on average, there would be many transgender people who would fall within the "cisgender range" and many cisgender people who would fall within the "transgender range." It is unlikely that scientists will identify a single brain region or group of regions that could be used to tell who is transgender and who is not because our brains, identities, and experiences are incredibly diverse and complex.

TRANS REPRESENTATION IN RESEARCH

Alexis Chavez, MD (she/her) is a psychiatrist for a newly created LGBTQ specialty service at the Department of Veterans Affairs and the former medical director for The Trevor Project.

Much of the research on trans people historically focused on looking for differences in brain structure, like a gender identity scavenger hunt. These researchers, inevitably, described how their research showed that trans people are either more like men or more like women. They proclaimed that trans people are valid in their affirmed gender because their brains look a particular way. Although well-intentioned, such research fails to recognize that validation of trans identity does not just come from a brain scan and not from someone else. Validation comes from an individual knowing their truth.

Another issue with this type of research is that it buys into the idea that being a (cis)man or (cis)woman are the gold standards, rather than understanding the variety of gender identity that exists in all people. Further research needs to incorporate more diversity in measuring gender identity and gender expression, especially in research that is not targeted toward trans people.

The research question should not be, "Are trans people different?" but rather, "In what meaningful ways can we improve the lives of trans people?" Some research has been moving in that direction. For example, we know that trans people are more likely to experience unemployment, homelessness, or living below the poverty line. Research has helped us understand how such discrimination against trans people directly results in increased amounts of mental health challenges such as depression, anxiety, and thoughts of suicide. Conversely, when trans people are supported in their gender identity, we see those increased risks go away.

Research can shape clinical care as well. The first NIH-funded study of trans youth was started in 2015 and is helping trans youth across the country. Further research can guide hormone prescribing in a more particular way for those who desire it, which makes more doctors feel able to do this and thus expands access to these services for many people.

Another way that research can meaningfully improve trans lives is to provide scientific evidence against unethical practices. For example, conversion "therapy" has been linked with many lasting, damaging effects on young people. As the evidence grows, more professional organizations are taking a stand against it. In turn, many states have now banned this discredited practice.

Overall, research with trans people is growing in very exciting ways. As we continue to develop broader inclusion and dimensionality of gender identity in research, it can only lead to better outcomes for all people.

GENDER DEVELOPMENT IN CHILDHOOD: PSYCHOLOGICAL MODELS

Once we are born, our social environment begins to shape our identity, through social norms and personal relationships with our parents and friends. Many researchers have studied the ways in which children develop a sense of gender, both personally and in the world around them. There are multiple theories about how this process happens. Unsurprisingly, nearly all psychological theories of gender identity development assume a cisgender identity. Such theories may or may not be applicable to transgender identity development.

COGNITIVE DEVELOPMENTAL THEORY

The cognitive developmental theory of gender identity, introduced by American psychologist Lawrence Kohlberg,[14] proposes that children's understanding of gender progresses through three stages.

Gender labeling occurs around two to three years of age, when children are building their vocabularies very quickly. During this stage, they become good at giving names to things—including gender. Children are often very insistent about using labels, even before they completely know what these labels mean.

Gender stability develops around three to five years of age when children begin to understand the notion that gender typically stays the same from childhood to adulthood (i.e., that most boys grow up to become men and most girls grow up to become women). They still do not typically understand, however, that gender usually does not change if someone's clothing, hairstyle, or activities change. For example, children this age may believe that if a man grows his hair long, he will turn into a woman.

The three stages in the cognitive developmental theory of gender identity are gender labeling, gender stability, and gender constancy.

When I was four or five years old, I knew something was wrong. Being born in the 1950s, and growing up in the 60s and 70s, there was no way to search for information that would help me to understand. As a result, I proceeded with my life, figuring that I had no choice. I was married and had children, all the while knowing what was wrong, but I could not share that knowledge with anyone.

I had a couple of nonbinary friends by the end of college that helped sort of . . . solidify the fact that I could be nonbinary, but I don't actually know what the progression was, necessarily. It was always less of an identification and more of a long, slow sigh of relief. The concept of gender euphoria was something I encountered relatively late in the game, after I was already identifying as trans and nonbinary, but that really helped solidify some of the more physical aspects of my transition and gender identity in particular, as well. And it's still changing and still malleable, and I'm not entirely sure it's ever going to stop doing that.

By about age six or seven, children develop gender constancy, and are able to see that appearances are not always the same as underlying characteristics. Kids at this age often find Halloween a lot less scary because they realize that people do not actually become monsters when they put on a Frankenstein mask!

Cognitive developmental theory demonstrates that children do not automatically understand the role of gender in society but, instead, have to be taught the rules of gender. Cognitive developmental theory explains that the process by which children learn about gender is consistent with how they learn about their world in general. How children come to understand gender depends on their individual experience and what they have learned about gender from their family, community, peers, and others.

GENDER SCHEMA THEORY

Like cognitive developmental theory, gender schema theory also focuses on the way children learn about gender as a concept. Jean Piaget, a Swiss developmental psychologist, introduced the term "schema" to describe a framework that helps us understand one specific aspect of the world.

For example, we all have a schema for a bird. We have an idea of what birds look like, what they sound like, and what they do. When we see a bird we have never seen before, our schema for birds is automatically activated and helps us understand and remember this new information about a bird that we are seeing for the first time. If the new bird is similar to our current schema for birds, we will simply assimilate the new information, leaving the schema rather unchanged. If the new bird is dramatically different (e.g., a penguin), we might accommodate the new information into our schema (i.e. include the information that "some birds do not fly") or we might leave our schema unchanged but consider penguins to be exceptions. In the face of a new example that contradicts our schema, we are much more likely to ignore the new information and maintain our schema, unchanged. Gender schema theory suggests that children learn to understand gender through this process.

Ava Ladner is a māhū wahine PhD candidate (defending Fall 2020) in the American Studies department at the University of Hawai'i whose dissertation examines southern culture and sports. She also developed and taught the first transgender studies class at the school with a focus on representation and place. (EunBin Suk)

According to gender schema theory, children develop schemas for gender that link certain behaviors and traits together under the schemas for male (or "boy") and female (or "girl.") Parents and teachers, as well as other people who spend time around children, can influence the way that these gender schemas develop. Children's schemas then, in turn, influence how they experience events and how they interact with the world. This process can have an impact on shaping future behavior, preferences, and skills.[15]

From a young age, I had feelings of curiosity about girls but witnessed the ramifications others experienced for breaking societal expectations, so everything got buried, and I became an exceptional chameleon. I spent 25 years never even asking the question of whether I was trans.

Imagine that a sister and a brother are living in an apartment with their family and are home when a repair person comes over to replace a broken cabinet door. If these children have learned over time to identify physical tasks with their schema for "male" behavior, the boy will be more likely both to pay attention to the steps that the repair person is following to replace the door and to try and tackle similar projects on his own in the future.

Of course, children must be able to identify themselves as boys or girls in order to apply their schemas to themselves. They must learn to label themselves, likely through a process similar to cognitive developmental theory. Even without yet being able to label themselves, they may still be able to start forming gender schemas.

Researchers have found that people have a much more specific and deep schema about their own group (known as the own-gender schema) compared to their schema about another gender (the other-gender schema). This schema development may be because they pay more attention to those behaviors or characteristics they see as relevant to their gender. This process is socially reinforced, but can also be self-directed. For example, it could be that, even if someone is perceived to be a boy, they might preferentially attend to the gender norms for girls if they have a female gender identity.

No one follows the "rules" of gender exactly or at all times. People vary in terms of how gender schematic they are, which is likely based on how rigidly they were taught to think about gender as children, as well as individual differences in their personality. Those who are highly gender-schematic focus strongly on the gendered nature of the people, behaviors, and characteristics of those around them. For these people, gender strongly influences the way that they see the world. Other people have much weaker gender schemas, meaning that gender is not as key a factor in the way they see the world.

I began to take on more masculine mannerisms in the way I sit, talk, and walk while also keeping airy aspects of femininity. I still wear makeup often, but I make an effort to wear it in a way I not only love, but one that is not traditionally feminine. Shaved eyebrows, hard lines, odd contouring, strange shapes. Anything that isn't exclusively feminine or masculine gives a very alien look, and that's about the closest I can come to my gender identity, because it is, it feels very alien in a heavily gendered world.

THE ONLY REASON I DON'T HAVE RAPID-ONSET GENDER DYSPHORIA: MY MOM ISN'T A RAGING TRANSPHOBE

Florence Ashley (they/them)

My favorite quote from Lisa Littman's controversial 2018 study on rapid-onset gender dysphoria (ROGD) goes: "Therefore, there is no evidence that the study sample is appreciably different in their support of the rights of transgender people than the general American population."[16]

That may be true. Is the general American population similarly hateful toward trans people as members of websites dedicated to anti-trans animosity? *4thWaveNow*—one of the three anti-trans websites where participants were recruited—is bad. So are J. Michael Bailey and Ray Blanchard. But doesn't the general public *also* believe that trans women are men with weird fetishes?

Rapid-onset gender dysphoria says that there is a large slew of psychologically vulnerable people pushed into falsely believing that they are trans by trans-positive sources and for whom social and medical transition is harmful. The study attempts to establish its existence through parental reports.

It is irrelevant whether the study sample is comparable to the general public—for three reasons. Firstly, the study primarily seeks to compare itself to past gender identity clinic samples. Those samples aren't representative of the general public on a number of metrics, most notably socioeconomic class. Secondly, reports are biased by the attitudes of participants whether or not those participants are representative of the general public. The question isn't whether they are representative but whether they are biased. And thirdly, their anti-trans attitudes can help us interpret the causal direction of various reported factors without referring to bias.

The most blatant way in which anti-trans attitudes impact interpretation of causality can be found in measures of well-being. Parents in the study reported that their children's well-being deteriorated, along with the parent-child relationship, following coming out as trans. For Littman, this is evidence that kids believing they are trans is making them worse off.

We do know, however, that parental support for gender is strongly correlated with mental well-being.[17] Trans people whose parents don't respect their gender identities fare much worse than those whose parents are respectful of their gender. When *4thWaveNow* is encouraging parents not to validate the gender identities of their teens, I expect a breakdown of the parent-child relationship. I expect their mental health to get worse. Lo and behold, this is what the study reports.

Lisa Littman's affirmations that the parents aren't singularly trans-antagonistic is a red herring. Those measurements aren't evidence of a new and dangerous "transgender trend." They're evidence of what we've known all along: *We need parental support.*

SOCIAL THEORIES OF GENDER DEVELOPMENT

Social theories of gender development focus on how we learn gender from our social interactions. A great deal of evidence shows that girls and boys are positively reinforced or rewarded (by parents, peers, teachers, and even strangers) when they engage in behavior that is considered typical for their sex (gender-typed behavior). There is also a great deal of evidence showing that girls and boys may experience negative consequences (or punishments) when they engage in behaviors that are considered typical for the other sex and not for their own sex (cross-gender-typed behavior).

Social learning theory, developed by American psychologist Albert Bandura,[18] emphasizes the importance of observation for people's learning of social behaviors. Social cognitive theory, also developed by Bandura,[19] suggests that three basic processes are important to gender development: children model the gender-related behavior of others; experience consequences for their gender-related behaviors or characteristics; and are directly taught information about gender roles.

> *I remember expressing myself very femininely as a small child because it got me praise from my family. In high school, I started dressing more neutrally, but my parents were constantly after me to dress "nicer" (read: femininely). In college, once I realized I was gay, I thought my more masculine gender expression was simply a "gay woman" thing, and once I could truly buy my own clothes, my wardrobe became much more masculine. Since then, I've realized I'm nonbinary, and that gender expression makes a lot more sense to me in retrospect.*

Conversion therapy is discouraged by the American Psychological Association, American Psychiatric Association, and American Academy of Pediatrics. It is illegal to practice conversion therapy with minors in multiple states in the United States.

Despite the fact that we learn behaviors through reinforcement and punishment, it is worth noting that reparative therapy or conversion therapy, in which a mental health practitioner uses behavioral techniques to reward and punish patients for their behaviors, is not effective in changing either sexual orientation or gender identity, and it is emotionally damaging.

It is unclear if social cognitive theory can account for transgender identity, given that many transgender people persist in an identity that is not socially reinforced. Furthermore, Bandura's theory does not distinguish among gender identity, gender role, and gender expression. For many people, cisgender and transgender, gender expression, identity, and role do not align in the socially prescribed manner. Bandura's framework also does not account for gender nonconformity or nonbinary identities.

> *It took a very long time for me to realize I was trans. As a child in the 1980s and 90s, especially growing up in West Virginia, I was largely unfamiliar with*

the LGBTQAI + community. I often wonder what things would have been like had I had an understanding of being trans, especially being nonbinary, as a teenager. Coming into contact with more trans people and learning there was more than the surgery/assimilation into straight culture path of transition really let me understand who I am. Looking back, it is very obvious that I was trans, but I didn't have the cultural context to understand myself.

More recent social theories specifically describe gender identity development for transgender people.[20] These theories acknowledge that transgender people often do not have transgender-specific models for our gender identity development. This lack of access to transgender models, coupled with the trauma of enforced social norms for gender, can mean that many transgender people suppress or hide our gender identities. Because of this, models of transgender identity development that use a staged framework often emphasize a period of confusion and turmoil, followed by a period of exploration and experimentation, culminating in a period of identity acceptance and integration. Although such models may describe the process of developing a transgender identity for many people, it is important to remember that these models do not describe transgender identity development itself, but rather, transgender identity development in a transphobic society.

Although I may have been faintly aware that I had questions about my gender identity and my sexual orientation, I buried those ideas so deeply that I wasn't aware of them. I developed the most toxic form of masculinity to stay closeted instead.

PSYCHOSOCIAL AND ENVIRONMENTAL INFLUENCES ON GENDER DEVELOPMENT

Children learn about gender from the many environments in which they participate. Families, peers, and the media impact children's gender development. Each of these groups has the potential to affect the ways that we label gender, understand gender constancy, form gender schemas, and model our behavior after others. In other words, we can apply many of the gender development theories to the environments in which we are raised.

In my day, there were no words to describe who I was, and I certainly did not see anyone like me in the media. My parents were ashamed and deeply concerned about my gender incongruence but would not explain to me what was going on. It wasn't until my late teens that I finally made contact with the community, primarily through their early community publications, and it is there that finally I could find the vocabulary to describe myself.

FAMILIAL INFLUENCES

The family is the first context of children's development, and parents' ideas about their child are influenced by the child's sex even before the child is born. Studies have asked couples that knew the sex of their fetus to view an ultrasound image and rate the characteristics of the fetus. On average, they rate female fetuses as smaller, softer, weaker, and more beautiful than male fetuses. After birth, parents perceive male infants to be bigger, stronger, and better coordinated, and female infants to be softer and more delicate.

These differences in perception can have long-term effects on how children develop. When parents believe that boy babies are tough and strong, they are more likely to be physically rough with them. Likewise, when parents believe that girl babies are delicate and emotional, they are more likely to hold them close and talk softly to them. Through these early interactions with parents, boys may get used to being handled roughly and learn to interact with others roughly, whereas girls may get used to being held closely and learn to interact with others in a gentle way.

Reed Brice is a non-binary comedian and actor.

Fortunately, research shows that in the United States most parents provide a similar amount of warmth, discipline, interaction, and encouragement of achievement to their children regardless of their sex. Sex does play a major role, however, in the types of activities that parents encourage. Parents provide different types of clothing and toys to their daughters than they do their sons, and they encourage them to participate in different activities at home and at school. Research also suggests that male parents are more likely to treat children differently based on their sex than female parents are.

By providing children with different opportunities and expectations based on their sex, parents influence their children's perception of what sorts of behaviors and activities are appropriate for girls and boys. The effects help shape individuals' attitudes and lives, as well as reinforcing larger cultural expectations and assumptions about gender.

I announced to my parents on more than one occasion that I was a boy. They assumed I wanted to imitate my older brother. This began when I was around three or four years old. Although transition wasn't something any of us were familiar with, I was allowed access to any activities I wanted. I knew at puberty that I wasn't developing how I wanted or saw myself, and I kind of disconnected from my body for years as a result.

How do parents treat children who do not conform to societal norms of gender? In a western context, parents are more accepting of daughters who do not adhere to norms of femininity than of sons who do not adhere to norms of masculinity. Particular gender nonconforming behaviors may be more or less accepted, and there are differences in tendencies of female parents versus male parents to accept gender nonconforming behaviors. Research shows that female parents often support boys' interest in domestic chores, such as cooking, and their displays of nurturance or empathy. Many female parents, however, do not support their sons' interest in feminine clothing or toys such as dolls. Male parents, as a whole, typically respond more negatively to gender nonconformity displayed by their sons than daughters, and they are particularly concerned with their sons' displays of passivity or emotion, such as crying. Of course, research only gives us averages, and there are many male parents who are extremely accepting of their sons' gender nonconforming behaviors and many female parents who are not.

PEER AND SOCIAL INFLUENCES

Elementary-aged children spend approximately 40% of their waking hours with their peers. Although the immediate family may be the primary social influence during infancy, toddlerhood, and the preschool years, some developmental researchers believe that peers have a greater impact on children than their parents once they reach school age.

Children as young as two and three years old show a preference for playing with same-sex peers, and this preference gets stronger as they move toward the school years. By the age of six, they may spend up to 10 times as much time with same-sex peers as they do with other-sex peers. There are probably many reasons that this segregation takes place, and much of it may have to do with social learning and modeling, which can not only shape our ideas about ourselves, but also about whom we are supposed to spend time with.

> I have always felt different from my peers. I participated in activities like dance, sewing, and cooking that were often seen as cross-gender play. I had difficulty connecting with other boys and often connected with those who also didn't easily fit binary assumptions of gender. Girls often excluded me because of their perceptions of me as a boy, but I felt safe and comfortable with girls who included me.

Segregation by gender is strongest during the early elementary school years and declines as children move toward adolescence. Some researchers argue that girls' and boys' peer groups are so different that they really represent two distinct cultures.[21] Other researchers, however, believe that the two-cultures idea overlooks the many similarities between girls' and boys' peer groups. Regardless, studies indicate that girls and boys do, on average, engage in different types of activities, have different styles of play, and have peer groups of different sizes and with different leadership styles. Boys, more than girls, tend to enforce these groupings by gender, and they are more likely not to allow girls to enter their groups than vice versa. In elementary school, both boys and girls tease their peers about contact with those outside of their gender group.

What happens when a child does not want to play with the children that everyone expects them to be playing with? Or, what if children prefer to play the games that children of the other sex typically play? Children can be cruel to those who are different, and intolerant of children who do not conform to expected gender roles. Research generally shows that peers, like parents, tend to respond more negatively to boys who do not conform to norms of masculinity than to girls who do not conform to norms of femininity. Children respond most negatively to boys' violations of gender norms when they relate to appearance—boys are judged harshly for having clothing or hairstyles that are perceived as feminine. This treatment of boys is likely because masculinity is a more valued trait in our society than femininity, so boys who enjoy feminine activities or display feminine behavior are more stigmatized.

I WAS BORN THIS WAY

Ms. Phoebe Renee Halliwell is a transgender advocate and activist in prison in Oklahoma. She writes to us with the assistance of the Sylvia Rivera Law Project's Prisoner Justice Project.

I am a trans woman, and no qualifications should be placed on the term "trans woman" based on a person's ability to "pass" as female, her hormone levels, or the state of her genitals—after all, it is downright sexist to reduce any woman (trans or otherwise) to her body parts or to require her to live up to certain societal ideals regarding appearance. What really gets under my skin is when someone tells me that if I have a penis still that makes me a man. Let me tell you what I tell them, "It takes a lot more than having a penis to make you a man, and I don't have a penis, I have a 9-and-a-half inch clit." They usually leave me alone after that.

Whatever you do, never let anyone tell you that being transgender is wrong, against the Bible, or that we are an abomination or blasphemy against God. The truth is that God does not make mistakes, so since we were born this way, it cannot be an abomination or blasphemy against God. However, because of the Christians' hatred toward my being a natural born transsexual female, I left Christianity, and now I'm an Elder in the Wicca Religion. I am now truly happy with my religion.

When you come out to your friends and family, if they leave you or disown you, then you deserve better, and they never loved you to begin with. You see, I was born in the body of a boy, but I have the brain of a female. Since I was two years old, I told my mother to quit buying me boy clothes and boy toys. My mother thought it was just a phase. In kindergarten, when the teacher said, "boys line up here and girls line up there," I got in line with the girls. The teacher said, "No, you belong with the boys." I just told her "there must've been some mistake because I'm a girl." I ended up getting kicked out of kindergarten—having to repeat it the next year because I got in trouble for using the little girl's room.

Keep your heads up and stay strong. Don't be afraid of who you are, because each and every one of you are very beautiful people, and being trans does not change anything. So listen to me, ladies, stand proud to be a trans female—as some say it is the best of both worlds.

CONCLUSION

There is a great deal of variation in our bodies and identities, and social influences determine what our bodies mean to us and to others. How we are perceived and how we identify may not match, and our identities may not align with our anatomy in the expected ways.

We do not have to divide the world according to whether we have certain types of genitals. On the other hand, we may miss important information if we assume that gender is completely social. Our genetic makeup and the hormones that we are exposed to as fetuses have the potential to affect our gender identities. Though gender is thought of as a social concept, there is some evidence that biological components may contribute to our gender identities.

As trans people, we have a wide range of experiences and thoughts related to how our gender identities develop. We often disagree about the relative influences of biology and culture. Some of us spend a considerable amount of time thinking about these issues, while others of us find them less important to our sense of who we are. There is no one right way to understand the many influences on our gender identities. In addition, no matter how far science advances toward isolating influential factors, we will always be a community rooted in our own experiences—and no one will be able to tell us who we are except ourselves.

I think coming to identify as trans was really about me feeling like I was allowed to want things. I was allowed to want my body to be different, want my life to be different. Wanting something is a good enough reason, and that was a hard realization to come to.

NOTES

1. Diamond, M. (2006). Biased-interaction theory of psychosexual development: "How does one know if one is male or female?" *Sex Roles, 55*(9), 589–600.
2. Veale, J. F., Lomax, T. C., & Clarke, D. E. (2010). The identity-defence model of gender-variance development. *International Journal of Transgenderism, 12*, 125–138.
3. Butler, J. (1990). *Gender trouble: Feminism and the subversion of identity*. New York: Routledge.
4. Bauer, G. R., Hammond, B. A., Travers, R., Kaay, M., Hohenadel, K. M., & Boyce, M. (2009). "I don't think this is theoretical; this is our lives": How erasure impacts health care for transgender people. *Journal of the Association of Nurses in AIDS Care, 20*(5), 348–361.
5. Bettcher, T. M. (2014). Trapped in the wrong theory: Rethinking trans oppression and resistance. *Signs: Journal of Women and Culture in Society, 39*(2), 383–406.
6. Levay, S. (1996). *Queer science: The use and abuse of research into homosexuality*. Cambridge: MIT Press.
7. Altemeyer, B. (2008). Changes in attitudes towards homosexuals. *Journal of Homosexuality, 42*(2), 63–75.

8. Herek, G. M. (2008). Beyond "homophobia": A social psychological perspective on attitudes towards lesbians and gay men. *Journal of Homosexuality, 10*(1–2), 1–21.

9. Feder, E. K. (2014). *Making sense of intersex: Changing ethical perspectives in biomedicine.* Bloomington: Indiana University Press.

10. Intersex Society of North America. (1993). Intersex Society of North America. https://isna.org/.

11. Dorner, G., Gotz, F., Rohde, W., Plagemann, A., Lindner, R., Peters, H., & Ghanaati, Z. (2001). INVITED NEL REVIEWS: Genetic and Epigenetic Effects on Sexual Brain Organization Mediated by Sex Hormones. *Neuroendocrinology Letters, 22*(6), 403–409.

12. Mueller, S. C., Wierckx, K., Boccadoro, S., & T'Sjoen, G. (2017). Neural correlates of ostracism in transgender persons living according to their gender identity: A potential risk marker for psychopathology? *Psychological Medicine, 48*(14), 2313–2320.

13. Case, L. K., Brang, D., Landazuri, R., Viswanathan, P., & Ramachandran, V. S. (2017). Altered white matter and sensory response to bodily sensation in female-to-male transgender individuals. *Archives of Sexual Behavior, 46*(1), 1223–1237.

14. Kohlberg, L. (1966). A cognitive-developmental analysis of children's sex-role concepts and attitudes. In E. E. Maccody (Ed.), *The development of sex differences* (pp. 82–173). Stanford, CA: Stanford University Press.

15. Bem, S. (1981). Gender schema theory: A cognitive account of sex typing. *Psychological Review, 88*(1), 354–364.

16. Littman, L. (2018). Parent reports of adolescents and young adults perceived to show signs of a rapid onset of gender dysphoria. *PLoS One, 13*(8), e0202330.

17. Simons, L., Schrager, S. M., Clark, L. F., Belzer, M., & Olson, J. (2013). Parental support and mental health among transgender adolescents. *Journal of Adolescent Health, 53*(6), 791–793. https:// doi.org/10.1016/j.jadohealth.2013.07.019

18. Bandura, A. (1977). *Social learning theory.* Englewood Cliffs, NJ: Prentice Hall.

19. Bandura, A. (2001). Social cognitive theory: An agentic perspective. *Annual Review of Psychology, 52*, 1–26.

20. Levitt, H. M., & Ippolito, M. R. (2014). Being transgender: The experience of transgender identity development. *Journal of Homosexuality, 61*(12), 1727–1758.

21. Maccoby, E. E. (1999). *The two sexes: Growing up apart, coming together.* Cambridge, MA: Belknap Press.

SECTION 2
LIVING AS OURSELVES

COMING OUT
Reid Vanderburgh

7

Coming out is one term used to describe the process of acknowledging our authentic selves, whether in terms of our gender or other aspects of our identities. Coming out can mean acknowledging something to ourselves as well as to others. This may not be a one-time process; there are always new people to whom we may choose to come out, and we may continue to discover new layers within ourselves to explore and embrace. For those of us who are transgender or gender expansive (T/GE), coming out refers to acknowledging to ourselves and to others our experience of gender. There is no consensus on terminology; those of us who don't identify as part of the gender binary may feel pressured to use terms that describe who we are *not* because there isn't yet language to accurately express who we *are*. Gender nonconforming, gender creative, and genderqueer are some terms that describe a gender identity outside the binary, and there are many more. Throughout this chapter, we will use the terms "trans" "gender expansive," and "nonbinary" to encapsulate many trans experiences, though these may not apply to everyone.

The term "coming out" has been widely used by white gay culture for over 50 years, and its usage has spread to other communities within the LGBTQ + acronym. There is no singular coming out experience, however, and many of us hold various intersecting identities that add complexity or altogether subvert the predominant "coming out" narrative. Some of these intersectional identities include race, class, religion, disability status, and neurodiversity, to name a few. The various identities some of us hold present us with our own unique path when it comes to sharing our experience of gender with those in our lives. For instance, some may experience a dilemma of feeling it would be okay with one of their communities to consider some form of transition, but not with a different community to which they belong. How each of us decides to navigate "coming out" within our other identities and communities is entirely our own to create in whatever way works best for us.

When we announce our true gender and it differs from the expectations and assumptions of others, this changes the nature of all our relationships. And we may want it to! If we ask people to change what pronouns they use for us—for instance, from "he" to "she" or "she" to "they"—this may also be accompanied by a change in social boundary between us. This may include how close we stand to people, how free we are to touch others, or the subjects of our conversations. There is a component of gender assessment in all of these boundaries. This autopilot process—these boundaries—are the kinds of things we begin learning when we're first meeting other children outside our family. We learn these things so young that we aren't aware that we are learning a cultural gender system—and these systems can differ depending on the culture(s) within which we are raised.

Gender boundaries we've learned within our particular culture and upbringing become apparent to those of us who change our gender presentation. It is a midtransition issue to learn the new social boundaries, as we begin meeting people who never knew us before our transition and don't know we are trans when we first meet them. Although we may want that change in social boundary, it can also lead to a sense of loss. We may have to let go of the relationship we used to have and develop a new one with a different social boundary. Some of the people in our lives may feel awkward and confused, not quite knowing what the rules of engagement are any longer.

Growing up as we do in a world that does not readily honor and respect trans and gender expansive identities, it can be challenging to see anything to celebrate in our coming out. Some are lucky enough to come of age in communities that embrace T/GE identities

Justin Vivian, 54, New York, NY, 2017. (Jess T. Dugan). From "To Survive on This Shore: Photographs and Interviews with Transgender and Gender Nonconforming Older Adults," a project by Jess T. Dugan and Vanessa Fabbre.

as something to celebrate (some indigenous cultures, for instance), but most of us don't grow up with a positive vision of T/GE identity. However, living as our authentic selves, whatever that might mean for each of us, *is* something to celebrate.

> *Since coming out I have made many more friends. It was like a weight lifted off of my shoulders. For the first time in my life I felt authentic and real.*

TRANSITIONING IN THE PULPIT

Reverend Debra Hopkins (she/her) is the founding pastor of Essentials for Life Ministries, a nondenominational ministry that focuses on spiritual renewal and wholeness in a fragmented world. Debra serves as founding director of There's Still Hope, a nonprofit transitional housing program for Transgender adults. Pastor Hopkins is also the proud parent of three adult children and eight beautiful grandchildren.

I transitioned in the pulpit while I was pastoring my first church back in 1991. I shared my decision to come out with the chairman of my deacon board. He suggested that I speak to the offices of the church, and they suggested I share this information with the congregation. I sat for hours writing a painstaking eight-page letter with photos and books that would help provide some clarity and understanding.

I was so afraid—afraid of the unknown! As a child of the Creator, however, I knew I had nothing to fear because the scriptures tell me that I'm created in God's image and likeness. Scriptures go on to say that I'm beautifully and wonderfully made. The God I serve is a God of Love!

When it came time to address my church congregation, what started out as a simple 90-minute business meeting turned into a six-and-a-half-hour affair. I explained in detail what I was in the process of doing, and I answered every question. Finally, as a very long afternoon turned into evening, the congregation that remained said, "Pastor we don't fully understand everything that you're doing but we love you, and we love what you have done for us as our pastor and we support you!" Within months, I got the same response from my oldest sister, my wife, and one of my children.

Changes like this, while liberating, are not always easy. This journey has brought me a lot of happiness, but I'm not saying life has been easy, because it has not. Transitioning has cost me some friends and most of my family. I also endured three suicide attempts, each worse than the one before. I have been followed by people, cat called on the streets, and sexually assaulted during a brief time in jail for a crime I did not commit.

People often ask why would I make this choice to transition? My answer: "It isn't a choice; it's a matter of life or death." I still make the choice to live instead of taking my own life. Why would someone choose a life that puts their life at risk even more? Why would someone choose to live in fear that they might be brutally beaten up or murdered? I would rather live my life as authentically as possible than go on living as something I'm not.

Since coming out, I have been received warmly throughout my work in ministry. I'm respected and treated with the utmost dignity and respect anyone could ask for. Now that's not to say that there haven't been moments of anger, hatred, bigotry, or discrimination, but I've learned through the grace of God to rise above the evil that's ever-present in this world and show humankind what God really looks like if we would allow the presence of a spirit to dwell among us.

As a transgender woman, I'm often reminded to be my authentic self and to understand that we are gifted, beautiful people. We have been in the mist since the beginning of time.

COMING OUT IS A PROCESS

Our first coming-out process begins with coming out to ourselves. Once we've realized who we are, then we face the question of how to tell others. We might feel our place in our family and among our friends is at risk if we come out. If we share a marginalized identity with family or friends, we might feel we will lose that "we're all in this together" support if we tell them who we are. Those of us who aren't white may have felt it was possible we would not receive support for our trans or nonbinary identity from within our particular community of color. We may feel "between communities," with our trans or nonbinary identity not accepted by our family and our identity as a person of color setting us apart among white people with whom we share a trans or nonbinary identity.

Our friends and family members have their own coming-out processes to navigate. For instance, others may ask them about changes in our gender presentation. Transition often involves dramatic changes in the way we present ourselves to the world; changing our presentation of this most deeply personal identity is not typically a process that can be undertaken completely privately, though we might wish for privacy.

There are various arenas in which we come out, each with its own considerations and implications; taken as a whole, coming out may feel overwhelming. Coming out at work may have financial implications. Will we lose our job? Will we be able to find work at all? Our religious community may be as important in our lives as the family that raised us. Part of the point of religion is to present one's whole true self to a higher power. Will we be faced with the dilemma of hiding our true selves at the expense of participation in our religious community? If we change our social presentation of gender, how will this affect our friendships? We may lose all, a few, or none of our friends, and yet we are still starting over in some ways with each friendship and creating new social boundaries based on gender. In some aspects, we may *want* our friendships to change this profoundly, as this means our friends are changing their perception of our gender in line with our own perception. And at the same time, that's a lot of change to go through all at once, and it may be accompanied by a sense of loss or closeness.

Coming out can be proactive—telling others as we begin our process, on our own timeline. It can also be reactive—answering questions raised by new behaviors, a new appearance, or information shared unexpectedly by someone who already knows. For many T/GE individuals, coming out is some combination of all these experiences.

Aaron Devor, a Canadian sociologist and trans man, proposes a 14-stage model of trans identity formation (*Journal of Gay and Lesbian Psychotherapy*, 2004, 8, 41–67).

THE FIRST COMING OUT: TO OURSELVES

Most of us grow up without trans role models and with little experience of other trans people. Many of us begin our process by questioning our own interpretation of ourselves. "Is this what it feels like to be trans?" or "Am I nonbinary?"

The model that was out there was that trans people feel that they are trapped in the wrong body and have always known they were actually a different gender. I didn't fit that model and I didn't know anyone who identified as neither man nor woman, both butch and femme. I was afraid of being judged for claiming a label

Untitled. (Chucha Marquez)

that wasn't mine to claim; I was afraid of appropriating a culture that wasn't mine: trans culture. It took years to feel confident in my gender and in my ability to name it and claim the labels that felt right. It took meeting other people with fluid genders and being seen and validated by close friends and lovers.

Some of us have known who we truly are since childhood, or perhaps we always knew there was something different about ourselves but did not understand why. Some of us never realized anything felt different until adulthood.

On the first day of kindergarten, our class went out to the playground and the teachers told the boys to go over here and the girls over there. I dutifully went with the girls. There was much giggling. The teacher tried to gently correct me, but I insisted I was a girl and refused to go with the boys. This led to a lot of trouble; finally I ran off by myself rather than go with the boys.

These days, there are more mainstream depictions of T/GE people in movies and on television. Although this may enable some of us to recognize our identity earlier than we might have otherwise, it might also make us feel we shouldn't do anything about it if our family members or friends mock the character, having no idea what effect such a reaction has on us. Such an experience might actually set us back in our process, reinforcing feelings of shame, rather than helping us by giving us a role model.

Particularly those of us who are white may have felt a great pressure to conform and fit into mainstream gender norms as a young person—to "act like a lady" or to not be a "sissy." As a result, some of us worked very hard to adopt the gender role expected of us. Others of us may have felt particularly vulnerable also being part of another marginalized community. We may have feared that facing our true selves would make ours and our family's lives overly difficult because we would be confronting multiple forms of oppression. We may have felt obligated to continue in the gender assigned to us at birth, supporting others at the expense of ourselves.

Mai-Chin, a friend of this chapter's author, is a 32-year-old trans man originally from Korea. He chose his name because it means "persists to the end." He laughs when he considers his birth name, Jeong. "Even if it wasn't a girl's name, how could I keep using a name that means 'silent and chaste?' Silent no more is a goal of mine, as much as I can." Mai-Chin has lived in the United States for 11 years, moving to Boston to pursue a master's degree in computer engineering. He remained in the United States on a work visa and has a high-paying job in the tech industry. He lives frugally, sending half his income back to his family in Korea. Though he identifies as a trans man, and has always known he would be happier if he could transition, he has chosen not to pursue any physical form of transition, or legal changes to his documentation. As he put it, "My family has no idea of trans anything. This would upset the older generation so much, and it's not my place to do that. I'll pursue transition once the last of that generation has died." Within his culture, choosing self-actualization at the expense of family harmony would be considered selfish and immature. He has taken transition as far as he can, asking his U.S. friends to use "he" and "him" pronouns, and introducing himself to others by his chosen name. "I'm stuck in the middle—my friends don't understand why I don't take hormones if I'm really trans, and my family doesn't understand why my hair is so short."

For some of us, recognizing our T/GE identity catches us by surprise. Perhaps some incident or reference to trans or nonbinary identity comes our way at just the right time, or with just the right language, and we have a sudden deep feeling of identification, resulting in an "Aha!" moment. Some of us adopted the defense of denial, repressing our identity at a young age so we no longer knew who we were. Human beings are the only species capable of lying to ourselves, a talent that gets us through childhood. As we mature, however, denial becomes less adaptive and eventually holds us back. How can we be in true relationships with others if we aren't in a true relationship with ourselves? At some point, we may find our denial lifts and everything in our previous life seems to make sense in a new way.

No matter when or how we begin to recognize ourselves as T/GE, coming out is not a static process. Our understanding of ourselves is always changing and maturing. Coming out does not mean we are committing irrevocably to a specific process. Some of us desire a social transition path that does not involve physical body modification. Some of us would like to undertake medical or surgical procedures that affirm our gender identity. Some of us don't undertake any changes to our daily lives or appearance, because of existing relationships, economic barriers, or other factors.

The self-discovery of my gender was basically the same as that of my sexuality.
I started out with the assumption that I matched the "norm" simply because it

Preston, 52, East Haven, CT, 2016. (Jess T. Dugan). From "To Survive on This Shore: Photographs and Interviews with Transgender and Gender Nonconforming Older Adults," a project by Jess T. Dugan and Vanessa Fabbre.

was the "norm." When I discovered there were other options, I began to try on labels as I discovered them, each more accurate than the last.

CenterLink hosts a directory of LGBTQ centers around the country, many of which have trans support groups.

Some of us come out as nonbinary and later decide that a physical transition toward living as men or women is right for us. Conversely, some of us start down the path of physical transition toward "woman" or "man," thinking that is "the way" to transition, only to discover we feel more comfortable with a nonbinary identity. Some of us realize "he" or "she" is a good fit for us, but are still what others might call nonbinary; our version of "he" or "she" doesn't exactly fit gender norms as many people see them. There is no one-size-fits-all path of transition; the only thing we have in common is that we are calling into question the gender assigned to us at birth. Each of us answers that question differently. There is no right or wrong—transition is a matter of each of us figuring out our own right path.

I was a big butch dykey Carhartt-wearing, Indigo Girls-listening, Subaru-driving lesbian before transitioning. I never really transitioned into being a dyke. I just always was one. I never remember being attracted to men or being girly at all. I came bursting out of the womb wearing rainbow suspenders while Melissa Etheridge played "Come to My Window" in the background. Interestingly, I have turned into a very feminine boy. I am much more girly now than I ever was when I was female bodied. I am also attracted to men now. Go figure.

SUPPORT SYSTEMS

Online Resources

There is a comforting anonymity to the Internet, allowing us to explore when we might not feel ready to talk to anyone in person about who we are. We are able to find information about the practicalities of T/GE identities: hormones, surgeries, how to change our name in the state we live in, and so on. The Internet can also connect us to online communities where we can learn from others' experiences, folks who have gone before us. Other people's stories can help us clarify for ourselves how we conceptualize our identities, which in turn helps us develop the language we use to come out to the people in our lives.

As we connect online, we may encounter others who put forth a "one-size-fits-all" path, as if there is only one right way and only one correct next step. We may find such folks criticizing our decisions, or our interpretation of our identity. When we are figuring out who we are, questioning our past and uncertain of our future, we may be vulnerable to this kind of feedback; we may find ourselves second-guessing our own conclusions and tentative decisions. Keep this firmly in mind: your experience is unique, and what works for someone else might not be the right fit for you.

We sometimes find ourselves scared backward by others' stories of negative reactions and dangers they have faced. It may help to remember that people are much more inclined to share bad things that have happened, and may not think to share the smile of encouragement they received from a casual acquaintance. As you move forward, it's worth keeping in mind that you might want to share the positive things that come your way from friends, people you work with, and family members.

Face-to-Face Support Groups

There is power in sharing within a support group setting, with people who will nod their heads in recognition of your experience, going through similar experiences themselves. Support groups can remind us that we are not alone. There are two types of support groups: peer-led and therapist-moderated.

Peer support groups comprise exclusively T/GE people, with a facilitator who is themselves T/GE. Such groups tend to focus on the real-world aspects of coming out and transitioning. Groups of this sort are most valuable to those early in their process. Most of the issues brought up are those of early transition (whether physical or not), such as how to deal with legal name changes. The power of this support system is such that even many years into transition, folks who participated in this kind of group may look back on their fellow group members with a special fondness, perhaps referring to them as "litter mates."

Self Portrait. "An illustration of the artist's struggle to express his identities in a world where his self expression is often deemed to be an abomination." "Cris Wolf, FtM, is involuntarily committed to the California Department of State Hospitals' system. He faces an on-going struggle to open a dialog and educate his care providers about self-identity in general and specifically. He confronts and pushes against stigma toward his diagnoses of gender dysphoria and Dissociative Identity Disorder daily. He is striving to be safer and healthier than before. After 11 years of legal, medical and mental health advocacy by and for him, he has finally been granted access and is preparing for gender confirmation surgery."

Therapist-moderated groups are often more focused on the emotional aspects of coming out and transition, such as how our families are reacting, how we are coping with the day-to-day stresses of living as our authentic selves, and what we are noticing about our relationships and identities. These groups often go deeper into emotional content than peer-led groups. Therapist-moderated groups may also be scheduled for specific eight- to ten-week periods, while peer support groups are generally ongoing.

Peer support groups tend to have a turnover rate. If you attend a group after an absence of a few years, the group will be composed of different people. Even the facilitator may have changed. Because these groups tend to deal primarily with early issues of coming out and transition, the need to attend generally lessens as each person moves on in their transition and other issues come to the forefront. Thus, the people attending are usually earlier in their coming out process, and the issues brought up typically remain those of early transition. Therapist-moderated groups may be focused on specific issues, such as invisibility and isolation—more of a midtransition than early-transition issue. Each type of group can be beneficial, but with a slightly different focus.

If you are more introvert than extrovert, you may find online support feels more helpful to you than a face-to-face support group. It is important to remember that what you're building is *your* support system, and that what works for someone else might not be the right fit for you. If you feel supported, then you have found what works for you.

Psychology Today is not only for finding individual therapists. Try choosing the "support group" category and "transgender," then entering your zip code. Be aware that websites like this may not be vetted, but they can be a starting place for research.

Difficulties Finding Support

In some places and situations, it may be hard to find a face-to-face support system. Small towns may have limited or no options for face-to-face support, or there may be privacy concerns. Some of us like living in small towns, or in rural settings, and don't want to move to a city, despite the lack of access to face-to-face support. The Internet is a godsend to those of us in this situation who have regular access to it. Some of us who want in-person experiences explore the resources available in the city closest to us and then make arrangements to visit that city once in a while. Perhaps we pool resources with others we find online who live in our area. These days, there are various trans-specific conferences; many offer scholarships for those who can't easily afford to attend. If you have connected well with others online, conferences may be a way you can arrange to meet in person.

COMING OUT TO OTHERS

For some of us, unsafe home situations, job loss, loss of family security, and loss of housing are realistic possibilities as we begin telling those around us who we are. For others, our primary fears are rooted in shame or guilt. Prior to coming out to anyone, many of us live in fear of others' reactions. As we begin telling people our stories, however, we often find the result is not as dreadful as we feared.

> *Coming out was extremely frightening until I said it, and then it was extremely relieving.*

It is hard to start these conversations, yet coming out to others can be an important step in taking our lives in new directions. If we choose to live our lives full-time in a new gender, it is inevitable that the people we know will find out, whether we have talked about it or not. Coming out to others can allow us to eventually live more full and complete lives as we progress with our transition process. When we are living the life we have chosen, we will often be happier—and that can benefit everyone in our lives.

> *It doesn't matter as much what others think about me when I come out to them. They will either accept me, or they will not. I have faced the fear of losing everything and I now know that not all will be lost. The fear of the unknown decreases the more I speak my own truth.*

For those of us with nonbinary identities, it may be especially difficult to explain how we see ourselves. For many of our friends and family, nonbinary identities exist far outside their realm of experience and worldview, which is rooted in a predominantly binary "male or female" framework of understanding gender. Their initial reaction may involve an additional challenge because they are not just changing their assumptions and perceptions about our gender, but they may also be confronted with confusion as to how to understand a gender that is not simply male or female. Our task of coming out is made even more difficult by the limitations of language, where we may feel forced to use terms such as "nonbinary" to describe our identity, which isn't a positive, proactive word, but a negative, "this is who I'm not" term. Some may prefer to use other terms to describe themselves,

The Knights and Orchids (TKO) Society "strives to build the power of the TLGB community for African Americans throughout rural areas in Alabama and across the south."

Untitled. (Chucha Marquez)

Living As Ourselves

such as "gender expansive," "genderqueer," "agender," or many more terms that exist or have yet to be created. Language limitations may present additional challenges for those of us trying to describe ourselves to family members or friends who speak languages other than English, as the element of translation may present additional complexity and challenge. Or, in some cases, the lack of a precise language translation may actually be beneficial, allowing for a more nuanced expression of our gender that does not depend on the limited number of available English words.

THE SPACE BETWEEN

justin demeter (he/him) is an Oakland, California-based, queer insomniac and hopeful romantic who dabbles in painting and poetry when he's not too busy climbing walls.

When you asked what I'm living as now, you had only two options in mind—and it was clear that unicorn wasn't one of them. if I could choose inanimate object right now, I would. if I could hold a needle in my callused right hand, my lover's hand in my left, and know that only magic would come of it, of course I would. when you asked if it's their privilege I'm after, and I respond by puncturing fingernails through my inner thigh, I have not acquiesced to your politics.

Instead I have bound in another layer of shame for you, beneath fabric, glands, and tissue.

I have left this body in the waiting room, on the sidewalk, in the back seat, and in the bedroom, so many times for you. when you give a face of faux recognition, and I heartbeat a smile, I would still choose the space between, every time, even if that renders me invisible to you—I would still choose our luminous, self-made bodies, over the broken binary system that you so rigidly cling to.

What to Expect

The way that we frame our coming-out process to others will affect the way they see it. If we have expectations of loss or rejection, this may become a self-fulfilling prophecy. On the other hand, if we approach coming out as a positive change in our lives, our families and friends may follow our lead. Those who had an initial negative reaction may become more accepting over time, though some may not. We may eventually conclude we have to let go if repeated reactions continue to be negative.

There is a spectrum of possible reactions to our revelation:

Negative attitudes				**The gray area**		**Positive attitudes**	
Hostility	*Anger*	*Denial*	*Resignation*	*Tolerance*	*Acceptance*	*Support*	*Congratulations*

Negative attitudes of hostility, anger, denial, and resignation are easily recognized; these are the attitudes most of us expect when we come out to others and thus we spot them easily. Tolerance is more insidious; it is negativity cloaked in a seemingly positive response: "I am a tolerant person." How positive is that, to feel someone is remaining part of your life in spite of who you are, rather than because of who you are? You are being tolerated. Acceptance may carry the subtext: "I accept this new identity of yours, isn't that big of me, and aren't you proud of me?" There is an undercurrent of distaste in tolerance and an undercurrent of condescension in acceptance. It might seem counterintuitive, but acceptance is the bridge between negative and positive. Sometimes we feel well-supported when someone says, "I accept you." Other times we might feel let down. Our reaction can sometimes determine whether a seemingly accepting response is positive or negative.

Unfortunately, we rarely encounter the congratulatory response: "That's great! Good for you! Congratulations!" The closer we are to someone, the longer they've known us in our birth-assigned gender, the less likely we will hear this as a first response. Our friends and family members have their own process to go through, involving some component of loss and grief. We need to allow them space to have this experience; if they don't let go of the old, how can we expect them to embrace who we are becoming? Though our friends and family need to go through this letting-go process, it's still hard to witness them grieving what we may be moving away from as fast as we can.

You may feel your friends and family aren't supportive of you if they are crying or hostile or otherwise resisting your transition. Give them time to go through their letting-go process. Fortunately, most of us do not lose our entire family, but many of us do lose a few people as we move forward into living as our authentic selves. It is hard to let go, but if we have a friend or family member who refuses to transition with us, who continues over time to use an inappropriate pronoun or name, or is hostile every time they use our new name or pronoun, we may feel we have to back away from the relationship. It is possible, however, to do so in such a way that the door is open if they have a change of heart down the road. It may be that at some point, perhaps with the help of more supportive friends or family members, they come around.

In these cases, it is all too easy to take a self-righteous stance of being hurt by their lack of support and to lash out at them in anger. It is harder, but in the long run often better for our psyche, if we can step back and see that they are reacting from their own socialization of gender as fixed reality. Holding a place of sympathy for their plight may help us keep the door open for a future relationship while creating a self-protective boundary for the present. We can track their progress through other friends or family members.

Telling people I was male was like telling them that there is no such thing as gravity: My experience is that people generally take gender to be immutable.

Friends and family interested in becoming allies to trans communities may want to check out the *Trans Allyship Workbook: Building Skills to Support Trans People in Our Lives* (written by Davey Shlasko and illustrated by Kai Hofius, Think Again Training, 2017.)

Onyx Star, 32, Los Angeles. Staff attorney, Public Counsel. (They, them, theirs). "There are so many words going around now. Genderqueer is something that I also identify with, but nonbinary trans feels the most authentic... I've always been gender nonconforming. For me, it was always about 'woman' being not what society said it was. I feel like my identity was more political because it was wrapped up in fighting against stereotypes... Society has now seen binary trans folk. When there's representation like that, your brain makes space for that. For me, moving through this world, I am always feeling like a fraud. Like, am I queer enough? Am I trans enough? Can I even use that label for myself? No matter where I go, I'm going to have to do a lot of work to prepare people to be more inclusive." (Zackary Drucker)

No matter how we identify, it is not easy to talk about feelings we may have felt we had to hide for years. It takes practice. Some people we tell may have a lot of resistance to the idea and may continue to use our old name and pronoun. Alternatively, they may be a bit too enthusiastic and start telling others before we are ready for our whole world to know who we are.

> *I found out when I came out that some people who said they would be with me through my coming out and early transition quickly left me. I experienced that some of the people who I suspected would disapprove, shunned me. I also had people who I barely knew at work and such come up to me and say things like, "I know we haven't been friends, but I just wanted to let you know that my brother is gay," or they'd say, "my daughter is bisexual, and you can come talk to me anytime you want."*

If you can stay centered in knowing the truth of your identity, you can approach most situations with grace and courage, allowing others the space to acknowledge the enormity of your journey and honor you for it. Certainly, there will be times when you will be met with hostility or derision rather than honor, but this is the time to remember how sad it is for some people that they feel that way.

CATCHING UP WITH A FRIEND YOU HAVE YET TO COME OUT TO

Zoë Johnson (they/them) is a complicated thing, being queer, nonbinary trans, neurodivergent, indigenous, and generally an overly earnest human being. For them, writing is as much trying to make the world see there are people like them out here as it is kind of pleading into the void for someone to tell them they're not the only one to have ever felt or existed in the ways they have.

You're sitting cross-legged on the floor and he says, "And that's all well and good but, I mean, I just think that 'they' as a pronoun sounds unnatural."

I actually meant to tell you . . . The words: *-that I just started using "they" pronouns myself* crumble—ash from the tip of a burning cigarette—and you close your lips around the hopeful wreckage.

You manage a weak, "Oh."

"Like just pick 'he' or 'she,' " he continues, because your downturned face and mouthful of cinders are apparently smaller and more hidden than it feels like from your end. "Why do they have to make it so hard on people, you know?"

They. You want to snatch the pronoun from the air, to hold onto it, to feel its solidity press back against your palm as you curl your fingers around it, to squeeze hard and have its ridges marked into your skin.

You want to press the word down across the seam of his lips like a piece of tape.

He lets out an exaggerated sigh as you play with a loose thread on your sweater. You keep pulling and pulling and it unravels around the hem as he laughs. You wrap the thread around your hand in loops and keep pulling, twisting your arm around to your back to keep unspooling your sweater from the bottom up.

"Anyway, what have you been up to?" he asks, light and unbothered and comfortable and not making it hard on people, you know?

You continue your unwinding and rewinding until the coils of the thread bite into your hand, slicing across the soft skin of your palm and fingers.

"Oh, not much," you say as you feel your fingertips starting to lose circulation.

Planning Transition

There are logistics involved in coming out to friends and family who are part of a close-knit group. If everyone is not informed at the same time, is there a possibility someone may find out through others in the group? Will you lose control of your coming-out process? Will someone be hurt because they were not told personally?

Inevitably, someone will have to be the first person told. This should be a person who won't immediately pick up their phone or turn on their computer to broadcast your transition. This should be a person you can brainstorm with about ways to tell others you both know. This should be a person who will be an ally to you as you move forward, someone you trust to have your back. Others may very well ask your ally questions, rather than approach you.

The person you choose to be first still has their own adjustment process to undergo before they can be a wholehearted ally. They also have to let go of who you used to be. This is one reason peer support is crucial. It is possible when you think about who to come out to first, a particular person you've known for a long time comes to mind. Yet, while they go through their adjustment process toward becoming your ally, you still need support. You may not have known your T/GE peers nearly as long as you have the person you're disclosing to first, but they will also not need to go through any grief process as you move forward on your journey.

Once you tell that first person, you now have someone you can talk with about who should find out second, third, and so on down the list. You can practice new names on your first person, if you haven't already settled on one. You can practice the experience of receiving support for your true self. No matter how carefully you plan and practice, however, situations arise that can't be scripted in advance. You may find yourself in a group of friends, suddenly realizing you don't know precisely who knows your new name/pronoun and who doesn't. You may find a friend frantically trying to catch your eye, not sure how to refer to you when a casual acquaintance approaches. You may have to take a deep breath and say to the casual acquaintance, "I'm not sure if you've heard . . . "

Somos Familia is a Bay Area organization with the goal to "create support and acceptance for Latina(o) lesbian, gay, bisexual, transgender, queer or questioning youth and their families" through educational workshops, support groups, and social activities.

When people we know slip up (and it will be "when," not "if"), they are probably not doing it to hurt us. It's not possible to count the number of times we use pronouns during the course of our day. Assigning gender is an autopilot process in most cultures; we are asking our family and loved ones to turn off an autopilot they weren't even aware they had. This isn't an easy adjustment! We slip on our own pronouns; it's unfair to our loved ones to expect quick change of this nature. Further, nonbinary identities are outside their framework, and it is even harder for them to make the adjustment if the pronoun we are requesting is neither "he" nor "she." Patience is required.

One of the most difficult aspects of transition is to allow it to unfold in its own way and time without trying to direct traffic. We are revisiting a core aspect of our identity and taking it in a whole new direction; we can't possibly predict in advance where the journey will take us. Make a plan—and hold it lightly. Transition is akin to driving down a dark road at night. Your headlights only illuminate the next 50 feet in front of you. You can drive 1,000 miles down that road only ever seeing the next 50 feet.

Educating Others

Many cisgender people are not going to understand on their own precisely what it means to be trans or nonbinary. And even if they have been allies to other trans or nonbinary people in the past, our journey isn't precisely like anyone else's. The education our friends and family need pertains not only to understanding trans or nonbinary identities in general, but also understanding what our unique path is. There are multiple levels to being an ally, from the sociological and political understanding of the meaning of bathroom bills to supporting our individual journey toward authenticity.

Keep track of websites that you think could help your friends and family understand you better. Connecting these resources with face-to-face conversations can be helpful. You might share a website, article, or book with a friend or family member, then invite them to talk about it with you over a meal.

In larger cities, you will be able to find support groups of various kinds; some groups may be specific to family members and some specific to trans or nonbinary folks. These groups may even meet at the same time, allowing you to travel with your friend or family member and meet up with them again afterward. This is a time to check in with yourself, and for your family members to do the same. Support groups allow us to bring forth our feelings about what's been going on for us. Sometimes, "what's been going on" involves our family member attending a support group in the room next door. Depending on what is happening in our lives, it might be better to travel separately to the support group

Untitled. (Chucha Marquez)

meeting. More often, you will be attending meetings on your own, not with family or friends along. It may be helpful to check out what other groups might be available for your friends or family members.

As we begin to share our stories, we will face difficult questions, some of which may feel too personal. When we're feeling unsure of our path, it can be hard to maintain our boundaries; with our identity shifting, we may find ourselves a bit at sea, wondering what our boundaries should be. Those of us who have grown up with shame and guilt may not feel entitled to establish a boundary, especially if there are many people in our lives giving us the message: "This is terrible! How could you do this to us?" This is a self-centered reaction that places their feelings at the center of our process. Please remember: It's your life. It's your identity. Not theirs.

I'm tired of feeling like I have to give a lesson about gender before I can have a meaningful conversation with my best friend.

Yes, we want our friends and family to adjust and be part of our lives as we move forward with this huge change. Some of our family members and friends may send the message that what we're expecting is above and beyond what they should have to do and therefore we need to hold their hand every step of the way. Their change is theirs. We aren't responsible for their change.

One invaluable resource for friends and family members is PFLAG, with chapters in all 50 states in the United States and in many countries worldwide, providing our loved ones support as allies. PFLAG used to stand for Parents, Families, and Friends of Lesbians and Gays, but the name is now simply the acronym. Many of those who seek support from PFLAG do so because they have a trans or nonbinary person in their lives.

FREEING THE WILDCAT: COMING OUT VIA LETTER

Sabene Georges (she/her) is a trans woman living in Colorado.

In June of 2017, at the age of 54, I finally came out—to everyone. My wife and closest friends had known for years, but now it was time to make it real with family and my friends. I posted this letter on Facebook and sent an abbreviated version to professional contacts, extended friends, and family. Needless to say, it was a tense time dealing with fear of rejection.

Coming Out . . . no easy way to say it at long last:

I am transgender.

I am starting my transition with the goal to begin living as my authentic female self early next year. For some of you, this may come as a shock. Others will think "well duh." A few of you already know.

Being trans and in the closet is like having a wildcat in a bag. I put the cat in a bag in order to survive as a child. I put the cat in a bag in order to have a career, to retain societal acceptance, and to enjoy what I perceived as "the fruits of life." I put the cat in a bag in order to continue a marriage to a wonderful person. And . . . for the last 7 years, even when all other barriers have been stripped away, I have kept the cat in the bag out of fear.

But every time I find a reason to put that cat into yet another bag, it gets larger. That cat grows fierce, and now that cat no longer fits in any bag I can construct.

And so here I am. I hope you will all try to understand why I need to do this, and what it has cost me to hide, deny, and repress my authentic self for 53 years. I waited for many reasons, but mostly it comes down to fear.

And I am still scared, . . . terrified to be exact. But it is finally time to come out and to take my place within the LGBTQ + community. My own vital needs—and events in our country—are compelling me past the point of my fear.

If you are reading this, you are my friend or my family. I want you all to know that I love you. I hope you can stay with me through this change, but if not, then I wish you love and happiness.

There, now I have said it. Now I just have to finally live it.

So there it was, out and open for all to see, to judge, and to determine in their own minds what it meant for their future relationship with me. The wildcat was, of course, fear, dysphoria, and the pressure of constantly hiding who I really was. That can really mess with your head over time. One of the ways I dealt with the wildcat was by putting it off. I spent decades in "Maybe someday . . . " mode, but the sheer sense of relief I felt at having let that wildcat out was an overwhelming force. I spent days in spontaneous tears. I felt it was the start of something wonderful . . . and that has indeed proved to be the case.

BEYOND PERSONAL RELATIONSHIPS

Each of us has a unique ethnic, cultural, and religious background, with various norms and beliefs about gender, gender roles, and sexuality. This context is an important piece of how we view our own identity, and it will influence how our friends and family respond to our coming-out process. For example, some cultures value family connection over individuality, which can make our decisions to come out or to transition difficult if our family is (or is likely to be) unsupportive. Some of us have decided to put our transitions on hold until the older generation of our family has died, not wishing to create a family schism. Many people may encourage us to pursue a transition path despite these concerns. The idea of self-actualization as the epitome of maturity is a white concept that originated in western culture, and it may not fit with the way we see our role in our various communities.

> My parents hate it, my fiancée is coming to terms with it, and most of my friends wonder what took so long.

For many of us, religious communities are also an important factor in coming out. Some religious traditions extend far beyond the actual worship service and are rooted in daily home life. Within these traditions, we may form our closest social ties with others who share our religious practice, and sometimes we have no friends outside our religious community. It is common in these situations that some people are supportive, others are not, and many aren't sure if they should be supportive or not. We will quite possibly lose our place in our religious community, no matter how supportive individuals may be. Some of us are surprised to find our religious family members find ways to accept our transition.

Within religious communities, even if some of our friends and family are supportive, it is likely that many of their friends are within the same religious community, as was once true for us. Though our friends and family may wish to be supportive and remain in contact, we may drift apart over time because we don't participate in the community as much anymore. For those of us transitioning within the binary gender system (moving from "he" to "she" or vice versa), it may be that over time, perhaps a long period of time, we may be able to return to our religious community in a new gender role. It may be harder to reintegrate for those of us who are nonbinary, as religious communities that are this close-knit also tend to be associated with older spiritual traditions, deeply entrenched in traditional gender roles.

> Even my uber-Christian family members have in subsequent years relayed to me that now they've come to believe that god has answered prayers about me and my well-being with testosterone, name change, and medical technology.

A transmasculine person getting a beer at a bar. (Zackary Drucker, The Gender Spectrum Collection, VICE/Broadly)

Some of us have lived our lives within lesbian or gay communities before coming out as trans or nonbinary. We may find that our worldview has been shaped by our participation in lesbian or gay communities such that we can hardly see ourselves as "straight" after transition, even if others perceive us that way based on who we form relationships with. We may gravitate toward language such as "queer" to define our sexual orientation. Many of us find that we do not lose our individual gay or lesbian friends. What we lose is our place within that community. The trans man who once participated in lesbian community may no longer be part of that community on the other side of transition, regardless of how much support he may receive from his lesbian friends. Those of us who were connected with a queer community to begin with may not lose our place within our community as we move forward, given that "queer" is a gender-neutral word to begin with, thus gender assignment may not be a criteria for membership in this community as it is within lesbian or gay communities.

Ray, a friend of this chapter's author, had been a founding member of a primarily lesbian chorus for nine years when he realized that he needed to transition to male. "I hadn't had any idea I was a trans man; I thought I was a lesbian with a lot of anxiety. I had a really hard time accepting that I needed to transition because I knew I'd have to leave the chorus. I wailed to the universe, 'Why does it have to be my voice???? Why couldn't I have been a tuba player???' But once I realized who I was, I couldn't stay at the expense of my true self. I stayed nearly two years longer, postponing my own journey because I wanted my name and voice on the first CD the group was going to record, in honor of their 10th anniversary." Ray's closest friends were all members of the chorus. His best friend was so upset at losing him, Ray didn't talk about his own internal process with her. She didn't want him to choose a male name, so she suggested he rename himself "Erin" instead of "Ray," which could be construed as "Aaron." Another friend, the woman he'd sat next to in rehearsals for years, said to him, "Do you have to leave? Can't you stay? I mean, we'd all know, but we wouldn't have to tell anyone." He said to her gently, "It just doesn't work that way." The afternoon of his last concert with the chorus, Ray held an open house at his apartment, announcing to the chorus that anyone who wanted could stop by to say goodbye. He received many cards and gifts that day. "The best present was a geode, one of the best metaphors for trans identity I've ever come across—plain rock on the outside, beautiful crystal inside. That came to me from my best friend, the one who initially wanted me to choose Erin as my name. Another chorus member gave me an antique mustache cup, telling me she'd been to four different antique stores looking for one. And this message someone wrote in a card encapsulates the sentiments of the vast majority of the group: 'What an incredibly exciting period this must be for you. Congratulations on a huge step forward. Here is a quote that seemed perfect for an end which is really a beginning. It is attributed to Anais Nin who was a French lesbian: "And the day came when the risk it took to remain closed in a bud became more painful than the risk it took to blossom." You are blossoming beautifully.' Leaving that group was the most painful part of my early transition time." Ray now sings in his local gay men's chorus. His lesbian friends welcomed him back into a singing circle with them for a performance. He says of himself, "I'm an honorary lesbian trans man singing baritone in a gay men's chorus and married to a woman. All me, all the time."

Many of us feel "stuck" between communities. Moving between these communities can be lonely, and we may not feel fully "seen" in either one. For instance, those of us who are Black may feel a lack of support coming our way from Black communities, while at the same time experiencing racism within trans communities. It may help to find others, through conferences and online forums, who share being Black and trans. Though our experiences will have differences, we may feel less alone and isolated.

In some cases, we may find that coming out to our families and partners changes our plans for transition. We may choose to delay making some kinds of social or physical transitions to ease relationships with our school-age children, to avoid confrontation with aging relatives, or out of a desire to accommodate our intimate partners' needs. Some of us have faced criticism for choosing to prioritize such relationships over our own desire. However, our culture, relationships, and sexuality are also core parts of our identity, and we navigate our needs alongside those of our family and partners.

Many people (trans or otherwise) may judge us harshly for transitioning while our children are young, feeling we should do what is best for them and put our own needs and desires on hold until they are on their own. There is no evidence, however, that transitioning while our children are young makes things harder for them. In fact, having a parent who is happier and more secure in their identity can have a positive influence on a parent-child relationship. Further, becoming one's true self is a wonderful example for a child of living in authenticity; the child will grow up with the message that whoever they realize themselves to be will be just fine.

Follow the Native Out Facebook page for information on in-person and online gatherings of Indigenous LGBTQ people.

CLOSE FRIENDS

Our closest friends may be the first people we come out to. Many of us are afraid of losing the relationships that we have had for years, of not being accepted by those with whom we have shared so much and perhaps grown up with. If we list our friends prior to transition in order of who we feel closest to, many of the names will stay on the list, but the order may change as we move forward. Many of us discover that the people we thought would take it the worst took it the best, and the people we thought would take it the best took it the worst.

I was surprised how much of a nonissue it was. True friends will always be true friends no matter what.

The gendered nature of relationships is apparent in our close friendships. If your best friend is a cisgender female and you transition from female to male you may remain best friends, but the social boundary may be different.

The best coming out experience was a male friend I came out to, who shortly thereafter asked me out on a date; it made me feel absolutely wonderful, and I felt so bad that I couldn't accept since I'm just not attracted to men.

FAMILY

Transitioning can be profound when the relationship has been life-long—either all of our life, or all of theirs. Many family relationship labels are associated with gender. In

English, for instance, one of the only family labels that is gender-neutral is "cousin." In some languages, such as Spanish, *all* family labels are gendered. It's not easy to say to one's brother, "I've always been a sister to you, but now I'm becoming your brother." In English, in the case of the nonbinary family member, a sister could become the nonbinary "sibling." There is, however, no nonbinary equivalent for the "uncle" or "aunt" relationship. How would one refer to a nonbinary "niece?" "Oldest child of my sister?" Family relationship labels highlight the language difficulties nonbinary people face in finding terminology with which to refer to themselves. Those to whom these labels apply are morphing English. For example, "nibling" is a nongendered term to replace "niece" or "nephew," and "pibling" is a replacement term for "aunt" or "uncle." (The "p" refers to "parent generation.")

My mom had some initial trouble . . . but then my grandma put her right on it. Told her that most women don't get to have a son and a daughter in one lifetime without having to give birth twice, so she needed to get over herself. I love my grandma a lot.

It may be difficult for family members who are close to us to believe our new identity is real, because they have not recognized it themselves, despite our closeness. It may be hard for close family to accept that we have had something this big going on inside us and they never knew. Sometimes they will express guilt for not "seeing" it at earlier times in our lives, though in reality, we may have been doing all we could to hide our true selves. Many of us find our families don't take us seriously at first, or realize how far down the path we are by the time we tell them. For them, it seems out of the clear blue when, in fact, telling our families is usually nowhere near our first step. While we may have been contemplating this transition for quite a while, our families are just beginning their process. And in truth, some of us do downplay the seriousness of it all at first, not wanting to deal with family emotionality.

Everyone said that I went too fast. But the question is: "Too fast for what, for whom?" I'd been 36 years in the wrong sex. I'd like to say it wasn't that fast.

In some cases, families and friends may change their reactions once we begin to make our transition, recognizing the positive effects of us living in our affirmed gender.

All my family but my sister took it well. She took some time away from me and didn't see me for a few months. I had at that point started hormones. The family got together for a funeral, and she told my mom there was no way she could be against it anymore because she had never seen me so happy. Since then I have had 110% support from my family.

Unfortunately, sometimes it does not get better.

I came home for Christmas one year and my mom refused to go out in public with me because she was embarrassed by me. She said the coat I was wearing made me look "like a woman." I said, "That's because I am a woman," and she literally screamed. I locked myself in a room and cried for hours until I drove myself into a panic attack. My mom told me I was sick, possessed by Satan, and was going to hell and then didn't speak to me for hours. Then she decided she didn't want me to "ruin Christmas" so we pretended like nothing happened, but I wasn't allowed to tell my dad or siblings to maintain the status quo. For months after that, my mom would call me and pretend like nothing ever happened. I finally wrote them a letter saying basically look, this isn't a phase . . . I'm on hormones, etc. They wrote back and told me I was never allowed to come home again because I was a threat to their "remaining children." This hurt me more badly than all the transphobes who ever bashed me, because I love my siblings more than anything in the whole world.

Untitled. (Chucha Marquez)

Turning to other support systems, practicing good self-care, and creating new, chosen families can be helpful as we grieve our losses. In some cases, transition fractures our families, with some family members adamantly refusing to support our process and others completely on board.

PARTNERS AND SPOUSES

Regardless of the type of transition you are considering, or the length of your relationship, it's never easy coming out to a spouse or partner. Partners often experience an overwhelming set of conflicting feelings as they sort through their reactions to a possible transition. They often find their own identity challenged: "If you've always felt like a man inside, then who am I?" Relationships that survive transition emerge all the stronger for the opportunity presented to all concerned to explore their own sense of self perhaps more deeply than at any other time.

FAMILY OF CHOICE

Many people find that as they come out, they begin to form friendships based on a sense of shared identity. The feeling of "family" develops over time. A long time. When we are first coming out, first emerging into our true selves, every relationship is new. Old friendships morph gradually as our friends adjust to a new gender boundary with us. New friends never knew us in any gender other than who we are now. No need to watch new friends go through a gender adjustment. It takes a long time before the people we meet at the beginning of our journey fall into the category of "old friend." It takes a long time before friends who knew us long before transition have come to know us even longer as our true selves.

bklyn boihood is made up of black and brown queer and trans bois. Activities include bike rides, annual retreats, camping trips, and "critical workshops exploring our role in redefining what masculinity is."

Many of us don't lose our entire family of origin, though we might have to let go of some family members who won't transition with us, who continue to use our old name and the wrong pronoun. For those of us who are able to have relationships with our family of origin going forward, there is still often a different quality to the sense of "family." It's a rare and lucky person who can say there is much overlap between who is part of their family of origin and who is their family of choice; many of us wouldn't choose our relatives if we were given a choice! Creating chosen family is well worth the effort, it just takes time.

COMING OUT TO CHILDREN

Many children are more open-minded about gender than adults and may accept our new identities more easily than other family members. The most important consideration in how to talk with children about our gender identity is the child's developmental age.

Young Children

Children learn about various aspects of gender at different times, and how children will understand and accept gender transitions differs over time.

Young children are concerned about loss of consistency, loss of continuity, and loss of love. Children's concerns are linked to what our new identity means for them and the family. They may have questions like:

"Can I still call you 'mommy' (or 'daddy')?"

"Are you going away?" "Are you getting a divorce?"

"Where are you going to live?" "Where am I going to live?"

If they ask whether your transition means they will grow up to be a different gender themselves, most will be reassured by the explanation that your gender identity is not going to affect theirs. One message that your transition sends is that whoever they are is just fine; if their birth gender assignment doesn't work for them, it's OK to tell you.

Once word gets out that we are transitioning, children who spend time in day care, school, religious, or community groups may hear gossip and unkind remarks about us. At younger ages, children do not have a large enough worldview to understand history and the transmission of misinformation and prejudice through generations. They will take things personally that are in no way personal to them or their family. Reassure them that there is nothing wrong with them or with you. Give them space to talk through the experiences they are having, and putting aside whatever pain it may cause you, be there for them. As children mature, it may become helpful to provide them with more historical education, placing discrimination in a cultural context.

COLAGE is a support network for LGBTQ + parents and their children. Every year at COLAGE's Family Week, LGBTQ + parents bring their children to learn, meet others, and have fun.

MY SNEAKY LITTLE NIECE

Kaylee V. Goins (she/her) is just a woman trying to make a difference in the world, even if it's one person at a time!

I came out as transgender at age 40. Not long after, my father passed away. The first person I came out to was my best friend of 35 years. Although he understood, he was a little disappointed that I had not said anything to him sooner. His girlfriend at the time immediately asked, "Perhaps this is all because your father just died?" "No," I told her, "I've known I wanted to transition since I was 20." Over the next few weeks, I came out to my cousin, mother, and sister. Most everyone knew that I was a little bit queer and that I "dressed up" on Halloween. I figured that most of them would be easy, and for the most part that was true, but how do I explain this to my 12-year-old niece?

I thought about this situation for a few weeks. I even wrote out what I wanted to say to her. The best way I could explain it so she would understand.

Hoping for some feedback, I sent a copy of my letter to both my sister and mother. I waited patiently for a reply from both, expecting to tell my niece when she and my sister arrived at home. The reply though . . . wasn't from my sister!

It seems that my sneaky little niece was poking around in my sister's phone, and she came across my message. She obviously read it and replied to me with a simple, "I love you anyway." When they arrived home, I sat her down, and I asked if she had any follow-up questions, to which she answered no. We said our goodnights, and the second I laid down in bed, I received a message from my niece, asking me . . . questions. We messaged for a short time, and when she was satisfied, we both went to sleep.

She's been one of my biggest supporters, and when her father once deadnamed me, she jumped all over him about it. He hasn't made a mistake since.

I love that kid!

Adolescents

Adolescents value honesty and straightforward information. They have developed the capacity for abstract thinking, and they may be more engaged with the idea (in both positive and negative ways) of our transition. When coming out to adolescents, it is helpful

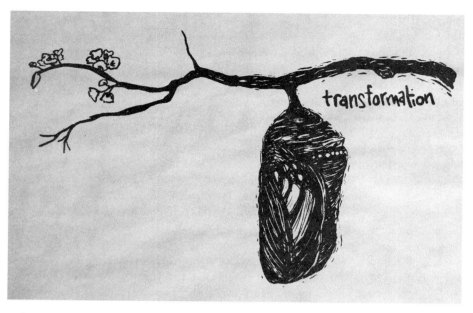

Transformation. (Sha Grogan-Brown)

to explain our experiences, as well as the nature of the process, as we understand it. In essence, teens need the explanation given to adults *and* the reassurance given to children, as they are in a bridge period in their lives.

As with younger children, reassurance of stability and continuity can go a long way toward reconciling the adolescent toward the idea of a parent or close adult in their life transitioning. Reinforce that your identity has no bearing on the adolescent's gender and sexual identities.

Adolescence is the time when the need for peer acceptance and approval is at its highest. It is important to reassure adolescents that as much as possible, it is their choice whether to tell their friends and teachers about our transition, and that we will do what we can to make them comfortable among their peers. The school milieu belongs to the adolescent, and we can help teens weather our transition by keeping our distance from the school setting until they are ready for our presence there.

Although some teens may see our transition as embarrassing at first, others may feel that having a trans parent somehow gains them "cool points" with their friends. Talk with them about your own goals and timeline for coming out, and make sure they understand when and with whom you are comfortable sharing this information. As is true with everyone else you are close to, it's their transition, too; keeping them in the loop will help them feel a part of your process and that you are not leaving them behind as you move forward.

Adolescence is also a time of coming to understand social issues on a broader scale than is possible for younger children. Adolescents begin to form a worldview at this point in their lives, adopting political opinions and taking stances on various issues. Their views are often polarized, with "black and white" or "right or wrong" judgments about issues. Some adolescents may see the social discrimination against trans individuals as a civil rights issue and be appalled at the pariah status of trans people. Others may continue to see gender as polarized; the "black and white" thinking that characterizes adolescence dovetails unfortunately well with the gender binary concept. Sometimes adolescents withdraw from a transitioning parent on this basis, only to come around later in their lives, when their worldviews have evolved.

Adult Children

Many of us who transition midlife have had full lives in our birth-assigned sex, often including marrying and having children, who are now adults with their own lives. Though they are now adults, this conversation isn't like telling other adults in our lives; these are still our children.

Many of us lived with depression, anxiety, or other mental health issues in trying to avoid facing our true selves; in some cases, we self-medicated with drugs or alcohol. In turn, our now-adult children may have felt neglected, helpless, or responsible for our health and well-being; they may now feel a great deal of anger and bitterness, learning as adults the reason behind their childhood experience. Having lived through their entire childhood with an unhappy parent, it can be difficult for the adult child to forgive the parent, and we may find ourselves having to make amends for quite some time. In other cases, our adult children may be delighted to see us taking control of our lives.

> *I anguished a long time, fearing what would happen when I came out to my daughters. I knew that if they accepted me, from there on out it would be much easier. Although I thought I would be coming out to my oldest daughter first, it turned out to be the youngest who guessed I was transgender from all the clues I'd been giving for so long. When I came out, trembling, she walked over, embraced me, and said, "I LOVE YOU UNCONDITIONALLY!!!" At that moment, I knew that even if the rest of the world despised me, I was going to be OK.*

Even with this level of acceptance, the adjustment is still a process, as for all family relationships. For example, if you transition to living as female, your children may still see you as "dad." They will (probably) over time change the way they refer to you, wanting to respect your transition, but may also experience a certain natural grief over this level of change. Over time, you and your adult children will find your own language. Some adult children may send Mother's Day cards addressed to "dad," meaning no disrespect at all; "dad" was the role we played early in their lives. In sending a Mother's Day card so addressed, their implicit message is: "You were my dad, you are still my dad, and I now see you as a woman so am sending you a Mother's Day card."

Stuck in the Middle with You: A Memoir of Parenting in Three Genders (New York: Crown Publishers, 2013) combines Jenny Boylan's personal narrative with interviews of others.

One conversation to have pertains to the public presentation of gender. How would it feel to be taken out to lunch on Mother's Day and then called "dad" in front of strangers? The family acknowledgement of gender is one thing; how we present gender out in the world is another. No matter what our past relationship with our adult children, or their initial reaction, coming out creates an opportunity to establish a new relationship with them—one that has an opportunity to be even closer, because it is based in authenticity.

ON THE JOB

The workplace is one of the most challenging milieux in most people's attempts at maintaining privacy during transition. If we transition on the job, this most personal of information comes into the workplace, and in a setting where it's generally not OK to talk about personal issues. We can't really talk about this most profound shift in our sense of self, and yet we often spend more time with our coworkers than we do with anyone else in our lives. Coworkers are brought into our transition process as they experience us making changes in our names and pronouns, the bathroom and locker room we use, and our gender presentation. And yet in many workplaces, there is no forum provided for talking honestly about the transition process, helping coworkers understand how to be supportive, and explaining exactly what's going on. It's no wonder that work is often one of the last places many of us come out, perhaps the last step on our journey toward living as our true selves.

For a quick rundown for allies on "How to Be a Trans Ally at Work," listen to Tuck Woodstock (host of the podcast "Gender Reveal") interview lawyer Chase Strangio on National Public Radio's Life Kit podcast.

WORD SPREADS

When we begin the process of coming out, information can often spread beyond our control. The desire for complete privacy can quickly become unrealistic. Our friends and family may have reached out to their support networks and disclosed some of our information, and news may have traveled through our informal community networks as rumor or gossip. We don't know exactly what others know at this point—what have they been told?

A non-binary femme using an eyelash curler. (Zackary Drucker, The Gender Spectrum Collection, VICE/Broadly)

It's likely those who hear about our process from others weren't privy to the information exactly as we would have presented it.

Some of us are outed by others in ways that dictate the course of our transition and family adjustment process.

> *I came out to my parents in 1985. My mom immediately rejected the idea and instructed me to not tell my father. When I changed my name, I had to publish the name change in the paper for three weeks. A local radio personality read the announcement on the air to be funny. My cousin heard it and called her mother (my aunt), who called her mother-in-law (my grandmother), who called her daughter-in-law (my mother), who called me and told me I was destroying my family. It was years before I reconciled with my parents, but by the time I went for surgery, my parents and one of my brothers drove me to the airport.*

Early in our process, it's difficult to know exactly how others are perceiving us. Our friends and family are going through the upheaval of changing how they refer to us, and we honestly don't know how strangers are seeing us.

> *To complete strangers I may not meet again, I usually just go with whatever their first impression is. It is a good gauge of how I'm perceived by others.*

Some of us want our friends or family members to help us spread the word. We may be feeling overwhelmed by the number of people who need to know and may want to be able to focus more on our own internal processes. If this seems like the right course for you, you may want to help them come up with answers to likely questions. In some cases, even if we are ready for others to begin sharing our information, they may still be in the middle of their own adjustment process. Be prepared to help them navigate these difficult conversations.

And what about friends or family members who find out before we have had a chance to tell them? If someone feels they are the last to find out and is hurt to hear about our transition through other people, it can help to tell them, "It isn't because you don't matter—it's because you matter so much." We often think our close friends and family members know this automatically, but this is not always true.

Casual Acquaintances

Interacting with casual acquaintances can be awkward and uncomfortable early in transition. Casual acquaintances are not close enough friends to have earned our trust. They are the people we work with occasionally, or the fellow student we study with sometimes. They are the grocery store clerk we see every other day, the person we most often buy coffee from or sell coffee to.

Casual acquaintances may not feel close enough to us to ask questions or even acknowledge our transition. Sometimes these relationships become close friendships over time, but while the person is still in the category "casual acquaintance," we might wish they did not have to know something this personal about us. It can feel awkward to the casual acquaintance to have this level of intimate knowledge about someone with whom they are not close. Many of us who transition find ourselves avoiding casual acquaintances for a while, if we can, to ease the tension.

Some of us come out to a casual acquaintance and are pleasantly surprised to receive great support and admiration. Sometimes the person eventually ends up in the category of "close friend" as a result of the disclosure. On occasion, you may find a casual acquaintance approaches you, offering support. Perhaps the relationship would have blossomed into close friendship anyway, but it was catapulted forward by the depth of intimacy involved in coming out.

The best reaction was from a woman I had known casually for years as a man. When she saw me en femme with a long streaked salt and pepper wig on, she asked if my hair had always been streaked.

"HELLO FRIENDS!": ADVENTURES IN MISGENDERING

Dara Hoffman-Fox, LPC (they/them) is a queer-identified gender therapist in private practice in Colorado Springs. Dara is the creator of the "Conversations with a Gender Therapist" YouTube channel as well as the author of the Amazon bestseller, You and Your Gender Identity: A Guide to Discovery.

I had a highly rewarding conversation with a server at one of my favorite restaurants regarding her use of "ladies" when addressing my wife and me.

Backstory: I've been working a lot lately on letting servers know that (as a nonbinary person) it is uncomfortable when I'm addressed as "ladies" or "ma'am." It's a tricky challenge, because I know that the servers more than likely have used those terms over the course of their entire lives in an effort to be respectful and polite. When I go out to eat, however, I enjoy feeling connected to the server, so having this conversation with them tends to result in a more pleasant dining experience for all.

So, because the server addressed us as "ladies" while taking our order, I brought up the subject. I could tell that she was thrown off a bit, and over the course of our meal we weren't sure how she took it (by the way, I asked what her pronouns were, which is why I'm using she/her).

When she dropped off the check, she knelt down and asked us if she could talk with us more about her using "ladies" to address her customers. She said that after I brought that up (just an hour earlier), she began to wonder if she was making other people uncomfortable by saying that. She asked what she could use instead, and by the end of the conversation she said she would Google "gender neutral language" to learn more about it. Additionally, when I was walking to the bathroom, I heard her talking to a coworker about it, and in a very positive way.

This encounter showed me how much this is all about taking our time to really see one another: me seeing her as a kind, non-trans person who really wants to learn; her seeing me as a nonbinary person whom she accidentally made uncomfortable; and my wife contributing to the conversation and witnessing the entire exchange with delight.

By the time we left, the server asked if she could now greet us with, "Hello friends! What can I start you off with to drink this morning?"

Reconnecting with Our Past

I attended my 40th college reunion in my new identity. After the banquet, we each were invited to tell the class what we had been doing personally and professionally. I began with the words, "Well, there have been a few changes. . . . " which immediately got me a big laugh followed by a standing ovation.

As we move on with our lives, situations change. We are out of school. Change jobs. Establish relationships. Maybe have kids. Maybe we joined the military young and are now in civilian life once again. Perhaps some friends remain part of our lives throughout, but many do not; we may have friends of proximity, people who only remain part of our lives because we live near them, work with them, go to school with them, or our kids are friends.

As we move on with our lives, coming out begins to feel done. Every now and then, however, someone from our past may come into our lives again, a reminder that coming out is never really in the past tense. As we center into our true selves, though, coming out also becomes more manageable and may feel easier. It usually feels less overwhelming, as the people we need to come out to become far fewer in number. Many more people know about our path than don't know.

I've had a good response from my Naval Academy classmates and will attend our 50th class reunion in October. I out myself now and then to people we meet. It is often the Naval Academy connection which provokes the, "I didn't know that women. . . . . . " question. "Well, actually, they didn't. I was a man back then."

The "Need to Know" Category

Regardless of how much privacy we might desire, there are some situations in which it can be extremely important to disclose our history. Medical providers, in many, but not all, situations, need to know that we once transitioned, in order to fully understand our physiology and medical needs.

Femmes Can Be They. (Art By Emulsify)

I wouldn't have the faintest idea what it's like to be "out." I live in deep stealth, which means my GP (general practitioner) is the ONLY person who knows of my medical history, and I intend upon keeping it that way! I was raised with the idea of social decorum. To me this is a VERY personal issue and in the words of my mother, "no one's damned business but my own!"

It may also be wise to inform certain professionals, such as attorneys, caseworkers, therapists, and accountants, who are providing us with legal or medical services. We may not be able to foresee in advance a way in which our transition might prove relevant, but it may, in fact, be important down the line. As an example, transition-related medical care may be tax deductible, and an accountant knowledgeable about our trans status can help us use this to our advantage.

For those of us who live in states that will only respect our identities if we have had certain forms of gender-affirming surgery, we may need to come out to our attorney, our tax preparer, and our health provider. These are the people who can best advise us of all our rights and what is available to us—but only if they know exactly what our status is under state law. And they can only know that if they know we are trans.

DESPITE ALL OF THAT

Laura Kelly (she/her) transitioned after age 60. She is the art museum and chamber music type of old lady. She is proud to be trans!

Despite being terrified out of my mind and yet having to feel my way through the booby-trapped legal and medical and social maze of transition; despite the hateful gatekeeper to whom I first outed myself; despite, just to survive, having to almost overnight acquire a detailed knowledge of women's clothing, hair care, and cosmetics that a cisgender woman had her entire adolescence to master—and often getting it all embarrassingly wrong;

Despite those who told me that I would be hideously ugly and would never be anything but a despised object of ridicule that no one could ever love; despite those who told me that I had no taste and insisted that I would spend the rest of my days dying of friendless loneliness; despite the friends who exited my life when I took off the mask and let them meet the real me for the first time; despite the family members I will never see again;

Despite the so-called medical professional who felt free to laugh at me for being transgender; despite the horrible people who think it a fine joke to come up to me and say the cruelest things they can think of; despite the condescending people who see me as nothing but a token they can collect to show how progressive and open minded they are;

Despite knowing that when I am read as a cisgender woman I am seen as a soft target for robbery or rape, and that when I have been clocked I am a target for murder; despite knowing that on any given day I might have to cope with either the smug sexism of males or the open hatred of the transphobic; despite knowing that I have joined a tiny minority group that has been targeted for destruction by powerful religious and political organizations;

Despite all that, transitioning and living as myself has been so, so worth it!

When I engage with others as myself, they may love or hate me, but at least it is *me* they love or hate, not the mask I was forced to create. I can be spontaneous and playful now! And I know joy, so much joy, for the very first time!

DOWN THE ROAD

When we are just beginning our coming-out process, it may seem impossible that we will reach a point when we can simply live in our affirmed gender. But for many of us, a time comes when we are seen as our true selves, without question.

Some of us, especially those of us who identify as women and transition somewhat later in life, may have more difficulty being seen as our true genders. Perhaps testosterone has been our dominant hormone long enough that many of the physical changes can't be entirely changed to allow us to be perceived as women. Our process then becomes one of serenely owning that we know who we are and others' reactions don't negate the truth of us.

Those of us who are nonbinary travel a different road, one of a lifetime of misgendering. We will be called "he" or "she," neither of which is correct. Our life path is one of making decisions about when it matters to us to correct the pronoun, to attempt to be seen as our true selves. As non-binary identities gain recognition, we may encounter fewer puzzled looks when we do come out; nevertheless, we will continue to face "he" and "she" as default pronouns applied to us automatically.

For those of us who are perceived in public spaces as our true identity, disclosing our trans status becomes a choice. Some of us choose to integrate our personal history into our current lives, being out when it feels safe and relevant. We come out to new friends as a matter of course, believing that no one can truly become a close friend without knowing our history. Our identity becomes not "man" or "woman," but rather "trans man" or "trans woman." We may use slightly different terminology, but the trans piece of our identity is included. For many of us, this is a means of giving back, remembering our own early transition time and wanting to be of service to those coming along behind us.

Others of us see the present as where we live, with the past left behind. We claim "man" or "woman" as our identity, and only disclose our trans status to intimate partners. Disclosure is on a "need to know" basis, and the list of those who need to know is very short. For the person who transitions, however, every use of the right name and pronoun affirms our identity. Choosing to be private about how we got there is a decision based on individual boundaries around privacy.

The boundaries around disclosure are unique to each individual. There is no right or wrong answer; the path unfolds before us as we proceed with transition.

CONCLUSION

Coming out is an ongoing process. As we begin our journey, our internal upheaval is compounded when we face challenges in our relationships. Staying centered in this time of complete change is not easy. The touchstone of peer support, and maybe that of a pet, who cares nothing about our gender, can provide the comfort we need to navigate this overwhelming time. Reaching out to others who have gone before, hearing their stories of life moving along, seeing the truth of their lives going on, can also provide deep comfort. "Oh, . . . others have done this before. I can do it, too."

As we proceed, coming out may become a choice. For some, it remains an ongoing necessity. For some of us who could be invisible, authenticity means disclosing our identity to new people in our lives, providing education as needed. For others of us, authenticity is achieved through transition and not through sharing our identities; we may choose to live a life of low disclosure. And for some, who aren't able to be seen as their intended gender, the goal is to acquire and maintain serenity in the face of living in a trans-hostile society. For all of us, the aim is to achieve a centeredness in the knowledge of who we are, and the peace of mind that comes from living in authenticity.

Letters for my brothers: Transitional wisdom in retrospect (2010) is a book by and for trans men, edited by Megan M. Rohrer and Zander Keig.

SOCIAL TRANSITION

Florence Ashley and Avy A. Skolnik

8

From clothes to haircuts, piercings to names, society genders human beings in a multitude of ways, beyond the physiological. For many transgender and gender expansive (T/GE) people, social and medical transition involves actively intervening to change our appearances and modes of interaction. Some of us may want to adopt a gender expression that will facilitate acceptance of our gender by broader society. Others might deliberately adopt a nonconforming gender expression that befuddles gender norms. The choice is deeply personal and is motivated by our background and cultural considerations such as gender identity, sexual orientation, race, religion, interests, political beliefs, age, and more. Some trans and gender expansive people do not socially transition in any way, whether because they have no desire to, or because external factors made them choose not to. The collection of ways in which individual trans people alter their gender expression is often referred to as social transition. Social transition can exist alongside or independently from medical transition, which involves interventions that affect primary and secondary sexual characteristics such as hormone replacement therapy, facial hair removal, and surgery.

> *I consider myself to be low-disclosure. My family, close friends, and trans acquaintances know that I am trans, but I do not disclose that I am trans to colleagues or less-than-close friends. I choose to be low-disclosure because it means that in general, people see me as "just a man," with no qualifiers. However, I hate that out in public, other trans and queer people have no way of knowing that I am one of them.*

The aspects of gender expression that we change during social transition are not inherently gendered but are instead gendered through social processes. Nothing makes pink, for example, inherently a "girly" color and its gendered perception varies across time and cultural groups. Nonetheless, it is widely perceived as feminine in Euro-American cultures, and this can have implications for trans people's choices. One trans man might abstain from wearing pink to avoid being misgendered, and another might deliberately wear pink to challenge gender norms and be read as gender nonconforming. There is no good or bad choice in social transition, only choices that are well-suited or ill-suited to unique individuals based on their wants and needs.

> *I don't like to describe my coming out as "transitioning." There is very rarely a "gender A to gender B" transition for nonbinary people and for me personally, there will never be a point where I'm "done" transitioning.*

The notion of social transition can be particularly challenging for nonbinary and gender nonconforming trans people, given that past conceptualizations have tended to focus on hegemonic—dominant or powerful groups'—gender roles, which are often binary and tightly regulated. One of the points of tension is the emerging distinction between expressing one's gender and producing a certain impression or image of gender for others. Those two aspects do not always converge, and many people may find themselves wanting to authentically express their gender in ways that will produce a gendered perception of them, which they may at times simultaneously resent. This may be all the more challenging, given the variations in gender norms across space, time, and communities. What's considered feminine in San Francisco will not be the same as in New Delhi. What was considered masculine just 20 years ago is not the same as what is considered masculine today.

DEVISING YOUR SOCIAL TRANSITION

Transition is a loaded word for nonbinary people. Some of us transition toward a more androgynous look, and some of us don't transition at all. I chose to transition a little bit. The roles, however, changed significantly. Sometimes I can pass as a man, and the sudden power dynamic that passing as a man has was startling and unsettling.

There is no cookie-cutter social transition, and the process of figuring out when to transition and what socially transitioning will include is deeply personal. Some of us begin socially transitioning with a clear idea of what we wish to change, whereas others do not and happily figure it out along the way. Nor does having a clear idea preclude future changes: Feelings and identities are never foreclosed, and some of us might find both our gender identity and desired gender expression evolve over time in a way that will have implications for how we present ourselves. Ultimately, social transitioning is about figuring out what works for you.

FEELING GENDER

Gender dysphoria and gender euphoria are commonly used guides to social transition. Many trans and gender expansive people are uncomfortable presenting a certain way and are overjoyed when specific pronouns are used for them. For instance, trans women frequently experience happiness being called "she" and distress being called "he." Sometimes, it will be clear which way gender dysphoria and/or euphoria are pointing. Other times, it can be difficult to know exactly what best suits us, because the feelings can

Precious Brady-Davis, 33, Chicago. Regional communications manager, Sierra Club. (She, her, hers; diva). "There needs to be more than one narrative of transness. We need to see trans people who are out, trans people who are not. Trans people who are airplane pilots, teachers, working at McDonald's down the street, trans people who are CEOs and executives, sisters, brothers, parents. We need to show that we are part of the fabric of society, part of humanity. There's a thought that transness is just glamorous, and, yes, there's a beauty to being your authentic self. But it's also gritty in the navigation of that experience, especially as a professional. The support of social networks is so important. I want trans kids to know you can bring your authentic self to whatever you do." (Zackary Drucker)

be complicated or because they may fluctuate or vary based on context. For some, this may indicate gender fluidity, whereas for others, it may be a very conscious strategy to navigate transphobia in different contexts. Still for others, it means that further introspection may be necessary to figure out what suits them best.

> *I have a complicated relationship with passing. I think that the idea of passing in the abstract is not desirable. I don't want to live my life constantly trying to attain a binary, colonial version of normality. I am not interested in assimilation. I do recognize, however, that passing is very often a matter of safety. Sometimes, if I want to get home safe, I need to pass.*

How we feel is not always concordant with societal expectations. Gender dysphoria and gender euphoria are, in a sense, indomitable: They feel however they feel, and although social norms may play a role in defining their contours, they can also fly in the face of social norms altogether. It is possible for someone to have, say, euphoria from being called "he" yet be perfectly happy with a traditionally feminine name. Others may be most happy when their gender presentation confuses others.

Sometimes, navigating social transition is a more creative process. For some people, socially transitioning is more of an artistic process wherein you arrange various components to make yourself into the gendered person you want to be. Your person is the most wonderful canvas for painting your gender. Just because you don't have gender dysphoria or euphoria about certain things doesn't mean that you don't have preferences and feelings about how to best (re)present yourself.

Finally, socially transitioning can be even more mundane. Picking names, pronouns, and appearances doesn't always have to be grounded in gender and how we feel about gender. Maybe I'm wearing a loose band T-shirt just because I really like that band. People have preferences and interests of all sorts and those can be just as helpful in figuring out how to present.

ON PASSING

Lillian Maisfehlt (she/her) is a trans lady and academic librarian living in Connecticut. She is a proud parent, a lapsed bassist, and a collage artist. She chose to transition openly and visibly at work and in her community, and she is eternally grateful to be able to make that choice.

I've never particularly liked the word *passing*. The opposite of *pass*, after all, is *fail*, and for myself, I refuse to consider any part of my transition, my body, or myself a failure, *especially* as judged by others. I've waited too long for the chance to transition, and I've poured too much of myself into it, and I love myself as I really am too much to let anyone but me say whether it's been valid. I didn't set myself free to win anyone's approval.

I prefer *blending*, which I define as *being accepted as the gender you are without having to state your gender explicitly.* That can mean the person you interact with doesn't realize that you're trans, they realize you're trans but don't care because they recognize your true gender on an unconscious level, or they realize you're trans and make a conscious effort to address you correctly out of politeness or respect. The important thing is the interaction, not the mind of the other person, because what they think can't be controlled, and trying to divine someone's mind, and whether you measure up, leads to heartache.

But even if *blending* is preferable to *passing,* and even if the definition is expanded to allow for being recognized as trans, I still find it to be an unsatisfyingly binary concept. One believes they either blend or not. But if I interact with everyone I meet as a woman, for days or weeks or months on end, and one person calls me *Sir,* does that one misgendering invalidate everything that came before it? Earlier in my transition I was misgendered frequently, but would then interact with someone who made it clear they weren't even considering the possibility that I was trans. Did that one instance of blending not count for something?

Of course I want to look like the person I know myself to be, and of course I want other people to see her, but more than that, I want and deserve to be accepted and respected for who I am. And I've found that if I carry the expectation that I will be, generally speaking, I am. And the more I'm accepted, the more I come to expect that I will be accepted, and the cycle continues.

And it becomes less about *passing* as myself, and more about *being* myself that way.

BLENDING IN AND CLASHING OUT

We are always in relationship to others, and how others perceive us or dictate social norms inevitably influences how we approach social transition. Being visibly trans or gender non-conforming can be hard in society, and many people understandably wish to minimize being identified as such by others for safety reasons, to facilitate social interaction, or because the thought of others knowing makes them dysphoric. Because of this, some people tailor their social transition around the aim of being generally perceived as a cisgender person.

When I first transitioned, I was very concerned about "passing" as a binary woman. I dressed in a hyperfeminine manner. For many years, I wore only skirts and dresses, never pants.

The desire to blend in with cisgender society is elevated to the status of a norm in some trans spheres. It is important to remember that there is nothing wrong with being readily identified as trans or gender expansive and that it doesn't make us less valuable, less important, or less lovable. Some people deliberately clash with norms of gender expression. This can be done for a wide range of reasons including political commitments, personal beliefs, or just because we feel good that way.

I haven't really taken any actions to limit others' awareness of my trans identity because I prefer to be out and proud about it. I never used to think I could pass, but now that I do pass sometimes it feels kinda weird. When I pass, people place the same expectations on me as a cis woman and that's not always welcome. I get really tired of the mansplaining, being talked over, and the sexual harassment that comes along with passing.

MODELING AND TRYING ON

My behaviors are a mix and mash of various masculinity and femininity as I grew up an outcast from both worlds, and so Mr. Rogers was the role model I had as a kid; I wanted to show love toward everyone the way Mr. Rogers did in his PBS show.

When trying to figure out how we want to socially transition, it can be helpful to look to others. Role models are all around us, be it within our communities, families, friend groups, or in media. Trans communities hold great wisdom. We can ask elders from our communities or people who have been out longer how they navigated social transition. Fictional characters can also inspire. Even just going through fashion magazines can be helpful in figuring out how we might want to present.

DapperQ is a queer style magazine that hosts an annual fashion show at the Brooklyn Museum in Brooklyn, New York.

I really haven't changed my gender expression because I've always been very butch in my presentation, even before I realized that's what it was, and I've been fortunate enough that my family didn't care enough to enforce specific standards about the way girls are supposed to dress in anything but the most formal occasions. I would say recognizing my gender and being validated in it by others has made me feel more comfortable in exploring femme/fag presentations when I'm interested in doing so, but my everyday dress/mannerisms have not really changed at all.

There are many archetypes in the social imaginary. While reading the words high femme, butch, goth chick, suspenders hipster, or bear, you probably have images popping into your head. For many, socially transitioning is not just about expressing gender, but also expressing it in a specific way that matches an archetype that speaks to us. Some trans women are butch lesbians. Some trans men are bears. Figuring out your social transition can also mean figuring out which "style" best fits you.

For a while, I tried to be more feminine, to wear make-up, dresses, skirts, grow my hair out, et cetera. I found a lot of this very dysphoria-inducing,

Taj Taylor. "In this photo, I had just finished doing my makeup and felt a little more confident than usual, so I decided to grab my camera and take some cute photos!"

uncomfortable, and deeply violent, as it was steeped in misogynistic expectations placed upon women. Eventually, I realized I could be a woman and still be masculine. That felt off limits for so long because of my transness. I felt like I had to be a gender conforming woman in order to be "actually" trans.

Exploring gender is something we can do through social transition. If we are not sure whether a name, pronoun, or clothing style will suit us, there is nothing wrong with trying it out. People often go through multiple names, pronouns, and styles before finding the ones that suit them best. Depending on context and social support, we can choose who to involve in our exploration and how many different options to explore. Maybe we want to use a name and pronoun combination with a friend for a day or two, or maybe we want to try it out in all spheres of our life for an extended period. Even if an approach doesn't end up working out for you, any trying on or exploring that helps you figure out how to be most comfortable is a success.

There are a number of transfeminine "finishing schools" or "immersion programs" that can help us explore our femme selves such as our sense of style, mannerisms, and speech patterns in a safe environment. They include Miss Vera's Academy and Neauveaushe in New York City, "Le Femme" in New Jersey, and The Transgender Institute in Kansas City.

GENDER, TRAFFIC, AND OTHER SUCH ANNOYANCES

Anna Burns (she/her) is a graduate student at Alabama A&M, where she studies psychology, specializing in sex and gender. She likes otters and psychology, and has more knowledge of Star Trek than may, strictly speaking, be wise.

One of the curious things about being trans is that we—sometimes temporarily, sometimes permanently—get to exist in a liminal space between genders. Mid-way into my own transition, prior to full-time, I got to engage in a bit of fun with that. I was driving home late from seeing my friends in girlmode, and got stuck in a massive traffic jam. The guy in the car next to me gets out to check the traffic and stretch. In the process he saw me and gave me *that look*, and kept glancing my way for a while. Finally, the cars start to move and we get going. Well, by this point I really needed to just use the restroom (thanks spiro), and I pull off the first exit with a gas station that I see. Being stared at had shaken my confidence a bit, so, as it was dark by then, I parked behind the McDonald's and quickly changed clothes back to a button-down shirt and my school lab coat in my car before racing in to use the restroom. As soon as I left the restroom, I saw that same guy, except this time he looked confused—Could this respectable looking "man" be the girl he saw earlier? So, as I was leaving, I gave him a wave.

Honestly, those small moments where someone is just plain confused about me being trans are moments I've come to enjoy. I haven't always taken a lot of pride in my identity—I've even tried to run away from it. I get that being trans doesn't make me less of a woman. It simply changes the narrative a little—just like how tall and short women have different experiences; both are valid. But these experiences are special to me now. Well, I mean, most of these experiences—some particular ones I could live without—as they have helped inform who I am. Besides, when isn't it fun to wink at some confused cis man, when it's safe?

LIFE CIRCUMSTANCES

Various external factors play a role in how and when we elect to socially transition. Each of us comes to social transition from a different place. Family, age, race, culture, religion, gender assigned at birth, geographical location, social class, finances, disability, and a plethora of other factors intersect to shape an individual's access to a healthy and safe transition.

> I think being fat and being nonbinary is a hard intersection. Being fat makes people think they can be mean to me without it being socially unacceptable. It also means that they see my curves as a sign of womanhood. If I don't bind, my boobs are so big that people immediately assume that there is nothing I could be other than a woman. This intersection hurts me a lot.

Disability plays a significant role in shaping the contours of social transition. Social transition may include clothing (which must be changed), makeup (which must be put on), packers, breast forms, binders (which must be put on, and which can significantly compress your chest), and demeanor (which must be adopted). Those of us who have a more limited range of movement or manual dexterity than average or who experience pain or difficulties breathing from binding may have to plan our social transition differently.

Support from family, friends, and communities is one of the leading determinants of well-being and frequently one of the foremost concerns of people considering social transition. Dependence on partners or parents for financial or immigration reasons, for instance, may make it difficult to socially transition at the time and in the manner desired. These factors intersect with race and culture. For instance, Black people and many other communities of color are often subject to increased scrutiny and judgment, which can complicate social transition.

Because safety can vary across communities and geographical locations, some of us wait until we can move before socially transitioning. If we cannot get out of a particular situation at the moment, we may choose to socially transition using less conspicuous approaches.

> I think I'm at that in-between point now where most people are unsure of my gender or just have to take wild guesses. It's not really by choice, because due to my stepfather's views, I'm not in a place safe enough to begin to medically transition. It's awkward and uncomfortable at times, though I'm happier now than when I had to pretend, and I know things will get better with time.

Social transition can be expensive. Job security, social class, and income are factors that often come into play when people think about socially transitioning. Not everyone is in a position to undertake a full wardrobe change and, although alternatives exist, such as clothing exchanges, some specific to trans people, it isn't always easy to find clothing, makeup, binders, packers, or other necessary tools for free or cheap. The threat of unemployment is a challenge, with low-paying jobs often being the ones with the highest risk of discrimination, especially in jurisdictions where anti-trans discrimination is legal. Many trans people also report a sense of being put "on hold" after they come out in the work-place, with employers being reluctant to promote trans people or help them advance in the company because socially transitioning is perceived as a time of instability that runs counter to capitalist productivity. These assumptions are typically wrong and reflect an underlying cisnormativity (or transphobia).

The idea of "trans time" refers to the different relationship that trans people have to time; much of transitioning occurs in waiting: waiting for hormones, waiting for surgeries, waiting for employers to get used to us being trans, waiting for birth certificate changes to go through, and so on. Trans time, to some, might mean waiting to socially transition until being able to medically transition. This may entail waiting until being able to move or obtain insurance coverage.

TIRED

Adrian Horsley (they/them) is a senior at Hopkins School in New Haven, Connecticut. This piece was originally a speech given at the Day of Silence assembly at school. They hope their experience resonates with others and perhaps helps someone else put their feelings into words.

I get more and more tired every single day. Existence is exhausting.

I am tired of arguing that I am a real person. I'm tired of hearing that I'm not really a boy because I wear skirts, or that I'm not really nonbinary because I don't fit a checklist that someone made up to describe the perfect enby. I am tired of looking at myself in the mirror and seeing the ghost of a girl that doesn't exist. I am tired of feeling like an imposter in my own body. I'm tired of feeling like a cosmic mistake. I am tired of choosing the women's bathroom in public places because I don't feel safe using the men's. I'm tired of introducing myself with my pronouns because no one will use the right ones on instinct. I am tired of not introducing myself with my pronouns be-cause the conversation that will follow just doesn't seem worth it.

I am tired of trying to decide between a baggy hoodie that hides my chest or a pretty shirt that I look good in. I am tired of feeling the weight on my chest that screams to the world that I have two X chromosomes. I am tired of holding a dress in my hands and repeating "this doesn't make you a girl" over and over until my skin stops crawling. I am tired of the burning, clawing beast in my stomach that calls itself dysphoria. I am tired of looking at my friend and knowing that he has had to fight even harder than I have. I am tired of looking at my friend and knowing that they have a longer battle than mine ahead of them. I am tired of commiserating over being utterly miserable to-gether. I am tired of knowing that none of us can afford to fix the bodies we're stuck in. I am tired of being trapped in this skin that doesn't fit me. I am tired of not having a guarantee that I can ever shape this body into something that does fit.

I am tired of hating myself.

But most of all, I am tired of being tired.

So I am standing here today, telling all of you all of this, because I am tired of not standing up for myself. I am tired of being silent.

I am done being silent.

(Thank you.)

COMPONENTS OF SOCIAL TRANSITION

Terms Used to Address Us

One of the ways that many of us begin to socially transition is to change the terms we ask others to use to address us. These may include our names, pronouns, and other gendered labels.

NAMES

Names identify us and represent us. Because names are gendered in many cultures, trans people are often uncomfortable with the name they were given earlier in life. Choosing a name that fits us can be an important part of social transition, and we can take as little or as much time as we need to find it. It will be easier for some—we may already have a favorite name, we may have already used a different name in the past, our name may be unisex, or maybe our name can be re-gendered satisfyingly by changing just a few letters. Others may take a long time and go through various names before finding one that they really like. Getting used to our name can take a while and not everyone experiences an immediate connection to their chosen name.

There are many ways to find a name for yourself. Some people who have good relationships with their family might ask them to rename them or ask what name they would have been given had they been assigned a different gender at birth. This approach reproduces the dynamic of name attribution experienced by many cisgender people, although you will likely have the option to reject a name that you dislike. Asking friends and family for suggestions is also a possible way of finding inspiration.

We may want to pick a name that reflects our cultural background. Gender is part of our identity, but so is ancestry, race, and culture. Changing our name can be an opportunity to keep or make visible other parts of our personal identity. Taking the name of a deceased family member can be a way of honoring their memory while reasserting belonging in a long line of men or women. It's important to keep in mind that taking a name from a culture you don't belong to may be disrespectful.

The Internet is replete with lists of male-coded, female-coded, and unisex names. Going through those lists can help narrow down possible names. Looking to other trans people can also be a way of finding a suitable name. For those who have a publication record, using a name with the same first letter can help maintain publication continuity given that many citation styles only use the first letter of your first name.

Keep in mind that cis people don't always have names that fit them perfectly. Having mixed feelings about our name is normal and doesn't necessarily mean it's an ill-fitting

Written and illustrated by Rowan S. Hampton, a disabled and bisexual non-binary illustrator and cartoonist rooted in Fort Worth, Texas.

Living As Ourselves

Written and illustrated by Rowan S. Hampton, a disabled and bisexual non-binary illustrator and cartoonist rooted in Fort Worth, Texas.

name. The perfect name might not exist. Part of life is giving meaning to our name by experiencing the world with it. Overthinking our choice can lead to unnecessary distress.

PRONOUNS AND GENDERED LABELS

Perhaps the most common way in which people are gendered is pronouns. English, like many other languages, has gendered pronouns, including he, she, they, and ze. Some of these pronouns are part of standard English and widely recognized. Some, like "they," are increasingly seen as valid, while others, like "ze," are only common in some nonbinary and genderqueer spaces. Because pronouns are strongly associated with gender, trans people often want others to change the pronouns they use when they talk about them. Trans women commonly favor "she" and trans men "he," whereas nonbinary people vary wildly in the pronouns they use: "he," "she," "they," and other pronouns are all common. Some repudiate pronouns altogether, asking that people use their first name or a monosyllabic nickname instead.

> *Not being out can be safer in some circumstances, and there are certainly places in my life where I don't bother to mention pronouns.*

Like names, finding pronouns that suit us is a deeply personal endeavor that may involve trying things on for size. Which pronouns we wish to use may change over time. It is common, especially among nonbinary people, to use different pronouns in different contexts or spaces, or give people multiple options either for their ease or because we are comfortable with multiple different pronouns. Gender-neutral pronouns other than "they" remain uncommon, and outside of nonbinary spaces it may be unfortunately difficult to have them respected.

We may grow tired of explaining which pronouns people should use when, and simply take the easier path by letting people use whichever pronoun they want or electing to use a pronoun that people will more readily respect even if it's not our favored one. If your gender presentation doesn't match what people expect those who use your pronouns to look like, misgendering can occur more often. Using a pronoun pin can help, although misgendering is often unavoidable.

The term "neopronoun" refers to pronouns that are new in English. Neopronouns include gender-neutral pronouns (i.e. theythey, xe/xym) as well as pronouns that do not reference gender (sometimes called "noun-self pronouns," such as cloud/cloudself or vamp/vampself). Noun-self pronouns can reflect a person's connection to nature, fandom, or other interests, and are highly individualized.

It is important to consider how we want to communicate our pronouns to others. If you're unsure which pronouns feel the most comfortable, trying on different ones with close friends, partners, or family members can be a good way to explore your feelings. If you're considering adopting gender-neutral pronouns, it's important to think about how these pronouns will make you visible as trans or nonbinary, which you may or may not be comfortable with. If you are uncertain about which pronouns best suit you, it's helpful to think about how people around you will react if you do change again; while your close friends might be supportive, your workplace might not be. This doesn't mean that we shouldn't try different pronouns, but our decision should take into consideration the unfortunate risk of negative reactions if we change our pronouns or name multiple times.

In some languages, adjective and verb endings, or even second-person pronouns are gendered. This creates many more opportunities for both gender recognition and misgendering. A trans person who speaks Spanish at home and English at work or school may find it easier to change their pronouns in one of the two contexts. Some multilingual trans people may find that different pronouns resonate with them in different languages. For people who are not speaking their first language, switching pronouns at the request of a trans or nonbinary person may be more challenging than if they were speaking their first language.

Pronouns and names are not the only way we are gendered. Gender labels (e.g., man, woman, genderqueer, agender) are obviously gendered, but so are a wide range of terms. Some of those terms are obvious, such as "prince," "princess," or "lesbian," whereas others are more subtly gendered: "handsome" and "pretty" are mostly applied to men and women, respectively. Preference for those gendered terms can be more difficult to communicate than pronouns. Our comfort with them might be context-dependent, too: Cis gay men often call each other "girl," and a queer trans man might be comfortable with being called "girl" in gay male spaces yet be deeply uncomfortable being called "girl" elsewhere. Like all other aspects of social transition, there is no right or wrong way to feel about gendered terms. Although you may feel a pressure to figure out your gender and how you feel about different gendered terms, it's perfectly fine to be comfortable with uncertainty.

GETTING MISGENDERED OR DEADNAMED

When someone uses gendered terms that differ from those we want them to use, they are misgendering us. Commonly, this takes the form of using pronouns or gendered terms associated with the gender one was assigned at birth. Whether intentional or accidental, it can be invalidating of our gender identities. For nonbinary people, misgendering frequently means being put in a binary box based on appearance. Closely related to misgendering is the phenomenon of deadnaming, which involves calling someone by a name they no longer use and which often clashes with their current gender identity.

Some people don't really mind being misgendered or deadnamed, while some are really distressed by it. Being misgendered by those we care about and love the most can be particularly upsetting. It's even more upsetting that those people can have the hardest time respecting our pronouns and name because they are more used to our previous name and pronouns.

> I have experienced microaggressions, most of which include the misuse of pronouns or use of an incorrect name. I work really hard to give folks the benefit of the doubt and minimize the aggressor's need for sympathy or care-taking if they apologize. It's not my duty to make an aggressor feel better about themselves for apologizing for their mistake. I can acknowledge what they've said and move on—and ask them to do the same.

Thinking about how we navigate being misgendered is important. Correcting people can be seen as rude, and can feel intimidating or tiresome. Being angry is a reasonable reaction, but can exacerbate interpersonal tensions. One way to teach people to respect your pronouns is describing how it makes you feel and telling them how you expect them to react if they catch themselves misgendering you or if you correct them. Obsequious apologies are rarely appreciated, especially in public spaces. Interacting with people who repeatedly misgender you can be distressing, and it is important to take the time to take care of yourself. Setting limits and clearly explaining how you will respond to future misgendering can help your mental health.

Having strong allies correct others can be extremely helpful. If you know people who can play that role for you, it may be helpful to tell them whether you want them to correct others, whether you want them to do so when you are there and when you are absent, and how you want them to do it. Having them correct others by saying, "they, not she" or "she, not he" will often have a stronger impact than just repeating the right pronoun, though having friends simply model the right pronoun usage can be powerful, too.

If you are particularly worried about being misgendered or people identifying you as trans, your reaction might be to blame yourself and despair at the possibility of it reoccurring in the future. In those moments, it is healthy to take a step back. Cis people also get misgendered and with the increase in trans visibility, many cis people are misidentified as trans. It's important not to set up unattainable goals in terms of (in)visibility and to find a balance between being comfortable with ourselves and in the world. Don't put too much pressure on yourself.

THE CHASE

Sam Allen (they/them) is a writer in the Central Valley city of Stockton, California. They would like all trans and gender-creative folk to know that they're fine just as they are. They've been published in their local weekly and in The Interfaith Observer.

"Do not be afraid of the terrors of the night, nor the arrow that flies in the day".
—Psalm 91:5, New Living Translation.

I was standing at Golden Gate Avenue and Main Street at twilight, just a few blocks away from downtown Turlock, California. On the corner to my left, I saw a group of guys in their twenties and one girl who was pushing a baby carriage. I could tell they were agitated. The guys in the group were in white T-shirts and jeans, too baggy for their age, and I instinctively backed up a little from the corner. I chastised myself: *Not all guys in baggy clothes are bad, Amy.* (I was still going by my birth name in those days.) I toed the edge of the corner.

There was a "heh, heh, heh," like a witch's cackling, on the guys' side. It was the kind of laughter that instinctively told me something bad was about to happen: "Hey man, is that your girlfriend?" One of the guys teased his friend. "Hellllll Nah," he loudly denied. *You've got that right*, I silently thought to myself. I was newly coming out into myself and knew that I was only into boyish girls at that point. Then I heard a shout, "Let's get her!!!!"

I booked it. They chased me down Main Street with a menacing swagger. Having the advantage of an extra corner to cross, I was ahead of them a bit. Frantically, I ducked into a Jack in the Box restaurant nearby. I waited a minute before sneaking out the side exit. The boys waited for me up front, imaginary chains in hand. Their fists were palpable—even though they never touched me. The girl in the group with the baby carriage was the worst, however; her silence was such a betrayal of our basic humanity, our shared existence. I looked at a passing butch in a truck—maybe just a farmer—with desperation. *How the hell do you live in this town?!* I silently pleaded to them as I escaped.

For years I blamed myself. My outfit from that night, part of a grand experiment in gender, sat in a pile on my bedroom floor—even after I moved to Stockton. I didn't call the police because I was just coming out as a dyke, later a trans boi, and, in my mind, there was nothing to report. Now I see that there was everything to report, but my internalized phobias prevented me from knowing that.

Despite that horrifying experience, I still call Turlock my heart's home. My feeling of belonging there is stronger than their fists. I continue to go out—even at night—but either with a handy getaway plan (usually my bicycle) or with someone as my safety partner. Blaming the chase on my clothing choice that night somehow provided a sense of security: If I keep those first boy clothes—an orange sweater and carpenter jeans—slumped on the floor and not on my body, I'll be OK. If I just cover myself with a hat on the day of the Marriage Equality decision, then I'll be safe. But to this day, The National Day of Silence rings in my ears as National Fuck Up a Queer Day, and whenever I see the mug shots of female hate crime suspects, I'm instantly brought back to the terror of that night.

APPEARANCE

I started painting my nails and sometimes wearing makeup again. Thanks to my friends and partners, I've started to wear long skirts in public, which I really love. I have also been more aware of how much space I take up in public, how often I talk in class, and how I hold my body when I sit or stand. I play around with taking up less space and acting more "female," sometimes to see how people react.

Our appearance is often the initial basis on which people gender us. Our appearances can serve to express our gender as well as manage how others perceive it. It's often one of the first things that people want to change as part of their social transition. For some, this means adopting a strongly feminine or masculine presentation, whether because it's the style that suits them best or because it makes others recognize their gender more readily. Others might adopt a more casual approach or carefully craft a more androgynous appearance for themselves.

It's not uncommon for people to dress in ways that used to feel off-limits in their youth because of their assigned gender. Many trans women who grew up in the 1990s and 2000s didn't get to experience the trend of chokers, emo, or scene subcultures and want to revisit them once they socially transition. Our gender expression can also be a way of processing grief toward the life we didn't get to have when we were younger.

Reflection. Charcoal on Paper on Wood Panel. (Devon Reiffer)

As your confidence and comfort with your gender increases over time, you might find that your relationship to your appearance changes and becomes less motivated by gender than by personal stylistic preferences. Medical transition can also make it easier to avoid misgendering despite a less starkly gendered style. Your appearance is not something you have to commit to for the rest of your life. Feel free to experiment with different styles as you try to find a home for yourself.

Clothing

One of the easiest ways of playing with gender expression is through clothing. The type of clothing we wear, its color, and its cut are all gendered aspects of clothing that can be taken into consideration when choosing how to dress. Whether a piece of clothing is masculine or feminine depends on fashion trends and perspective. Crop tops could be perceived as feminine or feel like a 1980s retro masculine piece of clothing. Awareness of fashion trends and what is popular where you live is helpful when deciding what to wear.

The easiest way to find clothes you like is simply to look around. Everyone wears clothes, even mannequins! Gathering the clothes and arranging them in a coherent style is often the more challenging part. Clothing shops are unfortunately very gendered, which can be a challenge. Knowing how sizing works, how shops divide clothes by gender and by style, and whether the shop has different fitting rooms for men and women can help appease the anxiety of shopping.

If you have fears related to shopping in a physical store, online shopping can be a relatively anxiety-free alternative. It's important to become familiar with clothing sizes, and with male-coded and female-coded styles being sized differently and varying wildly across brands. Buying a tape measure can be of help with online shopping, given that many websites have sizing charts. Still, you might have to return items and may want to avoid final sales unless you are familiar with that brand's sizes.

Rebirth Garments are "gender non-conforming wearables and accessories for people on the full spectrum of gender, size and ability. Instead of being centered on cisgender, heterosexual, white, thin people, Rebirth Garments is centered on Queer and Disabled people."

For low-price or free clothing, check out the Facebook group "Trans & Non-Binary Clothing Swap."

For people who are exploring wearing a bra, finding the right size can be challenging. Many cis women also struggle with it and wear the wrong sizes. If you are sufficiently comfortable, employees in lingerie stores are often happy to measure you for bra size. If you are undergoing estrogenic hormone replacement therapy, it may be best to err toward a larger size rather than smaller one, because your chest may continue to grow.

Some gender neutral clothing companies include The Phluid Project, Kirrin Finch, One DNA, VEEA, FLAVNT, Big Bud Press, Official Rebrand, Gender Free World, and TomboyX among many others.

Many trans and gender expansive people are afraid of customers' and employees' reactions when shopping at a physical store. Bringing a friend along can help appease some of that anxiety, though it can also increase scrutiny, especially for people of color. Discuss with your friend how you want them to approach advocating for you if staff members are reluctant to allow you to use the changing room that you are most comfortable using. Cis people have diverse appearances and shop for many reasons. You may not stand out as much as you think.

Although shopping at thrift stores is more work, it's cheaper and often more comfortable. Staff may be less intrusive, and, because people often go to thrift stores for costumes, employees are less likely to be judgmental about your clothing and shopping choices. Many trans community organizations and online groups organize clothing exchanges where transfeminine people and transmasculine people can trade their old clothes. Although these can be hard to find, and sizes can make it more difficult, few spaces are as accepting of gender identity as trans-led ones.

There are number of online stores for transfeminine folks where the clothing is often better cut and designed for our bodies than clothes designed for cis women. These include En Femme (enfemmestyle.com), Janet's Closet (janetscloset.com), and Cross Dress (cross-dress.com).

Honestly, my gender expression is still a bit of a work in progress. I got a lot of "tran-me-downs" (donations of clothes from one trans person to another) from a couple FTM friends, and I bought a few more clothes to complete a wardrobe change. Everything else is a work in progress.

Finding your size can be difficult, especially when it comes to shoes. Specialty stores exist for larger sizes, and salespeople can often order them if the brand carries that size. Many women's shoe brands go up to size 12. Discount stores are often organized by size, which can facilitate shopping. For smaller sizes on the masculine side, it can be difficult to find suitable work shoes, but many kids' brands carry formal footwear. There are almost certainly cis people who wear the same size as you and they do manage to find clothes: it's a matter of figuring out where.

NonConforming. (Armani Dae)

LIVING AS OURSELVES

I get a lot of people who know my situation correcting themselves and I try not to show offense, but that is really deflating. Like if I am carrying a purse, and they go "I love your purse—I mean satchel!" I just want to be like "No, you were right the first time."

Accessories are an important part of clothing, and a practical reality. Feminine clothing tends to either have no pockets or much too small ones, making purses and bags a necessity. The presence or absence of pockets is a surprisingly common topic of discussion and bonding among women. For people who opt for more masculine clothing, accessories such as larger wallets, keychains, ties, and belts are part of the fashion landscape. Learning to tie a tie can be challenging but tutorials are readily available on YouTube and achieving a dapper look can be highly rewarding.

Suit companies that cater to transmasculine, nonbinary, and butch people include Bindle & Keep, Sharpe Suiting, Saint Harridan, Wildfang, Haute Butch, and many more.

TRAVELING WHILE TRANS: SECURITY AND THE TSA

Faith DaBrooke (she/her) is one of the hosts of the Gender Rebels podcast.

No one wants to deal with airline security. It's a hassle. For trans and gender nonconforming people, it can also be invasive, terrifying, and humiliating. Thankfully, there are some steps you can take to make your navigation through airport security as smooth as possible.

Travel with your legal ID and book your ticket under your legal name, even if it doesn't really match your current appearance or preferred name.

Remember that you have a right to request a "pat down" instead of scanners. You also have the right to request a private screening.

For trans women, tucking securely can help speed you through security. Though you may not prefer to tuck, the scanners are based on traditional ideas of male and female body types. Your genitals can show up as an anomaly and that may lead to additional searches.

Don't wear breast forms, pads, or packers through the TSA. Trans people often depend on these items, but they can look suspicious on scanners. Instead, pack them at the top of your luggage. If asked, use the term "medical prosthesis." TSA agents may not know what a packer is, so using their language will help to avoid confusion. You can bring these items in a carry-on bag, and put them on in a restroom once you've passed through security.

If you get pulled aside, stay calm and be polite. Remember that you have done nothing wrong and have broken no laws. If you are subject to a more invasive search, you have the right to request an agent of the same gender. Do your best to stay calm, be courteous, and follow any legal directions. You may also request to have a police officer present during any screening.

If you feel that you are being subject to unlawful directions, harassment, prejudice, or assault, you can "opt out" at any time. This will mean missing your flight, but it is your right.

Document everything. You may be prevented from electronically recording the incident, but take notes of any and all details when you are able to. Who were the persons you interacted with? What day and time? What location? Ask to speak with a supervisor. You can also request video of the incident.

Though it is unfair, remember that you will not win an argument with the TSA while going through security. If you are mistreated, do your best to remain calm and courteous. You will get the best results by going through the proper channels.

Remember that thousands of transgender and gender nonconforming people travel every day. It is unlikely that you will experience any issues with security. But be prepared and know your rights.

Makeup

Using makeup can be exciting and daunting. Doing it well is a knowledge-intensive endeavor and many transfeminine people weren't taught how to use it growing up. The makeup artistry subculture is large. Websites and YouTube videos explaining how to use makeup and which products to acquire abound. You can also visit specialty stores and ask staff for help. They are knowledgeable about makeup and will happily do your makeup for a fee, which is often reduced or waived if you buy products.

Makeup can be expensive. With some help, you can find good quality makeup at the pharmacy at a lower price. Friends and family may also have products that they don't use and are willing to give away. You should nonetheless consider getting your own concealer and foundation, since they must match your skin tone.

Increasingly, workshops are being held specifically to help transfeminine people learn how to use makeup. These can be helpful to learn trans-specific tips, such as softening sharp facial features and applying color correction to beard shadow. You can also

Sephora offers free "Classes for Confidence," providing makeup tips and advice for transition.

find tips and help online. These tips can help you avoid standing out too much due to what some consider "mistakes," such as using bright colors instead of matching colors to your skin tone or using a dark eyeshadow that makes your eyes look deeper.

Although people who opt for more masculine gender expressions often shy away from makeup, it can be used to accentuate masculine features. Many trans men and nonbinary people also use makeup in more feminine styles; the choice is highly individual and people of all genders should feel free to use makeup if they so desire.

The biggest concrete change, within the past year, has been painting on facial hair—from a light mustache shadow that is unclockable to a full painted-on drag beard.

Hair

Hairstyles are another gendered and culturally mediated aspect of our appearance. In many cultures, longer hair is perceived as more feminine, and shorter hair as more masculine. In some Indigenous cultures, hair length may carry significant meaning but is not a gender signifier. Beyond length, the cut itself matters, as short hair can be further subdivided between masculine cuts and "pixie" cuts, which are considered more feminine. Some haircuts are more flexible than others in terms of gendered perception and may be perceived as androgynous. When deciding which style you want, you should consider how much product and maintenance the hairstyle will require.

When getting your hair cut short, it can be helpful to specify whether you're looking for a more masculine or feminine cut, given that it will have an impact on how the barber or hairdresser shapes it. Coming to the hairdresser with pictures of what you want helps them get a better sense of what you are hoping for and avoid making mistakes because of assumptions. You're a client, so don't be afraid to ask for what you want. Hair salons are unfortunately often strongly gendered with different price points based on gender rather than hairstyle or length; be prepared for this and decide in advance whether you want to challenge them if they misgender you. When growing out your hair, receiving occasional haircuts can help you avoid split ends and maintain a more fashionable hairstyle that grows evenly, which may be worth the extra time it will take to grow it out.

If you want longer hair, you might be interested in buying a wig. This is common for those who have baldness patterns influenced by hormones. Wigs come at different price points depending on their quality and type. Cheaper wigs can be an opportunity to try out different styles before buying a higher quality one. Numerous online resources explain the various types of wigs and the advantages and disadvantages of each. If you can afford them, wigs made from human hair look the most natural. Nevertheless, many wigs made from synthetic hair look natural, and not everyone cares or wants hair that looks natural. Shopping for wigs in a physical store, even if you don't plan to buy any, can help you get a sense of the elusive elements that make a wig feel and look best on you, and employees at the store are often knowledgeable about the benefits and disadvantages of various models. Like wigs, hair extensions and weaves come in many styles and materials, each with unique benefits and drawbacks. You can get them professionally installed at a salon or do them yourself, and the Internet is replete with information about them.

Hairstyle isn't just a question of gender, but also intersects with questions of sexual orientation and race. Hair with atypical colors such as blue, pink, or purple is often read as a sign of queerness, which you may either want to avoid or deliberately adopt. The natural texture of hair varies based on race, making hair styling a political matter. Black people routinely face discrimination for adopting hairstyles that best suit their natural hair texture, such as dreadlocks, cornrows, hair twists, and afros, and Black women and other women of color face strong pressures to straighten their hair and treat it chemically with hair relaxers. Afros and dreadlocks have become associated with political movements such as Black pride and can stand as a form of rebellion against white supremacy for Black people. Adopting them if you are not Black may be seen by many people as disrespectful.

Nervous about shopping for makeup in boy mode? You can tell the attendant that you're an actor to minimize attention or embarrassment. Male actors use makeup all the time!

Strands for Trans is a searchable network of trans-friendly hair salons and barber shops.

Beyond these political aspects, the natural texture of hair also impacts how you should take care of your hair. If you want to have healthy hair, it is important to know your hair texture and how to care for your type of hair. Charts are available online to determine your hair texture. These charts typically divide hair between 12 textures ranging from 1a to 4c, each corresponding to their own care and styling considerations.

Packers, Stand-To-Pee Devices, and Breast Forms

I pack and would really struggle if I couldn't do that.

Packing refers to the practice of wearing padding or other items in one's underwear to create a crotch bulge. Soft packers, which can sit loosely in briefs, are usually made of a soft silicone material and emulate the size and shape of a penis and testicles. Hard packers are worn with a harness and can be used for penetration. Cheaper alternatives such as rolled up socks also exist.

Stand-to-pee (STP) devices can come in the form of a penis-shaped prosthetic that doubles as a packer, but there are many portable devices that can be carried in pockets. Medicine spoons can be altered to make an STP device. One do-it-yourself option is to cut a flat disc from a plastic yogurt or coffee lid. To use it, roll it into a funnel and hold it at the opening of the urethra. This can be easily carried in a back pocket and is simple to dry after use. Before using an STP device in public, practice in the shower. Once you've mastered peeing without spills, practice with your home toilet. Soon, you'll be ready for public stalls and urinals. Many tutorials can be found online.

Transfeminine people often use breast forms or stuff their bra to give the appearance of larger breasts, especially if they are not undergoing estrogenic hormone replacement therapy or find their breasts are smaller than they would like. Padded bras can also help give off the appearance of larger breasts. Filling water balloons with seeds, gels, or powder can be a good way of stuffing bras. Many people simply opt for socks or tissues. It's also possible to buy breast forms online or at lingerie stores that are designed specifically for the purpose of creating a larger chest. They are worn under bras or directly on the skin.

PACKING WITH PUPPETS

Eppchez! (ey, em, eir) is a Cuban and Jewish Quaker, theater artist, designer, and musician in Philadelphia. Ey travels with several solo performances about historical gender self-determiners, how Whiteness and class privilege function, and a one troll show witnessing rivers, rails and all that passes along them.

How do you make space for yourself? Your imaginary, very real parts. For me, I invent my gender. I've invented all kinds of language. I call myself a darb—an onomato-poetic utterance. Equal parts clown and troll-fae. For me, trans is about manifesting new kinds of authenticity in the space my body holds. I became a doula to my own rebirth.

I'm trying to remember what I used to think about that place where my penis might protrude. What did I feel about that space? Not much.

It had existed on the other side of an impermeable public barrier: my pants. I never really afforded myself enough room in that space to wonder. There are plenty of flaccid silicone penises I could buy, but that's not me. That flaccid "nude" shape never did much for me. In my endless restless experimenting, I had started packing and stuffing all kinds of things in my jock. For a while I used a clown nose, which was a joy to whip out for the timely punch line. Soon my packing ambitions outgrew this gag (the nose I was using started breaking), and I moved on to packing with parts from old puppets that I had lying around.

Soon, I started designing my own junk for spiritual and physical comfort. I cut shapes from memory foam—leaving room for my growing dikclit. I covered the shapes in soft fabrics. The design possibilities were as endless as gender. A local art gallery had an open call for visual work dealing with queer representations. I entered several designs and was fortunate to show three of the original Darb Parts as wearable art objects. This work was very well received.

The spark ignited. I surely wasn't the only gender rebel who could benefit from this project. So here I am, working to bring this concept to others who may be struggling with similar dysphoria as what I have experienced as a transmasculine nonbinary person. I founded DarbGarb to expand as a metaphorical doula, helping others through rebirth. I have some designs ready to go, but I am most interested in taking commissions and holding consultations with interested nonbinary and gender nonconforming bad-asses to inquire, discover, and realize what their parts are like. For myself, I like bad penis puns: pocket rocket, one eyed monster, slow poke the snail. With a gender totem secure in my jock . . . out in the world, I feel seen. Visible. Proud. Refusing to be invisible again.

Binders

My main thing was beginning binding, which made me feel so much better. I have terrible chest dysphoria and while it's still not great and I definitely want top surgery, my binder has given me so much freedom to be more comfortable in public and wearing clothing that isn't huge and thick and obscuring of all of me.

Binders are a type of snug-yet-stretchy compression undergarment used for the purpose of flattening the chest. Chest binding has been practiced throughout history by a variety of cultures and certainly has a long history among transmasculine people. Binding techniques each have their upsides and downsides. When initiating binding, there may be some trial and error involved. People who have dysphoria toward their chest often report feeling more comfortable, especially in public, when binding. A good binder can smooth out the chest even beneath a T-shirt and can be worn comfortably for up to six to eight hours. Some people find binding can increase their awareness of their chest, especially in the beginning. Most people eventually get used to the binder, while others may not and choose not to bind. Some see binding as a necessity until they can access top surgery, while others only bind on occasion. Whether you view binding as a necessity or a choice, ensuring that you're binding safely and comfortably is essential.

Point of Pride has a binder donation program that has donated thousands of chest binders to people in all 50 states and 50 + countries.

Binders come in a variety of types, styles, colors, and sizes. Some binders resemble an undershirt, tank top, or sports bra, while others are styled more like crop tops. Some are plain and made to hide like an undershirt, while others are colorful and noticeable. Some can stretch past the hips and be tucked in, while others are shorter and extend only to the waist. Choosing a binder is less about chest size than body type and personal preference. They can be bought online or in physical stores. Most websites list size charts, so it's good to know your measurements. If you have worn a bra before and remember your bra size, it can come in handy. Otherwise, measure the circumference of your chest at the widest part, over clothing, with a tape measure. Write this number down and then take a second measurement underneath the pectoral area where the crease is. Add those two numbers together and divide by two. This number should work with most brands of binders. It may be tempting to get a smaller size for a tighter fit, but this increases the risk of being extremely uncomfortable and, in some cases, unsafe.

Binders range in cost and not everyone can afford to buy a new one. Some people give their binders away after getting top surgery and many community organizations offer

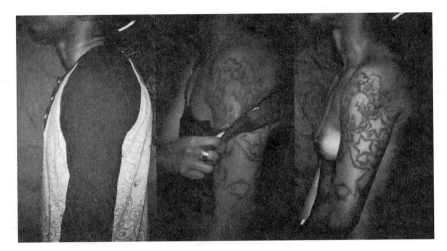

BinderTruth. (Armani Dae)

them for free or cheap. Some binder vendors also organize binder buybacks for people needing binders.

Use of tights, leggings, or control-top pantyhose as binders can be a more affordable option for some. Simply cut the legs to the desired sleeve length and cut a hole in the crotch where your head will go. These range in price, too, but start much cheaper. As with binders, it's important to find the right size for you. If the compression is too tight, breathing can be affected, muscles can become sore, and skin can get irritated. Other do-it-yourself options, such as ACE bandages and duct tape are not usually considered safe. They can cause bruising, skin irritation, and other health problems.

> *I occasionally bind my chest, but usually only for special occasions because my body can't handle it for more than a day or two once in a while.*

Binders can take some getting used to. When starting, increasing gradually from one or two hours a day can help your body adjust. In general, it is best to wear a binder for no longer than eight hours per day. Take it off for sleeping and for physically demanding activities. Sports bras are the ideal substitute when exercising, but if it's not enough for you, wearing a stretched out or larger binder will be better for breathing than your usual binder. You should be able to breathe normally while wearing a binder during everyday activities. If breathing feels difficult or restricted, the binder is too small.

Listen to your body. If you are fatigued or sore from the binder, try to take a brief "binder break" in the restroom. Massages and stretching when not wearing the binder help with recovery. Learn to breathe with your diaphragm instead of your chest. In diaphragmatic breathing, your belly expands while breathing, rather than your chest. You can inhale and exhale more fully with your diaphragm, which is especially useful when binding given that binders constrict your chest.

Depending on how often you wear a binder, it is best to clean it daily or every other day when possible, as binders absorb sweat and bacteria, which can irritate the skin and aggravate acne. Hand wash your binder with warm water, gentle antibacterial soap or gentle laundry detergent and leave it to air dry.

gc2b is a trans-owned company that makes comfortable, safe binders designed by and for trans people.

TIPS FOR SAFE BINDING

Frances Reed, LMT (they/them) is a genderqueer massage therapist, who specializes in transition-related bodywork. Through courses, their website, and their upcoming book on safe binding, they promote self-care, harm reduction, and pain management while binding.

Tips on how long to wear a binder:

- It is recommended that you not bind for more than eight hours per day, except in unavoidable conditions.
- If you must bind for longer than eight hours, take a break from the binder at least every eight hours.

Tips for taking breaks from your binder:

- Get to a public restroom stall, remove your binder and stretch your chest by placing your arms against the sides of the stall and taking deep breaths.
- If dysphoria makes it hard to remove your binder even at home, try switching to a looser compression garment than you wear during the day: a sports bra, a binder that is one to two sizes larger, or a sportswear compression tank top (for runners, triathletes, etc.).

Tips for choosing a binder:

- Take the measurements of your chest and follow the sizing instructions provided by the binder maker. Wearing a binder that is too small does not improve the visual results and will increase the pain and health risks.
- Binders with compression fabric located on the front only and not the back allow for more muscle, rib, and lung movement and still provide excellent outcomes for flattening the chest.
- If you are in need of a binder but cannot afford one, there are many programs that will assist you in acquiring one. Wrapping ACE bandages or tape around your torso is dangerous and should not ever be used as a method of binding.

Binding can be a lifesaver, but it can also cause serious complications in the upper body leading to pain in the shoulders, rib cage, upper back, neck, and jaw. Breathing is notoriously strained when wearing a binder, especially—but not exclusively—with strenuous physical activity. Self-massage and stretching can counteract the worst of these symptoms. If done regularly, it can prevent the worst of the pain, facilitate easier breathing, and decrease the incidence of complications in the upper body.

For the following symptoms, stretching and self-massage are advised:

- Upper body muscle pain or discomfort
- Rib pain
- Occasional tingling in the arms with various arm positions
- Manageable resistance when taking a deep breath

The risk of fainting and heat stroke are heightened when wearing a binder. If any of the following symptoms occur, get to a safe place and remove your binder.

- Throbbing headache
- Dizziness and light-headedness
- Lack of sweating despite the heat
- Nausea and vomiting
- Rapid heartbeat (strong or weak)
- Rapid, shallow breathing
- Confusion, blurred vision, or sensation that the room is moving
- Ringing in the ears

If these symptoms do not alleviate quickly, get to a cool place, drink room-temperature water, have someone stay with you, and call for medical attention.

For the following symptoms, medical attention is advised because these may be signs of serious medical conditions:

- Bluish discoloration of your hands or fingers
- Arm pain and swelling, possibly due to blood clots
- Cold fingers, hands, or arms
- Sustained numbness or tingling in your fingers
- Throbbing lump near your collarbone
- Inability to take a deep breath when the binder comes off

With the COVID-19 pandemic, respiratory health has been on everyone's mind and since binding limits your ability to clear phlegm from your lungs, binding increases the risk of respiratory infections. Hence, it is important to pay special attention to your lung health:

- If you have been exposed to COVID-19, avoid binding (or bind for the shortest time possible) until you can confirm you are negative.
- When you remove your binder, take three to five rib-expanding breaths and cough to help clear up any fluid in your lungs.
- If you test positive for COVID-19, avoid binding to minimize lung damage or infection.

Tucks, Gaffs, and Hip and Butt Padding

I use tucking, along with a gaff, for a smooth frontal appearance. I use attachable breast forms to enhance my figure. I use additional support garments to change the appearance of my waist and hips.

Tucking involves positioning the penis and testicles in a way that creates a smooth crotch profile. Gaffs are an alternative to tucking, using a specifically designed garment to produce the same effect. Some people also opt to use hip and buttock padding to create the appearance of larger hips or buttocks, which can be perceived as more feminine.

The most common way of tucking is by pushing the testicles back into the inguinal canals, through which the spermatic cord runs, and pulling the penis between the legs and fastening it. The penis placement keeps the testicles in place. Fastening the penis can be done with tape or tight panties. Many people find that wearing a pair of slightly smaller than usual panties underneath a more comfortably sized pair suffices to keep the penis in place. Others use tape. Shaving helps the tape stick better. Using medical tape is recommended, because duct tape is irritating and can cause skin reactions. Snug underwear over the tape helps keep the tuck in place.

To find the inguinal canal, put your finger on the testicular skin, pushing your testicle aside, and lift your finger upward toward your pubic bone. You should feel an area that is circle-shaped and through which you can slightly push inside your body. This is the entrance to your inguinal canal and where you want to push your testicle. Be careful, though, as not everyone is able to push their testicles inside their inguinal canals, especially if their testicles have not shrunk due to hormones. Pushing the testicles inside your inguinal canals can be uncomfortable, especially at first, but should not be painful. Some people enjoy the practice of tucking since the inguinal canals are full of nerves and pushing the testicles back into them can be a soothing sensation.

Callen-Lorde's Health Outreach to Teens (HOTT) program has an online Safer Tucking Guide.

I tuck my penis back, but I don't tuck my testicles into my inguinal canal because it's too painful.

Though they don't usually create as smooth a profile as tucking, gaffs, dance belts, and specially designed underwear can also be used for the same purpose. Dance belts can be found in theater and dance shops and are intended for cisgender men. Gaffs, as well as underwear designed specifically for transfeminine people, can be bought online and tend to be offered in more feminine designs. Padding for hips and buttocks is also used by some trans people. Padding can be designed to wear under underwear or clothing or be integrated in underwear. It is widely available for sale online or at lingerie stores because many cis women also use padding.

Bodily Modifications

The role of tattoos and piercings in social transition is often underestimated. Various piercing and tattoo placements and designs can be used to express gender or be read in a certain manner. Flowers, for instance, are coded as feminine and having flowery tattoos can make you appear more feminine. It is common for cis girls to have their earlobes pierced at a young age, and transfeminine people often want their earlobes pierced, too. Navel piercings tend to be seen as more feminine, as are lower back tattoos, whereas bicep tattoos are perceived as more masculine.

Some people choose tattoos that make their sexual orientation or transness visible. The trans symbol (⚧) is a common tattoo, as is "t4t," which was popularized by Torrey Peter's *Infect Your Friends and Loved Ones* (Seattle, WA: Amazon/CreateSpace Independent Publishing Platform, 2016), a sci-fi novella about a future where no one can produce hormones and everyone has to make a choice about their gender. For people who are not read as trans in everyday life, these tattoos can be a way to communicate pride in transness. Double

Gay. "Part of a series on trans male homosexuality. Gay trans men don't have a place in society and tend to be either infantilized or fetishized. We're not allowed to have sexualities." (Sammi Bradley @madradiohead on twitter, madradiohead on tumblr)

Venus (♀) and double Mars (⚣) communicate gender at the same time as they do sexual orientation and can be adopted to affirm the validity of trans folk's sexual orientations.

Piercings and tattoos hold great significance in some cultures. Many Māori women, for instance, proudly bear chin tattoos, known as moko kauae, to represent their family heritage, their true identity, and their connection to the spiritual world. In a world defined by ongoing colonialism, tattooing can be used to politically assert cultural resistance and identity. Given their cultural importance, many trans people find affirmation by adopting culturally specific piercings and tattoos best corresponding to their gender identity. People outside those cultures should refrain from adopting culturally specific patterns, because it can be disrespectful.

BEHAVIORS

Our names, pronouns, and appearance aren't the only way we express our gender. Behaviors—which activities we partake in, and how we do them—also feature in our gender landscape.

Demeanor

Where do I keep my arms? My hands? How do I walk? Depending on your desired gender presentation, you might answer these questions differently. Looking around and doing some respectful people-watching is a good way to learn how people carry themselves and how it varies by gender. Although adopting a new demeanor may feel awkward at first and require conscious effort, it typically becomes more natural over time.

> I'm also trying to sort of loosen up my behavior patterns to be more relaxed, and I take cues from what the guys are doing—hands in their pockets, how they talk and listen, how they sit, how they eat, and walk.

Gendered aspects of behavior also show up in spheres that are more traditionally private, such as flirting, sex, and dating. Going for a cutesier demeanor might be a way to express your femininity, for instance. Sexual interactions are deeply gendered and involve sexual roles that carry a slew of expectations and scripts, the gendered aspects of which will vary based on whether you are dating queer people or straight people. Feminine people are often expected to be the receiving partners in penetrative sex, and to be submissive in Bondage & Discipline/Domination & Submission/Sadism & Masochism (BDSM) contexts, and conversely, being the receiving partner or submissive might itself be read as feminine. Ultimately, the choice of whether or not to conform to these expectations is yours.

Learning and Navigating Gender Norms

Gender norms are an unavoidable part of the social landscape. One aspect of social transition may involve learning and navigating new gender norms. Some gender norms are relatively mundane and may be pleasant to follow. For instance, women tend to go to the bathroom in groups and chat. Other gender norms may be problematic, such as the expectation of emotional and domestic labor from women or the perception that men should be isolated and unemotional, which can make seeking mental health services or emotional support difficult for transmasculine people.

We typically learn gender norms over time. Unlike appearances, they are not visible. Some gender norms are stated explicitly through rules and stereotypes (e.g., men should be providers; women are bad drivers). Others are implicit and rarely stated overtly, existing instead as tacit assumptions that underpin social interactions. This can make them challenging to learn, especially for those who are not as relationally aware, such as neurodiverse people. It can be helpful to have friends accompany us in learning new gender norms, discussing them as they come up.

Gender norms are not the same everywhere. They vary based on culture, race, age, and social class. Going against the gender norms of one's own community or family may be viewed not only as gender transgression, but also as a rejection of culture. Depending on one's cultural values, having the support of your family and community may be especially important. Double consciousness or code switching refers to the process by which people of color negotiate the differing cultural expectations between one's neighborhood, community, and family, and those of school, work, or other environments, which may be dominated by white, Eurocentric norms. Social transition may require a triple or even quadruple consciousness, as unspoken behavioral norms of another gender within multiple cultural contexts must be learned. Trans men of color may experience more aggression from cis men than their white counterparts, given that men of color are subject to stereotypes about criminality and aggression. Learning and adopting the gender norms of one's culture can also be empowering, validating, and moving, particularly when it results in greater connection to one's community. Although some gender norms carry racist and sexist overtones, not all gender norms are inherently oppressive.

> *My religious community is completely segregated. Men are separate from women. Men pray in the men's section. Men have access to higher religious learning and learn in men's classes. Men dance with other men, never with women. Men lead and are expected to know how to lead publicly. Men wear special religious garb. I did not have access to these things or how to do them and had to learn how to do all these things. It still bothers me that women are not equal to men in my religious community.*

It's important to know which gender norms you will be held to, because it can help you decide which ones you want to conform to and which you want to reject or oppose. Awareness can help you set boundaries with others. Gender norms have

Robin (aka Hiro) is a trans guy from France. He is a CGI student at ESMA. He loves art in many forms, photography, drawing, dance, freerun, and even more. (Mathilde Bailley)

a relational aspect, and the norms people self-impose vary based on who they are interacting with. For instance, trans women who date men might suddenly find that their partners expect more domestic labor from them once they transition. This is important to keep in mind in relationships, because it can be a source of interpersonal tension and inequity.

Gender norms present a double bind for trans people. If you don't follow them, some people will claim you are not really your gender; if you follow them, others will criticize you for acting in stereotypical ways. There's no winning in cisnormativity, but each of us can decide for ourselves how we want to navigate the balance between conforming to the norms we want and opposing gender policing.

Being in male spaces is a learning curve. Learning Black male gender rules is ongoing. I ask questions of cis male friends or try to be very observant. I miss the women's community that was such a big part of my life and am saddened that I move through that world and am met with wariness or fear.

Refuge Restrooms is an app that provides information on trans-friendly restrooms across the country.

Beyond behavior, altering thought patterns may also be part of our social transition. Some people feel invalidated by their own thoughts. For gender-related reasons, some transmasculine people wish to become more confident, and some transfeminine people wish to become more empathetic and compassionate. Some transfeminine people can be uncomfortable with having sexual arousal patterns centered on visual stimuli rather than emotional connection. The invalidation we feel vis-à-vis our own thought patterns can be particularly challenging because thoughts are difficult to change and make us feel as though we are betraying ourselves. Keep in mind that cis people vary in how they think and that thinking a certain way doesn't make you less of a man, woman, or nonbinary person.

> There's just so many years of toxic masculinity that have been instilled into me, and it's gonna take a while to unpack all of that. I was never, however, a "man's man."

It's important to navigate gender norms in a way that is not harmful to others, and that avoids imposing gender norms (or their rejection) onto others. People are not any less valid in their gender because they refuse or fail to conform to gender norms. Conversely, although it is important to oppose all oppression, trans people aren't more responsible for the world's sexism than cis people, and we should be wary not to impose higher standards on ourselves than on cis people, especially given the dangers of nonconformity for trans people.

ONLINE CULTURE OF DISCRIMINATION PERPETUATES OFFLINE HATE

Michael Eric Brown

Millions of Americans use Facebook. Millions of people who are both reflecting their own cultures and creating new cultures through status messages and posts. Research suggests the motivations of why people respond to posts and status messages include expertise, the relationship to the person posting, desire to connect socially, obligation or indebtedness, humor, ego, and the feeling of earning social capital.[1] People communicate through their social media interactions, spreading their messages to their wider networks, reflecting, and creating a new ethos. A culture of discrimination toward transgender individuals is being reflected in online social media discourse, and due to this discourse, the online culture is creating and perpetuating additional deleterious values, beliefs, and behaviors in real life toward the transgender population.

This form of media interaction allows users the opportunity to experiment with alternate identities. Because anonymity provides individuals the opportunity to express themselves more openly, many feel at liberty to express what they otherwise wouldn't voice. Anonymous posts may reflect their true values and beliefs, including when it comes to sensitive or controversial issues such as racism, religion, same-sex marriage, or the transgender population.

This online anonymity allows people to be more explicitly transphobic.[2] In using social medica to communicate bigoted perspectives and hate-filled discourse, people connect with others and create a larger network of people who think and feel the same way. Anonymity provides them the ability to have a voice even when that voice is radical, profane, and vulgar.[3]

When dominant narratives in social media discourse misrepresent what it truly means to be a transgender person and perpetuate negative stereotypes through misrepresentation, these stereotypes become factual in society's eyes. American culture then finds it more acceptable to actively discriminate against transgender people, because, in their eyes, it is our fault that they find us disgusting, because we are the ones who are "pretending" to be someone we're not. Social media spreads this cultural sentiment, and the rippling effects of this cultural discrimination appear in real life in all social institutions, and continue to propagate the hatred we are forced to encounter because we have chosen to live authentically.

It is time to create new culture. Join me?

Spaces and Activities

> I have used women's restrooms for three years now. The sense of relief I feel is still palpable. Women are more talkative in bathrooms than I knew; it was beyond my experience, so now I feel included. This is true of how I feel included by my female coworkers now, and by women in general just walking on the street. I'm included in a sisterhood that I didn't really know existed but did yearn for.

Many spaces and social groups are explicitly or implicitly segregated by gender. Navigating gendered spaces is often a significant part of social transition. Gender-exclusive spaces include restrooms, locker rooms, sports teams, homeless shelters, shelters for people dealing with intimate partner violence, jails, prisons, colleges, clubs, choirs, social groups, and support groups. In some faiths, specific times or areas are designated for different genders to worship. In some countries, public transit may be gender segregated at certain times of day. Other spaces are implicitly gendered. Barbershops, salons, and bars may fall into this category, as do many social groups, board rooms, and cliques. You may be made to feel like you don't belong, even though it won't be stated outright.

Gendered spaces are often justified by safety, privacy, or comfort, although whether they succeed at their stated goals is debatable. These spaces can be troublesome for trans and gender expansive people, who may feel like they are imposing themselves into the space, or are impostors within it. For nonbinary people, the absence of spaces tailored to your gender can be invalidating and make it difficult to know which option would be best. Trans people unfortunately disproportionately face mistreatment, harassment, violence, and threats within gendered spaces, making them uncomfortable or unsafe. In some jurisdictions, it may be illegal to access spaces corresponding to your gender identity. But on the flip side, being welcomed in gendered spaces can also be validating.

> *My partner is a cis man and has been my compass for men's spaces. Sometimes I come home with a lot of questions about the rules.*

Trans individuals are impacted differently by gendered spaces. Some may face uncomfortable situations only occasionally, such as when using public restrooms, while others may experience them persistently (e.g. those working within gendered military structures). For binary trans people, the problem is often not that spaces are separated by gender, but that they are only constructed with cis people in mind, as evidenced by anti-trans "bathroom bills." Nevertheless, there are many examples of inclusive shelters, gyms, schools, and organizations. Trans-affirming policies and trans-only spaces are becoming increasingly common, and can offer reprieve from cisnormative pressures. Although navigating gendered spaces and activities may at times feel like a strenuous aspect of transition, these spaces can also provide affirmation and community.

Voice Training

> *I have done voice training in theater—it was not specifically meant for trans people, but the techniques built my range and comfort in different voices, and helped me find the voice that felt most like me.*

Our voice is another feature that gets us categorized by gender. A wide array of factors including pitch, intonation, articulation, resonance, and word choice, dictate whether someone's voice is perceived as more feminine or more masculine. For people who take testosterone, the changes to the vocal box and chords can sometimes suffice to make their voice sound masculine. Estrogen and antiandrogens, however, don't have a comparable feminizing effect, and many people want a more masculine voice without taking testosterone or in addition to taking testosterone.

Although anatomy puts constraints on the sound of our voice, it is usually possible to attain a significantly more feminine- or masculine-sounding voice through training. If we can afford it, some of us opt to do this with the help of a speech-language pathologist or voice communication therapist. Exercises involve learning how to use your head voice or chest voice, for a more feminine or masculine sounding voice respectively; how to shorten or lengthen your larynx—smiling works surprisingly well for shortening; and getting used to speaking at a higher or lower pitch.

Christella Antoni, a UK-based Speech & Language Therapist has an app called Christella VoiceUp with tips and advice for voice feminization.

Bound to Barbasol. Charcoal on Gesso on Canvas. (Devon Reiffer)

If you are interested in voice training, there are a number of videos available on YouTube that explain the underlying anatomical and acoustic principles and offer vocal exercises. Voice training apps also exist for phones, and often include pitch and resonance analyzers, which can provide helpful feedback as you learn how to speak differently. In addition, some speech and language pathologists specialize in helping trans and gender expansive people.

> *I trained myself, by listening to recordings of women in movies who I thought*
> *had similar voices to mine, then recorded myself and compared side by side, 'til*
> *I knew how it felt when it sounded right.*

Although voice training can radically change what we sound like when we speak, it does not have a large effect on our vocal range and thus has a limited impact on singing, although changing your resonance can help make your singing voice sound more feminine or masculine.

TransVoiceLessons is a popular YouTube channel for learning about voice training.

HOW DOES SOCIALLY TRANSITIONING MAKE YOU FEEL?

Social transition makes people feel a wide range of emotions. It's not true that if you're really trans, socially transitioning should only feel joyful or happy. Joy and happiness are common emotions when socially transitioning, but some other feelings are equally common.

Social transition can involve feelings of uncertainty. Sometimes we feel unsure about what we want or how we're feeling. When confronted with the infinite ways we can socially transition, compounded by the process of balancing what we want with staying safe, our whole life might seem permeated by uncertainty. Uncertainty isn't always a bad thing, however, and many people grow comfortable with it. Some even refuse to figure out their gender and aren't worse off for it!

> Lucille Sorella hosts a website called Femme Secrets with a long list of resources for transfeminine people who are transitioning.

I lived between genders during transition, which took years before people routinely read me as female. It was very, very difficult, and I constantly felt exposed, unsafe, and under great scrutiny. I resented being looked at like a freak or a pervert, being seen as invalid and a "less than." I could not read people's expressions very well: Were their smiles friendly, or amused, or pitying? Deeply frustrating and exhausting.

Fear and sadness are also common experiences. People's reactions to our social transition can be polarized. We may wonder who in our lives will be accepting and who will respond with anger or even violence. We may be anxious about losing jobs or apartments. We may fear going into the bathroom that best suits us due to harassment or violence. For those who engage in activism, getting harassed or doxxed—people revealing personal information such as your address or phone number—is a worrisome possibility.

PREAMBLE

Madeleine Terry's (she/her) experience walking both sides of the tracks reveals itself in her various roles including the one she cherishes the most—as a mom to her 14-year-old daughter. Exploring subjects such as spirituality, privilege, and vulnerability, she writes in the intersection between poetry and prose where economy and form open a space without having to fill it.

Though I'd flirted with women's clothing throughout my life and had fantasies about living as a woman, my true self hadn't broken through the hermetic seal I'd placed around my conscious self. Even after I'd started wearing my clothing of choice at home, there was always a reason I made for it, other than turning my questioning eye inward. It wasn't until she, my true self, came to me, cloaked in the guise of a man, that suddenly and without question, I knew who I'd been my entire life.

In my dream, I was dressed as myself—as a woman. I was perched upon the first porch step of a small house in an empty neighborhood adjacent to this industrial area where I worked, when he approached. The sky was light with hues of dusk, which made his face and features vague. His voice broke the malaise.

"Ma'am," he started earnestly. His words continued, but dropped to a dull murmur beyond my focus. *Ma'am.* It sunk in immediately. I'd been ma'am'd before, but instead of recoil, relief washed over me. He saw me for who I truly was: A woman. I woke up immediately.

"You've been a woman your entire life," I said to myself with crisp certainty. "A middle-aged woman." My own laughter followed sarcastically. This changes everything.

Suddenly, so many shards of my life's experiences which I couldn't quite fit in my own story comfortably and perfectly fit, especially my contradictions. The next three days, I didn't leave my apartment. I barely ate. With the false equilibrium I knew giving way so quickly, my relief was mingled with nausea. It was the longest sigh—finally exhaled.

This was my preamble.

It can be frustrating not to be able to blend in despite wanting to. Being outed in background checks or because of your publication footprint can be disheartening. Visibility is context-dependent and comes in degrees, and even those who try hard to be invisible may sometimes be identified as trans. Unfortunately, people often view and treat you differently once they know you are trans. You may feel more vulnerable if you have been mistreated prior to transition, or if you experience other forms of oppression, given that transitioning can alter one's visibility, sometimes shifting the frequency and/or severity of experiences of racism, classism, and other forms of oppression.

Frustration can also occur when it's not possible to be the way you want to be due to limitations on your ability to socially transition or because of the gendered codes prevalent in society. Nonbinary people are often frustrated when they are persistently gendered as male or female due to their gender presentation. Often, society is the problem and there's little we can do about it. One avenue of coping with the frustration is to use it to fuel antioppressive work.

It gets tiring to be constantly afraid or angry or to be treated as a trend because of the rising visibility of trans people in the media. But, as time goes on, people often find that their gender identity becomes less and less of a focus in their life, and with this shift in focus, fear, sadness, and fatigue may diminish. Others simply learn to accept these emotions in their life and funnel them into productive activities such as advocacy or art.

Although the experience is relatively rare, some feel discomfort with or regret about social transition. This may lead them to return to a gender role corresponding to the gender they were assigned at birth. Most often, this is due to external factors such as fear of discrimination and violence, but for some, it is simply because socially transitioning wasn't for them. If you feel like socially transitioning wasn't the right choice for you, that is a perfectly valid feeling and you should feel free to reverse it if you so desire. Social transition isn't just about the end goal but also about the process. We explore through transition and this means that we might realize it just wasn't for us. Often, people who reverse their social transition report gratefulness at the opportunity to explore their gender, despite ultimately realizing that transition didn't suit them.

Transitioning can bring grief. Sometimes, it is grief for a childhood we never had or for not transitioning earlier. Other times, it is grief at leaving behind an easier life as a cis person, even if transitioning was the right choice for us. Leaving behind a past identity can also bring feelings of loss. Despite it not suiting them, many people have developed a complex attachment to their past self. People navigate grief in many ways. Some try to hold onto mementos of their pretransition life, for instance by keeping their previous name as a middle name. Rituals, remembrance ceremonies, and taking time for mourning can also be helpful in processing our feelings of grief. If you experience grief related to transition, it's important to know that these feelings do not invalidate your gender identity or your transition. These feelings are normal.

Socially transitioning is also about finding community. We find love, friendship, laughter, loss, and joy. We live the full range of human emotions with other trans people. For many, the community found in other trans people is one of the most positive aspects of transition. Hanging out with trans people can mean feeling understood for the first time, and that feeling can be ecstatic. Social transition is often accompanied by increased recognition of one's gender by others (e.g., people using your correct name and pronouns or reading you more often as your identified gender). This can be extremely liberating and comforting. It can help clarify questions you had about your gender identity and illuminate feelings about medical transition. Social transition can happen over any time span or at any age. There is no minimum or maximum age to transition.

Chella Man is a multimedia artist who identifies as Deaf, trans, Jewish, and Chinese. Before learning the language to process and express his life experiences, art was a loophole and catharsis when coming to terms with his emotions and views on gender, race, sexuality, and disability. (MaryV)

Despite the difficulties associated with social transition, most trans people would tell you that it was one of the best choices they made in their life. Being happy or content with socially transitioning doesn't mean that we feel great about every single aspect. Few things only bring one feeling along with them, and having mixed feelings is a quintessential part of the human experience. Social transition might mean feeling less at home in the world at times, but typically means feeling more at home in ourselves. The homeliness of the self is an ineffable emotion that transcends the binary of happiness and sadness: I'm finally home.

NOTES

1. Morris, M. R., Teevan, J., & Panovich, K. (2010). What do people ask their social networks, and why?: A survey study of status message q&a behavior. In *Proceedings of the SIGCHI conference on human factors in computing systems* (pp. 1739–1748). ACM. Retrieved from http://teevan.org/ publications/papers/chi10-social.pdf

2. McInroy, L. B., & Craig, S. L. (2015). Transgender representation in offline and online media: LGBTQ youth perspectives. *Journal of Human Behavior in the Social Environment, 25*(6), 606–617. doi:10.1080/ 10911359.2014.995392

3. Baran, S. (2014). *Introduction to mass communication: Media literacy and culture updated edition* (8th ed.). McGraw-Hill Learning Solutions, VitalBook file.

WORK AND EMPLOYMENT

Lily Zheng and Jillian Weiss

9

INTRODUCTION

When we think of work, we might imagine sitting behind a desk in an office typing away at a computer, or driving vehicles in a construction site, or standing behind a counter serving customers. Although employment is certainly an important kind of work, it's far from the only kind that we do. Trans communities engage in an enormous diversity of work, and the reality is that only some of it is valued enough by our society to become a potential source of income. Those of us who work as caretakers and peacemakers, organizers, rabble-rousers, lovers, learners, and at other jobs that don't result in cash or a check are no less valid than those of us who work as accountants, consultants, tech workers, cashiers, or farmers. As trans people, we have already done an enormous amount of work to get to where we are today. This chapter will focus on employment and its joys and challenges, but know that the many kinds of work you have done and continue to do are all important. It is our hope to empower working trans people as part of a larger goal of creating economic liberation for all.

EMPLOYMENT

There are many reasons we might seek out employment, or paid work. We might be looking to start or reimagine our professional careers and seek out work to further our dreams. We might be working to earn money to put food on the table and keep roofs over our heads, to pay for medical care or school, or to otherwise survive. We might be hoping to create for ourselves a sense of meaning by doing important work for our communities and society. For all these reasons and more, trans people find themselves seeking employment in a vast number of industries, workplaces, and professions.

Looking for a Job

As trans people look for jobs, we join millions of people in America seeking a new place of employment. Some of us will be looking for our first job. Some of us will be hoping to change careers or make a fresh start in a new city, state, or country. Most of us will be job-hunting while we are also looking for housing, taking care of families or loved ones, navigating health care, or otherwise holding down the rest of our lives.

Looking for a job can feel daunting. Although there are many places to locate job listings, such as classified ads in newspapers, online, and through word-of-mouth from friends and acquaintances, it can sometimes feel like finding the "right" job is impossible. As trans people, many of us worry about finding jobs where we can avoid discrimination and have our identities validated, a difficult task given the large number of jobs and employers out there.

> *I have established a goal to work at a part-time job that would allow me to present as female.*

Some employers post job listings as a formality *after* already identifying who they want to hire. Other employers prioritize hiring from inside the company, or through events such as job fairs, or partnerships with colleges. As trans people, how can we effectively and efficiently navigate this complicated landscape?

- *Expand and make use of your personal network and resources.* Many of us are connected in today's digital world, and Facebook, LinkedIn, and other forms of social media allow us to meet and engage with dozens of people every day.

Waverly Evans is an artivist, author and LGBTQ+ Youth Advocate from Columbus, Ohio.

Although these people may be our friends and acquaintances, they can also be valuable professional connections. Staying connected to a big network helps us see information about new job openings, learn about opportunities outside our comfort zone, and gain potential allies and references to get our "foot in the door" when applying for jobs. Trans-friendly professional communities and resource groups, whether in nearby towns and cities or on the Internet can recommend workplaces, which, based on experience, are inclusive places for trans people to work. For larger companies, online corporate equality indexes can tell you which companies have trans-friendly policies and benefits. In general, the more people we know, the more information we can gather on the best places to work for our interests and skills.

- *Know your areas of excellence (but take risks, too).* Reflecting on your own strengths and abilities can help you gain insight into the jobs you might be able to do well. Don't be afraid to tap into your unique life experiences! Often, reframing challenging circumstances as "skills learned" can be both a professionally rewarding and emotionally healing exercise. At the same time, allow yourself to take risks. If you see a job you like that you don't believe yourself to be qualified for, apply anyway. You may surprise yourself and at the very least learn more about how you can become a competitive candidate.

- *Ask yourself what you're looking for.* It's important to not only look at our ability to do the job but also whether the job meets our personal, financial, and professional needs. When considering jobs, ask yourself:
  - "Would this job make me happy?"
  - "Does this job pay me enough?"
  - "Is this job setting me up for the career I want?"

Sometimes the right thing is continuing to look for jobs we know how to get. Sometimes the right thing is to seek more education or trade skills to pursue a new career. Whatever our decision, it's important to know our long-term goals so we can continually work toward them.

ON BEING AN OUT TEACHER

Skylar Case (she/her) is a science teacher in Upstate New York. She came out as a transgender woman in 2018 and began the process of hormone replacement in February of 2019. Being a teacher who is transgender has not always been easy for her, but she hopes to continue to be a positive role model for LGBTQ + youth as she grows as an educator.

Even before I completely came out at work, I was an advocate. I wanted the students in my classroom to know they were safe no matter who they were. I put safe-space posters on my walls; I took part in my school's gay-straight alliance; I wore rainbow during spirit week; and most importantly, I tried to be a safe ear when students came out of the closet.

So, when one of my students came out as a transgender boy last October, the first thing I did was smile, and say, "Nice to meet you properly." Once I made sure I could use his name and pronouns in class, I knew I wanted to be the teacher he could trust would *always* get his name and pronouns right.

I wanted him to know that, despite anything going on with his other teachers, his classmates, or at home, he was going to be safe and respected for who he is in my classroom. Toward the end of last year, he said to me, "I've known for three years that I was a boy, but I didn't tell anyone. I didn't feel safe enough to do it until you were here."

To this day, after telling the world I am a woman, I still get cards, notes, and artwork from students telling me that they're glad I do what I do as a teacher and as an advocate for LGBTQ + students in the school. I try to make them feel safe to be themselves. I try to prove to them that maybe things will work out OK for them in the end.

Teaching can sometimes be a thankless job, but these are the moments that remind me why I do what I do. Students pay attention to who really cares—and to whom they can really trust. We teachers can have a profound impact on the lives of our students, beyond the scope of the curriculum we teach.

It reminds me that teachers have the power to change lives.

Applying for a Job

Applying for jobs takes up the bulk of the time needed for any job search. Often, we will be applying to many jobs at once and dealing with what can feel like a never-ending cycle of applications and interviews until we get a hit. Sometimes we get lucky and a recommendation from a friend turns into a new job overnight. Other times we can spend weeks, months, or years in the job application process without success. Securing a job quickly is about the peculiarities of the job market and the positions being listed and applied to, but also about luck.

> *When I began to look for a new job, I put my pronouns on my resume and feel strongly that had a lot to do with how few callbacks I got. I had not had that problem the last time I looked for work. However, it also acted as a detection system to weed out places I shouldn't have been working at anyway!*
> *I typically do not disclose my sexuality or gender during interviews.*

The job hunt is difficult for everyone, but trans people often have added worries. We may be concerned about prior names or pronouns appearing on our resumes or in conversations with our references. We may worry that interviewers will discriminate against us based on our gender identities or gender expressions.

> *I usually put my name and pronouns in my cover letter, which could have an impact. It certainly took longer to find a job after transitioning, but there's no proof it was due to my trans identity.*

"My name is Sam Vertosick, I am from the Pittsburgh area, and I am non-binary. Currently, I am a part-time English instructor at Westmoreland County Community College and ABD in the Literature & Criticism doctoral program at Indiana University of Pennsylvania where I focus on LGBT issues in young adult literature."

As trans people, we have a wide range of life experiences and identities and will be applying for a wide range of different kinds of work. There is no one-size-fits-all approach to ace the job application process, but there are several helpful tips and strategies we can use to make things easier and help us land the job.

- *Be strategic about your identity.* Disclosure can be a tricky issue to navigate. Different pieces of information can communicate our trans status to potential employers and expose us to potential discrimination. For example, an employer might call a reference at a past job and hear that reference use a different name or set of pronouns for us than the one we've listed on our resume. Although we should never lie on our resumes or during interviews, making decisions around what information we choose to share is an important step of the application process. Our volunteer experience at an LGBTQ community center may have been important to us, but mentioning it on a job application for an administrative assistant position may not be ideal (unless the volunteer job was as an administrative assistant!) It's important to note that the concept of a "legal name" is fuzzy. Every U.S. state has a law permitting the use of any name so long as it is not for the purpose of fraud.[1] The name on your birth certificate, passport, or driver's license is not your "legal name," and a court order is not required to use a different one. That being said, employers have concerns about using new names for social security and tax purposes. If an employment application asks for previous names, keep in mind, in deciding what you wish to disclose, that a background check might bring up previous names.
- *Prepare documentation.* It is similarly important to consider the various forms of documentation we possess, and the names/genders listed on them. The application process for most workplaces goes most smoothly when the name and gender listed on school records/transcripts, resumes, driver's licenses, and health insurance match. Documentation that "doesn't match" typically introduces more delays into the application process and may potentially expose us to discrimination. Depending on the laws and policies in your state and city, you may decide to prioritize name and

Living as Ourselves

gender changes before the application process. Organizations like the Transgender Law Center or other local trans groups can help you with the name and/or gender change process in your state.

- *Be prepared to answer (appropriate) questions.* During the job application process, we may be asked to fill out forms or answer questions that end up outing our trans identities. Interviewers may ask questions about name changes, gender changes, or gaps in your employment history; having answers planned out in advance allows you to spend more interview time talking about your skills. Use your own discretion when disclosing details. In some workplaces, you will want to mention the bare minimum before moving on, while in others it may be OK or even beneficial to mention your trans identity in more detail. For example, a human resources (HR) representative may ask you questions about your gender identity for the purposes of payroll and benefits. Some employers ask for prior names on job applications. You may provide this information if you feel comfortable, but you always have the option of leaving this blank. Dishonesty on a job application, however, may provide a reason to later terminate you. Although answering questions about the legal name and gender on your documents is reasonable, answering questions about your transition history, surgical procedures, or dating life is not. Know that asking questions about your medical history is inappropriate unless it is necessary for your job.

- *Be consistent, confident, and competent.* Whatever the choices we make regarding the gender identity and expression we take through the application process, it is important for us to appear consistent, confident, and competent. For example, if you choose to use the name "Alex" during your interview, make sure you also use "Alex" in your resume and include a professional e-mail with the name "Alex." For in-person interviews, choose the gender expression that best allows you to be confident and display your professional skills. If you choose to disclose information your employer or interviewer may not be familiar or comfortable with, make sure to share that information as consistently, confidently, and competently as possible. For example, you might introduce yourself with they/them pronouns, followed by a sentence about how to use them correctly, and another sentence about your experience as an LGBTQ educator, if relevant. If you're unsure about the interview process, role-playing or practicing with friends is a great way to gain more familiarity and ease with presenting yourself in this way.

- *Be kind to yourself.* Job hunting is tough. As trans people we may be relearning how to interview with a different gender identity or gender expression, balancing authenticity with safety during the application process, or experimenting with new careers, industries, or identities. Looking for a job can be a drawn-out process and doing so as a trans person can be even more challenging. Having a supportive network of biological and/or chosen family and friends can help provide motivation and care throughout the process. Understand that your worth as a person and as a member of a community is not dependent on your having a certain kind of job or even a job at all.

I AM NOT A MISTAKE

Chaplain Andrés Herrera (he/him) is a 33-year-old Transgender man, a Latinx, a Christian, and a Chaplain.

I chose to do ministry when every bone in me told me it was a crazy idea. Yes, I felt—and still feel—called by God to do the work I do as a chaplain. I love being a chaplain. I love serving others and showing them the love of God. I want them to feel loved and accepted for who they are because for many years I didn't feel that way.

As I continue my spiritual journey, there are days when I am not sure if God called me at all or if it's just that this is what I want to do. But I keep listening and praying and God shows me the way to go. As I walk through the hospital halls, no one knows I am a transgender man, unless I have previously told them. Many days this is a relief. I can just exist in this world without having to justify my existence. Other days, I feel invisible—like my experience of being seen, raised, and treated like a woman has been erased. But it hasn't. I am the same person.

As I reflect on these thoughts, I realize that I am privileged. Yes, I am a minority. I am transgender. I am Latino. I am an immigrant. But I have family and friends who love me. I have a church that supports me and my ministry. I speak English. I have two college degrees. I have been able to medically transition. I have been able to legally be me. And to the world I am a heterosexual man, which gives me more privilege.

This is why I share my story. There is power in speaking my truth. There is more to me than what you can see and assume and guess. The same is true for you. In the end, whether chaplaincy chose me or I chose chaplaincy, it's what I love to do. I am a witness and a voice for those who are in pain, who are lonely, who are afraid, who are rejected, who are dying. I see their faith, their resilience, their love, their patience. I see and hold their pain and how they choose to share it with me. These precious sacred moments are a constant reminder that I am not a mistake.

Working While Trans

My colleagues didn't notice I was transitioning, but now that I've told them they've been good about using my new name and pronouns. HR has been ineffectual; I told them and received no support but no discrimination either.

Trans people across the country and around the world experience success in a variety of workplaces and professions. Building a successful career for yourself will require different steps depending on your industry, job title, workplace culture, management, and region of the country, but as the visibility of successful trans people rises, so, too, do opportunities for our communities. Employment victories for trans people at the local, state, and national level continue to push back against prejudice and stigma, and more and more employers are taking steps to reduce and eliminate workplace discrimination.

When I was doing temp work, the jobs I had were not supportive. I didn't dare come out due to how easily they'd drop the contract and not give a reason. I live in an "at-work" state, so no reasons have to be given for ending contracts of temp workers.

At the same time, discrimination remains a pressing problem for many workplaces. The Supreme Court ruled in 2020 that employment discrimination based on sexual orientation or gender identity is illegal.[2] Most state laws will likely follow suit, though not all have caught up yet.

I have a really great supervisor who was all on board with honoring my pronouns. He had me do a pronoun etiquette training for the leaders of our Money department, which helped them to be more kind and accepting toward the other trans folks at my workplace.

Izzy Jayasinghe is an optical microscopy developer and a cell biologist, currently working in the University of Sheffield. As a trans woman of color and the lesbian partner to another academic, Izzy is also interested in promoting equality, diversity and inclusion in higher education.

Even in areas of the country where trans people have been legally protected, trans employees continue to experience harassment, wage discrimination, and micromanagement at work. Below are some tips on not only minimizing negative workplace experiences, but also making the most out of your workplace for your personal and professional growth.

- *Proactively manage your disclosure.* Some of us go to work with the expectation that no one will know of our trans status, and that we will remain *stealth* indefinitely at work. Others go to work expecting that everyone in the office knows that we are trans. Many trans people lie somewhere in the middle. Regardless of how "out" we choose to be at work, it is important for us to be proactive and intentional about who we tell about our trans status. For example, if you are looking to keep your trans identity under wraps, it may be useful to communicate with HR about whether the workplace's technical infrastructure requires a legal name and gender to be displayed. If you want only your team to know about your trans status, it may be useful to discuss with your team members your expectations for their behavior and follow up with your manager or supervisor.

  My legal name appeared in the employee directory as an alternate name (as folks' maiden names or other names do), so it was no secret. That had a lot of follow-up and was a mess to deal with, but has also opened up conversations/opportunity for me to get involved in things that I wouldn't have otherwise.

- *Find allies in positions of power.* Especially because not every workplace will have HR or official policies on trans people, it is always beneficial to cultivate strong allies at work who will vouch for your ability and stand up for you in a pinch. A good ally is an individual you trust to represent you and advocate on your behalf. Building strong work networks of allies, especially those in management-level positions or other positions of power, gives you added protection and support if challenges arise at work.

  I have only told my boss and my HR rep, and my boss has been really accommodating. He worked with my schedule to make it easier to do things, and it has paid off. He said in my performance review he has noticed how much happier I seem and how the work is improving.

- *Learn to code-switch.* People of color are used to code-switching, or changing the way they speak and interact, on a daily basis in order to survive in white-dominated workplaces. Not everyone in every workplace will be someone you want as a friend or can talk to in the ways you would a friend or another trans person. As you navigate workplace social situations, office politics, and the day-to-day of work, you will find people you trust more and feel more comfortable around, as well as people you trust less and feel less comfortable around. You may find that it's easier to handle these groups of people if you speak a different language, or code, with each. With your friends you might make more jokes about your trans identity, for example, while with strangers you might be more formal so as to not invite unwanted humor.

  Management has gone out of their way to tell me that they want work to be a safe space for me and my gender identity and that anyone who makes me uncomfortable or unsafe will be asked to leave. After I experienced a minor hate crime on my way to my car, the general manager offered to give me her parking pass so I didn't have to go outside as often.

- *Balance safety and authenticity.* We are all dreaming of and working toward a world in which all trans people can bring their authentic selves to work and feel safe

In the case of *Bostock v. Clayton County, Georgia*, decided on June 15, 2020, the United States Supreme Court addressed the question of whether employees fired because of their sexual orientation and gender identity were protected by the federal Civil Rights Act, which prohibits sex discrimination. In a 6–3 decision, the court held that action taken on the basis of sexual orientation or gender identity necessarily means that the action was taken on the basis of sex. The opinion potentially gives to trans and queer people the protections of every statute prohibiting sex discrimination.

doing so. In workplaces that are less friendly, however, we may have to consider balancing our authenticity and safety by dressing or presenting in certain ways. We may decide to dress more "professionally" in the office, or to break the ice with humor. In some cases, we may choose to hide our gender identities entirely. Although using these strategies can help reduce discrimination, it's important to know that, for many people, suppressing authenticity at work can be emotionally draining and stressful over the long-term.

I never came out at work because there was a lesbian couple who worked there who had been fired for being gay. My coworkers would often rag on trans people whenever there was a big news story about us. I would just keep quiet and hope no one found out.

- *Be aware of your options for conflict management.* Discrimination is unacceptable, but every workplace occasionally has moments of conflict or discomfort that may straddle the border of acceptable behavior. Knowing the right avenues to resolve this conflict will help defuse these situations if and when they come up. Is it best to go to your manager with complaints, or do they not seem to get it? Does HR have a good conflict mediation process, or is it best to do it some other way? Although not optimal, in some workplaces the lack of good conflict management means that potential discrimination may not be addressed well. In these situations, you may decide not to pursue a resolution.

Since I was the first transgender employee at my place of employment, the Human Resources department didn't quite know how to proceed. They did OK.

SELECTIVE SEX

Jackson Reinagel (he/they) is a trans veteran working on a bachelor's degree in Gender Studies to make sense of my life and the world around me.

The state registered me for the military draft when I legally transitioned in Virginia because state law requires 18 to 25-year-old males to consent to having their information forwarded to the Selective Service in order to receive a driver's license. I wasn't worried about conscription since the War on Terror, recession, and neoliberal job market have secured enough voluntary recruitment to sustain the military industrial complex for years to come. Also, I'd already been in the Navy for five years. My draft card arrived right before I deployed to the Persian Gulf in 2015. I put it in my folder of name- and gender-proving documents: court order, surgeon's letter, birth certificate, government passport. After years of social and medical transition and countless hours spent navigating complex bureaucracies, everything finally matched my identity.

Consigned to live with 102 female roommates for 10 months, I was subjected to constant scrutiny by people who demanded to know why I was entering women's spaces without announcing "male on deck" as required. I submitted all of these documents with my request to move to the male living area onboard the ship, but none of it was enough to convince the captain to acknowledge my reality. Each time our daisy-chained toilets overflowed, I struggled to relieve myself in another bathroom without incurring punishment. I was forbidden from entering male spaces, but my gender presentation prevented me from using female restrooms without being confronted by security, senior personnel, or anyone else who suspected me of misconduct.

When we pulled into ports, members of the same sex and similar rank could stay off the ship upon approval of a group liberty plan. I was only allowed to sign out with "other females" so after my friends and I submitted our request paperwork, they each had to explain to their supervisors why they were checking out with a guy. I didn't have the right to exist, let alone privacy, so my transgender status became known throughout the department. Many didn't consider me man enough to respect my pronouns, yet I was a bit too masculine for them to feel comfortable signing off on overnight stays in separate hotel rooms with women who slept within feet of me onboard. Hard-pressed to justify denying both, I was permitted to spend one precious night a month outside of gendered spaces.

I wonder—when the next war comes, will I be fit for the draft?

Coming Out at Work

I announced my transition in an e-mail to my department colleagues at the beginning of the summer, telling them that I would be living with my "new" identity and name when school started again in the fall. I got quite a few very supportive e-mails back. Thankfully, I never experienced discrimination, at least not that I know of.

Some of us may choose to transition, or otherwise vary the gender identity/pronouns or the gender expression/appearance we take with us to work, while currently employed. We may choose to remain employed while transitioning for several reasons: we may value the workplace's track record or reputation for supporting transition, we may have a preexisting network of allies who can facilitate the process, or we may value the financial stability of the job and be unwilling or unable to take time off to transition or apply elsewhere.

I transitioned on the job without any trouble, and my employer at the time had clear policies and precedents for how the process would work, and a directory system that allowed them to change my name everywhere visible to colleagues before my legal paperwork went through.

For ideas for coming out at work, take a look at *The Complete Guide to Transgender in the Workplace* (Vanessa Sheridan, 2009) and *Transitioning in the Workplace: A Guidebook* (Dana Pizzuti, 2018).

Whatever our individual reasons for coming out while in a particular job, there are a few things we may want to consider:

- *Do your homework.* Before transitioning at work, it is helpful to know the resources available to you inside and outside the workplace. If your workplace has other trans employees, they can help give you a sense of what it's like being trans at that workplace. Talking to a trusted HR professional, when possible, can additionally give you a better understanding of any policies or guidelines available for workplace transition. Organizations outside the workplace, such as the Transgender Law Center, can provide additional help in working with you to know your rights and create a plan for action. Some things to consider as part of your plan:
  - The name/pronouns you want to go by at work
  - The clothing you want to wear at work

Donna Rose, 60, Phoenix. Enterprise LAN/WAN infrastructure program manager, American Airlines. (she, her, hers). "One of my frustrations is that there's so few of us at management or executive levels. It says that you can only go so far in your career as a trans person. There's a very real glass ceiling. Over the course of the last two decades, I've left jobs over trans issues. I've lost jobs over them. I'm sure I've been denied jobs because of them. But regardless, I realize I am far more fortunate than most." (Zackary Drucker)

- The bathroom/locker room facilities you intend to use at work
- The name you would like used for logistics and administrative purposes, including payroll and benefits
- The degree to which you want to "come out" or disclose your identity at work

Making this plan can give you insight into which individuals or groups to ask for help as you begin to transition.

- *Prepare a script.* In workplaces with existing HR transition policies, HR will often take the lead in facilitating a successful workplace transition. However, many of us transition in workplaces without such policies, and will often be working with a less-informed HR professional or manager. In these situations, other employees may come to you or your allies with questions and concerns. Having a script you can rely on for the "frequently asked questions" you receive can help you and your allies better manage transition-related attention.
- *Set and maintain your boundaries.* Everyone who transitions at work does it differently. Some may want a relatively quiet transition experience and only provide education to the extent necessary with the people who need to know. Others may want to become educators and advocates at work and use their transition experience to push for changes in their organization. Regardless of what you want out of your transition experience, remember that your boundaries are your own, and that you are never obligated to answer invasive questions about your body, medical history, or identity at work, even from a manager.

My transition was gradual enough that it was never an issue—again, I suspect because I didn't make it one. I didn't make an announcement when I had chest surgery. I just said I was having a fairly major medical procedure, and would be back in a week. It was nobody's business that I was having my breasts removed, any more than it would be anybody's business if I had had a breast augmentation. My coworkers could tell things had changed when I went back to work—but nobody had the nerve to ask me about it, which was fine by me.

NAVIGATING DISCRIMINATION

Employment discrimination remains a possibility in even the most progressive workplace. Discrimination can present in a number of ways, and each may require different tools for navigating it.

Hiring/Firing/Disciplinary Discrimination

I used to be a high school science teacher. Tenured. When I started living authentically, and the district had a solid two years to prep, I suddenly found myself on a teacher improvement program. I was suddenly a teacher they needed to fix. Three years later, I was given the option to resign or be fired.

For more information on transgender workplace discrimination, check out *Gender Ambiguity in the Workplace: Transgender and Gender-Diverse Discrimination* (2018) by Alison Ash Fogarty and Lily Zheng.

Although everyone occasionally experiences hardship around the hiring, firing, and disciplinary processes at work, discrimination on the basis of sex (which has now been clarified by the United States Supreme Court to include sexual orientation and gender identity) is unacceptable.

Common types of discrimination we may face as a result of our identities include:

- We are denied promotions or raises we deserve
- We are suspended or demoted for unjust reasons
- We receive threats of termination or demotion

- We receive biased negative evaluations or references
- We are rejected for a position in favor of a less-qualified candidate
- Our performance is viewed with a different standard compared to others

TWO TRANS ONE VAN

James (he/they) and Katherine (she/they) Blake are devoted partners, parents, and transgender activists. Through their work with initiatives such as Planned Parenthood, Rise Up Austin, Food Not Bombs, transKids Safety Network, Trans Empowerment Project, and Trans Lifeline, both have been able to create awareness of LGBTQ issues and advocate for marginalized populations of our nation. When they are not working in outreach, they are homeschooling their two beautiful children.

In 2014, my partner, Kat, and I both came out while living in Mississippi. Kat worked as a crew leader, in landscaping. I was recently postpartum from having a high-risk pregnancy with our youngest child. Shortly after coming out, Kat was attacked by a coworker. The person assaulted them with a shovel. Kat was extremely fearful, and reported to the supervisor, who stated, "Well this is Mississippi, what did you expect?" There was no support for Kat or consequences for the coworker.

Over the next weeks, Kat searched without any luck for employment to avoid going back to a dangerous work environment. Our bills fell behind; our electricity was shut off. We reached out to charities, churches, family, and friends for help with the bills—no one would help. Many of our friends and family had disowned us at this point. When we couldn't keep our place, we made a plan to move to a more trans-affirming area of the country.

I would love to tell you our first relocation was a success; however, we are still writing our success story. We've traveled over 10,000 miles seeking refuge, safety, and affirmation. We moved to Colorado, to Washington, to Oregon, to California, and to Nevada; we felt like refugees in our own country.

While on the road, we worked odd jobs: gigs on Craigslist, a car auction house, a temp agency, housekeeping, yard work, a hotel, a casino, and a couple of call centers. Kat also worked full-time volunteering as a hotline operator for Trans Lifeline, the only transgender suicide hotline.

For three years, pretty much wherever we went was awful for one reason or another, if not for the homelessness, then for being transgender. We were frequently traumatized by police officers—harassed for sleeping in the middle of the night. Thankfully, Kat was offered the first full-time staff operator position at Trans Lifeline. After three years of traveling to find an affordable place to start over, we moved to Nevada, where we found an apartment within two days, and now we have been re-housed for over two years! We've worked hard to get to where we are, and we have a lot more work to do to get to where we want to be, but we are eternally grateful for the people who showed their support, understanding, and compassion.

A transfeminine executive meeting with a non-binary employee. (Zackary Drucker, The Gender Spectrum Collection, VICE/Broadly)

Harassment and Hostile Work Environments

Customers were my primary concern and I had several experiences where I had to just deny someone service and disengage.

If someone says or does something unwelcome to you because of your gender, this is called harassment. A series of these incidents, or a fairly severe one, can constitute a hostile work environment. You are entitled to have a work environment free from hostility based on your gender identity.[3] Behavior that is considered harassment includes:

- Oral or written comments about our bodies, clothing, or mannerisms
- Disparaging or prejudiced comments about transgender, gender expansive, and nonbinary people
- Sex-based jokes, innuendos or chat
- Viewing or posting pornographic material at work
- Physical touching or blocking movement
- Ogling, leering, or laughing at you; or making demeaning gestures or facial expressions

I had one coworker who was on a mission to just make my life miserable. I introduced myself by my preferred name and preferred pronouns, but she knew I was trans and just refused to call me "he" even though I started hormones shortly after being hired. She would use the wrong pronouns in front of others, and I would correct her as I stood right by her. She would laugh and say, "no, she" and walk away laughing. It really hurt. Even when reporting it to my supervisors with witnesses it didn't change anything.

Microaggressions

Since we ran into each other in the men's washroom, a coworker who isn't on my team, but still on my floor, refuses to acknowledge my existence or gives me dirty looks on a daily basis.

A microaggression is defined by Merriam-Webster as "a comment or action that subtly and often unconsciously or unintentionally expresses a prejudiced attitude toward a member of a marginalized group." There is no legal definition and the law does not distinguish between microaggressions and harassment. If it bothers you, and it's based on gender, it probably crosses the line into something about which you can properly complain. Behavior that may be considered a microaggression includes:

- Misgendering that occurs constantly from an individual who always apologizes but never changes her behavior
- Someone rolling their eyes and nudging the person next to them anytime someone mentions LGBTQ + topics
- Exclusionary comments such as "ladies and gentlemen . . . oh, and whatever you are."
- Someone asks personal and invasive question about our bodies

I had a coworker bug me for weeks to tell her what my birth name is, she didn't understand that I didn't want to sacrifice my comfort just to sate her curiosity.

JUST NOT SURE WHAT YOU ARE

Shay (he/they) is just a real queer trans man.

Almost a year ago I asked my supervisor if she knew what transgender meant. She said yes, and I breathed a sigh of relief, because at least I wouldn't have to define a concept to her that I barely had a grasp on myself. I proceeded to tell her that the girl she just met a month ago wasn't actually a girl; she hugged me and promised to try her best to remember my new name and pronouns. The next day she gave me a new blank name tag, so I wouldn't have to display my birth name anymore. I asked if she wouldn't mind spreading my new identity around. Soon almost everyone was calling me my chosen name, but to this day she is one of three people that uses he/him pronouns and sir instead of ma'am.

I've been taking testosterone for over four months; my face has stubble; my voice is significantly deeper, and yet most of my coworkers let "young lady," "she," "ma'am," and bizarrely enough, "ladybug," slide out of their mouths like it's nothing. No one has been outrightly disrespectful, but hearing how easy it is for them to still see me as a woman feels like a sucker punch to the gut every time.

One of our regular customers told me not to become a boy as if the opinion of some guy who irritates me once a week is one that I should really consider when it comes to how I live my life. Last week a customer called me "ma'am" and then corrected himself to "sir." Then told me he just really couldn't tell, and I simply replied, "most people can't."

Christian Oropeza, 34, Washington, D.C. Vice President for Commercial Insurance, Long & Foster. (he, him, his) "I was transitioning [while working at the animal hospital]. My manager didn't believe in gay people but did believe in trans people. She believed it was possible we were wired as the wrong sex, but she only thought you could be a trans guy liking women... My gender identity doesn't play at all right now. I'm never like, 'Hey, I'm Christian. I'm trans.' Instead, I'd say, 'I grew the company 300 percent. Give me a raise.' When Chelsea Manning was transitioning in jail, I had a colleague that said, 'I don't believe that someone can transition.' I told her, 'You know I'm transgender?' Then they ask a lot of questions usually. The first question is always, 'What organs do you have?' Then they ask, 'Are you male or female?' 'How? When?' I guess because it's so innocent, in a way I don't feel uncomfortable." (Zackary Drucker)

Retaliation

If you make a complaint of discrimination, oppose discriminatory practices, or support someone else's discrimination claim, and you are punished and/or fired as a result of that, it is called retaliation. Retaliation is illegal. Some examples of retaliation:

- Being demoted or fired from your position after making a complaint
- Suddenly experiencing micromanaging after supporting a coworker's complaint
- Being excluded from staff meetings or consulted less at work after speaking up about workplace issues
- Receiving poor work evaluations in response to filing a complaint

Sexual and Physical Violence

I was sexually assaulted at one workplace because I was in a men's space; it was where I worked and there shouldn't have been any problem with me being there, but three cis guys thought it would be hilarious to do this because I was "ugly" (read: masculine). There was no support for it. When word got out the administration made *me* avoid the area and did nothing to the three guys who did it.

Any unwanted touching or act that places a person in reasonable fear of unwanted touching, whether sexual or not, is considered a criminal act. Examples of sexual and physical violence include:

- Asking for sexual acts to be performed
- Rape
- Coercing a sexual act under threat of termination, or with promises of promotion
- Physical intimidation or threats of violence

Getting Help

Discrimination is always unacceptable, and all people are entitled to respect, dignity, and safety at work. If you experience discrimination at work, know that there are many ways to get help. Depending on what you've experienced, you have numerous options available to resolve the situation. Making the system work for you can be challenging if you find yourself in a situation involving harassment or discrimination. Keep in mind that employers vary, and the law is complex. The tips listed here are for general information, and may not apply to your specific situation. You should consult a lawyer for more specific legal advice.

Human Resources

Almost every employer has a person or department tasked with addressing issues affecting human resources. In the case of federal employees, each agency has an Equal Employment Opportunity office. You may make a complaint to HR about the discrimination you experienced, though this is probably most useful if you are continuing to work at the employer. If you haven't been hired, or have been fired, as a result of discrimination, your next best step is to file a legal complaint outside of the employer. However, if you have no intention of filing an outside complaint, and you want to notify the company of what happened in the hopes they will take action for future situations, you can certainly do so.

Before making a complaint, do your best to compile any notes or documentation you have about the discrimination. This can include screenshots, pictures, written documentation, e-mails, or any other documentation you have. If there is a video camera operated by the employer in the area, alert them that they should review the recording before it is erased and preserve it. If you have video or audio of the incident, you may decide to

Helpful guides for employers include *Transgender Employees in the Workplace: A Guide for Employers* (Jennifer Kermode, 2017) and *Gender Diversity and Non-Binary Inclusion in the Workplace: The Essential Guide for Employers* (J. Fernandez and Sarah Gibson, 2018).

Paige Flanagan is an academic librarian living in Pennsylvania, who loves who she is and enjoys spreading that love to friends and strangers alike.

provide it. Note that recording conversations without consent may or may not be legal in your state or under employer workplace rules. Other kinds of evidence that can be included are your good performance reviews, your employer's failure to follow company policy, heightened scrutiny of your work, or the employer's changing explanations for your termination or discipline.

When you file a complaint with HR, they will investigate your complaint. Your complaint should be made in writing, and you should keep a copy of it. The benefit of making a complaint to HR is that the employer is then on notice of the problem, and can take action to remedy it. They may also have had other complaints against the perpetrator, which will allow them to take more serious action. It will also document what happened, so that if something more serious happens to you, there is a paper trail showing that the problem involves more than one incident and that the company should take action.

> *The people in my workplace have been very supportive, and I am working with a person in HR who is trying to build explicit transition guidelines for the business. We have a transgender group that has advocated for improved medical benefits, which I am now using.*

Human resources specialists can consult *Transgender Workplace Diversity: Policy Tools, Training Issues and Communication Strategies for HR and Legal Professionals* (2007) by Jillian T. Weiss.

Remember that HR's job is to protect the employer first. If they discover clear evidence of discrimination, they will most likely take some action, because otherwise the company may face a lawsuit. If the evidence is less than clear, however, they may find your complaint "unsubstantiated," which means there was not enough evidence to satisfy them that discrimination occurred. Note that HR may have a policy to not tell you what their investigation showed or what action, if any, they took as a result. In addition, if you admit to wrongdoing, HR may discipline you. It is possible that those who are notified of the complaint may retaliate against you, though that is illegal. You should think about the risks and benefits of making a complaint to HR.

> *My boss followed me into the restroom, repeatedly told me that I belonged in the women's restroom, and told me to show him my genitals. I'm looking for a new job.*

Although going to HR will not allow you to recover damages, it may be able to help you in other ways. You can request to not work with the offending employee(s), to have the offending employee(s) moved, or to relocate yourself to another location. You can also ask that they review their policies to ensure that discrimination of this type does not happen again, or seek remedial training to fill a gap in their policies. If you were unfairly denied raises or promotions as a result of discrimination, you can request that the raise or promotion be reconsidered.

> *The only major issue I've run into at one of my workplaces so far is that I wasn't able to get an ID badge with my chosen name. The system they have in place for HR, payroll, etc., only allows one's legal name to be used on any ID or documentation. It took me about five months to formalize my legal name change and obtain my new government ID.*

Filing a Complaint

The next step, if you are not satisfied with the employer's response, is filing a formal complaint. You may file a complaint with the United States Equal Employment Opportunity Commission (EEOC) or your state or local fair employment practices agency. Such agencies usually have people who can help you to write up your complaint and gather your evidence. Alternatively, you can file your complaint in court, though federal courts require that you go through the EEOC first. The process of agency investigation and/or a lawsuit in court is generally lengthy, and likely will extend over a year or more. It is often helpful to reach out to organizations such as the Transgender Law Center, Lambda Legal, the ACLU, and other legal services organizations for help filing the complaint and working with a trans-friendly lawyer.

Some people prefer to quit their job immediately if they encounter discrimination. This may not be the best course of action unless you have another job lined up, because if you want to bring a complaint, quitting lets the employer argue that you didn't take enough time to fix the problem. Quitting could also affect your ability to recover lost income, and make it harder to collect unemployment benefits. To recover damages, you may have to prove that the conditions were so intolerable that any reasonable person would have to quit—a difficult standard to meet. Quitting may be appropriate, but if you can, check with a lawyer first.

It is often best to find an attorney who specializes in employment discrimination law in your local area. An example of a helpful website for this is findlaw.com, although there are many others. Attorneys who specialize in employment-discrimination law often work on a contingency fee, meaning that they do not collect a fee unless they recover damages for you. Although contingency fees vary, most attorneys take one third of the recovery, plus expenses. Employment lawyers are always on the lookout for good cases, and generally do not charge for an initial consultation. Think carefully before paying for an initial consultation. If an attorney is not sure whether your case will involve enough damages so that they are paid for the dozens or hundreds of hours they will likely spend on your case, they will not take it, and may instead offer to represent you on an hourly basis. The hourly fees for most lawyers are in the hundreds of dollars per hour. If you are trying for a quick settlement, this arrangement may make economic sense. Otherwise, the fees during administrative and/or court proceedings will likely be in the tens of thousands of dollars. For this reason, it may be good to talk to several lawyers before choosing one.

Dee Dee Ngozi, 55, Atlanta, GA, 2016. (Jess T. Dugan). From "To Survive on This Shore: Photographs and Interviews with Transgender and Gender Nonconforming Older Adults," a project by Jess T. Dugan and Vanessa Fabbre.

QUESTIONS TO ASK AN EMPLOYMENT LAWYER

If you are thinking about working with an employment lawyer, it can be important to find out some information in advance, including:

- How many employment cases have they handled?
- How long do they expect the case to take?
- What do they think the case is "worth" monetarily?
- Do they think the case merits a quick settlement or extensive litigation, in hopes of a larger settlement or different verdict?
- What is their understanding of trans issues, including any courses they have taken or books they have read? Do they know it is different from sexual orientation, and that it is covered under sex discrimination statutes?
- Are they aware of the kinds of things that create a hostile work environment? (i.e., misgendering, failure to correct records even without a court order or government ID, failure to allow use of correctly gendered facilities, and failure to have trans-inclusive health insurance policies).

Going to the Police

You may consider bringing up a discriminatory incident to law enforcement, especially if you've experienced sexual assault, harassment, and/or physical violence. If you decide to go to the police, try to do so as soon as you are able. If you are injured, even in a minor way, for example, with scratches, bruises, or minor lacerations, and you are able to, you should take close-up, clear pictures of the injury. You should also note any witnesses and contact them as soon as you are able after the assault. It may take a few days after speaking with the police for the police report to be ready, and you can ask them how to go about getting a copy. You may consult a lawyer or legal organization to assist you in getting the police to write up an incident report.

You may feel uncomfortable interacting with law enforcement, especially if you are unsure of your safety while interacting with the police or have experienced discrimination from law enforcement before. Friends, loved ones, community members, and nonprofit organizations may be able to provide some of the help and support you need, especially if you are no longer in immediate danger.

RESOURCES FOR HELP WITH EMPLOYMENT DISCRIMINATiON

Many nonprofit organizations work on trans employment issues. Their websites and help desks can often provide assistance, guidance, and further resources for trans people and their allies. Here is a sampling of some of the best-known organizations from around the country:

ACLU LGBT & HIV Rights Project, New York, New York (affiliates in all states)—aclu.org/issues/lgbt-rights

Chicago House, Chicago, Illinois—www.chicagohouse.org/employment

Gender Justice, Minneapolis, Minnesota—genderjustice.us

GLBTQ Advocates and Defenders, Boston, Massachusetts—glad.org

Lambda Legal, New York, New York (additional offices in Atlanta, Chicago, Dallas, Washington, DC, and Los Angeles)—lambdalegal.org

Mazzoni Center, Philadelphia, Pennsylvania—mazzonicenter.org

National Center for Lesbian Rights, San Francisco, California (with additional offices in Washington, DC)—nclrights.org

National Center for Transgender Equality, Washington, DC—transequality.org

Sylvia Rivera Law Project, New York, New York—srlp.org

Transcend Legal, New York, New York—transcendlegal.org (specializing in health insurance issues)

Transgender Law Center, Oakland, California—transgenderlawcenter.org

Transgender Legal Defense & Education Fund, New York, New York—transgenderlegal.org

Whitman-Walker Legal Services, Washington, DC—whitman-walker.org/legal-services

---

NONTRADITIONAL WORK

The rise of companies such as Uber and Lyft has made nontraditional work more visible than ever before. These jobs vary immensely in their type, scope, legality, length, and other factors, and may challenge some of the traditional assumptions or expectations related to looking for work, applying for work, and carrying out actual work. In general, nontraditional work tends to be more flexible while sacrificing some of the stability or safety of a traditional nine-to-five. It is important for those looking to make a living out of nontraditional work to understand the various risks and rewards associated with the work they choose.

The Gig Economy

Because I could not hold a straight job, and the person I lived with wanted me out of the sex life, I opened my own delivery service and had that going for nine years straight. It was a modest income, but I view the whole thing as a success. I was 100% out to all my customers and wore dresses and skirts.

Those of us who work as independent contractors, part-time shift workers, temporary workers, and freelancers may do so because these kinds of jobs allow for greater freedom than traditional work. Examples of these jobs include rideshare driver, temp worker for an agency, exotic dancer, and tutor. Some of these kinds of jobs allow us to choose our own hours, and others permit us to choose our own clients. A drawback of these jobs is that the absence of a full-time employer typically means that we are unlikely to qualify for benefits from the job, and may even be expected to absorb the full cost of our work, including supplies and transportation.

Discrimination in the gig economy can be a challenge. In some jobs, we may have little recourse when clients harass us except to refuse the gig or quit the position. Repeatedly turning down jobs, however, can result in situations where we don't have enough work to make a living wage. Most antidiscrimination laws apply to employers, and do not protect independent contractors. Major exceptions are New York City and San Francisco, where the laws protect independent contractors. Without benefits or other employee perks, discrimination can cut our profits to a degree that makes working in the gig economy unsustainable. We can better our chances of success in the gig economy if we keep in mind some important tips:

- *Set realistic expectations.* Working in the gig economy will not single-handedly work miracles for your financial situation. The work carries with it some advantages over nine-to-five work, but also comes with some disadvantages. Expect to spend some time acclimating to the new work so you can take advantage of the benefits, and accept that you will experience challenges, too. Discrimination is a possibility in the gig economy, just as it is a possibility with more traditional work.
- *Take advantage of your flexibility.* One of the benefits of gig work is having more flexibility than traditional work. If you have time-consuming obligations such as school, caretaking, or part-time jobs, filling the extra space with gigs can be easier than trying to accommodate these obligations within a traditional workplace. Optimizing your schedule to take advantage of this flexibility will allow you to earn more, during hours that work for you. Keep in mind, though, that being your own employer means that you will need to set your own boundaries well.
- *Create a safety net.* The gig economy rarely comes with employer benefits. In the absence of tax withholding, medical insurance, and retirement savings, make sure to create this safety net yourself by being proactive with your earnings. Research a health insurance plan that works for your needs. Set aside money from each paycheck in a separate bank account that you don't look at until tax season. Be proactive about seeking new opportunities for better-paid gig work when you are able.

The Underground Economy

The underground economy, also known as the black market or the informal economy, is the portion of the labor market that operates outside of the law. Some underground work is "underground" because while the work is legal, it isn't reported as taxable income to authorities. This encompasses both unreported self-employment and under-the-table employment with an employer. Some underground work is "underground" because the work itself is illegal. This includes certain types of sex work, the drug trade, smuggling, gambling, and fraud.

We may see underground work as desirable for a number of reasons. Sex work, for example, may provide important physical and emotional affirmation for our gender identities and be a lucrative source of income. Other kinds of underground work may help give us meaning, help us feel important or connected to our communities, or offer convenience and flexibility we need.

Lil scraps of what we gotta do to push through while being true to ourselves and queer fam. Tai Ma and Queer Fam. Elliot is a "Genderfucked mechanic with epilepsy. I run a lil queer center supporting our underground QTPOC local dreams."

Many of us who participate in the underground economy do so because there are few other options available to us. We may be unable to work in other jobs, even those we are qualified for, due to our lack of social networks or documentation. We may struggle to find other jobs due to discrimination, lack of qualifications, or other factors, and be forced into underground work as our only option. For many of us, negative experiences within underground economies are unfortunately common. Without regulations and oversight, the potential for employers to discriminate against employees is higher, and few avenues exist for reporting discrimination to authorities. Some employers will take advantage of underground employees by paying them under minimum wage, withholding benefits, or otherwise exploiting their labor. Some types of underground work, including sex work and the drug trade, put workers at risk of physical violence and bodily harm from clients. All types of underground work, due to their illegal nature, put workers at risk. Police raids and crackdowns can result in jail time, misdemeanor or felony offenses, fines, and potentially in deportation.

Undocumented Labor

Undocumented trans people in the United States face a combination of challenges due to the intersection of their undocumented status and trans identities. Undocumented workers are constantly at risk of having their citizenship status discovered during routine interactions with employers or law enforcement, or during unexpected Immigration and Customs Enforcement (ICE) raids. Trans people are more likely to face discrimination, harassment, and profiling that may place them in proximity to law enforcement or the prison system. To address these risks, undocumented trans people may acquire fake Social Security cards to work at traditional jobs, may become independent contractors, or may seek under-the-table work with employers or family members. Some useful tips that can make surviving and thriving as an undocumented trans employee easier include:

- *Don't be afraid to ask for help.* Organizations such as the Transgender Law Center and Lambda Legal have posted extensive resources for transgender immigrants on their websites. Additionally, local organizations that can help provide support, community, and resources exist in many states. Searching for local trans-friendly organizations in your area on the Internet can help you find the help you need.
- *Be aware of the laws and your rights.* All people living in the United States, including people without documentation, have rights protected by the U.S. Constitution. For example, if ICE officers come to your workplace, they must have a valid search warrant to enter non-public areas, such as your desk, warehouse, or vehicle. Visit the websites of the Transgender Law Center, American Immigration Lawyers Association, and the Immigrant Legal Resource Center for more detailed information on these laws and your rights.
- *Create a support network.* Having a supportive community, friends, and/or family can help keep you more physically and emotionally safe as you navigate not only work but also social, economic, and political life. Know that you are not alone and that a range of organizations, communities, and individuals exist that care about you.

Sex Work

I have done a small amount of sex work. I have a Twitter where I have followed a lot of trans people. To be completely honest, sex work has really helped me find who I am. The trans sex work community is extremely kind. They have helped me feel more comfortable in my expression and in my body. I have not had a single negative experience yet. In fact, everything I have experienced has been positive.

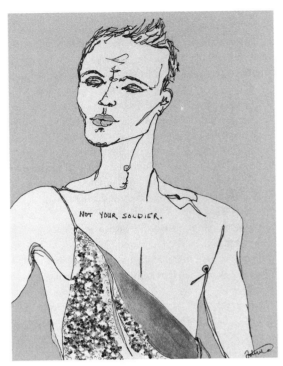

Not Your Soldier Signed. Justin Demeter is an Oakland, CA based queer insomniac and hopeful romantic who dabbles in painting and poetry when he's not too busy climbing walls.

Sex work is an umbrella term encapsulating a broad range of services, performances, or other work of an intimate nature done for pay. Some examples of sex work include webcamming, professional BDSM work, street work, escorting, and pornographic film modeling. Some, such as webcamming and phone sex, can be done remotely, while others, such as street work and film modeling, are done in person. Some types of sex work, such as escorting or stripping, are similar to independent contractor work done through an agency and offer varying levels of pay and safety depending on the employer, while other types of sex work, such as professional BDSM work, require a setup similar to starting a small business.

TRANS PEOPLE ARE THE GEMS OF HUMANITY

Tavia-Ann Kim (she/her) is a trans lady. Out since 1977, she is a survivor of human trafficking and opioid addiction. She is now a Certified Recovery Specialist who works with the LGBT community. She is grateful to be able to share her story. Curtsy to you all!

Being a survivor of human trafficking is just as much a life-defining event as being a transgender lady. Both identities are at the core of who and what I am. It is my identity.

It was a beautiful early summer evening in 1977. I was walking from the Thunderbird Motel to a little restaurant on the edge of downtown Detroit to get a gyro. I was feeling good. I had a roof over my head for a couple of weeks now and I had money for food. I had just been living on the street and was still hungry, cold, dirty, and depressed from being homeless. Pushed out of my parents' house, I was "too in touch with my feminine side," my mother wrote in a note. "It would be better if you left." Being young (and in a dress), I could not get work. Cishet people would just shut me out. They made it clear that I was unwelcome. Charities, shelters, soup kitchens, and especially the Christian missions would not let me in or help at all.

But a pimp came to my rescue. Yes, he had his own self-interests and motivations, but I still saw it as a rescue. He set me up with a motel room, makeup, and food. He put me with one of his ladies, a crossdresser, who taught me how to be a prostitute (which is what we called sex workers at that time) and how to get customers. I was even allowed some pocket money from some of the tricks I turned. Selling myself was an easy transition for me. As a feminine child, adult men took advantage of me and abused me sexually starting when I was in the fourth grade. This occurred so often, they sometimes brought me little gifts. So being a sex worker already came naturally—I just had to be fine-tuned.

At the Detroit restaurant, a couple of people took notice of me, and as I was coming out of the restaurant with my gyro, I was knocked to the ground, duct taped, cable tied, and tossed into the trunk of a car. This started my captivity in human trafficking for five years and nine months. Less than 10% of human trafficking victims are snatched and grabbed like I was. They physically tortured me, frequently tied me up, forced me to sleep either standing or on a box sitting down with no room to move. Sometimes they gave electric shocks with a wand—just to remind me that I was owned. They forced me on heroin and made me prostitute for them. I never got a penny.

I did finally make my escape—just by dumb luck—in just a black dress, with no shoes, ID, or money. I did not know what town or state I was in. I asked for help from passersby on the street. No one would help—most laughed at me or insulted me. However, one cis woman, Dominique, took me in. I spent years at her house healing from the physical and emotional pain. It took almost 10 years.

In time, I started to help other victims of human trafficking and opiate use disorder—mostly other LGBT people, with a focus on transgender people. The clinic I worked with, however, said I needed some kind of degree or certification, which I did not have. I was crushed. A month later, they set me up with a scholarship to become a Certified Recovery Specialist. I could continue my work as a community health worker and be a support for LGBT victims of human trafficking, abduction, torture, confinement, and addiction. This is now my passion, and people say I have a knack for it.

Now in the autumn of my life, I am still out on the streets, but this time working as a Certified Recovery Specialist. Dominique now has failing health, so I try to take care of her the best I can, with the support and help of my life partner, Michelle, who is also trans.

Love wins. My life may have been hell, but looking back, I would not change a thing, and I am so grateful and thankful to the Divine, to the universe, and to nature that I was born transgender. It lets me see the world and humanity as few can. It lets me see the transgender people in our community as the rare gems of humanity.

I did survival sex work when I was 20. It was an overall neutral experience for me at the time. I have considered doing it again because my household is poor, but it is so much more difficult to convince anybody to pay me for sex, as a man. The behaviors aren't even different. People think my sexuality is worth "less" as a man. Simultaneously, they might also misgender me. So I haven't been able to get back into sex work now that I've transitioned.

The risks and benefits of various types of sex work differ widely. Webcamming and online work offer flexibility and the potential for lucrative pay, but require a good Internet connection, strong brand management, and work outside of camming hours to maintain an audience. Although relatively safe, it is impossible to control what audiences do with produced content, which may remain on the Internet indefinitely. Professional BDSM work has the potential for lucrative pay, but requires brand and customer management as well as training. Escorting, pornographic film modeling, and stripping vary in safety, pay, and other factors depending on the employer or agency involved. Street work, or sex work done in-person on the street, tends to be the type of sex work that is most accessible to new sex workers, though the risks tend to be higher and the pay lower.

I used to dress "masculine." I'm a sex worker now and lots of my presentation has had to veer "feminine" to access conventional sex work. This has not changed my gender identity at all, although I am now almost always (mis)read to be a cis woman.

In 2018, Congress passed laws known as FOSTA-SESTA. These laws hold websites responsible for posting sex work ads, and have resulted in the shutdown of most online sex work ads in the United States. Supporters of these laws argue that this will help prevent sex trafficking, while others point out that the Internet makes it easier for sex workers to do their work safely. Although some providers have created offshore web platforms not subject to these laws, the disappearance of online options for sex work has pushed many sex workers into riskier street work.

I've had both positive and negative experiences with sex work. A lot of my clients are fetish chasers. I've had many abusive clients and even had some stalk me to my residence and attempt to assault me. I now carry a weapon for self-defense.

No matter the type of sex work we engage in, some tips can improve our well-being and success:

- *Find and utilize community.* There is strength in numbers. Finding communities of other sex workers like you can provide a sense of community, professional camaraderie, and emotional support. Sex workers acting together, especially on the streets, are less vulnerable to theft, assault, or harassment compared to sex workers acting on their own.

- *Set your own boundaries.* Although you may not have full control over the sex work you do (e.g., being able to host on a certain domain), know that ultimately you are the one offering services to your customers, and that you decide what to offer. It's OK to be more or less comfortable with some services and to refuse to perform a service, even for a customer you like.

I've only ever traded sex for a place to stay. I don't regret it, sex work is work.

- *Keep safety, health, and dignity in mind.* Sex workers and their allies have posted a number of best practices online that support the safety, health, and dignity of other members of the community. Knowing these practices will help you minimize the risks you may encounter while doing sex work.

berkeleyneed.org offers a resource manual called "Tricks of the Trade" that provides health and safety information for sex workers.

EMPOWERING ESCORTS, DEMANDING REVOLUTION

Stevie Trixx is an escort, writer, and queer history nerd based in Brooklyn, New York.

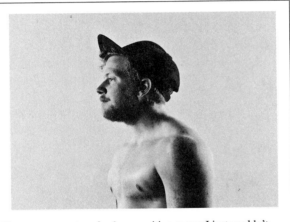

My ownership of my sexuality as a trans person is empowering for me and for the people who see my work. I moved to New York in 2012 to start a master's program in gender studies at NYU. Like many other trans folks at the time, seeing Reina Gossett's retrieval of Sylvia Rivera's historic "Y'all Better Quiet Down" speech from the archive had set me on fire. I felt ambivalent about the "equality" politics of the moment that suspiciously excluded trans people. However, realizing that 40 years earlier, just outside my classroom window, a Latinx trans sex worker stood up to a primarily white, cis crowd and demanded a revolution—that gave me hope.

I had originally planned to go on to a Ph.D. program, but my studies pointed me directly *away* from academic life. Years of putting myself through school—slinging coffee—gave way to a freelance writing career I just couldn't get off the ground. Although writing and research had their place, I felt real, palpable change lay in acts of protest, in acts of sex at the margins, and in acts of defiant existence. A stack of rejection letters sealed the deal for me. By 2017, I was so firmly embedded in a community of fierce sex workers that it made sense to try it. I saw a chance to work for myself, and I took it.

And what timing! On one hand, the possibility of decriminalizing sex work felt surprisingly close at hand as state governments and even presidential candidates gave it considerable thought. On the other hand, sex workers and civilians alike faced an increasingly repressive reality.

The 2018 passing of FOSTA/SESTA made things even more repressive. Although it was meant to protect survivors of sex trafficking, the new laws made it difficult for escorts to use safer online resources. It even forced some providers to return to dangerous street work. FOSTA/SESTA also impacted the average Joe, heralding the end of services such as Craigslist personals and the beginning of increasing restrictions on online sexuality.

When Sylvia Rivera fought her way on stage 40 years ago, she called the crowd's attention to her world—to the contributions that she, Marsha P. Johnson, and the STAR people made despite so many obstacles. As the gay lib movement shifted toward respectability over equality, Rivera demanded a revolution for a new, better world for everyone—not just the most privileged.

Trans people and sex workers—and those of us who are both—have inherited a better world because of people like Sylvia Rivera. It stands to reason that the world today would greatly benefit from tapping the knowledge and political savvy of sex workers instead of viewing us as victims or vixens.

But, I'd ask that people also take that one step further and acknowledge the services that we sex workers provide. My clients get a chance to explore their sexuality without judgment, to ask questions in a safe environment, and to experience intimacy in a world that's only getting colder. In doing what we do, we trans sex workers are creating a world that's not only more equitable, but also more compassionate, sexy, and kind. That's revolutionary.

CONCLUSION

Working while trans can be difficult for many of us, and navigating what can feel like an intimidating economic landscape, job market, and legal system can be tough. A number of trans and trans-friendly organizations across the country are available to help us secure financial stability, respect, equity, and dignity at work no matter who we are or what we do. We work to support ourselves and our loved ones, for personal meaning, to better our community, and to make it through to another day. And, as important as work is to our daily lives, we should recognize not only the joys and challenges of the work we do, but also that we are whole human beings, and that we are so much more than our jobs. We live, work, and dream so that each community that comes after us has a better shot at surviving and thriving.

NOTES

1. States recognize a person's right at common law to change names through use and passage of time, without resort to judicial procedure, with the exception of Hawaii, Louisiana, and Maine. Julia Shear Kushner, Comment, The Right to Control One's Name, 57 UCLA L. REV. 313, 318, 328 n.79 (2009).

2. *Bostock v. Clayton County, Georgia.*

3. *Meritor Savings Bank v. Vinson*, 477 U.S. 57 (1986) (Federal law affords employees the right to work in an environment free from discriminatory intimidation, ridicule, and insult).

LEGAL ISSUES

Sasha Buchert and Ezra Young

10

INTRODUCTION

For better and for worse, the law continues to play a unique role in the lives of trans and gender expansive (T/GE) people. In the first edition of *Trans Bodies, Trans Selves*, our esteemed colleagues Kylar W. Broadus and Shannon Price Minter painted a rich picture of the legal landscape for U.S.-based trans folks as things stood in 2014. We expand on their work by contextualizing issues and pointing out advances and obstacles that will garner our collective attention for the coming decade. We also aim to provide frameworks, tools, and examples that help illustrate the tremendous progress our community has won, ever mindful that far more work lies ahead.

We approach this chapter cognizant of the changing social condition of our community as well as our incredible diversity. There are a growing number of out trans and gender expansive folks in the United States, each of us carving out a life and livelihood as unique and diverse as the communities we call home. There are some common needs and experiences that unite us. For example, most of us seek legal recognition of our name and gender and need access to tools to redress discrimination in school or at work. However, differences in socioeconomic status, race, age, disability, religion, gender, how we define and experience being trans, and a host of other statuses shape the legal barriers and problems we face.

Defining Trans

We use the term *trans* as an umbrella term to refer to a diverse range of people including those who identify as (and/or have experiences of being labeled) transsexual, transgender, agender, genderqueer, or nonbinary. Where differences in identity or experience are pertinent to a particular legal issue, we specify the subgroup we are discussing.

Law is a powerful tool of social change, one that many of us need to turn to for help. Trans and gender expansive people are likely to interact with legal institutions, such as courts and agencies, during their lifetimes. Whether it is because we have experienced employment discrimination or simply because we are seeking recognition of our names, we are often required to navigate complicated legal processes. This chapter endeavors to demystify the American legal system and give you tools that empower you to learn more. We also share information that will help you better understand how and when your trans status comes into play in legal proceedings, highlighting areas of opportunity for community and legal advocates alike.

Knowing that the trans rights movement will make key advances through the law, we also share frameworks and tools that will help us meaningfully and critically engage with important legal battles both underway and on the horizon. To that end, we intentionally emphasize the diversity of the trans community in the United States, teasing out the unique challenges faced by vulnerable subsets of our diverse communities. We do this because we believe it is important that T/GE people support one another, especially those among us who face the steepest path to equality.

HOW OUR LEGAL SYSTEM WORKS

Our legal system is complicated! In this section we aim to help demystify how laws, courts, and agencies work. This is not intended to replace (nor could it) the advice you can get from

This chapter provides an overview and update of key legal issues for trans persons in the United States. The information provided is necessarily general and cannot take into account each individual's circumstances or changes in law. The information in this chapter should not be construed as legal advice. If you need legal help or advice, consult with an attorney or legal organization that can provide you with specific, detailed guidance based on your individual situation and the laws where you live.

a lawyer. But we hope that this overview will help you better understand the legal world around you. At the end of this section, we sketch out two all-too-common legal issues for trans folks (name changes and employment discrimination), and explain how these kinds of cases progress through our legal system.

Laws

When we talk about "law" we are referring broadly to principles and rules. There are different kinds of laws. For example:

A ***constitution*** is a written set of fundamental principles that describes and determines the powers and duties of government among various political units. In addition to the U.S. Constitution, each state has its own constitution. It is typically extremely difficult to amend a constitution.

A ***statute*** is a law passed by a legislative body (e.g., U.S. Congress). A law that is under consideration but not yet passed by a legislature is called a ***bill***.

A ***regulation*** is a rule created by an agency tasked with enforcing a particular statute. The agency gets its power to make rules by statute, and it can only make rules within the scope of that same statute.

In most courts, an earlier issued court decision forms part of the body of ***case law***, which establishes a principle or rule that should guide other cases with similar issues or facts. Case law may interpret a constitution, statute, or regulation. Sometimes case law speaks to something called the ***common law***, which refers to the body of judge-made law derived from precedent (i.e., old court cases and ancient rights).

Courts

We have two main, parallel court systems in the United States—federal and state courts.[1] Typically, federal courts have jurisdiction over issues that impact the U.S. Constitution or other federal law whereas state courts have jurisdiction over cases that arise under state constitutions or other state laws.

HOW CASES MOVE THROUGH COURT

In the federal and most state systems there are three levels of courts—trial courts, intermediate appellate courts, and courts of last resort.

Court of Last Resort

↑

Intermediate Appellate Court

↑

Trial Court

Trial Courts. Federal and state court systems work very similarly. In both systems, cases are initiated in trial courts. Some states have special trial courts that only hear certain kinds of cases whereas others hear any case that arises within its geographic boundaries. For example, some states have separate trial courts for civil and criminal cases. Trial courts are the work horses of our court systems. They hear the initial disputes between the parties, supervise the parties' exchange of information about the case (called "discovery"), and make findings of fact and law pertinent to the dispute. Trial courts typically assign one judge to oversee each case. Sometimes courts assign additional helper judges, often called "magistrate judges." Only trial courts have jury trials, and not every case is heard in front of a jury. In both systems, the vast majority of cases are resolved at the trial court level. If a party is unhappy with the trial court's decision, however, they can make an appeal to a higher court in the same system.

Intermediate Appellate Courts. The federal system has intermediate appellate courts that sit over the trial courts but are below the U.S. Supreme Court. These courts are called U.S. Courts of Appeals. Most (but not all) states have similar intermediate appellate courts. In both systems, intermediate appellate courts hear appeals directly from trial courts in a specific geographic area, although some types of cases are only heard by specialized intermediate appellate courts. So long as an appeal was filed in a timely fashion and other rules are met, intermediate appellate courts must hear the case. Intermediate appellate courts usually assign a panel of judges to decide an appeal. In the federal system, three judges sit on a panel. If a party is unhappy with the decision of an intermediate appellate court it can appeal it to a court of last resort. However, in the federal system, because the U.S. Supreme Court only hears a small fraction of petitions, most decisions of the U.S. Courts of Appeal are final.

Court of Last Resort. Both the federal and state court systems have courts of last resort. Courts of last resort are typically the last opportunity within the court system to overturn a decision made by a trial court or an intermediate appellate court. In the federal system there is one court of last resort, the U.S. Supreme Court. Nine justices sit on the U.S. Supreme Court. By law, the U.S. Supreme Court has discretionary review authority, meaning it can pick how many and which cases it hears every year. In a typical year approximately 7,000–8,000 requests for review (certiorari) are filed in the U.S. Supreme Court, but only around 180 of those are accepted for review.[2] State courts of last resort function a bit differently. Some states, like Texas, have separate courts of last resort for criminal and civil cases. Some state courts of last resort have discretionary review, so, like the U.S. Supreme Court, they hear only a handful of the petitions filed.

FARMER V. BRENNAN, 511 U.S. 825 (1994)

The first out trans person to ever bring a case to the U.S. Supreme Court won her case! Dee Farmer, a Black trans woman who is HIV+ and was a long-term federal prisoner sued claiming that guards failed to take reasonable steps to protect her from other prisoners' sexual assaults. In 1994, the Supreme Court ruled Farmer's Eighth Amendment right to be free from cruel and unusual punishment had been violated on the rationale that guards had a duty to protect prisoners, such as trans women, who are especially vulnerable to sexual violence.

Administrative Agencies

Administrative agencies are arms of the government that work in a specialized area. Typically, agencies are created by special laws called organic statutes, which expressly spell out the agency's powers and what it can (and sometimes can't) do. Different agencies have different jobs. Some agencies can investigate complaints and issue regulations (also known as "rulemaking") in a certain area of law. In some instances, agencies can even hear cases sort of the way courts do. There are many different federal and state agencies.

Most agencies are headed by political appointees, people selected by the executive branch—the president in the federal system or the governor in a state. As a result, agencies and their work can become politicized by the party that is in control of the executive branch. This can be a good and bad thing for trans people. If we vote people into office who support our rights, then we can expect to see pro-trans political appointees leading our agencies. If we don't vote or don't hold our politicians accountable, then important agencies might be staffed with political appointees who do not support our rights.

The Affordable Care Act (ACA) is a federal law that, among other things, bans discrimination in health care and insurance. In 2016, the U.S. Department of Health and Human Services (HHS) issued a regulation that clarified trans people are protected by the ACA. In 2020, HHS finalized a new regulation that stripped trans people of protection. Why the about face? Notably the law didn't change, but the presidential administrations did. HHS switched positions on a trans rights issue because the Trump Administration did not want trans people to be protected by the law. At the time of this book's publication, the Biden Administration has indicated it will switch positions yet again, affirming trans people are protected.

Piecing It Together

So, you're probably wondering how on earth real problems are solved through our legal system. This is where we help you piece it all together. The following are two examples of legal problems you might encounter, one that can be solved through the state court system and another that is solved through a federal agency and courts.

STATE COURT EXAMPLE: NAME CHANGE

Many T/GE folks choose to change their names. Most who do so want a court order recognizing their new name. Name change orders are handled exclusively by state courts. The process differs slightly from state to state. If you live in Florida, your first step would be to file a petition (a formal request) in a state trial court asking for it to recognize your new name. Florida, like many other states, requires that you publicize your name change and submit fingerprints for a criminal records request. After that, there is a hearing—a day in court—where you appear in front of a judge and they consider your petition. If the judge accepts your petition, they issue a court order—this piece of paper officially recognizes your new name. Once you have a court order, you can use it to change your name on identification documents (driver's license, Social Security card, passport, birth certificate, etc.). If the judge does not accept your petition, you can appeal the denial to a higher court.

FEAR AND THE LEGAL PROCESS

Eden Alison Shurman (she/her) is a journalist and author from New York.

Many find the legal process of changing their name and completing other legal documents quite overwhelming. Don't let it hold you back, for help is out there! There are websites that can help navigate the process of filling out forms, free of charge. Additionally, the local court's website (or whichever agency you're working with) may have a downloadable list of what forms are needed.

Do not be afraid to go to any of these agencies in person and ask questions. You may be able to place a phone call and reach someone quickly. Some offices will even let you print blank forms at no charge. In my experience, I found that although I had the option of filing legal forms online, it was better to do so in person. I learned more about the process, and I believe my name change petition was processed faster.

In the case of my name change, a charge was incorrectly listed on the website I used to complete name change forms. At the police station, the cost was less. At the station, I experienced no transphobia in working with the one 30-something gentleman who was probably some kind of officer. I was treated with indifference. Later, I was advised that although a particular form was legally required, I could probably go forward without it. However, this turned out not to be true.

When completing forms online using a free website, validate the online information with your local agency. Rules change frequently, rendering some websites inaccurate. Double checking will avoid frustration and wasted time.

FEDERAL AGENCY AND COURT EXAMPLE: EMPLOYMENT DISCRIMINATION

Employment discrimination is a common issue for T/GE Americans. If you are harassed, demoted, fired, or not hired because of who you are there are options to fight back. One way to do that is to file a charge of discrimination with the U.S. Equal Employment Opportunity Commission (EEOC). The EEOC is a federal agency specially charged with enforcing federal employment discrimination laws. The EEOC has field offices all over the nation.[3] You can learn more about how to file a charge of discrimination online.[4] There are special rules for "timeliness," so you should file a charge as soon as possible.[5] At the EEOC stage, investigators can assist you in gathering evidence and otherwise help you try to settle your case with your employer.[6] If your employer refuses to settle, the EEOC might sue them or you can go ahead and do that in a federal trial court. If you lose at the trial court level, you have the option to appeal your case to a higher court.

CHAVEZ V. CREDIT NATION AUTO SALES, 641 FED.APPX. 883 (11TH CIR. 2016)

Jennifer Michelle Chavez (she/her) is a Latina trans woman, automotive technician, and pioneering trans rights advocate. In 2009, Chavez transitioned on the job. In early 2010, she was taunted by coworkers, unfairly disciplined by managers, and terminated under suspicious circumstances. Chavez went to the EEOC immediately, but she was turned away because she is trans. Not being deterred, Chavez went back to the EEOC repeatedly over a two-year period insisting that she had a right to have her case investigated. Eventually, the EEOC admitted its error and started an investigation. But Chavez's employer refused to settle. In 2013, Chavez filed a federal lawsuit. Unfortunately, in 2014, a federal trial court dismissed Chavez's case on the pretense that there wasn't enough evidence showing discrimination. Chavez knew better. She appealed that decision to the U.S. Court of Appeals for the 11th Circuit. In November 2015, Chavez sat in the front row of the courtroom where three federal judges at the 11th Circuit heard oral arguments in her case. In January 2016, the 11th Circuit ruled that Chavez did have enough evidence of discrimination and clarified that trans Americans are protected by sex discrimination laws. Chavez's case settled shortly thereafter.

Learn more about Chavez's long fight for justice by watching the short film *Trans in America: Jennifer Chavez.*

KEY LEGAL DEVELOPMENTS

Kylar Broadus and Shannon Minter's original "Legal Issues" chapter in the first edition of this book is a rich and very thorough survey of the law as it stood in 2014, much of which is still accurate today. In this section we provide information on key legal developments and endeavor to highlight a handful of issues that speak to legal hurdles T/GE folks might encounter across the arc of life. We hope this section will help you better understand options available to you and how the law is changing to accommodate us. We caution that our assessment is intended for informational purposes only. If you are facing a serious legal problem, we encourage you to seek out a lawyer.

Jury Selection and Service

It is a bedrock principle of American law that if someone's life, liberty, or property are at stake they must be afforded a fair and impartial hearing. Put another way, if you find yourself in court the only thing that should matter is the facts of the case and the law. Right now, lawmakers, lawyers, and courts are trying to do a better job ensuring trans and nonbinary folks are treated fairly.

In our legal system, juries decide some of the hardest and most important cases. In both state and federal courts, juries are often tasked with hearing evidence and applying the law. In both civil and criminal cases, juries can be empowered to decide who wins a case. In civil cases, juries can often order the loser to pay the winner money. In criminal cases, in addition to deciding if someone is guilty of a crime, juries are often asked to recommend a punishment such as prison time or even death. The stakes can be high to say the least.

If you are on trial, you have a right to a fair jury. Jurors are not supposed to be predisposed to rule against you because of who you are. There are tools that your lawyer can use to help figure out if potential jurors are biased, such as *voir dire*, a special kind of hearing during which the judge or lawyers can ask potential jurors questions designed to reveal biases that make them unsuitable for your case. In some situations, judges will proactively strike a juror when a bias is revealed. If that doesn't happen, your lawyer might be able to exercise something called a preemptory challenge, which allows an attorney to strike a potential juror for any reason.

By a similar token, if you are called to jury duty, you have a right to serve free from discrimination. So long as you are willing and able to hear the evidence presented and decide the case based on the law, the fact that you are trans or nonbinary is not a legitimate reason to strike you. Some federal case law supports that notion, including a 1994 decision from the U.S. Supreme Court that recognizes that the U.S. Constitution does not permit sex discrimination in the selection of juries.[7] Recently, some federal courts have clarified that the U.S. Constitution doesn't permit gay people to be struck from juries simply for being gay.[8] Many advocates believe these cases mean that trans people cannot be excluded from juries simply because of who they are.

There have been some efforts to formalize discrimination protections in jury service. For instance, some states have laws that expressly prohibit gender identity discrimination in jury selection. There are also efforts to enshrine protections in federal law. As one example, in 2019 a bipartisan coalition of senators introduced the Jury Non-Discrimination Act and Jury ACCESS (Access for Capable Citizens and Equality in Service Selection) Act, which if passed would formally amend jury selection rules to expressly prohibit sexual orientation and gender identity discrimination in jury selection.

Learn more about jury selection and service at Lambda Legal's Fair Courts Project portal.

MAKING JURY SERVICE ACCESSIBLE TO ALL

Judge Mike Jacobs (he/him) is a state court judge in DeKlab County, Georgia.

During *voir dire* in a civil case in early 2019, I had a transgender man in one of my jury pools. Our court's jury management office generates a list that provides biographical information to the judge and the lawyers regarding each prospective juror. For this juror, the list included a female gender marker and female name. Early in the jury selection process, I call on each juror to provide their name, partly for the jurors to introduce themselves and partly to verify that all the jurors are present in the courtroom and seated in the correct order. When I called on the transgender juror, he gave the female name that was listed in the biographical information.

This juror was fortunate to be in the courtroom of the only openly LGBTQ trial judge in our county. The way I conduct *voir dire*, the jurors are divided into smaller groups of six for specific questioning later in the process. When this juror's group was brought into the courtroom for specific questioning, I called him to bench. With the juror standing in front of me, I looked at him and asked the simple question, "What are your pronouns?" The juror's eyes lit up and he responded, "he/him." I added, "And what's your name?" The juror answered with a male name that was different from the one in his biographical information. I sent the juror back to his seat, called the lawyers to the bench, and corrected the information they would be using for this juror.

Thereafter, everything went smoothly for the juror. He was able to live his truth in a setting in which he originally did not feel comfortable. The juror left my courtroom with a big smile on his face, maybe because he was not selected for the jury, but probably because of how he was treated. This experience underscored the importance of educating judges about respecting gender identity, including how to ask for and use pronouns. Unlike the juror in my courtroom, most citizens interact with the justice system in the courtrooms of trial judges who are not members of the LGBTQ community. All citizens who enter a court of law nevertheless should feel completely comfortable so that they can focus on the important reasons they are there in the first place.

Discrimination Protections

No one should be targeted for mistreatment because of who they are. Discrimination laws are one important tool to help keep us safe. These special laws are designed to prevent discrimination against groups on account of a particular protected status in specific contexts such as employment, health care, and education. Most of these laws are crafted such that the person who is mistreated and/or the government itself can sue the wrongdoer in court. The idea is that threat of a lawsuit will encourage people to treat others fairly and, if not, that proceeds from the suit will heal the victim's injuries and disincentivize future violations.

Trans people have a complicated relationship with discrimination laws. At the federal level and in many states there are no statutes that expressly indicate that trans people are protected. Most courts and experts agree, however, that we are protected by generally applicable laws, such as sex discrimination statutes, because discrimination against us as trans people is based on our sex. Many also believe that trans people with gender dysphoria are protected by disability discrimination statutes.[9]

For maps of nondiscrimination laws, check out the website for the Movement Advancement Project.

BOSTOCK V. CLAYTON COUNTY, GEORGIA, 590 U.S. ___ (2020)

Bostock is one of the most important transgender rights cases ever decided in the United States. In it, the U.S. Supreme Court held that Title VII of the Civil Rights Act of 1964—a federal law that prohibits discrimination "because of . . . sex" in employment—protects transgender and gay people. Employment protections are important, but *Bostock* does far more than just clarify why Title VII protects trans folks. Before *Bostock*, many courts simply presumed that transgender people could not reap the privileges of generally applicable laws unless expressly named as subjects of protection. According to Justice Neil Gorsuch, who wrote *Bostock*, that is not true. According to Gorsuch, *Bostock*'s "simple but momentous message" is this: that unless there are clear exceptions written into a law, exclusion of disfavored groups, such as trans people, cannot be presumed. Consequently, going forward, all federal and state laws that can be fairly read as protecting everyone—such as sex and disability laws—should now be construed as protecting transgender people.

Public Accommodations

Everyone should be able to make use of public spaces regardless of who they are. Public accommodations laws aim to help people do just that. These special laws prohibit discrimination in places of public accommodations, generally defined as facilities, both public and private, used by the public. Examples include retail stores, restaurants, hotels, theaters, pharmacies, and parks.

Unfortunately, there are only limited protections in force right now. At the federal level, you might be protected under the Americans with Disabilities Act (ADA), which prohibits discrimination in public accommodations if you have or are regarded as having a disability.[10] A growing number of authorities, including some federal agencies and courts, view trans people with gender dysphoria as qualifying as disabled for the purposes of the ADA.[11] Some states and localities have more protections on the books. For instance, both California and the City of Chicago expressly prohibit discrimination on account of gender identity in public accommodations.[12]

DOE V. BOYERTOWN AREA SCH. DIST., 897 F.3D 518 (3D CIR. 2018)

Cisgender students in Pennsylvania sued their public school after it adopted a trans-inclusive restroom policy. The trial court dismissed the suit, reasoning that cisgender students' rights were not violated by the trans-inclusive policy, a decision ultimately upheld by a federal appellate court.

There is also a growing trend to pass special public accommodations laws that zero-in on a narrow access issue. By far, restroom access is the most popular. Gender segregated restrooms have long created problems of convenience, fairness, and safety for T/GE people. One solution is to change the default and make all single-user restrooms gender neutral, given that there is no need to segregate them. To this end, some states and localities, such as California, New York City, and Washington, DC, have experimented with laws that require establishments with single-occupancy restrooms to mark them as gender-neutral.[13]

Gender Recognition

I couldn't get a job until I changed my documentation. No one would hire me because my appearance didn't match the gender and birth name on my ID.

For many of us, our gender identity is an integral part of who we are. It's key to how we understand our inner selves and hold ourselves out in the world. A piece of paper with the right gender marker on it doesn't make or break who you are on the inside, but it can be very important if you need to navigate the world around you. It's thus no surprise that many of us wish to have our gender legally recognized. But what exactly does that mean and what are our options?

Nearly one third of trans people report being harassed, denied services, and even attacked because they did not have an ID that matched their presentation.[14] When people don't have accurate ID, they find it difficult to find employment and housing. Whether going to the gym, a bar, or getting on an airplane, having accurate ID has an enormous impact on one's quality of life.

I magically got an M on my new ID when they sent it to me because they saw Jason as a male name and thought it was a mistake.

There is no such thing as a legal gender. Or at least, not in the way most nonlawyers think of it. Though American law has always recognized men and women as distinct classes of people (and, in some instances, third gender persons), there was never a single, formal mechanism by which people were legally recognized as such.[15] Put a different way, historically the law treated men and women differently, but there were no rules that governed whether someone was a man or a woman. Thus, if you held yourself out as being a man, the law treated you as such. Today American law functions mostly the same way. There is no one-stop shop to have your gender legally recognized for all intents and purposes.

ARROYO V. ROSSELLÓ, 305 F.SUPP.3D 327 (D.P.R. 2018)

A group of Puerto Rican trans folks, including out trans Latina lawyer Victoria Rodríguez Roldán (she/her), the Senior Policy Manager at AIDS United, sued the government for the right to amend the gender markers on their birth certificates. In 2018, a federal trial court ruled that it is unconstitutional for Puerto Rico to refuse to allow trans folks to amend their gender markers.

Binary gender changes. Depending upon your needs and resources, you can obtain IDs and sometimes even court orders that recognize your gender. Most states allow you to obtain a driver's license or identity card that reflects your gender identity without proof of surgery, though many do require documentation from a medical professional attesting to your gender transition and/or require showing that you underwent some form of medical treatment to effectuate a change in gender. Since 2010, the U.S. Department of State has permitted binary trans folks to obtain a passport reflecting their gender identity with proof of treatment from a medical provider. Some state courts will issue gender recognition court orders to anyone who lives in the state (even if they weren't born there).[16] Other states, such as Oregon, let persons with Oregon birth certificates skip the courthouse altogether and handle document amendment requests through an administrative agency for a small fee.[17]

When I registered to vote, I refused to put down a gender (it was optional), and I can say it was one of the most empowering and uplifting moments of the past two years when I got my registration card and it said, "no preference" in the gender slot.

Nonbinary gender changes. Many nonbinary folks desire identity documents without M or F gender markers. Some seek an X or a similar alternative mark intended to represent a nonbinary gender. Others want identity documents that list no gender marker at all. At the time of publication, fewer than 30 states have options for third gender markers. This is, however, a quickly developing area of law.

Learn more about changing identity documents at the National Center for Transgender Equality's Documents Center.

I have had my gender ignored, made fun of, and invalidated. The systems in place in the school are based off of a binary understanding of gender. Changing gender markers and your name requires expensive legal documentation and many professor[s] dead name students in classes because of it.

Name Changes

Many T/GE folks decide to take a new name. Because we live in a highly gendered society, having a stereotypically masculine or feminine name has a significant impact

Stay up to date on state laws affecting nonbinary persons at the Intersex Recognition Project's State Laws Resources Portal.

on the way in which people are treated in a myriad of contexts. Having the freedom to choose one's name and hold oneself out to the world with that name is deeply empowering.

Unlike gender recognition, there are more formal rules that govern how one goes about getting legal recognition of a name change. In most states, there are two ways to change your name.

Court order. You can go to court and file a petition to change your name. Different states have different rules that govern this process and charge different administrative fees. Once you complete all the steps, a court will issue you an order recognizing your change of name. When you have that court order you can use it to prove your name change to other courts, agencies, and authorities.

Common law change. Some states permit you to change your name without going to court. This is called a "common law name change." Rules vary, but in jurisdictions that allow this you can change your name by holding yourself out as your new name for a certain period of time. Most jurisdictions require that you use your new name consistently and exclusively in all aspects of your life. Common law name changes are free and don't require going to court, and are thus a great option for some people. It can sometimes be difficult, however, to prove your common law name change. The best practice if you go this route is to keep records that reflect you have held yourself out under your new name. These may include copies of bills, paystubs, snail mail, magazine subscriptions, or anything else that shows you have asked others to call you by this new name and others have responded in kind. If you run into trouble down the line proving your common law name, you always have the option of getting a court order formally recognizing your name change.

Learn more about name change options in your jurisdiction at the National Center for Transgender Equality's Documents Center.

TRANSGENDER BUREAUCRACY BLUES

Remy Patterson is an electrical engineer from Nebraska who enjoys writing poetry for fun.

Hi ho, hi ho
to the DMV we go
a mechanical thing
of timber and string
and three little words in a row
Hi ho, hi ho
the man at the desk lets me know
that I'm in the wrong line
I say that it's fine
as I feel my nose starting to grow
To the SSA building we drive
feed the meter a buck twenty-five
I foresee I'll expire
before I retire
but Uncle Sam wants me alive
Here the certified paper inspector
calls me "ma'am" and I dare not correct her
and the small silver locket
I keep in my pocket
has set off the metal detector

Criminal Justice Reforms

The criminal justice system plays an important role in our country, but often falls short of what we need. Maintaining law and order sounds like a good thing to most of us. Unfortunately, the criminal justice system in our country disproportionately criminalizes and mistreats marginalized groups, such as transgender people, who are accused and convicted of crimes. Our criminal justice system also does a terrible job at protecting us from crime. In fact, many T/GE people report serious problems trying to get police, prosecutors, and courts to enforce criminal laws that should protect us. There is some hope on the horizon. Over the last couple decades, trans folks have pushed to reform our criminal justice system both for those who are accused and convicted of crimes and for victims.

> *I have been arrested. In my state even with my updated gender marker, I am put in the male population even though I am a trans woman. I was treated appallingly. I was harassed, sexually assaulted, and raped in police custody. A judge refused my case and dismissed it in court.*

Housing. If you are serving a prison or jail sentence, you have a right to be safely housed. We've seen some modest improvements in housing conditions of incarcerated trans folks recently. Federal, state, and local prisons and jails are empowered to set their own housing policies. Historically, prisoners were housed according to their birth-assigned sex. Some prisons, however, have correctly recognized that it can be psychologically and physically harmful to house trans prisoners this way. Among other things, as the U.S. Supreme Court itself has recognized, trans people are especially vulnerable to sexual assault.[18] Indeed, it is estimated that 40% of incarcerated trans people are sexually assaulted, which is 10 times the national average for incarcerated people.[19] Safer housing options—placing trans folks in housing aligning with their gender identity, as one example—can go a long way toward correcting the problem. Unfortunately, as of 2018, it is the policy of the Federal Bureau of Prisons to house trans persons according to their birth-assigned sex, although some case-by-case exceptions are made.[20] Luckily, some state lawmakers have stepped up. For instance, California, Connecticut, and Massachusetts have all enacted laws that make it a legal presumption that prisoners are to be housed according to their gender identity.[21]

DOE V. MASSACHUSETTS, DEP'T OF CORRECTIONS, 1:17-CV-12255 (D. MASS. 2018)

Jane Doe, a trans woman incarcerated at a state men's prison in Massachusetts, sued so she could be housed in a women's prison. In 2018, the prison transferred her to a women's prison.[22] Doe's lawyers, including out trans lawyer Jennifer Levi (he/him), believe the transfer was the first of its kind in the country.

> *I was arrested with 15 other people in a protest a few years ago. Many of us are gender-nonconforming and/or trans. It was pretty horrible, they basically broke us up according to our gender markers on our IDs and so a couple trans guys were in a cell with me and other folks with F on our IDs and some trans femmes were in the men's cell.*

Identity Documents. There is some forward momentum in the fight to ensure that currently and formerly incarcerated persons have unencumbered access to accurate identity documents. Historically, prisoners were barred in many jurisdictions from changing their name while incarcerated. Some states even went so far as to bar persons with felony records from changing their names after reentry. That approach was hugely problematic. Not only did it deprive trans people a modicum of personal dignity while incarcerated, but it also made reentry more difficult when someone's IDs did not match their chosen name and gender presentation. Thankfully, many courts and lawmakers have intervened. For instance, in 2015, the Supreme Court of Virginia (Virginia's court of last resort) held that prisoners had a right to use the courts to change their name so long as it was done for a legitimate purpose and further recognized that a gender transition is one such purpose.[23]

Lawmakers in some states, such as California and Delaware, have amended name change laws to make clear that prisoners have a right to petition for court orders recognizing their names.[24]

If you have a criminal record and want to change your name, check out the Trans Lifeline's Name Change Guide for People with Criminal Records.

I am very afraid of getting arrested—I don't know where I'd be put. Don't want to be in isolation, but the men's prison isn't safe (I'd be raped, attacked), and I don't belong in the women's as a man. I also worry how I'd get access to my testosterone.

EDMO V. CORIZON, 935 F.3D 757 (9TH CIR. 2019)

A trans woman, Andree Edmo, sued her Idaho state prison claiming its refusal to give her access to genital reconstruction surgery violated her Eighth Amendment rights. She won in a federal trial court, and her win was upheld on appeal.

Health Care is another area where we have seen positive developments for incarcerated trans folks. Some federal courts have recognized that gender dysphoria is a legitimate medical condition and consequently have ruled that it violates the Eighth Amendment's prohibition on cruel and unusual punishment to deprive incarcerated trans folks of adequate medical treatment including, but not limited to, permanent hair removal, hormones, surgery, and "gender affirming" canteen items.

GET WOKE

Janetta Johnson (she/her) is the executive director of the TGI Justice Project

The atrocities trans people experience and the way we get beaten down is a system that is not conducive to rehabilitation for anybody—and just imagine trans people being at the bottom of that totem pole. You have traumatic experiences that will always live with you. It leaves you scarred in a way that you always have to have someone who experienced those systems help you navigate.

I'm a firm believer in de-carceration, and we have to start somewhere. If I had the call, I would immediately release all low-level offenders, and money in the criminal justice system would be given to reentry services so people have an opportunity to gain a paycheck. I would say we completely demolish all private prisons and not replace them with housing, because I wouldn't want people to live in that cesspool of trauma where so many people have served time.

Get woke, stay woke, pay attention, and stay a part of the movement. Make sure you love yourself.

Reentry. There are many collateral consequences associated with being convicted of a crime. One very important area is known as reentry, the transitional period between leaving jail or prison and reintegrating into society. Many courts put conditions on where and on what terms a person is released from prison or jail. Sometimes you are directed to participate in a specific reentry program, many of which are strictly gender segregated and limit the kind of health care you can access. Unfortunately, if you refuse to comply with the rules of reentry programs, you could be sent back to jail or prison. Though reentry programs are technically different than jail or prison, you should have similar rights to safe, gender-appropriate housing and access to gender-affirming health care.

Trans Panic Defense. No one deserves to be victimized because of who they are. Unfortunately, some people accused of committing crimes against trans people argue that it is our fault we are targeted. In essence, the accused asks the judge or jury to absolve them of their crime not because they are innocent, but because the fact that the victim is trans should excuse their crime. This is called a trans panic defense. These so-called trans panic defenses are "Rooted in transphobia and send the wrong message that violence against LGBT people is acceptable."[25]

At present, neither federal law nor the laws of any of the states formally recognize the trans panic defense. However, it is still routinely raised in court. For instance, in a 2016 jury trial in New York City a cis man accused of murdering Islan Nettles, a Black trans woman, claimed that he was "tricked by a transgender" and that this justified his fatal beating of Nettles.[26] Fortunately, there has been some progress made in this area. In 2013, the American Bar Association, the nation's preeminent professional association for lawyers, issued a unanimous resolution calling on federal, tribal, state, and territorial governments to prohibit the trans panic defense.[27] As of the time of publication, 11 states, including New York, have passed laws prohibiting use of the trans panic defense in criminal cases.

If you want to connect with grassroots activists working to abolish prisons and, in the meantime, improve conditions, check out the organization Black & Pink.

Learn more about efforts to ban the trans panic defense at the National LGBT Bar Association's portal on Gay and Trans Panic Defense.

I tried to recall the events of that night: I had recently graduated with a master's degree from Harvard in May 2018, but I was still on the hunt for a teaching job. While I knew I wouldn't find this job at the bottom of a glass of beer, it served as a temporary relief from my anxieties of being a Mexican-American trans guy from Texas who moved to Boston—a city known for its racism—for grad school and a career in academia. I was discussing this with a fellow Latino at the bar that night. I also spoke to a bartender that night about my growing beard. I am out as a trans man to everyone who works at all the local shops and restaurants. I had no reason to not feel safe being out in my usual haunts.

Before I left, I spoke with a gentleman about current events in Spanish. My parents immigrated from Mexico in the late 1970s, and we talked about the difficulties he had emigrating from Colombia during the Trump administration and the horrors that were happening. At that time, families with children, many seeking asylum from the gang violence in Honduras, had just been gassed at the Mexican border. It felt unreal this was happening in America in 2018.

I began walking home, which usually takes fewer than 10 minutes. I live in Jamaica Plain, known for its BLGTQ + inclusiveness and gentrification in recent decades. I became just one of a couple of people of color (POC) still living on my block; however, I have always felt safe. The irony isn't lost on me.

I believe someone heard something they didn't like. Toxic masculinity, transphobia, and racism can kill. But even if this was simply a random act, I have a hard time absorbing the fact that I could have been killed in a queer-friendly, formerly Latinx-populated part of Boston. It just doesn't compute.

In my recovery from my traumatic brain injury (TBI), I endured speech therapy, physical therapy, and daily cognitive exercises. Like Humpty Dumpty, I was determined to be put back together again. I'm grateful I'm still alive to tell my story. The fact that I am able to write this now is nothing short of . . . well, I won't say a "miracle," as that doesn't coincide with my belief system, but it is extraordinary.

I was originally named after my mother, who, herself, was named after a Biblical character. I gave her first dibs in renaming me when I first came out publicly as transgender two years ago. She chose to rename me "Noah," partially as a nod to her Christian faith. For her, the rainbow symbolizes God's promise to Noah to protect him from future floods. It is especially fitting now. The communities to which I belong are full of survivors of a deluge of metaphorical, mostly man-made "floods."

I am now one of those survivors, and I'm proud to be a part of the trans tribe, the Latinx tribe, the anxiety/depression/PTSD tribe, and now, the TBI tribe. Their survival and resilience have been my anchors, keeping me ashore while my body and soul repair—one piece at a time. Healing from physical and emotional trauma doesn't just take time. It requires community.

Some Lessons I've learned on how to deal with police in the aftermath of an assault:

- **Record What Happened:** As soon as you are able, write down everything you remember before the attack. Add details as you remember them. With head injuries, it's common to remember pieces of the puzzle later.
- **Reach Out Sooner Rather Than Later:** After an assault, a trans POC may not feel comfortable going to law enforcement right away for help. That is understandable. However, the sooner the incident is recorded, the sooner witnesses and suspect(s) can be found.
- **Find a Buddy:** It can be triggering to have to physically go to the police department to recount what happened. I went alone, but wish I had brought a friend for moral support.
- **Find Advocates:** I had a hard time getting the police to investigate my case. They did not do so for two months. Through the Violence Recovery Program at Fenway Health in Boston, I was put in touch with the LGBTQ liaison for the local police department (PD). They finally forwarded my case to a detective. Check if your local PD has someone like this on staff, or at the least, a violent crime advocate in the community to help with next steps.
- **Involve the Community:** If the local PD doesn't take your case seriously, which sadly is possible with trans/POC victims of violent crimes, inform the community. Members of my community and neighborhood called and pressured the local PD to start an investigation. Although there was no satisfactory outcome in my case, we can hope that no one else in that community will again have to wait so long for their case to be taken on by law enforcement.

I reclaim my voice not just for myself, but for all of us. Although my body and brain are still healing, I'm not planning to leave myself anchored forever. As corny as it sounds, ships are meant to sail, and my journey isn't over yet. Someday, I will make it home.

Military Service

Trans and gender expansive people have served in the U.S. military since the birth of our country. However, we have not always been able to serve openly. Right now, we are amidst what is hopefully a permanent shift in how the military accommodates and supports T/GE service members and veterans.

End of Trans Ban in U.S. Armed Forces. Every person willing and able to serve should be permitted to do so. Unfortunately, for a long time, transgender Americans were barred from enlisting and faced the prospect of being discharged if they tried transitioning while serving. In 2016, the Obama Administration's U.S. Department of Defense ("DOD") announced it would lift the trans ban on service in the Air Force, Army, Coast Guard, Marine Corps, and Navy, allowing currently serving but closeted trans personnel to serve openly. Unfortunately, in mid-2017, the Trump Administration put a new trans ban in place. Under that ban, some then currently serving trans people were permitted to serve openly, but no new trans personnel could enlist.

There has been some significant progress recently. In early 2021, President Biden issued an executive order lifting the Trump trans ban.[28] Later that year, the Pentagon issued regulations implementing fully inclusive service.[29] The overarching aim of the Biden open service policy is to ensure that ready, willing, and able trans people who wish to serve can serve as their authentic selves. Be aware, under the Biden policy, in order to transition while you serve, you *must* receive a diagnosis of gender dysphoria.

Learn more about the fight for a trans-inclusive military at the Palm Center, an independent research institute that advocates for a trans-inclusive military.

TRANS LAWYERS LEAD IN CHALLENGES TO TRANS BAN

Shannon Minter (he/him) is Legal Director of the National Center for Lesbian Rights and one of the lead attorneys in the cluster of cases challenging the Trump Administration's trans ban. Minter recognizes how important it is for openly trans lawyers to lead the way. As per Minter, "It's very gratifying to be able to use everything I've learned from the past 25 years to work on an issue that I care about so much. While the most important thing is the arguments we're presenting, I do think that it makes a difference to the court and the community itself to have transgender attorneys be the lead attorneys on this case. It's harder for any judge to ignore the humanity of a group of people when the attorneys that are in front of her are themselves members of that group. It underscores just how senseless it is to exclude an entire group of people and say that they are unfit and unable to serve, when in the very case itself you can see that transgender people are perfectly able to function in society and play a constructive role."

Excerpted from: Meredith Talusan, *Meet the Trans Lawyer Who Led the Fight Against Trump's Military Ban*, them. (Oct. 31, 2017).

Health Care. To fully implement Biden's open service policy, the military is presently adjusting healthcare policies for currently serving T/GE military members and dependents as well as veterans.

For current service members, you should be able to use your health insurance, TriCare, to obtain a diagnosis of gender dysphoria, receive hormone treatments, and coordinate care to access medically necessary transition surgeries. The Biden Administration has not yet issued any guidelines speaking to whether dependents, such as military spouses and children, may use TriCare for gender transition health care.

For veterans, you should be able to access some transition health care at Veterans Administration (VA) facilities. At the time of publication, you can access hormonal care, mental health services, and some postsurgical care. Starting in early 2021, the Biden Administration directed the VA to review its policies to ensure that transgender veterans have access to transition-related surgical care within the VA system.

Correcting Military Records after You Serve. The National Center for Transgender Equality estimates that there are more than 134,000 trans veterans in the United States. Having records that accurately identify you is important, especially if you are trying to access military benefits. If you transitioned *after* you left the military, you can update your service records to reflect both name and gender changes. To change your name on your DD214 Military Discharge Record, you can file a DD Form 149. To update your name and gender in the Defense Enrollment Eligibility Reporting System (DEERS), you can apply to your branch's Board of Correction.

SPART*A is an advocacy organization for trans, nonbinary, and gender nonconforming service members, veterans, partners, and allies.

Learn more about how to change your name and gender marker on your military records at the National Center for Transgender Equality's Military Records portal.

Landon Marchant (they/them) is a veteran of the United States Air Force, former plumber's apprentice and community college student, Williams College alum, and part-time storyteller.

Swimming is harder, now. My body is heavier, my coordination is different. Water feels heavy and is not my friend. This is the price of adding muscle and testosterone, turning willowy girlish curves into lean muscle. Today, however, every stroke and breath felt powerful: my body obeying, moving, succeeding. No matter how quickly I swam, though, I could not shake the memory of another pool. One I never made it to.

He let me leave because my sergeant had called. I was late for my supervisor's child's birthday party at the base pool. He let me leave because he didn't want anyone to come looking or ask where I had been. He called himself my friend; he was my friend. The only person I knew on base outside of work.

As I left, he said words that must have seemed flattering, words that I was not allowed to repeat while testifying at trial. They would have changed the nature of the case; it is already hard enough to convict a young white man of sexual assault. My body was up for judgment and found worthy of respect only within specific parameters. Parameters I was not allowed to set.

Five years later my body is again up for judgment and has been found lacking. It is difficult, now, to be comfortable in the silent locker rooms where I had just begun to feel safe. The mentality that breeds sexual entitlement is the same mentality that polices my identity. My body is not my own. Perhaps it has never truly been my own. I find myself wondering if it is safe for me to change in a school locker room without a friend around—or even at all. I find myself wondering if I need to carry identification with my gender marker or how best to navigate the Transportation Security Administration (TSA). I find myself wondering what kind of career I will have, and what kind of future is possible for someone like myself. I find myself wondering why strangers can determine my worth based on the body I inhabit. For the first time in years, I wanted to change in a bathroom stall. To hide. Instead I stood at my locker, claiming that small space as mine.

Today, swimming was not the difficult part.

Health Insurance

Trans and gender expansive Americans widely report experiencing health insurance discrimination. In one of the largest national surveys to date, an astounding one in four T/GE Americans reports being denied coverage for transition-related care or nontransition-related routine care in the past year.[30]

Learn more about how you can fight insurance denials at the National Center for Transgender Equality's Health Coverage Guide portal.

The high incidence of insurance denials is driven primarily by what are colloquially known as trans exclusions. These exclusions take various forms, but ultimately aim to exempt from coverage care sought by trans persons to treat gender dysphoria. Some exclusions impose categorical bars—meaning they exempt from coverage all treatments for gender dysphoria. Some exclusions are partial—meaning they cover a subset of care but totally bar other care without regard to whether a patient can show medical necessity. Whether categorical or partial, these exclusions deprive trans patients of health benefits otherwise covered by the plan.

FLACK V. WIS. DEP'T OF HEALTH SERVS., 395 F.SUPP.3D 1001 (W.D.WIS. 2019)

Wisconsin's Medicaid program had a longstanding trans exclusion. Two trans women—Cody Flack and Sara Ann McKenzie—sued, claiming it violated federal law. A federal trial court ruled for the women, finding the exclusion violated the Fourteenth Amendment's Equal Protection Clause.

Although trans exclusions are still prevalent, most courts and agencies have ruled that categorically excluding coverage of gender dysphoria care is illegal. For instance, some courts and agencies deem trans exclusions as unlawful sex discrimination on the theory that they single out trans people for disparate treatment because of their sex.[31] Others have ruled in the public benefits context (e.g., Medicare and Medicaid) that where a patient shows that gender dysphoria treatment is medically necessary that it is arbitrary and capricious for the insurer to deny care.[32] Similarly, some courts have ruled that public benefits cannot deny care by claiming the care is "cosmetic" where evidence reflects the care is medically necessary.[33] Where health benefits plans are provided by employers as a benefit of employment some courts and agencies have concluded that trans exclusions on those plans are forms of employment discrimination.[34]

Conversion Therapy

Conversion therapy or reparative therapy is an umbrella term that describes sustained efforts that seek to discourage behaviors associated with a gender other than the one assigned at birth and/or to promote gender identities that are aligned with one's gender assigned at birth.[35] It is estimated that one in seven trans Americans has been subjected to conversion therapy.[36]

Conversion therapy is harmful. Experts have long concluded that it is impossible to change someone's gender identity. Despite this, proponents of conversion therapy subject trans people to a wide range of discredited interventions that are designed to humiliate and psychologically terrorize them into rejecting their gender identity.

Thankfully, there has been considerable progress using the law to fight back against conversion therapy. At the time of publication, 20 states have laws on the books that prohibit licensed mental health practitioners from subjecting minors to conversion therapy.[37] Additionally, Washington, DC and Puerto Rico have also banned conversion therapy.[38]

Other legal avenues to fight back exist. Lawyers are experimenting with using old laws to solve new problems like conversion therapy. For instance, in 2015, a state trial court jury in New Jersey found that a conversion therapy organization's work constituted consumer fraud.[39]

Marriage

Love and companionship are the cornerstones of some of life's most important relationships. Marriage is one way that we formalize our commitments. Being legally married confers a number of special benefits that help you and your loved one navigate life together. Among other things, you are eligible for special federal tax benefits, you have next-of-kin status with your partner, which means you can visit them in the hospital if they get sick and make medical decisions for them if they are unable to do so, and you can inherit your partner's estate automatically in most jurisdictions.

There are two ways to get married in the United States. When most of us think about marriage, we picture a happy couple coming together in a ceremony and, of course, some paperwork. This is called a *celebrated marriage*. Every state has its own rules, but typically they require partners with the legal capacity to marry (e.g., of legal age and not already married) to get a marriage license, have a public celebration with witnesses, and file the marriage license with the appropriate registry so it is recorded. This kind of marriage is usually the best choice for couples because its public nature and documentation makes it easier, down the road, to prove the existence of the marriage.

Some, but not all states, have a second option called *common law marriage*, which recognizes as married couples who otherwise meet the legal requirements of marriage and hold themselves out to their friends, family, and community, to be married even though they never had a public ceremony or filed the appropriate paperwork with the government. Common law marriages can be a good fit for couples in jurisdictions that recognize them (at the time of publication this includes only eight states and Washington, DC) because they are free. They can sometimes be problematic, however, if the couple later moves to a jurisdiction that doesn't recognize common law marriages.

Find out more about state and local insurance nondiscrimination laws at the Movement Advancement Project's Healthcare Laws and Policies portal.

The Trevor Project's "50 Bills, 50 States" project addresses laws against conversion therapy across the country.

To learn more about the fight against conversion therapy check out the National Center for Lesbian Rights' Born Perfect campaign.

Thankfully, the fact that you are T/GE is no longer a barrier to marriage in the United States. In the past, many T/GE folks had difficulties because states had laws that prohibited same-sex marriage. During that period, some T/GE people were unable to get married or risked having their marriage deemed void because they underwent a gender transition. This is no longer a problem in the United States. In 2015, the U.S. Supreme Court ruled in *Obergefell v. Hodges* that everyone, regardless of sex, has a fundamental right to marriage. As a practical matter, this means that neither your or your partner's sex assigned at birth nor your or your partners' gender transition matters for the purposes of marriage. If you married your partner before 2015—even if you entered into a same-sex marriage before they were technically legal in your jurisdiction—your marriage is deemed retroactively valid today.

OBERGEFELL V. HODGES, 576 U.S. 644 (2015)

"The nature of marriage is that, through its enduring bond, two persons together can find other freedoms, such as expression, intimacy, and spirituality. This is true for all persons, whatever their sexual orientation. . . . There is dignity in the bond between two men or two women who seek to marry and in their autonomy to make such profound choices."

Divorce

If you transition *after* you get married, it is a good idea for you to consult a family law lawyer or legal services office to amend important documents to recognize your transition. In some states, you can amend your marriage certificate to reflect your new name and gender. In other states, you cannot amend your marriage certificate, but a lawyer can draw up official documents that explain your name and gender change.

To dissolve a marriage in the United States, you must formally divorce. Divorce is governed by state law, meaning rules vary from place to place. Today, all states allow you to file for something called "unilateral no-fault" divorce, meaning you need not prove why you want a divorce. Some states, including Mississippi and South Dakota, require your spouse to consent to no-fault divorce. Other states don't require spousal consent, but do mandate that you spend a period in formal "separation" before granting your divorce.

We recognize that many T/GE people are afraid of divorce because it requires going to court and they have had bad experiences there in other contexts. However, we have seen significant progress by judges and family law courts around the nation over the last few years. Many more judges understand who transgender people are and do their best to respect us, especially in sensitive proceedings like divorce. If you are worried about how you will be treated by the judge or court personnel, it's best to discuss your concerns. directly with your lawyer before the first time you go to court.

Each jurisdiction has special rules, but all require court proceedings that divide up assets (e.g., money and property). Some jurisdictions also award spousal support or maintenance—an obligation for one partner to pay the other a certain sum of money for a period of time—something that is meant to help equalize the partners at the time of separation.

The decision to get a divorce can be very difficult, but it need not be an adversarial process. Many jurisdictions allow partners to work out the details of their separation outside of court through a process called **collaborative divorce**. In collaborative divorce, the partners work with lawyers and others with special training to help the couple make collaborative decisions about how they will divide assets, how they will talk about one another with others, and anything else the partners want to resolve through the divorce. At the end of the process, the partners' lawyers prepare and file papers memorializing the uncontested divorce. This filing both begins and ends the court process.

Another option is **mediated divorce**. This is also a nonadversarial approach to divorce, wherein instead of going to a judge and lawyers, the partners work with a mediator who facilitates discussion between the spouses and assists in helping them come to agreements necessary to resolve their differences and end the relationship. At the end of the process, the partners have a tailored divorce agreement, which is then submitted to the court. Like with collaborative divorce, this filing both begins and ends the court process.

We realize that some T/GE people enter into marriages before they transition and their transition is a big factor in their divorce. If you are in this situation, it's best to seek help from a lawyer or legal services agency to navigate special challenges you might face. If your spouse no longer wishes to be married to you because you are T/GE, that is their right, even if it is upsetting or hurtful. However, if you are in this situation, you might want to think strategically about how best to approach the proceedings. For example, if your spouse is angry about your transition, it might be a good idea to try a collaborative or mediated divorce, either of which could help you privately work through your separation without having to air sensitive information about your gender transition in open court.

Children

For T/GE parents, relationship transitions often give rise to custody disputes. If you are currently considering divorce or separation we urge you to seek advice from a family law attorney with experience representing T/GE parents as soon as possible. Consulting with an attorney will help you better understand and protect your rights as a parent.

Although we have seen some important progress in family law courts' treatment of T/GE parents over the years, it is still possible that you will face bias by judges or lawyers involved in your case. You should flag this issue for your attorney early on. You may potentially need to retain experts who can educate the judge about what being transgender does and does not mean for you as a parent and why being transgender has no impact on a person's ability to be a good parent.

Parents who are actively transitioning during the custody dispute should be especially cautious. In custody disputes, it is always important that parents make decisions in light of the best interests of the children. Major life events, like a transition, can be stressful for all involved and courts may worry about whether the T/GE parent is making decisions and communicating with the children about transition in sensitive and age-appropriate ways. There are techniques to mitigate against risk here. You can take steps that evidence that your children are equipped to hear about your transition directly from you. For example, you might seek out and follow the advice of experienced professionals with expertise in child welfare and development, such as a child therapist, about how much and when to tell your children about your transition. It is also a good idea to inform the other parent of your transition and communication plans and, where possible, to involve them in the process.

We are seeing a growing number of children openly embrace being T/GE. We encourage all parents to support their T/GE children and explore, where necessary, legal and medical steps that might help the child affirm their identity. If your T/GE child has two parents and both support transition, there are no major legal obstacles to helping your child socially transition, obtain new identity documents, and pursue medical transition in most jurisdictions.

In situations where parents are divorced or separated and disagree about transition next steps, some problems arise. Just as in any other custody dispute, we urge parents to try to work out their differences before turning to the courts for help. If a custody dispute is unavoidable, we urge supportive parents to seek out help from professionals who know about T/GE children. Where resources allow, parents can seek advice from mental health and medical professionals, document this advice, and attempt to include and otherwise share information with the other parent. If a supportive parent winds up in a custody battle, the court is very likely to scrutinize everything the supportive parent has done very closely—if you're in that situation, it's important that you show you were following expert advice, not acting on your own.

If you are the parent of a T/GE child and the other parent isn't supportive of transition, you should seek out legal advice as soon as possible. If you cannot find a local attorney who has worked with T/GE children before, try reaching out to national LGBTQ or trans advocacy organizations—many of them give advice or provide informational materials.

To learn more about T/GE youth rights, check out the online Trans Youth Handbook created by the Harvard Law School LGBTQ+ Advocacy Clinic and the National Center for Lesbian Rights.

Intimate Partner Violence

Intimate partner violence (IPV) is a pattern of behavior where one partner coerces, dominates, or isolates another to maintain power and control over the partner and the relationship. IPV can manifest in various ways, including psychological and emotional abuse, physical abuse, verbal abuse, sexual abuse, cultural abuse, isolation, and intimidation.

According to the National Coalition of Anti-Violence Projects, T/GE people are disproportionately impacted by IPV.[40] It is estimated that trans folks are 1.7 times as likely to experience any IPV, 2.2 times more likely to experience physical IPV, and 2.5 times more likely to experience sexual IPV than cisgender folks.[41]

Historically, T/GE survivors have faced systemic barriers to accessing IPV services. Thankfully, we have seen significant progress recently. At the federal level, the Violence Against Women Act (VAWA) supports help for all survivors of IPV and has, since 2013, prohibited discrimination in services based on gender identity. This means that any program or agency that accepts VAWA cannot deny you services simply because you are trans.

INTERSECTIONALITY AS A TOOL

Trans Americans face staggering rates of discrimination. Far too often, popular media, the courts, and even trans activists diagnose the underlying problem as being that of pure transphobia. In other words, they believe that it is possible to make all trans people equally better off if we narrowly focus on eradicating a supposedly universal kind of bias that all trans folks equally face. Unfortunately, discrimination and bias are more complicated than that.

Discrimination is complex. To cure discrimination, we need to attack it on multiple fronts all at the same time. Put another way, the systemic, institutional, and even interpersonal animus trans Americans face cannot be fixed by narrowly focusing on what sets trans Americans apart from our peers if we do not also take into account how other facets of our identities and experiences shape discrimination.

How we experience being trans and the kinds of discrimination we encounter are shaped by our other identities. Imagine you are a Black trans woman and you are fired from your job shortly after you transition. If someone wants to solve that problem, how would they go about it? Some people might say you need special laws protecting trans people at work. Others might say existing laws prohibiting sex discrimination apply. Still others might say that existing laws prohibiting race discrimination apply. Each of those people is assuming that only one of your identities triggered the discrimination. Who is right? It's a trick question.

Intersectionality is an important tool. Law and policy work is often driven by the need to solve a particular problem, such as trans people being discriminated against at work. It's a good thing to want to solve big problems. But sometimes we go about thinking about these problems too narrowly and miss the bigger picture and thus the solutions we propose miss the mark. Intersectionality can help fix this.

Intersectionality is a framework that explains that discrete instances of discrimination cannot be fully understood by looking at only a single facet of the victim's identity. Intersectionality recognizes that folks with multiple marginalized identities often experience discrimination on multiple fronts, sometimes simultaneously. Put otherwise, if a trans person is discriminated against it might be her trans status that triggered the mistreatment or it could be one or more of her other identities, such as her race or gender, or even a combination of these.

Intersectionality helps us map problems, such as discrimination, by taking into account a victim's whole set of identities and lived experiences. By centering a particular group, we can investigate what issues that group faces as a whole and, most importantly, assess whether some members of that group are worse off in specific contexts.

If you or someone you know is in a violent or abusive relationship, contact the National Domestic Violence Hotline via phone at 1-800-799-SAFE, text START to 1-800-799-SAFE, or chat live at TheHotline.org. The Hotline can be called toll-free from anywhere in the United States. Calls are answered in English and Spanish, with interpreters available for an additional 200+ languages. They can also refer you to the intimate partner violence services closest to you

To learn more about your legal rights as a survivor of IPV, go to the National Center for Transgender Equality's Know Your Rights: Survivors of Violence portal.

Intersectionality is a framework that allows us to identify and map how people are vulnerable to and experience discrimination in light of their multiple identities (e.g., race, sex, religion). Lawyers can use intersectionality as a tool in policy work and litigation to capture how discrimination operates within institutions, structures, and politics.

"There is no such thing as a single-issue struggle because we do not live single-issue lives."[42]
—Audre Lorde

If a Black trans woman is discriminated against because of who *she is*, laws covering trans folks, women, and Black folks should all protect her equally. And, if she is already protected by one kind of law, she shouldn't have to wait for new laws to be passed.

Intersectionality was first articulated in 1989 by Kimberlé Williams Crenshaw, a Black feminist legal scholar.[43]

THE SYLVIA RIVERA LAW PROJECT

Sasha Alexander is a nonbinary trans, Black/South Asian, artist, educator, and healer who works as the Membership Director at the Sylvia Rivera Law Project (SRLP) in New York City. Sasha uses the pronouns she/they/he and insists that you mix it up or use their name.

The Sylvia Rivera Law Project (SRLP) works to guarantee that all people are free to self-determine their gender identity and expression—specifically centering low-income people and people of color who face persistent harassment, discrimination, and violence. We are a collective organization founded on the understanding that gender self-determination is inextricably intertwined with racial, social, and economic justice. For over 16 years, we have worked to increase the political voice and visibility of low-income people and people of color who are transgender, intersex, or gender nonconforming. SRLP works to improve access to respectful and affirming social, health, and legal services.

SRLP's work seeks to address both the root causes and effects of discrimination and violence on the basis of gender identity and expression. We believe that in order to create meaningful political participation and leadership, we must have safety from violence and access to basic means of survival. We are focused on maximizing political voice and power while providing desperately needed services.

We believe that justice does not trickle down and that those who face the most severe consequences of violence and discrimination should be the priority of movements against discrimination. Our agenda focuses on those in our community who face multiple intersections of state and institutional violence: people of color, incarcerated people, people with disabilities, people living with HIV/AIDS, immigrants, homeless people, youth, elders, and people trying to access public benefits.

Diagnosing problems. Even though many T/GE people face inordinate barriers to thriving, some clusters of our community are disproportionately burdened. Thus, if we want to fix anti-trans bias we must also be sensitive to the various ways bias manifests and remain cognizant of how our different identities and experiences shape it.

Intersectionality helps lawyers better understand what roadblocks to equality need to be dismantled, aids in triaging systemic problems by helping us identify which groups need the most help, and ensures that we invest time and resources where they are most needed. This is a powerful tool and, given the great diversity within the trans community itself, intersectionality is the exact right tool for the job.[44]

One important area where intersectionality has been deployed is in assessing the staggering rates of violence against the trans community. For a long time, we tended to talk about and propose solutions to anti-trans violence on the premise that all trans folks are equally vulnerable to violence. But that's not right. Intersectionality has helped us figure out what was actually going on.

Over the last decade, rights groups and advocates have invested considerable resources trying to measure rates of violence, with particular focus on homicides in trans communities. In the last few years, advocates have pushed for measures that take into account a victim's gender and race on the hunch that those factors disproportionately put trans folks at risk for homicide. It turns out that it's true—Black trans women are disproportionately targeted.[45] For example, of the 102 documented murders of trans people between 2013 and 2017, 88 were trans women and 75 were Black.[46] These numbers reveal that vulnerability to violence is influenced not just by being trans but also by one's race and gender. Though those statistics are chilling, they are important to know so that we can proactively work to improve the life outcomes of our Black trans sisters. Seeing, in stark numbers, how disproportionately they are targeted gives us the kind of information that we need to work on legal and advocacy solutions alike.

Another recent example of intersectionality being used to diagnose problems is a report by the African American Policy Forum, which revealed that the factors that make Black women as a group particularly vulnerable to police violence (including homicide) impact non-trans and trans Black women alike.[47] Pioneering work like this helps us understand that if we want to help Black trans women our trans rights work must redress factors that make Black folks and women as a whole vulnerable to police brutality. That is to say, we can't turn a blind eye to race and gender issues if we want to help Black trans women. They are vulnerable because of their cluster of identities—just focusing on the fact they are trans misses the bigger picture.

Making better arguments in court. Intersectionality is used in cutting-edge impact litigation cases, including those brought by this chapter's authors.

One of the biggest fights we've had in court recently is whether existing, generally applicable statutes protect trans people despite not expressly stating that they do. For a long time, courts took the position that if statutes did not expressly state trans people were protected, they weren't. Courts operated in this way because they believed trans people were exceptional. That is to say, they thought trans people should be relegated to a special legal category that had few, if any, protections under the law. Many courts demanded that trans people fight for additional statutes that specifically stated that the old statutes protected us.

Trans Day of Resilience 2016. Digital Media. (Rommy Torrico in collaboration with Familia TQLM and Strong Families)

Living as Ourselves

Of course, when your community is so marginalized that the courthouse doors are slammed like that, it's safe to assume you don't yet have the political power to create special statutes ratifying the old laws. So, what is a trans rights litigator to do?

Intersectionality is the solution. Intersectionality helps us explain why it is wrong to think trans people should be treated differently than other groups. It helps us show that where a law is generally applicable (meaning it applies to everyone), it is the court's job to make sure everyone who can be is protected. Trans people shouldn't be treated as exceptional.

With intersectionality, we can explain that courts don't require other groups to get special laws that name them if old statutes already cover them. For example, it wouldn't make sense to say that a woman who wears a red shirt to work is not protected by sex discrimination laws simply because a statute is silent as to whether red shirt wearers are protected. Everyone is supposed to be protected—that's the whole point of general laws.

We can also explain that general laws don't permit courts to limit protections to pro-totypical victims. This means that just because a court has only seen a certain kind of case brought by one kind of person in the past, that doesn't mean that other kinds of people aren't allowed to bring similar cases.

What recently happened in *Bostock v. Clayton Country, Georgia*, a case decided by the U.S. Supreme Court in 2020, is a great example of how intersectionality can help. As we discussed earlier, in *Bostock*, the Supreme Court had to decide whether a federal law that prohibits sex discrimination in employment protects trans people. The law, Title VII, only says that discrimination "because of sex" is prohibited. It's silent about who is or isn't protected from sex discrimination. Ultimately, the Supreme Court decided trans people are protected because the statute doesn't say we aren't protected. Justice Gorsuch, who wrote the *Bostock* opinion, called it a "simple, but momentous message" that our nation's laws protect everyone equally. This means that judges cannot impose special burdens on trans people that aren't imposed on other groups.

Crafting better legal strategies. Intersectionality can be used to make our legal strategies better. In the past, many important T/GE rights cases were brought on behalf of white trans women. Those women absolutely deserve legal protections. Too many of our cases, however, focused only on the narrow set of experiences white trans women face.

Intersectional trans rights litigators recognize that when we are picking cases to advance our community's rights we must pick wisely. We cannot just pick cases involving white trans women. If we want courts to truly understand that trans people aren't exceptional and laws protect us all equally, we need to bring cases on behalf of all sorts of trans people to drive that home. Put another way, if our big court wins are only won in the name of white trans women, later courts might not understand that other kinds of trans people have the same rights. Courts need to see the diversity of our community so they can make the right conclusions about who is protected and what trans rights can and should look like on the ground.

TUDOR V. SOUTHEASTERN OKLAHOMA STATE UNIV., 5:15-CV-324 (W.D. OKLA.)18-6102 (10TH CIR.)

Rachel Tudor is an English professor. She is also Native American and a citizen of the Chickasaw Nation, a sovereign tribe in Southeast Oklahoma. In 2010 and 2011, Tudor applied for tenure at her university but was denied in suspicious ways, complained, and was eventually fired. Tudor uncovered evidence that her university discriminated against her because of her sex and retaliated because of her complaints. In November 2017, a federal jury in Oklahoma City ruled in Tudor's favor and awarded her damages of $1,165,000. At the time, many thought it impossible for a woman who is Native and trans to win such a trial. Tudor and her jury proved that fair-minded people can do the right thing. Tudor's case is currently on appeal. As of the time of publication, Tudor is asking that the 10th Circuit order her employer to give her the job she earned. Tudor's employer is asking that the jury's verdict be tossed out because Tudor is transgender.

TRANS IN THE LEGAL PROFESSION

In the popular imagination, the biggest legal battles for trans rights are fought by allies, and T/GE folks are conceived of solely as clients. But that image doesn't wholly capture how our rights are won inside and outside of the courthouse. For several decades, a growing number of trans lawyers have lived their truth openly and harnessed their talents to reshape the national legal landscape and our profession for the better.

There are tremendous barriers to entering let alone thriving in the legal profession. In most jurisdictions, lawyers must complete a four-year undergraduate degree and a three-year graduate degree in law, pass a state bar exam, and complete continuing education classes yearly to maintain a law license. The steep cost of school and demands of the profession are difficult for many to grapple with, trans and non-trans alike. However, trans lawyers face an uphill battle getting hired, keeping a job, and obtaining promotions. Unfortunately, the same biases that trip up members of our community in other sectors plague the legal profession, too.

NONBINARY ON THE FRONT LINES

Shawn Meerkamper (they/them) is a senior staff attorney at the Transgender Law Center.

"I was lucky enough to publish one of the first law review articles about nonbinary folks in 2013. It's been remarkable to see how much progress we've made since then. Only four years later, I got to work on a bill in California that became one of the first state statutes to allow nonbinary gender markers."

I'm now retired. But, in the county in which I practiced law, I experienced prejudice and discriminatory behavior, by both other counsel and members of the bench and judicial administration.

There are very few out T/GE judges in the United States. As of publication, we have had five trans women serve as judges at the local and state trial court level. No out T/GE judge has served on an appellate court. Not a single T/GE person has openly served in the federal judiciary at any level. Though we have seen a handful of out trans lawyers become partners at medium and large law firms in recent years, their successes are outliers. Law students and early career lawyers still report difficulties getting internships and first jobs if they are openly T/GE. Trans and gender expansive lawyers face similar barriers to success in the nonprofit world. To date, even LGBTQ and trans rights legal organizations are woefully behind in hiring and promoting openly trans attorneys, creating a kink in the career pipeline that has made it nearly impossible for many trans lawyers to get the necessary training and support to do high-level trans rights work.

Despite this somewhat bleak picture, not all hope is lost. Bit by bit, out trans lawyers have pushed and will continue to strive to break down barriers to advancement in the legal profession. Over the last decade, trans law students and lawyers have banded together at the national level through organizations like the LGBT Bar Association and, more recently, the National Trans Bar Association, to organize, collaborate, and bring attention to barriers that stand in the way of our professional advancement. Trans and gender expansive lawyers are also working together at the local level to support one another as they seek employment, negotiate discrimination protections with their employers, and create supportive communities to help one another navigate professional challenges.

Diana Flynn (she/her) has dedicated her life's work to civil rights. For several decades, Diana served in the U.S. Department of Justice's Civil Rights Appellate Section, more than 30 of those years as Chief—the government's top appellate civil rights lawyer. Diana transitioned on the job

in the mid-2000s, a high-profile transition in the midst of the George W. Bush administration that made her the first openly trans person to hold such a senior position in federal government. In 2018, Diana left DOJ for Lambda Legal, where she is committed to using her skills to promote LGBTQ rights litigation and train the next cohort of trans litigators.

Reflecting back on her career, Diana's only regret is not transitioning sooner. She knows firsthand how valuable it is to have out, trans attorneys doing civil rights work. Though her own transition had its ups and downs, Diana was able to navigate it successfully in large part because she had already established herself as a good colleague who did quality work. There were no other out trans lawyers at DOJ at the time—indeed, there still aren't. This is something Diana hopes to help remedy.

Since moving to Lambda Legal, Diana has striven to build a professional pipeline for trans lawyers. Diana has proactively hired trans lawyers at all career stages with an eye toward ensuring there is a robust stock of trans lawyers who can go into government and public practice down the line and lead. To Diana's eye, having trans advocates on the front lines isn't just about optics—it is key to changing hearts and minds. "When you see an able trans advocate and when the public sees it happening, that as much as legal argument changes perceptions. For that reason it's very important that trans identified lawyers step in and be lead lawyers in our cases." A student of history, Diana sees that many of the biggest Civil Rights victories won by Black Americans were made possible because organizations invested in training, credentialing, and promoting the leadership of Black lawyers. Diana thinks the trans rights movement must make similar investments. It's not enough that ally lawyers be willing to take on our cases—"they must also make room for us at counsel's table and on the bench."

The legal profession is immensely rewarding and, for trans people in particular, can be a particularly important place for us to work to better ourselves and our communities. Though there will be challenges, we are a tight-knit group and always strive to make room for more folks to join us. Our shared commitment to doing justice and making a difference in our world brings us

closer together as we work together for a better tomorrow. If you want to make a meaningful difference, there's a place for you in our profession.

CONCLUSION

In our lifetimes, we have witnessed breathtaking advances in the law and suffered difficult and painful setbacks. But one through thread is our community's fierce and ongoing struggle for equality and dignity. We have worked tirelessly to win legal protections and shift public opinion so that we can live openly, safely, and without fear. Each of us, lawyer and nonlawyer alike, has a role to play. We need not be relegated to the margins of society. We need not hide in the shadows. Nor must we take "no" for an answer. We must keep pushing forward. We have an obligation to continue that fight for the next generation.

Organizations Providing Trans Legal Resources

American Civil Liberties Union (aclu.org) has an LGBTQ rights project.

Freedom for All Americans (freedomforallamericans.org) is a bipartisan campaign to secure full nondiscrimination protections for LGBTQ people nationwide.

Gender Justice (genderjustice.us) is a Minnesota-based organization that fights discrimination based on sex, gender, sexual orientation, or gender identity.

GLAD aka GLBTQ Legal Advocates & Defenders (glad.org) is an LGBTQ civil rights organization in New England.

Lambda Legal (lambdalegal.org) is a national organization dedicated to LGBTQ civil rights.

National Center for Lesbian Rights (nclrights.org) is a national organization dedicated to LGBTQ, not just lesbian, rights.

National Center for Transgender Equality (transequality.org) is a social justice organization dedicated to advancing the equality of transgender people.

National LGBTQ Task Force (thetaskforce.org) trains activists and organizes pro-LGBTQ legislation.

Southern Poverty Law Center (splcenter.org) is a nonprofit civil rights organization dedicated to fighting hate and bigotry, and to seeking justice for the most vulnerable members of society, including trans people.

Sylvia Rivera Law Project (srlp.org) in New York City works to guarantee that all people are free to self-determine gender identity and expression, regardless of income or race, and without facing harassment, discrimination, or violence.

Trans Women of Color Collective (twocc.us) is the nation's leading advocacy and policy organization promoting the rights of trans women of color.

Transgender Law Center (transgenderlawcenter.org) is a national trans-led organization advocating for a world in which all people are free to define themselves and their futures.

Transgender Law and Policy Institute (transgenderlaw.org) works on law and policy initiatives that benefit transgender people.

Transgender Legal Defense and Education Fund (tldef.org) is committed to ending discrimination based upon gender identity and expression and to achieving equality for transgender people through public education, test-case litigation, direct legal services, and public policy efforts.

Transgender Resource Center of New Mexico (tgrcnm.org) provides support, community, and connection to trans, gender nonconforming, nonbinary, and gender variant people and their families through advocacy, education, and direct services.

Whitman-Walker Health's legal services division (whitman-walker.org/legal-services) works with patients in its Washington, DC facilities on insurance issues, work disputes, discrimination, disability applications and appeals, public benefits appeals, immigration matters, powers of attorney and wills, elder issues, and identity documents for trans and gender expansive clients.

Organizations for Trans Legal Professionals

American Bar Association's Commission on Sexual Orientation and Gender Identity (SOGI Commission) (americanbar.org/groups/diversity/sexual_orientation) leads the ABA's commitment to diversity, inclusion, and full and equal participation by lesbian, gay, bisexual, and transgender persons in the ABA, legal profession, and society.

The International Association of LGBTQ + Judges (lgbtjudges.org) is the world's preeminent association for LGBTA + identified judicial officers.

LGBT Bar Association of Greater New York (LGBTbarny.org), with focus on the greater New York metropolitan area, is dedicated to improving the administration of the law, ensuring full equality for members of the LGBT community, promoting the expertise and advancement of LGBT professionals, and serving the larger community.

National LGBT Bar Association (lgbtbar.org) is the nation's preeminent bar association for LGBTQ + legal professionals.

National Trans Bar Association (transbar.org) promotes the advancement of trans and gender nonconforming legal professionals.

Oregon Trans Law Caucus, a division of OGALLA (LGBTQ Bar Association of Oregon) (ogalla.org) promotes the fair and just treatment of all people under the law regardless of sexual orientation.

NOTES

1. For our purposes, we use the term "state courts" throughout to refer to local tribunals, including court systems in U.S. territories and districts such as Puerto Rico and Washington, DC, as well as the courts of sovereign Native American tribes.
2. *The Justices' Caseload*, U.S. Supreme Court, https://www.supremecourt.gov/about/courtat-work.aspx (last visited Apr. 19, 2021).
3. *Field Offices*, U.S. Equal Employment Opportunity Commission (last visited Aug. 29, 2019), https://www.eeoc.gov/field/.
4. *How to File a Charge of Employment Discrimination*, U.S. Equal Employment Opportunity Commission (last visited Apr. 19, 2021), https://www.eeoc.gov/employees/howtofile.cfm.
5. *Time Limits for Filing a Charge*, U.S. Equal Employment Opportunity Commission (last visited Aug. 29, 2019), https://www.eeoc.gov/employees/timeliness.cfm.
6. *What You Can Expect After You File a Charge*, U.S. Equal Employment Opportunity Commission (last visited Apr. 19, 2021), https://www.eeoc.gov/employees/process.cfm.
7. *J.E.B. v. Alabama*, 511 U.S. 127, 129 (1994) ("We hold that gender, like race, is an unconstitutional proxy for juror competence and impartiality.")
8. *SmithKline Beecham Corp. v. Abbott Labs*, 740 F.3d 471, 484–87 (9th Cir. 2014).
9. *See, e.g., Rosa v. Park West Bank & Trust Co.*, 214 F.3d 213, 214–15 (1st Cir. 2000); *Schwenk v. Hartford*, 204 F.3d 1187, 1202 (9th Cir. 2000); *Smith v. City of Salem*, 378 F.3d 566, 575 (6th Cir. 2004); *Chavez v. Credit Nation Auto Sales*, 641 Fed.Appx. 883, 883 (11th Cir. 2016).
10. *See generally* Kevin M. Barry and Jennifer L. Levi, *The Future of Disability Rights Protections for Transgender People*, 35 Touro L. Rev. 25 (2019).
11. *See, e.g., Doe v. Mass. Dep't of Corr.*, 17-12255-RGS, 2018 WL 2994403 at 5*–8 (D. Mass. June 14, 2018) (prison context); *Blatt v. Cabela's Retail, Inc.*, 5:14-cv-04822, 2017 WL 2178123 (E.D.Pa. May 18, 2017) (employment context).
12. Cal. Civ. Code § 51; Chicago Mun. Code §§ 2-160-020(f) (defining gender identity) and 2-160-070 (prohibiting public accommodation discrimination).
13. Cal. Health & Safety Code § 118600 (2017); New York City Admin. Code § 28-315.9; District of Columbia Mun. Regs., 4 DCMR § 802.
14. Sandy E. James et al., Nat'l Ctr. For Transgender Rts., THE REPORT OF THE 2015 U.S. TRANSGENDER SURVEY 89 (2016) [hereinafter 2015 TRANSGENDER SURVEY], https://transequality.org/sites/default/files/docs/usts/USTS-Full-Report-Dec17.pdf.
15. For a deeper dive, check out Dean Spade, *Documenting Gender*, 59 HASTINGS L. J. 731 (2008).
16. *See, e.g., In re Heilig*, 372 Md. 692, 714 (Md. Ct. App. 2003).
17. Ore. Admin. Rules § 333-011-0272.
18. *Farmer v. Brennan*, 511 U.S. 825, 848–49 (1994).
19. Allen J. Beck, Bureau of Justice Statistics, U.S. Dep't of Justice, SEXUAL VICTIMIZATION IN PRISONS AND JAILS REPORTED BY INMATES, 2011–12: SUPPLEMENTAL TABLES: PREVALENCE OF SEXUAL VICTIMIZATION AMONG TRANSGENDER ADULT INMATES (Dec. 2014), https://www.bjs.gov/content/pub/pdf/svpjri1112_st.pdf.
20. Federal Bureau of Prisons, U.S. Dep't of Justice, *Transgender Offender Manual* (2018), https://www.bop.gov/policy/progstat/5200-04-cn-1.pdf
21. Conn. Gen. Stat. § 18-81ii (2018); Mass. Gen. Laws ch. 127, § 32A (2018).
22. GLAD Legal Advocates and Defenders. *In Groundbreaking Development, Incarcerated Transgender Woman is Transferred from Men's to Women's Prison in MA* (Jan. 30, 2019).
23. *In re Brown*, 289 Va. 343 (2015).
24. Del. Code tit. 10, § 5901 (2019); Cal. Civ. Proc. Code tit. 8, § 1279.5 (2018).
25. Jordan Blair Woods et al., Williams Institute, MODEL LEGISLATION FOR ELIMINATING THE GAY AND TRANS PANIC DEFENSES 3 (2016), https://williamsinstitute.law.ucla.edu/research/model-legislation/.

26. Diana Tourjee, *Man Accused of Killing Trans Woman Says He Was 'Tricked by a Transgender,'* VICE (Apr. 1, 2016), https://www.vice.com/en_us/article/3dx3d8/man-accused-of-killing-trans-woman-says-he-was-tricked-by-a-transgender

27. American Bar Association, Resolution 113A (2013), https://lgbtbar.org/wp-content/uploads/2014/02/Gay-and-Trans-Panic-Defenses-Resolution.pdf

28. Exec. Order No. 14,004, 86 Fed. Reg. 7471 (Jan. 28, 2021), *reprinted* https://www.whitehouse.gov/briefing-room/presidential-actions/2021/01/25/executive-order-on-enabling-all-qualified-americans-to-serve-their-country-in-uniform/

29. *Biden Policy on Transgender Troops is a Welcome Continuation of 2016 Rules*, Palm Center https://www.palmcenter.org/biden-policy-on-transgender-troops-is-a-welcome-continuation-of-2016-rules/ (last visited Apr. 19, 2021).

30. 2015 TRANSGENDER SURVEY at 95.

31. *See, e.g., Darin B. v. Office of Personnel Management*, EEOC No. 0120161068, 2017 WL 1103712 (EEOC Mar. 6, 2017).

32. *See, e.g., In the Case of Claim for UnitedHealthcare/AARP Medicare Complete*, M-15-1069, 2016 WL 1470038 (HHS 2016).

33. *See, e.g., J.D. v. Lackner*, 80 Cal.App.3d 90, 95 (Cal. Ct. App. 1978); *Flack v. Wis. Dep't of Health Servs.*, 395 F.Supp.3d 1001 (W.D.Wis. 2019).

34. *See, e.g., Boyden v. Conlin*, 341 F.Supp.3d 979, 995–97 (W.D. Wis. 2018).

35. Florence Ashley, *Reparative Therapy*, in THE SAGE ENCYCLOPEDIA OF TRANS STUDIES VOL. 2, 713–17 (2021).

36. Jack L. Turban et al., *Psychological Attempts to Change a Person's Gender Identity From Transgender to Cisgender: Estimated Prevalence Across US States, 2015*, AM. J. PUB. HEALTH e1–e3 (2019).

37. MOVEMENT ADVANCEMENT PROJECT, *Conversion Therapy Laws*, https://www.lgbtmap.org/equality-maps/conversion_therapy (last visited Apr. 19, 2021).

38. *Id.*

39. Susan K. Livio, *Group Claiming to Turn Gay Men Straight Committed Consumer Fraud, N.J. Jury Says*, NJ.COM (June 25, 2015), https://www.nj.com/politics/2015/06/gay_conversion_therapy_fraud_trial_verdict.html.

40. *See generally* Nat'l Coalition of Anti-Violence Programs, Lesbian, Gay, Bisexual, Transgender, Queer and HIV-Affected Hate and Intimate Partner Violence 2017, http://avp.org/wp-content/uploads/2019/01/NCAVP-HV-IPV-2017-report.pdf.

41. Sarah M. Peitzmeirer et al., Intimate Partner Violence in Transgender Populations: Systemic Review and Meta-analysis of Prevalence and Correlates, 100 Am. J. Pub. Health e1 (2020).

42. Audre Lourde, *Learning from the 60s*, in SISTER OUTSIDER: ESSAYS AND SPEECHES 138 (2012).

43. Kimberlé Crenshaw, *Demarginalizing the Intersection of Race and Sex: A Black Feminist Critique of Antidiscrimination Doctrine, Feminist Theory and Antiracist Politics*, 1989 U. CHI. L. FORUM 139. *See also* Jane Coaston, *The Intersectionality Wars*, VOX.COM, May 28, 2019, https://www.vox.com/the-highlight/2019/5/20/18542843/intersectionality-conservatism-law-race-gender-discrimination.

44. *See* Ezra Young, *Demarginalizing Trans Rights*, in DEPLOYING INTERSECTIONALITY: LEGAL, INTELLECTUAL, AND ACTIVIST INTERVENTIONS (Kimberlé Crenshaw et al., Eds., New Press, forthcoming 2021).

45. Gina Martinez and Tara Law, *Two Recent Murders of Black Trans Women in Texas Reveal a Nationwide Crisis, Advocates Say*, TIME, June 6, 2019, https://time.com/5601227/two-black-trans-women-murders-in-dallas-anti-trans-violence/.

46. Mark Lee, Hum. Rts. Campaign & Trans People of Color Coalition, A TIME TO ACT: FATAL VIOLENCE AGAINST TRANSGENDER PEOPLE IN AMERICA 34–36 (2017), http://assets2.hrc.org/files/assets/resources/A_Time_To_Act_2017_REV3.pdf.

47. Kimberlé Crenshaw and Andrea Richie, African American Policy Forum and Center for Intersectionality and Social Policy Studies, SAY HER NAME: RESISTING POLICE BRUTALITY AGAINST BLACK WOMEN 8, 32 (2015), https://tinyurl.com/o5gxzr7.

SECTION 3
HEALTH AND WELLNESS

GENERAL, SEXUAL, AND REPRODUCTIVE HEALTH

11

Nick Gorton and Hilary Maia Grubb

INTRODUCTION AND HISTORY OF TRANSGENDER HEALTH CARE

When talking about communities with limited access to health care, the focus is often on illnesses and diseases that are more common or more severe in those communities. Discussions about transgender and gender expansive (T/GE) health often concentrate on our higher rates of HIV, lack of access to primary care, vulnerability to interpersonal violence, and silicone injection. It is critical to address these conditions that threaten our health and welfare. It is also important, however, to understand T/GE health in terms of physical, mental, and social well-being. Health is a positive state of wellness, strength, and stability, not simply the absence of illness. Our health is impacted by our environments and communities. These include where we grow up, live, work, and seek healthcare services. Many healthcare providers, researchers, and educators have focused on these areas, which are also called the "social determinants of health." For example, if we cannot a find job due to being T/GE, we may be unable to afford food or safe housing. We might then need to access underground methods of survival, such as sex work, to have our basic needs met. This then exposes us to increased risk of violence, HIV, other sexually transmitted infections (STIs), and mental health concerns such as depression and post-traumatic stress. Social determinants of health in our community include stable employment, a safe home and environment, availability of T/GE-competent and affirming health care, access to healthy food choices, and opportunities to exercise.

> *A particular experience that sticks out to me is when I was establishing care with a new doctor after moving to a new city and at the end of the visit, he said something like "you are a lot more interesting than I thought when I saw '29yo M to establish care' on my charts for the day." I knew that he was referring to my transgender status. This guy at a later visit also referred to me with female pronouns outside of the room (not knowing I could hear) and the medical student corrected him. I myself am a healthcare provider, and while this made me hopeful for the future because of medical students like this one, I couldn't help but still feel shitty. If someone like me, who has the privilege and knowledge to advocate for myself in these types of environments could feel this way, what about those who aren't in my position? Needless to say, I found a new doctor eventually.*

Some social determinants of health are unique to T/GE people. One of the most important is access to health care that is safe, competent, and affirming of our T/GE identity. This includes access to gender affirming hormone therapy, gender affirming surgeries, mental health care, and provider support in changing our identity documents, if these are what we desire. We have health care needs similar to cisgender people, too, including routine vaccinations for preventable illnesses, treatment of chronic health conditions such as high blood pressure, asthma, and diabetes, and routine screening for diseases such as breast, cervical, and colon cancer. Unfortunately, we are less likely than cisgender people to have these needs met, and we may face more barriers when trying to access health care. Many of us have delayed or avoided health care and health maintenance screenings because of negative interactions within the healthcare system or fears of such.[1,2,3] We may have experienced uncomfortable questions about our bodies, had invasive exams, or been denied care because a provider refused to see us or our insurance company would not pay due to our T/GE identity. Bias and discrimination in healthcare settings are not only unethical but also violate law and policy in many areas. Luckily, times are changing and the healthcare system is, too. There are more and more T/GE-competent and affirming healthcare providers, as well as more T/GE-identified healthcare providers who are changing systems of care to combat transphobia and improve our access to quality health care. Not only should healthcare providers respect us, but they should also have a basic knowledge of social, medical, and surgical transition and be aware of the specific health concerns of our communities.

> *I almost cried the first time I walked into Howard Brown clinic. I don't know how they made the environment feel so welcoming, but they did. I instantly knew I was safe in that building. They had information, their documentation made sure that preferred name and pronouns were addressed and respected, they had queer history on display. It was wonderful.*

To improve our general health, it is important to focus not only on hormones and surgery but also to address our environments and communities. We need T/GE-focused job fairs, T/GE-friendly homeless and domestic violence shelters, T/GE cultural competency education for social services agencies and police departments, and access to appropriate identity documents. The past decade has seen significant improvements in all of these areas in the United States due to the hard work of our communities and allies who work in health care, research, and social services. Moreover, despite a history of bias, discrimination, and stigma in our interactions with healthcare systems, our communities are resilient! We have the ability to seek out competent, affirming, and sensitive providers who support us in all aspects of our health and wellness. We can feel empowered by advocating for our own health, as well as the health of our partners, families, and communities. There is still progress to be made, but the future of T/GE health care is bright!

> *I think the most helpful ways to make healthcare environments more inclusive for transgender people are to provide basic education for everyone in the clinic, including nurses and receptionists, and allow people to indicate their preferred name and pronouns on their records. The most uncomfortable experiences I have had happen when the people I interact with don't understand my trans identity.*

RAD Remedy is a nonprofit organization with a nationally collaborative referral network identifying care providers who serve trans, gender nonconforming, intersex, and queer folks nationwide.

A transgender woman meeting her doctor in the waiting room of doctor's office. (Zackary Drucker, The Gender Spectrum Collection, VICE/Broadly)

Kellan Baker (he/him) is a health services researcher in the Department of Health Policy and Management at the Johns Hopkins School of Public Health.

Policy is a tool to build real protections, benefits, and resources for our communities. Policy can range from international treaties between countries to protocols within a single organization. Important actors in U.S. health policy include the White House, Congress, the courts, governors, state legislatures, mayors, city councils, tribal governments, and international organizations such as the World Health Organization. Stakeholders such as hospitals, insurance companies, healthcare providers, and advocates, including each one of us, are also crucial players in creating health policy.

Effective policymaking requires advocates and policymakers to share a common language that describes what our communities need and explains why we have to take action. One useful term to describe policy that supports trans communities is *health equity*, which means that all people in all communities have everything they need to be healthy. This is not just medical care and health insurance; it also includes healthy food, safe neighborhoods, strong educations, good jobs, and full civil rights protections. Health equity reminds us that equality—that is, providing the exact same resources to everyone—is not enough because different communities have different needs.

By participating in policymaking, we as trans advocates can share our hard-won knowledge about the ways that systems from health care to immigration to criminal justice treat trans people and about the specific resources and protections that we need to live our best lives. Together, we can oppose policies that seek to harm us and assist policymakers in understanding their responsibility to help us build a better world.

You don't need to be a professional advocate in order to participate in creating policy. Some ways to make your voice heard include:

- **Keep in touch:** Call or visit your elected representatives on your local city council, school board, and county board of supervisors, as well as those in state and federal government. Remind them that you are their constituent and that your voice matters.
- **Keep track:** Follow organizations that work on issues that matter to you, and keep an eye out for opportunities to communicate with your elected representatives about a specific issue, to comment on policy proposals, or to write letters or op-eds.
- **Talk about the intersections:** Many trans people have experienced the ways that multiple forces of oppression—such as racism, sexism, and transphobia—work together to push us toward the margins. Share that knowledge with advocates and policymakers who might not have the same understanding.
- **Don't give up hope:** The world today is frightening, but we are continuing to push ahead and make progress in ways that our ancestors could have only dreamed of.[4,5]

HISTORY OF TRANSGENDER AND GENDER EXPANSIVE HEALTH CARE

T/GE people have existed throughout history, but only in the past century has the medical profession been able to provide assistance in changing our bodies to match our gender identities. In 1917 in the United States, Dr. Alan Hart underwent hysterectomy and eventually mastectomy to live his life as a man. In 1930, Lily Elbe had the first of five surgeries in Germany to transition from male to female. Almost as soon as synthetic sex hormones were available, they were used for T/GE medical transition. Christine Jorgensen's public transition in the early 1950s increased awareness about T/GE people. From then until the 1980s, trans-related health care was available at specific academic medical centers in the United States.

In the early 1980s, however, almost all academic medical centers in the United States closed their doors to T/GE people seeking transition-related care. This was set in motion by biased research by Jon Meyer and Donna Reter, under the direction of Dr. Paul McHugh, then-chairman of the first and most well-known American Gender Identity Clinic at Johns Hopkins University School of Medicine. McHugh, who espoused anti-trans sentiments,[6,7] oversaw research at Johns Hopkins on trans women to discredit gender affirming surgery, which he saw as a "misdirection of psychiatry."[8] Research by Meyer and Reter[9] compared transgender women who did and did not have gender affirming surgery. Criticisms highlighted the study's bias and that its conclusions were motivated more by politics than science.[10,11,12] In addition, the paper did not conclude that transgender women did worse with gender affirming surgery. In fact, trans women had the same or better outcomes in each area measured in the study, but the amount of improvement did not reach statistical significance, so they concluded surgery was of no benefit. After the study was published, the program at Johns Hopkins Gender Identity Clinic ultimately closed, and most other academic gender programs followed suit.

Meyer and Reter's research conclusions are at odds with the now much more vast research on transgender people who have access to gender affirming surgical interventions. Because this study came from the first and biggest U.S. academic medical center providing gender affirming care, it had tremendous influence and was even reported in the popular press at the time. The study was used to justify the closure of every other gender program in U.S. academic medical centers, except for the University of Minnesota Program in Human Sexuality. After the closure of academic gender programs, most care for T/GE people in the United States was provided in community medical settings.

GLMA: Health Professionals Advancing LGBTQ Equality and the World Association for Transgender Health (WPATH) are two organizations where healthcare professionals can learn about LGBTQ health. They also both offer online provider directories to help find providers in your area.

Planned Parenthood has been essential in me getting hormone treatment. While I have seen them occasionally deadname people, they do seem to be doing their best, and all the nurses I have dealt with have been friendly.

Around the same time, what little insurance coverage that existed in the United States for transition-related care was eliminated. Over the last two decades this has begun to change due to the efforts of countless advocates, activists, and the Affordable Care Act. Currently 24 states and the District of Columbia prohibit insurers from excluding coverage for transition-related health care.[13] Twenty-three states, Washington, DC, and Puerto Rico also explicitly cover transition-related treatment under Medicaid.[14] In 2014 the Center for Medicare and Medicaid Services (CMS) invalidated a National Coverage Determination from 1989 that prohibited coverage of gender affirming surgery for T/GE people with Medicare, and now surgery can be covered when medically necessary.[15] The U.S. Veterans Administration also provides medical transition care and is currently determining whether or not to cover surgical care. Many T/GE people in the United States and across the world, however, still have no insurance coverage for medically necessary care.[16,17]

DID YOU KNOW?

23%
of transgender people avoided going to a doctor when sick or injured out of fear of discrimination in the past year.

33%
of transgender people who saw a health care provider in the past year were harassed, denied care, or even assaulted.

Data from the *2015 U.S. Transgender Survey*

Statistics from the 2015 US Transgender Survey. (National Center for Transgender Equality)

My doctor asked my pronouns when my mom was out of the room so I was more comfortable.

The shift in location of trans health care (away from academic medical centers into community settings, where people paid for their own care) had some unintended benefits. For example, the power differential in the doctor-patient relationship changed. Patients who did not fit normative ideas of what medicine thought trans people were had the chance to get care, if they could afford it. This ultimately encouraged development of a more patient-centered model of trans medicine in the United States. Activists and trans-affirming medical providers are continuing to advocate for insurance coverage of transition-related care.

THE GENDER WELLNESS MODEL: DEPATHOLOGIZING TRANSGENDER HEALTH CARE[18]

Elias Lawliet (he/him)

In the United States, health care for transgender and gender expansive individuals is based on a model of pathology. Hormones and surgery are provided to those who meet stringent and often-shifting diagnostic criteria based on a loose mix of psychology, medicine, and stereotypes. As these policies have solidified, a pathologic view of transgender identity became the standard of care. Today, transgender identity is measured in the distress caused by the sex assigned at birth. Little serious attention is given to other essential dimensions of gender identity—for example, the relief, joy, and benefit that often accompanies transition. Today's model fails to meet the needs of those who require medical support to obtain gender wellness and fails those who don't want medical support, but could instead benefit from community engagement and psychosocial support. However, because our current model of health care is built on a model of illness and subsequent treatment, proposals to depathologize gender identity are often met with fear and concern. Without a pathological understanding of transgender identity, how will insurance companies be held responsible for coverage?

In recent years, the nursing and public health fields have begun to shift from a model of illness to a model of health promotion. The World Health Organization defines health as "a state of complete physical, mental, and social well-being and not merely the absence of disease or infirmity." Hence, instead of merely treating illness, medical professionals and public health initiatives have begun to proactively seek a maximum state of health. By including gender wellness as a dimension of one's holistic state of health, we can create a framework that fully grasps the diversity of experiences, desires, and needs within the transgender population.

In order to shift our pathology-focused model into one that focuses on wellness, I propose the *Gender Wellness Model* (GWM). The goal of the GWM is to increase one's subjective peace, satisfaction, and congruency with one's gender identity. This model affirms that everyone has an ideal gender wellness state, and different individuals require different interventions to attain this state. For example, a person questioning their gender identity may need to speak to a gender-affirming therapist or pursue some medical intervention. A transgender person who fully knows what interventions they need will need the support and specialized knowledge of a medical professional. A cisgender person would not require any gender-affirmation interventions at all, because their gender wellness would already be in its optimal state. Furthermore, the GWM is multidisciplinary and expansive enough to address the entire spectrum of need, treatment, and support. This multidisciplinary approach includes primary care, mental health, sexual health, reproductive health and preservation, complementary and alternative medicine, and social support through community events, housing assistance, employment programs, and support groups.

The GWM avoids pathologizing gender. Providers can partner with their trans and gender expansive patients to optimize gender wellness. This creates an environment of mutual respect that honors a patient's experiences and self-knowledge, seamlessly integrating with existing informed consent models. If we continue to conceptualize transgender identity as pathology, healthcare and policy interventions will be incapable of fully addressing the needs of our transgender and gender expansive communities. The GWM represents one way in which this disparity could be addressed.

GENERAL HEALTH

Accessing Health Care

Although many people in the general U.S. population are uninsured, T/GE people are less likely to have insurance than cisgender people.[19] There are many reasons for this, but the most significant is that we are less likely to be employed than cisgender people, and most people in the United States are insured through an employer. In addition, because we have more difficulty obtaining identity documents with the appropriate name and gender, we may have a harder time applying for public insurance.

For those of us who have insurance through an employer, we may still have policies that exclude transition-related care. Luckily, this is changing, with more and more employers offering inclusive insurance even in states that still allow insurance to exclude transition-related care. According to the Human Rights Campaign's (HRC) Corporate Equality Index, 853 private companies currently offer a trans-inclusive healthcare plan. This represents 83% of companies offering coverage—up significantly from 9% in 2010.[20] However, even when an employer offers insurance that covers T/GE medical care, it may be difficult for us to find a provider who both provides the care we need and also takes our insurance. In addition, because of copayments or travel expenses to see specialists, there can still be a considerable cost associated with accessing necessary care.

OutCare maintains an OutList of LGBTQ healthcare resources in all 50 states, including primary care, mental health services, youth groups, shelters, support groups, and testing for sexually transmitted infections (STIs).

I have a very kind and respectful doctor who I see for my general medical care, and she has been a good doctor in general to me. But, almost every time that I see her I have to explain some aspect of my gender or sexual identity, and that can be annoying and energy-consuming. I would not consider switching providers because I have heard too many horrible stories of transphobic doctors, that my doctor seems like the best option despite her ignorance.

Fearing denial of care, those of us with insurance exclusions may not inform our insurance providers of our T/GE identity. This can be risky because if insurers subsequently discover our T/GE status, they may retroactively deny care and seek repayment. Hiding our T/GE identity from our insurance can also be difficult to sustain because insurers receive a great deal of information about us from various sources in order to pay for our health care. Information comes from healthcare providers, pharmacies, labs, and others. Because insurers use gender designations on insurance forms to determine what care is needed, we are faced with choosing which designation is most appropriate for us. For example, if we identify as a woman and were assigned male at birth, and select "F" (for "female") on our insurance forms, we may be able to obtain coverage for estrogen prescriptions and mammograms, but we may be denied care for prostate issues. Likewise, if we identify as a man and were assigned female at birth, and select "M" (for "male") on our insurance forms, our insurance may cover testosterone prescriptions, but may reject claims for a PAP smear for cervical cancer screening. This can happen even with insurance that covers T/GE health care, and generally requires calling our health insurance company to resolve the discrepancy.

The first time I went to my general practitioner after changing my name and gender marker I checked in, quietly and calmly explained to the receptionist why my name was different on my ID and insurance card, and had the appropriate paperwork with me in case they needed to verify it. All went smoothly until I went and sat at the back of the waiting room and moments later very loudly and clearly hear the second receptionist asking about how "he was a she but now he is a he." I went over and very pointedly asked if she knew that she was violating HIPAA laws by discussing my private information loudly enough for the entire waiting area to hear. As much as I liked that doctor, I have not returned to that practice.

With the full provisions of the U.S. Patient Protection and Affordable Care Act (ACA), many of us have been able to obtain public or private insurance. Each state under the ACA can determine the minimum necessary benefits (in addition to the federal standard) that must be included on policies available on the health insurance exchange in that state. This means that some states require coverage of transition-related care while others do not. The ACA includes language that protects against discrimination based on sex, which during the Obama administration had been interpreted as including gender identity. Under President Obama, the U.S. Department of Health and Human Services (HHS) issued guidance that insurers under the ACA cannot limit coverage for transition-related care if those same services are provided for other indications in cisgender people. For example, if an insurer pays for hysterectomies to treat abnormal bleeding or cervical cancer in cisgender women (or in transgender men, for that matter), the insurer must also pay for hysterectomies in transgender men to treat gender dysphoria. Unfortunately, under the Trump administration, this guidance changed, but the Biden administration has reinstituted it.[21]

In addition to the ACA providing access to private insurance, it also increased the number of people eligible for Medicaid, which is public health insurance for those of us living at lower income levels. Included in the ACA is a Medicaid expansion that encourages states to insure more people under the Medicaid program. In states that participate in the expansion, Medicaid covers everyone with incomes up to 133% of the federal poverty level. Because T/GE people are more likely to live at or below the poverty level than our cisgender peers, many more of us became eligible for Medicaid under the Affordable Care Act.

There is a one stall bathroom in the back at the clinic I went to which is nice. Single stall bathrooms are fantastic for me, as I don't feel comfortable using men's or women's bathrooms. However, I'm generally seen in relation to my body and sex rather than my gender, which can be difficult and uncomfortable at times. Using my actual pronouns (they/them) makes me a lot more comfortable. Especially since that's not common, it tells me they're educated and aware about trans identities at least a little bit. It's uncomfortable when they deadname me, or mis-pronoun me. All the healthcare experiences that particularly stick out to me have to do with the medical mistreatment I've received as a disabled person. The trans stuff has always been secondary to that.

Out2Enroll is a national initiative to connect LGBTQ people with health insurance coverage options available under the Affordable Care Act.

Fortunately, even without legal mandates, insurers now have years of data to inform them that providing transition-related care improves patient outcomes and can be cost-efficient for the insurance company. For example, the cost of treating one suicide attempt can be more than providing a transgender man with a mastectomy, which might prevent him from becoming suicidal. The California Department of Insurance investigated the actual cost of transgender care relative to the savings (such as improved HIV treatment adherence, avoidance of the complications of silicone pumping, and "overall improvement in mental health and reduction in utilization of mental health services.") They concluded that ending insurance exclusions for transition-related care "will cost little or nothing in the short run and may produce longer-term cost savings and improved health benefits for transgender people."[22]

Preventive Health Care

I do have a primary health care provider, and so far she is excellent. She has other trans patients, but still needs help with medical issues and cultural competence; however, she is eager to learn. I bring in research and medical sites for her reference. I had to call around town a lot to find her, asking medical practices if they take trans patients.

Preventive care is proactive health care to prevent illness, diagnose and treat illnesses early on to prevent complications, and identify harmful health-related behaviors early enough to avoid an illness or poor outcome. Some of the leading causes of preventable death in the United States include poor diet and physical inactivity, tobacco use, alcohol and drug use, and sexually transmitted infections, including HIV. Like many groups experiencing discrimination, our T/GE communities have higher rates of harmful health-related behaviors than the general population. The greater prevalence of these behaviors in our communities is related to the stress we experience from the bias, discrimination, harassment, and violence that we face in society.

I finally do have a family physician for basic medical care. I found them through Mayo Clinic. Other than an inclusive question about gender and

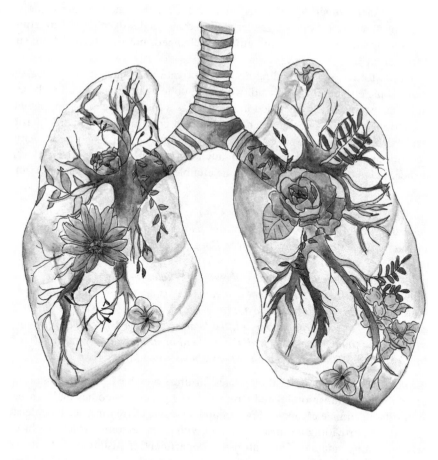

Regrowth. Watercolor and Ink on Watercolor Paper. (Eli Schleisman)

> *orientation in my profile, only one of my multitude of doctors even attempts to use my chosen name or gender.*

Establishing a Primary Care Provider

> *I found my primary care provider through a local trans helpline that helps trans folks to find affirming care that will meet their needs. My doctor doesn't just oversee my overall health and well-being, she also prescribes and monitors my hormone replacement therapy. Though my doctor is cisgender, she does her best to understand my needs and she has always respected my identity. I once called her out for gatekeeping and she immediately course-corrected and changed her standards.*

Primary care is our first stop in the healthcare system. Primary care providers (PCPs) are trained in comprehensive care to diagnose and treat common healthcare problems. PCPs provide ongoing care for chronic problems, offer preventative services such as vaccines and cancer screenings, coordinate specialist care, advocate for patients, and focus on treating the whole person.

> *I found my primary care doctor sort of by chance. She came in when my former primary doctor (who was great) moved to a new office, and it turned out that she was actively working with one of the main trans-friendly endocrinologists in my state to learn and promote trans-competent care throughout the hospital system that her office is under. She helped me navigate the path to gender*

Health and Wellness

confirmation surgery and has been completely committed to providing me the best care she can possibly provide, in all aspects of my health and wellness. All doctors should be as good as she is (also, she wears the funkiest, coolest shoes).

For T/GE people, having a PCP is especially important. Although increasingly more providers are sensitive to and knowledgeable about our needs, many remain un- or under-educated. Because of this, advocacy and care coordination by PCPs is even more important. For example, if we need to see a cardiologist, our PCP can direct us to a known trans-knowledgeable and affirming cardiologist if one exists in our area, or can speak with the cardiologist beforehand to ensure that the specialist will treat us respectfully and affirm our gender identity. Additionally, because some of us have avoided health care due to negative past experiences or fear of negative encounters, a PCP who provides comprehensive care can decrease the amount of care we have to obtain elsewhere, allowing us to receive the majority of our health care in a safe and familiar space. For example, a PCP trained in gynecologic procedures can provide this care for trans men instead of referring out to a gynecologist.

I got this provider when I got the initial Klinefelter diagnosis and was referred to a specialist as they were one of the few LGBT-friendly doctors in the area. They are one of the few medical practitioners who has ever shown me respect in that regard and I am very grateful for them.

Nutrition and Physical Activity

In our body-obsessed culture, size can be something that we use against one another and against ourselves. Medical providers are often trained to prioritize the body mass index (BMI)—used to categorize people as "underweight," "healthy weight," "overweight," or "obese"—as a measure of health. However, people with BMIs above or below the "normal" range can be healthy. Fat-positive activists seek to challenge fatphobia in our society just as we might challenge transphobia, cissexism, racism, classism, and other forms of personal and institutionalized bias. Part of staying healthy is determining a healthy size for ourselves as individuals, rather than being driven by media portrayals of a feminine or masculine ideal.

I have very seldom had good/affirming experiences accessing care. I had a forcible gynecological exam by a male doctor. I also had a female doctor insist that my body hair was a sign of poor mental health. I feel that most doctors are disgusted by my body, as a fat GNC person.

Although there is evidence that lesbian-identified women are at increased risk of obesity compared to their heterosexual peers, there are limited data regarding obesity risk in T/GE people. Taking either estrogen or testosterone is correlated with weight gain and can be associated with increased risk of developing certain conditions such as diabetes and heart disease.[23,24] Therefore, when starting gender affirming hormone therapy it is especially important for us to embrace balanced nutrition and healthy exercise regimens. For some of us, the process of initiating gender affirming hormone therapy or gender affirming surgery helps us value our bodies more and we may feel more motivated to improve our overall health and physical wellness.

My doctor's office is both Health at Every Size and does trans-affirming medical care. Having paperwork that includes spaces for pronouns and chosen names is a great way that medical practices can be supportive. I also very much enjoy paperwork that is designed not to gender experiences like menstruation, pregnancy, various genital configurations, etc. Gender neutral restrooms are also fantastic, as is being sure that automatic reminders and staff have my correct name and pronouns.

Many guidelines recommend moderate-intensity exercise for 30 minutes, 5 days per week. "Moderate intensity" may mean we are able to carry on a conversation while exercising, but not able to sing a song. Moderate intensity exercise generally involves breaking a sweat. Walking briskly is an easy, inexpensive way to engage in moderate-intensity exercise. For those of us with busy schedules, we may feel like we do not have 30 minutes

The Department of Veterans Affairs (VA) LGBT program includes Veteran Care Coordinators (VCCs) who assist veterans in connecting to services across the country.

The third annual Women's March LA at Pershing Square in downtown on Jan. 19, 2019. (Luke Harold)

per day to devote to exercise. Evidence shows that walking for 10 minutes, three times per day has similar benefits for weight loss and cardiovascular health as walking for 30 minutes continuously. Getting off the bus a stop early and taking the stairs make a difference.

One additional factor that we need to consider in constructing our diets and exercise plans is bone health. There are a number of ways to improve our bone health and prevent osteoporosis (decreased bone density that can lead to fractures), including taking in enough calcium and vitamin D, as well as doing weight-bearing exercise. As T/GE people, our bone health can be affected by our gender affirming hormone therapy and/or surgeries that remove our gonads (ovaries or testicles). Estrogen is known to be protective for our bones, and taking either estrogen or testosterone may help to protect our bones because some testosterone is converted to estrogen in our bodies. T/GE people assigned male at birth who have had orchiectomies (removal of the testicles) and are not taking estrogen, and T/GE people assigned female at birth who have had oophorectomies (removal of the ovaries) and are not taking testosterone, are at greater risk of osteoporosis because their bodies do not have the protection of estrogen. We should talk to our PCP and/or endocrinologist about whether we should undergo an osteoporosis screening test, or should change our dietary habits, exercise, or take medication to treat osteoporosis.

HOW FITNESS TRANSFORMED AND SAVED ME

Tristan Martin (he/him) is currently pursuing his PhD and is a couple and family therapist specializing in clinical issues with the transgender population. His passions outside of helping others include spending time with family, his dogs, and the gym.

My personal journey of transition has instilled the utmost perspective of positivity in my life. However, despite my strong resiliency, stress from gender dysphoria, social strains, and everyday tasks continuously knock at my door. Depression and anxiety often accompanied my gender dysphoria—possibly exacerbated by societal rejection. My mental health was in jeopardy. The spiral of anxiety and depression is an underreported mental health issue for trans men—and the transgender population as a whole.

Transitioning is not always easy; it's a physical and mental journey. It's about finding what saves you. In order to be my best self, I needed an outlet that could save me from myself and give peace and clarity to my life. That's when the gym saved me. Physical fitness became a positive gateway to addressing mental health concerns. As a former collegiate athlete and military service member, I have always focused on athletics.

My love for fitness expanded, however, when I was able to channel my struggles into exercise and build my body. Being able to physically alter my body and replicate my internal gender identity became a sole confirmation of self. With dedication and discipline, I built a method of self-care that will always be my escape.

My fitness journey has evolved throughout the years. I didn't realize the strength of my desire for physical fitness until I was at a standstill at the end of my basketball career. I needed a new passion. I researched fitness on my own. I started with bodybuilding, Olympic lifting, and Crossfit, and now I implement a combination of all three. Starting small was the key; I tried different routines, gyms, and programs until I saw the results benefited my mental health and reduced my dysphoria. There were many moments where I felt uncomfortable—especially early on in transition. I often compared myself to other men who were lifting more weight than I was. However, instead of making comparisons, I found that focusing on getting the job done and on using the other men as a source of motivation propelled my success.

When weightlifting, I personally focused on key points on the male physique such as broad shoulders and chest (V-Taper), which help reduce my dysphoria. I focused on my entire body while adding heavy weight to stimulate muscle mass. Research has shown that staying within the eight to twelve repetitions range is optimal for muscle growth. It is important to implement periodization (alternating programs to induce muscle confusion) and progressive overload (gradually adding more weight) for muscle hypertrophy. There are endless exercises available, and you can use more advanced movements as time goes on, but you should build a foundation first. Resources I used include: BodyBuilding.com, T-nation.com, Men's Health magazine, and *The New Encyclopedia of Modern Bodybuilding* by Arnold Schwarzenegger.

You'll also need to select an environment for exercise, which can often be distressing. I have used multiple gyms from old-school to new-school. In my experience, the environment that motivates you the most will be the best fit for you. However, some folks may feel unsafe in gym environments due to transphobia or homophobia. Many gym branches have "Diversity & Inclusion" statements that provide a safety net (e.g., Planet Fitness, YMCA) but they are not always enforced. Workouts can be completed at home or outdoors with minimal equipment (e.g., dumbbells, pull-up bar) or via bodyweight exercises available online for free. If you can afford it, there are many trans personal trainers available either locally or remotely.

SUBSTANCE USE

Because most studies of tobacco, alcohol, and drug use have not included questions about gender identity, data about substance use in our communities is limited. Some recent studies of T/GE people in several large urban areas across the United States have identified substance abuse as a substantial concern.[25,26]

Tobacco

Tobacco use in our communities is much greater than the general population. Since the mid-1990s, tobacco companies have made themselves highly visible in our communities via advertising, sponsorships, and promotions. In 1995, R.J. Reynolds actually created a campaign, internally named "Project SCUM" (an acronym for "Project Sub-Culture Urban Marketing,") which targeted LGBTQ and homeless people. Tobacco use is a major risk factor for heart attacks, strokes, chronic obstructive pulmonary disease (COPD), and multiple types of cancer. On average, smokers lose about a decade of life expectancy due to tobacco use. Fortunately, quitting smoking can significantly improve lung function, reduce cancer risk, and reduce the number of years of life expectancy lost. For those of us on estrogen for gender affirming hormone therapy, smoking is an even greater risk. Smoking while on estrogen increases the risk of developing a blood clot—also called a deep venous thrombosis (DVT) in the legs or elsewhere in the body—that can migrate to other parts of our body, including the lungs (called a pulmonary embolism), heart (i.e., heart attack), or brain (i.e., stroke), all of which can cause significant disability or death.

Resources for queer and T/GE smokers wishing to quit are available at smokefree.gov/lgbt-and-smoking

For those of us who want to quit smoking, medical treatments are available, including nicotine replacement therapy such as nicotine patches, gum, and lozenges; nicotine-free medications such as bupropion (Zyban, Wellbutrin) and varenicline (Chantix); and integrative treatments such as acupuncture and hypnotherapy. PCPs can give us prescriptions for these medical interventions and can be excellent resources for information about local programs that support smoking cessation.

Alcohol and Drugs

Use of alcohol and drugs such as methamphetamine and heroin are significant problems in our communities. In addition to the risks of the drugs themselves, injecting drugs carries an increased risk of contracting HIV and hepatitis. Those of us who use drugs are at increased risk of arrest and prosecution. Jails and prisons are dangerous places for anyone, but especially so for queer and T/GE people. In addition to the serious dangers associated with being housed in a jail or prison based on our sex assigned at birth, such as physical and sexual violence, we may also be deprived of our gender affirming hormone therapy, thereby risking further emotional trauma and regression of the effects of hormones.

Treatment for alcohol and substance use disorders exists throughout the country. Many inpatient and residential alcohol and drug recovery programs require rooming based on sex assigned at birth. However, there are also treatment programs that are knowledgeable and affirming of our T/GE identities and will make appropriate rooming and bathroom accommodations for our needs. Those of us who attend T/GE-inclusive treatment programs are more likely to complete treatment than those of us in noninclusive treatment programs.[27]

ENCOURAGING RECOVERY FROM ADDICTION IN TRANS COMMUNITIES

Kevin Johnson, MD (he/they) and Alann Weissman-Ward, MD (he/him) are addiction medicine physicians based in Syracuse, New York.

Those within our trans communities are three times more likely to use substances than cis folks.[28] This higher rate of substance use is secondary to enduring increased minority stressors within the worlds we live and survive. In addition, we are also less inclined to pursue substance use treatment—and it often relates to fear of discrimination or rejection (either for being trans or for having a substance-use problem).

Currently most addiction treatment programs are neither educated nor informed about transgender and nonbinary folks. Most addiction treatment programs are segregated along a gender binary and do not make space for people who do not identify within the two-gender system. Furthermore, while many programs may advertise an LGBTQ-oriented treatment program online or in their brochures, in reality, often no such services actually exist within the brick and mortar. There are, however, at least four to five such programs that offer trans and LGBTQ-specific addiction treatment services, and these are located in cities including New York, San Francisco, Los Angeles, and Minneapolis.

Conversely, many medical and mental health clinicians who are T/GE-competent are not comfortable either treating addiction or making the appropriate referrals. Our hope is that these providers who are already serving our community will make the effort to get comfortable treating addiction.

Regardless of what may be available in your region, getting help is key. Addiction is a deadly illness and we've all lost too many people along the way.

Some tidbits to keep in mind:

- *Medication Assisted Treatment (MAT) Can Help:* MAT includes medications designed to assist with cravings for alcohol, tobacco, opioids, and even cocaine and methamphetamines. Speak with your healthcare provider if this is something you're interested in.
- *Twelve- Step Programs (such as Alcoholics Anonymous or Narcotics Anonymous) Work for Many People:* Meetings are free; meetings are abundant; and meetings can be a source of support for those who feel they are alone in their addiction. There are often LGBTQ-oriented meetings that can be more welcoming to trans folks depending on the region. There are also LGBTQ online twelve-step meetings available via www.intherooms.com
- *Our Community Should Work Together to Support Recovery:* Although we can (and should) place the responsibility for addiction recovery treatment on medical professionals, all of us (in the community) should take responsibility for supporting those in need of safe, sober spaces. Some examples of this include: Avoid hosting events/gatherings in places where alcohol and/or drugs are abundant (i.e., bars) or be mindful of how those spaces can be triggering for folks in recovery. Don't pressure others into drinking or using if they decline. Respect their boundaries. Encourage folks who are struggling to get help—even offer to go with that person to a meeting or to treatment. And work on your biases/personal feelings about addiction.

A note on the words "addict" and "alcoholic": Those of us who attend twelve-step programs may hear people self-identify as addicts or alcoholics. Some find these terms to be affirming and normalizing; however, some consider these terms to be pathologizing, labeling, or demeaning. Be careful labeling others with those terms without their permission. We all have a responsibility to support those in need of safe, sober spaces for recovery.

HIV AND OTHER SEXUALLY TRANSMITTED INFECTIONS

As T/GE people, we are at increased risk of STIs (including HIV) for various reasons, which may include engagement in sex work or survival sex, lack of access to safe sex methods such as condoms and pre-exposure prophylaxis (PrEP) medications to prevent HIV, and/or lack of access to affirming and trans-knowledgeable health care. We may face more barriers when trying to get tested for STIs, including HIV, than our cisgender peers. A thorough sexual health assessment can identify our risk of STI and HIV exposure based on our sexual behaviors and the body parts involved in our sexual practices. STI screening is guided by our actual risk level. High-risk sexual practices include receptive anal or vaginal sex without a condom ("barebacking"), sex with multiple partners, sex with anonymous partners, and having sex while drunk or high. If we engage in these behaviors, STI screening is recommended every three to six months, and PrEP to protect against HIV may be a strong consideration. If we engage in lower risk sexual behaviors, it may be OK to be screened annually. Depending on our risk factors and where we go for care, STI screens may include penile, vaginal, and/or anal swabs, urine tests, and bloodwork to check for gonorrhea, chlamydia, syphilis, trichomonas, herpes virus, hepatitis A, B, and C, and HIV.

It is important to remember that although medical providers will ask us whether we are experiencing any symptoms that would indicate that we have an STI (such as burning when we pee, rectal pain or bleeding, or genital discharge), it is also possible to have an STI without having any symptoms at all, and failure to treat some STIs can lead to long-term effects. Thus, it is of utmost importance that we find a medical provider we can be honest with about our sexual behavior so that we can be screened and treated appropriately. Our sexual behavior may change over time, and we might shift from high-risk to low-risk categories or vice-versa.

HIV

In our communities, the rate of HIV infection is higher than the national average. Almost one in ten of us in the T/GE community is HIV positive. In a review of U.S. studies from 2006 to 2017, the overall rate of HIV among T/GE people was 9.2%, but it was higher in trans women (14%) than trans men (3%) and was disproportionately highest among Black trans people (44%).[29] It is important to remember that these worrisome statistics are related to social determinants of health. If we are unable to obtain other employment, we may be more likely to engage in sex work, which puts us at much higher risk of infection with HIV and other STIs. Additionally, we are more likely to abuse alcohol and drugs due to factors related to our experiences of societal discrimination and violence. Use of alcohol and/or drugs while having sex can lead to increased sexual risk-taking, thus putting us at higher risk of acquiring STIs, including HIV. Fortunately, there are steps we can take to decrease our risk of contracting STIs. In addition to participating in safer sex with condoms, dental dams, gloves, and washing dildos and sex toys, Pre-Exposure Prophylaxis (PrEP) can significantly decrease our risk of getting HIV. PrEP involves taking a daily pill that contains two HIV medications: emtricitabine and tenofovir. There are currently two FDA-approved brands of this medication combination—Truvada and Descovy. PrEP is highly effective in preventing HIV infection if taken regularly, reducing the chance of becoming HIV positive by 86%.[30] Studies of those of us who are transgender women show that we may be less likely than others to take PrEP regularly.[31] Even when taking these medications regularly, HIV infection can still happen, so if we engage in sexual activities that are deemed to be high risk, it is recommended that we continue to use a barrier method like condoms in addition to taking PrEP. Furthermore, for those of us with a uterus, ovaries, and vagina who engage in penile-vaginal sex, PrEP does not function as birth control, so we may want to use condoms and/or other birth control methods to prevent pregnancy if we do not want to become pregnant.

> *I was really strongly encouraged to get on PrEP when I told my doctor that I was trans and having sex with men.*

The Centers for Disease Control and Prevention (CDC) website (cdc.gov) has up-to-date information about PrEP and PEP.

If you think you have been exposed to HIV and need PEP, immediately contact your Primary Care Provider or your County's Health Department to find out where PEP can be obtained. If these measures will involve a significant delay (e.g., if your doctor's office is closed on the weekends), go to an Emergency Room or Urgent Care Center to get on PEP as soon as possible.

In addition to PrEP, Post Exposure Prophylaxis (PEP) is available and can be taken if we fear we may have been exposed to HIV through a recent sexual encounter. This treatment involves taking HIV medicines for 28 days after we are exposed to HIV or have engaged in high-risk sex or needle sharing. PEP can reduce the chance that we will become infected with HIV. PEP should be started within 72 hours of suspected HIV exposure, but the sooner it is started the better.

OTHER SEXUALLY TRANSMITTED INFECTIONS

Hepatitis

Although the data is limited, there is evidence that we, as T/GE people, are at higher risk than others of acquiring STIs—including syphilis, gonorrhea, chlamydia, human papillomavirus (HPV), hepatitis A virus (HAV), and hepatitis B virus (HBV)—based on data from cisgender men who have sex with men (MSM) and smaller studies of T/GE people. Transgender people who have sex with cisgender men may be at higher risk than the general population for contracting HAV and HBV, viruses that attack the liver. HAV can be transmitted by unprotected anal-oral contact during sex ("rimming"), and HBV can be transmitted through exposure to infected blood, semen, or vaginal fluid. Hepatitis A and B vaccinations are now given in childhood, but those of us who did not get them as children should talk with our PCPs about getting vaccinated. Additionally, it is possible for the immunity conveyed through vaccines to lessen over the years, thus we may need a booster hepatitis vaccine. Our PCP can check a hepatitis panel or hepatitis A and hepatitis B titers to see if we need a booster. Hepatitis C virus (HCV) is another virus that attacks the liver. HCV is spread through blood-to-blood transmission, such as blood transfusions, sharing needles for injections, unclean tattoo or piercing instruments, or certain types of sexual practices such as fisting or rough anal sex during which we may be exposed to our sexual partners' blood. Treatment for hepatitis C has drastically improved in both access and effectiveness in recent years. If we are at risk for acquiring HCV, we should be regularly tested for the virus, and if we test positive, there are now medications that can treat HCV.

QTPOC Birthwerq Postcard. (Artwork and Graphic Design Commissioned by QTPOC Birthwerq Project)

Pelvic Inflammatory Disease

There is evidence of underrecognition of STIs—including chlamydia, gonorrhea, herpes simplex virus, HPV, and trichomonas ("trich")—in cisgender women who have sex with women (WSW). It is reasonable to assume from this that anyone who shares sex toys, engages in oral-vaginal sex, or vaginal-vaginal sex/rubbing is at-risk of acquiring these infections. Chlamydia, gonorrhea, and trich are especially dangerous to those of us with a uterus, fallopian tubes, and ovaries. Though these infections can be treated with antibiotics, if left untreated, they can lead to Pelvic Inflammatory Disease (PID), which is when the infection spreads from the vagina to the uterus, fallopian tubes, and ovaries. This is a dangerous, at times life-threatening, infection that, even if treated, can lead to long-term consequences such as chronic pelvic pain and infertility. PID may present with vaginal discharge, foul-smelling vaginal secretions, pelvic pain, fevers, nausea, and vomiting. STIs that cause PID may not present with any symptoms at all, however, which is why regular sexual risk assessment and screening by a medical provider are of utmost importance, so that asymptomatic STIs can be diagnosed and treated appropriately.

Human Papilloma Virus

It is important to remember that healthcare screening is based on the organs that we have. In other words, if you've got it, check it! Those of us with a cervix, regardless of how we identify, need to get PAP smears and STI screening for our sexual health and physical wellness. We should have PAP smears according to the same screening criteria and recommendations as those for cisgender women to screen for cervical cancer, which is most often caused by exposure to the Human Papilloma Virus (HPV). Though not all strains of HPV cause cervical cancer, HPV is the most common STI, and there are over one hundred different strains of the virus. Some of the strains cause genital and anal warts, and other strains can cause cervical and anal cancer. HPV infections are acquired through sexual skin-to-skin contact (including hand-genital contact) with a person who is already infected. Anyone with a cervix who is sexually active can contract HPV and risks developing cervical cancer, regardless of the sexual orientations or gender identities of our partners. It is a misconception that HPV can only be transmitted by penis-vagina sex between cisgender men and women.

Human Papilloma Virus is often asymptomatic, and thus many people do not know when they have been exposed. Unfortunately, barriers do not protect against HPV transmission as well as they do against other STIs. Because of this, it is important to get routine cervical and anal health screening to catch HPV early before it becomes cancerous. Current screening recommendations for people with a cervix are to get PAP smears every three years (if normal screens) from the ages of 21 to 65, or PAP smears with HPV testing every five years (if normal screens and HPV negative) from the ages of 30 to 65. If there are any abnormal cells or indication of HPV, more frequent screening is recommended and a procedure called colposcopy may be needed for more in-depth screening of the cervix for cancerous lesions and biopsy, if indicated.

> I got my first PAP smear/well person exam a few weeks ago, and was prepared for the worst. However, the nurse who gave me the exam was incredibly competent—asking me about binding, birth control methods to stop my periods, plans for top surgery. She explained every part of the procedure. I felt extremely comfortable the entire time.

Cervical cancer prevention is a good example of how powerful preventive health care is. Before Georgios Papanikolaou discovered that PAP smears could detect early changes that lead to cervical cancer, cervical cancer was the number-one cause of cancer death in cisgender women. Since then, because of the implementation of routine cervical cancer screening with PAP smears, deaths caused by cervical cancer have been reduced by 98%.[32] We also now have an HPV vaccine to protect against some of the more dangerous strains of the virus.

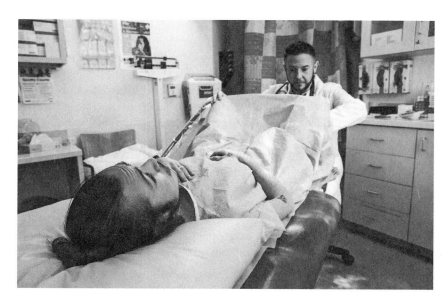

A genderqueer person in a hospital gown looking up and receiving a pelvic exam. (Zackary Drucker, The Gender Spectrum Collection, VICE/Broadly)

The HPV vaccine (Gardasil) is now recommended for everyone, regardless of gender or body parts, from the ages of 9 to 45. If you have not received the HPV vaccine, talk to your PCP about getting it. Cervical cancer is more likely to occur in people who smoke, those with compromised immune systems, and those who do not get regular PAP/HPV tests.

> I just met my new PCP, who when I showed discomfort with the idea of a future PAP smear told me of several different ways she can make the procedure less traumatizing. She also emphasized that I don't have to do it if I don't feel up to it at my next appointment, and that it's OK to bring someone/take an antianxiety med/get local anesthetic. None of these were offered to me at my previous PAP smears, or when I got my IUD put in!

Human Papilloma Virus can also infect the cells of the anus, causing changes to the cells, which if not detected and treated early, can develop into anal cancer. Anal cancer caused by HPV is more common in people who are HIV positive, anyone who has had precancerous changes of their cervix due to HPV exposure, and anyone who has receptive anal sex. Recent data show that anal cancer is up to 80 times more common in cisgender men who have sex with men than in the general population. While little data exist regarding the incidence of anal cancer in transgender populations, it is important for anyone who has receptive anal sex, has had anal warts, is HIV positive, has a condition that weakens their immune system, or has had precancerous lesions of the cervix or vulva to get anal PAP smears as part of preventive sexual health care and health maintenance screening. The HPV vaccine Gardasil also helps prevent anal cancer, so if we are under the age of 45, we should ask our PCP about getting the vaccine for protection against anal cancer in addition to cervical cancer prevention.[33]

CANCER RISK AND SCREENING

In addition to obtaining PAP smears to decrease our risk of developing cervical and anal cancer, other cancer screening tests are important for our overall physical health. There are limited data on the cancer risks we may face as T/GE people as a result of hormone replacement therapy, although several organizations (including Rainbow Health Ontario, the Endocrine Society, and the UCSF Center of Excellence for Transgender Health) have examined the data that currently exist and have developed cancer screening recommendations for our communities.[34,35]

I appreciate when clinicians are open about gaps in their knowledge and/or clinical research, and treat me as an expert in my own care. In general, I'm concerned about the lack of knowledge around reproductive health for trans men as it relates to the consequences of long-term HRT on ovarian cysts, cancer, etc. Short of getting an invasive ultrasound, it doesn't seem like there's a good deal of knowledge around diagnosing and levels of risk.

Breast Cancer

Screening for breast cancer is necessary for T/GE masculine-spectrum people regardless of medical or surgical history. Those of us who have had top surgery—even bilateral mastectomy—may have some residual breast tissue that is susceptible to breast cancer. T/GE individuals on the masculine spectrum who have not had top surgery require breast cancer screenings based on guidelines for cisgender women, which includes yearly mammograms starting at the age of 40 or 50, depending on family and personal health history. Those of us with a family history of breast cancer or the BRCA gene mutation may need to start getting mammograms at an earlier age. We should speak to our PCP to determine when is the right time for us to start yearly breast cancer screening. Annual clinical breast examinations and monthly self-examinations are no longer recommended for anyone at average risk for breast cancer who has not had a mastectomy.

Certain forms of breast cancer are increased by exposure to estrogen. In theory, gender affirming hormone therapy with testosterone could potentially increase our breast cancer risk due to the conversion of excess testosterone to estrogen in our bodies. Similarly, those of us who take estrogen for gender affirming hormone therapy are at a theoretically increased risk of breast cancer, though the data on breast cancer risk in T/GE people is limited. Although breast cancer screening is not required after mastectomy for those of us at average risk, any lumps felt in the chest or armpits should be reported to our PCPs promptly, because these could be signs of developing disease. Breast cancer has been reported in transgender women as well as transgender men, even after mastectomy.[36] If we have had top surgery to remove breast tissue, mammography is often not possible, in which case we may need to have an ultrasound, MRI, and/or biopsy if we have signs or symptoms concerning for breast cancer.

Those of us who are on the T/GE feminine-spectrum and over the age of 50 with additional risk factors should also have screening mammograms. The Rainbow Health Ontario Guidelines recommend mammograms every two years after the age of 50 if we have been on estrogen for more than five years, with earlier screening needed if we have additional risk factors, which include progestin use (especially if cyclic—taken only a few days every month instead of daily), positive family history of breast cancer, body mass index (BMI) greater than 35, and tobacco use.

Any of us who have a family history of breast or ovarian cancer—especially if in multiple relatives or if occurring in our relatives at younger ages—should discuss our risk with our providers and will likely need to start earlier breast cancer screening. In some cases, screening for genetic mutations (such as the BRCA gene) that increase breast cancer risk can identify those of us who are at even greater risk and indicate earlier intervention needs. Some of us may be scared to do this because we fear that our medical provider might not give us hormones. Hormone treatment can still be provided to T/GE people despite these increased risks as long as we are informed of the risks versus benefits and have the capacity to make an informed decision. Knowing that we are at an increased risk might mean we have more frequent or intensive screening, or, in the case of those of us on the masculine spectrum, obtain a bilateral mastectomy for cancer prevention.

Ovarian Cancer

Those of us with ovaries and a family history of ovarian cancer should have screening for ovarian cancer, particularly if we have a first-degree relative (i.e., parent or sibling) with

Jay, 59, New York, NY, 2015. (Jess T. Dugan). From "To Survive on This Shore: Photographs and Interviews with Transgender and Gender Nonconforming Older Adults," a project by Jess T. Dugan and Vanessa Fabbre.

ovarian cancer, or a known history of one of the genes that increases risk of ovarian cancer (i.e., BRCA1 or BRCA2 gene mutation). There is no data to suggest that ovarian cancer risk is increased or decreased in T/GE people who retain their ovaries. Because of the limited size of our community and the infrequency of ovarian cancer, there are statistical and medical research limitations to obtaining accurate data on this topic. When we are weighing the risks and benefits of surgery to remove our ovaries, we should consider the same risks that cisgender women have after removal of their ovaries, such as infertility, osteoporosis, menopausal symptoms (even if we are on testosterone), and the general risks of surgery and anesthesia.

Uterine Cancer

Those of us with a uterus who use testosterone for gender affirming hormone therapy may have a higher occurrence rate of abnormal changes to the endometrium (the lining of the uterus that is shed during menstruation) than cisgender women. Testosterone has been shown to cause the endometrium to grow more than usual (hyperplasia).[37] This can increase our chances of abnormal bleeding and of the growth of abnormal cells (dysplasia) that can become cancerous. There are no studies showing increased rates of endometrial cancer in transmasculine individuals. However, similar to ovarian cancer research, because of the limited size of our community and the infrequency of uterine cancer, there are statistical and medical research limitations to obtaining accurate data on this topic.

The most common initial symptom of uterine cell changes and uterine cancer is vaginal bleeding. However, most bleeding in those of us with a uterus is not caused by cancer. If we do have bleeding after a year or so on testosterone, have a recurrence of bleeding after our menses had previously stopped, or have bleeding after the age of what would have been our menopause (even if we are not on testosterone), we should see our PCP or gynecologist to be evaluated for the cause of our bleeding. In this case, our medical provider may order a pelvic or transvaginal ultrasound, or perform a uterine biopsy to assess for cancer or other uterine abnormalities. If we have difficulty with pelvic exams, we may want to inquire if our medical provider can perform these procedures under sedation, or refer us to someone who has this capability.

Prostate and Testicular Cancer

Screening for prostate and testicular cancers is unfortunately not very effective in either cisgender or T/GE individuals at average risk for these diseases. The United States Preventive Services Task Force (USPSTF) recommends against routine testicular cancer screening in people assigned male at birth.[38] The reasoning behind this is that testicular cancer is rare, generally found by patients without a testicular exam by a medical professional, and even when testicular cancer is present and has spread from the testicles to elsewhere in the body, it is usually very treatable. Therefore, routine screening has not been shown to prevent death from testicular cancer. Additionally, routine testicular screening might find noncancerous lesions, causing the patient undue stress and potentially leading to unnecessary additional testing and surgery. Because the risks of testicular screening outweigh the benefits, the USPSTF recommends against routine screening for testicular cancer.

Screening for prostate cancer is also not strongly recommended, even for people of the age most likely to benefit from this screening (55–69 years old). In individuals who are at average risk of prostate cancer, the harms of screening, similarly to testicular screening, may outweigh the potential benefits. This is because the tests for prostate cancer, which include a blood test for the prostate-specific antigen (PSA) and a digital rectal exam (feeling the prostate by inserting a finger into the rectum), may not detect cancer early and may be abnormal even if no cancer exists, leading to potentially unnecessary and invasive tests and surgical procedures. Even if the screening tests for prostate cancer were more accurate, not all prostate cancer is life-threatening. Prostate cancers usually grow so slowly that most people die *with* them rather than *from* them. The USPSTF recommends that people with a prostate between the ages of 55 and 69 discuss the risks versus benefits of screening with their PCP to decide whether or not they should be screened for prostate cancer.[39]

Gender affirming hormone therapy with estrogen can falsely lower the PSA blood test, even if cancer is present. Thus, the PSA screening test is less accurate in transfeminine individuals on feminizing hormones than in cisgender men.[40] Those of us who are at higher risk of prostate cancer (those of us of African descent and/or with a family or personal history of prostate cancer, for example) may benefit from prostate screening. This is a decision that we should make in collaboration with our healthcare providers. If we and our providers feel that screening with a PSA test could be beneficial, the usual normal range of 4.0 ng/ml used in cisgender men should be lowered to 1.0 ng/ml in transfeminine people on gender affirming hormone therapy and/or those of us who have had an orchiectomy (removal of the testicles).[41]

In almost all cases, having a vaginoplasty does *not* involve removal of the prostate gland. This is because removal of the prostate is a more dangerous procedure and can result in serious damage to the colon and/or chronic problems with incontinence (leaking of urine). It is important that we disclose to our healthcare providers that we have a prostate, regardless of whether we have had a vaginoplasty or other bottom surgery procedures. Cancer screenings and guidelines are based on the body parts and internal organs that we have; they are not based on our gender identity.

If we have had a vaginoplasty, a prostate exam may be better performed by our medical provider by inserting a finger into our vagina than the usual rectal exam, because the prostate sits on top of the new vagina instead of directly on top of the rectum. The best position for this exam is similar to a gynecologic exam for cisgender women and transmasculine individuals: laying with stomach facing up, buttocks just off the edge of the exam table, feet in adjustable brackets ("stirrups"), and knees spread slightly apart.

SAFETY, VIOLENCE, AND TRAUMA

Staying healthy also means staying safe. Unfortunately, T/GE people are more frequently the victims of physical and sexual assault than our cisgender peers. The U.S. Transgender Survey found that almost half (47%) of us reported at least one sexual assault in our lifetimes, 48% had been denied equal treatment, verbally harassed, or physically attacked *in the past year*, and 54% had experienced violence from an intimate partner in our lifetime.[42] If we are unemployed and/or share finances with our partner(s), it can be more difficult to leave an abusive relationship. Or we may worry about finding other partners because we have experienced discrimination and rejection in the past, which may motivate us to stay in unhealthy relationships. Domestic violence programs and shelters may not be knowledgeable about our T/GE identities or needs. If we, or someone we love, is in an abusive relationship, we can seek support from a national LGBTQ antiviolence organization, such as the National Coalition of Anti-Violence Programs.[43] Additionally, more and more domestic violence programs are becoming aware of and seeking training for LGBTQ + client needs, and thus we may be surprised to learn that our local domestic violence organization is LGBTQ-affirming and equipped to meet our needs.

UNPLANNED AND SPECIALTY CARE

I needed an emergency appendectomy and both my primary physician and spouse took very good care to ensure I was treated respectfully.

In addition to the care that is provided at a primary care office, we may need care at other locations such as an emergency room (ER), hospital, radiology center, or at a specialist's office. We can do several things to help ensure we get the care we need and minimize our exposure to discrimination. An important first step is to enlist our primary care provider's help: A call from a PCP to a specialist or ER can smooth the process and lay the groundwork for trans-informed care. If we need treatment such as a planned surgery or hospitalization, it may be possible to tour the facility ahead of time.

> *I have been refused care at the ER, discriminated against at the endocrinologist, and had several other terrible healthcare experiences. But I've also had wonderful experiences, like my obgyn/surgeon staying in the hospital with me until 10 pm after a difficult surgery and making sure the entire staff respected my gender identity and expression while in the hospital.*

Unscheduled health care may be able to be provided in a PCP office, but at times, requires treatment in an urgent care or ER, where we may not know any of the health care providers or their trans-competency. This can be scary for anyone, cis or trans. This is especially true for us as T/GE people because our bodies and identities do not necessarily fit within the typical medical binary of sex and gender,[44,45,46] and we may have heard stories about discrimination in medical settings or may have experienced difficulties ourselves in the past. It is important, however, to take our health care needs seriously, even if that means a trip to the local hospital ER. Although this may seem daunting, there are things we can do to help us have a safer and more comfortable experience.[47]

> *I needed a brain MRI as I have severe migraines, and my doctor wanted to make sure there wasn't anything seriously wrong. I let the technicians know that I was trans, that I had dysphoria, that I was aware of the rule about cotton-only fabric in the machine, and that my undergarments and shirt were 100% cotton. They let me keep my cotton clothes on, gave me pants (which I dubbed sexy pants, because they looked so terrible), and a cotton blanket. I used the blanket to wrap around myself, walking to the machine, and they helped lay it over my chest once I was laying down. They were amazing!*

One of the most important things we can do when we go to the ER is to bring a friend or loved one who can advocate for us. It is important to choose this person wisely: This should be someone we trust to be with us in vulnerable situations such as after taking sedating medicines or while having invasive physical exams. This person should also be someone level-headed and with good communication skills in order to be a good advocate in case we find ourselves in a challenging situation. Finally, this person should ideally be someone who is able to drive us or escort us on public transit or in a ride-share to get home after the visit.

THE TRANS BUDDIES PROGRAM AT VANDERBILT

Shawn Reilly, MEd, (they/them) is an educator and divinity school student living in Nashville, Tennessee. They are the program coordinator for the Trans Buddy Program at the Program for LGBTQ Health at Vanderbilt, and they co-coordinate the GLSEN Tennessee SHINE activism team, working in partnership with young people to make schools and communities safer for LGBTQI youth across the state.

In 2014, transgender organizer and healthcare professional Kale Edmiston had a vision for a transgender healthcare initiative, one that would provide transgender patients with emotional accompaniment during doctors' appointments and inpatient hospital stays. Modeled after The Doula Project in New York and informed by a reproductive justice framework, our supportive community of transgender people and their allies works to provide trans people with increased access to resources and care, an initiative now known as the Trans Buddy Program at the Program for LGBTQ Health at Vanderbilt. Since its inception, the program has received institutional support from Vanderbilt University Medical Center, has been continuously staffed by a transgender coordinator, and has been supported by a team of dedicated volunteers.

In order to access our service, transgender people call our Trans Buddy hotline, which is staffed by a trained patient advocate 365 days a year. During onboarding, our volunteers go through an intensive eight-hour training. During these biannual orientation sessions, new volunteers explore their own values, practice conflict resolution, learn healing-centered practices, and engage with transgender patients and current Trans Buddy volunteers. Once volunteers join the team, they engage in quarterly continuing education workshops, which are developed in response to emergent needs of our patients and volunteer force. Workshops have covered topics including caring for transgender patients through pregnancy and birth, mental health first aid for LGBTQI youth, and supporting persons experiencing suicidality.

Once a patient calls our line, our volunteers work to connect them with resources and supports that meet the patient's needs. The Buddies provide emotional and logistical support through offering referrals for local organizations and healthcare providers, for both transition and nontransition-related care. Patients may also request an advocate to accompany them during healthcare appointments and inpatient stays. During such appointments, advocates can wait in lobbies and examination rooms alongside patients. They are trained to intervene if a staff member uses the incorrect name or pronouns, to speak with unsupportive family members, and to support providers in correctly charting the patient's information.

As a nonbinary person, I know firsthand that transgender people, especially transgender women of color, face enormous barriers when attempting to access health care. The Trans Buddy program tries to ease transgender patients' well-founded anxieties when facing these barriers and support them in successfully accessing the services they need to survive and thrive.

Most healthcare providers in ERs genuinely want to help everyone who comes in. It can be hard to do this in crisis situations when crucial pieces of information are missing, thus it is important that we make sure we either have the following information written down or are able to state it reliably and completely, including:

1. All medications we take, including our hormones, over-the-counter medicines, and supplements, and the doses and frequency of each
2. All allergies we have (to medications, foods, latex, etc.), including what reaction these allergies cause (i.e., nausea/vomiting, rash, swelling, anaphylaxis)
3. Our complete medical and surgical histories, including hospitalizations and gender-affirming surgeries
4. Any tests we have had relating to our current or past medical problems
5. A copy of our government ID and insurance card, if we have insurance
6. Names and contact information for people we would like contacted in case of emergency, our primary care provider, specialists we may see, and our health care proxy (surrogate medical decision-maker) if we have one
7. If our emergency concern is related to a surgical issue, our surgeon's name and contact information
8. A copy of an advance healthcare directive or durable healthcare power of attorney, if we have one
9. If the emergency concern is a trans-related health issue, we may want to come equipped with a few resources in case the treatment provider has not had experience with T/GE care

When we first arrive in the ER, we will be triaged by a nurse who will assess our main concern with a brief history, exam, and checking our vital signs (i.e., temperature, heart rate, blood pleasure, oxygen level, and weight), to determine the acuity of our needs. Triage means "to sort"—the triage nurse is sorting us into a category based on the perceived severity of our illness/concern. Generally speaking, ERs see people in the order in which they come, but people who are sicker (or who have a higher risk of quickly deteriorating) get bumped to the front of the line. This may mean that if we have a less serious issue or are deemed to be medically more stable than other patients in the ER, we may have to wait to be seen until the more serious patients/illnesses are managed first. This can sometimes appear arbitrary, but we should keep in mind that we do not know what other patients are presenting with or what their medical history is. Additionally, patients do not always look as sick as they are found to be in triage.

If a problem arises in the ER, we can ask to talk to someone to see whether our issue can be addressed. It is important, however, to realize that although some problems may be resolved on the spot, others may not. We can start by addressing the issue with the medical assistant or nurse caring for us, or the triage nurse if we are in a waiting room. Our advocate can help with this. If the issue is not an emergency, we may need to wait before a nurse or doctor can talk with us. For example, the triage nurse may have to triage another patient before they can come and address our issue. If the nurse is unable to resolve the problem, we can ask to speak to a patient advocate or a nursing supervisor. We must be prepared to wait to speak with such an individual, because these staff persons may have to be called to the ER from another part of the hospital, or they may be offsite.

When we see the emergency room physician, physician's assistant, or nurse practitioner who will be providing our care, we should be prepared to answer lots of questions. The questions may not always seem relevant to us, but are usually important for our care. For example, if a trans man comes to the ER with a possible concussion, it may not be clear to us why the provider is asking if we have sex with cis men or have had a hysterectomy. The provider is probably asking this question to determine whether a pregnancy test is needed before performing a head computed tomography (CT), due to the risk of radiation exposure to a potential fetus.

> *If you're the "out" trans person in the ER, and there are eight residents who have not seen a trans person before, everyone wants to run into the room to be part of that evaluation.*

The question, "Have you had any surgeries?" is asked of every patient when taking a thorough and complete medical history. This question does not just refer to gender-affirming surgeries, but *all* surgeries. For example, if a patient comes into the ER with acute stomach pain, it is important to know which organs may or may not be causing the problem—such as if the person has had surgery to remove their appendix, gallbladder, ovaries, or uterus. Residents (physicians in training) and medical students frequently ask more questions than more senior physicians, because as part of their training, they are expected to take a more extensive history. If we think a question may not be appropriate, it is always OK to ask why the question being asked is relevant to our care.

> *Although it's probably uncomfortable for me, it's less uncomfortable for me than it would be for someone who's just starting out their process or transition. So I would rather be the "guinea pig," and almost take one for the team that way. Next time those students come across someone in any of our situations, they are better equipped to address it respectfully.*

In general, although we may be apprehensive about unscheduled care in an ER, assuming the best but being prepared for hiccups is generally a good plan. Unpleasant experiences may be due to discrimination, but may also be due to miscommunication or simply a busy ER.

RIGHT BODY

Casjen Griesel (he/him) studied Literary Writing and Editing (M.A.) and German and Gender Studies (B.A.) in Germany. He is an editor, podcaster, writing coach, sensitivity reader, and co-editor of a magazine by trans people for trans people.

I hate it when people say trans people were "born in the wrong body." I hate this statement because for me it is simply wrong. Whenever I hear people talk about trans people being "born in the wrong body," I want to grab them and shake them until they realize how much damage they are causing.

This body I live in is my body and will remain so forever. I am grateful for it because it allows me to do so many wonderful things. I have always been in this body and will never be able to leave it or live my life in another body. For some people, my body may not be perfect. Some people may see my body as too "male" or too "female" to be non-binary. Some parts may be a little too hairy, a little too fat, a little too scarred in the eyes of others. But the love I have for my body is endless.

I've made a few changes to my body that make it look the way I want it to look—that make it function the way I need it to function. Because when something doesn't work the way we want it to, sometimes we're lucky enough to be able to improve it by making changes. Because I've had surgeries and take hormones, people say I'm in the "wrong body." But because I wear glasses to make my eyes work properly, no one tells me I have "wrong eyes" and need new ones.

My body tells my story, the story of my transition but also the story of my life, my desires and dreams and successes, my defeats and rejections and deepest downs. I have tattoos and piercings, scars, wrinkles, rough edges. My body shows who I am.

These changes that my body has gone through since I was born do not mean that I was born in the "wrong body." They only show that I am always working on becoming and being myself.

SEXUAL AND REPRODUCTIVE HEALTH

Sexual Health

Just like general health, sexual health is a positive state of soundness, strength, and stability, not simply a lack of illness. Sexual health includes physical, emotional, mental, and social well-being with respect to sexuality. Good sexual health requires an approach to sexuality and sexual relationships that is respectful of ourselves and our partners. We should be able to engage in sexual experiences free of coercion, discrimination, and violence. Our sexual health is a crucial aspect of our overall health. Talking about sexual health includes prevention and early diagnosis of STIs, as well as birth control, when desired/needed. Sexual health also includes screening for cancers and other conditions that might get in the way of our sexual function.

Consider these examples:

1. A genderqueer person who has less interest in sex because of side effects of a medicine they are taking
2. A transgender man who wants to enjoy vaginal penetration but has pain that prevents him from doing so
3. A transgender woman who wants to maintain an erection but is unable to do so as a side effect of hormone therapy
4. A nonbinary person who wants to enjoy stimulation of their nipples but has lost erotic sensation due to top surgery

When we have issues with our sexual health such as these, it is important to seek out help, which can come from our primary care provider, sex therapist, and/or mental health providers. Turning to trusted members of our communities who have experienced similar issues may also be helpful.

I had a particularly negative experience trying to get gynecologic care and a supposedly "LGBT friendly gyno" saying that I was still technically a virgin because I hadn't had "sex with a man yet" (i.e., implying I was not a man and that cisgender sex with a penis and vagina was the only real sex).

SAFER SEX

Though it may seem difficult, communicating and negotiating around safer sex is of utmost importance. At times we may feel less empowered to assert boundaries around our sexual safety, or be more invested in engaging in certain sexual activities that we feel are affirming of our gender.[48] In T/GE communities, societal bias and stigma are associated with an increased risk of engaging in unsafe sexual activities and acquiring HIV.[49,50,51] Communication about safer sex is key to not only our enjoyment of sex, but to our physical and emotional safety. Communication helps ensure that we engage in pleasurable and safe sexual practices, and reduces the chances of acquiring and transmitting STIs, including HIV. Just as gender is a spectrum, safer sex is, too.

Reproductive Justice. (Art By Emulsify)

Sexual safety is relative to the sexual activities that we engage in and the protections that we may or may not use. For example, engaging in anal sex without a condom is three times riskier for HIV transmission for the receptive partner ("bottom") than it is for the insertive partner ("top"), whereas anal sex with proper condom use is three times *less* risky for the bottom than anal sex without a condom is for the top.[52] We can use barrier methods, avoid use of alcohol or drugs during sex, engage in open and honest communication, and take PrEP to decrease our risk of acquiring HIV. Barriers can include latex condoms, internal condoms (also called female condoms), and latex dental dams. Condoms and other barriers are one of the most important ways to protect ourselves from STIs. When using latex condoms (or any other latex barrier), it is very important to only use water-based lubricants. Oil-based lubricants or Vaseline can break down latex and make it ineffective against the transmission of HIV and other STIs. The internal condom currently available (FC-2, AKA "the female condom") is named such because it can be used by cisgender women during vaginal penetration. However, the FC-2 can be used by anyone who is having vaginal or anal intercourse regardless of gender identity.[53] An additional advantage of an internal condom is that it can be inserted prior to the start of sexual activity, giving the receptive partner control over protecting their own sexual health as well as that of their sexual partner(s).

A pleasurable and healthy sex life, however we conceptualize it, starts with sexual health. The bottom line is that sex and sexuality can and should be pleasurable, fun, and safe. Sexual health, for those of us who desire and want sexual relations with others, is an important part of our well-being.

Reproductive Health

Reproductive health care includes the ability to make informed choices about whether and when we would like to have children. These are two very important decisions for us to make. For those of us with a uterus, if we do not want to be pregnant, we should be able to prevent pregnancy through birth control options that suit our needs. If we desire to become pregnant, we should be able to get connected to obstetrical care and, if needed and

The National LGBTQIA + Health Education Center (a program of the Fenway Institute in Boston) provides training and technical assistance to health centers as well as online learning modules for individual healthcare providers.

desired, assisted reproductive techniques and technologies (ART) that can improve our chances of getting pregnant and having a successful pregnancy.

Every technique or method of assisting people with reproductive health has benefits, risks, and varying success rates. In many ways, these techniques are the same for cisgender and T/GE people. For example, condoms are condoms and their efficacy is based on body shape and function as well as technique of use, rather than gender identity. There are, however, special needs that we as T/GE people have and need to take into account when trying to become pregnant, such as the effect of gender affirming hormone therapy on our ability to get pregnant. As medicine and technology advances, more options for contraception and fertility may become available for our communities.

CONTRACEPTION FOR TRANSMASCULINE SPECTRUM PEOPLE

One of the most important things to remember is that testosterone is **NOT** birth control. In some of us assigned female at birth, testosterone may decrease fertility, but this is not reliable and has not been tested clinically. Unintended pregnancy has occurred in T/GE individuals assigned female at birth (AFAB) on testosterone for gender affirming hormone therapy.[54] Unintended pregnancy in T/GE individuals AFAB is also complicated by the fact that, unlike cisgender women, those of us on testosterone often do not menstruate, so unintended pregnancy may be detected later in the course of the pregnancy because there is no missed menstrual period to alert us that we are pregnant.

> Most of my bad experiences with contraceptives involve how focused on cis women the industry is. I am not a cis woman, but I still need to learn my options in a way/environment that isn't erasing a huge part of my identity.

The Food and Drug Administration (FDA) classifies medications in pregnancy as category A, B, C, D, or X depending on the risk to the developing fetus. Medications in class A and B are generally regarded as reasonably safe to the fetus. Medications in class C and D are known or suspected to cause harm to the fetus, but in some circumstances their use may be justified. Category X is reserved for medications that are known to cause harm to a fetus and whose use is never justified in pregnancy. Testosterone is a United States FDA "Pregnancy Category X" medication. Due to these risks, good contraception is important for those of us AFAB with a uterus and ovaries taking testosterone who enjoy receptive vaginal sex with a partner who produces sperm.

In addition to testosterone, finasteride, a medication that can be used to treat balding, is also pregnancy Category X.

> I don't have sex that has the possibility of pregnancy, but I have used contraception to try to reduce my dysphoria around menstruation. I tried a lot of different formulations of birth control pills, taking them without the one-week sugar pill break. Sometimes this caused issues with insurance not wanting to cover the next pack. I now have a hormonal IUD, which has helped but not eliminated the problem. When I still went to doctors as a cis woman, I used to get a lot of anxious pushback: "Are you sure you don't need contraception?" even though I only ever had sex with women. It's weird how now the fact of me being on "birth control" seems to alleviate medical practitioner anxiety.

There are many options for cisgender women to prevent pregnancy, and many of these are very reasonable options for us as well. Current recommendations for transmasculine spectrum people who have the potential for pregnancy is that they should be offered contraception, which includes all forms of contraception offered to their cis female counterparts. Barrier methods such as the traditional condom or internal condom are effective at preventing both pregnancy and sexually transmitted infections. If condoms are used 100% correctly during every penile-vaginal intercourse in a year, studies show that 2 out of 100 sexually active cisgender women will become pregnant. However, we know that condoms are not used correctly 100% of the time. In the way that condoms are typically used, the number can be as high as 15 pregnancies per 100 people. It is unclear what the rates of pregnancy with condom use in T/GE individuals AFAB are.

I ASKED SIX HEALTH CARE PROFESSIONALS

IS THERE ANY REASON NOT TO TAKE HORMONAL BIRTH CONTROL IF YOU'RE ON T?

I'M NOT SURE. LET ME ASK AROUND.

MAC E.R. DOCTOR

MADDY HEALTH EQUITY ALLIANCE

MARGOT MED STUDENT

PENNY FAMILY PHYSICIAN

KATIE THERAPIST AT THE GENDER CLINIC

LUCAS R.N.

HERE'S WHAT THEY FOUND:

THERE'S NOTHING TO SUGGEST IT'S UNSAFE AND TRANS GUYS HAVE BEEN USING IT FOR A WHILE, BUT OUTCOMES ARE NOT STUDIED

ANY BIRTH CONTROL IS SAFE AND EFFECTIVE TO USE

NOT DANGEROUS BUT PEOPLE DISAGREE ON WHETHER THE ESTROGEN IS AN ISSUE OR NO DIFFERENT THAN WHAT THE BODY MAKES ANYWAY.

AN ARTICLE PUBLISHED JUNE 2018 IN THE JOURNAL CONTRACEPTION SAID,

"TO OUR KNOWLEDGE, THERE IS NO CURRENT RESEARCH DEMONSTRATING POSITIVE OR NEGATIVE EFFECTS OF LOW DOSE HORMONES FROM CONTRACEPTION ON EXOGENEOUS TESTOSTERONE USE."

COMING FROM OUTSIDE THE BODY

SO IF ANY METHOD IS SAFE AND EFFECTIVE—

WHAT ARE THE BARRIERS TO GETTING BIRTH CONTROL?

"I AM MISGENDERING MYSELF BY OPENING YOUR FRONT DOOR."

WOMEN'S CLINIC

—KRIS NONBINARY, QUEER IN A "TRANS" CATEGORY

"THE MEDICAL INDUSTRIAL COMPLEX."

—KATIE GENDERQUEER

"I WAS ON CONTINUOUS BIRTH CONTROL TO STOP MY PERIOD BUT WAS TOLD I HAD TO STOP IN ORDER TO START T. THIS GAVE ME SUPER BAD DYSPHORIA."

—ANONYMOUS NONBINARY, NOTHING, WOMAN

"IF A WOMAN COMES INTO MY OFFICE I WOULD ASK, 'WHAT ARE YOU DOING FOR BIRTH CONTROL?' IF A TRANS MAN COMES, I MIGHT NOT ASK."

—PENNY FEMALE

"LACK OF KNOWLEDGE AND COMFORT FROM PROVIDERS."

—MADDY NONBINARY

"IT SEEMS LIKE BIRTH CONTROL IS HORMONAL AND PROBABLY DOESN'T WORK IF YOU'RE ON T. NO ONE REALLY KNOWS ANYTHING."

—OSCAR TRANS MAN

"I HAVE NO IDEA IF I NEED TO USE PLAN B. AND NO IDEA HOW IT WOULD INTERACT WITH MY HORMONES."

—LEO IT'S COMPLICATED

"THE SENSATIONS AROUND HAVING AN IUD TRIGGERED SO MUCH DYSPHORIA I HAD TO GET IT OUT."

—LUCAS TRANS GUY

"PRIMARY CARE PROVIDER EDUCATION"

—BO TRANSFAG

"A comic about my journey as a trans person with a uterus trying to find information about and access to birth control." "Will makes wacky, dark, funny comics about their life, politics, and flightless birds. He lives in Boulder and is working on their MFA in comics from California College of the Arts. Will teaches math, mentors trans youth, and is very friendly. (Will Betke-Brunswick, willbetkebrunkswick.com)

I don't want children right now, so I use the Depo shot. I didn't want too many hormones so I was trying to find a contraception that would work for my body. It has been traumatizing though, because my OBGYN I go to constantly misgenders me and gives me "women" documents. Only recently, after complaining, did they not display my gender on my medical bracelet.

Traditional hormonal contraceptive methods (e.g., "the pill") have not been studied in transmasculine people, but some OB/GYNS recommend that they can be used.[55] Other reasonable options for us for birth control include treatment with progestins such as the DepoProvera shot (which lasts about three months), or Nexplanon, which is implanted in the arm and lasts for up to three years. These birth control methods can be used for those of us on testosterone as well as those of us who are not. These methods may decrease or eliminate our menstrual periods whether we are on testosterone or not, a welcome effect for many of us. Another birth control option is an intrauterine device (IUD). IUDs are a highly effective and safe method of birth control, a benefit of which is that they can safely remain in place for several years. Options for IUDs include those with and without hormones. The progestin hormone containing IUDs decrease ovulation and significantly decrease vaginal bleeding. For those of us who have sex with partners with a penis that makes sperm, and who also have residual vaginal bleeding on testosterone, progesterone IUDs can provide highly effective contraception and help decrease our vaginal bleeding.

I've been using hormonal IUDs since before I came out as trans. On the one hand, I really like how they cease my menstruation; on the other hand, I wonder how having all this extra progesterone in my body is changing my body's appearance and my mindset—I've been on hormonal birth control for basically as long as I've been an adult, so I have no idea what I would be like without it, and that bothers me a little bit. I think I would like to stop using hormonal birth control, but I haven't yet found a form of nonhormonal contraception or sterilization that would stop my periods and also be safe for me.

Emergency contraception (the "morning-after pill") may be effective for T/GE people with a uterus and ovaries, although it has not been specifically tested. Emergency contraception is available over the counter in the United States to people of all ages and can be taken up to 72–120 hours after sex, depending on which medicine is used. If you are T/GE with a uterus and ovaries and think you may be pregnant, stop taking testosterone (and finasteride) immediately and contact your primary care provider or gynecologist for further testing and medical recommendations. Do not restart these medications until advised by a medical provider if you are considering carrying the pregnancy to term, because these medications can cause serious harm to a fetus.

I have used contraception. I have an arm implant so it's not too dysphoric, but I've needed plan B before and the idea of pregnancy makes me nauseous and panicky.

For those of us AFAB who do not desire to retain our ability to produce genetic offspring, surgical sterilization is an option for permanent birth control. A common method of surgical sterilization is a tubal ligation (having our "tubes tied"). This is done through a surgical procedure that ties off, clamps, or cuts the fallopian tubes, preventing eggs from reaching the uterus. Other options include a hysterectomy (removal of the uterus) and/or oophorectomy (removal of the ovaries). These surgical procedures may be done as part of gender-affirming surgical care for those of us who desire it. Typical methods of surgical sterilization now include laparoscopic procedures, in which instruments and a camera are introduced into the abdomen through small surgical incisions, which allows for faster recovery time and less postoperative pain. There are also surgical methods in which the sterilization is performed by entering through the vagina into the uterus and inserting the sterilization device into the fallopian tubes.

> *I use birth control for purely mental health reasons as a supplement to psychiatric treatment. This does not trigger my dysphoria as it helps my over-hormonal mood swings.*

CONTRACEPTION IN TRANSFEMININE SPECTRUM PEOPLE

Those of us assigned male at birth who retain our testicles can potentially produce a pregnancy in a cisgender female or transgender male who retains their sexual organs and is not on adequate birth control. Estrogens and spironolactone may decrease our sperm count and the viability of our sperm, but enough of our sperm may remain and can result in a pregnancy. The best nonpermanent contraceptive option currently available for us is condoms. In addition to decreasing the risk of impregnating a partner, condoms also decrease the transmission of STIs.

If pregnancy in a partner does occur while we are on estrogen and spironolactone, there is no risk of harm to the fetus. If we are using finasteride to decrease hair loss, however, it is very important to keep the medication away from our pregnant partner due to risk to the developing fetus. Pregnant people should not even touch finasteride pills.

For those of us who do not desire to produce offspring, there are relatively easy, permanent contraception options such as a vasectomy. This is an office-based procedure in which the ducts that carry sperm are cut and tied off to prevent sperm from exiting the body. Another option is to have an orchiectomy (removal of the testes), which can be done alone or in conjunction with a vaginoplasty as part of our surgical transition, if desired. There are added benefits to an orchiectomy including simplifying our hormonal treatments (we no longer have the need to take testosterone-blockers and often require lower estrogen doses) and improving our ability to "tuck."

FERTILITY OPTIONS FOR TRANSMASCULINE SPECTRUM PEOPLE

Some of us AFAB may desire to have genetic offspring. We may seek out fertility, either by carrying a baby ourselves or donating an egg to be fertilized and implanted in a partner or surrogate. Some of us who desire gender affirming surgery that involves a hysterectomy (removal of the uterus) or oophorectomy (removal of the ovaries) may first wish to preserve our eggs for future options for fertility.

Pregnancy in T/GE individuals AFAB who retain their uterus and ovaries is possible, though transmasculine individuals may face issues with fertility as the effect of testosterone on future fertility is not certain. Testosterone may reduce or eliminate one's fertility even after treatment is stopped. However, there are T/GE individuals who were on testosterone, stopped it, and were able to get pregnant. If we want to become pregnant, we must be off testosterone for a sufficient period of time for our sex hormone levels to return to a cis female range. In those of us on topical testosterone, this process may take a relatively short time (days), whereas in those of us injecting testosterone, this may take weeks to months. Even after menstruation has restarted, testosterone levels may still be too high to become pregnant safely. Those of us who wish to become pregnant should have our testosterone levels tested before attempting to get pregnant. In addition, we should have a visit with our primary care provider or an obstetrician/gynecologist before pregnancy for further prenatal testing. Anyone who is considering becoming pregnant should take 0.4–0.8 mg of folic acid daily in order to help prevent birth defects.[56]

For those of us who wish to preserve fertility for the future, options are available, though these options can be expensive and are not always successful.[57] The standard technique is to harvest oocytes (egg cells) from the ovaries. This requires taking hormones to increase ovulation, and making an increased number of eggs. The egg cells are then retrieved by an in-office surgical procedure. The retrieved eggs may be frozen by themselves or may be fertilized with sperm either from a known or anonymous donor to produce

The organization Family Equality helps with LGBTQ family building as well as connecting LGBTQ families to one another.

embryos, which are then frozen until desired for conception. In general, pregnancy success rates are higher when embryos are frozen than when eggs alone are frozen. Over the past decade, however, freezing unfertilized eggs (oocytes) without sperm has become a much more viable option with newer technology called vitrification (flash freezing). The primary benefit of freezing egg cells as opposed to embryos is that a sperm donor does not need to be identified at the time of fertility preservation. The major drawback for both techniques is cost, which is often $10,000–$20,000 with additional fees annually to store the preserved eggs or embryos (generally less than $1,000). Given the cost, many of us who desire to have genetically related children opt to preserve our fertility by keeping our uterus and ovaries and either delaying taking testosterone or taking it and hoping that it does not impact our fertility.

THE GYNECOLOGIST

Margaret Nickens (they/them) is a genderqueer writer and educator based in Denver, Colorado.

The doctor pushes me back and asks me to scoot forward until the bottom of my butt is hanging off the edge of the exam table. She spreads my legs quickly. Without warning, I feel the hard edges of a speculum spread me open, and a moment later, she slides two wet fingers into me.

I feel the pressure deeply inside of me and blink at the ceiling to distract myself. When I turn my head to the side, I'm staring at a poster of a mother and child standing under the title "The Benefits of Breastfeeding."

I take a deep breath and open my mouth, talking more to the mother than the doctor between my legs.

"I, um . . . wanted to ask you something about childbirth," I mutter quietly.

I feel her fingers slide out of me, leaving a trail of lubricant against my thigh and the sheet below me.

"Sure. You can sit up now," she responds.

When I push myself to sitting, she's walking over to the sink to wash her hands.

"I'm thinking of, uh, trying to have a baby," I say over the sound of the running water.

"That's wonderful," she smiles over her shoulder. "From your cervical exam, you look healthy. I could do a few other tests to check for fertility if you would like, though."

I shake my head, trying to ignore the lube continually dripping from my vagina to the sheet below and wishing I'd wiped myself before starting this conversation. Maybe put some clothes on. Maybe asked over the phone instead.

"No, it's actually . . . I'm also thinking of getting top surgery." I say the words before I can take them back. She furrows her eyebrows, confused, so I look at my hands before continuing. "Like having my breasts removed."

"OK," she says slowly, drawing the last syllable into a question.

"Like is it safe? To get the surgery before conceiving? Will the pregnancy hormones mess it up?"

I speak quickly again, and I'm afraid she'll ask me to repeat the questions. Twisting my hands in my lap, I'm not sure I could force the words out again.

"Well, you wouldn't be able to breastfeed," she responds pointedly.

"I mean, I know *that*," I sigh, "I just want to know if it is safe for me to have a baby after getting the surgery."

"I think you should be wondering, not if it's safe, but is it best? For the baby." She purses her lips and clasps her hands in front of her.

After I don't respond for a moment, she continues, "I'll let you get dressed. Here are some tissues for your . . . "

She trails off and gestures at my lap, before turning quickly and walking out the door. I stand up and slide my gown off, catching a glimpse of my reflection in the mirror. With a grimace, I step to the side, staring at the sink instead as I wipe the tissue between my legs.

Originally published in The Thought Erotic: A Sex Thinktank. https://thethoughterotic.com/2018/11/18/the-gynecologist/. Republished with permission of the journal.

FERTILITY OPTIONS FOR TRANSFEMININE SPECTRUM PEOPLE

Fertility preservation in those of us AMAB is much easier and less expensive compared to transmasculine individuals. The process of obtaining semen for preservation is simple and the cost for preservation for up to five years is in the range of $1,000–$2,000. Sperm can be frozen for longer periods of time with additional annual costs. For those of us who wish to use this technique, we should consider preserving sperm before starting gender affirming hormones, as we may become less fertile on hormones.

For those of us already on gender affirming hormones, we may need to stop hormones for long enough to enable our sperm counts to rise to viable levels. This is an option in many cases and likely increases our chances of future successful insemination of a partner. However, hormone use can reduce fertility permanently in some of us, even if hormones are paused. Estrogen may also have the effect of reducing our libido, erectile function, and ejaculation, thus impacting our ability to inseminate a partner through sexual intercourse.

I completely changed all of my medical care when I transitioned, moving to providers who I believed would be supportive and educated about trans health needs. So far, I have been happy with the care I have received. When I stored my sperm before beginning hormones, the doctor at the fertility clinic said something that really impressed me. "I have to ask you these questions, and I know they are terrible questions, and we have already given feedback to the relevant government agency about why they should be changed." Having already taken action to try to get the legally required questionnaire changed showed me that they really were supportive.

CONCLUSION

It is important to remember that health is a positive state of wellness, not merely the absence of disease, and includes physical, emotional, mental, spiritual, and social well-being. As we continue to work to eradicate the bias and stigma our communities face in healthcare systems and in society at large, we should also acknowledge our resilience and strength as individuals and as a community to get where we are today. As we look to the future of T/GE health, let us empower ourselves and each other to nourish all aspects of our health.

NOTES

1. Jaffee, K. D., Shires, D. A., & Stroumsa, D. (2016). Discrimination and delayed health care among transgender women and men. *Medical Care, 54*(11), 1010–1016.
2. Seelman, K. L., Colón-Diaz, M. J., LeCroix, R. H., Xavier-Brier, M., & Kattari, L. (2017). Transgender noninclusive healthcare and delaying care because of fear: Connections to general health and mental health among transgender adults. *Transgender Health, 2*(1), 17–28.
3. Samuels, E. A., Tape, C., Garber, N., Bowman, S., & Choo, E. K. (2018). "Sometimes you feel like the freak show": A qualitative assessment of emergency care experiences among transgender and gender-nonconforming patients. *Annals of Emergency Medicine, 71*(2), 170–182.
4. 9 Secrets to Getting Congress to Listen, Straight from Someone Who Worked There: https://www.popsugar.com/news/Best-Way-Contact-Congress-42794889
5. Advocacy Toolkit from Prosperity Now: https://prosperitynow.org/ advocate/toolkit
6. https://www.glaad.org/gap/paul-mchugh
7. McHugh, P. (2004). Surgical sex. *First Things: A Monthly Journal of Religion and Public Life, 147*, 34–38. Retrieved January 2014, from https://www.firstthings.com/article/2004/11/surgical-sex
8. McHugh, P. R. (1992). Psychiatric misadventures. *American Scholar, 61*(4), 497.
9. Meyer, J. K., & Reter, D. J. (1979). Sex reassignment follow-up. *Archives of General Psychiatry, 36*(9), 1010–1015. doi: 01780090096010.
10. Lombardi, E. (2010). Transgender health: a review and guidance for future research—proceedings from the Summer Institute at the Center for Research on Health and Sexual Orientation, University of Pittsburgh. *International Journal of Transgenderism, 12*(4), 211: Thirty years of international follow-up studies SRS: A comprehensive review, 1961–229.
11. Pfafflin, F., & Junge, A. (1998). Sex reassignment: Thirty years of international follow-up studies SRS: A comprehensive review, 1961–1991. http://web.archive.org/web/20070503090247/http://www.symposion.com/ijt/pfaefflin/1000.htm
12. Lothstein, L. M. (1982). Sex reassignment surgery: Historical, bioethical, and theoretical issues. *American Journal of Psychiatry, 139*, 417–426.

13. https://www.lgbtmap.org/equality-maps/healthcare_laws_and_policies

14. https://www.lgbtmap.org/equality-maps/healthcare_laws_and_policies/medicaid

15. https://transequality.org/know-your-rights/medicare

16. Canner, J. K., Harfouch, O., Kodadek, L. M., Pelaez, D., Coon, D., Offodile, A. C., Haider, A. H., & Lau, B. D. (2018). Temporal trends in gender-affirming surgery among transgender patients in the United States. *JAMA Surgery, 153*(7), 609–616.

17. Roach, A. P. (2018). Global Health for Transgender Individuals. In Dorman, R. & De Chesnay, M. (Eds.) *Case Studies in Global Health Policy Nursing*, 169.

18. Reference materials used to develop this piece:

    Beemyn, G. (2011). Transgender history in the United States. In *Trans bodies, trans selves: A resource for the transgender community* (pp. 1–49). New York: Oxford University Press.

    Drescher, J. (2010). Queer diagnoses: Parallels and contrasts in the history of homosexuality, gender variance, and the Diagnostic and Statistical Manual. *Archives of Sexual Behavior, 39*(2), 427–460.

    Meyerowitz, J. J. (2009). *How sex changed*. Cambridge, MA: Harvard University Press.

    Reisner, S. L., Bradford, J., Hopwood, R., Gonzalez, A., Makadon, H., Todisco, D., . . . & Mayer, K. (2015). Comprehensive Transgender Healthcare: The Gender Affirming Clinical and Public Health Model of Fenway Health. *Journal of Urban Health*, 1–9.

    Riggle, E. D., Rostosky, S. S., McCants, L. E., & Pascale-Hague, D. (2011). The positive aspects of a transgender self-identification. *Psychology & Sexuality, 2*(2), 147–158.

    Sallans, R. K. (2016). Lessons from a transgender patient for health care professionals. *AMA Journal of Ethics, 18*(11), 1140.

    Schuster, T. L., Dobson, M., Jauregui, M., & Blanks, R. H. (2004). Wellness Lifestyles I: A theoretical framework linking wellness, health lifestyles, and complementary and alternative medicine. *The Journal of Alternative & Complementary Medicine, 10*(2), 349–356.

19. James, S. E., & Herman, J. (2017). The Report of the 2015 US Transgender Survey: Executive Summary. National Center for Transgender Equality.

20. Human Rights Campaign. (2019). Corporate Equality Index 2018. Human Rights Campaign. https://assets2.hrc.org/files/assets/resources/CEI-2019-FullReport.pdf

21. https://19thnews.org/2021/05/biden-restores-transgender-aca-protections-ending-trump-era-of-uncertainty/

22. https://transgenderlawcenter.org/wp-content/uploads/2013/04/Economic-Impact-Assessment-Gender-Nondiscrimination-In-Health-Insurance.pdf

23. Gooren, L. J., Giltay, E. J., & Bunck, M. C. (2007). Long-term treatment of transsexuals with cross-sex hormones: Extensive personal experience. *Journal of Clinical Endocrinology and Metabolism, 93*(1), 19.

24. Gooren, Wierckx, K., Elaut, E., Declercq, E., Heylens, G., De Cuypere, G., Taes, Y., Kaufman, J. M., & T'Sjoen, G. (2013). Prevalence of cardiovascular disease and cancer during cross-sex hormone therapy in a large cohort of trans persons: A case–control study. *European Journal of Endocrinology, 169*(4), 471–478.

25. Santos, G. M., Rapues, J., Wilson, E. C., Macias, O., Packer, T., Colfax, G., & Raymond, H. F. (2014). Alcohol and substance use among transgender women in San Francisco: Prevalence and association with human immunodeficiency virus infection. *Drug and Alcohol Review, 33*(3), 287–295.

26. Reback, C. J., & Fletcher, J. B. (2014). HIV prevalence, substance use, and sexual risk behaviors among transgender women recruited through outreach. *AIDS and Behavior, 18*(7), 1359–1367.

27. Lyons, T., Shannon, K., Pierre, L., Small, W., Krüsi, A., & Kerr, T. (2015). A qualitative study of transgender individuals' experiences in residential addiction treatment settings: Stigma and inclusivity. *Substance Abuse Treatment, Prevention, and Policy, 10*(1), 1.

28. James, S. E., Herman, J. L., Rankin, S., Keisling, M., Mottet, L., & Anafi, M. (2016). The Report of the 2015 U.S. Transgender Survey. Washington, DC: National Center for Transgender Equality.

29. Becasen, J. S., Denard, C. L., Mullins, M. M., Higa, D. H., & Sipe, T. A. (2019). Estimating the prevalence of HIV and sexual behaviors among the US transgender population: A

systematic review and meta-analysis, 2006–2017. *American Journal of Public Health, 109*(1), e1–e8.

30. McCormack, S., Dunn, D. T., Desai, M., Dolling, D. I., Gafos, M., Gilson, R., Sullivan, A. K., Clarke, A., Reeves, I., Schembri, G., Mackie, N., Bowman, C., Lacey, C. J., Apea, V., Brady, M., Fox, J., Taylor, S., Antonucci, S., Khoo, S. H., Rooney, J., . . . Mackie, N. (2016). Pre-exposure prophylaxis to prevent the acquisition of HIV-1 infection (PROUD): Effectiveness results from the pilot phase of a pragmatic open-label randomised trial. *The Lancet, 387*(10013), 53–60.

31. Deutsch, M. B., Glidden, D. V., Sevelius, J., Keatley, J., McMahan, V., Guanira, J., Kallas, E. G., Chariyalertsak, S., & Grant, R. M. (2015). HIV pre-exposure prophylaxis in transgender women: A subgroup analysis of the iPrEx trial. *The Lancet HIV, 2*(12), e512–e519.

32. DeMay, M. (2007). *Practical principles of cytopathology* (Rev. ed.). Chicago, IL: American Society for Clinical Pathology Press.

33. Huyett, J. (2011). Love your hole: An ass manifesto. *Radical Faerie Digest*, Winter, 148.

34. http://sherbourne.on.ca/wp-content/uploads/2014/02/Guidelines-and-Protocols-for-Comprehensive-Primary-Care-for-Trans-Clients-2015.pdf

35. Hembree, W. C., Cohen-Kettenis, P. T., Gooren, L., Hannema, S. E., Meyer, W. J., Murad, M. H., Rosenthal, S. M., Safer, J. D., Tangpricha, V., & T'Sjoen, G. G. (2017). Endocrine treatment of gender-dysphoric/gender-incongruent persons: An Endocrine Society clinical practice guideline. *The Journal of Clinical Endocrinology & Metabolism, 102*(11), 3869–3903.

36. Brown, G. R. (2015). Breast cancer in transgender veterans: A ten-case series. *LGBT Health, 2*(1), 77–80.

37. Grynberg, M., Franchin, R., Dubost, G., Colau, J.C., Bremont-Weil, C., Frydman, R., & Ayoubi, J.M. (2010). Histology of genital tract and breast tissue after long-term testosterone administration in a female-to-male transsexual population. *Reproductive Biomedicine Online, 20*(4), 553–558.

38. US Preventive Services Task Force. (2004). Screening for testicular cancer. https://www.uspreventiveservicestaskforce.org/Page/Document/UpdateSummaryFinal/testicular-cancer-screening

39. https://www.uspreventiveservicestaskforce.org/Page/Document/RecommendationStatementFinal/prostate-cancer-screening1

40. Makadon, H., Mayer, K., Potter, J., & Goldhammer, H. (Eds.). (2007). *The Fenway guide to lesbian, bisexual and transgender health*. Philadelphia, PA: American College of Physicians.

41. Trum, H. W., Hoebeke, P., & Gooren, L. J. (2015). Sex reassignment of transsexual people from a gynecologist's and urologist's perspective. *Acta Obstetricia et Gynecologica Scandinavica, 94*(6), 563–567.

42. https://transequality.org/sites/default/files/docs/usts/USTS-Full-Report-Dec17.pdf

43. https://avp.org/ncavp/ or call Call the Hotline: 212-714-1141

44. Polly, R., & Nicole, J. (2011). Understanding the transsexual patient: Culturally sensitive care in emergency nursing practice. *Advanced Emergency Nursing Journal, 33*(1), 55–64. doi: 10.1097/TME.0b013e3182080ef4

45. Schaffer, N. (2005) Transgender patients: Implications for emergency department policy and practice. *Journal of Emergency Nursing, 31*(4), 405–407.

46. Samuels, E. A., Tape, C., Garber, N., Bowman, S., & Choo, E. K. (2018). "Sometimes you feel like the freak show": A qualitative assessment of emergency care experiences among transgender and gender-nonconforming patients. *Annals of Emergency Medicine, 71*(2), 170–182.

47. Gorton, R. N., & Berdahl, C. T. (2018). Improving the quality of emergency care for transgender patients. *Annals of Emergency Medicine, 71*(2), 189–192.

48. Sevelius, J. (2010). There's no pamphlet for the kind of sex I have: HIV-related risk factors and protective behaviors among transgender men who have sex with non-transgender men. *Journal of the Association of Nurses in AIDS Care, 20*(5), 398–410. doi:10.106/j.jana.2009.06.001

49. Herbst, J. H., Jacobs, E. D., Finlayson, T. J., McKleroy, V. S., Neumann, M. S., & Crepaz, N. (2008). Estimating HIV prevalence and risk behaviors of transgender persons in the United States: A systematic review. *AIDS and Behavior, 12*(1), 1–17.

50. Nemoto, T., Operario, D., Keatley, J., Han, L., & Soma, T. (2004). HIV risk behaviors among male-to-female transgender persons of color in San Francisco. *American Journal of Public Health, 94*(7), 1193–1199.

51. Kosenko, K. A. (2011). Contextual influences on sexual risk-taking in the transgender community. *Journal of Sex Research, 48*(2-3), 285–296.

52. NAM. (2013). HIV transmission and testing. http://www.aidsmap.com/Estimated-risk-per-exposure/page/1324038/

53. Planned Parenthood. (2013). Birth control. http://www.plannedparenthood.org/health-topics/birth-control/female-condom-4223.htm and http://www.plannedparenthood.org/health-topics/birth-control/condom-10187.htm

54. Light, A. D., Obedin-Maliver, J., Sevelius, J. M., & Kerns, J. L. (2014). Transgender men who experienced pregnancy after female-to-male gender transitioning. *Obstetrics & Gynecology, 124*(6), 1120–1127.

55. https://www.acog.org/About-ACOG/ACOG-Districts/District-VII/Contraception-for-Transmasculine?IsMobileSet=false

56. US Preventive Services Task Force. (2009). Folic acid to prevent neural tube defects. https://www.uspreventiveservicestaskforce.org/uspstf/recommendation/folic-acid-for-the-prevention-of-neural-tube-defects-preventive-medication#fullrecommendationstart

57. De Roo, C., Tilleman, K., T'Sjoen, G., & De Sutter, P. (2016). Fertility options in transgender people. *International Review of Psychiatry, 28*(1), 112–119.

12

MEDICAL TRANSITION
A.C. Demidont, Paul Irons, and Jamie E. Mehringer

INTRODUCTION

As transgender and gender expansive (T/GE) people, we have the choice to pursue medical interventions to change our bodies to better align them with our gender identity—if we so desire. The term "medical transition" refers to using hormones or other medications to change our physical body. In this chapter, the use of hormones for transition is referred to as gender-affirming hormone therapy.

HORMONES AND MEDICAL TRANSITION

Hormones are chemicals made naturally within our body that act as messengers to various tissues and organs. Hormones are involved in many complex processes within our body, including metabolism, growth, and the development of our secondary sex characteristics. The effects of hormones can be immediate or take a significant amount of time to generate change within our bodies. For example, there are hormones that act quickly to tell us we are hungry, full, or tired, and then, there are others, such as sex hormones, that take time to bring about changes. Those hormones referred to as "sex hormones" are involved in creating features and characteristics (i.e., hair growth patterns, body fat distribution, etc.) typically viewed by society as either feminine or masculine (although "sex hormones" also have functions unrelated to sex/gender).

Medical transition involves using medications such as exogenous (created outside of the body) hormones to add or block certain hormones in order to bring about physical changes to our bodies to better align them with our gender identity.[1] If we are children or adolescents, we may use hormone blockers to stop our body from progressing through puberty in a way that would have created external sexual characteristics that may not be fitting with our gender identity. In adulthood, we may use hormones to create more typically feminine or masculine characteristics, or to get our bodies to a point of somewhere in-between. The goals of gender affirming hormone therapy are unique to each of us. Some of us pursue gender-affirming hormones to transition along a binary, from one end of society's gender spectrum to the other, while others of us use gender affirming hormones to reach a place of more comfort in our nonbinary or gender expansive bodies and identities.

Examples of sex hormones include testosterone, estrogen, dihydrotestosterone (DHT), and progesterone.

HOW A FLAT CHEST HELPED ME FIT INTO A DRESS

Markus "Star" Harwood-Jones (he/they) is a space-case and day-dreamer living in Tkaronto. As an author, illustrator, and filmmaker, Star's main artistic works include the all-trans documentary "Mosaic," the "Confessions of a Teenage Transsexual Whore" zines, a collection of short stories titled, "Everything & All at Once," and the companion novels "Romeo for Real" and "Just Julian."

"I've seen those transsexuals before, they don't look real, they look like half-men, is that really what you want?!" I look down, my face hot with anger and shame. We talk about my life like it's up for debate, like the way we argue over the translation of bible verses or the political climate. I know he doesn't understand and, to be fair, I don't understand him either. Though, also to be fair, I'm not trying to stop him from living in his body as he sees fit.

Five years later, I'm sunbathing in nothing but pink short-shorts. He calls out, teasing, "Sort of femme, don't you think?" I turn back with a smile, toes dipped in the soft pull of lake water against stone, sun bouncing off my radiant chest. I am confident in my gender identity no matter what I'm wearing.

Throughout my transition, I kept a black skirt as a secret. I would wear it only when alone, usually drunk. With so many people lining up to tell me I couldn't "really" be a boy, I marched staunchly into aggressive masculinity. I was a no-homo homo, a queer driven by fear.

Losing the last toe of my footing on stable housing, I traveled through a myriad of liminal spaces. Trans people were always the ones who would take me in, help make sure I was fed. Long nights talking gender and borders, paired with long days alone on sidewalk corners, I found myself a gender existentialist. Those words rang in my head again—"half-man." I wondered if this really was the beginning of a huge regret.

Accepting insecurity, I drew on childhood heroes from old cartoons and tips I picked up in my dreams. Bringing out my stubborn passion, I dove to galaxies of dresses, leggings, and accessories, while holding space for my flannel and skinny jeans. "Are you detransitioning?" an acquaintance asks, looking over my black knee-highs, pleated miniskirt, and "Fuck the Cis-Tem" top. I laugh—I am getting more trans by the minute!

None of this would have been possible without access to medical transition. For me, having a flat, fuzzy chest was what I needed so I could pull on a low-cut sweater-dress. Now, it doesn't matter what anyone says—I have the body, hair, and wardrobe of my dreams. It is always growing, changing, and shimmering, just like me!

WHO UNDERGOES MEDICAL TRANSITION?

Gender dysphoria is a medical term that refers to discomfort or distress that some of us feel in our physical bodies as a result of our sex assigned at birth and physical characteristics not matching our gender identity. Many, but not all, T/GE people experience dysphoria. Some of us have an extreme amount of dysphoria, while others may not have any dysphoria at all. For some of us, the discrepancy between our sex assigned at birth and our gender identity leads us to seek out medical transition to help alleviate some or all of this discomfort or distress. Going through medical transition may help us feel more comfortable or authentic in our own skin and in how we present ourselves to the world. For those of us who choose to pursue gender-affirming hormone therapy, there is variability in which medications we desire and in what effects we are looking for. Everyone's gender journey and transition is unique to their needs and desires. There is no one particular medication or treatment that is right for all of us.

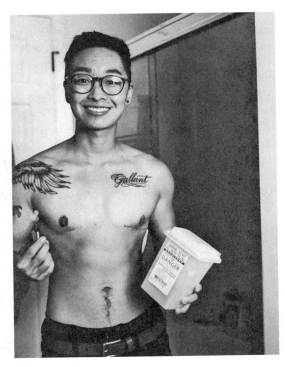

Noah (@quinoahpowersalad), 2 years on testosterone and living life authentically.

I have taken feminizing hormones for the past 15 months (estrogen, progesterone, and an anti-androgen). Mostly I've enjoyed a far better mental outlook and peace of mind since starting hormone therapy.

HOW DO I KNOW I'M READY FOR MEDICAL TRANSITION?

The decision to undergo medical transition varies greatly from person to person. Some of us do not feel we need medical interventions, while others of us feel we need gender-affirming hormone therapy to live as our authentic selves. Some of us begin our journey with social transition and no medications or surgery, whereas others may start with hormones. There is no one way or "right" way to transition or to be T/GE. We are unique individuals with different goals, desires, and life situations that drive our decisions around our gender identity and transition.

I was the first gender nonconforming individual that my provider had dealt with. But she had a ton of great information about what kind of changes I could expect if I did want to try hormone therapy or other more permanent bodily changes. I have not chosen to pursue anything yet.

There are many things we may take into account when we are planning to start gender-affirming hormone therapy. We may consider our own needs, desires, and well-being; our relationships with family members, partners, chosen family, and friends; our school or work situations, finances, and health insurance in order to determine when the time is right for us to start our transition. Although we all want to find the "perfect" time for starting medical transition, this rarely exists. Instead, we need to think about what is the best time given the realities of our individual life situations. Talking with people close to us, with a therapist, and/or with fellow members of the T/GE community may help us navigate obstacles along the way. Overall, the decision to start medical transition is a very personal one. We should not feel rushed or have pressure placed upon us by others. The decision is up to us, unless we are either underage or deemed not to have the capacity to make an informed decision. In this case, in most circumstances, we would need our parent, caregiver, or guardian's approval.

It is a myth that using gender affirming hormones or having certain surgeries is what defines being trans. In reality, as T/GE people we are all different, and we have a wide range of experiences, needs, and gender and life goals. There is no particular medication, surgery, or treatment that any of us require to be "trans enough." It is also a myth that "passing" is the end goal for all of us. It is important to note that although some of us desire to "pass," there are many of us who do not necessarily desire that ability. There are also those of us who do desire to "pass," but may not be able to for any number of reasons, such as genetics, physical characteristics, finances, relationship needs, and so on. Additionally, it is not uncommon for our transition goals and desires to change over the course of our transition, whether that is one year from now, five years from now, or ten years from now. Feeling "trans enough" or "passing" should not be our only motivation for transitioning.

Many nonbinary people consider taking lower doses of hormones or taking them for a short period of time and then stopping. After considering the pros and cons, we have the right to decide for ourselves if these options are appealing to us, and healthcare providers should not pressure us into making a binary transition if that is not what we desire.

I didn't do medical transition as it would impact too much on my life and well-being in a way that could undermine the level of success I've had being genderqueer.

I'M READY FOR MEDICAL TRANSITION. NOW WHAT?

Once we have decided that medical transition is the best course of action for our own individual needs and desires, we will need to figure out how to access gender affirming medical care. It is important for us to seek out a medical provider with experience providing gender affirming medical care and with whom we can feel safe and comfortable.

Depending on where we live, our finances, our insurance status, and other factors, it may be challenging to find such a medical provider.

I see a clinician for my transition, but I must travel 45 minutes to get to him. I do not have a closer doctor or any other medical professional that I can reliably see for my medical transition because there are none in my area and testosterone is a controlled substance, so I can't go to a minute clinic or urgent care to receive my treatments.

Researching on the Internet, talking with other T/GE community members, or calling gender affirming clinics or community resources may be the best way to find knowledgeable and affirming providers in our geographic area.

I had to identify all specialists myself in the beginning of my transition. They were identified through word of mouth within the community.

Over the past few decades we have seen more and more medical providers seeking training in gender affirming health care, as well as an increasing number of insurance companies and health systems covering the costs of gender affirming health care. Additionally, the informed consent model for medical transition has given us more bodily autonomy to choose when and how we want to transition. There is still plenty of progress to be made for all of our T/GE community to be able to access the care that we desire and deserve. We are hopeful that the strides made will continue on until full T/GE healthcare equality is reached.

The clinic that did my hormone treatment was fantastic—they had no issues with me being nonbinary, with wanting to start on a low dose, and with stopping hormones with the option to start again later if I decided to.

The Remedy: Queer and Trans Voices on Health and Healthcare is a diverse collection of real-life stories from queer and trans people on their own healthcare experiences and challenges (edited by Zena Sharman, Arsenal Pulp Press, 2016).

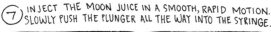

"How To Inject A Galaxy" is a short comic Noah made to celebrate six years on T, mediate their anxiety with self-injecting, and spread body positivity. Noah Grigni is a non binary comic artist, writer and organizer from Decatur, Georgia, currently living in Boston, Massachusetts. Their art is a reminder to heal, a conversation with fluidity, and a playful celebration of queer love. (noahgrigni.com, IG: @ngrigni)

TRANSITION-RELATED MEDICAL ISSUES FOR PEOPLE OF COLOR

Asa Radix, MD, PhD, MPH (he/they) is the Senior Director of Research and Education and an internist/infectious disease specialist and research scientist at the Callen-Lorde Community Health Center in New York City.

Some important transition-related medical issues predominantly affect people of color. For starters, people of color may experience additional barriers to medical care due to the structural racism that impacts all aspects of our lives, including discrimination in education, housing, employment, earnings, and health benefits. The direct result is that trans people of color can find it harder to access respectful and patient-centered health care, especially providers who understand the effects of hormones and other gender affirming interventions on our bodies.

Estrogen—and to a lesser extent progesterone—can cause uneven skin pigmentation, called *melasma*, mainly on the cheeks and the forehead. The skin condition predominantly occurs in people with darker skin tones, and it may affect up to 20% of those who initiate hormones. Sunblock (at least SPF 30) can be used daily for prevention of melasma when starting hormones. Treatment for this condition includes prescription skin creams to reduce the increased pigmentation.

Acne is a common issue affecting transgender men who start testosterone. In people of color, especially those of African descent, acne may result in darkened spots, called *postinflammatory hyperpigmentation*. These spots may resolve on their own, but they may require prescription-strength creams to treat the areas. Many acne medications, such as benzoyl peroxide, are available without a prescription, or you can request a prescription-strength treatment from your medical provider.

Pseudofolliculitis barbae, or razor bumps, can occur in trans men who use testosterone. The condition mainly affects people of African descent and those with naturally curly hair. After shaving, the hair curls and re-enters the skin, causing bumps. If the condition continues, it can result in hyperpigmentation (dark spots), infection, and keloids (bumps and scarring). Prevention techniques include allowing facial hair to grow, utilizing single-blade (avoid double- or triple-blade) razors, using depilatory creams or powders (such as Magic Shave), and shaving along the grain. Early treatment of infection is also important.

People of color may be more prone to *keloids*, or abnormal growth of scar tissue, after undergoing surgery. Keloids predominantly affect people of African, Asian, and Latinx descent, but they can affect anyone with darker skin tones. Keloid formation after top surgery is especially concerning for trans men. For those with a history of scar formation, the surgeon may opt to reduce the risk of keloids by injecting steroids or using silicone elastomer sheeting. Once keloids have occurred, treatment may involve steroid injections, surgical revision of the scar, and topical treatments.

PUBERTY 101

To understand how hormones such as estrogen and testosterone affect our bodies, it can be helpful to take a step back and examine how these hormones affect us during puberty. Puberty starts deep inside the brain at two areas called the hypothalamus and the pituitary gland.[2] These areas of the brain control many types of brain and bodily functions, including puberty, which is the development of adult sexual characteristics. Puberty generally starts between the ages of 9 and 13 years old. The hypothalamus signals to the rest of our body that it is time to begin puberty—similar to a puberty alarm clock. The hypothalamus makes two types of hormones: LH and FSH, which travel through the body. For those of us born with testicles, LH and FSH tell the testes to start maturing and to make the hormone testosterone. The testosterone made by the testes causes further growth of the penis and testes, an increase in body and facial hair, deepening of the voice, and the development of sperm. For those of us born with ovaries, LH and FSH tell the ovaries to start maturing and to make the hormone estrogen. The estrogen produced by the ovaries causes breast development, menstrual cycles (periods), a redistribution of body fat (typically more fat around the thighs and buttocks), and the ability to become pregnant.

Puberty Blockers

Puberty blockers are medicines that can be used to pause the progression of puberty. The medical term for puberty blockers is gonadotropin releasing hormone (GnRH) agonists. They work by telling the hypothalamus and pituitary gland to stop making LH and FSH—as if the blockers are hitting the snooze button on the puberty alarm clock.

For T/GE youth born with testes, puberty blockers prevent the testes from making as much testosterone, thus preventing the effects of testosterone such as development of facial and body hair, further growth of the penis and testes, and deepening of the voice. If someone has already had a lot of puberty changes before they start taking blockers, the blockers are not able to undo all of these changes. If blockers are started after facial or body hair has already developed, they won't eliminate the hair, but they will make the hair grow in more slowly and prevent further expansion of facial and body hair growth. If the voice has already deepened, blockers will not be able to change this.

For T/GE youth born with ovaries, puberty blockers prevent the ovaries from making as much estrogen, thus halting additional breast growth, menstrual cycles (periods), and further development of the ovaries. If someone has already started having periods, blockers will still be able to stop periods moving forward. For youth who have already had breast development, however, blockers will not be able to reverse this, but will prevent further breast growth.

As long as a young person continues taking puberty blockers, their pubertal development will be paused—the blockers will keep hitting the snooze button on the puberty alarm clock. The effects of puberty blockers are *completely reversible*. If the puberty blockers are stopped, the alarm clock will go off again, and puberty will pick up where it left off before the initiation of puberty blockers.[3]

Bobby, Eleanor, Dakota, and Hudson. "To our brave and bold boys—you are amazing humans and we're proud of you today and always for your courage and compassion!" (Captured by Candace Photography)

How Are Puberty Blockers Given?

There are two main types of puberty blockers available. Both of these work in the same way and equally well. Which type of puberty blocker we are prescribed depends on the availability of the medication, personal preference, and affordability or insurance coverage.

1. **Injection (shot).** There are a few different types of injectable puberty-blocking medicines available. The shots are usually given once every three months, though the frequency of shots varies, depending on which particular medicine is used and what dose is prescribed.
2. **Implant.** With an implant, the puberty blocking medicine is contained in a tiny plastic rod, about the size of a matchstick. The implant can either be inserted in a medical office with an injection of a local anesthetic to numb the area, or it can be done with sedation in a hospital. To place the implant, a very small hole is cut in our skin and the implant is inserted under the skin of our upper arm. The implant holds enough medication to last for at least a full year, though oftentimes it can last even longer. After one to two years, the implant will need to be taken out by making a tiny cut in the skin and removing the rod. A new implant can be inserted at the same time if we are going to remain on blockers.

When Can We Begin Puberty Blockers?

We can begin puberty blockers once our body has started to undergo early puberty changes, such as the development of breast buds, genital hair, and/or testicular growth. The blockers cannot be started before puberty has begun because it is important to know that our brain and body parts involved with puberty are all working properly before starting a medicine to pause them. If we have already reached the end of puberty, blockers can still be used. The blockers won't be able to alter the irreversible body changes caused by puberty, such as our voice dropping, facial hair development, or breast growth that has already occurred. Some young people who are already at the end of puberty may be able to begin gender affirming hormones (estrogen or testosterone) without taking puberty blockers.

Before starting puberty blockers, we will need to have a physical exam with our medical provider and bloodwork drawn to measure our hormone levels. We will also need to have consent from our parent(s) or guardian(s) if we are younger than 18 years old. Many medical providers may also require that we first be evaluated by a mental health professional before starting puberty blockers to confirm that the medication is in our best interest.

The Seattle Children's Hospital and UCLA Health YouTube channels have informative videos on puberty blockers.

Side Effects and Risks

Overall, puberty blockers are very safe and well-tolerated. But every medicine, even those that can be bought over the counter, has potential risks and side effects. One of the most common side effects of puberty blockers is hot flashes, which often go away over time. Some of us on blockers may also notice that we have a decreased sex drive or less energy than we did before taking the medication. One of the most serious concerns that has to be considered when starting puberty blockers is our bone health. The sex hormones estrogen and testosterone aren't just important for puberty changes, they are also important for making strong bones. If we were to stay on puberty blockers for many years and not start gender affirming hormone therapy (i.e., estrogen or testosterone) or let our body's innate puberty take place, we would eventually develop weak bones and be at risk for osteoporosis and fractures. Typically, though, we will be ready to begin gender affirming hormone therapy long before our bone health is in jeopardy. Medical providers will monitor our bone density periodically while we are on blockers.

Fertility

Puberty blockers themselves do not have any long-term impact on our fertility. If we were to stop taking puberty blockers, our ovaries or testes would continue maturing, and we would expect to be able to produce mature ova (eggs) or sperm that would enable us to have a baby. Our fertility may be affected, however, once we start taking gender affirming hormones (i.e., testosterone or estrogen). If we begin taking blockers before we are done going through puberty, our ovaries or testes become paused in an immature state. If we later start taking gender affirming hormones while our ovaries or testes are still immature, these hormones may stop our ovaries or testes from ever fully maturing, preventing our sexual organs from producing eggs or sperm needed to create a pregnancy. If we start blockers before our body has finished going through puberty, we need to think about our future goals and preferences for building a family. For those of us who want to maximize our chances of being able to have a child with our own genetics in the future, we may want to consider coming off of blockers and undergoing fertility preservation (such as freezing sperm or harvesting eggs) prior to starting on estrogen or testosterone. If our ovaries or testes are not yet mature, sometimes this means that we have to allow our biological puberty to progress further to allow for fertility preservation. When making the decision about whether or not to undergo fertility preservation, we and our families/guardians need to take into consideration our personal goals for family building, our comfort (or lack thereof) with undergoing fertility preservation procedures, the cost (it is rarely covered by insurance), and the potential risks of stopping the blockers, which would allow our biological puberty to continue.[4]

> *I'm not sure if I want children or not in the future, but I am really sad that I didn't consider it more prior to transition or that people didn't inform me more about those choices. I've since looked into fertility options but not sure if I want to pursue them at this time.*

How Long Does It Make Sense to Stay on Puberty Blockers?

How long we stay on puberty blockers depends on a number of factors: our goals for our medical transition, when gender affirming hormones are started (or not), our bone health, and our access to the blockers. For those of us on blockers who begin testosterone, testosterone alone is usually enough to keep our periods away and prevent our biological puberty from restarting. Blockers are often continued for several months to a year after starting testosterone, or discontinued as we reach a stable adult dose of testosterone. For those of us on blockers who begin estrogen, oftentimes the estrogen alone is not enough to keep our biological puberty from restarting. Those of us who start estrogen typically will stay on puberty blockers or begin spironolactone to suppress our body's testosterone production in order to avoid further growth of body/facial hair or other undesired puberty changes, unless we have had our testes removed, which would prevent our biological puberty from kicking back in.

Other Medicines for T/GE Youth

For those of us born with testes, spironolactone is another medicine that may be used to decrease the effects of our body's testosterone. Although it isn't a puberty blocker, spironolactone may still offer some benefits—especially for those of us who aren't able to start blockers due to cost/insurance coverage or other impediments. Spironolactone is a pill that is taken once or twice a day and is described in more detail later in this chapter.

For those of use born with ovaries who aren't on testosterone or blockers, there are a few different medications that can be used to stop our menstrual periods. All of these medications contain a hormone called progesterone, which helps to stop menstrual periods by thinning out the lining of the uterus and stopping the ovaries from releasing eggs. Some of these medications may also include a very small amount of estrogen. All of these medications are typically known as "birth control" methods, but are used for a variety of other medical reasons as well. These medications can be given in several different ways: pills, patches, injections, or as an IUD (intrauterine device). These medications can stop periods, but they won't prevent other puberty changes from happening, such as breast growth. In most states, because these medications are typically used for birth control and sexual health, medical providers are able to prescribe these medications to youth under 18 without notifying or needing permission from a parent/guardian. Information on these medications is available in the General, Medical, and Reproductive Health chapter.

> *I currently take a birth control pill, both to prevent pregnancy and because it helps me experience less painful menstrual cycles. I have very severe cycles and I've had them since I was super young. So for me being able to take the pill, it's helped my dysphoria subside quite a bit.*

QMed, started by Dr. Izzy Lowell, a Family Medicine physician, was founded to improve access to hormone therapy for trans* patients in the Southeast through in-person and telemedicine visits. QMed accepts patients of all ages and provides puberty blockers for those yet to enter puberty. QMed is now operating in Georgia, South Carolina, North Carolina, Alabama, Tennessee, Mississippi, Florida, Virginia, West Virginia, Kentucky, and Maine, with more New England states coming soon!

INFORMED CONSENT

In recent years, medical providers and transgender healthcare guidelines have moved to informed consent models of care for providing hormone therapy. Informed consent improves our ability to access gender affirming hormones and empowers us to have more

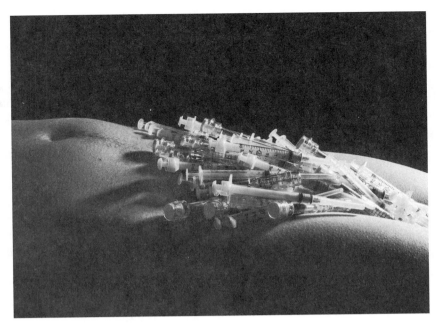

Syringes. "All of the syringes I've ever used on my body, for my body." (Cai Quirk, caiquirk.com)

control over how to align our physical bodies with our gender identities. Informed consent also helps break down barriers to care and gatekeeping requirements previously commonplace in transgender health care. Informed consent works to expand access to gender affirming hormones and decrease the lag time between when we decide we want/need hormones and when we are able to obtain these medications from healthcare providers. Informed consent recognizes that the transition process is different for each of us, and medical transition may precede social transition.

Previous transgender care models required that we socially transition and live as our true gender for a specified period of time (generally a year) before we could access gender-affirming hormone therapy. This arbitrary requirement was created by a community of cisgender medical providers who did not fully understand our needs and the dangers associated with forcing us to attempt to fit into societal gender roles and presentations without the benefits of hormone therapy for those of us who desired/needed these medications. It is emotionally and physically unsafe for many of us to live in society as our authentic selves when our bodies are visibly mismatched with our gender identities. Thus, the gatekeeping models of care created additional dangers for us and often caused rifts and distrust between us and our healthcare providers.

> It should not be difficult or expensive to get the care we need, and we should not have to prove who we are or what we want to other people.

The Informed Consent Model for Hormone Therapy

Informed consent is a relatively simple process. It requires that our treating healthcare provider counsels us on the risks and benefits of gender affirming hormone therapy, and assesses our capacity to make an informed decision about treatment. This allows most of us to make a voluntary and informed choice to begin or not begin gender affirming hormone therapy. Informed consent originates from the legal and ethical right of patients to decide what happens to their bodies, and from the ethical duty of the physician to involve the patient in their own healthcare decisions.

The informed consent model only applies to adults 18 years of age or older who are able to make their own healthcare decisions. The decision-making process for youth or those with significant emotional or intellectual disabilities generally requires a multidisciplinary approach with mental health assessment and parent/guardian or family involvement.

WHAT ARE THE ELEMENTS OF INFORMED CONSENT?

The most important part of informed consent is that we have the opportunity to be active and informed participants in our own health care decisions. With regard to gender affirming hormone therapy, it is generally accepted that informed consent includes a discussion of the following elements:[5]

- The nature of gender-affirming hormone therapy
- Available medical options for gender affirming hormone therapy
- The relevant risks, benefits, and uncertainties related to each option for gender affirming hormone therapy
- The timeframe for effects
- Assessment of our understanding of the risks, benefits, potential side effects, and limitations of gender affirming hormone therapy
- An informed decision and acceptance of gender affirming hormone therapy by the patient
- Voluntary consent, meaning that there was no coercion or undue outside influence pressuring our decision-making around starting gender affirming hormone therapy

The informed consent model for gender affirming hormone therapy works to empower us within the medical system to access necessary and potentially life-saving hormones. Informed consent allows us to be active participants in our own health care decisions around gender affirming hormone therapy and encourages us to collaborate with our medical provider in affirming our gender through medical transition.

My first effort at getting services was at a local Planned Parenthood clinic. They were concerned about starting me on HRT due to some other risk factors (age and blood pressure mainly). When I went to the clinic where my PCP practices, they were more prepared to work with me and operate under "informed consent" guidelines and allowed me to decide.

DON'T PUT YOURSELF IN DANGER

Aydian Dowling (he/him) is a trans rights activist, philanthropist, model, and entrepreneur. Aydian received national attention for being the semifinalist for the November 2016 "Ultimate Men's Health Guy" contest for Men's Health *magazine. This monumental event marked Aydian as the first transgender man to be featured on the cover of a mainstream magazine.*

Oddly enough for me, when I first came out as trans, I had no intention of starting hormones or getting any kind of surgery. I was scared to do anything medical to my body because there was not enough research or information on the long-term effects of HRT or surgeries on transgender bodies. My plan was to try to "naturally transition" as they called it back then. I used weight lifting, supplements, voice lessons, and other things to help me feel more comfortable in the body I was born into. That didn't last long.

After some underground research, I discovered the upkeep of this kind of transition would cost hundreds of dollars per month. The supplements that I was told would help me were not only expensive but also extremely dangerous. These supplements were neither FDA approved nor appropriately regulated, which meant I could be altering my body unaware of what was really happening inside of me. They could lead to liver damage or heart disease, and some were literally over-the-counter steroids that have since been pulled off of the shelves. I'm happy I knew internally that doing things like getting T off the black market was an unsafe and risky thing to do. But many transgender people feel too lost, too broke, and too broken to find the services (if any) available to them.

If you don't have professional, reliable, and knowledgeable trans-friendly support on how to align your internal self with your body, you put yourself at risk. That's why it's important we, as trans people, continue to advocate for ourselves within our healthcare system. We also desperately need our cis allies to step up and request this kind of research, information, and training.

If you're a transgender person who needs to change to feel more empowered within your body, you deserve the medical assistance you need. You do not need to put yourself in danger. You are worthy of the money and time it takes to have these changes made. Your voice is powerful enough to join us in the advocacy for our healthcare needs.

How Else Are People Getting Hormones?

Unfortunately, the ability for some of us to start gender affirming hormone therapy may be delayed for various reasons, such as not having health insurance, not being able to afford our copays for the medications, and/or not having an accessible T/GE-knowledgeable and affirming medical provider in our area. As a result, some of us seek out alternative ways of obtaining gender affirming hormones.

> *I was taking injections of testosterone for six months. I noticed more body hair and facial changes as well as weight loss during that time, but stopped treatment because of homelessness.*

Some of us may access hormones off the street or from other T/GE people we know. Others of us may obtain hormones from other countries or by ordering them off the Internet. It is important to recognize that if we use these means of obtaining hormones, there are many risks, including that we may not be getting the medication or quality of hormones that we think we are getting. Also, we may face legal repercussions if caught obtaining hormones in this way. Although estrogen, progesterone, and spironolactone may be obtained for individual use from other countries with limited legal repercussions, testosterone is a different class of medication, deemed a "controlled substance." Getting it off the street, through the mail, or from another country is a felony in the United States. Additionally, using hormones or other medications without monitoring by a healthcare professional comes with further risks. If we are using injectable hormones, we should ***never*** share needles. Sharing or reusing needles puts us at risk of acquiring life-threatening infections, such hepatitis B and C, and HIV/AIDS.

Getting hormones prescribed by a medical provider and distributed through a pharmacy with a prescription in our name is the only way to guarantee that the medications we are getting are safe, which means that they are what the provider says they are, that they are of the right concentration and dosage, and that they are not expired or contaminated. A medical provider can also monitor how hormones are affecting us with regular laboratory testing and check-ups to assess potential complications of hormone use. Rare but serious health risks can occur, even from proper use and dosages of gender affirming hormones.

> *I have been on HRT for three years. My first eight months were on the black market and I felt unsure of what I was getting, so I finally went to the LGBT center to see an endocrinologist and get a new GP. She basically put me on exactly the same things and dosages that I put myself on after a year of research. I was on estradiol tablets, finasteride, micronized progesterone, and spironolactone. I had an orchiectomy and have been taken off of progesterone and spiro. As far as changes to my body, they have been very miniscule in comparison to a person half my age. The most changes have been in my face.*

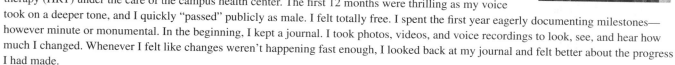

Tobey Tozier (he/him) is a social entrepreneur, founder of Transcapsule, and a transgender graphic designer from rural Maine.

Unlike a lot of the trans community, I didn't know that I was trans as a young child. Given how I always dressed, however, I was all-too-familiar with the question, "Are you a boy or a girl?" For most of my childhood, I simply saw myself as a tomboy, which was the closest word I knew that best described my identity. In my junior year of college, I learned what it meant to be transgender. I attended a talk about gender identity by a trans person who had been taking hormones for a number of years, and suddenly it clicked. I wasn't just a tomboy. Identifying as male was something that had always been a part of me, but I didn't know how to express it until that moment.

I started my transition from female to male as a senior in college, and I began hormone replacement therapy (HRT) under the care of the campus health center. The first 12 months were thrilling as my voice took on a deeper tone, and I quickly "passed" publicly as male. I felt totally free. I spent the first year eagerly documenting milestones—however minute or monumental. In the beginning, I kept a journal. I took photos, videos, and voice recordings to look, see, and hear how much I changed. Whenever I felt like changes weren't happening fast enough, I looked back at my journal and felt better about the progress I had made.

As time went on, changes became more gradual and the initial excitement faded into routine. I found it difficult to remember to continue documenting physical and emotional changes. Over time, everything became very disorganized and was all stored in different locations. It was impossible to see everything in one place on a linear timeline. Realizing that there had to be a better way, I started surveying the trans community and found that I wasn't the only person struggling to keep track of my transition. That's when I came up with the idea for Transcapsule, a mobile app tailored specifically to the trans community to document all aspects of transition. From taking photos and videos to recording body measurements and audio, Transcapsule offers a way to keep track of all of this data. The mission for Transcapsule is to help the trans community reflect on personal growth and live healthier, happier lives.

GENDER AFFIRMING HORMONE THERAPY

Everyone has varying amounts of estrogen and testosterone in their bodies. In those of us with ovaries, our bodies naturally produce higher levels of estrogen. In those of us with testicles, our bodies naturally produce higher levels of testosterone. Higher levels of estrogen are generally considered to give us what society views as more feminine features, while higher levels of testosterone give us more features considered by society to be masculine.

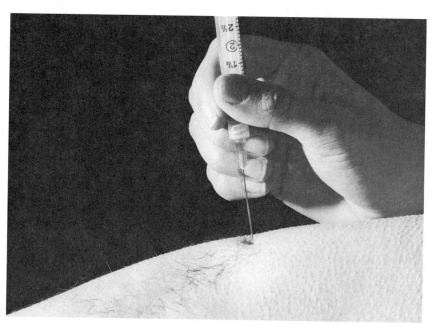

Inject. (Cai Quirk, caiquirk.com)

Gender affirming hormone therapy is generally considered either masculinizing or feminizing based on the hormones we are taking and their effects on our bodies, though these medications can also be used by those of us who identify as nonbinary or gender expansive to attain some bodily changes but not others. Gender affirming hormone therapy comes in various forms, including injectable shots, pills, skin creams, and patches. Not all methods of delivery are available for each of the medications.

Some of the bodily changes from gender affirming hormone therapy are irreversible, meaning that our bodies will not go back to the way they were prior to starting hormones, even if we stop taking the hormones. Those of us considering medical transition may want to familiarize ourselves with which effects are reversible versus irreversible, given that this can help us in our decision-making process.

Many of the changes with gender affirming hormone therapy depend on what types of hormones we take. Some things, however, do not change no matter which hormones we use. As children we have areas in our bones called growth plates where new bone is added to increase the size and length of our torso, arms, and legs. We continue to grow at these points throughout childhood and adolescence. As puberty moves toward completion, our growth plates seal together preventing further lengthening of our bones. For this reason, T/GE adults starting gender affirming hormone therapy will not experience any changes in height, limb length, or bony structure of the face/skull. The shape of our face does often change with gender affirming hormone therapy, but this is due to changes in fat deposition in our face, not due to bony change.

Howard Brown Health and the University of Iowa have posted instructional YouTube videos demonstrating hormone injection techniques. Fenway Health also has an online brochure detailing hormone injection.

EMBRACING WHO YOU ARE

Kristy Golba (she/her) is a retired Marine Corps veteran, transgender advocate, and spokesperson. She found out that courage wasn't only on the battlefield but in everyday living.

In June 2012, I retired from the Marine Corps after 31 years of service. I had decided it was finally time to embrace who I truly was. It was time to focus on me. I focused on what I needed to do for my transition. Little did I know what tragic effect my transition would have on myself and my family. As I worked with my mental health specialist, my endocrinologist, and my other doctors, I realized it was time to come out to my family. I told them about my transition thinking that they would support me. Unfortunately, I was completely wrong. My family members couldn't understand how somebody who was in the Marines for 31 years suddenly wanted to be a girl. I tried multiple times to explain myself, but they couldn't or wouldn't understand.

Shortly after I came out, on July 2, 2013, I took a shower at home, and some family members had placed an emergency medical call to the local police department falsely stating that I was suicidal and they were concerned for my safety and those of others. Two police officers found their way into the bathroom, where I was showering, and took me to the local hospital for a psychiatric evaluation. Eventually, after having the evaluation, I was released.

My family still hasn't accepted me to this day. I don't think they understand the personal cost that comes with transitioning or coming out within the LGBTQ community. People you've loved your entire life don't love you back anymore. You're forced to find new family and friends, which eventually happens over time. I think one thing everyone learns in the LGBTQ community when coming out is you'll find out who actually, cares, supports, and loves you. I hope that with education, knowledge, and time, my family and friends will come around to caring about and supporting me. The person never changed, just the gender, which comes with Embracing Who I Am.

I'll continue to work with the National Center for Transgender Equality and participate in veterans' panels and advocacy work for the Transgender and LGBTQ Community.

Feminizing Hormone Therapy and Effects

"Estrogen" is a common umbrella term used to describe feminizing hormones, but in reality, multiple hormones in the body can be considered estrogenic and not all hormones prescribed for feminization are estrogenic. The estrogenic hormone with the strongest effect in the body is called estradiol. Estradiol is the main medication used for gender affirming hormone therapy for those of us looking to develop more typically feminine bodily characteristics such as breasts, softer skin, and redistributed body fat toward the hips and thighs.

The effects of testosterone on the body are strong. For this reason, feminizing hormone therapy can require a combination of medications, usually estradiol plus a medication that blocks the effects of testosterone. In the United States, the most commonly used medication to block the effects of testosterone is spironolactone, often shortened to "spiro."

I'm on spironolactone and estradiol. I'm very happy with the feminization results of seven years. I'm able to get generic versions of these meds with insurance copays.

Another medication class known as 5-alpha-reductase inhibitors, which includes the medications finasteride and dutasteride, can also be used. These two medications specifically help combat scalp hair thinning and "male-pattern" baldness.

Finasteride did help grow back some of my hair, as well as minimized body hair greatly.

Progesterone is another hormonal medication that has some effect as a testosterone blocker, but it is mostly prescribed with the intent of increasing breast size. Research on the use of progesterone in the T/GE community is sparse; thus, the risks and benefits of this medication are uncertain. Progesterone's effectiveness is highly variable from person to person.

GnRH agonists (commonly known as puberty blockers), used in T/GE young people, can also be used in adults who want to block the effects of their body's internally produced testosterone.

I take the standard U.S. cocktail, spironolactone and estradiol (tablets), plus medroxyprogesterone. Insurance covers my endocrinologist visits, the labs he orders, and the prescription cost (which is minimal).

Aubrey "MF" Davis. "Mini photo shoot in my new apartment, feeling like the goddess I am."

EFFECTS ON BODY SHAPE AND COMPOSITION

We will experience changes in muscle mass and redistribution of fat throughout our body while on feminizing hormone therapy. These changes gradually occur as hormone therapy gets underway and is continued. Within a few months of starting estrogen, fat often gets redistributed to the hips and buttocks. It can take a couple of years of estrogen use for this redistribution to reach its greatest potential. Estrogen also causes a decrease in muscle mass and makes it more difficult to gain muscle. These changes can affect how we perform during physical activity or athletics. We should not be alarmed if we begin to experience some difficulty with more strenuous daily activities or workouts due to these changes.

> *I've been on estrogen about 22 months. I'm pleased with the results, my facial features have softened, and my body (especially the top) has become noticeably feminized.*

Our body shape and weight are also affected by how much we eat and how quickly our body processes food and converts it into energy, a process known as metabolism. Our metabolism generally slows down when we have lower levels of testosterone. As a result, those of us starting estrogen or testosterone blockers may notice that our appetite is decreased, and gaining or losing weight may become more difficult. Metabolic changes are individualized to both the person and the hormone regimen. Regardless of the possibility of changes in our weight and physical fitness, it is recommended that we stick to a consistent workout routine, because physical exercise is beneficial for our physical and mental wellness. Exercise is important for maintaining all aspects of our health, regardless of whether we are on gender affirming hormone therapy or not.

> *My skin has mostly changed over and gotten soft. Hips and cheeks are slowly filling out and my muscles are much weaker and no longer huge and bulky.*

EFFECTS ON SKIN

Increased estrogen levels in the body and decreased testosterone generally causes the skin to feel softer and less oily. Sebaceous glands in our skin generate and release oils that keep our skin from drying out. Testosterone activates these glands while estrogen makes them less active. Our acne may clear up and our skin may soften within a few months of starting feminizing hormone therapy. However, we may also experience dry skin due to decreased moisture and oil production. Similarly, testosterone also stimulates the sweat glands. Increasing estrogen levels in the body and lowering testosterone results in decreased sweating and changes in body odor.

EFFECTS ON HAIR

The hair on various areas of our body may be affected differently by gender affirming hormone therapy. For those of us born with testes, an increase in testosterone levels at puberty generates hair growth on the face and body. Testosterone stimulates the hair follicles to create thick, coarse hair. This hair growth and pattern continues regardless of estrogen use, though the hair does thin and growth is slower when we take estrogen. When we start estrogen or testosterone blockers, we generally experience slower hair growth and thinning of our facial and body hair within a few months. An overall decrease in body hair may occur after many years of continued feminizing hormone therapy.

> *My body hair has gotten thinner, but I still want laser/electrolysis to permanently remove my facial and body hair.*

Estrogen may thin body hair, and the addition of a testosterone blocker can provide further assistance. However, our faces and bodies continue to grow hair even while on feminizing hormone therapy, which may be a source of enduring discomfort or dysphoria for us. Conservative measures of hair removal, such as shaving, are a relatively inexpensive option to deal with unwanted hair, but can be a hassle. Some of us seek out procedures to more permanently address hair growth, such as electrolysis or laser hair removal. For more information on these methods, see the Surgical Transition chapter.

> *My beard growth didn't bother me before, but it certainly does now. I know that the cost of laser hair removal and/or electrolysis both for one's face and for the surgical site can be prohibitively expensive since it is not covered by insurance.*

For those of us who have already developed thinning scalp hair or balding patterns, use of estrogen or testosterone blocking medication will not regrow our hair. If we desire a fuller head of hair, some options include wearing a wig or consulting a surgeon who can perform a hair transplant.

DHT BLOCKER

Aislin Neufeldt (they/them) is an MA in sociology and is very queer. They have since been able to grow out their hair thanks to antiandrogen medication, and they are looking forward to new and holistic changes and growth.

Don't tell me my hair isn't thinning
I will show you each deficit
To which you will say
"Well, it isn't that noticeable."
I do not care. Your comment is rendered insincere.
What is apparent to me, isn't to you.
Your perceptions don't consider
My hairline's recession as bodily retaliation
Against my intentional recession of what little masculinity I once had.
My thinning has a name: male pattern baldness,
A pattern shared by the penis-holstered men
of my mother's and father's respective lineages.
Don't tell me my hair isn't thinning
Because it isn't the phallus that offends me
But rather the DHT Dysphoria
in that damn hairline of mine
I want all hair. Or no hair.
Don't tell me my hair isn't thinning
And while you are at it,
Don't ask why I shave my head.
Though the answer is simple:
I'm the amorphous
Girl – Boy – Alien
Of my Sci-Fi and liberation dreams.
Though you can call me trans,
Because I'm also that.
But (cis)gen(d)erally,
I'm unsure you could understand,
But if you can,
I'll acknowledge who you are
And not comment on your hair,
Unless it is cute,
Which, inevitably,
It will be.

EFFECTS ON VOICE

Our voice can impact how we are perceived by society before, during, and after medical transition. The pitch of a person's voice, how high or deep it may sound, depends on the length and thickness of the vocal cords. Exposure to testosterone causes the vocal cords to grow longer and thicker resulting in a deeper voice. These changes are permanent. Thus, for those of us with a deeper voice, the use of estrogen and/or testosterone blockers will not change our voice characteristics. Some of us alter the way we speak to make our voice sound higher, at a pitch that is not necessarily the one with which we would naturally speak. Sustaining this forced pitch can strain the vocal cords and risks long-term damage to our voice. We can try vocal coaching and/or work with a speech and language pathologist to purposefully manipulate certain qualities of our voice. Voice coaches and speech and language pathologists can teach us techniques to more safely and effectively change how our voice is projected, putting less strain on our vocal cords. Some of us also seek out surgical procedures to change the pitch of our voice.

Speech-language pathologists can help with a number of areas of speech that can potentially be gendered, including pitch, resonance, intonation, rate, volume, word choice, and nonverbal sounds.

EFFECTS ON THE CHEST

During puberty, estrogen is the hormone responsible for causing the budding and progressive development of breast tissue. Those of us born with testes typically did not have high enough levels of estrogen during puberty to develop breasts. Starting gender affirming estrogen should cause breast growth and enlargement of the nipples within a few months. Breast growth will continue gradually over time as hormonal therapy is sustained, plateauing within a couple of years. Breast growth can be uncomfortable, with intermittent tenderness of the chest and nipples, which should lessen over time. The time frame for full development and ultimate breast size varies significantly between individuals.

> *I take estradiol and spironolactone. After five months I bought my first bra. One year later I bought a bigger one and they are a solid B and still growing.*

We may be able to get an idea of our breast growth potential by considering that of our female family members, but there is no truly accurate way of predicting this. Breast growth is considered an irreversible change associated with estrogen use, and can only be reversed with a surgical procedure. Some of us choose to have breast augmentation surgery with or without hormone therapy.

> *I take estradiol and spironolactone, and I am finally starting to grow the breasts that have been missing all my life.*

CHANGES TO GENITALS AND REPRODUCTIVE ORGANS

The topic of genitals may cause significant discomfort or dysphoria for many of us, given that it dominates much of what the media and society view as the determining factor of our gender. Surgery is often considered the most direct and permanent way to change our genitals to "match" our gender, but this type of thinking does a disservice to those of us who do not want surgery, cannot have surgery for various reasons, or who do not identify with society's gender binary. Medical transition does cause changes to our genitals and reproductive organs, and may make us feel less discomfort or dysphoria.

Gender affirming hormone therapy with estrogen or a medication that blocks testosterone can cause a decrease in the size of the testicles and penis for those of us born with these body parts. Feminizing hormone therapy causes a substantial drop in how often erections or ejaculation occur, which may impact our sexual activity and sexual pleasure. We should discuss dosage changes or additional medication options (such as medications that induce erections) with our medical provider to mitigate these effects if they are undesirable.

Sildenafil (also known as Viagra) and similar medications can be an option for transfeminine people who want to retain the ability to have erections while on gender affirming therapy.

ORCHIECTOMY AND UNEXPECTED CONSEQUENCES

Nancy Nangeroni (she/her) is a longtime transgender activist who transitioned in 1993. She founded and cohosted GenderTalk Radio, chaired the Massachusetts Transgender Political Coalition, and led Boston's Transgender Day of Remembrance for many years.

My orchiectomy had been a long time coming. As a trans woman, I'd long wished someone could wave a magic wand and make my body female. But sex reassignment surgery hadn't been an option since a motorcycle accident in 1981 left me with too much scar tissue in the wrong place. No decent surgeon would risk performing a vaginoplasty on me. My closest option would be a penectomy and labiaplasty: to have my penis removed and a vulva—labia with no vagina—crafted. I seriously considered this for a few years. Then I fell in love with a woman with whom I share great physical sexual chemistry and a lifetime commitment. A penectomy and labiaplasty would put that at risk. Not happening.

I can live with a penis. It shrinks down and compresses nicely, so it's fairly invisible under most clothes. Testicles, though, are something else. They're hard, and contrary to what I was told, estrogen didn't make them much smaller for me, even after two decades. The uncomfortably tight underwear I wore to hide them made me hyperaware of their presence. There was nothing I liked about them.

After much discussion and research, my partner and I agreed I'd get an orchiectomy, a surgery to remove the testes. Because the testes produce most (though not all) of the body's testosterone, my blood testosterone levels would be greatly reduced. If this affected our sexual relationship, as reported by some people, I could take testosterone by prescription. So I underwent the surgery one January.

After I'd healed, my partner and I found our sexual connection undiminished. But that spring, I began to suffer from increased joint pain all over, unrelated to any specific activity. My doctor and specialists ran many tests, but all came up empty. Finally, it dawned on me that I was beginning to suffer from an affliction that affected many of the women, but none of the men, in my family: arthritis. Could the arthritis have been held at bay by my natural testosterone? I tried taking testosterone—about 20% of a normal dose—and sure enough, the joint pain receded.

I'd been prepared to take testosterone following the orchiectomy if my sexual functioning suffered. However, I never imagined needing testosterone for an affliction that attacked only the women in my family. I wonder how many other trans women have encountered this issue? And what other sex-linked problems might someone trigger when they change their hormone chemistry? Those considering hormonal transition might want to look into their family's gender-specific medical history for such issues.

Masculinizing Hormone Therapy and Effects

Since starting testosterone four years ago, my voice has dropped, I've grown a beard, and I did end up essentially going through a second puberty. I don't have insurance, and my medicine costs about $90 for a six-month period, and I go to a doctor for blood tests about every six months, which is $50.

Testosterone is the main hormone in the body that produces typically masculine characteristics. Increases in this hormone lead to the development of features such as a deeper voice and body and facial hair. Unlike feminizing hormone regimens, testosterone is generally the only hormone used for the majority of us who wish to develop features that are considered by society to be more masculine. Testosterone is a powerful hormone that can override the effects of estrogen produced by the ovaries.

I am still taking hormones, after starting in December 1970. I take subcutaneous injections of testosterone enanthate weekly. I have had beard growth, body hair growth, male pattern balding, deepening of my voice, fat redistribution, increase in muscle strength and mass, mood improvement, and increased libido.

EFFECTS ON BODY SHAPE AND COMPOSITION

Testosterone causes fat redistribution, with more fat settling around the abdomen and waist. Muscles may begin to look more defined as the amount of fat in certain areas decreases. Testosterone also causes an increase in muscle mass itself. This may make it easier to do certain aspects of physical activity, but we must be cautious to not overdo any particular workout or physical activity due to risk of an overuse injury to our muscles, ligaments, and/or tendons. Fat redistribution and muscle mass changes may begin within the first few months of hormone use, but can take upwards of five years to reach their maximum.

Testosterone is also likely to speed up our metabolism, causing an increase in appetite. We often feel more energy with greater levels of testosterone, but this is not guaranteed, and some of us may actually feel fatigue after starting testosterone.

EFFECTS ON SKIN

Sebaceous glands in our skin generate and release oils that keep our skin from drying out. Testosterone activates these glands, making our skin and hair oilier. The increase in oil production triggered by testosterone can lead to clogged pores causing bacterial growth and acne. This makes breakouts and pimples more frequent and widespread, even in places we may not have experienced acne before, such as the chest or back. Additionally, testosterone activates sweat glands, thus we may feel sweatier when taking masculinizing hormones, and experience more body odor and/or changes in body odor. These changes usually start early on with testosterone therapy, and can occur not just during intense workouts, but even with simple day-to-day tasks. It can take months to years for our skin to adjust to our gender affirming hormone therapy. We may need to establish new skin care and grooming habits or seek out medications to treat painful and persistent acne.

I have been on testosterone for a month. Changes that I've seen so far include: acne, the beginning of facial and body hair, facial shape change, increased libido, oily hair and skin, voice dropping, and mood changes.

Jaden. Leo Sun, Scorpio Moon, Capricorn Rising. Poet. Survivor. Collector of stories. Cannabis Enthusiast. Lover of bellies. Full of gender. Ol' Thick n Nasty. He/Sir. (Destin Cortez)

EFFECTS ON HAIR

Testosterone may trigger the growth of more diffuse body hair. This can include new and thicker hair growth of the face, chest, back, abdomen, buttocks, arms, and legs. Once hair follicles have started producing hair, they usually do not stop, even if testosterone use is later stopped. We should keep this in mind when deciding whether or not to start testosterone, because the hair growth is irreversible without medical interventions such as laser hair removal or electrolysis.

While testosterone can increase hair growth of the face and body, it can also cause hair loss of the scalp commonly referred to as "male pattern balding." This is due to dihydro-testosterone (DHT), a hormone derived from testosterone. DHT levels are unique to each individual and their genetics, though DHT levels generally rise with increasing levels of testosterone in the body. Hence, those of us on testosterone may notice our hair thinning and/or hairline receding, even to the point of total baldness of the scalp. This is usually a gradual progression over the span of several years—dictated by our genetics. Family history of balding may be an indication of what we can expect, but this is not a reliable prediction. Once hair thinning and loss have started to occur, regrowth may be difficult or impossible. A dermatologist or primary care doctor can prescribe a class of medications known as 5-alpha-reductase inhibitors (e.g., finasteride, dutasteride), which can provide some hair regrowth or limit further hair loss. Many of us embrace our hair loss, while others choose to wear a wig, toupee, or hair transplant to achieve a fuller head of hair.

It has made me hairier (I was a bit hairy anyway, but this made me hairier) and most importantly, has allowed me to grow a beard. This, more than anything, I think has allowed me to not get misgendered, except for on rare occasions.

EFFECTS ON VOICE

Some of us assume that speech-language pathologists are only helpful for transfeminine people because testosterone causes the voice to drop. There are, however, many elements of speech aside from pitch, and working with a SLP can also sometimes be helpful for trans men.

While feminizing hormone therapy generally has no impact on the vocal cords, testosterone does affect our voice. Testosterone enlarges the vocal cords, deepening the voice. Depending on testosterone dosing, this process generally begins around three months after starting, and the deepening tends to complete within a year of consistent hormone use. While our vocal cords are changing, we may experience hoarseness or episodes of our voice cracking when we try to project speech or reach high pitches that were within our previous voice range.

I have been taking testosterone for a few years now. Medicaid covers it, thankfully. It has lowered my voice, though I see it in my singing voice more than my speaking voice.

Vocal cord enlargement is irreversible. Voice coaching or work with a speech and language pathologist is also an option for those of us interested in training our voice to sound a certain way, especially for those of us who enjoy singing or work in music.

I took T for a year (I gave it up when I stopped being able to afford it, and I've never had insurance that would cover it). My favorite change, the deepening of my voice, is one that doesn't revert even when the hormones are stopped, so I'm happy about that.

EFFECTS ON THE CHEST

Testosterone does not directly affect breast tissue. Once breast tissue is enlarged, whether due to puberty or use of medications, surgery is needed to remove the tissue. With testosterone, breast tissue may become less dense and size may decrease slightly, but overall, the breast tissue will remain.

CHANGES TO GENITALS AND REPRODUCTIVE ORGANS

Within a few months to a year of starting testosterone therapy, the clitoris will likely increase in size. The growth is generally within the realm of a centimeter or two and is often not enough to allow for vaginal or anal penetration. This genital growth is irreversible. Those of us with a vagina are also likely to experience vaginal dryness as our body's estrogen level decreases. Vaginal dryness is a reversible change. It is also easily treated with lubrication and/or prescription creams if it is bothersome, causes recurrent urinary tract infections, or if we enjoy receptive vaginal penetration during sex.

> *I have used testosterone injections. I have obtained a more masculine silhouette, more hair in the groin, enlarged clitoris, cessation of menses, deepening of my voice, increased muscle strength, facial hair, somehow more hair on my forehead hairline, and a more masculine facial structure.*

Another notable change is testosterone's effect on our menstrual cycle. For those of us with functioning ovaries and a uterus, testosterone should stop our menstrual cycles and associated bleeding within three to six months. If stopping our periods is desired, but is not achieved by six to twelve months, we should speak with our healthcare provider about checking our testosterone levels and/or altering our hormone dosage. For some of us, even high levels of testosterone do not stop our menstrual cycles completely. In these cases, we may opt to use birth control options such as oral contraceptive pills, progesterone shots, or IUDs to stop bleeding. Another option is to add a GnRH agonist, or hormone blocker, to stop our body's estrogen production.

OTHER EFFECTS OF GENDER AFFIRMING HORMONE THERAPY

Sex and Sexuality

Many of the changes that occur with gender affirming hormone therapy can have a dramatic effect on our sex lives, especially if we start to feel more comfortable in our bodies and minds. We may experience differences in how often we desire sex, how we like to have sex, and who we desire to have sex with. Testosterone typically causes an increase in our sex drive; whereas estrogen and/or androgen blockers frequently cause a decrease in sex drive. The impact of gender affirming hormones on our sexual desires, behaviors, and intimacy may require learning new ways to derive pleasure from sexual activity.

Those of us with a uterus and ovaries who have receptive vaginal sex with people who make sperm need to be mindful of our risk of pregnancy. Testosterone does *not* prevent pregnancy, so we need to take other steps to prevent pregnancy if this isn't our desire or intention. Fortunately, there are lots of methods available for preventing pregnancy that are

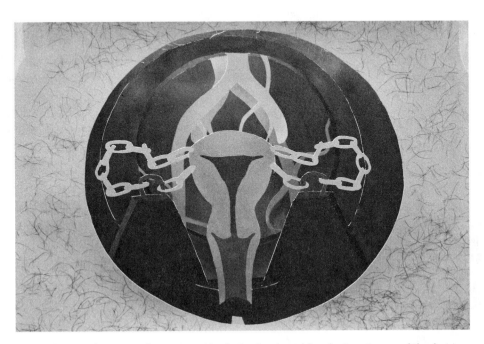

Tunnel Book Artwork. "Excerpt from a tunnel book about male and female stereotypes and the decision I might have to make about my ovaries being removed." Killian Blehm is a BFA student at Siena Heights University. "With the encouragement of my professors, I make most of my artwork on the theme of gender/identity/transition/transience."

safe and effective even for people on testosterone. If we are interested in becoming pregnant, we *must* stop taking testosterone during the pregnancy, because doing otherwise could cause birth defects.

Emotional Changes

We experience many different emotions when we medically transition. The experience is exciting, but can also be anxiety producing. Additionally, we may experience fluctuations in our mood or how we feel because of the effects of gender affirming hormone therapy on our brain and body. This may be more noticeable or dramatic for those of us with underlying depression, anxiety, or other mental health conditions.

The most immediate change was in the depth of my emotional response.

Some people report that higher levels of estrogen can cause mood swings or cause them to more easily feel upset or cry in situations that previously may not have made them feel that way. Some find that higher levels of testosterone can cause irritability, impatience, quickness to anger, or aggression. It is important to note that these emotional changes are not experienced by everyone starting gender affirming hormone therapy, and such changes are influenced by many things including our genetics, our individual temperaments and personality characteristics, our mental health conditions, stressors in our lives, and hormone levels. Many of us will notice improvements in our anxiety and depression associated with our gender dysphoria as our bodies become better aligned with our gender identities. Some of us will not experience changes in our emotions and mental health at all on gender affirming hormone therapy.

What *Not* to Expect

Gender affirming hormone therapy may alleviate some of the discomfort we feel from our physical bodies not matching our gender identity, but it may not alleviate *all* of our discomfort or dysphoria. Gender affirming hormone therapy will not cure our underlying anxiety, depression, or other mental health conditions unrelated to our gender. As we continue on gender affirming hormone therapy, we may notice that new forms of discomfort or dysphoria arise around aspects of our bodies that were not bothersome to us before. We may adjust our transition goals based on these changes in feelings.

The physical changes of gender affirming hormone therapy do not happen overnight. Some of the things we want to occur quickly (such as voice changes, breast development, and facial hair) actually take months to years to occur. Increasing hormone dosages above therapeutic levels does not cause bodily changes to happen any faster, and, instead, can make changes slow down and put us at higher risk of serious or life-threatening medical problems such as blood clots. For example, when levels of testosterone are too high, the body actually starts converting the excess testosterone to estrogen, decreasing the masculinizing effects we desire from a higher testosterone level. We should never try to increase recommended medication doses on our own and should always consult with our medical provider if we don't think our hormone dosages or levels are where we want them to be. A medical provider is able to check blood levels of estrogen and testosterone to ensure our hormone levels are in an appropriate range to cause the physical changes that we desire without going overboard to risky levels. Our medical providers will also check other bloodwork to monitor our blood count, kidney function, liver function, and cholesterol levels to make sure our gender affirming hormone therapy is not negatively affecting our body in any way.

Dr. Madeline Deutsch at the University of California—San Francisco's Center of Excellence for Transgender Health has posted detailed videos online about transmasculine and transfeminine hormone therapy.

What Happens If I Don't Stay on Gender Affirming Hormone Therapy?

Once gender affirming hormone therapy is started, many of us may desire to continue it for life to maintain the changes that help us feel more comfortable in our bodies. Over the years, we may switch delivery methods (such as from injections to gels or oral medications) to help us better adhere to our hormone regimens. Some of us choose to stop gender affirming hormone therapy for various reasons, such as changing desires around our gender transition, lack of access to affirming medical care, finances, complications of hormone therapy, new or chronic medical conditions, or other reasons. If we have had our ovaries or testicles removed, it is highly recommended that we take some type of sex hormones for the rest of our lives, because without these body parts our bodies are no longer able to produce sufficient amounts of these hormones on their own, and all bodies need a certain level of sex hormones to function properly.

The irreversible changes of hormonal therapy include:

- Testosterone: voice dropping, increase in body hair, facial hair growth, and clitoral growth
- Estrogen: breast development
- All gender affirming hormone therapy: possible infertility

Stopping hormone therapy will not reverse these changes to the body, but changes to our skin, fat distribution, and muscle definition will, over time, revert back.

I stopped taking the medication because I felt happy with the changes, which are permanent, and was experiencing much less gender dysphoria than when I began.

GENDER-AFFIRMING TELEHEALTH: REMOVING BARRIERS AND CELEBRATING OUR TRANS IDENTITIES

Jerrica Kirkley, MD (she/her) is a physician, parent, and bicycle enthusiast among other things. She has taught widely and established protocols for gender-affirming care across the country at academic institutions, community health centers, private clinics, and national conferences. Jerrica is the cofounder and chief medical officer of Plume, a virtual gender-affirming care medical service, created to provide trans people the care they deserve by leveraging amazing technology.

Gender-affirming medical care includes the process of prescribing medications to help align one's body and hormones with one's gender identity. Not all trans folks have a need for medical transition, but for many, it can be the difference between life and death. The current status quo of gender-affirming medical care is relegated to the brick and mortar clinic in the traditional American healthcare system, which is filled with providers and staff with limited clinical competence and cultural awareness, insurance restrictions, intolerant waiting room experiences, dead-end phone trees, long waitlists, hours on hold, the inability to actually talk to your doctor when you need to, and overall, a very nonaffirming negative experience—all for something that at its core is defined by euphoria, liberation, and a sense of well-being often never experienced before in one's life. I know this because I have gone through all of it myself both as a medical provider and a patient.

Telehealth offers one solution to these issues. I started Plume to create a virtual environment for gender-affirming care, which not only tears down all of these barriers to entry, but also flips the system on its head to create an affirming, supportive, convenient, and safe experience for trans people. The amount of courage and perseverance it takes to step out and truly live your life as your authentic self should be celebrated, not underestimated. My cofounder, Dr. Matthew Wetschler, and I worked to form an incredibly talented team of primarily trans folks, to develop a digital platform that will enable a virtual medical evaluation for gender-affirming care through a video visit, text communication for any follow-up (no visits needed), lab monitoring at a local blood draw site, and home medication delivery—all for one transparent, flat, monthly fee and accessible with an Internet connection.

We know that being trans is just one component of being human, and we hope this will support our community to easily fit hormones into our lives, instead of the other way around. We are leveraging technology to not only radicalize how we deliver gender-affirming care, but health care in general, and truly meeting both patients and medical providers where they are to create a care delivery system based around their needs and desires—something I have yet to encounter in the American medical system over the last 12 years since entering medical school.

Is It Dangerous to Stay on Gender Affirming Hormones Forever?

Gender affirming hormone therapy is generally considered safe, though as with any medication, there are risks associated with long-term use. Gender affirming hormone therapy causes changes inside our bodies that are hard to detect without blood monitoring, and can potentially lead to health problems down the road, if not monitored and treated appropriately.

For instance, estrogen use may increase the risk of developing a blood clot that can affect the arms, legs, lungs, heart (heart attack), or brain (stroke).

> *I suffered a pulmonary embolism and required hospitalization. The doctors there, with all good intentions, were suggesting that since estrogen carries a somewhat elevated risk of blood clots, discontinuing my HRT would be a simple way to solve the problem. I stressed to them that this was simply not an option, but it remained on the table. I called my endocrinologist, and she came in the very next morning, and made it absolutely clear to the doctors that hormones were absolutely medically necessary and non-optional.*

Spironolactone not only blocks testosterone's effects, but also acts as a diuretic that works on the kidneys to cause frequent urination. The diuretic effect of spironolactone can lead to dehydration with symptoms of dizziness, headaches, and muscle cramping. If we are on spironolactone, we must be sure to drink enough water to counteract the potential dehydrating effects of the medication. Spironolactone can also cause our kidneys to keep too much potassium in our blood, sometimes to life-threatening levels. Mild to moderately elevated potassium levels can lead to muscle cramps. Very high levels of potassium can affect the way the muscles in our heart are able to pump blood, which is a life-threatening emergency.

> *I have been on HRT for more than four years. It was steps for me. I started with only estradiol. Later spironolactone was added. Finasteride for my hair loss after another year, then progesterone less than a year ago. I had to push my various endocrinologists for each of these, there being a risk to each one. Estradiol gave me some changes to my face. Spironolactone made me very ill, so I had to stop taking it, and had an orchiectomy instead.*

Testosterone can cause increases in cholesterol, a fatty substance in our blood that can lead to a greater risk of heart disease, heart attack, or stroke.[6] Testosterone also tends to increase the number of red blood cells in our bloodstream. This elevation can cause

Cell Shifter. (Sha Grogan-Brown)

Health and Wellness

the blood to thicken, putting extra strain on our hearts and increasing our risk of blood clots, which can affect our limbs, lungs, heart (heart attack), or brain (stroke). Elevated red blood cells can be treated by lowering our testosterone dosage and/or donating/giving blood. Many medications, including testosterone and estrogen, go through the liver to be broken down in the body. This may put stress on our liver function and should also be considered when using these therapies, especially if we have underlying liver disease (e.g., hepatitis, fatty liver) or are heavy alcohol drinkers. No research, however, has shown a significant impact on long-term liver function in healthy T/GE populations.[7]

Consistent follow-up with a healthcare provider is important to monitor for possible side effects to ensure no unnecessary harm is being caused. Regular bloodwork to monitor the effects of hormone therapy usually includes checking our blood cells (complete blood count, or CBC), electrolytes, kidney, and liver function (comprehensive metabolic panel, or CMP), and cholesterol (fasting lipid panel). Routine bloodwork may also include following our levels of testosterone and estrogen to track how we are responding to our particular medication dosing, to make sure our levels are neither too high nor too low. Bloodwork is often checked more frequently early on in the course of gender affirming hormone therapy, generally every three months. As use of hormone therapy continues and our levels stabilize, healthcare providers may decide to decrease the frequency of these check-ups and bloodwork to every six to twelve months. This decision depends on our bloodwork and underlying medical conditions.

In the beginning I was paying for my testosterone out of pocket since it wasn't covered under my insurance . . . around $20 a month. I saw a provider every three months and got my labs completed, which was an additional cost. However, it was all worth it to get to where I am.

Overall, the medications prescribed for transition are safe and effective. They have been used for many years as gender affirming hormone therapy and for other medical reasons unrelated to transition. Some of us choose to stop gender affirming hormone therapy for personal reasons, or may have to if a particular medical issue arises. These decisions are very personal and individual to each of us.

CONCLUSION

The experience is ongoing and full of delays and complications, but overall I am grateful for the process.

Gender affirming hormone therapy is generally safe and effective for those of us who desire to medically transition. There are different medications, dosages, and methods of delivery to achieve the bodily changes that we desire. Some of the bodily changes from gender affirming hormone therapy are reversible, while others are irreversible. How and when we access gender affirming hormones is up to us as individuals, in collaboration with our healthcare providers. However, not all of us desire or have access to gender affirming hormone therapy. Gender-affirming hormone therapy is not right for everyone, but for those of us who choose to start it, we do best when we stay informed about how the medications are affecting our bodies and minds, and when we have routine bloodwork and follow-up appointments with our healthcare providers for monitoring.

NOTES

1. Hembree, W. C., Cohen-Kettenis, P. T., Gooren, L., Hannema, S. E., Meyer, W. J., Murad, M. H., Rosenthal, S. M., Safer, J. D., Tangpricha, V., & T'Sjoen, G. G. (2017). Endocrine treatment of gender-dysphoric/gender-incongruent persons: An Endocrine Society*clinical practice guideline. *Journal of Clinical Endocrinology and Metabolism*, *102*(11), 3869–3903. https://doi.org/10.1210/jc.2017-01658.
2. Wolf, R. M., & Long, D. (2016). Pubertal development. *Pediatrics in Review.* 37(7): 292-300. https://doi.org/10.1542/pir.2015-0065.

3.   Rafferty, J. (2018). Ensuring comprehensive care and support for transgender and gender-diverse children and adolescents. *Pediatrics, 142*(4), e20182162. https://doi.org/10.1542/peds.2018-2162

4.   Mehringer, J., & Dowshen, N. (2019). Sexual and reproductive health considerations among transgender and gender-expansive youth. *Current Problems in Pediatric and Adolescent Health Care, 49*(10).

5.   World Professional Association for Transgender Health (WPATH). (2009). *Standards of care for the health of transsexual, transgender, and gender nonconforming people* (7th version), 120. https://doi.org/10.1080/15532739.2011.700873.

6.   Velzen, D. M. V., Paldino, A., Klaver, M., Nota, N. M., Defreyne, J., Hovingh, G. K., Thijs, A., Simsek, S., T'Sjoen, G., & Heijer, M. D. (2019). Cardiometabolic effects of testosterone in transmen and estrogen plus cyproterone acetate in transwomen. *The Journal of Clinical Endocrinology & Metabolism, 104*(6), 1937–1947. doi: 10.1210/jc.2018-02138.

7.   Velho, I., Fighera, T. M., Ziegelmann, P. K., & Spritzer, P. M. (2017). Effects of testosterone therapy on BMI, blood pressure, and laboratory profile of transgender men: A systematic review. *Andrology, 5*(5), 881–888. doi: 10.1111/andr.12382.

SURGICAL TRANSITION

Gaines Blasdel and Nathan Levitt

13

INTRODUCTION

When transgender and gender expansive (T/GE) people seek gender affirming surgical procedures, we do so for our own reasons and personal needs. We don't have to understand another T/GE person's reasoning behind a surgical choice to support their autonomy and the dignity of their body. Not all of us desire surgery, but those of us who do are living at a time of unprecedented access to gender affirming surgical care and types of surgeries available. As access expands, there will be more stories about what it is like to be a T/GE person before, during, and after surgery. Our movement has achieved greater insurance coverage and individual decision-making power about access to medical treatment. Legal precedent regarding T/GE surgery has made it clear— when we fight, we win!

As a community, we are celebrating these victories. In some places, we are even achieving access to state-sponsored coverage (i.e., free for low-income people) for necessary care we previously thought would always be considered "cosmetic," such as hair grafting, prosthetic packers, and facial procedures. Other wins include the ability to be open about our nonbinary identities while accessing surgery, and technical advances such as being able to have surgery to create one set of genitals without having to give up the set we had previously. This new wave of coverage is helping many people, but can also be confusing and hard to navigate. Some of us are still left out and unable to access care.

> I'm truly upset with the VA and this administration for taking surgery options off the table for transgender veterans. I can't afford civilian insurance, so I'm stuck trying to find some way to get what needs to be done.

Increased coverage is creating access to a greater diversity of stories of surgical gender affirmation. Over time, this will help us gather personally relevant information for more nuanced decisions about the procedures available. There is not one surgery that is the most important, nor one particular surgeon who is the best. We all have personal goals for our bodies and life experiences that impact the way we research, undergo, and recover from gender affirming surgery. We need to learn and plan with our own needs in mind in order to decide what is best for each of us.

> After my NP completed my surgical readiness assessments, I had to ask my GP for a surgical referral for chest reconstruction. It took a lot of back-and-forth, and I had to take time off work to make an appointment to make the request for the referral. It's a messy system that can be frustrating, time consuming, and slow. And I live someplace where trans health care is considered above average.

Sometimes we address discomfort in our bodies through one surgery, only to find that another discomfort emerges. Having surgery will not necessarily end our experiences of gender-related discomfort. We may still have a body we perceive to be a sign of our T/GE history. No matter the surgical technology now, or how it improves in the future, surgery will always be a tradeoff, with risks and benefits.

One benefit of surgery is that it has the potential to help us feel more comfortable in our bodies. One of the risks is that surgical complications and/or the need for extended postoperative care can worsen discomfort in our bodies. This is a normal response to the trauma of surgery, and it is generally a temporary period in the healing process. Many of us have

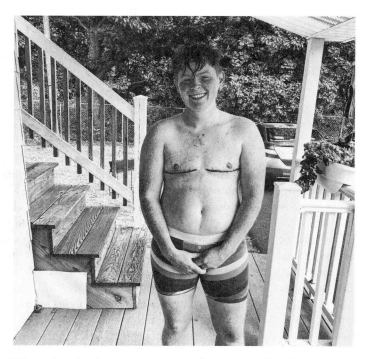

Asher Havlin. "This was 2 weeks after top surgery and my first time outside without a binder. Hard to explain how much joy I get from my flat chest, especially knowing all the work it took to get me to this place."

mixed emotions around the experience of having a gender affirming surgery. Usually the tough moments are one step in the path toward more comfort in our own skin. We generally feel more confident and positive in our sense of self, but we may also experience feelings of compromise, loss, or grief in our surgical transitions. This is to be expected, considering what we have had to give up or go through in order to access gender affirming surgery.

Many of us who have undergone gender affirming surgery experience joy about our outcome and resolution to our distress. Some of us may then focus on different aspects of our lives and move into new communities. It can be difficult to connect with or find information about T/GE people who have been living for years or decades as their authentic selves, perhaps living stealth—a community term that refers to telling few or no people about your gender history—or in a way where being T/GE is no longer at the forefront of their minds.

> *I had chest surgery in September 1972 at Stanford University Medical Center. I had phallus type bottom surgery there, started at the same time. In December 1972 I had the remainder of phallus surgery done, along with a total hysterectomy and revision of chest surgery on one side. In March 1973 I had a scrotum created, urinary revisions and testicle implants done. In September 1973 I had a revision of scrotum surgery and an abdominoplasty for removal of excess skin from the phallus tissue donor site. The total cost for four hospitalizations and all the surgeries was about $7,800. My health insurance paid nothing at all. At the time I had phalloplasty, no other surgical options were discussed with me as being available. I am generally satisfied with the overall result, even compared to the improvements made in surgeries since then. I probably would have chosen to have metoidioplasty instead, were it available.*

WHAT SHAPES OUR SURGERY CHOICES

It is hard to make informed choices about surgery when our knowledge about procedures and access to providers is limited. In the time before widespread insurance coverage, the only people who were able to obtain gender affirming surgeries were those with access to considerable amounts of resources and money. Beyond finances, gatekeeping has historically and often continues to get in the way of access to gender affirming surgery. Approval for gender affirming surgery is often granted by cisgender medical professionals or insurance company employees who may impose their own ideas about gender on us, restricting our access to appropriate surgical care.

> *I had to see a counselor before they would perform the top surgery . . . which was infuriating to me. That I, a grown adult, can't make a decision regarding my own body without someone else's permission, in essence. But she was stellar and helped me get the permission. The only other doctor I've seen specifically for that was the surgeon who did the top surgery. He was OK. All business, which was fine. He did the job.*

The decades of inequality in access to surgical care has led to knowledge gaps in our community. We may not have peers to turn to who have had the surgery or surgeries that we desire. Even mental health and medical providers who serve our communities may lack knowledge or training on our needs, including what surgical methods are available, complication rates, and how short- and long-term healing progresses. Due to biases and roadblocks in the medical system, it can be even harder to access resources for surgery when we are a person of color, a disabled person, and/or a nonbinary/gender-expansive person.

> *My PCP has referred me for SRS. I hated having to jump through hoops and be psychologically evaluated for SRS. It's humiliating, and involved disclosing information I would not otherwise want on record. Other people don't have to be psychologically evaluated for their health care.*

ON THE DAY MY BREASTS EVAPORATE FROM MY BODY

Senia Hardwick (they/them) is a nonbinary poet and part-time locust swarm living in New York City. They received their MFA from Queens College in the spring of 2019.

a stag will be born in a field somewhere;
I will tattoo his antlers across my collarbones.
a satyr's lips will be sewn shut.
a single eagle will descend from the sun.
there will be no pink scars, twin brothers,
along the length of my ribs.
a fox will release a ghost from its jaws.
I will love the curve of my stomach.
Dionysus calls me, on the phone,
and I agree to pick up.

INSURANCE AND FUNDING

Insurance coverage for gender affirming procedures has changed rapidly in recent years. Through activism, education, regulations, and laws enacted in the United States, we have proven that refusing to cover our health care is discriminatory. In the United States, our rights and access to insurance coverage were mandated in the Affordable Care Act, but different federal administrations have enforced these federal protections differently. Each state in the United States also oversees insurance in that state and 51% of LGBT people in the United States now live in a place where state-funded plans are required to cover T/GE health care, including surgery.[1] National health systems in other countries have started covering a wider range of procedures, such as facial gender affirming surgery in Sweden.[2]

Every year, out2enroll.org evaluates insurance plans on various state exchanges for coverage of transgender services and procedures.

We need to continue to hold our insurers and governments accountable for covering our necessary surgical transitions, advocating to expand coverage to every type of gender affirming procedure available.

For Americans who do not have insurance, it may be cheaper to purchase insurance on the Affordable Care Act exchange than to pay for surgery out-of-pocket. Some of us choose to get jobs with employers that provide these benefits. Many large corporations, from coffee chains to retail businesses to technology companies, are increasingly offering comprehensive T/GE insurance benefits. The Human Rights Campaign (HRC) maintains a list of companies that offer some form of T/GE benefits in their health care.[3] However, the questions HRC asks to determine inclusion on this list are not specific, and the plans offered may still make gender affirming surgery unattainable, by imposing discriminatory cost caps (i.e., $75,000 lifetime max) or excluding specific gender affirming procedures by arbitrarily deeming them to be "cosmetic." Some of us, including those of us from outside of the United States, may choose to enroll as students in an American university that offers T/GE-inclusive medical coverage in order to access gender affirming surgery.

> *I had insurance through the marketplace, and recently I qualified for a high deductible plan with my employer. None of my insurance covered the "cosmetic" surgery I had. I used an online crowd-sourcing platform to raise about $6,000 for surgery. I saved the rest of the $3,000 on my own. I got lucky and qualified for a credit card that gave something like 2% to 3% back on medical-related costs, so I paid for my surgery on the credit card and reinvested the cash back in surgery as well. I cancelled the card immediately after surgery was paid for and never carried a balance on the card.*

Some of us take out a medical loan or pay out of pocket to cover our gender affirming surgical costs. The prices for paying out-of-pocket can range greatly from $5,000 to $10,000 for chest surgery to more than $100,000 for phalloplasty. For some of us, it may be cheaper to travel internationally for our desired gender affirming surgery, a practice known as "medical tourism." If we do decide to go overseas, it is important for us to consider language and cultural barriers. Even if the surgeon speaks our language, there may be other communication or cultural barriers that impact our care. Some of us have found it helpful to bring or hire an advocate who speaks the local language and understands the culture, to communicate more effectively with our surgeon, care team, and the local residents. If we decide to travel for surgery, whether outside our local area or internationally, it is extremely important to make sure that we have postoperative care set up in advance of our return.

How Do You Know If Your Plan Covers Surgery?

UNITED STATES MEDICARE

Medicare is a federal insurance plan that covers those over age 65 and some people with disabilities or serious medical conditions. Since 2015 (and in the period before 1982) Medicare has covered gender affirming surgeries. It can be difficult, however, to find a surgeon willing to accept Medicare due to low reimbursement rates and because Medicare does not allow surgeons to "pre-authorize" gender affirming procedures. What this means is that surgeons cannot be certain that the surgery will be covered by Medicare until they bill for the procedure, which is done after the surgery is completed. Surgeons associated with large academic hospitals tend to be more likely to accept Medicare, though some who take Medicare for other procedures may refuse to accept Medicare for gender affirming surgeries, or may keep a separate, longer waitlist for Medicare patients because of issues with guaranteeing payment from the insurer. One way to get around this is to enroll in a Medicare Advantage plan (also known as Medicare Part C). Medicare Advantage plans are managed by private insurance companies, and can potentially allow access to that company's network of surgeons. This could either expand or further restrict our options for surgeons, depending on which plan we choose. The process of researching and picking a Medicare Part C plan can be quite confusing. Having a Medicare Advantage plan can enable a surgeon to obtain pre-authorization for gender affirming surgery, to confirm that the procedure will either be covered by the insurance or denied, allowing for an appeal before the procedure.

UNITED STATES MEDICAID

Medicaid is a health insurance program that is jointly funded by the federal government and each individual state. To make it even more confusing, many states contract with private companies or nonprofits to "manage" their Medicaid programs, requiring most individuals with Medicaid to enroll in a managed Medicaid option of their choosing, though some people, depending on their medical conditions, may be eligible for "straight Medicaid," run directly through the state. The specifics of Medicaid coverage of gender affirming surgeries vary from state to state. If Medicaid covers a medical service or surgery, the patient may not pay any costs for the procedure. Several states have no regulations or explicit restrictions on gender affirming surgery coverage. However, even in these states, there have been cases in which specific Medicaid managed plans have paid for gender affirming surgeries. It is best to connect to T/GE advocacy groups in our specific state for up-to-date information about gender affirming surgery coverage.

The Movement Advancement Project[4] maintains a map of state rules governing Medicaid coverage for T/GE care.

INSURANCE LITERACY WORKSHEET

healthy/trans

Googling the name of the company that handles your insurance plan and "transgender surgery" is not a way to find accurate info about coverage!

Log on to the website for your insurance company and download your personal:

➡ **Summary of Benefits and Coverage** *aka: quick guide to costs*

➡ **Certificate of Coverage** *aka: "Summary Plan Description" or "evidence of coverage." Should be a 30+ page .pdf*

You can also call your insurance to ask these questions. This is easier for costs, but it is common for phone representatives to know nothing about transgender-specific coverage, and there is no guarantee that you are getting accurate responses from them. If you do try to learn about trans coverage this way, try calling back and asking the same questions to multiple representatives. For more step by step help with insurance, go to: **https://video.transcendlegal.org/**

➡ **Does my certificate of coverage say that transgender surgery is covered?**
–Get to this section by searching the document for "gender" and "sex." It will tell you what your support letters need to say for surgery to be approved.
–If this section says transgender surgery is not covered, or that the specific procedures you want are cosmetic, it could be illegal discrimination.
–If there is no section making a statement either way, your surgeon can put a test claim through to see what happens

☐ YES ☐ No information ☐ Not covered, I need to look into local laws and advocates

➡ **What co-pays do I have for consultations with surgeons? Is there a hospital co-pay?**

➡ **What amount is my deductible, the costs I am expected to pay for surgery before my plan starts paying anything?**

➡ **Do I then have a co-insurance, or a portion of costs I pay after I meet the deductible?**

➡ **What is the out-of-pocket-maximum, or the limit on costs I pay in a plan year?**

➡ **Do I have out-of-network benefits? Are the deductible or out-of-pocket maximum separate for out-of-network providers?**

➡ **What is the date every year that my deductible and out-of-pocket maximum reset?**

www.HealthyTrans.com

Insurance Literacy Worksheet. (Healthy Trans, www.HealthyTrans.com)

WHAT IF MY PLAN DOESN'T COVER GENDER AFFIRMING SURGERY, OR IS DENYING AN ASPECT OF MY SURGICAL CARE?

It is very common in gender affirming surgery and all nonemergency medical care for insurance companies to deny initial pre-authorizations. Although you can initiate a preauthorization yourself (this might be called a *pre-service review*), it is generally the job of the surgeon's office to initiate the insurance preauthorization process. The surgeon's office should also help you appeal any denials. It is very important to stay on top of your insurance mail. When a denial occurs, the company should tell you in writing the reason stated for denial, what your next steps are for appealing, and the time frame you have for filing an appeal. If you have to appeal an insurance denial, there are usually two layers of internal appeals, which is when you or your surgeon's office asks your insurance company to reconsider your case and to take another look at the materials submitted. Additional materials may be needed, such as more letters of support or more information added to your existing letters of support to prove that you meet the plan's standards for surgery coverage. If the insurance company continues to deny you coverage after two internal appeals, there is always a third level of appeal which goes to an external review body. If you get to this step, it is helpful to have a legal advocate, but it is also possible to advocate for yourself through this process.

I'm in a health insurance gap at the moment, as I'm no longer covered by my parents but won't begin work until July. Insurance has been very difficult to navigate as a trans person and my original coverage (through my parent's job) fought with me at quite literally every step of the way. Initially, they did not cover any transition-related mental health (even though I had MH coverage), my testosterone, or my top surgery. After hundreds of hours of work, I got them to relent on the top surgery.

PRIVATE INSURANCE PLANS

Plans provided by an employer or university can fall into several legal categories. State laws around trans- related medical coverage may not apply to private insurance plans in your state. If there is a blanket exclusion on trans- related care in your insurance certificate of coverage, or an exclusion in your state's Medicaid policy, you will likely need professional legal advocacy in order to move forward to try to get coverage for gender affirming surgery. Some people in this position are able to access gender affirming procedures that are also needed for other reasons that are covered, such as a chest reduction surgery or the removal of reproductive organs if these areas of the body are causing pain.

They would not pay for chest reduction surgery unless I could prove my back was severely impacted.

GALAP: THE GENDER AFFIRMING LETTER ACCESS PROJECT

GALAP is a network of mental health providers collaborating to shift the culture of compulsory letters by eliminating the share of cost from our clients. It was started in early 2019 by a group of trans/nonbinary mental health providers based in the San Francisco Bay Area who have witnessed the highly unethical exploitation of trans people through the requirement of mental health "assessments" and letters. GALAP is not an organization, nor is it a source of income for any of us. The work we have done to create this resource and spread the word about it is a labor of love. We recognize that this movement is only an intermediary step toward a more ethical, just, and accessible model of gender-affirming care.

The long-standing practice of requiring letters for gender-affirming medical care has been defended by paternalistic, ableist, and pathologizing groups of professionals. It causes a significant financial burden for people in trans communities who, as a whole, experience employment discrimination, poverty, and other barriers to financial resources at much higher rates than the general public. Putting mental health providers in a position of gatekeeping negatively impacts the client-provider relationship and leads to abuses of power. Furthermore, therapy services should always be consensual; requiring clients to pay for services which they are, in some cases, not needing or wanting, is unethical. **This is not client-centered care.** The outrage that we felt toward this injustice fueled the GALAP movement.

We advocate for an informed consent model as it would apply to any medical service or surgery, with the emphasis on our community having the right to information in order to evaluate risks and benefits and feel empowered in their medical decision-making. We are aware that people who do not fit a certain narrative about what it means to be "transgender" often receive subpar care and face more barriers to receiving the care they need. We acknowledge that this particularly impacts people of color, those in indigenous communities, nonbinary people, and neurodivergent people.

We also acknowledge that trans and nonbinary youth often experience additional barriers and gatekeeping in accessing gender-affirming care, including extensive assessment and psychological testing. Although the basic principles of informed consent can be applied to working with minors, guardian consent is still a requirement in most places. The role of a gender-informed therapist can be in helping support family acceptance and readiness. We urge mental health providers working with youth and adults to abandon outdated notions of being able to "verify" if someone is transgender by asking arbitrary and intrusive questions that are based on colonialist ideas of gender.

Mental health providers who have signed onto the GALAP pledge have made a commitment to:

1. Stop participating in and profiting from a cycle that is physically, emotionally, and financially damaging, exploitative, unethical, and disempowering to transgender and nonbinary people. We urge those who are not a member of historically marginalized communities—particularly those with cisgender and/or white skin privilege—to reflect deeply on their practices and take action that is in solidarity with the self-determination and sovereignty of people in trans and nonbinary communities.
2. Publicly commit to providing gender-affirming care for medical transition without undue gatekeeping practices.
3. Provide **pro bono assessments and letters** to people who are seeking our services solely for this purpose. As mental health providers, our ethics codes state that we should be providing some pro bono work. For clinicians who truly care about social justice, financial redistribution, and improved access to care, this is a way to align our values with our clinical practice. Providers must commit to completing at least one free letter a month (based on demand), refrain from charging a fee for any additional letters, and refer to the GALAP network if they are not able to write any more letters in a given month.
4. Form networks to provide free or low-cost training to other mental health providers who would like to perform this service. We view this as capacity building that can support quality service provision.

The GALAP website (www.thegalap.org) and online pledge launched in August 2019 and the organizers presented the movement/pledge at the USPATH conference in Washington, DC the following month. Within three months, almost 200 pledge signers representing over 25 U.S. states have signed on. We are excited about the many possibilities the greater networking and access can do to help our communities.

Navigating insurance coverage for surgery can be a long and anxiety-provoking process. It is important not to get discouraged and to know that sometimes it's just a matter of calling the insurance out on the discriminatory nature of their exclusions. Insurance companies typically put up more of a fight when dealing with procedures that are considered "cosmetic" for cisgender people, which, unfortunately, often include breast augmentation and facial feminization procedures.

Even if our insurance plan covers our desired surgery at no cost, getting surgery can still be too expensive. Time off work, time during which we are unable to care for our family (i.e., childcare, care for our loved ones with disabilities), and time during which we may not be able to use our normal modes of transportation (cars, bicycles, public transportation) and perform activities of daily living (cooking, laundry, cleaning) can drain our finances and put a strain on our support networks. In the United States, the Family Medical Leave Act (FMLA) protects our jobs while we or a family member are experiencing medical issues. Once we have been working at our job for a certain amount of time (around one year full-time), FMLA helps ensure that we are able to take leave and helps keep our job for our return. However, FMLA does not mandate that we are paid during our leave.

National organizations that can help T/GE people navigate insurance coverage include TransFamily Support Services and the Trans Health Project of the Transgender Legal Defense & Education Fund.

I'm still waiting on bottom surgery until I can be FMLA approved, and insurance will pay.

If we have other insurance coverage such as short-term disability, which might be mandated in our state or offered by our employer, this can pay some percentage of our salary while we are off work for medical leave. The paperwork for short-term and long-term disability varies and might be much more detailed than FMLA paperwork, risking outing of our T/GE identity to our employer. However, many surgeons are able to describe our medical need in a way that does not disclose our T/GE identity. If being outed to your employer is a concern for you, you should discuss this directly and specifically with your surgeon. Sometimes the paperwork can be routed directly to the disability company offering the coverage rather than through our employer.

I would like to have bottom surgery, but I'm not emotionally or financially ready to have it yet.

Some of us may also be eligible for Temporary Assistance for Needy Families (TANF) (also known as "welfare") during our surgical recovery. If we don't have a job with disability benefits or leave protections, or live in a region without accessible TANF benefits, the costs for our recovery are entirely up to us. In addition to budgeting and saving money, working more, or hosting fundraisers, some of us may be eligible to apply for gender affirming surgery scholarships.

Some organizations that offer surgery scholarships include the Jim Collins Foundation and CKLife.

I would like to see more medical or medical-related treatments be covered by insurance. For myself, three of my four medications that I take for HRT are covered (and that one can be expensive depending where I get it), top and bottom surgery are covered, but facial feminization surgery (FFS) is not typically covered, and permanent hair removal is not covered. This means that even with what is covered, my expenses are quite a bit and will likely total in the 10's of 1,000's if everything is not covered.

Peel. "Many transgender people I know wish they could just step out of their skin into a new body." (Cai Quirk, caiquirk.com)

ACCESS TO SURGEONS

Although more surgeons are offering gender affirming surgery and coverage for these surgeries is growing, many of us are limited in our choice of surgeon by factors such as our insurance network or geographic location. It can be disappointing and confusing to be pushed toward a surgeon we've never heard of or don't feel comfortable with. Some of us choose to pay out of pocket, or use more expensive out-of-network insurance benefits instead of going to the in-network surgeon, where more of the costs would be covered by insurance. If possible, it is best to have several in-person surgeon consultations to feel comfortable with our choice and know all available surgical options before making up our mind.

> *Comfortable: having knowledgeable doctors and surgeons who have worked with trans patients before, plus clear and easy approval processes for procedures. Uncomfortable: being misgendered in records or by nurses helping prep for transition-related surgery.*

Although word-of-mouth, online reviews, and postoperative pictures are very helpful, extremely satisfied and dissatisfied people are the most likely to share their experiences. Some of us who have had surgery only disclose part of what happened during recovery or how we feel about our bodies, because we do not feel safe sharing the information that is more difficult to tell, or more difficult for the listener to hear. Surgeons who are not widely reviewed on the Internet might have excellent training and experience to offer, and similarly, just because a surgeon is widely known does not mean that our experience with them is guaranteed to be positive. Some surgeons claim to use novel techniques available only with them, when in fact they have put a "brand name" on an existing method. It is important to trust our own firsthand experience, and choose a surgeon based on our own priorities for our body and how comfortable we feel with the surgeon. Surgeons are also members of larger healthcare teams, and especially for genital surgeries, there might be other surgeons from additional specialties helping out in the operating room whom we might not have met during our consultation. Hospital staff where the surgery is being performed, from clerks to nurses to on-call doctors who could help with an emergency overnight also affect our experience with surgery.

> *Before my name change all documents had notes with my correct gender and name, and I was treated with utmost care and respect. When I went for surgery, I was treated as a female down to the point that they helped me with my wig and bra before opening the curtains in the recovery area.*

Geographic Restrictions

Some insurers only have contracts with surgeons in a limited geographic area. Medicaid often restricts us to our own state. National health systems outside of the United States may restrict gender affirming procedures to as few as one surgeon in the entire country.

> *I needed to see a psychiatrist for provincial insurance to pay for top surgery. The waiting list for top surgery is years long, but it gives me hope that I might eventually pass.*

If we are insured, and our insurance covers gender affirming surgery, but has no surgeon "in-network" to provide the service, we can claim a "network deficiency" or ask for a "network exception" to access the service outside of the limited area dictated by our insurance. Additionally, this strategy can be used when the surgeons in-network do not offer the surgical technique or outcomes that we desire. Using this argument, T/GE people who desire gender affirming surgery have been able to access surgeons outside of their insurance networks and even outside of their country's national health system.

> *Another issue was finding a doctor who would remove my testicles. None of the 21 in-network doctors would do the surgery.*

Traveling for surgery adds further expenses, such as needing to pay for food and housing during a required postoperative stay in the local area, and can limit our access to our caretakers and support networks. This leaves many of us in an uncomfortable position of having to wait until the surgery becomes available in our local area.

Training and Experience

There is no standard establishing how much training is required for a surgeon to perform gender affirming surgeries. Recent research has put the "learning curve" as high as 40 procedures for vaginoplasty[5] before operating times and complication rates start to decrease. There is very little T/GE health content covered in plastic surgery and urology residency training.[6] Many of us and our healthcare providers have noticed that with the increasing availability of insurance coverage for gender affirming surgeries, some T/GE patients have had poor surgical outcomes due to providers offering surgery without having had enough training or providing insufficient postsurgical care.[7] There is no professional body that certifies surgeons as competent to perform gender affirming surgery, other than those procedures that have a direct equivalent for cisgender people, such as hysterectomy and orchiectomy. Currently, it is entirely up to us as prospective patients to gather the information we need to make informed decisions about surgeries. This may include requesting to review pre- and postoperative pictures, as well as asking direct, specific questions to potential surgeons and their institutions about a surgeon's experience in performing surgery, number of surgeries completed, percentage of patients who have had complications, and any other questions that are important to us, our bodies, and our medical care.

Sensitivity to Nonbinary Identities and Choices

Surgeons are starting to acknowledge that surgical methods and research need to address nonbinary identities more directly.[8] The current version of the WPATH Standards of Care acknowledges that gender affirming surgery is a necessary part of care for those of us seeking nonbinary gender transitions. Along with growing awareness and understanding of nonbinary identities, some surgeons are also starting to offer more varied surgical options than traditionally sought, such as creating a penis without closing the vagina, or creating a vagina while retaining the penis, to better meet the needs and desires of our diverse identities and communities.

CONSIDERATIONS FOR SURGERY

Relationships and Sexuality

Deciding to undergo gender affirming surgery impacts not only ourselves but our loved ones as well. It may be complicated to navigate our intimate relationships before and after surgery. Some of us even put off pursuing gender affirming surgeries due to the desires of, and impact on, our lovers. Some of us worry about a decrease in sexual functioning or desirability to our partners after surgery. Other times, the perception of our partners is what leads us to consider surgery in the first place. In order to make the best choices, we must do what will make us feel at home in our bodies. Many people, T/GE and non T/GE alike, undergo a learning and understanding process about what is realistic to expect from surgery. Supportive people in our lives should ultimately honor our informed choices about our futures.

Even in strongly supportive relationships, concerns may come up over our changing body's ability to satisfy the needs of our partner(s) or our own sexual needs. Having surgery on our genitals and/or reproductive organs may require a prolonged time of sexual abstinence in the postoperative recovery period to allow for proper healing of the area. Many of us who have surgery find that we benefit from individual therapy and/or couples counseling with our partners to cope with the changes to our bodies, sexual selves, and

The Transgender Professional Association for Transgender Health (TPATH) is a healthcare organization headed by trans-identified health care professionals. TPATH was created as an outgrowth of conversations held by trans professionals and activists at the 2016 WPATH conference in Amsterdam.

intimate relations. Recovering from the trauma of surgery and relearning our bodies can change the sexual practices we previously enjoyed. Some of us may not have had previous positive sexual experiences due to discomfort with our bodies and previous body parts. Thus, after gender affirming surgery we need to learn how to have a positive sexual relationship with ourselves as well as others.

Individual Health History

Various health conditions may impact a surgeon's decision to approve us for surgery. Depending on the surgery we desire, the procedure may take several hours and have varying risks of complications, so our baseline health is a hugely important factor to take into consideration to ensure that anesthesia and surgery can be performed safely. Surgical teams typically consider sleep apnea or other breathing issues, weight and body mass index (BMI), heart and liver function, and other medical conditions in order to minimize our potential risks.

Our chronic health conditions and the medications we take affect our surgical risk, anesthesia risk, and healing capability, and thus must be discussed with our surgical team openly and honestly from the start of our engagement in care. If we are being cared for by a specialist, or have chronic conditions such as diabetes, heart disease, a clotting disorder, or HIV, surgeons usually request clearance from our specialists to ensure that our conditions are well managed and will not place us in danger during the surgery or recovery period.

For example, smoking cigarettes or consuming nicotine in any form, including vaping or chew, can impair healing. Many surgeons require a period of no smoking or nicotine consumption before surgery, and will perform lab tests to confirm that we have not consumed nicotine. Misuse of drugs and alcohol can also create danger with surgery, including risk of life-threatening withdrawal during our hospital stay or a decreased ability to care for ourselves well after surgery. It can be incredibly difficult to change the way we use substances, which is why it is important to plan ahead and start early to reduce consumption or change our relationship to the substance before surgery.

There are very few absolute contraindications to gender affirming surgeries, and many surgeons will work closely with us to develop a plan for a safe surgical process even if we have medical issues that can make things more complicated.

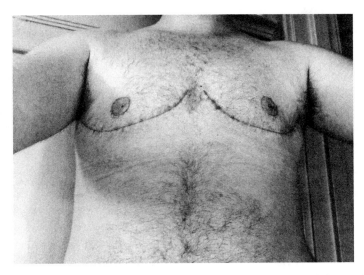

Top Surgery Healing. "This photo is of my chest as I am healing from top surgery and the complication of a hematoma on my left side. It is a visual representation of my healing process in that one moment." Ewan Duarte is a writer, photographer, filmmaker, and is becoming a therapist. Ewan holds his MFA in Cinema from San Francisco State University. He is currently pursuing his MSW. Ewan identifies as queer and trans.

Reproductive Capacity

Many gender affirming surgeries involve the alteration or removal of our reproductive organs, affecting our fertility, often irreversibly. Relieving the discomfort in our bodies is a priority and compels us to pursue gender affirming surgeries. Sometimes this decision is at odds with our desire to have biological children of our own. There are fertility-preservation options available. Unfortunately, many of us face financial barriers to preserving our fertility, as it is rarely covered by insurance and can be quite pricey. Some of us choose to delay gender affirming surgery until after we have children. Those of us who desire and can afford it may take other proactive steps[11] such as sperm or egg banking. There are also experimental procedures to harvest reproductive material during a hysterectomy or orchiectomy procedure.

Those of us born with a uterus and ovaries have been able to carry healthy children to term, and sometimes even breastfeed after masculinizing chest surgeries. It is rarer for transmasculine individuals to carry children after metoidioplasty or phalloplasty surgery, because this surgery usually involves a narrowing of the vaginal opening, creating anatomical limitations to birthing a baby.

Age

Although the current WPATH standards of care acknowledge only one type of surgery (chest reduction surgery) in minors (people younger than 18 years of age), it is clear that T/GE people under the age of 18 have accessed gender-related surgeries, including bottom surgeries,[12] and have even been able to get these procedures funded by insurance. While someone is a minor, their legal parent or guardian must provide consent for hormones and gender affirming surgeries. As we continue to accumulate evidence that gender affirming surgery can be safe and effective for T/GE minors, we expect that the guidelines around providing surgery to T/GE minors will continue to evolve.[13]

For supportive information about surgery and pregnancy, the Facebook group "Birthing and Breast or Chestfeeding Trans People and Allies" is a good resource.

Advanced age can also have an effect on our medical eligibility for surgery and the surgical choices available to us. Older trans people should be able to access gender affirming surgery, though they may have higher risk factors, such as high cholesterol, heart disease, or other medical conditions that are more common as we age. Surgeons often perform additional exams, such as cardiac tests, for those of us who seek gender affirming surgery later in life. This is to ensure that we are at optimal health status before surgery to decrease the risks associated with undergoing anesthesia and surgery.

THE SURGERY PLANNING PROCESS

Once we have decided we want a gender affirming surgery, we begin the process of researching techniques and providers, making consultation appointments, and finally, preparing for the surgery and postoperative recovery period.

Online Information

There are many online platforms that our communities have used over the years to share information about surgery and surgeons, and to view pictures of surgical outcomes. From early dial-up Internet bulletin board systems to e-mail listservs and now-defunct websites, we have continually reinvented the wheel with community support online. Online spaces are ever-evolving!

Accessing Pictures

A picture is worth a thousand words, and can be very helpful in helping us to navigate our surgical options and to interpret medical lingo. How big is 500 ccs? What do you mean by more feminine jawline? What does a "hidden scar" look like? Two people (even two surgeons) may use the same words to mean different things, and so it is important for us to ask for pictures to understand what a surgeon is describing and to provide evidence to back up their claims about results. A surgeon should be able to show us a portfolio of before and after pictures of the gender affirming procedure we desire.

Websites with information on surgeons include: transbucket.com (create an account to see pictures), radremedy.org, mytranshealth.com, transca-resite.org, transgenderpulse.com, and outcarehealth.org.

It is helpful to keep a few things in mind when looking at preoperative/postoperative pictures. Every picture represents a real person with their own body shape, genetics, health history, needs, and desires. Other people's results might not be achievable for our own body. When looking at postoperative pictures, it is important that we consider the person's demographic information (i.e., age, race, ethnicity), body structure, and how much time has passed since their surgery. Every person heals differently and not everyone follows postoperative instructions as advised, which can negatively affect surgical outcomes. A month, or even a year, is a short time in the life of a scar! Additionally, the person whose pictures we are looking at might have made specific requests of their surgeon to achieve a particular outcome, such as curvy scars, or a "plastic" appearance. Ultimately, pictures cannot replace in-depth conversations with surgeons and community members who have had the procedure we desire. It is important to know that some surgeons who work for academic medical centers and hospitals do not have control over their own web presence, whereas surgeons who work in private practice can put whatever they want online as long as their patients consent. If you can't find pictures of a surgeon's work on the Internet, that does not mean they are brand new. Usually surgeons can show you before and after pictures during an in-person consultation, even if they are not allowed to share pictures online. Keep in mind that surgeons often include their best results in the portfolio they show patients. Surgeons might also pay to advertise on for-profit plastic surgery review websites, affecting the reviews and pictures that we see. That is why looking at online T/GE surgery reviews, pictures, and talking directly with others in our communities is very helpful in guiding our choice of surgeon.

In-Person Information

Many T/GE and LGBTQ + conferences have in-person workshops for gathering information on gender affirming surgeries. These may include presentations by surgeons on their techniques, community-led sessions discussing surgery, and organized community "show and tells" to see postsurgery bodies firsthand. Some surgeons do free, personal, mini-consultations at these conferences. Information obtained at these events may give us a different perspective than information and pictures found online. Even if pictures online are accurately labeled for time after surgery, they are still cold medical images—single snapshots in time. Getting to see a whole person in front of us is a different experience. Additionally, people are less likely to participate in online communities years after surgery when they are no longer thinking about surgery on a regular basis. Connecting with other community members at in-person spaces gives us the opportunity to hear from people who have had surgery in the distant past as well as more recently, giving us more information and sources of comparison for consideration of what is best for our own body and desires.

There are also growing numbers of in-person support groups providing space for those of us seeking and recovering from surgery, particularly genital surgery. These spaces are generally found in major metropolitan areas, such as New York, San Francisco, and Toronto. If there isn't a support group in our area, we may want to consider forming one ourselves! Support groups give us a space to share emotional and logistical resources for ourselves and others as we work to navigate our decision-making process, insurance coverage, and recovery. Having community support can be a healing and empowering tool in our physical and emotional journeys.

Consulting with Surgeons

A surgical consultation is the beginning of a relationship that could last over the course of years, depending on the gender affirming surgery we are seeking, aftercare required, and revisions we may end up needing. It is best to talk to multiple surgeons before deciding on a surgeon. This helps us to gather firsthand information about various surgical options, compare portfolios of pictures, and assess our comfort with different communication styles and office environments. Together, we and our surgeon will decide what procedure(s) are best for our desired outcomes, body, and health history. Our surgeon will help us weigh what risks are worth taking in order to meet our individual surgical transition goals. Although "bedside manner" is more important to some people than others, it is crucial that we feel comfortable and safe with our surgeon. We need to be able to discuss all of our surgical desires and concerns with our surgeon, and not feel rushed or silenced in the doctor-patient partnership. At the end of the day, surgeons are also people, and sometimes we just get along better with some personalities than others. It is important to trust our gut and be critically engaged in the process of consulting. A surgeon may be positively reviewed online and still be a poor choice for our own personal needs, or they may have a communication style that is difficult for us to engage with. Even the most technically gifted surgeon has complications (in fact, it is a red flag if a surgeon claims to have none), and it is important that they have a plan for taking care of us if complications do occur.

TOP SURGERIES

Gender Affirming Chest Reduction, or Masculinizing Chest Surgery

DOUBLE INCISION

This is a procedure to remove breast tissue and fat that results in two scars under the line of our pectoral muscles. This procedure is better for bodies with more extra skin or larger chest sizes. Nipples must be re-placed (*grafted*) onto the body. The nipples are either entirely cut from the body and reattached (*free graft*), or they may be repositioned with nerves and

Health and Wellness

Surgery Consultation Questions. (Healthy Trans, www.HealthyTrans.com)

blood supply intact (*pedicle graft*). With a pedicle graft, preservation of nipple sensation is more likely, but not guaranteed. Sometimes the pedicle graft is marketed as a "buttonhole" or "t-anchor" procedure. Most surgeons are able to perform a version of the pedicle graft, but will have differences in the amount of flatness they can achieve depending on our chest size before surgery. Some of us do not get nipple grafts at all, sometimes because of insurance coverage (nipple grafts can be falsely deemed by some insurances as "cosmetic"), or because we want nippleless chests or plan to get nipples tattooed on later.

PERIAREOLAR

This is a procedure that does not involve cutting and removing skin under the line of our pectoral muscles. Instead, this procedure involves cutting the area around (*peri-*) the nipple (*areola*) and removing breast tissue and fat through this smaller incision. Variations of this procedure have been called *keyhole, circumareolar*, and *minimal scar*. Peri procedures leave just a small scar around the nipple, but are only recommended for smaller chest sizes. If this procedure is used with larger chests, we can get skin puckering and chests that are not as flat as we wanted. Because this procedure is less invasive than the double incision, it has the best chance of preserving nipple sensation. Not everyone is eligible for this procedure, and it is appropriate for those of us who are small-chested (usually A or B cup) and have less loose skin in the area. This is often determined by the

For more on top surgery, check out *Top Surgery Unbound: An Insider's Guide to Chest Masculinization Surgery*, by Drake Sterling (2016).

Another Chest is Possible. (Sha Grogan-Brown)

surgeon by taking measurements and looking at our chest composition. Some surgeons are more comfortable than others operating on "borderline" candidates, those of us who are on the edge of being eligible for periareolar procedures in that surgeon's practice.[14] If you are "borderline" but really want a periareolar surgery, you might need a second revision surgery in order to be satisfied with your final result. Emerging research on this surgery shows that this version of top surgery is associated with higher risks of bleeding-related complications, because the surgeon has a smaller "window" to work through.[15]

RECOVERY TIMELINE

The recovery from masculinizing chest surgery tends to allow a return to a desk job within two to four weeks, and a return to physical activity within a few months. During recovery, most surgeons instruct patients to limit the range of motion for their arms. Most of us will have drains to assist in healing and fluid draining for the first one to two weeks after surgery, and have to wear a postsurgical compression vest to limit swelling and fluid buildup. Some of us are able to care for our daily needs after these surgeries with some modifications, such as planning ahead by placing items on a countertop rather than a high shelf, but activities like walking a dog or caring for small children are too strenuous in early recovery. For double-incision surgeries, the contour of the final result is visible nearly immediately. For periareolar methods, the skin continues to retract and tighten over the course of as much as a year, thus the final result will not be apparent right away. If we find that we still have excess skin after significant healing has taken place, there is the option of having a second, less intense operation to remove excess skin.

COMPLICATIONS

Complications of masculinizing chest surgery can include the formation of a *hematoma* (pocket of internal bleeding) or *seroma* (pocket of fluid). Hematomas may appear immediately after surgery and often require urgent surgical intervention, in which case a second operation is performed to drain the blood and stop the bleeding. More minor hematomas and seromas can show up in the days following surgery. Drains are often used to keep these fluids from building up in the body. When we have had a nipple graft, there can be complications in healing and establishing blood supply to the grafted nipples. If healing and/or blood supply to the grafted nipples are impaired, we risk losing a portion, or more rarely, all of the nipple(s). Other recovery setbacks can include contour imperfections near

For detailed information on "dog ears" with top surgery, watch Dr. Scott Mosser's YouTube video "What are FTM/N Top Surgery Dog Ears?"

the armpit section of the scar, commonly known as *dog ears*, which can be addressed in small, secondary procedures. We may encounter problems with wound healing including keloids, or stretched or more pronounced scarring.

NIPPLES

Anonymous

> I never paid much attention to them
> before mine were plucked off
> sliced up
> and sewn back on
> in someone else's interpretation of a nipple
> Now they are all I can think about,
> my own passing numbness,
> sometimes dark brown coins
> under pink lace
> Every once in awhile
> electricity sparks
> as nerve endings re-attach themselves.

Gender Affirming Breast Augmentation, or Feminizing Breast Surgery

This is a procedure that increases the breast size by inserting a medical implant under the breast (*inframammary*), through the armpit (*transaxillary*), or around the nipple (*periareolar*). The implant then sits either between the breast tissue and the muscle (*subglandular*), or partially under the chest muscle (*subpectoral*). There is no single best or most "natural" place to put the implant, as different bodies and goals will require different methods. If our implant is placed under the chest muscle (*subpectoral*), some ways of moving our arms can squeeze the implant. With all techniques, it is possible to lose sensation in the nipple and breast that we previously enjoyed. Surgeons do recommend that if we plan on taking estrogen, we do so for a few years prior to surgery, in order to know how much breast tissue we can make on our own. Breasts have a primary growth spurt in the first few years of being on estrogen, then continue to change in shape throughout the lifetime.

Implants are most often made of a silicone shell with salt water inside. The salt water can be absorbed into the body without harm if there is a rupture of the implant. Recently, implants that are filled with silicone gel all the way through (referred to as "gummy bears" by some) were approved by the Food and Drug Administration (FDA), and some people are starting to use them. These new silicone implants are different than an older generation of silicone implants that were filled with liquid silicone, which could cause health problems if leakage into the body occurred.

RECOVERY TIMELINE

The recovery after breast augmentation surgery tends to allow a return to a desk job within two to four weeks, and a return to physical activity within a few months. During recovery, many surgeons have patients wear a specific postsurgical bra. Some of us are able to care for our daily needs after these surgeries with some modifications, such as planning ahead by placing items on a countertop rather than a high shelf, but activities like walking a dog or caring for small children are too strenuous in early recovery.

At first, the skin will be very tight around the breasts and ache from stretching to fit the new implant. Massaging the breast once the surgeon clears you to do so, as well as allowing for extra healing time before returning to activities, will help to relax the skin and the breast will "drop" to its final location.

COMPLICATIONS

Complications of feminizing chest surgery can include the formation of a *hematoma* (pocket of internal bleeding) or *seroma* (pocket of fluid). Hematomas may appear immediately after surgery and often require urgent surgical intervention, in which case a second operation is performed to drain the fluid and stop the bleeding. More minor hematomas and seromas can show up in the days following surgery. Longer term risks can include infection, which in some cases can occur well after the initial surgery, or *capsular contracture*, where the body forms too much scar tissue around the implant. If capsular contracture occurs, it can move the implant or affect the appearance of the breast in an undesirable way. There may be other issues with placement and appearance of the implants, for which a revision can be performed. We may encounter problems with wound healing including keloids, or stretched or more pronounced scarring.

Breast implants are not made to last a lifetime. Although many people happily live with their implants for decades, it is important to discuss with your surgeon the timeline for replacing the breast implant. Implants can also leak or burst, especially as they age. With salt-water-filled implants, this is very noticeable, and will immediately cause a different appearance. The salt water is harmless and will be absorbed by your body. With implants filled with silicone, a break in the implant will have more mild signs, or might not be noticeable at all, but can eventually be dangerous to your health. It is important to discuss any new symptoms such as changes in sensation or lumps/hardening with your surgeon and/or primary care provider.

Another complication of this surgery can be a desire for a different size of breast after surgery. Some of us experience back pain and discomfort from the extra weight, and would like to decrease the size. Others of us find that our first implant size helped, but that we would like more.

BOTTOM SURGERIES

Orchiectomy

Sometimes called "castration," this is a surgery that removes the testes, shutting down our internal testosterone production. An orchiectomy can be done as a single procedure, or at the same time as a vaginoplasty. Some ways of performing the procedure may limit the available skin for a future vaginoplasty, if desired, thus it is important for us to see a surgeon who is familiar with T/GE care or willing to learn. Waiting multiple years between orchiectomy and vaginoplasty may lead to shrinkage of the skin and thus less skin available for vaginoplasty.

Having an orchiectomy means that we no longer need to be on testosterone blockers such as spironolactone, because our body will no longer produce testosterone when our testes are removed. Some people with low testosterone levels, including cisgender women and T/GE people, choose to add very low doses of testosterone to their hormone regimens in order to help with mood and sex drive. Regardless of this choice, long term, everyone needs some sex hormones, either testosterone or estrogen. Without testicles, if we are also not on or not able to take estrogen, we are likely to start to experience low energy and depression and increased aging. Eventually, over the course of years, our bone density will decrease and we will be at greater risk of breaks and fractures.

> *I had an orchiectomy. I needed something more permanent than HRT treatment. The orchi did it. Insurance paid. I'm extremely satisfied with the results.*

Once orchiectomy is performed, we no longer have sperm to potentially use for reproduction. If our desires and finances allow, we can choose to freeze our sperm in advance to have the option of having biological children in the future. If we have not yet started estrogen, it can be a good idea to consider sperm-banking prior to starting, because many people lose the ability to produce viable sperm once on estrogen. Some of us are able to stop estrogen and produce sperm again, but this is not true for everyone.

Untitled. (Markus "Star" Harwood-Jones)

RECOVERY TIMELINE

Orchiectomy is a fairly simple procedure when performed on its own. We will likely go home from the hospital or surgery center the same day and can return to a desk job within a few days.

Our surgeon will instruct us on how long to refrain from sexual contact to ensure the surgical site heals fully.

COMPLICATIONS

As surgeries go, an orchiectomy is a relatively simple and low-risk procedure. Complications of an orchiectomy are those of any other surgical procedure, including bleeding, infection, and pain.

Hysterectomy and Bilateral Salpingo-Oophorectomy

Sometimes people use the word hysterectomy to refer to the removal of all internal reproductive organs: the cervix, uterus, fallopian tubes, and ovaries. In medical language, however, "*hysterectomy*" technically means only the removal of the uterus. Getting all parts removed at once is called a "*total hysterectomy with bilateral salpingo-oophorectomy.*" Depending on how the surgery is done, the cervix may or may not be removed. Some of us choose to keep our cervix because it helps decrease further the small postoperative risks of collapsing vaginal walls (*vaginal prolapse*) and incontinence. If the cervix is left in our body, we need to continue to get routine PAP smears to screen for cervical cancer. Closure of the vagina (*vaginectomy*) is not a required part of a hysterectomy or other genital surgeries (*metoidioplasty* or *phalloplasty*), but if we are planning to get a vaginectomy, a hysterectomy must be performed. This can be done either in advance of or at the same time as the vaginectomy. If we desire a vaginectomy, our cervix must be removed with our uterus, because we would no longer be able to have PAP smears done to assess for cervical cancer.

Currently there is no evidence to suggest that we have to have a hysterectomy if we take testosterone. We may choose to have a hysterectomy if going through the procedure will help us feel more comfortable in our gender identity, to address cramping and pelvic pain,[16] as a form of permanent birth control, to change our internal hormone mix, and/or to address medical issues that all people with these body parts are at risk for (i.e., cervical cancer, ovarian cancer, uterine bleeding).

When having a hysterectomy, some of us choose to keep one or both of our ovaries to allow our body to produce estrogen in case we decide to stop taking testosterone or lose access to testosterone in the future. The scientific evidence for keeping an ovary mostly comes from studies of cisgender women who will not be on testosterone supplementation after hysterectomy. Thus, more research is needed for guidance that specifically applies to us as T/GE people. Long term, everyone needs some sex hormones, either testosterone or estrogen or a combination of the two. Without ovaries, if we are also not on or not able to take testosterone, we are likely to start to experience low energy, depression, and accelerated aging. Eventually, over the course of years, our bone density will decrease and we will be at greater risk of breaks and fractures.

Some transmasculine people choose to keep their ovaries in order to retain reproductive material (i.e., eggs). If a hysterectomy has already been performed, however, harvesting this material can become more difficult and more expensive, and the individual would not be able to carry the pregnancy themselves.

RECOVERY TIMELINE

A hysterectomy is often performed *laparoscopically,* which involves a few small incisions in the abdomen and use of a fiber optic camera and tools inserted into the small incisions for visualizing, cutting, removing the organs, and sealing the internal cuts. Depending on your body and the reason for the surgery, it could also be performed *vaginally,* without any incisions in the abdomen, or as an open surgery requiring a large cut through the abdomen. Recovery from laparoscopic surgery is fairly quick and postoperative pain is less compared to having an open surgery, which will have a longer recovery with more physical restrictions. Most people can plan to return to desk jobs within a week or two after a laparoscopic surgery. Engaging in more strenuous physical activity will take a month or more. After a hysterectomy, our surgeon will instruct us to refrain from receptive sex (both vaginal and anal) for several months to ensure proper healing, and to prevent infections or *dehiscence* (wound separation).

COMPLICATIONS

Immediate, urgent complications of a hysterectomy include a *hematoma* (pocket of blood), uncontrolled bleeding, infection, wound separation, and more rare but life-threatening injuries such as damage to the bladder or rectum during surgery. You must be able to urinate before your surgeon will release you from the hospital. This is to ensure that your bladder and urinary tract have not been damaged by the surgery. Occasionally the surgery impacts the tissue and muscles around the bladder, which can cause long-term issues with bladder control (incontinence). Less serious, but nonetheless bothersome long-term effects may include vaginal dryness, pain with intercourse, or chronic abdominal pain from internal scar tissue.

GENITAL SURGERIES

Penile Inversion Vaginoplasty

Vaginoplasty involves creating a *vagina* (inner female genitals) and *vulva* (outer female genitals). The bulk of the *corpus cavernosum* (erectile tissue of the penis) is removed. To create the vagina, an incision is made in the *perineum* (the space between our external genitals and anus), and a space is created between the rectum and prostate for the new vaginal canal. The vaginal canal is made from the skin of the shaft of the penis and scrotum. The urethra (where we pee from) is made shorter and placed near the vaginal opening.[17] The outside portion of the new genitals, called the vulva (which includes the labia majora and labia minora), is made using scrotal or other skin. The clitoris is created by making the *glans* (head of the former penis) smaller, while keeping it attached to the nerves that provide pleasurable sensation. Vaginoplasty always involves an orchiectomy (removal of the testes), if one has not already been performed, thus ending our ability to create genetic children unless we have done sperm-banking ahead of time. Vaginoplasty *does not* create a womb or ovaries, thus we cannot carry a child. Currently there is no surgical procedure or scientific technology that would allow a trans woman to carry a child within her own body, though uterine transplants have been performed in a small number of cisgender women born without a uterus.

Any hair that is present on skin that is being used in the new vagina will also be present in the new vagina unless hair removal is completed. For most of us, this means removing hair from the base of the penis and most of the scrotum prior to surgery. It can be an extremely painful, embarrassing, and expensive process, and not everyone is able to start or complete hair removal. Most surgeons do "follicle scraping" or weaken and destroy as many hairs as possible during surgery. The scientific evidence about hair, along with community experiences of long-term vaginoplasty, indicates that this treatment during surgery is not sufficient to remove all the hair.

Male to Female Vaginoplasty

A vaginoplasty uses the skin and tissue of the penis and scrotum to form a new, functional vagina.

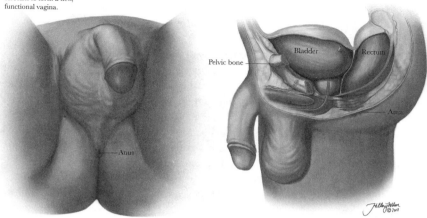

Pelvic bone

Bladder

Rectum

Anus

Anus

1 of 4 in series

Male to Female Vaginoplasty

The tissue of the penis is separated from the structures underneath to form a skin tube. The **bundle of nerves and blood vessels** on the top of the penis remain attached to the glans tissue

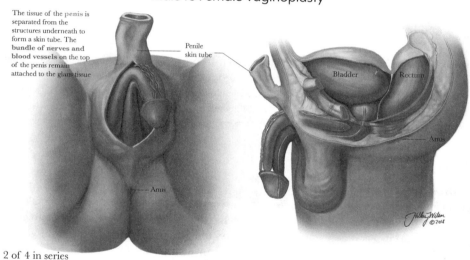

Penile skin tube

Bladder

Rectum

Anus

Anus

2 of 4 in series

Male to Female Vaginoplasty

A skin graft is taken from the scrotum and attached to the end of the penile skin tube.

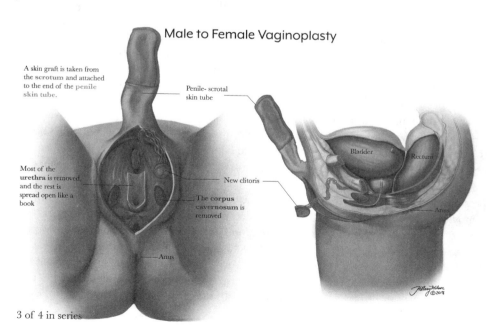

Penile- scrotal skin tube

Most of the **urethra** is removed, and the rest is spread open like a book

New clitoris

The corpus cavernosum is removed

Bladder

Rectum

Anus

Anus

3 of 4 in series

Male to Female Vaginoplasty

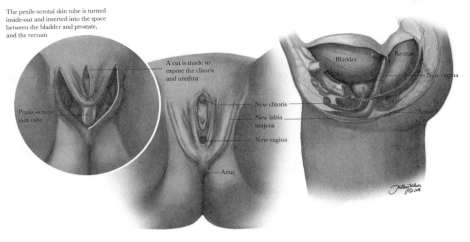

The penile-scrotal skin tube is turned inside-out and inserted into the space between the bladder and prostate, and the rectum

A cut is made to expose the clitoris and urethra

Penile-scrotal skin tube

Bladder

Rectum

New vagina

New clitoris

New labia majora

Anus

New vagina

Anus

4 of 4 in series

MTF Vaginoplasty Series 1-4. The procedures portrayed in these illustrations are techniques used by Dr. Devin O'Brien-Coon, which may differ from techniques of other surgeons. (Hillary Wilson)

DILATION

Dilation, which involves inserting a piece of medical equipment similar to a dildo into the new vagina, ensures that the new vagina remains open. After surgery, dilation is required multiple times a day for several months. Dilating regularly is not only about stretching the skin and keeping the new vagina from tightening due to scarring, but also about relaxing the muscles of the pelvis to allow for pleasurable penetration if so desired. For most of us, dilation is very uncomfortable and unpleasant during early healing. The space that is created for the new vagina passes through the *pelvic floor*, the muscles and connective tissues our body has spent our whole lives using to control urine, posture, and other important functions. This is a new configuration for these muscles, and dilation is also a process of the brain and body using these muscles in different ways than before. Pelvic floor physical therapists, who specialize in the way this part of the body affects sexual function and other areas of health, are starting to use their skills to help T/GE people who have had vaginoplasty.

Although some surgeons are more comfortable than others with getting to a certain depth within the pelvis during surgery, the amount of depth one can achieve postoperatively also depends on the shape and size of our pelvis, the position and angle of penetration, and our ability to relax our pelvic muscles. After several months, at the direction of our surgeon, we will change to dilating once a day, and eventually once a week. Long term, the vagina must be penetrated at least once a week to remain open, which can be done by penetrative vaginal sex with a partner, sex toys, or traditional dilation devices. Even with regular sexual intercourse, some of us choose to continue our dilation routine. Our sexual partner(s) may change and sexual intercourse alone does not always guarantee that we are able to maintain the amount of depth and degree of vaginal opening that we desire.

LUBRICATION

Many people with vaginas, including those created by vaginoplasty, find that they need to use lube in order to experience pleasure during receptive vaginal sex. All bodies have the capacity to produce "pre-cum," which is the release of fluid from the urethral opening when sexually aroused, but this is not always enough wetness to allow smooth and pleasurable vaginal sex. Some of us may experience more "pre-cum" or wetness than others after vaginoplasty. Penile inversion vaginoplasty does not result in vaginal tissue that produces its own lubrication. Some techniques for surgery (other than penile inversion) that line the new vagina with different tissue, such as peritoneal and colon vaginoplasty, mean that the vagina will produce more fluid. This fluid is not the same texture as pre-cum, and added lubrication will still make vigorous penetration more enjoyable.

HEALING TIMELINE

Because a vaginoplasty is an extensive surgical procedure, the healing time postoperatively is quite long. Most people can return to a desk job six to eight weeks after the surgery. During the initial healing period, it is very common to experience small areas of *dehiscence* (wound separation), bleeding, and fluids coming from the vagina. These should always be discussed with and evaluated by a surgeon or primary care provider. Normal post-op swelling often makes urine spray. It is also normal to have zaps, jolts, and strange or uncomfortable sensations as nerves reconnect.

If our new vagina is healing well and we are not experiencing any postoperative complications, our surgeon will clear us for sexual activity with our new vagina after a few months. Regardless of how wound healing is progressing, it is common to experience a setback in progress with dilation a few months postoperatively. This is because as long-term healing progresses, it is common for the vagina to tighten. Additionally, at some point in our lives we might stop dilating, then choose to start again, and experience difficulty regaining the previous depth and girth. Those of us who struggle with tightness and pain with dilation after vaginoplasty may benefit from working with a physical therapist who specializes in the pelvic floor musculature, and to learn scar massage and relaxation techniques.

After a few months, when the major swelling is gone, we may find that we desire a second minor procedure to make the inner labia more pronounced. Some sensation is immediately available but relearning how to pleasure our body and reach orgasm as nerves continue to reconnect may be a process. Additionally, the hormonal changes from orchiectomy performed before or during vaginoplasty may change our sex drive, orgasm, and mood. Some people with low testosterone levels, including cisgender women and T/GE people, choose to supplement with very low doses of testosterone to help with this. After surgery, the prostate is located between your lower belly skin and your vagina, and is sexually stimulated by vaginal sex. The prostate can also now be examined by a primary care provider inserting a finger in the vagina, as they may have done before by inserting a finger into the anus.

COMPLICATIONS

Complications that can occur during any surgery, such as infection or bleeding, can negatively affect the way the new vagina heals and functions. The new vagina will have an odor while the tissue inside is healing. This is to be expected. If the odor continues, changes in smell, or is accompanied by bleeding or discharge, we should call our surgeon or primary care provider immediately as this may indicate a healing issue, wound breakdown, or infection. Problems with healing may include delayed healing, *dehiscence* (incision opening) or formation of *granulation tissue* (abnormal wound healing, often causing bleeding, rawness, and sensitivity). If the odor persists and none of these issues are present, our surgeon may prescribe an ointment to be used on the dilator to help the area heal. Additionally, if our surgeon leaves too much erectile tissue in our body, this excess erectile tissue can swell when we get aroused, leading to pain and discomfort. If this occurs, an additional surgery can be done to reduce or take out this tissue. In addition to bleeding, dehiscence, and granulation tissue, other, very serious complications may occur. The major organs in our pelvis (i.e., our intestines, bladder, etc.) can be injured during the surgery, which would require immediate correction and thus a prolonged surgery. Damage to our other organs during surgery, even when fixed correctly, can cause chronic medical problems. Another possible complication includes a *fistula,* which is the formation of an unnatural tunnel. For example, fistulas can form between the rectum and the vagina, or between the urethra and the vagina. Fistulas need to be surgically fixed to prevent infections and allow for proper ability to urinate. Additionally, we may face complications with the new opening of our urethra. Scar tissue and swelling may cause our urine to come out in a spray formation instead of a steady stream. In some cases, scarring or swelling may create a blockage (called a stricture) that makes it difficult or impossible for us to pee. This is a medical emergency that requires immediate surgical intervention. It is important for us to have clear communication with our surgeon and/or local urology team to understand what symptoms are normal healing and what is a complication of surgery and/or a medical emergency.

Zero Depth or Limited Depth Vaginoplasty

"Zero depth" or "limited depth" vaginoplasty is an option for those of us who are certain that we do not want to have receptive vaginal sex. The procedure involves creating the external parts of a vagina—the clitoris and labia—but not the creation of a vaginal canal into the pelvis. Some surgeons create a shallow opening or dimple, in what is known as a "limited depth" vaginoplasty, which still does not allow for sexual penetration. Healing with these procedures tends to be faster, though similar complications related to wound healing, infection, and issues with urinary stream remain risks of this procedure. Dilation is not necessary after this surgery, and, in fact, should not be attempted since there is no vaginal canal created.

Other Options for Vaginal Construction

Although most evidence and surgeon experience support the use of the penile and scrotal tissue to create a new vagina, there are other bodily tissues that can be used. The majority of scientific literature about these other techniques comes from performing vaginoplasties on cisgender women born without a vagina, or, occasionally, as a second procedure after major complications from a penile inversion vaginoplasty. In both cases, there are no external genitals (penis and scrotum) to use to create the new vagina. Additionally, some people may require these procedures (if they desire bottom surgery) after being on puberty blockers, because their genitals may not have grown enough to provide enough skin for the lining of the new vagina. In the past, people in these situations have had their vaginas lined with a section of their colon or skin. Newer techniques are emerging that use cells from the inside of the mouth[18] and peritoneal tissue.[19] Those of us who desire these newer procedures should proceed with caution and ask in-depth questions of our surgeons, given that the full scope of complications and outcomes is still being explored. The alternative technique to inversion vaginoplasty with the most evidence and long-term outcomes in T/GE people is colon vaginoplasty. In this surgery, a section of the colon is cut out and used to create the vaginal canal. Possible complications include serious infections that can result from the bacteria that is naturally in our bowels, problems with rejoining of the colon, issues with wound-healing of the colon, and inflammation of the colon tissue in its new location. One possible benefit of this surgery is that long-term regular dilating may be less important because the colon tissue is more stretchable. However, serious complications from not dilating after colon vaginoplasty have been observed, thus dilation of the new vagina will always be recommended. Another benefit is that the colon tissue produces fluids, though this is generally a constant low flow rather than an arousal response during sexual activity. Peritoneal tissue also produces some fluid in this manner, though less so than with a colon vaginoplasty. It is often necessary to wear panty liners on a day-to-day basis to manage the fluid flow with colon vaginoplasty. The fluid is also a different thickness than "pre-cum," and people having this surgery will still likely need lubricant for vaginal sex.

Vaginoplasty without Penectomy

Some surgeons are starting to offer vaginoplasty without altering the penis. In the surgeries that have been performed thus far, an orchiectomy was done at the same time and the scrotal skin was used to construct the vulva. The internal part of the vagina was lined with skin grafts. Because the penis remains intact, the urethra and urinary function continues unchanged through the penis.[20]

Metoidioplasty

Metoidioplasty is a surgical procedure that creates a small penis by releasing the ligaments that hold the clitoris against the body. In order to increase the size of our penis, some of us do daily "pumping," which involves applying vacuum pressure to our clitoris/penis both before and after surgery. Sometimes pumping is done in combination with taking erection enhancing medications such as Viagra or applying DHT cream to our genitals. Pumping devices and medications should only be used under the guidance of a surgeon or primary care provider, as incorrect use can cause serious injury and long-lasting problems to our sexual organs. The metoidioplasty procedure to create the new penis shaft involves only release of the clitoral ligaments and repositioning of the clitoris. This can be done as a stand-alone procedure sometimes called a "simple" metoidioplasty. It can also be combined with other procedures, including: urethral lengthening to allow for urination from the new penis, *vaginectomy* (removal of the vagina), *scrotoplasty* (creation of a scrotum), testicular implants, and *monsplasty* (pubic lift/reduction). There is no surgery that allows us to produce sperm.

There are procedures that can be done at the same time as a metoidioplasty to increase girth (width) by using nearby tissues like labia to add to the bulk of the penis. Surgeons have used brand naming at times to explain these methods to patients, but most surgeons perform variations on the same procedures to incorporate more girth into the new penis. Some surgeons also use a product called *Alloderm* (derived from human skin) to add further girth. Penis length is dependent on our individual bodies and how much growth we have had from testosterone. Surgery could make internal erectile tissue more available, adding slightly to our length, but not substantially so.

Ability to penetrate partners during sex using the new penis created during metoidioplasty depends on a few factors. This includes amount of growth experienced on testosterone, the firmness of erections, the person receiving penetration, and the positions available to the people having sex. Some ways of doing metoidioplasty and freeing more length, by cutting the *suspensory ligament*, a band of tissue that connects from the top of the new penis, can change our erections. Erections after surgery might be less firm, or point down without these supportive ligaments. Many of us who have metoidioplasty continue to use prosthetics for penetrative sex.

HEALING TIMELINE

After a "simple" metoidioplasty, the new penis heals quickly, allowing return to sexual activity within months, and there are typically few complications other than those associated with any surgery.[21] Sensation remains generally the same, and often increases as more erectile tissue is available outside the body and happiness with genitals increases. Complications such as tissue loss or abnormal scarring could decrease sexual sensation. Adding procedures to a simple metoidioplasty can add more stages to the surgery, and increases healing time and possible complications.

COMPLICATIONS

A metoidioplasty alone is a relatively low risk surgery. Complications of a metoidioplasty are similar to those of any other surgical procedure and include risks of bleeding, infection, pain, and damage to nearby sensory nerves. It is possible to lose penile length after surgery due to scar tissue contracture. It is also possible, even if the surgery is a technical success, to not meet our goals from the surgery, such as standing to urinate or having penetrative sex. Depending on placement of the penis, size after surgery, and complications, it might not be possible to stand to pee at a urinal through the fly of pants. Some of us find that we need to drop our pants more to fully expose the new penis, or that we are more comfortable peeing into a toilet in a stall, while sitting or standing. If we decide to have urethral lengthening, we may experience other complications as described later in the Urethral Lengthening subsection.

For first-person accounts of bottom surgery, pick up a copy of *Hung Jury: Testimonies of Genital Surgery by Transsexual Men*, by Trystan Cotton (Transgress Press, 2012).

Transthetics and Gendercat both produce prosthetics for penetrative sex designed specifically for people who have had a metoidioplasty.

5 am

For almost two years, Lou Bigelow (he/him) had the life-changing opportunity to live at two different yoga centers, meditating a lot, and connecting with his inner self. Now, living back in the city with a full-time job working with trans youth, his goal is to share what he learned and to find that same spirituality in every part of life.

I'm scheduled to have bottom surgery in two months. I wake up at 5 AM drenched in worry. I heard an alarming story at work about someone who was treated terribly by the nursing staff after their bottom surgery. My thoughts race. Will that happen to me? What if I have complications? What if everything goes wrong? I try meditating in bed, but the worrying continues. My partner scoops her arm around me, and she dozes off while I try to be comforted. But the problem is in my mind, and her sweetness can't touch it.

"Fine, fine," I tell the higher part of myself, and scoot off the bed toward my meditation corner. In this little space dedicated purely to meditation, I sit cross-legged on a firm cushion, and watch my breath come in and go out. Every time the racing thoughts come, I gently refocus my mind on my breath—a practice so simple and yet so difficult. After a while, my nerves calm a bit, and my body relaxes.

How do we take the risks needed to better our lives? With our worries and our fear of the unknown, it's hard to pursue new things that could turn out great. For me, there are only two options: The first option is to stay in the comfort of the body I've known for so long and attempt to distract myself from the dysphoria that steals my energy and brightness. The second option is to take life's next big risk; for me, that's bottom surgery. I will go under anesthesia, and a surgeon will shift my genitals and reshape them to better suit me. The surgeon will cut the old innie's chains free to reveal a new outie ready to meet the world, and that extra hole will be sealed up—sewn together with healing light. This will be followed by a several-month recovery process to let everything mesh and meld together.

Bottom surgery will likely make me feel better than I've ever felt. I will likely feel more whole, more grounded, more embodied, and more confident. It's likely to take away at least some of the nagging feeling that everywhere I go, something's not quite right. I believe it'll help me feel better than anything I've ever experienced about the current body I'm in.

So here I sit at 5 AM meditating, watching my breath. The worries wash over me. I don't have to go with them. They are OK. They are not me. The meditation soothes the emotional turmoil and brings back my faith. Though by the end of it, I realize not even meditation will save me. There will be pain and there will be pleasure, and that's OK. Somehow that's the answer I was looking for—the grain of truth at the end of the tunnel.

Phalloplasty

A phalloplasty is the creation of a new penis using skin and tissue from other parts of our body.[22] Common sites used are the forearm, thigh, back, and abdomen. Any hair or tattoos on the skin will be on the new penis, unless we remove the hair or tattoos in advance. The size of the new penis is dependent on our individual preference, the size available from our donor site, and surgeon comfort. There are significant factors to this surgery that we must consider. The penis created from a phalloplasty does not have the ability to get erect from sexual arousal—it remains the same size and firmness in all situations, unless an erectile device is used. Using a thigh donor site generally results in a penis with a wider girth. Depending on the fat we carry on our thighs, we may end up with a penis that is too big for our liking, or that is heavy and too large for our body, clothing, or sexual partners.

If our penis was created using skin and tissue from the arm or the thigh, a second skin graft is needed to cover the area of the donor site. Surgeons either use a half layer of skin called a *split-thickness* graft, which will have a scarred appearance over the long term and will not grow hair, or a *full-thickness* graft of skin taken from a larger area that can be easily resewn together, such as extra belly skin or skin from below the butt cheeks.

In a phalloplasty, the original erectile tissue (*clitoris*) can be "buried" under the new penis, or left exposed. Specialized plastic surgeons use microsurgery techniques to connect the blood supply and sensory nerves from our existing genitals to the blood supply and sensory nerves in the donor tissue that makes up our new penis. If this procedure is successful, the erotic sensation in our genitals extends through some or all of our new penis. Regardless of whether microsurgery of the nerves is successful or not, if the clitoris is buried within the new penis, we will have erotic sensation at the base of our penis. Phalloplasty can be done alone or combined with urethral lengthening to be able to pee out of the tip of the penis, *vaginectomy* (removal of the vagina), *scrotoplasty* (creation of a scrotum), testicular implants, insertion of an erectile device, *glansplasty* (creation of a head for the penis), or *monsplasty* (pubic lift/reduction). There is no surgery that allows us to produce sperm.

We might also choose to get medical tattooing done on the new penis to add coloration that matches the rest of our genital skin and/or add the appearance of veins. Usually phalloplasty surgeries are carried out in several separate procedures, called stages, months apart. This ensures better success and allows for any complications with one step to be handled before proceeding to the next step. This typically prolongs the process of surgery to over a year or more. Some surgeons will do almost all of the surgery at the same time, but complications can still happen, and can require a multi-year process.

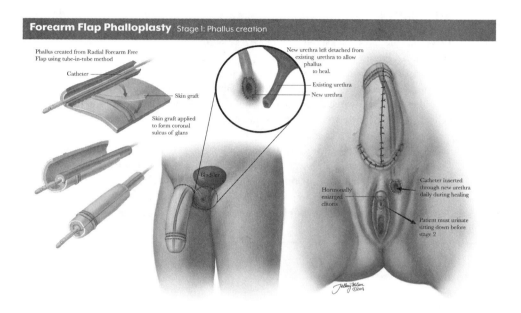

Forearm Flap Phalloplasty Stage 1: Phallus creation

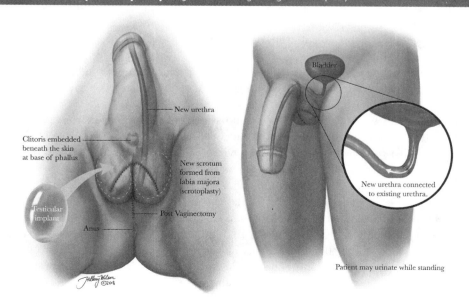

Forearm Flap Phalloplasty Stage 2: Urethral lengthening and scrotoplasty

Health and Wellness

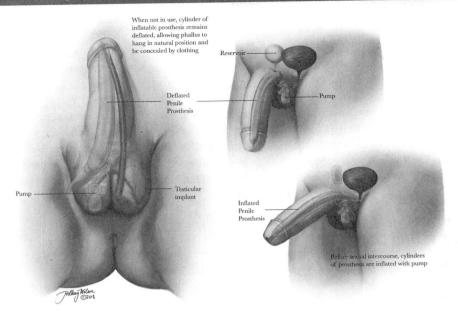

When not in use, cylinder of inflatable prosthesis remains deflated, allowing phallus to hang in natural position and be concealed by clothing

Reservoir

Deflated Penile Prosthesis

Pump

Pump

Testicular implant

Inflated Penile Prosthesis

Before sexual intercourse, cylinders of prosthesis are inflated with pump

FTM Phalloplasty Series 1-3. The procedures portrayed in these illustrations are techniques used by Dr. Devin O'Brien-Coon, which may differ from techniques of other surgeons. (Hillary Wilson)

HEALING TIMELINE

The first several days after phalloplasty, the penis is watched closely to make sure that the blood vessel connection is successful, otherwise we risk losing some, or more rarely all, of our new penis and having to have that portion removed. All tissues in our body need a blood supply to survive. Most phalloplasty procedures take place in multiple stages to ensure proper healing and decrease risk of complications. For example, *glansplasty*, the creation of the ridge below the head of a circumcised penis, is more successful in a later stage. Another reason for multiple stages is that any implants, such as testicular prostheses and erectile devices, have a greater risk of infection and rejection by the body (*erosion*) if inserted during the first stage of surgery.

An erectile device can be placed nine or more months after the initial phalloplasty procedure, once enough sensation is regained to protect the penis from damage. An erectile device enables us to more easily use our penis for penetration, though some of us find that we don't need an erectile implant to have penetrative sex with our new penis. That might be because our penis is thicker or firmer to begin with, or we might experiment with using penis extenders, wraps, and other external aids in order to use our penis for sex.

The sensation in a phalloplasty penis will take years to fully mature. The first signs of a successful nerve connection might be zaps or jolts, and may occur months to a year after the initial surgery. Sensation includes many specific details that will come in slowly over time, including pain, pressure, surface touch, vibration, and hot/cold, with a different final result for different people. Which nerves were connected, if any, during the procedure, and individual healing will impact sensation. Frequent self-testing and exploration helps to build the mind-body connection.

COMPLICATIONS

Complications of phalloplasty increase with the number of surgeries, or stages, desired or needed (i.e., urethral lengthening, insertion of an erectile device). As with any surgery, phalloplasty carries the risk of bleeding, infection, pain, and nerve damage. It is a common complication for small sections of the penis (such as the base or tip) to have insufficient blood flow, resulting in patches of dead tissue and increased scarring. Loss of the entire penis due to blood flow problems is very rare, but can occur. Nerve connections may not be successful, thus some of us may not experience sensation in our new penis aside from the area of our buried clitoris. If we decide to have urethral lengthening, there can be other complications as described later. Additionally, if we have an erectile device implanted, we risk having the erectile device erode through the penis and stick out. This is a medical emergency as it risks damaging and compromising the integrity of the penis, and can lead to infection and scarring that can cause further problems.

Complications can also include dissatisfaction with the size or appearance of the new penis. If the new penis is too large, it can be reduced in length, and somewhat in girth, in secondary procedures. If the penis is too small or too thin, there are few options for changing the size, other than adding an erectile device to increase the bulk of the penis. Some people who have major complications with their first surgery end up restarting with an entirely new graft to create a new penis.

ADDITIONAL PROCEDURES WITH METOIDIOPLASTY OR PHALLOPLASTY

Scrotoplasty and Testicular Implants

Scrotoplasty creates the *scrotum*, the pouch that holds the testicles.[23] Testicular implants are then inserted to fill the scrotum. Some of us opt to fill the scrotum with fat from other areas, or leave the scrotum unfilled. There are a few different methods of creating a scrotum. One method involves inserting implants into the existing labia majora. This version of scrotoplasty increases risk of the implants settling too far back, creating discomfort with sitting or bike riding. Another, more complex method, involves cutting and rotating the labia to create a higher, more forward scrotum. Scrotum size can range from very small to medium, depending on the procedure and the amount of tissue before surgery.

HEALING TIME

Scrotoplasty is usually performed at the same time as metoidioplasty or phalloplasty. In order to minimize risk of complications, many surgeons add testicular implants in a second surgical stage. If complications do not occur, return to physical activities and sexual contact is possible six to eight weeks after surgery.

COMPLICATIONS

Testicular implants, like any foreign object put into the body, can introduce an infection. Other possible complications include the implant working its way through the skin (*erosion*) and misplacement or migration of the implant to outside of the scrotum. Both initial scrotoplasty and later testicular implants can cause swelling, bruising, bleeding, infection, discomfort in this sensitive area, and postoperative pain. Particularly when our scrotum skin has been moved during a complex scrotoplasty, it is possible to have patches of numbness or less sensation. Some of us experience pain or discomfort with where our testicular implants end up lying after swelling has reduced, leading us to seek a revision of testicular placement or removal of our testicular implant.

Urethral Lengthening

The process of creating a longer *urethra* (the tunnel through which we pass urine) that extends through the new penis is one of the most difficult parts of a phalloplasty or metoidioplasty.[24] It is usually performed by a urologist, a surgeon who has gone through special training and focuses on the penis and urinary system. Some urologists have additional training in genital reconstruction, and specialize in fixing a urethra that has been damaged by trauma. Urethral lengthening is needed for us to be able to pee through the tip of the new penis. Not everyone who gets metoidioplasty or phalloplasty decides to

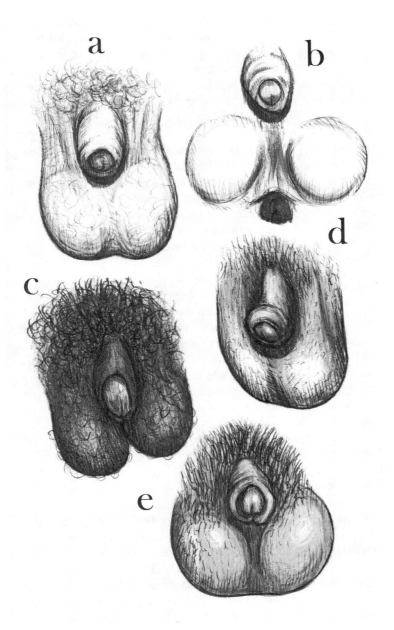

Diagram depicting various outcomes of different scrotoplasty methods along with a healed metoidioplasty: a.) V-Y scrotoplasty result; b.) a bifid scrotum without vaginectomy; c.) a bifid scrotum; d.) another variation on the V-Y method; e.) joined bifid scrotum. Sami Brussels is a medical and commercial illustrator and a multidisciplinary artist whose work deals with homosexuality, eroticism, disability, the intersection of art and medicine, and lived experience as a transsexual man. He is a fourth-generation West Philadelphian, and recently published the first volume of an illustrated surgical memoir, The Metoidoplasty Diaries. (IG: @transsexualwerewolf)

get urethral lengthening. If we choose not to, our urethra is either left entirely alone, or slightly altered during *vaginectomy* (closure of the vagina). Any tissue used to create the urethral canal of the new penis needs to undergo hair removal before surgery. Urethral lengthening in phalloplasty is often done in multiple stages. One method that many surgeons use is to first create a section of the urethral canal that moves urine to the front of the body, and then, in another surgery, to lengthen the urethra through the entire new penis. Surgeons often use a portion of the vaginal lining to create the lengthened urethra. For this reason, and other factors that could increase urinary complications, most surgeons require that someone getting urethral lengthening also get a vaginectomy.

HEALING TIMELINE

To allow for proper healing of the urethra, we will need to have a *catheter* (a tube put through the urethra to our bladder, which collects urine in a bag outside of our body). The catheter will remain in place until our surgeon feels that our urethra is properly healed. The surgeon will safely remove our catheter when the time is right. We should never attempt to remove a catheter on our own, as we risk causing damage to our bladder, urethra, and penis.

COMPLICATIONS

With any urethral lengthening procedure, there is a high risk of forming a *fistula* (unnatural tunnel), which can cause leakage of urine into the vagina or colon/anus. *Strictures* (narrowing or complete blockage of the urethra) are also common. Strictures can prevent us from being able to pee properly or entirely, which is a medical emergency. The majority of issues with urinating will show up in the year after surgery. Rarely, strictures can appear years after our initial surgery if scar tissue continues to form, which can cause new fistulas or other complications. Fistulas and strictures often require corrective surgeries and lead us to need a catheter for a longer period of time. Catheters are necessary for proper healing, but are often uncomfortable and increase our risk of urinary tract infections and bladder weakness, especially if in place for a longer amount of time. We may have to carry around a bag of urine hidden in our pants during everyday life, and sometimes leaks or spills occur. If we get recurrent strictures and fistulas, these can cause more problems and complications over time, including worsened scarring, inability to recreate the urethra and pee through the end of our penis, or even tissue loss. We may need multiple surgeries to treat these complications. The catch-22 is that the more surgeries we have, the higher the risk of complications. In worst-case scenarios, if the urethra cannot be extended through the entirety of the penis, it may be rerouted to the perineum (the area between our external genitals and anus). If this is done, we would have to sit to pee or use a stand-to-pee device. This option, called a *perineal ure-throstomy,* is also offered to cisgender men who have ongoing issues with urethral strictures.

Vaginectomy

Vaginectomy, also known as a *colpectomy*, is a surgical procedure in which the vagina is removed and the external genital opening is closed, leaving a smooth *perineum* (space between our external genitals and anus). There are a few ways to perform this procedure. We should discuss the risks and benefits of the procedure that our surgeon prefers when we have our consultation. Often vaginectomy is required by our surgeon if we desire urethral lengthening with our metoidioplasty or phalloplasty. This is because the area near the vagina is prone to fistulas, and performing a vaginectomy allows the surgeon to place more bulk and tissue in that location in order to prevent leaks. There are a few surgeons who will try to lengthen the urethra without closing the vagina. This raises risks of fistulas and can cause significant narrowing of the vaginal canal that often makes receptive vaginal sex difficult or painful. Dilation or regular stretching after surgery can be performed to address the narrowing.

If we desire to give birth to children, we must retain our vagina and uterus. If we have had a genital surgery that causes our vaginal canal to be narrower, this can cause problems during labor and prevent us from having a vaginal birth, requiring a cesarean section (c-section) instead.

HEALING TIMELINE

Due to the intensity of the surgery and unpredictable complications, healing times are highly variable with a vaginectomy. Return to a desk job, more intensive exercise, and sexual activity generally takes at least six to eight weeks at a minimum.

COMPLICATIONS

Vaginectomy is a surgery on an area inside our pelvis that has many blood vessels, nerves, and important organs nearby. High blood loss during surgery is common and may require a blood transfusion. Due to the high concentration of nerves in the area, we are likely to experience postoperative pain for many weeks.[25] Initially, a surgical drain may be placed to help drain blood and other fluids, and to promote healing and closure. More rarely, surgeries inside the pelvis such as vaginectomy can injure the nearby organs of the bladder or rectum. Surgeons monitor for these serious and life-threatening complications during the immediate postoperative period, before we are discharged from the hospital. It is possible, especially if we experience strictures in our urine stream, to have this area open back up, and for urine to flow into this space. This *vaginal remnant* can be removed in a later repair surgery.

FACIAL GENDER-AFFIRMING SURGERIES

Facial gender-affirming surgeries are also known as "facial feminization" or "facial masculinization" surgery. These are general terms for a group of procedures designed to change the bone structure of our face and reshape our facial features. A frequent abbreviation for facial feminization surgery is FFS, which may include: creating more female features through recontouring the forehead by shaving the exterior surface of the facial bones; cutting and repositioning bones (*osteotomy*); reducing the size of the jaw bone and repositioning it; and/or reducing the size of the chin. Other FFS procedures include shaping of skin and cartilage, such as lifting the upper lip; adding fat to our cheeks; reconstructing our nose (*rhinoplasty*); bringing our hairline further forward; and/or removing our Adam's apple. These procedures can also be performed to create more male features in facial masculinization surgery. Nonbinary people sometimes also get these procedures in order to alter their features in gender affirming ways.

Facial gender-affirming surgeries are typically outpatient procedures, meaning you leave the hospital the same day. They may be done under local or general anesthesia, depending on which and how many procedures we are having done at the same time. Recovery is also dependent on the amount of work done, which can vary greatly.

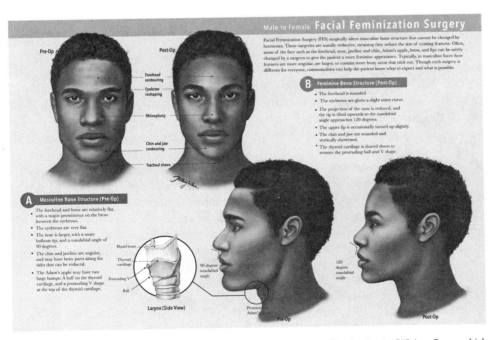

FFS 1. The procedures portrayed in these illustrations are techniques used by Dr. Devin O'Brien-Coon, which may differ from techniques of other surgeons. (Hillary Wilson)

Bone Reduction

Bone reduction may involve shaving down the outer edges of the bones, or a more intensive procedure of cutting sections of the bones out and reattaching them like puzzle pieces. This cutting and repositioning is called an *osteotomy*. These methods are used to reduce the prominence of our facial bone features on the forehead and jaw. Osteotomy procedures on the forehead are sometimes referred to in online forums and among patients as a "type III." This was a name used by Dr. Douglas Ousterhout who pioneered and popularized the use of facial reconstructive surgery techniques for our T/GE needs. Many surgeons caution against going to a provider who does not routinely perform osteotomies, because while just shaving or grinding the facial bones might be the right technique for some people, it does not work for everyone's goals and anatomy. It is best to consult with a surgeon who is skilled in multiple surgical techniques to reach our desired outcomes. Surgeons who perform facial gender-affirming surgery have usually had special training in facial reconstruction (craniofacial or maxillofacial fellowship) after a traditional otolaryngology (ear, nose, and throat) or plastic surgery residency.

HEALING TIMELINE

Bone reduction work is more invasive than soft tissue work, and requires general anesthesia. Any surgery that involves cutting inside the mouth, such as jaw reduction, requires a special liquid diet for a week or more after surgery. Most of us will experience significant swelling and bruising after bone surgeries, but will be able to interact with the world without obviously appearing as if we just had facial surgery within a month after the procedure. Others of us take more time to heal and for swelling to decrease. Waiting for swelling to go down can be quite nerve-racking and difficult for us psychologically, given that we may worry that the surgery has not met our goals. Additionally, we may feel isolated and disconnected from others if we don't feel comfortable going out in public while we are healing.

Augmentation and Fillers

Some surgeons and T/GE community members caution against going to surgeons who only offer *augmentation* (making larger) procedures, given that using both augmenting and reducing techniques together generally creates more natural-appearing outcomes. As with everything in art, beauty, and gender, there are multiple unique, individualized ways to successfully achieve the outcomes we desire. Facial skeletal augmentation uses implants created from different specialized surgical materials including silicone, Teflon, and plastic. These can be inserted into the cheekbones or chin to change the shape of our face. Surgeons may also use permanent fillers that they attach to the bone surface to change the angle of the forehead and fill in depressions at the temples. Additionally, our own fat can be taken from elsewhere in our body and placed into areas of the face.

It is also possible to achieve our goals using temporary dermal fillers, sold under brand names such as Juvederm and Voluma. Dermal fillers are injected under the skin to change the contours of our face. These are not permanent changes, and depending on the formulation, last anywhere from months to years. Dermal fillers are expensive, and it is incredibly rare to have them covered by insurance. Temporary fillers can be used in advance of more permanent procedures to "try out" what the outcomes will look like. All procedures that change the contour of our face can be used to feminize (such as by creating larger cheeks) or masculinize (such as by creating a stronger jawline), depending on our own individual facial features and gendered goals.

HEALING TIMELINE

Implants generally require more invasive procedures that add to healing time. There is usually significant swelling before the final result is visible. Dermal fillers have a quicker and typically painless recovery time, and show results immediately.

The book *Facial Feminization Surgery: A Guide for the Transgendered Woman* (by Dr. Douglas Ousterhout, Addicus Books, 2010) includes photos and detailed explanations of various forms of facial feminization surgeries.

COMPLICATIONS

The major concerns with these procedures include infection and misplacement or migration of implants. Some implant materials are more difficult than others to remove if they do migrate or shift in position.

SILICONE

Cecilia Gentili (she/her) started Trans Equity Consulting after serving as the Director of Policy at GMHC from 2016 to 2019. From 2012 to 2016, she managed the Transgender Health Program at the Apicha Community Health Center. For fun, she loves performing at storytelling and stand-up comedy events where she talks about her life experiences as a Latina, a sex worker, and a transgender woman.

In early 2018, I was called to read for a TV show, *POSE*, which was being filmed in New York City. I had just a couple of pages of script with the lines for the character I would be reading for: Ms. Orlando. I quickly understood I would be reading for a role I have played in real life in the past—that of a back-alley silicone provider.

My own relationship with silicone began at age 17 with the very first trans woman I've ever met. I saw her at a bar and immediately started to follow her around, desiring to absorb anything she shared so that I would have the chance to be like her. In one of our very first meetings she said to me, "If you choose to live this life, there are three things you must know: You are going to be a whore, you are going to get high, and you are going to die young."

For me there was no other choice, and so if my life was to come with sex work, drugs, and death then so be it.

She accepted me as her student. I quickly learned how to do makeup and hair, how to find clothes that flattered me, and how to hustle. She told me what was possible with surgery and what I could expect from hormones, but she did not tell me where she had gotten her huge ass and beautiful hips. "Silicone, of course!" she answered when I asked. As she told me about the injections, my eyes followed her hands as she touched her body. I was filled with envy. Silicone was not a medical procedure one got from a doctor, but something that the girls in the community did for each other. And yes, she would introduce me to one . . .

A few years later, my friend Claudia and I made the decision to get silicone together. I had some luck with hormones, but my breasts were still very small, and for me, the secret to womanhood lay in having a big juicy ass, and of course, I couldn't ignore that it would bring me more clients. We decided Claudia would go first and that I would take care of her afterward. She hired a trans woman—our very own Ms. Orlando—who arrived at the apartment with two big bottles of a gel-like substance. She held them in the air. "This is your right, and this is your left darling," she exclaimed, "and together they will bring you success in life!"

She spread an array of big syringes and even bigger needles across the bed sheet next to Claudia. "Are you ready bitch?" she asked.

Claudia took a big breath. With all the needles in place she asked me to fill the syringes. As I filled them and passed them to her, she injected the silicone into Claudia's accepting body. Like magic, her ass grew in front of my eyes. "Help me push down the syringes," she demanded of me, "It feels like her body does not want to take any more!" Claudia moaned in pain, but she knew what it meant. Surviving this would translate into a figure that says, "I am a woman." A figure that says, "I am beautiful."

"Don't you stop!" Claudia yelled in between screams, "I want the whole two liters in."

When we finished, the woman instructed us to massage the silicone into place. As I pressed my palms against her ass, I could feel it settling under her skin. It felt like playdough, like I was making a ceramic figure.

When my time came, the woman came to the house where I was staying, the domain of "La Correntina" —an older trans woman who opened her house to all the working girls. The process was similar to Claudia's. The pain was intense, but I knew how the results would look, and so I suffered in silence. When she finally finished, they walked me in front of the mirror. "I am beautiful," I first thought.

We girls only talked about how great we would look with silicone. I knew there were risks, but I chose not to look into them. Nobody said, "Hey, this silicone may travel to your heart and collapse it!" or "Bacteria can go inside your body with the silicone and kill you." We didn't even talk about how it could move around and look horrible. Why would we? We existed in a world that was about thriving in the present and accepting the likelihood of an early death. If I could have hips now, then what else was there to think about?

When La Correntina started getting sick all the time, we all knew. We did not talk about her health. If she didn't invite the conversation, neither would we. I also knew that if we even mentioned HIV or AIDS it would bring a cloud of judgment over her, over the home where we lived, and over the whole family.

So, without mentioning why, she asked me: "Maria Cecilia, I need to look healthier. I need to look more . . . robust. I eat and eat and eat and I don't gain any weight, and I put my faith in you because you are the only one I trust."

I owed her so much. How could I say no? "If you get the silicone, I will do it for you," I answered.

She brought home bottles of industrial silicone. "I cannot hide my arms in summer and they are too skinny. I need them to look bigger, to look healthier," she pleaded.

We sterilized all the syringes, and I cleaned her body with alcohol. I pinched the skin and pushed the needle in. I felt the sound of her skin breaking. When no blood flooded in, I held my breath and pushed a couple of big syringes of silicone into her right arm. I took the needle out, put crazy glue over the wound, and then started massaging the silicone into her shoulder and bicep. Together we looked down at the work. "This is what I needed," she said. "Do the left one, and do more." I came to repeat the ritual in her legs, in her chest, and in her face so she could look healthier.

After Correntina died, I moved to the United States. I got more silicone. I still avoided looking into the risks, but I couldn't help hearing about friends whose silicone traveled down their legs or about a girl who was disfigured by a bad job. One girl died of it, and another became very ill. One of my best friends now struggles with kidney issues because of silicone. Another friend lives in constant pain and has to take antibiotics all the time. Despite trying to avoid it, I learned how much can go wrong anyway.

However, even after all that, I continued to get silicone. More and more—always chasing that figure.

Nowadays, I know that life can be much longer than expected. We now know about Brazilian butt lifts, fillers, and fat transplants. Many people talk about seeking safe alternatives, but those procedures are very expensive. If you don't have health insurance—and even if you do—your insurance may not cover it. If you are undocumented or don't know how to navigate the coverage process, it is so difficult.

However, silicone is always there and doesn't need prior authorization.

These days, horror stories continue to surround me. I know what has happened to my community and what could happen to me. And still, when I don't see the shape that I want in the mirror, I cannot stop thinking of my first time—a teenage girl staring back at her reflection, finally believing, "I am beautiful . . . ."

Chondrolaryngoplasty

What is commonly referred to as "tracheal shave" is not actually an operation on the trachea, but rather, a procedure that cuts back the thyroid cartilage, known in medical terminology as a *chondrolaryngoplasty*. During this procedure, the surgeon makes an incision either in the front of the neck directly onto the protruding Adam's apple cartilage, or higher up in the fold of skin where neck and jaw meet. The cartilage is cut back, removed, and the incision is closed. An operation can also be done to create an Adam's apple for those of us seeking masculinization. In this surgery, cartilage from the rib or elsewhere in our body is cut out and attached in our neck to create the feature of an Adam's apple.

HEALING TIMELINE

Adam's apple surgery itself is a minor outpatient procedure with quick recovery time. It can also be combined with voice surgery or other facial gender-affirming surgeries, which would significantly increase recovery and healing time. Complete recovery is expected within weeks. During the healing period we can expect some soreness, along with difficulty swallowing and speaking.

COMPLICATIONS

As with any surgery, there is risk of bleeding, infection, and damage to surrounding tissue or organs. Because the area undergoing surgery is close to where our vocal cords attach, there is the risk of temporary or permanent damage to our voice.

Neurotoxins

Neurotoxins, such as brand name *Botox,* are injected into areas of the body to paralyze minor muscles in order to remove wrinkles and make a person look younger. They can also be used to alter gendered facial features. For example, neurotoxins can be used to raise the eyebrows and change the appearance of our eyebrow ridge. Neurotoxins can also be used to decrease the size of the masseter muscle, one of the muscles of the jaw that makes the lower jaw appear square.[26]

HEALING TIME

No anesthesia is needed for neurotoxin injections and the results are immediate. Healing time is very quick. There may be a few days of swelling or redness immediately after the injection. The effects of neurotoxins typically last for three to seven months.

COMPLICATIONS

We should only go to certified beauticians or plastic surgeons for Botox injections, not under-ground beauticians, because we risk causing permanent nerve damage and disfigurement if the procedure is done incorrectly or if we are injected with a fake or impure substance.

HAIR TRANSPLANTS

Some of us get hair transplants as part of a gender affirming surgical path to replace hair loss for a more societally feminine hairline. Others of us get hair transplants to replace hair loss on our scalp caused by our use of testosterone. Hair transplantation can also be used to create facial hair in those of us who desire more typically masculine facial hair patterns. Our surgeon will help us select a donor site from which our hair follicles will be moved. The donor sites typically used include the side or back of the head. Various techniques can be used, such as transplanting a strip of hair-bearing skin from one location on our body to a new location (known as *follicular unit strip surgery*), or transferring each hair follicle individually to a new location (known as *follicular unit extraction*). Hair transplants never have a 100% success rate. For example, if a hundred hair follicles are transferred, 75 might regrow. Thus, some of us may need multiple surgeries to reach our hairline goals.

Healing Timeline

Before surgery, surgeons may recommend massaging the scalp to increase the stretch of the skin of the donor site. Some surgeons may prescribe a medication to use preoperatively that prevents hair loss. After surgery, a bandage is kept on the scalp at least overnight. We will be advised not to shampoo the area of the hair transplant for at least 48 hours. After that, we must be cautious and gentle when we shampoo our hair. For the first several days, great care should be taken to limit swelling in the scalp by limiting movement of our scalp muscles (such as by raising our eyebrows or squinting). Showering is typically not recommended until about one week after surgery. Sutures are generally removed in eight to ten days. Regrowth of successfully transplanted hairs should be visible in nine to twelve months.

Complications

Risks of this procedure include swelling, ingrown hairs, infection, increased or decreased scalp sensation, temporary hair thinning, visible scarring, and unsuccessful transplantation.

VOICE SURGERY

Voice therapy with a trained speech and language pathologist is expected before we are deemed a good candidate for voice surgery. As we learn about the various elements of voice and speech, and the way they communicate gender, we can begin to alter the portions of our voice that we have control over. This will give us a better understanding of whether voice surgery would be an effective treatment for us. Voice surgery can alter pitch, but it does not affect other elements of our voice. There is an overlap in pitch range between societally dictated "masculine" and "feminine" voices. Some of us do not wish to approach our transition in such a binary way. Studies of voice surgery focus more on pitch as an outcome than patient satisfaction.

> *My PCP has referred me to one specialist inside of the same organization, who also supports trans health care: a voice therapist. I am part way through my voice therapy, and they also seem well-educated and aware of my specific needs.*

Various procedures have been described in the literature that alter the pitch of the voice by changing the tension on the vocal cords, shortening the vocal cords, or reducing the mass of the vocal area.[27] Often the procedures are sought out to raise pitch, but pitch can also be lowered by vocal surgery. It is best to go to a trained vocal surgeon, usually an otolaryngologist with a subspecialty in vocal cord surgery. Another benefit to working with a speech and language pathologist is that they are often in contact with vocal surgeons and can give recommendations about the training and competency of surgeons in your area.

Healing Timeline

During recovery we will have to undergo a period of "vocal rest" in which we do not use our voice at all. We must have complete vocal rest (i.e., no speaking or making noises) for the first few weeks after surgery. Then we will gradually be allowed to use our voice as healing progresses. Continuing to work with a speech and language pathologist after surgery helps us to heal safely and to learn how to use our new pitch range.

Complications

Possible complications include infection, difficulty swallowing or breathing, throat pain, scarring, decreased ability to speak loudly, reduced quality of our voice, and/or permanent vocal cord damage.

BODY CONTOURING AND FAT GRAFTING

Body contouring procedures change the silhouette of the body by removing fat from unwanted areas, and if desired, adding the removed fat to a different part of our body (known as *grafting*) to make these areas larger or curvier. When fat is grafted, much of it is reabsorbed by the body. Because of this, our ideal results might require placing an initially larger amount of fat than desired or repeating procedures. Some surgeons may also use synthetic implants to add volume to areas such as the hips. It is hard to get insurance to cover these procedures because they are often misconstrued by insurance companies as "cosmetic" rather than medically necessary procedures.

Healing Timeline

After body contouring, a compression garment is worn over the area to assist in healing and fluid drainage for weeks or months afterward. These compression garments can be very uncomfortable to wear. Healing time is dependent on each person's body and how much body contouring and fat grafting was done in a single procedure.

Complications

Body contouring can cause significant swelling and bruising. There is also risk of bleeding-related complications. When fat is removed and then replaced (grafted) into the body, the fat cells can die, causing *fibrosis*, or unusual lumps and hard spots. Large implants can also be uncomfortable, even after healing is complete, and issues with infection, incorrect placement, or migration of the implant can occur.

PREPARING FOR SURGERY DAY

Once we have decided on what surgery or procedures we want, and have chosen a surgeon, often times we must wait for an extended period for our surgery date to arrive. In the United States, the most reputable and experienced surgeons providing genital surgery who also take insurance currently have years-long waitlists. Similarly, countries with national health systems have multiyear processes in order to access bottom surgery. Finding out how long we have to wait for surgery, or even for just a consultation, can be incredibly disheartening. We can use this wait-time to prepare for the eventual surgery, and make sure our overall health and well-being is in optimal condition for the best possible surgical outcomes. This is the time to make sure our lifestyle and support system are stable so that our recovery can be as free of stress as possible.

We should work with our primary care providers on management of our other health conditions, such as getting our weight within the range required by our surgeon, quitting smoking, eating healthy, and exercising. Conditions such as diabetes and HIV will need to be well-controlled to lower our risk of complications during and after surgery. Some genital surgical teams have found that for people with existing pelvic floor problems, working with a pelvic floor physical therapist before surgery can have a positive impact on the vaginoplasty process.[28]

Hair Removal

Hair must be permanently removed from areas that are going to be used for our genital surgery. This can be done through electrolysis or laser hair removal, depending on our skin and hair tone. It is best to start the hair removal process as soon as possible to achieve total destruction of the hair follicles, which may take several hair growth cycles. Complete hair removal from the area can take well over a calendar year, even if we go to regular appointments every four to six weeks. Currently, prevailing advice is to allot a period of two years for full hair removal treatment. Not doing hair removal in advance raises our long-term postsurgical risks; there are documented cases in which postoperative hair growth created minor and major complications after genital surgery.[29,30]

The areas that can cause complications are the sections of skin that will be internally located and hard or impossible to access after surgery, such as the lining of the new urethra and the lining of the new vaginal canal. The exact area that will become internal varies based on surgical technique and our own anatomy, and thus may be hard to predict with complete certainty before surgery. It is best to ask our surgeon in the consultation what areas they suggest we begin hair removal on. Some surgeons' offices will even provide this guidance in advance of a consultation, or have diagrams on their websites. Often, hair removal professionals who have experience working with T/GE people preparing for bottom surgery will know where to start. Hair removal can be a painful process. A numbing cream containing lidocaine can be purchased over the counter, or prescribed in higher strengths by primary care providers and surgeons, to be applied to the area of skin 45–60 minutes before our hair removal appointments. Being well-hydrated before treatment and taking over-the-counter pain medicine such as ibuprofen or acetaminophen can also help decrease pain.

LASER HAIR REMOVAL

Laser hair removal works best on people with hair that is significantly darker than their skin tone. Laser treatments are more effective for treating a large area with dense hair follicles. It will weaken and thin the hair, ideally to complete hairlessness. Laser hair removal is often sold in "packages" of multiple treatments. Six treatments weeks apart is the minimum amount of treatments that might be needed. Most of us will need far more than six treatments to achieve significant hair reduction necessary for surgery. Lasers in a specific wavelength, including nd:YAG lasers, are more effective for darker-skinned people. One considerable risk to laser hair removal is that it can change the pigment of our skin in the treated area. This risk is higher in people with darkly pigmented skin.

ELECTROLYSIS

Electrolysis is a method of damaging hair follicles one-by-one by delivering electricity directly to the root of the hair follicle using a handheld needle attached to the electrolysis machine. Electrolysis is the only FDA-approved method for permanent hair removal. Like laser hair removal, it requires multiple treatments over time to ensure total clearance. Electrolysis is a longer, and more painful process than laser hair removal, because each hair follicle is treated individually. It may be difficult to find a certified electrolysis provider who is comfortable working on the genital area.

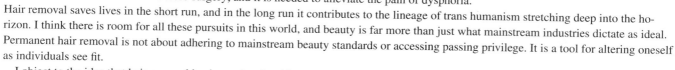

Claire Russell (she/her) is a queer, polyamorous trans woman who was born in San Diego, California. She is an artist, writer, comedian, activist, entrepreneur, cofounder of San Diego Trans Pride, sole proprietor of Auntie Claire's, and current sitting president of The T-Spot Inc. in San Diego.

Electrolysis, a permanent form of hair removal more potent than laser, falls into an unusual intersection in my life and the lives of other trans people. For those seeking genital reconstruction surgery, it's often a vital preparatory step. It's also the preferred hair removal method for trans women looking to eliminate facial hair. I was trained in this field to understand it as a cosmetic trade, where trans women are mentioned in one brief aside, and other trans people are ignored entirely. In addition, some people have confronted me with the idea that permanent hair removal isn't body positive and plays into mainstream beauty standards. My entire career, however, is built around body positivity and the needs not just of trans women but of the trans community as a whole.

For myself and a lot of trans people, electrolysis is about beauty, medical necessity, and self-actualization. It is often needed before surgery, and it is needed to alleviate the pain of dysphoria. Hair removal saves lives in the short run, and in the long run it contributes to the lineage of trans humanism stretching deep into the horizon. I think there is room for all these pursuits in this world, and beauty is far more than just what mainstream industries dictate as ideal. Permanent hair removal is not about adhering to mainstream beauty standards or accessing passing privilege. It is a tool for altering oneself as individuals see fit.

I object to the idea that hair removal begins and ends with societal peer pressure to live up to a projected image of beauty, simply because it often overlaps with current mainstream beauty standards. We all have the right to self-actualize. It is nobody's business what someone else does to their body, and there is no room in a compassionate world for shaming others for those bodies. There is no difference between having your nails done, muscles strengthened, teeth whitened, skin tattooed or tanned, taking hormone therapy, or implanting computers into one's limbs. Nor is there a difference between growing fur, feathers, scales, altering pupil shape, height, permanent hair color, and more modifications that may become available to us in the future, whether what they are doing conforms to mainstream beauty standards or not.

I take strides to emphasize to my clients that no body hair needs to be removed by virtue of its existence. There is no such thing as wrong hair, only undesired or painful hair. Occasionally people leave my consultations deciding not to pursue hair removal. They discover what their true desires for their hair are, realizing that the pressure to remove it was coming from external forces. Other times, people have a stoked confidence in their decision. My openness and lack of judgment may not always be the best business decision, but it's a good human decision. When it comes to altering human bodies those are the decisions that are most important.

RECOVERING AFTER SURGERY

Creating a Support Team

Although the limited long-term research that currently exists shows that those of us who want surgery are generally happy with our surgery,[31,32] there can be frustrating and scary moments as we adjust to our new bodies. No matter how much we research and prepare for surgery in advance, there will always be some aspects that are outside of our control. It is common for anesthesia used during the surgery and postoperative pain to negatively affect our mental health. In addition, spending significant periods in bed, having to be away from our normal routine, being isolated from others, and feeling unable to physically take care of our own needs can also contribute to postoperative depression. It is important that we plan ahead to have friends and family support us physically and emotionally after surgery. If we are having a same-day surgery under general anesthesia, we will need someone to escort us home and stay with us for a few hours to make sure we are OK. For more intensive surgery with higher risks and longer recovery periods, many surgeons require that we designate a person to be our support throughout the postoperative period, when it may be difficult to take care of our own physical needs, including wound care, personal hygiene, toileting, and obtaining and cooking food. Some surgeons may want us to go to a skilled nursing facility after discharge from the hospital until we are able to provide care for ourselves. This could be an added expense, and may risk being an unpleasant experience if the skilled nursing facility is not T/GE competent and affirming. We should research skilled nursing facilities and ask specific questions about trans care and staff

Embrace. (Armani Dae)

trainings before we decide on a place. It is also possible to hire a personal caretaker for after surgery. Some T/GE people have recently started offering this as an in-community hired service.[33]

It is important to remember that all surgeries have risks. However, worrying excessively about something going wrong can be detrimental to our well-being. Our surgeon will give us instructions on how to contact them in case of a complication or urgent need after surgery. Depending on the situation though, we might have to go to an emergency room if we experience a complication that is a medical emergency. After surgery, our new parts will require medical care throughout our life.

Medical Support

Our local primary care provider (PCP) will likely be asked to do a routine preoperative physical exam for surgery clearance. If our PCP provides care to many T/GE patients, they may be a valuable resource for making decisions about surgery and getting feedback about local surgeons. Our PCP can also help us after surgery, even taking on postoperative care tasks such as removing surgical drains or sutures, if our PCP is comfortable doing so and our surgeon has given them permission. PCPs are responsible for our long-term preventative screenings such as PAP smears, prostate exams, and chest exams that may still be needed, depending on the surgery we have had and what organs and tissues remain in our body.

If we are traveling out of our local area for bottom surgery that will affect our urinary system, it could help to establish care with a local urologist near our home before we leave for our surgery. This way, we will be an established patient and have an easier time getting an appointment to be seen for postoperative care needs, especially those that may arise unexpectedly. It is best that our surgery team and PCP are allowed to communicate for any postoperative concerns or follow-up care.

Immediately after surgery, I had to see numerous health professionals because I was having a lot of problems. When I spread my legs they tended to look at it like Will Smith looking at the woman giving birth to an alien in Men in Black! It's very clear that normal practitioners are extremely hard pushed to try and treat any trans-specific surgeries. It was a very testing time because their default cures were contrary to how trans women should be treated (e.g., catheter should not be removed in the case of a UTI because it may never be able to be reinserted, but it is normal practice to do so). There was also the misdiagnosis of a hematoma by a nurse as a Bartholin's cyst—trans women don't have Bartholin's glands, they've got a prostate!

Emotional Support

Those of us who experience emotional difficulties after surgery may feel isolated and misunderstood by our community. Others may place their own expectations on us as to how we should feel after surgery. Having surgery creates complex emotions, and it is normal to have ups and downs during our recovery. In addition to having a primary support person to help with our daily activities, we should also have a network of support in place that we can access for our emotional needs. Some of us may only have one person to care for all of our needs after surgery. This can be a difficult experience for our caretaker and cause them emotional fatigue. It is best to be proactive before surgery to create a plan for postoperative support from a variety of sources.

If we do not routinely receive mental health care, the therapist who wrote our letter for surgery may be able to serve as a resource after surgery. We may plan to engage in short-term therapy after surgery to help us through the rough patches and address our postsurgical expectations. Online and in-person peer support groups can also be helpful to normalize our experiences and provide camaraderie and community support. It is hard to predict what feelings will come up after surgery. Sometimes it can bring up past traumas and make us feel disconnected from our body. If our trauma history involves medical care or the parts of the body that are being operated on, we may want to make a proactive plan about how we will address these potential triggers.

If it is hard for us to access professional and social support, we can still plan for ourselves in order to take care of our emotional well-being. Are there hobbies or projects we can do from bed or with our mobility limitations? Are there books, television shows, or music that we know will be entertaining and a good distraction for us? If we cannot be physically active during our recovery, keeping an active mind can help us feel better and provide a distraction during challenging moments. Before surgery, we can make a written list of activities or media that we can engage in, and loved ones and community members that we can reach out to for support. It can be helpful to keep this list near our bed so it is easily accessible during our recovery period. This visual will help remind us of our options for changing how we feel if we experience postoperative blues.

Complications and Revisions

Advocating for our needs after surgery through the process of complications and revisions can be frustrating. Even the most experienced of surgeons have had surgical complications, because complications are a part of even very routine, common procedures. The best way to judge a surgeon is not just by their complication rates, but also by how they respond and make themselves and the larger care team available if something does not go as planned. Surgeons should be willing to coordinate with our PCPs and specialists. Surgeons who have completed a large volume of cases are more likely to have had former patients who were dissatisfied with their surgical outcomes, because the surgeon has treated so many patients and not everyone will be satisfied with their results, regardless of how good the surgeon is. Word of mouth from the community, while very valuable, should not replace our own carefully conducted research. It is also hard to rely purely on what a surgeon quotes as their complication rate without knowing certain details, such as how long after surgery they follow their patients, and how they are defining "complications." For example, is the surgeon only counting complications that require a surgical fix? Many T/GE people travel to specialized surgical centers, thus many surgeons never hear back from patients once they are cleared to return home. In these cases, the patients get follow-up care, even for complications, closer to home.

There is a broad power dynamic between T/GE people and our surgeons due to the lack of options available to us and financial barriers to access our desired surgeries, which adds to an already existing power imbalance in provider-patient relationships. Many of us who have accessed surgical care may feel pressured to not speak badly about providers who are the only option available in our area. As hard as it is to find information about surgery, it is even harder to find information and support for what to do after a first surgery does not go as planned.

> *I had top surgery. Insurance covered it. Doctor botched it to the extent that I would call it a hate crime. Head of surgery said he would fix it. He made it better, but it is far from fixed. My chest is ruined and insurance will not pick it up. It is too late to sue.*

Research into trans surgery is starting to be taken more seriously by the mainstream medical establishment, and surgeons are developing tools that center the voices of T/GE people in deciding what counts as a success or a complication.[34] The currently existing data on T/GE procedures focuses on very specific complications such as infection and re-operation. Data collected about overall satisfaction, sexual function and pleasure, and postoperative pain, is often gathered via questions that assume a cisgender, heterosexual norm.

GETTING TO KNOW OUR BODIES AGAIN

Scars

Scars are permanent marks on the skin that result from trauma, whether that be a chosen intervention like surgery, or accidental cuts and scrapes, or self-injury. Scarring is a very individual process affected by genetics, location of injured area, sun exposure, and the way we use our bodies after surgery. Some scars become *hypertrophic,* or raised and bunchy. It's impossible to predict exactly how a scar will heal, but looking at previous scars on our own body can give us an idea. People with darker skin have a higher chance of forming *keloid* scars, which is a kind of hypertrophic scarring. Raised and keloid scars may be treated by our surgeon or a dermatologist with steroid injections to make the scars heal flatter.

The pigment of scars is also hard to predict, and is dependent on our genetics, location, skin pigmentation, and sun exposure. Exposing scars to the sun within the first year of healing causes them to be more noticeable long term. Wearing sunscreen and keeping the scar covered with UV-protective clothing is advised in order to minimize pigmentation changes. Surgeons or dermatologists can also use lasers to decrease the redness of scars and help the skin soften. Sometimes, scars adhere to the underlying bodily tissues, limiting movement, creating dimples or indentations, and/or causing discomfort. This

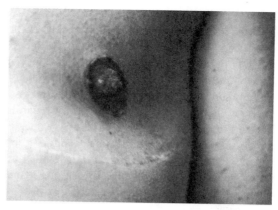

Scar. (Cai Quirk, caiquirk.com)

can be treated in a variety of ways: with physical therapy, acupuncture, massage, mobility exercises, ultrasound therapy, and/or manual manipulation. Scars can also be revised with minor secondary surgeries.

I also don't want to have a massive scar on my forearm. As more people get access to surgeries, more cis people are aware of what the scars mean. My top surgery scars still haven't faded, and I have a hard time being shirtless in public. I was even approached at a pool once and outed in front of everyone by someone who said they were an "ally" and wanted to know if I could offer advice for their friend. I am not willing to have an even bigger scar on a more visible part of my body. The last thing I want is for some cis person to notice the scar on my arm and know exactly what it means.

Nerves and Sensation

Any surgery runs the risk of disrupting nerves in the area of the body where the surgery is being performed, and may result in a change in sensation temporarily or long-term. One possible change is a complete lack of feeling. More often, these changes involve a combination of numbness, tingling, painful or sharp sensations, hypersensitivity, and/or loss of specific elements of sensation such as hot/cold or light surface touch. Small superficial nerves often regrow and reconnect over years. However, factors such as age and health conditions affect healing time and nerve regeneration. It is normal to experience electric zapping sensations in the period immediately after surgery as the nerves heal. It also takes time for our brain to learn how to interpret stimulation in a new area, such as in a newly created vagina or penis.

Sexuality

Discomfort or dissatisfaction in our bodies can be a huge barrier to having an enjoyable and fulfilling sex life. After surgery, we may be able to explore the joys of sex with less gender-related discomfort, but we may also experience frustrations with waiting for healing to take its course and having to relearn our bodies. The vast majority of people who could achieve orgasm before genital surgery are able to do so after bottom surgery.[35,36] Some people who had difficulty achieving orgasm before surgery are able to do so after.[37] There have been cases where the ability to orgasm was made more difficult or even lost after bottom surgery, but this is not a frequent occurrence and is linked to more significant surgical complications and medical trauma. Although sensation may be reduced in the short- or long-term by surgery, many T/GE people experience an overall increase in pleasure and sexual health because we are able to enjoy the sensations we do experience with less, or no, gender-related distress. Even when our discomfort has disappeared and pleasurable sensation is present, it still takes time and intentional effort for our mind-body connection to fully enjoy and give in to our sexual experiences.

We look forward to more community-led research on the impact of surgery on holistic sexual health. In the meantime, connecting online or in person with other T/GE people who have had similar surgeries can help us learn more about the complex and personal experience of sexuality after surgery.

CONCLUSION

The process of planning and recovering from surgery is long, and our surgical results might not be "perfect." The outcome will, however, be perfectly ours, to take care of and enjoy for the rest of our lives. We may end up grieving the loss of some physical parts and sensations in order to make space for the new ones we seek. When considering the trade-offs of acting on the desire for surgery, we must also consider the compromises we are currently making by not getting surgery. As T/GE people, we have the ability to change our physical body and take informed risks in order to affirm our gender. For many of us, surgery is a necessary step in order to honor and support our identity, emotional health, sexual health, spiritual wellness, and/or personal vision for our future.

NOTES

1. Healthcare Laws and Policies. Movement Advancement Project. http://www.lgbtmap.org/equality-maps/healthcare_laws_and_policies
2. Lundgren, T. K., Isung, J., Rinder, J., Dhejne, C., Arver, S., Holm, L. E., & Farnebo, F. (2016). Moving transgender care forward within public health organizations: Inclusion of facial feminizing surgery in the Swedish National Treatment Recommendations. *Archives of Sexual Behavior, 45*(8), 1879–1880.
3. Corporate Equality Index. Human Rights Campaign. https://www.hrc.org/resources/corporate-equality-index-list-of-businesses-with-transgender-inclusive-heal
4. Healthcare Laws and Policies. Movement Advancement Project. http://www.lgbtmap.org/equality-maps/healthcare_laws_and_policies
5. Falcone, M., Timpano, M., Ceruti, C., Sedigh, O., Oderda, M., Gillo, A., Preto, M., Sibona, M., Garaffa, G., Gontero, P., Frea, B., & Rolle, L. (2017). A single-center analysis on the learning curve of male-to-female penoscrotal vaginoplasty by multiple surgical measures. *Urology, 99*, 234–239.
6. Morrison, S. D., Dy, G. W., Chong, H. J., Holt, S. K., Vedder, N. B., Sorensen, M. D., Joyner, B. D., & Friedrich, J. B. (2017). Transgender-related education in plastic surgery and urology residency programs. *Journal of Graduate Medical Education, 9*(2), 178–183.
7. WPATH Open Letter. https://wpathopenletter.wordpress.com
8. Esmonde, N., Heston, A., Jedrzejewski, B., Ramly, E., Annen, A., Guerriero, J., Hansen, J., & Berli, J. (2019). What is "nonbinary" and what do I need to know? A primer for surgeons providing chest surgery for transgender patients. *Aesthetic Surgery Journal, 39*(5), NP106–NP112.
9. Brown, H. (2015, March 24). Planning to go on a diet? One word of advice: Don't. https://slate.com/technology/2015/03/diets-do-not-work-the-thin-evidence-that-losing-weight-makes-you-healthier.html
10. Chodosh, S. (2018, January 10). There are better ways to measure body fat than BMI. https://www.popsci.com/there-are-better-ways-to-measure-body-fat-than-bmi/
11. Mitu, K. (2016). Transgender reproductive choice and fertility preservation. *AMA Journal of Ethics, 18*(11), 1119–1125.
12. Milrod, C., & Karasic, D. H. (2017). Age is just a number: WPATH-affiliated surgeons' experiences and attitudes toward vaginoplasty in transgender females under 18 years of age in the United States. *The Journal of Sexual Medicine, 14*(4), 624–634.
13. Olson-Kennedy, J., Warus, J., Okonta, V., Belzer, M., & Clark, L. F. (2018). Chest reconstruction and chest dysphoria in transmasculine minors and young adults: Comparisons of nonsurgical and postsurgical cohorts. *JAMA Pediatrics, 172*(5), 431–436.
14. Bluebond-Langner, R., Berli, J. U., Sabino, J., Chopra, K., Singh, D., & Fischer, B. (2017). Top surgery in transgender men: How far can you push the envelope? *Plastic and Reconstructive Surgery, 139*(4), 873e–882e. https://doi.org/10.1097/PRS.0000000000003225

15. Wilson, S. C., Morrison, S. D., Anzai, L., Massie, J. P., Poudrier, G., Motosko, C. C., & Hazen, A. (2018). Masculinizing top surgery: A systematic review of techniques and outcomes. *Annals of Plastic Surgery, 80*(6), 679.https://doi.org/10.1097/SAP.0000000000001354

16. Grimstad, F., & Gray, M. (2018). Assessing the ache: A survey to assess new onset abdomino-pelvic pain after initiation of testosterone therapy in female to male transgender and gender non-binary persons. *Journal of Pediatric and Adolescent Gynecology, 31*(2), 180. https://doi.org/10.1016/j.jpag.2018.02.057

17. Berli, J. U., Knudson, G., Fraser, L., Tangpricha, V., Ettner, R., Ettner, F. M., Safer, J. D., Graham, J., Monstrey, S., & Schechter, L. (2017). What surgeons need to know about gender confirmation surgery when providing care for transgender individuals: A review. *JAMA Surgery, 152*(4), 394–400. https://doi.org/10.1001/jamasurg.2016.5549

18. Dessy, L. A., Mazzocchi, M., Corrias, F., Ceccarelli, S., Marchese, C., & Scuderi, N. (2014). The use of cultured autologous oral epithelial cells for vaginoplasty in male-to-female transsexuals: A feasibility, safety, and advantageousness clinical pilot study. *Plastic and Reconstructive Surgery, 133*(1), 158–161.

19. Jacoby, A., Maliha, S., Granieri, M. A., Cohen, O., Dy, G. W., Bluebond-Langner, R., & Zhao, L. C. (2019). Robotic Davydov peritoneal flap vaginoplasty for augmentation of vaginal depth in feminizing vaginoplasty. *The Journal of Urology, 201*(6), 1171–1176.

20. I am recovering from a non-standard vaginoplasty: I kept my penis. Ask me a couple things. (Serious, NSFW) https://www.reddit.com/r/asktransgender/comments/9csb92/i_am_recovering_from_a_nonstandard_vaginoplasty_i

21. Frey, J. D., Poudrier, G., Chiodo, M. V., & Hazen, A. (2016). A systematic review of metoidio-plasty and radial forearm flap phalloplasty in female-to-male transgender genital reconstruction: Is the "ideal" neophallus an achievable goal? *Plastic and Reconstructive Surgery. Global Open, 4*(12), e1131. https://doi.org/10.1097/GOX.0000000000001131

22. Frey, J. D., Poudrier, G., Chiodo, M. V., & Hazen, A. (2017). An update on genital reconstruction options for the female-to-male transgender patient: A review of the literature. *Plastic and Reconstructive Surgery, 139*(3), 728–737. https://doi.org/10.1097/PRS.0000000000003062

23. Selvaggi, G., Hoebeke, P., Ceulemans, P., Hamdi, M., Van Landuyt, K., Blondeel, P., De Cuypere, G., & Monstrey, S. (2009). Scrotal reconstruction in female-to-male transsexuals: A novel scrotoplasty. *Plastic and Reconstructive Surgery, 123*(6), 1710. https://doi.org/10.1097/PRS.0b013e3181a659fe

24. Nikolavsky, D., Yamaguchi, Y., Levine, J. P., & Zhao, L. C. (2017). Urologic sequelae following phalloplasty in transgendered patients. *The Urologic Clinics of North America, 44*(1), 113–125. https://doi.org/10.1016/j.ucl.2016.08.006

25. Groenman, F., Nikkels, C., Huirne, J., van Trotsenburg, M., & Trum, H. (2017). Robot-assisted laparoscopic colpectomy in female-to-male transgender patients: Technique and outcomes of a prospective cohort study. *Surgical Endoscopy, 31*(8), 3363–3369. https://doi.org/10.1007/s00464-016-5333-8

26. Ascha, M., Swanson, M. A., Massie, J. P., Evans, M. W., Chambers, C., Ginsberg, B. A., Gatherwright, J., Satterwhite, T., Morrison, S. D., & Gougoutas, A. J. (2019). Nonsurgical management of facial masculinization and feminization. *Aesthetic Surgery Journal, 39*(5), NP123–NP137.

27. Song, T. E., & Jiang, N. (2017). Transgender phonosurgery: A systematic review and meta-analysis. *Otolaryngology–Head and Neck Surgery, 156*(5), 803–808.

28. Manrique, O. J., Adabi, K., Huang, T. C. T., Jorge-Martinez, J., Meihofer, L. E., Brassard, P., & Galan, R. (2019). Assessment of pelvic floor anatomy for male-to-female vaginoplasty and the role of physical therapy on functional and patient-reported outcomes. *Annals of Plastic Surgery, 82*(6), 661–666.

29. Suchak T., Hussey, J., Takhar, M., & Bellringer, J. (2015). Postoperative trans women in sexual health clinics: Managing common problems after vaginoplasty. *Journal of Family Planning and Reproductive Health Care, 41*(4):245–247. Doi: 10.1136/jfprhc-2014-101091

30. Zhang W., Garrett, G. L., Arron, S. T., & Garcia, M. M. (2016). Laser hair removal for genital gender affirming surgery. *Translational Andrology and Urology, 5*(3): 381–387. doi: 10.21037/tau.2016.03.27

31. Horbach, S. E., Bouman, M. B., Smit, J. M., Özer, M., Buncamper, M. E., & Mullender, M. G. (2015). Outcome of vaginoplasty in male-to-female transgenders: A systematic review of surgical techniques. *The Journal of Sexual Medicine, 12*(6), 1499–1512.

32. Horbach, S. E., Bouman, M. B., Smit, J. M., Özer, M., Buncamper, M. E., & Mullender, M. G. (2015). Outcome of vaginoplasty in male-to-female transgenders: A systematic review of surgical techniques. *The Journal of Sexual Medicine, 12*(6), 1499–1512.

33. T4T Caregiving. https://transcaregiving.weebly.com/

34. Klassen, A. F., Kaur, M., Johnson, N., Kreukels, B. P., McEvenue, G., Morrison, S. D., Mullender, M. G., Poulsen, L., Ozer, M., Rowe, W., Satterwhite, T., Savard, K., Semple, J., Sørensen, J. A., van de Grift, T. C., van der Meij-Ross, M., Young-Afat, D., & Pusic, A. L. (2018). International phase I study protocol to develop a patient-reported outcome measure for adolescents and adults receiving gender-affirming treatments (the GENDER-Q). *BMJ Open, 8*(10), e025435. https://doi.org/10.1136/bmjopen-2018-025435

35. Hess, J., Hess-Busch, Y., Kronier, J., Rübben, H., & Neto, R. R. (2016). Modified preparation of the neurovascular bundle in male to female transgender patients. *Urologia Internationalis, 96*(3), 354–359.

36. Horbach, S. E., Bouman, M. B., Smit, J. M., Özer, M., Buncamper, M. E., & Mullender, M. G. (2015). Outcome of vaginoplasty in male-to-female transgenders: A systematic review of surgical techniques. *The Journal of Sexual Medicine, 12*(6), 1499–1512.

37. Capelle, R., & Massault, E. (2017). Comparative study: Free radial forearm flap phalloplasty versus anterior lateral thigh flap phalloplasty. Dissertation. Ghent University. https://libstore.ugent.be/fulltxt/RUG01/002/350/038/RUG01-002350038_2017_0001_AC.pdf

14

MENTAL HEALTH AND EMOTIONAL WELLNESS

Sand C. Chang and Nathaniel G. Sharon

INTRODUCTION

Perspectives vary widely on what mental and emotional wellness looks like, how we seek help and emotional healing, and how our mental health is affected by our transgender and gender expansive (T/GE) identities, cultural identities, and societal influences. The concepts of "health" and "wellness" are culturally bound and defined. If we consider the available representations of health within our family, culture, or society at large, we can reflect on what messages we have come to internalize, which ring true for us personally, and which we are seeking to unlearn or dismantle. There are many different ways of thinking and talking about mental health. What is "healthy" for one person may not apply to a different person. There may be terms in this chapter that feel "right" for you and others that do not. As with anything else, we want to empower you to find your own language to describe your experiences and identities.

> At the time when I realized I was trans, I was seeing a counselor for anxiety. Even though I didn't seek to interrogate issues of gender, I happened to find a counselor who ended up being experienced with transition and such questions, and she was an invaluable resource in helping me come to some important conclusions on my path.

Mental health can be framed in a variety of ways, from more formal medical diagnoses and treatment to more behavioral, social, or spiritual forms of care. Even the idea of "treatment" itself can be limiting, because it can assume that mental health concerns must be cured or alleviated versus accepted as an expression of human variation or diversity.[1] We encourage an appreciation for the many ways that people choose to view and respond to their mental and emotional health needs. We all deserve the dignity to choose whatever is most helpful for us.

Trans Lifeline (877-565-8860) is a "trans-led organization that connects trans people to the community, support, and resources they need to survive and thrive."

> For the first several therapists, it was I who had to educate them on gender identity issues. Frankly, I got tired of paying them to listen to me train them. I was glad to find a therapist who was not only well-educated on trans issues, but had a ton of experience. Of late, I have not needed gender-related mental health help but on a more personal level dealing with my parents (I live w/them as they are both in their mid-nineties).

Mental health involves our behaviors, emotions, thinking, self-care, and relationship with ourselves and others. Mental and emotional wellness, or the lack thereof, can impact every aspect of our lives, from being able to perform our jobs to being able to communicate with others effectively. Our mental health needs can also change as we progress through the lifespan. As children, having a safe and nurturing environment that supports our learning and development is crucial to healthy brain and emotional development. Family love and acceptance is essential to children's well-being. In middle-age, our emotional well-being is often supported by engagement in things we find productive and satisfying, such as work, education, or building a community of supports. We may enrich our spiritual lives or social connectedness, or build families or legacies of service and giving. As we grow older, our desires and life goals may change direction. At times, we may need to rely

Solomon and Dodger. Picnic at Old Forge.

on others for physical support and companionship. We may desire to pass down to others the knowledge we've gained from our years of living. Despite societal oppression that we may experience throughout our lives, we as T/GE people are resilient and supported by community, strength, and visibility, along with a collective voice that can strengthen our mental health and create lives worth living.

ON DYSPHORIA

Eden Squish Mackenzie (they/them) is a genderqueer writer and essayist, and considers themself a student of identity. They use writing to explore their struggles with the subject and uncover new ways to see the world. Eden is from Birmingham, Alabama and is working toward a Fiction BFA at Columbia College Chicago.

Within the trans community, we talk a lot about dysphoria. It's understandable. Dysphoria is a real, inescapable part of the lives of many transgender people. I myself am coping with my own as I write this piece—acutely aware of the traditionally masculine meatiness of my hands.

However, I've watched my trans siblings weaponize dysphoria against one another—claiming that the pinnacle of trans identity is dysphoria. That to be trans is to hurt.

Treating dysphoria with this level of priority only builds arbitrary barriers, separating people without severe dysphoria from a community that should give them the same solidarity it has given the rest of us. A community we—or at least I—love being a part of.

Dysphoria becomes dangerous when we forget to talk about its specifics or its opposite.

Most times dysphoria is mentioned, it implies *physical* dysphoria—distress caused by the incongruence between gender and the body. Again, physical dysphoria is real for many trans people. It exists alongside our common understanding of the word *transition*. Medical. Physical.

Social dysphoria, however, is seldom mentioned. It can be just as painful as its physical counterpart, revolving around how a person's gender is perceived by those around them. Being misgendered, for example, is a common trigger of social dysphoria. It doesn't necessitate bodily discomfort. A social transition differs from a physical one—be it changing names, changing presentation, or changing or accepting different pronouns.

We as a community also need to make room for the voices of those who recognize transness before, or without, dysphoria.

"But Eden," you say, "how can you know you're trans sans dysphoria?"

I'm glad you asked, nonexistent other half of this conversation.

While the community prioritizes dysphoria, we never mention euphoria—the feeling of comfort or satisfaction caused by being gendered correctly. Although some trans people have dysphoria, some don't, and they experience transness through gender euphoria. Not through pain, but pleasure.

In the same breath as they weaponize dysphoric experiences, people often say things like, "being trans isn't fun" (usually with the aid of excessive clapping emojis). Although there is truth to that—the trans experience isn't easy nor should it be trivialized—I've had a lot of fun being trans. Knowing who I am, being able to embrace myself, becoming a part of a wider community that validates me. It's fun to be whole. And why shouldn't it be?

MENTAL HEALTH STIGMA AND ABLEISM IN TRANS COMMUNITIES

I had one bad experience recently where I was seeing a therapist (who was a cis lesbian) and when talking about my partner's gender identity she got really hung up on it. I mentioned it in passing, but she kept coming back to them being trans and started trying to explain that some of their struggles, which I was seeking support in helping them with, were because they were trans. She also talked a lot about this one trans friend she has and his experiences, which was totally irrelevant. I'm also a social worker and I was really taken aback by this borderline TERF-iness. But I was also super triggered because she was my therapist, and I was in a super vulnerable emotional state. I ended up terminating services and telling her why, after which she continued to contact me (and tokenize her one trans friend in our communication). It was pretty disappointing and made it harder for me to trust my next therapist.

In many places, having mental health concerns and seeking treatment for them can come with stigma, shame, and fear of judgment. It may be especially difficult for us as T/GE people because we already face social stigma based on our trans identities. Having mental health needs may add to the stigma we experience. We may internalize this stigma by feeling the need to keep our mental health diagnoses a secret or hide that we see a therapist or psychiatrist. We may fear losing our jobs or our connections to a religious community that may not be accepting of mental health treatment. We may fear discrimination in religious, legal, and medical systems due to our mental health needs and/or T/GE identity. Fortunately, there are many local and national organizations working to counter mental health stigma by providing education and support, such as the National Institute of Mental Health, National Alliance on Mental Illness, and The Icarus Project. LGBTQ + organizations, including The Trevor Project and Trans Lifeline, also play a role in reducing the shame around mental health care for queer and T/GE people.

I've been with the same therapist for at least five years. Coming out to her was a little scary because I really depend on her, but she obviously took it well. It isn't a specialty for her, so when I asked her for a letter for HRT she just did her best, but it means a lot to me that I can count on her to always do that for me.

We may experience distrust or fear when seeking mental health care due to the role mental health systems have historically played in gatekeeping access to gender-affirming medical care for our communities. Many of us are required to see a mental health provider to access various gender affirming medical interventions—particularly surgeries—which may create an uncomfortable power dynamic. Luckily, there has been a shift away from a

Sadness. "Sadness, loss, and grief has weight and is held in our bodies as trans, non-binary and GNC people."
(Elliot Kukla)

gatekeeping role, and more and more mental health providers are striving to take a collaborative stance in support of our communities' needs both for physical and mental wellness.

> *The psychotherapist who worked with me before my transition knew that my gender identity was the main reason for my referral to her, but the work we did was much more far-reaching. Without that extensive self-examination, my transition wouldn't have been possible.*

Unfortunately, our identities have historically been pathologized in mental health systems. In the United States, the desire to change our physical traits or social role to align with our gender identity has been listed as a mental health disorder in the *Diagnostic and Statistical Manual of Mental Disorders (DSM)* since 1980.[2] The prior diagnostic term "gender identity disorder" utilized a limited, hetero- and cis-centric narrative of gender, and conflated a desire to change physical traits with differences in gender identities and expressions. As the diagnosis has evolved to "gender dysphoria," it has focused more on the desire to change physical traits and the medical necessity for this care.[3] The continued classification of "gender dysphoria" as a mental health condition is rife with conflict both in medical systems and within our own communities. Many advocate making changes that would remove "gender dysphoria" as a mental health diagnosis and categorize it as a medical condition.[4,5] Others argue for the diagnosis to remain as is for various reasons including insurance coverage, access to mental health treatment, and familial acceptance/support, while others prefer no label or classification at all.[6,7]

Rest for Resistance is a New York City-based organization that runs meditation sessions for BIPOC LGBTQIA + people and publishes written pieces that create healing space for trans and queer people of color.

> *Make gender dysphoria a medical diagnosis rather than a psychiatric one. Create greater access to medical transition for those who seek it. HRT should be something any general practitioner or LIP can initiate and monitor and patients should be able to access it with an office visit and informed consent form so long as it is not medically contraindicated. I also believe GCS should be similarly available to adults.*

The *International Classification of Diseases (ICD-11)*, published by the World Health Organization (WHO), formerly used the diagnosis gender identity disorder but now contains a new diagnosis called gender incongruence that is no longer in the mental health section and instead in a new medical section called "Conditions Relating to Sexual Health." The current World Professional Association for Transgender Health (WPATH) Standards of Care and other professional mental health organizations emphasize that simply being transgender is not a mental health disorder.[8,9]

> *I understand that including gender dysphoria as a medical condition is useful for insurance coverage purposes. However, this does still pathologize trans people (as stated by the WHO), and in an ideal world it wouldn't be necessary. I was lucky enough to find a doctor who works with low income patients through payment plans and uses informed consent instead of requiring recommendation letters for trans-related health care.*

The Trevor Project provides support for LGBTQ youth under 25 years of age facing suicidality and other difficult issues through the Trevor Lifeline (866-488-7386), Trevor Text (text START to 678-678), and Trevor Chat (online instant messaging).

Unfortunately, some mental health providers have tried to "cure" or change our genders to match our sex assigned at birth rather than support and affirm our identities and bodily autonomy. We may have endured conversion therapies or psychiatric hospitalizations to try to force us to change our gender identity or expressions or sexual orientations. It is now well established that conversion therapy causes great harm to our well-being. Most mental health professional associations have declared conversion therapy ineffective, unethical, and harmful. In many states, mental health providers can lose their licenses for performing conversion therapy.[10]

> *I feel strongly that transgender identity is not pathological in itself. Gender dysphoria, however, is distressing and can severely impact quality of life, therefore, it necessitates treatment. Therefore, in my opinion, gender dysphoria is a psychopathology, the treatment for which is transition.*

We may avoid seeking mental health care because of stigma or fears of being judged within our own families or communities. Acknowledging our fears, our past experiences, and internalized messages about mental health care, and discussing these with our mental health providers is one way to address our concerns, allowing us to start a dialogue about our wants and needs and facilitate a collaborative and empowering relationship with our mental health provider. It will likely take time to open up about our more vulnerable experiences and develop a sense of trust and assurance that we will not be labeled or judged. That is OK and understandable. A therapeutic mental health provider will see us through these difficult beginnings and allow us time and space to open up. We can empower ourselves with a list of questions to ask our mental health provider prior to seeing them to help ensure we are working with a collaborative and affirming person. A supportive mental health provider will not personalize our protective responses, but rather be open to exploring them with us and will understand why we may have deep-rooted concerns about engaging in mental health care.

> *I do not agree with transgender identities being categorized as a psychiatric diagnosis. This implies that people must suffer from their transgender identity/experience and need to be fixed, rather than the distress coming from the social stigma and inability to align one's physical/social reality with one's gender identity.*

Headcase: LGBTQ Writers and Artists on Mental Health and Wellness is a collection of personal reflections and artistic representations illustrating the intersection of mental wellness, mental illness, and LGBTQ identity, as well as the lasting impact of historical views equating queer and trans identity with mental illness (edited by Stephanie Schroeder and Teresa Theophano, Oxford University Press, 2019).

Some of us may resist and advocate against being labeled as mentally ill, while others of us may find having mental health diagnoses to be helpful in understanding our experiences and promoting hope. For those of us who identify as having mental health concerns and seek out treatment for them, we may experience shame or internalized ableism. There is nothing wrong with having mental health concerns. Denying the severity or significance of our mental health concerns can hurt us and get in the way of us seeking the care and healing that we need to live our lives fully and happily.

> *I am not a big fan of the medical industrial complex as a disabled person. On the one hand, transness isn't a defect. On the other, as a trans and disabled and neurodivergent and mentally ill person, fighting to get transness classified as something other than a psychiatric illness doesn't really help me in any way. Like, OK,*

Self Portrait. Watercolor on Paper. Asher Machado is a Massachusetts based artist with a focus in watercolor and acrylic painting.

even if it's not a psychiatric diagnosis, where does that leave the rest of me? When abled trans people fight that fight, I'm what they're trying to distance themselves from. They don't want to stand next to me and claim me as a member of their community. They want the distance from the stigma that I cannot escape. It isn't helpful. As far as healthcare professionals go, I have to fight to get proper care in any context, although the trans clinic specifically has so far been wonderful.

CURRENT TECHNICAL TERM

Nash Keyes is a nonbinary student from Columbus, Ohio. They study applied mathematics and climate physics while also holding onto passion for art, poetry, and queer issues. They hope to do good for the world through research and activism, as well as create deep connections and beautiful things along the way. They use they/them pronouns as of now, although they are somewhat pronoun agnostic.

for this feeling is essentialized
as the core of any experience
that prefers or demands more
for this burns in me like any chemical
like tampon, like cup, like cock
for this rubs wrong everywhere, mostly nowhere
between shoulders and knees is okay
for this requires six bullet points

> of specific criteria
> for this the page of the DSM-5
> cannot tell me which of the following
> i check off the list
> for this the symptoms
> carry on their slow progress
> without regard for diagnosis

FACTORS AFFECTING MENTAL HEALTH AND EMOTIONAL WELLNESS

Difficulties managing our emotions, behaviors, or thinking can impact our day-to-day functioning, social connections, and ability to reach or maintain our goals. Our mental health is intricately connected to our environment and our bodies, particularly the brain, nervous, and endocrine systems. The health of our brain and the impact of our environment can alter the ways we think, feel, perceive, behave, and socially interact.

Some mental health concerns such as bipolar disorder and schizophrenia are likely to develop regardless of what happens in our environment, and we tend to understand these problems as more influenced by genetics and the brain. Other mental health symptoms or concerns may be temporary and result from particular stressors such as grief or loss of a job. Stress can also "trigger" ongoing or lasting changes in the brain's functioning and chemistry, especially when we have a familial/genetic tendency for particular mental health symptoms or concerns. For example, a person prone to anxiety may develop social anxiety disorder after a history of extensive bullying, or someone prone to depression may experience their first episode of depression after failing a semester of college. For most mental health concerns, there is usually not one exact cause, but multiple factors, given that behaviors and emotions are complex. We may understand our mental health symptoms differently based on our religious, regional, ethnic, or other cultural lenses. Mental health symptoms and concerns may present in different ways depending on our culture. Additionally, what may feel distressing for one person may not feel that way for another.

When considering ways to improve our emotional well-being, we may consider which parts of our lives can be adjusted or changed. Social factors such as employment, the presence of a social community to connect with, housing, and access to mental health services can promote mental wellness, while lack thereof can impact the development and persistence of mental health concerns. Many people underestimate the role of basic self-care, such as getting enough sleep or having our nutritional needs met, in mental and emotional wellness. Additionally, overuse of alcohol or drugs can greatly impact our mood and emotional wellness. Although there may be some factors we cannot control (i.e., having a predisposition toward mental health concerns), there are others that we can (i.e., developing coping skills, mindfulness, and self-efficacy).

THE IMPACT OF HAVING A STIGMATIZED IDENTITY

DeHQ is an LGBTQ Helpline for South Asians (908-367-3374).

Research shows that our communities have higher rates of depression, anxiety, trauma, and suicide when compared to the general population[11,12] due to the daily stressors of stigma and discrimination.[13,14] Simply being a member of a stigmatized group can put us at risk for medical and mental health concerns. The accumulation and effect of having a marginalized identity is referred to as minority stress.[15,16] Minority stress can be compounded for those of us who experience discrimination based on other aspects of our identity, such as physical/mental abilities, ethnicity, gender, sex, religion, nationality, and economic status. Our community experiences high levels of violence and discrimination based on our identities, including emotional, physical, and sexual abuse.[17,18,19] We may run into challenges within religious, medical, mental health, legal, and other systems with which we interface on a routine basis. We may face difficulties obtaining proper government identification to access care, securing trans-affirming insurance to cover our care, or be turned away from care when we seek it. These negative experiences and accumulated stressors can take a toll on our mental health. Societal discrimination may limit our ability to participate in educational goals, find employment opportunities, or develop community connectedness and pride in our identities, and in turn, negatively impact our emotional and physical well-being.

It is well known that many of us experience high levels of violence and discrimination,[20] which negatively affect mental health. We may also experience secondary or "vicarious" trauma when we repeatedly bear witness to our friends and loved ones being victims of violence. Those of us who provide peer or professional support to others in our communities that have been hurt can accumulate secondary trauma.

Research into mental health symptoms and conditions in transgender communities is limited. Some studies indicate that we have the same prevalence rates of mental health conditions as cisgender populations, while others show our community as having higher rates.[21] The rates of mental health conditions in our communities are difficult to ascertain because research methods have been poor and frequently without a matched cisgender control group and research has focused primarily on those of us seeking care in medical or mental health settings, rather than looking at T/GE people in the general population. This approach may artificially inflate numbers and influence what types of mental health conditions are captured.

STRENGTHS AND RESILIENCE
Though our community faces a multitude of social, emotional, financial, and housing trials and tribulations, we have developed profound strength, resilience, and coping strategies to rise above. The ability to "bounce back" in the face of life challenges is known as resilience.[22] For T/GE youth, family acceptance, feeling connected to peers, and a supportive academic environment have been shown to reduce suicidal ideation and increase psychological well-being.[23,24,25] For transgender adults, the same themes apply. Peer and family support, identity pride, community connectedness, and access to affirming healthcare environments can all improve psychological well-being and empowerment.[26,27]

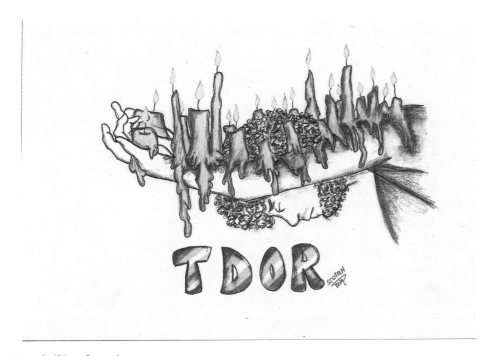

Artwork. (Diego Barrera)

Looking for strategies for developing resilience? Check out *The Queer and Transgender Resilience Workbook: Skills for Navigating Sexual Orientation and Gender Expression*, (by Anneliese Singh, New Harbinger Publications, 2018).

Individual sources of resiliency are person-centered and may include asking for help, learning how to set boundaries, finding productive ways to protect ourselves, developing effective and healthy coping strategies, and advocating for our needs and our communities. Sometimes, however, there is only so much we can do as individuals, and we need to look to our external environment to help support and protect us. Feeling supported by others can have an enormous impact on our sense of well-being. Some of us may have supportive families of origin, while others of us may rely on our peers or "chosen family" to get support and belonging. Some of us are able to access T/GE support groups, which can be incredibly helpful in validating our experiences and building our collective strength. In geographic areas without such support groups, online communities can provide us support and community-connectedness. A sense of community resilience is also fostered by taking care of one another, helping one another access resources, sharing knowledge and skills, and advocating for legal rights and protections for all members of our communities.

THESE DAYS

Hailing from the Sierra Nevada foothills, Lane Lewis (they/them) doubts they'll ever be able to shake the feeling of the forest as home. But that doesn't stop them from trying. You can find them in San Francisco these days, looking for sunshine to soak up and working on a book they're co-writing with their father.

Some days I wish I had a full beard—coarse, thick hair to run fingers through and shape my face.

Some days I want to paint my nails—pinks, purples, teals.

Some days I cringe at the sound of my voice—I try not to talk much on these days.

Some days I want to grow my hair out long, to braid it and put it in a bun—beautiful, handsome, glorious, wavy tumbles of hair.

Some days I see pictures of cis men and I crumple like a paper bag because I'll never be that and it feels like the end of the world—all the air leaves my body and it folds in on itself.

Some days I want to bind my chest so flat that I can't breathe—secure in this too-small fortress.

Some days I want to wear sparkly lipstick and shine for days.

Some days I feel happy when I look in the mirror.

Some days I avoid the mirror at all costs.

Some days I just want to run—somehow, I can escape all of the feelings if I can just get far enough away from them.

Some days I don't want to move—crushed underneath the despair of too much and not enough.

Some days I want to scream—to explode, to refuse to hold it all in.

Some days hormones and top surgery feel so out of reach that I want to just give up.

Some days I feel like I'm making progress—an inch feels like a mile, and I can fly over it all.

This back and forth can be kind of hard to navigate.

Some days I'm good at it.

Some days I'm not.

COMMON MENTAL HEALTH CONCERNS

In this section we provide a brief discussion of common mental health concerns as they affect our communities. The following conditions are described using western understandings of mental health based on the *Diagnostic and Statistical Manual (DSM)*, National Institute of Mental Health (NIMH), and the World Health Organization (WHO). Some mental health conditions such as major depressive disorder, bipolar disorder, and schizophrenia are recognized globally and impact people regardless of background or culture. Other mental health conditions can be understood or manifest in different ways depending on culture and environmental influences. Not every mental health symptom or condition is covered in this chapter; however, the most common ones are reviewed to provide education and empowerment for mental health and well-being.

Mood Disorders

Fluctuations in our mood and emotions occur naturally throughout the day in response to what we are experiencing and do not tend to cause problems in our daily living. We may experience more intense times of fear, anxiety, or sadness that resolve once our external circumstances improve. Some mood changes, however, can be persistent, prolonged, or have a severe impact on our ability to care for ourselves, perform our daily goals, and interact with others. The two most common mood disorders are major depressive disorder (MDD) and bipolar disorder (BD). The World Health Organization[28] cites depression as the leading cause of disability around the world. Those of us with these conditions usually experience our first mood episode between adolescence and adulthood, typically in our teens or twenties. MDD and BD impact not only mood, but also our thinking, motivation, sleep-wake cycle, energy level, and stress hormones. Mood episodes of MDD and BP can last for weeks or even months, and can take significant time to recover from, even once better.

In episodes of MDD, our emotions are consistently sad, down, blue, or irritable—even without an apparent reason. Our thinking may be slowed; we may struggle with proper sleep; we may either not want to eat or we may resort to stress-eating. We may feel constantly tired and sluggish, have a hard time getting motivated, find that our daily self-care and hygiene fall by the wayside, and lose our sex drive. For some of us, the depression gets so severe that we experience hopelessness and thoughts of suicide.

Bipolar disorder (BD) is characterized by separate depressive and manic episodes. The depressive episodes are similar to those in MDD. During manic episodes, we may experience a decreased need for sleep but have excessive energy and feel on top of the world or very irritable. We may talk, think, and move much faster than is usual for us. Our emotions may fluctuate drastically from euphoric to angry. We may become impulsive and do things that are out of character for us such as engaging in shopping sprees, gambling, participating in risky sex, or using alcohol and drugs to excess. Sometimes mania can get so severe that we hallucinate (hearing or seeing things that other people do not), believe we have special powers or abilities, or think people are out to harm us. Only about 3% of the population has BP, but a much higher percentage of people have been told that they have or might have this disorder. That is because trauma can cause fluctuations in mood that are often misdiagnosed as BP. Many of us have difficulty regulating our emotions, which can change rapidly in response to social interactions, sometimes multiple times a day. These types of symptoms are a result of trauma rather than bipolar disorder, and are treated differently.

Treatment for major depressive disorder and bipolar disorder looks different for different people and may depend on how the condition is impacting our daily lives. Many of us find it helpful to keep a daily routine, exercise regularly, and engage in healthy sleep habits to regulate our mood. Many of us may also pursue therapy and medication. Our mental health providers will ask about our medical history and drug and alcohol use, because these can cause mood changes that resemble MDD or BP. There are times when we may need to seek out a psychiatric hospitalization during a mood episode if we are unable to maintain our safety, take care of our daily needs, or if we are unsafe to those around us. Many of us work with a mental health provider to track our mood episodes, identify what factors contribute to our mood changes, and determine what helps promote our mood stability.

Anxiety Disorders

Anxiety is a common experience for all human beings. Anxiety lets us know when to stay alert and motivates us toward action. A little anxiety can be important when studying for an exam or stepping on the brakes to avoid a car accident. Our T/GE communities may experience greater levels of anxiety due to societal discrimination and trauma. Even when all is well, we may anticipate rejection or violence by others because of how we identify or express our genders. Fearing bad things may happen to us and being more aware of our surroundings may be protective if we are in unsafe environments.

Alone. "As a visible, often shunned member of society (and families) the rejection can cut deep and leave transgender people alone and isolated." (Robin Rose)

Although at times helpful, excessively high levels of anxiety or persistent anxiety can interfere with our lives and daily well-being regardless of our gendered experiences. Problems with anxiety often start in childhood and can present in various ways. Those of us with generalized anxiety disorder experience persistent, excessive worries or nervousness. We tend to overthink situations —even the "small stuff." Physical restlessness, headaches, stomach upset, and muscle tension are common. Our racing thoughts and physical symptoms can make it hard to focus and sleep. These symptoms can get in the way of our schooling, work, or relationships.

Panic disorder is a condition in which we experience brief episodes of intense terror and dread. These episodes are accompanied by sweating, nausea, difficulty breathing, chest pain, racing heart, shakiness, and, sometimes feeling we are going to die or we need to escape. Panic attacks can occur randomly or in response to a particular trigger. Some of us have difficulty leaving our homes due to fear of when the next panic attack may occur.

A specific phobia is when we have excessive anxiety or fear of a specific object or situation, such as blood or flying. Phobias can impact our self-care (e.g., fear of needles making us avoid getting our blood drawn for our medical care).

In social anxiety disorder, anticipated or actual encounters with other people create large amounts of fear and anxiety in us. We may fear judgment by others, or feel that we will say or do something wrong. Even while desiring connection with others, social anxiety stops us from engaging. Although we may have good reason to fear discrimination and public judgment, social anxiety disorder tends to be generalized to all social environments, even around others who love and affirm our authentic selves.

Eliminating anxiety altogether is neither feasible nor desirable, but reducing it from impairing levels to adaptive levels can be life-changing for us. There are different approaches

When experiencing mood or anxiety symptoms, it may be helpful to see a medical provider to rule out underlying medical conditions. For example, having increased or decreased thyroid hormone levels can influence these mental health symptoms.

to treating anxiety disorders, which may depend on the type and severity of our condition. Exposure-based therapies can help fear-based responses in phobias and social anxiety while cognitive behavioral therapy can help address ways our anxiety impacts our thoughts, feelings, and behaviors. Medications can be used daily or as needed to help with anxiety symptoms. Support groups, meditation, and exercise can also help us manage our anxiety.

Post-Traumatic Stress and Trauma Responses

As T/GE people, we are frequently exposed to trauma and adverse experiences throughout our childhood and adult years.[29,30] Undergoing traumatic experiences can lead to multiple different mental health conditions, including difficulties with safety and attachment to others, depression, anxiety, substance misuse, and post-traumatic stress disorder (PTSD). Research suggests our community has much higher rates of PTSD related to the minority stress of compounding traumatic experiences and discrimination that we face in our daily lives.[31,32] Accumulation of individual trauma experiences, particularly in childhood, can have a profound impact on our mental and physical health.[33] For example, family rejection is a kind of attachment trauma that may create challenges in feeling safe in friendships or intimate relationships. For all people, the more adverse life events someone has in childhood, the more at risk they are for substance use problems, high risk sexual behaviors, suicide attempts, and depression as they grow older.[34]

Our innate responses to trauma are based on evolutionary responses to danger or threats to our life or safety. These include fight, flight, and freeze responses that are regulated by our nervous system. A "fight" response may look like anger, attack, or confrontation. A "flight" response may look like avoidance, phobias, isolation, or shutting down emotionally. We may dissociate or blank out during a "freeze" response. In PTSD, these responses are frequently out of our control and can occur when triggered or at unexpected times. We may experience persistent negative emotions, nightmares, memories, or

Sleep Carnival, Page One. (Colin Laurel)

flashbacks of our trauma; feel on-edge and unsafe; and avoid people or places that remind us of getting hurt. Trauma reminders may cause us to feel physical symptoms such as difficulty breathing and racing heart. We may abuse drugs or alcohol as a way to numb our negative emotions or stop bad memories. We may even avoid medical or mental health care due to past negative experiences.

Trauma that occurs repeatedly over time during childhood and adolescence is sometimes referred to as "complex trauma," and those who have experienced these types of events, including many of us in T/GE communities, are often diagnosed as having "complex PTSD." Similar symptoms are sometimes given the label "borderline personality disorder" (BPD). While BPD can be a stigmatized diagnosis, it may also be helpful for some of us who feel that its symptoms match our experiences. Some of these symptoms include interpersonal difficulties, unstable relationships, fear of rejection, rapid mood swings, feelings of emptiness, intense anger, and self-harm.

Although some aspects of PTSD are our mind's way of keeping us safe from danger, many of the symptoms of PTSD can become debilitating and interfere with our everyday functioning and relationships. Because PTSD symptoms have served, in part, to protect us, we may not even be fully aware of our trauma reactions or the ways in which trauma has impacted our daily lives. Having medical and mental health providers who are aware of how trauma impacts our reactions and sense of safety is important for us to be able to stay engaged in the care we need. There are several treatment approaches specifically geared toward treating trauma, including eye movement desensitization and reprocessing (EMDR) therapy, prolonged exposure (PE) therapy, somatic experiencing (SE), cognitive processing therapy (CPT), dialectical behavior therapy (DBT), and trauma-focused cognitive behavioral therapy (TF-CBT). These interventions not only help us better understand the ways in which our trauma experiences impact us, but also help reduce the intensity of our trauma responses and increase our feelings of safety and connectedness with others. Medications can be helpful in treating various symptoms of PTSD, such as problems with our mood, anxiety, sleep, and nightmares.

The National Coalition of Anti-Violence Programs (212-714-1141) provides LGBTQ-affirming support.

BEING MANY: NORMALIZING THE PLURAL-TRANS EXPERIENCE

The Crisses (Rev. Criss Ittermann) (they/them) are nonbinary gender fluid plural activists, run Kinhost.org, offer self-help materials to the public, & produce the Many Minds on the Issue podcast.

Being plural is the experience of being many. Plurals experience being more than one (part, person, consciousness, soul, etc.) sharing their body. They may each identify as being different genders.

Expressions of plurality include mental health issues such as dissociative identity disorder (DID), other dissociative disorders, & spiritual experiences. When a plural is troubled, anxious, disjointed, unable to achieve their goals, or experiences internal arguing or fighting, they may decide to seek support from licensed practitioners or experienced peers, or they may use self-help resources.

Many may be plural without significant problems. People who are either trans or plural may feel marginalized & stigmatized, & those who are both may feel additionally targeted. There are few, if any, acceptable role models for plural experience; there is, however, a growing plural community that offers positive ongoing support & excellent role models for newly aware plurals, & psychology is starting to recognize living as an internal community as a viable option.

Do you relate to plural experiences? Here are some tips:

1. The symbol for plurals is "&" (ampersand).
2. You might just be becoming aware of your plurality, but it's not new. They were with you long before you were aware of it.
3. You're all in this life together. Collaboration is more productive than fighting.
4. Be compassionate with one another. It's likely you're all trauma survivors & could use safety & understanding.
5. If you find any internals frightening, maybe they are hurt & trying to defend themselves from something in your past; they may not be capable of understanding what they're doing.
6. Don't trust the media about plurality (just like you shouldn't trust the media about much else). As a rule, books, TV shows, movies, articles, & documentaries about plural people are stigmatizing & inaccurate. Seek accurate, healthy, self-affirming resources.

7. Online community resources can be found by searching for *plural*, *plural pride*, *dissociation*, or *dissociative*. Beware of toxic communities; seek out nurturing & inclusive support.
8. If you have trouble finding a specialist in dissociative disorders, seek a trauma specialist who is queer- or trans-friendly, especially when trauma or anxiety is involved.
9. Don't panic. You've got this. Y'all always have.

As you get to know yourselves better & learn to work as a team, being plural can become a rich & rewarding experience—a missing link in the vast diversity of human experience.

Substance Use and Other Addiction/Compulsive Behaviors

Substance use disorders (SUDs) involve using drugs or alcohol in excess to the point that we experience problems from them such as getting physically ill when not using, not being able to cut back our use even though we may want to, having intense emotional fluctuations, missing work and important events, experiencing relationship problems due to our use, and/or running into legal problems stemming from our substance use. Drugs can include legal and illegal substances such as cigarettes, marijuana, cocaine, prescription pain pills, heroin, and amphetamines. SUDs can not only damage our physical and emotional health, but can also cause problems with our relationships, jobs, housing and the legal system. Substances can impair our decision-making and affect how alert we are, making us more vulnerable to experiencing trauma or engaging in harmful behaviors. As in other marginalized communities, rates of substance use are higher in T/GE communities and this link is related to our higher rates of societal discrimination and trauma.[35,36] We may use substances to self-medicate negative feelings or to help us feel more at ease in social settings. If we have family members who have problems with drugs and alcohol, we may be more vulnerable to developing a substance use problem. It is not only substances that can draw us into addictive or compulsive behaviors. We may also find ourselves engaged in other behaviors, such as spending hours online with video games or pornography, or engaging in frequent sexual encounters with others. Although no one behavior is necessarily pathological, we may notice excessive time spent in an activity, or in search of that activity, such that it gets in the way of our self-care, daily life, employment, interpersonal relationships, or other priorities.

Seeking help for addictive behaviors can be difficult. At times we may not recognize that our use is causing us harm. Stigma and shame around our substance use or addictive behaviors can make it hard for us to seek the help we need and deserve. We must give ourselves compassion and find our own motivations for change. Those of us who struggle actively with misusing substances or with addictive behaviors may benefit from a harm reduction approach. Harm reduction involves nonjudgmental and noncoercive approaches to shifting behaviors that are the most concerning to us and minimizing the consequences that our substance use has on our lives. Harm reduction recognizes and honors our autonomy and the complexities of our histories that contribute to our addictive behaviors. Harm reduction may involve reducing the amount or frequency of our use, or complete abstinence. Some of us find outpatient support groups and programs to be helpful in building community and social support for our recovery, while others of us benefit from engagement in more intensive drug or alcohol treatment programs, such as inpatient detox or rehab, or outpatient drug and alcohol therapy. There are also medications available that can help support our path to recovery, particularly for problems with cigarettes, alcohol, and opioids. If we are interested in medications for our substance use issue, we can ask our primary care provider (PCP) if they provide medication-assisted therapy (MAT) or ask for a referral to a specialist who does.

Trans Folx Fighting Eating Disorders is a collective of trans and gender diverse people who believe eating disorders in marginalized communities are social justice issues. Their website offers online support groups and other resources.

Disordered Eating and Body Image Concerns

Eating and body image concerns occur at significantly high rates in trans communities.[37,38] Recent studies have suggested trans people may be up to eight times more likely than cisgender women to report an eating disorder.[39] Reasons for engaging in disordered eating or exercise behaviors may be different for trans people, because there is often a significant overlap between gender dysphoria and a desire to control our body shape, size, or appearance.[40] Additionally, it can be difficult to feel a sense of agency in the face of medical gatekeeping, fatphobia, or binary gender ideals. This can lead us to engage in problematic eating behaviors to seek control or self-soothe.

Common symptoms of eating disorders include food restriction, binge eating, purging, and/or over-exercising. Formal and more commonly recognized eating disorder diagnoses include anorexia nervosa, bulimia nervosa, and binge eating disorder. However, at least a third of the people who suffer from disordered eating or body image concerns do not meet full criteria for these disorders.[41,42] The result is that our struggles and a need for medical or mental health treatment may go unrecognized. Disordered eating exists along a spectrum, and if you are struggling with how you feel about your weight, shape, or size, it can be helpful to seek care from a provider who is versed in Eating Disorders, utilizes the therapeutic techniques of Intuitive Eating (IE)[43] or Health At Every Size (HAES),[44] and understands the complexities of what it means to have an Eating Disorder as a trans person. In some instances, when we are able to access gender-affirming medical care, this can both reduce a sense of dissatisfaction with our bodies and decrease our disordered eating.[45]

Suicide

Sadly, our community is all too familiar with suicide. Many of us have considered suicide or attempted it at some point in our lives.[46,47,48,49] Others have been impacted by the loss of our friends and community members from suicide. On average, one out of two transgender people have thought about suicide and a third have attempted suicide at least once.[50,51] Suicide rates are much higher for us compared to non-trans people and are related to our experiences of discrimination, trauma, and rejection.[52] Going through challenging life events increases our chances of having depression, low self-worth, social isolation, and substance abuse,[53,54,55,56] all of which are risk factors for suicide. Having other marginalized identities (e.g., being a person of color, being disabled) can increase our odds of having negative life experiences and contribute to higher rates of suicide attempts.[57]

Although we face many challenges in our environment, we can also increase our strengths to help during times of crisis. Finding ways to increase our social supports by engaging with others in transgender communities, building families of choice, and serving as mentors and role models can help buffer the effects of discrimination and violence. Having others around us who affirm our gender as well as being able to access needed medical services for transition can also reduce our risk of suicide.[58,59,60,61] Our community is rising up to support one another through peer crisis services such as the Trans Lifeline, a crisis hotline started in 2014 with all trans operators. We are working as individuals and collectively to reduce suicide attempts by putting an end to discrimination in political, medical, religious, and legal systems. Accessing support from affirming mental health professionals can help with depression, trauma, and suicidal thoughts. We may work with our mental health provider(s) to create a safety plan for what coping skills to use or positive things to do when we experience suicidal thoughts. We may want to consider psychiatric hospitalization as part of the plan to help keep us safe and get increased supports and faster access to needed mental health care and medications. Talking ahead of time with our therapist and/or psychiatrist about previous suicidal thoughts and making preventive plans about possible future crises can assist us in creating a safer and more trusting relationship to discuss these difficult topics.

Self-Injurious Behavior

Some of us may hit, bite, burn, or cut parts of our bodies without intending to die. This is known as self-injury or self-harm, and is different from acts of bodily modification such

Untitled. (Chucha Marquez)

The GLBT National Hotline (888-843-4564) and the GLBT National Youth Talkline (up to age 25) (800-246-7743) are LGBTQ-affirming services for concerns about suicide or other mental health issues.

as tattooing, piercing, and scarification. We may hurt ourselves for many reasons: to deal with difficult emotions, as a physical release of emotional pain, or because of discomfort with our physical bodies. Studies show that 37% to 53% of trans people have self-harmed at least once in their lifetime, particularly trans youth and masculine spectrum people.[62,63,64,65,66] Although we may not intend to die by cutting or harming our bodies, self-injurious behaviors carry a risk of harm such as infection, serious bodily injury, and accidental death. Although there are many reasons to self-harm, our community is more likely to self-harm because of social isolation, low self-esteem, poor body image, conflicts in interpersonal relationships, and a perception of stigma coming from others.[67,68,69,70] We experience higher rates of depression, anxiety, and other mental health diagnoses that contribute to self-harming behaviors. Feeling discomfort with our bodies can also lead to self-harm.[71]

Talking to friends, family, or a professional about self-harming can be difficult because of stigma and shame. Relying on people who listen to and accept our painful emotions creates a safer space to share what we go through. We can then work on finding more positive ways than self-injury to cope with overwhelming feelings and emotions. We may need to take some time to explore why we self-harm so we can become empowered to address the underlying causes. Staying socially connected by attending a support group, having a friend come with us to our medical appointment, or getting help with bullying at work through human resources are all ways to specifically tackle the stressors we go through that can contribute to self-harming behaviors. For youth, finding a teacher at school who stands up for us, or working with a therapist to help improve family acceptance, can go a long way toward reducing self-injurious behaviors.[72] Getting psychiatric care and/or medications for trauma, depression, anxiety, or other mental health problems can also reduce self-harming thoughts and behaviors. Specific therapies have been designed to help improve relationships and reduce self-harming behaviors. These include interpersonal psychotherapy (IPT), cognitive behavioral therapy (CBT), and dialectical behavior therapy (DBT).

HOPE

Allison Whitaker (she/her) is a business professional and writer living in New Jersey. She recently published her first book, Sometimes it Hurts: A Transgender Woman's Journey, *and is currently writing her next book. Nearly three years ago, she came out to the world as transgender and hasn't looked back since. She is exploring who she was always meant to be and is living her life to the fullest.*

Note: This essay discusses depression, suicide, and self-harm in ways that can be triggering for some readers.

My life, and the lives of so many other trans people, are fraught with depression and oftentimes suicide—this has been the case for me my whole life. Every day, I make a conscious choice to live my life as it exists in this moment. After I transitioned from male to female almost three years ago, each day became an opportunity to be a better version of myself. Being my authentic self relieved the depression that came from living a lie as the male that I was assigned to be at birth. However, other feelings of depression endured. Although for the first time in my life I was finally happy with how my body looked and felt, I continued to deal with some difficult feelings—even on my happiest days. This is what depression is for me: an illogical feeling of hopelessness and a loss of who I am.

I've acted out my depression by isolating myself, by crying, and by sometimes resorting to self-harm. I don't know why I do this. As I write this, I remind myself that I cut myself last night. Fifteen hours ago, I fell apart, crying more and more, wishing for the pain to stop, and I eventually fell asleep.

Last night, however, I did something I've never done before. After going through all these stages of depression, I actually reached out to someone on my own for the first time ever. My friend stayed on the phone with me as long as I needed until I stopped crying and hating myself. I reached out because I knew something in my life needed to change. I really don't *want* to end things, but my depression keeps pushing me there. Sometimes it's just unbearable.

I'm on a journey, and my destination is unknown, but because of the help of friends who are like family, I know that I'll eventually be OK. Some days are really hard, harder than any day ever, but I can do this. I know I'll be OK. I have to because life is far too precious.

Schizophrenia and Psychotic Disorders

Schizophrenia is a complex disorder with symptoms that include hallucinations (perceiving things that are not there, such as sounds and visions), delusions (fixed beliefs that are untrue), problems with thinking and speaking clearly, unusual behaviors, physical motor impairments, cognitive problems (memory, attention, planning), and difficulties with emotional expression and social interactions. Schizophrenia impacts 21 million people worldwide and research estimates 0.25%–0.64% of the United States population has schizophrenia.[73,74] It is associated with multiple problems in brain functioning and gene expression, but there is no one known cause. Schizophrenia typically starts in late adolescence but can begin as late as the mid-thirties. For those who are going to develop schizophrenia, use of marijuana in adolescence is known to trigger the illness and worsen its course.[75] There are no blood tests or brain imaging that can help diagnose schizophrenia. The diagnosis is made by a mental health provider trained in assessing the symptoms, such as a psychiatrist. Schizophrenia ranges from mild episodes to chronic and severe symptoms that can make social interactions, employment, housing, and self-care challenging.

Most people with schizophrenia benefit from medication (typically antipsychotics) throughout their lifetime to help reduce symptoms and improve life function and quality of life. Medication can reduce hallucinations, delusions, and unusual thinking. Medications, however, do not help as much with cognitive problems, emotional expression, and social interactions. Unfortunately, part of the illness may include not being aware of the symptoms of schizophrenia. Due to this lack of awareness, some people with schizophrenia have a hard time staying on medication, resulting in a recurrent need for hospitalizations. Some people with schizophrenia choose to use long-acting injectable medication to help reduce symptoms, frequency of recurrences, and hospitalizations. Cognitive behavioral therapy has been shown to provide ways to better manage hallucinations but cannot eliminate them. Cognitive enhancement therapy (CET) can help with the cognitive effects and interpersonal challenges associated with schizophrenia. Community interventions and social support services help people with schizophrenia increase social interactions with others, pursue employment opportunities or life goals, stay engaged in medical care, and obtain stable housing.

Personality Disorders

We are all born with unique personality traits. Our personalities refer to fundamental ways we experience our own identities and emotions, how we direct our dreams and goals, and ways we relate to others. Our personality traits also impact how we understand or interpret other's emotions and behaviors. Our personality tends to stay stable over time, even as we may change in abilities, goals, or stages of life. Personality traits may emerge from trauma responses that we have developed in order to keep us safe, and certain personality traits involving attachment and emotional safety with others may be amplified by the trauma we go through. Differences in personalities are what make us strong, giving us different perspectives and strengths as a collective. Some personality traits, however, contribute to profound difficulties in how we see ourselves, regulate our emotions and behaviors, and relate to others. We may struggle with feeling numb or feel emotions that are too intense to handle. We may act impulsively when angry or hurt, or perseverate on how to accomplish a task to the point it never gets done. We may be overly suspicious of others or avoid intimacy altogether. Because we are often so "at home" in our own personalities, it can be difficult to recognize some of the challenges in our relationships and work that our personality traits may create.

Getting help for personality traits that are creating difficulties in our lives can be life-changing, helping us with boundaries, interpersonal conflict and intimacy, emotional regulation, and attunement to ourselves and others. While one aspect of our personalities may cause us harm in some situations, the same trait may hold strengths and positive aspects. Therapy can be helpful for managing personality traits that are putting

Rainbow Heights Club in New York City is a support and advocacy organization for LGBTQ people with severe mental illness such as bipolar disorder and schizophrenia, providing a space for socialization, meals, events, and trips in a safe and supportive environment.

stumbling blocks in our way, by learning more helpful ways to see ourselves and interact with the world around us. Dialectical behavior therapy (DBT), a therapy approach initially intended to treat borderline personality disorder, is aimed at helping with emotional validation and regulation, interpersonal conflict, impulsive self-harm behaviors, and being present in the moment.

SELF-CARE IN THE AFTERMATH OF SEXUAL VIOLENCE AND TRAUMA

Reo Cosgrove (they/them) is a queer nonbinary trans researcher and student. Their work covers topics around sexual violence and the trans community. They is also a lone parent but is part of a queer community household.

Self-care is important. It can be done in many ways, big or small. Everyone's forms of self-care, support, and healing are different. What may work for some may not work at all for others.

As dull as it sounds, trying your best to eat and drink the right amount every day can improve your general well-being. You might find taking time for yourself each day or each week to relax is beneficial. After experiencing sexual violence, time can feel too fast, too slow, or not real at all. This can be a challenge for people who take medication. Forgetting to take medication is common, so frequent reminders can help you take control of this issue. One can set recurring alarms, leave a note pinned to your bedroom door or bathroom mirror, or ask a reliable friend.

Sexually Transmitted Infections (STIs) are common after experiencing a sexual assault, but getting tested can feel retraumatizing and dysphoric. There may be a service or charity local to you that has a clinic suited specifically for trans people. If this is not the case, a trusted friend can call up the clinics in your area and ask about trans inclusion. They can also accompany you to the appointment. During the exams and tests, it is OK to tell the nurse that you are nervous or scared. It may feel painful, terrifying, or remind you of your traumatic experience. Remember: In this moment, you have already survived.

After an assault, some people find it extremely difficult to look at or touch their body. This can be especially hard if the sexual violence heightens dysphoric feelings, prompting bodily detachment. Keeping clean can really help people to feel more comfortable, grounded, and empowered. If you're feeling as though you cannot touch your skin or look at your body while it is naked, it may help to wear clothing or swimwear while bathing. If we only feel able to wash one body part, the feet are a great place to start. We may remove clothing in the water as we become more comfortable.

Some of us may start the healing process by writing about our feelings and experiences in a journal. Some write stories, both fiction and nonfiction, that contain their experiences, their feelings, and their identity. Others prefer to write poetry. Making music is a great way of releasing pent up energy while being emotional and expressive. Many like to draw or paint. It doesn't need to be artistically great; it is a beautiful expulsion of your feelings and your perception.

Sports are another way we can release energy while staying healthy and active. Exercise keeps our bodies and minds in tune with each other—movement and control promote healing from sexual violence. Keeping active tends to ensure that you eat the right amount and drink a good amount of water, which may help with feelings of anxiety or depression. Keeping active can help you to reconnect to your body by being in control of the movements that you make in the water, on the court, or running along the sidewalk. Sexual violence seeks to take power and control from you. The journey of healing is about reclaiming that control back for yourself.

Healing is always a process, no matter how long it takes. Every step we take is huge, and it helps us manage, cope, process, and understand our emotions. It can be painful. It can be rewarding. We all deserve support, no matter what form it is in.

The Autism Spectrum

People with autism may be referred to as being on the autism spectrum or having an autism spectrum disorder (ASD). People with autism have diverse communication styles and ways they experience and process sensations, and sometimes refer to themselves as "neurodiverse." People on the "spectrum" may enjoy or know a lot about a singular topic or interest. Transitions to new places or unexpected events can feel particularly overwhelming, and consistent routines can help us feel more at ease. Loud noises or different textures of food or clothing may cause anxiety and irritation. Autism is considered a spectrum because some people with autism experience more challenges than others, such as having communication difficulties, self-injurious behaviors, and intellectual disabilities. Sometimes autism can make things such as planning, paying bills, and being organized more difficult. Being on the autism spectrum can also be challenging because most of the world does not account for differences in communication or sensory processing, requiring neurodiverse people to adapt instead. Autism should not be confused with social anxiety from past negative experiences or having a shy personality. Neuropsychological testing by a trained psychologist or assessment by a psychiatrist is usually required to diagnose autism. For some, this is helpful because it opens up access to things like community supports and assistance with education, employment, and housing.

Recent research, particularly with children, has suggested a possible correlation between the gender diverse and trans experience and being on the autism spectrum.[76,77,78,79] Clinically diagnosed autism in gender diverse people is four to seventeen times higher than in the cis population.[80] In fact, some studies suggest that when the negative mental health effects of transphobia and discrimination are teased out, the only mental health concern that is significantly elevated in our communities is ASD.[81] What this means is that trans people may be more likely to be autistic, and autistic people may be more likely to be trans. More research is needed to assess this possible relationship due to methodological concerns in existing research, such as lack of appropriate comparison groups and using measures of traits of autism rather than autism itself. We also need to include the voices of people with autism in research to avoid further stigmatization and marginalization of people with autism.

There is an unfortunate history of providers trying to "figure out" if someone is either trans *or* autistic rather than recognizing that some people are both. Some of us have been told that our gender identities, expressions, likes, and preferences are simply "stereotyped interests" that often occur for someone on the autism spectrum.[83] Having autism does not negate our gendered selves nor our autonomy in our care.

Gender diverse and trans people on the autism spectrum are collectively using their voices to advocate for their rights in care, including in "The Rights of Transgender and Gender Non-Conforming Autistic People," a document produced by the Autistic Self Advocacy Network.[82]

TRANSITIONING AND MENTAL HEALTH

Changing our physical appearance, either through medical services (e.g., hormones and/ or surgeries) or through changes in how we present ourselves to others (e.g., clothing, hair, binding) is a complex process that can impact our emotions, relationships, and every fabric of our lives. For many of us who seek transition-related care, our quality of life and emotional well-being can significantly improve. Rates of depression and anxiety are frequently lessened with transition.[84,85,86] Still, various social challenges of transition such as loss of housing, jobs, and relationships can continue to take a severe toll on our mental health even when we feel more aligned with our true selves.[87,88] While transition can help improve our psychological sense of well-being and self-esteem, transition does not always "cure" mental health concerns such as major depressive disorder, generalized anxiety disorder, post-traumatic stress disorder, bipolar disorder, or schizophrenia. Being cared for in a psychiatric hospital or having an acute "flare up" of a mental health problem is not a reason for anyone to stop their medical care, including hormones. Hormone therapy can impact our sleep, sex drive, mood, and energy. We may need to let our medical or mental health provider know if we suspect hormones are contributing to negative mood effects (i.e., too high or too low hormone levels); adjustments can be made to help improve our overall well-being.

Having a mental health concern or getting mental health care should not inhibit our access to transition-related medical services unless is it causing clear impairments in our ability to make informed decisions. Obtaining hormones and surgeries requires us to be able to give informed consent, that is, to indicate that we understand why we are using the interventions, what the benefits and risks are, and what other options we may have to consider. Occasionally, when symptoms of mental health problems such as schizophrenia, bipolar disorder, substance use problems, or recurrent suicidal behavior or self-injury are not well-managed, they can impair thinking and judgment, making it difficult to participate in informed consent about medical care, including hormones and surgery. They can also get in the way of our ability to emotionally manage through surgery, pain, and post-operative recovery needs. In general, it is best to not make any major medical decisions during times when our thinking is severely impaired. Once our mental health symptoms

Kalki Subramaniam is a celebrated artist, actor, poet and transgender rights activist from India.

are better controlled, we can more actively participate in collaborative decision-making with our medical providers.

If we are seeking gender-affirming medical interventions, our providers may ask us about our substance use. This is particularly the case with smoking and surgery, because nicotine constricts blood vessels and impairs healing, which can negatively affect our surgical outcomes or other aspects of our physical well-being. Additionally, smoking and taking feminizing hormones (estrogen) can result in an increased risk of blood clots. Sometimes, substance misuse can impair our decision-making abilities or our ability to follow through with medical care we may need for positive surgical outcomes. To maximize our health and healing, our providers may have other guidelines about the use of, or abstinence from, substances of abuse. For those of us in recovery from substance use disorders, having to take prescription painkillers after surgery can create a great deal of anxiety. We may also struggle with substance use reminders based on the need to inject our hormone medication. Many of us find it helpful to establish a structured safety plan around the use of these medications, often with the support of a sponsor, counselor, or medical provider.

BODY-MIND FREEDOM: COUNTERTRANSFERENCE IN ACTION

Jake Heath Jacobsen (he/him) is a native New Yorker, a psychotherapist, a visual artist, and a writer living in Portland, Oregon. Transitioning at 54 years old has been one of his greatest adventures.

I'm grateful I decided to work with transgender and gender variant youth as a psychotherapist. For positive change to unfold in the therapeutic relationship, however, it's essential to identify, explore, and effectively use countertransference –a therapist's own emotions affecting the relationship. For example, my youngest client, a nine-year-old trans boy, unearthed my countertransferential feelings of grief over my own lost boyhood. Week after week he twisted and turned his small body on my office rug in anger and grief at not being a "real boy" with a "real penis." It was painful for me to witness. I had repressed my own feelings of grief and loss at not being cisgender for decades, and I almost allowed those feelings to stop me from transitioning. Like this child, I had a clear visceral feeling that I was a boy when I was five years old in 1965. Working with this client, I realized that I had initially decided not to work with trans youth to avoid my feelings of grief.

I explored my client's thoughts about "realness" and brought up the idea of "trans is beautiful," which really missed the mark with him. My client clearly needed a more immediate concrete change rather than an emotional revelation. "Trans is beautiful" would have to wait. I learned that he was not exploring the Internet like my teen clients and so, he was unaware of STPs (a stand-to-pee silicone prosthetic penis). His parents were totally on board with his social transition and the introduction of an STP was another potential option for the healthy integration of his sense of self and body. Within a week he had mastered using his STP. The following week he bounded up the stairs to my office exploding with sheer joy as he told me he peed at a urinal with his father at the movies and peed with his male friends on a tree in the woods. Looking at me, in an instant, he sensed that I had not yet peed in a urinal. "Oh Jake, you've got to do it, you've just got to pee in a urinal, you're going to love it!!" Several feelings shot through me: embarrassment, pride, jealousy. In that moment I chose to share his joy, because I understood that it was truly *our* shared joy. His shift from anger and grief to joy at having developmentally appropriate experiences from the integration of his mind and body was clearly psychologically life-enhancing and saving.

SEEKING PROFESSIONAL HELP

Many of us seek professional help, and our reasons for doing so vary based on our individual concerns. Some of us feel it is a choice to seek care, while many of us feel forced to meet with mental health professionals in order to seek necessary medical care. Some of us have had positive or even lifesaving experiences in mental health care, while others have been treated poorly by mental health providers. In this section, we discuss some of the factors that are important to be aware of when interacting with mental health providers and systems.

Confidentiality and Trust

Confidentiality is our right to privacy when seeking healthcare services. Mental health providers are legally and ethically bound to maintain our privacy. That means that they are not allowed to share anything about who their clients are, what their diagnoses are, and what is discussed in the professional exchange. It is important to mention that there are times when our privacy may be compromised, and it is good to be aware of this risk. For example, if we are on someone else's health insurance plan (e.g., parents, partner), this person may receive statements in the mail that indicate the services we have received and the corresponding diagnoses. This should be taken into consideration, especially if you have not disclosed being transgender to people you live with or are dependent on for insurance coverage.

> It is valuable in the context of insurance coverage but should not be a prerequisite for accessing care. Diagnoses should be for things causing distress or dysfunction, and dysphoria isn't necessarily an integral part of the trans experience.

There are some exceptions to confidentiality. Providers are mandated to break confidentiality when a person is in immediate danger of hurting themselves or others, or if there is a case of minor or elder abuse or neglect. Knowing that a provider has a responsibility to notify authorities when someone is in danger can raise anxiety for many of us. We know from survey research that thoughts of suicide or self-harm are high in our communities.[89] It is not uncommon for us to doubt the quality of care we will receive if we are voluntarily or involuntarily taken to emergency departments or hospitalized. These are valid concerns. An informed provider will ideally be aware of this and take this into consideration when making decisions regarding our safety and well-being. We recommend having conversations with providers about confidentiality and its limits, as well as whether they have a typical protocol for responding to imminent risk or safety concerns. We may want to ask about what would result in a provider needing to involuntarily hospitalize us and ways we can maintain autonomy in our safety plan. We may ask our providers in advance to vet affirming inpatient care facilities, should we need to be hospitalized at some point in time.

A transgender woman sitting on a therapist's couch and listening. (Zackary Drucker, The Gender Spectrum Collection, VICE/Broadly)

Trans communities, whether in person or online, can be small and intertwined. Many of us have concerns about other members of our communities learning personal information about us. For example, if we seek counseling services at a local LGBTQ community mental health center, we may be worried about running into people we know. We acknowledge that there may be a sense of stigma or shame in seeking mental health services, but we also want to challenge our communities to reject internalized ableism and to prioritize getting the help we need and deserve for ourselves, our friends and family, and our communities.

Mental Health Professional Roles and Approaches

Mental health providers may play numerous roles in our process of growth, healing, or transition. Regardless of the reason for seeking out a professional, you will want to choose someone who has a trans-affirming stance and approach. Being affirming means respecting trans people for being trans, believing that we are who we say we are, and not trying in any way to pressure us to conform to the expectations that others have placed on us based on our sex assigned at birth. When you are looking for a provider, it can be helpful to interview them on the phone to ask what their experience or approach is in working with trans people. It is harmful to us to have to interact with nonaffirming professionals, whether they are ignorant but well-meaning or blatantly transphobic. It pays off for us to take our time, research various options, seek community recommendations, and trust our intuition.

There are a number of different treatment modalities within mental health, including individual counseling, couples/family/relationship counseling, and group therapy. Providers may use a variety of treatment approaches, from somatic approaches to psychoanalysis to manualized or structured treatments such as cognitive behavioral therapy (CBT), interpersonal psychotherapy (IPT), internal family systems (IFS) therapy, dialectical behavior therapy (DBT), eye movement desensitization and reprocessing (EMDR), and/or medication management. Other providers may incorporate spiritual counseling or direction. In addition to more western approaches, we may seek holistic or non-western approaches to healing or treating emotional concerns, including acupuncture, mindfulness practice, reiki, or herbalism. We may also turn to our religious or spiritual advisers to guide us through adversity.

For some of us, it is helpful to work with professionals who provide psychotherapy or counseling. The concerns that motivate us to ask for help may warrant different treatment approaches or healing modalities. There is no one-size-fits-all approach to any of our problems or stressors. When we look to professionals to help us with mental health concerns, whether short-term or chronic, we look for clinicians who do not blame gender for all of our problems. We will want someone who can be attuned to the ways in which our gendered experiences and our emotional distress *might* be related, but it is not helpful to work with people who assume that *everything* about us is due to being trans.

Another role of mental health professionals is to provide gender- or transition-related counseling. Many of us find it helpful to have someone to talk to regarding gender, whether it be past experiences, goals for the future, exploring medical options, or navigating aspects of social transition at work, home, or in public. It can be very useful to have the space to explore thoughts and feelings before making big decisions. Even if we feel very clear about our path, talking through our thoughts and feelings with a professional can provide added clarity and support.

Some mental health professionals consider or market themselves as *gender specialists* or *gender therapists*. This is a term that has been put forth by WPATH, because they recommend that trans clients find gender specialists to work with. In our communities, there are mixed feelings about this term. It can be very uncomfortable to think that there are (typically cisgender) people who specialize in *us* or pose as experts on *our experience*. We recommend focusing more on the provider's experience and approach rather than the label they apply to themselves or others apply to them. When interacting with providers who have invested significant time and care into learning how to work with our communities, we typically respond better when these providers demonstrate a willingness to truly *listen* to us rather than assume they understand everything there is to know about trans identity or experience.

The National Queer and Trans Therapists of Color Network (nqttcn.com) has an online directory to search for therapists.

Behaviors of affirming mental health providers:
- Utilize the language and perspective that we use in describing our body and identity
- Use correct name and pronouns
- Apologize and correct mistakes when they happen
- Understand that gendered experiences are influenced by culture
- Include and affirm nonbinary experiences and views of gender
- Refrain from making assumptions about our sexuality and affirm that there are many valid expressions of sexuality
- Recognize that there is more to us than a diagnosis
- Recognize the longstanding history of pathologization of T/GE identities in health care
- Recognize their own privilege and how this can impact the therapeutic relationship

Behaviors of nonaffirming/pathologizing mental health providers:
- Use pathologizing language
- Refuse to use our correct name and pronouns
- Do not apologize when mistakes are made and/or repeatedly make the same mistakes
- Do not affirm our intersectional identities
- Deny or dismiss the validity of nonbinary experiences
- Make assumptions about our sexuality and deem certain forms of sexual expression "healthy" or "unhealthy"
- Treat our trans experience as a diagnosis to be fixed
- Deny or invalidate the longstanding history of pathologization of T/GE identities in health care

Hormones and Mental Health Concerns

Hormone therapy to address gender dysphoria has been shown to improve quality of life and psychological wellness and reduce rates of depression and anxiety associated with gender dysphoria.[90,91] When hormones are at appropriate physiological levels they do not have significant impacts on mood. However, hormones are known to impact physical health in ways that can affect mental wellness, including libido, energy levels, and sleep/wake cycle. When testosterone is at *higher* levels than physiological norms, sleep can become disrupted and mood can become irritable. Mood disorders are also known to impact similar systems, and if you are working with a client with a mood disorder, it may be helpful to have them monitor for any changes in energy, sex drive, and sleep cycles while on hormones. If a person is experiencing significant changes to mood including marked energy changes or depression, consider having hormone levels checked to ensure hormone levels are not below or above physiological norms. Adjusting frequency and dosing schedules of hormones may help provide a more consistent mood state due to improved consistency in hormone blood levels. A person's hormones should not be discontinued due to worsening mental health concerns or for an acute exacerbation of a mental health illness. Psychiatric hospitalization is never a reason to discontinue a person's hormones, although levels should be checked to ensure they are not exceeding physiological limits.

Informed Consent and Mental Health

Having a mental health disorder should never preclude a person's access to gender affirming medical interventions such as hormones and surgeries. Prohibiting a person from accessing medically necessary interventions to address gender dysphoria solely due to a mental health condition is considered "gatekeeping" and excludes the ethic of autonomous decision-making in medical care for adults. There may be times when mental health problems impair capacity for informed consent to medical care or make it difficult for a person to follow up with medically necessary care, which should be addressed collaboratively with the individual. Capacity for informed consent should be something all medical and mental health providers are trained in assessing; however, impaired decision-making due to a mental health problem is best assessed by a mental health professional. Capacity for informed consent involves a person being able to communicate their choice, understand the information given (including the reasons why the intervention is being proposed, ways it may help, ways it may hurt and alternatives), be able to repeat the information given, and make a consistent and rational choice.[92] A person should also be able to explain why they have made a choice.

I would love for people to not have to lie about having a binary trans identity in order to get the affirming health care that they need. I would also love to see gender affirming care be more affordable and covered (along with all the other kinds of health care that aren't affordable or covered, like dental).

Sometimes mental health conditions or fear of interacting with medical systems impede a person's ability to participate in self-care, such as coming in to get cholesterol monitored or being able to follow postsurgical care instructions. A mental and medical health care model that involves harm reduction should be considered to promote a patient's autonomy in their care needs as well as to ensure no harm is done. If there is concern that a mental health problem, such as a mood disorder or a substance use disorder, is impairing a person's ability to engage in collaborative decision-making and medical care, mental health providers can be integral in helping a person make positive life changes to move toward their overall health and transition goals.

I'd like to see trans people be allowed our surgeries because we want them, not because they'll cure us of gender dysphoria. Being trans hasn't made me happy, and as long as improved prospects of happiness are the gate to trans surgeries, somebody can close it with the reason, "This person wouldn't be made enough by surgery"—like in the Johns Hopkins study, an evaluation of how "successfully" you'd transition. Back then, success was passing. Now it's passing and being happy.

STANDARDS OF CARE FOR REFERRALS AND LETTERS FOR GENDER AFFIRMING MEDICAL INTERVENTIONS

Many surgeons, physicians, medical systems, and insurance companies adhere to the WPATH Standards of Care. Certain requirements from past versions of the Standards of Care are outdated or have been discontinued. For example, mental health support may be recommended, but there is no longer a *requirement* that people seeking gender affirming medical interventions engage in psychotherapy or counseling for a minimum length of time. The WPATH Standards of Care Version 7 (SOC7) are meant to be used as flexible guidelines, so medical systems often use their discretion in how closely they follow the guidelines and when they make exceptions informed by other rationale. WPATH and the Standards of Care are controversial, and perspectives vary widely in terms of their applicability and appropriateness; we acknowledge that these standards have a great deal of power in determining what is possible for us, as a community, to access.

The criteria posed by WPATH SOC7 vary based on the specific service being requested. You have likely heard that in order to access surgery or hormones, you need to get a letter or, in some cases, two letters from mental health professionals. There is no absolute standard way of providing transition-related or gender affirming health care, so different providers or insurance companies may have different requirements. This can be confusing, and some of us have felt at times like we were perpetually jumping through hoops to get the care we need. A fairly universal aspect of this process is getting a diagnosis of gender dysphoria in order to access gender affirming medical care. Some providers may only ask us to tell them enough to be able to justify giving us this diagnosis, while other providers may ask us to recount lengthy histories of our gendered experiences and feelings dating back to early childhood. Some of us find this to be intrusive and gatekeeping, and we do not feel that we need to justify our gender identities or our desires for medical care by giving evidence of our gender nonconformity. For many of us, this can bring up dysphoria and the uncomfortable feelings of seeking approval from providers who are in a position of power based on professional status, but also often due to holding other privileged identities.

> I currently have health insurance through work, and I'm extremely fortunate in that it completely covers my HRT and transition-related surgeries. I wouldn't have been able to afford to medically transition out of pocket. Before I got this job, I did not have benefits through work. The first couple years of the ACA actually hurt my access to care, because my state refused to expand Medicaid but insurance premiums for private insurance went up significantly. Once my state expanded Medicaid, I was able to qualify for that and thus get coverage again. I support upholding the ACA, but I think it's important for people across the political spectrum to recognize how it does genuinely place a burden on some vulnerable people, and work to fix that gap.

Mental health providers writing recommendation letters for gender-affirming care will also ask us to share our mental health histories, whether we have been diagnosed or received treatment for mental health symptoms or disorders, and if and how these concerns are currently affecting us. These providers are typically trying to get a sense of whether our symptoms are managed well enough to not impair our decision-making for informed consent or contribute to life-threatening problems in our care. Having major depressive disorder should not prohibit anyone from surgery, but if it is impairing a person's ability to get out of bed and perform basic self-care, certain surgeries pose greater risks because of the immense self-care needed for a positive outcome and healing. Of course, we often find a double bind in having to be distressed enough to justify medical care but not so distressed that we are seen as a danger to ourselves. Though many providers are not aware of this, we in our community know that oftentimes medical interventions *are* mental health interventions. Many of us find it helpful to work with providers who use an informed consent approach and center the discussion on whether we have all the information we need to make informed decisions and are aware of the risks and benefits of the specific medical service we are seeking. With an affirming, knowledgeable, and experienced provider, going through the process of getting a letter can be a supportive or positive experience. It can be helpful to talk to other trans people to learn about how different providers work so that we know what to expect and, if possible, choose the option that best suits our needs.

> I had to see a therapist for a year in order to get on hormones. She was very familiar with binary trans things, but had no clue when it came to other identities. She refused to let me get hormones unless I fell into her expected narrative, so I had to fake it. My therapist now knows very little about gender identity, but I see her for depression and anxiety. I spend a lot of time teaching her about gender, which is exhausting, but at least I don't have to pretend to be something different.

A genderfluid person burning sage above an altar. (Zackary Drucker, The Gender Spectrum Collection, VICE/Broadly)

MEDICATIONS

We may consider taking medications to support our mental health (sometimes called psychotropic medications). Psychotropic medications can help us get control of our mental health symptoms, thus improving our life function, and can be lifesaving for many. Medications vary in terms of the symptoms they treat and associated side effects. The desire or need for psychotropic medication may depend on the severity and nature of our mental health symptoms. Many mental health disorders respond best to a combination of treatment or healing approaches (e.g., psychotherapy, mindfulness practice, and exercise) plus medication. Making a decision to start psychotropic medication can be complicated due to internalized stigma and misperceptions, social stigma, cultural background, religious beliefs, and potential side effects. The decision is ultimately up to us in collaboration with our provider, with whom we can review the pros and cons of medication options.

If we are considering medications, it is important to have a conversation with the provider (psychiatrist, primary care physician, nurse practitioner, physician's assistant, or in some states, psychologist) about what the medication is for, the benefits it can offer, possible side effects, and alternative options. Some medications may impact our weight or sex drive. The pros and cons of side effects for each person should be considered prior to starting a medication. Alternative options can include other medications, forms of self-care, and/or psychotherapy. We do not have to decide on a medication immediately. We can request a handout to take home and read over, talk to our support system, or ask more questions before making a decision. If we decide to start psychotropic medication, regular visits with our provider are important to follow up on how the medication is working and assess for possible side effects. Some medications require blood work to monitor for potential effects on our organs (e.g., kidney, liver, thyroid) and levels of the medication in our body. If we decide to stop medication, we should talk to our provider about the risks versus benefits of this decision, and how to do so safely. Suddenly stopping medication without speaking with a provider can lead to worsening of mental health symptoms, side effects, or withdrawal symptoms and is highly advised against.

We may already be on medications for other health problems or on hormones. Telling our provider about our health problems and other medications we are taking is very important to make sure there are no interactions with the psychotropic medications we are about to start or are already taking. Of note, few psychotropic medications interact with gender affirming hormone therapies. Some interactions are known, however, and it is important to discuss with your prescriber if you are on hormones or other medical therapies for gender affirmation.

The Association of LGBTQ + Psychiatrists (aglp.org) can help find a trans-affirming psychiatrist.

BLOODY CHRYSALIS

Regan Ryder (she/her) has always written . . . but now she really has a story to tell.

Note: This essay discusses self-harm and other mental health struggles in ways that can be triggering for some readers.

I only have one mirror in my house, and more than half of the time I don't like to use it. It triggers something to see my body, something jarring and painful. I am the Thing That Should Not Be; not a person, but an "it." In one way or another, everyone important in my early life told me so—parents, ex-wife—exemplified by my first girlfriend's parting remarks: "You're a monster. I hate you, and I never want to see you again."

So, no mirrors or pictures, because I never want to see that body again, either.

For longer than I like to admit, I've known on a primal, subconscious level that something is locked inside my flesh, screaming. Until recently, I had never understood how to consciously release it and that's led to some ugly episodes. Sometimes the impulse is simplistic: I just want to shred myself. The body I see in that one damnable mirror makes me want to puke: hairy chest, potbelly, gangly limbs improperly shaved. Sometimes, the impulse is to hurt this wrong body; scar and mangle it, perhaps? I have a hard time getting those thoughts out of my head.

There's been a glimmer of hope in this morass of self-loathing. About a year ago, I finally put a name to my anger and pain: gender dysphoria. I consciously accepted the concept of "trans" into my personal lexicon.

The admission freed something: a stuck cog or a splinter in the brain, I don't know, but it came with a lot of tears and curiosity. I bought some breastforms. They came in a heavy, nondescript cardboard box, and they smelled of cornstarch and vanilla oil. They went inside the bra I had walked into Target and bought like there was nothing wrong—even though I was screaming inside that I was going to be punished. Over that went the beautifully soft chibi Wonder Woman T-shirt that I would never have worn before for fear of retribution.

And I cried because I looked down and saw my shape, the shape I needed to see. Not the monster. Seeing the affirming shape doesn't solve all of my problems, but it sure helps.

ACCESS CONCERNS

The kinds of support available to us depend greatly on our geographic location. Some of us have to travel a long distance to meet with qualified or affirming providers. Many of us have found online resources or telemedicine to be helpful when we cannot locate a local provider.

Access to financial resources and/or health insurance may also impact our ability to seek and receive the care we need. State policies vary with regard to coverage of gender-affirming care, and the political climate can lead to significant fear for many of us. Insurance plans that cover gender-affirming medical services may require us to have a diagnosis of gender dysphoria. Whether this diagnosis fits us or not, receiving it can bring up concerns about our medical records and how this information may be used. It can be important to discuss these concerns with our medical or mental health providers as part of the process of collaboration and informed consent.

CONCLUSION

Mental health and emotional wellness are unique experiences for each of us, and depend on our backgrounds and current situations. Being aware of the forces that affect our mental health, such as a history of trauma, and current discrimination, can help us to understand our mental health concerns. In some situations, trained mental health professionals can be valuable in helping us to piece together the symptoms we are experiencing and find treatment modalities that help. We may also turn to other forms of mental health support, such as peer support groups and community organizations. Many of us have felt alone in our mental health concerns, but we are not alone, and there are many ways we can connect with other T/GE people to work together to improve mental health and wellness for all of us.

NOTES

1. DuBrul, S. A. (2014). The Icarus project: A counter narrative for psychic diversity. *Journal of Medical Humanities, 35*(3), 257–271.
2. American Psychiatric Association. (1981). *Diagnostic and statistical manual of mental disorders. DSM-III.* American Psychiatric Association. Washington, DC.
3. American Psychiatric Association. (2013). *Diagnostic and statistical manual of mental disorders (DSM-5).* American Psychiatric Association. Washington, DC.
4. Drescher, J., Cohen-Kettenis, P., & Winter, S. (2012). Minding the body: Situating gender identity diagnoses in the ICD-11. *International Review of Psychiatry, 24*(6), 568–577.
5. Robles, R., Fresán, A., Vega-Ramírez, H., Cruz-Islas, J., Rodríguez-Pérez, V., Domínguez-Martínez, T., & Reed, G. M. (2016). Removing transgender identity from the classification of mental disorders: A Mexican field study for ICD-11. *Lancet Psychiatry, 3*(9), 850–859.
6. Beek, T. F., Cohen-Kettenis, P. T., Bouman, W. P., de Vries, A. L., Steensma, T. D., Witcomb, G. L., Arcelus, J., Richards, C., De Cuypere, G., & Kreukels, B. P. (2017). Gender incongruence of childhood: Clinical utility and stakeholder agreement with the World Health Organization's proposed ICD-11 criteria. *PLoS One, 12*(1), e0168522.
7. Vargas-Huicochea, I., Robles, R., Real, T., Fresán, A., Cruz-Islas, J., Vega-Ramírez, H., & Medina-Mora, M. E. (2018). A qualitative study of the acceptability of the proposed ICD-11 gender incongruence of childhood diagnosis among transgender adults who were labeled due to their gender identity since childhood. *Archives of sexual behavior, 47*(8), 2363-2374.
8. American Psychological Association. (2015). Guidelines for psychological practice with transgender and gender nonconforming people. *American Psychologist, 70*(9), 832–864.
9. Coleman, E., Bockting, W., Botzer, M., Cohen-Kettenis, P., DeCuypere, G., Feldman, J., Fraser, L., Green, J., Knudson, G., Meyer, W. J., Monstrey, S., Adler, R. K., Brown, G. R., Devor, A. H., Ehrbar, R., Ettner, R., Eyler, E., Garofalo, R., Karasic, D. H., . . . Zucker, K. (2012). Standards of care for the health of transsexual, transgender, and gender-nonconforming people, version 7. *International Journal of Transgenderism, 13*(4), 165–232. https://doi.org/10.1080/15532739.2011.700873
10. Substance Abuse and Mental Health Services Administration. (2015). Ending conversion therapy: Supporting and affirming LGBTQ youth. Rockville, MD: Substance Abuse and Mental Health Services Administration.
11. Beckwith, N., McDowell, M. J., Reisner, S. L., Zaslow, S., Weiss, R. D., Mayer, K. H., & Keuroghlian, A. S. (2019). Psychiatric epidemiology of transgender and nonbinary adult patients at an urban health center. *LGBT Health, 6*(2), 51–61.
12. Su, D., Irwin, J. A., Fisher, C., Ramos, A., Kelley, M., Mendoza, D. A. R., & Coleman, J. D. (2016). Mental health disparities within the LGBT population: A comparison between transgender and nontransgender individuals. *Transgender Health, 1*(1), 12–20.
13. Bockting, W. O., Miner, M. H., Swinburne Romine, R. E., Hamilton, A., & Coleman, E. (2013). Stigma, mental health, and resilience in an online sample of the US transgender population. *American Journal of Public Health, 103*, 943–951.
14. Goldblum, P., Testa, R. J., Pflum, S., Hendricks, M. L., Bradford, J., & Bongar, B. (2012). The relationship between gender-based victimization and suicide attempts in transgender people. *Professional Psychology. Research and Practice, 43*(5), 468–475.
15. Hendricks, M. L., & Testa, R. J. (2012). A conceptual framework for clinical work with transgender and gender nonconforming clients: An adaptation of the Minority Stress Model. *Professional Psychology: Research and Practice, 43*(5), 460.
16. Meyer, I. H. (2003). Prejudice, social stress, and mental health in lesbian, gay and bisexual populations: Conceptual issues and research evidence. *Psychological Bulletin, 129*, 674–697.
17. Grant, J. M. M. L., Mottet, L., Tanis, J., Herman, J. L., Harrison, J., & Keisling, M. (2010). National transgender discrimination survey report on health and health care. National Center for Transgender Equality and the National Gay and Lesbian Task Force. Washington, DC.

18. James, S. E., Herman, J. L., Rankin, S., Keisling, M., Mottet, L., & Anafi, M. (2016). The report of the 2015 U.S. Transgender Survey. Washington, DC: National Center for Transgender Equality. http://www.ustranssurvey.org

19. Wirtz, A. L., Poteat, T. C., Malik, M., & Glass, N. (2018). Gender-based violence against transgender people in the United States: A call for research and programming. *Trauma, Violence, & Abuse*, 1524838018757749.

20. James, S. E., Herman, J. L., Rankin, S., Keisling, M., Mottet, L., & Anafi, M. (2016). The Report of the 2015 U.S. Transgender Survey. Washington, DC: National Center for Transgender Equality.

21. Dhejne, C., Van Vlerken, R., Heylens, G., & Arcelus, J. (2016). Mental health and gender dysphoria: A review of the literature. *International Review of Psychiatry, 28*, 44–57.

22. Singh, A. A., Hays, D. G., & Watson, L. (2011). Strategies in the face of adversity: Resilience strategies of transgender individuals. *Journal of Counseling and Development, 89*, 20–27. doi:10.1002/j.1556-6678.2011.tb00057.x

23. Johns, M .M., Beltran, O., Armstrong, H. L. Jayne, P. E., Barrios, L. C. (2018). Protective factors among transgender and gender variant youth: A systematic review by socioecological level. *The Journal of Primary Prevention, 39*(3), 263–301.

24. Ryan, C., Russell, S. T., Huebner, D., Diaz, R., & Sanchez, J. (2010). Family acceptance in adolescence and the health of LGBT young adults. *Journal of Child and Adolescent Psychiatric Nursing, 23*(4), 205–213.

25. Watson, R. J., Veale, J. F., Gordon, A. R., Clark, B. A., & Saewyc, E. M. (2019). Risk and protective factors for transgender youths' substance use. *Preventative Medicine Reports, 15*, 100905.

26. Singh, A. A., Hays, D. G., & Watson, L. S. (2011). Strength in the face of adversity: Resilience strategies of transgender individuals. *Journal of Counseling & Development, 89*(1), 20-27.

27. Singh, A. A. (2018). *The queer and transgender resilience workbook: Skills for navigating sexual orientation and gender expression.* New Harbinger Publications. Oakland, CA.

28. World Health Organization. (2018). Depression (Fact Sheet). https://www.who.int/news-room/fact-sheets/detail/depression.

29. James, S. E., Herman, J. L., Rankin, S., Keisling, M., Mottet, L., & Anafi, M. (2016). The Report of the 2015 U.S. Transgender Survey. Washington, DC: National Center for Transgender Equality.

30. Kosciw, J. G., Greytak, E. A., Zongrone, A. D., Clark, C. M., & Truong, N. L. (2018). *The 2017 National School Climate Survey: The experiences of lesbian, gay, bisexual, transgender, and queer youth in our nation's schools.* New York: GLSEN.

31. Shipherd, J. C., Maguen, S., Skidmore, W. C., & Abramovitz, S. M. (2011). Potentially traumatic events in a transgender sample: Frequency and associated symptoms. *Traumatology, 17*(2), 56–67.

32. Reisner, S. L., White Hughto, J. M., Gamarel, K. E., Keuroghlian, A. S., Mizock, L., & Pachankis, J. E. (2016). Discriminatory experiences associated with posttraumatic stress disorder symptoms among transgender adults. *Journal of Counseling Psychology, 63*(5), 509–519.

33. Felitti, V. J., Anda, R. F., Nordenberg, D., Williamson, D. F., Spitz, A. M., Edwards, V., Koss, M. P., & Marks, J. S. (1998). Relationship of childhood abuse and household dysfunction to many of the leading causes of death in adults. The Adverse Childhood Experiences (ACE) Study. *American Journal of Preventative Medicine, 14*(4), 245–258.

34. Gilbert, L. K., Breiding, M. J., Merrick, M. T., Thompson, W. W., Ford, D. C., Dhingra, S. S., & Parks, S. E. (2015). Childhood adversity and adult chronic disease: An update from ten states and the District of Columbia, 2010. *American Journal of Preventative Medicine, 48*(3), 345–349.

35. Glynn, T. R., & van den Berg, J. J. (2017). A systematic review of interventions to reduce problematic substance use among transgender individuals: A call to action. *Transgender Health, 2*(1), 45–59.

36. Keuroghlian, A. S., Reisner, S. L., White, J. M., & Weiss, R. D. (2015). Substance use and treatment of substance use disorders in a community sample of transgender adults. *Drug and Alcohol Dependence, 152*, 139–146.

37. Watson, R. J., Veale, J. F., & Saewyc, E. M. (2017). Disordered eating behaviors among transgender youth: Probability profiles from risk and protective factors. *The International Journal of Eating Disorders, 50*(5), 515–522.

38. Witcomb, G. L., Bouman, W. P., Brewin, N., Richards, C., Fernandez-Aranda, F., & Arcelus, J. (2015). Body image dissatisfaction and eating-related psychopathology in trans individuals: A matched control study. *European Eating Disorders Review, 23*, 287–293.

39. Diemer, E. W., Grant, J. D., Munn-Chernoff, M. A., Patterson, D. A., & Duncan, A. E. (2015). Gender identity, sexual orientation, and eating-related pathology in a national sample of college students. *Journal of Adolescent Health, 57*(2): 144–149.

40. Cella, S., Iannaccone, M., & Cotrufo, P. (2013). Influence of gender role orientation (masculinity versus femininity) on body satisfaction and eating attitudes in homosexuals, heterosexuals and transsexuals. *Eating and Weight Disorders, 18*, 115–124.

41. Machado, P. P., Machado, B. C., Gonçalves, S., & Hoek, H. W. (2007). The prevalence of eating disorders not otherwise specified. *The International Journal of Eating Disorders, 40*(3), 212–217.

42. Vo, M., Accurso, E. C., Goldschmidt, A. B., & Le Grange, D. (2017). The impact of DSM-5 on eating disorder diagnoses. *The International Journal of Eating Disorders, 50*(5), 578–581.

43. Tribole, E., & Resch, E. (2012). *Intuitive eating.* New York: Macmillan.

44. Bacon, L. (2010). *Health at every size: The surprising truth about your weight.* Dallas, TX: BenBella Books.

45. Testa, R. J., Rider, G. N., Haug, N. A., & Balsam, K. F. (2017). Gender confirming medical interventions and eating disorder symptoms among transgender individuals. *Health Psychology, 36*(10), 927.

46. Haas, A. P., Rodgers, P. L., & Herman, J. (2014). *Suicide attempts among transgender and gender non-conforming adults: Findings of the national transgender discrimination survey.* Los Angeles, CA: The Williams Centre.

47. Grossman, A. H., Park, J. Y., & Russell, S. T. (2016). Transgender youth and suicidal behaviors: Applying the interpersonal psychological theory of suicide. *Journal of Gay Lesbian Mental Health, 20*(4), 329–349.

48. McNeil, J., Ellis S. J., Eccles, F. J. R., Mizock L., & Mueser, K. T. (2017). Suicide in trans populations: A systematic review of prevalence and correlates. *Psychology of Sexual Orientation and Gender Diversity, 4*(3), 341–353.

49. Toomey, R. B., Syvertsen, A. K., & Shramko, M. (2018). Transgender adolescent suicide behavior. *Pediatrics, 142*(4). e20174218; DOI: https://doi.org/10.1542/peds.2017-4218

50. Adams, N., Hitomi, M., & Moody, C. (2017). Varied reports of adult transgender suicidality: Synthesizing and describing the peer-reviewed and gray literature. *Transgender Health, 2*(1), 60–75.

51. García-Vega, E., Camero, A., Fernández, M., & Villaverde, A. (2018). Suicidal ideation and suicide attempts in persons with gender dysphoria. *Psicothema, 30*(3), 283–288.

52. Romanelli, M., Lu, W., & Lindsey, M. A. (2018). Examining mechanisms and moderators of the relationship between discriminatory health care encounters and attempted suicide among U.S. transgender help-seekers. *Administration and Policy in Mental Health, 45*(6), 831–849.

53. Clements-Nolle K., Marx R., & Katz M. (2006). Attempted suicide among transgender persons. The influence of gender-based discrimination and victimization. *Journal of Homosexuality, 51*(3), 53–69.

54. Klein, A., & Golub, S. A. (2016). Family rejection as a predictor of suicide attempts and substance misuse among transgender and gender nonconforming adults. *LGBT Health, 3*(3), 193–199.

55. Testa, R. J., Michaels, M. S., Bliss, W., Rogers M. L., Balsam, K. F., & Joiner, T. (2017). Suicidal ideation in transgender people: Gender minority stress and interpersonal theory factors. *Journal of Abnormal Psychology, 126*(1), 125–136.

56. Wolford-Clevenger, C., Frantell, K., Smith, P. N., Flores, L. Y., & Stuart, G. L. (2018). Correlates of suicide ideation and behaviors among transgender people: A systematic review guided by ideation-to-action theory. *Clinical Psychology Review, 63*, 93–105.

57. Perez-Brumer, A., Hatzenbuehler, M. L., Oldenburg, C. E., & Bockting, W. (2015). Individual- and structural-level risk factors for suicide attempts among transgender adults. *Behavioral Medicine, 41*(3), 164–171.

58. Lytle, M. C., Silenzio, V. M. B., Homan, C. M., Schneider, P., & Caine, E. D. (2018). Suicidal and help-seeking behaviors among youth in an online lesbian, gay, bisexual, transgender, queer, and questioning social network. *Journal of Homosexuality, 65*(13), 1916–1933.

59. Moody, C., Fuks, N., Peláez, S., & Smith, N. G. (2015). "Without this, I would for sure already be dead": A qualitative inquiry regarding suicide protective factors among trans adults. *Psychology of Sexual Orientation and Gender Diversity, 2*(3), 266–280.

60. Testa, R. J., Jimenez, C. L., & Rankin, S. (2014). Risk and resilience during transgender identity development: The effects of awareness and engagement with other transgender people on affect. *Journal of Gay & Lesbian Mental Health, 18*(1), 31–46.

61. Trujillo, M. A., Perrin, P. B., Sutter, M., Tabaac, A., & Benotsch, E. G. (2017). The buffering role of social support on the associations among discrimination, mental health, and suicidality in a transgender sample. *International Journal of Transgenderism, 18*(1), 39–52.

62. dickey, l. m., Reisner, S. L., & Juntunen, C. L. (2015). Non-suicidal self-injury in a large online sample of transgender adults. *Professional Psychology Research and Practice, 46*, 3–11.

63. dickey, l. m., Singh, A. A., & Walinsky, D. (2017). Treatment of trauma and nonsuicidal self-injury in transgender adults. *The Psychiatric Clinics of North America, 40*(1), 41–50.

64. Jackman, K. B., Dolezal, C., Levin, B., Honig, J. C., & Bockting, W. O. (2018). Stigma, gender dysphoria, and nonsuicidal self-injury in a community sample of transgender individuals. *Psychiatry Research, 269*, 602–609.

65. Marshall, E., Claes, L., Bouman, W. P., Witcomb, G. L., & Arcelus, J. (2016). Non-suicidal self-injury and suicidality in trans people: A systematic review of the literature. *International Review of Psychiatry, 28*(1), 58–69.

66. Peterson, C. M., Matthews, A., Copps-Smith, E., & Conard, L. A. (2017). Suicidality, self-harm, and body dissatisfaction in transgender adolescents and emerging adults with gender dysphoria. *Suicide and Life Threatening Behavior, 47*(4), 475–482.

67. Arcelus, J., Claes, L., Witcomb, G. L., Marshall, E., & Bouman, W. P. (2016). Risk factors for non-suicidal self-injury among trans youth. *The Journal of Sexual Medicine, 13*(3), 402–412.

68. Claes, L., Bouman, W. P., Witcomb, G., Thurston, M., Fernandez-Aranda, F., & Arcelus, J. (2015). Non-suicidal self-injury in trans people: Associations with psychological symptoms, victimization, interpersonal functioning, and perceived social support. *The Journal of Sexual Medicine, 12*(1), 168–179.

69. Davey, A., Arcelus, J., Meyer, C., & Bouman, W. P. (2016). Self-injury among trans individuals and matched controls: Prevalence and associated factors. *Health and Social Care in the Community, 24*(4), 485–494.

70. Jackman, K. B., Dolezal, C., Levin, B., Honig, J. C., & Bockting, W. O. (2018). Stigma, gender dysphoria, and nonsuicidal self-injury in a community sample of transgender individuals. *Psychiatry Research, 269*, 602–609.

71. Ibid.

72. Eisenberg, M. E., Gower, A. L., McMorris, B. J., Rider, G. N., Shea, G., & Coleman, E. (2017). Risk and protective factors in the lives of transgender/gender nonconforming adolescents. *The Journal of Adolescent Health, 61*(4), 521–526.

73. National Institute of Mental Health. (2018). Schizophrenia (Statistics). https://www.nimh.nih.gov/health/statistics/schizophrenia.shtml.

74. World Health Organization. (2018). Schizophrenia (Fact Sheet). https://www.who.int/en/news-room/fact-sheets/detail/schizophrenia.

75. Murray R. M., Quigley H., Quattrone D., Englund A., & Di Forti M. (2016). Traditional marijuana, high-potency cannabis and synthetic cannabinoids: Increasing risk for psychosis. *World Psychiatry, 15*, 195–204.

76. de Vries, A. L. C., Noens, I. L. J., Cohen-Kettenis, P. T., van Berckelaer-Onnes, I. A., & Doreleijers, T. A. (2010). Autism spectrum disorders in gender dysphoric children and adolescents. *Journal of Autism and Developmental Disorders, 40*(8), 930–936.

77. Hisle-Gorman, E., Landis, C. A., Susi, A., Schvey, N. A., Gorman, G. H., Nylund, C. M., & Klein, D. A. (2019). Gender dysphoria in children with autism spectrum disorder. *LGBT Health, 6*(3):95–100.

78. Janssen, A., Huang, H., & Duncan, C. (2016). Gender variance among youth with autism spectrum disorders: A retrospective chart review. *Transgender Health, 1,* 63–68.

79. Nobili, A., Glazebrook, C., Bouman, W. P., Glidden, D., Baron-Cohen, S., Allison, C., Smith, P., & Arcelus, J. (2018). Autistic traits in treatment-seeking transgender adults. *Journal of Autism Developmental Disorders, 48*(12), 3984–3994.

80. Strang, J. F., Janssen, A., Tishelman, A., Leibowitz, S. F., Kenworthy, L., McGuire, J. K., Edwards-Leeper, L., Mazefsky, C. A., Rofey, D., Bascom, J., Caplan, R., Gomez-Lobo, V., Berg, D., Zaks, Z., Wallace, G. L., Wimms, H., Pine-Twaddell, E., Shumer, D., Register-Brown, K., Sadikova, E., & Anthony, L. G. (2018). Revisiting the link: Evidence of the rates of autism in studies of gender diverse individuals. *Journal of the American Academy of Child & Adolescent Psychiatry, 57*(11), 885–886.

81. Shumer, D. E., Reisner, S. L., Edwards-Leeper, L., & Tishelman, A. (2016). Evaluation of Asperger syndrome in youth presenting to a gender dysphoria clinic. *LGBT Health, 3*(5), 387–390.

82. ASAN, NCTE, and LGBTQ Task Force Joint Statement on the Rights of Transgender and Gender Non-Conforming Autistic People. (2016). Autistic Self Advocacy Network, National Center for Transgender Equality, and National LGBTQ Task Force. https://autisticadvocacy.org/wp-content/uploads/2016/06/joint_statement_trans_autistic_GNC_people.pdf

83. Strang, J. F., Powers, M. D., Knauss, M., Sibarium, E., Leibowitz, S. F., Kenworthy, L., Sadikova, E., Wyss, S., Willing, L., Caplan, R., Pervez, N., Nowak, J., Gohari, D., Gomez-Lobo, V., Call, D., & Anthony, L. G. (2018). "They thought it was an obsession": Trajectories and perspectives of autistic transgender and gender-diverse adolescents. *Journal of Autism and Developmental Disorders, 48*(12), 4039–4055.

84. de Vries, A. L., McGuire, J. K., Steensma, T. D., Wagenaar, E. C., Doreleijers, T. A., & Cohen-Kettenis, P. T. (2014). Young adult psychological outcome after puberty suppression and gender reassignment. *Pediatrics, 134*(4), 696–704.

85. Keo-Meier, C. L., Herman, L. I., Reisner, S. L., Pardo, S. T., Sharp, C., & Babcock, J. C. (2015). Testosterone treatment and MMPI-2 improvement in transgender men: A prospective controlled study. *Journal of Consulting and Clinical Psychology, 83*(1), 143–156.

86. White Hughto, J. M., & Reisner, S. L. (2016). A systematic review of the effects of hormone therapy on psychological functioning and quality of life in transgender individuals. *Transgender Health, 1*(1), 21–31.

87. Dhejne, C., Lichtenstein, P., Boman, M., Johansson, A. L., Långström, N., Landén, M. (2011). Long-term follow-up of transsexual persons undergoing sex reassignment surgery: Cohort study in Sweden. *PLoS One, 6,* e16885.

88. Nobili, A., Glazebrook, C., & Arcelus, J. (2018). Quality of life of treatment-seeking transgender adults: A systematic review and meta-analysis. *Reviews in Endocrine and Metabolic Disorders, 19*(3), 199–220.

89. James, S. E., Herman, J. L., Rankin, S., Keisling, M., Mottet, L., & Anafi, M. (2016). The Report of the 2015 U.S. Transgender Survey. Washington, DC: National Center for Transgender Equality.

90. Colizzi, M., Costa, R., & Todarello, O. (2014). Transsexual patients' psychiatric comorbidity and positive effect of cross-sex hormonal treatment on mental health: Results from a longitudinal study. *Psychoneuroendocrinology, 39,* 65–73.

91. De Cuypere, G., Elaut, E., Heylens, G., Van Maele, G., Selvaggi, G., T'Sjoen, G., & Monstrey, S. (2006). Long-term followup: Psychosocial outcome of Belgian transsexuals after sex reassignment surgery. *Sexologies, 15,* 126–133.

92. Appelbaum, P. S. (2007). Assessment of patients' competence to consent to treatment. *New England Journal of Medicine, 357*(18), 1834–1840.

SECTION 4
RELATIONSHIPS AND FAMILIES

INTIMATE RELATIONSHIPS

Andie Leslie, Micah Rea, Sarah E. Belawski, and Carey Jean Sojka

15

INTRODUCTION

Our relationships come in all shapes and sizes. Just like there is no one way to be trans, there is no single way to engage in intimate or romantic relationships. How we interact with others in this realm may vary widely based on who we are, our life experiences, what our relational needs are, and how we choose to get these needs met. We live and love like everyone else, but being transgender or gender expansive can also add some unique joys and challenges to our relationships—sometimes both at the same time.

We have an incredible amount of diversity in our relationships. We start relationships before, during, and after we come out as trans or start to transition. We have straight relationships, same-gender relationships, queer relationships, monogamous relationships, polyamorous relationships, and nonsexual relationships. Some of us are married or have domestic partnerships, while others of us do not want or cannot attain legal recognition of our relationships. There is no one model for our relationships. However, there are basic strategies we can use to ensure that our relationships are healthy for us and our partners.

DATING AND TRANS IDENTITY

For those of us who are dating or interested in dating, there can be many steps to finding the types of relationships we desire. For some of us, our gender identities and expressions may not affect our dating relationships any more than other aspects of ourselves. For others, our trans or gender expansive identities may be incredibly impactful on how we perceive and pursue intimate relationships. We may enter new dating pools, perhaps finding a different set of potential partners than before social, medical, and/or legal transition. We may attract or be attracted to new kinds of people. We may wonder whether the people attracted to us are attracted for the right reasons. We may need to learn new ways of interacting in dating cultures as we transition and discern if or how to disclose our trans status to potential partners.

Loving Our Bodies

Trans and gender expansive bodies are beautiful. Of course, we are all on our own journeys to becoming the most authentic versions of ourselves, and we may struggle with self-esteem due to our culture's views on desirability. We must build awareness about what transphobic, homophobic, androcentric, racist, ableist, and body size-related messages we have internalized from the society we grew up within, and challenge narratives that tell us we are not magnificent just the way we are, inside and out. When we enter relationships without a healthy self-image, those challenges may be reflected in the relationship. For example, it can be hard to set and maintain healthy boundaries with others when we feel less confident.

> *My partner has been increasingly owning the nonbinary label since I've come out and it has been somewhat challenging for our relationship as we both discover how to best be ourselves. It is also bonding.*

We may spend a significant amount of time and effort working to deconstruct societal expectations and building our self-esteem, and we may be confronted with discrimination

Want to read more about trans people in relationships? Check out *Trans Love: An Anthology of Transgender and Non-Binary Voices* (edited by Frieya Benson, Jessica Kingsley Publishers, 2019).

Sujay Abhilash and Erick Jackaman (@transingabout).

based on any aspect of our identity, gender-related and beyond. This is hurtful, and it can lead us to feel alone and isolated, creating barriers to seeing our value and beauty.

Of course, many people are attracted to trans people, and many of us find loving, secure, and sexually fulfilling relationships, but it can be hard to seek out these supportive relationships with others when we do not feel confident and when we do not treat ourselves with love and compassion. Building our self-esteem can help us feel good about ourselves and invest in relationships where we are treated with the kind of respect and care we know we deserve. Strengthening our self-esteem is an ongoing process. It involves challenging deeply ingrained messages and narratives about trans experiences, as well as navigating our ever-changing perceptions of who we are in relation to ourselves and others. This process deserves self-compassion, gentleness, and patience.

> *Since coming out, I've met my girlfriend. It has been nice to navigate this relationship as a non-binary person—I feel powerful, equal, and respected. My partner loves how I look and dress and will always tell me I look good when I feel good. She listens when I complain about how I'm treated or what my dysphoria feels like or when I just want to give up.*

Julia Serano, Glenn Marla, Amos Mac, Silas Howard, and many others contributed to Morty Diamond's *Trans/Love: Radical Sex, Love & Relationships Beyond the Gender Binary* (Manic D Press, 2011).

Although many of us struggle with building self-esteem and experience gender dysphoria, there are many transgender and gender expansive folks who experience gender euphoria, finding joy and power in their trans experience. Gender euphoria comes from the elation of experiencing gender congruence and gender affirmation, and from living our lives authentically. Gender euphoria plays an important role in the depathologization of the trans experience by shifting the narrative away from one of deficit and toward one of centering the pleasure and joy in being trans. Being trans is beautiful, and it is important to honor both the beauty and challenges that we navigate daily in society. Even so, dysphoria is a real experience that affects many of us day to day and within relationships. For many of us it can be helpful to aim for the balance between finding appreciation for our bodies while also acknowledging that sometimes, because of dysphoria or trauma, it can be hard to do so.

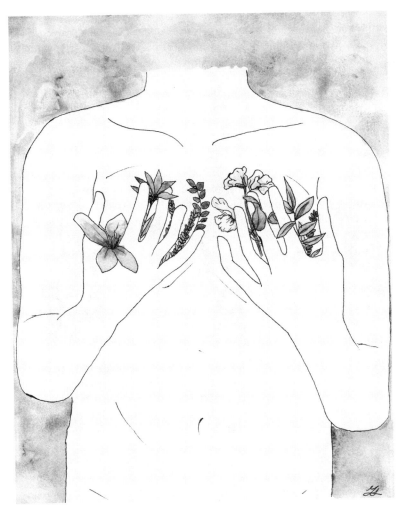

It's Mine to Define. Watercolor and Ink on Watercolor Paper. (Eli Schleisman)

LET'S TALK ABOUT FEAR

Sabene Georges

Fear for me took many forms and it evolved over time. I was a foster kid; my parents died when I was young. The foster system teaches a child to conform, to not rock the boat, to fit in. I was passed from a stepfather to a sister, and finally to an outside family from age 11 to 18. I learned the lessons of fear, conformity, and fitting in. I habitually adapted myself to everything and everyone around me. It is a survival mechanism against my fear of rejection. It is why I could not bring myself to risk the rejection from coming out as trans until I was well into my fifties.

In 1984, at age 20, fear took the form of the AIDS epidemic. Young gay men were dying. I was in a relationship with another trans woman. Seeing the ever-increasing death rate and how society treated both the epidemic and the suffering people kept me firmly in the closet and pushed me toward heterosexual relationships.

In 1990, at age 26, fear took the form of wanting to have a career and understanding that coming out would mean I would be, in essence, unemployable. A gay colleague came out to me in 1993 during a late-night work session. It was an act of bravery and trust then because if it were known he was gay, he would have absolutely been fired. Me too . . .

In 2000, at age 36, fear evolved into a disconnection from my life. I would have a freak-out about every six months, and then I would subsume again. I was in a marriage with a wonderful person who had trouble accepting my "girl side," and we had reached an uncomfortable and ultimately destructive "détente" of "don't ask, don't tell." I need to stress that my wife at the time tried very hard and did everything possible to come to grips with it. Ultimately, the heart wants what it wants, and she bears no blame.

Finally, in 2008, I met a wonderful woman who woke me up. She lovingly saw and accepted all of me. Fear finally came home to rest in my own heart, but I spent the next decade wrestling with my need to conform. When you are rejected and ejected from your home as a 9-year-old kid, and again as a 14-year-old teenager, that affects you deeply, but it was finally time for me to deal with it.

In June of 2017, I came out in a Facebook post, and I finally . . . finally, started my journey. "Someday . . . " for me became "every day." If you are a closeted trans person reading this, please know that even though the distances may seem vast, and the circumstances completely impossible, "someday" can become "every day" for you, too. Keep doing the work and you will get there.

Meeting Potential Partners

As trans and gender expansive people, we may have a hard time meeting potential partners, given that being trans can limit the spaces in which we can safely meet partners. This varies drastically depending on where we are located geographically, what the widely held political and social beliefs are, and our own intersectional identities. For example, the San Francisco Bay Area is likely to have more spaces intentionally created for trans folks to build community, whereas small rural and/or politically conservative towns may have very few spaces for safe trans community-building.

> *It has been extremely hard to develop any intimate or romantic relationships as a trans person. I don't live in a large urban center and while the culture here is liberal, there is a fairly small queer community. Many of the straight cis-gender women I meet are afraid to form a relationship with a trans man.*

Often, trans and queer spaces center alcohol, which makes these spaces inaccessible to many of us who do not use substances or are in recovery, creating another barrier to meeting people. Access to specifically designated "trans spaces," such as mixers, speed dating, dancing nights, or play parties may provide us with unique opportunities to meet partners without worrying about disclosure, or cause trepidation if we do not wish to find partners solely based on one aspect of our identity.

The rise of social media and use of dating apps has significantly changed our ability to meet people across geographic lines, and to seek out people with specific identities. Queer dating apps make it easier to connect with people with similar identities, wherever you live. Dating app profiles also present an opportunity to disclose our gender and other identities, without dealing with the potential of a negative in-person reaction. Dating apps help to filter out people who are not attracted to our identities or expression, which is often challenging to do when navigating social situations in person. Dating apps are also used to build community and meet new people outside of romantic or sexual relationships.

Disclosing While Dating

Some of us are not necessarily read as trans in public, and we may not be in private either. When we are forming new relationships, we have to decide for ourselves when (or if) to disclose our transgender or gender expansive identity to potential partners.

> *I navigate [dating] with a great deal of care. I'm straightforward and come out immediately, because I need to know immediately if someone will accept me or not. Seeking out relationships with men has been especially difficult, because I've dated men in the past that were ashamed of my identity, and I find it hard to trust that any guy, trans or not, won't do the same thing. I didn't really start trusting my boyfriend until we had dated for over a month, but now I do and it feels nice. I was probably a little too forward in establishing my boundaries, like areas that he isn't allowed to see/touch (my chest), because I've had male partners who disregard it.*

For many of us, our identity as trans is just as large a part of our core being as other parts of our identity, and it may be very important to us that a potential partner understand our trans identity and experiences. We may be left feeling that a part of ourselves is missing from a relationship if we do not disclose.

> *I briefly considered dating and went so far as to make plans to go out with a few people. I disclosed my trans identity up front and would probably do so even if I was passing—I prefer not to hide things from others whenever possible and, for me in the world we live in now and having come out so late in life, I feel like I couldn't talk about myself or my history at all without tipping my hand.*

The "if and when" of disclosure depends entirely on our personal comfort. It is not dishonest to choose not to out ourselves to everyone we date. The expectation that we must out ourselves to every potential partner or that we are otherwise being dishonest is problematic. If trans people are expected to disclose their trans status at the beginning of a relationship and no equivalent expectation exists for cisgender people, a potentially dangerous cissexist power dynamic is created.

Safety should always be a top priority. Although it can be difficult at times to work up the courage to disclose, it can be dangerous to keep this information from someone who might discover it while we are alone with them and vulnerable to being hurt. Leaving our trans status to a partner to discover in the heat of a sexual encounter can be awkward at

A Rose By Any Other Name. . . Charcoal, Acrylic, and Gesso on Canvas. (Devon Reiffer)

best and dangerous at worst. It is up to us to decide for ourselves whether it is right, when it is right, and how it is right for us to disclose our trans identity to our partners. The timing of disclosure can be tricky, and as a result, some of us develop clear personal guidelines as we gain experience in the sphere of dating.

> *When I seek out a new relationship, I ask three questions before I proceed. Do you know how to use they/them/theirs pronouns? Do you support trans women? Do you get tested for STI's? If they answer all questions in the positive, we get to know each other. If not, we go our separate ways. There can be no compromise with respecting my identity.*

The "how" of disclosure can be challenging in the moment. It is helpful to keep in mind that many people, trans and cis alike, experience the burden of disclosure when they start getting to know a potential partner. We might not be the only one on the date who is worried about disclosing certain personal information, including information that pertains to physical intimacy such as fetishes, aspects of the body that are different than expected, HIV status, or chronic illness.

> *Meeting new persons of interest is always stressful. I have gotten to the point that after interacting a bit, if I think I may want to date this person I go ahead and explain I am TG. Everyone is surprised and confused, but then curious. I tend to date cis hetero women. Most come to terms with the news pretty easily. As one said, "I really liked you before I knew, why should that change?" But I don't wait too long so they don't feel they are being deceived. Trust is an important part of any relationship. And it is this trust concept that is more important than any TG issues.*

Sometimes we are pleasantly surprised by dates who have already dated trans or gender expansive people, who have strong trans-awareness, or who are even trans themselves.

> *My partner recently told me he is a demiboy! It has been so wonderful and exciting for me. I love that we share this relationship with gender and this understanding that gender is not a cut and dried thing. I always feel very honored when people feel comfortable enough to come out to me, and I love to support and celebrate them.*

Other times, we find ourselves having to teach Trans 101 to a date who has no reference point for or experience with trans identities. In these cases, we can engage however we feel most comfortable. Some of us are happy to answer a slew of questions, while others of us might share some basics but then suggest consulting outside resources, or propose that deeper conversations about gender wait until future dates. All we can really do is approach a potential disclosure knowing what we want to communicate (and how) and being prepared for various responses.

Effects of Gender Norms and Socialization on Dating

If and/or when we transition, we may notice that our experiences with gender impact how other people relate to us. This happens in both casual and more serious intimate relationships. We may or may not change how we act during a transition, but people may change how they act toward us because of binary gendered norms and expectations. For instance, transmasculine people may find that our partners expect us to initiate more in the relationship—from being the one to ask someone else on a date to initiating sexual intimacy. Transfeminine people may notice that others expect us to take up less space in conversations or that other people invade our personal space more often. These changes may be minor annoyances or major problems. In either case, it can be important to be aware of how people may interact differently with us and how this influences our dating experiences.

MY PARTNER'S SCARS

Sage Russo (they/them) wants pizza, donuts, and free health care and housing for all. They spend most of their time contemplating abolishing ICE, prisons, and corporate cooptation of "diversity." When not dousing themselves in biodegradable glitter and dancing the night away, Sage loves to cuddle animals and sing too loud.

My partner's scars are oceans
filled with currents of pessimistic hopes
that snake under cresting waves of fervent dreams,
deep in excess of comprehension,
a compilation of navigations and needs,
fulfilling a space that is anything but empty.
My partner's scars are never still.
They run late to the train,
they quiver with fear
and I rock them to sleep.
They expand with the promise of continued life
and shrink with the relief of a deep sigh.
They stretch.
My partner's scars recreate time
With memories of passing and holding and slipping and busting,
Dali's clocks make all the more sense as they (and we) drip
into selves beyond our own.
My partner's scars are careful.
They are meticulous research, too many conversations you shouldn't have to have, and a
    collage of complexities I may never know.
They are early morning appointments and listening extra hard and trying to write down
    every single word the doctors say so that you can be doctor when no one else is
    around, and they always deserve the very best care.
They are frantic but never questioned.
They are intentional.
My partner's scars are an emblem
of the daring trust we bestow upon each other reminding me I am not alone.
They teach me how to be the pillar of strength they think I am—that being leaned on is
    an endurance exercise in generosity and patience.
They insist that we are not one sided.
My partner's scars are beautiful,
an inspiration,
A masterpiece,
A living, breathing piece of art,
An ocean,
A treasure chest,
A new understanding of time, of love, of multiplicity, and of joy.

Falling into binary gender roles may feel comfortable for some of us, while others feel boxed in, sometimes in ways that are uncomfortable.

> *I sometimes feel like I have to fulfill more masculine roles such as paying for dinner, bringing in all or most of the groceries, or know more about sports just because I'm a man and I "should" know or do these things.*

Sometimes we may adhere to binary gender roles based on how people treat us because we want to please potential partners or because we don't feel safe expressing ourselves in more nonconforming ways (even if it feels more authentic to us!). It's important

For interesting takes on various kinds of relationships, check out *Expanding the Rainbow: Exploring the Relationships of Bi +, Polyamorous, Kinky, Ace, Intersex, and Trans People* (edited by Brandy L. Simula, J. E. Sumerau, and Andrea Miller, Brill | Sense, 2019).

A transmasculine gender-nonconforming person and transfeminine non-binary person cuddling. (Zackary Drucker, The Gender Spectrum Collection, VICE/Broadly)

to approach ourselves with self-compassion and patience as we navigate forming new relationships (not just romantic ones). Perhaps we have some spaces where we feel we can experiment and express ourselves more authentically as our identities and expressions change (such as on a college campus), while there are others where we feel like we must play a part to be safe or accepted (such as at a partner's family home.) Everyone's gender journey is different, and what we need to feel congruent in relationships will change based on many factors.

Potential Partners

Dating presents many challenges and many opportunities for joy and growth. We may face discrimination and fetishization as we navigate intimate partnerships. Fetishization refers to when someone is interested in us based only on our gender identity, expression, and/or body, sometimes without interest in other parts of ourselves. Being fetishized may make us feel like we are objectified or dehumanized, worthy of interest only if we express our gender in certain ways, such as medically transitioning in a particular manner, having sex in a certain way, or wearing our hair or clothing in a way that pleases our partner.

A person who is primarily attracted to transgender and gender expansive people should not necessarily be dismissed as someone with a fetish. Implying that there is something wrong with being attracted to trans bodies is the same as saying there is something wrong with having a trans body. The problem occurs not when someone is attracted to our bodies, but rather when the attraction comes without respect for who we are: whole people with unique desires. There is a history of fetishization of our bodies, particularly for those of us who are transfeminine. People have historically viewed those of us who are transfeminine as sexual objects and expressed shame for having relationships with us, often keeping the relationship behind closed doors. A healthy relationship involves our

FOR A MAN FROM KIEV

Arden Eli Hill (he/they) is a lecturer at the University of Nebraska-Lincoln and a tutor at South-
east Community College. He has had work published in places like the short story collection
Women's Work, *the essay collections* First Person Queer *and* Second Person Queer, *as well as*
journals such as Willow Springs, Western Humanities Review, JoslynNOW, *and* Kaleidoscope.
Arden's manuscript in progress is Bloodwater Parish, *which wrestles with inheritance in terms*
of the intersections of race, gender, disability, and adoption in southern Louisiana.

I am a gender immigrant
with mothertongue still salt in my mouth.
Even with the needle's last shadow on my face,
serum transformed to muscle, I bleed at the moon.
I wetten at desire. The glistening bud shifts.
I am nothing that does not want to take you in
to blossom on the curved stem of your cock
until you make milkweed sap and pollen.
You are an immigrant of cities–
the blue and gold domes of Kiev,
tumesce to a New York skyline that
fell around you as you misplaced English.
No mother gave us our names.
Is yours real you ask on our first date, as if I might
only use it for meeting strangers.
As real as anything, I say, and later when you tell me
I look fifteen, and late at night when you remark
on how slender my hands are, I know you do not know
where I am from any further than geography,
a lisp I lost in grade school, my house full of dykes,
and what you, at forty-seven, have never touched
hidden like a root between the borders of my thighs.

partners loving us in a holistic way that values who we are and not just how we appear or express ourselves.

Dating Other Trans People

My significant other and I have similar feelings about gender. However, I'm farther along in my coming out process and I have more confidence in my identity. It's really great having someone who feels similarly and who I know understands and believes me. But sometimes it's tough that I am more "out" and accept my identity more. I feel a little guilty for the progress I've made.

Partnering with someone who shares many of the same experiences of being trans or gender expansive and going through transition can reduce some of the stress associated with dating. Other trans people are more likely than cis people to have an understanding of the experience of being transgender, though no two trans experiences are alike.

The person I was dating when I came out as trans came out as trans around the same time—we didn't know about each other's gender identity when we started dating, but we helped each other explore our identities and test out things like pronouns and terms for each other, and that was a tremendous support.

The increasing visibility of trans movements, the creation of trans-specific spaces, and the rise of online communities have greatly increased our ability to find and connect with other trans people. We cannot assume that other trans people will always understand our experiences, but finding and partnering with other trans people can create a greater likelihood that our partner "gets it."

The trans erotica author Patrick Califia discusses the personal and the political in *Sex Changes: The Politics of Transgenderism* (Cleis Press, 2003).

My partner is a transgender man who started his transition before I met him. In some ways this has been helpful, because we can talk about negative experiences and fears and celebrate the awesome parts about being transgender. (There are so many awesome parts about being transgender! But they don't get as much attention, at least in the dominant stories about transgender identities.) But on the other hand, I felt like it was hard to take my own path in transition because I was always comparing myself (or being compared) to my partner.

Dating within Queer Communities

Some of us may never have dated in queer communities and may not be interested in doing so. Others of us, however, have participated in queer communities before, during, and after a transition, and we may continue to seek relationships in these spaces. Many queer spaces can be safe and welcoming for us as trans people. However, not all LGBQ spaces are trans-friendly. Transphobia, trans exoticization, and trans invisibility can occur in these spaces and can potentially negatively influence our dating experiences.

Despite some of these challenges, many queer spaces are trans-inclusive. Many trans and gender expansive people find cis queer-identified partners in queer spaces, who may identify as the same gender or a different gender than they do. Queer spaces may offer a wide range of possible intimate connections where expansiveness in gender, sexuality, and partnership style are better understood, or even assumed. Queer culture also provides space for folks whose identities are in flux, who are part of queer subcultures like the leather scene, or whose sexual identities may not seem to match their dating lives as seen by cis/hetero culture (e.g., a lesbian-identified cis woman who exclusively dates trans men).

SueZie, 51, and Cheryl, 55, Valrico, FL, 2015. (Jess T. Dugan). From "To Survive on This Shore: Photographs and Interviews with Transgender and Gender Nonconforming Older Adults," a project by Jess T. Dugan and Vanessa Fabbre.

Relationships and Families

Trans-Friendly Dating Communities

There are some spaces that are not specifically trans or queer, yet have an increased likelihood of trans inclusion. Multiple cultures exist that not only accept but encourage challenging gender norms. In goth culture, for example, femininity is valued in all genders. Many trans women have found that goth culture provides a nonjudgmental space in which to experiment with our gender expression. Someone assigned male can feel comfortable entering many goth spaces wearing makeup, skirts, and fishnet stockings. In such a space, where the rules of normative gender expression are already subverted, we may be less likely to encounter harassment. Other examples of subcultures where queer themes have had a long-existing influence include: art scenes, punk culture, drag culture, anime culture, alternative educational communities, and communities focused on advancing social justice. In spaces like these, we may find increased inclusion and acceptance that can influence our dating experiences.

TRANS FAMILIES OF CHOICE

Nik Lampe (they/them) is pursuing a master's degree in applied sociology at University of Central Florida. Their research focuses on health, gender, and sexualities in the experiences of transgender and gender nonconforming populations.

Much like my trans and nonbinary siblings, I have coped with the relative absence of my family of origin by creating a family of choice. Families of choice are familial relationships that we create intimately, emotionally, or socially when we choose to treat certain people in our lives as family. Families of choice take many forms and can provide fuller satisfaction for individuals when families of origin fail to do so. These families are even more important to trans and nonbinary people who face rejection from their families of origin. In my case, I sought out others who would see me in full. The friendships and intimacy I created provided me the security and comfort I needed to feel fulfilled.

My family of choice does what my family of origin was ill-equipped to do. I don't have to save myself anymore. Instead, I have my family of choice to provide a safety net of sorts as I continue to grow and pursue my goals. People who are privileged enough to find affirmation in their families of origin often talk about this safety net when they speak of the meaning of family. By opening myself up completely and forming emotional intimacy with people who matter to me, I became fully myself again as a loud and proud trans warrior. In these ways, I centered my transness with others via forming my own familial relationships.

Having Multiple Partners

Exploring our authentic sexuality is an ongoing, fluid process. It often requires an internal deconstruction of messages we were taught growing up, including the assumption that we will be monogamous—that is, we will date and partner with one person at a time. We may have a desire to experience a variety of different types of relationships with a variety of people in order to find what is right for us. For some of us, having multiple partners is a core part of our identity and a way we express our authentic sexuality.

> *I have started two new relationships since I started transitioning and living as who I am. Both of my partners are queer, one is a trans man and the other is nonbinary (and prefers not to label their gender at all) so in both cases I have had no trouble "disclosing" my identity because I avoided dating people who might potentially have a problem with me being trans. Since all three of us have different experiences with gender it does make navigating our intimate times and conversations more complicated. We have to be aware that each of us has a different relationship with our body and how we talk about/relate to it.*

The impact of colonization and the domination of white Christianity has created a hierarchy in many cultures that privileges cis, straight, married relationships as more valuable than single, queer, and/or non-monogamous relationships. Some of us may want to maintain multiple relationships for a limited period of time, while others hope to build multiple relationships that last a longer portion of their lives. Perhaps we have one relationship that we consider primary while exploring other connections with varying degrees of depth and commitment. For others of us, we may be more interested in nonhierarchical relational structures. Perhaps we maintain multiple serious long-term relationships. Perhaps we maintain several casual relationships for a long period of time. Maybe some of these relationships are sexual, while others are not. Maybe multiple partners are involved equally in one relationship, or maybe there are multiple hubs of interrelated relationships. Some people refer to such a network as a polycule.

More and more people are exploring what relationship structures are right for them without an assumption of monogamy. What is acceptable, and with whom, varies widely depending on the people involved and their agreements. Sometimes non-monogamous relationships are called "open" relationships. Polyamorous relationships usually imply a greater degree of emotional intimacy and commitment between partners within multiple relationships, although this is dependent upon the individuals involved.

Regardless of what structure(s) are right for you, having multiple partnerships means navigating gender exploration and/or transition with several people, each with their own understandings of sexual and gender identity. It can be beneficial to have multiple people supporting us as we experiment, explore, and make decisions about our gender—offering more than one perspective on our journey and perhaps a wider network of support during intense times, such as after surgeries.

> *I have two partners who were assigned male at birth, and who now identify as something other than strictly "men" . . . though neither one has undergone, or plans to undergo any kind of medical/surgical intervention. They're mostly happy just to paint their nails when they feel like it and reject the cis/het models of manhood they were offered as kids. Even though my own gender path has involved a lot more investment, physical risk, and permanent alteration of my body, I'm totally uninterested in ranking or policing anybody else's "right" to identify or express their own gender landscape. The more the merrier, I say.*

For therapists working with trans clients, especially in non-monogamous relationships, check out *Sex Therapy with Erotically Marginalized Clients: Nine Principles of Clinical Support* (Damon M. Constantinides, Shannon L. Sennott, and Davis Chandler, Routledge, 2019).

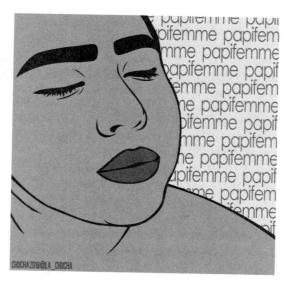

PapiFemme. (Chucha Marquez)

As with every relationship, clearly communicating desires, expectations, and boundaries is important. Special considerations for relationships where there are multiple partners include agreements about communication between partners, STI/HIV testing, sexual boundaries, and how to revisit and revise existing relationship agreements to meet the needs of all partners. Additionally, partners in relationships may want to openly discuss the impact of new relationship energy (sometimes termed "NRE") when one or more partners are establishing new relationships.

Asexuality and Aromanticism

We may invest in intimate relationships that include sexual activity and attraction, be interested only in romantic relationships without sex, or be interested in relationships that do not include sexuality or romantic elements. In many social contexts, we are assumed to experience sexual attraction and to desire sexual and/or romantic relationships. However, many people do not. Asexuality generally refers to those of us who do not have and/or are not interested in sexual relationships, while allosexuality refers to folks who experience and act on sexual attraction.

Asexuality is a spectrum that can range from abstinence and complete lack of desire for sexual relationships to varied sexual engagement and some desire for sexual intimacy. Asexual folks sometimes shorten "asexuality" to "ace." Some asexual people have a desire for romantic relationships and may identify based on the kinds of romantic relationships they want, such as asexual and homo-, hetero-, or panromantic (or other terms describing romantic interest based on the other person's gender). Other asexual people may not desire sexual or romantic relationships, and may identify as an aromantic asexual person. Graysexual people may feel low levels of sexual attraction, may experience sexual attraction but not want to act on it, may be interested in sex in specific circumstances, or may have ambiguous feelings toward sexuality.

Aromanticism refers to the lack of desire for romantic relationships. As is true with asexuality, aromanticism is a range and each of us will express our aromanticism differently. Like other identities, some people identify as asexual and/or aromantic for a lifetime, and others for specific periods of time. For some people, this will overlap with their comfort with their gender, and for others, it has no connection to their gender.

> *I would say that I'm lucky to have found the person that I am currently with. His life experiences are different from mine, but we are very similar as people when it comes to our morality. With everything that has been going on, my significant other has been 100% supportive. Every problem that I have, he listens. Every experience that I go through, he tries to understand. There are some things that I am definitely still figuring out, and I know that he will be there to support me through it no matter what. Ultimately, I think people just need to find either a friend or loved one to help them with what they have to go through. That doesn't necessarily mean it has to be someone that you're also in a sexual relationship with, but someone that you love and trust. Those are the most important relationships, in my opinion. Luckily, I was best friends with my significant other before we started dating. It's important to find somebody you're a kindred spirit with. Someone who lets you know, "I'll be there for you through these kinds of things, no matter what." They're not easy, but it feels a little easier when you have somebody that loves you right by your side.*

Deciding Not to Have Sex

Some of us are not asexual but temporarily opt out of sexual relationships. This may be simply because we do not feel like being sexual, or because we are in a stage where we are adjusting to our identity. We may wish to wait until after a medical transition to begin a relationship that could include sexual intimacy because we feel we will then be more comfortable with our bodies. Others of us may fear the reaction of a potential partner toward either our gender identity or our body. Whatever our reason for not wanting to have sex at a particular point, it is valid.

SHARE MY LIGHT

Cinda Gonzales is stumbling in the dark, running into the coffee tables of self-realization. Still not sure. Plenty insecure. She writes to us with the assistance of the Sylvia Rivera Law Project's Prisoner Justice Project.

I'm confused enough as it is with these curves in my hips, my butt, and my breasts. I don't need you to remind me that I've got a dick. You make a reason to strip search me just to be sure. What are you hoping to see?

I live this life, it didn't happen today, but it happens. I've learned to maneuver my way through and around the weirdos who want to see the "freak," the one that got mixed up when Mother Nature was distracted by God—their little inside joke. Sometimes, it's hard to laugh and find the humor in the hate I receive because I was born a male but feel like I'm female. Sometimes, I don't even notice. I'm just me.

Then there's the sidelong glances, stares, whispers, and pointing, but I started it. I told them to begin with because apparently no one would've known. They think I'm angry. I'm just reserved. I have them at face-value. Once they know, it's the last time I hear their voice—besides in whispers.

God is good. Good is great. Keep a good mood and suffer the hate.

There's love out there though—a postcard here, a cut-out heart there. Turns out I'm not alone. There are more people that deal with these same things—even worse. They don't just love you, but need love, too. When you're the only positive person, the only one sharing the light, the shades of darkness can overwhelm you.

To the people reading these words: You are not alone! Share my light.

COMMITTED RELATIONSHIPS

Some of us are in committed relationships. They may have begun before, during, or after our transition. They may be extremely healthy or may have problematic power dynamics. Many relationships have significant challenges, and we have to learn how to communicate well and respect our partners in order to have fulfilling, lasting partnerships.

Building Healthy Relationships

I was terrified of intimacy before realizing how connected it was to my dysphoria. As I transition, that fear has lessened, though it will still take some work.

Healthy relationships are not always easy—they take work. There is no universal definition of what constitutes a healthy relationship, but relationships that thrive are typically those with foundations of mutual respect. There are a number of ways to create respectful relationships, including maintaining appropriate boundaries, establishing effective communication, being emotionally attuned and available, paying attention to enactments of power and privilege, and being accountable when we fall short of our ideals.

Setting and maintaining boundaries with our partners can contribute to healthy relationships. Our boundaries impact our own emotional health. For instance, we may want our partners to understand when and how we can talk about particular issues. We may have certain situations in which we are happy being out about our trans identity, and others in which we want our partners to understand that we would prefer not to be. Boundary setting is a mutual process, given that our partners will also have needs and expectations. Boundaries can change from day to day and will need to be continually reassessed throughout the relationship. Respecting these changes is important for our relationships. Some trans and gender expansive people may have trouble feeling empowered to set boundaries if they have not felt safe and supported in their formative family and social environments. Sometimes, surviving these oppressive situations means hiding our true desires for fear that we will lose significant relationships. Seeking support through peer support groups, couples and individual therapy, 12-step programs, and relationship classes may help us to practice identifying and articulating what we need.

We can also nurture healthy relationships through effective and empathetic communication with our partners. Prioritizing empathy with our partner(s) may help increase honest communication of relational needs. This, in turn, will allow us to better respond to our partners' needs and desires. Healthy communication does not mean that we will never argue with our partners—disagreement can be a positive way to clarify our own needs and learn to effectively work through conflict. One aspect of healthy communication is the capacity to acknowledge when we make mistakes or hurt someone we care about, communicate that we are sorry, and articulate what we will do differently next time.

Trans and queer communities experience high rates of trauma, and the impact of these traumas may present itself in the context of a relationship, creating new needs as we move through healing. Maintaining boundaries that allow us to take care of ourselves, while also risking some degree of safety in favor of being vulnerable about our past can be helpful in navigating trauma in intimate relationships with others.

Trans People in Love is a collection of stories about trans people and relationships (Tracie O'Keefe and Katrina Fox, Routledge, 2008).

Intersectionality, Power, and Privilege

Our gender identity and gender expression are not the only salient identity categories we must pay attention to in our intimate partnerships. Each person in the relationship may have a number of meaningful identities, such as their race, ethnicity, socioeconomic status, educational background, family structure, documentation status, body size, native language, ability, and religion. These can all affect the ways we each navigate the world. Each of these identity characteristics affords us a relative amount of power and privilege. There can be issues with trust, understanding, and alignment in our goals in partnership in situations where we carry more or less privilege based on our combinations of identity compared to our partner(s). Furthermore, where we live and our access to community resources impacts the kind of support we can access in navigating our different experiences in society.

Most of us are used to the amount of power and privilege in our individual lives. A white, college-educated person who has family support, and who passes as a man in society, may be used to communicating needs directly, with an expectation that they will receive what they want. If they are in a relationship with a Black, nonbinary, formerly incarcerated person who is not always read as their true gender in society, the white person may not realize their partner does not feel as comfortable speaking up for what they want in the relationship. They may not know how to support someone navigating multiple social systems that regularly oppress them based on identities other than gender, and this can result in a serious power imbalance. It is the responsibility of people with more privileged identities—especially white trans and gender expansive people—to learn more about their privilege and interrupt dynamics that further devalue other trans and gender expansive people in relationships.

Though power structures and dynamics can affect all relationships, there are specific ways in which these dynamics can show up in non-monogamous relational structures, and they must be addressed consciously in order to avoid enactments of oppression. For example, people of color and women/femmes getting involved with a partner who already has a "primary" partnership (in the case of hierarchically structured systems) or "nesting" partner may have certain feelings come up if treated as a second-class citizen within these

Two Men Hugging. (Noah B. Sullivan)

structures. In order to practice relationships responsibly in these situations, partners who hold forms of privilege must truly reflect on how they are treating everyone involved so as not to create a dynamic in which anyone feels dehumanized, invalidated, or used. None of these dynamics are easy to navigate, but in committing to relationships it is important to try our best to face whatever challenges get in the way of us showing up with care and respect for ourselves and others.

Intimate Partner Violence

Healthy relationships are an ongoing process. We may work through some difficult times. We may sometimes find ourselves in relationships that are harmful to us or to our partners.

The Anti-Violence Project (212-714-1141) is an LGBTQ antiviolence organization and hotline.

> *Getting pregnant has been a real fear of mine. It is difficult to get partners to use protection. One partner even wanted to impregnate me and I left them when I realized I didn't trust them not to try covertly.*

Intimate partner violence (IPV) is a deliberate pattern of assaultive and coercive behaviors perpetrated by one partner (or ex-partner) to gain power and control over the thoughts, feelings, and behaviors of another partner. This abuse may occur in intimate, romantic, and sexual relationships. Abusive dynamics can happen in all kinds of relationships, including between people who are married, non-monogamous, dating, hooking up, divorced, broken up, or platonic. Abuse in a relationship can include: verbal abuse (such

As trans people become more visible in the media and in communities across the country, more trans people are able to name and understand their own experiences and may feel safer and more comfortable sharing them with others. Being open about one's gender identity and living a life that feels truly authentic can be a life-affirming and even life-saving decision.

The transgender movement is part of a long tradition of social justice movements of people working together to claim their civil rights and better opportunities in this country. These challenges are connected. Discrimination that we face is compounded by racism, and lower-income trans people face economic challenges and classism. I believe that progress toward transgender equality requires a social justice approach that fights all forms of discrimination.

In the context of this, it can be difficult for people who are not transgender to either imagine what being transgender feels like or understand what they can do to help the cause. So for our cis friends, family, and significant others here are some things you can do to be supportive of us:

- Educate yourself about transgender issues.
- Be aware of your attitudes concerning people with gender-atypical appearance or behavior.
- Use names and pronouns that are appropriate. If in doubt, ask their preference.
- Don't make assumptions about our sexual orientation, desire for surgical or hormonal treatment, or other aspects of our identity or transition plans.
- Don't confuse gender dysphoria with gender expression. For example, gender-dysphoric males may not always appear stereotypically feminine and not all gender-variant men are gender dysphoric.
- Be available by keeping the lines of communication open.
- Get support in processing your reactions. It can take some time to adjust to seeing someone close to you transition in a new way. It will be an adjustment and can be challenging, especially for partners, parents, and children.

Together, we can help put an end to transphobia, discrimination, harassment, social stigma, mistreatment, abuse, and violence toward all transgender and gender-variant people.

---

as insulting or criticizing), physical abuse (such as hitting or shoving), financial abuse (such as withholding or controlling finances), emotional or psychological abuse (such as threatening or intimidating), and sexual abuse (such as forcing or coercing sexual encounters).

> *Not long after coming out, I met someone and started dating them. They insisted on outing me to every member of their family and friend group. They said it was because they wanted to make sure everyone gendered me properly, but all it did was make everyone see me as "other." Had they not outed me, I doubt there would have been any problems with those people gendering me correctly.*

As trans people, we are vulnerable to specific methods of abuse. These tactics include ridiculing or belittling our identities, dictating self-expression, denying access to medical treatment or hormones, eroticizing or fetishizing our bodies without consent, and threatening to out us to others.[1]

FORGE is a national transgender antiviolence organization that provides resources for survivors.

> *I have been in a physically/sexually/emotionally abusive relationship in the past. One relationship targeted my gender identity and started out as a D/s dynamic. Part of that dynamic was referring to me by my dead name in order to "feminize" me and verbally degrading parts of my body and/or physically abusing me during sex/scenes.*

Over time, we may begin internalizing and believing negative messages from abusers, resulting in a diminished sense of self-worth and feelings of disempowerment. This can further hinder our ability to find support.

Discussing IPV is not easy. This is due to many factors, including the emotional impact that discussing trauma can have on the individual, and also because of the real fear of negative responses to sharing the experience. People of color often face additional marginalization when discussing their experiences of IPV, which creates added oppression at an already vulnerable time.

When IPV occurs within queer relationships, there may also be real or perceived fears of making the community look bad, or losing protection and support from the community.

I was in an abusive relationship where another trans person used her identity and status to isolate and hurt me. I couldn't tell people about it for fear they would think all trans women are dangerous. (They're obviously not! Just this woman was.)

Many gay and bisexual men have been afraid to speak out about IPV because of the assumption that men cannot be the ones who are abused, and many lesbians and queer women have been afraid to speak out because a woman does not fit the typical profile of an abuser. On top of that, some lesbian, gay, queer, and bisexual people fear that public acknowledgment of IPV in same-gender relationships will only perpetuate negative and false stereotypes that lesbian, gay, queer, and bisexual people cannot form healthy, lasting relationships.

Getting Help with Intimate Partner Violence

If you are someone who is in an abusive relationship, there are a number of things you can do:

1. *Find specialized support.* You may wish to speak with a therapist or contact an organization, such as a local organization working against intimate partner violence, or a national hotline. It can be helpful to have a list of organization phone numbers available in case you need them. Contacting these organizations can provide a place for you to discuss your experiences with someone who understands, and they can help you to figure out your options.
2. *Identify your support system.* Who are the people in your life, such as friends, family members, or neighbors, whom you can trust and who will support you?
3. *Create a plan in case you need to leave.* Think about things such as where you would go, who could lend you money, how you would support your children, and who would care for your pets. You may also wish to have a packed bag with essential items handy and hidden so that you can leave at a moment's notice if necessary.

If you have a friend you think might be in an abusive relationship, there are many ways you can help. First, never underestimate the power of listening. Having someone to listen in a nonjudgmental way can be very helpful for a person experiencing abuse. Second, try to avoid giving advice about what they should do, even if your friend asks for it. A person in an abusive relationship may already be accustomed to not having choices, and one of the most empowering things can be for them to make choices for themselves. Instead of giving advice, you can offer options and resources. Help them brainstorm possible ways to respond. Do research for your friend to find contact information for a local, trans-friendly nonprofit working to end IPV or find the number of a 24-hour hotline. If possible, you may want to offer your home as a safe place for them and their dependent(s) to stay.

Even if your friend leaves their abusive relationship, be prepared for them to potentially return. Many people return to their abusive partner at least once after leaving, some many more times. The most important thing for you to do is to support your friend

Intimate partner violence happens in our communities, too. Check out the book *The Revolution Starts at Home: Confronting Intimate Violence Within Activist Communities* by Ching-In Chen, Jai Dulani, and Leah Lakshmi Piepzna-Samarasinha (South End Press, 2011).

Need someone to talk to about intimate partner violence? Call the 24/7 National Domestic Violence Hotline (1-800-799-SAFE).

Relationships and Families

through their decisions, and be there to listen to them when they need it again. Each time someone leaves an abusive relationship, it can help to empower them to eventually leave for good. It is important to remember that returning to abusive relationships reflects how deep and ingrained the manipulation and abuse has been.

WHAT CAN BE DONE AND WHERE DO WE TURN?

Jules Purnell, M.Ed. (they/them/theirs) is the Associate Director of Prevention Education at Muhlenberg College. They have been teaching on sexuality, relationships, and gender for 10 years, specializing in intersectional analysis, LGBTQIA + concerns, kink, non-monogamy, and safer sex.

Sexual, gender-based, and intimate partner violence impacts people of all genders, sexual orientations, and relationship configurations (single, partnered, non-monogamous, etc.). These problems, however, disproportionately affect transgender and nonbinary people, especially those who are also people of color. Although appropriately representative samples can be difficult to obtain and study, what we do know suggests the problem may be even larger than we realize. We also know there are specific ways in which misunderstandings about these communities intersect with institutional trauma. For example, those who respond to domestic violence calls may automatically assume that the person who presents in a more masculine manner, or is taller or larger-bodied, is the aggressor in an abusive relationship and treat that person accordingly.[2] Depending on the definition of rape, it may or may not apply to the kinds of sexual violence trans and nonbinary people experience. In addition, homo- and transphobia on the part of social service providers, law enforcement officers, and the larger carceral system can make it harder for victims/survivors to find support and for perpetrators to access rehabilitation.[3]

So what can be done? First, we need a deeper and further-reaching study of how and why these populations are experiencing this violence. Both FORGE[4] and the National Center for Transgender Equality[5] are leaders in research on this topic. Second, anyone having professional contact with victims/survivors and/or aggressors, including police, forensic specialists, rape and intimate partner violence crisis counselors, social workers, and nurses, needs mandatory training that includes the specific skills required to work with these populations. This will require a massive, multidisciplinary effort and will include work such as implicit bias training, the proper use of pronouns, how to discuss body parts of trans and nonbinary survivors, and a basic understanding of the dynamics of queer relationships (such as how things like outing a person or insisting they present their gender in a certain way can be used as manipulation and control tactics). This is no small undertaking, but it must be done to effectively serve our communities. In addition to educating providers, we need more inclusive sex education in K–12 schools. We cannot wait until college to begin discussing gender identity, sexual orientation, pleasure, healthy relationships, and safer sex methods specific to queer and trans relationships (e.g., condoms on toys, using gloves and dental dams, using terms like "people with penises" instead of "boys" or "male-bodied"). This education must include how sex can be pleasurable post-abuse, offering avenues for healing and positive sexual exploration.[6]

Finally, we need to believe those who have been victimized while also acknowledging the humanity of the person who caused harm—especially unwittingly—and encourage that person's ability to grow and do better. Encouraging growth requires deep "heart work," which is some of the most difficult work. We have to be willing to recognize that young people by and large are not given adequate tools to ensure their relationships and sex lives are healthy, and this is doubly true for transgender and nonbinary students who never hear about their bodies, relationships, or sexualities. We have to be deeply invested in meaningful education and reform for those who cause harm—especially if the harm was caused out of ignorance and if the person does not pose a threat to our communities. This should be preferred over relying on the prison industrial complex or on social isolation to simply create disposable people.

Taking a Relationship through Transition

Those of us in relationships prior to identifying as or coming out as trans may be in strong relationships that we want to continue as we transition. Some of us may already be out to our partners in some way before we tell them everything we understand about our identities. For others of us, our partners may not be as prepared. Finally, for some of us, there may not have been language available to describe or understand our identity until we were in a relationship. The experience of coming to terms with our own identity can be jarring enough as a single person. Navigating our gender exploration and exploring trans communities while already in a committed relationship can lead to additional challenges.

Gender Outlaws: The Next Generation includes a number of essays about relationships and sexuality (edited by Kate Bornstein and S. Bear Bergman, Seal Press, 2010).

Coming Out to a Long-Term Partner

Our relationships are healthier if we are treated with respect and embraced in all of our identities. The stress associated with pretending to be something other than ourselves can hinder healthy communication and connection. There is a wide spectrum of how out we may be to a partner before transition. Some of us may feel uncomfortable adhering to traditional gender roles, or we may act in ways around our partners that communicate an androgynous or ambiguous style without voicing a trans identity. Some of us directly disclose an intent to transition to our partners, even if we are not ready to do so yet, or if barriers exist that prevent us from moving forward. Even if we are not planning to socially, medically, or legally transition, we may want to talk with our partner(s) about questioning our gender.

> *My significant other was excellent and supportive when I came out. His response was, "Well, then I must not be straight." It was the best, most helpful thing for me.*

Making an announcement to the people in our life about our identity, our desire to transition, or that we have already begun transitioning, is an act of bravery and honesty. Disclosing our status as trans, or communicating that our presentation is not aligned with our identity and we do not have a strong connection to our sex assigned at birth, can potentially end a relationship, greatly strengthen the connection with our partner, or fall somewhere between.

> *My fiancé has recently come out as gender nonconforming. It's comforting to know that the person I will be spending my life with is also part of the same community that I am.*

Partners can be great allies and advocates. Even without fully understanding the complex emotions of gender dysphoria, gender euphoria, or gender minority stress, partners may provide vital affirmation and support. Some partners, however, may be less than supportive. In some cases, perhaps especially before a person is settled into or comfortable with sharing their identity, a partner may exhibit resistance or resentment for behavior deemed "gender nonconforming." This can be extremely hurtful and distressing. In some cases, a partner may grow to be more accepting. In other cases, however, it may prove emotionally or even physically unsafe to remain with an unsupportive partner.

HOW I FOUND MY VOICE AS THE PARTNER OF A TRANS PERSON

D. M. Maynard (she/her) has been an educator in New York for more than 30 years and has used her expertise in teaching to create workshops. She has presented internationally to empower the voices and help navigate the journeys of the partners who are in a relationship with individuals who are questioning their gender or now identify as transgender and/or nonbinary.

I remember feeling alone and scared of all the unknowns. I wondered how my spouse's newly understood transgender identity would affect our individual lives and the future of our relationship. My emotions came in waves, and for much of the time, I felt like I was drowning. As an educator, I quickly realized that questioning myself, learning all I could about transitioning, and reflecting my thoughts in writing would be the remedy for keeping me afloat.

Were there other couples who were experiencing all of these changes too? If so, how could I find them? As I began to search for information back in 2010, I soon discovered that most books related to transgender relationships focused on the person in transition. And when I did find materials that primarily pertained to the partners, they were in the form of memoirs. Rarely, if ever, were there any resources that provided a place for partners to process their own personal journey throughout the transition.

Finding a space that respected my voice became critical to me, and so I attended a conference that concentrated on trans issues. Though most of the workshops centered on those in transition, there was one workshop for partners. I cried throughout the entire workshop, yet I did not want it to end. I quickly realized I was not the only one who felt that way. I left that conference stronger and more determined to find my own voice and then create a way to help other partners do the same. I understood that the needs and wants of the partners had to be as essential and valued as the needs and wants of those who identify on the transgender spectrum. I also recognized that every partner deserved a tool that would enable them to figure out if they could remain in their relationship or not, and regardless of their decision, begin to comprehend how this would all look for them.

I returned to the same conference the following year and presented my own workshop using all the knowledge I had gained both from my own research and from personal journaling. Using my skills as veteran teacher, I began to write down numerous questions, a list of activities that would assist partners to reflect on their own journey, and games that would aid participants in absorbing all the vocabulary and terms that entering this new venture entailed. Much to my surprise, attendees requested a workbook that included all I had shared with them at the conference. I honored their wishes and wrote the book I wish I had had for myself when my spouse began to transition.

I have now published the first workbook for and about the partners of those in transition, which is titled, *The Reflective Workbook for Partners of Transgender People: Your Transition as Your Partner Transitions*. This vital resource focuses on all the topics that partners have stated were relevant to them as they navigated their own transition as their partner transitioned. As a vocal advocate for partners, I am humbled by the fact that I continue to be afforded the privilege to present my workshops and classes throughout the world in order to promote a platform that respects and honors the voices of partners.

Being Out as a Couple

When we are in long-term relationships, our relationships are often known to others in our lives. As such, every time we out ourselves, we also out our partners, and vice versa. We may need to discuss with our partners whether we are comfortable being out as trans in various situations. We may be comfortable being out with our partner's extended family but not with work friends, and we need to be able to discuss and negotiate these differences.

We also need to consider whether or when our partners are comfortable being out, because every time we come out as transgender or gender expansive, our partner is also outed as the partner of a transgender or gender expansive person. At times our needs can conflict, with one partner wanting more or less visibility than the other. Our partners may even find themselves the targets of discrimination or violence. There is no simple answer when one person's needs or safety are in conflict with another's, but it is often possible to negotiate a comfortable and safe situation that will work for both people.

I was in a relationship with my girlfriend. She was very supportive and, knowing me personally, we had many conversations and she helped me clarify my thoughts and our relationship is stronger now that I feel I can be more authentic. I consider her support part of the reason I was able to find myself and come out. Our relationship was still the same after my transition, and she loves that I can be who I am and we can be us together. Her extended family is less supportive of trans and gay people, and we had previously been stealthing as both straight, so me coming out as trans "forced the issue" and caused her to be outed to her extended family as bisexual and that she was dating me, a trans woman. This was difficult for us to deal with, but she is a lot happier knowing she doesn't have to hide and we are both happy.

Looking for a resource for families, partners, or friends? Pick up a copy of *Trans-Kin: A Guide for Family and Friends of Transgender People* (Eleanor A. Hubbard and Cameron T. Whitley, Bolder Press, 2012).

There are always outside influences on our romantic relationships. Our friends and families matter in the support they give to our relationships. Our communities matter, too. Religious communities, racial and ethnic communities, queer communities, and so on, can all play a part in shaping our relationships. The challenge is to seek out the people in our communities who will support us and help us to build healthy relationships.

S/HE by Minnie Bruce Pratt is a memoir about the author's life and relationship with trans activist Leslie Feinberg (Ithaca, NY: Firebrand Books, 1995).

Changing Sexuality through Transition in a Partnership

Some people experience a shift in their sexual or romantic desires during a transition. Some of us experience changes in our libido, our interest in specific sexual practices, and even the types of people to whom we are attracted. It can be confusing to understand what our new desires mean for both our existing and our future relationships.

Mannakins. (Glori Tuitt)

Those of us who are in relationships may have many questions, such as: *Can my partner help me fulfill my new sexual desires? What if they are not interested in my body anymore?* Although we may not be able to anticipate our partners' reactions, one of the best things we can do is to be honest with ourselves and clearly communicate our feelings.

Many of our relationships thrive after disclosing our identity as trans or our intention to transition. Not all of us, however, find that our existing relationships are a good fit once we transition. Some of us find that our own desires change and no longer include our existing partner. For others of us, our partners' desires do not include the new us. A partner who identifies as strictly homosexual or heterosexual may consider a transition to be extremely threatening, or an immediate reason to end a relationship. Our sexual orientation can be much more than an indication of our attractions. It can also be a core part of our identity, representing not only how we see ourselves but also how we want to be seen by others, as well as which communities we go to for support.

Supporting Our Partners

While we struggle with being our authentic selves, our partners have their own challenges and concerns, and they may need our support. Their lives often change as ours do. They may now need to be out to others in a new or different way. They may have new questions about their identity as we disclose ours. Our transition can be a whirlwind experience for our partners. We can give them support in the same ways we would like to have support: by listening without judging, asking questions, and making an effort to understand our partners' perspectives and needs.

It is important for partners of trans and gender expansive people to take responsibility for educating themselves and seek individual support. There are many e-mail lists, community groups, and resources where partners can share experiences, learn from one another, and discuss joys, fears, challenges, or frustrations. Our partners need support from others in addition to us.

Relationships with Our Families of Origin in Our Partnerships

Trans people have widely varied experiences with their families of origin. While some of us have been accepted and even celebrated, outright rejection and disownment is still not uncommon. Between these extremes is a wide spectrum of experiences, ranging from subtle microaggressions to blatant invalidation, rejection, and violence. This can leave

We recognize that some readers of this book are not trans themselves, but are the partners of trans people seeking to become better allies. Thank you for making this effort! As a partner of a trans person you may find yourself confused, upset, or concerned about the implications of your partner's transition. It is important not only to learn about the various things being "trans" may mean, but also to talk to your partner about their experience, as each person is unique. Flexibility is extremely important, because your and your partner's feelings may shift as the transition process (physical and/or social) progresses.

It is also important to balance genuine care for and acceptance of your partner with self-honesty and honesty with your partner. As with any life transition, the transition of a partner can (and likely will) shift some dynamics and roles within your relationship. You may find yourself questioning whether your relationship can go on. Some people find that they are no longer attracted to the body of their partner. It is important to discuss with your partner what that will mean for sexual contact, if you intend to have continued sexual interactions with your partner. It is also important to discuss how changes for your partner may prevent the relationship from continuing in a genuine, honest, loving, and supportive way. This can be a very painful choice for you or your partner, and often it will be painful for anyone involved.

For this reason it is important to evaluate the reasons you have for remaining in the relationship and any reasons you may be considering for leaving the relationship. Are you concerned that your partner will no longer be attracted to you after transition? Are you concerned that you will no longer be attracted to your partner? Are you concerned about how sexual contact may change? Have you spoken with your partner about modifications or additions that might allow you to preserve your relationship, if that is something both of you are interested in? Have you spoken to your partner about, and do you understand what changes (physical and social) they want to make, and how these will affect you both? As you have these conversations, it is important to keep an open mind, and to avoid making assumptions about what transition means for your partner. You may find that with some minor modifications to your relationship, it can continue in an even healthier and more fulfilling way.

If you have already been in a relationship with a trans person, it is important to remember when entering a relationship with a different trans person, that everyone's experience of transness is different. As with any relationship, some things that worked for your previous partners may not work with your new one. Some things may continue to work. Respectfully approaching your new partner with some specific and educated questions may allow you and your partner to invite new understanding and value into your partnership.

an individual with the difficult question of how to engage with a family of origin that is unsupportive. Some transgender and/or nonbinary people may choose not to come out to unsupportive family members. Others may continue contact despite hostility. There is no perfect way to navigate these situations. Power dynamics come into play here as well. In some cases, transgender and nonbinary people may continue to rely on family for financial

Two transmasculine people sitting together and having a serious conversation. (Zackary Drucker, The Gender Spectrum Collection, VICE/Broadly)

or other resource needs. Conversely, someone who has been cut off from their family of origin may depend much more on intimate relationships, chosen family, and community for support.

As we develop our relationships to include intimate partners, we also have to decide how to include our partners within our family of origin structures, if at all. Introducing a partner into our families of origin can prove helpful or make things more difficult. For example, if a family was concerned their transgender or nonbinary child would not "find love," bringing a partner home may have a positive effect. In other circumstances, an intimate partner may become the target of intrusive questions or hostile behavior. Each person has to navigate their own feelings regarding family.

Ensuring that partners are in agreement about interactions with their families of origin is necessary to provide safety and security. When partners are not "out" to each other's families, but contact is still desired, partners may wish to discuss appropriate pronoun use around their families to avoid accidentally "outing" each other. Likewise, when a person is out to their family of origin, it may be useful to discuss how their partner can most effectively be an ally. Partners might consider discussing how they plan to handle interactions with families of origin. There is no "right" arrangement to have, but when one or more partners in a relationship are transgender, nonbinary, and/or genderqueer, it is important to make space for the possibility of altering or limiting family interactions that could be harmful for those people.

FAMILY INTERACTION QUESTIONNAIRE

Consider taking some time with or without your partner(s) to explore your feelings about engaging with families of origin. The following questions may serve as a useful guide:

Is it appropriate to correct your parents/siblings/extended family if they misgender you or use the wrong name?

Should family unity be prioritized over correct name and pronoun usage?

Which family gatherings are safe to attend? How many family gatherings can you each safely commit to attending every year? Do both of you feel comfortable saying, "No" when you cannot attend a family gathering?

What kind of flexibility will you have for last-minute cancellations, if one of you is feeling overwhelmed or unsafe?

What signals or cues can you each use to indicate to each other that you need to excuse yourself for a time, or even leave a family engagement?

Legal Partnerships

Some of us marry legally, and some of us have other legal partnerships such as domestic partnerships or civil unions. Some of us form partnerships without ever having the government recognize them but still choose to make our commitments to each other public, whether this is with our friends, families, and/or within religious communities. Some of us do not prioritize public or legal recognition of our relationships.

Whether or not we have legal recognition of our relationships, we may still want to consider legal protections within our partnerships, such as securing the right to healthcare visitation, second parent adoptions if we have children, or completing a will. Taking these extra steps can protect us not only from discrimination by people outside of our relationships, but also from potential vulnerability if a relationship ends.

CONCLUSION

Relationships require continually reassessing our needs and our partners' needs as we navigate the many challenges and joys to being our full and authentic transgender, gender expansive, and nonbinary selves. Working toward mutual respect, open communication, and being true to ourselves can help us to create and maintain healthy, happy relationships of all kinds. No matter what our identities, our relationships have the possibility to contribute to our lives in meaningful and fulfilling ways. In all of our intimate relationships, we deserve to be valued and loved.

NOTES

1. Forge. (2013). Trans-specific power and control tactics. https://forge-forward.org/wp-content/uploads/2020/08/power-control-tactics-categories_FINAL.pdf

2. Baker, N. L., Buick, J. D., Kim, S. R., Moniz, S., & Nava, K. L. (2013). Lessons from examining same-sex intimate partner violence. *Sex Roles*, *69*(3-4), 182–192.

3. Langenderfer-Magruder, L., Walls, N. E., Kattari, S. K., Whitfield, D. L., & Ramos, D. (2016). Sexual victimization and subsequent police reporting by gender identity among lesbian, gay, bisexual, transgender, and queer adults. *Violence and Victims*, *31*(2), 320–331.

4. FORGE Empowering. Healing. Connecting. Retrieved from https://forge-forward.org/anti-violence/

5. James, S. E., Herman, J. L., Rankin, S., Keisling, M., Mottet, L., & Anafi, M. (2016). *The Report of the 2015 U.S. Transgender Survey.* Washington, DC: National Center for Transgender Equality.

6. Haines, S. (1999). *The survivors guide to sex: how to have an empowered sex life after child sexual abuse.* San Francisco: Cleis Press.

16

SEXUALITY

Tobi Hill-Meyer, Mx Nillin Lore, Jiz Lee, and Dean Scarborough

INTRODUCTION

Sex can be a sensitive subject for trans and gender expansive (T/GE) people. Much of the sex-related information we receive centers on sex that occurs between two cis, heterosexual people. Like everyone, trans people often internalize and believe implicit messages about the kinds of sex we are "supposed" to be having. We face messages that imply the shape of our genitals determines what we are "supposed" to do with them. We're told that certain kinds of sex might invalidate our genders. But the reality is that whatever kind of sex works for us is the kind of sex we are "supposed" to be having.

MYTHS AND MISCONCEPTIONS ABOUT SEX

Myths and misconceptions breed freely in the confusion of our cultural messages. Some of us have been taught to view sex as dirty, bad, or wrong. We may have learned to feel shame, fear, and guilt about our bodies, our desires, and our sexualities. It can be hard for us to find or even understand good information about healthy sexuality.

Many of us first learn about sex from our parents or our schools in the form of sex education. Some of us are led to believe that the only thing that counts as "sex" is when a cisgender man penetrates the vagina of a cisgender woman. (And depending on where we were educated, some of us were taught that sex should only happen after marriage and for the sole purpose of procreation—and that anything outside these lines is a sin.) This "traditional" concept of sexuality, however, paints a dangerously narrow picture of what healthy sexuality can look like. The truth is there is no "normal" when it comes to sexuality or sexual relationships.

> I'm coming out of a place of religious deconstruction where I'm tearing down my concepts of purity culture and sexual ethics.

Some of us first learn about sex from pornography, much of which can deepen and reinforce societal misconceptions about our sexualities. Transfeminine people are commonly represented either as sexually voracious, dominant, penetrative predators waiting to violate unsuspecting cis people, or as demure, receptive sex kittens available solely for the sexual pleasure of cisgender men. Transmasculine people are barely represented in mainstream porn at all, and nonbinary people aren't even alluded to as a possibility. There are many more options available than are typically found in mainstream porn. Queer- and trans-made porn can provide us with a wider range of representation.

> I don't really have a good model for what sex and intimacy for someone with my anatomy can look like. Pornography isn't the best guide for a number of reasons, and it's not like there's much porn out there featuring people with bodies like mine to begin with. I sometimes have trouble believing anyone could want me, since I've never seen anyone like me portrayed as an object of desire.

Distinguishing accurate information about sex from fantasy and stereotype can be difficult—especially because most currently available information is directed exclusively at cis people. Relying on this information often means tolerating trans erasure and exposure to potentially triggering language.

Self Portrait. (Reed Brice)

I do believe that societal expectations and norms, including toxic masculinity,
made it infinitely more difficult for me to accept my gender and sexuality.

Some of us may only be aware of very limited ways to have sex—for example, genital penetration and oral penetration. If that doesn't work for us or our partners because of dysphoria or other reasons, we may feel we have no options. This limited framework has been shaped by generations of social conditioning that is laden with shame, puritanical views of chastity, and misogynistic control over bodily autonomy. This impacts people of all genders but is especially harmful for us T/GE people. Sex can exist in many different forms. Sex does not have to involve penetration. Sex doesn't even have to involve genitals. As we learn about our own sexuality, we can map our own body's responses and desires.

THIS ONE (AFTER GREY VILD)

Silen Wellington (they/them) is a sculptor of sound, artist of people, storyteller, witch, activist, genderqueer shapeshifter, and lover, among other things. Avidly interdisciplinary, they like to combine poetry with other art mediums, be that music, visual art, ritual performance, loud and fiery eye contact, otherworldly and melting trysts, or something else entirely.

I met this one at camp three summers ago. He had that radiant blond boy smile that seemed to grab everyone in the room. This one would talk to me for hours about sex and scars and it seemed safe because I called myself a lesbian at the time. This one loved that I wanted to kiss him. This one loved helping people and in the worst interpretations saw me as a charity case, but this one loved me, really loved me, but also loved enacting his identity as a healer. Three years later, this one picked me up in the airport, radiant-as-ever-blond-boy-smile. This one asked how to refer to me. Maybe this one would have even tried the pluralistic pronouns if I'd asked him to. This one romanticizes birth and wombs and menstruating as if the divinity of "womanhood" lies only in fertility. As if the divinity of my body exists only if I identify as a woman. This one didn't mind that I liked sleeping naked and that we were sharing a bed. This one loves platonic cuddling. After two days, this one gets honest and shares all the stirrings in his heart and head and sacral. This one admits he projects his insecurities onto my unreadable expressions. This one asks how sharing a bed has been. This one says, "Yes and there's also been some sexual tension." He says, "I think it's just the familiar comfort of a female body." This one says he's been masturbating in the shower. This one asks if it's a problem that he sees me as a girl. This one only asks this in the context of sex and not in the context of our friendship. This one identifies as bi. This one wants gentle and slow sex. This one doesn't like pain. This one wants to make something "meaningful" out of lust. This one doesn't want to be obliterated by sex. This one has softer facial hair than I imagined. This one can't sustain an erection with a condom. This one assumed we would have sex in the morning. This one said, "Other women I've slept with . . ." while we were having sex. This one says, "You have to pick and choose your battles." "I'm not saying trans people are too sensitive, just that . . . maybe there needs to be a learning of resilience." This one shuts me down immediately. This one dismisses Trans Day of Remembrance as further evidence of Americans' overall obsession with violence. This one doesn't realize that it is a privilege to "pick and choose your battles." This one still has sex with me that night. This one was weak on his knees after orgasm. This one said "Really?" when I told him he fingered too abrasively. This one doesn't know how testosterone affects the clitoris or how queerness affects sex. This one hasn't messaged me in months. This one I lost for self-love.

BODY POSITIVITY, SEX POSITIVITY

The more confident and at home I feel in my genderqueer femme identity, the more interested I am in exploring sex with myself, my partner, and other people. It's great.

As the radical trans activist Mark Aguahar once said, "Bodies are inherently valid." The same could be said of sexuality. As long as it's consensual and safe, there is nothing invalid, wrong, or bad about the many ways we desire to have sex. Our bodies and sexualities are inherently valid, worthwhile, and good.

I have an intersex body that, despite childhood surgery, is capable of sexual feeling. Many other intersex people do not because infant surgery took away their sensation.

For a fat-positive take on sex and relationships, pick up a copy of *Big Big Love, Revised: A Sex and Relationships Guide for People of Size (and Those who Love Them)* (Hanna Blank, Random House, 2011).

Dealing with all the world's messages about our sexuality, it's easy to sometimes feel like sex is an uphill struggle through layers of shame, self-doubt, confusion, and misinformation. But it is possible for us to have fulfilling sex lives as T/GE folks despite the negativity we've internalized. Asserting our limits and boundaries around the sex we *don't* want to have is also an important part of feeling positive about sex. Our "yes" is only meaningful if we're able to say "no" whenever we need or want to.

I normally describe my gender as nonbinary and trans masculine. In more detail, my masculinity is inextricable from my homosexuality; I'm not a man without being a gay man. I also identify as tritiya prakriti, which is a South Asian concept of third sex (literally "third nature").

ALTERNATIVES TO SEX

I have been somewhat sexually reticent since I realized my transness, which happened around the time that I ended a long-term relationship and realized I had been having sex for attention/out of obligation for my entire life.

It's also OK for us to not have sex. We don't need to explain to anyone why we don't want sex or why we are not ready to have sex—any reason is valid. There are many reasons that sex may not be what we want or need. We may be asexual. We may have never had sex before. We may be young. We may be recovering from trauma. We may have just started transition and feel uncomfortable. We may be taking medication that diminishes our sex drive. We may have had some other major shift in our lives.

I can't masturbate or have sex. I don't want anyone to see my parts, and I don't want to see them or touch them. Maybe testosterone will help that, but until I have a penis I don't think I'll ever be comfortable.

There are a wide range of options for physical intimacy, including kissing, licking, hugging, cuddling, groping, or other forms of sensual touch. We are all going to have some kinds of touch that we like and others that we don't. We can just engage in the activities we like without having to do anything else. It is also OK for us to decide for ourselves what counts as sex to us. Some of us may believe that kissing or cuddling counts as sex, while others may not consider it sex until additional acts or activities take place. Sex is an individual construct. Instead of only one strict thing that counts as sex, there can be thousands of options. The result is limitless and can be incredibly freeing! Sex is a "choose your own adventure" journey that we can explore with ourselves and other consenting partners. We can create lists of activities that excite us and turn us on. We can partner with people who share our excitement and curiosity, and we can negotiate which activities we want to explore together. Anyone who expects us to have a "good" explanation for why we don't want any particular kind of touch or activity is not acting in our best interests. All forms of physical intimacy can constitute sex, and are valid ways to be sexual.

PEOPLE OF ALL GENDERS CAN HAVE SEX WITH OTHER PEOPLE OF ALL GENDERS!

I have become attracted to a wider range of gender identities. Also, I have become more confident about exploring more adventurous sexual activities.

Getting access to medical transition often requires proving ourselves to therapists and doctors. A big part of proving ourselves has been explaining what kind of sex we have or want to have. In the past, doctors were only interested in working with patients who would meet society's ideals after transitioning. It was even common for doctors of transfeminine patients to consider their own attraction to them as a criterion. If the (presumably straight male) doctor wasn't attracted to the patient, she wasn't *really* a woman.[1] That would be counted as a strike against her transitioning.

Some of us had to demonstrate that we would be "straight" after transition. Being gay, lesbian, or bisexual after transition was not considered acceptable. We were also required to hate our genitals and hate the idea of using them for sex before genital surgery—even masturbating was considered a taboo. All of this was codified into a two-type diagnosis system: transsexual or transvestite. True transsexual or secondary transsexual. Transgender or crossdresser. Over time, the language has changed, but the idea has been consistent: The "real" trans person deserves support, care, and medical transition, while the one who isn't "real" enough does not.

When trans support groups were first created, one of their major functions was to prepare people to navigate this medical gatekeeping system. They shared advice and tips—including how to talk about sexuality or how to behave sexually. When someone acted in a way that would likely be rejected by the doctors, the group would discourage them. We began policing ourselves to make sure we could prove ourselves to be "real" enough. Our communities still carry a lot of shame, judgment, and anxiety about fitting the gatekeeper's ideal image. When it comes to having sex, it's easy to get swept up into fears about having the wrong kind of sex or what the sex you have says about how you identify. But the reality is that people of all genders have all kinds of sex. The most important thing is that we are having (or not having) the sex that we want to be having.

I have always had a clear sense that I was sexually attracted to a lot of different types of people, and that did not change with my transition. However, the way I want to touch and be touched, talk about bodies and relate to bodies has changed a lot with my understanding of my gender.

Coming Out on Top. "This single-page comic faces, and then belittles, the notion that genitalia determine how queer/trans people have sex (front hole translating to bottom, big clit to top), reminding the reader that sex for us is both exploratory (serious, self-affirming) and experimental (fun)." Ulysses "Liz Tetu" Texx is a white bi cub from Minnesota who draws gag comics and eats more pineapple than is strictly necessary. His graphic narratives about trans sexuality (and romance) appear in collections like *Exposure: Queer Masculine Sexuality* and *Callisto Speaks* as well as his own zine *Spacebian*. He has a BA in Creative Sexual Communication.

QUEERS RULE AND I DROOL

El Wilson (they/them) is a nonbinary disabled human who graduated from Oberlin College with a B.A. in psychology and creative writing. They enjoy podcasts, pets, and diet pop.

I kissed their neck before inching my lips down to their nipples. Their body thrust against mine. They smiled in between loud gasps. I felt on top of my sexual game until I paused to let them catch their breath. I looked down at their chest only to realize that they were soaking wet. Their skin glistened in the glow of the string lights lining my dorm room. I had drooled all over them.

I shouldn't have been surprised. I have cerebral palsy, which means that my brain can't control my body the way a typical person's does. I spend most of my time in a manual wheelchair, have a speech disability, and drool. I quite like being disabled. I love bombing hills in my wheelchair and always being recognized on the phone.

Growing up, people told me that my disability eliminates jerks from my dating pool because my partner would have to "look past" my disability. Considering that my disability affects everything but my genitals, this isn't reassuring. Even as disabled representation in the media increased, my body image did not. Not only do I not look like any of the able-bodied celebrities, I don't look like the disabled ones either. They don't drool and are almost all cisgender. I'm a nonbinary afab person. Before I started testosterone, everyone said that the sexiest parts of me were my boobs and hips, which triggered extreme dysphoria.

Yet, my drool caused far more discomfort in the bedroom than my dysphoria did. Unlike some people with CP, I don't drool continuously, but rather when I'm fixated on something or when I'm very excited. Good sex is fixating and exciting, so it leads to lots of drooling. Before the evening when I drooled all over that partner's chest, I would prepare for sex by dehydrating myself so that my mouth would be dry.

But sex that night had been spontaneous, and I was as hydrated as ever. I sat on top of them, waiting for their look of pleasure to become one of disgust. It never did. After a few seconds, they looked up with a smile on their face, waiting for more. Making out with a human lube factory feels really good.

When it comes to sex, normal is just another word for boring. If someone says you're unsexy, spit on them. They might like it.

CHANGING PREFERENCES

After a few years of socially transitioning I went from considering myself exclusively gay to being pansexual. The way I relate to women and other non-men entirely changed.

Sexual preferences shift over time for many of us. This may mean a shift in whom we are attracted to, how we choose to identify our sexual orientations, or what types of sexual activity we prefer. Changes in sexual preference are especially common in the context of transition. Just because we used to have sex a certain way in the past doesn't mean we should be expected to do it again, and it's also OK for us to change our minds about having sex in ways we never thought we would. As we transition, the contexts in which we date and have sex naturally shift. What was once uncomfortable for us before transition might become comfortable after transition—or vice versa. For many of us, having our true genders recognized changes our relationship to our sexualities.

Being sexually attracted to men as a trans woman has been a lot more comfortable to me; it feels right, and I am no longer as anxious about the prospect, as I want men to see me not as a man but as a woman. I am still bisexual, but more comfortable with it.

Being interpreted as a woman in a lesbian relationship is different than being interpreted as a man in a straight relationship. Similarly, being viewed as a trans person in a relationship can be different than being viewed as a cis person of any gender in any relationship. Even if it's the same people in the relationship as it was before one partner transitioned, the feeling of the relationship (and what we do in it) may totally change. The kinds of sex we are comfortable having and the people with whom we want to have that sex may evolve as the way we are perceived changes. For many of us, this may look like a shift in sexual orientation.

Coming out and transitioning made me more comfortable with being gay. Before, I tried to force myself to be attracted to women, because I thought that liking men would make me straight.

All aspects of sexuality may be up for change, not just whom we are having sex with. As we transition (with or without hormones or surgeries), we may find some kinds of sensation or some kinds of sex may start feeling different. It can sometimes be a struggle if the kinds of stimulation we're used to no longer work, but that can just mean it's time for us to reexplore our bodies and find new things that turn us on.

I was a heterosexual male. Upon transitioning, to my shock and surprise, I found myself to be a heterosexual female. After talking this aspect of transition out with my therapist, it was, or became, not much of a surprise.

Some trans-positive erotic anthologies include *Nerve Endings: The New Trans Erotic* (edited by Tobi Hill-Meyer, 2017), *Take Me There: Trans and Genderqueer Erotica* (edited by Tristan Taormino, 2011), *Best Transgender Erotica* (edited by Raven Kaldera and Hanne Blank, 2002), and *Sovereign Erotics: A Collection of Two-Spirit Literature* (edited by Qwo-Li Driskill, 2011).

PORN AND EROTICA

I watch a lot of queer porn and see myself in it, which is something I never felt with gay/lesbian porn.

Many of us enjoy sexually explicit material as part of our fantasy lives, masturbation, or partnered sex. This might include erotic stories, adult graphic novels, photos, or videos. We may watch photos or videos while masturbating or with a partner, read erotic stories aloud to our partner(s), or write them ourselves. Porn and erotica that are trans-inclusive and portray trans people in affirming ways can be difficult to locate. But there are now a few transgender erotica anthologies on the market and several film producers who are themselves trans and create inclusive, affirming porn.

TRANS PORN: WHERE TO START

This list was compiled by trans performers' recommendations. It is by no means exhaustive. The state of porn on the Internet is in constant flux. There are now thousands of trans and non-binary performers creating content and custom videos, independent of established porn studios. Please consider this list just a starting point!

- AjaPornFilms
- AORTAFilms.com
- Black Swan Productions
- Bonus Hole Boys
- Chelsea Poe
- Cookie Cosmos
- CrashPadSeries.com
- Doing it Ourselves: Trans Woman Porn Project
- Eddie Wood
- Foxhouse Films
- FTM Fucker
- FTM.XXX
- Handbasket Productions
- HeavenlySpire.com
- Icy Winters
- Indie Porn Revolution
- James Darling
- Jaysen Drake
- JockPussy.com
- Kink.com
- Lyric Seal
- Mandy-Mitchell.com
- Michelle-Austin.com
- Papi Coxxx
- PinkLabel.TV
- QueerPorn.TV
- Ramses Rodstein
- Sexing the Trans Man XXX
- Skyler Braeden Fox
- Slanted Tendency
- TS-BaileyJay.com
- TSNaturals.xxx
- TransPOV.com
- TwoTGirls.com
- Venus-Lux.com
- William October

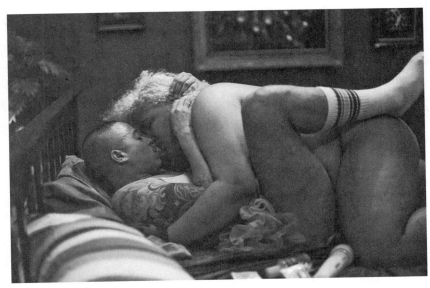

Papi Coxx and Golden Curlz. (Photo by Tristan Crane for CrashPadSeries.com, directed by Shine Louise Houston)

DESIRE: OUR NEEDS AND WANTS

Needs versus Wants

Needs and wants play an influential role in our emotional wellness—both for us and our partner(s). Knowing the difference between the two can help us more clearly and confidently express ourselves.

Needs are things we absolutely require in our relationships either emotionally, romantically, affectionately, or sexually. For some of us, this might mean strong communication, honesty, not being abused, or living in a certain geographic region. Needs may also revolve around sexual requirements—including "hard no's" on specific sex acts, certain words, or types of touch that we may find traumatic or invalidating. One way to determine our needs is to ask ourselves what we require from our relationships—sexual or otherwise—to feel most comfortable, supported, encouraged, and fulfilled.

Wants are things we could potentially go without in a relationship or may be subject to compromise. A want might look like going on more dates, receiving certain types of pleasure (such as oral sex), or experiencing certain types of play (such as public sex or watersports, where one partner urinates on another). If we're okay with possibly not getting something, it isn't a need. While having our wants met would certainly be wonderful, we could accept it if our partner(s), lover(s), or play friend(s) didn't want those same things.

> *My former wife and I wanted children. She was willing to engage in role play that allowed me to become aroused enough to have intercourse with her. After our second child we used other means to pleasure one another that did not involve my penetrating her with a penis.*

It's important for us to openly discuss both our needs and wants in our relationships. Not doing so can cause us frustration, bitterness, unrealistic expectations, overburdening, or relationship toxicity. As we understand our needs and wants more, we must also be mindful that everyone we become involved with will have needs and wants of their own, too.

What (or Whom) Are You Looking for?

Developing your sexual needs and wants can be a daunting task—even in the best of times. Our desires are not only informed by our personal experiences but also by what is socially and culturally desirable. What we seek is shaped not only by our own intimate fantasies but also cisnormative and heteronormative ideals of intimacy. For some of us, this can lead to unrealistic—even conflicting—expectations of the sex we wish to have as well as the partners that we hope to have it with. While working toward a better understanding of our sexual selves it is important to create personal boundaries for ourselves, to acknowledge the boundaries of potential partners, and to be open to compromise should conflicts arise.

> *I describe myself as polysexual generally, because I am attracted to many genders, but at least up to now, have not been attracted to all genders. Also the distribution of how much I'm attracted to different genders is significantly uneven. However, I often use gay casually, and will describe myself as bi often for simplicity's sake. I also identify with the word queer.*

If you're looking for some ideas and inspiration, check out *The Good Vibrations Guide to Sex: The Most Complete Sex Manual Ever Written* (Cathy Winks and Anne Semans, Cleis Press, 2002).

Our needs and desires are not static. They shift, change, and evolve either due to transition or numerous other internal and external factors. Although this can at times feel overwhelming—even scary—change isn't necessarily a bad thing, and being open to change can lead to even more exciting experiences.

> *Before coming out, I thought that I was a cis lesbian. After coming out, I have realized that I'm more into men than women and that I was trying to play the part of a butch lesbian.*

OUR BODIES, OUR PORN: A TRANS-POSITIVE GUIDE

Jiz Lee (they/them) is a nonbinary erotic artist who has worked in the adult film industry for over a decade, advocating for sexual health and sex worker rights around the world. As an author and editor, they created "Coming Out Like a Porn Star," an anthology of intersectional essays by porn professionals on the stigma attached to working in porn.

In the following interview, trans performers and producers come together to present a resource of erotic and explicit materials that reflect a broad array of trans, gender expansive, and nonbinary desires—while supporting sex workers who gain financial stability and life-affirming benefits through adult film production. Quotes have been edited for clarity and length. For full interviews, see PinkLabel.TV.

How Do You Find Trans Porn?

Rooster Xray: The best way to find media that represents us is through queer and trans-specific film screenings and festivals.

Q: I am a big fan of asking your friends or in online groups or forums that you're a part of. So many people, trans or otherwise nonconforming, still have no idea that there is actual quality, authentic, hot trans sexual media readily available.

Mahx Capacity: Instagram is currently where we're connecting with other indie makers.

Papí Coxxx: Using ONLY the word/identifier *trans* may not result in including any trans person whom society does not see as trans. I believe the use of *feminist, queer,* and *sex positive* broadens the search for trans women/femmes, trans lesbians, trans fags, gender fuckers, and all trans no/op, pre-op, and post-op folks.

Ex Libris: If you find a porn star you really like, hit them up on Twitter or another platform and ask them what they would recommend. You'd be surprised how often you will get a fast and thoughtful response.

Luna Loveless: The only place that healthy trans* porn can be found is produced by the people it represents: us. Look to what the models are producing themselves. I have great admiration for performers' ability to weave fantastic storylines and sensual content.

What If You Want to Make It Yourself?

Viktor Belmont: You must ask yourself a few things. Are you OK with your coworkers seeing your porn? How about your mother? Your sibling? Your ex? If you feel comfortable with the outcome of anyone and everyone finding out you do porn, then hurray! You're in a place where you can make sexy content for excited viewers.

Eddie Wood: Don't feel like you need to wait until you're in better shape, more famous, or further along in your transition. Of course, do what you feel comfortable with, but you might as well start today, because the road is long!

Courtney Trouble: Don't get discouraged by this, but it may take a while before your work gets appreciated the way you fantasize it to. Be patient. And show everyone. It may surprise you how little people talk about porn or respond to your work face to face, but if you make something wonderful you could change someone's life.

Michelle Austin: I was told early on that I would never sell. So, I self-produced everything I did. Sometimes the word "No" is powerful enough to spark a fire in you to prove people wrong.

Bailey Jay: It is impossible *not* to have a place somewhere in this industry. So many aspects of our silly human bodies can be fetishized and therefore porn as an entity is authentically inclusive even when the industry is, more often times than not, socially ignorant.

Caleb Daniels: Don't overthink it. Just start filming and get comfortable around the camera. Watch scenes you like and notice what you like about them. Reach out to other porn creators and ask for their advice.

Alyx Fox: Learn as much as you can from people who are already making porn that's similar to the kind that you want to make. Take workshops and attend festivals if possible. Our community is full of incredible resources. Many of us do support each other in a way that is rare in the entertainment world.

Parts Authority: As with any craft, you learn as you go. Try not to be too precious about your first attempt and use it as a learning experience. You can start small! The three of us spent several years doing annual nude photo shoots on Valentine's Day, and through that, I think we all gained information about what made us feel sexiest on camera.

Why Trans Porn?

Tobi Hill-Meyer: We don't often get to see other trans people's bodies and it's easy to compare yourself to an impossible standard or imagine the only way to look good is to look cis. We all have things about our bodies that make us feel terrible, but sometimes it's easier to see someone else with the same hips, brow, jawline, or shoulders, and realize that they are beautiful—and if they can be beautiful, maybe you are, too.

Venus Lux: Porn has helped me find security in my queerness and given me a newfound confidence in myself, my body, and expression of who I am. Through porn I was able to learn how to navigate consent, respect one another, leave shame behind, and be empowered by the work I do.

TYPES OF SEXUAL RELATIONSHIPS

I always thought I was Asexual. I never had feelings of dating or having relationships. As soon as I started Hormone Replacement Therapy I started thinking about relationships and feelings and started to feel more attracted towards anyone who I thought was beautiful inside and out. I still think I am Asexual, but also Pansexual.

Every relationship brings out different aspects of the people within it. When looking for a relationship, there are three major aspects for us to consider: sex, intimacy, and romance. Not everyone is interested in all of these.

I am asexual, in short. This means I do not experience sexual attraction to anyone. More specifically, I am a sex-averse asexual.

Some of us are asexual (sometimes abbreviated as "ace") and, hence, experience little to no sexual attraction to other people, prefer nonsexual forms of intimacy, or simply have little interest in partnered sex. Some of us are aromantic, which means we experience little to no romantic attachment or attraction to other people. We may be asexual but interested in romance. We may be aromantic but interested in sex. Or we may be both asexual and aromantic. Some of us might want just sex, just intimacy, just romance, or any combination of the above. We may also want different relationship configurations with different partners. All configurations are valid as long as there is consent among everyone involved.

I am less attracted to people for their bodies and more for their minds and the way that we relate and the way they make me feel. To many, this means an emphasis on emotional connection, which many define as demisexual.

Just like with sex, many of us have different needs and wants with regard to our individual experience of a fulfilling relationship. That's why it is so important to have explicit conversations to ensure that everyone is on the same page. Conflict often arises when the expectations and wants of one person do not align with those of another.

For example, for those of us who are highly sexual, we may expect sex to be a core aspect of our relationships. If a person we are interested in does not have that same want, we would need to either find common ground or discuss whether or not the relationship should continue. Pressuring, guilting, or expecting others to fulfil our needs against their interests wouldn't be fair to either party.

That being said, just because somebody can't fulfill *all* of our needs, doesn't necessarily mean that the relationship has to end. Many of us find polyamory or non-monogamy preferable to monogamy in order to have our needs met by more than one person.

Polyamory is a form of relationship configuration in which we can be romantically, sexually, emotionally, or otherwise intimately involved with multiple individuals simultaneously. This requires the full knowledge and consent of everyone involved. A poly relationship that includes a romantic, sexual, or emotional network of people may be called a polycule. Each person in the polycule may be partners with everyone or only with some. While polyamory generally refers to a form of relationship involving multiple people, being polyamorous is a romantic orientation wherein a person experiences love, affection, or attraction for more than one person at a time.

Non-monogamy is the practice of sexual or intimate activity outside of an existing relationship dynamic—such as being in an open relationship that allows for sex with others, swinging with a partner and other couples, or participating in group sex. Polyamorous relationships, like one-partner relationships, may be closed off to or may allow for outside sex.

As we explore our ideal relationship configurations, it can be tempting to compartmentalize our relationships—intentionally or not. This act of secrecy can be construed as deceitful, nonconsensual, and even traumatizing for others. If we hide lovers or play friends, even if it's just an occasional hookup, from our other partner(s), it does not allow for everyone to ensure that they feel comfortable, safe, and content. Keeping quiet about having an emotional or romantic bond with someone outside of our relationship can cause significant pain or even trauma to everyone once the truth comes to light.

Although some of us enjoy and choose to have polyamorous or non-monogamous relationships, some of us prefer monogamy for emotional reasons, time concerns, or personal preference. Either way, it is paramount that all individuals involved in any relationship configuration, be it monogamous, non-monogamous, or polyamorous, are informed and consent to the structures and activities therein.

A good intro to non-monogamy is Tristan Taormino's *Opening Up: A Guide to Creating and Sustaining Open Relationships* (Cleis Press, 2008).

The website *polyfriendly.org* provides lists of professionals with experience working with poly clients, including therapists, physicians, lawyers, and financial advisors.

The National Coalition for Sexual Freedom is a trans-friendly organization that advocates for political, legal, and social change for greater acceptance of BDSM and polyamory.

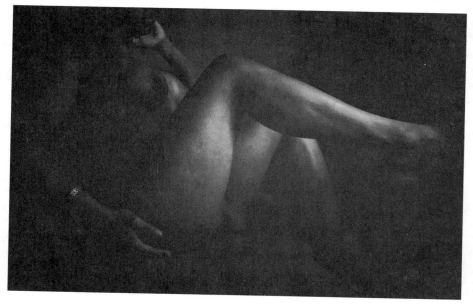

Desire. (Armani Dae)

When Things Don't Mesh

Sometimes, despite all of our efforts to ensure that our needs and the needs of those we care about are being respected, things still don't work out. Although compromise is an important part of any relationship, be it sexual, romantic, or emotional, there is a big difference between finding middle ground versus giving so much that we lose our sense of safety, identity, or comfort.

Should we find ourselves in situations where we feel we're giving an awful lot without getting much in return, where we are being guilted into doing things that distress us, or where we are punished for not meeting our partner's expectations, we may be experiencing relationship toxicity—or even abuse. Likewise, it is never appropriate for us to guilt, manipulate, threaten, demean, or otherwise intimidate any of our partners into getting what we want. We must always be mindful of bodily autonomy and the consent of both ourselves and whomever we are involved with.

If our needs are not being met by an individual, or if our wants and desires are not being considered in a respectful and thoughtful way, and if conversation has come to an impasse, then it may be time for us to consider moving on rather than staying in something that isn't fulfilling. We cannot force anyone to do what we want them to do, respond how we want them to respond, or generally be how we want them to be.

OUR SEXUAL BODIES

Our Body Map: Reconceptualizing Sex and the Body

Developing our sexual selves often requires us to imagine our own body map: an image of what our body feels like when we close our eyes. It may mean avoiding types of sex that don't match our body map, and it may mean physically recreating our body map to accommodate the types of sex we do have. For example, some of us have a clear experience of having a cock where no flesh organ is present. In some cases, this cock can be stimulated with hand gestures alone or with the wearing of a prosthetic cock.

> [After transition], I am more likely to fantasize about myself in a male / penetrative role and also to masturbate with phalluses/in a phallic motion than I did before.

A body map may structure how we think about our bodies and the words we use (or don't use) to describe various parts of our bodies. There's no right or wrong set of words, and people in our T/GE communities have been quite creative at coming up with terms. This isn't just an issue for T/GE people, either. Many cis people cringe at gendered words used about their bodies. It's all very individual. For example, some cis women will be turned off by the word "pussy" but love the word "cunt" (or vice versa). Whatever sexual parts our body maps include (or don't include) are the parts that are right for us. Acknowledging our desired sexual experiences, including experiencing genitals that may or may not be visibly present, allows us to seek out more fulfilling sexual opportunities.

Dysphoria, Triggers, and Dissociation

There are two major kinds of gender dysphoria that can impact sexual activity: social dysphoria and body dysphoria. The former is external in origin. This is what we experience when people mispronoun or misgender us through their language or behavior. The latter is internal in origin. This is when the body we have doesn't match our desired body map, and this mismatch can cause distress.

Dysphoria of both kinds can be traumatic. It may cause us to isolate ourselves, become depressed, or feel intolerably anxious in relationships. Without the skills to cope with it, sex and dysphoria may cause some of us to dissociate. Dissociation is when we consciously or unconsciously separate from, ignore, or minimize our feelings, environment, or experiences. Dissociation can be very extreme, such as feeling like we've left our body, or very subtle, such as telling ourselves that what our partner is doing during sex *should* feel good even when it really doesn't.

> *I don't enjoy playing with penises or seeing pre-cum or ejaculate, so I had some dysphoria there. It was mild enough I was able to distract myself in the moment, but it did grow stronger in memory and with repeated sexual activity. I'm not sure what to do about that.*

Our Bodies as a Place We Want to Be

Embodiment is the opposite of dissociation. Becoming embodied means accepting that our feelings are valid and it's important that they be recognized, felt, and respected—including by ourselves. If our feelings seem intolerable or if we believe we're wrong or bad for having them, learning to pay attention to and honor our feelings can be very difficult. But in order to have safe, fulfilling sex we have to learn to tolerate or cope with our feelings to some degree. Our body and emotions may feel unmanageable sometimes, but with care, gentleness, and patience it is possible to learn to accept our feelings.

For many of us, our habitual response to strong emotions or intense physical sensation is to dissociate, distract ourselves, or use drugs and alcohol to limit our capacity to feel. This can be compounded by other negative messages society tells us about our bodies when we don't match up to white beauty expectations, aren't skinny enough, or have a body that doesn't function the way able-bodied people expect it to function. We may have a lot of unlearning to do before we can stay embodied during sex. The first step is to take notice of when we dissociate, what makes us dissociate, and in what ways we dissociate. Some of us seek the help of a mental health provider to explore our patterns of dissociation.

> *I was so afraid of my body that I channeled my frustrations into meeting just my partner's needs, and it still shows in my service topping.*

Sky, 64, Palm Springs, CA, 2016. (Jess T. Dugan). From "To Survive on This Shore: Photographs and Interviews with Transgender and Gender Nonconforming Older Adults," a project by Jess T. Dugan and Vanessa Fabbre.

Many of us are used to having sex that is uncomfortable and frightening, and we may even be used to having our sexual boundaries and preferences violated either intentionally or through ignorance. If this is true, one option is to take a step back from sex until we're in a better headspace or find a partner who is safer and more understanding. We can also work on staying present and embodied during masturbation before trying partnered sex again. If we're unable to stay present during masturbation, it's unlikely we'll be able to stay present enough to set safe boundaries during sex.

Learning about my body and understanding my dysphoria triggers has helped me have more fulfilling sex.

For those of us who want medical transition, this may be a key element of making our bodies a place we want to be. Hormone therapy can change everything from the way we smell to the way we are able to have orgasms, all of which can have a profound effect on our sex lives. When we have a body that feels like our own, many of us are more capable of embodiment and receiving pleasure. Sometimes surgery or hormones can mean relearning our bodies, however, as we may no longer respond in the way we did before. We must be patient with ourselves, learn how we work, and keep experimenting!

I have had to be open to letting go of old favorites that no longer seem to fit me, be more conscious of my dysphoria and euphoria, and constantly experiment and communicate.

Not all of us want or have access to hormone therapy or surgery. Being treated as the correct gender regardless of our hormonal or surgical status is vital. This includes during sex, even if it's masturbation. Most of us will be able to stay more present and self-aware during sex when the language and kind of touch used is what's right for us and our bodies.

I think the freedom of being the woman I wanted to be for so long has made me really take the time to enjoy my womanhood. My wife and I have about the same level of sex as before but it has definitely changed and is much more feminine and feels more like lesbian sex than before. Our sex life feels more equal and like we are on the same page.

Survivors and People with Traumatic Histories

Sadly, many of us have survived some sort of abuse, bullying, or violence. Every kind of abuse (including cultural/institutionalized abuses such as racism, sexism, fatphobia, etc.) affects those of us who survive it. Whether it was emotional, psychological, verbal, spiritual, physical, or sexual, violence or abuse may impact the way we deal with intimacy or sex. Many of us may be traumatized by what we have survived. Some of us have post-traumatic stress disorder (PTSD), depression, or anxiety disorders as a result.

I'm more interested in sex but feel less able to seek it out (with casual or serious partners) as there's still a lot I don't know about how my body will work and what will work for it; I need that exploration to be with people I can trust deeply.

For many of us, trauma-related triggers can be much like dysphoria-related triggers and can be handled in similar ways. One strategy that works for some of us is breathing. If we notice ourselves feeling like we're leaving our body, it may be helpful for us to take a moment to take in our surroundings and find out what caused us to dissociate in the first place. If we're having partnered sex, our partner can help us by checking in and reminding us where we really are. If we're triggered while masturbating, some of us try to slow down, stay present, and stop if needed. Remember, sex is for us. If we're not enjoying it, we have the right to stop at any time.

Healing Sex: A Mind-Body Approach to Healing Sexual Trauma explores how to get in better touch with our own desires after trauma (Staci Haines, Cleis Press, 2007).

SEXUAL VIOLENCE: A GUIDE FOR THE TRANS COMMUNITY

Reo Cosgrove (they/them)

Sexual violence can happen to any person at any time in their life. All sexual violence is a traumatic violation of your body, your trust, and your right to exist peacefully.

Although it is widely accepted that sexual violence is a gendered violence—with more women experiencing sexual violence and more men perpetrating it—trans people are disproportionately affected. Despite this, there is a lack of trans-specific resources available for understanding and coping with sexual violence, as well as many barriers to accessing support after an assault.

During an assault:

People react to assault in many ways—all normal and valid. Most have little control over their reactions, which may include:

Fight: In fight mode, our bodies are filled with adrenaline with the aim of shoring up additional energy and power in dangerous situations. We may instinctively try to defend ourselves. This might translate as screaming or shouting at the perpetrator. We may try to escape by pushing, kicking, biting, or scratching the perpetrator out of self-defense.

Flight: In flight mode our bodies want to run away from the threat. This is not always possible and the built-up adrenaline sometimes becomes stuck inside our bodies.

Freeze: Freezing is the most common reaction to sexual violence and is the result of pathways in the brain becoming overwhelmed. If we freeze during an assault, our bodies may feel stiff or stuck in a certain position. Freezing can be terrifying; however, it can also be a necessary survival instinct. Becoming tense may reduce the risk of further harm.

Flop: When our bodies are threatened, they might flop or feel droopy. This feels like the opposite of freezing; we may lose control over our limbs or muscles. Again, this can be a vital survival instinct.

Friend: Our bodies may react by entering friend mode, where we might start a dialogue with the perpetrator. This might include negotiating or reasoning with them. Some people describe friending as an attempt to comply with the demands of the perpetrator in a nonconfrontational way, to reduce the risk of further harm. It is a survival method and does not imply consent.

Every reaction is valid, and it is common to experience multiple reactions during the same assault. Each reaction is extremely energy consuming and exhausting. It is important to rest and engage in self-care immediately afterward to help restore balance to the nervous system and brain.

Immediately after an assault:

If you are able, move to a safe area away from the perpetrator. Try to do this as soon as you can. If the perpetrator is in the house, try moving to a different room—the bathroom is usually a good option. We may have to contact a friend to meet us or pick us up. If we are outside or in a public location when the assault occurs, we can try to find our bearings by looking around for something familiar. This may also help us feel more grounded. We may need to ask someone nearby for help getting home or to find out where we are. They do not need to know what has happened.

If we are injured:

It can be very difficult to check our bodies for injury—especially after an assault. It is normal for our body parts—especially our genitals—to feel sore and painful after a sexual assault. It is important to check for any bleeding, which is common after rape or sexual assault. We can use toilet tissue to wipe or dab the affected area gently to look for blood. It is advisable to seek medical help if we are in excruciating pain or are bleeding excessively. If we do, we are not obligated to disclose to anyone what happened to us. It is our choice to tell what happened.

Managing Our Emotions:

Our feelings and emotions can range from mild to distressing after an assault and can affect us in a multitude of ways. We may feel rage, anger, devastation, depression, grief, confusion, numbness, violation, fear, shame, guilt, self-blame, disgust, anxiety, panic, hopelessness, helplessness, and heartbreak. Our feelings are valid and normal. It can be helpful to learn how to identify our emotions, which can help us to work through them or manage them more efficiently. Emotions may feel debilitating at times; it is important to acknowledge how they affect our lives and to acknowledge that they will eventually stop. Feelings change all the time and no state of emotion will last forever, as much as it feels like it will.

Accessing support and healing:

As trans people, we are likely to encounter more barriers to supportive services after we experience a sexual assault. We may fear being outed, judged, or not being believed because we are trans. We may fear medical procedures. We may fear reporting another trans or LGBTQ + person for sexual violence—especially if we belong to the same community as the perpetrator and fear losing that community.

We deserve support after experiencing sexual violence. There are a variety of support services that you can access. Some people prefer talk therapy. This varies depending on the type of therapy, but it may help to talk to someone impartial about your experiences, to allow yourself to feel the emotions that you have around what happened, and to make sense of the situation for yourself. Other types of therapy include art therapy, drama therapy, and EMDR (eye movement desensitization and reprocessing), a specialized type of psycho-therapy specifically used to help people with PTSD that employs movement, light, and imagery in order to process past experiences and alleviate distress.

Support groups can also be helpful. Some areas have multiple support groups specifically for survivors, and some may be trans-inclusive or trans-specific.

Finally, there is no substitute for friends. We are never obliged to tell anyone what has happened, but being able to confide in a friend that you trust and love can be a huge relief. Sometimes just saying the words out loud can help you feel less distressed, scared, or guilty.

Sexuality and Hormones

Hormones can change many aspects of our bodies and our sex lives. Some changes are subtle, such as the scent of our armpits or how much we sweat. Some changes may be more dramatic. For example, the kinds of stimulation we used to enjoy may no longer work, and we may have to seek new types of stimulation.

> *Medically transitioning changed my experience of sex and masturbation, and I did discover new things.*

POSSIBLE EFFECTS OF ESTROGEN ON OUR SEX LIVES

Taking estrogen (with or without testosterone blockers) may stimulate breast and nipple growth and increase nipple sensitivity. During the growth process, breast tissue may become hard to the touch and our chest may even be painfully sensitive. Some people may enjoy that sensitivity while others will want to limit or restrict stimulation.

The kinds of stimulation we like and the way we like to reach orgasm may shift for some of us. Some kinds of touch that used to work for us might not anymore, and some of us may need to discover new ways of interacting with our body that we like. We may also find that our experience of orgasm changes. Some of us no longer ejaculate when we orgasm, or we may do so only rarely. It's also possible that the refractory period (the time after orgasm and before we are able to orgasm again) will decrease, and the ability to have multiple orgasms will appear. All of this varies greatly from individual to individual.

> *One of the best parts of being on estrogen and testosterone blockers was losing the nearly uncontrollable urge to be sexual. I have very little libido these days.*

Many AMAB trans people experience decreased sex drive from estrogen and/or testosterone blockers. Switching our bodies to an estrogen-centric hormone balance may decrease sex drive; however, for some of us, having the right hormones and having a body that feels more like *us* allows us to be more present and connected to ourselves and thus experience increased sexual desire.

> *This is a complicated subject. My sex drive and physical/mental arousal have greatly decreased since starting hormone therapy, but my want for them has stayed the same. I have actually considered stopping hormone treatment several times because I miss enjoying sex so much.*

The ability to get and maintain erections will also likely be affected, but the degree to which this happens varies greatly. Some of us are no longer able to get erections at all after starting estrogen, while, for others, erections merely take a little more work to achieve. This difference may be affected by how often we exercise this physical response. Whether we specifically want to *cease* having erections or want to *keep* having erections, many of us are able to influence that by how often we "practice" doing each.

"I remember thinking to myself 'Wow, I'm going to have figure out how to be strong to follow through with my transition.' But, it was my transition that showed me that I was already stronger than I thought I was." - Gabrielle Inés

Spironolactone, a common testosterone blocker (sometimes known simply as Spiro), has libido-suppressing and erection-suppressing effects in addition to lowering testosterone. For some of us, ceasing spironolactone after removing the gonads (as a result of orchiectomy or vaginoplasty) can result in increased sex drive despite having lower testosterone levels. Some of us who are unhappy with our sex drives try low doses of supplemental testosterone or progesterone, and many find that this boosts our libido up to where we want it to be.

POSSIBLE EFFECTS OF TESTOSTERONE ON OUR SEX LIVES

For many of us, starting testosterone therapy can have quite dramatic sexual effects. Many of us find that it radically increases our sex drive. For some of us, this may mean suddenly fantasizing about everyone and everything we see, all the time, uncontrollably. We may want sex almost non-stop. For some of us, the increase is much smaller, and we might only want sex a little more often than before.

My libido is through the roof, testosterone is amazing! I have been seeking more men for sexual experiences but haven't necessarily engaged with others more often than I used to, just a lot of masturbation. I typically use anal insertion rather than my front hole like I used to.

The way in which sexual arousal occurs may also change for some of us on testosterone. We may need more visual stimuli to become aroused, meaning a greater interest in visual porn than before. Some of us report being able to become physically aroused without emotional engagement in the situation, where before testosterone the two were inextricably linked. Some of us may find casual sex easier to engage in, because sex no longer feels as automatically emotional. These are, however, completely individual changes. In fact, some of us find ourselves *more* emotional about sex than before or more emotional in general. As always, transition involves so many factors that it is hard to for us to determine what is a result of hormones and what is the result of other major life changes.

> *After the physical change of testosterone and gaining a lot more confidence in my gender expression, I didn't feel that slight aversion to masculine partners anymore.*

For some of us, orgasm becomes easier to achieve while taking testosterone. For others, we may lose the ability to have multiple orgasms or find each orgasm less intense. For example, before testosterone, some of us may have been able to have multiple huge orgasms or have continuous orgasms for long periods of time; after starting testosterone, some of us may start to instead have a pattern of several small orgasms leading up to one larger one. Some of us on testosterone therapy also experience abdominal cramping immediately after orgasm. The cause of this is unknown.

> *After I came out to myself as transmasculine, I was exclusively interested in relationships and sex with other men, and pretty exclusively interested in bottoming. Since I started testosterone and began having sexual experiences, though, I've had more verse feelings.*

For AFAB people who go on testosterone, the stimulation needed to achieve climax may also change. Some of us may begin to prefer more external than internal stimulation, or we may suddenly prefer anal penetration to genital penetration, or vice-versa. Growth of genital erectile tissue is stimulated by testosterone. This means that many of us may experience major shifts in the size and shape of our external genitals with testosterone. The bundle of tissue commonly referred to as the clitoris—which many AFAB trans people call their dick, cock, or dicklet—may double, triple, or quadruple in size from testosterone. As a result of the change in size, erections may become clearly visible for the first time. Color as well as rigidity may shift with arousal.

The mucus membranes on the inside of the front hole tend to thin and become more delicate as a result of testosterone therapy. They also produce less lubrication. As a result, penetration of the front hole may cause some bleeding and may feel a little rougher or rawer. This effect can be mitigated by using an estrogen cream or by engaging in regular penetration of the front hole. The tissues of the front hole seem to follow a "use it or lose it" rule without estrogen to keep them supple, so if we use the hole often, we may be able to retain greater elasticity and tissue strength.

Possible Effects of Surgery on Our Sex Lives

Those of us who have had surgeries may notice that our bodies now respond in different ways. For those of us who have top surgeries, the sensitivity we retain in our chests can differ significantly depending on the type of surgery and our individualized process of postsurgical recovery. For those of us who have bottom surgeries, we may have to relearn ways of stimulating ourselves or achieving orgasm. It may be as easy for us to become aroused or achieve orgasm as before surgery, or it may be a long process of discovering what feels good and works for us. It can be frustrating to feel like we are starting all over again.

For those of us who have had a phalloplasty (creation of a larger phallus), there are several different surgical techniques, some of which allow our phallus to become erect and others that do not. For those of us who have had a vaginoplasty, our vagina might not be able to produce its own lubrication—different surgical techniques yield different results, and some of us find that we produce some lubrication. Many of us find that store-bought lubrication is helpful or necessary for penetration. We may also have to maintain regular use of a dilator—a tool used to help create more flexibility in the muscles and tissues inside the vagina. This can allow for easier, more comfortable penetration.

It is normal for it to take some time after surgery to regain sexual function. After surgery, our nerves may be distributed slightly differently, so our bodies may respond somewhat differently. One of the best ways to start exploring our new bodies is by ourselves, where we can experiment in a safe and comfortable environment. For those of us with supportive partners, we may want to try new positions or ask them to stimulate us in new ways.

If it is taking longer than expected to recover sensation, speak to a medical provider. There are many different kinds of surgery, and techniques differ by surgeon. It may be helpful to speak with the surgeon about the technique used and ask for any advice based on how our anatomical parts are now arranged.

ORGASMS AND TRANSITION

Suzi Chase (she/they) is a post-op nonbinary transgender woman. She is a high school teacher, sex educator, speaker, writer, and activist.

Orgasm was different after starting E and T-blockers. Before, it was just a squirt. A really, really good squirt, but all the feeling was centered in that one body part. From my first day on E, it changed, becoming more like an explosion of warmth all through my body. It was harder to achieve. I needed to become mentally aroused in a way that did not used to be necessary. But it was worth it. The feeling was so powerful it always left me completely drained.

After surgery, I found I did not reach climax at all. I had full arousal, sensation, and stimulation, but couldn't manage to pull the trigger. A sex therapist specializing in trans clients made all sorts of suggestions, including vibrators, books for anorgasmic cisgender women, and a few other interventions that didn't help. A gynecologist who had experience with post-op women declared my neovagina "well constructed" and told me there was no structural problem. After fighting with doctors and insurance for more than a year, I finally was approved to try testosterone. On my first hit of T, within ten minutes of trying, I was able to achieve a certified grade A orgasm. As long as I had even a little bit of T in my body, orgasm was possible. For the next year, I allowed myself a "T date" every couple weeks where I applied T gel and then enjoyed my body. I could usually mange two O's that day before the T wore off.

For some reason, about four months ago I was unexpectedly able to climax without T. I'm not sure what changed, but miraculously I no longer seem to need the T-gel. I'm free to enjoy the delicious release of female orgasm without pharmaceutical help. That experience in my new body is so wonderful that afterward I'm often left thinking I've gotten away with something.

FLIRTING, HOOKING UP, AND DATING

Trans Amorous

> *I think I tend to favor more non-straight, non-binary, and non-cis gendered folk after coming out. I think this is mostly because we have the experience of coming out in common.*

Some of us are trans amorous, or chiefly or exclusively attracted to T/GE people. We may prefer partners or lovers who are T/GE like us and thus are more able to provide intuitive empathy based on our shared experiences.

> *I am married to a transgender man and find other transgender men attractive though am not attracted to cisgender men. Being demisexual/demiromantic, I have never developed feelings of sexual or romantic attraction to cis men.*

Just because we are T/GE ourselves doesn't mean we will have the same experiences of our identity as those T/GE people we are interested in dating. Additionally, there are often power dynamics built into our relationships, even if both parties are part of T/GE communities. For example, trans men who are newly out may receive increased sexual

Malito. (Chucha Marquez)

attention, and can easily, often unintentionally, move into roles that resemble the toxic masculinity of some of their cis male counterparts, especially in relationships with trans-feminine people.

I have grown attracted to other trans women, having a new appreciation for them and finding beauty in how their expressions mirror my own or what I hope to be.

Chasers: When Flirting Becomes Transphobic

Chasers are people who engage in inappropriate or exploitive behavior as they pursue sex or relationships with T/GE people. The same dynamic occurs with any number of marginalized populations. Fat folks, people with disabilities, and people of color all deal with a range of exotification and manipulation. When it comes to trans chasers, some of us may think of chasers as a positive resource for easy sex, and some of us may view chasers as an abusive and unavoidable problem.

One common issue is when the chaser is attracted to a generic image of a T/GE person and, hence, treats all T/GE people as representations of that image instead of as individuals. The assumptions a chaser might make can vary greatly. A chaser may look for a specific kind of sex and lose interest in any T/GE person who does not engage in that particular act. A chaser may project certain qualities onto a T/GE person, who is not comfortable having their body or behavior interpreted in those ways. For example, a chaser might assume all trans women are hyperfeminine. Upon meeting a butch trans woman, the chaser may assume that she wants to be more feminine but doesn't know how and offer to "help" with her makeup. In this example, the chaser isn't actually attracted to her but to their image of a generic trans woman.

Chasers might say things like "trans people are the best of both worlds!" or "I like dating trans people because of [a sexist assumption about gender roles]." They may even

The *Fucking Trans Women* zine by Mira Bellwether gets real about anatomy, sexuality, and pleasure.

457

view trans people as desperate, needy, or having lower standards and, thus, being easier to manipulate or take advantage of. This is the kind of behavior that might get someone labeled a creep or abuser in other contexts, but it is useful to recognize how chasers will specifically target T/GE people's insecurities and vulnerabilities.

People of any gender—cis or trans—can engage in the inappropriate behavior associated with chasers. Nonetheless, it is worth being aware that the term has a history of specifically referencing straight or bi-identified men who are interested in trans women—with lots of sexism and transmisogyny wrapped up in that history. Some chasers assume that trans women are more sexually available, less likely to object to sexism or boundary crossing, more desperate for validation, and more likely to have sex with anyone who flatters them a little. A surprising number of such individuals will respond with shock and disbelief when turned down by a trans woman, because in their worldview, trans women are always available.

Some queer cis women's communities allow for chaser behavior. These spaces may encourage the fetishization of trans men via a variety of assumptions. These may include the transphobic idea that trans men are a "lite" version of men and less likely to engage in sexist or abusive behavior. Some queer cis men's communities see trans men as the ultimate bottoms—always willing to be penetrated. Certain radical communities see gender expansive or nonbinary folks as inherently subversive or revolutionary. Even "positive" assumptions can sometimes become serious problems.

Location, Location, Location

Although finding partners as a T/GE person can seem daunting or downright impossible, there is a time and place for everything, and that is arguably most true of flirting. Although we might really crave a sexual or romantic relationship with someone, not every space or circumstance is appropriate for making advances.

For instance, hitting on someone at an emotional support group, during a Transgender Day of Remembrance ceremony, or while engaging in advocacy activities, such as a rally or sit-in, could be construed as inappropriate, trigger someone's trauma experiences, or result in community members feeling unsafe. Being mindful of location and context can help minimize a lot of misunderstanding.

> In a rural state, the queer dating/hookup population is small. Casual hookups with cis people feel pretty impossible as a masc person with a vagina.

Dating websites or apps are one option many of us use to find partners. Every site or app is different and has its good points and bad points. Some are specifically for trans women and AMAB nonbinary people. Some of us may find this welcoming and safe, while some of us may find it fetishizing and gross. It depends on who we are and what (or whom) we're looking for. Many generic dating sites may not accept openly trans people, and navigating them may be an exercise in going stealth. Those of us who are kinky may feel comfortable looking for partners on a site for other kinksters or fetishists. The Fetlife website includes lots of personals groups, which you can use to look for hookups or regular partners.

> I find it easier to find people for casual sex via apps rather than in bars or clubs. This is because I look a lot younger than I actually am, but also because I don't have to actively tell them I'm trans—it's there in my profile.

Bars are also common spaces to find hookups and potential partners. Meeting people in bars gives us an opportunity to read others' body language and facial expressions in order to judge their reactions throughout the conversation. If we choose to disclose our T/GE status, we can gauge their reaction to that as well. It can be harder, however, for us to filter for trans-accepting partners and many people we encounter may hold harmful assumptions about trans people. This can be true for both straight bars and queer bars.

In a few major cities, there are bars or theme nights specifically for the trans community, though, in many cases, these spaces are specifically for trans women and cis male "admirers." Dating events may be an option depending on where we live—some locations have events like Poly Speed Dating. Some of us may feel safe or comfortable attending these as an open trans person while some may want to go stealth.

I do feel pretty strongly that a partner would need to be queer, because I can't imagine a cishet person being able to understand where I'm coming from.

Safety is often a concern for us—especially when meeting people we don't know well. There are a number of precautions we can take to minimize risk and maximize safety. When meeting someone from online, one option is to meet in a public place first (such as a coffee shop, library, or restaurant). For those of us not comfortable with giving away our home address or with going to someone else's place, getting a hotel room and splitting the cost may be a suitable option. It may be helpful to tell a friend where we are going and when to expect us back as a safety precaution. For those of us with a smartphone, there are GPS tracking programs that allow for a friend to instantly find our location if we go missing or don't respond to messages. If we have the kind of friends that we can simply bring with us to the date or hookup, there is always safety in numbers.

Other Avenues to Seeking Sexual Fulfillment

Beyond flirting and hooking up, some of us desire sexual outlets to express ourselves and receive sexual satisfaction. Some of us use ethical exhibitionism communities online. For example, Reddit has a number of sexually explicit, user-submitted content forums, such as r/TransGoneWild or r/LGBTGoneWild, where users can post nudes or engage with others who have similar interests. Some of us use other social media platforms such as Twitter, Kik, or Snapchat; however, these platforms are not always reliable. Many have fallen prey to the whims of queerphobic and sexphobic legislation or changing company policies.

Tragón. (Chucha Marquez)

There have been a number of changes to online platforms since the passage of the Stop Enabling Sex Traffickers Act (SESTA) and the Allow States and Victims to Fight Online Sex Trafficking Act (FOSTA). Although the original intent of these laws was to stop sex trafficking, they have resulted in further stigmatizing, criminalizing, and endangering of those engaging in sexual activity and services online by conflating all forms of consensual sex work with human sex trafficking. FOSTA takes things an additional step by making websites, social media platforms, and hosting services criminally liable for anything deemed to be an exchange of sexual services. As a result, many major social media platforms have cracked down on adult content to varying degrees of severity, by removing specific pages and resources, by heavily policing community members with invasive policies and algorithms, or by completely purging anything they deem to be "adult" or "sensitive" content. Craigslist discontinued its personals section in anticipation of SESTA, and Tumblr banned the posting of nudity. Both actions wiped out countless adult communities, resources, and safe sharing spaces for T/GE folks.

Where there is Internet, however, there will always be folks exploring and sharing their sexuality, so don't be afraid to take a look around on whatever platforms may be the hot new thing. Chances are we can find folks like us hooking up, having fun, flirting, sexting, or complimenting each other's photos. When sharing, some of us may be concerned about being outed or recognized, so it may be helpful to take precautions to hide key aspects of our identity—such as our faces, tattoos, birthmarks, or unique details of our environment.

Those of us with the financial freedom to have an entertainment fund might consider setting some of that aside for hiring a trans-affirming or inclusive sex worker or escort. In addition to in-person dates or sexual encounters, many trans and queer sex workers also offer online services such as sexting, private cam shows, "girlfriend/boyfriend" experiences, custom videos tailored to our liking (including saying our name), or personalized "ratings" of our own nudes. It may be helpful for us to explicitly ask for an affirmative experience if that's what we want. Before seeking out sexual services, familiarize yourself with the laws regarding sex work in your region. In some places, paying for any sort of sexual services can result in an arrest, fine, or criminal prosecution.

Sex workers have friends, partners, and relationships just like everyone else. If you are considering hiring a sex worker, if you have a friend who is doing sex work, or if you are dating a sex worker, there are some useful things to keep in mind:

- *Respect their boundaries.* Do not pry for gossip if they do not seem interested in talking about their work, and do not tell others about their work without their permission.
- *Do not project your judgments.* You might think that sex work is horrifying or that it is the coolest thing in the world, but they might not see it that way. It is important to let them define their experience for themselves.
- *. . . but don't hide your feelings.* If you have insecurities, fears, or other difficult feelings come up, find an appropriate time to discuss them.
- *Sex for work can be different.* A lot of sex workers make a strong distinction between sex for work and sex in their personal life. This can look different for different people, but for the most part clients and partners are not interchangeable, nor are they in competition.
- *Be willing to listen.* It is good not to have things feel like a secret. We all need to vent about work sometimes. If they talk about having a bad day at work, it does not mean things are horrible and they need to be rescued from their job.
- *Do not fall for the stereotypes.* Just because someone does sex work does not mean they are hypersexual. They might not be up for sex sometimes, and that is fine.
- *Learn the issues.* Sex worker organizations and advocacy groups are constantly involved in political issues, support projects, or community building. From protesting condom confiscation by police to organizing storytelling and performance spaces, there are a lot of things you can get involved with.

ENVY

Konner Jebb (he/him) is a transmasculine agender man, poet, and activist. His work has been published in Trans Cafe, Strange Horizons, *and* Poems2Go.

Men taunt me
with their chests—flat
as cardboard–triangled torsos.
I lust
for broad shoulders with pinpointed freckles in the clavicle—
pecs bare. Embossed goosebumps.
It's like my breath whispered
to each follicle
a love song.
Lured by a straightened waist without childbearing hips,
thick vocal chords that strum
tenor tones out of a veined neck, a rectangular jawbone
that strengthens
my smile, the ability to be naked. I don't want
this body to be
a tombstone, but a sculpture.
I fall in love
with what should be
mine

Responding to and Moving On from Rejection

Not everyone is going to be interested in starting a relationship or having sex with us, and some people may start to date or have sex with us and then change their minds. It is imperative to know when to disengage. Some individuals will be straightforward if they aren't interested; however, others may feel too shy, anxious, or nervous about turning someone down. Body language can be a really good indicator of interest, or a lack thereof. If someone fidgets a lot, looks around the room anxiously, fails to hold up their end of a conversation, fixates on their phone rather than you, or some combination of these things, then it could mean that they aren't really interested or aren't comfortable with your flirting.

Rather than pushing, we may consider placing the ball in their court and say something along the lines of: "Hey, thanks for talking with me! It was great meeting you. If you want to chat more I'll be around for a little while still. If not, have a great night." This can provide a polite "out" from a potentially awkward situation of unrequited flirting while also leaving the door open for them to still approach you if they'd like to. Of course, leaving the door open doesn't guarantee that anyone is going to go through it. Learning to accept and move on from disinterest, dismissal, or rejection is key to looking after our mental health and wellness.

Rejection never feels good. Putting ourselves out there and being emotionally vulnerable is scary enough. When we're told that somebody isn't interested, that can sting. It's valid to feel hurt after getting turned down. However, we are not entitled to anyone's time, affection, or body just because we like them or are attracted to them—just as we are not required to engage with or reciprocate anyone else's advances.

Some of us may feel tempted to take rejection personally. However, getting turned down doesn't make us ultimately unattractive or unlovable. It may be helpful for us to prioritize self-care and avoid internalizing rejection as an absolute or defining experience. For some of us, this can take a lot of time and require a lot of patience with ourselves. Some of us may seek the assistance of a close friend or therapist to process and explore our feelings. Regardless of how we cope, responding to rejection with yelling, insulting, threatening, guilt-tripping, manipulating, or using physical force is never appropriate and can result in traumatizing others, being shunned from establishments or communities, or even being charged with a criminal offense.

Disclosing T/GE Status

Disclosing the fact that we are T/GE to potential partners can be awkward, scary, and even dangerous. We may hear many different opinions on when we "have to" tell someone. We may even hear some people claim that dating without immediate disclosure is a violation of consent because they would not have chosen to date or have sex with a particular person if they had known their T/GE status. There are some practical considerations if it's likely a person will find out our T/GE status before we disclose, but there really is no simple rule about disclosure and what makes the most sense can vary from situation to situation.

Some of us prefer to disclose first thing—in a dating profile, for example. This way, we can avoid rejection and promote safety by steering transphobes away from us to begin with. It can also help remove the anxiety of figuring out when to disclose. Some folks we meet may not read our dating profiles ahead of time, however, so we can't assume everyone contacting us will know our trans status.

Some of us may prefer to wait until shortly after beginning a conversation, allowing for an emotional connection first before disclosure. Having the opportunity to have an in-person discussion can also give space for others to overcome transphobic stigma that would have otherwise been a deal-breaker. Some of us may find ourselves in situations where we might not feel safe being publicly out or open—online or otherwise, and waiting might feel like the only option. It may be helpful for us to keep in mind that, even if we wait, we may have to have several difficult conversations that could still end in rejection. Some of us choose to never disclose, especially if we have a series of short-term relationships or one-time sexual encounters; it can sometimes be more dangerous to disclose than keep our T/GE status private.

So much of disclosure comes down to stigma: The stigma of being a trans person and the stigma of dating a trans person. However, someone might choose not to date us if we are or aren't a vegan, a Republican, an abuse survivor, an alcoholic, or an infinite number of other things. It may be helpful to remember that it is not our responsibility to immediately disclose everything about ourselves that a partner or potential partner might care about. If they care about it enough, they can be responsible for asking or for not assuming until they get confirmation. Many of us might choose not to date a transphobe, but, oddly enough, there has never been a case where someone was accused of being deceptive when they withheld the fact that they were a transphobe.

When first meeting someone, there are some ways we can "test the water" while keeping ourselves safe. For example, we can talk about a television show that we like, such as *POSE*, or bring up a situation or character who is trans, and gauge the other person's reaction to the character and their awareness of trans issues. If we are worried someone might respond poorly or violently, it might be a good idea to have this conversation in a public space, plan an escape route, avoid sharing our home address, ensure that a friend knows what is happening, and, perhaps, prepare to have that friend check in afterward. It's usually safer and more effective to have this conversation when neither person has been drinking or using drugs.

If we are in a longer-term relationship, there may come a point where we feel it is important to open up about our trans status. Disclosing our status to a long-term partner may be important to us as a way of demonstrating or building trust, or it may be relevant information to a partner who desires to have children in a traditional manner. Waiting to tell a long-term partner about our transition history can pose challenges, and we should prepare for some difficult conversations.

Even if a partner is supportive of T/GE identities and attracted to us, getting news that our body is different than they expected, or finding this out during a sexual encounter, can be a surprising and confusing experience. People have different reactions to finding out about our T/GE status in the middle of a sexual encounter. Some may have experience with other T/GE partners or feel otherwise unconcerned by potential differences in our anatomy or gender identity and be comfortable continuing. Others may want to slow things down and take time to process their feelings. In some cases, a partner who wants to be supportive may feel pressured to continue having sex so as not to hurt us, appear transphobic, or send a message that we are not attractive—even if they would rather take some time to think through things. In some cases, people who find out about our T/GE status in the middle of a sexual encounter may become very angry that we did not tell them and our physical safety may be at risk.

Some of us have bodies that are not recognizable to most people as T/GE bodies. For example, we may have had breast augmentation and vaginoplasty, and we feel we are at low risk of a partner finding out that we are T/GE without our telling them. The point at which we choose to discuss our status with a partner is up to us—and many of us feel that we have no obligation to tell anyone about our history. Keep in mind that we are not to blame if someone else uses violence against us. There have been innumerable assaults and murders attributed to the "trans panic" of someone realizing their date is trans. In many of those cases, however, they actually already knew, and the violence occurred after their friends found out and they felt they needed to pretend they hadn't known.[2,3] Disclosure is a personal decision for each of us, and should absolutely never result in violence, though, sadly, in our society, it sometimes does.

EQUIPMENT

Lots of different "equipment" can be used during sex, both for masturbation and with others. People of all genders and sexual orientations use sex toys for stimulation and fun. Certain toys and other products can be especially useful for T/GE people to learn about.

Lubricants

Not all kinds of sex require lubricant (lube), but many of us benefit from it. Lube can be an issue of safe sex as well. Lube cuts down on friction and irritation, which, in addition to feeling unpleasant, can create small tears in the skin and increase our risk of getting a sexually transmitted infection (STI). Dry condoms often equal broken condoms, as friction can cause them to tear. Many T/GE folks need lube even more than cis folks. Taking testosterone reduces the natural lubrication in a front hole. Many of us who have had a

Sex shops known for being good at helping trans customers with toy suggestions for different bodies and using gender affirming language include The Smitten Kitten, Pleasure Chest, Early to Bed, Babeland, and Good Vibrations.

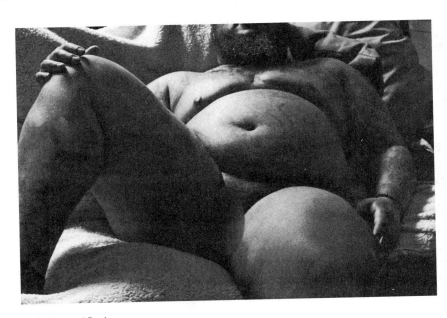

TeddyBearb. (Armani Dae)

vaginoplasty will find our vaginas are not self-lubricating. And the anus doesn't produce any natural lubrication.

Knowing what is in our lube is important. Oil-based lubes will break down latex and should be avoided when using condoms and other latex barriers. Water-based lubes are the most common, and are condom and barrier safe. They can dry out during sex, however, and it can be beneficial to have a cup of water (or a spritzer bottle) nearby to rehydrate the lube when needed. Silicone-based lube is also condom and barrier safe, but requires soap to wash off. It is more expensive, but some of us prefer it because it is less likely to dry out.

Some of us will have an allergic reaction to certain kinds of lube. If that's a concern, we could consider spot-testing a lube on the inside of the wrist. We should also be wary of lubes containing glycerin. It's added as a sweetener to many flavored and even some unflavored lubes. However, as a form of sugar, it may increase our risk of yeast infections if used for front hole penetration. Applied anally, glycerin can act as an anal suppository laxative, which encourages defecation. Both are side effects we may want to avoid.

Vibrators, Dildos, Strap-Ons, and Prosthetic Cocks

Vibrators are sex toys that vibrate. They come in many shapes and sizes. The stimulation from vibrators can be used on a wide variety of erogenous zones. Some vibrators are designed to be used primarily for penetration. Some of these are specifically made to reach areas where vibration may feel especially powerful, such as the prostate (a gland in AMAB people) or the urethral sponge (a cushion of sensitive erectile tissue around the urethra in all people, also known as the party ridge or g-spot). Other vibrators are designed for external use, and may be much smaller. They can be used on external genitals, the perineum, nipples, feet, or anywhere else. Those of us who experience dysphoria may find vibrators a good way to receive genital stimulation without having to have a lot of direct interaction with our anatomy.

Dildos are sex toys that are designed for penetration. Some are shaped like a phallus. Some are also vibrators. Dildos can be strapped on with a harness, used by hand, or attached to objects/surfaces. Dildos can sometimes feel very gendered and can be used in ways that feel validating for us, but for some of us, dildos can also lead to dysphoria. One trans man might love the opportunity to penetrate a partner with a strap-on, while another might feel expected to wear a strap-on even if he doesn't want to. One trans woman might feel too much dysphoria to engage in any type of penetration, while another might love using a strap-on to penetrate a partner because of how strap-ons are often associated with cis women. If using a dildo causes dissociation or discomfort in any way, it may be helpful to check in with ourselves and discuss what meanings or associations they have for us and for our partner(s).

Prosthetic cocks are phallus-shaped dildos that can be worn over our other bits. They can be used or worn by people of all genders, sexes, and identities—and there are various types created for different bodies. They are sometimes called "packers" or "packs." They can be hard or soft, and they can be worn throughout the day or put on before or during sex. Some packers allow the user to stand and pee.

Everybody can use dildos, strap-on harnesses, and prosthetic parts for penetration, regardless of their gender identity, the sex they were assigned at birth, the shape of their genitals, or what they'd like to do with those genitals.

Masturbation Sleeves

Many sex toy manufacturers produce toys that are called masturbation sleeves. They are designed to be pleasurable to penetrate, often with textured patterns on the inside. Some of them have openings made to resemble genitals, anuses, or mouths. Others have nondescript openings. Sleeves may be made of silicone or jelly rubber like other sex toys.

Trans women or others assigned male might appreciate these toys. Difficulty with erections or dysphoria might become problems, but some sleeves are made in a small egg shape and may work more easily without erections or for anyone with smaller genitals. For

Sex toys are made from many different materials. Nonporous materials such as hard plastic, silicone, glass, and steel can be sterilized. Porous materials, like most plastic and latex, have small pores that can trap dirt and bacteria and can never be fully sterilized. They are usually cheaper but if used without a condom can spread STIs, yeast, or bacterial infections. Toxic materials such as jelly rubber, polyvinyl chloride (PVC), and many plastics are unfortunately common among cheaper toys because there are no federal safety regulations.

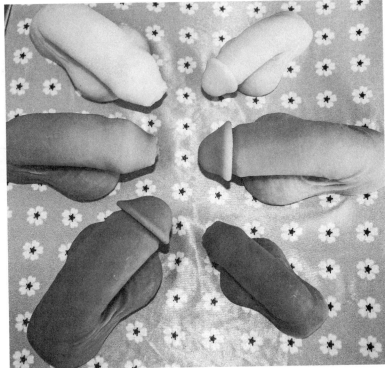

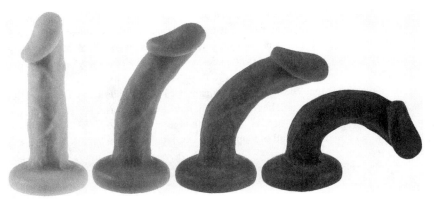

Images of Packers and Dildos. (New York Toy Collective)

those who cannot tolerate penetration but want to please their partner by providing it, or who want to be penetrated in the front but cannot be, one option is to place a masturbation sleeve between our thighs and have our partner penetrate the sleeve.

Pumping and Extenders

Hand-operated pump systems include a clear cylinder that is used to create suction to enlarge body parts and engorge them with blood. Pumps can be used on external genitals, nipples, genital openings, or the anus. Pumping can create increased sensitivity and an intense tugging sensation, which some find very pleasurable. Pulling blood into the area can help create erections and temporarily increase genital size.

We can even detach the tube and pump while leaving the cylinder suctioned on to play with. One creative option some people use is to then slide an erection-enlarging sheath, also called an extender, over the cylinder to use for penetration that also stimulates them. Extenders are marketed for cis men who want bigger genitals, but they can be used by other folks as well with a little creativity.

We can test the pump on our thigh to become familiar with how it works, especially the quick release valve. Be sure to go slowly and experiment when you are first using a pump. If you overdo it, pumping can desensitize you or cause burst capillaries. If you notice blue or purple marks or bumps under the skin where you've been pumping, remove the pump immediately and ice the area to decrease swelling. After removing the pump, the area will continue to be extra sensitive for a while.

TRANSGENDER FOLKS AND SEXUAL PERVERSION

Tobias Wiggins (he/him) is an assistant professor of Women's and Gender Studies at Athabasca University (AU). His research centers transgender mental health, queer visual culture, clinical trans-phobia, community-based wellness, and psychoanalysis. His recent research has been published in Transgender Studies Quarterly, The Psychoanalytic Study of the Child, *and the anthology* Sex, Sexuality and Trans Identities: Clinical Guidance for Psychotherapists and Counselors.

Perversion is a dirty word with a long, strange history. Today, we might hear the term used in a number of fashions. It could condemn sex acts considered seriously offensive or violent: "That exhibitionist in the subway was a total pervert." Or, we could use it as a friendly jab, aimed at a friend's peculiar desires: "Oh Caiden, since T you only think about sex, you're such a pervert!!" In most cases, the language of perversion is a powerful tool that labels the sexual things that sit outside of people's comfort zones. Because of its flexible and sometimes unpredictable associations, the sex that gets branded as "perverse" can tell us something important about stereotypes in our current social world.

Much like homosexuality, transgender people have been officially linked with sexual perversion since the beginning of their appearance in popular Western psychiatric manuals. For example, the first classification for gender difference in the *Diagnostic and Statistical Manual for Mental Disorders* was "transvestism," found listed under "Sexual Deviations" and sandwiched between "homosexuality" and "pedophilia." Much has changed since 1952, and although, in most cases, transgender people must still get a diagnosis to access many gender-affirming treatments, transgender identity is no longer categorized as sexually deviant or as a psychological illness.

The now outdated idea that specific people or sexual desires are naturally perverse has still managed to have a lasting impact on many transgender people's lives. When the famous bathroom panics started to occur in the United States, conservative politicians manipulated the stereotype of transgender perversion. They used the media in toxic, transphobic ways, constructing trans women as violent sexual predators. Yet another impact of the association of gender difference with perversion is that transgender people's diverse, authentic sexuality and sexual expression have often been overlooked. This has especially been true if their sexual desire falls outside of society's various norms, such as heterosexuality and penis-in-vagina penetration.

Some transgender people have chosen to *reclaim* the word perversion. The act of reclaiming a word means that the community that has been called that offensive thing chooses to fight back by using that same word, but in their own, more positive ways. For example, some trans people might enjoy sex acts that fall outside of society's expectations—such as sex without bottom surgery or rope bondage—and they might themselves, lovingly, call that sex "perverse." Our community is full of wonderfully diverse bodies, desires, and unique ways to describe them. There is no one right way to be sexual.

Working with Limits, Consent, and Boundaries

It's important that sex happen under consent of all parties. That consent must be informed and must not be coerced. It also must be freely given and able to be withdrawn at any time.

Many of us know how important it is to ask for consent, but can still find it intimidating. Especially if we know—or think we know—that our partner wants to have some form of sex, it might seem unnecessary for us to ask about something specific. Asking for consent may also be intimidating. What if the person says "no"? Will we feel embarrassed or ashamed? Will we feel undesirable, ugly, or unloved? It's important for us to be able to both give and receive consent with the acceptance that rejection is a possible outcome. After all, rejection is part of consent. We cannot have "yes" without the possibility of a "no," a "not right now," or a "how about we do this instead?"

When seeking consent, it may be helpful for us to consider that a "no" isn't a personal rejection or reflection of our desirability. A "no" is an expression of someone respecting their boundaries and sexual autonomy.[4] If they feel safe communicating with us, it is also an expression of respect and trust. Feeling rejected may hurt, but it doesn't have to be personal. Ahead of time, it may help to practice both saying and hearing "no" to prepare for potential emotional reactions we might have when negotiating sex.

When we hear "no," it is also key for us to understand that the person's choice is definitive. We shouldn't push them to give in or try to emotionally manipulate them to change their mind. Instead, try saying something like, "thank you for taking care of yourself," or "I appreciate that you are aware of and upholding your boundaries," or simply, "OK, I understand." This will show the other person that we respect their bodily autonomy.[5]

If we're asked to do something that makes us feel uncomfortable, it can be scary for us to say "no" because we may want to avoid the unpredictable emotions of our partner(s). We may not want to hurt their feelings, make them upset or angry, or jeopardize the relationship. We may feel tempted to go along with what they want—perhaps feeling it is our only option if we want to remain safe, to stay in a relationship, or to continue having sex. By stating our boundaries, however, we are engaging in consent and playing an active role in our safety and our pleasure. Being able to express boundaries builds trust between partners and can improve confidence in communication, which can ultimately lead to safer and more satisfying sexual experiences and relationships.

Given that saying or hearing "no" can feel challenging, a helpful exercise is to practice. Take turns asking your partner, "can I hold your hand?" and replying, "no, thanks" or "instead of holding my hand, would you massage my shoulders?" After a few rounds, you'll see that it gets easier.

But how might you know what someone's likes or dislikes are in the first place? Although there's no one right way to go about navigating boundaries, there are a few tools that can be used as a helpful starting place. One such tool is the "yes, no, maybe" list, in which participants list the activities they like as "yeses," activities they don't like as "no's," and activities that might depend on the situation as "maybes" or "depends." To create this list, write down things that turn you on, as well as the things that don't. It may be uncomfortable to think about the things you really dislike, but it's important to be able to identify and communicate these things to prevent them from happening without your consent. If there are things you're curious about and have never tried, you might put these things in the "maybe" category. Remember that all of these activities can shift back and forth from yeses to no's or maybes at any time. Some people get really detailed with the list, making extensive spreadsheets organized by type of sensation, and put activities on a scale from 1 to 10. The "yes, no, maybe" list is often used for people who explore BDSM, but it can be adapted to almost any sexual or sensual encounter. You don't have to build this list from scratch; there are a number of examples online or in sex education books to get the ideas and conversations flowing. Share the list with your partner, or write it out together to help guide a conversation about your boundaries and exploration.

How exactly can we ask questions about a partner's desires? And how can we ensure that we seek active consent before, during, and after sex? This can actually be achieved through a surprisingly diverse range of creative, yet still very direct and clear, questions that frame asking for consent and respecting boundaries as a part of "dirty talk" and flirting. For example, here are a variety of things that you can ask while making out, caressing each other, or engaging in any number of sexual acts:

- "How does this/that feel?"
- "Do you like this/that?"
- "Is there anything that you want to do to me right now?"
- "Is there anything that you want me to do to you right now?"
- "I'd really like to make you feel good. How could I do that for you?"
- "I can't stop thinking about [sexual or sensual act], would you like that too?"
- "I think it would be really hot if we [sexual or sensual act], what do you think?"
- "I'd really like to _____ you right now, can I do that?"

These are just a few examples, though there are so many other ways, too, and they can be adapted to any situation. For example, while leading up to fingering someone we can ask "How many fingers would you like inside of you?" and during the act we can ask, "Are you ready for another finger?" or "How hard do you want me to fuck you?" as a means of allowing our partner or lover to decide how they are comfortable receiving pleasure from us.

After we've shared a sexual or sensual experience with someone there are also a myriad of ways to check in and make sure everyone felt comfortable, respected, and fulfilled. You might do this more directly by saying, "That felt really great to me, did you enjoy yourself?" or you can take a more conversational approach such as "I really liked it when you [insert action]. What did you like? Was there anything that you didn't like?"

Don't be afraid to check in again days later as well! Following up with our partner(s), lover(s), and/or play-friend(s) on discussions of consent, boundaries, limits, desires, needs, and wants, are integral parts of developing strong communication, trust, honesty, and respect.

Sex is not just for able-bodied people! Check out *The Ultimate Guide to Sex and Disability: For All of Us who Live with Disabilities, Chronic Pain and Illness* (by Miriam Kaufman, Corey Silverberg, and Fran Odette, Cleis Press, 2007).

KINK AND BDSM

We do not have to like latex, leather, or whips to be kinky. There are many elements of kink that we use in our sex lives without realizing it. If you have ever given or received a hickey and liked it, then you enjoyed marking or biting your partner. If you have ever liked consensually holding someone down or being held down yourself, then you have enjoyed a form of dominance/submission and power exchange. If you have ever used handcuffs or blindfolds, you have experimented with erotic restraint and sensory deprivation. "Kinky" people are often just those who have created names for certain types of intimacy and experimented with them more.

On hormones, I've had to rediscover how I like sex. Before, I played a dominant role, now I play both a dominant and submissive role.

Fully expanded, BDSM represents a combination of multiple acronyms including B/D (Bondage & Discipline), D/s (Dominance & Submission), and S/M (Sadism & Masochism). The acronym BDSM is used as a catch-all umbrella term for a whole variety of behaviors, relationship styles, fetishes, and kinks. What it boils down to is people enjoying a variety of different sensation types, consensual power dynamics, and sex fantasies.

Many of us have had fantasies that involve power, domination, submission, or role dynamics, such as teacher/student or boss/employee. Many people think of these as "just fantasy" and never realize that such scenarios can be safely and responsibly acted out in real life without any real authority figures being involved.

It was only after transition that I realized I could enjoy being sexually submissive, whereas before I had always seen myself as naturally dominant.

For those of us who do not desire genital sex, kink can be a great substitute. For those who do, it can be a fun addition to our repertoire. Giving and receiving consensual pain, for example, can create intense intimacy and give both parties the same kind of emotional "high" as orgasm. Although kink may not always result in the specific kind of physical pleasure we call climax, kink can give some of us feelings of intense euphoria, pleasure, connectedness, and passion in much the same way that genital sex might.

For an introduction to power play, look for *The Bottoming Book: Or How to Get Terrible Things Done to You by Wonderful People* and *The Topping Book: Or Getting Good at Being Bad* (Dossie Easton and Catherine A Liszt, Greenery Press, 1998).

circle of sexual pleasure

This is a visual drawing of how to have pleasure-orientated sex. Instead of a goal or finish line that you're trying to reach, it's a circle with as many arms as you can think of. Each arms contains a behavior that you consider both sexual and pleasurable. And they are all "real" sex. You can do any of these activities and you're having "real" sex or you can do a bunch at once and you're still having "real" sex. There's no right order and there isn't one way to have "real" sex!

Here's one example of what could be on the circle of sexual pleasure. For this person a hot date could be holding hands and cuddling, or it could be making out and watching porn, or it could be oral sex and orgasm. Any combination is a good date with less pressure and more pleasure!!

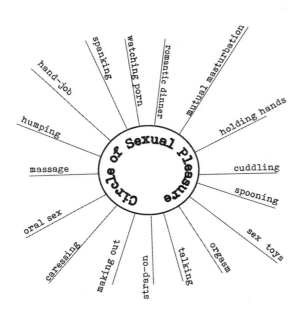

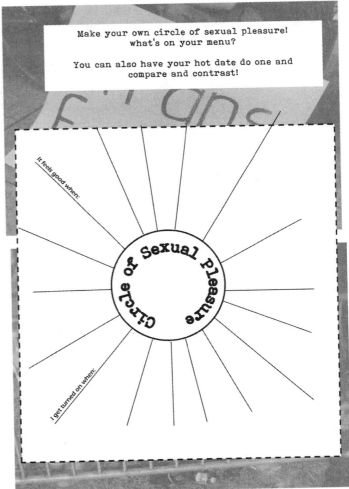

Make your own circle of sexual pleasure! what's on your menu?

You can also have your hot date do one and compare and contrast!

yes/no/maybe list

One of the most amazing things about being trans, and also sometimes the most frustrating, is that when it comes to sex there are no rules. There is no one way to have sex. And there is no way to know what each person (or yourself for that matter) likes and feels comfortable with until you ask. This is where the yes/no/maybe list comes in.

Below is an example of yes/no/maybe list and on the next page is a blank one for you to fill out. Or, make a copy and fill it out with a special friend. Think about what feels really good, what sometimes feels good, and what you're not comfortable with. If you and your boo both complete the lists you can compare notes. It's ok to say what doesn't feel good and expect that be respected.

Your yes/no/maybe list can also include things like taking a bath, getting a massage, watching porn together, being tied up, or spanking.

ACTIVITY	YES	NO	MAYBE	NOTES
giving oral sex	x			!!!!
receiving oral sex			x	Depends how I feel about my body that day
being penetrated			x	Only with people I know well
penetrating partner	x			
having my chest touched		x		

yes/no/maybe list

ACTIVITY	YES	NO	MAYBE	NOTES
giving oral sex				
receiving oral sex				
being penetrated				
penetrating partner				
having chest touched				
having genitals touched				
touching genitals				
kissing				
having body kissed				
using a strap-on				
receiving a strap-on				
giving hand job				
receiving hand job				
giving anal sex				
receiving anal sex				

Trans Sex Zine activities (first 4 pages). (Damon Constantinides)

Certain types of play are more dangerous than others. If you are interested in experimenting with something comparatively risky, such as needles, seek in-depth information from experienced sources. Everything that goes into making safe, consensual, and fulfilling sex is true of kink as well: Be careful about consent, negotiate before you play, have check-ins, and give each other aftercare. Practice good communication with your partners and negotiate safe words before beginning play.

SAFER SEX

For many of us, the risks associated with sex can sometimes seem far off or improbable. This is especially true for those of us who live with a significant amount of day-to-day risks—including discrimination, harassment, and violence. When validation and support seem scarce, it can seem difficult to insist on safer sex when it might mean rejection from a sexual partner. Support does not need to be scarce. Being aware of potential health issues around sex and making informed decisions to minimize risk is an important part of taking care of ourselves and our partners.

There are a number of different sexually transmitted infections (STIs) out there, many of which are treatable if identified. Infections often spread when bodily fluids such as blood, semen, or ejaculate from one person get into bodily openings or mucous membranes of another. One of the best safer sex strategies is to engage in sexual activity that reduces or eliminates fluid transfer. This might involve mutual masturbation, use of toys, engaging in nongenital sex, or using barriers such as condoms, dental dams, and gloves to stop fluids from mixing.

The three main tenets of safer sex are communication, testing, and barriers. Communication can include disclosing our STI status; discussing our boundaries and desires; having regular check-ins during a sexual experience; and being open about both mental and physical needs. Incorporating regular STI testing into our personal care is important, but discussing our STI status can be challenging because there is a lot of misinformation and stigma around sexual health. However, the more we educate ourselves and the more honest discussions we have with one another, the less this stigma can negatively impact our communities and our relationships. If we learn that we have contracted an STI, it does not make us "dirty," sexually invalid, or undeserving of a satisfying sex or love life. It is important for us to learn how to communicate about our status so that we can continue to engage in safer sex for ourselves and others.

Barriers include internal and external condoms and dental dams. Other forms of STI prevention include pre-exposure prophylaxis (PrEP) and post-exposure prophylaxis (PEP), which are antiretroviral medicines we can take before or after sex to prevent transmission of HIV.

An element of sexual health that is often overlooked is sexual hygiene. Proper care includes washing hands and genitals to prevent infections caused when feces or other contaminated materials make contact with mucus membranes of our genitals, mouths, and eyes. There are many tutorials and guides online to help illustrate the proper techniques of thorough hand-washing and cleaning of the skin folds of our genitals with gentle soap, as well as the administration of enemas.

Risk Management and Harm Reduction

There is no one way to do safer sex that works for everyone. What's important is finding ways to reduce the risk to a level that feels reasonable. For some of us, that might mean using barriers for every single sex act. For others of us, that doesn't fit with our desires or situation, and we make compromises. For example, many of us choose to engage in oral sex rather than genitally penetrative sex because oral sex is considered a lower-risk activity. Although the risk of HIV transmission is far lower, it is still possible to transmit HIV, as well as a number of other STIs, via oral sex. That may be an acceptable risk for some people. It is important for us to assess our own comfort and risk levels to make decisions about our sexual behavior. Because all sexual activity comes with some level of risk, we must use the information available to us, along with communication and sexual negotiation with our sexual partners, to make informed decisions that can reduce potential harm.

> I have used barrier contraception methods with all my (cis) female partners, because I have used barriers against STDs with *all* my partners. Growing up as a queer "boy," I was very acutely aware of the risks, and I have used barriers assiduously for my entire sexual life.

Some of us may also form "fluid bonds," where we choose to allow fluid exchange in one relationship but take additional precautions to make sure that neither have any infections that could be sexually transmitted. It's important to remember that frequent testing, sexual exclusivity, and/or consistent use of barriers with other sexual partners are what make this strategy effective, not just how much we care about our partner or how much our partner cares about us.

Making Barriers Work for Us

Barriers come in many varieties: traditional "external" condoms, receptive-partner "internal" condoms (aka the "female condom"), gloves, and dental dams (latex squares used for oral sex). Barriers are most commonly made out of latex, but nonlatex options are available for those of us with latex allergies. We may have a latex allergy if we sneeze, get a runny nose, have itchy eyes, break out in a rash, or have other allergy symptoms around latex products.

> *I don't think I'm fertile anymore and I don't want children, but I still use contraceptives for STI protection. I don't like to use external condoms though. I use a large finger cot on my penis, which works because it prevents erection which would give me dysphoria.*

Making barriers work can sometimes be tricky. We are told so often that condoms and dental dams are for cis people of particular genders that it can feel invalidating or de-gendering to use them. More importantly, they often aren't designed to work with our bodies and the activities we want to do. For example, those of us with big bits may be unable to use a condom because condoms require us to maintain an erection at a certain size.

> *My genitals don't work very well with condoms (uncircumcised, borderline phimosis). This has been an impediment to me topping before, and perhaps that influences my gender identity.*

We often need to get creative to maintain barriers. Remember that the bottom line is to prevent fluid transfer. For example, we can alter a glove for a variety of different uses. We can create what some call "the cape," where the thumb of the glove can be used to wrap around small bits or non-erect large bits with a barrier covering the surrounding area for oral sex. This can work very well for those of us with smaller bits who are trying to create the experience of receiving a blow job. Those of us with larger bits can stretch the thumb of the glove open and put it over our bits, which might be especially useful if getting erect is difficult, if condoms are too loose, or if we want to experience our bits being reshaped in a new way. Another technique for altering a glove can be creating a dental dam with finger holds. Dental dams and receptive partner condoms can also be used creatively. For those of us with long or rough fingernails, we can put cotton balls, tissue, or toilet paper in the fingers of the glove for added protection from scraping.

> *I have not needed to use medical contraception for a good majority of my life (due to my sexual activity prior to 2016 being afab/afab). I do use condoms now, but not for birth control—rather safety from STIs.*

Pregnancy and Birth Control

The heterosexist and cissexist way pregnancy is often talked about can make it easy for us to forget that many trans people are also capable of becoming pregnant or getting someone else pregnant. It is also often assumed—even among trans people—that wishing to give birth or impregnate someone somehow makes us less trans. This is simply not true. It is just as valid for us to want to produce our own children as it is to want to avoid it. Discussing the issue of pregnancy with a partner can be difficult for us, but it's important nonetheless.

> *Sometimes I feel excluded from lesbian jokes about not being able to get pregnant. Since I have a uterus, I am at risk for pregnancy because I'm in a long-term relationship with a trans woman. I am, in fact, a lesbian who can experience a pregnancy scare.*

For those of us who are capable of getting pregnant, birth control can be an uncomfortable topic, and it can be difficult to find good information. For those of us on testosterone who no longer menstruate, it can be tempting to assume that there is no risk of pregnancy, but that is not the case. Although there is a decreased risk of pregnancy while on testosterone, there is no good data on what that risk is. Some of us on testosterone have gotten pregnant, even without menstruating. Testosterone can be damaging to a fetus and should be stopped immediately if we find out we are pregnant and intend to keep the pregnancy.

"Big bits" and "little bits" are not euphemisms for "non-op trans women" or "non-op trans men." They refer to exactly what they say: people with larger or smaller genitals regardless of their surgical status or gender designation at birth.

Many hormonal forms of birth control contain estrogen, progesterone, or some combination of the two. Ideally, this prevents ovulation, which makes pregnancy unlikely. Putting these hormones into our bodies can also lead to side effects including decreased libido, mood changes, or weight gain—especially in the thighs and chest. It can sometimes be an overwhelming experience for those of us already dysphoric about our body shape. For others, hormonal birth control doesn't have many noticeable side effects, especially if we are taking testosterone at the same time.

Some of us may choose barrier protection to avoid pregnancy. The use of spermicide or spermicidally lubricated condoms can further reduce the risk of pregnancy, but they are not a surefire method. Spermicides can also cause skin irritation and break down the tissue lining inside our various holes. Such irritation or damage to the mucous membranes may render us more susceptible to STI transmission. (Plus, spermicide tastes horrible!) However, if we consider harm reduction, some of us may decide to use a spermicidally lubricated condom instead of no condom at all.

CONCLUSION

Stigma and a lack of trans-inclusive information on sex can make researching information about sexuality feel invalidating of our genders and sexual orientations. However, sex can be a way for us to feel empowered in our bodies and our genders. We owe it to ourselves to be informed of our needs, wants, risks, and health status so that we can be our own best caregivers. We deserve a healthy and happy sexuality, and we are worthy of love, pleasure, and care. What feels right to us is what is right for us.

NOTES

1. Denny, D. (1992). The politics of diagnosis and a diagnosis of politics: The university-affiliated gender clinics and how they failed to meet the needs of transgender people. *Chrysalis Quarterly, 1*(3), 9–20. doi: http://dallasdenny.com/Writing/wp-content/uploads/2013/12/The-Politics-of-Diagnosissmallpdf.com_pdf

2. Belcher, M. (2017, July 11). 2008 Greeley murder back in national spotlight. https://www.thedenverchannel.com/news/local-news/2008-murder-of-transgender-greeley-woman-brought-back-into-national-spotlight

3. Allen, S. (2018, February 21). Why did Joshua Vallum kill Mercedes Williamson, his transgender girlfriend? https://www.thedailybeast.com/why-did-joshua-vallum-kill-mercedes-williamson-his-transgender-girlfriend

4. Dr. Nerdlove. (2013, March 29). Getting a yes (instead of avoiding a no): The standard of enthusiastic consent. *Paging Dr. Nerdlove.* http://www.doctornerdlove.com/2013/03/enthusiastic-consent

5. Yourlesbianfriend. (March 22, 2013). Un-memorizing the "silence is sexy" date script. *Queer Guess Code.* http://queerguesscode.wordpress.com/2013/03/22/un-memorizing-the-silence-is-sexy-date-script

17

PARENTING
Junior Brainard and Morgan Weinert
Based on first edition content by Kel Polly and Ryan G. Polly

INTRODUCTION

Parenting is an incredible experience that allows us to create a connection with a child and have a part in shaping a life. Parenting can take many forms: as a teacher, a mentor, a family member, or in a close relationship with the child of a friend. Families with children can have lots of different configurations, and may include single parents, parents in a partnership, or more than two adults raising and parenting together. As transgender and gender expansive (T/GE) people, we have the opportunity to teach the youth in our lives about gender diversity and model living authentic lives outside of the gender binary. The desire to parent may be lifelong, or develop only after creating a new relationship with a partner or child. No matter how the decision to parent comes along, there are many ways to start the journey. Although many transgender people come out as trans after already having children, this chapter focuses primarily on information that will be useful to transgender people who want to plan how they have children and build a family.

> *I do not have children, but I am an "entle" (gender neutral to aunt/uncle) to children of both blood and choice.*

"My husband and children saved my life. I had a life full of confusion and depression and then my husband came and showed me how to be loved and gave me two beautiful babies. That has forever changed my life. This is what true happiness looks like, Transmom and Transdad, the New Normal." (Kennedy and Mya Power)

CONCERNS ABOUT PARENTING AS TRANS PEOPLE

I definitely think I want to have children one day, but the societal expectations of gender make it a little difficult to decide. I do think I want to continue taking testosterone and living "professionally" (at work, etc.) as a man, and worry about what would happen if I decided to carry a child, as I imagine I would have to be off hormones. Dysphoria is a small concern, but I more so worry about how others would perceive me.

T/GE people are capable of parenting successfully, and being trans does not mean that you will be unable to raise happy, healthy children. There are, however, some reasonable concerns that we may have about how we are perceived by society, or how our children may be impacted by these societal perceptions.

I do not want to have children. Since most of the world sees me as a woman, I am expected to want to have children. This seems doubly unfair to me, since I am not actually a woman to begin with.

Our visibility as T/GE people may impact how cisgender people interact with us and our children. For example, parents who are perceived as male but are visibly pregnant may experience confusion or scrutiny from people who believe that only cisgender women can be pregnant. Although transgender people are often accustomed to being more highly scrutinized by cisgender people, it may feel more intense or dangerous when it involves our children. Where we live, where we work, and what our community support looks like can all impact our experience parenting. Other parts of ourselves, such as our race, class, and/or ability may also intersect with our transgender identity and impact the level of scrutiny we face as parents. It is our choice as transgender people to choose to adjust, or not adjust, how we present ourselves in the world in order to protect ourselves and our children, and some of us have greater or lesser ability to change our presentation and how we are seen in the world. It is important to remember that it is OK to do what you need to do in order to feel safe and successful in raising your child.

I am very happy and content without children. I have never had the urge to have them and, in fact, the mere thought that I had the physical capability to become pregnant was the biggest trigger for dysphoria. I am very happy that my hysterectomy sterilized me.

We may worry about how our children will respond to us being transgender. Even if you have been out as transgender since your child was an infant, social pressure from other children may cause your child to question why you aren't like "other" parents. It is normal for children to ask these sorts of questions as they learn where they fit in the world. Coming out to your older child can also be a challenging experience, especially if they have been used to you presenting in another gender for most of their life. There is no "right" way to have these conversations, but perhaps it is reassuring to remember that the way we talk to our children about our genders, and how our unique families were formed, can help set the stage for our children to grow into accepting, caring adults.

I have two adult daughters, ages 35 and 37. My youngest daughter has disowned me and cut off all contact. My oldest daughter expressed some initial concern and then accepted me. As to other parents, be yourself, allow your children to do likewise. You cannot force them to accept you. As the parent it is our job to support our children, even if that means respecting their decision not to have us in their lives.

OPTIONS FOR BECOMING A TRANS PARENT

When we reach the point in our lives when we begin to consider whether to become a parent (the timeline of which varies widely from one person to the next), one of the

A *Womb of Their Own* is a 2017 film by Cyn Lubow that follows "six diverse masculine-identified people" as they become pregnant and "are challenged by binary gender constructs in mainstream culture, and even in the LGBTQ community."

Legal resources for trans parents include Lambda Legal's *FAQ about Transgender Parenting*, ACLU's *Protecting the Rights of Transgender Parents and Their Children*, and the National Center for Lesbian Rights' *Family and Relationship Resources*.

Ten month old Irie Storm with parents Simon and Maxx, and four legged sibling Oso.

Thinking of starting a family? Check out Family Equality's online *Family Building Guide*, exploring paths to parenthood for LGBTQ people.

questions we must ask ourselves is how we will do so. Some of us also become parents in less intentional ways and navigate being a trans parent without having necessarily decided to do that ahead of time. Regardless, some of the most common ways that people become trans parents include the following: becoming a parent by combining our lives with a partner or spouse who is already a parent themselves, adopting or fostering a child, or planning a biological family.

Parenting a Partner's Child

Many of us begin relationships with people who have children. As we get to know our partners, we may also become part of their children's lives. We may unofficially begin to parent them, or we may officially take steps to adopt them. Becoming a parent to a partner's child can be a wonderful way to add a child to our lives and build a family, and being trans and parenting a partner's child can provide unique opportunities. For children who already grew up with a parent who is trans, their prior experience may be helpful in terms of having a framework for understanding our own gender, and may be a point of connection or familiarity. For children who have never had a parent who is trans before, our status as a trans person may make it easier, in some ways, to create an entirely new role for ourselves in the family that is distinct from any other parent the child may have.

I don't have kids, though one of my partners has two young sons (ages 12 and 10), and we spend time together fairly often. They've been raised in a very open, queer-accepting household full of engaged, supportive adults, so while they seem to be both straight and cis, they're extremely cool, easygoing kids who can hold a conversation with just about anyone.

Parenting a partner's child can also pose challenges, many of which are not unique to being a T/GE parent. Parenting a partner's child requires building a relationship with a child over time that works with all of the other family dynamics and relationships in place. What that relationship looks like varies greatly, and often depends on factors such as how old a partner's child is when you enter into their life, whether the child has another parent, and what that other parent's relationship is with the child and your partner. Parenting a partner's child means participating in child- and family-related decision-making, which often requires negotiation about who has the power to decide what. Parenting a partner's child often means doing so without legal protections.

I have stepchildren whose lives I have been in since they were early teens. They were not comfortable with the lesbian nature of my relationship with their mother. But, as time went on, we navigated the difficulties, and I have ended up with very close relationships with them. My transition was not a surprise to them, nor did they have any trouble with it.

In addition to the hurdles that many parents face when they begin to parent their partners' children, we also have concerns that are unique to us as trans people.

- We may wrestle with when and how to tell the child about our transgender identity, and we may have fears about how to do this within an existing family structure. Although how we come out (or don't) depends on many factors, making sure that we have a support system, including our partner, to navigate this is important.

- If there is any custody battle happening with the child's other parent, we may need to consider whether our status as a trans person could be used to deny our partner custody, regardless of whether it is legal to do so. It may be useful to ask for legal advice.

- For a variety of reasons, including transphobia, many cisgender people assume that trans people are not parents; we are sometimes seen as too young and/or too queer, or our families are not heteronormative enough. Parenting a partner's child can sometimes exacerbate these challenges. From school pick-ups to interactions at the playground, there may be more of a need to assert ourselves as parents or to explain our relationship to the child.

I recently became a co-parent to my genderqueer partner's 12 year old. Their child is also trans and is exploring his gender identity. We both constantly provide advice and insight from our own experiences with gender to help him navigate his own gender journey.

BIRTHING JUSTICE

Darius McLean (he/him) is the Director of Empowerment Programs at the Arcila-Adams Trans Resource Center as part of the William Way Community Center in Philadelphia, PA.

I am Black, queer, trans, and assigned female at birth. I am a parent and a partner; I am a healthcare worker and advocate. I am an Indigenous American; I am also a first-generation Jamaican American. I understand that these identities cannot be separated and placed into a hierarchical structure. These identities are fluid and shape my experiences in life.

Recently I have been exploring what it means to continue building my family as a Black trans man. As a family, we have decided that I will carry our next child. It was not an easy decision, and I will be in the process around this for the rest of my life. I continue to have conversations with myself where I question what Black masculinity is. How do I want to manifest this in myself? What do I want and not want from this? Prior to considering carrying a child, I often found myself disappointed by my trans masc. peers who perpetuate toxic masculinity and violence against trans women. Yet in the process of making this decision, I've found myself having fears of losing my newly gained "Black Man" status. I've feared the potential judgment from Black Cis Het folks, and from my TGNC and LGB community. There is a social taboo against the pregnant man, and society often believes that different groups of people have a set of characteristics that make us who we are and different from one another. The essentialist view of pregnancy assumes that only women can birth, that they by nature want to be and should be mothers. This approach denies and excludes TGNC people and denies AFAB women individual autonomy.

Being in transition has forced me to make decisions around my body that I was not always ready to make. In the state that I was born, you need genital surgery to change the gender on your birth certificate. To have a gender affirming lower surgery requires trans people to undergo sterilization. This is a form of gatekeeping repo and passive eugenics by means of medical and legal frameworks of transitioning. This assumes you're not fully a "man" or "woman" until your body looks a certain way; it only acknowledges medical transition and reinforces the idea that organs = gender identity. As an AFAB Black man, I can't help but consider the historical devaluing and misuse of the Black Fem body and its implications for trans inclusivity in the reproductive justice movement.

I have found power in making this decision and importance in being visible for those of us who cannot during this process. The intersections of my identity force me to make my body my politic.

Adoption and Fostering

Melissa Regan's *No Dumb Questions* is a 2001 film described as "a funny and touching exploration of gender and sexuality through the eyes of 6, 9, and 11 year old sisters" who are learning about their uncle transitioning to female.

There are many children around the world who need parents because their birth parents are unable to care for them. Transgender people can become parents temporarily through fostering or permanently through adoption. Transgender people should not be excluded from fostering or adopting, but may face barriers to both, especially if working with private organizations.

> *Being trans and nonbinary has changed how I think about parenting. Who does what work and how I want to relate to my future children is not based on rigid gender roles, but on the unique relationship I and my partner(s) will have with each child. It has been freeing, but I also know that adopting children as a queer person is going to be an uphill battle.*

It is important to consider the intersections of your identities and how they might impact raising a child who may not share those identities. For example, white parents who foster or adopt a child of color should consider how they can ensure their child of color remains connected to communities that share the child's racial/ethnic identity. Many foster and adoption agencies offer classes and other resources to address the issues that can arise in transracial adoption. It is important, however, that people who are considering adoption do their own work to learn about the racist/colonialist history of the foster/adoption system and consider how they can ensure their child feels empowered and supported in their racial/ethnic identity.[1]

> *I personally don't want children, but I have a partner who wants to adopt or foster at some point. We're both nonbinary, and our relationship is not sexual, so bio-kids are definitely not happening, but I have considered adopting or fostering with this partner/our polycule, if they really want it.*

Fostering

A foster parent is someone who provides temporary care for children in foster care. A foster parent or parents can be an individual, couple, or family that may be related to the child or have no previous relationship with the child. Foster parents play a critical role in the life of foster children by providing an environment that promotes a feeling of safety and well-being. Fostering is usually done through local governments, but can also be facilitated by private organizations. Foster parents must go through home inspections, classes, and evaluations before having children placed with them. The goal of a foster parent is to provide a nurturing environment while child welfare organizations work to safely reunify children with their families. In some instances, reunification is not a possibility and other options are explored, including legal guardianship or adoption.

As transgender people, we may expect additional questions about our gender, but our identities should not prevent us from becoming foster parents. Private foster organizations

Image from TransFertility. Mr. Leo Mateus (he/him) is a transgender illustrator based in the UK who focuses on body positivity and diversity. This illustration was part of a series for a transgender fertility information hub online. (Leo Mateus, IG: @mrleomateusart, mrleomateusart.com)

may deny transgender people the ability to foster, especially if they are funded by conservative organizations. Most government foster programs should not discriminate based on gender or sexual orientation, although subtle forms of discrimination can be difficult to prevent.

> I want to become a foster parent, specifically to queer and trans youth, which is directly connected to my experience growing up trans and queer, and not having any supportive people around me.

Fostering a child may be short-term (a few weeks or months), or long-term (a few years). Some foster agencies will let you set parameters for the types of children you want to foster (i.e., certain age groups). Often, foster agencies are eager for foster parents who are willing to foster children with special needs—such as neonatal withdrawal from parental drug use, or physical or mental disabilities—and will provide extra training so foster parents are prepared to help children with these needs. Foster agencies may also be excited for transgender identified parents who are willing to foster LGBTQ children!

Fostering children sometimes comes with challenges. Children are often placed urgently, with little or no warning or time to prepare. Foster children may be coming from difficult experiences, and could arrive with trauma they need to be supported through. Some children may have been through many foster placements, and are distrustful of the experience of a new placement. Foster agencies should provide plentiful training for these scenarios, and should have support in the form of case managers if other issues arise. Whatever the background of the child, transgender people can be loving, supportive foster parents.

Adoption

Adoption is the process of bringing a child in need of a permanent home into your life and taking on the role of their legally recognized parent. Some adoptions take place after a family has fostered a child for a period of time, but adoptions can also take place outside of the foster system. There are many ways to be connected to children in need of adoption. There are government agencies looking for adoptive families, and many private agencies assist in placement, too. Private agencies may have more restrictions on who they allow to adopt, and may restrict LGBTQ identified people from adopting. There are, however, many private agencies that are welcoming to LGBTQ families and who may even specialize in placing LGBTQ children.

I'm already a dad. Now I want to finally be the mom I always wanted to be. To that end I'd happily adopt.

The first step in adopting a child is determining the route you are most comfortable pursuing. Some options are working directly with an adoption attorney, finding a full-service agency that will orchestrate all the requirements of adoption, and fostering to adoption. There are also kinship adoptions where you adopt a child who is related to you in some way in order for the child to stay connected to family. There are open adoptions (where the child and birth parents are able to stay in contact) and closed adoptions (where the birth parents are not able to stay in contact with the child). All adoptions require a home study, and creating a family book to share photos and information about you with

Trans Lives Matter. "This child of a trans activist grew up in social justice community from a young age." (Jamila Headley)

birth families is very much encouraged. Many agencies find families for children instead of children for families, centering the agency of the birth parent to choose parents for their child.

My adult daughters are my partner's biological children from a previous relationship. My sons were adopted by my partner and I when they were infants.

The Human Rights Campaign (HRC) website has a list of adoption agencies that welcome LGBTQ families and children.

If you are looking to adopt an infant, the process may feel very competitive. Expectant birth parents who have chosen to make an adoption plan for their infant look through profile books/online profiles of families hoping to adopt and choose who they want to adopt their child when they are born. When possible, the prospective adoptive parent(s) chosen will be given some advance notice that they've been chosen before the child is born, but sometimes the adoptive parent(s) are notified when the birth parent is in labor or has already given birth. The baby may be born in a different state than the one you are living in, which means you may have to quickly travel to where the baby is waiting. There is often a waiting period during which you must stay in that state before you are able to travel home, and there are other legal processes that must be observed, such as a "revocation period" during which the birth parent is able to decide that they want to rescind the adoption. It is also important to remember that the baby may need to stay hospitalized if it is born with a health condition.

I am very conflicted about having children because I am asexual (so I don't want to have sex), and I think that being pregnant would make me dysphoric. I think I would want to adopt one day.

If you choose to adopt an older child, there may be more flexibility and less cost. Adoption agencies will show you a list of children who are waiting to be adopted, and will help facilitate meeting the child and bringing them home. With any age child, legally adopting them is a process that must happen in court and may not happen until many months (or years) after the child is brought into your home. Costs vary widely for adoption. If you adopt from a foster agency you may not pay any money, but if you adopt privately or internationally the costs may run into the tens of thousands to cover travel, expenses for the birth parent, court costs, and other fees.

MY BREASTS, MY AUTHENTICITY

Lara America (she/they)

It was when I reintroduced testosterone into my body. I cycled through hormone changes and gender dysphoria in an attempt to produce sperm again. An article went viral about a transgender woman who was able to breastfeed her child. I realized her NYC doctor was the same as mine. I could breastfeed, too. I, a transgender woman, could achieve a milestone of womanhood that many cisgender women never experience.

I learned that the process of breastfeeding involves altering your hormone levels to match the estrogen levels of a pregnant person. You raise your estrogen levels and then you lower them as much as possible. This simulates the hormone changes that happen when you give birth. Your body is tricked into thinking you had a baby and you begin to produce milk.

My breasts and I were introduced by accident. I imagined our first encounter on a princess bed with pink and white pillows. Instead, we were united by an attempt to catch a spilling soda can. As I brushed against the newly developed flesh, I felt a new pain. A sharp, gender affirming twinge. Physical evidence that my body was slowly inching closer to my authenticity.

A giant outdated plasma tv cast a blue glow on my skin as plastic carpet fibers imprinted on my freshly shaven knees. Estrogen was flowing through my body and I knew conceptually that I would gain secondary physical characteristics similar to cisgender women. I couldn't have prepared myself for the euphoria that would come from becoming myself—physically.

It was time for the women in my family to surround me and teach me all the secrets of femininity and womanhood. They take you into a room with shut doors and teach you things men were forbidden to know. I touched my newly developing nipples and wished for this experience. Instead, I was alone, clutching an old stuffed bear given to me by an ex-partner.

I cried tears of joy knowing that my body was beginning to reflect my true self. My journey into femininity would be a lonely one and that was OK. Caterpillars in the chrysalis are alone, too. I knew I would emerge from my chrysalis with a new identity and an undeniable authenticity.

Years later, I fell in love with a human bundle of laughter, Italian food, and hand gestures. The love of my life, Joanne. We were inseparable as soon as we met. Walking together down a path of sex, activism, and rock music, we decided we wanted a child. After a grueling, year-long fertility journey, Joanne became pregnant.

To my relief, my breasts began to return after a year starting estrogen treatments again. The same gender euphoria came but there were no tears of joy. My time on testosterone taught me lessons about myself. I learned to embrace my masculinity. Parts of me that were locked away. I became a whole person.

Images of myself breastfeeding and producing milk played in my mind. An archaic book titled, *The Womanly Art of Breastfeeding*, returned to my memory. Providing my child not only with life lessons earned through trauma and triumph, but also immunity to disease. Did I want to breastfeed to provide for my child or did I want to breastfeed to affirm my gender identity? I couldn't answer this question.

Our child came and I hadn't moved forward with treatments to produce breast milk. My partner went through the naturally occurring stages of milk production and started to excrete colostrum. I was thankful that my mind and body were at their peak. I endured a year of waking nightmares due to hormone changes. It was nice to meet my child with the correct estrogen levels.

At three in the morning, I bottle feed my child breastmilk produced by my partner. She pumped right before going to bed. I knew I made the right decision. And if I had decided to create supplemental breast milk, I would also have made the right decision. The challenges would have been different but the love for my child would be the same. What my baby needs more than breastmilk is me. My love and support. There will always be an endless supply.

Planning a Biological Family

The choice to have a child who is biologically related to you or your partner may seem a bit more complicated than it can be for straight and cisgender people. There are many ways to have a biological child, however, and many transgender people have been able to have biologically related children even after years on hormone replacement therapy.

> *I want to carry my own children in the future, but because my partner and I are both assigned female at birth, I would have to be artificially inseminated (which I am fine with). However, I experience a lot of pressure to adopt in the future rather than pursue artificial insemination, more so than I see straight and cisgender people getting. If a woman in a cisgender, straight couple gets pregnant, nobody says she is selfish for carrying her baby to term instead of adopting. But it's different for me.*

FERTILITY CONSIDERATIONS

There is no real data that confirms to what degree transgender people can regain fertility after hormone use, or if all ovaries exposed to testosterone, or testes exposed to estrogen are able to produce healthy eggs and sperm. Many transgender people, however, have successfully used their eggs or sperm to conceive healthy children after stopping hormones for a period of time.

There is no way to know if any individual will or will not be capable of conception after being on hormones, and no amount of time on hormones that we can consider "safe" to retain fertility. Just as cisgender people can lose fertility for a variety of reasons, so can trans people—and fertility loss may or may not be due to hormone use.

If you and your partner have sperm, eggs, and a uterus and are trying to conceive a child through intercourse, keep in mind that, on average, it takes people six months of trying to successfully conceive. If you have tried for six months or longer, consider finding a fertility specialist to troubleshoot.

If parenting a child that is biologically related to you is important, and you have not yet started hormone replacement therapy, you may want to consider egg or sperm banking. Sperm or egg banking involves harvesting your sperm or eggs and having them preserved at a facility for future use.

Insurance coverage for fertility procedures varies greatly, often depending on whether you live in a state that mandates fertility coverage or not. Some health insurance plans

Bri and Rylee.

cover almost all fertility treatments, others cover some aspects of the treatment, such as medications, and others cover none at all. Some insurance requires that you show that you and your partner have an "infertility" diagnosis, which can present some challenges for couples who simply don't have both sperm and eggs between them. If you are going to be using insurance, working with a provider who is familiar with transgender patients, or even same-sex couples, can be helpful.

If you have already started hormone therapy, and are considering conception in the near future, here are some important things to think about:

For transgender people with a uterus and ovaries:

- If you are using testosterone for HRT, you should discontinue the testosterone before you start trying to conceive. Testosterone is "category X" in pregnancy, which means it can cause significant harm to the fetus. You can still ovulate (produce fertile eggs) while on testosterone, even if you're no longer menstruating. Always use a backup method of birth control if you have sex with someone who produces sperm to prevent pregnancy until you have stopped taking testosterone.
- There is no agreed-upon interval for how long you should be off testosterone before attempting to conceive, but many providers feel that after you have three "normal" menstrual cycles, you can begin attempts at conception. However, you may regain fertility very soon after stopping testosterone, even before you start getting a

The website *Queer Conception Stories* includes a number of stories of trans people creating families.

"My queer family cheesing before attending a queer wedding in Montauk. One month later, my second parent adoption would be finalized, just in case anyone were to doubt that this goofball was mine forever." —Jackson (L-R: Mariah, August, and Jackson)

menstrual cycle again, so it is important to use back-up birth control methods unless you are OK with a "surprise."

- Once you start your menstrual cycle again, begin tracking your cycle to see when you are ovulating. Ovulation is when you are most likely to conceive. There are many ovulation tracker apps available, and you can buy ovulation test strips to get confirmation of when you may be ovulating.

For transgender people with testes:

- There is no guarantee that you will regain fertility after coming off HRT. There is also no official interval for how long you have to discontinue hormones in order to regain fertility if you are able, although anecdotally three to six months is sufficient for most people.[2]
- Depending on how long you have been on HRT, and what dose you're taking, you may still produce viable sperm even while on HRT. Always use a back-up method of birth control when having sex with a partner with a uterus and ovaries, unless you and your partner are ready for conception.
- You can have your sperm tested for viability by a fertility specialist after you have discontinued HRT for a few months to see if you are producing viable sperm again.

FAMILY PLANNING WITH AN HIV-POSITIVE PARENT

Incredible advancements in medications and technologies have made it possible for HIV-positive people to have HIV-negative children without exposing their partner(s) to HIV. Given that transgender people are disproportionately affected by HIV, it is important that we are aware of these technologies.

HIV-positive people with uteruses can utilize "artificial" insemination with sperm from an HIV-negative partner or donor. The sperm can be inserted with a syringe at home, or via intrauterine insemination (IUI) or in-vitro fertilization (IVF) in a clinic. HIV medication is taken by the HIV-positive gestating parent during pregnancy to keep the viral load "undetectable," which helps protect the baby from HIV during childbirth. Even if the birth parent has a detectable viral load, they can be treated with HIV medication during labor, and the baby can be treated shortly after birth to drastically reduce the baby's odds of getting HIV. HIV-positive people who make sperm can have their sperm "washed" in order to remove the semen (where the HIV virus may be) from the specimen before it is inserted into the vagina or uterus of the partner/surrogate. The Centers for Disease Control have announced that an undetectable viral load means a person cannot pass on HIV to their sexual partners. If a person with HIV is taking antiretroviral medication and has their viral load successfully suppressed, they cannot transmit HIV. This is great news for HIV-positive people and their partners!

HIVE, "a hub of positive reproductive & sexual health," shares videos and resources for sexual wellness and safe pregnancies for people with HIV.

HARVESTING EGGS OR SPERM

Harvesting eggs or sperm is the process by which sperm or eggs are taken out of the body. They may be stored for later use. Harvesting sperm is generally a simple, nonintrusive process. It usually involves collecting ejaculate in a sterile container at a provider's office or sperm bank, but can also be done at home and then brought into an office or mailed into a sperm-banking company. Typically, after collecting sperm, a provider will perform a semen analysis in which they examine the sperm under a microscope to assess its overall count and quality for fertility purposes.

> Our current children were all conceived naturally pre-transition. We banked sperm before my orchiectomy, and will use that to attempt one more child soon.

Harvesting eggs, on the other hand, is a complicated, costly, and physician-assisted process. The first step is often a set of lab tests, as well as a pelvic exam and ultrasound. Once the decision is made to proceed, the next step is daily injections of hormones that stimulate the ovaries to increase the number of eggs available for harvest. For a few weeks, your provider will require you to come in for frequent visits in order to monitor how your egg follicles are developing, which is done through bloodwork and vaginal ultrasounds. After this, your provider will perform an egg retrieval in a surgical setting. During the procedure, you are put under sedation and the provider uses a long needle to remove eggs from the ovaries via the vagina. You will then go home to rest for the day. The procedure does result in some pain afterward, primarily from cramping. Some people are able to return to normal activity the next day, and others are still in pain and prefer to rest for an additional day. Egg retrieval cycles are much more expensive than the process of sperm-banking.

STORING EGGS, SPERM, AND EMBRYOS

Cryogenic storage or freezing of sperm, eggs, and embryos is one way to preserve fertility over time or delay a pregnancy. Freezing techniques have improved in recent years, and many fertility clinics now have almost no difference in the success rates from frozen embryos versus fresh embryos. Cryobanks may be found online, and they generally have storage rates that vary depending on the length of the storage contract. The cost of storage is sometimes comparable, regardless of whether we are storing eggs, sperm, or embryos, but some facilities charge more for eggs and embryos than they do for sperm. Depending on the facility, prices typically work out to $30 to $70 per month, but require a payment of six months or several years at a time, with cheaper monthly rates for longer storage commitments. Embryos, made from combining eggs and sperm prior to freezing, are more likely to result in a pregnancy and live birth than egg freezing alone. However, if you do not have both the sperm and egg you want to use to create a child in the future, you can freeze your sperm or eggs alone, rather than as part of an embryo, or purchase or obtain donor sperm/eggs before freezing. Frozen sperm can later be used for intrauterine or intracervical insemination, while frozen eggs and embryos require IVF.

Some Facebook groups for trans people planning families include *Birthing and Breast or Chest Feeding Trans People and Allies; Queer Parents Network; Non-binary Pregnancy and Parenting Support; Gender Neutral Parenting Support Group; and Transgender Parenting.*

Purchasing Sperm or Eggs from a Bank

There are many companies that collect sperm and eggs from donors so people trying to conceive are able to access them for conception. These "banks" usually have a database of donors that includes information such as their height, weight, race/ethnicity, hobbies, and more. Most banks charge a fee to view their databases, a fee to purchase the sperm or eggs, and a fee to store these materials if they will not be used right away. Some banks require the material to be sent directly to a provider's office instead of released to the person who bought it. The cost to buy sperm is usually around $1,000 per sample (this cost varies depending on many factors), and the cost to buy eggs is around $15,000 (again, this cost varies).

Some LGBTQ-friendly cryobanks include California Cryobank, Pacific Reproductive Services, Sperm Bank of California, and Seattle Sperm Bank.

Using a Known Sperm Donor

If you have a friend who produces sperm who is willing to donate, you may be interested in involving this person in your family-building process. You may also be able to save on the cost of donor sperm, although using a known donor can sometimes be just as expensive or even more expensive than buying sperm, because you may have to pay for your friend's sperm bank visits and labs. Asking friends if they'd be willing to donate sperm may feel a little awkward, but many people are very understanding about being asked when they know it's to help a family grow. Even if your friend says no, the conversations that come out of asking may lead to strengthening of a friendship.

Two children by birth—one with a man when I was 18 and one with a woman when I was 36. The second one I used a known donor from a personal ad!

Gabriel, Katherine, Charlie, and Gregory hanging on the beach in late spring.

Before you ask potential donors, be sure to think about what sort of relationship you want the donor to have with your child and family. Do you want the donor to be a co-parent, or do you want them to have a different sort of relationship? Be sure to ask the person what they want their level of involvement to be, too! It is good to research the laws in your area about known donors. If your donor does not want any legal liability for the child, or you do not want them to have parenting rights, you may need to do all inseminations through a provider's office and/or get a contract written up by a lawyer that explicitly lays out the donor's relationship with your family. Other families will choose to do home inseminations, which are typically less expensive and have less medical intervention, although home insemination may come with more legal liabilities for both parties. Even if you and the donor are close friends, and agree on the type of relationship the donor will have with the child, it is important to set the legal groundwork that will protect you and your donor. In some areas, the government will pursue child support payments from your donor if you ever apply for government aid, unless you have successfully severed the donor's legal liability.

The Known Donor Registry is a free online tool outside of the cryobank system to connect those donating sperm, eggs, or embryos to those looking for them. This can be a cheaper way to start a family, but does not ensure quality control or legal protections.

PREGNANCY

Some of us are interested in being pregnant, have a partner who is interested in being pregnant, or want to use a surrogate to build or expand our family. For any of us considering pregnancy, there are medical, logistical, and legal questions about the process of becoming pregnant, as well as emotional and psychological issues to consider. Some of us may be in partnerships that include sperm, eggs, and a uterus, while for many of us, we will need one or more from a donor or surrogate.

Transparent is not just a TV show. It is also the title of a 2005 documentary by Jules Rosskam about 19 trans men who give birth.

> *Labels are an issue. We decided to use "mom" and "he," "my mom is a guy." They still lapse into "she" when talking with family. They change to "dad" and "he" when talking with outside folk. They decide which of their friends get to know my trans status or not. It's a bit awkward if a friend doesn't know and they call me "mom."*

Artificial Insemination

If someone in the relationship has a uterus, there are a number of ways to start and carry a pregnancy. Some of these methods involve a lot of involvement from medical professionals, but some can be done at home with no intervention, or with the help of a midwife.

Intra-Vaginal Insemination

Intra-vaginal insemination (IVI) is the simplest form of conception. The partner hoping to become pregnant tracks their cycle to find out when they are ovulating (most fertile). When ovulation is occurring, sperm can be deposited into the vagina of the person with the uterus through sexual intercourse, if the sperm-producing person is present and intercourse is something both parties are OK with. Alternatively, if you have a sample of fresh or thawed sperm, you can deposit the sperm into the vagina using a clean syringe. It is important to deposit the sperm as close to the cervix (the opening to the uterus that is at the end of the vagina) as is possible. The person with the uterus, or a helpful friend or partner, can insert the sperm.

Intra-Uterine Insemination

Intra-uterine insemination (IUI) is when a sample of fresh or thawed sperm is deposited directly into the uterus by inserting a very small tube through the cervix. This procedure can be done by a midwife at home, or at a medical clinic by trained staff. It is very important that the sperm being used is "washed" to ensure no bacteria are introduced into the uterus, which could cause infection. Washed sperm is available for purchase at sperm

Image from TransFertility. (Leo Mateus)

banks, but sperm can also be washed in a clinic before the procedure. IUI is a more afford-able way to increase the chances of conception, but there is still a cost involved because it requires medical intervention. IUI cycles can cost $1,200 to $1,800 per cycle.

In-Vitro Fertilization

Another potential option for help with initiating a pregnancy is In-vitro fertilization (IVF). In IVF, the sperm and egg are introduced in a laboratory setting, then transferred into the uterus as an embryo by a healthcare professional, or stored in a cryogenic bank for later use. The egg and sperm may come from the intended parents or from anonymous or known donors. For couples who both have eggs and a uterus, reciprocal IVF may be an option. This means harvesting eggs from one partner, fertilizing with donor sperm, and then transferring the embryo into the other partner's uterus. The average cost for an IVF cycle in the United States is $12,400, according to the American Society of Reproductive Medicine, with a typical range of $10,000–$15,000 per cycle.

Queer midwives doing home IUI and providing options outside of fertility clinics include: Maia Midwifery (Seattle, Skype), Restore Midwifery (Oakland), Taproot Midwifery (Sacramento, Skype), Horizon Midwifery (Los Angeles), Motherbloom Midwifery (Austin), Mandala Midwifery (Minneapolis), and Refuge Midwifery (Philadel-phia, South Jersey, Skype).

Although IVF is considerably more expensive than other artificial insemination (AI) techniques, it is sometimes more effective, or the only viable option, for people experi-encing fertility challenges. In an IVF cycle, the goal is to harvest multiple eggs and then fertilize them in a laboratory. Without IVF or fertility drugs, most bodies with ovaries typically produce one egg per month. Because egg quality is so critical, increasing the number of eggs per cycle increases the chances of one or more eggs being viable. IVF can also be combined with ICSI, or intracytoplasmic sperm injection, where sperm is injected directly into an egg, rather than simply putting sperm and eggs together and allowing the sperm to make its way into the egg. ICSI can be particularly useful for people with compromised sperm quality. Fertilized eggs that result in embryos can be evaluated by an embryologist and in some cases genetic testing can be done on the embryos prior to transferring them into a uterus. IVF also comes with the option of transferring more than one embryo into the uterus in order to increase the chances of a live birth, but that decision should be made in consultation with a provider, because it also carries risks, such as both embryos developing and having twins, which is more stressful on the body.

Relationships and Families

LACTATION FOR TRANS PARENTS

Jacob Engelsman (he/him) is a doula and training to become an International Board Certified Lactation Consultant (IBCLC).

Lactating is an emotional experience, and the potential complications that come with being a trans-parent tend to make it more so. How will you feed your child? How will your family/friends/society react? How will this make you feel about your body? These are questions that all nursing parents must consider—and trans parents especially so. It is important to remember that if you are deciding whether to nurse your child, your own mental health takes priority. Although trans women often find nursing to be a gender-affirming experience, trans men more often report feelings of gender dysphoria. If you do decide to nurse, remember that regardless of your gender identity, whether or not you were the gestational parent of your child, or whether or not you are producing significant amounts of milk, a nursing relationship is possible and healthy for all parties involved. Nursing provides not only sustenance for the child but also increased levels of oxytocin, a hormone released by the pituitary gland, which plays a role in birth and milk production, and also produces feelings of love and happiness.

Transfeminine Breastfeeding

As of this writing, it is not possible for a transfeminine person to become pregnant (although it is worth mentioning that advances in uterine transplantation mean it may be possible in the not-too-distant future). One can induce lactation, however, through a combination of nipple and breast stimulation and taking medications/herbs. One could also provide comfort to their baby with non-nutritive sucking—when infants suck the parent's nipple reflexively for comfort instead of food. This is why babies and toddlers suck on their thumbs and fingers. There is no reason to feel that offering the baby your nipple if you are not lactating is an attempt to trick or deceive your child. If they are actually hungry and not just sucking for comfort, they will let you know! Although there are few documented cases of trans women producing enough milk to feed their baby exclusively, remember if your goal is to produce any milk at all, then even a small amount is a success. It is not uncommon for trans women to lactate spontaneously when starting or changing their hormone replacement therapy regimen. If you are having trouble producing milk, another technique is to use a supplemental nursing system (SNS). A small feeding tube is connected to a container of milk or formula at one end and the other end is taped near the nipple so the baby receives nutrients while suckling. *Breastfeeding Without Birthing*, a book by Alyssa Schnell, IBCLC, provides detailed information on the various protocols used to induce lactation.

Transmasculine Chestfeeding

Problems with lactating tend to be more emotional than physical for those on the transmasculine spectrum. Even if they have had surgery to reduce chest tissue, a transmasculine person who has recently given birth may start lactating automatically. Fortunately, they will have had several months to assess how this will make them feel and whether it is an avenue they would like to pursue. There is nothing wrong with ceasing lactation if it becomes uncomfortable. Remember, there are plenty of healthy options for feeding a baby, and a parent's mental and emotional well-being is just as important to the well-being of a child as how the child is fed. Perhaps the most well-known work on the topic of chestfeeding is Trevor MacDonald's memoir *Where's the Mother? Stories from a Transgender Dad*. It provides an account of MacDonald's transition, pregnancy, and chestfeeding relationship with his first child.

Carrying a Pregnancy

For those of us with a uterus, we may consider carrying a child ourselves. Along with all of the questions pregnancy might raise for a cisgender woman, we are likely to have questions and perspectives that are unique to being trans. We may have carried a child in the past when we had a different understanding of our own gender and wonder whether or how it will be different now. We may wonder whether we will be able to remain emotionally healthy through a year of intense female hormonal fluctuations, in addition to not taking testosterone for a year or longer, depending on how long it takes for us to get pregnant. Some of us may wonder whether pregnancy will cause heightened gender dysphoria. Others of us may approach the experience as an expression of the power of our bodies or simply something we are physically able to do, rather than as a gender-specific experience. Some of us will need to out ourselves or will be outed in spaces where we were not out before, such as our workplace, because of being visibly pregnant. For others, this may be unnecessary due to differences in our body shapes and sizes and genders. Some of us may experience more transphobia as a result of being visibly pregnant and trans. After the fact, some of us feel glad that we were able to play this role in building our family, while others would prefer never to repeat the experience, regardless of the immeasurable depth of love that we feel for our children.

> *I decided to be "mom" because I gave birth to her and pregnancy was an empowering female experience. I decided even if I passed as male and lived as a man I would still want to be "mom." As she has grown up, she has been more influenced by media and her environment than I realized she would be. I*

Transbirth.org is "a directory created to connect trans and gender nonconforming people and their families to midwives, OBGYNs, and doulas who provide welcoming care to our communities."*

was not very forthright in asserting my gender identity with her, so now (age 6) she has trouble understanding that mom is not a girl. When I told her that I had a boy soul and a girl body she laughed and said that was silly because she thought it was a joke.

It's important to provide yourself space to figure out whether pregnancy is the way you want to become a parent or expand your family. For those of us who carry our own child, doing as much as we can to build a supportive, trans-competent support system and medical team is important. Here are a few ways you can begin to do so:

- Consider an obstetrician-gynecologist (OBGYN) or midwifery practice that specializes in queer or trans health, or that has put resources into trans-competency training for the practice.
- Keep in mind that most OBGYN and midwifery practices cannot guarantee a specific person who will be on-call during your delivery, so make sure that you feel comfortable with the practice as a whole and not just one provider.
- Consider joining a support group if there are pregnancy support groups that are queer and trans friendly, potentially through a local LGBTQ center, or finding online support through Facebook groups.

Trystan Reese conducts in-person and online trainings for birthworkers who would like to learn more about working with trans clients.

Surrogacy

If you or your partner do not have a uterus, or if you do but no one is willing or able to carry a pregnancy due to medical issues or dysphoria, it is possible to find a surrogate to carry a pregnancy using the genetic material of one or both of the people who want the baby.

I want to have biological children, but I can't have kids the way I would like to. I can't get anyone pregnant, and the thought of me becoming pregnant seriously distresses me. I would not be able to handle the dysphoria that would come with pregnancy. I want to freeze my eggs and put them in a surrogate with donor sperm. In some ways I feel cheated out of having the family I want.

Surrogacy costs a great deal of money because your genetic material and/or that of your partner must be harvested and then introduced into the uterus of the surrogate through reproductive technology such as IVF. In addition, surrogacy typically includes a large payment to the surrogate for carrying the baby. Surrogacy, however, makes it possible to produce a child who is genetically related to one or both partners without either carrying the child. There are situations where a close friend or relative is willing to be a surrogate for the prospective parent(s), and so the total cost can be much lower.

The Birthing Process and Postnatal Considerations

Whether we are supporting our partner, giving birth ourselves, or intend to be present when our surrogate or gestational carrier goes into labor, the birthing process can be an intense emotional and physical journey. For those of us giving birth, our bodies may be pushed to our physical limitations at the same time we welcome new life into our family. For transgender people, it may be an even more joyful and exciting time if the birth comes after a long period of fertility challenges or attempts to build a family. It may also be complicated by having to advocate for ourselves or our partner in additional ways because of being trans.

Some trans-friendly doulas include: Jenna Brown (Austin), Charlie Monlouis (New York City), Moss Froom (Washington, DC; Baltimore), and Rainbow Doula DC (Washington, DC). Many also conduct sessions online for those not in their areas.

One of the main ways to reduce stress and advocate for our needs during and after a birth is through a birth plan, which you and/or your partner create and share with your provider and the relevant hospital staff or midwife ahead of time. A birth plan is a document in which you write out the details of what you would like to happen during and immediately after the birth. Attending childbirth education classes can be helpful in terms of providing an overview of some of the options and approaches to

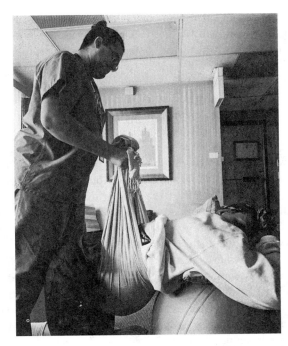

"My name is Luar and I am Full Spectrum Doula, a Certified Childbirth Educator, and a Certified Breastfeeding Counselor serving all pregnant people in their reproductive wellness. I believe in a practice that serves all gender identities as well as utilizing gender inclusive language/care/support for all clients, while operating in the framework of reproductive and birthing justice. I am a Trans NonBinary Person of Color and use They/Them and She/Her pronouns, so it is very important for me to reflect who I am into my practice to be inclusive and welcoming to folks who are on the LGBTQIA+/QTGNC+ spectrum to have access to a doula who will advocate and offer support centered in their identities."

childbirth. There are also sample birth plans on the Internet. Here are a few specific issues that you may want to include in your birth plan and discuss with your providers ahead of time:

- Include the name and pronoun you and your partner use, and other details that will be helpful for medical providers who may be at the birth but not have met you or your partner before.
- Consider hiring a trans-competent doula to be an additional advocate for you during the birth. Some doulas also provide childbirth education classes, as well as other supportive visits during your pregnancy. If you are going to hire a doula, include that in your birth plan.
- Consider what you or your partner will want to wear during the delivery and after the baby is born. Most hospitals will allow the birthing parent to wear their own clothing (unless they need surgery), so discuss this in advance.
- Decide who will hold the baby when the baby is first born. Typically, the baby is given to the birthing parent immediately after they are born, but this does not have to be the case.
- Decide how and what to feed your baby. Babies can be breastfed or chestfed, or can get formula or donor milk in a bottle, or through a Supplemental Nursing System. There are also a variety of options for who feeds your baby; for example, it is possible for some nonbirthing parents to breastfeed their baby, and it is also possible for some trans people who have had top surgery to chestfeed their baby. Nongestational parents with breasts can also induce lactation, including trans women. Discuss these options ahead of time with your partner, provider, and possibly a lactation specialist.

- Parents who want to nurse their baby but who do not produce enough milk, or who need to artificially induce lactation, can use a Supplemental Nursing System to feed their baby. These devices allow a parent to nurse their child on their chest using formula or donor milk that flows from a small container through a length of flexible narrow tubing. The baby learns to latch onto the parent's nipple while also getting milk or formula through the tube, which fits into the corner of their mouth while latched.
    - Some hospitals will supply donor milk if you make it clear that is a need ahead of time. If you want to use your own formula, find out in advance if the hospital will allow you to bring it or if you will be required to use theirs.

- It's also helpful to have a plan for the birth certificate. Be prepared for the birth certificate to use gendered language that may or may not reflect your and your partner's gender identity. Some states do provide the choice of a parent/parent designation on the birth certificate, but most still only provide a mother/father designation. Typically, the birthing parent is listed as the mother on the birth certificate, but you may have other options depending on the legal name and gender of the birth parent. You may also want to consider legal name and gender changes prior to your child's birth in order to have a birth certificate that better reflects you and your partner's preferred names and titles. You may also opt to do that after your child is born, and go through a legal process to have the birth certificate amended. If you and your partner are not both the biological parents of the child, you may opt to do a second-parent adoption after the child is born in order to add legal protections. There are additional legal steps you will need to take if you are using a surrogate. You may want to consult a lawyer well before your baby is born about how to maximize the legal protections for your family.

Birth for Every Body is an organization of midwives who provide compassionate and holistic care for people of all backgrounds, including trans clients and people of color.

- You also may want to discuss what information you will share about the conception/insemination ahead of time. You are not required to share information about sperm or egg donors or about the details of the conception or insemination with your medical providers at your birth, although you may choose to do so. For example, you may share the details of your insemination with your OBGYN, but decide not to discuss this with the staff attending the delivery.

BECOMING A TRANSGENDER OR NONBINARY BIOLOGICAL PARENT: GETTING STARTED

Hez Wollin (they/them/their) is a trans/nonbinary queer clinical social worker/therapist and healer living in the San Francisco Bay Area/Ohlone/Chochenyo Land. Hez is passionate about working with queer and trans folks going through the family-building process, as well as increasing access to gender affirming care by training mental health and medical providers in best practices. They are also a lecturer at the University of Washington School of Social Work. When Hez is not working, they enjoy making pottery, reading fiction, and spending time with loved ones (including their cat).

Are you trans or nonbinary and want to have a baby? Congratulations! You've taken the first step on a remarkable journey. There aren't too many models out there of trans folks who have gestated babies or contributed their genetic material in order to become parents, and we have our work cut out for us because of transphobia and (cis)sexism. Choosing medical providers who are trans-competent, compassionate, and knowledgeable can help make this journey a little easier. Here are some tips to help you get started:

Assemble your team. Consider reaching out to your primary care provider and asking them for a recommendation. Planned Parenthood in your area may also have some trans-competent medical providers. Additionally, sites such as *mytranshealth.com* and *transcaresite.org* allow you to search by specialty and by geographic area to find a provider.

Advocate for yourself. Ask your providers directly about their experiences working with trans and nonbinary patients on fertility and reproduction. If you feel uncomfortable with a provider, you don't have to go back to see them. Ever. It may take a little longer to put your care team together, but you deserve competent and affirming care no matter what. If you feel up for it, you can tell a professional that they mis-stepped or offended you, but it's not your job to educate your providers about your experience. This is a demanding journey, and you want to feel empowered as you are imagining your little one into being.

---

492   Relationships and Families

Don't go it alone! There are a few online support groups through Facebook that can help you to connect to others who are going through this or have been through it before. Support groups may alleviate the feelings of loneliness, with people who understand the challenges we face. Your nearest LGBTQ center may have some ideas about where to go for more support. We need to hold each other closely during this time—especially since we have to imagine alternate models of family-building than that of our straight and/or cis coworkers, friends, and family members. Finding a supportive therapist to listen to your feelings, help you make sense of it all, and be with you through this time can be relieving and empowering.

Self-compassion is key. You may experience some new feelings of dysphoria you've never experienced before. This is normal. Roll with those even though they might feel impossible at the time. Be gentle with yourself, and reach out for support as an antidote to feelings of shame and frustration. Consider what gives you life as you are trying to create life.

Under our cis-centric, binary system, we might not feel like we have a lot of choice. Remember, no matter what kinds of changes you go through in this process, you can have and deserve choice and agency around your care.

BEING A TRANS PARENT

I have a four-year-old child who was born after I began my transition. He doesn't have a strong understanding of gender, as far as I can tell, though he has lately been saying more to indicate he's working things out. He knows that there are boys, girls, and nonbinary people. He knows I am transgender. But I'm also just daddy to him, so I'd say it's going to be some time before he works it all out.

The joys and difficulties of parenting are universal, regardless of the parent's gender identity. Parenting is both a challenging and incredible experience, and our transgender identities should not subtract from that reality. As transgender people who parent, we may come up against confusion or discrimination from people who do not understand how our transgender identities can coexist with our identity as parents. It is important to remember that our experiences as transgender people can only enrich the lives of our children as we model living as our authentic selves.

I have a daughter who is 28 years old. She hasn't spoken to me in 10 years due to my transition. I send her Christmas and birthday cards every year hoping someday she'll respond. I transitioned when she was 9 on the advice she would have an easier time accepting it instead of waiting till she was a teenager. Went to therapy together for a year while I was changing. Still didn't help ease her pain of losing her mom. To this day, I sign my cards as mom, because I am always going to be. I don't give advice in this area because it's too painful for me.

What Should Our Children Call Us?

My children were very young when I transitioned. At first I asked them to call me Mommy-Daddy as a transition to Daddy. They've now called me Daddy for years.

Mom and dad can feel like gender affirming, exciting titles to take on for some trans people. But for others, being called mom or dad may feel dysphoric or part of a binary system that doesn't apply to us. Just as we should be able to live in our authentic gender identity and choose our new names and pronouns, we should also feel empowered to choose a parenting name that feels right for us. Some parents choose to go by a traditional name, some like to make up a new name, and some like to see what name their child makes up for them. Explore other languages, play with nicknames, ask friends for their ideas—there's no wrong way to pick your new name as a parent. Just make sure you like how it sounds because you'll be hearing it a *lot* from your child!

My kids are now 15 and 10. They are New York kids, so they accepted my transition but still call me "dad." I'm going to let them as it doesn't make me feel too dysphoric.

Transgender Parents is a 2014 film by Remy Huberdeau that explores parenting experiences of a number of trans people and their partners.

COLAGE is an organization for children of LGBTQ parents. COLAGE hosts a Family Week every summer in Provincetown, Massachusetts.

Paul Hill's 2003 film, *Myth of Father,* explores his relationship with his trans parent.

GENDER OPEN PARENTING

reese simpkins (he/him) and Adinne Schwartz (she/her) have been parenting their 4.5-year-old together without assigning a sex or gender. They created Theyby Parenting, an organization that supports other parents doing the same.

Within the journey of parenting, there are so many decisions to make about how to raise a child—everything from the type of diapers to the way to introduce solid food. One of the more significant decisions we made was that we didn't want to force our child into a sex or gender.

reese: As a queer trans person, I knew firsthand what it was like to be misgendered from birth, and knew I didn't want the same harm to come to our child. I also knew that our child's genitals indicated nothing essentialist about who our child could be in terms of their gender, sexual orientation, interests, or personality.

Adinne: As a queer cis person, I didn't want our child to be subjected to numerous stereotypes people would make based on our child's genitals alone, and as a trans ally, I also understood the importance of not equating sex and gender with genitals.

For these reasons, we decided to do what we call "gender open parenting" (sometimes called "gender neutral" or "gender creative" parenting). We decided to leave our child's gender and sex open for them to identify on their own terms, and to use they/them pronouns until our child decided if another pronoun fit them better.

In preparation for Emry's birth, in June 2014, we shared a zine with our community to explain how and why we were doing gender open parenting. We explained that by not assigning a sex or gender, we are letting Emry be exactly who they are from the start. Some people think that raising a child gender open means only having them wear yellow and green, but far from it! We dressed our baby in all the colors of the rainbow. We gave our baby trucks and dolls and blocks and books. The goal isn't to eliminate gender but to provide as many diverse experiences as possible to help our child discover who they are. We followed their lead and supported their interests. When people would ask us if we had a boy or a girl, we would say "We don't know—we're waiting for them to be able to tell us!" and as Emry got older, we let them know that the world is full of boys and girls and nonbinary people and we'll love whoever they are.

The journey turned out to be much simpler than we expected—we're lucky to be part of a diverse, supportive community. We didn't know anyone doing gender open parenting when Emry was first born, but here and there, we've learned about other families across the world raising their children in similar ways. Adinne started a Facebook group for parents raising children who have lovingly been nicknamed "theybies," which now has hundreds of members.

To Disclose or Not: Providers, Schools, and Friends

The YouTube channel Queer Kids Stuff has age-appropriate videos that helped along with the children's book, Red: A Crayon's Story, and the teachers at their school were receptive when I clarified my pronouns and preferred parenting terms.

Frankie Shelton-Testone, Glennda Testone, and Jama Shelton at home in Asbury Park, NJ.

For some of us, being "stealth" and simply passing as the gender we identify with is an option. For others of us, including some nonbinary people, coming out as trans may be important to avoid misgendering; for example, we may feel it is important to tell a teacher our identity and what our child calls us so the teacher is able to adjust curriculum to be more inclusive of our family structure.

I have two children and the preschooler has been the most enthusiastic about the transition. My older child doesn't get what the big deal is or why other people care. He knows what gender identity and gender expression are and that I identify as trans.

It may be important to make a child aware of our pronoun preference, our name, or other aspects of our gender that are not immediately obvious to them. Regardless of how our gender identity is perceived by a child, we may decide to come out or not to come out. This often means including our partner in a conversation about a developmentally appropriate way to do this. Coming out as trans to a child usually is not a one-time event and happens in various ways over time.

My advice is present in front of your kids as soon as possible. If that is too hard, do it in stages. I started with make-up, hat, and no hair. Then slowly introduce a wig or clothing, etc. They will adjust, and it will get better. Later in life they will thank you for being honest with them. I can't answer that for sure, but I think honesty is important in families.

CONCLUSION

T/GE and queer people have historically built families and found ways to parent, even if those were not always recognized in legal or other official ways. The scientific advancements of cryogenic preservation and other fertility techniques now provide even more reproductive opportunities than existed in the past, and, slowly, we are pushing the medical community to provide trans-competent care in all aspects of our lives, including reproductive health and fertility. There are many nontraditional ways that transgender people have created—and continue to create—families. When we use donor sperm or eggs, or foster or adopt, we continue to prove that it need not be blood that defines a family. There is no reason to deny ourselves the opportunity to become parents, if doing so is something we wish to experience.

Through talking with our children openly about gender, gender roles, and gender expression, we are empowering them with the tools they will need to navigate challenging conversations with peers about their trans family. This can only work to strengthen the bond between us and our children. We should take care to surround ourselves with friends, supporters, and allies—people we can rely on—and we should encourage our children to do the same.

NOTES

1. Special thanks to Christopher Flores-Adams, Carley Flores-Adams, and Sophia Perez-Cruz for their help on the fostering and adoption sections!
2. Amato, P. Fertility options for transgender persons. UCSF Transgender Care. https://transcare.ucsf.edu/guidelines/fertility

SECTION 5
LIFE STAGES

CHILDREN

Aidan Key and Micah Vacatio

18

INTRODUCTION

As individuals and communities who care for and engage with trans and gender expansive (T/GE) children, we have the enormous honor of encouraging and affirming their intersecting identities through support and empowerment. T/GE children who are encouraged to explore gender learn to embrace their whole selves, nurturing their ability to face adversity. Families of T/GE children, however, often experience a challenging journey in learning to support our children, as we can feel isolated and unsure of how to approach certain topics, much less how to find knowledgeable providers and other caregivers who are having similar experiences. In addition, families of T/GE children can face multiple and intersecting barriers to supporting their loved ones due to systemic mechanisms that organize the distribution of power and resources differentially across lines of race/ethnicity, gender identity, gender expression, class, sexual orientation, ability, and other dimensions of identity. Therefore, there are a wide variety of factors to consider when supporting T/GE children. Above all else, the most important task is unconditional love and acceptance of all children for their whole selves.

This chapter is written for parents, families, and other caregivers who are supporting trans or gender expansive children before the onset of puberty. Chapter 19 (Youth) explores issues that may arise for young people entering puberty, specifically adolescents and teenagers.

RECOGNIZING T/GE CHILDREN

Many caregivers have an idea early on that the child they are raising is transgender or gender expansive based on the child's toy or clothing preferences, playmates, or specific identity statements. For others, it can be a shock to hear a child say they do not identify with the gender they were assigned at birth. Although there is no checklist to determine a child's gender identity, we can do our best to pay attention and to listen to T/GE children as closely as possible. They may say things like:

- *I'm not a boy, I'm a girl.*
- *God made a mistake. I am supposed to be a girl.*
- *When is my penis going to grow in?*
- *Why do they keep calling me a girl? I'm a boy.*
- *I don't want to be a mother—I want to be a father!*

Common behaviors families have observed from their children who later identify as T/GE adults include:

- Expressing anger at a parent for "correcting" someone who perceives the child to be a gender other than the gender assigned at birth
- Allowing or encouraging other children to believe they are a different gender

Bailey McCafferty (they/them) is 7 years old and wants to live in a double decker tree house one day with their tiger friend.

- Announcing to parents, family, and friends that they have a new name that is typically associated with another gender
- Adopting the identity of an animal such as a dog, bear, or kitten, or a fictional creature like a unicorn or dragon, in order to have a nongendered identity and experience

These behaviors are certainly not the sole indicators of a child's gender identity but could point to a T/GE identity that should be actively addressed and explored.[1] Identity rejection can result in depression, low self-esteem, self-harming behavior, and even suicidality. Many times, none of the aforementioned examples are evident. Some parents feel blindsided when, seemingly out of nowhere, their child announces that they are T/GE and that they wish to change genders. It is not uncommon for a parent to say that there were no signs at all.

Supporting a T/GE child while they navigate their gender can feel like a huge decision for most adults. It can be even more difficult to consider that there may not be a definitive endpoint. A child's gender may actually be a blend of genders, or that child may experience gender fluidity that changes often, even day to day. Some important points to consider include the following:

- Children do the best they can with the words available to them. It is important to understand that binary language such as boy/girl, masculine/feminine, and pink/blue offer children restrictive words with which it may be difficult to describe the full spectrum of their experience.
- Some children have a gender identity that is a bit of both girl and boy, neither, or one in which they experience varying degrees of fluidity.
- Gender, like life, can be a journey, not a destination.
- Gender does not exist in a vacuum. Two questions any T/GE person faces are "Who am I?" and then "Who am I in relation to the world?"

When a T/GE child does not make a definitive statement such as "I am really a boy," or "I am really a girl," it is difficult for many of us to know what to do. In some cases, caregivers cling to fluidity as an indicator that the child is not really T/GE. In other cases, they may ignore the child's statements that they feel themselves to be a blend of genders and press the child onward to a gender transition before they are ready, or when this is not the child's desire. Both scenarios are ways to relieve the adult's discomfort with uncertainty. Day by day, it is important to be mindful and fully present for the sake of the child.

DEAD NAME

Lucia (she/her), age 10, loves soccer and naked mole rats. She lives with a loving family and her dogs, Fredge and Skronk.

I had a name that wasn't mine
I had clothes I didn't want
I had a body I did not like
I had feelings nobody knew about

I had a name that wasn't mine
But that was my dead name
Now myself is more like me
Now I'm a she and not a he

For more on how to create a supportive environment for children exploring their gender, check out Diane Ehrensaft's book, *The Gender Creative Child: Pathways for Nurturing and Supporting Children Who Live Outside Gender Boxes* (The Experiment Publishing, 2016).

IS THIS A PHASE?

One of the questions most commonly asked by caregivers, teachers, and counselors is whether gender nonconformity could be a phase. The simplest answer, at any given moment, is, "We don't know." The only way to really determine whether a child's interests are short-term is to allow the passage of time. Experts often refer to the presence of an insistent, consistent, and persistent gender identification over time when determining whether a child is experimenting or stating a stable identity. This means the more insistent a child is, and the longer that insistence lasts, the less likely they are to change their mind about their gender identity and/or expression. Whether a child, who may or may not be T/GE, is going through a phase, is not really the point. What's important is a nonjudgmental and supportive response during all the stages of the child's gender journey. This affirming approach lets them know they are loved, heard, and supported unconditionally.[2]

The gender-affirming model of care increases the psychosocial well-being of T/GE children.[3] In recent research with T/GE youth, those who reported their immediate family as being encouraging and supportive of their gender identity and expression in childhood endorsed more positive overall mental health, fewer depressive symptoms, higher self-esteem, and greater overall life satisfaction in later adolescence compared with those whose families were nonsupportive.[4,5] Equally important, in a gender affirmative model, gender identity and expression are given license to unfold over time, as a child matures, allowing for fluidity and change. Hold space for your child to listen to their own inner self, and consider the following:

- A child may identify as another gender early in life because they have not had the freedom to explore and express their gender. If a child is provided greater latitude to step outside of restrictive gender expectations, they may find their gender assigned at birth is not limiting.
- A child may recognize the distress of others and take self-sacrificing steps to decrease or eliminate that distress even if it is at their own expense. If a child feels that their parents will not love them, or that their parents might divorce over the issue, they may be scared enough to minimize the importance of their own needs.

"Jodie Patterson and Tiq Milan live in Brooklyn with 3 of Patterson's 5 children where she co-raises them with love, education and family solidarity. Jodie is an author and activist, holding the position of Chair of the Human Rights Campaign Foundation Board, our nation's largest LGBT organization."

- Some T/GE children have experienced daily bullying and violence and can see no other way to make it stop except to "go back." Others find that they are isolated or rejected by their peers at school or within their neighborhood and understand that if they compromise their own identity, they may regain some of that acceptance and inclusion they so deeply desire.

- Children who feel themselves to be more fluid in their gender identity may find difficulty "landing" on a single gender. Our current options of either "male" or "female" may feel limiting. If a parent or counselor does not recognize a T/GE child's gender-fluid identity and a child is restricted by only two options, that child may feel like they have no choice but to "settle" for one over the other, finding neither one to be a perfect fit.

SEARCHING FOR AN ANSWER

Many parents ask themselves, "Have I somehow caused this?" The search for a definitive answer is natural, but the answers are elusive and the search itself can be potentially quite damaging. It can cause rifts between parents (assigning "blame," for example) and cause parents extreme amounts of guilt and shame. Although we do have some basic understanding about the origins of gender identity development (explored in Chapter 6), we have a way to go before we can make conclusive determinations.[6] There are those who might consider gender and sexuality differences to be somehow unnatural, but this ignores the interactive complexity of human body development, brain differentiation, and external influences. We cannot control whether a child will or will not be trans or gender expansive, but we can change how they will navigate the world—whether they will be proud of themselves, take care of their health, and retain close connections with their families.

GENDER IDENTITY VERSUS SEXUALITY

The difference between gender identity and sexual orientation is important to think about in relation to children. Assuming that a child is dealing with an issue of sexuality when, in actuality, the difference is related to gender expression, can result in a caregiver missing

Life Stages

a chance to connect with the child and support them. The best approach is to be open and affirming of any gender expression that children seem to be exploring without making assumptions about the child's sexuality.

Talking about gender with children is different than talking about sexuality. Conversations about gender are appropriate for children of all ages. For the most part, issues of sexuality can be saved for the beginning of adolescence, but there are many non-sexual ways to talk with children of all ages about attraction, relationships, and families. We can talk with children about same-sex and different-sex couples and explain that some men love other men, or some women love other women, laying the groundwork for healthy conceptions of both gender and relationships.

HOW CHILDREN UNDERSTAND GENDER

The ways in which children understand the concept of gender are closely linked to their age, race/ethnicity, language, culture, and developmental level, as well as their exposure to information.[7] As children, teens, and then as adults, we learn many things about the world, including our current framework of gender. To understand the world in the same way the adults in their lives do, children must learn these same concepts. For example, in the United States, we, as adults, primarily experience two genders in the world. We then equate the genders of male and female with particular body parts. We also understand that (without hormones or surgeries) our bodies will remain the same with respect to those body parts. We know that people have certain expectations placed on them because they have either "male" parts or "female" parts. Children do not come into the world knowing these things. Many children grow up in different cultures around the world that have gender roles and identities that are much more expansive than the typical western European framework. Dual-gender and third gender identities are prevalent in communities across the globe throughout Asia, the Americas, Africa, Australia, and some places in Europe. Although many of these differing gender identities are now stigmatized, in part due to western colonization, this was not always the case. Preservation of these nonbinary identities is vital to our global understanding of the long-standing acknowledgment and acceptance of nonbinary gender identities.

The award-winning film, *Kuma Hina*, is a documentary exploring the Māhū culture of Hawai'i through the experiences of a teacher and student.

EXPLORING GENDER

Identity exploration is a natural part of all childhood. This includes exploring bodies, language, clothing, games, and music. An exploration in clothing choices, where a child seemingly "crosses" gender lines, may not be about that child's gender identity. It might simply have to do with the child's color preferences or a tactile interest in certain fabric textures. Some children are very imaginative, while others are physically active; some are emotionally expressive, while others are introverted. These are not characteristics of gender but are qualities of being human. Exploring identity and how to express that identity is a natural part of the healthy development of any child. Gender expression is simply one aspect of that exploration.[8]

Toys, colors, clothing, hairstyles, and activities do not have a gender of their own. They are given a gender designation by our society. A girl may have a preference for pants and a boy may enjoy wearing a dress. Neither outfit will "make" a child desire to change their gender. For a child, it is the arbitrary societal rules assigning gender to nongendered items that are confusing.

> *My dad said that boys don't belong in the kitchen. That makes me sad because I really love to cook with my grandma. She's sad, too.—9-year-old T/GE boy in chapter author Aidan Key's third-grade classroom discussion of gender*

This chapter uses affirming language. A "T/GE boy" refers to a child assigned female at birth who identifies as male, while a "T/GE girl" is a child assigned male at birth who identifies as female.

Emotions do not belong to one gender over another. Our society values toughness and resiliency in boys, but these qualities are beneficial for girls as well. Sensitivity to others is encouraged in girls, but boys could benefit from it, too. These propensities are attributes of a well-balanced child. For a child to develop strong mental health, it is important to allow that child to experience the full array of emotional expression.

Magic catman. (Evan, age 9)

GENDERQUEER

Aiden (they/them) is a high school student in Franklin, Tennessee. They're a GLSEN SHINE team member who is passionate about LGBTQ youth activism and is on a seemingly infinite quest to start a GSA (Gender and Sexuality Alliance) at their school. They are a science nerd who enjoys Star Wars and Doctor Who.

I have a very distinct memory of my eight-year-old self sitting alone on the playground, watching the boys and girls around me. *I'd rather be a boy. But I don't mind being a girl. Well, maybe I don't want to be a boy. But I also don't want to be a girl.* This mental tug-of-war continued until I decided it didn't matter anyway because I was a girl, and that was that. Nobody had told me I could be a boy if I wanted or that I could be neither boy nor girl. That was never an option until it was.

I've known I was genderqueer since age eight, and I've known about genderqueer as an identity since sixth grade, but I didn't connect *genderqueer* with *my identity* for a long time. I blame this paradox on the popular trans narratives that society loves to promote: that the trans experience is an experience of pain, of being trapped in the wrong body, of a cosmic mistake, of a life of suicidal ideation and suffering until medical transition can finally be achieved. While I do experience dysphoria, I've never felt particularly "trapped in the wrong body," because what is the right body? According to many cis people, a trans person's "right body" is always an unachievable and picturesque body of the "opposite sex." If that's true, then what is the right body for nonbinary individuals? These narratives used to assure me that I couldn't possibly be trans, because I've never been consumed by self-hatred or daydreamed of another body. What I did feel was a subtle discomfort when called "she," a strange disconnect from my birth name, and an occasional wish that I wasn't a girl. None of that could possibly be enough to make me trans, right?

My criticism of this narrative isn't meant to dismiss anyone whose experiences align with what I've described. I aim only to present an alternative narrative—one that allows me to admit and accept who I am. I didn't cry when I first bound my chest or heard my chosen name, but I did finally feel *comfortable*. Comfortable enough to do my homework and hang out with friends without also lending headspace to my gender identity. If I'm sad or stressed on any given day, it's probably because of my Spanish grade and not some cosmic mistake to which I have fallen victim.

IMPACT ON FAMILY

Most caregivers feel considerably uprooted upon first learning of their child's gender status. Although they may not be able to specifically articulate why, we should not dismiss the significance of their response. Almost without exception, this will be uncharted terrain for caregivers as well as for any spouse, sibling, extended family member, friend, or coworker. Most parents are not able to imagine any positive outcome for their child or within their family. Supporting a child's gender journey can bring about stress, hardship, and volatility for everyone. It might seem obvious to state that anti-T/GE bias is at the source of everyone's distress; yet, it doesn't end there. The fears a white parent might experience may include the potential bullying and ostracism of their T/GE boy, while the parent of a Black T/GE girl may be petrified that their child will not even make it to adulthood due to the astronomical violence directed at T/GE Black women. Social class also has an influence, because families with greater resources and/or education have more direct access to knowledgeable T/GE providers and ability to pursue and prevail in legal battles. They may even be able to make geographic moves to find a more supportive environment in which to raise their child.

The intersections of both external and internalized cissexism, heterosexism, racism, sexism, xenophobia, and other oppressions make for deeply complicated pathways for which very few have the road map. Systems of oppression and privilege occur simultaneously and serve to provide opportunities for some and barriers for others. Inequality is multidimensional and requires multidimensional measures and interventions. Medical providers, counselors, educators, and others who are connected with any particular family should have a compassionate, encompassing approach, recognizing that an entire family system is in need of their full support.

The family acceptance project® is directed by Dr. Caitlin Ryan at the Marian Wright Edelman Institute at San Francisco State University, where multiple studies have suggested that family acceptance is a key resilience factor in reducing suicidality, substance abuse, depression, anxiety, and other mental health stressors for LGBTQ youth.

STAGES OF ACCEPTANCE FOR CAREGIVERS

Parents can experience a high degree of mixed emotions in relation to their T/GE children's gender expression and identity. In families with two parents, one parent may experience hope and optimism, while the other parent is resistant, only to find that they switch experiences later on. Seeking out parent support groups or individual or family counseling can be extremely valuable in learning how to acknowledge all of the family's needs.

Even parents who are supportive of their T/GE children can experience conflicting feelings, given that it may not be easy, especially at the beginning, to support and advocate for a T/GE child. In addition, caregivers of T/GE children come from all walks of life—liberal and conservative, religious and atheist, wealthy and working class, able-bodied and disabled, and from all races, ethnicities, and cultures. Gender expectations and gender roles are often deeply intertwined with these other identities, and it is rare to find parents who do not need to reexamine their own hearts and minds as they move into acceptance and support of their T/GE children. Not all parents of T/GE children process in the same ways, but there are some common stages that many caregivers experience.

Denial and Fear

Rarely will you encounter a family that, at least initially, considers it a blessing to have a T/GE child. Part of being a good parent is keeping your child fed, warm, and safe from harm. Although attitudes are changing, T/GE people have historically experienced ridicule, ostracism, contempt, and violence. What parent wants to support their child's innate gender identity and expression when the repercussions of this "acceptance" can lead to such social marginalization? It is no wonder that many parents, teachers, counselors, and others who are caring for these children are fearful.

Denying the presence of a gender identity difference is quite common. Many parents point to their child's level of femininity or masculinity as proof that their child is not really T/GE. For example, if their child is active in Boy Scouts, on the basketball team, and has

Families of T/GE children each have their own journeys. To read about some of them, pick up a copy of Rachel Pepper's *Transitions of the Heart: Stories of Love, Struggle and Acceptance by Mothers of Transgender and Gender Variant Children* (Cleis Press, 2012).

Jaime and Dempsey. "My daughter is love, light, happiness and hope - it all just radiates from within."

a girlfriend, they may insist that it is impossible for their child to identify as a girl. This parent has made the mistake of equating their child's gender expression with their gender identity. Of course, a child can like the Scouts (embrace group activities), play basketball (enjoy team sports), and like girls (have a lesbian sexual orientation). Another form of denial can include hanging tightly to the belief that a child is going through a "phase." Very common explanations for children's behaviors include the following:

- She'll do anything for attention!
- This is just one more thing in a long list of things he's done to drive us crazy!
- This is a "white" thing!
- This gender stuff isn't her issue—she is easily influenced by friends and always dives into new things without thought.

Coming to terms with a T/GE child's identity can be heartbreaking for some parents and much easier for others. It takes a caring, brave caregiver to embrace and support a child when the fear of societal judgment and stigmatization can be so high.

Grief

Those who champion the cause of a child they know and love may be quite surprised to discover they have profound grief. On one hand, they recognize the value of support and may even see immediate improvements in both temperament and self-esteem of their T/GE child. On the other hand, this was a child they loved—deeply—for exactly who they perceived them to be. Despite the living, breathing presence of their child, the loss is present and is important to acknowledge. Moving through grief allows for a person's sense of loss, and it also makes room for the rediscovery of hopes and dreams.

Although everyone's experience is different, there can be an even deeper sense of grief for parents whose T/GE children are older. This may simply be because they have had a greater number of years raising their child, cultivating particular visions of their child's future family and legacy. They may believe these dreams are unattainable now that their child is T/GE. Therefore, learning to use new names and/or pronouns, not to mention discarding any gender-influenced hopes and dreams for that child, is very painful. Additionally, older T/GE children may request to remove family photos from the walls, or get rid of any other evidence of the gender that caused them so much anguish. It is not an exaggeration to say that, for some parents and other family members, it can feel like a death in the family.

Guilt

In a culture that has not provided gender options beyond "male" and "female" and operates on the assumption that anatomy equals gender, most adults raising T/GE children take this gender "truth" for granted. Many parents feel guilty about not seeing their child's gender nonconformity, and many judge themselves for not listening to their child earlier.

> *My five-year-old trans daughter is struggling with the fact that people keep telling her that she "used to be a boy." Her response is anger and frustration, and she says, "No, I was ALWAYS a girl." When I tried talking with her about this, explaining that we had "made a mistake" when we assumed she was a boy, she got really angry. I realized how hard it is for her that we didn't understand earlier that she wasn't a boy. I told her that it was OK to be angry and apologized that I had been mistaken in her gender. She is obviously having a hard time with this, and clearly feeling betrayed and frustrated. I don't see how I could have known sooner, but really, should I have been able to see this? She certainly thinks so and the pain and hurt in her eyes is hard to see. I am feeling so guilty. It breaks my heart that I have unwittingly hurt her.—Mother from a Gender Diversity support group*

Not every parent will experience all the emotions expressed here. There are as many ways for a parent to respond to a child's gender journey as there are parenting styles. Feelings that are sometimes considered negative are an important part of a parent's process of acceptance. Parents and other family members need time and space to express denial, anger, grief, and fear before they are able to step into acceptance, support, and advocacy for their children. A parent can be fully supportive while deeply wishing their child's gender "issues" would just disappear.

Acceptance and Willingness

Increased distress experienced by a T/GE child is often what propels a caregiver to finally seek outside help. T/GE children readily perceive and internalize pressure from peers, reprimands from parents or teachers, reproachful looks, and disapproving comments. This can result in the child having angry outbursts, elevated frustration, increased anxiety, depression, withdrawal, violent behavior, and threats of or actual self-harm. For many adults, this distressing behavior from a T/GE child can launch them from a place of resistance to one of acceptance (which sometimes begins as resignation.) The bottom line is that we do not want to see our children in pain. Regardless, it is necessary to become willing to take the next step—to accept the child as they are and identify the ways in which they may need support.

HBO's documentary series *15: A Quinceañera Story* features a young trans woman, Zoey Luna, whose quinceañera serves as both a welcoming to adulthood and a gender-affirming coming out ceremony.

Celebration and Gratitude

As parents roll up their sleeves to learn more and get past early confusion and fear, they quite often come to a place of delight and gratitude for the positive changes in their T/GE child's life, as well as their own. While agreeing that it is challenging, and sometimes painful, many parents ultimately declare they would not have had it any other way. They recognize their child as an amazing and beautiful gift—someone who teaches them about bravery, authenticity, and acceptance. Many name their child as the hero in their lives.

> *If you had told me a year ago that I would be the proud parent of a trans boy, I would have told you you were crazy! Now I can honestly say that it's the best thing that ever happened to me!—Father of a 10-year-old trans boy at a Gender Diversity parent support group*

Vivian, age 4, swimming in the Wenatchee River.

This may be a time of celebration and public affirmation of the child's gender, which can be supported by reclaiming cultural, social, and religious spaces. Revisiting "coming-of-age" ceremonies in a T/GE context can bridge a person's cultural heritage with their gender identity, all the while increasing social consciousness and reducing stigma within the communities in which they were raised. Examples of these ceremonies are Jewish Bar and Bat Mitzvahs; Mexican/Chicanx/Latinx Quinceañeras; Japanese Seijin-no-Hi ceremonies; Chinese Confucian traditions of Ji Li and Guan Li; the Apache Nation Sunrise Ceremony; and Indian Ritu Kala Samskara, to name just a few. Whatever comprises your family's celebration, ritual, or rite-of-passage, consider helping your child to embrace it as their true self.

> We wanted to share some good news. While our child's name was legally changed a long time ago, there were still missing connections with the community that he grew up in. Recently, we decided to do a "Naming Ceremony" in Indian Tradition. A priest from temple came to our house and performed the ceremony. This is the ceremony we usually do when kids are born. We felt it made perfect sense to do it now for a fresh start and integrating with society again. Close family and friends attended this and everyone felt so good. We're so glad we did this!—Letter from a Gender Diversity support group family

Keep in mind that naming or coming-out ceremonies centered around family or community may not be available to everyone. Coming out to one's family or community can create unsafe situations for some. For example, trans people of color may deal with both racism within LGBTQ communities and cissexism within communities of color, leading them to feel conflict between their identities. This conflict can give rise to internalized shame and anti-T/GE bias, thus reducing or eliminating the celebration of gender affirmation.[9] Parents, caregivers, families, schools, and communities need to expand their notions of gender and challenge societal norms by creating affirming spaces for all children along the continuum of gender expression.[10]

Life Stages

Suzanne Opp (she/her)

As the mother of a young adult who came out as a transgender woman last year, I have had to confront my own perceptions and constructs of what that means for her, me, my spouse, and her siblings. Just as no coming out story is the same, our family ripple is surely different also.

When she first came forward, I did everything to support and help make external changes—the "logistics." A new haircut, manicure, make-up tutorials, finding a hormone doctor, shopping for clothes, attending as many pride events as possible, and so on. All the trappings of what I perceived to be "womanly." Being what I have always thought of as progressive, this was the easy part.

But, more deeply, it was staggering to feel the radical seismic shift in the foundation of what I thought of as family. I was shocked and surprised by my own emotional reaction, and the level of grief and regret that came in those early months.

It was not only *her* identity that was becoming more authentic to her, but my own identity which needed to transform in order to become aligned. As a mother of four boys, this challenged everything in my parenting up until then. I was absolutely unprepared and blindsided by the amount of processing it took for me. Of course none of that is to minimize the extraordinary efforts my daughter faces daily.

Then, as the holidays approached, our usual greeting card task loomed ahead and I struggled with exactly how to convey the news to more extended family and acquaintances. Ultimately, we all dressed in various shades of pink, and created a simple statement, which may help provide wording inspiration for other families as they move through this remarkable passage:

> *You may have noticed the pink . . . We've had a big change in our family and wanted to express solidarity. After much soul searching, our number two child has realized an incongruent gender. We would like to take the opportunity to introduce you to Ellie. It's been an extraordinary journey so far. But the only thing consistent in life is change, growth, and transformation. We thank you in advance for your kind thoughts, prayers, and support as our family undergoes this adjustment.*

Happily, our friends and family have been completely compassionate and lovingly accepting. I wish the same for other families who are sharing their own story.

T/GE-AFFIRMING PARENTING

It can be difficult to set clear boundaries and expectations for a T/GE child while working through the many different emotions a parent or guardian experiences. It is important to recognize that consistent, strong parenting, on all issues (gender-related or otherwise) provides children with feelings of security and safety.[11] Ideas for maintaining consistent parenting in gender-related areas include:

- Do not use gender-related care as a reward for good behavior or as punishment for bad behavior. Acknowledgment, support, and transition-related care are not items to dangle in front of a child in order to encourage good behavior, nor are they things to withdraw in the case of bad behavior. A parent would not withhold medical or mental health treatment if a child brought home bad grades. Gender-related care should be no different.
- Do not use your T/GE child as a sounding board for your distress, grief, anger, or confusion. Parents can have a hard time navigating their feelings regarding their child's gender identity or expression. This can be compounded by the fact that so many have to navigate their feelings in isolation. The lack of societal understanding, difficulty finding an experienced therapist, spousal conflicts, and loss of friendships and other bases of support can leave a parent with only one outlet for their feelings—their child. This is not the appropriate outlet. Children can and do internalize the challenging feelings expressed by their parents and feel guilty, responsible, shameful, anxious, and confused. A parent should find an adult with whom they can address their feelings. Keep looking until you find a supportive, caring person or group who can help you care for your own heavy heart, but do not burden your child with it.

- When confused about what to do, take gender out of the equation. Because the "gender issue" can take center stage in a family's life, sometimes for a lengthy period of time, it is easy for a parent, teacher, or counselor to assume gender is a factor in situations where it may not be. This can result in overexplaining, defensiveness when none is needed, and an inability to see solutions to problems. One way to address a situation where the solution is not clear is to frame a scenario where gender is removed as a factor. Imagine if the T/GE child of a friend were in a similar situation. What advice would you give to that parent? Replace the gender piece with another aspect of identity. Does that help develop a better perspective or solution?

When Parenting Approaches Differ

Depending on their upbringing, socioeconomic status, cultural ideals, and experience with oppression, parents may have differing positions on raising their T/GE child.[12] With this in mind, it is important for each parent or member of the child's care team to get in touch with both sides of the "accept/adapt" equation as the first step to improving family unity. When parents are more unified, they can make decisions with, instead of against, each other. This informs an affirmative approach where parents realize that acceptance translates to the best care, protection, and advocacy for their T/GE child.[13] Some considerations for parents who are coming into conflict within themselves or toward each other about parenting styles include:

Some affirmative spaces for parent support include Trans Families (transfamilies.org), Gender Diversity (genderdiversity.org), Transforming Family (transformingfamily.org), and the Gender Odyssey Conference (genderodyssey.org).

- Seek out a counselor skilled in negotiating parental conflict as well as one who is familiar with T/GE children.
- Approach differences of opinion with mutual trust that each parent comes from the same foundation of wanting what is best for their T/GE child.
- Recognize that each parent may have their own timeline for understanding T/GE issues, navigating personal barriers, and making determinations on the best course of action for their T/GE child. For example, one parent may need to move faster than they might like while the other could consider slowing their pace, ideally allowing everyone the ability to move forward as a family.
- Know that the T/GE child's distress may override any timetable or course of action that the parents decide. If you have a child considering self-harm, waste no time getting professional help and put the needs of your child first and foremost.
- Reflect on the timeline of a T/GE child's gender expression and identity. If your child has consistently asserted their gender presentation over time, do not try to convince the other parent (or yourself) that your child is going through a phase. Days, weeks, or even a few months may constitute a phase. A year or more is significant and should not be dismissed.
- Invite both parents to seek information, knowledge, and resources. If one parent has more knowledge on the issue than the other, it can create an even wider chasm when important decisions need to be made.
- Set aside relationship differences as much as possible. For parents who are divorced or separated, know that bringing a T/GE child's gender into a courtroom can serve to prolong the proceedings and can be painful to experience as courts seek to educate themselves on what, for many, is still a very unfamiliar topic.

Seeking Support

One of the first steps that many parents take when realizing their child is T/GE is to search for others who are grappling with the same issues or find service providers who have experience working with T/GE children. It can be lonely and isolating to face these issues on our own, and many people make wonderful connections that enhance their ability to be the best caretakers possible.

Self portrait by Milo, age 7.

Parent Support Groups and Children's Play Groups

Several organizations provide support for families through in-person groups for both parents and T/GE children. Ideally, a parent group occurs at the same time and place, in a separate room, from the children's group. Some children's groups have volunteers who engage children in imaginative play while guardians have time to express their fears, frustrations, and triumphs to understanding ears. Other parent groups have e-mail lists and chat rooms that provide online connections for those who live far away from in-person groups. As T/GE children grow older, there are also online resources for them. In addition, annual conferences like Gender Odyssey provide places for parents to connect with one another and for children to meet and play with other gender diverse children.

Nurturing Resilience

One of the greatest gifts we can give a T/GE child is to help them build their emotional and psychological resilience. Resilience is the capacity to cope with adversity, stress, and other negative events. The world can be a tough place for a T/GE child, even those children whose families are fully supportive. Therefore, it is critical to build healthy coping skills. If a T/GE child is aware of how they feel and has the tools to move through their intense emotions, they will have acquired a skill that will last a lifetime. In order to help children recognize their emotions, we, as adults, need to spend time thinking about the underlying causes for a child's emotions and talking to them about how to identify their feelings. Many times, an angry outburst actually comes from a place of fear or shame.

In addition to teaching children about their own emotions, we have to teach them about the emotions of others. T/GE children who are taught that insensitive comments often result from ignorance can be sad and disappointed but also compassionate. It is important that we guide our children toward a place of understanding informed by empathy. By developing this practice, a child can better activate self-regulating and coping skills, have healthy boundaries, build strong connections, practice self-care, be less impulsive, be willing to understand the needs of others, appreciate uniqueness and genuine expression, not engage in bullying, and have enhanced self-esteem and self-worth.

As adults, we can model this kind of resiliency when dealing with comments from other adults in front of children. We should be ready to address or deflect comments in ways that show confidence and support for a T/GE child. If we are having difficulty doing this, it can be important for us to spend time talking with family members, friends, or our own mental health providers about the feelings we are having, while continuing to model appropriate responses for our children.

Teaching Body Awareness and Affirmation

Many, but not all, T/GE children have negative relationships with their bodies, or specific parts of their bodies, feeling a sense of betrayal that their bodies are not in alignment with how they feel. These T/GE children may have an extremely difficult time developing attuned body awareness. Efforts should be made from an early age to encourage T/GE children to participate in dance, sports, martial arts, or any other activities that can serve to put them in touch with their bodies and gain a sense of pride in their bodies' accomplishments. Encourage T/GE children to explore what their body can do at different stages of development. Talk about the importance of loving their body and taking care of it. Additionally, remind them that all bodies are different, unique, and special.

While we work toward greater societal acceptance of gender expansiveness, what can any parent or caregiver do to best support a T/GE child's relationship with their body? One simple step can be to stop assigning a gender designation to specific body parts. If a T/GE girl is told that the sole reason she is not a girl is that she has a penis, it is understandable that she may come to see her penis as what invalidates her core identity. Many young children immediately find it relieving to hear that some girls have penises and some boys have vulvas.

Parents often worry about T/GE children experiencing dysphoria in relation to their bodies. Cisgender parents of T/GE children can feel helpless in this because they feel they cannot personally relate to their child's experience. It is often assumed that a child will have some level of body dysphoria simply because they are T/GE. This is not a given. There are some unique differences to consider, but the reality is that unhappiness with one's body is experienced by many children and to varying degrees.[14] A child may be distressed with their skin, hair, height, the shape of their nose, weight, level of attractiveness, and so on. Parents can take steps to improve and empower their child's relationship with their body by:

- Playing an active role in encouraging T/GE body positivity and acceptance. All bodies are different! Many people later embrace the very differences that once caused them distress. Share the stories of people with a wide array of bodily differences. Let children see how others address these differences and accompanying challenges. Help them draw parallels to their own lives.
- Teaching them how to address inappropriate questions from others, such as: "Please don't discuss my private parts" or "My parents say that I don't have to answer that kind of question." You can also instruct them to simply walk away and find a supportive adult.
- Helping T/GE children understand that adults and kids alike are often unaware that people with diverse gender identities exist. At the very least, a child can recognize that ignorance is at play rather than internalizing a message that there is something inherently wrong with them.
- Finding opportunities for a T/GE child to engage with other T/GE children and teens. It is too easy to hate one's body if one believes no one else has that kind of body or experience.
- Finding physical activities that provide a T/GE child with empowering ways to engage with their bodies. Sporting opportunities are not the only way nor are all

Founded by an 11-year-old trans girl, Ruby, and her father, RUBIES sells form-fitting clothing, including bathing suits, for trans girls.

children interested in or physically able to participate in competitive activities. Also consider things such as yoga, dog-walking, dancing at home, playing at the park, or martial arts. Getting outside and limiting screen time is crucial for all children and, although these activities may not entirely eliminate a T/GE child's body distress, they can certainly decrease it.

TYEF: THE TRANSGENDER YOUTH SUMMER CAMP EXPERIENCE

Susan Maasch (she/her) is the director of TYEF Camps through the Trans Youth Equality Foundation.

In 2010, the Trans Youth Equality Foundation (TYEF), an advocacy organization for trans youth, began a youth camp. In those days, we knew of only one other camp for trans youth, and it had also just begun. We knew that trans youth needed an intensive and immersive experience with one another. They need to feel what it's like to not be the only trans person in a cisgender world. They need to feel the company of others—both campers and staff—on a real, cellular level. We began with a dozen kids in a rented house in Maine and held it one or two times a year. It was a hit from the start. Campers came from all over: Florida, Maryland, Texas, Ohio, New York, and every New England state.

Eventually our camp got so big we began to rent a large formal camp at a university. This was a significant camp with zip lining, kayaking, mountain climbing, swimming, and more. Kids returned each year. Many came more than once a year. TYEF camp is magical. By 2019, after moving on to a smaller camp site in New England, we completed our 13th camp. We have watched kids grow up, and many are now in college, done with college, and even counselors at camp.

Many refer to TYEF camp as *lifesaving*, which is different than just fun, though we do have a blast! A. J., one of our youth, sent the following testimonial: "Thank you Susan Maasch and Trans Youth Equality Foundation for having me back for my third camp this summer! (This time as a counselor!) I am proud to openly live as a trans woman and help this amazing organization, which saved my life in high school." We know that many come to camp feeling isolated and with few friends. Though this is not everyone's experience, it is for many, and camp allows them to build community. The best part is the lifelong relationships that have been built.

We decided early on that gathering trans and nonbinary kids without addressing their specific and unique needs would be a lost opportunity. Trans kids learn so much about their journey online. We incorporated workshops, and kids know when they sign up that this is part of camp. Some of our workshops include: Know your Legal Rights (most often offered by GLAD Boston), Know Your Medical Rights, How We Relieve Dysphoria, Sex Education Non-Cis Style, and general support groups.

We always note that when it is time to attend a workshop none of the kids complain or roll their eyes. Kids want this content. It helps them grow. In support groups, kids open up and share their most personal stories. I believe they feel safe because we create a safe and healthy atmosphere. We give them the chance to feel at home. This is where deep friendships are formed. The youth experience an all-trans environment with people who accept them, who love them, and who are living their own best lives.

Joy is in the shared experience of being in nature, playing games, singing, laughing, and connecting. We want to thank all past and present allies who helped us build one of the first and most fabulous all-trans camps in the country. We have trained other camps and want to spread our model by training groups elsewhere to start a trans camp where they are. The need is great.

Discussing Sexuality

Just because a T/GE child is not yet sexually active does not mean their parents are free from worry about their child's future relationships. Dating, bodies, disclosure, sex, and safety weigh heavily on the minds of caregivers even though sexual experiences may be years away. A good deal of resources are available on the Internet and in bookstores that can offer great guidance on age-appropriate conversations with young children about sex. Conversations should happen in a calm, matter-of-fact manner. How a parent talks to a three-year-old about where babies come from will be much simpler than the conversation an eleven-year-old needs. If bodies, love, affection, privacy, and boundaries are discussed at all ages, then there is no need for one big awkward "birds and bees" discussion.

When utilizing guidance from other sources, it is crucial to be on the lookout for any gender-proscribed language or framework. While conventional wisdom advises using the

L.O.L. Dolls - Trans Series. (Kai, age 11)

Author Cory Silverberg provides the youngest of readers with straightforward language that does not make assumptions about gender based on a person's body parts. Look for *What Makes a Baby* and *Sex is a Funny Word*. Children and adults can benefit greatly from Silverberg's simple and inclusive approach.

correct language for body parts rather than nicknames or euphemisms—a penis is a penis, for example—it is often stated that boys have penises and girls don't. A parent or any other adult should state clearly that many, but not all boys have penises but sometimes girls do as well. This can provide significant relief—as well as greater body acceptance—to a T/GE child who can then understand that they (and their body) have a place in the world.

Talk to T/GE children about their bodies and the many, many ways that bodies are different. Share with them that there are various different ways to have a family. Emphasize the importance of exploring their own bodies and finding the things that feel good. Consent, privacy, and boundaries with respect to bodies can and should be discussed with children of all ages. Parents of T/GE children should not forego or delay conversations about bodies and intimacy simply because they are intimidated or unfamiliar with gender diversity. Parents who engage in these conversations can foster a much stronger sense of self for their child. A child who knows and loves their body will have better success in finding intimate relationships with people who will do the same.

MAKING EARLY CONNECTIONS WITH PROVIDERS

There are providers such as pediatricians, child psychiatrists and psychologists, social workers, and family therapists who have experience working with T/GE children and their families. These people can be great resources in thinking about the many factors contributing to an individual child's identity. Establishing relationships with providers early on can also be important as a T/GE child approaches the age at which some families begin to think about possible medical intervention related to gender. Families who do not have established relationships with providers before this stage may end up in more of a rush to connect with providers as puberty approaches.

Mental Health Care for T/GE Children

We can do many things at home to assist children in developing good mental health. Often, for T/GE children, it is also helpful to bring in an experienced counselor. Mental health providers such as psychologists, psychiatrists, school-based counselors, social workers, and licensed mental health counselors can be wonderful allies to T/GE children and their families. Most parents and guardians have legal control over their child's medical care, so social service providers play a vital role in helping caregivers understand the implications of their decisions affecting their children as they navigate supportive care.[15]

Some of these providers specialize in working with T/GE children and can also be great resources to connect families with support groups and other services. They often work in conjunction with physicians, who manage children's general physical health as well as assist families with decisions about gender-related medical care. When selecting a mental health provider, look for one who is knowledgeable regarding gender diversity and T/GE issues. This provider should be one who can distinguish between a child's gender expression (interests, clothing choices, etc.) and their gender identity (innate sense of self). An optimal provider will be the one who starts with a holistic assessment of the T/GE child and their family to ascertain all variables that impact that child's life. To adequately assess a child's gender identity and state of exploration may require several sessions and include discussions with the child, parents, and sometimes siblings. The ideal provider will simultaneously be paying attention to the child's gender concerns, determining familial comfort or distress, assessing supportive networks for the whole family, and addressing issues of possible anxiety, depression, behavioral issues, and any other concerns regarding the child's health and well-being.

It can be extremely valuable to establish a relationship with a mental health provider early in a T/GE child's life. Not only can providers be important resources and supports for both the child and their family, but they can also be strong advocates for the child's needs when the child approaches a time that the family is considering puberty blockers or other medical interventions.[16] Most medical providers and insurance companies require a child to have a relationship with a mental health provider in order to start puberty-suppression and hormone-blocking medications, and sometimes families have found themselves rushing to establish relationships when puberty is starting.

T/GE children are, first and foremost, children. Like many other children in today's society, they can struggle with other issues that serve to complicate their lives. Some of the issues these children face are gender-related, while others may not originate from gender but can certainly be compounded by it. A percentage of T/GE children can struggle with depression, anxiety, eating disorders, and any other issues that all children may experience. Some T/GE children have developmental disabilities or are on the autism spectrum/neurodiverse.

Keep in mind that it can be common for providers, often unfamiliar with T/GE children, to first give attention to these other areas of concern simply because they are more familiar with the possible courses of treatment. Sometimes a provider is unable to recognize distress around gender. Other times, they may not feel they have the knowledge or experience to address gender issues. What can result is a situation where the potential core area of a T/GE child's distress is ignored, invisible, or is "put off" until other mental health concerns, such as depression or anxiety, are "under control."

It is important to look at a child's full experience—including any gender exploration—and not view their difficulties as items that should be dealt with sequentially, as in, "We'll get the anxiety in check first and then we'll address the gender concerns." Although it is understandable that any adult—parent or provider—might be inclined to put off the intimidating topic of a possible T/GE gender identity, what will be of deepest benefit to that child is to address these factors concurrently. Affirmation of a child's gender identity may not fully eliminate other behavioral challenges, but it can very often decrease the frequency and intensity of those challenges over time.

TRANS IS BEAUTIFUL

Noah Fritz-Sherman (he/him) is a 10-year-old trans athlete.

Separating kids by gender can hurt them and give them anxiety when they use boys' and girls' bathrooms, because they feel like they are different and not welcome there. I have always hated boys' and girls' bathrooms; they have this idea that if you don't have this body part you can't come in. I have always been scared and nervous when or wherever I use the bathroom, sometimes even at home, but it really racked me up to a new level of that stuff after this:

I remember it like it was yesterday (although I sort of wish I didn't). I was at this camp, and I was in the boys' changing room waiting in a line to change in the stall. I remember being pierced with a shout that has made me so careful ever since: "There's a girl in the boys' bathroom!" The room was instantly filled with boys looking around and shouting "Who?!" and "Where?!" I was so scared I fled out of the changing room silently crying and unnoticed. That made me consider I was "different" and not a real boy. I kept that in for a while, but eventually I told my mom who told me that I was a boy through and through—no matter what anybody said. Even though that helped me, I still lay awake at night wishing I was born a boy.

I used to think that being trans is like being in an egg or a butterfly trying to come out of its cocoon. But I was wrong—I was the butterfly with a loving family that accepts me. But really for a lot of people it is like they are trapped inside a rock that cannot be broken until the rock breaks itself. Many people—even when they die—won't have parents and family members who support them. They have to penetrate the rock until the family members finally realize who that person they were growing up with really is. Then finally the rock breaks.

Protect Trans Kids (translifeline). (Colin Laurel)

Life Stages

Gender-Related Mental Health Diagnoses

Among T/GE adults there is considerable debate over the categorization of T/GE identity as a mental disorder. The latest version of the *Diagnostic and Statistical Manual of Mental Disorders (DSM-5)* renames Gender Identity Disorder as Gender Dysphoria. Families who are raising a T/GE child often struggle with the ramifications of a child being diagnosed with gender dysphoria.

Gender dysphoria in childhood is defined as a period of at least six months wherein a child experiences a difference between their assigned sex and gender identity, and which causes significant distress or impairment. Although many parents recognize that there is nothing "wrong" with their child's mental health—only ignorance and bias in our society—the advice from medical, mental health, and legal professionals may be to obtain a gender-related mental health diagnosis. There are various reasons for doing so, which may include insurance coverage, access to hormone blockers, and even divorce or child custody issues. Arriving at a definitive diagnosis can also be comforting for many parents, because it is concrete and paves the way for specific actions such as identity document changes.

It is important to recognize that there are pros and cons to a child receiving a diagnosis of gender dysphoria. Diagnoses remain permanently in medical records. There are a number of opportunities, services, and situations where a mental disorder diagnosis could potentially prevent or greatly hinder someone's access to resources—either now or later in life. Insisting on a label could make a child feel like they must identify with a particular gender, and could potentially impede further attempts to find their authentic self if that challenges their providers' understanding of their gender. In an effort to decrease the discomfort of their parents and others, a child may make choices that are not aligned with how they actually feel. A diagnosis can also later lead to a situation where a child "changes their mind" or says they have "made a mistake" simply because they felt pressured to make a decision before they were ready. Each family should educate themselves as to the potential benefits and repercussions of obtaining a gender dysphoria diagnosis.

> *Our child disclosed that he was male at the age of 7 years old. As we stepped in to learn more and support him, we pushed hard against having him "diagnosed" with gender identity disorder. His father is a pilot and our child had expressed an interest in this profession as well. We knew a mental health diagnosis would prevent him from pursuing this career path. Once we supported him in his transition, he's doing just fine. Why would we allow a stigmatizing diagnosis that would then limit his life options?—Family from a Gender Diversity support group*

Medical Health Care Providers

The decision to pursue medical intervention with gender expansive youth can be complicated and is unique to each family. The possibility of medical intervention is important to talk about early, and with a supportive pediatrician, family physician, nurse practitioner, physician's assistant, pediatric endocrinologist, or other provider who is knowledgeable about hormones and children's bodies. Building relationships with experienced healthcare providers can be extremely helpful and doing this early can prevent feelings that a family is rushing at the last minute to explore options.[17]

General pediatricians working in communities often have little training in working with T/GE children. Some are eager to learn. Many families have established long-term relationships with their pediatricians and want to continue working with them, while others feel more comfortable finding new pediatricians who have more experience working with T/GE children. Children come into contact with other types of medical providers such as nurses and dentists on a regular basis, and it is appropriate to request and expect these providers to use the proper name and pronoun for a child during all interactions. If

"SR a year and a half after her social transition showing her true colors which before were hidden away."

Some hospitals providing medical treatment for T/GE youth include: the Children's Hospital of Los Angeles; UCSF Benioff Children's Hospital; Children's National Medical Center in Washington, DC; New York University; Boston Children's Hospital; Lurie Children's Hospital of Chicago; and Seattle Children's Hospital.

a pediatrician or other healthcare provider is not respectful of a family's wishes, it may be important to change providers.[18]

Pediatric endocrinologists are pediatricians who specialize in hormonal disorders such as diabetes and growth problems. Many pediatric endocrinologists are not familiar with treatments for T/GE children, although they use the same medications (puberty blockers) to treat growth disorders. Like many pediatricians, pediatric endocrinologists are often eager to learn about T/GE children, but this may be new terrain for them and will require the pursuit of additional medical knowledge. Many providers find that, with adequate resources, continuing education, or consulting opportunities, the endocrine care of preadolescents falls well within their scope of practice.

SOME OPEN-ENDED QUESTIONS TO ASK OF A POTENTIAL MEDICAL HEALTH CARE PROVIDER

It is an important part of any family's journey to find a medical provider who is open, willing to learn, affirming of your child's gender identity (whether binary or not), and who recognizes the importance of their role in the child's gender journey (without overstepping bounds). Consider the following questions:

- Have you treated any T/GE children within your practice? If so, how many and what ages?
- Are you familiar with the importance of gender-affirming care for T/GE children put forth by numerous medical and mental health professional associations (e.g., American Medical Association, American Psychological Association)? Can you elaborate?
- What do you think are the most important considerations that should be in place for a family like ours with a T/GE child?
- How would you define your role in our T/GE child's gender-affirming care team?
- Are you familiar with any current research regarding gender identity in children? If so, what?

- What gender-affirming training or continuing education have you had or are you pursuing?

EVOLVING OR CHANGING GENDER IDENTITY

One of society's greatest sources of hesitancy when considering the support of a T/GE child's identity is the specter of a child's change of heart. "What if my child changes their mind?" is easily among the top questions a parent, or any other adult for that matter, will ask. The fear is that a child may simply be going through a phase of gender exploration and that the Herculean steps of gender transition will have been a terrible mistake. This fear causes many parents, and even providers, to ignore what is happening or deny a child support. What happens if a child has transitioned to a different gender and then later says they want to "go back"? Does this happen? The answer is yes, but rarely. The reasons this may occur are not easy to predict but, if it does, the same course of action should be taken—providing love, support and validation. A positive, supportive approach to a child's gender exploration is the correct course of action regardless of whether a child changes their mind at a later date.

It can be helpful to understand a child's gender identity as having two major components. The first is their internal sense of their own gender—what gender they feel themselves to be in their heart and mind. Girl, boy, both, or neither are reasonable options, among many others. The second component is the level of supportive climate surrounding them. Are parents, siblings, and extended family members understanding and supportive? Is there resistance from teachers and/or other students? Is bullying a part of their regular experience? Are people of diverse gender identities visible to the child on a regular basis and, if so, are these people accepted or shunned and ridiculed? Each child is part of many communities—familial, faith, cultural, social, political, and regional—and each environment may differ in how it engages with, understands, accepts, or rejects gender diverse people. Imagine the struggles of a child when those environments are rejecting or isolating.

We know that family support has a direct, positive impact on the ability of a child to solidly step into their gender exploration. If supporting a child's exploration results in that child "trying on" different gender roles until they find what feels like the best fit for them—balancing their internal sense of self and negotiating possibilities in the external world—fantastic!

TRANS HANDEDNESS

A late bloomer, Erika Joyner (she/her) started transitioning in her late fifties and has found her true heart and soul as a trans woman. Transitioning has brought her the gift of self-awareness and self-acceptance. She has made it her mission to share this gift in as many ways as possible—not the least of which is through her poetry.

I've noticed a change in your handwriting lately.
It's so curvy and really too flowing.
Oh my god, son, have you been using your left hand!
What! You're telling me you are a lefty!
Such a disgrace upon our family.
Why would you choose to use your left hand in a world
    of rightness?
What do you mean it's not a choice? You were born this
    way?
Haven't we raised you to know that
right is right and left is wrong?

How can you say that handedness is non-binary!
We must cure this affliction.
I know, conversion therapy. Our minister says it works.
What do you mean all beings are equal in the eyes of God?
It says right here in the Bible that lefties are perverted.
We love you, son. Don't cry.
Here's a tissue but please wipe with your right hand.
Ok, you can use your left, but please don't use it in public.
What will the neighbors think?!
Why would you choose to give up the privilege of right dominance?
What do you mean you are a lefty born into a right-handed body?
Well, hopefully this is just a phase you are going through.
WHAT, YOU'RE MOVING OUT?!!

CONSIDERING SOCIAL TRANSITION

Whether caregivers are pursuing medical or mental health interventions related to their child's gender, many families come to a point where they feel that the best thing for a T/GE child will be to support the child in expressing their gender identity publicly. Parents may have already spent considerable time allowing the child to try out different clothes, names, or pronouns at home, or with select groups of peers and other parents. For parents considering social transition for their T/GE children, there are a few concrete steps to affirm a young child's gender. These can include all or some of the following:

- Changes in hairstyle, clothing, accessories, toys, and/or activities
- Name change
- Pronoun change
- Identity document changes
- A reversible, medical delay of puberty

For some parents, these tasks seem quite daunting. For others, especially those parents who tend to cope by finding solutions and implementing them as quickly as possible, having tangible, concrete actions to focus on can provide a sense of relief. It can be easy to focus on a "checklist" of transition-related tasks. It can provide a caregiver with what feels like a step-by-step pathway through unfamiliar territory. Moving quickly through these tasks may provide some comfort, or a sense of purpose, but it can also result in a bit of tunnel vision that can hamper a parent's ability to see other, more immediate, issues. It can also send a message that a child "needs" to transition fully when their gender identity is more fluid and transition is premature or not needed.

Even if all these tasks are necessary, it does not mean they are easy to accomplish. It is quite common to encounter barriers within systems (e.g., laws dictating ID document changes vary state by state). These barriers are often not insurmountable but can take an incredible amount of time and sometimes require legal assistance. It is important to pace ourselves in order to avoid burnout, financial hardship, or an overall drain on our day-to-day life experience.

For parents, teachers, and counselors ready to help T/GE children with social transition, one of the biggest fears expressed is that we are moving too fast, and that the child may yet "change their mind." A decision to transition a child's gender can feel like an irreversible course of action. When a trans adult transitions, some steps, like hormones and surgeries, do change the body in permanent ways. This is not true for a child pursuing a social transition. A T/GE child's transition primarily consists of steps where no permanent physical changes are made.

Many times, fears are larger than reality. It can be helpful to actually "play out" a scenario in which the child does change their mind. Say that a family supports their

Danaë is a Dutch company that makes underwear and swimwear for trans people and sells kids' binders, bikinis, and other clothing.

"This suburban family is not unlike other suburban families. Work, school, activities and sports keep them busy year round. For these parents, whether it's their transgender child or cisgender children, they want all three kids to have the opportunity to live their lives to the fullest potential."

T/GE child in a social transition. The T/GE child takes on a different name, perhaps changes their hairstyle, is supported in their clothing preferences, uses the bathroom that aligns with their gender identity, and everyone works very hard to get the new pronoun to easily roll off their tongues. Then the child comes home one day and says, "I want to go back!"

If a child states that they made a mistake or that they want to go back to the gender they were before, simply work the aforementioned steps backward. These steps are all reversible and it may not be as hard as it was during initial social transition. This is not to say that it will be easy. A parent will still be placed in the position of explaining to others why supporting their child includes gender transition and, if need be, a change "back." As those caring for gender expansive children, our fears about a child "changing back" may be more about our own shame at having been "wrong" than about concerns for the child's safety or well-being.

The American Academy of Pediatrics issued a policy statement in the fall of 2018 titled, *Ensuring Comprehensive Care and Support for Transgender and Gender-Diverse Children and Adolescents.* The important message of this statement is that "Transgender and gender-diverse children face many challenges in life, but, like all children, they can grow into happy and healthy adults when supported and loved throughout their development."

SAMPLE LETTER TO FAMILY MEMBERS ABOUT A CHILD'S TRANSITION

Dear Family,

We have some big news to share, so we thought it best to write to you personally. Our child, who you know as Lacey, has shared feeling like a boy since two-to-three years old. We have, in fact, learned we are not the parents of a little girl, but the parents of a little boy. Through long and careful exploration, discussion, prayer, counseling, family talks, and self-reflection, we have come to understand this new truth. We are proud and excited to introduce a new but old member of our family, Justin!

Justin (who uses he/him/his pronouns) is now known by everyone in our neighborhood and school as a boy. He is unbelievably happy and comfortable about this big change and so are we. As you are a very important part of our lives, we decided to also share this truth with you. We understand this may be confusing. In the beginning, we, too, felt confused. For years now, Justin has told us how he feels inside with the words he knew.

There is plenty of information available about transgender and gender expansive children—we invite you to explore this information as we have. There is quite a bit of information on the Internet. There are also several good books on the subject. We are happy to recommend some to you upon request.

We ask that you welcome Justin fully as part of our family. Please refer to Justin only with he/him/his pronouns and by his name, Justin. Despite any personal reservations you may have, we expect and hope you will be fully welcoming, respectful, and kind to Justin. All the experts we have consulted on this subject agree this is the right approach for maintaining Justin's mental health and happiness long-term. Transgender kids are much more prone to suicide, depression, and self-harm when they don't have the support and love of their family.

If you are no longer able to treat our child with complete respect, we will decline further contact until that changes. Regardless of personal beliefs, all of us as parents want our children to be happy and safe. Our friends, community, and Justin's school have been extremely helpful and supportive. Our love and support for Justin is complete. We hope yours will be also. We love you all so much and miss you.

Warm regards,
The Johnsons

Choosing a New Name

Many T/GE children are eager to shed the names assigned to them at birth. This can be a difficult task for a parent who may have put careful consideration into selecting their child's name. It is normal to feel an attachment to a child's name and grief at the thought of it changing. Many parents also worry that giving a T/GE child too much leeway in choosing their own name could result in a choice that the child is upset about later in life. Young children often choose popular names, such as those of Disney characters or other toys. The amount of influence the child has in decisions related to name changes depends greatly on the age and developmental level of the T/GE child.

Some parents feel it is important for their T/GE child to have a family name or one that fits well within their culture. Many families have trial periods, where the child's new name is used at home or among family members to be sure it is a good fit. Some children may try multiple names before settling on one. Gender-neutral names can sometimes be good choices because they allow children to explore their gender identity without making any big decisions. Some families have approached the prospect of a name change as a family affair, explaining to their T/GE child that "A parent is the one who picks out a name for their child. I recognize that I didn't get it right because I didn't fully understand your gender at that time. So, we'll pick out a name together that we all feel good about."

Legal name changes take time and money. Taking legal steps can be very important in many cases in order to affirm a T/GE child's identity. However, holding off on a legal name change does not mean that a child needs to be addressed by their birth name at school or in a health provider's office, given that these entities often have options for the use of a child's nickname or preferred name, and may be required to use the name a family requests even if it has not been legally changed. Changing a child's legal name generally follows the same process as that for adults, but it requires the approval of a parent or guardian.

Taking a Gender Vacation

Although not an option readily available to all, there are some families who will opt for a trial "gender vacation" for a T/GE child. If your family has a trip planned out of town or to someplace where you are not likely to run into people you know, consider testing the waters by giving your child an opportunity to adopt their preferred clothing choices, pronoun, or even a different name while away from home. Many parents have been quite surprised at how happy and at ease their T/GE child is as well as how uneventful the temporary "social transition" is as they see how society readily receives their "new" daughter, son, or nonbinary child.

Dawn Acero and family. Top: Arrow (7). Middle: Eliana (11) and Isaiah (9). Bottom: Tobias (13), Dawn, and Elias

Social Transition Progression—Not an All-or-Nothing

The best way to support a child's gender pathway is to view it as just that—a journey of many steps. Many parents worry about potential choices that are years down the road or potential hardships for their child that may never occur. That worry only serves to decrease sleep and increase stress. A parent, caregiver, or provider does not need to make a definitive gender determination in order to proceed. Agreeing to a pronoun and/or name change sends a message to a child that their request is heard and respected. Delaying puberty is not a step forward toward a cross-gender determination, it simply allows more time for discernment. Even cross-hormone care can be done in a slow, gradual manner to allow for all involved to gain greater clarity and direction. We do not need, nor can we obtain, extreme certainty for most of life's decisions. A gender transition is no exception. What a child needs is for their parents or caregivers to support and guide them through the necessary steps to solidly reach their authentic self. The end gender destination is for them to discover.

After the Dust Settles—Ongoing Considerations

Providing care for a T/GE child is a process that can have a steep learning curve. Most "how-to" parenting books have not addressed the topic of gender diversity in children. Nor is there anything beyond a handful of hard-to-find courses for providers that address this topic during the course of their education. Parents and providers alike can inadvertently believe that, with basic transition steps out of the way, a T/GE child will just go on to live a "normal" life in which their gender history is not an issue. However there are factors to consider such as where, when, if, and to whom to disclose one's gender history. T/GE bodies are unique and medical providers will, at times, need to know the full picture to provide a person with the best care possible. If later surgical options are pursued, appropriate and ongoing care may be needed to address any complications or unforeseen variables. Additionally, the systematic categorization of gender across multiple systems— school records, citizenship and naturalization documents, birth certificates, court records, and more—may be incongruent for reasons sometimes out of an individual's control. This incongruity can result in outing a child, or limiting their access to necessary services in the future. Possible disclosure of a child's gender journey will be a factor to consider for the duration of their life.

Dr. Lourdes Ashley Hunter (pronoun: Goddess) is the founder of the Trans Women of Color Collective and Shauna Gordon-McKeon (she/her) is an author.

Every story is an opportunity. Stories are a chance to see the world through someone else's eyes—someone different from you. With our stories, we can show people our lived experiences and highlight the commonalities among us. Within others' stories, we can see the humanity in ourselves.

Social constructions of gender inform every aspect of western life. Even before the day a baby is born, their entire life is coordinated according to physical anatomy. From blankets and bonnets to strollers and booties, from the color of a child's room to the toys within it, everything conforms to the sex assigned at birth. Children are conditioned to perform within gender roles and norms and rewarded for performing successfully in their assigned roles. However, they are chastised, teased, punished, abused, and even murdered when their performance is identified outside those assigned norms.

But what if parents had tools to affirm, protect, advocate for, and celebrate their gender expansive kids?

Super Princess Saves the Night is a story about a gender expansive child named Sam who assumes the identity of a superhero, Super Princess, to protect her family. But Super Princess doesn't protect people by fighting the dishes and clothes and books that have magically come alive at night. Instead, she listens to their stories, empathizes, and lets them tell her what they need. In the climax of the book, Sam's parents do the same.

The book has become a tool that works toward creating and strengthening relationships that celebrate, advocate for, protect, and affirm gender expansive kids, their families, friends, and others who are still trying to understand that there is more than one way to exist in the world. The process of writing and publishing the book created yet another relationship–ours: Shauna Gordon-McKeon and Dr. Lourdes Ashley Hunter.

The proceeds from this book are being donated to the Trans Women of Color Collective, which is a grass-roots global initiative led by trans and gender nonconforming people of color that works to uplift the lived narratives, experiences, and leadership of trans and gender nonconforming people of color, their families and comrades, while building toward collective liberation for all oppressed people through healing and restorative justice.

Through our collaborative effort we have journeyed toward curating opportunities for gender expansiveness in loving and joyful spaces. *Super Princess Saves the Night* is a tool that so many of us needed growing up in a world not yet designed to affirm our greatness and purposefulness.

Gender Disclosure

Many families find it helpful to approach the topic of gender disclosure as an ongoing skill to develop and hone rather than a one-time task. Whether a T/GE child lives "stealth" (i.e., their gender history is kept private) or their gender story is known, there will continue to be times where this disclosure may be necessary, unavoidable, or is knowingly or inadvertently disclosed by someone else. Because assigned birth sex designation can be so deeply rooted in our social systems, there can be occasions where a child's sex assigned at birth pops up despite everyone's best efforts. It is all too common for a child's former name, for example, to be listed on a class roster generated for a substitute teacher. Sometimes there are situations where it is medically necessary to disclose a T/GE child's gender history. Both parent and child can benefit from planning for unexpected disclosure, with the assumption that these times will happen rather than hoping they will not. Strategizing ways to navigate these situations will help minimize any negative impacts they may cause.

Many families find it helpful, even if their child's gender story is not known to most, to provide opportunities where their child can engage with other T/GE children in an open way. This could be in the form of a play or support group for T/GE children, arranging occasional playdates with other families who have T/GE children, or going to conferences or camps that support T/GE children. If a T/GE child has navigated environments where they can be open and be received positively, they will be less fearful and more confident during

Summer camps where kids can explore their gender identities include Camp Aranu'tiq, The Laurel Foundation, and Camp Indigo.

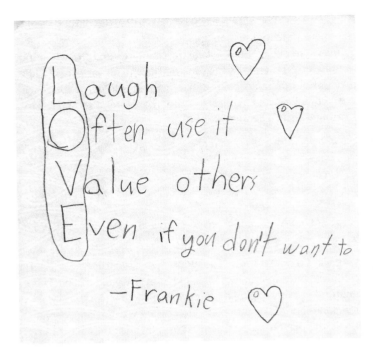

Artwork by Frankie, an 8 year old transgender boy.

times of inadvertent disclosure. It is important to acknowledge that these are options that are not always available to families due to geographic, financial, and other barriers.

Preparing Children for Questions from Others

It is critical to prepare T/GE children for questions, whether they come from an inquisitive child or an insensitive or unthinking adult. Some people will let their curiosity override their sense of what is appropriate to ask of a child. If you do not think an adult would ever ask a T/GE child if they are "going to have a sex change operation," think again!

Children typically ask questions that are simple and address immediate curiosities. Simple answers are highly effective. Adults may have a different agenda. They are more likely to couch their questions in politeness and express their discomfort or disapproval in more subtle ways. A T/GE child may sense an adult's inappropriate agenda but not be able to articulate what they perceive to others, including a parent or a counselor. This is where attentive, supportive adults in a T/GE child's life are critical. One option is to tell your child that they do not have to answer any gender-related questions from adults. Equipping T/GE children with a response like, "My mom says you shouldn't ask me questions but should come talk to her" can immediately relieve a child's pressure to respond and reduces their emotional labor. If the adult persists, tell the T/GE child to find their parents immediately.

There is no one-size-fits-all approach to the way a T/GE child should or shouldn't respond to questions from others. This is something that a caregiver can explore with a child considering factors such as their age, temperament, level of confidence, and any additional level of support from extended family, teachers, and more. Role-playing is beneficial to better discern what is reasonable and what falls outside of the optimal boundaries. In general, a T/GE child (or siblings) should not be the source of information for the curiosities of others.

ROLE-PLAYING

One activity shown to be highly effective for building resilience in children is role playing. This involves the acting out of any number of potential situations where a child might need to think on their feet. The parent or other support person plays the role of one person and the child practices potential responses.

A whole family can engage in role-playing exercises and the whole family can benefit. To start, brainstorm potential situations and list them on paper. These can include school scenarios highlighting particular dynamics the child may experience with students or teachers. It might include an upcoming family reunion and seeing relatives for the first time since affirming a child's gender.

> *My son who had socially transitioned at a young age was having a conversation recently with a friend who'd known him for a long time. His friend said, "Hey, didn't you used to have a girl's name?" My child just shrugged, rolled his eyes, and said, "Yeah, can you believe my parents named me that!" Both kids laughed at how silly adults can be and went on to something else. We've done a lot of role-playing and it paid off. He really thought on his feet.—Family from Gender Diversity support group*

Role-playing should not be limited solely to the gender diverse child. Parents need to be prepared to address questions at any time and with any person. That is not to say that an in-depth explanation—or any explanation for that matter—is necessary. Parents, however, need to envision a number of scenarios and determine what, if any, explanation is needed depending on who the person is, what degree of relevance they have in the family's life, how much time they have at that moment, and their assessment of that person's receptivity. Here is a sample scenario and possible responses:

Scenario: You are in a grocery store with your eight-year-old T/GE daughter and you see someone you know from your neighborhood. They say hello, seem confused when you mention your daughter, and then inquire about your son. You are a little caught off-guard and are not sure how much to say, but end up providing an explanation about how your daughter used to be your son, that you became aware that he was T/GE, and that now you support her in her true gender identity as a girl. Your neighbor has an uncomfortable smile on their face, comments on your bravery as a parent, says they wouldn't know what to do if they had a child who was like "that," and then moves on down the aisle. Your child seems to have been thoughtfully contemplating the cereal boxes the whole time and because your child says nothing, you say nothing.

This response to an unexpected situation was handled pretty well, though there is a little room for improvement. A brief, educational response may be just the thing for an unexpected supermarket interaction. It is important, however, to consider how this response might affect your child. There is a really good chance that the T/GE child was listening to all that was said. She could have easily stolen a glance or two at both you and the neighbor as the conversation progressed, felt the discomfort of both adults, and registered how quickly the neighbor moved away. The child can internalize this discomfort and develop a sense of shame about themselves. Because this was not addressed by the parent afterward, it could cause a child to conclude that their parent's own discomfort comes from a sense of shame they have about her. This unintended consequence, instilling shame and silence, can be long-lasting.

Here are two examples of responses to the above scenario that elevate family support and trust as the number one priority.

Example Response 1: You are in a grocery store with your eight-year old T/GE daughter and you see someone you know from your neighborhood. They say hello, seem confused when you mention your daughter, and then inquire about your son. Because you have done your own preparation, you are not caught off-guard. You say, "No, I only have a daughter" and that's it. You allow them their confusion as you excuse yourself and say, "Sorry I have to run. It was nice seeing you," leaving them with a quizzical look on their face and a very relieved child.

Example Response 2: Perhaps this is a family with whom you would like to discuss your family's journey, but you recognize that the grocery store is not an ideal place. You take the lead in the conversation and say how nice it was to run into them. Then you mention that you have been meaning to stop by and visit them and ask whether they are going to be around tomorrow morning. If they ask a question about your child, you gracefully state that you would love to catch up with them soon and if tomorrow does not work, you will call them to find another time.

Have fun with role-playing. Try out silly responses along with your serious ones; shout out some one-liners or speak them using your favorite accent. If a child is relaxed and having fun during the role-playing, chances are they will be able to bring some of those feelings into real-life situations.

SHINE: MAKING SCHOOLS AND COMMUNITIES SAFER FOR LGBTQI YOUTH IN TENNESSEE

Shawn Reilly, M.Ed. (they/them), is an educator and divinity school student living in Nashville, Tennessee. They are the program coordinator for the Trans Buddy Program at the Program for LGBTBQ Health at Vanderbilt, and they co-coordinate the GLSEN Tennessee SHINE activism team, working in partnership with young people to make schools and communities safer for LGBTQI youth across the state.

According to the 2017 National School Climate Survey conducted by GLSEN, 80% of Tennessee LGBTQ students hear antitransgender remarks from other students in school. The same report revealed that in Tennessee, most transgender students are unable to use the bathroom that aligns with their gender and are prevented from using their chosen name and pronouns in school. This is a reality that unfortunately extends beyond the borders of Tennessee and threatens the well-being of transgender students across the nation. Students experience harassment and discrimination not only from other students but also from the teachers, principals, and school districts that they engage with daily.

This is precisely the reality that the GLSEN Tennessee SHINE team works to shift. The team consists of student leaders collaborating to create safer schools and communities throughout Tennessee. SHINE members are committed to being inclusive and responsible. They are open to learning, and willing to examine their own privileges. Each summer, they come together for a weekend retreat, which includes an orientation to queer and trans histories, intersectionally minded organizing, and action planning and facilitation. The student leaders also meet regularly throughout the year to hone their activism skills, form a network with other youth leaders, and organize programs in their schools and communities promoting respect for LGBTQIA + students.

In the few years that I have worked with the team, they have accomplished extraordinary feats. They have planned and led the annual Tennessee LGBTQI youth summit. On Trans Day of Remembrance, they developed an online trivia game to teach histories of trans resistance and realities of trans existence. They spoke at the Nashville "We Won't Be Erased" rally and organized in response to the 2018 Health and Human Services memo outlining the Trump administration's plans to redefine gender and sex on a federal level. Last year, they worked to have a resolution passed *unanimously* through the Nashville City Council and Metro Nashville Public Schools that encouraged teachers to engage in professional development opportunities surrounding hate speech intervention in schools.

The young people I have had the privilege to work beside as a co-coordinator of the team are nothing short of incredible. This motley crew of students from across the state has conversations that are more transgressive and productive than any group of advocates with whom I have worked. By investing my time in these powerful youth advocates, I know that I am contributing to a safer and freer future.

T/GE CHILDREN AND SCHOOLS

Outside of the home, most T/GE children spend the majority of their time at school. Unfortunately, most K–12 schools have gender-conforming expectations built into their traditions, systems, and policies. The pressure to conform can come from peers and teachers alike. Even the most progressive schools can have practices that unintentionally marginalize or silence a T/GE student.

For many teachers and administrators, the desire to be inclusive within the school community is strong, but practical tools are limited. Many schools and districts are willing to help but need a road map for creating a gender-inclusive environment. Often, schools have the capacity to create an inclusive environment for T/GE students without any major overhaul. Administrators, teachers, and other staff can prepare to care for the needs of gender diverse children in a number of ways. Here are a few:

For more information on schools, check out *Schools in Transition: A Guide for Supporting Transgender Students in K–12 Schools* (Asaf Orr, Joel Baum, Jay Brown, Elizabeth Gill, Ellen Kahn, and Anna Salem, ACLU, 2015).

- Pursue gender-inclusive training for school staff, administrators, teachers, and parents from an organization such as Gender Diversity, Gender Spectrum, or HRC's

Elijah Campbell told his parents he was a boy inside when he was 3 years old. He lives in a small rural Ontario community where he is supported to live freely out and proud as his authentic self by his family and community.

Welcoming Schools. Informed and confident adults are key to the overall ease with which any school successfully incorporates gender-diverse students.

- Gain familiarity with specific questions that may arise from students or parents and become confident in providing knowledgeable answers about T/GE children.
- Address T/GE classroom situations/questions in a manner consistent with other areas of diversity.
- Create and/or implement T/GE-affirming school policies that specifically name gender identity and gender expression.
- Provide all-gender restrooms, changing rooms, and locker rooms where students can change and use the restroom in private. Additionally, allow students to self-select to use the facilities that conform with their gender identity. This can be as simple as changing signs on multistall restrooms or making single-stall restrooms all-gender. Ensure all teachers, assistants, and administrators are on the same page about restroom and locker room use.

Teaching Tolerance provides free resources to educators—teachers, administrators, counselors and other practitioners—who work with children from kindergarten through high school. Educators use their materials to supplement curricula, to inform their practices, and to create civil and inclusive school communities where children are respected, valued, and welcomed participants.

Some schools are excited to be on the cutting edge of T/GE student rights, but many are not, at least not at first. Some, however, are happy to ride on the coattails of schools that have successfully implemented T/GE-inclusive practices. Knowing that other schools have broken this ground with little controversy and to the benefit of all students can mean all the difference in the world. Fortunately, a number of schools have done this work and can provide other schools and districts with successful experiences and model policies.

CONCLUSION

Raising a T/GE child can be both exciting and scary. Being open-minded and supportive, seeking out resources, and connecting to community are vital in creating an optimal environment for exploration. Providing T/GE children with loving homes, acceptance, and emotional tools builds the resiliency and self-esteem that children of all genders need in order to live happy and fulfilling lives, while also exploring other important aspects of their identity (e.g., race/ethnicity, sexual orientation, social class, disability, and more). In addition to the work of individual parents and caregivers, it is also essential that we move towards increasing societal understanding and acceptance. As our communities become more supportive, we can much more easily provide T/GE children the space needed to discover and embrace their true selves.

NOTES

1. Ehrensaft, D. (2016). *The gender creative child. Pathways for nurturing and supporting children who live outside gender boxes.* New York: The Experiment Publishing.

2. Ehrensaft, D. (2016). *The gender creative child. Pathways for nurturing and supporting children who live outside gender boxes.* New York: The Experiment Publishing.

3. Ryan, C., Russell, S. T., Huebner, D., Diaz, R., & Sanchez, J. (2010). Family acceptance in adolescence and the health of LGBT young adults. *Journal of Child and Adolescent Psychiatric Nursing, 23*(4), 205–213.

4. Travers, R. Bauer, G., & Pyne, J. (2012). Impacts of strong parental support for trans youth: A report prepared for Children's Aid Society of Toronto and Delisle Youth Services. *Trans Pulse*, 1–5.

5. Simons, L., Schrager, S. M., Clark, L. F., Belzer, M., & Olson, J. (2013). Parental support and mental health among transgender adolescents. *Journal of Adolescent Health, 53*(6), 791–793.

6. Olson, K. R., & Gulgoz, S. (2018). Early findings from the TransYouth project: Gender development in transgender children. *Child Development Perspectives, 12*(2), 93–97. doi: 10.1111/cdep.12268

7. Sue, D. W. S. (2010). *Microaggressions in everyday life: Race, gender, and sexual orientation.* New York: John Wiley & Sons, Inc.

8. Adelson, S. L. (2012). Practice parameter on gay, lesbian, or bisexual sexual orientation, gender nonconformity, and gender discordance in children and adolescents. *Journal of the American Academy of Child and Adolescent Psychiatry, 51*(9), 957–974.

9. Robinson, B. A. (2018). Conditional families and lesbian, gay, bisexual, transgender, and queer youth homelessness: Gender, sexuality, family instability, and rejection. *Journal of Marriage & Family, 80*(2), 383–396. doi: https://doi.org/10.1111/jomf.12466

10. Singh. A. A., & dickey, l. m. (2016). Implementing the APA guidelines on psychological practice with transgender and gender nonconforming people: A call to action to the field of psychology. *Psychology of Sexual Orientation and Gender Diversity, 3*(2), 195–200. doi: 10.1037/sgd0000179

11. Tando, D. (2016). *The conscious parent's guide to gender identity: A mindful approach to embracing your child's authentic self.* Avon, MA: Adams Media.

12. Malpas, J. (2011). Between pink and blue: A multi-dimensional family approach to gender nonconforming children and their families. *Family Process, 50*(4), 453-470.

13. Hill, D. B., Menvielle, E., Sica, K. M., & Johnson, A. (2010). An affirmative intervention for families with gender variant children: Parental ratings of child mental health and gender. *Journal of Sex and Marital Therapy, 36*(1), 6–23.

14. Steensma, T. D., McGuire, J. K., Kreukels, B. P. C., Beekman, A. J., & Cohen-Kettenis, P. T. (2013). Factors associated with desistence and persistence of childhood gender dysphoria: A quantitative follow-up study. *Journal of the American Academy of Child & Adolescent Psychiatry, 52*(6), 582–590. doi:10.1016/j. jaac.2013.03.016

15. Olson, K. R., Durwood, L., DeMeules, M., & McLaughlin, K. A. (2016). Mental health of transgender children who are supported in their identities. *Pediatrics, 137*(3), e20153223. doi: 10.1542/peds.2015-3223

16. Durwood, L., McLaughlin, K. A., & Olson, K. R. (2017). Mental health and self-worth in socially transitioned transgender youth. *Journal of the American Academy of Child & Adolescent Psychiatry, 56*(2), 116–123. doi: 10.1016/j.jaac.2016.10.016

17. Temple Newhook, J., Winters, K., Pyne, J., Jamieson, A., Holmes, C., Feder, S., Pickett, S., & Sinnott, M-L. (2018). Teach your parents (and providers) well: A call for re-focus on the health of trans and gender-diverse children. *Canadian Family Physician, 64*, 332–335.

18. Pleak, R. R. (2011). Gender-variant children and transgender adolescents. *Child and Adolescent Psychiatric Clinics of North America, 20*(4), 1001–1016. doi: https://doi.org/10.1016/j.pcl.2015.04.013

19

YOUTH
G. Nic Rider and Colt St. Amand

Based on first edition content by Colt St. Amand and Lance Hicks

INTRODUCTION

As transgender and gender expansive (T/GE) youth, we do not experience our gender identities in isolation from other facets of our identities. Our gender is influenced by many other factors, such as our race, ethnicity, ability status, religious beliefs, age, body size, skin color, where we live, the language(s) we use, socioeconomic background, and immigration status. As T/GE youth, we are also impacted by the dominance of authority figures in our lives.

> *I always felt out of place. I'm awkward and throughout life thought it was that. Often it was. I frequently thought I was "not like other girls." Some of it was dumb patriarchy shit, AKA it is bad to be "like a girl." At this point I like to think I've unpacked most of that. I still find it hard to separate my feelings of being "other." Is it because I have strange interests? I'm awkward? I'm bi? I'm trans? I was raised Catholic? Raised in a small town? I'm "artsy?" I guess that is when we can do a deep dive into intersectional feminism. I've always felt out of place for whatever reason, but at least now I can tell when it is because I am nonbinary . . . because I know now who I am.*

SELF-EXPLORATION AND SELF-REALIZATION

Adolescence is a time when many of us are beginning to figure out who we are. During these years, we experience significant biological and social changes that usher us into adulthood. Puberty sets in and our bodies change—usually in ways that highlight sex differences. It is also when we experience increased gender segregation and even more pressure to follow gendered social norms. Parents, teachers, and other authority figures hold a great deal of power over our life choices. When we begin to express our identities in ways that are different or challenging to their assumptions, it can be hard for them to know how to react. They may write off our T/GE identities as rebellion, confusion, "just a phase," or otherwise invalidate our experiences. But having the freedom to explore our gender identities is an important part of becoming an adult. These are the years when we are learning what kind of adults we will be—and how we inhabit our genders is a big part of that process.

Shifting Identities

As T/GE youth, we tend to be inquisitive about the things we have been told about our identities and who we are as people. We have a drive for discovery and to know our own personal truths. We are curious and courageous in our questioning. For some of us, there may be a desire to decrease discomfort or a sense that "something is wrong." The journey to better understanding ourselves and our identities can be fairly short for some, and for others can be quite long, with a variety of adventures along the way. Some of us may try on a few different identities until we find the one that fits best.

Whereas the previous chapter focused on younger children, this chapter is for youth in adolescence.

"All of us are put in boxes by our family, by our religion, by our society, our moment in history, even our own bodies. Some people have the courage to break free."—Geena Rocero, model and founder of the Gender Proud media production company

Actress Zoey Luna. (Samuel Paul)

I just thought I was a lesbian for a long time. The things I later realized were dysphoria just registered as social anxiety or other vague "something's wrong." When I was a teenager, I was so obsessed with watching movies and trying to make myself look like the male leads, but I convinced myself it was because I wanted to be with the female lead. Turns out, no, I really did want to be the male lead.

For many of us, adolescence is a time of discovery, and for some, it is a time of exploring romantic, sexual, emotional, and/or physical attractions. Although some of us know from the beginning that our question is one of gender identity, others may first explore their sexual orientation. And some of us find our sexuality on the way to discovering our true gender.

I started identifying as nonbinary since I was 13. I did not always feel like a boy but I was still too scared to admit to myself that I wanted to be feminine. In the past year, I've become more comfortable with my femininity and have started to call myself transfem, along with nonbinary. I still feel like a man some days, though. I have referred to my sexuality as 'gay' since I was 8. The fact that I'm not a cis man did not change how I label my sexuality.

Want to dig a little deeper into your gender identity and have fun at the same time? Check out the *Gender Identity Workbook for Teens* by Andrew Maxwell Triska (Rockridge Press, 2021).

As we give ourselves space to discover our identities, they may shift over time. We may identify as a woman-loving woman and then realize that, in fact, we are genderqueer and romantically attracted to people of any gender. Our gender identities may take on a few different names and looks, or even a combination of names at once. Some of us will fit comfortably into binary girl or boy identities. Others may discover that we are both boy and girl, aren't quite a girl or a boy, or have a different gendered experience that is not captured by the terms T/GE girl or boy. As T/GE youth, our gender possibilities have no limits.

PAGES AND PROSE

Drew Mindell (he/him) is a writer, a student, and an activist from the woodlands of Connecticut. He is a proud advocate for equal representation in literature and media.

For as long as I can remember, I've loved to read.

When I was a baby, my mother would gather me and a pile of story books onto her bed, and she would read to me until I could no longer keep my eyes open. When I was old enough to read on my own, it was all I would do. I read at school under my desk, and home in the big recliner chair, even at birthday parties. I read book after book, page after page, losing myself in stories and linking myself to characters.

But in all those pages, in all those characters, I was alone. I had read stories of wizards and demigods and fairies, children fleeing the Nazis and children fighting dragons and children growing up and finding love. But none of them were like me. None of them were trans. And so I felt alone, even surrounded by my hundreds and thousands of fictional friends.

When I wrote my first story, I didn't know where it would lead. I didn't know how I wanted the plot to twist. I didn't know how I wanted the characters to develop. I didn't even know if I would finish it (I didn't, but I finished the next one). All I knew was that I wanted someone in the story to be trans. Their name was Adeline, they were the monarch of an entire kingdom, and not only were they trans, they were trans and in love. They were trans and in love and happy. Beautiful. And for the first time, I started to feel happy. Beautiful. And I knew, reading and rereading my own pages, my own prose, that I could never stop writing.

I have never stopped writing. I have kept going and kept creating. Trans characters and autistic characters and Jewish characters spilled from my fingers. These imperfect, beautiful people, these people drawn from my memory and my tears and my life, they dance out into the world searching for children like me. The ones who need friends. The ones who need reassurance. The ones who need to feel beautiful and happy and not alone.

As for me, all I can do is set them forth and hope they find a mark.

Butterfly. "The butterfly symbolizes transformation and nonconformity. When people think butterflies, often times they think feminity, but this butterfly symbolizes a transformation into one's true self, despite what others may think. As someone who is on the masculine side of the nonbinary spectrum, my goal is for people to see me for who I am and not as a certain gender, just as you would when you see a butterfly." (Alex Collins, he/they, age 16)

SELF-ESTEEM AND BODY IMAGE

I always felt wrong growing up, but I didn't understand why. When I hit junior high, I started noticing gender differences and separation, but I didn't recognize gender as the cause of my distress. I assumed I was not good enough at being a girl, or that my body was too fat, and that if I changed those things, I would feel better.

As young people, we all get messages about the "right" way to look and act from every angle—at school, from family, in our communities, and via the media. Our cultures shape our view of our bodies (often from a narrow binary and gender conforming perspective), what we should wear, where our priorities ought to be, and how to be successful. Our society's ideas about what girls and boys "should" be like make up a seemingly endless list dictating body shape and size, clothing, sexuality, career goals, and just about everything else.

I was very masculine from an early age, and had very few girl friends. I hit puberty when I was 8 and openly hated my breasts, so much to where my family would joke and chuckle about me wanting a flat chest when so many girls would love to have big boobs like me. They never considered I might actually be a boy though, and kept steering me towards femininity. My aunt spent hundreds of dollars on fancy bras for me, as if wearing a lacy underwire to middle school might make me feel better.

It is unfair and often not possible for us to meet so many unreasonable standards in order to gain basic respect. Each of us is an individual, with our own unique perspectives and experiences. Our differences are what make us uniquely beautiful.

I've known I was different ever since I can remember. I have always rejected traditional femininity and resented how I was boxed in by expectations that I would be a girl. At first it was little things, gender roles and such. I hated pink and loved Legos, although that is very much a stereotype . . . I was uncomfortable with my attraction to boys throughout my teenage years because I thought it reduced my masculinity and felt like I had something to prove. I wished from a very young age that I was a boy and started experiencing dysphoria even before puberty. Growing breasts was a nightmare. Menstruating was horrific for me in ways I couldn't even begin to understand. I never recognized myself in the mirror, especially when wearing dresses. My mother noticed all this and tried to force me to be more feminine, which made me shut myself off from femininity even more. I just assumed all girls felt the same way. I had no idea what trans people even were until I was 19.

COMING OUT

It was June (Pride) of 2018, and I had seen a post about many different sexualities and genders in my feed. I was a little bored and interested, so I began to really look into the LGBTQ community. I was shocked. Not only had many of the stereotypes I believed been wrong, but the truth seemed like it described me. About a month or two later, I realized I didn't really want to be a boy anymore. Now, I'm actually considering taking Estrogen, though I'm doing extensive research on what it actually does to a 14 year old's body.

Coming out is the process by which someone comes to terms with a sense of personal identity (in this case, T/GE identity) after the process of self-discovery, also known as "coming in"[1] or "clueing in."[2,3] There are a lot of steps to consider in coming out—it is an ongoing process rather than a single event. T/GE people of all ages have their own coming out experiences, and there are some special considerations for us as T/GE youth.

With increasing visibility, youth are coming out at earlier ages and in a variety of settings, from family to school. While visibility and validation are important, what is most crucial is our safety and survival. We often have to consider what the risks of coming out are, such as loss of a good education, relationships with family of origin, health care, social support, work, or housing.

"It's a tiny revolution to express yourself fully and be who you want to be, especially when systems tell you that you can't."—Amandla Stenberg, nonbinary actor and singer

"Self-definition and self-determination is about the many varied decisions that we make to compose and journey toward ourselves . . . It's OK if your personal definition is in a constant state of flux as you navigate the world."—Janet Mock, trans writer and activist

Photo of Melissa DeStefano and Aidan next to the trans flag at the Governor's Mansion in Harrisburg, PA during the launch of the first ever Pennsylvania Commission on LGBTQ Affairs in 2018.

If you are considering coming out to others for the first time, some preparation is needed in order to think through and make a plan. Before deciding when, how, and to whom to come out, it is important to consider the possible risks that could come with disclosing a T/GE identity. The risks that we, as T/GE youth, take when coming out will vary depending on our specific circumstances and whom we choose to tell. We may have to make the choice to tell some people and not others for various reasons. For example, coming out to a parent who pays for things like food, housing, and clothing has different—and possibly more significant—risks than coming out to a friend at school.

We wish that the expected response from everyone was to celebrate our identities. And this does happen for some of us. Many of us, however, have the experience of hearing people who we thought cared about us say very hurtful things to our face, over text or online, or through other people. When we experience this, we can feel disappointed, hurt, and/or scared. Other times, we may be met with acceptance. Acceptance does not necessarily mean that we will get a joyful, happy, two thumbs up response. It may still take a long time for people to understand what it means for us to be T/GE, to use our correct names and pronouns, or treat us in ways that feel affirming to our gender identities and expressions.

Whether someone is shocked and angry or supportive but unsure, we may need to educate our friends and family on how to be there for us. Sometimes people need time and space in order to become our allies. We also need to remember that there is pressure to come out to everyone in our lives, but in reality, it is our choice to whom and when to come out. It may even be a reality that we come out to certain people and rarely talk about it again. Ultimately, we have to make decisions about coming out that fit who we are and what we value.

Choosing Someone Safe

Knowing we are T/GE can be a huge weight to carry around, and we may want to come out to have someone we can talk with. Picking a safe person to come out to first can help us find support as we think about how we want to live our lives authentically. The first people that we choose to tell may *not* be our parents, guardians, or other people who ensure our access to housing, food, employment, health care, or education. Most of us choose a close friend, sibling, teacher, or counselor who we think will be safe to talk with.

> *I tried to talk to people regarding my gender, but they thought I was delusional. Only my Religious Studies teacher validated my feelings and told me I was fine as I was (he still misgendered me however).*

We can often figure out whether someone is safe by listening to how they talk about cisgender lesbian, gay, and bisexual (LGB) people or other T/GE people on TV or in our communities. If they speak negatively about cisgender LGB people, there is a good chance that coming out to this person may not be safe. However, even if they speak well of cisgender LGB people, they still might not be affirming of T/GE people. Some may even be OK with T/GE people in the community but not in their family. If they do not bring it up, we might try bringing it into casual conversation by asking whether they have heard of well-known T/GE people or how they feel about laws that relate to T/GE people. Their response can give us clues about whether coming out to them is safe.

Sometimes we have to make compromises. If we are going to interview for a job that we really want, we may have to make some adjustments in how we dress in order to get the job. Many of us have to dress a certain way to be allowed to stay in our parents' houses and have food to eat. We will not always have to make these sacrifices, and we will likely be better off in the future if we get our basic needs met in the present. We have to weigh the short- and long-term risks and benefits, keeping physical and emotional safety at the forefront of this consideration.

> *Both my parents fixated on my hair, but on different aspects of it. My dad hated it when I cut my hair short; he comments on it to this very day. On the other hand, my mom was insistent on policing my body hair, once I started growing it. She made it a rule that I couldn't wear sleeveless shirts unless I shaved my armpits. I hated this rule and would break it as often as possible. Eventually she wore me down with enough scolding and lecturing, but even when I caved and shaved, it felt like something wrong and shameful, so I actually did it in secret— even though it was what she wanted to happen! As I got older and started looking for internships and jobs, my mother took the lead in policing what attire was "professional." She insisted that I needed heels and skirts, even though I thought flats would look just as professional. We eventually compromised with very, very low heels.*

If we do not want someone we talk with to tell other people about our genders, it is good to make sure to say so before saying anything else. Some information may get shared with our parents or guardians when we are adolescents that we are not ready to share or don't necessarily want them to know. This especially goes for school counselors. Make sure to ask what the counselor's confidentiality policy is before disclosing. Although counselors in private practice cannot share most information about us with others, school counselors often are not held to the same strict standards. If we are currently supported by a parent or legal guardian, we should make sure the person we come out to realizes that keeping our information private may be a matter of our survival.

Understanding the Risks of Disclosure

It can be helpful for us to consider all the potential risks and benefits of coming out to the people in our lives. Here are some "what if" considerations that could be good for us to reflect on as we plan if, when, and how to disclose our gender to others.

- *Find a short-term place to stay.* If you are concerned that you may not be welcome or safe in your home, it can be comforting to have planned ahead. Some of us may have friends, classmates, or relatives who we may be able to stay with over a short-term period. In some places, youth or LGBTQ-focused shelters may be able to provide a safe place to sleep, as well as access to support services.
- *Plan a budget for the long-term.* Find out how much money you could make at a job and how much it costs living in an apartment, getting furniture, having electricity and water, buying groceries to have three meals a day, doing laundry, using transportation, wearing decent clothes, and buying things like toothpaste and toilet paper. Keep in mind that as a young person, it may be challenging (or impossible) to rent an apartment without a cosigner for a lease, and you may be limited in the kinds of jobs you can have or the number of hours you are allowed to work.
- *Pack a bag.* Even if you are relatively sure things are going to be OK, it is never a bad idea to have a bag packed just in case. Include some clothes, a toothbrush, and anything you need for school. Make sure to bring important documents such as IDs and birth certificates, and any medications you take on a regular basis.

Some of us choose to wait to come out to our parents until we are more socially and financially independent. For some people, this may mean waiting until we no longer live with our parents, while for others, it may mean waiting until we have finished our education. If we choose to wait until we have more independence, we may be able to maintain better control over our own transition process. That may feel like an option for some but not all of us.

Self-portrait by Lizzy Jay, age 17. Pen and ink.

Disclosure: Private versus Secret

In some cases, we do not have to come out to people if we do not want to or if keeping our T/GE status private will keep us safe. If we are not sure if we identify as T/GE or we are not sure what kind of T/GE identity fits best, telling everyone we know can add a lot of pressure we may not be ready to deal with. Also, if we find out that someone we thought was safe turns out not to be, we might feel discouraged and invalidated. Instead of isolating, be sure to continue to reach out to others if that person did not work out. If no one in your community seems safe to come out to, you might try reaching out to other T/GE people online.

For some of us, it is important to be "out" or to be open about being a T/GE person in all areas of life. On the other hand, some of us prefer to keep that part of ourselves more private. We get to determine the level of openness that is right for us. Most T/GE youth do, however, end up telling at least a select few trusted friends about their identity. Being selective about telling others about our T/GE identity does not mean it is a *secret*; it is our *private information* to share.[4] Secrets tend to be those things that we don't want others to know because we might feel ashamed about them and are keeping them to ourselves. We do not need to be ashamed of being T/GE. But we do get to decide who gets to know that part of us.

Coming Out to Parents and Guardians

We all have different relationships with the adults who are responsible for our care, and their reactions will vary widely and may be difficult to predict. Although some of us are fortunate to have caregivers who embrace our gender identity immediately, many of us find that they need time to adjust. Even though parents may initially express fear, anger, guilt, sadness, or confusion, they can ultimately become our biggest supporters. If we can give them some time and space to experience their feelings, they may come around. Sometimes we may have to set boundaries with them. It is really difficult to be patient during these times, but a little patience may pay off in the long run. It may also be helpful to provide them with resources.

> [My parents] recognized me as a tomboy and that was seen as just fine. However, I was forced into feminine clothing and roles from time to time for formal occasions. What I hated most was when it became official that I was a "girl." I would roughhouse with my male cousins and run around with them, but as puberty came along the adults forced me to spend more time with the girls because "the boys are too rough and strong for you to play with." It was devastating.

Providing our families with information and resources can help them understand our needs and concerns. PFLAG, formerly called Parents, Friends, and Families of Lesbians and Gays, has an online "Support Guide for Families and Friends of Transgender and Gender Non-conforming People" where we can refer our families. Additional challenges may arise for those of us whose parents' first language is not English, but PFLAG and the American Psychological Association both have resources available in multiple languages. Gender Spectrum and the Family Acceptance Project are additional resources for parents that can be accessed online.

If we do not know where our family stands on being T/GE, we can try to test the waters before coming out. Casually bring up queer or T/GE issues with family members and gauge their reaction. Are they generally queer- and T/GE-positive? Do they have personal or religious stances on queer- and T/GE- issues? Remember to factor in the level of your current relationships. It may be beneficial to come out to people individually rather than in a big group. We might choose to send some people a coming out letter, email, or text if we are uncomfortable telling them in person.

Looking for a way to organize your thoughts about your gender identity? Check out *The Gender Quest Workbook: A Guide for Teens and Young Adults Exploring Gender Identity* (edited by Rylan J. Testa, Deborah Coolhart, and Jayme Peta, Instant Help, 2015).

NEVER GIVE UP

Lucas Wehle (he/him) is a trans man who works as the Trans Services Division Manager at a local nonprofit in St. Petersburg, Florida. He adores his niece and nephew and cuddling with his cat, Shark.

Growing up, I always knew I was not a girl. What I did not know was how difficult it would be to convince people otherwise. Until I went to college and got involved with the PRIDE student organization, I had never heard the term transgender or known there was a community of people who felt the way I did. In my second semester, I realized I was trans and wanted to live as male. When I realized this, I immediately knew that my family was going to have a hard time accepting it. However, I kept pushing and persisting.

My parents did not accept me when I came out as a lesbian, so I knew that coming out as trans was going to be a much bigger hurdle. However, after 18 years of struggling with severe dysphoria and depression, I could not hide who I was for another day. When I told my parents I was male and wanted to be called Lucas, they immediately went into denial and refused to use my name and pronouns. Their denial was extremely confusing for me considering I had presented masculine for about 90% of my life. My parents could not wrap their minds around the fact that I was so uncomfortable being perceived as female that I needed to change my physical appearance in order to live happily, or to live at all. They fought my gender identity for a very long time. To say we struggled would be a tremendous understatement. At one point, I had to move out of their house to show them how uncomfortable and toxic it was to be around their constant misgendering and deadnaming. However, I did not cut them out of my life or write them off completely. I continued to keep communication open with them, but distanced myself a little and allowed them more time to adjust.

I knew my family loved me very much, but I was 99% sure they were never going to come around. However, I never gave up, and thankfully, I was very wrong. Six years later, when I was named grand marshal of our city's Pride Parade, my family started referring to me as Lucas and using he/him/his pronouns for the very first time. I am happy to say that my family has since respected my name and pronouns for almost two years, and my mom is now an active member of our local chapter of PFLAG, which is an organization that unites people who are lesbian, bisexual, transgender, and queer with their families, friends, and allies. So if there is ever a time where you think things may never turn around for you or your family, do not lose hope. You never know how perfect your life could turn out to be.

Coming Out at School

The decision about when—or whether, or how—to come out at school is something that many of us spend a long time grappling with. Many of us want to share our identity so we can be seen as a complete person and live authentically. At the same time, we may be afraid of the challenges we will face. The decision to come out at school is very personal and should be based completely on our level of comfort, access to support networks, and safety.

My high school was a part of a collection of schools across several states in the Southwest of the U.S. My mom still teaches at one of them, and my step-dad works for their administration. I have heard terrible stories about their "Diversity Club" that had to form and meet in secret. They came out with policies stating that faculty and staff had to address students by their legal gender on their birth certificates, though not all teachers followed those rules. And the administration celebrated the day Trump was elected, saying that they wouldn't have to worry about the trans students and their families kicking up such a fuss anymore. When I was in their school, I never saw how blatant their erasure of trans experiences was, but now that I am outside of it I can see that they did everything they could to encourage us to fall in line with white, cisgender expectations. They refused to host sex ed or health classes, even as an elective, post-school hours session. They told us we were not allowed to use the words "penis" or "vagina" in biology when learning about reproductive systems, and had a rule that we could not bring up anything that was "pop-culture" (which meant anything more recent than 50 years ago) in class.

Coming out at school is usually a long process. It is unlikely that our school will be willing to have a giant mandatory assembly where we can stand in front of everyone in the

Two non-binary students looking at each other in a school hallway. (Zackary Drucker, The Gender Spectrum Collection, VICE/Broadly)

school and come out to all of them and then never have to do it again—nor would many of us want that. The reality for most of us is that we will find ourselves coming out to people one by one, in small groups, or in a class setting. We will have conversations with teachers and administrators, coaches and counselors. When thinking about coming out to any of these adults at school, it can be useful to go into the conversation with some talking points prepared. This means thinking ahead of time about what we want to say to this person and what we hope to get out of the conversation.

School settings can be giant rumor mills. The more people we tell, the higher the chance that someone will tell someone else who we may not want to know. We can think through how we might deal with this with a supportive adult at school or a close friend before disclosing to anyone. If we are out at school, it is also likely that our parents or guardians will find out. It can be helpful to have the support of a counselor or other ally when coming out to our families, but we may also risk losing control of when and how we come out to them. We should understand what confidentiality we are guaranteed when speaking with school staff and know that information can travel quickly through the community, even if we have only told a few friends.

SOCIAL TRANSITION

Social transition is the process of making nonmedical changes to how we look and live in order to feel more at ease with our gender. Just like everything else about being T/GE, there is no one right way to approach social transition. Some common steps include making a name change, switching pronouns, wearing different types of clothing, cutting our hair differently, or making nonmedical physical alterations such as binding our chests or wearing a bra with breast forms.

Our transition process typically happens in a school setting, where we have different challenges and opportunities. We may encounter problems with peers, teachers, administrators, or school policies. As minors we have more "gatekeepers" who control our access to medical, mental health, and legal services, and are more likely to face economic constraints in our transition process.

Trans Student Educational Resources (TSER) is a youth-led organization dedicated to changing the educational environment for T/GE students.

My schools mostly did not care about my ambiguous gender presentation, but I'm sure it would have been an issue had I wanted to use a different bathroom or change my name. Teachers started to separate me from the boys starting in first grade when changing for gym class or during sports activities.

As youth, if a person in a position of power over us (teacher, principal, parent, coach, pastor, etc.) is not respecting us, we need to decide what we are willing to compromise on and what we are not. For example, if we really want to play on the sports team and can play only under the wrong name and pronouns, we are faced with a decision. Some of us may feel comfortable using different pronouns in different contexts, while others may decide to take legal action or address the issue with the school board. We get to decide what is important to us. Not all of us will make the same decision.

In high school I knew there was something going on with me in terms of my gender because I felt frustrated and confused about it. Being a girl was weird and not quite right but I also knew I was not a man. I just remember wearing a favorite black jacket in front of a mirror and feeling like something was off and I couldn't figure out what. I also started liking wearing sports bras in high school and didn't know that that was basically because I was binding. In my first year or so of college I was with my mom in a coffee shop when my mom was talking to her friend about me. When my mom said "she" when talking about me I had this awful reaction inside like, "Ew, why did you just call me that??" but I had no idea at the time that there were even more than two genders.

YOUNG LGBT LIVES

Eddy Funkhouser (they/them) is a gardener and volunteer coordinator in San Francisco, where they currently live.

I came out when I was twenty
people don't talk about before that
it's too hard for them to mince around my name my
    pronouns
my entire childhood and adolescence
erased
everywhere except my own memory

it's hard to hold onto
who I am
without acknowledgement or remembrance
of who I was

I remember
an entire childhood and adolescence
full of fear and confusion
without knowing trans people existed
how could I know who I was
without any reflection
however distorted
of people like me
how could I know I was not alone
without an image of trans adulthood
how could I know that I had a future
how could I know that I would get to grow up

it took time but
I did grow up
come out
transition
find community
explore who I am
I got to find space to hold who I was

people struggle when telling stories about me in the past tense
when they're talking about my childhood
my "girlhood"
they stumble over my name my pronouns

if I had a nickel for every time
I heard "when she was a little girl"
sometimes followed by
"that was your name back then I don't get what you're so upset about"
or "I support you please forgive me"
I'd be able to donate a lot more to The Trevor Project

I donate what I can
I hold and value myself
past
current
future
I tell the stories others cannot tell
because they are too scared of stumbling over my name my pronouns
I use the right name right pronouns
I tell the right stories
they end in hope

The Pressure to Pass

The ability to present our gender in such a way that we are consistently seen as our authentic gender identity is frequently called "passing" or "cis-passing." Some of us take pride or pleasure in "passing," while some of us do not. Many of us have rejected the term because it suggests that we are not *really* the gender we present as or that we are deceiving others. The pressure to "pass," or to blend in as cis, can be very real, especially for binary trans youth. Society often imposes heavy expectations on us as T/GE people to live up to cisnormative gender roles.

The pressure can be particularly strong during adolescence, when all of our peers are shaping their own gender identities as well. As a result, we receive many messages about the "right" way to express our gender, whether from cisgender family and friends or from T/GE peers. Many T/GE youth feel astounding pressure to prove we can fit into preexisting gender categories in our society and to prove we can live up to the standard of a "real" man or woman.

"Because whether or not I present hyper-masculine or not, at the end of the day, I'm still [me], I still feel masculine, I still feel like I only want to use he/him pronouns and nothing changes that."—Ian Alexander, trans actor known for his role on *The OA*

> *The only problem I have is that some [trans] guys are not as accepting of gender variance. They think you have to have this really typical trans narrative, want to do as much to transition as possible, and be really stereotypically masculine in order to fit in. They are always pointing out people who "make the community look bad." That makes me nervous, because I do some things that others think make the community look bad (I'm sometimes very feminine; I am dating a lesbian; I call myself a lesbian sometimes.) I'm afraid*

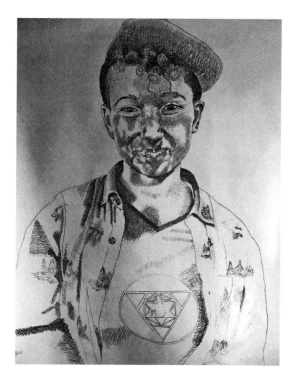

Portrait of Megan Small. Activist Portrait Series. (Syrus Marcus Ware)

that admitting that I go by female pronouns sometimes is going to get me kicked out of the core community.

Being read correctly is just one experience of living as our authentic selves. It is wrong for others to impose their ideas of gender on us, and we should work on unconditionally accepting and encouraging each other. There are as many ways to be T/GE as there are T/GE people in the world.

Gender-Segregated Spaces

When we are coming out at school, issues we may want to discuss with school administrators include the use of gendered spaces, such as bathrooms and locker rooms, and participation in gendered activities such as sports teams, cheerleading, and school clubs. These are points of anxiety for almost all T/GE people.

I frequently felt detached from my peers, especially once I got a bit older and social activities became sex segregated, but I mostly just assumed it was because I was shy.

One of the most feared gender segregated places is the public bathroom. This can be especially problematic for T/GE students because we spend eight hours a day in a school where it might not be safe for us to use the bathroom.

My teachers were horrible. I was forced to use the girls changing rooms where I was attacked and ridiculed. Couldn't use the bathroom at school without the fear of being attacked or tossed out.

Choosing bathrooms, locker rooms, or other facilities that correspond to the gender we are transitioning into is a personal decision. We might come into conflict with peers who are uncomfortable or surprised to see us in those spaces, and we might not get support from all teachers and school officials. There may be concerns raised about our right to be in those spaces, and we may be put in a position of having to advocate for ourselves in order to access them.

Growing up my teachers knew nothing. In my first high school I was forced to tell them and one of my teachers outed me to the entire class and made an already unsafe situation even more unsafe.

We might also have to make a compromise in order to show the school that we are willing to work with them. For example, while using the nurse's bathroom can be a real pain, it may be the safest possible option, at least for a short time.

Gender is something that comes up in all sorts of ways. At school dances, such as homecoming and prom, there are typically students chosen to be gendered "royalty," and our school might also have a policy on who we can go to a dance with. To find out more about our school's policies on gender, we might consider joining the Gender and Sexuality Alliance (GSA). If the school does not have one, we can use resources at the Gay, Lesbian, and Straight Education Network (GLSEN) and the GSA Network to create one. Not just high schools, but many middle and elementary schools also have LGBTQ support groups. Even if we are the only T/GE student in the group, we can still learn a lot from other students as well as the adult mentor. At the same time, we might have to do more outside research, education, and networking than the cis LGB students. In the end, it is more important for us to be safe than to be right about the school's policies.

Sometimes we feel like we have no support at school. If you are feeling this way, reach out to a national organization such as the Trevor Project (866-488-7386), the GLBT National Help Center (800-246-7743), or Trans Lifeline (US: 877-565-8860; Canada: 877-330-6366). The Transgender Law Center also works with schools and families to advocate for our right to be safe in school.

Building Community

I did not know any transgender people personally, but I was very aware of the amazingly bad-ass Puerto Rican trans women in my neighborhood . . . as I was growing up!! They were super fierce and always had each other's backs!! I was super impressed by them as they were so brave (!) and still think about them to this day!

One of the most helpful things we can do for ourselves when we first come into a T/GE identity is to find our own communities. As youth, we are often restricted by things such as transportation, our families' rules, money, or other issues. We all do the best we can with what we have. For some of us, knowing that T/GE people live in our neighborhoods can be exciting. We might have a desire to reach out to someone who is considered an elder or who can be a mentor. If we have access to the Internet, we can try searching for resources such as YouTube videos, blogs, or forums where we can connect with other T/GE youth.

A group of friends of varying genders taking a photo at a party. (Zackary Drucker, The Gender Spectrum Collection, VICE/Broadly)

I wish I had known trans adults as a child or teenager; I probably would have figured things out quicker if I had.

As youth, some of us live in a culture where posting personal material in public forums is a reality, and we may desire to document our transition process and share it with others online. Many of us appreciate and find community through others who do so. Cultural and legal practices around the privacy of online information are changing rapidly, however, and we want to spend some time thinking about our privacy limits.

I'm mostly involved in the transgender YouTube community, which is really huge. I have a vlog where I talk about gender, and I'm subscribed to a ton of transguys and their partners. It is a nice community, very supportive.

Bullies, Rumors, and Problems with Peers

Bullying takes many forms, from verbal and emotional harassment to physical intimidation and violent attacks. No matter what form it takes, bullying is never OK. Some people may tell us that bullying is just teasing or a normal part of growing up, but this is not true. Bullying is dangerous and has very real and lasting effects on our safety and self-esteem. Those of us who are bullied are more likely to experience depression and more likely to think about or attempt suicide. In fact, recent studies have shown that suicide attempt rates in T/GE youth are significantly higher than in their cisgender peers. Being misgendered contributes to depression and suicidality.[5] Bullying is incredibly serious and something that needs to be treated as such.

If we are being bullied, it is important to get as much support as we can. One way to make sure that we are heard is to document everything that is happening at school—from the bullying and harassment to the response (or lack thereof) from teachers and administration. This log should include as much information as possible, including the dates, times, names of the people involved in the incident, our attempts to get help, and how the adult(s) responded. For example, "On Thursday, December 7, I was sitting in my homeroom class when Rob and Steve started calling me a fag. They did not stop when I asked them to stop. I then told the teacher, Ms. Wortham, what they said. She told me to be quiet and sit back down." When we experience trauma, it is actually very difficult for our brains to encode memories as well as usual. It is helpful to record what happened as soon as possible because these experiences can be traumatic.

Hombre Trans. (US Embassy Mexico)

Life Stages

Even when we know that the bullying we experience is wrong, it can be easy to take the messages we hear from bullies personally. It is important to remember that what is happening is not our fault, and just because we hear these terrible messages does not mean that any of them are true. All students deserve to have a safe learning environment where we are not harassed, and our schools have an obligation to make sure that we have a safe place to learn.

Sometimes resolving the issues we are having at school can be as simple as a meeting with people in power. This is more likely to happen if we have a supportive administration and counselors at our school who are concerned about the safety of all students. We might try speaking with the assistant principal or the principal of the school. We can talk to them about the bullying we experience at school and the negative impact it has on our lives.

> *By senior high school I was being bullied by two different physical education teachers because I refused to take showers in a communal shower area. I was also "put down" by a school counselor for being "too masculine" in behavior and appearance. None were supportive at all. However, my age peers were friendly and not at all mean to me.*

Unfortunately, sometimes teachers and administrators do not do anything about the bullying and harassment that we experience. When they do not do anything, it seems as if they are supporting what is going on. In some cases, adults in schools are directly harassing us. In other cases, they are indirectly participating in our harassment by failing to work with us to increase our safety at school or by being unwilling to accept that there is even a problem occurring. In these situations, we sometimes need to go to someone in a higher position, such as the school district superintendent or the school board. We might also choose to reach out to local community groups who can support our efforts to advocate for ourselves.

If you are being bullied at school, it may be helpful to first create a plan to ensure your immediate safety. From there you can begin thinking about ways to improve the overall situation at your school. You can also identify an ally who will help you stand up against the discrimination you are experiencing. This could be a friend, counselor, social worker, teacher, parent, or guardian. This person should be willing to support you in what you are going through and to assist you in advocating for your safety with school administrators.

One of the best things we can do to arm ourselves is to learn about our rights. Contact local and national organizations such as the Transgender Law and Policy Institute, the Transgender Law Center, the Southern Poverty Law Center, the Sylvia Rivera Law Project, and the National Center for Lesbian Rights. Memorize the laws that apply to you, and share the information with other T/GE people in the community.

The National Center for Transgender Equality website has a free resource that explains how Title IX, a federal law that is part of the Educational Amendments Act of 1972, protects T/GE youth in schools.

T/GE YOUNG ADULT LITERATURE

A short piece by Jackson Radish on trans young adult literature appeared in the first edition of Trans Bodies, Trans Selves. This new version was created by this chapter's authors, but builds on similar ideas and themes.

Have you ever had a moment when reading a book or watching something on TV where you saw yourself in a character? A trans researcher, Dr. Aaron Devor, calls this experience "mirroring."[6] Mirroring is where we see a part or parts of ourselves reflected by another person. This can also happen when we meet other T/GE people or other folks who share similar identities with us. Mirroring is less likely to happen for those of us with minority identities, especially in the media or in books. It can be challenging for some of us to find characters who seem to resemble us or reflect our lived experiences. They do exist though; we just have to search a little harder to find those characters who are like us. Some examples include: Xemiyulu "Xemi" Manibusan, an Indigenous, Two-Spirit theatrical director, actor, and author; Andraya Yearwood, a Black transgender girl high school student athlete; Ian Alexander, an Asian-American transmasculine actor; and Garcia, also known as Josiah Victoria Garcia, a transgender nonbinary Latinx actor.

Young adult (YA) literature for T/GE youth continues to grow. Consider looking for books written by T/GE authors and finding information about the context of the book or perspective of the author. *How to Understand Your Gender: A Practical Guide for Exploring Who You Are* by Alex Iantaffi and Meg-John Barker serves as a guide to exploring gender identity and sexuality and offers reminders to readers to pause and breathe or take a break if necessary. One of our trans elders, Kate Bornstein, has written books that guide identity exploration (*My Gender Workbook*) and coping with bullying and depression (*Hello Cruel World: 101 Alternatives to Suicide for Teens, Freaks and Other Outlaws*).

I started to notice how different I felt from my peers when we went through puberty. My friends were excited about breasts and periods, but I was terrified and it made me feel so sick to even think about. I started writing and making characters that I expressed these feelings through and I pretended that those things were them and not me to try and cope with the dysphoria I was feeling. I didn't have any of the knowledge or language to explore why I was feeling that way until quite a bit later.

Even though more and more T/GE characters are showing up in books, there's still plenty of room for more characters, especially those with diverse identities and ways of being. Many of us find it healing or therapeutic to write our stories, whether for ourselves or others. For example, *Stacey's Not a Girl* is a children's book written by Colt (one of the authors of this chapter) who channeled his child self and what would have been helpful to know at a young age. He combined his own story and those of his friends to create literature for and about T/GE youth.

LGBTQ YOUTH PROGRAMS

LGBTQ youth organizations like Hetrick-Martin in New York City may offer activities, food, clothing, counseling, and housing support.

LGBTQ youth programs, such as peer support groups and drop-in centers, can provide us with opportunities to access resources and connect with community, especially if these are lacking in our schools and peer networks. These organizations provide safe spaces with affirming staff and volunteers and are populated with other youth who are grappling with similar problems and experiences. Oftentimes, these spaces offer fun activities such as queer prom nights or drag shows that youth can participate in. They may also provide resources like clothing and food.

LGBTQ-specific programming can be particularly important for those of us who are not getting emotional support from our families, teachers, or peers. Some of us feel extremely isolated in our homes, schools, and broader communities. We may feel like the people around us do not understand what we are going through. These spaces can become our surrogate families and homes, providing structure, safety, and a sense of belonging.

Lambert House, a community center for LGBTQ youth in Seattle, WA. "Women like me aren't often afforded many comforts, though I suppose those that are will never know the pleasant surrealness of crying in a stranger's arms. Trust me, it's amazingly cathartic, though I'd hardly call Lambert House a stranger. If anything, its more of a family to me than the one I was born into." (Alaska Miller)

The concept of a chosen family—individuals who are deliberately chosen to play important roles in our lives and to offer caring and support when it is otherwise lacking—is a crucial part of queer/T/GE communities and has been a source of resource sharing and relationship building for LGBTQ youth and adults for many years. LGBTQ youth programs are places where many of us have met people we now call our chosen family members.

LGBTQ youth programs can also be an important connection for those of us who are in need of social services or counseling. Most LGBTQ youth centers and programs offer free case management services that can help get us connected with other programs and agencies and possibly mental health providers. They also often provide a range of other life skills programs that can assist us with our self-esteem, HIV/STI prevention and intervention, and other aspects of health care specific to LGBTQ youth. In most instances, services from these programs can be accessed without parental consent. These services allow us a degree of autonomy over our own mental health, giving us access to resources within a supportive environment. Sometimes there are time limits or age restrictions on these programs, effectively limiting the amount of time we can utilize the services. However, these services can be lifesavers for many of us.

HOUSING INSECURITY

Housing insecurity among T/GE youth is extremely prevalent. Twenty to forty percent of the 1.6 million homeless youth in the United States identify as LGBTQ. According to the National Center for Transgender Equality, one in five T/GE people report having experienced homelessness in their lifetime, often as a result of family rejection, discrimination, and violence. Most youth experiencing housing insecurity are people of color.[7]

Housing insecurity takes a variety of forms. Some of us may be living on the street. Others may be couch surfing after having been kicked out of our homes. For those of us who do not have stable homes, accessing T/GE-inclusive and affirming shelters where we feel safe is extremely important. Unfortunately, most mainstream shelter programs do not have staff, policies, or procedures that meet the needs of transgender youth. There have been reported cases of T/GE youth being refused services by homeless shelters solely because we are trans.

Most homeless shelters that include youth-specific programs are gender segregated. Some places have policies that will allow us to be sheltered with others who have similar gender identities as us only if we have had genital surgery—that is, we can only shelter with others with similar genitals as us. This can present a serious barrier to us as we simply seek shelter. A possible compromise that we might make is to dress in more gender-neutral ways in order to survive the night. This is unfair, and puts us in a position where we express ourselves inauthentically in order to have a warm place to sleep. We may feel like we have to leave a shelter because being on the streets feels safer than experiencing harassment.

A life-saving alternative for us can be LGBTQ youth-specific shelters, which are becoming more prevalent within major cities across the United States. These organizations are designed specifically to meet the needs of LGBTQ youth. Within these shelters, we are able to have our identity respected and enable us to connect with other resources that can assist in our journey toward stable housing.

The Ali Forney Center, named after a homeless T/GE youth named Ali Forney who was killed in 1997, is a social service organization in New York City with multiple housing sites for LGBTQ youth.

FOSTER CARE

If we are under 18, or under 21 in a growing number of states, one option for accessing stable housing is to attempt to go into foster care. Some major cities like San Francisco, Los Angeles, and New York City have group homes for LGBTQ youth where we receive an allowance and are given help in applying for college. Each state has its own hotline to get into foster care. Search foster care hotlines and your state online in order to find what number to call to get into foster care. If you expect your stint to be shorter, and are under 23 and in a big city, a possibility is to call a Covenant House (most but not all are inclusive and affirming of T/GE youth). In a smaller town, call the Trevor Hotline or the GLBT

National Youth Talkline and find out what they suggest. Or get on the Internet and find the closest LGBTQ center. Call during open hours, tell them about being recently homeless, and ask them where to go.

As we age, it becomes more difficult to find foster care placements. In some places, we are put into group home settings as an alternative to foster homes. If they are not LGBTQ-specific, these group homes are nearly always divided by sex assigned at birth, often leaving us in the difficult position of being housed in ways that do not affirm our gender identity. The foster care system is not always well-equipped to provide T/GE inclusive and affirming service to us. In a survey commissioned by the New York City Administration for Children's Services, compared to non-LGBTQ youth, LGBTQ youth in foster care were less satisfied with their current placement, more likely to say that they experienced little to no control over their lives, more frequently heard staff or other people refer to them as "hard to place," and had more absent days without permission.[8] Fortunately, there are some cities with LGBTQ foster care programs. In these places, many of the adults who volunteer to be foster parents are LGBTQ themselves.

GENDER ACTIVISM IN HIGH SCHOOL

Dakota Adiel (they/them) is a high school senior interested in art and design. They have been a member of the Tennessee SHINE activism team for two years, working to make schools and communities safer for LGBTQI youth across the state.

When I was little, Halloween was my favorite holiday. I would dress up as whatever I wanted, from Belle to Tigger to Bob the Builder. My parents never understood why I would want to dress up as anything other than a girl, and I never knew how to explain it to them. Now, I realize it was because I felt like I had to dress up every other day of the year to be the "little girl" my parents told me I was.

Middle school was when I first started realizing that I wasn't straight. I spent so much time going through Tumblr threads of different labels for sexuality, and I eventually settled on bisexual. I thought that finding this label would make me feel more complete or at home, but I didn't find that sensation of fullness there. By this point, I had heard of transgender* identities, I just never thought that I was a part of that community. I liked makeup, pink, and flowers, so I must be a girl, *right?*

Not even close. Freshman year of high school I finally figured it out. I had made some friends through Twitter, and a couple of them had told me that they were nonbinary, and that they used they/them pronouns. This normalized the concept of gender nonconformity, and I was *so* enthralled. I spent hours online researching it, and at one point I sat down and asked myself, "Why on Hashem's green Earth am I so interested in this?" I looked at myself in the mirror and had a conversation with my reflection. It went a little something like this:

"Are you a girl?"

Mirror-me blinked, and slowly shook their head no.

"Are you a boy?"

More certain this time, mirror-me shook their head again.

"What is your name?"

This one took mirror-me time to process. But I gave them all the time they needed. Mirror-me instinctively wanted to say my deadname, but they stopped. They realized that that was not who I was.

Now, it took a lot more time and many more tears to actually acknowledge that I am not a girl. I am nonbinary. I am normal. I am valid. Eventually, I came to the conclusion that I am Dakota, and that feeling of completion I had longed for finally came to be. Now, Halloween is the only day that I have to dress up.

DATING AND SAFER SEX

In addition to all of the typical pressures and concerns of teenage dating and sexuality, as T/GE youth, we navigate situations and issues that cis youth do not consider. Youth and T/GE people constitute two social groups that many adults believe should not be sexually active, as they often see our sexualities as somehow "inappropriate." This unrealistic standard sets us up to enter into unhealthy relationships, to engage in riskier sexual behaviors, and to fear self-advocacy. Yet, the truth is that we can have safe, healthy, and fun dating and sexual experiences.

Dating

As youth, we often transition within our existing community. We may assume that our gender transition has been very public and that everyone has followed our changes along the way, but that is not always the case. As adolescents, we all have a lot going on, and we may not always be aware of what other people are going through. If we are flirting with someone from our school, they may or may not know about our gender identity. We may have to navigate disclosing, even if we wish we didn't have to.

If we are lucky enough to have access to a community of other T/GE youth, it wouldn't be out of the ordinary that we might have a crush on one of them at some point. With all the complications that come with dating cis people, many of us find it more comfortable to date other T/GE people, who may be more familiar with the ways we think about our gender identities, presentations, or bodies. As amazing as it can feel to date other T/GE youth, sharing parts of our identities doesn't mean we are safe from negative experiences. A shared T/GE identity is all too often mistaken for a license to ask inappropriate questions, cross boundaries without asking, or put unwanted meaning on a partner's body.

Sexual Orientation

One of the first questions many of us are asked after coming out is what gender we are attracted to. Because most people are presumed to be straight unless proven otherwise, most cis straight youth do not have to come out as heterosexual. After a young person comes out as T/GE, we might be asked more questions about our sexuality than our cis peers, and people may confuse our gender identity and our sexual orientation.

Because our gender identities tell us what gender we are and not what gender(s) we are attracted to, most of us end up coming out twice: once as T/GE and once as gay, straight, pansexual, queer, heteroflexible, omnisexual, lesbian, asexual, demisexual, questioning, or any of the countless other sexual identity labels. The label that best matches our sexual orientation may change over time.

A picture of Jay Brown and Emily Hill embracing and smiling three weeks post Jay's top surgery.

Disclosure of our sexual identity follows the same principle as does disclosure of our gender identity. We get to decide whom we tell, when to tell, and how much we tell. Sometimes we have to remind people, especially adults, that it is our story to tell. If we are not sure what our sexual orientation is, it's OK to say, "I'm not sure, but I'm figuring it out." Most of us go through a period of questioning and/or exploring our sexual orientation, and this may happen after we discern our gender identity. This is healthy and completely valid. We are not required to tell the world we are questioning if we do not want to.

I always felt different from my peers because I was a girl who was a big nerd, read a lot, didn't watch TV, and wasn't afraid of bugs. It didn't really become about gender to me until I started dating in my mid-teens. I was super attracted to men, but every relationship I was in just felt wrong somehow. Looking back on it, I think I was really resistant to be seen as a woman in a straight relationship. Now, when I'm hooking up with men (cis or trans), I feel good about it because they know I'm genderqueer and respect that. Even if we're physically or emotionally doing the same things, it feels different because my identity is seen and respected. I'm not expected to fill this role of cis woman that always felt deeply uncomfortable.

We are not the only ones whose sexuality may be in question. The people we date may experience a period of questioning, by themselves or others, about their own sexual identity when they date a T/GE person. Whether we identify as the gender(s) our partner(s) typically are attracted to or not, they may wonder if being attracted to us makes them any more or less gay or straight than they had originally imagined themselves to be. Sexual orientation is a fluid thing. For example, if we identify as female and our partner identifies as a gay cis man, we are allowed to make up our own rules, be together, and keep using the labels that we like for our own sexual identities.

Talking about Sex

As youth, we may find it harder to talk about what we do and do not want sexually. Maybe we haven't received clear sex education, maybe we're not sure what we like because we don't have experience, and maybe it just feels uncomfortable! The best way to get through the awkwardness of talking about physical intimacy and sex is to talk about it a lot. Really. Sex is a taboo topic in our culture. We are constantly bombarded with messages that we should not have sex until we are older and that sex might be more difficult for us because our bodies may be different as T/GE people. These combine to pack a pretty powerful punch. It follows that talking about physical intimacy and sex is often really awkward for us. For most people, it gets easier with practice.

Talking about sex is what enables us to practice good consent—a foundation to healthy sexual engagement. This involves both giving and asking for consent to engage in sexual activities. We can understand consent as given when there has been an emphatic, voluntary, and conscious yes; otherwise, it is a no. When we assume that our partner wants to be sexual when they have not said that they do, or we try new things without confirming that our partner is interested, we are not using good consent practices. These harmful behaviors are modeled for us all the time by adults.

Sure, the idea of sweeping in for a surprise kiss at the end of a first date can be romantic—but if it makes our date feel unsafe, or upsets them, that is not fun for anyone. What is even more romantic is knowing, without a doubt, that our date really wants that kiss, or (if we are on the receiving end) that our date cares enough about us to make sure we always feel safe and in control of our decisions and what happens to our bodies.

Try using open-ended questions such as "How would you like me to touch you?" "What would feel good for you?" or "What kinds of things have you liked doing in the past?" These kinds of questions give our partners an opportunity to tell us what they want, instead of feeling like they might have to say no. This is often called enthusiastic consent—and it can help build strong, sexy relationships between people.

Scarleteen is a website that provides "sex ed for the real world," and features detailed diagrams of bodies using gender-neutral language, as well as answers to all kinds of questions about sex.

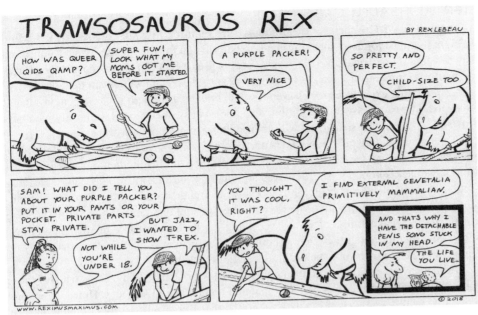

"This comic is part of a series I draw for Options Magazine, a free LGBTQ publication based in RI, and features a non-binary/genderqueer T.Rex and their mentee, a trans kid named Sam." "I'm a non-binary/genderqueer artist living in Newport, RI." (Rex LeBeau)

It is OK to say no or change our minds at any time. Just because we say yes to something one time does not mean that we are consenting to it at other times—even with the same person—even in the same sexual encounter. And just because we say no to something does not mean we cannot change our minds and try it later. It is definitely OK to *not* want to do certain things. Some of us only want to make out, keep clothes on, cuddle, or give or receive massages. Others of us have oral sex only, or manual sex but not oral sex, and still others want to experience many different combinations of sexual behaviors. Many of us do not want our genitals or chest area touched—or only sometimes, or only by certain people. Some of us have limits about certain parts of our bodies.

Safer Sex Practices

Not all of us are having sex or even want to have sex. Some of us are saving sex until we are in a long-term partnership. Many of us have limits as to what we will do physically with someone. Regardless of whether we are having sex, knowing about safer practices can increase the likelihood that we will have safe sex when we do decide to have sex.

No sex is ever completely safe, but being proactive about our sexual health and safety can be empowering and set us on the road to positive sexual experiences. Contrary to popular belief, safer sex is not as simple as using a condom. Safer sex is a lifelong process of learning about our body, the risks associated with the types of sex we like to have, and the different kinds of protection available to us. We can revisit what feels safe to us with every sexual encounter.

Survival Sex and Sex Work

Some of us may have engaged in sex work to support ourselves financially. "Survival sex" refers to the exchange of sex for food, shelter, or other basic survival needs. If we are engaging in sex work or survival sex, we have many more things to consider, when it comes to our safety, than those of us who are not engaging in these behaviors. Remember that being a sex worker does not mean we are any less entitled to set clear and firm boundaries or that our clients are any less obligated to ask for consent.

MENTAL HEALTH CARE

Although being T/GE does not mean that we are required to go to counseling, if we find the right therapist for us, counseling can be a helpful and fulfilling experience. Counseling may be a tool for personal discovery and acceptance as well as for accessing gender-affirming medical interventions such as hormones or surgeries. Counseling can be a productive and empowering experience for us even if we do not feel as though we have gender-related issues to address in session. In addition, it can be a very effective tool for family members or friends who may be struggling with their own feelings about our transition.

Having an adult to talk with who is not judging us may give us the freedom to explore our identities in new ways and may help us to develop and strengthen our resilience. As minors, we lack autonomy over our lives and many of our healthcare decisions. Because of this, it is extremely important for us to know our rights when beginning to access counseling. From there, we can advocate for ourselves, ensure that our confidentiality is being respected, and make sure that we are receiving the highest possible quality of services. Sure, some therapists out there are not competent in gender-affirming care, but many do "get it" and can be incredibly helpful to us and our well-being.

Adults have the ability to control many aspects of our lives. This holds true for those of us who are attempting to access medical and mental health services. However, mental and sexual health are two areas in which some states offer provisions for confidential care. Confidentiality is key for many people seeking individual counseling or gender-affirming medical care. Confidentiality means that what we say to a provider is kept private. If we are under 18, our parents may have to give consent for therapy and may have access to our confidential records. They may be able to talk to the counselor about what happens during sessions. That might limit what we talk to the counselor about, so it is a good idea to discuss with the counselor what they will and will not share with our parents.

There are things that our doctors and counselors are legally mandated to report. These things can be summed up as the "three hurts." A counselor must report (1) if we are in danger of hurting ourselves, (2) if someone else is hurting us, or (3) if we are hurting someone else. Counselors are also mandated to report if they suspect that child abuse is happening, even if it is not to us (e.g., if we talk about a sibling or friend who is being abused).

There are some counselors who practice "conversion therapy," also known as "reparative therapy," where they try to change our gender identity or sexual orientation. If this happens to you, seek out an adult you trust, as this type of counseling can be damaging. Many states have passed laws to outlaw conversion therapy for minors.

MEMOIR

Miles McIntosh, MD (he/him) received his degree in medicine from Chicago Medical School and is pursuing a career in psychiatry.

Look at the way she walks Jimmy. Look, she walks just like Sarah.

Mom stop.

I want you to go back there and walk towards me.

No.

Jimmy what do you think? Look at the leg hair.

Rose I think you should stop.

What? Come on she walks just like your sister, she is going to be just like her.

I am NOT! I am not going to be like Sarah stop watching me walk! Leave me alone.

We walk along the sidewalk and she keeps looking. She is watching me. She thinks I'm a "homo." She thinks I'm going to be mentally ill. My mother is behind me watching me walk. Why can't she just leave me alone. I just want to be left alone.

She judges me constantly. She compares me to every other kid on the planet. I don't think I will ever walk normal. How do I walk anyways?

I did not know my aunt Sarah very well. I had met her a few times when I was young. She was my father's older sister and as far as I could tell my mother did not think very highly of her. My father would tell me stories about how she decided to be "gay" and then became crazy. He would tell me that she was on so many medications that she would drool and could not walk. He would tell me how she had electricity passed through her brain with a machine and how she was put in beds that had restraints for her arms and legs. She was the only "gay" person I knew and from what I could tell, that was a bad thing. I did not want to be like her.

At this point I'm 10 years old. I wear a pair of baggy jean shorts that I gave to my dad for Father's Day, but that he gave back. On my slender frame hangs a Pearl Jam t-shirt my parents bought me in Dallas. The only thing I remember about Dallas is finding that shirt. It was the last shirt my mother would allow my father to buy me because if I did not walk and talk like a little girl then I would not have any clothing. My identity as a boy in school was the root of my problem. My psychiatrist told her that if she did not reward my male behavior that I would quickly transform into the little girl my mother wanted. If I could just be *normal* everything would be alright. The kids would not pick on me if I wore a cute outfit. I could not do it. It made me sick to think of being a . . . . girl.

MEDICAL CARE AND TRANSITION

As youth, whether or not we are T/GE, we have a lot to think about when it comes to medical care and physical well-being. Puberty comes with a lot of physical, mental, and emotional changes. For T/GE youth, these changes can kickstart new needs in a health care setting. For example, as we begin to experience physical changes related to puberty, our doctors may ask us more questions about our bodies, our genitals, and our sexual relationships. We may not feel comfortable with the words our provider uses to describe our body, or we may want to ask questions that are not on their radar. But we still need to take care of our health.

Coming Out to a Provider

If we already have a provider we see regularly who does not know we are T/GE, it may be a good idea to come out to them, even if we do not have any intention of accessing hormones or medical interventions to transition. They may be making incorrect assumptions about our body that could potentially lead to issues taking good care of our health. For example, we could be pregnant, and they do not think to test us for pregnancy. If your

Isaiah Stannard is an actor and artist from New York.

parent or guardian takes you to the medical provider, make a plan to ask the provider to speak privately during an upcoming visit. Before sharing your identity with a provider, however, it is important to verify their stance on confidentiality—especially if you are not out to your family.

Because gender-affirming care is not something all medical providers have a lot of knowledge about, we might want to help them learn about us. For example, we might want to teach them the language we use to talk about our bodies and gender identities. Educating our healthcare providers about T/GE people can be stressful. Many people find that it is helpful to provide some educational materials to their provider when they come out.

Puberty and Puberty Blockers

More and more of us are beginning medical and/or surgical transition as youth. Our options vary, depending on how far along we are in puberty. Puberty is a time when our testes and ovaries begin to produce large amounts of testosterone and estrogen (i.e., hormones) and our body begins to grow rapidly. Everyone has both testosterone and estrogen in their bodies, just in differing amounts. Although people usually start puberty between age nine and thirteen, not everyone starts puberty at the same age, because everyone's body is different.

Puberty is divided into a series of stages, known as Tanner Stages. There are five stages, and before puberty children are in Tanner Stage One. During Tanner Stage Two, we grow soft, light pubic and underarm hair and develop breast buds, or our testes begin to grow. People assigned female at birth (AFAB) tend to start earlier than people assigned male at birth (AMAB). Many people AFAB may begin menstruating (though others will not). In Tanner Stages Three through Five, our pubic hair will continue to become darker, thicker, and more prevalent. We will also get more hair under our armpits. The penis, testes, and scrotum will begin to grow. Some of us will experience spontaneous erections and ejaculation when sleeping or masturbating. By Stage Five, our genitals will be our adult size and shape, and we will have complete breast development.

Tanner Stage Two is the earliest stage that we are eligible to take puberty-blocking medication. Most Tanner Stage Two changes are reversible. If we have known that we are T/GE since we were very young and are fortunate enough to have our parents' support, we might be able to see a provider who can prescribe us medicine to pause our puberty around this time. See Chapter 12 for a more in-depth discussion of how puberty blockers work and for information about hormone therapy for those who have already gone through puberty.

THINKING ABOUT COLLEGE

The decision whether or not college is the right path for us is a difficult one for many of us. If we do decide to go to college, it is important to consider what role our gender identity and expression will play in our decision. Are we looking for a college experience where faculty and fellow students may already be aware of transgender people and issues? A place where there is a strong LGBTQ presence on campus with active out TG/E students? A college where we can be ourselves without disclosing our TG/E status to anyone?

There are LGBTQ-specific organizations that can be great resources to us when looking at colleges. Campus Pride, the largest national organization dedicated to LGBTQ students in college, publishes a yearly index ranking colleges on a variety of areas in terms of their friendliness and safety for LGBTQ students. They also host LGBTQ college fairs in cities across the country and publish lists of schools with gender inclusive policies on their website.

However, just because a school is described as "LGBTQ-friendly" does not mean that it is necessarily friendly to T/GE students. If we are interested in going to a campus that

amaze is an organization that creates short educational videos about puberty and sex. Their website includes videos related to gender identity and puberty for trans youth and is designed for both youth and parents.

Kayden Ortiz, just after getting a tattoo. Captured by his mom, Chaiya Mohanty Ortiz, who writes that seeing the "absolute joy and euphoria" on Kayden's face after he was allowed to stop wearing his compression vest following top surgery was "as good as a thousand Christmases rolled into one moment!"

is welcoming to T/GE students, or are curious about how our top choice schools rank, the Campus Pride "Trans Policy Clearinghouse" keeps tabs on which colleges and universities have gender-inclusive housing and policies, processes to change name and gender on campus records, and transition-related medical coverage.

If our schools of interest are not on the lists, there are some other ways to find out about them. Check the school's nondiscrimination policy (typically accessible online) to see whether it includes gender identity and expression. Find out if the school has an LGBTQ resource center, student group, or women's center, which may be able to provide information about T/GE issues on campus and connect you with other T/GE students. We may also want to look into how the school handles specific issues that we are concerned about, such as housing policies, campus activism, or student health services.

QUESTION 8

M List is a nonbinary high school student from Massachusetts.

Adorned with a red asterisk, the seventh question on the Common Application, an undergraduate general application for college admission, requires individuals to click one of two boxes to indicate their sex: male and female. The eighth question, with no red asterisk in sight, invites applicants to "share more about your gender identity below." The difference between the two queries is almost poetic: the first, being written for cisgender people to answer without giving pause, is required of all applicants, while the second is voluntary. A footnote. Inessential. It's similar to what is frequently the general public's view of the transgender community. A footnote. Inessential.

It is great to see a large institution like the Common App making steps toward equality by having a designated spot to input this information. My problem is not with Question 8. My problem is with how answering Question 8 is unrequired while my identity is indispensable.

My problem is with how few individual colleges ask students what pronouns they use. My problem is with how few schools offer gender-neutral housing and with how inaccessible those room and board programs generally are. My problem is with how much time and energy I have to spend researching these institutions to find out if my fundamental identity will be respected on campus. My problem is that, as a nonbinary and transgender person, I am forced to prioritize the opinion of others over all else in my life so that I'm not risking my safety. My problem is that in this world that I am living in my identity is a footnote. Inessential.

On my application, the box is filled with the word "non-binary," but I'm not sure if it will stay that way because disclosing this part of myself is a gamble. Admissions staff could be well-educated on the subject or be generally open-minded, but given how many people seem to think that the existence of my identity is up for debate, I think that some concern is justified. People like me have to go about their lives prepared to hide intrinsic parts of ourselves. We do not get the privilege of knowing we are judged solely by our qualifications. Instead, we are left to worry over political affiliations and the opinion of authority because of the tenets of marginalization, waiting for the day that Question 8 is considered just as mandatory as Question 7.

Paying for School

The costs of attending college can be a barrier for many students. As T/GE youth, we may face particular challenges. Coming out may have complicated our relationship with parents or guardians, and we may no longer be able to count on their financial support. There are many ways that we can pay for education, however, including the following:

- *Loans*: Many students across the country take out loans to pay for their education.
- *Scholarships*: There are many scholarships available for LGBTQ youth for undergraduate and graduate school. If your school has an LGBTQ resource center, they may have a list of LGBTQ scholarships.
- *Financial independence*: To qualify for financial aid, the Free Application for Federal Student Aid (FAFSA) requires us to report how much money our parents make until we reach the age of 25. If we can demonstrate that we have been financially independent of our parents for two or more years, we can be considered independently from our parents and qualify for additional grants and loans.
- *Employment*: Many students, of all backgrounds, work their way through school with full-time or part-time jobs.

Organizations offering college scholarships to LGBTQ students include the Point Foundation, the League Foundation, PFLAG, the Pride Foundation, and Live Out Loud.

Remember that we are not alone in struggling with the costs of our education. There are many excellent resources available online, as well as career and college counseling services in our schools and neighborhoods that can provide us with additional information about how to pay for school. Being T/GE does not mean that we cannot afford to continue our education.

Campus Housing

For many students, living in the dorms is an important part of the college experience. Others may not be able to afford to go away to college or may prefer to live with friends or relatives while attending. For those of us planning to live on campus, we often face specific concerns about what this experience will look like. Traditionally, college dorms are segregated into the gender binary. Roommates are typically assigned based on our legal gender. If we have not changed our legal documents or a particular state does not allow for a nonbinary (X or unspecified) gender marker on our legal documents, we will most likely be housed with a roommate who shares our birth-assigned gender. Depending on where we live and if we are in a physical transition, altering our legal gender may not be an option. Thanks to organizing and activism by transgender students and allies, this has been changing. If we are already out as trans, we may be able to address this before we are assigned to a dorm.

While we may be able to make housing requests for roommates of particular genders, there are other solutions as well. Some possible options include moving to a single room (and it is well within our right to advocate that we not be charged any additional fees), moving to on-campus apartments, if available, or arranging permission to move off campus, if we are at a school where students of a particular year are required to live on campus.

Many universities have loopholes in their housing policies that allow students with medical conditions to live in single rooms or make other housing arrangements, and it is illegal for them to discriminate. If it is what we want, a doctor's note advocating for a single room due to "gender dysphoria" may be a helpful tool for those of us who are willing to use it.

Many colleges and universities offer gender-neutral housing options. At these schools, students who apply to this housing have the option of living with other students regardless of gender. Colleges usually designate a floor or building as a space for gender-neutral housing. For many T/GE students, this is the option that makes them feel the safest and most comfortable on campus.

If we come out in the middle of a school year, additional issues may arise if we are already living with a roommate in a gender-segregated dorm. Socially transitioning in the dorms involves different levels of coming out not only to friends but also to people like our roommate and residential advisor (RA). If we are coming out in this setting, having a support network of allies in place—friends, the LGBTQ resource center, or other campus groups—can make the process much easier.

RECOMMENDED READING WITH TG/E CHARACTERS FOR YOUNG ADULTS

Fiction

I Wish You All the Best by Mason Deaver
Pet by Akwaeke Emezi
Felix Ever After by Kacen Callender
Dreadnought by April Daniels
When the Moon was Ours by Anna-Marie McLemore
Golden Boy by Abigail Tarttelin
Cemetery Boys by Aiden Thomas
Being Emily by Rachel Gold
Blanca & Roja by Anna-Marie McLemore
Spy Stuff by Matthew Metzger

Comix/Manga

Wandering Son by Shimura Takako
The Avant-Guards by Carly Usdin

Nonfiction

Beyond the Gender Binary by Alok Vaid-Menon
You're in the Wrong Bathroom": And 20 Other Myths and Misconceptions about Transgender and Gender Nonconforming People by Laura Erickson-Schroth and Laura Jacobs

Relationships/Sexuality/Love

Queer Sex: A Trans and Non-Binary Guide to Intimacy, Pleasure, and Relationships by J. Roche
Trans Love: An Anthology of Transgender and Non-Binary Voices, edited by Freiya Benson
Nerve Endings: The New Trans Erotic by T. Hill-Meyer (erotica)

College Athletics

Another site of potential struggle and opportunity for organizing within college campuses has been athletics. There are often very strict gender-segregated policies for participation in competitive sports. While individual schools may have their own policies about participation in intramural or recreational sports, the National Collegiate Athletic Association (NCAA) governs participation in competitive college athletics representing the school. The NCAA's policies on T/GE students' eligibility to play are as follows:[9]

- Trans female student athletes who are not taking hormones may participate on men's teams only.
- Trans male student athletes who are not taking hormones may participate on either a men's or a women's team.
- Trans female student athletes being treated with testosterone suppression medication for diagnosed gender dysphoria may continue to compete on a men's team. After one year of testosterone suppression treatment, they may compete on a women's team.
- Trans male student athletes taking testosterone for diagnosed gender dysphoria may compete on a men's team. They are no longer eligible to compete on a women's team.

Women's Colleges

Historically, the conversation about T/GE students at women's colleges has revolved around T/GE men coming out on women-only campuses. However, as T/GE youth have gained visibility and more of us are coming out at younger ages, a number of young trans women and nonbinary folks who were assigned male at birth have sought the opportunity to attend women-only colleges.

"My name is Mack Beggs and I am a student-athlete at Life University. I am also an advocate for the LGBTQ community. I believe that anything in this world is achievable through love, happiness, and hard-work."

Some schools have stipulations regarding admission based solely on the basis of legal sex. For those of us with M on our identification documents (e.g., ID, passport, or Social Security card), we may not be able to apply. Those designated male at birth, whether we identify as T/GE, may need to update our legal documents if we want to apply to certain women's colleges. Some colleges have changed their policies to admit T/GE women (e.g., Barnard College, Bryn Mawr College, Mills College, Mount Holyoke College, Scripps College, Smith College, Spelman College, and Wellesley College, to name a few).

Policy questions are only one aspect of the issue. For the past several years, attention and concern around the issues created by transgender men attending women's colleges have increased. Questions have been raised such as if T/GE men were right to apply to those schools in the first place and what is the most appropriate decision regarding students who come out as male who are already attending a women's school. With support from allies, many transmasculine people have made great strides in finding a place on these campuses. They have had some success in advocating for their rights to stay enrolled even while transitioning. The argument many of these transmasculine people use is that they feel safe in women's spaces. This is usually because they see their upbringings as important parts of their pasts and believe that they should have the right to continue their studies within that environment. However, other transmasculine people decide to transfer out of women's colleges to other schools after they transition, because they do not feel comfortable in the environment, they have been asked to leave, or they are concerned about outing themselves by stating they went to a traditionally women's college.

COMMUNITY BUILDING AND ACTIVISM

Young adults in the transgender community have a long and powerful history as activists, and, though often not credited, are responsible for much of the social change the LGBTQ community has seen. T/GE youth have often been at the forefront of activism and many of us continue to work tirelessly as activists and community organizers.

Historically speaking, T/GE youth were some of the leading voices in what we now think of as early LGBTQ activism in the United States. Gender nonconforming young people were involved in the Compton's Cafeteria Riot in San Francisco in 1966 as well as in the Stonewall riots in 1969. At Compton's, the T/GE community organized against police brutality, poverty, and social stigma that young, mostly gender nonconforming people were facing in that part of the city. They also produced a magazine spreading the word about these issues and the work that they were doing making communities safer for disenfranchised young people. Based on accounts from individuals who were in the Stonewall Bar, historians believe that the majority of active participants in the riot itself were young, homeless, and otherwise street-involved T/GE youth.

Intergenerational Activism

As youth, we may focus our activism on issues specific to us, but many of us also work in partnership with adults and many of us are actively working to make change for other marginalized groups and important causes (e.g., T/GE women helping others access safe abortion). LGBTQ youth have taken on important roles within broader LGBTQ social and political organizing. For example, we have worked on issues such as housing and employment nondiscrimination policies, as well as passing marriage equality.

In order to get involved with groups of activists, we must first find out about these groups. Most of them are easily accessed online. Some of them are focused on one political party, while others have a broad social justice focus. Examples of such groups include Solutions Not Punishment Collaborative, Black Trans Advocacy Coalition, The TransLatin@ Coalition, and the Asian Pacific Islander Queer Women and Transgender Community.

Within intergenerational activist settings, one issue that often comes up is ageism. Young T/GE activists and organizers may not be taken seriously by adult activists. This is not specific to T/GE youth—it is an issue faced by all youth organizers. Sometimes activist

Attendees at Pride in London, 2016. (Jwslubbock)

spaces provide a welcoming environment for us to feel like we are a valued part of a community. Sometimes, however, we can be used to do some of the most labor- and time-intensive work but might be removed from larger and more important conversations regarding strategy and from positions of power. Adults often talk over the perspectives or experiences of youth. At the same time, as youth, we sometimes ignore the advice or suggestions of older people, which is another form of ageism. Something important for any organization is to ensure that they are incorporating the voices of youth activists in a way that is not tokenizing. Organizations can actively utilize the talent and energy that youth organizers bring to issues and recognize that we come into situations with particular backgrounds and experiences that might be different from theirs due to generational differences. Both perspectives need to be recognized and taken into account when doing this sort of work.

Activism takes a variety of forms. Within activist communities there are differing opinions about which types of activism are the most helpful or important. For some of us, activism looks like working toward changing legislation. Others of us may feel that legislation will either take too long to pass or will be ineffective. Some people focus their work on community education or the creation of services. Others spend time working toward access and cultural humility within existing agencies. Some of us engage in direct actions, while others of us are opposed to direct action as an activist tool. For T/GE youth activists there are a variety of outlets for our passion and activist energies—it is simply a matter of finding the right fit.

CONCLUSION

As T/GE youth, we face unique challenges. We may sometimes feel like we are alone, but there are networks of thousands of adults and other youth in countries around the world who care very much about us and our futures, and are working to make the world a safer place for us to grow and thrive. We are growing up in a time when understandings of gender change rapidly. We can all be part of the change, now more than ever. There are so many ways for us to make our individual marks, and our voices are needed in the larger T/GE movement.

NOTES

1. Olson-Kennedy, A. (2017). *Gender dysphoria: Beyond the DSM.* Conference presentation presented at the 7th annual Gender Infinity Conference, Houston, Texas.
2. Chang, S. C., Singh, A. A., & dickey, l. (2018). *A clinician's guide to gender-affirming care: Working with transgender & gender nonconforming clients.* Oakland, CA: New Harbinger Publications, Inc.

3. Singh, A. A., Meng, S., & Hanson, A. (2011, September). *The resilience strategies of transgender youth: A qualitative inquiry.* Paper presented at the Biennial Symposium of the World Professional Association for Transgender Health, Atlanta, Georgia.

4. Brill, S. (2009). Health professional workshop. Presentation at the 9th annual Gender Odyssey Conference, Seattle, Washington.

5. Toomey, R. B., Syvertsen, A. K., & Shramko, M. (2018). Transgender adolescent suicide behavior. *Pediatrics, 142*(4), e20174218.

6. Devor, A. H. (2004). Witnessing and mirroring: A fourteen stage model of transsexual identity formation. *Journal of Gay & Lesbian Psychotherapy, 8*(1-2), 41–67.

7. James, S. E., Herman, J. L., Rankin, S., Keisling, M., Mottet, L., & Anafi, M. (2016). The Report of the 2015 U.S. Transgender Survey. Washington, DC: National Center for Transgender Equality

8. Sandfort, T. (2019). Experiences and Well-Being of Sexual and Gender Diverse Youth in Foster Care in New York City. New York City Administration for Children's Services (ACS) and Columbia University. https://www1.nyc.gov/assets/acs/pdf/about/2020/WellBeingStudyLGBTQ.pdf

9. NCAA Office of Inclusion, NCAA Inclusion of Transgender Student-Athletes, 2011. https://www.ncaa.org/sites/default/files/Transgender_Handbook_2011_Final.pdf

20

AGING
Leigh Anne Gregory and Pony Knowles

INTRODUCTION

There's no one way to be trans, and there's no one way to get older.

Aging is about more than just time passing. It is also a process of sea changes that affect our relationships to place, to family, to our sense of community, to our health and bodies, and to the ways that we experience all of our identities (e.g., race/ethnicity, social class, ability, sexual orientation, religious/spiritual affiliation, and others), as well as the social world around us. As transgender and gender-expansive (T/GE) people, we have intersecting identities and experiences that are themselves changing over time—and not always at the same pace.

> *I am older than most gender fluid people I know . . . . As I move past middle age, I see fairly few role models for elders in the gender fluid space and I don't know what that future holds for me.*

We use the abbreviation T/GE in its broadest and most general sense—encompassing nonbinary and nonconforming identities. However, it might not be the best fit for everyone. It is impossible for one word or phrase to capture the rich tapestry of what gender means to all of us.

> *I feel I can't relate to all the young trans folks who seem to be more nonbinary/ gender queer than I was raised to be. Like I'm being punished for being good at what I did—medically transitioning.*

Depending on when we came to know our gender as T/GE people, many of us may have found ourselves using words from medical terminology to describe our gender. Often, these terms suggested some form of "deviance," from *inversion* (pre-1920s) to *transvestism* (1930s) to *transexualism* (1960s). Some of us may have strong negative or positive reactions to these older terms or to newer terms that evolved after we came to understand our identities. We hope to embrace a cross-generational perspective that makes ample room for all of us to celebrate ourselves as T/GE elders or as T/GE people who will one day become elders.

GENERATIONAL COHORTS

> *I have a living memory of queer history that gives me a different perspective—but not always a better one.*

For the bulk of T/GE seniors or elders, multiple societal influences have shaped our respective sense of being and identifying as T/GE. In particular, the age at which we come out and/or transition has a profound impact upon our experience of T/GE culture. Aging is being aware that the way things are now are not the way they have always been. The choices and options we have had vary greatly over the time periods and places in which we have come of age. Aging also involves the passing of friends and family over the years. Depending on our own intersectional identities such as race/ ethnicity and social class, we may experience more rapid, frequent, and ongoing losses

To Survive on this Shore is a book of photographs and interviews with T/GE older adults (by Jess T. Dugan and Vanessa Fabbre, Kehrer Verlag, 2018).

Gloria, 70, Chicago, IL, 2016. (Jess T. Dugan). From "To Survive on This Shore: Photographs and Interviews with Transgender and Gender Nonconforming Older Adults," a project by Jess T. Dugan and Vanessa Fabbre.

of important people in our lives. In addition, many of us now in our fifties, sixties, and older lived through a time before there were any treatments or effective prevention efforts with regard to HIV/AIDS, and we experienced profound loss that still lingers in our communities to this day. Those of us who have made it through the trials and tribulations have much to be thankful for, and yet it is also common for us to continue to experience the grief of these times.

> *Although I am relatively new to the transgender community, most of the trans-gender people I know are younger than me. I feel both young and old. I do feel a responsibility to model that "it gets better" for my younger trans acquaintances, but I also try to foster places for them to be themselves in a way that I was never able to be.*

A major part of T/GE aging is determined by when you were born and what you have lived through. The roots of modern concepts associated with being T/GE in the west are closely tied to formal medical and social transition. In the 1940s and 1950s, sexologists such as Harry Benjamin and Alfred Kinsey laid the groundwork for understanding gender and sexuality more fluidly, and embarked upon the first course of treatment in the United States that affirmed a T/GE individual's gender. During the 1950s and 1960s, affirming medical support emerged not only in university medical centers, but also in large cities.

Jamie Shipman (she/her) is a transgender woman and regular contributor on Quora with over 1,400 answers and over a million viewers.

My story provides a different perspective on being transgender than most because of the age at which I transitioned. I knew I was different around the age of three. I thought I was a girl until I was eight years old. My mother fought me consistently and finally convinced me that I had to live as a male if I wanted to be "normal." Going through puberty was so bad that I tried to commit suicide at age 15. After puberty, my body was so badly damaged that I feared I would never be passable as a woman, so I lived in the closet most of my life dealing with depression, anxiety, and gender dysphoria.

By the time I transitioned, I was 63 years old. I was a business professional with both graduate and undergraduate degrees. I was also a Christian with a degree in ministry study. I had two grown sons, four beautiful grandchildren, and a loving wife of 10 years. I had every reason to be happy, yet I was in so much pain and conflict that at one point I thought I had to end my life.

I transitioned because I felt I had nothing to lose. Even though puberty screwed up my body physically, I no longer cared if I was passable as a woman. I had to be free of the lie I had been living my whole life. Coming out was humiliating. I lost family, friends, my career, finances, and a lot of respect. I faced shame, ridicule, and rejection from the people I had loved and cared about. But I also lost depression, gender dysphoria, and the conflict in my head. I am finally at peace with myself and for the first time in my life I actually like myself. I have never been happier. My only regret is that I let fear keep me from transitioning years earlier.

Today I am a full-time post-op transgender woman, and I can honestly say that the worst day of my life as a woman has been far better than the best day of my life as a man. Please take your children seriously when it comes to being transgender. Their happiness depends on it!

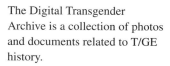

The Digital Transgender Archive is a collection of photos and documents related to T/GE history.

The 1960s saw the arrival of a number of trans-led protests and organizations, often in the larger context of the Civil Rights and women's rights movements. In places such as San Francisco's Tenderloin, young gay and T/GE people formed the Vanguard. In August of 1966, a powerful resistance to police arrests in the Tenderloin erupted at Compton's Cafeteria. The Stonewall uprisings in 1969 happened in large part because of "gender deviant" activists Storme DeLarverie, Marsha P. Johnson, and Sylvia Rivera. In all cases, the political and organizing actions of trans people—in particular people of color—formed the cornerstone of the contemporary movement for LGBTQ liberation.

In the 1970s and 1980s, the women's rights movement embraced efforts to seek equality through degendering elements of mainstream culture; for example, by introducing universal pronouns such as *ze* and *hir* or by substituting nouns like *chairman* with the unisex form *chair*. Ballroom culture, dating back to at least the early 1900s, sprang up in full force in the 1980s in predominantly Black urban communities and created space for gender expression that truly celebrated our identities.

In other ways, the 1980s and 1990s were also witness to a stifling of these overtures toward greater gender expression and affirmation. The role the HIV/AIDS crisis played in our T/GE communities was cataclysmic, and in its aftermath, we saw intense repression of T/GE identities within LGBTQ activist spaces. Insurance coverage for gender "disorders" was denied, gender clinics closed, and medical support became privatized among a very small group of doctors. On the other hand, hormone therapies became more available, and across mainstream life, jeans were no longer an exclusively male garment. The availability of unisex clothing produced a profound change in the mobility (both spatially and socially) possible for anyone who did not rigorously adhere to the gender assigned to them at birth.

For some T/GE people, the concurrent restraints and added mobility often engineered a notion of social and/or medical transition that meant leaving your family and home area to move—likely to a large city—and begin life afresh. "Transition" for transfeminine folks usually meant you accessed medical interventions (some safe, and others, like silicone injections, not), went stealth, and cut many relationships with family, former friends, and home. Medical interventions for transmasculine individuals lagged behind by decades, with hormone therapies not really becoming widely available until the late 1990s and early 2000s. Because of this, many transmasculine folks born before the 1970s and 1980s have undergone "later in life" transitions and had experiences that significantly delayed their sense of feeling socially affirmed as T/GE adults.

For many of us, over the course of the 20th century, one of the only viable options for living freely and authentically was to escape to a big city such as New York or San Francisco. In large cities, we could find vital community and support, as well as access to affirming procedures, both in and out of the medical mainstream. The need to move to a big city and start over was especially true for many people of color. In many ways, the birth of ballroom culture was a response to the need for housing for many T/GE individuals of color who found themselves on the street after making the move to cities. For white middle-class T/GE women, there was Tri-Ess, a national crossdresser organization that met in private settings and held retreats—though the rules dictated that members be both married and straight.

For so many of us, the only real choice was to remain closeted and questioning, and in many places it was illegal to present as any gender outside of your sex assigned at birth. Many T/GE men faced a choice to remain entrenched in lesbian communities—some of which were dominated by Trans-Exclusionary Radical Feminists (TERFs) who advocated against them and against the inclusion of T/GE women—or to fly stealth in mainstream straight masculinity. It is notable that most options for stealth and "successful" transitions forswore the notion that trans women could be lesbians and trans men could be gay, and gender fluidity was often frowned upon.

Bobbi, 83, Detroit, MI, 2014. (Jess T. Dugan). From "To Survive on This Shore: Photographs and Interviews with Transgender and Gender Nonconforming Older Adults," a project by Jess T. Dugan and Vanessa Fabbre.

For research on LGBTQ aging, check out *Still Out, Still Aging: The MetLife Study of LGBT Baby Boomers* (American Society on Aging, MetLife Mature Market Institute, 2010) and *LGBT Aging: A Review of Research Findings, Needs, and Policy Implications* (Soon Kyu Choi and Ilan H. Meyer, The Williams Institute, 2016).

Across the board, however, information on social and/or medical transition and T/GE-affirming resources was simply not widely available and depended upon word-of-mouth. Those of us who had the resources to seek out a psychologist or psychiatrist were formally diagnosed as "sexual deviants," and might find ourselves being forced into a promised "cure." In the old days, the cure was often electric shock treatments to punish those "evil thoughts" and push them out of your mind. One factor that could save you from these types of unethical "treatments" in a visit to a mental health professional was whether you were "latent" or "active." If you only thought about these "deviant behaviors" there might well be no need for a cure, so long as you did not act on them and remained latent. The super deep closet, which might have been as bad as the cure, likely led to the creation of the liberation button reading, "better blatant than latent."

Aging is an experience worth sharing. If nothing else, it has been a heck of a ride, and there are many things that have changed that seemed impossible even a few years ago. Everyone should have not only a sense of what T/GE elders have been through and are still going through, but a notion of how we can all act to improve the circumstances of aging for T/GE people.

THE ADVANTAGES OF AGING

I wish so much that I could have started earlier. It feels like so much of life was wasted. But it makes that which remains all the more precious. I have a whole lot of living to do and I do it every day to the utmost.

What does one get out of the aging process? Well, other than the obvious answer of being alive, with all the fond memories and joyful times, there is the experience of maturing and the depth of resilience that results from surviving as a T/GE person. For T/GE people, the experience of aging can be not just depressing and defeating at times, but also wondrous, as we grow into that beautiful butterfly that we knew was in our cocoon the whole time. By now, no matter which version of us we consider ourselves to be, we have acquired increasingly complex tones, flavors, and depth. We have confronted and solved multiple crises, both big and small, over a lifetime. We have learned that, thankfully, not every day will include an existential crisis. In short, we have the opportunity to live with much less drama in our lives, and that makes more room for thriving, not just surviving.

Age is a trip. I imagine half my life is over, and I spent the first half as a woman. I look forward to aging as a genderqueer person. There are no cultural benchmarks to follow, so I just get to be me.

IT AIN'T OVER UNTIL IT'S OVER

Linden Jordan (he/him) has had careers in law, mental health, and college teaching. He is happily living with his lovely partner in Marblemount, Washington, with three dogs and eight chickens (but who is counting?)

Over the years, I knew in my heart that I was transgender, but I never had the courage to act on it. I was assigned female at birth. I knew from the age of four that I was not a girl. I grew up in a small town in West Virginia in a Southern Baptist family. The church was the center of our world. I knew I liked girls by the age of 12, so I knew I was homosexual. I left the church at the age of 17. Given the paucity of resources and support, I lived as a closeted lesbian until the age of 26 when I moved to Seattle and came out.

When I retired at age 62, I figured I would just give up on the notion of transitioning in this lifetime. However, then I attended a forum featuring a trans man. He was so comfortable in his skin. I was hit with the realization that I wanted to spend the last part of my life honestly. I wanted to feel that comfort of looking in the mirror and seeing who I really am. I began testosterone at the age of 63. I had already had bilateral mastectomies due to an earlier breast cancer diagnosis. I am now 67 and have never been happier. I also found love again at the age of 66. Who knew? As they say, it ain't over until it's over.

As T/GE elders, we may have acquired the ability to more frequently remain calmer, to control our anger, to access a more even temperament. We may have also had more opportunities to learn and practice more effective social skills, from defusing situations to solving personal challenges. Because of our many experiences as T/GE people, we have become able to see things in a broader context of prior experience and knowledge. In addition, aging can be liberating, as our responsibilities change over our lives. We may have had children and families we were raising, and now we are free to explore other pursuits of our own. We may have retired and are now able to be more creative or reconnect with interests we have long forgotten. The annoyances of everyday life may decrease even as the nature of them changes. Worrying about how someone else sees or thinks of us can greatly diminish. Broad experience and memory of individual details are not the same thing. Memories make for ample trees and experience provides the depth and beauty of the forest.

At the same time, we also want to recognize that many of us in the aging T/GE community are still surviving the deleterious effects of anti-T/GE bias, racism, classism, xenophobia, heterosexism, and other oppressions. In this sense, some of our community has not been afforded the "privilege" of aging, as evidenced by the high rate of murders of Black T/GE women. In addition, some of us have clued into our gender identities much later in life, and we may regret not engaging in a social and/or medical transition sooner.

The Diverse Elders Coalition advocates for policies and programs that improve aging for racially and ethnically diverse and LGBTQ elders.

> *I did not transition until late in life. I don't know a lot of transgender people and consider myself more a member of the Queer and Lesbian community than the trans community. Most trans people are a lot younger than I. Transgender people who would be my age are mostly closeted or dead. Closeted by a lifetime of fear or dead from AIDS, suicide, or diseases of poverty.*

Some of us still hold our identities privately within ourselves (or share with a select few others), and do not express our gender identities because we want to maintain our families, partnerships, and community connections. Sometimes, losing these connections would be more devastating than not expressing our gender. So many complexities and harsh realities exist within our T/GE aging community, and we hold these with gentleness, compassion, and acceptance, because we know the most important aspect of life is to find ways that we can really *live* and feel good about the resilience of ourselves and our communities.

The positive skills and knowledge that come with aging can equip both the individual and the community at large with greater context and expertise. As mature T/GE people, we have found a home for ourselves in the world, in whatever sense that means for us. And we are not done living yet, so we look forward to new experiences, challenges, and delights of navigating an ever-changing world.

SOCIAL EXPERIENCES OF AGING: STAYING CONNECTED AND ACTIVE

> *Aging—I feel alone. . . . I don't look trans so I don't count/don't matter. Also, all the trans people online who are my age are newly transitioning, so I can't find anyone like me, who's my age, but transitioned 10–20 or more years ago. Feels very lonely, isolating.*

"We queer folk don't have a patent on growing old alone, but we definitely get a double dose of it because our support group is smaller."—Gen Silent: The Lives of LGBT Elders[1]

If we feel increasingly isolated as we get older, it is important to reach out, ask for help, and know we are not alone. Although one of the most terrifying aspects of aging is feeling isolated, nothing requires us to live that way. Over the course of our lifetimes, nearly everyone has intimate relationships (whether sexual, spiritual, or intellectual) and this holds true for us at any age. However, the mere fact of living longer can mean that those people who have been positive or negative influences on our lives tend to make a permanent exit. This means that without an infusion of new people entering our lives, the

Ceyenne Doroshow (G.L.I.T.S Founder/CEO), Black Trans Lives Matter March, Brooklyn, NY, June 14, 2020. (Cole Witter)

people upon whom we rely will become fewer and our sense of community can shrink. To make matters more difficult, the friends and family that we are growing old with also need help. For those of us who transition later in life, a sudden lack of support from family and friends can feel all the more extreme.

> At age 68, I am definitely a senior member of the transgender community. I only started transition at age 57 . . . I do not feel like I am aging. This is the best I have ever been and everything important in my life keeps on getting better all the time. . . . However, being nonbinary and a senior, I feel very isolated.

Why should we work so continuously to avoid isolation and being alone? Studies show an alarming increase in the health consequences—both physical and mental—for individuals who suffer from isolation. The risks increase even more dramatically for older adults, and those are tripled for older LGBTQ adults.[2,3,4,5,6]

> It took almost 50 years of life to find terms for who I am and people who get it. Sometimes it is hard, though, because the resources I want or need to heal are mostly for young people, even the crisis lines like Trevor Project. I don't know where older people who need to talk about this stuff are. We didn't have these resources, that I know of, when growing up and we are still left out because now we are too old for the resources we needed growing up!

As a T/GE person who is aging, how do we avoid social isolation and its negative health consequences? The earlier we recognize our own risk of isolation, the better. Identifying local services that can help support us socially is also key. Just because we are getting older does not mean that our social life must dwindle. Intimate relationships can and must continue, whether they be sexual or platonic. Being the life of the party does not end at a given age, nor does the joy of sitting quietly and reading a book. Whatever has given us pleasure will continue to give us pleasure. We may slow down and take longer to do some of the things we've always done, but we do not stop enjoying life. For those of us who get the chance to retire, we enjoy more time to pursue hobbies. For an aging trans person, the intimate relationships we nurture can be of crucial importance not only for the support they provide to us, but also because everything we do forges a way forward for younger generations of trans people.

I consider myself as an open/out/proud elder trans man. At 78 years old I am still active as an advocate, activist, educator, researcher, and now as a writer, serving folks across the spectrum of LGBTQIAA2s + communities. Now my own focus is on trans aging and trans history. I am often the oldest trans person at any of the events I attend. My partner and I both say that "old age ain't for sissies," while we are experiencing fatigue or pain. But, like the Energizer Bunny "who just keeps on going," we do the best we can from day to day.

The Movement Advancement Project has teamed up with SAGE to create a guide called, *Understanding Issues Facing LGBT Older Adults.*

CLOSURE

Rachel Lee Campbell (she/her) is a transgender woman who lives in Asheville, North Carolina. She writes to document her transition and has appeared on a number of panels and forums discussing transgender issues. She also performs her poetry at local venues.

"My name is fucking Rachel," I said
To my last remaining childhood friend, It is not
    Richard,
It is not RC, it's not hey there, hey you, or yo dude!
It's fucking Rachel!
Seems simple enough, not really so hard, is it?
My name used to be Richard,
I am a transgender woman and instead of suicide
I found the courage to transition.
As my hair grew longer, as my breasts grew larger, Richard no longer fit.
I love my name now, Rachel Lee Campbell
My hand flowing smoothly as I sign . . . .
I would swear I can hear it whisper thank you.
Not for an instant have I hesitated nor been tempted
To be Richard again, by failing memory or distraction.
I am Rachel, and I smile each time I say it.
I'm Rachel; I'm pleased to make your acquaintance.
It should be that simple, you approach those that know you.
You say, this is who I am now, and in fact it is who I have always been.
They say, it's going to be difficult getting used to that, I've known you so long,
There are those that will resist change to the bitter end
Expending their energy to convince me their truth is the authentic one.
That I must return them to the comfort of a reality that never was.
I cannot, I will not inhabit that world again.
Richard is dead, he is gone, and not coming back.
I will not play along; I cannot live as two anymore.
Lying and hiding for 60 years, to make others happy.
I've given all that I can.
What remains is mine.
I will mourn the passing of these lifelong friendships
But I am fucking Rachel.
I will not look back any longer.

New relationships may present themselves organically, but a commitment to actively seeking them out is crucial. The way we experience intimacy may very well change. Many people assume that interest in sex diminishes as we age, and for some that may be true, but often it remains stable or even increases. Physical and emotional closeness does not end with age; although it may not be sexual, some older folks may experience an even greater appreciation for the intimacy that nonsexual touch provides. Others become even more sexually adventurous as they age. We may have begun adult life when sexuality tended to be defined as either gay or straight and nothing in between. The world we live in has changed, and more options exist for us to forge common bonds with others that are deep and meaningful—whether those options be medical advancements that extend our sex lives, online communities, or apps that allow us to meet and stay in touch with people who live far away. Unless we practice early on the habit of saying yes to new social situations with the possibility of new relationships, we can find ourselves battling increasing isolation. For some, many our community connections may have centered on bars and clubs, and they can still be vital to avoiding isolation. But, it may be time to begin to expand our horizons.

If you live near an LGBTQ community center, check and see if they have programming for older T/GE adults. Look for age-related providers and your local American Association of Retired Persons (AARP) chapter to see if they have trans-friendly programming. If they currently don't, consider volunteering with them to develop groups and programs. If you build it, others will come! Resources from national advocacy organizations such as the National Center for Trans Equality, Services and Advocacy for LGBT Elders (SAGE), The National Center on LGBT Aging (a project of SAGE), Diverse Elders Coalition, the Human Rights Campaign, and AARP are good places for us to start looking for opportunities to connect with other older people.

Building connections across generations is of vital importance as we find ourselves and our closest friends in an increasingly challenging cycle of providing help to one another. Cross-generational friendships can be especially crucial for late-in-life transitioners. Spaces that allow for cross-generational interaction can imbue us with energy and enthusiasm, while learning new things and practicing old skills. We also have the opportunity to offer younger generations wisdom and affirmation that they

Hank, 76, and Samm, 67, North Little Rock, AR, 2015. (Jess T. Dugan). From "To Survive on This Shore: Photographs and Interviews with Transgender and Gender Nonconforming Older Adults," a project by Jess T. Dugan and Vanessa Fabbre.

may otherwise lack. That said, opportunities for cross-generational misunderstandings abound, and it can be hard to overcome the sense that people from other generations "don't get it."

No matter our current comfort level as T/GE elders, a continual commitment to pursuing new friends to replace the ones who have moved out of our lives will positively impact our lives for years to come. This can be as simple as undertaking new interests and activities—joining a church or religious community, participating in a group specifically for aging T/GE or LGBTQ people, attending conferences, visiting community centers, beginning new hobbies, and/or pursuing old ones. There are often groups centered around various subcultures and interests, especially in larger urban areas. Online communities such as MeetUp, Facebook groups, SAGE Table, or even online video games can provide age- and gender-affirming opportunities for us to make new friends and revolutionize our social experience. We can also participate in service to others in the community. Depending on where we are, the opportunities to volunteer can be extensive once we start to look around. Identifying organizations where we can volunteer our time in person is an incredible way to meet new people, deepen existing relationships, and allow others in our community to benefit from our lived experience and expertise.

Consider checking out SAGE Table or Generations Working Together for cross-generational dialogue.

Every June, the San Francisco Trans March hosts a youth/elder brunch to bring together older and younger members of the trans community for mutual learning and understanding.

HOUSING

Many of us are familiar with research illuminating the stark housing disparities for T/GE people. Depending on the intersections of oppression we are facing (e.g., racism, classism, heterosexism, ableism), we can encounter mounting pressures and losses with regard to housing. At the same time, even if we do have a home, sometimes the home that is a source of comfort and protection can become a dangerous trap in both a social and physical sense. For instance, as more delivery services and online shopping opportunities appear, the ability to order everything online can be as profoundly isolating as it is convenient. Few people want to give up their homes, but our homes can also become a source of isolation as we age.

Twenty-three percent of transgender older adults have faced some form of housing discrimination. More than one quarter (26%) of those who experienced homelessness in the past year avoided staying in a shelter because they feared being mistreated as a transgender person.[7]

> I fully expect to be homeless within five years, likely when I'm 60 years old. It's almost certain that asserting my womanhood (this language is far preferable to the gay closet terminology of "coming out") will precipitate the loss of my job which, in turn, will cause the loss of my house.

We all know that aging incurs a steady increase in physical limitations. Those stairs we never really noticed before may become increasingly daunting. Something as simple as a bathtub or shower can suddenly become a challenge with the threat of falling—and indeed, studies show that most dangerous accidents in the home occur in the bathroom. Some basic changes to our homes may need to happen, and it's best that they happen sooner rather than later. Bars and rails in the bathroom, safe counter access in the kitchen, an eye level microwave, and many other things that we may not think of, can make day-to-day life less exhausting and lengthen our independence. If we cannot afford to hire help, then we may need to ask friends, family, or neighbors for care and assistance from time to time.

Rossmoor in Walnut Creek, California, one of the largest retirement communities in the country, has a burgeoning LGBTQ Alliance with over 500 members.

Retirement communities may provide organized activities, a social life, and end-of-life care. For a select few with financial resources, such options are life-savers, but for many of us, class and racial or cultural experiences make living in these communities far less likely. And they bring with them their own baggage for trans individuals. Many such communities focus on providing services to religious or cultural minorities (for instance, in Florida—a state known for its high number of retirees—there are a number of Jewish and South Asian communities that provide care to older folks), and they may not be well-versed in how to serve aging trans folks in affirming ways.

POSITIVE DEVELOPMENTS FOR TRANS ELDERS

Loree Cook-Daniels is Policy and Program Director for FORGE, Inc. and founder of the Transgender Aging Network. Loree goes by any pronoun; though most people use she or they.

Federal policy related to trans elders has been a real roller coaster in the last few years: sickening drops followed by painfully gained highs, followed again by heart-pounding losses.

Luckily, we are again in the hands of an Administration that not only is pro-transgender, but in which actual transgender activists are Presidential family friends (Sarah McBride) and appointees (including Rachel Levine, Assistant Secretary of Health and Human Services). Indeed, less than nine months in, President Biden's White House sponsored a listening session on trans aging issues, inviting about 20 trans elders and advocates to advise personnel from 15 agencies on what else needs to be done to protect and serve us.

Between Biden Administration changes and advances made through the courts and the country at large, the situation for trans and non-binary elders has improved a great deal since the first *Trans Bodies, Trans Selves* was published in 2014.

Health care coverage. The Affordable Care Act's (ACA) provision forbidding discrimination against trans people is again in place, and many health insurance companies have eliminated their discriminatory trans exclusion policies. One of the most important successes has been Medicare coverage for routine preventive care regardless of gender identity, and the inclusion of hormone therapy and gender-affirming surgery as care that can be deemed medically necessary. As with other services covered by Medicare, "medically necessary" means providing care determined on a case-by-case basis. If a doctor deems hormones or surgery are appropriate, they will write-up the care that is needed and these services should be covered. Coverage under Medicaid is also expanding, although the rules vary from state to state. Many state employee health programs now also cover trans-related care.

Employment. For future elders and older adults who are still working, the 2020 *Bostock v. Clayton County Supreme Court* ruling gave us long-sought clarity that sex discrimination protections cover gender identity and sexual orientation. We are still working to pass through Congress the more comprehensive Equality Act, but Bostock provides critical protections in the meantime.

Marriage. It may surprise you, but we won marriage equality only between the first *TBTS* and this one – in 2015. Benefits associated with marriage are often particularly important later in life, when access to Social Security benefits, tax-free inheritance, and pensions becomes critical.

Housing. In 2012, the US Department of Housing and Urban Development (HUD) issued an Equal Access to Housing rule prohibiting owners and operators of federally-funded or federally insured housing, as well as lenders offering federally insured mortgages, from discriminating based on gender identity and sexual orientation. This rule includes elder housing and homeless shelters, and it also expands the definition of "family" to ensure that LGBT elders are allowed to live with partners and others who are not related by marriage or blood. (We lost this protection in one of those stomach-churning turns last Administration, but have it back now.) There has also been an explosion in communities building their own congregate housing for LGBT elders.

Military and veterans. Trans people can now finally serve openly in the U.S. military. New provisions make trans-specific health care more accessible, as well. The Veterans Administration continues to be a leader in providing pro-trans health care and supports.

Cultural competency. Over the past decade, much has been done to improve the ability of various professionals and agencies to provide respectful and competent care to transgender elders. One of the most important advancements has been the federally funded National Resource Center on LGBT Aging (NRC). From its inception in 2010, NRC has had an unwavering commitment to ensuring its materials, trainings, and resources are inclusive of and accurate about trans elders. Its extensive transgender resource list includes links to guidelines for transgender-affirming hospital policies, trans-specific best practices for front-line health care staff, advice on making LGBT organizations fully transgender-inclusive, a guide to being an ally to transgender elders, and a fact sheet for front-line nursing home staff on how to work with transgender residents. NRC has also trained thousands of aging program and long-term care staff. NRC's parent organization, SAGE, partnered with the Human Rights Campaign and multiple LGBT aging advocates to create a Long-Term Care Equality Index (LEI) designed specifically to improve policies and practices for LGBT residents of long-term care facilities. The first phase was released only in 2021, but the hope is that over time, the LEI will spark major improvements in that sector's care of LGBT elders.

Public awareness and acceptance. Awareness and acceptance of trans people, including trans elders, continues to steadily improve. The *To Survive on This Shore* photograph and essay project is an example of increasing public awareness. In addition, several anthologies on trans aging have recently been published.

Social connections. People of all ages benefit from social connections. LGBT Community Centers collectively offer more transgender programs than any other type of programming. More than half of them also offer programs for elders. There are many Facebook pages devoted to trans elders and/or trans aging issues. And ElderTG—a listserv founded in 1998 to provide peer support to elders age 50+—is still going strong.

We continue to make progress.

Sukie, 59, New York, NY, 2016. (Jess T. Dugan). From "To Survive on This Shore: Photographs and Interviews with Transgender and Gender Nonconforming Older Adults," a project by Jess T. Dugan and Vanessa Fabbre.

In one study, 89% of LGBTQ elders reported that they expected staff in long-term care facilities would discriminate against an elder who was out of the closet. More than three out of four elders thought other residents were likely to discriminate against them, and more than half expected staff to neglect or abuse them. Forty-three percent of respondents who were out as LGBTQ reported actual mistreatment by staff in long-term care facilities.[8]

SAGECare provides training for retirement communities on LGBTQ-competent care.

> As I write this, I will be eligible for early retirement (age 62) in 290 days—not that I am counting. I worry about finding a safe place for me to retire to. I worry about nursing home care. I worry what this Administration has planned for me. I have been fortunate in that I have been able to get health care at a facility that specializes in LGBTQ+ health care.

In an ideal world, no one should have to choose between affirming their cultural and gender identities, but a trans-identified potential resident may want to weigh the cost of what being out in such communities may entail, particularly as we face a decline in mobility and independence that demands greater reliance upon those around us. Although there are a few LGBTQ-specific retirement communities and long-term care facilities, existing facilities (including ones that cater to particular ethnic or religious groups) may have received enough training to be credentialed as culturally competent providers.

In general, the best course of action is to ensure that we're located in an age-friendly and trans-friendly community *before* we get older, even if we consider ourselves "underage," or are still working. If we are younger and reading this now, there are likely some good steps we can take now that will make our future years easier. Even if we are older, we may have experienced too much fear, anxiety, or even discouragement from others in our lives to begin exploring options. No matter what our age is, we can start by looking around where we live now with fresh eyes.

LGBT Long Term Care (lgbt-longtermcare.org) provides information on how to advocate for yourself if you have been discriminated against in a nursing home.

HEALTH AND MEDICAL CARE

I transitioned in order to be able to live a normal life as an ordinary woman . . .
I feel like I won't be able to get top surgery before it becomes a case of hanging
a chandelier in a condemned house.

We often talk about how it takes a village to raise a child, but it can also take a village to care for us as we age. Getting older requires enlisting the help of doctors, nurses, family, friends, and strangers—and for trans people, it also means being ready to actively advocate for ourselves in healthcare settings. All aging humans have increased healthcare concerns. It is no different for us, but we may have some unique concerns. For example, some silicone injection practices for trans women that were most prevalent in the 1970s and 1980s can result in serious health problems in later years as silicone hardens and bonds painfully to muscles or other tissues. Other concerns can stem from long-term lack of access to health care because of lack of insurance, being underemployed, or being unemployed. Additionally, there are few medical studies on the long-term effects of the use of hormone replacement therapy.

Aging has impacted my body and doctors just love blaming it on being trans.

As we grow older, many of us have to deal with something that cisgender people do not—a hesitation to seek out health care because of the expectation and fear that we may be met with discrimination and mistreatment. For many of us, especially T/GE elders, this stems from a long-standing troubled relationship with medical care. We are all products of what and who we have met over a lifetime. Even today, many providers and institutions have not acknowledged the need for training to properly treat T/GE patients. Some may refuse treatment altogether because they wrongly think treating a trans person is a specialty for which they are not equipped. Never mind that we have hearts, lungs, and all those other necessary human parts, just as everyone else does.

I transitioned 10–20 or more years ago. . . .I worry because medical standards
have changed so much since then—I wonder if what I was told back then is still
true now.

Transitions later in life can be a unique concern for aging trans and gender expansive people. After years, perhaps even decades, of questioning and deep discomfort, being mystified by what to do and where to go, older T/GE people may find that many medical resources are tailored for young people. However, access to gender-affirming care is greater than ever and growing year by year around the country.

BABY BOOMERS IN THE TRANS COMMUNITY

Michael Eric Brown (he/him) is the Founding Executive Director of TransMentors International, Inc., a nonprofit organization dedicated to the support of trans individuals. He is also a published author and editor of nonfiction books on trans and nonbinary experiences. His latest book is Aging With Dignity: A Transgender Perspective.

At 19, I was certain I would be dead by the time I was 35, so I vowed to enjoy life and live authentically as I had already been involved in activism within the gay rights movement. I fought the system and loved every moment, because I was angry at the injustice and how difficult it was to live in an unaccepting society. My thirties came and went, and now—over two decades later—the world is in a different place due to the work which we, the LGBT community, put into it, and all the continued work by subsequent generations.

Here I am just short of 60 years old and there is still a significantly under-researched and unexplored facet of transgender life: that of aging transgender individuals. There is a dearth of literature, and only now is there a large enough population of trans individuals to thoroughly research. I realized a few years ago when I passed the half-century mark that it's me and those who came before me—all who encompass the Baby Boomer generation—who are the guinea pigs for cultural competency in the arena of aging transgender adults.

As human beings age, we all face similar questions:

- Who will take care of me?
- Where will I live?
- Will I have enough money for health care and living expenses?
- Will I outlive my spouse or significant other?

Trans people have to ask more than the majority:

- Will I have to detransition in a nursing home in order to be treated with respect?
- Will I be treated with dignity in medical and other vulnerable situations, especially with a body or documents that might defy my gender identity?
- Will Medicare cover my trans-related medical care when I'm older?

Aging transgender people have these and other legitimate and serious concerns that need answers. Our fears and concerns are valid and we implore the medical community, social workers, caregivers, and all those who have devoted their lives to the care of the aged to become educated on the experiences of transgender people. Help ease our fears, and give us the same time, energy, and finances that you give to the majority, and show us you care about us as human beings.

We are the Baby Boomers in the transgender population. There are tens of thousands of us. How long will you continue to keep us invisible?

LEAVING OUR LEGACY: FROM RETIREMENT TO SUNSET YEARS TO END-OF-LIFE

One of the things that many aging people fear the most is losing control over our lives. Out of fear of the unknown, we may be afraid to ask for help. It is important for us to seek support and openly express our wishes, whether about final medical decisions, choosing the executor to settle our affairs after we pass, or ensuring that we are honored the way we want to be during memorial services remembering our life. We can do much to make certain we are the primary authors of the final chapter in our lives.

> As an older person I don't feel like I have a lot of role models. There are great younger nonbinary people, but their experiences are very different than mine. I had a lot of good queer rep when younger, but it feels different now. I guess I see myself as something for others to respect, like a promise they, too, can make it this far.

Our entry into retirement is highly individualized, depending on whether we are ending a long career, aging out of certain social support systems, or suddenly having life circumstances change because of our gender transition. We may strategically plan for and choose when we stop working, if we were working in the first place, or we may be the target of ageism, transphobia, queerphobia, racism, or other discrimination, which leads to ending employment. We may find ourselves in need of social services and other support that we never expected to need.

A 2014 SAGE study found that 50% of single older LGBTQ people had to continue working after retirement age, as compared to 27% of single non-LGBTQ people.[9] Retirement is far from guaranteed for the older T/GE community. Only recently have employment policies become supportive of T/GE people; so, the older we are, the greater likelihood that we have been underemployed and/or unemployed during our working lives. Some of us who transition later in life put off transition so as to avoid potential gender-related discrimination and maximize our benefits and security nets.

Galadriel stands in front of a cafe with clear windows while holding their leopard print cane. Galadriel is a queer non-binary Black writer, artist and social worker. (Disabled and Here. www.affecttheverb.com/disabledandhere)

Some of us may be coming out for the first time in long-established communities of neighbors, family, and friends who have known us in a different gender. Some of us may have made plans to join a retirement community before discerning our gender identity and must navigate whether, or how, to live our authentic gender within it. Others of us who work(ed) in gig or underground economies might not be eligible for Social Security benefits or have a nest egg for retirement, and must make difficult choices about how we will fund our older years. This could include applying for low-income housing, living with family or children who don't know about our gender or don't accept us, sharing resources with friends, or continuing to work past the time we intended.

Finances: Making the Most of What We Have

If we have been fortunate enough to have been employed, a portion of our lifetime income pays into the Social Security system. Generally, our benefits are determined by the amount of money we paid into the system, the length of our employment, the year we were born, and the year we decide to start drawing from Social Security.

If we have been employed, our employer may have offered a 401K, other retirement plan, or a pension. If this is the case, be sure to contact human resources or the organization that manages this account well in advance of an anticipated retirement. For those who have not been fortunate enough to have Social Security or another retirement plan, our options may be limited. Accessing social services becomes paramount, and we may need to reach out to a local AARP chapter, community center, or social services office to ask about what resources might be available to us on a sliding scale or no-fee basis.

Long-Term Care and Hospice Care

Long-term care may be the most daunting of all the challenges faced by T/GE people who are aging. There are many stressors that our T/GE community can face as we interface with long-term care and hospice care service and staff. We may have been open about our T/GE identity in many aspects of our lives, and all of a sudden feel pressure to "pass" and not talk about our T/GE identity. Or we may feel like we want to discuss our T/GE identity to ensure we receive respectful and affirming services, only to find there is little T/GE-awareness in the facility. Finally, for some of us, entering long-term care may happen after a sudden illness or injury that impacts our ability to communicate our wishes and advocate for our needs. This is why establishing networks of people who support our gender, and who have access to our healthcare paperwork and authorizations, is vitally important.

As the general population of older people continues to grow through extended life expectancy, there is an impending shortage of care facilities, other than for the prosperous. Even if we have financial resources and/or long-term care insurance, we may face discrimination and misunderstanding. National policies are in flux, pending further legal rulings, and state protections differ widely. For example, both Medicare and Medicaid provide coverage for long-term care, but they do not cover private rooms, so a roommate is required under this coverage. For T/GE people, this opens the door to discrimination, especially at nonpublic facilities. Even if admitted, we may be housed with someone based on our sex assigned at birth rather than our gender.

"The generation that fought the hardest to get out of the closet now thinks they may have to go back in the closet."—Stu Maddox, Gen Silent: The Lives of LGBT Elders[10]

As with retirement housing, there are some long-term care facilities specifically for LGBTQ people in later life, which are virtually all in major urban areas. Even in these facilities, staff training in T/GE issues may be lacking, given that we are often lumped in with the LGB community. Some states, such as Massachusetts and California, mandate LGBTQ training for certain kinds of facilities that provide care for aging people.

Preparing for the End of Life

What happens to us as we approach the end of life very much depends on the preparations we have made. Questions that come up include those related to end-of-life support, final medical decisions, how we wish our remains to be handled and our life memorialized, as well as who inherits possessions, money, and property. T/GE-affirming end-of-life support networks exist, particularly in faith communities. End-of-life doulas are also powerful sources of support as we face a very new kind of transition.

Legal documentation is an important part of the preparations we must consider as our health declines. Who will speak for us in the event we become medically incapacitated? Even if we do not have much, are there special things we would like to make sure specific people inherit? To make our desires clear and actionable, our wishes should be in writing, signed, witnessed, and preferably appropriately notarized. Often it is best to consult a lawyer to help us draft documents that detail how we want our estate to be handled. For more information, contact the local bar association that operates in your area. Local LGBTQ community centers and social services agencies may have specialized programs to help us with estate planning. In many places, local LGBTQ- or T/GE-identified lawyers may provide pro-bono assistance to us.

Sometimes we can fill out your own directives through websites such as Legal Zoom. Websites do their best to keep up with the various local requirements. However, although we may leave an autographic will and medical statement—which is just a handwritten document expressing our wishes—without advanced legal directives in place, there is no guarantee that our wishes will be honored. It is best if any legal documentation we sign is witnessed by neutral parties and notarized.

Important Paperwork: Wills, Power of Attorney, and Healthcare Authorizations

In many states, the minimum wealth level for estate taxes and settlement has been raised to the point that the vast majority of estates have no tax obligation, and can be relatively easy to deal with, if we have the right paperwork. The executor just executes the will. In general terms, if there is an estate, estates that do not have written directives, like wills,

Marilyn Mardi Pieronek. "58 year old survivor to thriver from a 1970s Teen Trans Experience"

have the inheritance distributed among the legal heirs by state statute by an executor selected by the probate court.

If we have no paperwork, the state will determine who inherits any property or financial resources we leave behind. This is done through descent and distribution, which means only legally recognized relations are eligible to inherit and the law determines who gets what. If you have a life partner, for example, but no legal recognition of that relationship, that person is usually excluded from inheriting.

With regard to paperwork, there are several documents that we as T/GE people should consider preparing:

- *Living will:* A written statement detailing our desires for medical treatment in circumstances in which we are no longer able to express informed consent. This is often called an "advance directive." This includes things such as when to stop medical treatment and specific desires, like "Do not resuscitate" orders.
- *Healthcare Power of Attorney/healthcare proxy:* A written statement that assigns the power to a designated person to make medical decisions for us in the event we are no longer able to express informed consent.
- *Visitation Authorization:* In the event a healthcare facility only permits visitation rights to members of the legally recognized family, we can make written preparations to allow others to visit.
- *Durable Power of Attorney:* This authorizes a chosen person to handle all of our day-to-day affairs should we become unable to do this ourselves. This document may go by different names depending on where we live.

It is important to keep a copy of these documents in a safe place in our home, but also to keep a copy with a friend, family member, and/or loved one(s) that we trust to carry out the directives of our wishes authorized by this paperwork. Numerous legal aid organizations can help us prepare this paperwork in advance, and a quick search of the Internet can also provide downloadable wills and other healthcare paperwork that are easy to complete. Because T/GE people experience so much societal discrimination that we cannot always control, it is important for us to prepare this paperwork earlier in our lives so our wishes will be honored by people we trust.

DYING WITH DIGNITY: CONSIDERATIONS FOR TRANSGENDER ELDERS OF COLOR

S. Aakash Kishore, PhD, (they/he) is a licensed clinical psychologist who was born and raised in the Midwestern United States. He now resides and practices in the Pacific Northwest. (Photo Credit: Yasmin Khajavi)

Transgender and nonbinary people of color may have some unique experiences as we get older. On one hand, significant barriers to health and well-being throughout our lives may pose an added set of challenges in later adulthood. On the other hand, we have many strengths to draw from that can help us age with dignity.

Barriers. Transgender and nonbinary people of color face systemic discrimination across many arenas of life. Discrimination in employment and housing in early adulthood, which particularly impacts Black and Latinx transgender individuals, can create many more problems that impact overall health as we age.[11] For example, being unemployed, underemployed, or unhoused can make it harder to get other resources, such as preventative health care and access to health-promoting foods. This can take a toll on our overall health and can put us at risk for things like heart problems and diabetes as we get older. It can also mean more exposure to diseases that may need to be managed throughout our lifespan. In addition, trans and nonbinary people of color experience interpersonal discrimination related to our gender identity and expression, our race and ethnicity, and the intersection of these identities. Black transgender women face particularly extreme levels of violence in intimate relationships, in the public domain, and elsewhere. Studies also show that day-to-day experiences of subtle discrimination, called *microaggressions*, are correlated with increased stress and poorer health.[12] Microaggressions can be especially common in the care facilities on which elders may come to rely, and this can leave transgender elders of color feeling especially vulnerable or isolated.

Resilience. We are also artists, innovators, and healers who have experience with growing even in the face of adversity. We call this resiliency. Cultures on every continent have historically had a place for people who might be called transgender or nonbinary today. Some transgender people of color have been able to draw from their cultural roots to stay connected to an ethnic community or to a family of origin. Others have created their own family, rites of passage, and traditions. These social and family networks are an important part of health and well-being for older adults. It can be helpful to talk openly with people you trust about a plan to support one another in older adulthood. It is also important for trans and nonbinary people of color to know our rights so that we can advocate for ourselves. The Transgender Law Center and the Sylvia Rivera Law Project have resources that can help. Staying informed about how to access care can help us to age with dignity.

Creating Our Own Legacy

When planning for the end of our lives, it can sometimes be easier to enumerate the tangible things we leave behind than the ways we have affected the people and circumstances around us, and left lasting imprints upon our surroundings that we may never fully grasp. Helping to plan our celebration of life after our death, whether a service, ceremony, or simply a gathering of our closest loved ones, can be one way we articulate what we wish to leave behind. For some of us, we may have already communicated how we wish to be remembered, and for many, we choose cultural and/or religious rituals. Perhaps we want people to gather and remember us; or perhaps we want our remains scattered in a special place.

Often, our loved ones may not be clear on how we want this to be handled. Details we may want to leave in writing for our loved ones include: what funeral services to use, where to be interred, whether to be buried or cremated, whether to have a religious service, whether to have an open casket, and, which speakers or music we would like at a ceremony. Some of us may see this as more of an event for those who survive us and their closure, rather than something for us. Grieving can take many forms, whether it be a quiet observance, a prescribed service and practice depending on religious faith, or a cultural practice. There is no correct way to mark the passing of a life in this world. There is only the way that is most comforting to those who come to honor our lives and mourn our passing.

Each of us leaves behind a personal legacy that is uniquely ours. Our personal legacy does not have to be a material legacy of money, property, or donations. It means a life well-lived, friendships made and lost, lovers fondly remembered or still treasured, and having done some good in the world during our time here. Even as we have met challenges as T/GE people, we believe helping others to overcome challenges, and find joy and affirmation in their gender, is a key part of a fulfilling life. Our work does not always have to include grand gestures or leadership, but can be found in the quiet times with others when we listened, wiped away tears, or comforted someone who was hurting. Wherever we may find ourselves, we hope we can all take time to enrich the people in our lives, and in so doing create more opportunities for those who follow.

CONCLUSION

Aging T/GE people are part of a generational legacy, as well as a personal legacy. Our lives have witnessed vast changes in our ability to live openly in society. Vocabularies and identities that did not exist when we were born, and often came along long after we entered adulthood, continue to evolve through the turmoil and triumph of our lives, from possible childhood confusion through realization to the final product that is uniquely each of us. We have been both participants and witnesses to a remarkable period of change. Today's older T/GE adults have borne burdens both privately and publicly, and deserve respect for the battles we fought that we hope younger generations do not have to fight. We recognize the broad legacy we are leaving for future T/GE communities.

NOTES

1. Maddux, S. (2010, February 18). *Gen Silent* [Documentary]. Interrobang Productions.
2. Fredriksen-Goldsen, K.I., et al. (2014). Successful aging among LGBT older adults: Physical and mental health-related quality of life by age group. *The Gerontologist, 55(1)*,154-168.

3. Fredriksen-Goldsen, K.I., et al. (2014). Physical and mental health of transgender older adults: an at-risk and underserved population. *The Gerontologist, 54(3)*, 488-500.

4. Emlet, C. A. (2016). Social, economic, and health disparities among LGBT older adults. *Generations*, 40(2), 16-22.

5. Grant, J. M., Mottet, L. A., Tanis, J., Harrison, J., Herman, J. L., & Keisling, M. (2011). *Injustice at every turn: A report of the national transgender discrimination survey*. Washington, D.C.: National Center for Transgender Equality.

6. Gandel, Cathie. AARP. (2018). Health Conditions & Treatments: Loneliness is Lethal. https://www.aarp.org/health/conditions-treatments/info-2018/loneliness-risk-death.html

7. James, S. E., Herman, J. L., Rankin, S., Keisling, M., Mottet, L., & Anafi, M. (2016). *The Report of the 2015 U.S. Transgender Survey*. Washington, DC: National Center for Transgender Equality.

8. National Senior Citizens Law Center, National LGBTQ Task Force, SAGE, Lambda Legal, National Center for Lesbian Rights, & National Center for Transgender Equality. (2011). *LGBT Older Adults in Long-Term Care Facilities: Stories from the Field*. https://www.lgbtagingcenter.org/resources/pdfs/NSCLC_LGBT_report.pdf

9. Espinoza, R. (2014). Out & visible: The experiences and attitudes of lesbian, gay, bisexual and transgender older adults, ages 45–75 (pp. 15–16). Services and Advocacy for GLBT Elders (SAGE). https://www.sageusa.org/wp-content/uploads/2018/05/sageusa-out-visible-lgbt-market-research-full-report.pdf

10. Maddux, S. (2010, February 18). *Gen Silent* [Documentary]. Interrobang Productions.

11. James, S. E., Herman, J. L., Rankin, S., Keisling, M., Mottet, L., & Anafi, M. (2016). *The Report of the 2015 U.S. Transgender Survey*. Washington, DC: National Center for Transgender Equality.

12. Sue, D. W. (2010). *Microaggressions in everyday life: Race, gender, and sexual orientation*. Hoboken, NJ: Wiley & Sons.

SECTION 6
CLAIMING OUR POWER

U.S. HISTORY

Andrés C. López and Qwo-Li Driskill

21

INTRODUCTION: CONSTELLATING TRANS HISTORIES OF RESISTANCE

Transgender and gender expansive (T/GE) history in the United States, and globally, is a complex web of people, communities, and political movements. There are many ways to tell the stories of T/GE people in the United States, and many have already been told. Some of these ways include tracing the history of people we would now consider transgender through major events such as the Compton's Cafeteria riot or the Stonewall uprising. We also claim particular people, such as Sylvia Rivera and Marsha P. Johnson, as central to transgender history.

> *I was 10 when I read about Christine Jorgensen and knew that I was not alone in the world.*

Scholars, historians, and activists such as Tourmaline (formerly known as Reina Gossett), Susan Stryker, Sasha Wortzel, and others have done important historical recovery work. This work contributes in essential ways to the formation of T/GE histories and the historical memory for trans people and communities. It also enables us to recover a view of the past in order to better understand our present and imagine future possibilities.

> *I read a lot as a kid, but never saw any trans characters, which is a shame. Exposure to trans people when I was younger would have really helped me be more confident.*

Our aim in this chapter is to complicate the traditional ways that our histories are told by shifting away from "major figures" and instead looking at T/GE histories as a multitude of stories that are sometimes contradictory and continue to be recovered. Rather than attempt to share one grand narrative, we want to look at trans histories through the process Malea Powell calls "constellating."[1] Constellating is a way of weaving histories and stories together that do not focus on one particular center. In this case, we move away from a fixed idea of what being "transgender" or "gender expansive" means. Instead, we put multiple stories together as part of a larger type of storytelling. Through constellating we can change our storytelling from the traditional ways we narrate history and shift it without the pressure of fitting into preconceived notions or ideas of what any of the categories we use (e.g., trans, community, history) might mean. Our telling of trans histories here is not meant to negate other tellings, but rather, to look at the multiple stories that are currently being told.

> *For me, I think about the Holocaust's pink triangles, I think of Stonewall, the AIDS crisis, the banning of trans troops, marches, pride month and parades, and I tie trans history to queer history and all history.*

Susan Stryker explores our pasts in *Transgender History: The Roots of Today's Revolution* (Seal Press, 2017).

Aurora Levins Morales's concept of "medicinal history," is a specific type of practice that is meant "not so much to document the past as to restore to the dehistoricized a sense of identity and possibility."[2] T/GE people, particularly people of color, are often erased from history. Part of the process of claiming our identities and building communities and movements is claiming our histories. The way we go about claiming those histories and imagining the past is important to our individual and collective senses of ourselves and being able to create the world we want to live in. "Medicinal histories" provide us with a

In June 2015, Jennicet Gutiérrez interrupted a White House gay pride event, with a call to end detainment + deportation of LGBTQ immigrants. For 500+ years, gender violence has been a key strategy of European Christian conquest + genocide in the Americas. Today, trans women fleeing violence are denied U.S. asylum, held with men + assaulted, and tortured in solitary. TRANS + QUEER Freedom means ending TORTURE + DEPORTATION.

Jennicet Gutiérrez. (Micah Bazant)

model for thinking about how histories can and do change the way our communities might see ourselves and, in turn, how finding ourselves within these histories might help us all heal from the trauma of ongoing violence.

FRAMEWORK

One of the ways in which T/GE history has traditionally been told is by centering a history of "major figures" within the context of the United States. This history, in turn, becomes the only history most people ever think about when they imagine transgender people in the past. Although this chapter focuses on transgender histories within a U.S.-specific context, transgender histories have always already been influenced by transnational politics, Indigenous sovereignty, and multiple histories of resistance—even if these factors have not always been associated with, or thought of alongside, transgender histories. It is important to question assumptions about the ways in which the United States—its borders, politics, and national identity—is often imagined as a cohesive and static whole. The United States is a settler-colonial state, rooted in genocide and the forcible removal of

Indigenous peoples from their traditional homelands. Today, colonization is still present and continues to perpetuate the genocide of Indigenous people for the purposes of maintaining white supremacy—a belief that white people, white culture, and whiteness are superior to people of other races and cultures. The dominant imagining of the United States too often erases the presence of Indigenous nations, which are defined by the colonizing government as "domestic dependent nations." U.S. colonialism and imperialism continue today outside of the North American continent. The United States has a total of 16 territories, two of which are disputed, with five inhabited, including Puerto Rico, Guam, American Samoa, the Virgin Islands, and the Northern Mariana Islands.

T/GE identities and experiences are not universal or consistent across time and space, but instead take place anytime people cross the boundaries of gender regimes. Gender regimes are governmental, cultural, and religious attempts to control and monitor people's bodies, communities, and lives. This control emerges from rigid sex and gender categories.

The United States is a settler-colonial state that has built an economy of land theft and enslavement, and exploited the labor of women, children, and racialized immigrants of all genders for the purposes of empire-building. Although the term "empire-building" has often been associated with older empires such as Rome or Greece, the United States also uses colonial strategies to gain, maintain, and exert power over other nation-states outside of and within U.S. borders. Transgender histories do not only take place within these contexts, but they also exist through them. Colonizing strategies, which construct social and legal understandings of gender, are used as a weapon to control and regulate entire populations of people and maintain systems of power and control. Trans people and movements create ruptures within these systems.

I believe we need more trans history books about our diverse communities and experiences.

T/GE histories are histories that have always been influenced and driven by specific movements for liberation. Rather than focus on individual figures, this chapter examines trans histories as parts of broad movements for social justice and revolutionary change in the United States. This way of approaching the past can help us reclaim histories of resistance to transphobia within a context of struggles against U.S. racism, settler colonialism, imperialism, misogyny, and homophobia. It also allows us to revise memories of the past with an intersectional analysis.

Language is ever evolving, so it's nice to see folks capture this in the [online] Trans Language Primer. People update it regularly and address the intersections of race, class, disability, and sexuality with trans identity.

Women of color feminists, and queer women of color in particular, provided intersectional frameworks of analysis before Kimberle Crenshaw coined the term "intersectionality." They articulated their experience of multiple or interlocking forms of oppression as a "triple jeopardy," meaning that women of color experience racism, sexism, and classism simultaneously. These experiences cause them to be impacted by oppression in multiple ways. Queer women of color further pointed out how homophobia created another layer of oppression that feminists broadly, and feminists of color in particular, needed to address and incorporate into their politics and activism if movements for radical social change were to be successful.

There is a tendency to try to separate our identities instead of looking at the ways in which race, gender, class, and sexuality have affected the multiple communities we belong to and recognizing the ways they are interconnected. This tendency leads to misrepresentations and assumptions that these differences create separate, distinct histories for trans people. It also functions as a way to reinforce whiteness within the histories that are told. By focusing only on gender as the primary center of power, trans histories run the risk of erasing intersectionality and ignoring the complicated ways in which power plays a factor in determining who gets to survive and who does not.

Two Spirit. A "digital woodcut" depicting We'wha, Fred Martinez, Idle No More, and Two Spirit pride. (Kevyn Breedon)

FIRST WAVES OF COLONIZATION OF THE AMERICAS AND GENDERCIDE

> *So many trans and gender non-conforming identities existed hundreds and hundreds of years before me (many being in communities of color and non-Western societies). Those people have been erased and taken advantage of for ages due to violent colonization and Westernization, imposing white-ideals on them; but, they have always been there, and have done/are doing so much of the work to get us the rights and recognition that we have now.*

In order to understand T/GE movements, we also need to understand the conditions that led to a need for resistance, particularly within the context of colonization. Christopher Columbus's invasion of Indigenous nations in the Caribbean marked the first wave of colonization of the Americas. During this time, Spain and the Catholic Church began to lay claim to Indigenous land, resources, bodies, and souls. The Columbus invasion took place within the context of the Spanish Inquisition, which emerged from earlier inquisitions led by the Roman Catholic Church. These inquisitions brutally enforced Church doctrines, which included gender and sexual norms. It was during these early inquisitions that Joan of Arc—a renowned figure from the peasant class in English-occupied France who helped lead the French army against the English—was executed for heresy for wearing the clothing of the "opposite" gender. These beliefs carried over to the Spanish Inquisition and particularly targeted Muslims and Jews as part of the Spanish Catholic "Reconquista" of the Iberian Peninsula from Muslim political dynasties. Similar genocidal practices by the Catholic Church transferred into the Americas, resulting in people being murdered on the grounds of "heresy" and "sodomy."

> *As a wee child I was told of the stories of Joan of Arc and of Amazon warriors. The fact that I'm 62 and still remember those stories tells me they were pretty significant.*

As Deborah A. Miranda explains in her article, "Extermination of the Joyas: Gendercide in Spanish California," the targeting of people outside of European gender binaries by European powers was part of larger physical and cultural genocidal projects against Indigenous people.[3] Miranda borrows and expands upon Maureen S. Heibert's term "gendercide" to include genders outside of European binaries. She then provides an example of Vasco Núñez de Balboa's 1513 mass murder of Indigenous "sodomites" in Panama as part of the broader practices of gendercide against Indigenous people.

Miranda also gives us a different understanding of how assumptions about homophobia and transphobia operate within Indigenous communities. She specifically refers to the Chumash people in her article and explains the erasure of *joyas*—a label used by Spaniards to describe folks in Chumash society who took on women's roles and who Miranda identifies as a third gender. Miranda shifts how we might think about contemporary homophobia within Native communities. She outlines how homophobia was learned through the California mission system where the extermination and active genocide of joyas was established and enforced. Miranda also points out that joyas were made into examples through violence and death as a way to contain and change Chumash traditional practices. As such, these mass murders of joyas within the mission system were not just instances of homophobia, but rather part of a larger project of gendercide. Reframing this violence as gendercide requires us to rethink how Indigenous communities were forced to assimilate to European cultural values. It also causes us to recognize how the joyas are a separate gender that does not fit within binary gender ideas imposed by European colonizers. As Miranda points out, the joyas were not gay men, nor were they specifically people we would now call transgender. The joyas were a gender all their own, and one that had specific community roles and responsibilities among the Chumash. Naming the violence joyas endured as a type of gendercide highlights the connections that gender roles, sexual practices, and community responsibilities have for Chumash people. It also names the violence that we might consider today to be homophobic or transphobic as being connected to a much longer history involving the policing of gender roles learned through colonization.

Colonization of Indigenous beliefs and cultural practices occurs in other ways, too. For instance, Two-Spirit identity has been appropriated and brought into transgender histories as a way to legitimize trans (and queer) identities in mainstream society. "Two-Spirit" is a term that represents a range of types of gender fluidity and gender roles among Indigenous communities. These Indigenous gender roles are often regarded as historical "evidence" for non-Indigenous nonbinary and transgender identities as being natural, normal, and valid. This phenomenon is what Evan B. Towle and Lynn Marie Morgan call "romancing the transgender native," which creates a "longing for the other" and imagines "a generic, seductive figure who lives in an idealized existence in a utopian place and time."[4] When non-Native and white people invoke nonbinary genders in non-western systems as evidence for their own legitimacy, it minimizes the multiple and varying gender roles that exist within various Indigenous cultures. It also erases the historical gendercide Indigenous people experience under colonization and it generalizes trans experience across difference. Such approaches to trans history ignore the lived realities and ongoing resistances of Indigenous people. They also perpetuate colonial and racist appropriations of Indigenous culture and identity.

A number of people assigned female at birth lived as men and married women from colonial times into the 20th century. For an in-depth look at their lives, pick up *Female Husbands: A Trans History* by Jen Manion (Cambridge University Press, 2020).

Mx Chris Paige (they/them) is an OtherWise-identified writer, educator, organizer, and coach, who authored "OtherWise Christian: A Guidebook for Transgender Liberation." Chris was founding executive director of Transfaith, a multitradition, multiracial, multigender advocacy organization by and for people of transgender experience. Chris continues as operations director for Transfaith and Dean of the Transfaith Institute. They have also launched OtherWise Engaged Publishing, where they provide a platform for prophetic, transgender, intersex, and OtherWise voices.

The appropriation of Christian religious traditions to validate and sustain systems of violence is Christian supremacy. Christian supremacy is one part of the larger project of European colonization. The ideology that insists on two and only two, mutually exclusive and unchangeable genders—defined strictly based on biology at birth—is closely tied to European and Christian settler-colonist values, which align with the violence of white supremacy and Christian supremacy. As such, movements for transgender liberation need to interrogate the brutal legacy of settler-colonial violence that still shapes the way many North Americans think about both gender and liberation.

When it was adopted as the official religion of the Roman Empire, Christianity became wrapped up with questions of power, wealth, and prosperity in ways that were antithetical to the teachings of Jesus. During this time period, the leaders of the new Christian Empire (called Christendom) similarly rejected the leadership of eunuchs even though this alternate gender had been affirmed and celebrated by Jesus. This same Western Christian tradition would go on to legitimize and even fund the colonization of what we now call the Americas. In that process, people (who would now be called Two Spirit) were specifically singled out for abuse and often gruesome slaughter. Later, residential schools similarly forced Western notions of binary gender on Native American children—under the banner of Christianity. The historic and ongoing suppression of authentic gender expression has had lingering effects both within and beyond Indigenous communities. Colonization is not just something that "happened" to Native Americans several hundred years ago. It remains a powerful and influential worldview that continues to thrive and adapt in the contemporary world.

Yet, Judeo-Christian traditions and hundreds of Indigenous cultures testify to more sophisticated and nuanced understandings of the diversity of human gender experiences. I call those perspectives "gender-full" worldviews and I use "OtherWise-gendered" to describe any gender identity or expression that resists the "two and only two" gender ideology of the Western tradition. The ancient world and the early church were gender-full; they were well aware of OtherWise-gendered people and understood them as a natural part of their society. We in the modern world, however, have been bamboozled. Knowledge of gender diversity through the centuries has been suppressed and stolen from us by the same people and traditions that align with white supremacy and Christian supremacy. This is one of many ways that colonization still shapes our world.

Movements for transgender liberation need to be deeply thoughtful about questions of race, religion, culture, and language. In particular, it is important to recognize the ways that Christianity has so often been co-opted as a moral justification for the oppression of OtherWise-gendered people, as well as a rationalization for systems of colonization, slavery, and genocide. However, even (and especially) people who identify as Christian can resist Christian supremacy by speaking out against the use of Christian teaching as a tool for domination and control by those in positions of power. Such resistance is essential if OtherWise-gendered people are to flourish.

Excerpt adapted from Paige, C. (2019). OtherWise Christian: A Guidebook for Transgender Liberation. OtherWise Engaged Publishing.

SLAVERY, SEGREGATION, AND CIVIL RIGHTS

White supremacy and the transatlantic slave trade of African peoples forced African people into chattel slavery, while simultaneously attempting to eradicate their social practices. All enslaved people, regardless of gender, were seen as a population to keep in perpetual servitude. Many African cultures had (and continue to have) nonbinary gender systems that exist outside of dominant European Christian definitions of gender. Even under (and in resistance to) the horrors of slavery, some of these nonbinary gender systems have survived or have reformed in the diaspora just as other African cultural features were retained within African American culture. For example, African diasporic religions such as Santeria and Vodun include deities who cross, balance, and/or transcend gender.

Within the context of slavery in what is now called the United States, Black people were characterized as subhuman and concern over gender focused on their ability to work and produce children. Beginning in 1662, children born into slavery inherited the enslaved status of their mothers, putting Black women at an increased risk of rape by white men. In the 1800s, a specific set of beliefs about womanhood and women's roles as wives and mothers started to emerge. Often referred to as the "cult of domesticity" or

In 2017, C. Riley Snorton published *Black on Both Sides: A Racial History of Trans Identity* (Minneapolis: University of Minnesota Press).

Aaron Devor founded the world's first Chair in Transgender Studies, the world's largest Transgender Archives, and the Moving Trans History Forward Conferences. He is also a professor of sociology, a national-teaching-award winner, and a former Dean of Graduate Studies at the University of Victoria, Canada. (photo © Blake Little)

the "cult of true womanhood," these beliefs emphasized piety, purity, submissiveness, and domesticity. Yet, these standards were only placed on white women and held in contrast to the subjugated status of enslaved Black women. Angela Y. Davis explained the specific position of Black women during slavery in her pivotal 1971 essay, "The Black Woman's Role in the Community of Slaves." Davis examined the ways in which Black women were excluded from "the ideology of femininity," as they were forced to perform "degrading household work" as well as work "in the fields, alongside the men, tolling under the lash from sun-up to sun-down."[5] In this sense, the concept of "womanhood" in the United States can be seen as being constructed in opposition to Black women.

Even under the brutality of slavery, cross-gender identification and gender-variant expressions existed. As historians such as C. Riley Snorton and Joan E. Cashin have pointed out, it wasn't uncommon for enslaved people to "cross-dress" in order to escape slavery, "sometimes changing gender identities several times to evade slave-catchers."[6] Historian Steeve O. Buckridge similarly points out a story from Jamaica about an enslaved person named Hurlock who in 1831, along with others, dressed as a woman and evaded guards to gather information from the militia to bring back to rebelling slaves. Buckridge remarks, "We don't know if cross-dressing was confined to periods of rebellion or whether it represented a sub-culture among slaves,"[7] but we do know that there were people who lived their lives outside of the gender they were assigned at birth while existing under a slave system.

In the 19th century, white physicians in the United States worked to define race and sex as biological categories in order to justify the racialized and gendered social order. As Marli F. Weiner explains, most Southern physicians "shared the assumption that Black (or African) bodies were fundamentally different than white (or European) ones."[8] Such assumptions led to the classification of bodies based on perceived physical differences and reinforced the belief that such differences made certain bodies naturally more superior to others by comparison. Similar thinking has been used to determine who is considered a "real" man or woman, invalidating the lived experiences of many transgender and nonbinary people. Perceived physical differences were used as "evidence" to support the supposed "natural" division of these biological categories, and some physicians and psychologists attempted to find "cures" for sexual or gendered behaviors deemed "unnatural" because they disrupted the social order.

> *Most of our history is erased and bent to say we are "just women dressed as men" or "just men dressed as women." It's hard to decipher who might have been trans and who might have been cis.*

The first person to dub themselves a "queen of drag" (now called "drag queen") was William Dorsey Swann, who was born into slavery in 1858 and in the 1880s held elaborate drag balls in Washington, DC.[9]

The classification of bodies to justify racial and gendered divisions continues to impact an array of people today. It is through the backdrop of slavery in the United States that we can understand how assumptions about a "normal" and "healthy" body (e.g., white, cisgender, and able-bodied) are often at the expense of other bodies considered "deviant" or of "lesser" value (e.g., Black, disabled, and trans). This is one of the ways racial hierarchies and gender binaries are constructed through white supremacy. Yet, through 246 years of slavery, followed by legal segregation and the re-enslavement of many through the convict leasing system, African Americans resisted, created communities, and built social movements that later shaped queer and trans activism and deeply transformed the place we now called the United States.

A SNAPSHOT OF TRANS MILESTONES

Year	"Milestone"
1886	We'wha, a *lhamana* (Two-Spirit) from Zuni, visits Washington, DC as an ambassador and meets President Grover Cleveland.
1959	Cooper Donuts Riot in Los Angeles.
1964	Reed Erickson starts the Erickson Educational Foundation.
1965	Dewey's Coffee Shop Protest.
1966	Compton's Cafeteria Riot in San Francisco. John Hopkins Medical Center opens the first Gender Clinic.
1969	The Stonewall Uprising in New York City. The founding of the Gay Liberation Front.
1970	Sylvia Rivera and Bubbles Rose Lee start STAR: Street Transvestite Action Revolutionaries. Marsha P. Johnson is invited to serve as Vice President.
1975	Minneapolis becomes the first city to pass a law prohibiting discrimination against transgender people. Gay American Indians is cofounded in San Francisco by Randy Burns and Barbara May Cameron.
1977	The Combahee River Collective, a collective of Black lesbian feminists, releases their collective statement, rejecting lesbian separatism and biological determinism. Instead they argue for a practice of resistance that understands how major systems of oppression are interlocking. Renée Richards wins landmark case when the New York Supreme Court rules in her favor that she is eligible to play tennis in the U.S. Open as a woman.
1981	Persephone Press publishes *This Bridge Called My Back: Writings by Radical Women of Color*, edited by Gloria Anzaldúa and Cherríe Moraga.
1987	American Indian Gays and Lesbians is founded in Minneapolis.
1991	FTM International, Inc. is established by Jamison Green. First Southern Comfort Conference in Atlanta, Georgia.
1992	Leslie Feinberg publishes *Transgender Liberation: A Movement Whose Time Has Come*. Transgender Nation forms.
1993	Minnesota becomes the first state to extend protections against discrimination to transgender people. Ricki Anne Wilchens, Denise Norris, and Jessica Xavier found The Transexual Menace, a transgender rights activist organization.
1995	First FTM Conference of the Americas. First Transgender Lobbying Day in Washington, DC.
1998	PFLAG adds gender identity to their mission. Bay Area American Indian Two-Spirits is founded.

1999	Gwendolyn Ann Smith founds the Transgender Day of Remembrance.
2000	Transgender Pride Flag, designed by Monica Helms, is first shown at the Pride Parade in Phoenix, Arizona.
2002	Sylvia Rivera Law Project founded by Dean Spade. Transgender Law Center opens.
2004	The Transgender Gender-Variant & Intersex Justice Project is founded to address human rights abuses and prison violence toward transgender people, specifically transgender women of color in prisons and detention centers. María Belén Correa, an exiled Argentinian living in the United States, creates Red Latinoamericana y del Caribe de Personas Trans, REDLACTRANS, which integrates organizations led by trans women in various countries in Latin America and the Caribbean. First all-transgender performance of the Vagina Monologues.
2005	California becomes the first state to mandate transgender healthcare coverage.
2008	Laverne Cox is the first transgender person nominated for a Primetime Emmy Award in the acting category.
2009	Bamby Salcedo and other activists start the TransLatin@ Coalition.
2010	Phyllis Frye becomes the first openly transgender judge appointed in the United States.
2012	Bay Area American Indian Two-Spirits holds the world's first public Two-Spirit powwow in San Francisco.
2013	Alicia Garza, Patrisse Cullors, and Opal Tometi found Black Lives Matter.
2014	Trans and queer immigrants, undocumented people and allies, youth leaders and parents found Familia: Trans Queer Liberation Movement.
2015	Annalise Ophelian releases the film *Major!* about Miss Major Griffin-Gracy's work as a Black transgender elder and activist who has been fighting for the rights of trans women of color for over 40 years.
2016	Water Protectors gather at the Standing Rock Indian Reservation to stop the Dakota Access Pipeline. Two-Spirit people are a visible presence, including the Two-Spirit Nation camp.
2018	Phillipe Cunningham is the first openly Black trans man and Andrea Jenkins is the first openly Black trans woman elected to public office in the United States. Danica Roem is the first openly transgender person to be elected to service in a U.S. state legislature (Virginia). Raquel Willis starts Black Trans Circles, a project that focuses on developing the leadership of Black trans women in the South and Midwest, and becomes the first trans woman to be executive editor of *Out Magazine*. Members of the TransLatin@ Coalition drop a giant Trans Pride flag at the World Series at Dodger Stadium in Los Angeles that reads, "Trans People Deserve to Live."
2019	*Vogue* cover features Estrella Vazquez, a Zapotec *muxe* from Oaxaca.
2020	Amidst renewed Black Lives Matter protests following the murder of George Floyd, a rally for Black Trans Lives draws thousands in Brooklyn.

THE STONEWALL REBELLION, GAY LIBERATION, AND INTERSECTIONAL TRANS ACTIVISM

There have been disagreements about the origins of queer and trans political organizing since the creation of the concept of "gay liberation." One starting point is the political work of the Gay Liberation Front (GLF), which was first established in New York City and then later grew nationally. Although there are other possible origin points, and other political activism that took place throughout the United States that are also part of these histories, GLF was central to an intersectional movement. Its organizers intentionally connected it to a global "Third-World" movement of non-Europeans against imperialism and colonialism. Even the organization's name intentionally invokes the language of a "liberation front"—language that was specifically used during the anticolonial movements in Vietnam, as well as Algeria, and throughout European-colonized nations. Language used by GLF also reflects the language of Black liberation from Black Power organizations such as the Black Panthers. This framing had already been created by the Women's Liberation Movement, which emerged out of Black Civil Rights organizing. The Stonewall Riots, a frequent flashpoint of "gay liberation," occurred within this larger context of movements for the liberation of "Third-World" peoples both within and outside of the United States. These were organized antiwar movements aimed against United States involvement in Vietnam—a fact sometimes ignored or erased within contemporary retellings of the legacy of Stonewall.

Most people think back to Stonewall in the U.S. when they think of LGBTQIA + history, and it is certainly one of the most prominent events I can think of.

Although Sylvia Rivera and Marsha P. Johnson are often credited for starting the Stonewall Riots, these claims are part of the mythology that has emerged since Stonewall. Some of these claims are based, in part, on Rivera's own stories. For instance, Rivera has remarked that she was at Stonewall the first night of the riots, later correcting these claims. Other times, such histories become revised, erasing certain parts and adding others. What remains clear is that there were trans people, including trans people of color, present at Stonewall during the police raid that started the riots. Butches and transmasculine people who were targeted for wearing men's clothing were also present at Stonewall, even though this history is often left out. Stormé DeLarverie, a Black and mixed-race butch who performed in masculine drag at the Jewel Box Revue and only wore men's clothing, claimed to be the butch lesbian seen by witnesses who resisted arrest and was struck in the head with a billy club. In response, DeLarverie punched the officer, which quickly led the already angry crowd outside of Stonewall to rebel. The Stonewall Riots lasted six days, and many more people participated in acts of resistance beyond the initial riot. While we attempt to recreate and recover the specific histories of Stonewall as one of the moments that created trans activism, what is important is that Stonewall gave rise to trans movements. The exact ways in which Rivera and Johnson were part of the Stonewall Riots is less important than the fact that they were both highly involved in organizing and creating the frameworks of an intersectional vision of liberation for trans people.

The NYC LGBT Historic Sites Project offers an online Transgender History tour of sites in New York City related to trans history.

It is significant to me that trans people were in the forefront of the "gay liberation" movement. I am thinking of the Compton's Cafeteria riot. Had it not been for the presence and arrest of trans people, Stonewall would have been just another police raid.

Sylvia Rivera at Gay Liberation Front's Demonstration at Bellevue Hospital, 1970. (Richard C. Wandel Photographs collection, The LGBT Community Center National History Archive)

At the time of the Stonewall Riots, the word "gay" was an in-community umbrella term for people we might not call "gay" now. Although there was certainly transphobia and misogyny within the gay community, the distinctions that are now articulated between "gay" and "trans" were not always as separately defined as they are today. In fact, the emergence of specific trans identities and movements occurred, in part, because white middle-class gays and lesbians distanced themselves from the struggles of poor trans people of color during the emergence of Gay Liberation. According to Ron Ballard, the Gay Activists Alliance (GAA) was formed specifically because white, middle-class people, mainly men, were angry that the GLF voted to financially support bail for members of the Black Panthers. Ron Ballard recalled in a 1995 interview:

> "[The GAA] was formed because of class and because of race. [. . .] the dirty little secret of the gay movement is how, and why, the GAA was formed, and that was because they wanted white power. And so they let the freaks—the artists, the poets, the drag queens, the street people, the street queens, and the Blacks [. . .] keep the GLF, we're going to form this thing that's going to change laws. That's a good idea—change laws, but it was mainly reformist. The vision was broken. The vision went."[10]

Although the GAA may have broken the original vision of gay liberation, GLF and its offshoots, as well as other movements and organizations, continued to organize for a vision of liberation that included an end to racism, capitalism, imperialism, sexism, and what we now call transphobia.

Second Christopher Street Liberation Day March, 1971. (Leonard Fink Collection, The LGBT Community Center National History Archive)

I remember the demonstration we held in 1967 outside of the Black Cat—a Tavern in Los Angeles, California. We were protesting the police raids that happened during New Year's Eve.

In the immediate wake of Stonewall, Sylvia Rivera and Marsha P. Johnson were highly involved in GLF organizing work, and they also attended GAA meetings and events. Although Rivera and Johnson are often held up as central to the formation of trans identities and political movements in the United States, they were part of a larger family and community that is often forgotten and erased, which included other trans women and transfeminine people. After a 1970 GLF protest at New York University in solidarity with gay students, Rivera and Bubbles Rose Lee began the Street Transvestite Action Revolutionaries (STAR), later inviting Johnson to serve as Vice President.

The 2017 Netflix film *The Death and Life of Marsha P. Johnson* (directed by David France) centers on activist Victoria Cruz's investigation into Marsha P. Johnson's death.

It is within this context of revolutionary social movements that critiques of gender, gender binaries, and visions for trans liberation emerged. For example, in 1971, the Third World Gay Revolution in New York City published the manifesto "What We Want, What We Believe" in a bulletin called *Gay Flames*. Declaring the manifesto as part of their revolutionary platform, the Third World Gay Revolution stated the following:

> "We want the right of self-determination over the use of our bodies: the right to be gay, anytime, anyplace; the right of free physiological change and modification of sex on demand; the right to free dress and adornment. [. . .] We believe that these are basic human rights which must be defended with our bodies put on the line."[11]

The manifesto calls for complete and total restructuring of society, and this part of their platform remains radical and still unrealized. The Third World Gay Revolution argued that it is a *basic human right* to receive *free* gender affirming medical care and to express gender in any way one wants, without being restricted by the U.S. medical industry's demand for diagnoses such as "gender dysphoria" (or the earlier term "gender identity disorder")—a struggle we continue to have today. Such statements both reflect and create a critique of conversations taking place in radical movements focused on the eradication of sexism, racism, capitalism, and all forms of enforced gender roles and sexual norms.

Sylvia Rivera, who was involved with the Young Lords and the Black Panthers, along with other members of STAR, was likely a coauthor of the Third World Gay Revolution manifesto. Similar language appears in STAR's manifesto, which calls for an end to all forms of oppression and articulates specific forms of antitrans violence perpetrated by nontrans people:

> "The oppression against Transvestites of either sex arises from sexist values and this oppression is manifested by heterosexuals and homosexuals of both sexes in the form of exploitation, ridicule, harrassment [sic], beatings, rapes, murders."[12]

STAR's work articulated a vision of trans liberation as part of larger visions for the complete transformation of society. These larger visions included a literal and cultural revolution following the aftermath of Stonewall, in which queer and trans people began to situate themselves and their queer and trans identities within revolutionary political agendas and movements.

According to a 1972 interview with Marsha P. Johnson, at the beginning of gay liberation, hostility toward transfeminine people organizing came primarily from gay men:

> "We still feel oppression by other gay brothers. Gay sisters don't think too bad of transvestites. Gay brothers do. [. . .] Once in a while, I get an invitation to Daughters of Bilitis and when I go there, they're always warm. All the gay

Street Transvestite Action Revolutionaries (STAR) at the Christopher Street Liberation Day March, 1973. (Leonard Fink Collection, The LGBT Community Center National History Archive)

sisters come over and say, 'Hello, we're glad to see you,' and they start long conversations. But not the gay brothers. They're not too friendly at all toward transvestites."[13]

However, despite some women's organizations being welcoming to early T/GE activists, other women increased their hostility, excluding trans and gender nonconforming individuals from their communities. For instance, by the time Sylvia Rivera insisted on speaking at the Washington Square rally in 1973, Jean O'Leary—a white lesbian feminist—countered Rivera's call for solidarity with jailed transfeminine people by engaging in what we might term today as Trans-Exclusionary Radical Feminist (TERF) behavior, which accuses transfeminine people of exploiting and mocking nontrans women. Early TERF beliefs also made their way through some lesbian separatist communities.

> *The current wave of attacks on trans identity by elements identifying themselves as feminist may, in retrospect, be very important in reversing civil rights progress, but it's far too soon to assess that impact. This issue is tied up with so many other retrograde movements in play right now.*

Later, in 1977, the Combahee River Collective—a collective of Black, feminist, socialist, lesbian activists—wrote their now famous "Combahee River Collective Statement."[14] In this statement, the Combahee River Collective explicitly critiqued lesbian separatism

Marsha P. Johnson at the First Christopher Street Liberation Day March, 1970. (Leonard Fink Collection, The LGBT Community Center National History Archive)

In 1973, at the Christopher Street Liberation Day Rally in Washington Square Park, Sylvia Rivera fought her way onstage to become the only trans person to speak. She called out the audience for ignoring the needs of trans people in jail. "The people," she said, "are trying to do something for all of us, and not men and women that belong to a white middle class white club."

by pointing to how it reinforces dangerous concepts of gender and lacks an analysis of racism and capitalism as sources of oppression:

> "As Black women we find any type of biological determinism a particularly dangerous and reactionary basis on which to build a politic. We must also question whether lesbian separatism is an adequate and progressive political analysis and strategy, even for those who practice it, since it so completely denies any but the sexual sources of women's oppression, negating the facts of class and race."[15]

In opposition to the "Combahee River Collective Statement," the emergence of TERF politics then and now reinforces essentialist notions of gender and frequently attacks trans women by claiming that only those assigned female at birth are "real" women. This kind of analysis of gender has underpinnings of white supremacy and classism as its roots.

MARSHA P. JOHNSON AND SYLVIA RIVERA WERE THE MOTHERS OF THE MOVEMENT, BUT HOW DO WE TELL THE STORY OF THEIR STRUGGLES WITH THEIR MINDS?

Anole Halper, MSW, MPH (they/them) is a genderqueer neurodivergent social worker, poet, and weirdo. They are dedicated to individual and collective healing from trauma and violence, and have worked in many areas of the field, including grassroots restorative justice processes, support group facilitation, training, and program design and evaluation. Anole wishes to thank Reina Gossett/Tourmaline for making this piece possible with her critical archival and creative work to bring Marsha P. Johnson's legacy to a new generation.

Note: This article discusses mental health, suicide, and psychiatric care in ways that may be triggering for some readers.

Marsha P. Johnson and Sylvia Rivera were trans femmes of color and lifelong dear friends who fought in the Stonewall riots and led intersectional movements for liberation before the word "intersectional" was born. They fought hard for us, demanding recognition and agency from a white straight world and a white gay movement that often ignored and disparaged them. Now, at long last, they have begun to be honored for their role in our liberation.

They met on the street when Marsha was 18 and Sylvia was 12. They were both homeless and engaged in sex work on and off from childhood, even as they mothered friends and movements. They cofounded Street Transvestite Action Revolutionaries (STAR), which housed young trans folks who lived on the street and fought for their rights because, according to Sylvia, "Marsha and I just decided it was time to help each other and help our other kids." Sylvia cofounded the Gay Liberation Front and Gay Activist Alliance and supported the Black Panthers and Young Lords, and Marsha was involved with ACT UP!

In addition to these achievements, there are experiences more private that are well-documented but complex to linguistically approximate. These experiences are often omitted from the mythology that is emerging about these remarkable people. In naming them, I will say what we know and try not to take any liberties:

According to Bob Kohler, a human rights activist and friend, Marsha P. Johnson would sometimes get picked up by the police for walking naked down the street, talking incoherently about her father and Neptune, and be "taken away" for a few months. She would return implanted with Thorazine and "would be like a zombie" for a month or so before returning to "the old Marsha." Marsha herself said she had her "first mental breakdown in 1970." Her nephew, Al Michaels, remembers her family taking her to the hospital during "spells." Sylvia Rivera, according to her, had "a drinking problem," used heroin, and attempted suicide at least twice in low periods.

Why are these facts often omitted? Perhaps we don't know what to make of them? As trans people, our very existence has been pathologized; maybe we worry it will invalidate us if our heroes also have pathologies of their own, if they struggled against internal pain as well as the forces of external oppression.

But one struggle does not erase the other. A brain that is hard to inhabit does not make the life it holds any less extraordinary. As Marsha herself said, "I may be crazy, but that don't make me wrong." Marsha and Sylvia may have been extraordinary, but in their struggles, they were like many of us.

Sylvia and Marsha already remind us of the beauty of our human wholeness, complexity, and messiness. As we hold these mothers of the movement in the light of our unfolding liberation, let us not leave this facet of them, or ourselves, in darkness.

So if we do not omit this part of their story—or our own—then how do we tell it?

We know Sylvia said that Marsha kept her alive, saving her life after a suicide attempt on the fourth anniversary of Stonewall, the night she was famously booed off stage at Pride. Marsha found her, got her to a hospital, and told her it was "not her time." After Marsha's mysterious death in 1992 caused Sylvia to lose stability and become homeless on the Christopher Street Piers, she somehow kept candles burning on an altar to Marsha inside her makeshift home. Sylvia said that meditating on Marsha and the Hudson River where her body was found kept her going through bouts of "hitting bottom" in her drinking.

Marchers at Christopher Street Liberation Day, 1973. (Rudy Grillo Collection, The LGBT Community Center National History Archive)

So it seems that the story of their mental suffering is partly a testament to the revolutionary power of queer and trans love, its ability to soothe immense psychic pain and keep us here to fight alongside one another. It is also important to recognize that Sylvia and Marsha probably skipped some meetings and protests (perhaps hungover or in a hospital) to accommodate mental and emotional cycles that did not always align with the political moment. We need to recognize this because, like so many people with mental illness coming up against their rhythms and limits, Sylvia and Marsha managed to accomplish a great deal while simultaneously challenging norms of endless, perfect productivity.

These remarkable individuals have done a lot to liberate us all. And when I imagine them holding each other safe, resting, away from the front lines, I feel liberated by that, too.

Article adapted from original publication on trans-survivors.com from June 25, 2019. Republished with permission from the author.

THE AIDS EPIDEMIC AND RESPONDING TO REAGANISM

In 1981, the Centers for Disease Control in the United States noticed outbreaks of pneumocystis pneumonia among gay men in Los Angeles. Initially called "Gay-Related Immune Deficiency" (GRID), the name of the syndrome was changed to Acquired Immune Deficiency Syndrome (AIDS) in 1982. The virus that causes AIDS was identified in 1983 in France and the United States and later named the Human Immunodeficiency Virus (HIV) in 1986.

Although the HIV/AIDS pandemic tends to be spoken of in the United States in terms of its enormous impact on cisgender gay, bisexual, and queer men, the AIDS crisis has always deeply impacted trans people and communities. Even into the 1980s and 1990s—particularly in many communities of color—divides between gay, lesbian, and bisexual identities and trans identities were not always clear. Further, because HIV/AIDS reporting was based on a gender binary system, many trans people were erased by reporting systems that used assigned sex at birth to categorize and classify HIV transmission as well as deaths caused by AIDS.

Sylvia & Marsha. "This painting is of Sylvia Rivera in her bedroom, with a photo of Marsha P. Johnson in the background. We tend to focus on this transestor in her public domain but Sylvia Rivera experienced mental and physical illnesses and was restored at home with her comfort objects." (Elliot Kukla)

The emergence of the AIDS crisis began at the same moment when there was heightened resistance against the limited gains of "gay and lesbian" movements for legal rights and protections. In 1977, Anita Bryant fought to overturn legislation in Dade County, Florida, and founded the organization "Save Our Children" to fight against "gay and lesbian" rights. Two years later, in 1979, Jerry Falwell began The Moral Majority, which worked against LGBTQ people on a national level. The following year, the 1980 election of Ronald Reagan to the presidency of the United States signaled a rise of the Far Right and a backlash toward the gains of people of color, feminists, and LGBTQ movements during the previous decades. In 1983, Patrick Buchannan—the White House Communications Director under Reagan—stated that AIDS was "nature's revenge on Gay men."[16]

The University of Victoria Transgender Archives is host to online materials as well as a conference called "Moving Trans History Forward."

I remember when Sandy Stone published her 1987 essay, "The Empire Strikes Back: A Posttranssexual Manifesto," which responds to Janice Raymond's attack of Sandy for being a transgender woman and part of a woman's collective.

COVID-19, TRANS LIVES, AND TRANS STUDIES

Red Washburn, PhD (they/them), is an Associate Professor of English and Director of Women's and Gender Studies at Kingsborough Community College. Red also teaches Women's and Gender Studies at Brooklyn College. This is a small portion of their contributions and thoughts from a panel about COVID-19 for the Center for LGBTQ Studies at the City University of New York (CUNY) held on April 3, 2020.

How are surviving pandemics and movements for transgender, gender-nonconforming, and queer people inter-connected?

Many prior pandemics have direct connections to LGBTQ communities. Naomi Replansky, a lesbian poet, age 101, has recently talked about embracing her confinement during the COVID-19 pandemic. She has reflected on living through the Spanish Flu, the Great Depression, and the Holocaust in this context.

The AIDS pandemic is often forgotten in the litany of pandemics. While it is often portrayed as a gay disease by the mainstream media, trans folks are very much a part of the AIDS pandemic and are without the same access to healthcare. I'm thinking about an ACT UP flyer that read, "Women don't have AIDS, but die from it." These issues are resurfacing now with COVID-19, as we don't have the same healthcare access under the Trump administration as we did under the Obama administration.

LGBTQ folks, historically, have also been pathologized as "sick," "perverse," and "monsters." Mike Davis, an American scholar, political activist, and historian, recently discussed capitalism using the metaphor of the "monster," and the first thought I had was about trans folks, including folks with disabilities, being deemed "monstrosities." The DSM only recently removed gender identity disorder from its manual, just a few years ago, for instance.

COVID-19 expands pandemics created and exacerbated by capitalism and neoliberalism (as well as white supremacy and cis-heteropatriachy) with its values of big pharma and prisons—profits and bailouts over people. Politicians and administrators often use sickness as a distraction with elections looming to promote their political agenda and fascist policies. Global warming is destroying land, animals, plants, and Indigenous and Two-Spirit lives (for instance, I'm thinking about the Amazon), and capitalism needs "disasters," what Naomi Klein calls "disaster capitalism," to thrive. Those folks especially targeted and harmed are those experiencing poverty, homelessness, starvation, unemployment/job discrimination, lack of healthcare or access to decent healthcare, educational struggles, food/hunger, social stigma, etc. Trans people have high rates of all of the above, in particular, as well as social isolation from family/kin, friends, depression, suicide, anxiety, and hate violence, including from the state. Trans folks' politics of everyday life and frequent injustice and microaggressions are merely exacerbated and made hypervisible with the recent pandemic. Whose life matters? Who is essential? Who is a human? These are questions philosophers like Judith Butler and George Yancy have been asking and are also addressed by activists in Black Lives Matter, led by Black queer women.

Does the COVID-19 pandemic present a unique challenge for our communities?

Yes. All the issues I mentioned are social justice issues that affect trans folks across the spectrum of difference. Some unique challenges coming up now: Thirty million people with no healthcare access, and those that do have it, often can't see doctors who treat them humanely—for example, don't want to touch or evaluate us—or have doctors who just can't see us for surgeries, hormones, etc., because of the quarantine. We can't go to court for name and gender changes. Lawsuits—including mine against my university—are on hold. These are some examples that can lead to increased violence that not only affects our physical health, but also our mental health. Trans folks are affected by intimate partner violence and toxic environments, are homeless/kicked out when they come out/are without work/are sex workers and living on the streets, are in prison and solitary confinement, state-sanctioned social distancing (for example, Layleen Polanco died/was murdered at Rikers and Chelsea Manning was just released because of mental health reasons), are around transphobic families and housemates, and/or are dealing with cyber bullying from bosses and colleagues. I'm thinking of Lorena Borjas's death, which shows the intersecting realities of trans folks and the harm being enacted on individuals and our communities.

What are our survival strategies?

We were never meant to survive, as Audre Lorde reminds us. Our recognition as humans has been stripped from us during the Trump administration—from healthcare, to housing, to the military. It started with his removing us from the White House website on his Inauguration Day and removing non-discrimination policies from the Affordable Care Act. The Hungarian government seeks to end the legal recognition of trans folks during this crisis. To survive, we have had to create our own communities and organizations from Sylvia Rivera's and Marsha P. Johnson's work with STAR to Trans Lifeline. We survive in community. We dissociate to survive as well as create care and support networks because we do not have access to many services. We create our own families and housing. Survival is our resistance.

In your teaching/research/advocacy how do you see transgender/GNC/queer communities being impacted by the COVID-19 pandemic? What is your experience with teaching trans/studies online?

In my Women's and Gender Studies classes, we have been talking a lot about rethinking knowledge and learning using multiple modalities and assessments/grading methods as well as connecting them to rethinking single-issue struggles and moving towards multiple issues. We have been talking about how to create a better world in and outside of the classroom for folks who are targeted now, including poor, working-class, women, trans and nonbinary folks, lesbian, bisexual, gay, and queer folks, folks with disabilities and immuno-compromised folks, and/or elderly folks. In particular, we have been talking a lot about racism targeted against Asian Americans in my classes because of COVID-19.

In class, I've also been talking about my own experiences with whiteness and privilege as a tenured professor with stable work and health benefits. I've shared my relief at having a shelter in a place that is safe, but my guilt thinking about prisoners (approximately 2 million in prison at high risk of infection) and homeless folks who are sick and dying. I've also shared my frustrations about lack of rights for delivery workers, doctors, nurses, and farmworkers, among others. I've also shared my relief about my experiences with less misgendering, less exposure to street violence, less bathroom policing, and less harassment at Kingsborough during the quarantine. I've been relieved that many students with disabilities and/or many working-class students—mainly students of color—have access to the learning they should have received along with accommodations and technologies in place with remote learning. I've shared my concerns about not being able to see medical professionals about my own health issues during my transition. I've been inspired by the empathy, generosity, and kindness in my classes—how students are being emotionally supportive to each other. I've been most excited by the discussions about making a new world—general strikes, rent moratoriums, mutual aid for food and medical depositories, and fighting for people's right to a life in ways capitalism can't provide through its value of corporations, the destruction of the environment and Indigenous communities, and the lack of stable work as the impact of COVID-19 takes us into a recession with rates of higher unemployment than the Great Depression.

What does a world look like without exploitative work, carceral and detention institutions, and inflated rent/gentrification, etc.? What are the possibilities of hope we can now create for a more just world? This is just the beginning of the current phase of the ongoing freedom struggle.

Amid a growing public panic about HIV/AIDS, which was fueled by the antigay rhetoric of the religious right, organizations such as Focus on the Family (based in Colorado) continued to create panic about both AIDS and "homosexuality." In 1992, voters in Colorado approved Amendment 2, which barred "gay, lesbian, and bisexual" people from legal protections. That same year in Oregon, Ballot Measure 9—led by Oregon Citizens Alliance—attempted to change the state constitution to include the following:

> "All governments in Oregon may not use their monies or properties to promote, encourage or facilitate homosexuality, pedophilia, sadism or masochism. All levels of government, including public education systems, must assist in setting a standard for Oregon's youth which recognizes that these 'behaviors' are 'abnormal, wrong, unnatural and perverse' and they are to be discouraged and avoided."[17]

While Ballot Measure 9 did not pass, propaganda around the measure resulted in horrific violence and harassment of LGBTQ people in the state, including the murder of Hattie Mae Cohen (a Black lesbian) and Brian Mock (a white disabled gay man) through a fire-bombing of their apartment in Salem. Although transgender people were not named explicitly in these laws, given that unified language around gender diversity and identity had yet to emerge, attacking "homosexual" or "bisexual" people (who were often imagined as gender nonconforming) implicitly also attacked trans people.

Brandon Teena's murder in 1993 and Leelah Alcorn's suicide in 2014 were significant moments in history for me.

The AIDS crisis and growing attacks on LGBTQ people gave rise to new radical organizing, such as the AIDS Coalition to Unleash Power (ACT-UP), Queer Nation, and the Lesbian Avengers. In 1992, Leslie Feinberg—a Jewish community labor activist—published the pamphlet *Transgender Liberation: A Movement Whose Time Has Come,* which argued for the uniting of all people outside of rigid gender binaries as a "gender" or "transgender" movement. The pamphlet also articulated "gender-phobia" as a system of oppression related to, but distinct from, other forms of oppression.

The start of Camp Trans, an annual demonstration protesting the Michigan Womyn's Music Festival's policy of excluding trans women from attending, was really important to me.

In 1993, trans activists Ricki Anne Wilchens, Denise Norris, and Jessica Xavier cofounded The Transexual Menace in order to protest the refusal of Stonewall 25—a New York City event marking the 25th anniversary of the Stonewall Riots—to include "transgender" in the title of the event. These forms of organizing garnered momentum, leading to the founding of more trans organizations that ranged from providing direct services and resources (e.g., gender clinics and support groups) to advocating for mainstream acceptance and inclusion.

The first Trans March, which was in San Francisco as part of Pride in June 2004, was an important moment for me. I was there.

The Digital Transgender Archive is an international collaboration among more than 60 colleges, universities, nonprofit organizations, public libraries, and private collections to expand access to trans history for academics and independent researchers.

ACT UP. (Richard C. Wandel Photographs collection, The LGBT Community Center National History Archive)

As the 1990s progressed into the early 2000s, the Internet became a space for trans people to connect, exchange information, provide resources, and organize. Yet, despite increased access to technology, accurate representations of trans lives remained sparse in mainstream media. Furthermore, many organizations that aimed to include trans folks continued to exclude their lived experiences, particularly the perspectives of trans folks of color. Even today, when speaking about sexualities and gender identities, discussions of race and the effects of racism are often ignored. As we move forward, it is crucial to understand the various ways in which trans visibility and representation can sometimes reinforce the very elements they attempt to undo.

Transy House (1995–2008) was a transgender collective in Park Slope, Brooklyn, run by Rusty Mae Moore and Chelsea Goodwin. Sylvia Rivera was one of its residents.

At the time of my transition, there were not a lot of comprehensive resources on nonbinary identities or transitions online. So, when I found Micah, who runs the website genderqueer.me, it was a hugely positive thing for me.

TIME KEEPS SLIPPING BACK TO THE PAST

A. Dionne Stallworth's (she/her) name appropriately begins with "A"—as her social justice resume boasts a bouquet of beginnings. She is one of the founding members of GenderPAC, the first transgender political action committee. She is also a founding member and original cochair of the Transgender Health Action Coalition. In addition, Stallworth has served as an officer and board member of the Pennsylvania Mental Health Consumers' Association. She has led the observance of the International Transgender Day of Remembrance (TDOR) in Philadelphia and was one of the original founders of the TransHealth Conference, under the leadership of Charlene Arcila-Moore.

As a child, I often heard these words come from my television with no real understanding of what they meant:

"Like sands through the hourglass, so are the days of our lives . . ."

As I get closer to my 61st birthday and reflect on my life and the events in it, I understand it more and, in some ways, yes, it totally freaks me out! I've seen a few transwomen of color become a standard of beauty, fame, and power in the world; a child's journey into her own identity become the subject of a docu-reality show; and more amazing things that I can't possibly list in the time that I have here. However, it is the essence of these "grains of sand" that I'm driven to speak to and about—as I find myself one of them.

I look at the struggle of gender variant people since the beginning of time, and I see one thing: We seem to have no history of our own. Every year at Pride celebrations, I see the celebrations of the so-called collective struggles of LGBTQI people and watch as we ignore what that cost us in life and loss. I've met young people, gay, lesbian, trans, cis, and straight who have never heard of Marsha P. Johnson, Miss Major, Lady Chablis, Leslie Feinberg, Dawn Wilson, Charlene Arcila-Moore, Sandy Stone, Kylar Broadus, Monica Roberts, Kortney Ziegler, Ethan St. Pierre, Jamison Green, Rev. Louis Mitchell, BT Transman, Sylvia Rivera, or me. Most of these people are young adults who will soon be responsible for preserving our history and the rights we continue to fight for every day.

Some of you will be curious enough to check out the names I've listed here and the stories behind them. I hope you do. We seem to learn nothing from the history of humanity. The truth is that either there's equality and history for everyone or there isn't any for anyone. Each of us is connected and that which we acknowledge (or not) does affect everyone else. We all either live by this universal truth or die by it.

CURRENT ISSUES

When I was in high school, I did see Zarf's coming out story on my mom's soap opera, All My Children, which has since been canceled. At the time, I thought it felt realistic, given what I was going through with my sexual orientation . . . The character was mostly temporary though and left the show after the coming out/transition arc. I think if anything, I wish the show had left her as part of the main cast . . .

Amanda Armstrong-Price is a historian of gender and labor in modern Britain.

In 2014, *Time* magazine released a cover with Laverne Cox, stating that "the transgender tipping point" had arrived. This "tipping point" seems to suggest that transgender rights have become the new civil rights struggle in the United States. *Time* magazine looked at the higher instances of media portrayals of T/GE characters, and the handful of transgender individuals in the spotlight, as proof that the time for trans issues was right.

Laverne Cox at L.A.'s Families Belong Together March. (Luke Harold)

The media has been doing a shit job for many years with representing trans and gender nonbinary people. Nowadays, I believe that more queer people are succeeding in making television and films. They are creating more space for better representation of trans and gender expansive individuals, but the efforts and successes of these people have been inconsistent at best and exclusionary/revisionist at worst.

Around the same time, however, there was an increase in news reports covering the murders of trans women. For instance, during the first two months of 2015 there were seven reported murders of trans women in the United States, most of whom were trans women of color. These numbers did not include folks who might have been misgendered by media sources. Although mainstream media sources often talked about these murders as a new problem, painting an image of diversity, inclusion, and equality, the murder of trans women (specifically trans women of color) is not a new phenomenon. As Sylvia Rivera reminds us in "Queens in Exile, the Forgotten Ones" the erasure of trans women of color's contributions to the contemporary LGBTQ movement, as well as the strategic forgetting of the violence enacted upon trans women of color, is an ongoing problem that queer and trans people of color (QTPOC) have been working against since before the Stonewall Riots.[18] Although hate crime laws have been passed, healthcare reforms have made access to hormones and surgery somewhat more accessible, and media representations have increased, these representations and inclusions have not necessarily addressed many of the core issues that QTPOC face on a day-to-day basis. Some of these issues include housing insecurities, employment issues, healthcare barriers, and, of course, the ever-present threat of violence.

The Transcripts Podcast is a production of The Tretter Transgender Oral History Project at the University of Minnesota.

I'm part of the newer generation and am well aware of what Marsha did, but it's the current media blitz of people like Mock, Jennings, Cox, and the litany of articles that have helped me.

As Dean Spade argues, the early 2000s neoliberal LGBTQ push for civil rights and hate crime prevention laws has obscured some of the various violences QTPOC experience as they navigate a society that wants them dead—both literally and figuratively.[19] Current hate crimes legislation, diversity language, expansions to health coverage from insurance companies, and increased visibility of trans people in dominant media have not addressed the multiple violences that transgender people, and specifically trans women of color, continue to face. These small protections are also not permanent but can easily be removed, amended, or changed. Spade names administrative violence as the way laws, policies, and practices make trans people vulnerable. Administrative laws, such as an ever-growing list of documentation to access gender affirming health care and the criminalization of sex work, can increase trans people's risk of violence.

Neoliberal is a complicated and debated term. It is often used in economics to describe a stance that encourages free-market capitalism and privatization, while decreasing taxes and government spending on social programs.

In 2013, the change in the Diagnostic and Statistical Manual of Mental Disorders (DSM) from "gender identity disorder" to "gender dysphoria" was really important to the trans and gender expansive community.

Belief in a gender binary that does not recognize T/GE people, coupled with anxieties about who belongs in single-gender spaces such as bathrooms, have led to multiple types of violence perpetrated against trans bodies.[20] These concerns are amplified when there are administrative barriers that restrict trans and gender nonconforming folks from acquiring and changing specific documents to match their gender presentation more fully.[21] Although these administrative barriers may not, at first glance, appear to be directly related to instances of hate speech and physical violence, the emphasis on "proper" gender expressions—first introduced through colonization—creates fear around a group of people who are regarded as not belonging in particular single-gender spaces. These beliefs and attitudes make trans and gender nonconforming folks more vulnerable to violence.[22]

A memorable moment in history for me was in 2013 when the Colorado Civil Rights Division ruled in favor of six-year-old Coy Mathis so she could attend school as a girl and use the girls' bathroom.

Andrea Jenkins is a writer, poet, educator, and public speaker. She has appeared on CNN, ESSENCE Online, LOGO TV, and in TIME Magazine. She is the Vice President of the Minneapolis City Council.

It's been over 30 years since I first publicly came to terms with my expansive gender identity. It was the early 1990s, and I was a bit naive. I thought the acronym GLBT actually included Transgender people. I quickly learned, however, that gay men thought of Trans women as drag queens and didn't take us seriously, and lesbian women (some, not all) thought of Trans women as imposters, not real women.

I learned that my struggle was not just with the heteronormative, cisgender, straight world. I also had to battle within the community that I thought of as my own. One of the tools I employed in my fight was my art. It brought me in community with groups like "Mama Mosiac"—a Black women performance company–and events like "She Rock." I wrote, performed, and created with *20% Theatre Company*. My art has created a lot of opportunities for me—including the privilege to be an oral historian, creating the world's longest archive of authentic Trans and GNC voices in the world. The project is online at the University of Minnesota, my alma mater.

I was recently in New York City as a participant in an event celebrating the 100th commemoration of the 19th Amendment, which gave white women the right to vote. After the panel a white woman who self-identified as a lesbian came up to me and asked, "What do you call a man that becomes a woman?" At the moment, she seemed genuinely interested, but as I thought about it afterward, it occurred to me that she was actually mocking me, letting me know that she doesn't think, understand, or consider me as a woman. This let me know that we still have a lot of work to do.

An example of the ways in which administrative violence creates vulnerability is the case of CeCe McDonald, who was imprisoned on charges of second-degree manslaughter for the death of Dean Schmitz. In 2011, Schmitz attacked McDonald and a group of friends for being trans women. Even though Schmitz was the one who initiated the altercation by using hate speech to incite McDonald and her friends, it was McDonald who was found guilty of manslaughter for defending herself during the physical attack that followed. Because McDonald fought back and Schmitz died, she was the one who was imprisoned. Additionally, McDonald was placed in a male facility and put in solitary confinement to allegedly "protect" her from attacks by other prisoners.[23] Her placement in solitary confinement at a male facility, regardless of her documentation or her gender presentation, compounded the disproportionate effects of her isolation and punishment.

> *I think of the shooting in Orlando, Florida at the Pulse nightclub as a significant historical event for the gay and trans communities.*

The McDonald case received a lot of attention and the "Free Cece" support campaign became one of the various strands of the prison abolition movement. With an online petition, multiple protesters at the Minneapolis courthouse showing support, and an onslaught of prominent trans people advocating for her release, McDonald's case quickly gained national visibility. Trans activist and author Leslie Feinberg wrote that "[t]he right of self-defense against all forms of oppressions—the spirit of Stonewall—is at the heart of the demand to free [McDonald]."[24] McDonald was released in 2014 after serving 19 months in prison. She has garnered national attention and has become an avid advocate of prison abolition, giving talks on her experiences with the criminal legal system.

> *Chelsea Manning deciding to come out in 2013 as a trans woman and transition in the face of her persecution and imprisonment was a significant moment.*

Another organization involved in the prison abolition movement is the Trans, Gender Variant, and Intersex Justice Project (TGIJP). TGIJP's mission is to "challenge and end

Cece McDonald. (Micah Bazant)

The NYC Trans Oral History Project is a collective, community archive working to document transgender resistance and resilience in New York City. It works in partnership with the New York Public Library.

the human rights abuses committed against transgender, gender-variant/genderqueer, and intersex people in California prisons and beyond."[25] In a conversation with Jayden Donahue, Miss Major Griffin-Gracy, a Black transgender activist and Stonewall veteran, outlines the ways in which TGIJP is not just working toward the abolition of prisons, but also creating support and care networks specifically for trans women of color who are currently incarcerated. TGIJP provides legal support, an ongoing pen pal program, and help for folks once they have been released from prison.[26] While Miss Major describes these efforts as not directly connected to ending the prison industrial complex, she deems these forms of support as necessary because "we can't just snap our fingers and [. . .] get rid of the system."[27] There needs to be something in place to help support those currently in prison and those who are adapting to life outside prison as the struggle for the abolition of prisons continues.

Passage of trans-protective civil rights legislation in California has probably been the most important historical event to me.

As conversations about prison abolition have become more prominent, so, too, have discussions of the intersecting struggles revolving around the mass incarceration of transgender people. In 2015, Jennicet Gutiérrez, a founding member and current Community Organizer and Advocate at Familia: Trans Queer Liberation Movement (FTQLM), interrupted President Obama at a White House reception "to protest his administration's

Miss Major, 74, Oakland, CA, 2015. (Jess T. Dugan). From "To Survive on This Shore: Photographs and Interviews with Transgender and Gender Nonconforming Older Adults," a project by Jess T. Dugan and Vanessa Fabbre.

deportation policies and their impact on trans immigrants and detainees."[28] Gutiérrez was booed by attendees, primarily representatives from LGBTQ organizations, and escorted out of the building. She received heavy criticism for this act of protest against the Obama administration. In taking a stand, however, she brought attention to the connections between the high incarceration rates of trans women throughout the country and immigration detainees who are held at facilities also run by prison corporations. Additionally, the video portraying the moment in which Gutiérrez interrupts President Obama was widely circulated. Upon watching the video, the consequent boos by those in attendance that day are reminiscent of the way in which Sylvia Rivera was booed on stage at the 1973 Washington Square rally.

McDonald's experience is but one contemporary example of the ways that the prison industrial complex affects transgender people, and specifically trans women of color, but this is not the first time trans organizers have tried to bring attention to the mass incarceration of transgender people. Rivera's speech at the 1973 rally is an important marker for understanding how this particular issue has been an ongoing struggle. Miss Major's work supporting transgender women in prison and Gutiérrez's work with FTQLM make connections between prison abolition and immigration struggles. Also, McDonald's various talks across the country about her experiences serve as moments in which we might remember that the ongoing fight against incarceration is one that is integral to trans movements for liberation. More than that, we should remember that these are not new issues. There is a long legacy of organizing against police brutality and incarceration. What this means is that transgender people have rich histories to draw upon and models to combat state suppression and violence.

California allowing a gender-neutral marker on birth certificates in 2017 and Canada allowing an "X" gender identifier on all legal documents in 2019 were important moments in history.

Black and Pink is a national prison abolitionist organization dedicated to abolishing the criminal punishment system and liberating LGBTQIA2S + people and people living with HIV/AIDS who are affected by that system, through advocacy, support, and organizing.

Yet another contemporary moment of connection between T/GE organizing and other liberation movements is the formation of Black Lives Matter (BLM). "In 2013, three radical Black organizers—Alicia Garza, Patrisse Cullors, and Opal Tometi—created a Black-centered political will and movement building project called #BlackLivesMatter." Garza, Cullors, and Tometi's hashtag was in direct response to "the acquittal of Trayvon Martin's murderer, George Zimmerman."[29] In a 2014 conversation in *Feminist Wire*, Alicia Garza explained the need to connect conversations about police violence against Black people to larger liberation movements across a number of differences. Garza stated that "hetero-patriarchy and anti-Black racism within our movement is real and felt. It's killing us and it's killing our potential to build power for transformative social change."[30] Garza, here, points to the ways queer Black women's work has been erased within anti-Black racism organizing. At its core, the movement for Black Lives is, and has always been, part of the fight for trans liberation. It is this attention to an intersectional model of organizing that generates possibilities for coalition building through difference; and, more importantly, it is this intersectional approach that leads to addressing the needs of people caught in-between identities that are often separated but whose histories are interconnected.

WORDZ: THE HIPHOP ARTIST THE TRANS COMMUNITY SHOULD GET TO KNOW

Often referred to as "a breath of fresh air," WORDZ (he/him) is a gifted lyricist, poet, and songwriter, delivering authentic hip hop and soul. With the release of 11 albums total so far, WORDZ is featured in numerous showcases and concerts throughout the United States and continues to provide listeners with music that is artistically pure and organic.

Growing up, I was constantly silenced—raised to believe my thoughts, feelings, and emotions were unimportant. I was very shy and withdrawn. At one point, I went a few years without verbally speaking to anyone. When I did speak, it was only a whisper. I lived an invisible life, lost in this world and in my mind. But that all changed when I was introduced to HipHop.

One thing that immediately drew me to HipHop was the power of the mic. When an emcee grabbed the mic, he got people's attention. When he spit into the mic, the people listened. Not having an outlet myself, I was instantly drawn to the art and the culture. For the first time in my life, I felt that what I had to say was important and did matter. No one cared about me off-stage, but on-stage, the very light within, that people overlooked daily, was able to shine and shine bright.

HipHop wasn't simply a type of music or artistic expression. HipHop gave us kids from the hood power, a sense of community, and a purpose. It allowed us to stand tall and grow—like roses in concrete. HipHop mended my heart and literally saved my life. It gave me the voice I always longed to have.

I was 15 when I started recording professionally. At the time, my stage name was Chris Gutter. It was actually the street name given to me by my former gang members in South Philadelphia. I was a hardcore, street-wise, butch lesbian rapper, whose rhymes told true tales of crime, drugs, violence, and idealized gangsta lifestyles. My fans enjoyed me because I spit just as hard and raw as the male rappers. It was my gimmick: hard, butch lesbian, gangsta rapper. But it wasn't who I truly was as a person or an artist. It just got me applause.

Soon, I was under the mentorship of Beautiful Black Children (aka BBC), a four-member all-male rap group from West Philadelphia. Although BBC was gangsta in appearance, their music spoke of community, pride, culture, and revolution. It was under their mentorship that I chose to no longer go by Chris Gutter and thus changed my stage name to Spoken Wordz, for I had evolved into a more conscious and lyrical female emcee.

My sexual orientation and gender expression were never an issue for me when performing. I think it's because, with artists like Queen Latifah, MC Lyte, Da Brat, and Missy Elliot, lesbians have always had a presence in HipHop, whether they were totally out or not. Being butch actually worked for me in many instances, because instead of being sexualized like my femme counterparts, I was simply respected for being a dope emcee.

Since my early years as a young, up and coming artist, I now go by the name WORDZ The Poet Emcee. "The Poet Emcee" was added as a tribute to the late Tupac Shakur, my favorite rapper, who was also a poet. I have released eight albums since my first drop in 2003. I perform as often as I can, have been in magazines, newspapers, and on major TV and radio shows. Since then, I have also medically transitioned to male. Many may believe my journey in HipHop to be easier as a transsexual male. The assumption is that because I am now perceived as male, not butch, I'm able to blend and simply fall in with the other male emcees. But that isn't the case entirely.

Many emcees approach HipHop as a competitive sport, rather than simply artistic expression. Prior to my medical transition, I admittedly felt no competition, as I was oftentimes the only female emcee in da buildin'. In the past, I would compete with my male counterparts in my head, but was never truly seen as a threat to their crowns as Kings of Rap. Today I am just that. So the respect I had once experienced has been replaced with envy, hatred, and anger by other male emcees and their squads. With the threat of man-on-man violence, safety is now an issue and concern.

The struggle also continues with my size, sense of style, and dress. My short stature, lean build, and vintage/tailored fashion statements cause many cisgender male rappers to label me as gay. From hearing whispers, to receiving weak handshakes, to being repeatedly shoved, I'm made to deal with the homophobia that taints HipHop culture—till this day. In these moments, no matter how great I perform, applause and appreciation are extremely limited if any occurs at all. The respect I was given while on stage prior to my medical transition has diminished, as many like to use my sets as opportunities to utilize the restrooms, talk loudly with friends, or exit the venue to smoke a cigarette. Although lesbians have had a presence in HipHop . . . appearing to be a gay male whether you are one or not is apparently not the move for "success."

HipHop artists such as Busta Rhymes, Talib Kweli, Erick Sermon, and Lil' Scrappy have been very vocal when asked if HipHop can handle transgender talent. They all have replied with a resounding "no," and many HipHop artists and fans would agree. So during the few rare times I am actually given props after a performance, I know that the respect I'm given is conditional.

My journey in HipHop is a courageous one. It's a revolutionary move and I often wonder if the world is ready. Until then, I'll continue to show up, giving my all, because I do have a place in HipHop as a Transsexual male and I do got barz.

CONCLUSION: FUTURE VISION

I think the Obama administration's acknowledgement of trans identities and value in the eyes of the government, however short-lived it was, was a big historical moment.

As the various movements for trans liberation have taught us, the struggle for freedom is one that is always mediated by constant gains and slippages. The "constellating" histories of trans people point to moments of connection and coalition building among communities that are often imagined as separate. These histories, especially those that are forcibly forgotten and erased, give us models for resistance. Recovering and remembering these often-erased histories and connections can give fruit to strategies for survival that may have been forgotten. In the act of retelling such histories, we are engaged in imagining a world that leads to a different future, one where true liberation for all can be achieved. It is through remembering the resilience of transgender movements and the ancestors who have come before us that we can find tools for helping us survive. The folks we have remembered here, and others who are yet to be remembered, imagined all of us in this current time. As such, it is our inheritance and responsibility to also imagine the future for those of us yet to come. Remembering how we got here allows for a different future to be possible.

NOTES

1. Powell, M., Levy, D., Riley-Mukavetz, A., Brooks-Gillies, M., Novotny, M., Firsch-Ferguson, J., & The Cultural Rhetorics Theory Lab. (2014, October 25). Our story begins here: Constellating cultural rhetorics. *Enculturation: A Journal of Rhetoric, Writing, and Culture.* Retrieved from http://enculturation.net/our-story-begins-here.
2. Morales, A. L. (2019). *Medicine Stories: Essays for Radicals.* Durham, NC: Duke University Press, p. 24.
3. Miranda, D. A. (2010). The extermination of the joyas: Gendercide in Spanish California. *GLQ: Gay and Lesbian Quarterly 16*(1–2), 253–284.

4. Towle, E. B., & Morgan, L. M. (2002). Romancing the Transgender Native: Rethinking the use of the "third gender" concept. *GLQ: Gay and Lesbian Quarterly 8*(4), 469–497, p. 477.

5. Davis, Angela Y. (1971, December). The Black woman's role in the community of slaves. *The Black Scholar: Journal of Black Studies*, 1–14, p. 5.

6. Cashin, J. E. (1995). Black families in the Old Northwest. *Journal of the Early Republic 15*(3), 449–475, p. 456.

7. Buckridge, S. O. (2004). *The Language of Dress: Resistance and Accommodation in Jamaica, 1760–1890*. Kingston, Jamaica: University of the West Indies Press, pp. 81–82.

8. Weiner. M. F., & Hough, M. (2012). *Sex, sickness, and slavery: Illness in the antebellum South*. Urbana: University of Illinois Press, p. 94.

9. Joseph, Channing Gerard. The first drag queen was a former slave. *The Nation*. January 31, 2020. https://www.thenation.com/article/society/drag-queen-slave-ball/

10. Dong, A. (Producer & Director). (1995). *The Question of Equality: Out Rage '69*. USA: Deep Focus Productions, Inc.

11. Jay, K., & Young, A. (Eds.). (1992). *Out of the closets: Voices of gay liberation* (20th Anniversary ed.). New York: New York University Press, p. 364.

12. Cohen, S. L. (2008). *The gay liberation youth movement in New York: "An army of lovers cannot fail."* New York: Routledge, p. 16.

13. Jay, K., & Young, A. (Eds.). (1992). *Out of the closets: Voices of gay liberation* (20th Anniversary ed.). New York: New York University Press, pp. 114–115.

14. Taylor, K.-Y. (2017). *How we get free: Black feminism and the Combahee River Collective*. Chicago, IL: Haymarket Books.

15. The Combahee River Collective. (1986). *The Combahee River Collective statement: Black feminist organizing in the Seventies and Eighties*. Latham, NY: Kitchen Table/Women of Color Press.

16. Southern Poverty Law Center. (2005, April 28). History of the anti-gay movement since 1977. *Intelligence Report, Spring*. https://www.splcenter.org/fighting-hate/intelligence-report/2005/history-anti-gay-movement-1977.

17. Measure No. 9. (1992). *Official 1992 General Voter's Pamphlet*. Salem, OR: Elections Division.

18. Rivera, S. (2002). Queens in exile, the forgotten ones. In J. Nestle, C. Howell, & R. Wilchins (Eds.), *GenderQueer: Voices from beyond the sexual binary* (pp. 67–85). Los Angeles, CA: Alyson Books.

19. Spade, D. (2011). *Normal life: Administrative violence, critical trans politics, and the limits of law*. Brooklyn, NY: South End Press.

20. Buist, C. L., & Stone, C. (2014). Transgender victims and offenders: Failures of the United States criminal justice system and the necessity of queer criminology. *Critical Criminology, 22*(1), 35–47, p. 41.

21. Spade, D. (2011). *Normal life: Administrative violence, critical trans politics, and the limits of law*. Brooklyn, NY: South End Press, p. 137.

22. Ibid., p. 138.

23. Erdely, S. R. (2014, April). The transgender crucible. *Rolling Stone, 1215*, 48–66.

24. Avery, D. (2012, June 4). Trans woman Chrishaun "CeCe" McDonald sentenced to 41 months for slaying attacker. https://www.queerty.com/trans-woman-chrishaun-cece-mcdonald-sentenced-to-41-months-for-slaying-attacker-20120604.

25. Donahue, J. (2011). Making it happen, Mama: A conversation with Miss Major. In E. A. Stanley & N. Smith (Eds.), *Captive genders: Trans embodiment and the prison industrial complex* (pp. 301–313). Oakland, CA: AK Press, p. 268.

26. Ibid., p. 271.

27. Ibid., p. 278.

28. Stryker, S. (2017). *Transgender history: The roots of today's revolution* (2nd ed.). New York: Seal Press, p. 221.

29. Black Lives Matter. Herstory. (n.d.). Retrieved from https://blacklivesmatter.com/about/herstory/.

30. Garza, Alicia. A Herstory of the #BlackLivesMatter Movement. October 7, 2014. https://thefeministwire.com/2014/10/blacklivesmatter-2/

22

ARTS AND CULTURE
Erica Chu, Arbor Archuletta, and Joseph Liatela

INTRODUCTION

For better or for worse, every person's views about gender identity have been shaped by artistic and cultural products. From television and film to the less mainstream, we consume written, visual, musical, and performance art presented in theaters and museums, bookstores and libraries, bars and clubs, rented warehouses, and conference centers. Some of the spaces we consume art and culture are online and found through social networks, search terms, hashtags, or algorithms. The most negative of these representations play a major role in teaching us what is and is not allowed by our culture's standards, and these representations shape beliefs about whose lives are and are not worth living. This is a heavy reality for transgender and gender expansive (T/GE) people, who experience high rates of mental distress, suicide, and violence. T/GE art and culture attempts to create a cultural unlearning of those life-threatening messages. It builds new narratives, images, questions, and demands that create space for the possibility of full and rich lives for all kinds of gender expansive people. But T/GE art and cultural products are not only tools for imagining our survival, they are also gateways to artistic and cultural communities that testify to our creativity, passion, and investment in our own joy.

> *Confessions of a Fox by Jordy Rosenberg helped me see, for the first time, that a transmasculine body can be sexy and beautiful and powerful on its own terms, not just relative to cis male bodies.*

REPRESENTATION: WHAT IS AT STAKE?

The negative portrayal of T/GE people in mainstream art and culture has been a weapon used to enforce transphobia among the public. Though positive representation of trans folks cannot resolve transphobia in and of itself, it is a powerful tool in shaping what is possible for T/GE people. This tool becomes even more empowering when trans people are involved in the production of these representations.

> *Media portrayals over the last several decades have influenced people to be incredibly cruel to trans people, especially trans women. I believe that this has a lot to do with the fact that most mainstream media content is produced by cis people. If this trend is to be ended, we need more trans people to be heavily involved in the writing and production of any media portraying us.*

Nonbinary actor Lachlan Watson plays a nonbinary character in Netflix's *Chilling Adventures of Sabrina.*

Misrepresenting Worth and Purpose

In U.S. popular culture, T/GE identities have often been associated with the dangerous subversion of norms. One representation is the character Norman Bates—the murderous villain in Alfred Hitchcock's iconic 1960 film, *Psycho.* Bates is characterized as having a dissociative disorder that causes him to dress as a woman when he is in a deranged and violent state. This framing is a problematic misrepresentation of mental illness, and it is particularly damaging to T/GE communities that experience high levels of mental distress due to an unaccommodating and transphobic society. In addition, Bates dressing as a woman, and regarding himself as one, becomes conflated with mental illness and violence. Within the history of popular culture, transfeminine characters are often seen as sick and dangerous villains. These negative representations, particularly of trans women, share

Brian Michael Smith. "I'm an artist and a performer. As an actor I look for roles that are complex, authentic, and that enable me to explore the challenges I faced in my own journey through life as a Black Trans man. I seek to create art that supports people in their quest for personal growth while challenging the existing biases and stereotypes about trans men and women in media and life." (photo © Coline Jourdana)

similarities with the ways mainstream society hypersexualizes transfemininity, reduces T/GE identities to deception, and enforces the view that being trans is inherently disgusting and worthy of violent reactions.

> *I think the media in general portrays trans people as either inspiration porn or a caricature.*

Other common stereotypes of T/GE characters are incredibly demeaning, and can endanger the lives of T/GE people because of the cultural attitudes they reinforce. Take, for example, the reaction of comedic characters when they realize a love interest is T/GE. In *Ace Ventura: Pet Detective* (1994), after kissing Einhorn—a transgender woman whose very name (translated from German: "one horn") reduces her identity to her genitals— Ace vomits repeatedly, then uses a plunger to help himself vomit further, brushes his teeth with an entire tube of toothpaste, sets his clothes on fire, sobs in a hot shower, and, finally, chews multiple packs of gum, to attempt to cleanse himself. Even though these responses are dramatized for comedic effect, this scene models expected negative responses when cis people "discover" they were attracted to a transfeminine person. The shame Ace experiences in this scene motivates his later actions to publicly remove Einhorn's clothing and expose her genitals in a fit of violent entitlement. These actions reproduce and justify the force cis men use when they abuse, and even murder, trans women to whom they have been attracted.

> *Most shows and movies that depict trans people do so incorrectly and/or with blatant prejudices. Trans characters are usually miserable and wind up dying gruesomely or tragically.*

TRANS REPRESENTATION IN MOTION PICTURE MEDIA: THE INTERSECTION OF ENTERTAINMENT AND ACTIVISM

Bode Riis (they/them) is an Agender Non-Binary Filmmaker from New Zealand.

Representation matters. As many audience members of minority experiences can attest, seeing a fictional character whose lived experiences closely align with our own can give us a sense of visibility and validity. But it is not enough to simply have trans characters in media if that representation is largely negative.

My own research into transgender representation in motion picture media began in 2014, when I published my first piece on the topic: *Transgender Reflections: Audience Studies on the Portrayal of Trans Characters in Film & TV.*[1] My essay painted a historically dismal, yet gradually improving, portrait of the portrayal of trans characters in motion picture media. At the time (2012), the most recent large scale media study on the topic had been published by GLAAD. They found that "Transgender characters were cast in a 'victim' role at least 40% of the time" and "were cast as killers or villains in at least 21% of the catalogued episodes and storylines."[2] This portrayal of trans characters as often being involved in violence, either as the villain or victim, but hardly ever as the hero, resulted in a cyclical reinforcement of negative media portrayals of trans people. This shaped negative public perceptions of trans people, which, in turn, influenced ongoing negative media portrayals.

Since that study, media representation of trans people has begun to flourish. A 2018 study concluded that "a way to reduce transphobia is to humanize transgender people by exposing individuals to information about them and representations of them,"[3] and 2018 saw an especially strong step toward that representation equity, with a main cast comprised largely of trans people of color on *POSE*, and the *Supergirl* Season 4 introduction of Nia Nal, the first transgender superhero on television.

Familiarization and normalization in representation can inform attitudes toward trans people both on and off screen. Positive representation fosters acceptance and celebration. By acceptance, I speak not only of a cisgender audience accepting trans people but also trans audiences accepting themselves. Because trans people make up such a small percentage of the population, media representation is often a young trans person's first exposure to other trans lives. If these representations are overwhelmingly negative and violent, one can understand that this may produce "mean world syndrome" and add to a negative self-image. Conversely, if trans characters are respected—and even the hero of the narrative—a generation of young trans folks will grow into a world where they feel valid and empowered, and they can start to see a growing potential for their own fulfilling future.

Disclosure: Trans Lives on Screen (directed by Sam Feder) is a 2020 documentary about trans representation in Hollywood.

Though we might expect progress as time goes on, a similar scene takes place in a 2010 episode of *Family Guy*. After Brian discovers the woman he had sex with was a trans woman, he vomits on screen for thirty continuous seconds, screams, then scrubs himself vigorously in the shower, and then stands shaking in front of a mirror. To make matters worse, the woman's son finds out they had sex and beats Brian furiously on screen as Brian tries to escape. The social message these representations send is not only that trans women are undesirable, but that attraction to them is shameful. It further reinforces the idea that it is the responsibility of cis men to violently punish those who are involved sexually with trans women.

A scene from *The Hangover II* (2010) reinforces a similarly toxic message when Stu, who doesn't remember the previous night, realizes he had sex with Kimmy. Stu is upset because he has cheated on his fiancé, but acknowledges Kimmy is a lovely woman. Yet, when Kimmy reminds Stu that he enjoyed having sex with her in part because she has a penis, he becomes inconsolable. Kimmy says their sexual encounter was special and beautiful, but the film treats Kimmy as a prop used only to shame Stu and make him feel less masculine. The film further disregards trans experiences when Stu calls Kimmy a man and his friend calms him by assuring him he can forget that the encounter ever happened. This scene encourages those who watch it to view attraction to, or sexual enjoyment with, a trans woman to be so shameful that even remembering it is potentially damaging. In so many mainstream portrayals of T/GE identities, T/GE people are exploited to further stories about cis people, while problematic narratives place T/GE people—especially trans women—at risk of physical harm. This risk of harm is very real. When trans experiences are invalidated and cisgender people are shamed for their attraction to trans people, these factors can contribute to the stress that makes T/GE people susceptible to suicide, substance abuse, homelessness, and physical as well as emotional harm from intimate partners. It also leads to cis folks being so ashamed of themselves that they kill their trans

Femme Blessins. (Art by Emulsify)

partner, or potential partner, to make it easier to forget their attraction ever happened or ever could have happened.

The fact remains that cis people are often attracted to T/GE people. The incredible popularity of pornography featuring transgender people supports this fact, even if those representations are seen as "sensational" or "exotic." Although there should be no shame attached to T/GE identities or to an individual's sexual attraction to transgender people, often the most accessible representations of sexuality involving trans folks are violent at worst and shameful at best. Both endanger the lives and well-being of T/GE people.

> *The media portrays us with a great degree of sensationalism. One of the first things you learn as a trans person on the Internet is to never read the comments on articles, Facebook posts, or YouTube videos because these comments are usually filled with outright hatred and disgust.*

Even when T/GE people are not being portrayed as the unstable villain, the hypersexual woman, or the shameful secret, they are often represented in ways that suggest they are less deserving of empathy, connection, and investment. In mainstream film and television, a similar trend is notable in representations of Blackness. Frequently, Black folks are portrayed as less complex, less interesting, less worthy of attention and empathy by the viewer, and as being included only to fulfill their expected purpose of providing assistance to white characters.[4] These problematic representations of Black communities are complex and warrant study in their own right. They are also relevant to how we discuss trans representations. Many of the misrepresentations we see about T/GE people share similarities with misrepresentations about Blackness, placing both populations at risk of physical and emotional harm.

Trap Door: Trans Cultural Production and the Politics of Visibility is a collection of essays, conversations, and archival explorations that unpacks trans representation within contemporary culture (edited by Reina Gossett, Eric A. Stanley, and Johanna Burton, The MIT Press, 2017).

In films such as *Angels in America* (2003), *Kinky Boots* (2005), *Dallas Buyers Club* (2013), and *Dumplin'* (2018), T/GE characters have little purpose except to provide support to cis characters.[5,6] Representations of "the tragic black character"[7] share much in common with representations of the "suffering trans person."[8] In films such as *Boys Don't Cry* (1999), *Rent* (2005), *Albert Nobbs* (2011), and *The Danish Girl* (2015), the audience is made to feel sympathy for these characters because their lives are seen as tragic and filled with suffering. It is no coincidence that many T/GE characters are also Black, given that they are often held in contrast to what is accepted in mainstream society as "normal"—characters who are straight, white, middle class, and able-bodied. These "normal" characters are often more complex, allowing the audience to connect to them and regard them as deserving of their empathy. In these contexts, transphobia works alongside white supremacy, homophobia, economic exploitation, ableism, and other oppressions to reinforce the idea that there are only certain kinds of people who matter. Solutions to any of these issues require us to invest in all vulnerable populations in ways that go beyond sympathy.

Unfortunately, characterizations of T/GE lives are often viewed as progressive when they do not equate T/GE people with being sick, deranged, or criminal. Yet, the message these representations send to the audience is ultimately too similar to those that do. This message is that living a fulfilling trans life is impossible. This damaging message helps explain the level of difficulty T/GE populations have with mental distress, addiction, self-harm, and suicide. When we don't see representations of T/GE people living full and complex lives, it is difficult to imagine or invest in our own trans lives.

TRANSCRIBEZ

Andrew Spiers (he/him) is a writer, musician, and social worker from Philadelphia, Pennsylvania. He founded the transcribez youth writing group along with poet Rachel Zolf.

Founded in 2016, transcribez is a free creating writing group for trans and gender nonconforming youth ages 14–24. Guided by poet Rachel Zolf, and supported by The University of Pennsylvania's Kelly Writers House, transcribez sprang from an identified need for Philadelphia-area trans youth to build community and share creative space. transcribez meets the second Saturday of every month, providing lunch, transportation fare, and writing supplies for all who attend. Youth are invited to participate regardless of writing experience.

Each transcribez session during the academic school year hosts a trans identified guest writer, and trans identified facilitators attend and support all groups. Guests writers have included Trish Salah, Lady Dane Figueroa Edidi, JD Stokely, Faye Chevalier, Tyler Vile, Annie Mok, Cat Fitzpatrick, Kayleb Rae Candrilli, Wo Chan, and Noor Ibn Najam, among others. During summer months, transcribez continues to meet regularly without guest facilitators, functioning as an informal writing community. Youth are given the opportunity to share their work, explore books by trans writers provided by support facilitators, and enjoy a trans-only social space. Current monthly facilitators include writer/musician Andrew Spiers; writer/percussionist Mariya Oneby; and poet Devin Esch, with past support from writers Darius McLean, Hazel Edwards, and Kavi Ade.

transcribez also publishes a compilation of youth writing each Spring. In 2018, with support from the Leeway Foundation, guest writers Davy Knittle and Levi Bentley collaborated with transcribez to produce a chapbook series. Over the course of five months, 11 youth composed, edited, and sequenced their manuscripts with guidance from writing mentors, including poet Kavi Ade; writer Nico Amador; Pew Fellow CA Conrad; writer/essayist Cyree Jarelle Johnson; Philadelphia Youth Poet Laureate Otter Jung-Allen; writer/artist Monk; and Philadelphia Poet Laureate Raquel Salas Rivera. Each youth received 20 copies of their chapbook and the full collection is available for individuals to view at local LGBTQ establishments.

To date, transcribez has conducted 42+ workshops and served over 100 unique young writers, averaging 8–11 youth per session, with work ranging from poetry to journalism, nonfiction to fantasy. transcribez serves as a safe space for young trans folks to imagine, play, and express their whole selves through language only trans people can truly understand. These workshops change the lives of the youth who attend, creating new bonds between attendees, many of whom have experienced homelessness, family rejection, bullying in school, and other hardships. Our group is a sacred and joyful space. I am so grateful it exists.

Hypervisibility, Invisibility, and Trans Possibility

Transfeminine folks are the most visible and hypersexualized of T/GE people, which makes them the most stigmatized. On the other hand, transmasculine and nonbinary identities are relatively invisible. Although invisibility makes them less of a target for ridicule in media representation, invisibility can also lead to negative health outcomes caused by T/GE people being unable to imagine that the life they want and need is possible. For cisgender men and women, imagining life as a man or woman is fairly easy because representations of livable lives for cis men and women are abundant among their family members, friends, teachers, the public, and within mainstream media. But trans men, trans women, nonbinary folks, and other T/GE people don't have as many opportunities for seeing what possibilities exist. When you find little to no representations of who you are, it is very difficult to articulate what you want and need—or to even know that something else is possible. Though current representations of trans women can be damaging, there is also some value in them. Whether demonized as villains, sensationalized on talk shows, exoticized in pornography, or presented as trans victims, trans women at least know that other people like them exist, and have a reference for what might be possible. Having a show, character, or term to look up in a search engine or on social media is extremely valuable as a T/GE person attempts to explore who they might be. It is a shame, however, that such opportunities also come with toxic messages about the nature of trans identity and can lead some to suppress who they are in ways that damage their physical and mental well-being.

> *The media doesn't portray trans men of color. There are more and more white trans men in media, but no people of color. Also, it would be great to see more nonbinary and gender nonconforming individuals in the media.*

Better representations would benefit T/GE people in ways that do not also put them at risk for distress and violence. For example, the Netflix sitcom *One Day at a Time* focuses on a multigenerational Cuban family living in Los Angeles. In a 2018 episode, the show introduces Elena's love interest, a nonbinary character named Syd who uses they/them pronouns. For many viewers, this was the first time the topic of pronouns had been represented on television in a way that normalizes the somewhat jarring experience of cis folks, like Penelope and Lydia (Elena's mother and grandmother), when they learn about gender neutral pronouns. For nonbinary viewers, storylines like this are affirming and contribute to the experience of feeling less invisible. Additionally, to T/GE viewers who may not even know how to describe who they are, such a storyline gives some context that gender expansiveness is possible. Witnessing Syd knowing who they are, and being supported by their friends, sends a strong message that nonbinary lives are possible. This message strengthens a sense of self that helps folks combat the alienation and internalized shame that comes with invisibility or stigma. Additionally, seeing Penelope and Lydia struggle but ultimately learn how to use they/them pronouns adds to a sense of what is possible. Even if members of one's own family cannot learn to see beyond their prejudice and lack of experience, it is possible to find community among those who can. This kind of hopeful, affirming, and life-saving representation is a testament to the power of T/GE people, such as *One Day at a Time* writer Michelle Badillo, being involved in how T/GE stories are told. As with any narratives about any kind of marginalized population, affirming representations are only possible when people with those identities and experiences are part of shaping the narratives. In the case of this episode of *One Day at a Time*, the input of T/GE Latinxs like Badillo are necessary in order to represent nonbinary and Latinx identities in affirming ways.

> *I first realized that being trans was OK through the TV show,* I Am Jazz. *She showed me that there is life and love after transition. I'm so thankful to Jazz, as her show was a thing my whole family watched, when we could. Her show aired when I was in seventh grade. Worst year of my life, I wanted to die, and here's someone doing something wonderful, which I had hoped to do as a kid, on TV. Of course, she's MTF and I'm FTM, but the message still resonated with me. There is life and love after transition.*

The Matrix (1999) movie, written and directed by sisters Lana and Lily Wachowski, has recently been confirmed by them to be a trans allegory. Both Lana and Lily are out transgender women, and they have confirmed that the idea of desire for transformation, through science fiction and genre-bending, helped shape the blockbuster movie to be the cultural phenomenon that it was. They also confirmed that the character of Switch was originally written to be trans, but they had a difficult time passing it through studio production.

TRANS BODIES, TRANS LIVES

Hannah Fons (she/they) is an editor, strength coach, and graduate student living in New York City. Her academic work focuses on the issues and concerns of LGBTQ youth, and of trans youth in particular. She is especially interested in mobilizing myth, legend, and folklore to inspire and empower trans individuals and communities. (Photo credit: Statia Grossman)

Last year, I presented a paper at a conference on trans, Two-Spirit, and gender-nonconforming lives in the arts at a prestigious Canadian university. In a nutshell, I suggested that today's trans and nonbinary/genderqueer folx (of which I am one) are the spiritual descendants of shamans, and that our position at the crossroads of sex and gender gives us unique access and insight into powerful archetypes; ancient universal ideas, symbols, and figures that show up in the stories, songs, art, and dreams of all human beings, regardless of language or culture.

For starters, I dug into the archetype of the *Androgyne*: the two-in-one being who changes or transcends gender, who is both (and yet neither) male and female. I talked about the universal figure of the *Trickster*: the quick-witted, boundary-breaking guardian of the crossroads who laughs at convention, defies arbitrary rules, and makes fools of the arrogant. And I explored the *Wounded Healer*: the one who gains wisdom and strength through understanding their own illness or suffering, and brings those gifts back to help others. I argued that trans and genderqueer folk are the living embodiment of these archetypes, that our experience of "transition"—whatever that may look like from person to person—is the modern equivalent of the shaman's spiritual calling.

Overall, my point was that there's a powerful, bright place in the gap between theory and theology—and we genderqueer people should feel right at home there. As scholars and theorists, we should also maybe consider whether our work is dragging us too far from that place, muting our ability to draw strength and courage from those archetypes—*our* archetypes—as we navigate a world that's not built for us.

Five minutes in, I could tell I was bombing. Alongside all the other presentations on, for example, *the speculative ontology of necropoetic subaltern performative praxis,* my quirky little paper was received with politely blank looks and subdued applause. I soldiered through to the end . . . then skipped the rest of the conference and went back to New York to hang out with my dog.

To be clear: I'm not dragging gender theory—hell, I've got a graduate degree in it. It's a crucial, revolutionary field, despite my snarky attitudes about necropoetics or whatever. But the field as it stands currently is missing something—a gauzy, wildly unfashionable thing: it's missing a Soul.

And that matters, because the Queer Soul—and the Trans Soul in particular—is A Thing, and a mighty one. There's an uncanny, almost holy quality that lingers around us genderfuckers. That's why, throughout history, figures like the Androgyne are a ubiquitous presence in the folklore and legends of peoples on every continent.

When I was coming of age as a deeply queer, nonbinary trans kid in a tiny farming town in Iowa, I didn't know what to call myself, or how to describe the existential distance I felt between myself and the other kids, but I knew that when I read about the Tricksters—like Coyote, or Loki, or Anansi the Spider—who gleefully embodied contradiction and lived to troll anyone arrogant enough to try them, I felt like I was reuniting with old friends. Later, when I encountered stories of Healers who drew strength from their own scars to navigate the shadowy places where others were too scared to go, I felt a rush of recognition. My own scars—two pale crescents across my chest—mark me as different from my fellow villagers, endowed with the perspective you can only get from sinking into sleep, crossing over a threshold, and returning to the waking world forever changed.

Despite what some folks seem to think, trans and nonbinary people aren't some brand-new social phenomenon. Sexually ambiguous figures decorate the walls of Bronze Age caves in China; Greek prophets change from male to female and back again; Afro-Brazilian Orishas appear as whatever gender they feel like in a given story; Sumerian gods create third-gender people to be priests and prophets; the Australian aboriginal Creator wears both male and female faces; and on and on.

The whole world is *full* of stories about us, and has been for as long as humans have had the power of speech. And my personal, slightly spooky position on that is that we genderqueers and transfolk are so strong in spirit that we inspire legends—just by existing, by being ourselves. Look anywhere, and there we are, always. *I'm* the two-in-one, the boundary-breaker, and the healer—and if you're reading this, you might be, too.

So by all means, explore necropoetics and the ontogeny of postmodernist ontology if it makes you happy, but if you happen to possess the gift of a Trans Soul, don't neglect the spirit in the flesh. Because as my late friend and trans pioneer Holly Boswell once said, "*We* are living proof of Spirit manifesting beyond the limited social constructs of gender. Evidence continually abounds of our flesh being informed and inspired by Spirit—and when Spirit moves, anything is possible."

Another example of how affirming trans representation can be when created by trans people is the 2016 Emmy-nominated web series *Her Story*, which follows the friendship of trans women Violet and Paige as Violet falls in love with a cis lesbian for the first time and Paige navigates the decision to disclose her trans status while dating a straight cis man. The connection to and investment in transgender community is what makes *Her Story* such a positive representation. Jen Richards and Jen Zak wrote, starred

A NEW SERIES FROM DIRECTOR **SYDNEY FREELAND**

JEN **RICHARDS**   ANGELICA **ROSS**   LAURA **ZAK**

Her**Story.**

WWW.HERSTORYSHOW.COM

Her Story is a web series about two trans women in Los Angeles who have given up on love, when, suddenly, chance encounters give them hope. Trans women in the media have long been punchlines, killers, indications of urban grit, pathetic tragedies, and dangerous sirens. Rarely have they been complex characters who laugh, struggle, and grow, who share strength in sisterhood, who seek and find love. Co-written by Jen Richards and Laura Zak, directed by Sydney Freeland, with cinematography by Bérénice Eveno, and produced by Katherine Fisher/Speed of Joy Productions, Her Story features predominantly LGBTQ women, on and off-screen.

in, and were executive producers of *Her Story*. Angelica Ross also starred in the production and Sydney Freeland directed it. Among these contributors, only Zak is cisgender. The trans experience of the writers, actors, and director add nuance and depth to the representation of these characters in contrast to other representations where cis actors play trans characters that are written primarily by and for cis people. In *Her Story*, trans women are not just plot devices but instead central characters whose desires and experiences drive the story forward. Unlike the lessons about trans people in productions such as *Psycho, Family Guy, Angels in America*, or *The Danish Girl*, *Her Story* demonstrates that trans women are complicated individuals who lead full and complex lives. Violet is a waitress, a survivor of gender-based violence, and is in recovery. As the story progresses, she explores her sexuality and what she wants in life. Paige is a lawyer with a commanding presence who is also in recovery. We see her as she tries to balance vulnerability and risk in her romantic life. Amidst all this complexity, these characters happen to be trans—a feature that is integral to their experiences, but is not the only defining factor.

Looking for transfeminine YouTubers to follow? Check out Kat Blaque, ContraPoints, Sonnis Love, and Mia Mulder.

Sense8 will forever be branded in my memory. I began watching Sense8 around the start of my transition and it was incredibly affirming to see a show written by two trans women that features a trans woman playing a trans role. The best part of the show is that Nomi's experiences as a trans woman are featured in the same degree as other aspects of her identity. She's shown as a human, not a trope of a trans woman.

Trans representations such as these allow cis viewers to gain more nuanced understandings of trans people and the nature of T/GE identities, which can lead to reduced entitlement, shame, and aggression in interactions with T/GE folks. They can also help cis people empathize with trans folks in ways that recognize trans individuals as peers deserving of connection, community, shared spaces, and resources. For T/GE viewers, this kind of trans representation provides a needed break from the onslaught of exploitative images and unlivable lives. It also allows them to see themselves and their communities in the characters and storylines, which can help them combat internalized transphobia and feel empowered. In addition, viewers who may not be ready to assert their T/GE identities can see that trans lives are possible and that they are beautifully complex, interesting, and worthwhile. When it comes to imagining one's own life, making commitments for one's own health and well-being, and making decisions about who should and should not be in one's life, witnessing such possibilities makes valuing who one is, or who one can be, more possible.

T/GE people having space to take more control of their own representation changes the quality of trans narratives and increases consciousness of the livability of T/GE lives. Trans folks speaking out, mobilizing, and creating art and cultural productions has had a big effect on the quality of trans representation, but this is not a new phenomenon. What is perhaps new is the level of visibility trans folks have gained and the increased number of folks in cultural industries learning to (and sometimes being forced to) listen to trans concerns.

ON CREATIVE WRITING AS ACTIVISM

Joy Ladin (she/her) is the first openly transgender employee of an Orthodox Jewish institution, Yeshiva University, where she holds the Gottesman Chair in English. She is the author of nine books of poetry and a memoir of gender transition, Through the Door of Life. *Her latest book,* The Soul of the Stranger: Reading God and Torah from a Transgender Perspective, *came out in November 2018 and was a finalist for Triangle and Lambda Literary Awards. (Photo credit: Lisa Ross)*

Without creative writing, I couldn't have survived decades of living as a male I knew I wasn't. The first book of poetry I published under my true name, *Transmigration*, is filled with poems I wrote to keep from giving into the suicidal despair that beset me during gender transition, when I was losing the life I had built around pretending to be a man but not yet able to build a life as myself. The act of writing poetry, feeling words and sounds take on new shapes inside me, the claiming of the power of creation in a world that often seemed to deny me the power even to be myself, made me feel deeply, ecstatically alive—and those sparks of life saw me through the darkest parts of gender transition, the process of dying and being reborn.

I started writing poetry—or rather, rhymes I thought of as poems—as soon as I learned to write. I'm not sure why—my family didn't read poetry or have poetry in the house. But from the first poem I felt something mysterious, powerful, and transformative happen when I put words together into lines and stanzas. Making rhymes felt like making magic: I was revealing the hidden kinship between words and meanings that seemed, from the outside, to be completely different. I suspect that rhyme felt to me like a way of symbolically overcoming the isolation I felt as someone who was seen as a boy despite my female gender identification. If rhyme could show that totally different words were the same inside, maybe the magic of language could reveal that I was really the same inside as the girls who saw me as a boy.

In a sense, my childhood wish was right on target: all trans people have is language, the magic of language, to enable others to see past our clothing and skin and the clumsiness of gender signifiers that weren't made for people like us, and begin to understand who we really are. When trans people write, we are not only creating poems, stories, songs, and memoirs—we are creating a new world, a world that understands and celebrates the fact that being human means more than being male or female.

Trans Arts and Culture as Entry to Trans Connection and Community

Despite the gains being made in mainstream representations of T/GE identities, the shame, stigma, invisibility, and presumed impossibility of trans lives exhibited in our culture will never be resolved by Hollywood, but rather in community with other T/GE people. Connection and community are ultimately the anecdote to the isolation and distress caused by negative perceptions of T/GE identities, because it is in these contexts that we can tell narratives that communicate the experience, value, and enjoyment to be found in T/GE lives. Mainstream film and television are among the most accessible forms of representation, but communities of T/GE folks help form empowering responses to the narratives told about us. Transgender artistic and cultural productions are the stories we tell about ourselves and the worlds we inhabit. They also have the power to counter the damaging narratives told about us. These stories happen only in community, and they provide the space and opportunity to help us process through the difficulties we face, access the resources we need to survive, and give us the power to celebrate ourselves in all our complexity and beauty.

Reading a variety of first-person narratives has helped me understand that people can be trans in many ways.

For many years, an individual's first entry into the T/GE community was almost always through a cultural event at a local queer bar, club, or other venue. Before "transgender" existed as an identity in the way it exists today, T/GE identities and expressions were (and, in some contexts remain) understood as part of the same category as sexual orientation. Costume balls featuring crossdressing were regular occurrences in New York since the late 1800s and were gathering places for gays, lesbians, and those not fitting the socially defined sexual and gender norms of the time.[9] Because of class and racial alienation among some in these groups, Black folks hosted their own drag balls. In the 1920s, influential Harlem Renaissance writers such as Langston Hughes were regular attendees of these events. Ball culture has further developed as a uniquely Black queer and trans community with voguing as an art form specific to that cultural group.[10] The documentary film *Paris is Burning* (1990) famously captured some of the Black ball scene and house culture of the 1980s, making it accessible to a wider public. The recent television series *POSE* (2018) further reflects on this time period, bringing the voices of trans women of color to the forefront. Today, ball culture is present in many U.S. cities, and balls allow queer and trans folks to gather, perform, and compete in an environment that is rooted in Black queer and trans culture and affirming to queer and trans folks of color.[11,12] Though attendees and competitors are not all T/GE, like the earlier drag balls of the Harlem Renaissance, gender exploration becomes more possible among community and chosen family who offer support, guidance, and emotional/physical space to explore gender expression and identity, all while having a good time.

Drag shows in queer bars, clubs, and other venues are common not just in big cities but also in rural areas. The structure of these drag shows and community groups are very different from the ball scene, but they share the opportunities for queer community and gender exploration in a fun environment. It is common, for instance, to hear T/GE folks

Vogue. (Armani Dae)

discuss the feelings they had in drag or cross dressing for a queer event, and how those feelings represented a significant part of their journey toward embracing their gender identity. Drag performances and competitions among primarily cis gay performers and, as represented on *RuPaul's Drag Race* (2009–2019), are unfortunately fraught with transphobic structures, histories, and environments.[13,14] Though these structures are sometimes slow in changing, attending and enjoying drag performances can still be a fun and powerful opportunity to witness different forms of gender expression and connect with others.

> *I understand the historical role of drag in trans and trans POC experiences, and I affirm anybody who finds that there now. However, my experience with it is overwhelmingly from cis gay men, and has not felt inclusive or, honestly, even really safe for me. One exception, that I'm not involved in but admire from a distance, is the Sisters of Perpetual Indulgence, whose work I deeply respect.*

T/GE communities have often found their physical space in gay bars and clubs and, in many areas, there are trans and nonbinary nights or other social events that become cultural networks for trans arts and culture. These include dance parties with trans DJs, performances featuring trans musicians, open mics, theater groups, writing groups, literary magazines, artistic collectives, and gallery events. More recently, social media has altered how these groups mobilize, which allows folks to simply search for trans-related events or groups of possible interest. It has also opened up new online venues to share artistic production, cultural space, and community.[15,16,17] These artistic and cultural events and spaces are not as easy to stumble upon as mainstream representations of T/GE people, but they are gateways to trans community. They also provide opportunities to access affirming representations of trans life, experience, and connection.

I will say that Instagram promotes a very white, skinny, androgynous leaning masc, afab image of being nonbinary, which was harmful to me. It wasn't until I met other enbies of color in real life who were femme and beautiful and funny and real that I was able to open up that part of myself.

The crossover between art and cultural events is often blurry as these collide and overlap with social events and activism. Trans-produced artistic and cultural events and spaces are vital for their ability to facilitate, develop, refine, and distribute trans creative work. It can even be said that trans folks experiencing trans art and culture is itself a form of activism because it offers us a testament to the fullness, complexity, and beauty possible in our lives. It also connects us to larger communities of T/GE people who have gone before us and who remind us of all that has been and can yet be possible. And, when the communities we belong to fail to offer us all that we need, these artistic and cultural spaces create opportunities to meet others who feel similarly and collaborate on making representations and narratives we have been longing for.

THE IMPORTANCE OF ART FOR COMMUNITY INCLUSIVITY

Alister Rubenstein (they/them) is a queer, nonbinary artist and activist. They use their artwork to uplift and affirm queer people, trans people, and others from communities that are often excluded or marginalized. When they are not creating art, they work in transgender health care, developing policies, managing trainings, and connecting HIV+ and low-income New Yorkers with gender-affirming services. They live in Queens New York with their nonbinary spouse and two rescue cats.

Art has always been an outlet for me, a way to escape from the oppression and misgendering I face on a daily basis.

Cisgender society doesn't recognize or celebrate trans milestones, resilience, and joy. As a queer, nonbinary, and trans survivor, I've experienced this firsthand. When I changed my pronouns or when I changed my name, the people by my side supporting me were mostly fellow community members: other queer and trans people. When my trans spouse and I got married, we received countless cards with inappropriately gendered messages . . . along with duplicate copies of one gender-neutral card.

It's important for us to affirm one another, to lift each other up in ways society doesn't. I created The Crafty Queer to specifically provide art and affirmations for trans and queer people. The Crafty Queer has a variety of products including cards, totes, T-shirts, trans flag earrings, and more. I focus specifically on making art that addresses marginalized people and milestones that are often left unrecognized by mainstream society such as name and gender marker changes, sobriety anniversaries, coming out, and celebrations of love that are not cis, het, and monogamy normative. My greeting cards are also a great starting place for cisgender allies who want to celebrate our milestones but don't have the right words or cards to turn to.

I design my art with my community in mind, and I believe it's important for trans and nonbinary artists to create art that will uplift the community and center their voices and experiences. Supporting the efforts of trans artists is just one of many ways to make the world a better place for trans people.

ACCESSIBILITY OF TRANS ART AND CULTURE

There is a scene in the movie *But I'm a Cheerleader* (1999) where Natasha Lyonne plays the newly out, totally in love, and recently abandoned lesbian youth, Megan, and, in all of her bewildered earnestness, Megan asks two gay elders: "I was wondering if you could teach me how to be a lesbian. You know, what they eat, where they live?" The exchange that follows is all about "being yourself." Although this advice holds true, there is undoubtedly a way to be visible as a lesbian. Neighborhoods we live in, bars we frequent, and cultural codes we adopt, can signal particular identities. Art and culture not only impact what we think of when we hear an identity term, but also shape how we

Leo Sheng. Activist, Public Speaker, Writer, Artist. "Born in Hunan, China, and raised by two moms outside of Ann Arbor, Michigan, I grew up as one of the only Asian kids in school. And, one of the only queer kids. I stood out from my peers, and for a while, I struggled to really embrace it. I came out as trans when I was 12 and started my social transition in middle school. With the support of a local group for queer and trans youth, I found a way to share my story. I learned how to tell my story in my own words. And later, I went public, documenting my transition online."

might *do* and *understand* that particular identity as it connects to our individual, lived experiences.

> *With Instagram, I have the freedom to share my stories and my identity publicly. My Instagram is meant to be affirming for other trans folks and informative for cis allies. It's incredibly empowering to have a space to put my narrative out into the world and demonstrate that there is diversity among trans folks.*

Unless we sift through various non-mainstream sources, the representations we find of T/GE people are fraught with negative stories. Luckily, with the rise of gadgets and the technologies they put at our fingertips, the new question isn't *where* to access trans representation so much as it is *which kinds* to access. Technology has also caused us to question what is even considered "mainstream" anymore, particularly when so many online communities exist and there are various ways to experience them. Where there is access, there is also power.

The children's show, *Steven Universe*, tackles issues of gender and sexuality and explores trans themes.

> *Tumblr has been really helpful to me in exploring both my sexuality and my gender identity. The Tumblr community, despite its many flaws, is very diverse in terms of gender and sexuality. It gave me models to consider as I thought about my own gender, examples of people living their best lives as nonbinary, and friends to talk to, both giving and receiving advice about identity, gender expression, and coming out. It has given me a safe place to vent about my frustrations when I'm not able to share these feelings with most people in my life, and a kind of testing ground to try out a new identity or set of pronouns before I was ready to share them with anyone in the face-to-face world.*

Play It Again

For so many of us, music is an emotional experience that we are drawn to early in life, and having representations of T/GE people in the music we listen to can be immensely powerful. Laura Jane Grace of *Against Me!* made a huge impact when she announced her coming out as a trans woman, particularly in the punk scene. Although punk is a counterculture genre, homophobia and transphobia remain ingrained in many punk scenes. Queer and trans punk bands and their members (e.g., *Limp Wrist, Pansey Division, HIRS*, and *Tribe8*) have addressed these issues in their music and interviews. However, Grace's coming out meant that a more well-known band was now bringing trans experience to the masses. Grace uses her albums to talk about what it means to be trans and how her identity and music connect. Other T/GE artists, like *Sophie*, who tragically passed away in 2021, have been out as trans but spoken less about trans identity, and there can be something nice about this, too.

> *I do karaoke a lot, and my gender expression has a great influence on that performance and vice versa. I primarily sing songs by male artists (a lot of hard rock/metal) and my clothing tends to reflect this, while being generally masculine-leaning. Then, when no one's expecting it, I'll break out my feminine range . . . the cognitive dissonance for the audience is delicious to me! Although this started as a solo affair, over time it's become a community—one or two NB persons, two MTF ladies, and many allies, supporters, and karaoke nerds, all brought together by our love of singing and performance.*

Websites such as Bandcamp have a "transgender" tag for musicians and this tag can be used to find lesser-known trans artists across genres. Some T/GE bands include *She/Her/Hers; Pidgeon Pit*; and *Dyke Drama*, fronted by Sadie Switchblade, previously of *G.L.O.S.S.* Trans musicians and producers have been around for a long time, but were not as easy to find. For instance, Plan-It X Records, founded by transgender DIY-er Samantha Jane Dorsett, provided an early platform for *Against Me!* At the time, if you wanted to find new artists, you had to pull a label's sheets of available records from a CD or record, checking off which titles or artist sounded interesting, and then mail in the form or bring the list into a record store. Today, the circulation of music, whether in the mainstream or self-produced and underground, is shared in a more rapid manner, allowing us to more easily access music about our communities and our lives.

MORE THAN FUTANARI: TRANSNESS IN ANIME AND MANGA

Haru Nicol (they/them) is a cultural critic originally hailing from Tokyo, Japan, who focuses on how their race and culture intersect with their gender and sexuality.

Transness in manga and anime is a subject that is, unfortunately, not as prevalent as it could be. However, there are still glimmers of hope with various titles trying to explore transness by either tackling it directly or by accidentally playing with gender identity.

The most widespread form of trans-adjacent representation in anime/manga is the often-pornographic *futanari*. In this trope (and fetish), an otherwise cis-feminine woman has a penis and engages in sex with either a cis man, a cis woman, or occasionally another futanari. This is mostly targeted at the cis-male consumer and, unfortunately, perpetuates trans women as sexual objects who are only desirable if they seem cis-passing. But in more queer spaces, futanari has been adopted as a form of trans acceptance and trans-positive sexuality.

Transness is not exclusive to pornography in Japanese pop culture; for instance, there is the classic *Ranma ½*. In this manga/anime, the protagonist changes genders whenever they have water poured onto them. Another example of gender transformation is the "Sailor

Starlights" characters from the latter portions of the *Sailor Moon* anime series. These three sailor scouts physically transform into men-in-disguise to look for their princess on earth. This interpretation of the characters, however, was only present in the anime series, because the manga author did not like this change to her work: originally they had only cross-dressed as men. These are both examples of the "gender-bend" trope, which is not intentionally trans-coded by the creators. These titles don't deliberately tackle the topic of transness; instead they have cis characters changing genders due to external circumstances.

There are, however, media that directly deal with the trans experience. For example, in the comedy idol anime *Zombie Land Saga*, one of the protagonists is an unambiguously trans girl. Lilly Hoshikawa, the character in question, has a very touching narrative surrounding her transness that is exceptionally well-written and worth watching. For a more trans-focused narrative, attention should be paid to *Wandering Son*. This slice-of-life anime/manga is unequivocally about the trans experience in modern-day Japan, with dual protagonists Shuuichi Nitori and Yoshino Takatsuki each dealing with their transness as the onset of puberty looms on the horizon for them. It may be uncomfortable, because they are deadnamed and misgendered a number of times, but it is one of the most touching and one of the best examples of transness in Japanese pop culture media.

Transness and trans lives are often either accidentally stumbled upon or used as a sexual prop. Trans narratives, however, are starting to appear more and more in various media outlets, giving hope that wider trans representation will continue to grow in these popular Japanese artforms.

Read Me a Story

I love Autostraddle and them, and used to follow Black Girl Dangerous. In terms of books, Stone Butch Blues makes me cry every time. I took a lot of queer and trans theory classes as an undergrad and also many of my Ethnic Studies classes were taught by nonbinary professors who included trans perspectives in every topic. The books and articles I read were countless and impossible to name all of them but it was a gift to spend four years in that environment.

Today there are innumerable T/GE artists, and our stories appear in novels, memoirs, graphic novels, zines, and blogs. Like music, books can give us access to discovering trans identities and experiences. We often align ourselves with trans characters and, in doing so, we find things out about ourselves. *Stone Butch Blues* by Leslie Feinberg has been taught in many college courses on queer and trans literature because it is a seminal and early work by a transgender pioneer. It is also an incredibly impactful story that traces the narrator's experience traversing working class lesbian butch communities to eventually making the decision to transition.

I have read a few books regarding trans and gender nonconforming people, and I love them. It's very helpful for me to read things that I can relate to. I absolutely love the Magnus Chase series by Rick Riordan with the genderfluid character, Alex.

Other books that focus on trans narratives include Casey Plett's *A Safe Girl to Love*, a collection of 11 short stories following various characters as they navigate love and lust, and Imogen Binnie's *Nevada*, in which a trans woman unravels as she tries desperately to coax a stranger she perceives as a closeted trans girl out of her shell. Books allow us to find ourselves in characters and engage with their experiences as we continue to define and redefine who we are.

The most helpful reading materials for me have been speculative fiction novels where the characters struggle with and ultimately remake themselves. I know that sounds weird, but books are an excellent reminder that we're not alone in whatever we're struggling with. I needed to know that there are lots of reasons that people decide to step away from the identities they were assigned, and that self reinvention is an inherent human right.

Faith DaBrooke (she/her)

Podcasts are audio recordings that are hosted online and listened to via a web browser or a phone app. A podcast audience can grow into a real community. Podcasts can be used to rally people to a cause that might not be getting coverage. They can be a vital tool in organizing community action and in providing healing after a tragedy. Your podcast can also help you grow your confidence, process your own concerns, and better develop your own identity. Getting started in podcasting is easy and inexpensive. To get started all you'll need is a phone (or laptop) and an idea. Your idea can be as simple as your extemporaneous thoughts, or it can be something more complex like interviewing people or sharing detailed research. Episodes can be as short as five minutes or as long as multiple hours. It's your podcast, and it can take any format you like.

Next, you'll need an app or a program to record. There are plenty of free voice memo and recording apps as well as loads of open-source (free) audio editing programs available for every platform. If you have the budget, you can invest in an external microphone, though it's not needed to get started. Once you've found a technical setup that works for you, it's time to start recording. Find a quiet place—preferably without too many flat, hard surfaces. These can cause echo and may reduce sound quality. Your own room—or even your closet—will likely work; although you may want to experiment with various setups and locations to find what sounds best to you.

There are numerous places online to host your podcast. With a little searching you should find lots of options, many free. When you host you'll be assigned an RSS feed. You can use this to post your podcast to different sites and apps. If you're just starting, try recording 10 episodes before you release any content. This way you'll have a backlog of material, which will give you time to record more. Keeping a regular schedule can also help grow an audience.

Recording your own podcast is a wonderful way to develop your unique voice, to share your thoughts and ideas, and to connect with others around the world. Because transgender and gender nonconforming people's stories are often absent from mainstream media, creating your own podcast gives you an opportunity to launch your unique voice and ideas into the world. It can also help you to connect with others who share similar experiences.

Gaming

While music can make us cry or dance, and books can give us visions to sculpt our imaginations, games allow us to literally play someone new. Games can be played on boards, video screens, or acted out (i.e., Live Action Role-Playing Games [RPGs], or LARPing). Whether they reflect playful fantasies or our personal identities, games can be exploratory and exciting, and the rules of games are up to the players involved. Some people attend in-person events, dressed as their characters, allowing for them to interact with others as a new version of themselves.

When it comes to video gaming, gender representation of characters is still very binary and predominately male-oriented. An increase in trans gamers and programmers, however, has led to the introduction of trans main characters, even in major games. In *Cyberpunk 2077,* players can now engage as a binary or nonbinary trans character. In 2020, Microsoft introduced the first trans lead character in a major video game. *Tell Me Why*—a game from the French studio Dontnod—tells the story of twins (one of whom is a trans man) who return home to Alaska to face events from their childhoods. Other video games with T/GE themes include *Dupli_City,* a cyberpunk narrative game centered around fighting a megacorporation's evil artificial intelligence, and *One Night, Hot Springs*, a visual novel game about a young trans girl in Japan. There are also realistic games such as the visual novel *Acceptance*, which is designed for allies and caregivers to learn about some of the day-to-day challenges of early transition.[18] Video games come in a diverse array of formats and can allow T/GE people, as well as cis people, to explore and experiment with gender.

Trans actor Ian Alexander appears in both the TV show *The OA* and the video game *The Last of Us Part II.*

Looking for more info on trans characters in gaming? Check out the YouTube video "A Brief Transgender History of Video Games" on Nerd Out with Jessie Gender.

A Touchy Subject

I think the websites with trans themes that I use most often would be OkCupid, Grindr, and PornHub.

Pornography, though stigmatized, is deeply embedded in our culture. Mainstream porn sites such as *PornHub*, however, can often provide degrading and unrealistic representations of trans sexualities, despite "transgender" consistently falling in the top 20 most searched-for categories.[19] Similar to mainstream media, mainstream porn frequently depicts trans characters without involving trans creators. If trans people are not equitably included in the creation, production, and dissemination of erotic materials, our bodies, narratives, and sexual experiences remain erased or are not considered valid.

There are several trans and nonbinary creators making their mark on the porn industry. Among them are Courtney Trouble (*Trouble Films*), James Darling (*FTM Fucker*) and Cyd St. Vincent (*Bonus Hole Boys*). All of these creators are trans or nonbinary-identified people who work more equitably to create content about trans bodies and sexualities, and do so for a trans and nonbinary audience, as well as those who are interested in having sex with trans and nonbinary individuals. The way sex and sexuality are presented on these sites allows for more affirming understandings. The content often includes asking for consent; ongoing communication during sex; engagement in or conversations about sexual health practices; and real depictions of pleasure being experienced by trans people.

Tobi Hill Meyer (founder of *Handbasket Productions* and creator of the trans woman-focused *Doing It Ourselves* series) not only creates erotic materials both in film and print formats (e.g., erotic zines), but on some of her websites has conversations around positive sexual representation. Meyer has also started exploring content material relevant to individuals who identify as asexual.

Most media does not portray trans people so I wish there was more of that with more trans POC and trans people with disabilities.

ON MYTH MAKING AND STORYTELLING

Frances Cordelia Beaver (she/her) is a video artist, storyteller, and professor working and living in Philadelphia, Pennsylvania.

Gender polymorphism is as old as civilization. Myths from all over the world include gender fluid characters. Consider a few for example: Inanna in ancient Sumer, Mawu-Lisa in West African lore, the Greek myth of Teiresias, the Hindu Hijra, Eunuchs of the Bible, and Mukhannathun in Islam. For further reading check out the works of Devdutt Pattanaik, Kay Turner, and Austen Hartke.

There is still debate about whether these myths can be read as evidence of historical social attitudes toward non-cis people, but we can at least see we were there and we can glean other paradigms from them. For example, some myths link trans-ness to sexuality—gender transformations in order to have sex without disturbing gender dimorphic cultural regimes—and some treat trans-ness as independent of sexuality. This is all worth studying for sure, but more interesting to me is contemporary myth making.

Transwomen in America sometimes characterize trans-ness as a "woman trapped in a man's body." This can be read as an indication of how American culture constructs a human-being from two major components: a soul/psyche and a body/vessel. I find this myth fascinating and frustrating. It is overly simple and may require the existence of a soul to be relatable.

In my 2016 film, SEX OF THE EARTH, I examine the relationship between biology and gender. In the film, a Pennsylvania borough council-member attempts to determine the municipal gender of his town by observing a subterranean geological formation exposed by an earthquake. He comes to believe this is the town masturbating after having a conversation with a satyr-esque park ranger. The ranger explains that the geological formation under the town is molten and remains shapeless until the town masturbates, resulting in an earthquake during which the geological-genital formation solidifies into a shape that is unique and has never occurred before. The council-member deduces that if the solid formations could be recorded over time, an average shape could be observed and a gender arrived at. His mission is all sparked from a session he has with a fortune teller who uses satire as a form of divination. In this myth, I explain how communication/miscommunication meddles in the complex, and culturally specific, relationship between biology and gender.

Remember, myths are made by mortals. We do not simply live in a world where myths exist, we live in a world where people make them!

POWER DYNAMICS OF ART AND CULTURE PRODUCTION

We are living in a time of heightened visibility of T/GE people. Simultaneously, we are living in a time of increased legislative, interpersonal, and structural forms of violence that impact T/GE people. These forms of violence disproportionately target people who are also harmed by classism, racism, ableism, and misogyny, such as low-income people, transfeminine people, and people of color. In a time when there is so much visibility of T/GE people in the arts and media, it is crucial to examine what role visual culture (and visibility in general) plays in a moment of concurrent increased violence.

Often, media that is labeled a "positive representation" of T/GE people is thought of as the main indicator of social progress. Representation and visibility *are* incredibly powerful. The possibility of being able to see a future for oneself and belonging to a larger community can be nothing short of life-saving. In order for there to be a cultural and structural shift that would be supportive of trans people, however, we must look beyond representation in visual culture as the *sole* way for this to be accomplished.

Since visibility is so impactful, it is important to consider how power dynamics are embedded in visual culture and how the category of "transgender" is depicted, consumed, and put out into the world. Here are some crucial questions to ask:

- Who is authoring this story or image?
- How might the distribution of this representation or image impact the T/GE community?
- Who is the intended audience to view this?

Trans people are frequently told they will benefit from being represented. With many cultural productions, however, it is often cis people who end up benefitting at the expense of trans people. For example, films like *The Danish Girl* (2015) and the television series *Transparent* (2014–2019), both cast cis men to play trans women—Eddie Redmayne as Lili and Jeffrey Tambor as Maura. *Transparent*, in particular, was applauded by the mainstream media as a landmark for trans representation and a symbol of acceptance. However, when cis men are cast in these roles to play trans women, it sends the false and

Making Fun of Mapplethorpe (with Juliana Huxtable) by Amos Mac.

damaging message to a wider audience that trans women are "really men" who are acting. The consequences of this false and dangerous message are nothing short of dire. When we consider the power dynamics of who benefits from the popularity of these productions, we see that Jeffrey Tambor and Eddie Redmayne both gained recognition and won awards for their performances, and that the creators of these two productions financially profited from their success. At the same time, transfeminine people experienced some increase in mainstream representation but also faced potentially harmful concrete effects. It is for this reason that the implications, power structures, and ramifications of representation are so important to consider when creating or consuming visual culture that represents trans identity.

Even when working within mainstream media, some T/GE people have been able to shift narratives and claim power. Laverne Cox from the Netflix television series *Orange is the New Black* is one such example. In various interviews, she has expertly redirected questions about her own body and transition toward larger trans struggles. For instance, Cox famously shut down Katie Couric's questions about her genitals by responding with the following:

> "I do feel there is a preoccupation with that. The preoccupation with transition and surgery objectifies trans people. And then we don't get to really deal with the real lived experiences. The reality of trans people's lives is that so often we are targets of violence. We experience discrimination disproportionately to the rest of the community. Our unemployment rate is twice the national average; if you are a trans person of color, that rate is four times the national average. The homicide rate is highest among trans women. If we focus on transition, we don't actually get to talk about those things."[20]

Such responses shift the narrative away from our physical transformations and allow us to refocus the story on our lived experiences. Doing so not only empowers us as trans people, but it creates a kind of cultural power that shapes how a cis audience hears and understands the stories we tell.

Another way that power can function in telling T/GE stories is in deciding who these stories are made for (i.e., their intended audience). Much of trans-related media is created by cis people for other cis people, sometimes with the seemingly positive goal of education. Visibility and representation in the media are often proposed as a broad way to "fix" transphobia, overlooking the complex overlapping social issues many trans people face, such as racial violence, lack of access to medical care, employment discrimination, and housing discrimination, in addition to gender-based violence. This logic of representation resolving social problems is made apparent in instances where works of visual culture are created with the main purpose of educating a non-trans audience that may have little or no contact with transgender people and our multiple, diverse communities. In an effort to portray trans people as more relatable to this audience, these works often oversimplify the many diverse experiences, cultural contributions, and ways of existing that trans people put forth into the world. These simplified narratives are used to "prove" trans people's humanity, while at the same time neglecting to acknowledge the ways institutions, history, and U.S. culture marginalize people who are T/GE or how they would need to change in order for trans people to lead livable lives.

When we consider our current moment and political climate of late capitalism, racism, income inequity, and continuously increasing levels of funding toward police and prisons, it becomes evident that representation and cultural production *alone* cannot deliver safety, rights, or protections to the majority of T/GE people.

Star Trek, a science-fiction franchise that spans eight television series and 13 films, has had a poor track record of addressing LGBTQ issues. The first prominent gay and lesbian characters only surfaced in 2017, and the first openly trans and nonbinary characters did not appear until late 2020. Star Trek has, however, obliquely addressed gender identity and expression in numerous ways. One of the earliest and most noticeable depictions took place in "The Outcast," a 1992 episode from *Star Trek: The Next Generation.* An androgynous race, that considers binary gender to be primitive and offensive, persecutes and forcefully "cures" one of their own for identifying as a woman. Although it had numerous issues, the episode addressed proper pronoun usage, the limitations of gender roles, the stress of coming out, the portrayal of variant gender identities as a form of illness, and the damaging impacts of societal transphobia.

BLACK TRANSGENDER MEN ARE UNDERREPRESENTED IN THE MEDIA

Ray Gibson (he/him) is an elderly black transmale veteran who is an activist, international mentor, writer, and chosen father of many. He is the executive Director-Founder of TMBLM, Inc. (Transmale Black Lives Matter) and has his own YouTube channel, TMXPollinator.

There have only been a few black transgender men represented in mass media to date. One is real-life activist Tiq Milan from MTV's 2007 reality series, *I'm From Rolling Stone*. The video interview, *Being Black & Transgender*, of Mr. Milan—written by Anslem Samuel of *Black Enterprise* on July 15, 2011—is no longer online. Samuel has a YouTube channel with only 145 subscribers, even fewer than mine does. People making YouTube videos of eating cupcakes get more support than non-celebrity black people do! My role model is Alexander John Goodrum, but look what little was written about him.

Then there was a *Law & Order: Special Victims Unit* episode, "Service," which aired on NBC, April 11, 2018, featuring a black transgender military sergeant named Preston (Marquise Vilsón). I cried at the end of that one as the soldiers in his charge saluted him. I am a black transgender disabled veteran who thought that was an incredible sign of respect I wish I had when I was serving my country in the 1970s as the *wrong* gender, in the *wrong* uniform, and in the closet. There was also a YouTube web series called *Eden's Garden* that featured a cast of black transgender men, starting in January 2015. This is only a handful of black transmen over the course of almost a decade.

We black transgender men have a different narrative, yet we are severely underrepresented. Nobody cares when black transmen are talking about transphobia, racism, and sexism. I have experienced and felt incredible push-back due to the lack of representation by the media—even on my own YouTube channel. I'm a "nobody" because I am a black transgender male who isn't a celebrity. These words are said to me by journalists, publicists, publishers, and editors.

I'm the eldest offspring of *Hall-of-Fame* St. Louis Cardinal baseball legend Bob Gibson. I live on a fixed-income and cannot afford a publicist, agent, editor, or a shiny advertising campaign. I almost got a story published by *The Daily Beast*; only to find out they were after my father. The editor stepped in and cock-blocked the whole thing. They never showed me the article, while telling me to trust them. Really? Even my father told me to read the article and determine for myself what is or is not "fake news" about it. They put a wedge between my father and me without even apologizing.

I am a strong pro-black transgender alpha male—not anti-white. Facebook employees won't leave me alone; they've put me in their group-jail consistently since 2017. They never tell me why they're doing this; they're allowing unknown people to report me. Everybody looks the other way while I am the target of racism, sexism, and bigotry. I'm 61 and a pioneer of a Pro-Black Transman who was raised during the Civil Rights Era. I'd rather stand for something, than fall for anything.

Article adopted from Gibson, R. (2018, June 23). Black Transgender Men Underrepresented in the Media. Medium.com. Re-published with permission from the author.

Visual Culture, Representation, and the State: Representation as Powerful and Necessary

There is no doubt that representation *is* powerful and necessary. If it weren't, there wouldn't be such a backlash to the heightened visibility of trans identity in visual culture. As media representation of T/GE people has increased, so has legislation to target T/GE people, such as North Carolina's HB2 "bathroom bill," since repealed. Laws such as the HB2 bathroom bill demonstrate how the state upholds and enforces gender norms by categorizing which bodies are seen as acceptable to be in public.

The backlash of antitrans legislation shows just how disruptive being visibly gender nonconforming in public is, and by extension its ability to destabilize state sanctioned ideas of "acceptable" gender presentation. Who is and is not visible to the state goes beyond solely one's transgender status. To be able to conform to legal and medical definitions of normative gender, a person must also be able to embody standards of racial, sexual, and economic privilege. To be gender conforming is to be, or be able to pass as, cisgender, white, middle class or higher, and heterosexual. There is a need for T/GE people to represent ourselves and make ourselves visible as a way to disrupt and challenge the dominant culture's ideas of gender. It is through transgender cultural production that such power can be reclaimed.

A non-binary femme in a gender neutral bathroom. (Zackary Drucker, The Gender Spectrum Collection, VICE/Broadly)

Representation in Visual Culture versus Lived Reality

The contrast between representation and the day-to-day lived reality for trans people is stark. In September 2017, The New Museum in New York opened "Trigger: Gender as A Tool and A Weapon." This show featured over 40 artists from different generations whose goal was to explore a range of gender expressions beyond the binary and consider gender's role in artistic representation. Despite the debut of such a diverse exhibit in a mainstream museum, the reality of T/GE people's lives at the time was not one of acceptance and inclusion. The exhibit opened shortly after the transgender military ban was proposed by the Trump administration, and closed the same month as the creation of the U.S. Department of Health and Human Service's Division of Conscience and Religious Freedom, which provided federal legal protections for healthcare providers who refused to treat transgender patients because of moral or religious objections.

Without structural change on a societal level, increasing trans representation has the potential to, instead of improving the lives of T/GE people, lead to new methods of surveillance and regulation of our communities.

REPOSE, REFIGURE, RESTORE: GRAPPLING WITH TRAUMA THROUGH ART MODELING

Álida Pepper (she/her) is a writer and model based in the San Francisco Bay Area. Out of the experience recounted here, she was inspired to found, with others, Visibility Drawing, *a Bay Area trans and nonbinary artist collective that organizes drawing events exclusively featuring trans and nonbinary models. (Photo credit: Mia Komel)*

I was falling. I moved my awareness toward that physical sensation as I began to take a static pose for an art group on New Year's Day. In the immediate aftermath of being physically assaulted, I was modeling nude, and the injuries from the assault were noticeable but not visible from every angle. The artists drawing me could still see the EKG electrodes from the ambulance. The distance they gave me from my body somehow felt comfortable. The doctor had told me I could model if I avoided putting too much weight on my left leg; besides, in figure modeling you get no sick days.

My body poured into my trauma as it poured out of me. I held myself upside-down, my weight concentrated over a small patch of my shoulders in contact with the modeling stand. I held my limbs in a frozen flail for the minute allotted to the pose; dangled another minute from supporting rafters holding up the ceiling, with the balls of my feet grazing the stand and supporting me; then balanced on my good hip in a squat as I raised my arms in self-defense. As that first hour proceeded, I fell through those gestures, coiled my knees, and soaked up my silent grief. I concentrated my pain into my shoulders and pressed it into the exposed rafters. I was supporting the heaviness of the roof, of the pain pressing into me. A relieving exhaustion settled warm and dense into my core. For my final pose, I twisted outer tension against inner tension, arranging my head, limbs, and torso into various planes as I lay pulling a cloth across myself. To an artist opposite my feet, my falling had turned into flying.

My relationship to my own body changed as I eased back into modeling. Cantilevering and holding my body in positions at the limit of my endurance had allowed me to discover athleticism and comfort with my body that had eluded me, even into transition.

Yet at the next booking, I experienced gender dysphoria for the first time during a pose. My face became pre-face, my breasts pre-breasts—the gazes of the artists around me somehow felt all-powerful in determining their substance beyond uncategorized flesh. A 40-minute pose based on the *Spinario*, an ancient Roman statue of a boy pulling a thorn from his foot, no longer produced for me the same transgressive vitality as before. Instead of the joy of queering a famous artwork, I felt simply uncomfortable.

I found my way out of that self-estrangement by doing the only thing I could. I focused intensely on the physical experience of posing. My body became both an originator and an endpoint of my internal dialogue. When I thought of the quality of my body's alignment within my poses, of how to turn my wrist, of how to extend the arch of my foot, I no longer thought from the perspective of an outside observer. I experienced that alignment organically, as a natural consequence of my body, not from precision or will, but from the emotions radiating from within my core.

I had become used to my body speaking a language I did not understand. Over the next couple weeks, I noticed a subtle shift in my poses: When I returned to a kneeling, doubled-over pose that I had once filled with pain and regret, I noticed my torso twisting, my head looking out, and right arm and fingers sweeping out into a position of purpose.

A pose of pain changed into a pose of power.

NEW WAYS OF RECOGNIZING

What does it mean to be a trans cultural worker who exists and creates work in this deeply contradictory moment of apparent celebration and heightened interpersonal, institutional, and legislative violence? In this "post-trans tipping point" moment, there is an apparent hunger for and fascination with trans imagery in popular culture. This fetishization of T/GE bodies and imagery in the "art world" and beyond is, of course, not new. An example of this is painter Jenny Saville's *Passage* (2004), which features a nude transfeminine figure. The model is posed sitting so that her genitals are the focal point of the image, and the rest of her body is painted with broad, abstract strokes that are characteristic of Saville's work. It is evident that Saville, who is a cisgender artist, spent the majority of her time painting the model's genitalia, which speaks to the othering and fetishization of trans bodies by a non-trans viewer. Instances like these raise the question of how to approach creating work within cultural systems or institutions that fetishize, tokenize, decontextualize, and/or reject trans identity.

In order to resist these cultural and institutional patterns, it is necessary to create new modes of identification, recognition, and visual vocabularies. An example of art produced in a cultural institution that disrupts dominant narratives around trans identity and identification is Patrick Staff's film, *Weed Killer* (2017), which was commissioned by the Museum of Contemporary Art Los Angeles. Inspired by Catherine Lord's memoir *The Summer of Her Baldness* (2004), which describes the author's experience with cancer and chemotherapy, *Weed Killer* uses the monologue from this written work to highlight the phenomenon of having to consume medicine that has both destructive and desired effects in order to survive. Chemotherapy can prevent people from dying of cancer, but its toll on the body is horrific. Similarly, hormone replacement therapy has allowed trans people to alter their bodies in ways that affirm their genders, yet the cultural conditions of transphobia and medical pathologization in the United States are severe.

Although it is not explicitly stated during the film, all people featured in it are transgender. Importantly, this film does not play into predictable tropes of reveals, undressing scenes, plot twists, "wrong body" narratives, or giving the viewer visual cues to indicate what the "true genders" of the performers are. By examining hormone replacement therapy next to chemotherapy, *Weed Killer* offers us new ways to think about how our bodies and identities are informed and regulated by pharmaceuticals and biomedical technologies. Patrick Staff offers us new ways of portraying trans existence and how that existence reckons with larger cultural and institutional frameworks in a manner that does not circulate the dominant images of transgender identity that reinforce one-dimensional narratives.

DISTORTED REALITY

Maggie Mae Pitchlynn (she/her) used to sing for a heavy metal band, for which she started writing poetry. She loves poetry, for it can mean something different to anyone who reads it.

Looking in the mirror
But only blind eyes see
A Perverted image
In a distorted reality
Dreams open the door
To secrets the mind hides
It's when we live those dreams
That we become truly alive
Fear is one emotion that can kill the dream
Bravery sometimes takes a lifetime to achieve
Be yourself even though you know society will stare
You'll find your courage has always been there
Authentic life in a world so fake
Being yourself will never be a mistake

CONCLUSION

Each photo, sculpture, video, cartoon, song, poem, production, performance, novel, and even meme that we produce as T/GE people is evidence of communities of trans folks who are making and sharing work that helps us survive, laugh, connect, dream, change, and make change happen. Because we are a diverse community, we must recognize that we are inevitably going to fail at representing all of us. Art labeled "transgender" that might, on one hand, be an earnest attempt to be inclusive and diverse, can simultaneously be invested in ableism, racism, colonialism, economic exploitation, and other forms of oppression. T/GE communities, and the arts and culture we produce, must strive to do better. At this point, we are failing as much as we are succeeding, but our continued efforts have a real impact on making trans lives more possible and fulfilling.

NOTES

1. Riis, B. (previously Lauritzen, B.) (2014). Transgender Reflections: Audience Studies on the Portrayal of Trans Characters in Film and TV. Copenhagen University. https://www.academia.edu/31051462

2. GLAAD. Victims or Villains: Examining Ten Years of Transgender Images on Television, GLAAD. http://www.glaad.org/publications/victims-or-villains-examining-ten-years-transgender-images-television

3. Flores, A. R., Haider-Markel, D. P., Lewis, D. C., Miller, P. R., Tadlock, B. L., & Taylor, J. K. (2018). Transgender prejudice reduction and opinions on transgender rights: Results from a mediation analysis on experimental data. *Research & Politics, 5*(1), 205316801876494. https://doi.org/10.1177/2053168018764945

4. Hughey, M. W. (2012). Racializing redemption, reproducing racism: The odyssey of magical negroes and white saviors. *Sociology Compass, 6*(9), 751–767. https://doi.org/10.1111/j.1751-9020.2012.00486.x

5. Copier, L., & Steinbeck, E. (2018). On not really being there: Trans* presence/absence in *Dallas Buyers Club. Feminist Media Studies, 18*(5), 923–941.

6. Ford, A. (2017). *The Dallas Buyers Club*: Who's Buying It? *TSQ: Transgender Studies Quarterly, 4*(1), 135–140. https://doi.org/10.1215/23289252-3711601

7. Houston, S. M. (2017). *Mudbound* vs. *The Underground Effect*: It's time for the spectacle of black suffering to evolve. *Paste Magazine*. https://www.pastemagazine.com/articles/2017/11/mudbound-vs-the-underground-effect-its-time-for-th.html

8. Groothuis, E. (2017). Stop killing trans characters in movies. *Bitch*. https://www.bitchmedia. org/article/stop-killing-trans-people-on-screen

9. Chauncey, G. (1994). *Gay New York: Gender, Urban Culture, and the Making of the Gay Male World, 1890–1940*. New York: Basic Books.

10. Loggans, R. (2016). Fantasies of opulence: Racial dynamics of drag balls in New York City, 1890–1969. *Academia.edu*. https://www.academia.edu/32755203/Fantasies_of_Opulence_ Racial_Dynamics_of_Drag_Balls_in_New_York_City_1890-1969

11. Bailey, M. M. (2013). *Butch Queens Up in Pumps: Gender, Performance, and Ballroom Culture in Detroit*. Ann Arbor: University of Michigan Press.

12. Glover, J. K. (2017). Reading came first: A book review of Marlon M. Bailey's *Butch Queens Up in Pumps: Gender, Performance and Ballroom Culture in Detroit. Text and Performance Quarterly, 37*(3–4), 277–278. https://doi.org/10.1080/10462937.2017.1328738

13. Hodes, C., & Sandoval, J. (2018). *RuPaul's Drag Race*: A study in the commodification of white ruling-class femininity and the etiolation of drag. *Studies in Costume & Performance*, *3*(2), 149–166. https://doi.org/info:doi/10.1386/scp.3.2.149_1

14. Riedel, S. (2018). A brief history of how drag queens turned against the trans community. *Them.* https://www.them.us/story/how-drag-queens-turned-against-the-trans-community

15. Horak, L. (2014). Trans on YouTube: Intimacy, visibility, temporality. *TSQ: Transgender Studies Quarterly, 1*(4), 572–585.

16. Raun, T. (2016). *Out Online: Trans Self-Representation and Community Building on YouTube*. London; New York: Routledge.

17. Miller, J. (2017). "I wanna know where the rule book is": YouTube as a site of counternarratives to transnormativity. *Women's, Gender, and Sexuality Studies Theses*. https://scholarworks.gsu.edu/wsi_theses/60

18. Dale, L. K. (n.d.). *Acceptance*. Itch.Io. Retrieved February 10, 2020, from https://laurakindie. itch.io/acceptance-jam-for-leelah-entry

19. PornHub Insights. (2019). The 2019 Year in Review. PornHub. https://www.pornhub.com/ insights/2019-year-in-review

20. Laverne Cox on *Katie* with Katie Couric, January 6, 2014.

23

ACTIVISM, POLITICS, AND ORGANIZING

Benji Hart and Kung Feng

INTRODUCTION

Transgender and gender expansive (T/GE) activism and organizing form not only the foundation of the modern LGBTQ movement, but they comprise the core of countless other liberation struggles, both historical and contemporary. The history of trans resistance helps us understand trans organizing as a pathway toward the liberation of all oppressed people.

> *I am a deeply political person, and I do my best to participate in activism on behalf of queer and trans folks, women, POC, differently abled people, and other marginalized communities, because queer identity is not just about gender and sexuality but also radically changing the structures of power.*

In leftist spaces, arguments often arise over whether justice will come through small steps (such as passing a bill that gives trans workers family leave), or large sweeping actions (such as abolishing prisons). It is important that we take small, immediate steps toward liberation, while at the same time being guided by a brave and radical vision for what trans freedom might one day look like. T/GE activists and organizers have long understood the need for harmony between their actions in the present, and their ultimate vision for a future where all trans people can live lives of safety, dignity, and autonomy.

> *I talk to my legislators, testify for state bills, push state government departments for better policies, lead community member groups at LGBT lobby days at the statehouse, and register voters to help the transgender community and its members.*

Rico Jacob Chace (He/Him), Director at TransActual UK, Producer & Activist. Recently starred in Black Rainbow documentary exploring the intersectionality between being Black & Queer. Producer & Host of the Against Racism radio series addressing racism in the UK.

TRANS RESISTANCE AS A DIRECT RESPONSE TO POLICE VIOLENCE

I have volunteered to do work with racial justice, food insecurity, and class struggle, and I believe that all of our liberation is tied up together, so in that sense it intersects with transness.

T/GE resistance is an inherently abolitionist struggle—one in direct opposition to state violence. *Abolition* refers to the total dismantling of oppressive institutions and their replacement with resources that offer support and healing. Most commonly associated with the 19th-century movement to abolish chattel slavery, this term can also be used to refer to the abolition of the systems that share a direct lineage with slavery (i.e., prisons, police, and all forms of systemic and institutional harm). *State violence* refers to harm of any kind committed by or on behalf of the interests of the nation-state. Many people think of this term when people are murdered by police. It can also be extended to encompass all forms of policing and incarceration, including deportation, solitary confinement, family separation, austerity measures, surveillance, and militarization. Modern T/GE history in the United States began with a series of police riots, and the founders of the trans movement fought against many of the same conditions—and for many of the same basic rights—as we do today.

Queer Trans War Ban is an abolitionist project founded by Dean Spade. Black and Pink is also a national abolitionist group that writes letters to T/GE prisoners in the U.S.

Many of us are familiar with the Stonewall Riots of 1969 in New York City, wherein queer and trans folks of color, like Marsha P. Johnson and others, famously sparked a melee during a police raid. For multiple days, they fought back against law enforcement agents arresting queer clientele at the Stonewall Inn. The days of rioting that ensued would lay the foundation for the Gay Liberation movement and the induction of LGBTQ identities into the political mainstream. Yet, the abolitionist history of these riots is regularly omitted.

The TGI Justice Project is a group of transgender, gender variant, and intersex people—inside and outside of prisons, jails, and detention centers—creating a united family in the struggle for survival and freedom.

T/GE people led the charge as community members militantly resisted the unjust practices that allowed them to be targeted by police. In commemoration of the riots the following year, Marsha P. Johnson and Sylvia Rivera participated in the first Christopher Street Liberation March. The gathering passed in front of the New York Women's House of Detention, drawing direct connections between the policing of trans women of color and the incarceration of survivors of violence at-large. Though Rivera and Johnson were important participants in the original march, Rivera had to fight her way onstage to become the only trans speaker at the rally three years later, because her message and tactics were deemed too disruptive. The march was ultimately rebranded as the Pride Parade, and became an opportunity to garner mainstream acceptance, rather than protest state violence.

My activism directly involves collaboration with trans artists to challenge the prison industrial complex.

The Stonewall Riots were not the first instance of militant trans resistance to policing in U.S. history. Cooper's Donuts in 1959 Los Angeles is the first known record of trans folks clashing with the police. Although it has been regarded as a somewhat isolated incident, it ushered in an era of parallel instances where queer and trans people have resisted state violence. For instance, in 1966, patrons of Compton's Cafeteria in San Francisco—an all-night restaurant and hub for the local trans community—erupted into violence after police attempted to eject a group of trans youth who had not made any purchases. Protesting patrons shattered the restaurant's plate glass windows and beat law enforcement agents with their purses and high heels, forcing police to leave without making any arrests.

The Sylvia Rivera Law Project is a collective organization that works to guarantee that all people are free to self-determine their gender identity and expression, regardless of income or race, and without facing harassment, discrimination, or violence.

Marsha P. Johnson. (Micah Bazant)

One of the many reasons Compton's Cafeteria was long-lost to history was because the officers at the scene never filed a report. As such, most local media did not pick up the story and the riot remained a fixture of local lore for decades. Yet, Compton's Cafeteria set the stage for many of the riots and protests that followed it, including a multiracial lunch counter sit-in protesting police harassment of trans and queer customers at a Dewey's franchise in Philadelphia (1968) and the Stonewall Riots the year after (1969). Just as the Black Lives Matter movement—a part of the modern Black liberation movement—can be seen as a catalyst for countless other groups currently re-engaging direct action to confront state suppression, trans people of color became emboldened by the riots and protests of the Civil Rights Movement of the 1950s and 1960s. Many of them adapted similar tactics to address police violence in their own communities, laying the groundwork for the modern transgender movement.

THE FIGHT CONTINUES

Miss Major (all pronouns) is a mother figure to countless trans and nonbinary people around the world. She currently lives in Little Rock, Arkansas, where she founded House of GG in 2018. Films and writing about her incredible life story have raised her profile since the first edition of Trans Bodies, Trans Selves, *but she's never stopped being the source of love and care she's always been—especially to her gurls.*

I tried retiring back in 2016. That plan failed.

For better or for worse, there's still a lot of work to do. I can still say with the utmost assurance that prison was the most frightening thing that ever happened to me. The harassment and abuse by the guards were the worst. They set up abusive situations between prisoners. They try to strip you of your dignity, which is hard when the rest of the world has already been trying. They strip away your privacy. They humiliate you—anything to make sure you know you are worth nothing and you don't exist while you're there. This is degrading for everyone, and it just makes the trauma deeper for transgender people who are dehumanized all the time.

So no, I wasn't thrilled when Alex Lee, the founder of the Transgender, Gender Variant, and Intersex Justice Project, convinced me to go back into prisons around California—back to the scene of the crime. But after you live through something like that, it feels like the thing to do: try and help the gurls inside to fight the isolation and danger and to make sure their humanness is seen.

The problem is the guards don't read the laws that are supposed to protect us—much less enforce them—so things don't change. The reason I kept going was because of the gurls who would write and call because they know that we're on the outside supporting their fight. We fight this together to build our pride and to help us all survive. We are survivors because we have survived with nothing (especially black trans women). We know how to live in the hole of solitary confinement for years and, yet, still muster enough respect for ourselves and decency for others.

They're still killing us and still trying to make us believe we're worth less than the dirt that they shovel onto the graves of our sisters and brothers and nonbinary family members. The only way I survived is because of the family I've got around me—whether they're gay, straight, or trans, it doesn't really matter.

Sometimes it's hard when the hatred is so real and the problems are so big, but at least we're trying.

And it's not just us. There are people outside the so-called community who care about us and recognize that our lives are important. I'm trying to recreate that sense of family that some of us don't have. We're trying to conform to what society tells us we should be: man, woman, or alien, or what we should have: dick, pussy, or if you're lucky, both. We're all trying to negotiate our way through this life. The only way to do that is to recognize our worth and give some rope to our enemies, so they can hang their damn selves with it and—more importantly—to give the next gurl a helping hand.

THE CRISIS OF YOUTH HOMELESSNESS

Shortly after the Stonewall Riots, Rivera and Johnson were leaders in the newly formed Street Transvestite Action Revolutionaries (STAR), created to combat many of the conditions they saw as leading to the original uprising. Although "transvestite" is now considered an offensive term, the founding of STAR predated the introduction of the term "transgender" and was the best word many had to describe their identities. STAR is often credited as the first trans-women-of-color-headed project in U.S. history. Its most well-known contribution was the creation of STAR House.

Beginning as a trailer in a Greenwich Village parking lot, STAR House took shape when the organization's members acquired a property in the Lower East Side, reclaiming it as a hangout and haven for homeless youth. Though the building had no running water or electricity at the time, STAR took up residence and its members quickly got to work renovating it. In this space, STAR was able to provide housing, hot meals, and other forms of community support. At one point, when police attempted to evict the residents, members famously tipped a refrigerator onto them from an upper-story window.

The Audre Lorde Project is a Lesbian, Gay, Bisexual, Two-Spirit, Trans and Gender Non-Conforming People of Color center for community organizing, focusing on the New York City area.

Early on in its analysis, STAR recognized connections between youth homelessness, housing inequality, and mass incarceration. The group's manifesto not only decried state violence in the forms of discriminatory policing, harassment, and sexual abuse faced by trans people in shelters and jails, but also demanded a sweeping redistribution of resources and the introduction of targeted social services (e.g., trans employment, health care, and free education) as the solution to combat such violence. These radical stances, which sought collective empowerment rather than individual acceptance, not only distinguished STAR from the other budding gay and lesbian organizations of the time, but foreshadowed trans struggles for decades to come.

In our current era, where a staggering 40% of homeless people 18 years of age and younger are trans or queer,[1] the crisis of youth homelessness is still regularly portrayed as the result of lapsed morality in poor, Black, Brown, and immigrant communities. Frequently, transphobia and homophobia in marginalized populations is blamed for LGBTQ youth homelessness, rather than housing discrimination, the defunding of public education, hyper policing, wage theft, and the unwillingness of employers to hire T/GE workers. Such an approach not only fails to place accountability for the trans homelessness crisis on the social, political, and economic structures that depend on trans marginalization and impoverishment to thrive, but it demonizes other oppressed communities suffering under those same systems. Those with these views tend to provide solutions that work to further harm queer and trans people of color instead of protecting them.

STAR called for an uprooting of transphobia in all the places from which it emanated—individual families, partners, and neighbors, but also systemic factors such as policing,

Sylvia Rivera. (Micah Bazant)

TrueChild is a network of experts and researchers dedicated to helping funders, policy-makers, and practitioners challenge rigid gender norms through intersectional approaches that reconnect race, class, and gender.

incarceration, housing and job discrimination, and ultimately, capitalism itself. This call extended beyond just words and ideas, leading STAR members to establish what we might regard as the first trans shelter in U.S. history. STAR members took immediate action to create the kinds of support and resources on a microlevel that they longed to see be made available to trans people at every level of society. Programs like the Broadway Youth Center in Chicago and Ali Forney in New York City now provide through the nonprofit system the same wraparound services once demanded by and implemented at STAR House. Each of these programs stems from a direct lineage with the grassroots activism of the original STAR members.

WAGING LOVE THROUGH SPIRITUAL JUSTICE

Emmanuelle Emani Love (she/her) is an agriculturalist, spiritualist, vocalist, and writer. She is the founder and director of Wage Love Apothecary, a cross-cultural healing justice initiative, and does hospitality work in the tradition of the Catholic Worker Movement.

    I understand *spiritual justice* as a movement against the forces that perpetuate oppression through spiritual abuse and the lies that conceal spiritual truths. I remember seeing a sticky note somewhere with the words *spiritual justice*, and since then, I've been consciously and subconsciously processing what it even means! There are many ways to say the same thing. When I say spirit, someone else says energy; a different person says quantum physics; another suggests the distinction between appearance and reality—or metaphysics. Spiritual justice affirms that we are fighting a spiritual fight, and therefore, spirit is in everything. Spiritual justice is for those traumatized by limited dogma who dare to be optimistic about the possibility of trauma recovery. Spiritual justice targets systemic reticence of spiritual knowledge and the spiritual implications and intersections of our movements; it acknowledges and affirms all spiritual paths and disciplines, and it envisions their harmonious coexistence.

Religious trauma for me looked like being taught to think transness holds no spiritual precedence or significance and that my understanding of self is absolutely incorrect, and that my most high God could never accept me . . . I have learned so much from Black trans women who endure their oppression, fight in the name of Jesus, and make it. I exist in a community chock-full of victims of church hurt. I see all of the ways in which individuals, partnerships, and families are transgressed by spiritual collectives. There is a vexation of the spirit caused by misinformation, ignorance, judgment, spite, malice, envy, and so on . . . There is demonization of young mothers who have sex and kids out of wedlock; demonization of the souls who dare to identify as anything other than cis-het; demonization of sex workers and those dependent on street economies. In my experience, perpetration of religious trauma is rooted in hypocrisy and perpetuated ignorance, which to me, is worse than sin.

I'm a Catholic Worker, and I deeply resonate with the philosophy of Dorothy Day, an intellectual, radical catholic, who, with her abyss of knowledge, dared to focus her contemplation on solutions to the physical and spiritual suffering she saw, studied, felt, worked to alleviate, and could do little about. She eloquently declared, "The only solution is love." Love is a transformational experience with a price. Love is joy, pain, and sacrifice. Love is a noun. Love is a verb. Love is the most powerful force. If we fail to understand the force of love well beyond romanticism, eroticism, charity, and affection then we are truly doomed. Spiritual justice offers us a path to true love, divine Love, and it is how I've personally chosen to reclaim the power I've lost through trauma, poor choices, abuse, and the absorption of the judgment and lovelessness of my past. We can acknowledge the sacred, scattered history of trans people and the spiritual arts. We can acknowledge and honor that spirituality is not now, nor has ever been singular. Collective liberation requires loving interconnectedness.

Banner created by Sasha Alexander, Founder/Co-Director of Black Trans Media, for the Queer Liberation March in 2019.

SEX WORKER POWER

Another crucial component of STAR's mission was advocacy for and protection of sex workers. Both Johnson and Rivera identified as sex workers and were open about the ways they had relied on sex work to support themselves when their subversive gender identities and histories of incarceration made it difficult for them to find housing and employment. STAR House was seen not only as a place for its members to eat, sleep, and relax, but fundamentally as a respite for trans youth who were constantly profiled and harassed by police as sex workers—regardless of their participation in the sex industry.

> *I am forced to advocate constantly for myself, but I feel the importance to also advocate for others. I have a gift of advocacy and I choose not to use it only on myself.*

A commitment to sex worker rights is just as radical in the current political moment as it was in the 1970s. Queer, trans, and feminist movements continue to struggle with the idea that sex work is something that can be engaged in consensually. Progressive conversations about sex work can enable us to envision the bodies of cis women, trans women, and those from across the gender spectrum as autonomous, allowing individuals to make their own decisions about when and how they engage in sex. As these questions once again reach a critical boiling point, the work of STAR remains instructive and necessary in our contemporary conversations.

In 2018, President Trump signed the Senate bill Stop Enabling Sex Traffickers Act (SESTA) and the House bill Fight Online Sex Trafficking Act (FOSTA). Although the titles of these bills suggest a positive goal (i.e., ending sex trafficking), the legislation contained in them has had negative effects on individual sex workers, and less of an effect on those who engage in sex trafficking—mostly wealthy and powerful men. SESTA/FOSTA criminalizes some of the tools that keep sex workers safe, putting their lives in greater danger. The most visible result of FOSTA, for example, has been the shuttering of personal ad pages on sites such as Craigslist and Backpage. A host of sex worker activism, often led by trans and queer sex workers, has fought to instruct the public that online platforms are the safest way for sex workers to screen clients, conduct their business independent of outside exploitation, and build networks of support with other sex workers. By removing these platforms, they argue, those engaged in sex work are pushed further to the margins, making it more likely that they will experience abuse and wage theft, and potentially get caught up in actual sex trafficking.

I definitely try to stay informed, and I'm figuring out what activism in my area is possible.

STAR's radical platform reminds us in the current moment that support, not criminalization, is what keeps sex workers safe. Robust social programs (e.g., a living wage, free child care, affirming health care, affordable food, and housing) should be seen as the first steps in supporting and empowering sex workers and all survivors of systemic violence.

The Transgender Law and Policy Institute is a nonprofit organization dedicated to engaging in effective advocacy for transgender people in our society.

Bay Area American Indian Two-Spirits is an organization that exists to restore and recover the role of Two-Spirit people within the American Indian/First Nations communities.

NURTURING ACTIVISM: FROM MARCHES TO MENTORING LGBTQ + YOUTH

Cole Foust (he/him) is the LGBTQ+ Program Manager at Metro Inclusive Health.

As a young activist, I found civil rights rallies and protests invigorating. Walking side by side with people who had stories that intersected with mine both filled me with purpose and cemented my understanding of solidarity. After several years of lobbying and motion, I realized that activism isn't always an organized crowd marching purposefully through the streets. There is another form of activism: nurturing oneself and one's community.

In January 2017, I worked for a federal agency in Mississippi. I could feel my transgender identity bursting at the seams as I tried to fit into the cisgender, heteronormative persona I built to survive in the conservative South. One night, I lay in bed wondering how thousands of LGBTQ+ youth were doing the same thing. I dreamed of an environment where LGBTQ+ youth wouldn't have to pretend to be anything other than their authentic selves. I applied to the LGBTQ+ Youth and Transgender Program Coordinator position at Metro Inclusive Health in St. Petersburg, Florida, and I was quickly offered the job. After starting at Metro in July 2017, I came out as transgender, began my medical transition, and received a promotion to LGBTQ+ Program Manager. I encourage those who access our programs and services to pursue their unique, beautiful, queer paths. I study local community resources so that LGBTQ+ youth know where to go when they are presented with a challenge. There is nothing more rewarding than when a young person tells me they've found a home at Metro Youth Nights, where youth ages 13–17 are invited to drop-in for creative and fun activities. At our programs, LGBTQ+ youth are infused with confidence through art and expressive projects while bonding with peers and facilitators.

Nurturing isn't sensational. It isn't a body of people chanting for justice, and it doesn't usually make the headlines. However, nurturing creates a lasting and impactful effect. There are LGBTQ+ youth all over the nation who are seeking spaces that allow them to be themselves. Those spaces have to be run by educated, empowering, and compassionate people who can teach youth how to advocate for themselves and others. For every LGBTQ+ young adult that grows up with a place to belong and a future to hope for, another strong and inclusive future leader is born. I still attend rallies and lobby for change, but my activism today feels more complete. I'm grateful for the activists who came before me, and I am eager to see the evolution of activism for the youth of today.

HEALTH CARE

In 1995, a hit and run car crash in a Washington, DC neighborhood left 24-year-old Tyra Hunter injured and bleeding profusely. What happened next led to her death. Emergency responders were treating her when they discovered she was transgender. They stopped providing her medical assistance to talk and joke about her in derogatory ways. When she was finally taken to a hospital, emergency room doctors also failed to provide her the care she needed. She died at the hospital of treatable injuries.[2]

What happened to Tyra Hunter was not an isolated incident; rather, this was another case of the often-deadly violence trans women of color face. It was also an example of the life and death stakes for transgender people needing health care. In 2015, a national survey reported that in the year prior to taking the survey, one in three transgender people had at least one negative experience with a healthcare provider, such as being harassed or refused care because of their gender identity.[3] Discrimination, disrespect, or even abuse from providers meant many more people avoided seeking healthcare treatment in the first place. Insurers often do not cover transition-related health care, making it difficult or impossible to get. Even getting basic preventative services such as Pap smears can be a struggle for transgender people because the services approved for their gender marker by insurers may be different than the services needed for their bodies. Additionally, transgender people in jails, prisons, or detention centers, including the 47% of Black trans people who have been incarcerated, are subject to inadequate and inhumane treatment.[4] As a result, poor health care can be a death sentence for people who are locked up.

> *I provide support services for other trans and nonbinary people who are actively involved in the fight.*

Many T/GE people are among the 27 million people in the United States who lack any healthcare coverage at all.[5] For transgender people to get the care they need to live and be healthy, it is necessary not only to improve the healthcare system, but fundamentally

The Intersex Society of North America and interACT are organizations that advocate for intersex people's human rights and autonomy.

Community is Home. (Art by Emulsify)

change it in ways that will ultimately help make health care universally available for all people. Almost all other wealthy nations have universal coverage, providing free or low-cost services through a national health system (as in the United Kingdom, Spain, or New Zealand) or a single-payer system that publicly finances services (as in Canada, Denmark, Taiwan, or Sweden). In comparison with other wealthy nations, the United States has the lowest life expectancy and the highest infant mortality rate despite spending twice as much on health care. Even Cuba, a poor socialist country surviving a U.S. embargo, utilizes a tenth of what the United States spends on health care and manages to achieve world class health outcomes.

> *I work in reproductive justice. People don't always see the connection, but sexual health care and abortion care is super important for trans people, and especially making sure it's done respectfully. That's something I try to ensure happens at my job as much as I can.*

In the past few years, the movement to revolutionize our healthcare system has taken off. Congressional representatives are successfully campaigning with a Medicare for All platform. If we work toward a transformative vision of health care as a right for all people, we can help make sure that *all* transgender people, especially transgender people who are disproportionately poor, have adequate health care. Trans activism, in this sense, is a part of realizing a fuller life for all people.

WHEN HEARTBREAK SPARKS ACTION

Kim Leighton (they/them) is Pride Foundation's Regional Philanthropy Officer in Montana. Kim was born and raised in Montana. They identify as queer and nonbinary, and they have a passion for uplifting the voices of transgender and nonbinary people and the issues impacting them, particularly in rural and remote areas. In their spare time, Kim enjoys exploring photography, adventures with their spouse, and hanging out with their misfit cadre of rescue animals.

I looked both students in the eyes and asked, "How are you doing? I hope I didn't just overwhelm you more with this information. I know you both are feeling so much right now."

They looked at each other, looked at me, sat back, and each let out a long exhale. One of them said, "Thank you so much, I feel a lot better knowing there are people who care and are willing to help."

The day before, I'd received an e-mail from their teacher and GSA (Gender and Sexuality Alliance) advisor, whom I know well. He knew these teenage students needed help. One of them had been kicked out of their home, and the other was living in a tense environment where it might not be safe to come out as trans. Although the teacher believed the high school senior who had been kicked out was now safe with a friend whose parents are supportive of trans youth, he wanted to know if I knew of any local resources.

Hearing this news from their teacher, my heart immediately sank. It had been snowing for two consistent days—the tail end of a long, arduous winter here in Helena and across Montana. I simply couldn't wrap my head around this idea that a parent would tell their child they couldn't live at home anymore. Not only did this youth's father kick them out in the snow, but it was also Spring Break week, so they didn't even have school to rely on for warmth.

In one vein, I knew I shouldn't be that surprised. We hear it all the time in our community— parents and families who can't reconcile another family member's identity as a trans or queer person. This is my community. I grew up here. I live here. This reality felt far too sharp to understand—and I felt it deep in my heart.

Officially, there are no services for emergency housing for youth—particularly LGBTQ+ youth—in Helena. So, while the news was in and of itself heartbreaking, I wrestled with the idea that there was very little referral or help I could provide. The reality is, queer and trans youth experience homelessness across Montana due to family rejection, and, as a result, they face housing instability at disproportionate rates.

On the flip side, the reality I quickly learned is that there are people across Montana who care deeply for one another—especially trans and queer youth who are being forced to look for temporary, or even longer-term, housing, often due to sudden and heart-wrenching circumstances.

My heartbreak and frustration quickly turned to action.

I put a message out into the world: *If needed, could anyone provide short- to long-term respite for one to two queer and trans youth who did not have supportive family?* The response was overwhelming. People I didn't even know saw my message and reached out. People shared it with their networks and connected me with folks they knew who could potentially help.

Gratitude overtook my feelings of helplessness and sadness. So many people were willing to help—and it reminded me of just how much good and hope is in this world.

People in Montana often say our state is just one large community connected by roads and highways, and I've never felt that more than I did in this moment. People from different areas of the state heard the call for help and reached out. Some for the immediate need and some to let me know that if this happens again in their community, they are willing to house LGBTQ+ youth who have been displaced by their families of origin.

Together, people in Montana are working to support trans and queer youth in their communities to make sure their experiences with housing instability are brief, temporary, and one-time. I feel incredibly grateful and hopeful for these relationships—because no youth or young adult should have to face this awful experience simply for being who they are.

MIGRANT RIGHTS

We need to support our global communities more from the U.S.

In July 2018, 14 transgender women walked free from an Immigration and Customs Enforcement (ICE) detention center in New Mexico. They were freed after a national campaign by advocates to release asylum seekers held at ICE's transgender detention unit. But not everyone there left alive. One woman named Roxsana Hernández Rodriguez would never make it out. Hernández Rodriguez left Honduras hoping to be free in the United States from the violence, abuse, and threats she faced as a transgender woman. Instead, she was held for five days in a freezing cold cell known as an "ice box" that ICE frequently uses to hold migrants. She was denied medical care for days, despite vomiting and having diarrhea. When Hernández Rodriguez was finally hospitalized, she died from severe dehydration and HIV-related complications. A later autopsy also showed evidence of physical abuse while she was in ICE custody. Advocates hold ICE responsible for her subsequent death due to her poor treatment and neglect.[6]

The UndocuQueer Movement is a movement that defends the rights of undocumented queer immigrants facing difficulties in the United States.

Organizations like Queer Liberation Front, Occupy ICE, and Black Lives Matter have been working hard to include trans folks and fight for their rights.

The third annual Women's March LA at Pershing Square in downtown on Jan. 19, 2019. (Luke Harold)

647

Later that summer, trans women leaders from La Familia: Trans Queer Liberation Movement, Transgender Law Center, Black LGBTQIA+ Migrant Project, and others protested in Albuquerque, New Mexico to demand justice for Roxsana Hernández Rodriguez. The action was not only a call to free transgender people from ICE detention, but also to abolish ICE and prisons—to end the caging of Black and Brown people altogether. The subsequent campaign to #AbolishICE built upon progressive campaigns to defund ICE, which gained mainstream visibility during the family separation crisis that year.

As a form of resistance to governmental restrictions and oppressive regimes, the UndocuQueer movement has been an important home for many queer and transgender youth. Many became immigrant rights activists during the fight for the DREAM Act to provide legal status for young people brought to the United States as children. With parallels to coming out as queer or transgender, many UndocuQueer youth organizers used coming out as undocumented to share their stories. Despite the personal risk of deportation and fear of state violence, those who used this tactic helped defy negative anti-immigrant narratives.

El/La Para TransLatinas is an organization that fights for the rights of TransLatinas.

Queerness and defying gender conformity have long been criminalized. As some queer and transgender people gain greater social acceptance, the question turns toward whether our movements will continue to fight for the freedom of immigrants, Black people, poor people, and others who continue to be locked away.

LUCKY

eliott jennieve jude gillooly (they/them) is a queer, disabled, nonbinary activist, poet, and creator of collages. They are currently working toward their MSW at UC Berkeley to continue their passion of improving resources for trans/nonbinary and disabled/chronically ill people.

trans people are not your props for "personal growth,"
we do not exist to make you a better person,
we are not your conversation piece, not your interesting fact,
trans people do not exist so that you may expand your world view,
just because we cause you to question all that you thought you knew
does not mean we must be here to guide you through it,
you are not a better person because you can learn to love us,
consider yourself fucking lucky if we love you.
trans love is revolution.

GETTING INVOLVED

If I had the time, I would love to be more involved in political advocacy and activism, and my hope is that someday I can.

There have been many moments in queer and transgender resistance where the fight for liberation is inclusive of struggles for queer youth, sex workers, immigrant rights, and racial justice. Becoming an activist is a way to become a part of this resistance and our future. There are many ways to get involved in activism. Different strategies to make change can shape how we get involved. Three important political approaches are community organizing, direct action, and voter engagement.

Being involved with activists and organizations who share my identity is a really important way that I build my personal support networks and my self-confidence.

Community Organizing

I mostly make spaces in my community where we can meet and feel safe. I help new students navigate the trans resources on campus and meet with supportive teachers and clubs.

Community organizing in its broadest sense brings people together around shared experiences and/or interests to accomplish common goals. Organizing in a community is different from providing services or advocacy for a community. For example, a health clinic for transgender people might provide services such as hormone treatments or counseling; a health advocacy group for transgender people might have policy experts issue a report demonstrating the need for certain kinds of health services; and, a community organizing group might hold meetings that bring together community members to understand what their healthcare needs are, then plan activities such as rallies or hearings that involve those members in winning access to needed services from a healthcare provider.

I created a nonprofit to help give more access to mental health services for trans and nonbinary folks.

A key characteristic of community organizing is the participation and leadership of ordinary people—especially people impacted by the issues being addressed and people who are most impacted because of the various forms of oppression involved. Community organizations may serve or advocate for people as well. Organizing, service, and advocacy can work together. But unlike traditional service and advocacy, organizing doesn't just provide better outcomes for a community, it changes how outcomes are decided and who has the power to determine the outcome. Organizing challenges existing power relationships by transforming people into active leaders of change and bringing groups of people together to build greater collective power. Organizing is unique in that it builds power in communities.

Familia Trans Queer Liberation Movement is an organization that works at local and national levels to achieve the collective liberation of trans, queer, and gender nonconforming Latinxs through building community, organizing, advocacy, and education.

Melania Brown (Sister of Layleen Polanco Xtravaganza, crossing arms in solidarity with the House of Xtravaganza) and Ianne Fields Stewart (Founder of Okra Project), Black Trans Lives Matter March, Brooklyn, NY, June 14, 2020. (Cole Witter)

I'm involved in student organizing, and I see my gender as integral to everything I do and how I move, because it's what I'll be hit with the hardest if something goes wrong.

Community organizing can be especially transformative for people who are kept in positions of little or no power in society. Young, mostly queer and trans people of color who were often homeless found community and a safe space in the 1980s, 1990s, and early 2000s on the historic Christopher Street Pier in New York City. When the city started construction in and around the waterfront, this community was left out of planning and development decisions while real estate interests pushed to transform the area through profitable high-end development. FIERCE, an organization of LGBTQ youth of color, worked with their members on campaigns to protect access to the piers and defend their community spaces from exclusionary redevelopment and aggressive racist policing. Their organization's power came from their base—the people in the impacted community who joined FIERCE and took action together. By bringing over 200 members to a community board meeting, FIERCE was able to defeat a proposal that would limit access to the Christopher Street Pier and impose an earlier curfew.

I bring my queerness to all activist work I'm engaged in. Currently I do Palestinian liberation organizing (IfNotNow and Palestine Solidarity Committee Austin) and hopefully more local housing justice work.

The National Center for Transgender Equality is an organization that advocates to change policies and society to increase understanding and acceptance of transgender people.

Another form of organizing with a long tradition takes place at the workplace. Many workers who organize do so as members of a union. A union is an organization that brings workers together to collectively struggle for better wages, benefits, and a voice on the job. Worker centers are another type of labor group that provides services to workers. These centers organize workers who have been excluded from formal employment and labor protections, such as domestic workers and day laborers. By joining together and organizing, workers build the collective power to achieve incredible changes. Just as unions fought to limit the workday to eight hours, today's Fight for $15 movement has organized waves of strikes by fast food and other low-wage workers. This movement passed a previously unthinkable $15 per hour minimum wage in dozens of locations in the United States and resulted in $68 billion in raises for 22 million workers. Workers can also use their collective power to win broader social justice demands. In 2014, UAW Local 2865, a union of over ten thousand graduate student employees at the University of California, won a new contract with their employer that provided raises, better parental leave and childcare benefits, support for undocumented students, and a mandate to provide all-gender restrooms.

SPART*A: ADVOCATING FOR TRANS MILITARY MEMBERS, VETERANS, AND THEIR FAMILIES

Laila Ireland (she/her)

Transgender people, like any other group of people in America, have become a solid part of the American fabric. They have been, are, and always will be part of the rich traditions of the military services that defend our country and our values. Through the struggles of discrimination from outdated policies and current administrations, SPART*A Trans was created.

SPART*A Trans is a 501c3 nonprofit organization that was founded in late 2012 and stands for Service Members, Partners and Allies for Respect and Tolerance of All. The organization exists online and was established by and for transgender service members. It is composed of unique individuals who are dedicated, honorable, and willing to serve—whose love of country calls them to accept the sacrifices and burdens of military service.

Today, there are over 900 Soldiers, Sailors, Marines, Air Force members, and Coast Guard members who are currently serving and openly identify as transgender. Our members represent the entire transgender spectrum, including nonbinary and gender fluid folks, even while the military does not recognize outside of the binary. SPART*A's purpose and mission is to advocate for our actively serving transgender military members, veterans, and their families. It provides our members with a peer support network, assistance in navigating military transgender policy and health care, and educational resources for their professional development. SPART*A actively coordinates and collaborates with other LGBT advocacy organizations to promote an inclusive military environment that values the contributions of all Americans with the desire to serve. It is a nonpartisan, inclusive, member-based organization that is committed to ensuring that the rights of all transgender service members, veterans, and their families are protected. SPART*A is also fully committed to equal opportunity for all service members regardless of race, national origin, religion, sex, sexual orientation, and gender identity and expression. SPART*A often educates key stakeholders and the public about issues that impact transgender service members, veterans, and their families in order to continue accomplishing our mission of strengthening the culture of inclusion and diversity within the United States military.

Direct Action

In the past I've been a part of labor organizing (Fight for $15), radical queer and trans groups that use direct action (Queer Rising NYC, Trans Task force Boston, Stonewall Militant Front Austin), housing justice work (Queer Rising and Boston Homeless Solidarity Committee), and immigration rights (Cosecha).

Direct action is a tactic and a strategy employed by activists and organizations to call attention to an issue. Often, direct action is mistakenly equated with protests that involve violence or property destruction. Many practitioners of direct action commit themselves explicitly to nonviolence, whether as a philosophy (like Gandhi or Martin Luther King Jr.), as a strategy (like the theories of Gene Sharp), or as a practice (like the countless environmental, antinuclear, antiglobalization, antiwar, and Black Lives Matter activists in the United States). Many activists using direct action point out that the debate over supposedly "violent" protests is a distraction from the deep and systemic violence being protested. Often, these debates detract from larger concerns like the war on Black people through police brutality and mass incarceration, wars on people abroad, the widespread pollution of our air and water, or the impoverishment of many communities in one of the richest countries in the world.

Direct action simply refers to actions that are taken for immediately effective results. In the face of the government's inaction around the AIDS epidemic that decimated the LGBTQ community in the 1980s, the group ACT UP employed direct action to intervene in a life-or-death crisis. To protest the price-gouging of a pharmaceutical company that manufactured life-saving drugs, ACT UP activists held a rally at the New York Stock Exchange. Some slipped inside and chained themselves to a balcony, dropping fake money and disrupting the opening bell of the stock market. This action captured national attention and, four days later, the pharmaceutical company lowered the price of its HIV-treatment drug.

The Ruckus Society describes four types of direct action: (1) protests to register dissent or sound the alarm about an issue, (2) noncooperation such as strikes or boycotts that withdraw something necessary for a system to function, (3) interventions that disrupt a system, such as blockading roads or disrupting meetings, and (4) creative solutions that develop a community alternative.[7] Another form of direct action that ACT UP took was establishing needle exchanges to provide clean needles to users and prevent HIV transmission. Distributing needles without a prescription was illegal, but activists did it anyway, creating a community solution that directly addressed the issue. Activists sometimes intentionally invited arrest, publicly distributing needles as a way of protesting

Black Lives Matter Rally in Washington Heights. (Laura Erickson-Schroth)

The Degenderettes is an international genderqueer agitprop (art for social change) club.

these conditions, which ultimately led to the change of a law that was taking people's lives. Civil disobedience is one kind of direct action that intentionally violates an unjust law in an effort to change it.

Most people are familiar with the civil disobedience practiced by those who took part in the Civil Rights Movement, sitting in at lunch counters that excluded Black people, riding segregated buses, and defying sheriffs who beat and hosed marchers. These actions are widely accepted and valued now for the changes they brought; however, at the time, most people felt negatively about them. A Gallup poll in 1961 found that over 60% of Americans disapproved of Freedom Riders who fought bus segregation. A majority also thought the Freedom Riders' actions were hurting their cause.[8] But, dramatic direct actions coupled with mass organizing directly led to victories such as the Voting Rights Act of 1965. Sometimes the impact of actions isn't immediately apparent and is only felt generations later as those visionary actions shift the political climate to change what is considered acceptable or possible. Politics has been famously described as the art of the possible, but for many activists, politics is the art of making the impossible, possible.

Claiming Our Power

TRANSLATING HATE

Jeffrey Marsh (they/them) is a nonbinary writer, actor, artist, activist, and social media personality, best known for making inspirational viral videos on Vine and other forms of social media. With over a quarter-billion views, Marsh has been described by CBS as "the internet's most beloved anti-bully."

Don't read the comments. Never.

I was recently quote tweeted by presidential candidate Elizabeth Warren. I made a video about working with her to create a national nonbinary rights policy. A friend of mine told me he was going to read some of the online responses to the video. "Oh don't do that," I said. "We don't ever read the comments."

I thought about trolls and why people—sometimes anonymously—write the most awful, inhumane, and evil things in comments. It's a well-known problem. I've dealt with it since I was famous on Vine years ago. The paradox of social media is especially burdensome for LGBTQ people. I would not have a career if it wasn't for the Internet and social media. But, in order to help people, spread kindness, and, yes, sell books, I need to encounter the worst hate known to humankind. And I'm not unique.

Many young LGBTQ people can only find community online. They find others like them, and they find recognition and respect. And sometimes it's only online that they find the language to describe what they have been feeling all their lives. At the same time, being online opens them up to the worst abuse possible. Another creator from Vine and I used to joke that if we took the worst possible thing we could think of to say and then multiplied it by 10, we still wouldn't be close to the hate on Vine. Twitter is no different. Instagram is no different. Facebook . . . don't get me started.

I have come to understand something I find comforting in regard to this hate. Queerphobia is very close to pain. I discovered that queer hate is a bulwark—a dam—against the rising tide of the hater's own self-hate and pain. Many of those who hate were likely taught to hate the queer or the queer-adjacent parts of themselves.

This notion is comforting—not because I delight in other people feeling pain but because it helps me make sense of why I am treated the way I am. If people like me are representative of pain, if we are walking reminders of pain, of course people will hate us. The only way I have found to deal with this situation is to do my best to represent the hope that arrives after someone has dealt with their pain.

Voter Engagement

I'll support most politicians who seek to further trans inclusion in public spaces and recognize our existence as people, not just amorphous targets to fight against.

Voting and elections are oftentimes the most visible form of political activity. Many people are apathetic or cynical when it comes to participating in elections because of the unfair influence of wealthy donors and corporate interests on elections, an active and racist exclusion of people from voting rights, a distrust of government cultivated by conservatives intent on cutting social services and public goods, and a general sense that the world and the people who make decisions about it aren't working for them.

I don't think politicians should be able to label themselves "allies." They should have to beg for our support and fight for us.

Yet elections remain an important part of efforts to make political change, build power, and have an impact. Some organizers describe their work as pursuing a coordinated inside/outside strategy of working within and outside of electoral politics. Sometimes winning an election is not about winning for a particular candidate or issue, but altering the terrain and political landscape, making other changes possible.

Christine Hallquist ran for governor in Vermont. I remember being at the Women's March 2019 in Vermont and seeing her right as I was starting to question my identity. I thought that if she could be that successful in politics, so could I as a nonbinary politician.

Idle No More SF Bay is a grassroots all-volunteer organization composed of Native and non-Native allies dedicated to climate change activism.

The struggle for voting rights was a defining landmark for the Civil Rights Movement, which catalyzed many other freedom struggles of the 60's and 70's. That struggle for full democracy is not over. Mass incarceration targeting Black and Brown people, coupled with laws disenfranchising people with convictions, means that more than six million people in the U.S. have their right to vote taken away from them. Many of these voter-suppression laws were explicitly created to uphold white supremacy after the Reconstruction Era following slavery. For example, in 2016, one in five Black residents in Florida did not have the right to vote.[9] Yet, that all changed in November 2018 when groups like the New Florida Majority, Color of Change, Planned Parenthood, the Service Employees International Union (SEIU), and many other groups worked together and succeeded in passing Amendment 4. This amendment restores voting rights to people with convictions, winning the largest expansion of the right to vote since the Civil Rights Movement and women's suffrage. To win, organizers and volunteers knocked on the doors of 1.5 million people to talk to them about their vote. The results on Election Day are not the only goal of voter engagement. Rather, its potential power is reaching people at a mass scale and building the broad support needed for systemic change.

Massachusetts Transgender Political Coalition is an advocacy, education, and community-building organization that works to end discrimination on the basis of gender identity and expression.

Seeing articles on Facebook about more trans people being elected to office made me feel more supported even though they weren't my elected officials. I'd love to see more trans politicians.

COVID-19 AND COMMUNITY SUPPORT: CREATING A VIRTUAL PANEL

Debanuj DasGupta is an Assistant Professor in the Feminist Studies Department at the University of California Santa Barbara and serves on the Board of Directors for The Center for LGBTQ Studies (CLAGS).

On April 3rd, 2020, I was privileged to bring together scholars and activists in the field of transgender studies with an intermedia event titled, *"COVID 19: Trans/Lives and Trans/Studies."* This coming-together was both a scholarly event and a survival attempt. As a gender nonconforming (GNC) scholar living in a small New England town, I was feeling isolated, unsafe, and helpless about the precarity faced by many transgender communities across the United States and South Asia. My conference travels and my summer travel plans to visit my parents in India were canceled. The changing geopolitics, travel bans, and daily restrictions on mobility triggered my own post-traumatic stress disorder symptoms, developed from being undocumented and an ex-detainee. The event allowed for virtual thinking and grieving within a dedicated transgender space in the wake of a global pandemic.

My research and activism involves questions of mobility, migrancy, regulation, and recognition of diverse gender identities across the United States and South Asia. Such research places my friendships with diverse transgender communities on various continents within variegated power-knowledge and regulatory formations. In the United States, I work with transgender and gender nonconforming asylum seekers, undocumented immigrants, and detainees. Many face severe restrictions on mobility across borders, restrictions within their everyday lives, and restrictions within detention facilities while COVID-19 continues to spread.

There has also been a lockdown in most South Asian countries since March 2020. The pandemic impacts transgender persons in South Asia. Many diverse communities (Hijra, Kothi, Khwaja Sira, Meti, Kinnar, Aravani) have lost income because many of them rely on daily wage jobs as house cleaners, beauticians, and masseuses. Hijra communities often rely on begging, dancing at weddings, and assisting with childbirth. Because of the pandemic (and Cyclone Amphan) several transgender community members have been rendered homeless without income or food. Activists are creating fundraising drives and distributing bags of rice, onions, and potatoes for many homeless transgender persons throughout South Asia.

Simultaneously, as a professor of Queer and Transgender Studies, I was required to start teaching online, converting lecture materials that were designed for face-to-face interaction into online-friendly equivalents. The lives of our students—especially international students, LGBTQ students, undocu/queer students of color, and survivors of domestic violence—were being thrown asunder as they were forced to leave campus.

Our virtual coming together was a way for us to emote, learn, and build collective trans/queer power. The event featured scholars and activists, including Dr. Susan Stryker, Amita Swadhin (Founder, Mirror Memoirs), Dr. Treva Ellison (Pomona College), Chanel Lopez (New York City Human Rights Commission), Dr. Red Washburn (CUNY Kingsborough), and myself. Dr. Washburn and I served as moderators, while our fellow CLAGS board member Dr. Laura Westenguard (CUNY Metro Tech) served as the web diva, managing security and chat functions on Zoom.

During the panel, Dr. Stryker first reminded us that pandemics are not new to transgender and queer people. We have been surviving the HIV/AIDS pandemic, and we have created community survival networks. Amita Swadhin has been increasing visibility through storytelling of LGBTQ survivors of child sexual abuse. Her organization, Mirror Memoirs, has been working to end child sexual abuse, and was about to unveil an archive of stories before the pandemic. Swadhin spoke about the queer and transgender mutual aid fund that she has created with co-panelist Dr. Treva Ellison. Further, Swadhin reminded us about the rise in domestic violence, intimate partner violence, and sexual abuse during shelter-in-place orders.

We explored other questions: How can we create accountability at this moment? What is safety for queer and transgender persons at this moment? Both Swadhin and Ellison spoke about pandemics as chronic conditions. Racism, neoliberal capitalism, and xenophobia are all pandemics that many of us are surviving. Chanel Lopez reported from New York City how several transgender persons were being treated for COVID-19 in New York City hospitals—including how their families of choice were unable to visit them. Dr. Washburn also noted that many were being told that top and bottom surgeries were being classified as "nonessential" and placed on indefinite hold.

Over 100 persons attended the event, and we were truly unprepared for such a high volume of interest. However, this CLAGS event was probably one of the first conversations about transgender lives and COVID-19 in the early moments of the pandemic. Although the pandemic has exacerbated the inequalities faced by transgender communities, our communities are creating innovative on-the-ground social networks in hopes of a livable life.

Using All the Tools in the Toolbox

Movements for change often incorporate elements of multiple activist strategies. When conservatives in North Carolina succeeded in 2016 in passing HB2, one of many recent bathroom bills to criminalize T/GE people for using bathrooms that aligned with their gender, outrage and organizing sparked a boycott of North Carolina that the Associated Press estimated would cost the state $3.7 billion in lost business by the year 2028.[10] Sports leagues, high-profile music stars, and major companies canceled events or plans to expand. Thousands of people decided not to travel or spend money in the state. Moreover, two thousand activists occupied the streets outside the governor's mansion for hours the day after HB2 was signed. Queer and trans people of color and Black Lives Matter groups blockaded streets and connected HB2's anti-trans hysteria to the murders of trans women of color, like Angel Elisha Walker, and the disregard for trans, Black, and Brown lives.

> When I was a call center supervisor who had trans employees, I heard some women talking crap in the lunchroom about transwomen using the restroom and I thought my head would explode. I did not sit silently by and I'm sure the entire room heard me yelling. I went straight to human resources and the HR director followed up and offered them the opportunity to use the single person restroom in the lobby for which you needed special access. While this is a perfect example of "separate but not equal," it was a huge step at the time. These women were grateful because at their previous call center they had to cross the street and use the toilet at the gas station when they were at work.

North Carolina's HB2 banked on stoking panic around trans women in women's bathrooms and played on racially coded calls to protect white womanhood from assault. It wasn't just a bathroom bill. HB2 also blocked local minimum wage increases and antidiscrimination policies. Trans people are already three times as likely to be unemployed, twice as likely to be in poverty, and far more likely to rely on criminalized work in the underground economy than their cis counterparts.[11] Structural racism and economic inequality mean more than half of Black and Latinx workers nationwide make less than $15 an hour.[12] As queer and trans people of color (QTPOC) activists in North Carolina pointed out, fighting for trans lives meant more than fighting HB2; it meant taking an intersectional approach that would tear down, as a whole, the interlocking structures of white supremacy, economic exploitation, and heteropatriarchy. These structures not only discriminate against trans people and keep them out of bathrooms, but they keep them in poverty, locked up in prisons, and at risk of being murdered.

Conservatives had hoped the topic of bathroom policing would energize their base, build their power, and become a wedge issue that would split their opposition. Over the course of the struggle against HB2, however, the bathroom issue became toxic because of effective direct action, dedicated organizing, and protest that built public opposition. The Republican governor who had led the bathroom bill was defeated in the election later that year. The election of a Democratic governor was not sufficient to fully repeal HB2. Though some important changes were made to the bill, the compromise with a Republican-controlled state legislature fell seriously short. Still, the power of the fight over HB2 served as a warning to other legislators and helped stall other bathroom bills around the country.

This fight is not over, as conservatives continue to drive an anti-trans agenda. Several of the current issues include: undermining protections from discrimination in schools and locker rooms; allowing doctors and healthcare providers to refuse to treat transgender and queer people; banning transgender military members; and, defining gender as biologically determined and immutable. Just as conservatives attacked same-sex marriage in recent decades for strategic reasons—such as when noted Republican strategist Karl Rove put measures opposing same sex marriage on the ballot in 11 states to drive socially conservative voters to the polls in favor of George W. Bush—the Far Right is now using this same strategy of inciting fear of transgender people to build their base, create a wedge issue, and gain political power. All those interested in any kind of progressive change have an interest in pushing back against this latest wave of dangerous antitrans attacks.

EPISTEMIC INJUSTICE AND TRANS LIVES

Matthew Cull (they/them) is a nonbinary philosopher and PhD student based at the University of Sheffield. They are interested in trans and feminist theory, and how the resources of analytic philosophy might be useful in building progressive political movements.

Trans people suffer injustices in all aspects of our lives. One category of such injustice is the *epistemic* injustices—injustices having to do with knowledge and our capacities as knowers. For instance, trans people often suffer a form of epistemic injustice that Miranda Fricker has called *testimonial* injustice, when attempting to tell others who we are. Testimonial injustice is the failure to give a speaker the appropriate level of credibility on the basis of some identity-based prejudice. The speaker is not believed when they ought to be believed, doubted when they should not be doubted. Trans people are the authorities on our own genders—we're the experts! Experts, moreover, should (in their area of expertise) be granted a high level of credibility; people should generally believe what they say. Yet trans people are often not afforded the high level of credibility we deserve when we assert our identities—our self-identifications are disbelieved, and we are misgendered. This effect is heightened given that, as Talia Mae Bettcher has pointed out, trans people and especially trans women are often stereotyped as evil deceivers, hiding their "true" sex, or "make-believers," deluding themselves about their gender.[13] These "controlling images," to use Patricia Hill Collins's terminology,[14] unjustly imply that trans people are not trustworthy. Of course, this injustice is just one manifestation of transphobia and must be fought like all others.

Another form of epistemic injustice faced by trans people is *hermeneutical* injustice. To quote Fricker, hermeneutical injustice involves having "one's social experience obscured from collective understanding" due to prejudice in society, creating a "gap" in our conceptual resources.[15] For a young nonbinary person, growing up in a binary gender system, and isolated from alternative ways of understanding gender, hermeneutical injustice manifests itself by preventing that person from accessing the concepts or labels by which they might understand their experience. Of course, through education, and *hermeneutic innovation*, whereby we, as trans people, develop new concepts to help us describe and share our experiences moving through our gendered lives, this kind of injustice can be overcome.

CONCLUSION

I'm an anarcho-socialist and feminist among other political identities. These politics are all about creating a world that's best for everyone and this includes trans people.

From fighting state violence, homelessness, and wage theft, to supporting sex worker power, worker rights, universal health care, and voter empowerment, activism within T/GE communities is varied and intersecting. That means there are many opportunities for us to take action and many movements we can take part in that will make a positive difference for our communities. Our struggle can be a force for change, not only in transgender communities, but for the liberation of all oppressed people. Organizing, direct action, and voter engagement can be complementary and critical strategies toward that liberation. These three approaches share a common principle—that people have the power to make change. We are the ones we have been waiting for.

NOTES

1. Durso, L.E., & Gates, G.J. (2012). *Serving Our Youth: Findings from a National Survey of Service Providers Working with Lesbian, Gay, Bisexual, and Transgender Youth who are Homeless or At Risk of Becoming Homeless.* Los Angeles: The Williams Institute with True Colors Fund and The Palette Fund.
2. District Settles Hunter Lawsuit for $1.75 Million. Press release jointly approved by the D.C. Office of the Corporation Counsel and attorneys for Margie Hunter. Thursday, August 10, 2000. GLAA. http://www.glaa.org/archive/2000/tyrasettlement0810.shtml
3. James, S. E., Herman, J. L., Rankin, S., Keisling, M., Mottet, L., & Anafi, M. (2016). *The Report of the 2015 U.S. Transgender Survey.* Washington, DC: National Center for Transgender Equality, p. 5.
4. Grant, J. M., Mottet, L. A., Tanis, J., Harrison, J. Herman, J. L., & Keisling, M. (2011). *Injustice at every turn: A report of the National Transgender Discrimination Survey.* Washington, DC: National Center for Transgender Equality and National Gay and Lesbian Task Force, p.163.
5. Berchick, E. R., Barnett, J. C., & Upton, R. D. (2019). *Current Population Reports, P60-267(RV), Health Insurance Coverage in the United States: 2018.* Washington, DC: U.S. Government Printing Office.
6. Garcia, S. E. (2018). Independent autopsy of transgender asylum seeker who died in ICE custody shows signs of abuse. *New York Times*, November 27, 2018.
7. The Ruckus Action Strategy Guide. The Ruckus Society: Actions Speak Louder Than Words. https://ruckus.org/training-manuals/the-action-strategy-guide/
8. Izadi, E. Black Lives Matter and America's long history of resisting civil rights protesters. *Washington Post*, April 19, 2016. https://www.washingtonpost.com/news/the-fix/wp/2016/04/19/black-lives-matters-and-americas-long-history-of-resisting-civil-rights-protesters/
9. Uggen, C., Larson, R., & Shannon, S. (2016). *6 Million Lost Voters: State-Level Estimates of Felony Disenfranchisement, 2016.* The Sentencing Project. https://www.sentencingproject.org/publications/6-million-lost-voters-state-level-estimates-felony-disenfranchisement-2016/
10. Dalesio, E. P., & Drew, J. (2017, March 27). AP Exclusive: Price tag of North Carolina's LGBT law: $3.76B. *AP News.* https://apnews.com/fa4528580f3e4a01bb68bcb272f1f0f8

11. James, S. E., Herman, J. L., Rankin, S., Keisling, M., Mottet, L., & Anafi, M. (2016). *The Report of the 2015 U.S. Transgender Survey*. Washington, DC: National Center for Transgender Equality.

12. Tung, I., Lathrop, Y., & Sonn, P. (2015). *The Growing Movement for $15*. National Employment Law Project. https://www.nelp.org/wp-content/uploads/Growing-Movement-for-15-Dollars.pdf

13. Bettcher, Talia Mae. (2007) "Evil Deceivers and Make-Believers" *Hypatia, 22*(3), 43–65.

14. Collins, Patricia Hill. (2000). *Black Feminist Thought*. New York: Routledge.

15. Fricker, Miranda. (2007). *Epistemic Injustice*. Oxford: Oxford University Press, p. 155.

AFTERWORD

A TRANSGENDER TOAST: MAY YOU LIE, CHEAT, AND STEAL

Jennifer Finney Boylan
Belgrade Lakes, Maine

September 2019

Years ago, the writer Gwendolyn Ann Smith invented what she called the "Transgender Documentary Drinking Game." You can imagine how this goes: one drink for a shot of a trans woman looking at herself in the mirror, combing her hair; another one for a shot of a trans woman doing anything in heels and a skirt that is obviously done better in jeans: changing the oil in her car, sweeping the ashes out of the chimney. If there's a shot of an embittered wife weeping as our heroine Tiffany Chiffon is wheeled off to surgery, you're supposed to down the whole bottle. Good times.

The great Helen Boyd, author of *She's Not the Man I Married*, had a version of it, too. And why not: the game reflects the weariness so many of us—trans people and the people who love us—have experienced, being constantly portrayed by the same old clichés of grief and sponge cake and "authentic selves." For a while there it seemed as if there was a new documentary being produced every couple of weeks, and every single one used the same old chestnuts, all presented in soft focus as melancholy new-age piano played gently in the background.

I wondered, sometimes, why they bothered making new documentaries in this genre, instead of just showing the same one over and over again.

I know I shouldn't talk, given that I was the centerpiece of more than a few of these shows when I came out almost 20 years ago. I still remember sitting there with Oprah, as she asked her audience whether they didn't think I was incredibly selfish, coming out as trans, and putting my own survival ahead of the happiness of my wife and children. And the audience all muttered, *yes, you're selfish*. I still remember how they titled that episode, "The Husband Who Became a Woman." Rather than "The Woman Who Became Herself." I also recall the time Larry King looked me in the eyes and said, "You've lost something." I literally had no idea what he was talking about. Finally, the penny dropped. "No, Larry," I said. "I've gained something."

Twenty years is a long time, though, especially measured in trans years, and I admit that I haven't seen the usual trans documentaries—the ones that inspired the drinking games—for a while. This may be because I've gotten to the point where I read more books than I watch TV shows, but it might also be because the idea that trans people are complex, that we are about more than our transitions, and that the same old clichés no longer reflect reality—well, who knows. Would it be too idealistic of me to hope that this idea has finally begun to sink in?

In part, this is because the media has gotten a little better at telling our stories—for which, in part, I thank GLAAD, the queer media advocacy group that I was associated with for most of the last decade. As a result of their work—and that of hundreds of other trans folks who have had the courage to become visible—things have changed. There have been other stories in the culture: from *Transparent* to *Sense8*, from *Orange is the New Black* to *Pose*.

As someone recently remarked to me, "It's not your grandfather's sex change."

That's a funny line, but even that language—*"sex change," ew*—feels antiquated and dated now. My friend, the great surgeon and activist Marci Bowers, once starred for a while in a reality show titled, "Sex Change Hospital," which was groundbreaking for its time and did a great job of capturing the drama and the triumph of people in surgical transition. But now, just a few years later, it's not uncommon for a young person, in hearing about the show, to scrunch up their nose and ask, "Seriously? They called it that?"

They did, Gandalf. They did.

The language has been changing at a dizzying pace. I rarely hear "transgendered" anymore; now people say "transgender." Other terms on the wane: "genderqueer," "transsexual," "post-op" and "pre-op," "MtF" and "FtM." More common to my ears now: "nonbinary," "gender fluid," or just plain "trans." And plenty of people don't even want to be bothered with labels any more. We just say *queer,* and leave it at that. All signs of progress, if you ask me.

In the Introduction to the first edition of this book, I wrote a little bit about the language that people then used to talk about their genders, and noted some of the tension in the community between some of its different wings—transsexuals (*sic*), drag queens, cross dressers, genderqueer people. I observed then that the diversity of the community is its strength, not its weakness, and that we should all be glad that there are so many ways of being us.

I still feel that way, no matter what words we choose to use for the things that are in our hearts.

Since that first edition was published, though, there've been other changes, too. For one thing, our lives are—on a good day—not quite as obscure as they might once have been to most cis people. Thanks to increasingly positive exposure in the media, there are better role models, and more visible examples of trans people living their lives—both the ways we struggle as well as the way we prevail.

But increased visibility has also meant increased risk, as the forces allied against us have begun to invent new ways of making our lives harder. The election of 2016, a national disaster by almost any measure, also gave new encouragement to anti-trans bigots of all kinds, and in the years since then the Trump administration moved heaven and earth in an attempt to erase us, and the people we love.

And yet, somehow, we are still here, living our lives with struggle, and passion, and grace. Just as the old civil rights hymn goes, "Just like a tree planted by the water, I shall not be moved."

Like all of you, I've been shaken by the pushback against the humanity of our people. But I refuse to lose my spirit, or my hope, or my love.

My dream is that in years to come the Transgender Drinking Game will continue—but with different rules. Maybe someday it will go like this:

- Access to health care—take a shot.
- Protections for trans people in the workplace—take a shot.
- Equal protection under the law—take *two* shots.
- Election of more trans people in statehouses, and in Congress, and to the White House—take a shot of champagne, for every last trans person serving their country with honesty and with pride.
- Freedom to serve in the military—take a shot.
- Freedom to live our lives with joy, according to our own lights, and according to the realities of our own complex human hearts: well, you can just drain the bottle, once and forever.

It may be that these goals seem unrealistic, like the kind of thing that could only take place in Aristophanes' *Cloud Cuckoo Land.*

But if you'd described to me 20 years ago the life I'm currently living, I'd have thought that this life was unreal, too. And yet here I am: still writing, still living, still fighting. And yes: still married—31 years now, 12 as husband and wife, 19 as wife and wife.

It's deeply moving to me to see the torch being passed to a fierce new generation. If you want evidence of the passion—and the struggle—of the next wave of trans people, well all you'd have to do would be to read this book.

There's so much more work ahead, so much evil to undo, so much love to bring to the world. In the years ahead, that work will continue. I know we're in good hands.

I raise my glass to my trans siblings, and their families, and I offer you this old Irish toast—may all of us, in the years to come, lie, cheat, and steal.

May we lie in a bed of roses.

May we cheat misfortune.

And may you steal each other's hearts, just as you have stolen mine.

Cheers.

CONTRIBUTORS

(Note: Short Piece authors and Artists have their bios included with their pieces.)

The members of the TBTS First Edition Survey Team were unintentionally left out of the first edition of this book. They include Katie Dibona, Ray Edwards (see bio below), Ira Gray, Nora Hansel, Kate Kourbatova, Caden Polk, and Elizabeth Spergel.

Colt St. Amand, PhD, MD (Youth Chapter Author) is a white transgenderqueer Two Spirit queer man, licensed psychologist, and physician who is completing a Family Medicine residency at the Mayo Clinic in Minnesota and teaches gender and sexual health at Baylor College of Medicine and the University of Houston.

Leigh Anne Gregory, PhD (Aging Chapter Author) is a trans woman and a retired Professor of History, who is active as a representative of and as a member of the Community Advisory Committee of LGBTQ Healthcare at Vanderbilt University Medical Center.

Arbor Archuletta, MA (Arts and Culture Chapter Author) is an educator on LGBTQ and women's studies, a trans artist and activist, and an all-around lover of bad bands who do great music.

Florence Ashley (Social Transition Chapter Author) is a transfeminine jurist and bioethicist from Tio'tia:ke (also known as Montreal) whose work spans a wide range of trans social, legal, and health issues, and who served as the first openly trans law clerk at the Supreme Court of Canada.

Alexandre Baril, PhD in Women's Studies (Disability Chapter Author) is a trans disabled man and an assistant professor at the School of Social Work at the University of Ottawa, specializing in diversity, including sexual, gender, (dis)ability, and linguistic diversity.

Sarah E. Belawski (Intimate Relationships Chapter Author) is a trans woman author, musician, and activist from Albany, New York.

Gaines Blasdel (Surgical Transition Chapter Author) is a transgender man who has worked with LGBTQ teens in New York City, written about T/GE health care for community and academic audiences, and currently does research on gender affirming surgery outcomes.

Jennifer Finney Boylan (Afterword) is the Anna Quindlen Writer in Residence at Barnard College of Columbia University in New York; a Contributing Opinion Writer for *The New York Times*; and a member of the Board of Trustees of PEN America. Her 2003 memoir, *She's Not There*, was the first bestselling work by a transgender American.

Junior Brainard (Parenting Chapter Author) is a transgender man in Philadelphia, where he teaches community college English, is a co-president of his local union, and lives with his partner and four-year-old kid.

Sasha Buchert (Legal Issues Chapter Author) hails from lovely Portland, Oregon and is now an attorney fighting for trans rights at Lambda Legal in Washington, DC.

Tamar C. Carmel, MD (Former TBTS Board Member, Health and Wellness Section Editor) is a community psychiatrist and program creator and Medical Director of Mental Health Services at an LGBTQ + health center in Pittsburgh, Pennsylvania.

Sarah Cavar (they/them) (Disability Chapter Author) received their BA in critical social thought from Mount Holyoke College in 2020; a writer and peer mentor, their interests sit at the nexus of queer, trans, disability, and Mad studies.

Sand C. Chang, PhD (they/them) (Former TBTS Board Member, Who We Are Section Editor, Mental Health and Emotional Wellness Chapter Author) is a Chinese American, Oakland-based, nonbinary, genderfluid psychologist and trainer who specializes in gender, sexuality, trauma, and eating disorders.

Erica Chu (Arts and Culture Chapter Author) is a visiting lecturer in Gender and Women's Studies at the University of Illinois Chicago; they also teach English and Global Asian Studies courses.

A.C. Demidont (Medical Transition Chapter Author) is a Connecticut-based AMAB, Transfemme identifying, femme-drogynously expressing, Queer Radical Witch and Infectious Diseases/Internal Medicine Physician. Her journey as a LGBTQ healthcare practitioner, researcher, academician, and innovator has given her the opportunity to participate in everything from individual patient care to teaching healthcare professionals TGNC/Queer medicine to writing Connecticut guidelines for ending the HIV epidemic to creating a new and innovative LGBTQ healthcare center in Connecticut. She currently serves as Gilead Sciences' Principal Medical Scientist for HIV Prevention, covering New England and Upstate New York, and the Medical Chair of the Board of Directors for Anchor Health Initiative.

Qwo-Li Driskill (U.S. History Chapter Author) is a (non-citizen) Cherokee Two-Spirit writer, performer, and activist and an associate professor in Women, Gender, and Sexuality Studies at Oregon State University.

Alan Dunnigan (Living as Ourselves Section Editor) is a queer trans attorney advocating on behalf of unhoused people with disabilities in Oakland, California, and has been serving the LGBTQ community since 2006 with the LGBT National Hotline.

Ray Edwards, MA (TBTS First Edition Survey Coordinator) is a public health researcher studying the intersection of health insurance and gender affirming care. They worked as Survey Coordinator for the first edition of *Trans Bodies Trans Selves*, analyzing qualitative and quantitative data on issues faced by the transgender and gender nonconforming (TGNC) community that are presented in this book.

Laura Erickson-Schroth, MD, MA (Book Editor, TBTS Board Member, Sex and Gender Development Chapter Author) is a psychiatrist working in emergency medicine at Columbia University and at Hetrick-Martin Institute for LGBTQ youth.

T. Evan Smith (Sex and Gender Development Chapter Author) is a trans man who has a PhD in developmental psychology and is an associate professor of Psychology at Elizabethtown College.

Ezra Young, Esq. (Legal Issues Chapter Author) is a visiting assistant professor of law at Cornell Law School.

Kung Feng (Activism, Politics, and Organizing Chapter Author) is the executive director at Jobs with Justice San Francisco, a labor and community alliance that builds power for working class communities.

Miqqi Alicia Gilbert (aka Michael A. Gilbert) (Sex and Gender Development Chapter Author) is a professor emeritus in the Department of Philosophy at York University in Toronto, and a lifelong committed cross-dresser.

Nick Gorton (General, Sexual, and Reproductive Health Chapter Author) is a gay and transgender physician. In addition to his Emergency Medicine practice, he volunteers weekly as a primary care provider for transgender patients at Lyon-Martin Health Services. He is a lead clinician for TransLine, the National Clinical Consultation Line. He has worked as a medical consultant for the Transgender Law Center, the Sylvia Rivera Law Project, the New York Legal Aid Society, the ACLU, the Northwest Justice Project, Lambda Legal, and the National Center for Lesbian Rights. He is an active member of the World Professional Association for Transgender Health.

Sha Grogan-Brown (Art Editor) is an antiracist white queer trans dad from the Washington, DC area. He is the Deputy Director of Grassroots Global Justice Alliance (GGJ), and has worked to strengthen movements for social justice since the late 1990s.

Hilary Maia Grubb, MD (General, Sexual, and Reproductive Health Chapter Author) is a genderqueer psychiatrist and educator who provides clinical care to trans* and queer communities in the San Francisco Bay Area and develops curricula in cultural humility with gender diverse populations for mental health professionals.

Vern Harner, MSW (Survey Team Member) is a femme, nonbinary, and chronically ill PhD Candidate in Social Welfare at the University of Washington whose work focuses on trans intracommunity support.

Benji Hart (Activism, Politics, and Organizing Chapter Author) is a Black queer femme writer, artist, and educator living in Chicago, advocating and organizing for police and prison abolition.

Stephanie Luz Hernandez (TBTS Board Member) is a queer Latinx trans-femme and gender health therapist that works with trans & non-binary youth and adults at Kaiser's Multi-Specialty Transitions Department in Oakland, California, as well as in private practice.

Tobi Hill-Meyer (Sexuality Chapter Author) is an indigenous chicana trans woman with 15 years experience working in nonprofits, serving on boards, and consulting in nonprofit management. She is editor of the Lambda Literary Finalist anthology *Nerve Endings: The New Trans Erotic*, author of children's books *A Princess of Great Daring* and *Super Power Baby Shower*, and director of the award-winning erotic documentary series *Doing it Online*. Currently, she serves as Co-Executive Director for Gender Justice League.

Maria Carmen Hinayon (Immigration Chapter Author) is a California-based Filipina-American civil rights attorney who represents clients from the transgender community, LGBTQ + community, and communities of color. Aside from her legal education and training, Ms. Hinayon draws inspiration and perspective from her lived experiences as a transgender woman of color, immigrant, and survivor of discrimination, poverty, homelessness, and violence.

A. Ikaika Gleisberg, PhD (TBTS Board Member, Claiming Our Power Section Editor) is a queer and trans mixed-race activist-scholar of Kanaka ʻŌiwi descent who teaches in the Sociology and Sexuality Studies Department at San Francisco State University.

Paul Irons, MD (Medical Transition Chapter Author) is currently a urological surgery resident in the South, who previously worked with LGBTQ patients throughout the Northeast while in medical school, and plans to continue working with transgender patients in his career.

Kevin Johnson, MD (TBTS Board Member, Relationships and Families Section Editor, Short Piece Editor) is a queer, multiracial (Black and Hawaiian), māhū-identified addiction psychiatrist who lives and works in Upstate New York.

Mira C. Jourdan, PhD (Our Selves Chapter Author) is a board-certified neuropsychologist and consultant based in Michigan, who is passionate about supporting autistic people and traumatic brain injury patients, and who engages in public and organizational education and advocacy around gender and sexual diversity.

E. Kale Edmiston, PhD (Sex and Gender Development Chapter Author) is a trans neuroscientist and an assistant professor at the University of Pittsburgh, where he researches the brain in anxiety disorders.

Harper B. Keenan, PhD (Our Selves Chapter Author) has worked in the field of K–12 education for more than a decade and is currently an assistant professor of Gender and Sexuality Research in Education at the University of British Columbia.

Aidan Key (Children Chapter Author) is a gender educator, speaker, and author whose work centers on K–12 gender diverse children and their families. He is the founder of the long-running Gender Odyssey conference; offers national school and workplace trainings through gender-diversity.org; and operates his newly launching family support program, transfamilies.org.

Pony Knowles (Aging Chapter Author) is a gay trans man with a deep love for intersectional and intergenerational organizing, formerly the National Engagement Manager at SAGE, and currently the U.S. Campaigns Director at Change.org.

Kai Koumatos (Assistant Survey Editor) is a queer transman who currently works with homeless veterans in Northern California.

Mel Kutner (Survey Team Member) is a trans scholar and doctoral candidate in Critical Studies of Educational Theory and Practice at The University of Georgia who holds a Masters in Conflict Analysis and Resolution and has a background in special education research, policy, and technical assistance.

Jiz Lee (Sexuality Chapter Author) is a porn polymath and a key player in the queer porn movement. In their many years in the adult film industry, Jiz has worked as an adult film performer, producer, author, and speaker.

Andie Leslie (Intimate Relationships Chapter Author) is a nonbinary Latinx/black mixed-race person of color working as a therapist and training to become a clinical psychologist.

Ethan Czuy Levine (Survey Team Member) is a transmasculine Jewish atheist who advocates for abuse survivors and currently works as an assistant professor at Stockton University in New Jersey.

Nathan Levitt (Surgical Transition Chapter Author) is a queer, white, transgender Family Nurse Practitioner who is the Director of LGBTQ and Gender Justice Learning at Yale University School of Nursing and has been working in transgender health as a health care professional, trainer, educator, and advocate for over 20 years.

Joseph Liatela (Arts and Culture Chapter Author) is an artist and trans person based in New York City who makes work about the institutional, cultural, and medico-legal ideas of what is considered a "complete" or "correct" bodily formation, and is currently an MFA candidate at Columbia University.

Andrés C. López (U.S. History Chapter Author) is an Afro-Latinx trans and queer writer, poet, musician, and scholar whose activism, pedagogy, historiographic work, and artistic projects center the lives and experiences of queer and trans folks of color.

Jamie E. Mehringer, MD (Medical Transition Chapter Author) is a pediatrician and adolescent medicine specialist, and a member of the trans community.

Mx. Nillin Lore (Sexuality Chapter Author) is a queer, nonbinary, polyamorous, award-winning sex blogger and erotica author who also provides LGBTQIA + diversity training and inclusive sex education around the Canadian prairies.

G. Nic Rider, PhD (Youth Chapter Author) is an Asian American nonbinary/transmasculine queer licensed psychologist who works as an assistant professor at the Program in Human Sexuality at the University of Minnesota Medical School and Co-Associate Director of Research at the National Center for Gender Spectrum Health.

Kelsey Pacha, MA, MDiv (TBTS Board President, Survey Editor, Religion and Spirituality Chapter Author, Relationships and Families Section Editor) is the owner of Kelsey Pacha Consulting, providing cultural humility training, group facilitation, and policy guidance with special expertise at the nexus of gender, sexuality, religion, spirituality, and mental health.

Jules Purnell (Survey Team Member) is a nonbinary, queer clinical psychology PhD student. Their focus is in neuropsychology and promoting inclusive research and clinical practice.

Micah Rea, LMFT (Intimate Relationships Chapter Author) is a psychotherapist who works with queer and trans communities in the San Francisco Bay Area.

Romeo Romero (Race, Ethnicity, and Culture Chapter Author) is a gender-fluid Boricua/Jewish poet, educator, and restorative + transformative justice practitioner currently residing in Western Massachusetts.

Dean Scarborough (Sexuality Chapter Author) is a white, queer, nonbinary trans guy from the Bay Area who does sex education in their spare time.

Nathaniel G. Sharon (Mental Health and Emotional Wellness Chapter Author) is a pediatric psychiatrist who works to promote trans health education and health initiatives in New Mexico.

666

Jama Shelton (Survey Team Member) is an assistant professor at the Silberman School of Social Work at Hunter College and the associate director of the Silberman Center for Sexuality and Gender.

Sy Simms (Race, Ethnicity, and Culture Chapter Author) is a Black, Transgenderqueer, Afrofuturist, scholar-practitioner examining the roles of race and gender in higher education.

Anneliese Singh (she/they) (Life Stages Section Editor) is a genderqueer femme, mixed-race South Asian, Sikh American who serves as Chief Diversity Officer at Tulane University in New Orleans and is author of *The Queer and Trans Resilience Workbook* and *The Racial Healing Handbook*.

Avy A. Skolnik, PhD (Social Transition Chapter Author) is a trans psychologist working in college counseling in western Massachusetts.

Carey Jean Sojka, PhD (Intimate Relationships Chapter Author) is an assistant professor of Gender, Sexuality, and Women's Studies at Southern Oregon University whose research and teaching interests include transgender studies, embodiment, intersectionality, feminist and queer theory, activism, gender, sexuality, race, disability, and fatness. Sojka also founded the Trans and Queer Training program at Southern Oregon University, which provides trainings and consultation services to the region.

Nicole Sowers (Legal Issues Chapter Intern) is an LGBTQ student at Brooklyn Law School, class of 2021, who hopes to work in Civil Rights Law after graduation.

Kai Cheng Thom (Foreword) is an award-winning writer, performer, community worker, lasagna lover, and wicked witch who resides in Toronto. Kai Cheng's books have been featured in *The New York Times*, Emma Watson's *Our Shared Shelf* feminist book club, and on the CBC. Kai Cheng has worked extensively in the areas of gender-affirming health care and social services, mental health, and transformative justice.

Anastacia Tomson (Sex and Gender Development Chapter Author) is a medical doctor, author, and activist, who provides healthcare services for trans folk in South Africa, as well as education for students, health professionals, members of the South African judiciary, and the public.

Micah Vacatio, MSW, LICSW (Children Chapter Author) is a nonbinary, queer social worker working with the LGBTQ + community in rural Washington.

Reid Vanderburgh (Coming Out Chapter Author) is an honorary lesbian transman, married to a cisgender woman and proud to be a baritone in the Portland Gay Men's Chorus; he is the LGBT + Inclusion Specialist at Friendly House in Portland, Oregon working to ensure local senior housing options are safe and welcoming environments for LGBT + seniors.

Morgan Weinert, AGPCNP (Parenting Chapter Author) is a white, queer, and gender queer nurse practitioner from Saint Paul, Minnesota.

Gavin Weiser (Survey Team Member) is a queer scholar who grew up in New Jersey, spent formative years of their life in the South, and now lives in the Midwest.

Jillian Weiss, JD, PhD (Work and Employment Chapter Author) is a lawyer representing trans people in discrimination cases in federal courts around the country.

Lily Zheng (Work and Employment Chapter Author) is a queer, Chinese-American trans woman and Diversity, Equity, and Inclusion consultant based in the San Francisco Bay Area.

GLOSSARY

ABLEISM A set of beliefs or practices that devalue and discriminate against people with physical, intellectual, or psychiatric disabilities and often rest on the assumption that disabled people need to be "fixed" in one form or another.

ABOLITION A term that describes the movement that was organized to end the practice of slavery in the United States. Also used as a general term to describe a goal of social justice work (e.g., ending the prison industrial complex, halting the deportation of undocumented immigrants).

ADMIRER A term that describes a person who tends to be romantically and/or sexually attracted to transgender or gender expansive people. Some (but not all) admirers may be considered "chasers" (*See* chasers).

AFFIRMED GENDER A term describing a person's gender identity. Affirmed gender may or may not correspond with that person's gender assigned at birth.

AFFIRMED MALE/AFFIRMED FEMALE These terms describe a person's gender identity, rather than their gender assigned at birth. An affirmed male is someone who identifies as male while an affirmed female is someone who identifies as female, regardless of their birth-assigned genders.

AGENDER A term that describes a person who does not identify with or conform to any gender.

ALLY A person who helps to advocate for a particular group of people, such as the transgender or the LGBTQ community. Allies may help build more supportive climates and are often knowledgeable about issues or concerns.

ANDROGEN BLOCKERS *See* DHT blockers.

ANDROGYNOUS When a person has a gender expression that isn't clearly or stereotypically male or female within the context of the observer's culture. Usually involves combining masculine and feminine elements or characteristics. This term can also refer to objects or styles that are difficult to "gender" easily.

AROMANTIC A term that describes a person who does not experience interest in romantic relationships. May or may not be asexual.

ASEXUAL A term that describes a person who does not experience sexual attraction. May or may not be aromantic.

ASSIGNED FEMALE AT BIRTH (AFAB) Describes a person who was assigned a female gender at birth, typically based on outward appearance of their genitals. Also sometimes referred to as "designated female at birth" (DFAB) or "female assigned at birth" (FAAB).

ASSIGNED GENDER The gender that is given to an infant at birth, most often based on that person's external genitals. This may or may not match the person's gender identity in adulthood.

ASSIGNED MALE AT BIRTH (AMAB) Describes a person who was assigned a male gender at birth, typically based on outward appearance of their genitals. Also sometimes referred to as "designated male at birth" (DMAB) or "male assigned at birth" (MAAB).

ASSIGNED SEX The biological sex (male, female, intersex) that is given to an infant based on the appearance of the external genitals. Most infants are assigned a sex and gender at birth that match.

BALLROOM CULTURE/COMMUNITY An LGBTQ subculture in which events are held (also known as "balls") during which people compete for prizes. Participants "vogue," dance, or compete in various genres of drag. Many people involved in ball culture belong to a house, which is led by a house mother and/or father.

BDSM An acronym that represents a combination of multiple acronyms including B/D (Bondage & Discipline), D/s (Dominance & Submission), and S/M (Sadism & Masochism). BDSM is a catch-all umbrella term for a wide variety of sexual behaviors, relationship styles, fetishes, and kinks.

BIGENDER A term that describes those who feel they have two genders. They may move between masculine and feminine appearances or behavior depending on their feelings, location, or situation.

BINDING The process of using an elastic band, cloth, or special clothing (binder) in order to flatten the chest.

BIOLOGICAL SEX A term that describes a person's sex (male, female, intersex) based on physical or medical methods of distinguishing, such as chromosomes, genitals, or secondary sex characteristics. Because there are also likely biological contributions to gender identity, many prefer the term "assigned sex." (*See* gender identity).

BLACK AND INDIGENOUS PEOPLE OF COLOR (BIPOC) A term used in some circles to center specific groups of people of color who have traditionally been marginalized or discriminated against.

BISEXUAL (BI) A person who has the capacity to form sexual, romantic, and/or emotional attractions to those of the same gender or to those of another gender. Some consider this term to be specific to those who are attracted to cisgender men and cisgender women, while others use the term "bisexual" in a more inclusive way, similarly to the term "pansexual."

BITS A gender neutral term for genitals. "Big bits" and "little bits" are not euphemisms for "non-op trans women" or "non-op trans men." They refer to exactly what they say: people with larger or smaller genitals regardless of their surgical status or gender designation at birth.

BLENDING Being accepted as the gender you are without having to state your gender explicitly. Sometimes preferred over the term "passing" (*See* passing).

BLOCKERS A shortened form of "puberty blockers" (*See* puberty blockers).

BOI A versatile term used in different communities to mean slightly different things. Nonbinary people or young trans men sometimes describe themselves as bois. In gay culture, it can also describe a younger male who prefers older men and engages in a "daddy boi" relationship. In lesbian culture, it can be a self-identifier for butch women. Being a boi can signify feeling young, carefree, and sexually explorative.

BOTTOM A slang term with two distinct definitions. One refers to the person being penetrated. The other meaning of being a "bottom" refers to someone who takes a passive or submissive role during a scene.

BOTTOM SURGERY A term that refers to surgeries performed to alter genitals or internal reproductive organs.

BREAST AUGMENTATION A form of top surgery during which implants made of either silicone or saline are used to enhance the size of the breasts (also known as *breast implants*).

BUTCH A term that describes a person who appears and/or acts in a masculine manner. Used in various ways within different cultures, such as gay male and queer women's communities.

CARRY LETTER A document written by a medical provider or therapist that is used to state a person's transgender status without having to explain it directly to the person asking questions. A carry letter can be used to "validate" a person's gender identity while traveling or when interacting with government institutions.

CHASER (AKA TRANNY CHASER) People who engage in inappropriate or exploitive behavior as they pursue sex or relationships with T/GE people. Often used to describe straight men who seek out transgender women but do not treat them with respect.

CISGENDER (CIS) A person whose gender identity matches their birth-assigned sex.

CISNORMATIVITY A term that describes the assumption that all people are cisgender or that those assigned male at birth grow up to be men and those assigned female at birth grow up to be women.

CISSEXISM A system of bias in favor of cisgender people.

CLITEROPLASTY A form of bottom surgery where a clitoris is created. Typically performed at the same time as a vaginoplasty.

CLOCK/ED When a person is identified as trans while trying to present as their affirmed gender (also known as *being read*).

COCK-IDENTIFIED Someone who knows they have a cock, regardless of their gender identity or the shape of their genitals.

COLONIALISM Also known as "settler colonialism." The history of European countries forcibly extending their authority over Indigenous people and their territories for economic gain. This was done through means of violent genocide, assimilation, white supremacy, and erasure of Two Spirit identities.

COMING OUT To take a risk by sharing one's identity, sometimes to one person in conversation, sometimes to a group or in a public setting. Coming out is a life-long process—in each new situation a person must decide whether or not to risk coming out. Coming out can be difficult for some because reactions vary from complete acceptance and support to disapproval, rejection, or violence (*See* disclosure).

CONVERSION THERAPY A harmful form of therapy that focuses on convincing LGBTQ people that they have a mental illness and that their proper gender identity and/or sexuality is cisgender and heterosexual. Research has long demonstrated that conversion therapy is not only ineffective, but also psychologically damaging (also known as *reparative therapy*).

CROSS-DRESS (CROSS-DRESSING, CROSS-DRESSER) Wearing the clothes typically worn by another gender, sometimes only in our own homes, or as part of sexual play, and sometimes at public functions. Some people who identify as cross-dressers see themselves as part of transgender communities and some do not.

DEADNAMING The act of referring to someone by the name they used before they transitioned. This can be deliberate or accidental.

DEMIGUY/DEMIGIRL A term that describes someone who partially (but not fully) identifies as a guy (or girl), whatever their assigned gender at birth.

DEMISEXUAL A person who only feels sexually attracted to someone once they have an emotional connection.

DETRANSITION When someone decides to stop or reverse medical and/or surgical transition. This can be done for a number of reasons, including frustrations with side effects, loss of desire to physically transition, or fear of harassment or discrimination with transition.

DHT BLOCKERS Medications that block the effect of DHT (dihydrotestosterone), such as finasteride or dutasteride. These can be used by anyone on the trans spectrum to prevent hormone-related (aka "male-pattern") baldness.

DIAGNOSTIC AND STATISTICAL MANUAL OF MENTAL DISORDERS (DSM) A diagnostic tool created by the American Psychiatric Association that provides clinicians with a framework for understanding mental health issues and diagnoses. Many trans community members oppose the inclusion of gender-related diagnoses in the *DSM*.

DICKLET One name for the phallus of a trans man on testosterone. Also known as a "cocklet," "little cock," "little bit" or, in a more medical context, an enlarged clitoris.

DIHYDROTESTOSTERONE (DHT) A hormone that promotes the growth of male genitals before birth and also contributes to "male-pattern" baldness. Some on the transmasculine spectrum use DHT creams to enhance clitoral growth; however, DHT creams are not currently available in the United States and there is no clear evidence for their use.

DILATOR A piece of plastic or silicone that is used to maintain, lengthen, and stretch the size of the vagina after vaginoplasty. Dilators of increasing size are regularly inserted into the vagina at time intervals according to the surgeon's instructions. Dilation is required less frequently over time, but is recommended indefinitely (*See* vaginoplasty).

DIS/ABILITY A socially constructed category that separates out some people whose bodies or minds are seen by society as in need of "fixing."

DISCLOSURE The act or process of revealing one's identity to another person. Within trans communities, the term "disclosure" is commonly used to discuss sexual or romantic situations (*See* coming out).

DISORDER OF SEX DEVELOPMENT (DSD) A controversial term describing a medical condition that affects the congenital (in the womb) development of genitals or reproductive organs. Many consider the concept of having a "disorder" to be offensive and prefer the term "intersex" or the phrase "difference of sex development" (*See* intersex).

DOUBLE-INCISION TOP SURGERY (OR MASTECTOMY) A form of reconstructive chest surgery in which two incisions are made to remove breast tissue and fat, resulting in two scars under the line of the pectoral muscles. This procedure is typically chosen for bodies with more extra skin or larger chest sizes.

DRAG The act of dressing in typically over-the-top gendered clothing and adopting gendered behaviors as part of a performance, most often clothing and behaviors typically not associated with the person's gender identity. Drag can be performed for entertainment, as a political commentary, or for personal enjoyment.

DRAG KING A person who dresses in stereotypically masculine clothing for performance. Many drag kings are cis women or trans men, but people of all genders can perform as drag kings.

DRAG QUEEN A person who dresses in stereotypically feminine clothing for performance. Many drag queens are cis gay men, but people of all genders can perform as drag queens.

DYKE Initially a derogatory term, "dyke" has been reclaimed by some queer women to describe themselves. It continues to be used by those outside these communities in a negative way.

DYSPHORIA A state of unease, unhappiness, or dissatisfaction. Within trans communities, often used as part of the phrase "gender dysphoria," which is also a mental health diagnosis in the *Diagnostic and Statistical Manual of Mental Disorders (DSM)* (*See* gender dysphoria).

ELECTROLYSIS The process of applying a tiny amount of electricity to hair follicles, which destroys their ability to grow new hair.

ENBY A slang term for someone who identifies as nonbinary. It is a phonetic pronunciation of NB (*See* nonbinary).

ENDOCRINOLOGIST A type of physician who specializes in conditions that involve hormones and affect the endocrine system. Some endocrinologists (in addition to primary care providers) prescribe hormones for transition.

ESTROGEN/ESTRADIOL Traditionally considered a "female hormone," even though people of all genders have estrogen in their bodies. Transfeminine people may take estrogen to develop more feminine characteristics, such as breasts, softer skin, and a more feminine fat distribution pattern.

FACIAL FEMINIZATION SURGERY A diverse set of plastic surgery techniques that are performed to alter the jaw, chin, cheeks, forehead, nose, ears, lips, or other parts of the face to create a more feminine facial appearance.

FAG Initially a derogatory term, "fag" has been reclaimed by some gay men to describe themselves. It continues to be used by those outside gay communities in a negative way.

FEMALE-TO-MALE (FTM, F2M) A term that describes someone who was assigned a female sex and gender at birth and currently has a male gender identity. People who are FTM may or may not have had surgery or taken hormones to physically alter their appearances. The acronym FTM is often used in medical or research communities (*See* trans man).

FEMININE A term that describes behavior, dress, qualities, or attitudes that one associates with women. What is considered feminine differs based on one's culture, race/ethnicity, and environment.

FEMINISM Belief in and advocacy for gender equality.

FEMINIZE The process of making someone or something appear or act more feminine. Examples include putting on make-up, dressing in women's clothes, or taking estrogen.

FEMME A person who takes on a traditionally feminine role or works to have a feminine appearance. In queer women's communities, the term is used to describe feminine appearing or behaving lesbians.

FRONT HOLE A term that can be used to describe an orifice in the genital region. Some people call it the vagina, pussy, cunt, snatch, box, or any number of other terms based on personal preference.

GAFF A type of tight underwear that helps keep the penis tucked between the legs (*See* tucking).

GATEKEEPER/GATEKEEPING The concept that a medical or mental health provider has the potential to restrict or restrain people from obtaining hormones or access to surgery to transition (*See* informed consent).

GAY A person who is attracted sexually/erotically and/or emotionally to people of the same gender. More often used to refer to a male identified person who is attracted to other men.

GENDER A set of social, psychological, and emotional traits, often influenced by societal expectations, that classify an individual as feminine, masculine, androgynous, or other identities.

GENDER AFFIRMING SURGERY (GAS) Surgical procedures that help us adjust our bodies in a way that more closely matches our gender identity. Not every transgender person desires surgery.

GENDER BENDING Playing with gender roles through personal gender expression, fashion, art, and media.

GENDER BINARY The concept that in our society there are only two genders, male and female, and that everyone has to be either one or the other.

GENDER CONFIRMING SURGERY (GCS) A variation on the phrase "gender affirming surgery."

GENDER DISSONANCE A distressed state arising from conflict between a person's gender identity and their sex assigned at birth.

GENDER DYSPHORIA A phrase used in different ways by various groups. Trans communities often use "gender dysphoria" to describe feelings of discomfort about one's body or assigned gender. Gender dysphoria is also a mental health diagnosis that is defined as a "sense of discomfort in one's body and with one's own gender identity." It has replaced gender identity disorder in the *Diagnostic and Statistical Manual of Mental Disorders (DSM)* and its presence in the *DSM* is controversial.

GENDER EUPHORIA The feeling of comfort or joy that accompanies being able to present as one's affirmed gender.

GENDER EXPANSIVE A term that describes people who identify or express themselves in ways that broaden the culturally defined behavior or expression associated with one gender.

GENDER EXPRESSION Refers to an individual's physical characteristics, behaviors, and presentation. This can include one's appearance, dress, mannerisms, speech patterns, and social interactions, which are linked, traditionally, to masculinity, femininity, or somewhere in-between.

GENDER FLUID Someone who embodies characteristics of multiple genders, or shifts in gender identity.

GENDER IDENTITY Our inner sense of being male, female, both, or neither.

GENDER IDENTITY DISORDER (GID) A previously used controversial diagnosis for those who may identify as T/GE. It was defined as having a "strong and persistent cross-gender identification," with "persistent discomfort with his/her sex or sense of inappropriateness in the gender role of that sex." It has since been replaced by gender dysphoria as a clinical diagnosis in the *Diagnostic and Statistical Manual of Mental Disorders (DSM)*.

GENDER INCONGRUENCE A diagnosis in the *International Classification of Diseases (ICD-11)* that replaces older diagnoses such as "transsexualism" and "gender identity disorder" and appears in a new chapter titled, "Conditions related to sexual health" rather than "Mental and behavioral disorders." Some feel that this new diagnosis decreases stigma while still ensuring access to gender-affirming health care and health insurance coverage of transition-related services.

GENDER MARKER A legal indicator of one's gender. This can include one's gender on a passport, birth certificate, state ID, or insurance card. Many of us have to jump through various legal hoops in order to change our gender markers on these documents.

GENDER NONCONFORMING An umbrella term that describes those who are not cisgender or who push up against gender norms.

GENDER NORMS Societal expectations, often grounded in cisnormativity, about how people of different designated genders are supposed to act, live, and look (*See* cisnormativity).

GENDER POLICING Enforcing gender norms and attempting to impose gender-based behaviors on another person.

GENDER PRESENTATION Gendered outward appearance and behavior, which may or may not match gender identity (*See* gender expression).

GENDER ROLES Positions we take in social relationships based on our genders, such as men being the income earners or women taking responsibilities for housekeeping. The masculinity or femininity of specific roles in our societies differs based on our cultures and/or geographic locations.

GENDER SCHEMA A psychological framework that helps us learn and understand the concept of gender. Children develop schemas for gender that link certain behaviors and traits together under the schemas for male (or "boy") and female (or "girl"). Their schemas then, in turn, influence how they experience events and how they interact with the world.

GENDER SPECIALIST A health professional who specializes in gender issues. Some of us may seek gender specialists to discuss gender issues, to help with transition, to find a place of comfort in whatever gender or body fits best, or to discuss coming out to others. There is no specific training program to call yourself a "gender specialist" and not everyone who advertises as a gender specialist is well-trained, but there are multiple online forums to find out more about a particular provider.

GENDER SPECTRUM The wide range of gender identities and expressions beyond the normative binary of "male" and "female."

GENDER STEREOTYPES Assumptions, expectations, or beliefs that a person will act or appear a certain way because of that person's gender or perceived gender.

GENDER THEORY The study of what is understood as masculine and/or feminine and/or queer behavior in any given context, community, society, or field of study (including, but not limited to, literature, history, sociology, education, applied linguistics, religion, health sciences, philosophy, and cultural studies).

GENDER VARIANT A term that describes those who dress, behave, or express themselves in a way that does not conform with dominant gender norms. Some people like the term "variant" while others find it offensive (*See* gender nonconforming).

GENDERFUCKING Refers to the act of "fucking with" or playing around with gender expression or gender roles. Includes purposefully playing with gender, wearing clothes we are not supposed to wear, or acting in ways that people don't expect. It can be done for fun and/or used as a political statement to mock the concept of a gender binary.

GENDER NEUTRAL Applying to all genders. Can refer to language (including pronouns), items (such as children's toys), or spaces (such as bathrooms).

GENDERQUEER A term that is sometimes used to describe someone who defines their gender outside the constructs of male and female (*See* nonbinary).

GENITAL RECONSTRUCTION Surgery that is directed at altering the physical appearance of one's external genitals (*See* gender affirming surgery).

HATE CRIME An act of violence or vandalism that is targeted against a social group or motivated by prejudice. In 2009, U.S. Federal hate crime legislation was amended to include sexual orientation and gender identity. Hate crime legislation is somewhat controversial due to its disproportionate enforcement against people of color. Those critical of mass incarceration believe that hate crime legislation perpetuates the prison industrial complex.

HETEROFLEXIBLE A term used to describe someone who is largely attracted those of another gender but expresses curiosity and/or interest in people of the same gender.

HETEROGENDER A term that refers to relationships that involve two people with different gender identities.

HETERONORMATIVITY The worldview or assumption that everyone is heterosexual until proven otherwise.

HETEROSEXISM A term that applies to attitudes, bias, and discrimination in favor of heterosexual sexuality and relationships. It includes the presumption that everyone is heterosexual and that heterosexual attractions and relationships are the norm and therefore superior.

HETEROSEXUAL A person who is attracted to those of another sex, gender identity, or expression. Sometimes shortened to "hetero" by queer communities when talking about straight communities.

HOMOPHOBIA The fear or hatred of people who are not heterosexual or don't appear heterosexual, which can lead to discrimination, rejection, and/or violence.

HOMOSEXUAL A person who is attracted to others of the same sex, gender identity, or expression.

HORMONE REPLACEMENT THERAPY (HRT) Medications that are similar to hormones produced by the body. HRT can be taken for transition or for other medical purposes, such as menopause.

HORMONE A chemical that serves as a messenger in the body. Hormones send instructions to various tissues and organs in the body and promote physical changes, including the development of gender-related characteristics such as breasts and body hair.

HOUSE (BALLROOM) *See* ballroom culture.

HYSTERECTOMY AND SALPINGO-OOPHORECTOMY (HSO) A form of bottom surgery that involves removing the uterus, ovaries, and fallopian tubes. This procedure is most often performed if there is concern for cancer, but can also be a gender-affirming procedure.

IMPERIALISM An ideology of extending a country's power and influence by military force, diplomacy, and/or economic control.

INDIGENOUS A term used as a broader category to define genealogical ties to original inhabitants/land/creation myths of a given area. May be used as a self-descriptor by those whose ancestors lived on the same land they do.

INFORMED CONSENT A model of care that assumes clients are able to make informed choices about their own health care as long as they do not have temporary or permanent conditions that prevent them from doing so. Clinicians who practice using informed consent models help their clients understand the risks and benefits of their healthcare choices (such as taking hormones or getting surgeries). This deviates from the controversial "gatekeeper" model of health care, which often requires mental health professionals to assess transgender people and decide if they are appropriate for hormone therapy or gender-affirming surgeries.

INTERSECTIONALITY A sociological concept that describes the ways in which different oppressive ideologies (e.g., transphobia, racism, homophobia, sexism, classism, ageism) interact with one another and are inseparable.

INTERSEX A general term used for a variety of situations in which a person is born with a reproductive or sexual anatomy that doesn't fit typical definitions of female or male. Examples include a person who is born with ambiguous external genitalia or a person who may appear female on the outside, but have male reproductive organs. Intersex people vary in how they self-define, some using the term "intersex" and others more comfortable with "disorder of sex development" or "difference of sex development" (DSD) (*See* disorder of sex development).

KIKI A subset of the ballroom community specifically started by and for LGBTQ youth in order to create a less competitive, fun space to enjoy themselves (*See* ballroom culture).

KINKY A descriptor of sexual desires and practices that are not generally considered normative. Many self-described kinky people, or those who engage in kink, are affiliated with BDSM communities.

LABIAPLASTY A form of bottom surgery where labia are created, typically as part of a vaginoplasty.

LASER HAIR REMOVAL A process of hair removal that involves using a laser to destroy hair follicles.

LATINX A person of Latin American origin or descent (used as a gender-neutral or nonbinary alternative to Latino or Latina).

LESBIAN An identity term used by some people who are female identified and who are attracted sexually/erotically and/or emotionally to other women.

LGBT/GLBT, LGBTQIA Umbrella terms that refer to people who identify as lesbian, gay, bisexual, transgender, queer/questioning, intersex, asexual, and/or allies.

MALE-TO-FEMALE (MTF, M2F) A term that describes someone who was assigned a male sex and gender at birth and currently has a female gender identity. People who are MTF may or may not have had surgery or taken hormones to physically alter their appearances. The acronym MTF is often used in medical or research communities (*See* trans woman).

MASCULINE A term that describes behavior, dress, qualities, or attitudes that one associates with men. What is considered masculine differs based on one's culture, race/ethnicity, and environment.

MASCULINE OF CENTER An evolving definition that recognizes the cultural breadth and depth of identity for lesbian/queer womyn and gender nonconforming/trans people who tilt toward the masculine side of the gender spectrum. This term includes a wide range of identities such as butch, stud, aggressive/AG, macha, dom, boys like us, trans masculine, boi, etc.

MASCULINIZE The concept of instilling or adding more masculine characteristics. This may include (but is not limited to) wearing masculine clothing, having masculine hair styles, growing facial hair, or taking male hormones (e.g., testosterone or DHT).

MEDICAL TRANSITION The process of taking hormones or going through surgical procedures in order to change one's body in a way that affirms one's gender identity.

METOIDIOPLASTY A form of bottom surgery that involves lengthening the clitoris (or phallus). The procedure may include a "urethral hookup," in which the urethra is extended through the phallus, allowing for standing urination. It may also include a scrotoplasty, which involves cosmetically reconstructing a scrotal sac with or without testicular implants.

MICROAGGRESSION A comment or action that subtly and often unconsciously or unintentionally expresses a prejudiced attitude against members of a marginalized group.

MINORITY STRESS THEORY A psychological theory that suggests that those who belong to oppressed, marginalized, or minority communities (including T/GE communities) are at greater risk of mental issues because of our higher risk of being subjected to chronic stress, stigma, discrimination, violence, and/or prejudice.

MISC OR MX Gender neutral titles that can be used in the place of Mr. or Ms. Misc and Mx are pronounced (misk) and (mix) respectively.

MISGENDER The act of incorrectly gendering someone either intentionally or unintentionally.

MISOGYNY The hatred, dislike, or distrust of women or girls. Misogynistic acts can include physical violence, discrimination, sexual objectification, or oppression.

MISPRONOUN Intentionally or unintentionally using the wrong pronouns to describe someone.

MONOGAMISH A term coined by advice columnist Dan Savage to refer to relationships that are primarily monogamous but may allow for sexual and/or romantic relationships outside the partnership on a limited basis.

MONOGAMOUS Having one sexual/romantic partner at a time.

MUFFING A slang term for penetration of the inguinal canal. The inguinal canal is the passage through which testes descend from the abdomen, and into which testes are typically pushed when tucking.

NEOPRONOUN A term used to classify "new" pronouns used in English. Neopronouns can include gender-neutral pronouns (i.e. theythey, xe/xym) as well as pronouns that do not reference gender (sometimes called "noun-self pronouns," such as cloud/cloudself or vamp/vampself). Noun-self pronouns can reflect a person's connection to nature, fandom, or other interests, and are highly individualized.

NEUTROIS The concept of having a neutral gender. As opposed to androgynous, which combines masculine and feminine characteristics, neutrois has neither. Some people who identify as neutrois seek to have gender neutral bodies (*See* agender).

NEURODIVERSE/NEURODIVERSITY A concept that emphasizes natural diversity in the human mind and depathologizes natural variance in information and sensory processing, as well as interpersonal communication.

NEURODIVERGENT/NEURODIVERGENCE A term used to describe those whose minds function in a way that diverges from the dominant societal standard of "normal." Neurodivergent individuals, such as people with autism, often face societal oppression compared to neurotypical individuals.

NONBINARY Can be used to describe terms such as titles or pronouns, or as a self-identifier. Those who identify as nonbinary may see themselves as not fitting into the gender binary or may oppose the idea of the gender binary.

NONGENDERED *See* neutrois or agender.

NON-MONOGAMOUS Used to describe people or relationships where there are other arrangements than monogamy.

OF TRANS EXPERIENCE (MAN OR WOMAN) A way of describing one's experience being transgender without forcing that person to label themselves as transgender. Some may identify as men or women "of trans experience," as affirmed males or affirmed females, or simply as males or females.

ORCHIECTOMY A form of bottom surgery that involves removing the testicles and, in some cases, the scrotal sac. This operation may eliminate the need for testosterone blockers by taking out the testes, which are the main site of production of testosterone.

OUT The concept of having others know your true sexual orientation or gender identity. Being out is not always all or nothing. One may be out to no one, to a few people, or to a larger group.

OVARY An internal organ that produces estrogen, progesterone, and other hormones, and is home to eggs for reproduction.

PACKING Putting things in the crotch of our pants to create the outward appearance of a penis and testicles. This look can be achieved with a pair of socks, and there are also "packers" made out of silicone or other materials.

PANSEXUAL Describes those who have the potential to be attracted to people of many sexes or genders.

PARTY RIDGE A nongendered term for the g-spot, also known as the urethral sponge. This anatomical structure is simply a cushion of sensitive erectile tissue around the urethra. Everybody has one, regardless of gender or genital shape.

PASSING When a person can appear in the general public and not be identified, read, or "clocked" as transgender. Passing can be a controversial concept, because it enforces cisnormativity, but can also provide safety from violence (*See* clock/ed and blending).

PATHOLOGIZATION The act of pathologizing something, making it into a diagnosis or a thing to be fixed or cured. In the context of trans health, many feel that having a gender-related diagnosis in the *Diagnostic and Statistical Manual of Mental Disorders (DSM)* pathologizes normal gender differences. Many trans community members and allies hope to depathologize trans identity.

PENECTOMY A form of bottom surgery that removes the penis with or without reconstructive efforts to create a labia or vagina. Penectomies are now rarely performed in the United States, having been replaced by vaginoplasties.

PEOPLE OF COLOR (POC) A term designed to be an umbrella or catch-all term for those who are not "white" or predominately of European descent. It includes a diverse group of people from multiple ethnicities, races, and backgrounds.

PERFORMATIVITY/PERFORMANCE The concept, developed by philosopher Judith Butler, that gender is socially constructed through repeated performance by many people over time in a society. Butler is not arguing that gender is not "real" or that we are consciously performing gender, but instead that, over time, throughout history, the concept of gender has been created and continues to be created by societies, rather than stemming from clear biological origins.

PERIAREOLAR (KEYHOLE) TOP SURGERY A form of top surgery that involves removing breast tissue and forming a male-contoured chest. In this specific procedure, primarily for those with small chests, tissue is removed by making a small incision around the nipple, and there is minimal scarring.

PHALLOPLASTY A form of bottom surgery that involves the creation of a penis using donor skin from elsewhere on the body.

POLYAMOROUS Having more than one sexual, romantic, or emotional relationship at a time. Polyamory generally involves consent from all parties and is not considered "cheating."

POST-OPERATIVE (POST-OP) A term that means "after surgery." It can be used to label someone who has undergone gender-related surgery. Many trans communities have stopped using this term because it can contribute to hierarchies and divisions and can suggest that some of us are not "really" trans if we have not had surgeries.

PREFERRED GENDER PRONOUNS (PGPs) *See* pronoun.

PREMARIN A form of estrogen that comes from horses, also known as conjugated equine estrogen.

PRE-OPERATIVE (PRE-OP) A term that means "before surgery." It can be used to label someone who has not undergone gender-related surgery. Many trans communities have stopped using this term because it can contribute to hierarchies and divisions and can suggest that some of us are not "really" trans if we have not had surgeries.

PRIVILEGE Refers to advantages conferred by society to certain groups solely based on a part of their identity, such as their gender, race, ethnicity, ability, social class, or financial status. These advantages are conferred by society and not seized by individuals, which makes it difficult to see one's own privilege.

PROGESTERONE A hormone that is sometimes taken by those on the transfeminine spectrum.

PRONOUN A word that can be used in place of a noun or a person's name. In the English language, some pronouns are associated with a particular gender identity (i.e., him, her, he, she, etc.) while others are gender neutral (i.e., they, hir, ze, zim, etc.) or do not reference gender (i.e. noun pronouns such as bun/bunself or kitten/kittenself). The term "preferred gender pronoun" (PGP) has fallen out of favor because the word "preferred" can suggest that pronouns are not important or that they are simply preferred rather than correct.

PROSTATE An organ responsible for secreting seminal fluid to nourish and transport sperm in those assigned male at birth.

PUBERTY BLOCKERS Medications that delay puberty by blocking the effects of hormones that initiate it. Blockers are sometimes prescribed to young people who identify as transgender and want to delay puberty (also called puberty inhibitors, puberty suppressors, or hormone blockers).

QUEER A term that has historically been used as a slur against those in the LGBTQ community. It has more recently been reclaimed by many communities and is used as a positive umbrella term/identity.

QUEER THEORY An area of academia/scholarship that analyzes various fields of study through a queer lens.

REAL LIFE EXPERIENCE (RLE) A period of time during which transgender individuals start to live full-time as their desired gender before starting hormone therapy or having gender-related surgery. Health providers used to require us to go through a real life experience in order to "qualify" for hormones or surgery. This requirement has since fallen out of favor; however, some providers and surgeons still insist on it (also known as real life test or RLT).

RECONSTRUCTIVE CHEST SURGERY A form of top surgery that involves removing breast tissue and forming a male-contoured chest (*See* double-incision and periareolar (keyhole) top surgery).

REPARATIVE THERAPY *See* conversion therapy.

SAME-GENDER LOVING (SGL) A term that describes someone who is sexually, romantically, or emotionally attracted to people of the same gender. The term is more frequently used in communities of color.

SECONDARY SEX CHARACTERISTIC A gendered part or characteristic of the body that develops during puberty. We often take hormones to help us develop secondary sex characteristics of our desired gender.

SEX Refers to biological, genetic, or physical characteristics that define males and females. These can include genitals, hormone levels, genes, or secondary sex characteristics.

SEX CHANGE (SURGERY) A term that may be considered offensive (*See* gender affirming surgery).

SEX REASSIGNMENT SURGERY (SRS) An older term that may still appear on some websites and brochures (*See* gender affirming surgery).

SEX WORKER/SEX WORK Adults who exchange consensual sexual services for money or goods. Many activists have organized around decriminalizing sex work to promote worker safety and human rights. Not to be confused with human trafficking, which includes nonconsensual acts such as violence, forced labor, or sexual exploitation.

SEXISM Discrimination based on a person's perceived sex.

SEXUAL ORIENTATION Who we are attracted or oriented to sexually, erotically, or emotionally.

SIGNIFICANT OTHERS, FAMILY, FRIENDS, AND ALLIES (SOFFA) Designation for people who are not necessarily trans-identified but who are close to us and part of our lives. May be used to search for support groups.

SILICONE Material that can be pumped into certain parts of the body (face, butt, breasts, thighs, etc.) to enhance appearance. Although the term "silicone" can refer to medical-grade silicone, it is also frequently used to describe other chemicals that are injected into the body, including bathtub sealant or fix-a-flat. This is controversial and often dangerous. Silicone is also a material that is often used to make sex toys.

SILICONE INJECTION Refers to the injection of silicone (and sometimes other substances) into certain parts of the body for enhancement.

SOCIAL CONSTRUCTION The concept that society has "created" or "developed" certain concepts that some may believe are from nature because of their long and entrenched history. For example, gender is a social construct that we continue to rely on to tell men and women how to act. Other socially constructed concepts include race, sexual orientation, and socioeconomic status.

SOCIAL TRANSITION Transitioning in the context of everyday life and social spaces, without necessarily taking steps to medically transition. Social transition can include using new names or pronouns, changing the clothes we wear, and making legal updates to our IDs and birth certificates.

SPIRONOLACTONE (SPIRO) A medication that is often used to block the effects of testosterone in transgender women. It may be taken in conjunction with estrogen.

STAND TO PEE (STP) DEVICE A device that aids the user in urinating while standing up. These may be do-it-yourself creations or store-bought.

STEALTH A term used to describe T/GE individuals who are not out to others or only out to some. Some may work very hard to "pass" or appear cisgender so they are not discovered. There are many reasons people choose to live stealth, including safety.

STRAIGHT Being attracted to people of the same gender or sex (i.e., heterosexual).

SURGICAL TRANSITION The process of going through surgical procedures in order to change one's body in a way that affirms one's gender identity.

SWITCH Someone who enjoys both topping and bottoming. This may also refer to someone who likes penetrating other people and being penetrated, or to someone who likes being both dominant and submissive.

TESTOSTERONE (T) The traditional "male hormone," though everyone has a certain amount of testosterone. T is often taken by those on the transmasculine spectrum to develop more masculine physical characteristics such as body hair, deeper voices, and a more masculine fat distribution pattern.

TESTOSTERONE BLOCKER Medications that block the effects of testosterone. The most commonly used in the United States is spironolactone.

T-GIRL A colloquial term used in some trans women's communities to describe themselves.

THEY/THEM The most commonly used gender-neutral pronouns.

THIRD GENDER/THIRD SEX A term that incorporates genders other than male or female. Third genders exist around the world and include the Fa'afafine in Samoa, Kathoey or Ladyboys in Thailand, Hijras in India and Pakistan, Two Spirit people in North America, and many more. Some people in the United States, especially in communities of color, use the term "third gender" to self identify.

TOP A slang term with two distinct definitions. One refers to the person doing the penetrating during penetrative sex of any kind. The other refers to the partner who takes an active role.

TOP SURGERY A term that refers to surgeries performed on our chests. These can include breast augmentation and reconstructive chest surgery, though the term "top surgery" is more commonly used in transmasculine than in transfeminine communities.

TRACHEAL SHAVE A procedure that minimizes the thyroid cartilage that makes up the Adam's apple. Also known as an Adam's Apple Reduction, Thyroid Cartilage Reduction (TCR), or chondrolaryngoplasty.

TRANNY A colloquial term used to describe T/GE people. It has a particular history of being used as a slur or insult toward trans women, though some trans women have adopted the term to describe themselves.

TRANS A shortened form of the word transgender.

TRANS AMOROUS A term that describes those who are romantically, emotionally, or sexually attracted to trans people, including T/GE people themselves.

TRANS AND GENDER NONCONFORMING (TGNC) A phrase used as an umbrella term to describe a spectrum of gender identities, often in the context of youth work and youth spaces.

TRANS BOY A young trans person assigned female at birth who identifies as male.

TRANS-EXCLUSIONARY RADICAL FEMINIST (TERF) A person who considers themself a feminist but excludes trans women from women's spaces and organizations, and does not advocate for the rights of trans women along with cis women.

TRANS FAG/TRANS DYKE Terms sometimes used by trans-identified people who also identify as lesbian, gay, bisexual, or queer.

TRANS FRIENDLY Describes a person or agency/business that is either an ally to transgender communities or tolerant/accepting of those who are transgender.

TRANS GIRL A young trans person assigned male at birth who identifies as female.

TRANS GUY A colloquial term for a trans man.

TRANS MAN A person assigned female at birth who identifies as male.

TRANS WOMAN A person assigned male at birth who identifies as female.

TRANS PEOPLE OF COLOR (TPOC) A phrase sometimes used to describe trans people who identify as people of color (POC).

TRANS* An asterisk is added to the word trans by some groups to signify a diversity of trans experiences.

TRANSFEMININE Describes those who fall on the feminine end of the trans spectrum. Most commonly refers to people assigned male at birth.

TRANSFEMINISM An approach to feminism that integrates trans politics and viewpoints.

TRANSGENDER A broad umbrella term that can be used to describe people whose gender identity is different from their sex assigned at birth. Transgender people may or may not choose to alter their bodies hormonally and/or surgically. People must self-identify as transgender in order for the term to be appropriately used to describe them.

TRANSGENDER AND GENDER EXPANSIVE (T/GE) The phrase this book uses as an umbrella term to describe our communities.

TRANSGENDERED A form of the word transgender that is considered incorrect or offensive by many transgender communities.

TRANSITION The process one goes through to discover and/or affirm one's gender identity. This can, but does not always, include taking hormones or having surgeries.

TRANSLATINA/O/@/X An identity that combines one's experience being trans and being Latinx.

TRANSMASCULINE Describes those who fall on the masculine end of the trans spectrum. Most commonly refers to people assigned female at birth.

TRANS-MISOGYNY A term coined by trans activist Julia Serano, which describes a form of misogyny directed at trans women.

TRANSPHOBIA Fear, hatred, or discrimination based on our status as T/GE people.

TRANSSEXUAL A older term that has been mostly replaced by the word transgender. In the past, it was used to refer to those trans people who had undergone surgeries, but over time communities fought against this type of hierarchy. This term is now considered offensive by some trans people, though others continue to use it to describe themselves.

TRANSVESTITE An older term originally describing someone who cross-dresses. In the 1960s and 1970s it was sometimes used as a self-identifier by transgender people before other terms became more popular. It has fallen out of favor and is considered offensive.

TUCKING The process of rearranging one's penis and testicles in a way that avoids the appearance of a bulge in clothing. This is mostly done to give the body a more feminine-appearing profile.

TWO SPIRIT An umbrella term used to describe Indigenous North Americans with a multitude of gender roles, identities, and expressions. Those who identify as Two Spirit tend to embody both masculine and feminine spirits and characteristics. Two Spirit is an example of a third gender category.

VAGINECTOMY A form of bottom surgery that involves removing the vagina. This surgery is less common than other bottom surgeries for those assigned female at birth.

VAGINOPLASTY A form of bottom surgery that involves creating a vagina. It is typically accompanied by a cliteroplasty (creation of a clitoris) and a labiaplasty (creation of labia).

WORLD PROFESSIONAL ASSOCIATION FOR TRANSGENDER HEALTH (WPATH) An international professional organization dedicated to transgender health. WPATH produces a "Standards of Care" document that is often used by medical clinics and insurance companies.

SUGGESTIONS

Trans Bodies, Trans Selves would love to hear from you about your experience with this book so that we can make each edition better. Please send comments and suggestions to info@transbodies.com.

INDEX

Tables and figures boxes are indicated by *t* and *f* following the page number

and trust in mental health providers, 399–401, 552

Confucianism, 120–21

congenital adrenal hyperplasia (CAH), 140–41

Congregation Beit Simchat Torah (CBST), 107

consent. *See also* informed consent
  sexual, 79, 447–49, 467–68, 550–51

constellating, 585

constitution, 240

contraception. *See* birth control/contraception

Convention Against Torture and Other Cruel, Inhuman, or Degrading Treatment or Punishment (CAT), 65–66

conversion (reparative) therapy, 147, 150, 255, 382, 552

Cook-Daniels, Loree, 566

Cosgrove, Azrael ("Az"), 79f

Cosgrove, Reo, 452–53

countertransference, 398–99

courts, 240–42. *See also* Supreme Court
  how cases move through the, 240
  intersectionality and making better arguments in court, 260
  state, 240–42

COVID-19 pandemic, xi, 204, 601–2, 654–55

Cox, Laverne, 61, 605f, 632

Coxx, Papi, 445f, 446

Crafty Queer, 625

creative writing as activism, 616–19

Crenshaw, Kimberlé Williams, 17, 34, 259

criminal justice reforms, 248–51

crisis hotlines, 258, 428, 430. *See also* hotlines; Trans Lifeline

critical disability studies, 69–71

cross-dressing, 30, 106, 591. *See also* drag queens

cryobanks and cryopreservation, 485–88. *See also* egg freezing; sperm freezing

Cull, Matthew, 656–57

Culley, Blake, 70

cult of domesticity, 590–91

cultural representation. *See* representation

culture, 33–34, 614. *See also* trans art and culture; *specific topics*
  acknowledging our transcestors, 30–31, 33

"cure," 77, 134, 382, 520, 566, 592. *See also* conversion (reparative) therapy
  disability and, 68–69, 72, 77, 80, 85
  enforcing normativity through cures and treatments, 80
  forging pathways beyond, 85

D

DaBrooke, Faith, 199, 629

Daoism, 120

DapperQ magazine, 188

dating (and trans identity), 413
  disclosing while, 416–18
  flirting, hooking up, and, 452–63
  gender norms, socialization, and, 419–0
  loving our bodies, 413–14
  other trans people, 421–22
  within queer communities, 422
  among youth, 548–49

dating communities, trans-friendly, 423

dating partners
  having multiple, 423–24, 448
  potential, 416, 420–21

Davis, Angela Y., 591

Davis, Benjamin, 130

Davis, Mike, 601

Day, Dorothy, 643

deadnaming, 195

deafness
  deaf, trans, and disabled, 84
  growing up transgender and deaf, 70

death. *See* dying with dignity

Death and Life of Marsha P. Johnson, The (film), 596

deferral of removal (immigration), 65–66

dehiscence (wound separation), 350, 354

DeLarverie, Stormé, 594

demeter, justin, 167, 235f

denial of child's gender identity difference, 505–6

Department of Health and Human Services (HHS), 242, 274, 527

depathologization. *See* pathologization

deportation, 58

depression, 387

dermal fillers, 364–65

desexualization, 78–80

Desi LGBTQ Helpline, 115

Desjardins, Amber, 77–78

de-transitioning, 22

"deviance," 562, 564, 566, 592

Devor, Aaron H., 161, 545, 597f

de Vries, Kylan Mattias, 143f

Diagnostic and Statistical Manual of Mental Disorders (DSM), 74
  DSM-5, 74, 517, 606

Digital Transgender Archive, 564, 603

dihydrotestosterone (DHT), 141
  DHT blocker, 320
  effects on hair, 324

dildos, 464, 465f. *See also* sex toys

Dillon, Michael, 117

direct action, 651, 652
  types of, 651–52

disability (and transness), 68
  "cure" and, 68–69, 72, 77, 80, 85
  and denial of health care, 81–83 (*see also* gatekeeping)

and diagnosing problems, 259–61
disabilities and, 71, 72, 79, 84, 86–88
importance, 42, 48, 258
lawyers' use of, 258, 259, 260
meanings and uses of the term, 17, 34
origin of the term, 17, 34, 259, 587, 598
power, privilege, and, 427–28
as a tool, 258–61

strengths and resilience, 385–86 (*see also* resilience)

transitioning and, 397–98

mental health care
    access concerns, 405
    seeking professional help, 399–1
    for youth, 552

mental health concerns, common, 386–397

mental health diagnoses, gender-related, 517

mental health professionals
    behaviors of affirming vs. nonaffirming/pathologizing, 401
    gatekeeping and, 336, 380–575
    open-ended questions to ask potential, 518–19
    roles and approaches, 400–1
    T/GE children and, 517–19

mental health stigma in trans communities, 380–83

mentoring LGBTQ+ youth, 644

Mesner, Kerr, 123

Methodist Church, 110

metoidioplasty, 356, 361*f*
    additional procedures with, 360–63

Metropolitan Community Church (MCC), 110

microaggressions, 579
    defined, 39, 226, 579
    overview and nature of, 39, 226

midwives, 481, 489, 490, 492
    queer, 488

migrant rights, 647–48

migration. *See* immigration

military ban, transgender, 253, 634

military service, 253, 566, 650–51
    correcting military records after you serve, 253–54

Mindell, Drew, 532

Minter, Shannon Price, 239, 243

Miranda, Deborah A., 589

misgendering, 77, 494, 495, 544
    defined, 17
    getting misgendered, 195
    health care and, 80
    overview, 17, 195
    pronouns and, 17, 194, 195
    and the term "ladies," 181

Miss Major. *See* Griffin-Gracy, Miss Major

Mock, Janet, 533

monogamy, 424, 448

monsplasty, 356, 359

mood disorders, 387, 402

Movement Advancement Project, 245, 255, 336, 569

movies. *See also* specific films
    Blackness represented in, 617–18
    featuring trans people of color, 40
    pornographic, 440, 446
    trans representation in, 616–18

Ms Ty, 19

MTF (male to female), 3, 6, 353*f. See also specific topics*

Muhammad, Prophet, 110, 111

mukhannath, 112

Muslim Alliance for Sexual and Gender Diversity (MASGD), 112

Muslims, 57, 110–13

Muslims for Progressive Values, 112

Muslim Youth Leadership Council, 112

myth making, 630

Myth of Father (film), 493

N

name change, 242, 247–48, 250
    for children, 522
    choosing a new name, 39, 522
    common law change, 248
    court order, 248

names, 221
    gender-neutral, 39, 192, 522
    social transition and, 191–92, 194

naming oneself, 34–36. See also name change

Nashville, Tennessee, 527

National Center for Transgender Equality (NCTE), 57, 247, 248, 254, 258, 264, 430, 545, 603, 650

National Collegiate Athletic Association (NCAA), 558

National Immigrant Justice Center, 61

National LGBT Bar Association, 264

National LGBTQIA + Health Education Center, 294

National Trans Bar Association, 264

Native Americans, 43–44, 122–23, 262, 589, 644

Native Out (Facebook page), 174

naturalization, 58

Navajo, 43, 122

necropoetics, 620

neo-Paganism, 118

neopronouns, 194

Neufeldt, Aislin, 320

Neumeier, Shain, 70*f*

neurodiversity/neurodivergence, 78–80, 83, 85, 396. *See also* autism spectrum

neuroqueer, 85

neurotoxins, injection of, 366–67

new religious movements, 123

New Thought, 123

Nickens, Margaret, 299

Nicol, Hara, 627–28

nipple graft, 344–48

nipples, 345, 347, 489

No Dumb Questions (film), 478

nonbinary (gender), 15, 25, 166, 589
    and the law, 247, 262
    navigating nonbinary identities, 247
    terminology and related terms, 166
    use of the term, 14, 166

physical activity, 277–78

physicians. *See* primary care provider; providers; surgeons

Piaget, Jean, 147

piercings, body, 205

Pitchlynn, Maggie Mae, 636

Planned Parenthood, 272, 314, 492

play groups, children's, 511

Plume, 327

plural-trans experience(s), 390

podcasting, 629

poetry, 247, 248, 333, 461, 616–17, 636

poets, 10, 100, 461, 610, 611, 618
    in TPOC communities, 32–33

Point of Pride, 202

police
    going to the, 231–32
    guidelines for dealing with, 231, 252
    people of color and, 33, 38, 60, 260, 610, 639
    in schools, 38

police raids, 30, 31, 225, 594, 596, 639, 641

police violence, 31, 38, 60, 248–49, 260, 609–10
    trans resistance as a response to, 639–40

policy, importance of, 271

political sphere, trans identity in the, 18–20

politicians, 647
    nonbinary and trans, 647, 654

polyamory, 424, 448

polycystic ovary syndrome (PCOS), 137

polysexuality, 446

polytheism. *See* goddesses and gods

pornography (porn), 440, 446, 447, 627, 630
    trans, 440, 446
    a trans-positive guide to, 446–47

POSE (TV series), 40, 47, 365, 623

possibility models, 41

postinflammatory hyperpigmentation, 308

post-trans tipping point, 635

post-traumatic stress disorder (PTSD), 73, 75, 451
    and trauma responses, 389–90

Powell, Annette (A), 88

Power, Mya, 474*f*

power exchange (BDSM), 468–69

power of attorney, 579

Pre-Exposure Prophylaxis (PrEP), 281–82

pregnancy, 472–73, 481–88
    carrying a, 489–90

preventive health care, 275–76

Pride Parade, 31, 560*f*, 603, 639. *See also* Christopher Street Liberation Day parade

primary care provider (PCP)
    establishing a, 276–77
    for medical support, 371–73

primary sex characteristics, 136

prisons, 249–51, 607, 641. *See also* Immigration and Customs Enforcement (ICE) detention center abuse and violence in, 241, 250, 280, 593, 607–8, 640, 641
    activism and, 153, 251, 607–10, 641 (*see also* Sylvia Rivera Law Project)
    identity documents, 249–50

prison abolition movement, 250, 251, 607–10, 648

prison guards, 241, 640, 641

prisoner housing, 249, 250, 280

prisoner reentry, 250–51

privacy, 180. *See also* bathrooms; confidentiality; disclosure
    disclosure, coming out, and, 161, 179, 537
    and finding support, 165
    online, 544
    vs. secrecy, 537

privilege, social, 40, 41
    intersectionality, power, and, 427–28

privileged identities, 17, 37, 38, 403, 427

progesterone, 297, 312, 318

progestins, 297

pronouns, 13. *See also* gender-neutral pronouns

prostate cancer, 287

prosthetics, 138*f*
    breast, 199, 201
    penis-shaped, 201, 356, 449, 464

prostitution. *See* sex work

providers. *See also* mental health professionals; primary care provider
    coming out to, 554
    disclosure to, 494–95
    T/GE children and making early connections with, 514–19

pseudofolliculitis barbae (razor bumps), 308–9

Psycho (film), 614

Psychology Today, 165

psychotherapy, 398–402. *See also* mental health

psychotic disorders, 395

puberty, 136, 309, 554

puberty blockers, 554
    and fertility, 311
    how long to stay on, 311–12
    methods of administration, 310
    overview and nature of, 309
    side effects and risks, 311
    when to begin, 310–11

public accommodations laws, 245–46

public awareness and acceptance of trans people, 566

Public Facilities Privacy & Security Act (HB2), 633, 655, 656

Pulse nightclub attack, 31

pumping devices, 356, 466

Purnell, Jules, 431

697

INDEX

transmasculine bodies, 138f

trans narratives, deconstructing and reconstructing, 133

trans panic defense, 251

Transparent (TV series), 57, 481, 631

trans parent, being a, 474, 493, 495. *See also* parenting
  adoption and fostering, 478–81
  concerns about parenting as trans people, 475
  gender open parenting, 494
  options for becoming a trans parent, 475–76
  parenting a partner's child, 476–77
  planning a biological family (*see* family planning)
  what children should call their parents, 493

trans people of color. *See* TPOC

transphobia, 391, 462, 614, 632, 641. *See also specific topics*
  on the Internet, 209
  race, people of color, and, 37, 44, 55, 100
  trans panic defense and, 251
  when flirting becomes transphobic, 457–58

Transportation Security Administration (TSA), 29, 199, 254

Trans/Portraits: Voices from Transgender Communities (Scultz), 10

transsexual, 4, 5, 441, 562

transsexualism (diagnosis), 74

trans sexuality, 15, 630. *See also* sexuality

trans spirituality, 23

Trans Student Educational Resources (TSER), 539

trans studies. *See* transgender studies

trans time, 191

TransTorah, 48, 103, 104, 106

transvestism, 466

trans woman, 7

trans women of color (TWOC), 30, 51, 603, 623, 641. *See also* Black trans women
  prison and, 607–8, 609, 639
  violence against, 37, 57, 606, 645, 655

Trans Women of Color Collective, 264, 524

Trans Youth Equality Foundation (TYEF), 513

trauma, 288. *See also* post-traumatic stress disorder; violence
  grappling with trauma through art modeling, 634–35
  self-care in the aftermath of, 396

traumatic brain injury (TBI), 71, 72, 252

traumatic histories, people with, 451

traveling while trans, 199. *See also* Transportation Security Administration

Trevor Project, 255, 380, 382

trial courts, 240

triggers, 449–51

tritiya-prakriti (third gender), 55, 114, 440

Trixx, Stevie, 237

Trump administration, 242, 253, 275, 527, 601, 602, 634

tucking, 199, 205, 298

Tudor, Rachel, 261

Tudor v. Southeastern Oklahoma State Univ., 261

tumtum, 9, 103

twelve-step programs, 280, 388

twin studies, 142

Two Spirit, 588f, 593
  Indigenous peoples and, 44, 122, 589
  meaning and scope of the term, 11, 122, 589
  use of the term, 122

Two-Spirit people, 122, 590, 593, 644

Ty, Ms, 19

TYEF (Trans Youth Equality Foundation), 513

U

underground economy, working in the, 233–34

undocumented labor, 234. *See also* immigrants, undocumented

UndocuQueer, 58

UndocuQueer movement, 647, 648

Unitarian Universalist Association (UUA), 123

United Methodist Church (UMC), 110

United Nations Convention Against Torture (UNCAT), 65–66

United We Dream, 60

urethral lengthening, 360–61
  complications, 362
  healing timeline, 362

U.S. history, 611
  AIDS epidemic and responding to Reaganism, 601–4
  confronting the historical legacy of colonization and Christian supremacy, 590
  constellating trans histories of resistance, 585–86first waves of colonization of the Americas and gendercide, 588–89
  framework, 586–87
  slavery, segregation, and civil rights, 590–92, 652
  Stonewall Rebellion, gay liberation, and intersectional trans activism, 593–98
  trans milestones, 592–93

U.S. Transgender Survey (1995), 71, 254, 272f, 288, 645

uterine cancer, 286–87

V

vaginal reconstruction, options for, 355. *See also* vaginoplasty

vaginectomy, 350, 356, 359, 361
  complications, 362–63
  healing timeline, 362
  overview and nature of, 362

vaginoplasty, 287, 348, 353, 353f
  types of, 355 (*see also* penile inversion vaginoplasty)

Veale, Jaimee, 130